MARTIN'S
POCKET CRIMINAL CODE
═══ 2021 ═══

MAT# 42729721

CANADA LAW BOOK

MARTIN'S
POCKET CRIMINAL CODE
2021

Forms of Charges by

Marie Henein, LL.B., LL.M.

**In Memory and Acknowledgement of his valued
contributions from 1995 to 2015:
The Honourable Mr. Justice
MARC ROSENBERG**

**In Memory and Acknowledgement of his valued
contributions from 1995 to 2014:
EDWARD L. GREENSPAN, Q.C.**

THOMSON REUTERS®

A cataloguing record for this publication is available from Library and Archives Canada

ISSN: 0527-7892
ISBN: 978-0-7798-9408-6

Printed in the United States by Thomson Reuters

THOMSON REUTERS®

THOMSON REUTERS CANADA, A DIVISION OF THOMSON REUTERS CANADA LIMITED

One Corporate Plaza
2075 Kennedy Road
Toronto, ON
M1T 3V4

Customer Support
1-416-609-3800 (Toronto & International)
1-800-387-5164 (Toll Free Canada & U.S.)
Fax 1-416-298-5082
Fax 1-877-750-9041 (Toll Free Canada Only)
Email CustomerSupport.LegalTaxCanada@TR.com

IN MEMORY OF
The Honourable Justice Marc Rosenberg
(1950-2015)

It is with great sadness that we commemorate the passing of The Honourable Justice Marc Rosenberg.

Justice Rosenberg was a highly regarded appellate advocate, judge and one of our greatest legal minds. His tireless commitment to legal judicial education, both nationally and internationally, was a great contribution. The Honourable Justice Rosenberg was a long-standing co-author and co-editor of *Martin's Annual Criminal Code*, *Martin's Criminal Code (Counsel Edition)*, *Martin's Related Criminal Statutes*, *Martin's Ontario Criminal Practice*, *Martin's Pocket Criminal Code*, *Martin's Online Criminal Code*, the *Dominion Law Reports* and the *Canadian Criminal Cases*.

It was a great honour to work with him and be the beneficiary, like so many in his profession, of his knowledge, compassion and great wisdom. He will be greatly missed.

Marie Henein

IN MEMORY OF
Edward L. Greenspan, Q.C.
(1944-2014)

It is with great sadness that we acknowledge the passing of Edward L. Greenspan, Q.C., one of the most celebrated criminal defence lawyers in Canada.

A tireless and passionate advocate, speaker and writer, Mr. Greenspan was a long-standing co-author of *Martin's Annual Criminal Code*, *Martin's Criminal Code (Counsel Edition)*, *Martin's Related Criminal Statutes*, *Martin's Ontario Criminal Practice*, *Martin's Pocket Criminal Code*, *Martin's Online Criminal Code*, *Canadian Charter of Rights Annotated*, and *Dubin Lectures on Advocacy 1998-2002*. He was, in addition, on the Editorial Boards for the *Canadian Criminal Cases* law report series from 1972 and the *Weekly Criminal Bulletin* from 1976.

It was a privilege and a pleasure to work with him on these career-long projects that he cared so deeply about. We are filled with great sadness at the loss of our colleague and dear friend.

Marc Rosenberg
Marie Henein

IN MEMORY OF
David L. Grossman, Q.C.
19??–2010

PREFACE

The *Martin's Pocket Criminal Code, 2021* contains the *Criminal Code, Canada Evidence Act, Canadian Bill of Rights, Canadian Charter of Rights and Freedoms, Controlled Drugs and Substances Act, Crimes Against Humanity and War Crimes Act, Firearms Act, Identification of Criminals Act, Interpretation Act* and *Youth Criminal Justice Act.*

This edition is updated with all statutory amendments up to and including those receiving Royal Assent on April 15, 2020. The text of any amendments which have not been brought into force are printed in shaded boxes.

Substantial amendments have been made to the *Youth Criminal Justice Act* which attempt to achieve the following:

- the modernization and enhancement of interim release provisions with special focus on Aboriginal accused, offenders from vulnerable populations, and those who commit violent acts against intimate partners;
- the provision of a judicial referral hearing to deal with failure-to-comply and failure-to-appear offences;
- the abolition of peremptory challenges of jurors and modification of the process for challenging jurors for cause;
- the restriction of preliminary inquiries to offences punishable for terms of fourteen years or more; and
- the re-introduction of the Victim Surcharge regime, which now permits the court to adjust amounts owing in the event of undue hardship or disproportionality.

For your convenience we have again included the *Regulations Prescribing Certain Firearms and Other Weapons, Components and Parts of Weapons, Accessories, Cartridge Magazines, and Projectiles as Prohibited or Restricted*, SOR/98-462, following s. 84 of the *Criminal Code*, and *Regulations Prescribing Public Officers*, SOR/98-466, following s. 117.07 of the Code. The texts of these regulations are found in shaded boxes.

The Forms of Charges for the *Criminal Code* and the *Controlled Drugs and Substances Act* have again been included and updated.

MARIE HENEIN, LL.B., LL.M.

Toronto, Ontario
June, 2020

TABLE OF CONTENTS

CRIMINAL CODE CONCORDANCE

This Table sets out all sections of the *Criminal Code*, R.S.C. 1970, c. C-34, as amended to December, 1988, and the corresponding numbering in R.S.C. 1985, c. C-46, as amended to April 15, 2020. References to subsections, paragraphs and subparagraphs appear only when the numbering has been changed in the R.S.C. 1985 Code. The numbers listed under the heading "R.S.C. 1985" reflect the numbering scheme set out in the main volumes of the Revised Statutes of Canada, 1985, the First, Second, Third and Fourth Supplements and amendments.

Locate the number under the heading R.S.C. 1970, c. C-34, and cross-refer to the number that appears in the opposite column under the heading R.S.C. 1985, c. C-46. Where a case cites provisions from the 1970 Code, consult the R.S.C. 1985 column for the corresponding 1985 Code section numbers. Where contemporary cases cite the 1985 Code, consult the R.S.C. 1970 column for the corresponding 1970 Code numbers.

Note: Users should bear in mind, however, that the Concordance is not a citator and has been assembled only as a guide to the numbering of the 1985 Code.

R.S.C. 1970, c. C-34	R.S.C. 1985, c. C-46	R.S.C. 1970, c. C-34	R.S.C. 1985, c. C-46
1	1	—	2 "criminal organization offence" [en. 1997, c. 23, s. 1]
2	2		
—	2 "appearance notice" [en. 2019, c. 25, s. 1]	—	2 "environment" [en. 2013, c. 13, s. 2(2)]
—	2 "associated personnel" [en. 2001, c. 41, s. 2(2)]	—	2 "government or public facility" [en. 2001, c. 41, s. 2(2)]
—	2 "audioconference" [en. 2019, c. 25, s. 1]	—	2 "intimate partner" [en. 2019, c. 25, s. 1]
—	2 "common-law partner" [en. 2000, c. 12, s. 91]	—	2 "justice system participant" [en. 2001, c. 41, s. 2(2)]
—	2 "criminal organization" [en. 1997, c. 23, s. 1]	—	2 "nuclear facility" [en. 2013, c. 13, s. 2(2)]

R.S.C. 1970, c. C-34	R.S.C. 1985, c. C-46	R.S.C. 1970, c. C-34	R.S.C. 1985, c. C-46
4	5	7(1)(b)	8(1)(a)
5	6	8	9
6	7	9	10
6(1.1)	7(2)	10	11
—	7(2.01)-(2.02) [en. 2005, c. 40, s. 2]	11	12
		12	13
—	7(2.21) [en. 2013, c. 13, s. 3(1)]	13	repealed
		14-33	14-33
—	7(2.32) [rep. 2019, c. 25, s. 4]	—	25.1 to 25.4 [en. 2001, c. 32, s. 2]
6(1.2)	7(3)	—	27.1 [en. 2004, c. 12, s. 2]
6(1.3)	7(3.1)		
6(1.4)	7(3.2) [rep. 2013, c. 13, s. 3(2)]	—	33.1 [en. 1995, c. 32, s. 1]
6(1.5)	7(3.3) [rep. 2013, c. 13, s. 3(2)]	34	34
		35	35
6(1.6)	7(3.4) [rep. 2013, c. 13, s. 3(2)]	36-42	36-42 [rep. 2012, c. 9, s. 2]
6(1.7)	7(3.5) [rep. 2013, c. 13, s. 3(2)]	43	43
6(1.8)	7(3.6) [rep. 2013, c. 13, s. 3(2)]	44	44 [rep. 2001, c. 26, s. 294]
6(1.9)	7(3.7)	45	45
6(1.91)	7(3.71)	Part II	Part II
6(1.92)	7(3.72)	46-55	46-55
6(1.93)	7(3.73)	—	49 [rep. 2018, c. 29, s. 1]
6(1.94)	7(3.74)		
6(1.95)	7(3.75)	56	repealed
6(1.96)	7(3.76)	57	56
6(1.97)	7(3.77)	—	56.1 [en. 2009, c. 28, s. 1]
6(2)	7(4)		
—	7(4.2) [rep. 2002, c. 13, s. 3(2)]	58	57
		59	58
		60	59
6(3)	7(5)	61	60
6(3.1)	7(5.1)	62	61
6(4)	7(6)	63	62
6(5)	7(7)	64	63
6(6)	7(8)	65	64
6(7)	7(9)	66	65 [renumbered as (1) and (2) en. 2013, c. 15, s. 2]
6(8)	7(10)		
6(9)	7(11)		
7	8		
7(1)(a)	8(1)(b)		

R.S.C. 1970, c. C-34	R.S.C. 1985, c. C-46	R.S.C. 1970, c. C-34	R.S.C. 1985, c. C-46
67	66 [renumbered as (1) and (2) en. 2013, c. 15, s. 3]	—	83.191 [en. 2013, c. 9, c. 7]
		—	83.201 [en. 2013, c. 9, c. 8]
68	67	—	83.202 [en. 2013, c. 9, c. 8]
69	68	—	83.221 [en. 2015, c. 20, c. 16]
70	69		
71	70	—	83.222 [en. 2015, c. 20, c. 16]
72	71 [rep. 2018, c. 29, s. 4]	—	83.223 [en. 2015, c. 20, c. 16]
73	72	—	83.231 [en. 2004, c. 15, s. 32]
74	73	—	83.28 [rep. 2019, c. 13, s. 145]
75	74		
76	75	—	83.29 [rep. 2019, c. 13, s. 145]
76.1	76	—	83.3(7.1), (7.2), (8.1), (11.1) and (11.2) [en. 2015, c. 20, c. 17]
76.2	77		
76.3	78		
—	78.1 [en 1993, c. 7, s. 4]		
77	79	—	83.31(1) and (1.1) [rep. 2019, c. 13, s. 147]
78	80	—	83.33(1) [rep. 2019, c. 13, s. 149]
79	81		
80	82	Part II.1	Part III (replaced 1995, c. 39, s. 139)
—	82.1 [en. 1997, c. 23, s. 2]		
—	82.2 [en. 2013, c. 13, s. 5]	82	—
—	82.3 [en. 2013, c. 13, s. 5]	83	—
		84	—
—	82.4 [en. 2013, c. 13, s. 5]	85	—
—	82.5 [en. 2013, c. 13, s. 5]	86	—
		87	—
—	82.6 [en. 2013, c. 13, s. 5]	88	—
—	82.7 [en. 2013, c. 13, s. 5]	—	—
81	83	89	—
—	Part II.1 (ss. 83.01 to 83.33) [en. 2001, c. 41, s. 4]	—	—
		90	—
—	83.181 [en. 2013, c. 9, c. 6]	91	—
		92	—
		93	—
		—	—

R.S.C. 1970, c. C-34	R.S.C. 1985, c. C-46	R.S.C. 1970, c. C-34	R.S.C. 1985, c. C-46
94	—	106.8	—
95	—	106.9	—
96	—	—	84
97	—	—	85
98	—	—	86
98(11) "appeal court"	—	—	87
		—	88
98(11)(a)	—	—	89
98(11)(b)	—	—	90
98(11)(b.1)	—	—	91
98(11)(c)	—	—	92
98(11)(d)	—	—	93
98(11)(e)	—	—	94
98(11)(f)	—	—	95
99	—	—	96
100	—	—	97 [not yet in force]
101	—	—	98
102	—	—	99
103	—	—	100
104	—	—	101
104 [1976-77, c. 53, s. 47(3)]	—	—	102
		—	103
104(3)	—	—	104
104(4)	—	—	105
104(5)	—	—	106
104(6)	—	—	107
104(7)	—	—	108
104(8)	—	—	109
104(9)	—	—	109(1)(c.1) [en. 2018, c. 16, s. 208]
104(10)	—		
104(11)	—	—	110
104(12)	—	—	110(2.1) [en. 2015, c. 27, s. 31]
105	—		
106	—	—	110.1 [en. 2015, c. 27, s. 32; rep. 2019, c. 25, s. 32]
106.1	—		
106.2	—		
—	—	—	111
106.3	—	—	112
106.4	—	—	113
106.5	—	—	114
106.6	—	—	115
106.7	—	—	116

R.S.C. 1970, c. C-34	R.S.C. 1985, c. C-46	R.S.C. 1970, c. C-34	R.S.C. 1985, c. C-46
—	117	122	133
—	117.01	122.1	134
—	117.011	123	135 [rep. R.S.C. 1985, c. 27 (1st Supp.), s. 17]
—	117.02		
—	117.03		
—	117.04	124	136
—	117.05	125	137
—	117.06	126	138
—	117.07	127	139
—	117.071 [en. 2017, c. 27, s. 61]	128	140
—	117.08	129	141
—	117.09	130	142
—	117.1	131	143 [rep. 2018, c. 29, s. 8]
—	117.11	132	144
—	117.12	133	145
—	117.13	—	145(5.1) [en. 1997, c. 18, s. 3(2)]
—	117.14		
—	117.15	133(7)	145(7) [rep. R.S.C. 1985, c. 27 (1st Supp.), s. 20(2)]
—	117.15(3) and (4) [en. 2015, c. 27, s. 34]		
		134	146
Part III	Part IV	135	147
107	118	136	148
108	119	137	149
109	120	Part IV	Part V
110	121	138	150
—	121.1 [en. 2014, c. 23, s. 3]	139	150.1
		—	150.1(2.3) [en. 2015, c. 29, s. 6]
111	122		
112	123	140	151
113	124	141	152
114	125	142-145	repealed
115	126	146	153
116	127	—	153(1.1) and (1.2) [en. 2005, c. 32, s. 4(2)]
117	128		
118	129	—	153.1 [en. 1998, c. 9, s. 2]
119	130		
—	130.1 [en. 2014, c. 10, s. 1]	—	153.1(2.1), (2.2) [en. 2018, c. 29, s. 10(1)]
120	131		
121	132		

R.S.C. 1970, c. C-34	R.S.C. 1985, c. C-46
147	154 [rep. R.S.C. 1985, c. 19 (3rd Supp.), s. 1]
148 and 149	repealed
150	155
151-153	156-158 [rep. R.S.C. 1985, c. 19 (3rd Supp.), s. 2]
—	156 [en. 2019, c. 25, s. 53]
154	159 [rep. 2019, c. 25, s. 54]
155	160
—	160(4)-(7) [en. 2019, c. 17, s. 1]
156	repealed
157 and 158	161 and 162 [rep. R.S.C. 1985, c. 19 (3rd Supp.), s. 4]
—	161 [en. 1993, c. 45, s. 1]
—	161(1.1) [en. 2005, c. 32, s. 5(2)]
—	162 [en. 2005, c. 32, s. 6]
—	162.1 [en. 2014, c. 31, s. 3]
—	162.2 [en. 2014, c. 31, s. 3]
159	163
159(6)	163(6) [rep. 1993, c. 46, s. 1(2)]
—	163(7) [rep. 2018, c. 29, s. 11(4)]
—	163.1 [en. 1993, c. 46, s. 2]
—	163.1(4.1) and (4.2) [en. 2002, c. 13, s. 5(3)]
160	164
160(8) "court"	164(8) "court"
—	164(8) "crime comic" [rep. 2018, c. 29, s. 12(3)]

R.S.C. 1970, c. C-34	R.S.C. 1985, c. C-46
160(8)(a)	164(8)(a)
160(8)(a.1)	164(8)(b)
160(8)(b)	164(8)(c)
160(8)(c)	164(8)(d)
—	164.1 [en. 2002, c. 13, s. 7]
—	164.2 [en. 2002, c. 13, s. 7]
—	164.3 [en. 2002, c. 13, s. 7]
161	165 [rep. 2018, c. 29, s. 13]
162	166 [rep. 1994, c. 44, s. 9]
163	167
164	168
165	169
166	170
167	171
168	172
168(2)	172(2) [rep. R.S.C. 1985, c. 19 (3rd Supp.), s. 6]
—	172.1 [en. 2002, c. 13, s. 8]
169	173
170	174
171	175
172	176
173	177
174	178 [rep. 2018, c. 29, s. 14]
175	179 [rep. 2019, c. 25, s. 60]
175(1)(a) to (c)	repealed
175(1)(d)	179(1)(a) [rep. 2019, c. 25, s. 60]
175(1)(e)	179(1)(b) [rep. 2019, c. 25, s. 60]
175(2)	179(2) [rep. 2019, c. 25, s. 60]
175(3)	repealed
176	180

R.S.C. 1970, c. C-34	R.S.C. 1985, c. C-46
178.21	194
178.22	195
178.22(2)(g.1)	195(2)(h)
178.22(2)(h)	195(2)(i)
178.22(2)(i)	195(2)(j)
178.22(2)(j)	195(2)(k)
178.22(2)(k)	195(2)(l)
178.22(2)(l)	195(2)(m)
178.22(2)(m)	195(2)(n)
—	195(2.1) [en. 2013, c. 8, s. 5(3)]
178.23	196
178.23(2)	—
178.23(3)	196(2)
178.23(4)	196(3)
178.23(5)	196(4)
—	196(5) [en. 1997, c. 23, s. 7]
—	196.1 [en. 2013, c. 8, s. 6]
Part V	Part VII
179	197
180	198 [rep. 2018, c. 29, s. 16]
181	199
182 and 183	repealed
184	200 [rep. R.S.C. 1985, c. 27 (1st Supp.), s. 30]
185	201
186	202
187	203
188	204
188(6.1)	204(7)
188(6.2)	204(8)
188(6.3)	204(8.1)
188(7)	204(9)
188(7.1)	204(9.1)
188(8)	204(10)
188.1	205 [rep. R.S.C. 1985, c. 52 (1st Supp.), s. 1]
189	206

R.S.C. 1970, c. C-34	R.S.C. 1985, c. C-46
190	207
—	207(4.1) [en. 2014, c. 39, s. 171]
—	207.1 [en. 1999, c. 5, s. 7]
—	207.1(4.01) [en. 2018, c. 29, s. 17(2)]
191	208 [rep. R.S.C. 1985, c. 27 (1st Supp.), s. 32]
192	209
193	210 [rep. 2019, c. 25, s. 73]
194	211 [rep. 2019, c. 25, s. 73]
195	212 [rep., with heading, 2014, c. 25, s. 13]
—	212(5) [rep. 1999, c. 5, s. 8]
195.1	213
—	213(1.1) [en. 2014, c. 25, s. 15(3)]
Part VI	Part VIII
196	214
—	214 "aircraft" [rep. 2018, c. 21, s. 13]
—	214 "operate" [rep. 2018, c. 21, s. 13]
—	214 "vessel" [rep. 2018, c. 21, s. 13]
197	215
198	216
199	217
200	218
201	repealed
202	219
203	220
204	221
205	222
206	223
207	224

R.S.C. 1970, c. C-34	R.S.C. 1985, c. C-46	R.S.C. 1970, c. C-34	R.S.C. 1985, c. C-46
208	225	228	244 [en. 1995, c. 39, s. 144]
209	226	—	244.1 [en. 1995, c. 39, s. 144]
210	227 [rep. 1999, c. 5, s. 9(1); re-en. 2016, c. 3, s. 2]	—	244.2 [en. 2009, c. 22, s. 8]
211	228	229	245
212	229	—	245(2) and (3) [en. 2016, c. 3, s. 6]
213	230 [rep. 2019, c. 25, s. 78]	230	246
214	231	231	247
214(6)	231(6) [rep. R.S.C. 1985, c. 27 (1st Supp.), s. 35]	232	248
		233	249 [(and heading) rep. 2018, c. 21, s. 14]
—	231(6.01) [en. 2001, c. 41, s. 9]	—	249.1 [en. 2000, c. 2, s. 1; rep. 2018, c. 21, s. 14]
—	231(6.1) [en. 1997, c. 23, s. 8]	—	249.2 [en. 2006, c. 14, s. 2; rep. 2018, c. 21, s. 14]
—	231(6.2) [en. 2001, c. 32, s. 9(2)]	—	249.3 [en. 2006, c. 14, s. 2; rep. 2018, c. 21, s. 14]
215	232	—	249.4 [en. 2006, c. 14, s. 2; rep. 2018, c. 21, s. 14]
216	233		
217	234	234	250 [rep. 2018, c. 21, s. 14]
218	235		
219	236	235	251 [rep. 2018, c. 21, s. 14]
220	237		
221	238	236	252 [rep. 2018, c. 21, s. 14]
222	239		
223	240	237	253 [rep. 2018, c. 21, s. 14]
224	241		
—	241.1 [en. 2016, c. 3, s. 3]	—	253.1 [en. 2018, c. 21, s. 2; rep. 2018, c. 21, s. 14]
—	241.2 [en. 2016, c. 3, s. 3]	238	254 [rep. 2018, c. 21, s. 14]
—	241.3 [en. 2016, c. 3, s. 3]	—	254.01 [en. 2018, c. 21, s. 4; rep. 2018, c. 21, s. 14]
—	241.31 [en. 2016, c. 3, s. 4]		
—	241.4 [en. 2016, c. 3, s. 3]		
225	repealed		
226	242		
227	243		

R.S.C. 1970, c. C-34	R.S.C. 1985, c. C-46	R.S.C. 1970, c. C-34	R.S.C. 1985, c. C-46
—	254.1 [en. 2008, c. 6, s. 20; rep. 2018, c. 21, s. 14]	—	270.03 [en. 2015, c. 34, s. 2]
239	255 [rep. 2018, c. 21, s. 14]	—	270.1 [en. 2002, c. 13, s. 11]
—	255.1 [en. 1999, c. 32, s. 4; rep. 2018, c. 21, s. 14]	246.1	271
240	256 [rep. 2018, c. 21, s. 14]	246.1(2)	271(2) [rep. R.S.C. 1985, c. 19 (3rd Supp.), s. 10]
240.1	257 [rep. 2018, c. 21, s. 14]	246.2	272
241	258 [rep. 2018, c. 21, s. 14]	246.3	273
—	258.1 [en. 2008, c. 6, s. 25; rep. 2018, c. 21, s. 14]	—	273.1 [en. 1992, c. 38, s. 1]
242	259 [rep. 2018, c. 21, s. 14]	—	273.1(1.1), (1.2) [en. 2018, c. 29, s. 19(1)]
243	260 [rep. 2018, c. 21, s. 14]	—	273.2 [en. 1992, c. 38, s. 1]
243.1	261 [rep. 2018, c. 21, s. 14]	—	273.3 [en. 1992, c. 38, s. 1]
243.2	262	246.4	274
243.3	263	246.5	275
243 [old provision]	264 [rep. R.S.C. 1985, c. 27 (1st Supp.), s. 37]	246.6	276
		—	276(4) [en. 2018, c. 29, s. 21(3)]
—	264 [en. 1993, c. 45, s. 2]	—	276.1-276.5 [en. 1992, c. 38, s. 2; rep. 2018, c. 29, s. 22]
243.4	264.1	246.7	277
244	265	246.8	278
245	266	—	278.1 to 278.91 [en. 1997, c. 30, s. 1]
245.1	267		
245.2	268	—	278.92-278.97 [en. 2018, c. 29, s. 25]
245.3	269	247	279
—	269.01 [en. 2015, c. 1, s. 1]	—	279(3) [rep. 2018, c. 29, s. 26]
245.4	269.1	—	279(1.21) [en. 2013, c. 32, s. 1]
246	270	—	279.01 [en. 2005, c. 43, s. 3]
—	270.01 [en. 2009, c. 22, s. 9]	—	279.01(3) [en. 2015, c. 16, s. 1]
—	270.02 [en. 2009, c. 22, s. 9]		

R.S.C. 1970, c. C-34	R.S.C. 1985, c. C-46	R.S.C. 1970, c. C-34	R.S.C. 1985, c. C-46
—	279.02 [en. 2005, c. 43, s. 3]	253	289 [rep. R.S.C. 1985, c. 27 (1st Supp.), s. 41]
—	279.03 [en. 2005, c. 43, s. 3]	254	290
—	279.04 [en. 2005, c. 43, s. 3]	255	291
247.1	279.1	256	292
—	279.1(3) [rep. 2018, c. 29, s. 27]	257	293
248	repealed	—	293.1 [en. 2015, c. 29, s. 9]
249	280	—	293.2 [en. 2015, c. 29, s. 9]
250	281	258	294
250.1	282	259	295
250.2	283	260	296 [(and heading) rep. 2018, c. 29, s. 30]
250.3	284	261	297
250.4	285	262	298
250.5	286	263	299
—	286.1 [en. 2014, c. 25, s. 20]	264	300
—	286.2 [en. 2014, c. 25, s. 20]	265	301
—	286.3 [en. 2014, c. 25, s. 20]	266	302
—	286.4 [en. 2014, c. 25, s. 20]	267	303
—	286.5 [en. 2014, c. 25, s. 20]	268	304
251	287 [rep. 2019, c. 25, s. 111]	269	305
		270	306
		271	307
251(6) "Minister of Health"	287(6) "Minister of Health" [rep. 2019, c. 25, s. 111]	272	308
		273	309
251(6)(a)	287(6)(a) [rep. 2019, c. 25, s. 111]	274	310
		275	311
251(6)(a.1)	287(6)(d) [rep. 2019, c. 25, s. 111]	276	312
		277	313
251(6)(b)	287(6)(c) [rep. 2019, c. 25, s. 111]	278	314
		279	315
251(6)(c)	287(6)(b) [rep. 2019, c. 25, s. 111]	280	316
		281	317
251(6)(d)	287(6)(e) [rep. 2019, c. 25, s. 111]	281.1	318
		281.2	319
252	288 [rep. 2018, c. 29, s. 28]	281.3	320
		281.3(8) "court"	320(8) "court"
		281.3(8)(a)	320(8)(a)
		281.3(8)(a.1)	320(8)(b)

R.S.C. 1970, c. C-34	R.S.C. 1985, c. C-46	R.S.C. 1970, c. C-34	R.S.C. 1985, c. C-46
281.3(8)(b)	320(8)(c)	—	320.3 [en. 2018, c. 21, s. 15]
281.3(8)(c)	320(8)(d)	—	320.31 [en. 2018, c. 21, s. 15]
—	320.1 [en. 2001, c. 41, s. 10]	—	320.32 [en. 2018, c. 21, s. 15]
—	Part VIII.1 [en. 2018, c. 21, s. 15]	—	320.33 [en. 2018, c. 21, s. 15]
—	320.11 [en. 2018, c. 21, s. 15]	—	320.34 [en. 2018, c. 21, s. 15]
—	320.12 [en. 2018, c. 21, s. 15]	—	320.35 [en. 2018, c. 21, s. 15]
—	320.13 [en. 2018, c. 21, s. 15]	—	320.36 [en. 2018, c. 21, s. 15]
—	320.14 [en. 2018, c. 21, s. 15]	—	320.37 [en. 2018, c. 21, s. 15]
—	320.15 [en. 2018, c. 21, s. 15]	—	320.38 [en. 2018, c. 21, s. 15]
—	320.16 [en. 2018, c. 21, s. 15]	—	320.39 [en. 2018, c. 21, s. 15]
—	320.17 [en. 2018, c. 21, s. 15]	—	320.4 [en. 2018, c. 21, s. 15]
—	320.18 [en. 2018, c. 21, s. 15]		
—	320.19 [en. 2018, c. 21, s. 15]	Part VII	Part IX
		282	321
—	320.2 [en. 2018, c. 21, s. 15]	283	322
		284	323
—	320.21 [en. 2018, c. 21, s. 15]	285	324
		286	325
—	320.22 [en. 2018, c. 21, s. 15]	287	326 [rep. 2014, c. 31, s. 14(2)]
—	320.23 [en. 2018, c. 21, s. 15]	287.1	327
		288	328
—	320.24 [en. 2018, c. 21, s. 15]	289	329 [rep. 2000, c. 12, s. 94]
—	320.25 [en. 2018, c. 21, s. 15]	290	330
		291	331
—	320.26 [en. 2018, c. 21, s. 15]	292	332
		293	333
—	320.27 [en. 2018, c. 21, s. 15]	—	333.1 [en. 2010, c. 14, s. 3]
—	320.28 [en. 2018, c. 21, s. 15]	294	334
—	320.29 [en. 2018, c. 21, s. 15]	295	335

R.S.C. 1970, c. C-34	R.S.C. 1985, c. C-46	R.S.C. 1970, c. C-34	R.S.C. 1985, c. C-46
—	335(1.1) [en. 1997, c. 18, s. 15]	306	348
296	336	—	348.1 [en. 2002, c. 13, s. 15]
297	337 [rep. 2018, c. 29, s. 33]	306(3)	repealed
298	338	306(4)	348(3)
298(1.1)	338(2)	307	349
298(2)	338(3)	308	350
298(3)	338(4)	309	351
299	339	310	352
300	340	311	353
301	341	—	353(1.1) [en. 1997, c. 18, s. 22(1)]
301.1	342	—	353(2.1) [en. 1997, c. 18, s. 22(2)]
—	342(3) [en. 1997, c. 18, s. 16(2)]	—	353.1 [en. 2010, c. 14, s. 4]
—	342(4) [en. 1997, c. 18, s. 16(2)]	312	354
—	342.01 [en. 1997, c. 18, s. 17]	—	354(4) [en. 1997, c. 18, s. 23]
301.2	342.1	313	355
—	342.1(1)(*d*) [en. 1997, c. 18, s. 18(1)]	—	355.1 [en. 2010, c. 14, s. 5]
—	342.1(2) "computer data" [en. 2014, c. 31, s. 16(4)]	—	355.2 [en. 2010, c. 14, s. 5]
—	342.1(2) "computer password" [en. 1997, c. 18, s. 18(2)]	—	355.3 [en. 2010, c. 14, s. 5]
—	342.1(2) "traffic" [en. 1997, c. 18, s. 18(2)]	—	355.4 [en. 2010, c. 14, s. 5]
—	342.2 [en. 1997, c. 18, s. 19]	—	355.5 [en. 2010, c. 14, s. 5]
—	342.2(4) [en. 2014, c. 31, s. 17(2)]	314	356
302	343	315	357
303	344	316	358
304	345	317	359 [rep. 2018, c. 29, s. 40]
305	346	318	360 [rep. 2018, c. 29, s. 40]
305.1	347	319	361
—	347.1 [en. 2007, c. 9, s. 2]	320	362
		321	363
		322	364
		323	365 [rep. 2018, c. 29, s. 41]

CONC.

R.S.C. 1970, c. C-34	R.S.C. 1985, c. C-46	R.S.C. 1970, c. C-34	R.S.C. 1985, c. C-46
324	366	—	380.3 [en. 2011, c. 6, s. 4; rep. 2015, c. 13, s. 11]
—	366(5) [en. 2009, c. 28, s. 7]		
325	367	—	380.4 [en. 2011, c. 6, s. 4; rep. 2015, c. 13, s. 11]
—	367(2) [rep. 1994, c. 44, s. 24]		
326	368	339	381
—	368(1)(c) [en. 1997, c. 18, s. 25]	340	382
		341	383
—	368(1)(d) [en. 1997, c. 18, s. 25]	342	384
		343	385
—	368(1.1) [en. 2009, c. 28, s. 8]	344	386
		345	387
—	368.1 [en. 2009, c. 28, s. 9]	346	388
		347	389
—	368.2 [en. 2009, c. 28, s. 9]	348	390
		349	391
327	369	350	392
328	370 [rep. 2018, c. 29, s. 42]	351	393
		352	394
329	371 [rep. 2018, c. 29, s. 42	—	394.1 [en. 1999, c. 5, s. 10]
330	372	353	395
331	373 [rep. R.S.C. 1985, c. 27 (1st Supp.), s. 53]	—	395(1.1) [en. 2019, c. 25, s. 152]
		354	396
332	374	355	397
333	375	356	398
334	376	357	399
335	377	358	400
336	378	359	401
Part VIII	Part X	360	402 [rep. 2018, c. 29, s. 44]
337	379		
338	380	—	402.1 [en. 2009, c. 28, s. 10]
—	380(1.1) [en. 2011, c. 6, s. 2]	—	402.2 [en. 2009, c. 28, s. 10]
—	380.1 [en. 2004, c. 3, s. 3]	361	403
—	380.01(1.1) [en. 2011, c. 6, s. 3(5)]	362	404 [rep. 2018, c. 29, s. 46
—	380.2 [en. 2011, c. 6, s. 4]	363	405
		364	406
		365	407

R.S.C. 1970, c. C-34	R.S.C. 1985, c. C-46	R.S.C. 1970, c. C-34	R.S.C. 1985, c. C-46
366	408	—	431.2 [en. 2001, c. 41, s. 13]
367	409		
368	410	388	432 [rep. R.S.C. 1985, c. 27 (1st Supp.), s. 58]
369	411		
370	412		
371	413 [rep. 2018, c. 29, s. 47]	389	433
		390	434
372	414	—	434.1 [en. 1990, c. 15, s. 1]
373	415		
374	416	391	435
375	417	392	436
376	418	—	436.1 [en. 1990, c. 15, s. 1]
377	419		
378	420	393	437
379	421	394	438
380	422	395	439
381	423	396	440
—	423.1 [en. 2001, c. 32, s. 11]	397	441
		398	442
—	423.1(2) [rep. 2015, c. 13, s. 12(2)]	399	443
381.1	424	400	444 [rep. 2018, c. 29, s. 52]
—	424.1 [en. 2001, c. 41, s. 11]	401	445
		—	445.01 [en. 2015, c. 34, s. 3]
382	425	—	445.1 [en. 2008, c. 12, s. 1]
383	426		
384	427 [(and heading) rep. 2018, c. 29, s. 50]	—	445.2 [en. 2019, c. 11, s. 2]
		402	446
Part IX	Part XI	403	447
385	428	—	447(3) [rep. 2019, c. 17, s. 3(2)]
386	429		
387	430	—	447.1 [en. 2008, c. 12, s. 1]
—	430(4.1) [en. 2001, c. 41, s. 12]	404 and 405	repealed
		Part X	Part XII
—	430(4.11) [en. 2014, c. 9, s. 1]	406	448
—	430(4.2) [en. 2005, c. 40, s. 3]	407	449
		408	450
387.1	431	409	451
—	431.1 [en. 2001, c. 41, s. 13]	410	452
		411	453

CONC.

R.S.C. 1970, c. C-34	R.S.C. 1985, c. C-46	R.S.C. 1970, c. C-34	R.S.C. 1985, c. C-46
—	462.38(2.1) [en. 2001, c. 32, s. 20(3)]	Part XII	Part XIV
		426	468
		427	469
420.19	462.39	428	470
420.2	462.4	429	471
420.21	462.41	429.1	472 [rep. R.S.C. 1985, c. 27 (1st Supp.), s. 63]
420.22	462.42		
420.23	462.43		
—	462.43(2) [en. 2001, c. 32, s. 24]	430	473
		431	474
420.24	462.44	431.1	475
420.25	462.45	432	476
420.26	462.46	433	477
420.27	462.47	—	477.1 [rep. 1996, c. 31, s. 8]
420.28	462.48		
—	462.48(1)(a.1) [en. 2018, c. 16, s. 215]	—	477.2 [en. 1990, c. 44, s. 15]
—	462.48(1)(c) [en. 1997, c. 23, s. 10]	—	477.3 [en. 1990, c. 44, s. 15]
420.29	462.49	—	477.4 [en. 1990, c. 44, s. 15]
420.3	462.5	434	478
Part XI	Part XIII	435	479
421	463	436	480
422	464	437	481
423	465	—	481.1 [en. 1996, c. 31, s. 72]
423(1)(c)	repealed		
423(1)(d)	465(1)(c)	—	481.2 [en. 1996, c. 31, s. 72]
423(1)(e)	465(1)(d)		
423(2)	465(2) [rep. R.S.C. 1985, c. 27 (1st Supp.), s. 61(3)]	—	481.3 [en. 1996, c. 31, s. 72]
		438	482
424	466	438(1.1)	482(2)
425	467	438(2)	482(3)
—	467.1 [en. 1997, c. 23, s. 11]	438(3)	not consolidated
		438(4)	482(4)
—	467.11 to 467.14 [en. 2001, c. 32, s. 27]	438(5)	482(5)
—	467.111 [en. 2014, c. 17, s. 9]	—	482.1 [en. 2002, c. 13, s. 18]
—	467.2 [en. 1997, c. 23, s. 11; rep. 2019, c. 25, s. 185]	—	482.1(6) [rep. 2019, c. 25, s. 187(2)]
		Part XIII	Part XV
		439	483

R.S.C. 1970, c. C-34	R.S.C. 1985, c. C-46	R.S.C. 1970, c. C-34	R.S.C. 1985, c. C-46
440	484	—	487.01(5.2) [en. 1997, c. 23, s. 13]
440.1	485	—	487.01(7) [en. 1997, c. 18, s. 49(2)]
—	485(1.1) [en. 1997, c. 18, s. 40]	—	487.018 to 487.0199 [en. 2014, c. 31, s. 20]
440.2	485.1	—	487.02 [en. 1993, c. 40, s. 15]
441	repealed	—	487.021 [en. 2014, c. 31, s. 20]
442	486	—	487.03 [en. 1993, c. 40, s. 15; rep. 2019, c. 25, s. 196]
—	486(1.5) [en. 2001, c. 32, s. 29(1)]	—	487.04 [en. 1995, c. 27, s. 1]
442(2.1)	486(2.1)	—	487.04 "secondary designated offence" (*a*.1) [en. 2018, c. 16, s. 216]
442(2.2)	486(2.2)		
442(3)	486(3)	—	487.04 "secondary designated offence" (*c*)(iv) [rep. 2018, c. 21, s. 18(1)]
442(3.1) [re-en. 1987, c. 24, s. 14(1)]; 1988, c. 30, s. 1	486(4)		
		—	487.04 "secondary designated offence" (*c*)(viii.2) [en. 2018, c. 21, s. 18(2)]
442(4)	486(5)		
442(5)	486(6) [rep. R.S.C. 1985, c. 19 (3rd Supp.), s. 14(2)]	—	487.04 "secondary designated offence" (*d*.1), (*d*.2) [en. 2018, c. 21, s. 18(3)]
—	486.1 to 486.6 [en. 2005, c. 32, s. 15]		
—	486.2(7) and (8) [rep. 2015, c. 13, s. 15]	—	487.05(3) [en. 1997, c. 18, s. 44]
—	486.31 [en. 2015, c. 13, s. 17]	—	487.051 to 487.058 [en. 1998, c. 37, s. 17]
—	486.5(2.1) [en. 2015, c. 13, s. 19(1)]	—	487.06 to 487.09 [en. 1995, c. 27, s. 1]
—	486.7 [en. 2015, c. 20, s. 22]	—	487.071 [en. 1998, c. 7, s. 20]
443	487		
—	487(1)(*c*.1) [en. 1997, c. 23, s. 12]		
—	487(2.1) [en. 1997, c. 18, s. 40]		
—	487(2.2) [en. 1997, c. 18, s. 40]		
—	487.01 [en. 1993, c. 40, s. 15]		
—	487.01(5.1) [en. 1997, c. 23, s. 13]		

R.S.C. 1970, c. C-34	R.S.C. 1985, c. C-46	R.S.C. 1970, c. C-34	R.S.C. 1985, c. C-46
—	487.091 [en. 1998, c. 37, s. 23]	—	490.02901 to 490.02915 [en. 2010, c. 17, s. 19]
—	487.092 [en. 1997, c. 18, s. 45; renum. 1998, c. 37, s. 23]	—	490.03111 [en. 2007, c. 5, s. 29]
443.1	487.1	—	490.0312 [en. 2010, c. 17, s. 23]
—	487.11 [en. 1997, c. 18, s. 46]	—	490.1 to 490.9 [en. 1997, c. 23, s. 15]
443.2	487.2	—	490.2(4.1) [en. 2001, c. 32, s. 31(4)]
—	487.2(2) [rep. 2005, c. 32, s. 16(2)]	—	490.41 [en. 2001, c. 32, s. 33]
—	487.3 [en. 1997, c. 23, s. 14]	—	490.8(3.1) [en. 2001, c. 32, s. 35(2)]
444	488	—	490.81 [en. 2001, c. 32, s. 36]
—	488.01 [en. 2017, c. 22, s. 3]	446.1	491
—	488.02 [en. 2017, c. 22, s. 3]	446.2	491.1
444.1	488.1	446.3	491.2
445	489	447	492
445.1	489.1	—	492.1 [en. 1993, c. 40, s. 18]
446	490	—	492.1(5) [en. 1999, c. 5, s. 18(2)]
—	490(1.1) [en. 2001, c. 41, s. 18; rep. 2001, c. 41, s. 130(7.1)]	—	492.1(6.1) [en. 2019, c. 25, s. 207]
—	490(3.1) [en. 1997, c. 18, s. 50(1)]	—	492.2 [en. 1993, c. 40, s. 18]
—	490(18) [en. 1997, c. 18, s. 50(4)]	—	492.2(5.1) [en. 2019, c. 25, s. 208]
—	490.01 [en. 1997, c. 18, s. 5; am. 1999, c. 5, s. 17]	Part XIV	Part XVI
—	490.011 to 490.032 [en. 2004, c. 10, c. 20]	448	493
—	490.016(3) [en. 2007, c. 5, s. 16(2)]	—	493 "appearance notice", "officer in charge", "promise to appear", "recognizance", "summons", and "undertaking" [rep. 2019, c. 25, s. 209(1)]
—	490.017(2) [en. 2007, c. 5, s. 17]		
—	490.023(1.1) [en. 2007, c. 5, s. 23]		
—	490.027(3) [en. 2007, c. 5, s. 25(2)]	—	493.1 [en. 2019, c. 25, s. 210]

CONC.

R.S.C. 1970, c. C-34	R.S.C. 1985, c. C-46	R.S.C. 1970, c. C-34	R.S.C. 1985, c. C-46
—	493.2 [en. 2019, c. 25, s. 210]	455.5	509
		455.6	510 [rep. 2019, c. 25, s. 222]
449	494		
—	494(4) [en. 2012, c. 9, s. 3(2)]	456	511
		—	511(3) [en. 1997, c. 18, s. 57]
450	495		
—	495.1 [en. 2019, c. 25, s. 211]	—	511(4) [en. 1997, c. 18, s. 57]
451	496	456.1	512
452	497	—	512.1 [en. 2019, c. 25, s. 224]
453	498		
453.1	499	—	512.2 [en. 2019, c. 25, s. 224]
—	499(2)(e) to (g) [en. 1997, c. 18, s. 53(1)]	—	512.3 [en. 2019, c. 25, s. 224]
		456.2	513
—	499(4) [en. 1997, c. 18, s. 53(2)]	456.3	514
		457	515
453.2	500 [rep. 1999, c. 25, s. 6]	457(2)(c.1)	515(2)(d)
		457(2)(d)	515(2)(e)
453.3	501	457(2.1)	515(2.1)
453.4	502	457(3)	515(3)
—	502.1 [en. 2019, c. 25, s. 216]	457(4)	515(4)
		—	515(4.1)(b.1) [en. 2001, c. 32, s. 37(1)]
454	503		
454(1.1)	503(2)	—	515(4.1)(b.2) [en. 2018, c. 16, s. 218]
—	503(2.1)(e) to (g) [en. 1997, c. 18, s. 55(1)]	—	515(4.3) [en. 2001, c. 41, s. 19(3)]
—	503(2.3) [en. 1997, c. 18, s. 55(2)]	457(5)	515(5)
454(2)	503(3)	457(5.1)	515(6)
454(2.1)	503(3.1)	457(5.2)	515(7)
454(3)	503(4)	457(5.3)	515(8)
454(4)	503(5)	457(6)	515(9)
455	504	—	515(9.1) [en. 2009, c. 29, s. 2]
455.1	505		
455.2	506	457(7)	515(10)
455.3	507	457(8)	515(11)
—	507.1 [en. 2002, c. 13, s. 22]	—	515(13) and (14) [en. 2015, c. 13, s. 20]
455.4	508		
—	508.1 [en. 1997, c. 18, s. 56]		

R.S.C. 1970, c. C-34	R.S.C. 1985, c. C-46	R.S.C. 1970, c. C-34	R.S.C. 1985, c. C-46
—	515.1 [en. 1997, c. 18, s. 60]	—	529 to 529.5 [en. 1997, c. 39, s. 2]
457.1	516	Part XIV.1	Part XVII
—	516(2) [en. 1999, c. 5, s. 22]	462.1	530
—	516(3) [en. 2019, c. 25, s. 227]	—	530.01 [en. 2008, c. 18, s. 19]
457.2	517	462.11	530.1
—	517(3) [rep. 2005, c. 32, s. 17(2)]	—	530.2 [en. 2008, c. 18, s. 21]
457.3	518	462.2	531
457.4	519	462.3	532
—	519.1 [en. 2019, c. 25, s. 230]	462.4	533
457.5	520	—	534 [rep. 1997, c. 18, s. 63]
457.6	521	Part XV	Part XVIII
457.7	522	463	535
457.7(2.1)	522(3)	464	536
457.7(2.2)	522(4)	—	536.1 [en. 1999, c. 3, s. 35]
457.7(3)	522(5)	—	536.2 [en. 2002, c. 13, s. 27]
457.7(4)	522(6)	—	536.3 [en. 2002, c. 13, s. 27]
457.8	523	—	536.4 [en. 2002, c. 13, s. 27]
—	523(1.2) [en. 2011, c. 16, s. 2(1)]	—	536.5 [en. 2002, c. 13, s. 27]
—	523.1 (and heading) [en. 2019, c. 25, s. 234]	465	537
458	524	465(1)(a)	repealed
458(4.1)	524(5)	465(1)(b)	537(1)(a)
458(4.2)	524(6)	465(1)(c)	537(1)(b)
458(4.3)	524(7)	465(1)(d)	537(1)(c)
458(5)	524(8)	465(1)(e)	537(1)(d)
458(5.1)	524(9)	465(1)(f)	537(1)(e)
458(6)	524(10)	465(1)(g)	repealed
458(7)	524(11)	465(1)(h)	537(1)(f)
458(8)	524(12)	465(1)(i)	537(1)(g)
458(9)	524(13)	465(1)(j)	537(1)(h)
459	525	465(1)(k)	537(1)(i)
459.1	526	—	537(1)(j.1) [en. 2002, c. 13, s. 28]
460	527		
461	528	—	537(1)(k) [en. 1997, c. 18, s. 64(1)]
462	529 [rep. 1994, c. 44, s. 52]		

R.S.C. 1970, c. C-34	R.S.C. 1985, c. C-46	R.S.C. 1970, c. C-34	R.S.C. 1985, c. C-46
—	537(1.1) [en. 2002, c. 13, s. 28]	482 "judge"	552 "judge"
—	537(2) [en. 1997, c. 18, s. 64(2)] [*new provision*]	482(b)	552(b)
		482(c.1)	552(d)
		482(d)	552(g)
		482(e)	552(e)
466	538	482(f)	552(h)
467	539	482(g)	552(f)
—	539(4) [rep. 2005, c. 32, s. 18(2)]	482(h)	552(i)
468	540	482 "magistrate"	552 "magistrate" [rep. R.S.C. 1985, c. 27 (1st Supp.), s. 103(2)]
469	541		
470	542		
—	542(3) [rep. 2005, c. 32, s. 19(2)]	483	553
471	543	—	553(c)(viii.1) [en. 1997, c. 18, s. 66]
471.1	544	—	553(c)(x) [en. 1997, c. 19, s. 72]
472	545	—	553(c)(xi) [en. 1997, c. 19, c. 72; rep. 2018, c. 16, s. 219]
473	546		
474	547		
474.1	547.1		
475	548	484	554
476	549	484(2)-(4)	554(2)-(4) [rep. R.S.C. 1985, c. 27 (1st Supp.), s. 105]
477	550		
478	551	—	554(2) [en. 1999, c. 3, s. 38]
479 — 481	repealed	485	555
—	Part XVIII.1 [en. 2011, c. 16, s. 4]	—	555.1 [en. 1999, c. 3, s. 39]
—	551.1 [en. 2011, c. 16, s. 4]	486	556
—	551.2 [en. 2011, c. 16, s. 4]	487	557
		488	558
—	551.3 [en. 2011, c. 16, s. 4]	489	559
—	551.4 [en. 2011, c. 16, s. 4]	490	560
—	551.5 [en. 2011, c. 16, s. 4]	490(5)	560(5) [rep. R.S.C. 1985, c. 27 (1st Supp.), s. 109(2)]
—	551.6 [en. 2011, c. 16, s. 4]		
—	551.7 [en. 2011, c. 16, s. 4]	491	561
		—	561.1 [en. 1999, c. 3, s. 43]
Part XVI	Part XIX	492	562
482	552	—	562.1 [en. 1999, c. 3, s. 44]

R.S.C. 1970, c. C-34	R.S.C. 1985, c. C-46	R.S.C. 1970, c. C-34	R.S.C. 1985, c. C-46
493	563	—	579.001 [en. 2017, c. 27, s. 62]
—	563.1 [en. 1999, c. 3, s. 45]	—	579.01 [en. 2002, c. 13, s. 47]
494	564 [rep. R.S.C. 1985, c. 27 (1st Supp.), s. 110]	—	579.1 [en. 1994, c. 44, s. 60]
495	565	509	580
—	565(1.1) [en. 1999, c. 3, s. 46]	510	581
496	566	511	582
—	566.1 [en. 1999, c. 3, s. 47]	512	583
497	567	513	584
—	567.1 [en. 1999, c. 3, s. 48]	514	585
498	568	515	586
499	569 [rep. R.S.C. 1985, c. 27 (1st Supp.), s. 111]	516	587
		517	588
		518	589
		519	590
—	569 [en. 1999, c. 3, s. 49]	520	591
		—	591(4.1) [en. 2011, c. 16, s. 5]
500	570	521	592
501	571	522	593
502	572	523-525	594-596 [rep. R.S.C. 1985, c. 27 (1st Supp.), s. 120]
503	573 [rep. R.S.C. 1985, c. 27 (1st Supp.), s. 113]	526	597
—	Part XIX.1	—	597(4) [en. 1997, c. 18, s. 68]
—	573 [en. 1999, c. 3, s. 50]	—	597(5) [en. 1997, c. 18, s. 68]
—	573.1 [en. 1999, c. 3, s. 50]	526.1	598
		527	599
—	573.2 [en. 1999, c. 3, s. 50]	527(1.1)	599(2) [rep. R.S.C. 1985, c. 1 (4th Supp.), s. 16]
Part XVII	Part XX		
504	574	527(2)	599(3)
505	575 [rep. R.S.C. 1985, c. 27 (1st Supp.), s. 113]	527(3)	599(4)
		527(4)	599(5)
506	576	528	600
507	577	529	601
507.1	578	530	602
508	579	531	603

CONC.

R.S.C. 1970, c. C-34	R.S.C. 1985, c. C-46
532	604 [rep. 1997, c. 18, s. 69]
533	605
534	606
—	606(1.1), (1.2) and (5) [en. 2002, c. 13, s. 49(1)]
—	606(4.1), (4.2), (4.3) and (4.4) [en. 2015, c. 13, s. 21]
535	607
535(6)	607(6)
536	608
537	609
538	610
539	611
540	612
541	613
542	614
543	615
543(2.1)	615(3)
543(3)	615(4)
543(4)	615(5)
543(5)	615(6)
543(6)	615(7)
543(7)	615(8)
543(8)	615(9)
544	616
545	617
546	618
547	619
548	620
549	621
550	622
551	623
552	624
553	625
553.1	625.1
554	626
—	626.1 [en. 2002, c. 13, s. 51]
555	627 [en. 1998, c. 9, s. 4]

R.S.C. 1970, c. C-34	R.S.C. 1985, c. C-46
556	repealed
557 [rep. 1985, c. 19, s. 129]	628 [rep. R.S.C. 1985, c. 27 (1st Supp.) s. 129]
558	629
559	630
560	631
—	631(2.2) [en. 2011, c. 16, s. 7]
561	632
562	633
563	634 [rep. 2019, c. 25, s. 269]
564	635
565	636 [rep. 1992, c. 41, s. 2]
566	637 [rep. 1992, c. 41, s. 2]
567	638
—	638(3) and (4) [rep. 1997, c. 18, s. 74]
568	639
569	640
570	641
571	642
—	642.1 [en. 2002, c. 13, s. 57]
572	643
—	643(1.1) [en. 2002, c. 13, s. 58]
573	644
—	644(1.1) [en. 1997, c. 18, s. 75]
—	644(3) [en. 2019, c. 25, s. 273]
574	645
575	646
576	647
576.1	648
—	648(3) [rep. 2005, c. 32, s. 21(2)]
576.2	649
577	650

R.S.C. 1970, c. C-34	R.S.C. 1985, c. C-46	R.S.C. 1970, c. C-34	R.S.C. 1985, c. C-46
—	650(1.2) [en. 1997, c. 18, s. 77]	594(3.1)	667(4)
		594(4)	667(5)
—	650.01 [en. 2002, c. 13, s. 61]	595	668 [rep. 1995, c. 22, s. 4]
—	650.02 [en. 2002, c. 13, s. 61]	596	669 [rep. 1995, c. 22, s. 4]
—	650.1 [en. 1997, c. 18, s. 78]	597	669.1
		597.1	669.2
578	651	—	669.3 [en. 1994, c. 44, s. 66]
579	652	598	670
—	652.1 [en. 2011, c. 16, s. 13]	599	671
580	653	600	672
—	653.1 [en. 2011, c. 16, s. 14]	—	Part XX.1
581	654	—	672.1-672.95 [en. 1991, c. 43, s. 4]
582	655		672.1(2) [en. 2005, c. 22, s. 1(3)]
583	656	—	672.121 [en. 2005, c. 22, s. 3]
584	657	—	672.16(1.1) and (1.2) [en. 2005, c. 22, s. 7(2)]
584.1	657.1		
—	657.1(2)(c.1) [en. 1997, c. 18, s. 79]	—	672.191 [en. 1997, c. 18, s. 81]
—	657.2 [en. 1997, c. 18, s. 80]	—	672.21(3)(c) [rep. 2005, c. 22, s. 12]
—	657.3 [en. 1997, c. 18, s. 80]	—	672.24(2) and (3) [en. 1997, c. 18, s. 82]
—	657.3(3) to (7) [en. 2002, c. 13, s. 62]		
585	658	—	672.33(1.1) [en. 2005, c. 22, s. 13]
586	659 [rep. R.S.C. 1985, c. 19 (3rd Supp.), s. 15]	—	672.38(3) [en. 1997, c. 18, s. 83]
—	659 [en. 1993, c. 45, s. 9]	—	672.45(1.1) [en. 2005, c. 22, s. 14]
587	660	—	672.47(4) and (5) [en. 2014, c. 6, s. 6(2)]
588	661		
589	662	—	672.5(5.1) [en. 2005, c. 22, s. 16(1)]
590	663		
591	664	—	672.5(5.2) [en. 2014, c. 6, s. 7(2)]
592	665 [rep. 1995, c. 22, s. 3]		
593	666		
594	667		

CONC.

R.S.C. 1970, c. C-34	R.S.C. 1985, c. C-46	R.S.C. 1970, c. C-34	R.S.C. 1985, c. C-46
—	672.5(8.1) and (8.2) [en. 1997, c. 18, s. 84(1)]	—	672.851 [en. 2005, c. 22, s. 33]
—	672.5(13) [en. 1997, c. 18, s. 84(2)]	—	672.852 [en. 2005, c. 22, s. 33]
—	672.5(13.1) and (13.2) [en. 2005, c. 22, s. 16(2)]	Part XVIII	Part XXI
—	672.5(13.3) [en. 2014, c. 6, s. 7(3)]	601	673
—	672.5(15.1), (15.2) and (15.3) [en. 2005, c. 22, s. 16(3)]	—	673 "sentence" (d) [en. 1996, c. 19, s. 74]
—	672.501 [en. 2005, c. 22, s. 17]	—	673 "sentence" (e) [en. 2018, c. 16, s. 220]
—	672.54 [en. 1999, c. 25, s. 12]	602	674
—	672.5401 [en. 2014, c. 6, s. 10]	603	675
—	672.541 [en. 2014, c. 6, s. 10]	—	675(1.1) [en. 1997, c. 18, s. 92(1)]
—	672.542 [en. 2014, c. 6, s. 10]	603(1.1)	675(2)
—	672.55(2) [rep. 2005, c. 22, s. 22]	—	675(2.1) [en. 1997, c. 18, s. 92(2)]
—	672.56(1.1) [en. 2014, c. 6, s. 11(2)]	—	675(2.3) [en. 2011, c. 5, s. 2]
—	672.64-672.66 and heading [rep. 2005, c. 22, s. 24]	603(2)	675(3)
—	672.64 [re-en. 2014, c. 6, s. 12]	603(3)	675(4)
—	672.79 [rep. 2005, c. 22, s. 26]	604	repealed
—	672.8 [rep. 2005, c. 22, s. 25]	605	676
—	672.83(2) [rep. 2005, c. 22, s. 29]	—	676(1.1) [en. 1997, c. 18, s. 93(2)]
—	672.84 [rep. 2005, c. 22, s. 30; re-en. 2014, c. 6, s. 16]	—	676(6) [en. 2011, c. 5, s. 3]
—	Schedule to Part XXI [rep. 2005, c. 22, s. 37]	—	676.1 [en. 1997, c. 18, s. 94]
		606	677
		607	678
		607.1	678.1
		608	679
		—	679(7.1) [en. 1997, c. 18, s. 95]
		608.1	680
		608.2	681
		609	682
		610	683

R.S.C. 1970, c. C-34	R.S.C. 1985, c. C-46	R.S.C. 1970, c. C-34	R.S.C. 1985, c. C-46
—	683(2.1) and (2.2) [en. 2002, c. 13, s. 68]	628	700
—	683(2.3) [en. 2019, c. 25, s. 281(2)]	—	700.1 [en. 1999, c. 18, s. 94]
—	683(5)(e) [en. 1997, c. 18, s. 97(2)]	629	701
—	683(5.1) [en. 2008, c. 18, s. 29(1)]	—	701.1 [en. 1997, c. 18, s. 100]
—	683(7) [en. 2008, c. 18, s. 29(2)]	630	702
611	684	631	703
612	685	631.1	703.1
613	686	631.2	703.2
—	686(5.1) [en. 1997, c. 18, s. 98]	632	704
		633	705
614	687	634	706
615	688	635	707
—	688(2.1) [en. 2002, c. 13, s. 68]	636	708
		—	708.1 [en. 1997, c. 18, s. 101]
616	689	637	709
617	690 [rep. 2002, c. 13, s. 70]	638	710
618	691	639	711
619	repealed	640	712
620	692	640(3)	712(3) [rep. R.S.C. 1985, c. 27 (1st Supp.), s. 153(2)]
621	693		
622	694		
622.1	694.1	641	713
622.2	694.2	—	713.1 [en. 1994, c. 44, s. 76]
623	695		
—	695(2) [rep. 1999, c. 3, s. 27]	642	714
		—	714.1 [en. 1999, c. 18, s. 95]
624	696	—	714.2 [en. 1999, c. 18, s. 95]
—	Part XXI.1 [en. 2002, c. 13, s. 71]	—	714.3 [en. 1999, c. 18, s. 95]
		—	714.4 [en. 1999, c. 18, s. 95]
625	697		
626	698	—	714.5 [en. 1999, c. 18, s. 95]
627	699	—	714.6 [en. 1999, c. 18, s. 95]
—	699(5.1) [en. 1997, c. 30, s. 2]	—	714.7 [en. 1999, c. 18, s. 95]
—	699(7) [en. 1997, c. 30, s. 2]		

R.S.C. 1970, c. C-34	R.S.C. 1985, c. C-46
—	714.8 [en. 1999, c. 18, s. 95]
643	715
—	715.01 [en. 2019, c. 25, s. 291]
643.1	715.1
—	715.2 [en. 1998, c. 9, s. 8]
	Part XXII.01 [en. 2019, c. 25, s. 292]
—	715.21 [en. 2019, c. 25, s. 292]
—	715.22 [en. 2019, c. 25, s. 292]
—	715.23 [en. 2019, c. 25, s. 292]
—	715.24 [en. 2019, c. 25, s. 292]
—	715.25 [en. 2019, c. 25, s. 292]
—	715.26 [en. 2019, c. 25, s. 292]
	Part XXII.1 [en. 2018, c. 12, s. 404]
—	715.3 [en. 2018, c. 12, s. 404]
—	715.31 [en. 2018, c. 12, s. 404]
—	715.32 [en. 2018, c. 12, s. 404]
—	715.33 [en. 2018, c. 12, s. 404]
—	715.34 [en. 2018, c. 12, s. 404]
—	715.35 [en. 2018, c. 12, s. 404]
—	715.36 [en. 2018, c. 12, s. 404]
—	715.37 [en. 2018, c. 12, s. 404]
—	715.38 [en. 2018, c. 12, s. 404]
—	715.39 [en. 2018, c. 12, s. 404]

R.S.C. 1970, c. C-34	R.S.C. 1985, c. C-46
—	715.4 [en. 2018, c. 12, s. 404]
—	715.41 [en. 2018, c. 12, s. 404]
—	715.42 [en. 2018, c. 12, s. 404]
—	715.43 [en. 2018, c. 12, s. 404]
Part XX	**Part XXIII**
ss. 644 to 686	ss. 716 to 751.1, as amended. *Please note: this Part was replaced as a whole by 1995, c. 22, s. 6. For in force information, see the list of amendments to the Code starting on page CC/1.
—	718.01 [en. 2005, c. 32, s. 24]
—	718.02 [en. 2009, c. 22, s. 18]
—	718.03 [en. 2015, c. 34, s. 4]
—	718.04 [en. 2019, c. 25, s. 292.1]
—	718.201 [en. 2019, c. 25, s. 293.1]
—	718.3(5), (6) and (7) [en. 2015, c. 23, s. 17]
—	718.3(8) [en. 2019, c. 25, s. 294]
—	720(2) [en. 2008, c. 18, s. 35]
—	722.1 [rep. 1999, c. 25, s. 18]
—	722.2 [en. 1999, c. 25, s. 18]
—	722.2(3), (4) and (5) [en. 2015, c. 13, s. 26]

R.S.C. 1970, c. C-34	R.S.C. 1985, c. C-46	R.S.C. 1970, c. C-34	R.S.C. 1985, c. C-46
—	729.1 [en. 2011, c. 7, s. 2]	—	745.2
—	731(3.1) [en. 1997, c. 17, s. 1]	—	745.21 [en. 2011, c. 5, s. 4]
—	732(6) [en. 2008, c. 18, s. 37]	—	745.3
—	732.1 [en. 1995, c. 22, s. 6]	—	745.4
—	732.1(2.1), (2.2) [en. 2014, c. 21, s. 2]	—	745.5
—	732.1(7)-(12) [en. 2011, c. 7, s. 3(2)]	—	745.51 [en. 2011, c. 5, s. 5]
—	732.11 [en. 2011, c. 7, s. 4]	—	745.6
—	737	—	745.6 (2.1) to (2.8) [en. 2011, c. 2, s. 3]
—	737.1 [en. 2015, c. 13, s. 29]	—	745.61
—	738(1)(d) [en. 2009, c. 28, s. 11]	—	745.62
—	739.1 [en. 2015, c. 13, s. 30]	—	745.63
—	742.3(1.1), (1.2), (1.3) [en. 2014, c. 21, s. 3; rep. 2019, c. 25, s. 303(1)]	—	745.64
—	742.3(4) [en. 2008, c. 18, s. 40]	—	745.64(1.1) [en. 2019, c. 25, s. 306]
—	742.3(5)-(10) [en. 2011, c. 7, s. 5(2)]	Part XXI	Part XXIV
—	742.31 [en. 2011, c. 7, s. 6]	—	747 to 747.8 and heading [rep. 2005, c. 22, s. 39]
—	743.21 [en. 2008, c. 28, s. 42]	687	752
—	743.4 [rep. 2002, c. 1, s. 184]	—	752 "designated offence" [en. 2008, c. 6, ss. 40, 61]
—	743.6(1.1) [en. 1997, c. 23, s. 18]	—	752 "long-term supervision" [en. 2008, c. 6, s. 40]
—	743.6(1.2) [en. 2001, c. 41, s. 21]	—	752 "primary designated offence" [en. 2008, c. 6, s. 40]
—	745.1	—	752.01 [en. 2008, c. 6, s. 41]
—	745.01 [en. 1999, c. 25, s. 21]	—	752.1 [en. 1997, c. 17, s. 4]
—	745.01(2) [en. 2011, c. 2, s. 2]	688	753
		—	753(1.1) [en. 2008, c. 6, s. 42(2)]
		—	753(4.1) [en. 1997, c. 17, s. 4]
		—	753(4.2) [en. 2008, c. 6, s. 42(4)]

R.S.C. 1970, c. C-34	R.S.C. 1985, c. C-46	R.S.C. 1970, c. C-34	R.S.C. 1985, c. C-46
747(c)	812(1)(c)	770	838
747(d)	812(1)(b)	771	839
747(e)	812(1)(a)	—	839(1.1) [en. 1999, c. 3, s. 57]
747(f)	812(1)(d)		
747(g)	repealed	772	840
747(h)	812(1)(e) [rep. 1992, c. 51, s. 43(2)]	Part XXV	Part XXVIII [replaced 2002, c. 13, s. 84]
747(i)	812(1)(h)		
—	812(1)(i) [en. 1999, c. 3, s. 55]	773	841 [replaced 2002, c. 13, s. 84]
—	812(2) [en. 1999, c. 3, s. 55]	773(3)	841(3)
		—	842 to 849 [en. 2002, c. 13, s. 84]
748	813	Forms 1 and 2	Forms 1 and 2
749	814	Form 3	Form 3 [rep. R.S.C. 1985, c. 27 (1st Supp.), s. 184(2)]
750	815		
751	repealed		
752	816	Forms 4 to 5.2	Forms 4 to 5.2
752.1	817	—	Forms 5.01 to 5.09 [en. 1998, c. 37, s. 24]
—	817(4) [rep. 2019, c. 25, s. 324(2)]		
752.2	818	—	Forms 5.001 to 5.0091 [en. 2014, c. 31, s. 26]
752.3	819		
753	820	—	Form 5.041 [en. 2005, c. 25, s. 12; 2007, c. 22, s. 23]
754	821		
755	822		
755.1	823	—	Form 5.061 [en. 2005, c. 25, s. 12; 2007, c. 22, s. 23]
756	824		
757	825		
758	826	Form 5.3	Form 5.3
759	827	Forms 6 and 7	Forms 6 and 7
760	828	Form 8	Form 7.1 [en. 1997, c. 39, s. 3]
761	829		
—	829(2) [en. 1999, c. 3, s. 56]		Form 8
762	830	Form 8.1	Form 9
763	831	Form 8.2	Form 10
764	832	Form 8.3	Form 11
765	833	—	Form 11.1 [en. 1994, c. 44, s. 84]
766	834		
767	835	Form 9	Form 12
768	836	Form 9.1	Form 13 [rep. 2019, c. 25, s. 337]
769	837		

R.S.C. 1970, c. C-34	R.S.C. 1985, c. C-46
Form 9.2	Form 14 [rep. 2019, c. 25, s. 337]
Form 10	Form 15
Form 11	Form 16
—	Form 16.1 [en. 1997, c. 30, s. 3]
Form 12	Form 17
Form 13	Form 18
Form 14	Form 19
Form 15	repealed
Form 16	Form 20
Form 17	repealed
Form 18	Form 21
Form 19	Form 22
Form 20	Form 23
Form 21	Form 24
Form 22	Form 25
Form 23	Form 26
Form 24	Form 27
Form 25	Form 28
—	Form 28.1 [en. 2000, c. 10, s. 24; rep. 2007, c. 22, s. 26]
Form 25.1	Form 29
Form 26	Form 30
Form 27	Form 31
Form 28	Form 32
Form 29	Form 33
Form 30	Form 34
—	Form 34.1 [en. 2011, c. 6, s. 5]
—	Form 34.2 [en. 2015, c. 13, s. 35]
—	Form 34.3 [en. 2015, c. 13, s. 35]

R.S.C. 1970, c. C-34	R.S.C. 1985, c. C-46
Form 31	Form 35
Form 32	Form 36
Form 33	Form 37
Form 34	Form 38
Form 35	Form 39
Form 36	Form 40
Form 37	Form 41
Form 38	Form 42
Form 39	Form 43
Forms 40 and 41	repealed
Form 42	Form 44
Form 43	Form 45
Form 44	Form 46
Form 45	Form 47
774	repealed
—	Form 48 [en. 1991, c. 43, s. 8]
—	Form 48.1 [en. 2005, c. 22, s. 40]
—	Form 48.2 [en. 2015, c. 13, s. 36]
—	Form 49 [en. 1991, c. 43, s. 8]
—	Form 50 [en. 1991, c. 43, s. 8]
—	Form 51 [en. 1991, c. 43, s. 8; rep. 2005, c. 22, s. 41; en. 2011, c. 7, s. 13]
—	Form 52 [en. 2004, c. 10, s. 21]
—	Form 53 [en. 2004, c. 10, s. 2]
—	Form 54 [en. 2010, c. 17, s. 27]

THE CRIMINAL CODE

R.S.C. 1985, Chap. C-46

Amended R.S.C. 1985, c. 2 (1st Supp.); brought into force January 1, 1990, as provided by R.S.C. 1985, c. 27 (1st Supp.), s. 188

Amended R.S.C. 1985, c. 11 (1st Supp.); proclaimed in force December 12, 1988

Amended R.S.C. 1985, c. 27 (1st Supp.); originally proclaimed in force as follows: ss. 1 to 35, 37 to 93, 96 to 126, 128 to 186, 188 and 203 to 208 proclaimed in force December 4, 1985; parts of s. 36 enacting ss. 249 to 253, 254(1), (3) to (6), 255(1) to (4) and 256 to 261 with the exception of s. 258(1)(*c*)(i) and (*g*)(iii)(A) of the *Criminal Code* proclaimed in force December 4, 1985; s. 258(1)(*c*)(i) and (*g*)(iii)(A) to come into force on proclamation (repealed before coming into force 2008, c. 20, s. 3); part of s. 36 enacting s. 254(2) of the *Criminal Code* proclaimed in force December 4, 1985 in each of the provinces; part of s. 36 enacting s. 255(5) of the *Criminal Code* proclaimed in force December 4, 1985 in New Brunswick, Manitoba, Prince Edward Island, Alberta, Saskatchewan, Yukon Territory and Northwest Territories, proclaimed in force January 1, 1988 in Nova Scotia, and to come into force on proclamation in the remaining provinces; s. 94 in force June 20, 1985 in New Brunswick, Manitoba, Ontario, Yukon Territory, Northwest Territories, proclaimed in force September 1, 1987 in Nova Scotia, P.E.I. and Saskatchewan and with respect to indictable offences in Saskatchewan, into force on proclamation in the remaining provinces; and s. 127 proclaimed in force September 1, 1988

Amended R.S.C. 1985, c. 31 (1st Supp.), s. 61; proclaimed in force December 12, 1988

Amended R.S.C. 1985, c. 47 (1st Supp.); proclaimed in force December 12, 1988

Amended R.S.C. 1985, c. 51 (1st Supp.); in force December 12, 1988

Amended R.S.C. 1985, c. 52 (1st Supp.); proclaimed in force December 12, 1988

Amended R.S.C. 1985, c. 1 (2nd Supp.), s. 213; proclaimed in force December 12, 1988

Amended R.S.C. 1985, c. 24 (2nd Supp.), ss. 45 to 47; proclaimed in force December 12, 1988

Amended R.S.C. 1985, c. 27 (2nd Supp.), s. 10, Sch. item 6(1) to (16); proclaimed in force December 12, 1988 (but see s. 11)

Amended R.S.C. 1985, c. 35 (2nd Supp.), s. 34; proclaimed in force December 12, 1988

Amended R.S.C. 1985, c. 10 (3rd Supp.); proclaimed in force May 1, 1989

Amended R.S.C. 1985, c. 19 (3rd Supp.), ss. 1 to 16; proclaimed in force May 1, 1989 (but see s. 19)

Amended R.S.C. 1985, c. 30 (3rd Supp.), ss. 1 and 2; proclaimed in force May 1, 1989

Amended R.S.C. 1985, c. 34 (3rd Supp.), ss. 9 to 13; proclaimed in force May 1, 1989

Amended R.S.C. 1985, c. 1 (4th Supp.), ss. 13 to 17; originally in force February 4, 1988

Amended R.S.C. 1985, c. 23 (4th Supp.); originally ss. 1 to 3 and 7 proclaimed in force October 1, 1988, ss. 4, 5 and that part of s. 6 which enacts s. 727.9 proclaimed in force July 31, 1989, s. 8 proclaimed in force November 1, 1989; that part of s. 6 which enacts ss. 725 to 727.8 repealed by 1995, c. 22, s. 11 (in force September 3, 1996)

Amended R.S.C. 1985, c. 29 (4th Supp.), s. 17; proclaimed in force November 1, 1989

Amended R.S.C. 1985, c. 30 (4th Supp.), s. 45; proclaimed in force November 1, 1989

Amended R.S.C. 1985, c. 31 (4th Supp.), ss. 94 to 97; s. 96 proclaimed in force September 15, 1988, s. 97 proclaimed in force February 1, 1989, remainder in force as noted

Amended R.S.C. 1985, c. 32 (4th Supp.), ss. 55 to 62; proclaimed in force November 1, 1989

Amended R.S.C. 1985, c. 40 (4th Supp.), s. 2; proclaimed in force November 1, 1989

Amended R.S.C. 1985, c. 42 (4th Supp.), ss. 1 to 8; proclaimed in force November 1, 1989

Amended R.S.C. 1985, c. 50 (4th Supp.); proclaimed in force November 1, 1989

Amended 1989, c. 2, s. 1; in force June 29, 1989

Amended 1990, c. 15; brought into force July 1, 1990 by SI/90-83, *Can. Gaz., Part II*, July 4, 1990

Amended 1990, c. 16, ss. 2 to 7; brought into force July 1, 1990 by SI/90-90, *Can. Gaz., Part II*, July 18, 1990 (but see s. 24)

Amended 1990, c. 17, ss. 7 to 15; brought into force September 1, 1990 by SI/90-106, *Can. Gaz., Part II*, August 29, 1990 (but see s. 45)

Amended 1990, c. 44, s. 15; brought into force February 4, 1991 by SI/91-18, *Can. Gaz., Part II*, February 13, 1991 (but see s. 20)

Amended 1991, c. 1, s. 28; in force January 17, 1991

Amended 1991, c. 4; in force January 17, 1991

Amended 1991, c. 28, ss. 6 to 12; brought into force October 3, 1991 by SI/91-136, *Can. Gaz., Part II*, October 23, 1991

Amended 1991, c. 40, ss. 1 to 20, 21(2) and 22 to 41; s. 28 brought into force March 26, 1992, remainder, except ss. 3, 5(1) and (2), 8, 10(1), 14, 18, 19(1) to (7), 20, 22, 23, 39, 40 and 42, brought into force August 1, 1992 by SI/92-138, *Can. Gaz., Part II*, July 29, 1992, *however*, by SI/92-144, *Can. Gaz., Part II*, August 12, 1992, s. 2(3) and that part of s. 2(6) which enacts s. 84(1.2) are brought into force July 27, 1992; ss. 5(1) and (2), 10(1), 23(1), (2), (3), (5) and 42 brought into force October 1, 1992; that part of s. 3 which enacts s. 86(3), ss. 14, 18, 19(1), (2), (5) to (7), 20, 22, 23(3), 39 (except s. 39(4)(*a*)) and 40 in force January 1, 1993; s. 19(3) and (4) were to come into force July 1, 1993 (see SI/92-156) but amended by P.C. 1993-1446, so that s. 19(3) and (4) came into force January 1, 1994 (see SI/94-7), s. 106(2)(*c*) as enacted by s. 19(3) in force (*a*), in Alberta, British Columbia, Ontario, Prince Edward Island, Quebec and the Yukon Territory on January 1, 1994, and (b), in Manitoba, New Brunswick, Newfoundland, Nova Scotia and Saskatchewan on April 1, 1994, however, the coming into force in Saskatchewan was deferred to September 1, 1994, the coming into force in the Northwest Territories was repealed by SI/98-80, *Can. Gaz., Part II*, July 8, 1998; the order bringing ss. 8 and 39(4)(a) into force on January 1, 1993 was amended so that s. 8 now in force as of January 1, 1995 and s. 39(4)(a) is to come into force on some future, unspecified date; that part of s. 3 which enacts s. 86(2) to come into force by order of the Governor in Council; however, s. 86(2) as enacted by s. 3 repealed by 1995, c. 39, s. 163 (brought into force December 1, 1998 by SI/98-93, *Can. Gaz., Part II*, September 30, 1998 (in force date amended by SI/98-95, *Can. Gaz., Part II*, September 30, 1998)); s. 34 repealed by 1995, c. 39, s. 162 (brought into force December 1, 1998 by SI/98-93, *Can. Gaz., Part II*, September 30, 1998 (in force date amended by SI/98-95, *Can. Gaz., Part II*, September 30, 1998)); s. 105(4) of the *Criminal Code* as enacted by s. 39(4) repealed by 1995, c. 39, s. 164 (brought into force December 1, 1998 by SI/98-93, *Can. Gaz., Part II*, September 30, 1998 (in force date amended by SI/98-95, *Can. Gaz., Part II*, September 30, 1998))

Amended 1991, c. 43, ss. 1 to 10; brought into force, except that part of s. 4 which enacts ss. 672.64 to 672.66, ss. 5, 6 and 10(8), February 4, 1992 by SI/92-9, *Can. Gaz., Part II*, February 12, 1992; ss. 5 and 6 repealed by 1995, c. 22, s. 12 (in force September 3, 1996); that part of s. 4 which enacts ss. 672.64 to 672.66 and 10(8) to come into force by order of the Governor in Council (repealed before coming into force by 2005, c. 22, ss. 24, 43(3) (in force January 2, 2006))

Amended 1992, c. 1, ss. 58 and 59; in force February 28, 1992

Amended 1992, c. 11, ss. 14 to 17; in force May 15, 1992

Amended 1992, c. 20, ss. 199 to 204, 215, 216, 228 and 229; brought into force, except s. 204, November 1, 1992; s. 204 repealed by 1995, c. 42, s. 61 (in force January 24, 1996)

Amended 1992, c. 21, s. 9; brought into force June 30, 1992 by SI/92-126, *Can. Gaz., Part II*, July 15, 1992

Amended 1992, c. 22, s. 12; brought into force July 24, 1992 by SI/92-134, *Can. Gaz., Part II*, July 29, 1992

Amended 1992, c. 27, s. 90(1)(i); brought into force November 30, 1992

Amended 1992, c. 38; brought into force August 15, 1992 by SI/92-136, *Can. Gaz., Part II*, July 29, 1992

Amended 1992, c. 41; in force July 23, 1992 (but see s. 7)

Amended 1992, c. 47, ss. 68 to 72; brought into force August 1, 1996 by SI/96-56, *Can. Gaz., Part II*, July 1, 1996

Amended 1992, c. 51, ss. 32 to 43; brought into force January 30, 1993

Amended 1993, c. 7; brought into force September 1, 1993

Amended 1993, c. 25, ss. 93 to 95; s. 93 deemed in force January 1, 1993; ss. 94 and 95 in force June 10, 1993

Amended 1993, c. 28, Sch. III, ss. 25 to 37; however, s. 27 repealed by 1995, c. 39, s. 192 and s. 35 replaced by 1998, c. 15, s. 20 (in force June 11, 1998); in force April 1, 1999; however, ss. 25(2), 28, 29, 31, 32, 34, 35.1 to 36 repealed 1999, c. 3, s. 12 (in force March 11, 1999)

Amended 1993, c. 34, s. 59(1); in force on the day after the day on which 1993, c. 34, s. 142 is brought into force (1993, c. 34, s. 59(1) in force December 15, 1994)

Amended 1993, c. 37, ss. 21 and 32; brought into force September 1, 1993

Amended 1993, c. 40, ss. 1 to 18; brought into force August 1, 1993

Amended 1993, c. 45, ss. 1 to 14 and 16 to 19; brought into force August 1, 1993 by SI/94-137

Amended 1993, c. 46, ss. 1 to 5; brought into force August 1, 1993

Amended 1994, c. 12, s. 1; brought into force July 1, 1994

Amended 1994, c. 13, s. 7(1)(*b*); in force May 12, 1994

Amended 1994, c. 38, ss. 14 and 25(1)(*g*); brought into force January 12, 1995 by SI/95-9, *Can. Gaz.*, *Part II*, January 25, 1995

Amended 1994, c. 44, ss. 1 to 84 and 103; brought into force, except ss. 8(2), 39 to 43 and 84, February 15, 1995; ss. 8(2), 39 to 43 and 84 brought into force April 1, 1995

Amended 1995, c. 5, s. 25(1)(*g*); brought into force May 13, 1995 by SI/95-65, *Can. Gaz.*, *Part II*, May 31, 1995

Amended 1995, c. 19, ss. 37 to 41; brought into force December 1, 1995 by SI/95-116, *Can. Gaz.*, *Part II*, November 29, 1995

Amended 1995, c. 22, ss. 1 to 12, 14, 15, 18 to 24 and 26; brought into force September 3, 1996 by SI/96-79, *Can. Gaz., Part II*, August 21, 1996, except that part of s. 6 that enacts ss. 718.3(5) and 747 to 747.8 (to come into force by order of the Governor in Council (that part of s. 6 that enacts s. 718.3(5) repealed before coming into force by 1999, c. 5, s. 30 (in force July 1, 1999); that part of s. 6 that enacts ss. 747-747.8 repealed before coming into force by 2005, c. 22, s. 39 (in force January 2, 2006); s. 7(2) repealed before conditions were satisfied by 2005, c. 22, s. 44 (in force January 2, 2006)); that part of s. 6 that enacted ss. 745.6 to 745.64 re-enacted 1996, c. 34, s. 2(2); brought into force January 9, 1997 by SI/97-12, *Can. Gaz., Part II*, January 22, 1997

Amended 1995, c. 27, ss. 1 and 3; in force July 13, 1995

Amended 1995, c. 29, ss. 39 and 40; brought into force November 1, 1995 by SI/95-115, *Can. Gaz., Part II*, November 15, 1995

Amended 1995, c. 32, s. 1; brought into force September 15, 1995 by SI/95-101, *Can. Gaz., Part II*, September 20, 1995

Amended 1995, c. 39, ss. 138 to 157, 163, 164, 188(*a*) and (*b*), 189(*e*) and 190; that part of s. 139 which replaces s. 85 and ss. 141 to 150 brought into force January 1, 1996, by SI/96-2, *Can. Gaz., Part II*, January 10, 1996; ss. 138, 139 (except to the extent that it replaces ss. 85 and 97 of the *Criminal Code*), 140, 151 to 157, 163, 164, 188(*a*) and (*b*), 189(*e*), 190 brought into force December 1, 1998 by SI/98-93, *Can. Gaz., Part II*, September 30, 1998 (in force date amended by SI/98-95, *Can. Gaz., Part II*, September 30, 1998); that part of s. 139 which replaces s. 97 to come into force by order of the Governor in Council; however, repealed before coming into force

Amended 1995, c. 42, ss. 73 to 76, 86 and 87; brought into force January 24, 1996 by SI/96-10, *Can. Gaz., Part II*, February 7, 1996 (see ss. 86 and 87)

Amended 1996, c. 7, s. 38; brought into force July 31, 1996 by SI/96-57, Can. Gaz., Part II, July 10, 1996

Amended 1996, c. 8, s. 32(1)(*d*); brought into force July 12, 1996 by SI/96-69, *Can. Gaz.*, *Part II*, July 24, 1996

Amended 1996, c. 16, s. 60(1)(*d*); brought into force July 12, 1996 by SI/96-67, *Can. Gaz.*, *Part II*, July 24, 1996

Amended 1996, c. 19, ss. 65 to 76 and 93.3; ss. 65 to 76 brought into force May 14, 1997 by SI/97-47, *Can. Gaz., Part II*, May 14, 1997; s. 93.3 in force December 1, 1998 as provided by that section

Amended 1996, c. 31, ss. 67 to 72; brought into force January 31, 1997 by SI/97-21, *Can. Gaz., Part II*, February 5, 1997

Amended 1996, c. 34, ss. 1 and 2(2); s. 2(2) in force January 1, 1997; s. 1 to come into force by order of the Governor in Council (repealed before coming into force 2008, c. 20, s. 3)

Amended 1997, c. 16, s. 2; brought into force May 26, 1997 by SI/97-66, *Can. Gaz.*, *Part II*

Amended 1997, c. 17, ss. 1 to 10; brought into force August 1, 1997 by SI/97-84, *Can. Gaz.*, *Part II*, July 23, 1997

Amended 1997, c. 18, ss. 1 to 115; ss. 107.1 and 139.1 in force May 2, 1997 by SI/97-60, *Can. Gaz.*, *Part II*, May 14, 1997; ss. 1, 23, 27 to 39, 99, 100, 109 and 140 in force May 14, 1997 by SI/97-62, *Can. Gaz., Part II*, May 28, 1997; ss. 2 to 22, 24 to 26, 40 to 98, 101 to 105, 108, 110 to 115 and 141 in force June 16, 1997 by SI/97-68, *Can. Gaz., Part II*, June 25, 1997; ss. 106 and 107 to come into force by order of the Governor in Council (repealed before coming into force 2008, c. 20, s. 3)

Amended 1997, c. 23, ss. 1 to 20 and 26; ss. 1 to 20 in force May 2, 1997 by SI/97-61, *Can. Gaz.*, *Part II*, May 14, 1997; s. 26 brought into force December 1, 1998

Amended 1997, c. 30; brought into force May 12, 1997 by SI/97-63, *Can. Gaz., Part II*, May 28, 1997

Amended 1997, c. 39, ss. 1 to 3; in force December 18, 1997

Amended 1998, c. 7, ss. 2, 3; brought into force May 1, 2000 by SI/2000-25, *Can. Gaz.*, *Part II*, April 26, 2000

Amended 1998, c. 9, ss. 2 to 8; brought into force June 30, 1998 by SI/98-79, *Can. Gaz., Part II*, June 24, 1998

Amended 1998, c. 30, ss. 14(*d*) and 16 (and see ss. 10 and 11); brought into force April 19, 1999 by SI/99-37, *Can. Gaz.*, *Part II*, April 28, 1999

Amended 1998, c. 34, ss. 8, 9 and 11; ss. 8 and 9 brought into force February 14, 1999 by SI/99-13, *Can. Gaz.*, *Part II*, March 3, 1999; s. 11 in force September 1, 1999 (as provided by s. 11)

Amended 1998, c. 35, ss. 119 to 121; brought into force September 1, 1999 by SI/99-75, *Can. Gaz.*, *Part II*, July 21, 1999

Amended 1998, c. 37, ss. 15 to 24; brought into force June 30, 2000 by SI/2000-60, *Can. Gaz.*, *Part II*, July 19, 2000

Amended 1999, c. 2, s. 47; brought into force March 18, 1999 by SI/99-25, *Can. Gaz.*, *Part II*, March 31, 1999

Amended 1999, c. 3, ss. 12, 25 to 58; s. 12 in force March 11, 1999; ss. 25 to 58 in force April 1, 1999

Amended 1999, c. 5, ss. 1 to 47; s. 9 in force March 11, 1999; s. 51 in force July 1, 1999 (as provided by 1999, c. 5, s. 51); s. 52 in force March 18, 1999 (as provided by 1999, c. 5, s. 52); ss. 6 and 7 brought into force March 15, 1999 by para. (*a*) of SI/99-24, *Can. Gaz.*, *Part II*, March 31, 1999; ss. 1 to 5, 8, 10 to 24, 26 to 28 and 43 to 47 brought into force May 1, 1999 by para. (*b*) of SI/99-24, *Can. Gaz.*, *Part II*, March 31, 1999; ss. 25 and 29 to 42 brought into force July 1, 1999 by para. (*c*) of SI/99-24, *Can. Gaz.*, *Part II*, March 31, 1999

Amended 1999, c. 17, s. 120; brought into force November 1, 1999 by SI/99-111, *Can. Gaz.*, *Part II*, October 13, 1999

Amended 1999, c. 18, ss. 92 to 95; in force June 17, 1999

Amended 1999, c. 25, ss. 1 to 27, 30, 31(3) and (5); ss. 1 to 27, 31(3) and (5) brought into force December 1, 1999 by SI/99-135, *Can. Gaz.*, *Part II*, December 8, 1999; s. 30 brought into force May 1, 2000 as provided by s. 30; (s. 29(2) repealed before conditions were satisfied by 2005, c. 22, s. 46 (in force January 2, 2006))

Amended 1999, c. 28, ss. 155 and 156; brought into force June 28, 1999 by SI/99-70, *Can. Gaz.*, *Part II*, July 7, 1999

Amended 1999, c. 31, ss. 67 to 69; in force June 17, 1999

Amended 1999, c. 32, ss. 1 to 6; brought into force July 1, 1999 by SI/99-73, *Can. Gaz.*, *Part II*, July 21, 1999

Amended 1999, c. 33, s. 346; brought into force March 31, 2000 by SI/2000-15, *Can. Gaz.*, *Part II*, March 29, 2000

Amended 1999, c. 35, s. 11; brought into force May 1, 2000 by SI/2000-27, *Can. Gaz.*, *Part II*, April 26, 2000

Amended 2000, c. 1, s. 9; brought into force August 1, 2000 by SI/2000-73, *Can. Gaz.*, *Part II*, August 16, 2000

Amended 2000, c. 2, ss. 1 to 3; in force March 30, 2000

Amended 2000, c. 10, ss. 13 to 24; brought into force June 30, 2000 by SI/2000-61, *Can. Gaz.*, *Part II*, July 19, 2000

Amended 2000, c. 12, ss. 91 to 95; brought into force July 31, 2000 by SI/2000-76, *Can. Gaz.*, *Part II*, August 16, 2000

Amended 2000, c. 17, s. 89; brought into force October 28, 2001 by SI/2001-88, *Can. Gaz.*, *Part II*, September 12, 2001

Amended 2000, c. 24, ss. 42 to 46; brought into force October 23, 2000 by SI/2000-95, *Can. Gaz.*, *Part II*, November 8, 2000 (however, s. 43 later replaced 2001, c. 34, s. 36, in force December 18, 2001)

Amended 2000, c. 25, ss. 2 to 4; brought into force March 15, 2001 by SI/2001-42, *Can. Gaz.*, *Part II*, March 28, 2001

Amended 2001, c. 26, s. 294; brought into force July 1, 2007 by SI/2007-65, *Can. Gaz.*, *Part II*, June 27, 2007

Amended 2001, c. 27, ss. 244 to 247; ss. 244, 246 and 247 brought into force June 28, 2002 by paras. (*f*) and (*g*) of SI/2002-97, *Can. Gaz.*, *Part II*, June 14, 2002 (however, s. 246 since repealed 2001, c. 32, s. 81(3)(*d*) in force June 28, 2002 as provided by the section); s. 245 to come into force by order of the Governor in Council (repealed before coming into force 2004, c. 15, s. 110)

Amended 2001, c. 32, ss. 1(1) to (5), 2, 4 to 8, 9(1), 10, 11, 12(1) to (4), (6), (7), 13 to 30, 31(1), (2), (4), 32 to 42, 45 and 46; ss. 1(1) to (5), 4 to 8, 9(1), 10, 11, 16, 24, 27 to 30, 31(1), (2), (4), 32 to 42, 45 and 46 brought into force January 7, 2002 by para. (*a*) of SI/2002-17, *Can. Gaz.*, *Part II*, January 16, 2002; ss. 2,

12(1) to (4), (6), (7), 13 to 15, 17 to 23, 25 and 26 brought into force February 1, 2002 by part (b) of SI/2002-17, *Can. Gaz.*, *Part II*, January 16, 2002

Amended 2001, c. 37, s. 1; in force December 18, 2001

Amended 2001, c. 41, ss. 2 to 23, 31 to 34, 80, 126(2), (3), 130(7.1), 131(2), 133(2), (5), (8) to (11), (13), (14) to (19), (21) and 143; ss. 80, 133(21) in force December 18, 2001; ss. 2 to 23, 31 to 34 brought into force December 24, 2001 by SI/2002-16; s. 131(2) in force December 24, 2001 (as provided by this section); ss. 130(7.1), 133(2), (5), (8) to (10), (13) to (19) in force January 7, 2002 (as provided by these sections); s. 133(11) in force February 1, 2002 (as provided by this section); s. 126(2), (3) in force June 28, 2002 (as provided by these sections); s. 143 in force July 2, 2003 (as provided by this section)

Amended 2002, c. 1, ss. 175 to 177, 179 and 181 to 186 brought into force April 1, 2003 by SI/2002-91, *Can. Gaz.*, *Part II*, June 19, 2002

Amended 2002, c. 7, ss. 137 to 150 brought into force April 1, 2003 by SI/2003-48, *Can. Gaz.*, *Part II*, April 9, 2003

Amended 2002, c. 13, ss. 2 to 4, 5(2), (3), (4), 6 to 15 and 17 to 85; ss. 2 to 4, 5(2), (3), (4), 6 to 15, 17 to 23, 47, 50 to 58, 60, 61, 63 to 65, 67 to 69, 73 to 78, 80 to 86 brought into force July 23, 2002 by para. (b) of SI/2002-106, *Can. Gaz.*, *Part II*, July 31, 2002; ss. 49 and 62 brought into force September 23, 2002 by para. (c) of SI/2002-106, *Can. Gaz.*, *Part II*, July 31, 2002; ss. 66, 70, 71 brought into force November 25, 2002 by para. (d) of SI/2002-106, *Can. Gaz.*, *Part II*, July 31, 2002; ss. 24 to 46, 48, 59 and 72 brought into force June 1, 2004 as provided by para. (b) of SI/2003-182, *Can. Gaz.*, *Part II*, December 3, 2003; s. 79 brought into force July 23, 2003 by para. (b) of SI/2003-127, *Can. Gaz.*, *Part II*, July 2, 2003

Amended 2002, c. 22, ss. 324 to 327 and 409(2)(b); s. 409(2)(b) in force June 13, 2002 as provided by this section; ss. 324 to 327 brought into force July 1, 2003 by SI/2003-47, *Can. Gaz.*, *Part II*, April 9, 2003 [Note: ss. 326 and 327 since repealed by 2002, c. 22, s. 409(2)(a) and (6) as provided in the section, in force June 13, 2002.]

Amended 2003, c. 8, ss. 2 to 8; s. 2(1) brought into force May 30, 2003 by SI/2003-114, *Can. Gaz.*, *Part II*, June 18, 2003; ss. 2(2) and 3 to 7 brought into force August 15, 2003 by SI/2003-144, *Can. Gaz.*, August 27, 2003; s. 8 to come into force by order of the Governor in Council (repealed before coming into force 2012, c. 1, s. 47)

Amended 2003, c. 21, ss. 1 to 21; brought into force March 31, 2004 by SI/2004-22, *Can. Gaz.*, *Part II*, February 25, 2004; s. 22 in force June 1, 2004, as provided by that section

Amended 2003, c. 22, s. 224(z.23), brought into force April 6, 2005 by SI/2005-24, *Can. Gaz.*, *Part II*, April 6, 2005

Amended 2004, c. 3, ss. 1 to 8; ss. 2 to 8 brought into force September 15, 2004 by SI/2004-119, *Can. Gaz.*, *Part II*, September 22, 2004; s. 1 brought into force September 15, 2005 by SI/2005-60, *Can. Gaz.*, *Part II*, June 29, 2005

Amended 2004, c. 10, ss. 20 and 21 brought into force December 15, 2004 by SI/2004-157, *Can. Gaz.*, *Part II*, December 15, 2004

Amended 2004, c. 12, ss. 1 to 7 and 9 to 17; ss. 1 to 7 and 9 to 16 in force on Royal Assent, April 22, 2004; s. 17 brought into force October 1, 2004 by SI/2004-131, *Can. Gaz.*, *Part II*, October 20, 2004

Amended 2004, c. 14, ss. 1 and 2, in force on Royal Assent, April 29, 2004

Amended 2004, c. 15, ss. 32 and 108; brought into force December 1, 2004 by SI/2004-158, *Can. Gaz., Part II*, December 15, 2004

Amended 2005, c. 10, ss. 18 to 25 and 34(1)(*f*), brought into force April 4, 2005 by SI/2005-29, *Can. Gaz., Part II*, April 20, 2005

Amended 2005, c. 22, ss. 1 to 8, 10 to 26, 27(2), 28 to 34, 36 to 41 and 64(2); ss. 1 to 7, 10, 11, 33 and 40 brought into force June 30, 2005 by para. (*a*) of SI/2005-56, *Can. Gaz., Part II*, June 15, 2005; ss. 8, 12 to 26, 27(2), 28 to 32, 34, 36 to 39 and 41, brought into force January 2, 2006 by para. (*b*) of SI/2005-56, *Can. Gaz., Part II*, June 15, 2005; s. 64(2) in force January 2, 2006 as provided by the section

Amended 2005, c. 25, ss. 1 and 3 to 13; s. 5 in force on Royal Assent, May 19, 2005; ss. 1, 3, 4 and 6 to 13 brought into force January 1, 2008 by SI/2007-108, *Can. Gaz., Part II*, December 12, 2007

Amended 2005, c. 32, ss. 1 to 7, 8(2) to (5) and 9 to 25; ss. 1 to 7, 8(2) to (5), 9 to 12, 24 and 25 brought into force November 1, 2005 by para. (*a*) of SI/2005-104, *Can. Gaz., Part II*, November 16, 2005; ss. 13 to 23 brought into force January 2, 2006 by para. (*b*) of SI/2005-104, *Can. Gaz., Part II*, November 16, 2005

Amended 2005, c. 38, ss. 58, 138(*e*) and 140(*b*); brought into force December 12, 2005 by SI/2005-119, *Can. Gaz., Part II*, December 14, 2005

Amended 2005, c. 40, ss. 1 to 3 and 7; ss. 1 to 3 in force November 24, 2005; s. 7 in force November 24, 2005 as provided by the section

Amended 2005, c. 43, ss. 1 to 7 and 8(3); ss. 1 to 7 in force November 25, 2005; s. 8(3) in force November 25, 2005 as provided by the section

Amended 2005, c. 44, ss. 1, 3 to 12; in force November 25, 2005

Amended 2006, c. 9, s. 246; brought into force March 1, 2007 by SI/2007-15, *Can. Gaz., Part II*, February 21, 2007

Amended 2006, c. 14, ss. 1, 2, 3(2) and (3), and 4 to 7, in force on Royal Assent, December 14, 2006

Amended 2007, c. 5, ss. 11 to 20, 21(2), 22 to 29, 30(2), (3) and 31; brought into force September 12, 2008 by SI/2008-93, *Can. Gaz., Part II*, September 4, 2008

Amended 2007, c. 9, ss. 1 and 2; in force on Royal Assent, May 3, 2007

Amended 2007, c. 12, ss. 1 and 2; in force December 1, 2007, as provided by s. 2 (received Royal Assent May 31, 2007)

Amended 2007, c. 13, ss. 1 to 11; in force on Royal Assent, May 31, 2007

Amended 2007, c. 20, s. 1; in force on Royal Assent, June 22, 2007

Amended 2007, c. 22, ss. 2 to 4, 7 to 26; ss. 2 to 4, 8(2) to (5), 9, 11(1), 13(1), 18, 19, 20(1) to (3), 21, 23 and 25 in force June 22, 2007; ss. 7, 8(1), 10, 11(2) to (4), 12, 13(2), 14 to 17, 20(4), 22, 24 and 26 brought into force January 1, 2008 by SI/2007-108, *Can. Gaz., Part II*, December 12, 2007

Amended 2007, c. 28, s. 1; in force on Royal Assent, June 22, 2007

Amended 2008, c. 6, ss. 2 to 44, 45(1), (2), 46, 47, 48(1) and 49 to 54; ss. 2 to 17, 28 to 38 and 54 brought into force May 1, 2008 by SI/2008-34, *Can. Gaz., Part II*, April 2, 2008; remainder brought into force July 2, 2008, by SI/2008-34, *Can. Gaz., Part II*, April 2, 2008

Amended 2008, c. 12, s. 1; in force on Royal Assent, April 17, 2008

Amended 2008, c. 18, ss. 1 to 26, and 28 to 45.2; ss. 1 to 6, 9 to 17, 22 to 26, 28, 30 to 34, 36, 41, 43, 45 and 45.2 in force on Royal Assent, May 29, 2008; remainder in force October 1, 2008 by SI/2008-71, *Can. Gaz.*, *Part II*, June 25, 2008

Amended 2009, c. 2, s. 442; in force March 12, 2010 by s. 444 of the Act

Amended 2009, c. 22, ss. 1 to 19; brought into force October 2, 2009 by SI/2009-92, *Can. Gaz.*, *Part II*, September 30, 2009

Amended 2009, c. 28, ss. 1 to 11; brought into force January 8, 2010 by SI/2009-120, *Can. Gaz.*, *Part II*, December 23, 2009

Amended 2009, c. 29, ss. 2 to 5; brought into force February 22, 2010 by SI/2010-9, *Can. Gaz.*, *Part II*, February 17, 2010

Amended 2010, c. 3, ss. 1 to 8; in force June 29, 2010

Amended 2010, c. 14, ss. 2 to 11; brought into force April 29, 2011 by SI/2011-23, *Can. Gaz.*, *Part II*, April 13, 2011

Amended 2010, c. 17, ss. 2 to 27; brought into force April 15, 2011 by SI/2011-35, April 13, 2011

Amended 2010, c. 19, s. 1; brought into force November 30, 2011 by SI/2011-99, *Can. Gaz.*, *Part II*, December 7, 2011

Amended 2010, c. 20, s. 1; in force on Royal Assent, December 15, 2010

Amended 2011, c. 2, ss. 2 to 5; brought into force December 2, 2011 by SI/2011-108, *Can. Gaz.*, *Part II*, December 21, 2011

Amended 2011, c. 5, ss. 2 to 5; brought into force December 2, 2011 by SI/2011-107, *Can. Gaz.*, *Part II*, December 21, 2011

Amended 2011, c. 6, ss. 2 to 5; brought into force November 1, 2011 by SI/2011-82, *Can. Gaz.*, *Part II*, October 12, 2011

Amended 2011, c. 7, ss. 2 to 13; brought into force March 31, 2015 by SI/2014-105, *Can. Gaz.*, *Part II*, December 31, 2014

Amended 2011, c. 16, ss. 2, and 4 to 16; ss. 2, 4 to 6, 7(2) and (4), 10, 11 and 14 to 16 brought into force August 15, 2011 by SI/2011-62, *Can. Gaz.*, *Part II*, August 17, 2011; remainder bought into force October 24, 2011 by SI/2011-62, *Can. Gaz.*, *Part II*, August 17, 2011

Amended 2012, c. 1, ss. 10 to 38, 47, 141(2) and (3), 143 to 146, 160(c), 200; s. 32(2), 141(2) and (3), 143 to 146 in force March 13, 2012; s. 147 brought into force June 13, 2012 by SI/2012-40 *Can. Gaz.*, *Part II*, June 20, 2012; ss. 10 to 31 and 35 to 38 brought into force August 9, 2012 by SI/2012-48, *Can. Gaz.*, *Part II*, July 4, 2012; ss. 32(1), 33 and 47 brought into force November 6, 2012 by SI/2012-48, *Can. Gaz.*, *Part II*, July 4, 2012; s. 34 brought into force November 20, 2012 by SI/2012-48, *Can. Gaz.*, *Part II*, July 4, 2012; s. 200 brought into force October 23, 2012 by SI/2012/48, *Can. Gaz.*, *Part II*, July 4, 2012; s. 160(c) brought into force February 28, 2013 by SI/2013-13, *Can. Gaz.*, *Part II*, February 27, 2013

Amended 2012, c. 6, ss. 2 to 8; brought into force April 5, 2012 by SI/2012-28, *Can. Gaz.*, *Part II*, April 25, 2012

Amended 2012, c. 9, ss. 2 and 3; brought into force March 11, 2013, by SI/2013-5, *Can. Gaz.*, *Part II*, September 12, 2012

Amended 2012, c. 15, ss. 1 and 2; in force on Royal Assent, June 28, 2012

Amended 2012, c. 19, s. 371; brought into force August 20, 2012 by *Can. Gaz.*, *Part II*, SI/2012-68, September 12, 2012

Amended 2012, c. 29, s. 2; brought into force January 13, 2013

Amended 2013, c. 8, ss. 2 to 6; s. 5 in force September 27, 2013; remainder in force March 27, 2013

Amended 2013, c. 9, ss. 2, 3(2) and 4 to 16; in force July 15, 2013 by SI/2013-67, *Can. Gaz.*, *Part II*, June 19, 2013

Amended 2013, c. 11, ss. 2 to 4; brought into force October 24, 2013 by SI/2013-112, *Can. Gaz.*, *Part II*, October 23, 2013

Amended 2013, c. 13, ss. 2 to 9; brought into force November 1, 2013 by SI/2013-108, *Can. Gaz.*, *Part II*, October 9, 2013

Amended 2013, c. 15, ss. 2 and 3; in force on Royal Assent, June 19, 2013

Amended 2013, c. 19, s. 1; in force on Royal Assent, June 19, 2013

Amended 2013, c. 32, s. 1; in force June 26, 2013

Amended 2013, c. 40, s. 174; in force on Royal Assent, December 12, 2013

Amended 2014, c. 6, ss. 2 to 20; in force July 11, 2014, three months after Royal Assent, April 11, 2014

Amended 2014, c. 9, s. 1; in force on Royal Assent, June 19, 2014

Amended 2014, c. 10, s. 1; in force on Royal Assent, June 19, 2014

Amended 2014, c. 17, ss. 1 to 16; in force on Royal Assent, June 19, 2014

Amended 2014, c. 20, s. 366(1); brought into force June 17, 2019 by SI/2018-100, *Can. Gaz.*, *Part II*, November 14, 2018

Amended 2014, c. 21, ss. 1 to 4; in force September 19, 2014

Amended 2014, c. 23, ss. 2 and 3; brought into force April 10, 2015 by SI/2015-26, *Can. Gaz.*, *Part II*, April 8, 2015

Amended 2014, c. 25, ss. 2 to 33, 46(2) to (7) and 48(5) and (6); ss. 2 to 33 in force December 6, 2014; s. 46(2) to (7) in force March 9, 2015; s. 48(5) and (6) in force July 23, 2015

Amended 2014, c. 31, ss. 2 to 13, 14(2), 15 to 26; in force March 9, 2015

Amended 2014, c. 32, s. 59 in force on Royal Assent, December 9, 2014

Amended 2014, c. 39, s. 171 in force on Royal Assent, December 16, 2014

Amended 2015, c. 1, s. 1; in force on Royal Assent, February 25, 2015

Amended 2015, c. 3, ss. 44 to 59; in force on Royal Assent, February 26, 2015

Amended 2015, c. 13, ss. 3 to 36; in force July 23, 2015, 90 days after Royal Assent, April 23, 2015; ss. 5(1), 18(3) repealed 2014, c. 25, s. 48(3), (8)

Amended 2015, c. 16, ss. 1, 3, 4; ss. 1 and 4 in force June 21, 2019; s. 3 to come into force by order of the Governor in Council

Amended 2015, c. 20, ss. 15-28, 34(2)-(4), 35, 38; ss. 15(1), 16, 19-23, 35 in force on Royal Assent, June 18, 2015; ss. 15(2), 17, 18, 24, 25-28 in force July 18, 2015, 30 days after Royal Assent, June 18, 2015; s. 27(2) repealed 2015, c. 20, s. 37(3); s. 38 in force July 23, 2015

Amended 2015, c. 23, ss. 2-19, 30, 31, 33; ss. 2-19, 33 brought into force July 17, 2015 by SI/2015-68, *Can. Gaz.*, *Part II*, July 17, 2015; ss. 30, 31; to come into force by order of the Governor in Council

Amended 2015, c. 27, ss. 18-34; in force on Royal Assent, June 18, 2015

Amended 2015, c. 29, ss. 6-12; brought into force July 17, 2015 by SI/2015-67, *Can. Gaz.*, *Part II*, July 17, 2015

Amended 2015, c. 34; in force on Royal Assent, June 23, 2015

Amended 2016, c. 3, ss. 1 to 6; ss. 1 to 3 and 6 in force June 17, 2016; ss. 4 and 5 in force June 17, 2017

Amended 2017, c. 7, ss. 54, 56, 58, 59(1), 60(1), 61, 64-68; ss. 56 in force on Royal Assent, May 18, 2017; ss. 54, 58, 59(1), 60(1), 61, 64-68 brought into force June 21, 2018 by SI/2018-46, *Can. Gaz.*, *Part II*, July 11, 2018

Amended 2017, c. 13, ss. 3, 4; in force on Royal Assent, June 19, 2017

Amended 2017, c. 22, s. 3; in force on Royal Assent, October 18, 2017

Amended 2017, c. 23, ss. 1, 2; in force on Royal Assent and conditions satisfied, December 12, 2017

Amended 2017, c. 27, ss. 61, 62; in force August 15, 2019

Amended 2017, c. 33, s. 255; brought into into force October 1, 2018 by SI/2018-83, *Can. Gaz.*, *Part II*, September 5, 2018

Amended 2018, c. 11, ss. 27 to 29; in force on Royal Assent, June 21, 2018

Amended 2018, c. 12, ss. 114, 403 to 405; ss. 403 to 405 in force September 19, 2018; s. 114 in force October 17, 2018

Amended 2018, c. 16, ss. 190, 207 to 225; ss. 207 to 224 in force October 17, 2018; if Bill C-28, introduced in the 1st session of the 42nd Parliament and entitled *An Act to amend the Criminal Code (victim surcharge)*, receives royal assent, then, on the first day on which both subsec. 2(1) of that Act and s. 222 of 2018, c. 16 are in force, s. 190 will come into force; s. 225 in force June 21, 2019

Amended 2018, c. 21, ss. 1 to 9, 12 to 23, 25 to 31; ss. 1 to 9 in force on Royal Assent, June 21, 2018; ss. 12 to 31 in force December 18, 2018

Amended 2018, c. 26, s. 23; brought into force September 1, 2019 by SI/2019-41, *Can. Gaz.*, *Part II*, June 26, 2019

Amended 2018, c. 27, ss. 28 and 686; in force on Royal Assent, December 13, 2018

Amended 2018, c. 29, ss. 1 to 72; in force on Royal Assent, December 13, 2018

Amended 2019, c. 9, s. 17; in force June 21, 2019; ss. 16, 18 to come into force by order of the Governor in Council

Amended 2019, c. 11, s. 2; in force June 21, 2019

Amended 2019, c. 13, ss. 140-145, 146(1), (3), 147-154; in force June 21, 2019

Amended 2019, c. 14, s. 58.3; in force June 21, 2019

Amended 2019, c. 15, s. 47; to come into force by order of the Governor in Council

Amended 2019, c. 16, ss. 122-124; in force June 21, 2019

Amended 2019, c. 17; in force June 21, 2019

Amended 2019, c. 25, ss. 1 to 353; ss. 51, 53, 54, 55(1), 60, 62, 63.1, 69.1, 69.2, 73, 77, 78, 89, 98-102, 111, 189, 190, 202, 251.1, 320 in force June 21, 2019; ss. 278, 301, 314 in force July 21, 2019; ss. 1(1), (2), 2, 3, 4(1), 6-23, 25-29, 33, 34(2), 35-46, 48-50, 52(2), 55(2), 56-59, 61, 63, 64-69, 70-72, 74-76, 79-88, 90, 92-97, 103-110, 112-156, 157(1), 158-181, 183-186, 187(2), 188, 191-201, 203-208, 216, 225(2), 237, 238, 239(1), (3)-(5), 240-244, 245(1), 246, 247, 250, 251, 252 and 253, 254(1), (5), 255(1), (4), 256-259, 260(1), 261-263, 265(1), (3), 267-275, 277, 281(1), (2), 282-285, 286(1)-(3), 290-294, 298, 299, 302, 305-307, 315-317, 318(1), (3), 319(1), (4), 321, 322, 329-333, 334(1), (2), 336(1), 338-344, 345(1), 346, 347, 348(1), (2), 349(1), (2), 350-353 in force September 19, 2019; ss. 1(3), 5, 24, 30-32, 47, 91, 157(2), 182, 187(1), 209-215, 217-224, 225(1), (3)-(7), 226-236, 245(4), 248, 249, 254(2), (3), 255(3), 260(2), 264, 266, 276, 279, 280, 281(3), (4), 287, 288, 295, 296, 297, 300, 303,

304, 308-313, 323-328, 334(3), 335, 336(2), 337, 345(2), 348(3), 349(3) in force December 18, 2019 [s. 402(11)(*b*)-(*e*), (14) conditions not yet satisfied] [s. 89 repealed before coming into force 2019, c. 25, ss. 402(4), (6), (9).] [s. 178 repealed before coming into force 2019, c. 25, s. 401(2)] [ss. 85-88 repealed before coming into force 2019, c. 25, s. 402(11)(*a*)] [ss. 38(2), 116(2), 158(2), 295 repealed before coming into force 2019, c. 25, s. 403(6), (11), (20), (25)]

Amended 2019, c. 29, s. 103; in force June 21, 2019

Amended 2020, c. 1, ss. 35 to 38; to come into force by order of the Governor in Council

An Act respecting the Criminal Law

SHORT TITLE

SHORT TITLE.

1. This Act may be cited as the *Criminal Code*. R.S., c. C-34, s. 1.

INTERPRETATION

DEFINITIONS / "Act" / "Associated personnel" / "Attorney General" / "Bank-note" / "Bodily harm" / "Canadian Forces" / "Cattle" / "Clerk of the court" / "Common-law partner" / "Complainant" / "Counsel" / "Count" / "Court of appeal" / "Court of criminal jurisdiction" / "Criminal organization" / "Criminal organization offence" / "Day" / "Document of title to goods" / "Document of title to lands" / "Dwelling-house" / "Every one", "person", "owner" / "Explosive substance" / "Firearm" / "Government or public facility" / "Her Majesty's Forces" / "Highway" / "Indictment" / "Internationally protected person" / "Justice" / "Justice system participant" / "Mental disorder" / "Military" / "Military law" / "Motor vehicle" / "Municipality" / "Newly-born child" / "Night" / "Offence-related property" / "Offender" / "Offensive weapon" / "Organization" / "Peace officer" / "Prison" / "Property" / "Prosecutor" / "Provincial court judge" / "Public department" / "Public officer" / "Public stores" / "Railway equipment" / "Representative" / "Senior officer" / "Serious offence" / "Steal" / "Street racing" / "Superior court of criminal jurisdiction" / "Territorial division" / "Terrorism offence" / "Terrorist activity" / "Terrorist group" / "Testamentary Instrument" / "Trustee" / "Unfit to stand trial" / "United Nations operation" / "United Nations personnel" / "Valuable mineral" / "Valuable security" / "Victim" / "Weapon" / "Wreck" / "Writing".

2. In this Act,

"Act" includes

  (*a*) an Act of Parliament,

(*b*) an Act of the legislature of the former Province of Canada,

(*c*) an Act of the legislature of a province, and

(*d*) an Act or ordinance of the legislature of a province, territory or place in force at the time that province, territory or place became a province of Canada;

"appearance notice" means a notice in Form 9 issued by a peace officer;

"associated personnel" means persons who are

(*a*) assigned by a government or an intergovernmental organization with the agreement of the competent organ of the United Nations,

(*b*) engaged by the Secretary-General of the United Nations, by a specialized agency of the United Nations or by the International Atomic Energy Agency, or

(*c*) deployed by a humanitarian non-governmental organization or agency under an agreement with the Secretary-General of the United Nations, by a specialized agency of the United Nations or by the International Atomic Energy Agency,

to carry out activities in support of the fulfilment of the mandate of a United Nations operation;

"Attorney General"

(*a*) with respect to proceedings to which this Act applies, means the Attorney General or Solicitor General of the province in which those proceedings are taken and includes his or her lawful deputy or, if those proceedings are referred to in subsection 2.3(1), the Attorney General of Canada or the Attorney General or Solicitor General of the province in which those proceedings are taken and includes the lawful deputy of any of them,

(*b*) means the Attorney General of Canada and includes his or her lawful deputy with respect to

  (i) Yukon, the Northwest Territories and Nunavut, or

  (ii) proceedings commenced at the instance of the Government of Canada and conducted by or on behalf of that Government in respect of an offence under any Act of Parliament — other than this Act or the *Canada Elections Act* — or any regulation made under such an Act, and

(*b*.1) [*Repealed*, 2019, c. 25, s. 1(1).]

(*c*) means the Director of Public Prosecutions appointed under subsection 3(1) of the *Director of Public Prosecutions Act* with respect to proceedings in relation to an offence under the *Canada Elections Act*;

(*d*) [*Repealed*, 2019, c. 25, s. 1(1).]

(*e*) [*Repealed*, 2019, c. 25, s. 1(1).]

(*f*) [*Repealed*, 2019, c. 25, s. 1(1).]

(*g*) [*Repealed*, 2019, c. 25, s. 1(1).]

Note: Subparagraph (*b*)(i) of the definition "Attorney General" had been replaced by 2002, c. 7, s. 137(1); however, before it came into force, the definition was replaced by 2001, c. 41, s. 2, and as such, there was no longer a subpara. (*b*)(i).

"audioconference" means any means of telecommunication that allows the judge or justice and any individual to communicate orally in a proceeding;

"bank-note" includes any negotiable instrument

    (a) issued by or on behalf of a person carrying on the business of banking in or out of Canada, and

    (b) issued under the authority of Parliament or under the lawful authority of the government of a state other than Canada,

intended to be used as money or as the equivalent of money, immediately on issue or at some time subsequent thereto, and includes bank bills and bank post bills;

"bodily harm" means any hurt or injury to a person that interferes with the health or comfort of the person and that is more than merely transient or trifling in nature;

"Canadian Forces" means the armed forces of Her Majesty raised by Canada;

"cattle" means neat cattle or an animal of the bovine species by whatever technical or familiar name it is known, and includes any horse, mule, ass, pig, sheep or goat;

"clerk of the court" includes a person, by whatever name or title he may be designated, who from time to time performs the duties of a clerk of the court;

"common-law partner", in relation to an individual, means a person who is cohabiting with the individual in a conjugal relationship, having so cohabited for a period of at least one year;

"complainant" means the victim of an alleged offence;

"counsel" means a barrister or solicitor, in respect of the matters or things that barristers and solicitors, respectively, are authorized by the law of a province to do or perform in relation to legal proceedings;

"count" means a charge in an information or indictment;

"court of appeal" means, in all provinces, the Court of Appeal;

"court of criminal jurisdiction" means

    (a) a court of general or quarter sessions of the peace, when presided over by a superior court judge,

  (a.1) in the Province of Quebec, the Court of Quebec, the municipal court of Montreal and the municipal court of Quebec,

    (b) a provincial court judge or judge acting under Part XIX, and

    (c) in the Province of Ontario, the Ontario Court of Justice;

"criminal organization" has the same meaning as in subsection 467.1(1);

"criminal organization offence" means

    (a) an offence under section 467.11, 467.111, 467.12 or 467.13, or a serious offence committed for the benefit of, at the direction of, or in association with, a criminal organization, or

    (b) a conspiracy or an attempt to commit, being an accessory after the fact in relation to, or any counselling in relation to, an offence referred to in paragraph (a);

"day" means the period between six o'clock in the forenoon and nine o'clock in the afternoon of the same day;

"document of title to goods" includes a bought and sold note, bill of lading, warrant, certificate or order for the delivery or transfer of goods or any other valuable thing, and any other document used in the ordinary course of business as evidence of the possession or control of goods, authorizing or purporting to authorize, by endorsement or by delivery, the person in possession of the document to transfer or receive any goods thereby represented or therein mentioned or referred to;

"document of title to lands" includes any writing that is or contains evidence of the title, or any part of the title, to real property or to any interest in real property, and any notarial or registrar's copy thereof and any duplicate instrument, memorial, certificate or document authorized or required by any law in force in any part of Canada with respect to registration of titles that relates to title to real property or to any interest in real property;

"dwelling-house" means the whole or any part of a building or structure that is kept or occupied as a permanent or temporary residence, and includes
  (a) a building within the curtilage of a dwelling-house that is connected to it by a doorway or by a covered and enclosed passageway, and
  (b) a unit that is designed to be mobile and to be used as a permanent or temporary residence and that is being used as such a residence;

"environment" means the components of the Earth and includes
  (a) air, land and water,
  (b) all layers of the atmosphere,
  (c) all organic and inorganic matter and living organisms, and
  (d) the interacting natural systems that include components referred to in paragraphs (a) to (c);

"every one", "person" and "owner", and similar expressions, include Her Majesty and an organization;

"explosive substance" includes
  (a) anything intended to be used to make an explosive substance,
  (b) anything, or any part thereof, used or intended to be used, or adapted to cause, or to aid in causing an explosion in or with an explosive substance, and
  (c) an incendiary grenade, fire bomb, molotov cocktail or other similar incendiary substance or device and a delaying mechanism or other thing intended for use in connection with such a substance or device;

"feeble-minded person" [Repealed, 1991, c. 43, s. 9.]

"firearm" means a barrelled weapon from which any shot, bullet or other projectile can be discharged and that is capable of causing serious bodily injury or death to a person, and includes any frame or receiver of such a barrelled weapon and anything that can be adapted for use as a firearm;

"government or public facility" means a facility or conveyance, whether permanent or temporary, that is used or occupied in connection with their official duties by representatives of a state, members of a government, members of a legislature, members of the judiciary, or officials or employees of a state or of any other public authority or public entity, or by officials or employees of an intergovernmental organization;

15

"Her Majesty's Forces" means the naval, army and air forces of Her Majesty wherever raised, and includes the Canadian Forces;

"highway" means a road to which the public has the right of access, and includes bridges over which or tunnels through which a road passes;

"indictment" includes

    (a) information or a count therein,

    (b) a plea, replication or other pleading, and

    (c) any record;

"internationally protected person" means

    (a) a head of state, including any member of a collegial body that performs the functions of a head of state under the constitution of the state concerned, a head of a government or a minister of foreign affairs, whenever that person is in a state other than the state in which he holds that position or office,

    (b) a member of the family of a person described in paragraph (a) who accompanies that person in a state other than the state in which that person holds that position or office,

    (c) a representative or an official of a state or an official or agent of an international organization of an intergovernmental character who, at the time when and at the place where an offence referred to in subsection 7(3) is committed against his person or any property referred to in section 431 that is used by him, is entitled, pursuant to international law, to special protection from any attack on his person, freedom or dignity, or

    (d) a member of the family of a representative, official or agent described in paragraph (c) who forms part of his household, if the representative, official or agent, at the time when and at the place where any offence referred to in subsection 7(3) is committed against the member of his family or any property referred to in section 431 that is used by that member, is entitled, pursuant to international law, to special protection from any attack on his person, freedom or dignity;

"intimate partner" with respect to a person, includes their current or former spouse, common-law partner and dating partner;

"justice" means a justice of the peace or a provincial court judge, and includes two or more justices where two or more justices are, by law, required to act or, by law, act or have jurisdiction;

"justice system participant" means

    (a) a member of the Senate, of the House of Commons, of a legislative assembly or of a municipal council, and

    (b) a person who plays a role in the administration of criminal justice, including

      (i) the Minister of Public Safety and Emergency Preparedness and a Minister responsible for policing in a province,

     (ii) a prosecutor, a lawyer, a member of the Chambre des notaires du Québec and an officer of a court,

    (iii) a judge and a justice,

    (iv) a juror and a person who is summoned as a juror,

(v)   an informant, a prospective witness, a witness under subpoena and a witness who has testified,

(vi)   a peace officer within the meaning of any of paragraphs (*b*), (*c*), (*d*), (*e*) and (*g*) of the definition "peace officer",

(vii)   a civilian employee of a police force,

(viii)   a person employed in the administration of a court,

(viii.1)   a public officer within the meaning of subsection 25.1(1) and a person acting at the direction of such an officer,

(ix)   an employee of the Canada Revenue Agency who is involved in the investigation of an offence under an Act of Parliament,

(ix.1)   an employee of the Canada Border Services Agency who is involved in the investigation of an offence under an Act of Parliament,

(x)   an employee of a federal or provincial correctional service, a parole supervisor and any other person who is involved in the administration of a sentence under the supervision of such a correctional service and a person who conducts disciplinary hearings under the *Corrections and Conditional Release Act*, and

(xi)   an employee and a member of the Parole Board of Canada and of a provincial parole board; and

(*c*) a person who plays a role in respect of proceedings involving

(i)   security information,

(ii)   criminal intelligence information,

(iii)   information that would endanger the safety of any person if it were disclosed,

(iv)   information that is obtained in confidence from a source in Canada, the government of a foreign state, an international organization of states or an institution of such a government or international organization, or

(v)   potentially injurious information or sensitive information as those terms are defined in section 38 of the *Canada Evidence Act*;

"magistrate" [*Repealed*, R.S.C. 1985, c. 27 (1st Supp.), s. 2(4).]

"mental disorder" means a disease of the mind;

"military" shall be construed as relating to all or any of the Canadian Forces;

"military law" includes all laws, regulations or orders relating to the Canadian Forces;

"motor vehicle" means a vehicle that is drawn, propelled or driven by any means other than muscular power, but does not include railway equipment;

"municipality" includes the corporation of a city, town, village, county, township, parish or other territorial or local division of a province, the inhabitants of which are incorporated or are entitled to hold property collectively for a public purpose;

"newly-born child" means a person under the age of one year;

"night" means the period between nine o'clock in the afternoon and six o'clock in the forenoon of the following day;

"nuclear facility" means

  (a) any nuclear reactor, including a reactor installed on a vessel, vehicle, aircraft or space object for use as an energy source in order to propel the vessel, vehicle, aircraft or space object or for any other purpose, and

  (b) any plant or conveyance used for the production, storage, processing or transport of nuclear material or radioactive material;

"nuclear material" means

  (a) plutonium, except plutonium with an isotopic concentration of plutonium-238 that is greater than 80%,

  (b) uranium-233,

  (c) uranium containing uranium-233 or uranium-235 or both in an amount such that the abundance ratio of the sum of those isotopes to the isotope uranium-238 is greater than 0.72%,

  (d) uranium with an isotopic concentration equal to that occurring in nature, except uranium in the form of ore or ore-residue, and

  (e) any substance containing any material described in paragraphs (a) to (d);

"offence-related property" means any property, within or outside Canada,

  (a) by means or in respect of which an indictable offence under this Act or the *Corruption of Foreign Public Officials Act* is committed,

  (b) that is used in any manner in connection with the commission of such an offence, or

  (c) that is intended to be used for committing such an offence;

"offender" means a person who has been determined by a court to be guilty of an offence, whether on acceptance of a plea of guilty or on a finding of guilt;

"offensive weapon" has the same meaning as "weapon";

"organization" means

  (a) a public body, body corporate, society, company, firm, partnership, trade union or municipality, or

  (b) an association of persons that

    (i) is created for a common purpose,

    (ii) has an operational structure, and

    (iii) holds itself out to the public as an association of persons;

"peace officer" includes

  (a) a mayor, warden, reeve, sheriff, deputy sheriff, sheriff's officer and justice of the peace,

  (b) a member of the Correctional Service of Canada who is designated as a peace officer pursuant to Part I of the *Corrections and Conditional Release Act*, and a warden, deputy warden, instructor, keeper, jailer, guard and any other officer or permanent employee of a prison other than a penitentiary as defined in Part I of the *Corrections and Conditional Release Act*,

  (c) a police officer, police constable, bailiff, constable, or other person employed for the preservation and maintenance of the public peace or for the service or execution of civil process,

  (c.1) a designated officer as defined in section 2 of the *Integrated Cross-border Law Enforcement Operations Act*, when

    (i) participating in an integrated cross-border operation, as defined in section 2 of that Act, or

      (ii) engaging in an activity incidental to such an operation, including travel for the purpose of participating in the operation and appearances in court arising from the operation;

   (d) an officer within the meaning of the *Customs Act*, the *Excise Act* or the *Excise Act, 2001*, or a person having the powers of such an officer, when performing any duty in the administration of any of those Acts,

(d.1) an officer authorized under subsection 138(1) of the *Immigration and Refugee Protection Act*,

   (e) a person designated as a fishery guardian under the *Fisheries Act* when performing any duties or functions under that Act and a person designated as a fishery officer under the *Fisheries Act* when performing any duties or functions under that Act or the *Coastal Fisheries Protection Act*,

   (f) the pilot in command of an aircraft

      (i) registered in Canada under regulations made under the *Aeronautics Act*, or

      (ii) leased without crew and operated by a person who is qualified under regulations made under the *Aeronautics Act* to be registered as owner of an aircraft registered in Canada under those regulations,

     while the aircraft is in flight, and

   (g) officers and non-commissioned members of the Canadian Forces who are

      (i) appointed for the purposes of section 156 of the *National Defence Act*, or

      (ii) employed on duties that the Governor in Council, in regulations made under the *National Defence Act* for the purposes of this paragraph, has prescribed to be of such a kind as to necessitate that the officers and non-commissioned members performing them have the powers of peace officers;

"prison" includes a penitentiary, common jail, public or reformatory prison, lock-up, guard-room or other place in which persons who are charged with or convicted of offences are usually kept in custody;

"property" includes

   (a) real and personal property of every description and deeds and instruments relating to or evidencing the title or right to property, or giving a right to recover or receive money or goods,

   (b) property originally in the possession or under the control of any person, and any property into or for which it has been converted or exchanged and anything acquired at any time by the conversion or exchange, and

   (c) any postal card, postage stamp or other stamp issued or prepared for issue under the authority of Parliament or the legislature of a province for the payment to the Crown or a corporate body of any fee, rate or duty, whether or not it is in the possession of the Crown or of any person;

"prosecutor" means the Attorney General or, where the Attorney General does not intervene, means the person who institutes proceedings to which this Act applies, and includes counsel acting on behalf of either of them;

"provincial court judge" means a person appointed or authorized to act by or pursuant to an Act of the legislature of a province, by whatever title that person may be designated, who has the power and authority of two or more justices of the peace and includes the lawful deputy of that person;

"public department" means a department of the Government of Canada or a branch thereof or a board, commission, corporation or other body that is an agent of Her Majesty in right of Canada;

"public officer" includes

(*a*) an officer of customs or excise,

(*b*) an officer of the Canadian Forces,

(*c*) an officer of the Royal Canadian Mounted Police, and

(*d*) any officer while the officer is engaged in enforcing the laws of Canada relating to revenue, customs, excise, trade or navigation;

"public stores" includes any personal property that is under the care, supervision, administration or control of a public department or of any person in the service of a public department;

"radioactive material" means any material that emits one or more types of ionizing radiation, such as alpha or beta particles, neutrons and gamma rays, and that is capable of, owing to its radiological or fissile properties, causing death, serious bodily harm or substantial damage to property or the environment;

"railway equipment" means

(*a*) any machine that is constructed for movement exclusively on lines of railway, whether or not the machine is capable of independent motion, or

(*b*) any vehicle that is constructed for movement both on and off lines of railway while the adaptations of that vehicle for movement on lines of railway are in use;

"recognizance" means a recognizance in Form 32 entered into before a judge or justice;

"release order" means an order in Form 11 made by a judge as defined in section 493 or a justice;

"representative", in respect of an organization, means a director, partner, employee, member, agent or contractor of the organization;

"senior officer" means a representative who plays an important role in the establishment of an organization's policies or is responsible for managing an important

aspect of the organization's activities and, in the case of a body corporate, includes a director, its chief executive officer and its chief financial officer;

"serious offence" has the same meaning as in subsection 467.1(1);

"steal" means to commit theft;

"street racing" [*Repealed*, 2018, c. 21, s. 12.]

"summons" means a summons in Form 6 issued by a judge or justice or by the "chairperson" of a "Review Board" as defined in subsection 672.1(1);

"superior court of criminal jurisdiction" means

(*a*) in the Province of Ontario, the Court of Appeal or the Superior Court of Justice,

(b) in the Province of Quebec, the Superior Court,

(c) in the Provinces of Nova Scotia, British Columbia and Prince Edward Island, the Court of Appeal or the Supreme Court,

(d) in the Provinces of New Brunswick, Manitoba, Saskatchewan and Alberta, the Court of Appeal or the Court of Queen's Bench,

(e) in the Province of Newfoundland and Labrador, Yukon and the Northwest Territories, the Supreme Court, and

(f) in Nunavut, the Nunavut Court of Justice;

(g) [*Repealed*, 2015, c. 3, s. 44(3)]

(h) [*Repealed*, 2015, c. 3, s. 44(3)]

"territorial division" includes any province, county, union of counties, township, city, town, parish or other judicial division or place to which the context applies;

"terrorism offence" means

(a) an offence under any of sections 83.02 to 83.04 or 83.18 to 83.23,

(b) an indictable offence under this or any other Act of Parliament committed for the benefit of, at the direction of or in association with a terrorist group,

(c) an indictable offence under this or any other Act of Parliament where the act or omission constituting the offence also constitutes a terrorist activity, or

(d) a conspiracy or an attempt to commit, or being an accessory after the fact in relation to, or any counselling in relation to, an offence referred to in paragraph (a), (b) or (c);

"terrorist activity" has the same meaning as in subsection 83.01(1);

"terrorist group" has the same meaning as in subsection 83.01(1);

"testamentary instrument" includes any will, codicil or other testamentary writing or appointment, during the life of the testator whose testamentary disposition it purports to be and after his death, whether it relates to real or personal property or to both;

"trustee" means a person who is declared by any Act to be a trustee or is, by the law of the province, a trustee, and without restricting the generality of the foregoing, includes a trustee on an express trust created by deed, will or instrument in writing, or by parol;

"undertaking" means, unless a contrary intention appears, an undertaking in Form 10 given to a peace officer;

"unfit to stand trial" means unable on account of mental disorder to conduct a defence at any stage of the proceedings before a verdict is rendered or to instruct counsel to do so, and, in particular, unable on account of mental disorder to

(a) understand the nature or object of the proceedings,

(b) understand the possible consequences of the proceedings, or

(c) communicate with counsel;

"United Nations operation" means an operation that is established by the competent organ of the United Nations in accordance with the Charter of the United Nations and is conducted under United Nations authority and control, if the operation is for the purpose of maintaining or restoring international peace and security or if the Security Council or the General Assembly of the United Nations has declared, for the purposes of the Convention on the Safety of United Nations and Associated Personnel, that there exists an exceptional risk to the safety of the personnel participating in the operation. It does not include an operation authorized by the Security Council as an enforcement action under Chapter VII of the Charter of the United Nations in which any of the personnel are engaged as combatants against organized armed forces and to which the law of international armed conflict applies;

"United Nations personnel" means

    (*a*) persons who are engaged or deployed by the Secretary-General of the United Nations as members of the military, police or civilian components of a United Nations operation, or

    (*b*) any other officials or experts who are on mission of the United Nations or one of its specialized agencies or the International Atomic Energy Agency and who are present in an official capacity in the area where a United Nations operation is conducted;

"valuable mineral" means a mineral of a value of at least $100 per kilogram, and includes precious metals, diamonds and other gemstones and any rock or ore that contains those minerals;

"valuable security" includes

    (*a*) an order, exchequer acquittance or other security that entitles or evidences the title of any person

        (i) to a share or interest in a public stock or fund or in any fund of a body corporate, company or society, or

        (ii) to a deposit in a financial institution,

    (*b*) any debenture, deed, bond, bill, note, warrant, order or other security for money or for payment of money,

    (*c*) a document of title to lands or goods wherever situated,

    (*d*) a stamp or writing that secures or evidences title to or an interest in a chattel personal, or that evidences delivery of a chattel personal, and

    (*e*) a release, receipt, discharge or other instrument evidencing payment of money;

"victim" means a person against whom an offence has been committed, or is alleged to have been committed, who has suffered, or is alleged to have suffered, physical or emotional harm, property damage or economic loss as the result of the commission or alleged commission of the offence and includes, for the purposes of sections 672.5, 722 and 745.63, a person who has suffered physical or emotional harm, property damage or economic loss as the result of the commission of an offence against any other person;

"videoconference" means any means of telecommunication that allows the judge, justice or chairperson of a Review Board, as defined in subsection 672.1(1), and any individual to engage in simultaneous visual and oral communication in a proceeding;

"weapon" means any thing used, designed to be used or intended for use

    (*a*) in causing death or injury to any person, or

    (*b*) for the purpose of threatening or intimidating any person and, without restricting the generality of the foregoing, includes a firearm and, for the purposes of sections 88, 267 and 272, any thing used, designed to be used or intended for use in binding or tying up a person against their will;

"wreck" includes the cargo, stores and tackle of a vessel and all parts of a vessel separated from the vessel, and the property of persons who belong to, are on board or have quitted a vessel that is wrecked, stranded or in distress at any place in Canada;

"writing" includes a document of any kind and any mode in which, and any material on which, words or figures, whether at length or abridged, are written, printed or otherwise expressed, or a map or plan is inscribed. R.S., c. C-34, s. 2; 1972, c. 13, s. 2, c. 17, s. 2; 1973-74, c. 17, s. 9; 1974-75-76, c. 19, ss. 1, 2, c. 48, s. 24, c. 93, s. 2; 1976-77, c. 35, s. 21; 1978-79, c. 11, s. 10; 1980-81-82-83, c. 125, s. 1; R.S.C. 1985, c. 11 (1st Supp.), s. 2, c. 27 (1st Supp.), s. 2, c. 31 (1st Supp.), s. 61; c. 1 (2nd Supp.), s. 213(4), c. 27 (2nd Supp.), s. 10, c. 35 (2nd Supp.), s. 34; c. 32 (4th Supp.), s. 55; c. 40 (4th Supp.), s. 2; 1990, c. 17, s. 7; 1991, c. 1, s. 28; 1991, c. 43, ss. 1, 9; 1991, c. 40, s. 1; 1992, c. 20, s. 216; 1992, c. 51, s. 32; 1993, c. 28, Sch. III, s. 25(1), (2) (repealed by 1999, c. 3, s. 12); 1994, c. 44, s. 2; 1995, c. 29, ss. 39, 40, c. 39, s. 138; 1997, c. 23, s. 1; 1998, c. 30, s. 14(*d*); 1999, c. 3, ss. 12, 25; c. 5, s. 1; c. 25, s. 1; c. 28, s. 155; 2000, c. 12, s. 91; 2001, c. 32, s. 1; 2001, c. 41, s. 2 and 131(2); 2002, c. 7, s. 137(2); 2002, c. 22, s. 324; 2003, c. 21, s. 1; 2004, c. 3, s. 1; 2005, c. 10, s. 34(1)(*f*)(i); 2005, c. 38, s. 58; 2005, c. 40, ss 1 and 7; 2006, c. 14, s. 1; 2007, c. 13, s. 1; 2012, c. 1, s. 160(*c*)(i); 2012, c. 19, s. 371; 2013, c. 13, s. 2; 2014, c. 17, s. 1; 2014, c. 23, s. 2; 2014, c. 25, s. 2; 2015, c. 3, s. 44; 2015, c. 13, s. 3; c. 20, s. 15; 2018, c. 21, s. 12; 2019, c. 13, s. 140; 2019, c. 25, s. 1.

FURTHER DEFINITIONS — FIREARMS.

2.1 In this Act, "ammunition", "antique firearm", "automatic firearm", "cartridge magazine", "cross-bow", "handgun", "imitation firearm", "prohibited ammunition", "prohibited device", "prohibited firearm", "prohibited weapon", "replica firearm", "restricted firearm" and "restricted weapon", as well as "authorization", "licence" and "registration certificate" when used in relation to those words and expressions, have the same meaning as in subsection 84(1). 2009, c. 22, s. 1.

ACTING ON VICTIM'S BEHALF / Exception.

2.2 (1) For the purposes of sections 606, 672.5, 715.37, 722, 737.1 and 745.63, any of the following individuals may act on the victim's behalf if the victim is dead or incapable of acting on their own behalf:

(*a*) the victim's spouse, or if the victim is dead, their spouse at the time of death;

(*b*) the victim's common-law partner, or if the victim is dead, their common-law partner at the time of death;

(*c*) a relative or dependant of the victim;

(*d*) an individual who has in law or fact custody, or is responsible for the care or support, of the victim; and (*e*) an individual who has in law or fact custody, or is responsible for the care or support, of a dependant of the victim.

(2) An individual is not entitled to act on a victim's behalf if the individual is an accused in relation to the offence or alleged offence that resulted in the victim suffering harm or loss or is an individual who is found guilty of that offence or who is found not criminally responsible on account of mental disorder or unfit to stand trial in respect of that offence. 2015, c. 13, s. 4; 2018, c. 12, s. 403.

CONCURRENT JURISDICTION / For greater certainty — Attorney General of Canada / For greater certainty — Director of Public Prosecutions.

2.3 (1) The proceedings for the purposes of paragraph (*a*) of the definition "Attorney General" in section 2 are

   (*a*) proceedings in relation to an offence under subsection 7(2.01), (2.3) or (2.31) or section 57, 58, 83.12, 103, 104, 121.1, 380, 382, 382.1, 400, 424.1, 431.1, 467.11 or 467.111 or in relation to any terrorism offence;

Note: Paragraph 2.3(1)(*a*) replaced, 2020, c. 1, s. 35 (to come into force by order of the Governor in Council):

   (*a*) proceedings in relation to an offence under subsection 7(2.01), (2.3) or (2.31) or section 57, 58, 83.12, 103, 104, 121.1, 380, 382, 382.1, 391, 400, 424.1, 431.1, 467.11 or 467.111 or in relation to any terrorism offence;

   (*b*) proceedings in relation to an offence against a member of United Nations personnel or associated personnel under section 235, 236, 266 to 269, 269.1, 271 to 273, 279 or 279.1;

   (*c*) proceedings in relation to an offence referred to in subsection 7(3.71) or in relation to an offence referred to in paragraph (*a*) of the definition "terrorist activity" in subsection 83.01(1) if the act or omission constituting the offence was committed outside Canada and is deemed under any of subsections 7(2), (2.1) to (2.21), (3), (3.1), (3.72) and (3.73) to have been committed in Canada;

   (*d*) proceedings in relation to an offence if the act or omission constituting the offence is a terrorist activity referred to in paragraph (*b*) of the definition "terrorist activity" in subsection 83.01(1) and was committed outside Canada and is deemed by virtue of subsection 7(3.74) or (3.75) to have been committed in Canada;

   (*e*) a proceeding in relation to an offence under section 811 that arises out of a breach of a recognizance made under section 810.01 or 810.011, if he or she has given consent to the information referred to in those sections; and

   (*f*) proceedings under section 83.13, 83.14, 83.222, 83.223, 83.28, 83.29 or 83.3.

(2) For greater certainty, the Attorney General of Canada or his or her lawful deputy may, in respect of an offence referred to in subsection (1) or an offence under any Act of Parliament — other than this Act or the *Canada Elections Act* — or any regulation made under such an Act, exercise all the powers and perform all the duties and functions assigned to the Attorney General by or under this Act, and those powers include the power to commence and to conduct

(a) a proceeding for conspiring or attempting to commit such an offence or for being an accessory after the fact or counselling a person to be a party to such an offence;

(b) a proceeding in relation to a criminal organization offence that arises out of conduct that relates, in whole or in part, to any offence for which he or she has the power to commence and to conduct a proceeding;

(c) a proceeding in relation to an offence referred to in section 354, 355.2, 355.4 or 462.31 that arises out of conduct that relates, in whole or in part, to any offence for which he or she has the power to commence and to conduct a proceeding or

out of any act or omission that, if it had occurred in Canada, would have constituted such an offence;

(d) a proceeding for the breach of any court order made in the course of a proceeding commenced or conducted by him or her;

(e) a proceeding for the failure to comply with any condition associated with the release of a person by a peace officer or other competent authority — including a condition to appear at a specified time and place — in relation to any offence for which he or she has the power to commence and to conduct a proceeding; and

(f) any ancillary proceedings in relation to any offence for which he or she has the power to commence and to conduct a proceeding.

(3) For greater certainty, in respect of an offence under the *Canada Elections Act*, the Director of Public Prosecutions, subject to the *Director of Public Prosecutions Act*, exercises the powers and performs the duties and functions of the Attorney General of Canada referred to in subsection (2). 2019, c. 25, s. 2.

DESCRIPTIVE CROSS-REFERENCES.

3. Where, in any provision of this Act, a reference to another provision of this Act or a provision of any other Act is followed by words in parenthesis that are or purport to be descriptive of the subject-matter of the provision referred to, the words in parenthesis form no part of the provision in which they occur but shall be deemed to have been inserted for convenience of reference only. 1976-77, c. 53, s. 2.

EFFECT OF JUDICIAL ACTS / Clerk of the court.

3.1 (1) Unless otherwise provided or ordered, anything done by a court, justice or judge is effective from the moment it is done, whether or not it is reduced to writing.

(2) Unless otherwise provided or ordered, if anything is done from the bench by a court, justice or judge and it is reduced to writing, the clerk of the court may sign the writing. 2002, c. 13, s. 2; 2019, c. 25, s. 3.

Part I / GENERAL

POSTCARD A CHATTEL, VALUE / Value of valuable security / Possession / Expressions taken from other Acts / Sexual intercourse / Proof of notifications and service of documents / Proof of service in accordance with provincial laws / Attendance for examination / Means of telecommunication.

4. (1) For the purposes of this Act, a postal card or stamp referred to in paragraph (*c*) of the definition "property" in section 2 shall be deemed to be a chattel and to be equal in value to the amount of the postage, rate or duty expressed on its face.

(2) For the purposes of this Act, the following rules apply for the purpose of determining the value of a valuable security where value is material:

- (*a*) where the valuable security is one mentioned in paragraph (*a*) or (*b*) of the definition "valuable security" in section 2, the value is the value of the share, interest, deposit or unpaid money, as the case may be, that is secured by the valuable security;
- (*b*) where the valuable security is one mentioned in paragraph (*c*) or (*d*) of the definition "valuable security" in section 2, the value is the value of the lands, goods, chattel personal or interest in the chattel personal, as the case may be; and
- (*c*) where the valuable security is one mentioned in paragraph (*e*) of the definition "valuable security" in section 2, the value is the amount of money that has been paid.

(3) For the purposes of this Act,

- (*a*) a person has anything in possession when he has it in his personal possession or knowingly
  - (i) has it in the actual possession or custody of another person, or
  - (ii) has it in any place, whether or not that place belongs to or is occupied by him, for the use or benefit of himself or of another person; and
- (*b*) where one of two or more persons, with the knowledge and consent of the rest, has anything in his custody or possession, it shall be deemed to be in the custody and possession of each and all of them.

(4) Where an offence that is dealt with in this Act relates to a subject that is dealt with in another Act, the words and expressions used in this Act with respect to that offence have, subject to this Act, the meaning assigned to them in that other Act.

(5) For the purposes of this Act, sexual intercourse is complete on penetration to even the slightest degree, notwithstanding that seed is not emitted.

(6) For the purposes of this Act, the service of documents and the giving or sending of any notice may be proved

- (*a*) by oral evidence given under oath by, or by the affidavit or solemn declaration of, the person claiming to have served, given or sent it; or

(b) in the case of a peace officer, by a statement in writing certifying that the document was served or the notice was given or sent by the peace officer, and such a statement is deemed to be a statement made under oath.

(6.1) Despite subsection (6), the service of documents may be proved in accordance with the laws of a province relating to offences created by the laws of that province.

(7) Despite subsection (6) or (6.1), the court may require the person who appears to have signed an affidavit, a solemn declaration or a statement in accordance with that subsection to appear before it for examination or cross-examination in respect of the issue of proof of service or of the giving or sending of any notice.

(8) For greater certainty, for the purposes of this Act, if the elements of an offence contain an explicit or implicit element of communication without specifying the means of communication, the communication may also be made by a means of telecommunication. R.S., c. C-34, s. 3; 1980-81-82-83, c. 125, s. 2; R.S.C. 1985, c. 27 (1st Supp.), s. 3; 1994, c. 44, s. 3; 1997, c. 18, s. 2; 2008, c. 18, s. 1; 2014, c. 31, s. 2.

CANADIAN FORCES NOT AFFECTED.

5. Nothing in this Act affects any law relating to the government of the Canadian Forces. R.S., c. C-34, s. 4.

PRESUMPTION OF INNOCENCE / Offences outside Canada / Definition of "enactment".

6. (1) Where an enactment creates an offence and authorizes a punishment to be imposed in respect of that offence,
    (a) a person shall be deemed not to be guilty of the offence until he is convicted or discharged under section 730 of the offence; and
    (b) a person who is convicted or discharged under section 730 of the offence is not liable to any punishment in respect thereof other than the punishment prescribed by this Act or by the enactment that creates the offence.

(2) Subject to this Act or any other Act of Parliament, no person shall be convicted or discharged under section 730 of an offence committed outside Canada.

(3) In this section, "enactment" means
    (a) an Act of Parliament, or
    (b) an Act of the legislature of a province that creates an offence to which Part XXVII applies,
or any regulation made thereunder. R.S., c. C-34, s. 5; R.S.C. 1985, c. 27 (1st Supp.), s. 4; 1995, c. 22, s. 10.

OFFENCES COMMITTED ON AIRCRAFT / Idem / Offences in relation to cultural property / Definition of "Convention" / Offences against fixed platforms or international maritime navigation / Offences against fixed platforms or navigation in the internal waters or territorial sea of another state / Nuclear terrorism offence committed outside Canada / Space Station — Canadian crew members / Space Station — crew members of Partner States / Proceedings by Attorney General of Canada / Consent of Attorney General of Canada / Definitions / Offence against internationally protected person / Offence of hostage taking / Jurisdiction / Offence against United Nations or associated personnel / Offence involving explosive or other lethal device / Offence relating to financing of terrorism / Terrorism offence committed outside Canada / Terrorist activity committed outside Canada / Offences by Public Service employees / Offence in relation to sexual offences against children / Offence in relation to trafficking in persons / Consent of Attorney General / Jurisdiction / Appearance of accused at trial / Where previously tried outside Canada / If accused not Canadian citizen / Definition of "flight" and "in flight" / Definition of "in service" / Certificate as evidence / Idem.

7. (1) Notwithstanding anything in this Act or any other Act, every one who
   (*a*) on or in respect of an aircraft
      (i) registered in Canada under regulations made under the *Aeronautics Act*, or
      (ii) leased without crew and operated by a person who is qualified under regulations made under the *Aeronautics Act* to be registered as owner of an aircraft registered in Canada under those regulations,
     while the aircraft is in flight, or
   (*b*) on any aircraft, while the aircraft is in flight if the flight terminated in Canada,
commits an act or omission in or outside Canada that if committed in Canada would be an offence punishable by indictment shall be deemed to have committed that act or omission in Canada.

(2) Notwithstanding this Act or any other Act, every one who
   (*a*) on an aircraft, while the aircraft is in flight, commits an act or omission outside Canada that if committed in Canada or on an aircraft registered in Canada under regulations made under the *Aeronautics Act* would be an offence against section 76 or paragraph 77(*a*),
   (*b*) in relation to an aircraft in service, commits an act or omission outside Canada that if committed in Canada would be an offence against any of paragraphs 77(*c*), (*d*) or (*g*),
   (*c*) in relation to an air navigation facility used in international air navigation, commits an act or omission outside Canada that if committed in Canada would be an offence against paragraph 77(*e*),
   (*d*) at or in relation to an airport serving international civil aviation, commits an act or omission outside Canada that if committed in Canada would be an offence against paragraph 77(*b*) or (*f*), or
   (*e*) commits an act or omission outside Canada that if committed in Canada would constitute a conspiracy or an attempt to commit an offence referred

to in this subsection, or being an accessory after the fact or counselling in
relation to such an offence,

shall be deemed to have committed that act or omission in Canada if the person is,
after the commission thereof, present in Canada.

(2.01) Despite anything in this Act or any other Act, a person who commits an act
or omission outside Canada that if committed in Canada would constitute an
offence under section 322, 341, 344, 380, 430 or 434 in relation to cultural
property as defined in Article 1 of the Convention, or a conspiracy or an attempt to
commit such an offence, or being an accessory after the fact or counselling in
relation to such an offence, is deemed to have committed that act or omission in
Canada if the person

   (a) is a Canadian citizen;

   (b) is not a citizen of any state and ordinarily resides in Canada; or

   (c) is a permanent resident within the meaning of subsection 2(1) of the
Immigration and Refugee Protection Act and is, after the commission of the
act or omission, present in Canada.

(2.02) For the purpose of subsection (2.01), "Convention" means the Convention
for the Protection of Cultural Property in the Event of Armed Conflict, done at
The Hague on May 14, 1954. Article 1 of the Convention is set out in the schedule
to the *Cultural Property Export and Import Act*.

(2.1) Notwithstanding anything in this Act or any other Act, every one who
commits an act or omission outside Canada against or on board a fixed platform
attached to the continental shelf of any state or against or on board a ship
navigating or scheduled to navigate beyond the territorial sea of any state, that if
committed in Canada would constitute an offence against, a conspiracy or an
attempt to commit an offence against, or being an accessory after the fact or
counselling in relation to an offence against, section 78.1, shall be deemed to
commit that act or omission in Canada if it is committed

   (a) against or on board a fixed platform attached to the continental shelf of
Canada;

   (b) against or on board a ship registered or licensed, or for which an
identification number has been issued, pursuant to any Act of Parliament;

   (c) by a Canadian citizen;

   (d) by a person who is not a citizen of any state and who ordinarily resides in
Canada;

   (e) by a person who is, after the commission of the offence, present in Canada;

   (f) in such a way as to seize, injure or kill, or threaten to injure or kill, a
Canadian citizen; or

   (g) in an attempt to compel the Government of Canada to do or refrain from
doing any act.

(2.2) Notwithstanding anything in this Act or any other Act, every one who
commits an act or omission outside Canada against or on board a fixed platform
not attached to the continental shelf of any state or against or on board a ship not
navigating or scheduled to navigate beyond the territorial sea of any state, that if
committed in Canada would constitute an offence against, a conspiracy or an
attempt to commit an offence against, or being an accessory after the fact or

counselling in relation to an offence against, section 78.1, shall be deemed to commit that act or omission in Canada

(a) if it is committed as described in any of paragraphs (2.1)(b) to (g); and

(b) if the offender is found in the territory of a state, other than the state in which the act or omission was committed, that is

(i) a party to the Convention for the Suppression of Unlawful Acts against the Safety of Maritime Navigation, done at Rome on March 10, 1988, in respect of an offence committed against or on board a ship, or

(ii) a party to the Protocol for the Suppression of Unlawful Acts against the Safety of Fixed Platforms Located on the Continental Shelf, done at Rome on March 10, 1988, in respect of an offence committed against or on board a fixed platform.

(2.21) Despite anything in this Act or anyother Act, everyone who commits an act or omission outside Canada that if committed in Canada would constitute an offence under any of sections 82.3 to 82.6, or a conspiracy or attempt to commit such an offence, or being an accessory after the fact or counselling in relation to such an offence, is deemed to have committed that act or omission in Canada if

(a) the act or omission is committed on a ship that is registered or licensed, or for which an identification number has been issued, under any Act of Parliament;

(b) the act or omission is committed on an aircraft that

(i) is registered in Canada under regulations made under the *Aeronautics Act*, or

(ii) is leased without crew and operated by a person who is qualified under regulations made under the *Aeronautics Act* to be registered as owner of an aircraft in Canada under those regulations;

(c) the person who commits the act or omission is a Canadian citizen; or

(d) the person who commits the act or omission is, after the commission of the act or omission, present in Canada.

(2.3) Despite anything in this Act or any other Act, a Canadian crew member who, during a space flight, commits an act or omission outside Canada that if committed in Canada would constitute an indictable offence is deemed to have committed that act or omission in Canada, if that act or omission is committed

(a) on, or in relation to, a flight element of the Space Station; or

(b) on any means of transportation to or from the Space Station.

(2.31) Despite anything in this Act or any other Act, a crew member of a Partner State who commits an act or omission outside Canada during a space flight on, or in relation to, a flight element of the Space Station or on any means of transportation to and from the Space Station that if committed in Canada would constitute an indictable offence is deemed to have committed that act or omission in Canada, if that act or omission

(a) threatens the life or security of a Canadian crew member; or

(b) is committed on or in relation to, or damages, a flight element provided by Canada.

(2.32) [*Repealed*, 2019, c. 25, s. 4(1).]

(2.33) No proceedings in relation to an offence referred to in subsection (2.3) or (2.31) may be instituted without the consent of the Attorney General of Canada.

(2.34) The definitions in this subsection apply in this subsection and in subsections (2.3) and (2.31).

"Agreement" has the same meaning as in section 2 of the *Civil International Space Station Agreement Implementation Act*.

"Canadian crew member" means a crew member of the Space Station who is
  (a) a Canadian citizen; or
  (b) a citizen of a foreign state, other than a Partner State, who is authorized by Canada to act as a crew member for a space flight on, or in relation to a flight element.

"crew member of a Partner State" means a crew member of the Space Station who is
  (a) a citizen of a Partner State; or
  (b) a citizen of a state, other than that Partner State, who is authorized by that Partner State to act as a crew member for a space flight on, or in relation to, a flight element.

"flight element" means a Space Station element provided by Canada or by a Partner State under the Agreement and under any memorandum of understanding or other implementing arrangement entered into to carry out the Agreement.

"Partner State" means a State, other than Canada, who contracted to enter into the Agreement and for which the Agreement has entered into force in accordance with article 25 of the Agreement.

"space flight" means the period that begins with the launching of a crew member of the Space Station, continues during their stay in orbit and ends with their landing on earth.

"Space Station" means the civil international Space Station that is a multi-use facility in low-earth orbit, with flight elements and dedicated ground elements provided by, or on behalf of, the Partner States.

(3) Notwithstanding anything in this Act or any other Act, every one who, outside Canada, commits an act or omission against the person of an internationally protected person or against any property referred to in section 431 used by that person that, if committed in Canada, would be an offence against any of sections 235, 236, 266, 267, 268, 269, 269.1, 271, 272, 273, 279, 279.1, 280 to 283, 424 and 431 is deemed to commit that act or omission in Canada if
  (a) the act or omission is committed on a ship that is registered or licensed, or for which an identification number has been issued, pursuant to any Act of Parliament;
  (b) the act or omission is committed on an aircraft
    (i) registered in Canada under regulations made under the *Aeronautics Act*, or
    (ii) leased without crew and operated by a person who is qualified under regulations made under the *Aeronautics Act* to be registered as owner of an aircraft in Canada under those regulations;

   (c) the person who commits the act or omission is a Canadian citizen or is, after the act or omission has been committed, present in Canada; or

   (d) the act or omission is against

      (i) a person who enjoys the status of an internationally protected person by virtue of the functions that person performs on behalf of Canada, or

     (ii) a member of the family of a person described in subparagraph (i) who qualifies under paragraph (b) or (d) of the definition "internationally protected person" in section 2.

(3.1) Notwithstanding anything in this Act or any other Act, every one who, outside Canada, commits an act or omission that if committed in Canada would be an offence against section 279.1 shall be deemed to commit that act or omission in Canada if

   (a) the act or omission is committed on a ship that is registered or licensed, or for which an identification number has been issued, pursuant to any Act of Parliament;

   (b) the act or omission is committed on an aircraft

      (i) registered in Canada under regulations made under the *Aeronautics Act*, or

     (ii) leased without crew and operated by a person who is qualified under regulations made under the *Aeronautics Act* to be registered as owner of an aircraft in Canada under such regulations;

   (c) the person who commits the act or omission

      (i) is a Canadian citizen, or

     (ii) is not a citizen of any state and ordinarily resides in Canada;

   (d) the act or omission is committed with intent to induce Her Majesty in right of Canada or of a province to commit or cause to be committed any act or omission;

   (e) a person taken hostage by the act or omission is a Canadian citizen; or

   (f) the person who commits the act or omission is, after the commission thereof, present in Canada.

(3.2) [Repealed, 2013, c. 13, s. 3(2).]

(3.3) [Repealed, 2013, c. 13, s. 3(2).]

(3.4) [Repealed, 2013, c. 13, s. 3(2).]

(3.5) [Repealed, 2013, c. 13, s. 3(2).]

(3.6) [Repealed, 2013, c. 13, s. 3(2).]

(3.7) Notwithstanding anything in this Act or any other Act, every one who, outside Canada, commits an act or omission that, if committed in Canada, would constitute an offence against, a conspiracy or an attempt to commit an offence against, being an accessory after the fact in relation to an offence against, or any counselling in relation to an offence against, section 269.1 shall be deemed to commit that act or omission in Canada if

   (a) the act or omission is committed on a ship that is registered or licensed, or for which an identification number has been issued, pursuant to any Act of Parliament;

   (b) the act or omission is committed on an aircraft

    (i) registered in Canada under regulations made under the *Aeronautics Act*, or

    (ii) leased without crew and operated by a person who is qualified under regulations made under the *Aeronautics Act* to be registered as owner of an aircraft in Canada under those regulations;

  (c) the person who commits the act or omission is a Canadian citizen;

  (d) the complainant is a Canadian citizen; or

  (e) the person who commits the act or omission is, after the commission thereof, present in Canada.

(3.71) Notwithstanding anything in this Act or any other Act, every one who, outside Canada, commits an act or omission against a member of United Nations personnel or associated personnel or against property referred to in section 431.1 that, if committed in Canada, would constitute an offence against, a conspiracy or an attempt to commit an offence against, or being an accessory after the fact or counselling in relation to an offence against, section 235, 236, 266, 267, 268, 269, 269.1, 271, 272, 273, 279, 279.1, 424.1 or 431.1 is deemed to commit that act or omission in Canada if

  (a) the act or omission is committed on a ship that is registered or licensed, or for which an identification number has been issued, under an Act of Parliament;

  (b) the act or omission is committed on an aircraft

    (i) registered in Canada under regulations made under the *Aeronautics Act*, or

    (ii) leased without crew and operated by a person who is qualified under regulations made under the *Aeronautics Act* to be registered as owner of an aircraft in Canada under those regulations;

  (c) the person who commits the act or omission

    (i) is a Canadian citizen, or

    (ii) is not a citizen of any state and ordinarily resides in Canada;

  (d) the person who commits the act or omission is, after the commission of the act or omission, present in Canada;

  (e) the act or omission is committed against a Canadian citizen; or

  (f) the act or omission is committed with intent to compel the Government of Canada or of a province to do or refrain from doing any act.

(3.72) Notwithstanding anything in this Act or any other Act, every one who, outside Canada, commits an act or omission that, if committed in Canada, would constitute an offence against, a conspiracy or an attempt to commit an offence against, or being an accessory after the fact or counselling in relation to an offence against, section 431.2 is deemed to commit that act or omission in Canada if

  (a) the act or omission is committed on a ship that is registered or licensed, or for which an identification number has been issued, under any Act of Parliament;

  (b) the act or omission is committed on an aircraft

    (i) registered in Canada under regulations made under the *Aeronautics Act*,

33

    (ii) leased without crew and operated by a person who is qualified under regulations made under the *Aeronautics Act* to be registered as owner of an aircraft in Canada under those regulations, or

    (iii) operated for or on behalf of the Government of Canada;

  (*c*) the person who commits the act or omission

    (i) is a Canadian citizen, or

    (ii) is not a citizen of any state and ordinarily resides in Canada;

  (*d*) the person who commits the act or omission is, after the commission of the act or omission, present in Canada;

  (*e*) the act or omission is committed against a Canadian citizen;

  (*f*) the act or omission is committed with intent to compel the Government of Canada or of a province to do or refrain from doing any act; or

  (*g*) the act or omission is committed against a Canadian government or public facility located outside Canada.

(3.73) Notwithstanding anything in this Act or any other Act, every one who, outside Canada, commits an act or omission that, if committed in Canada, would constitute an offence against, a conspiracy or an attempt to commit an offence against, or being an accessory after the fact or counselling in relation to an offence against, section 83.02 is deemed to commit the act or omission in Canada if

  (*a*) the act or omission is committed on a ship that is registered or licensed, or for which an identification number has been issued, under an Act of Parliament;

  (*b*) the act or omission is committed on an aircraft

    (i) registered in Canada under regulations made under the *Aeronautics Act*, or

    (ii) leased without crew and operated by a person who is qualified under regulations made under the *Aeronautics Act* to be registered as the owner of an aircraft in Canada under those regulations;

  (*c*) the person who commits the act or omission

    (i) is a Canadian citizen, or

    (ii) is not a citizen of any state and ordinarily resides in Canada;

  (*d*) the person who commits the act or omission is, after its commission, present in Canada;

  (*e*) the act or omission is committed for the purpose of committing an act or omission referred to in paragraph 83.02(*a*) or (*b*) in order to compel the Government of Canada or of a province to do or refrain from doing any act;

  (*f*) the act or omission is committed for the purpose of committing an act or omission referred to in paragraph 83.02(*a*) or (*b*) against a Canadian government or public facility located outside Canada; or

  (*g*) the act or omission is committed for the purpose of committing an act or omission referred to in paragraph 83.02(*a*) or (*b*) in Canada or against a Canadian citizen.

(3.74) Notwithstanding anything in this Act or any other Act, every one who commits an act or omission outside Canada that, if committed in Canada, would be a terrorism offence, other than an offence under section 83.02 or an offence referred to in paragraph (*a*) of the definition "terrorist activity" in subsection

83.01(1), is deemed to have committed that act or omission in Canada if the person

    (*a*) is a Canadian citizen;

    (*b*) is not a citizen of any state and ordinarily resides in Canada; or

    (*c*) is a permanent resident within the meaning of subsection 2(1) of the *Immigration and Refugee Protection Act* and is, after the commission of the act or omission, present in Canada.

(3.75) Notwithstanding anything in this Act or any other Act, every one who commits an act or omission outside Canada that, if committed in Canada, would be an indictable offence and would also constitute a terrorist activity referred to in paragraph (*b*) of the definition "terrorist activity" in subsection 83.01(1) is deemed to commit that act or omission in Canada if

    (*a*) the act or omission is committed against a Canadian citizen;

    (*b*) the act or omission is committed against a Canadian government or public facility located outside Canada; or

    (*c*) the act or omission is committed with intent to compel the Government of Canada or of a province to do or refrain from doing any act.

(3.76) [*Repealed*, 2000, c. 24, s. 42.]

(3.77) [*Repealed*, 2000, c. 24, s. 42.]

(4) Every one who, while employed as an employee within the meaning of the *Public Service Employment Act* in a place outside Canada, commits an act or omission in that place that is an offence under the laws of that place and that, if committed in Canada, would be an offence punishable by indictment shall be deemed to have committed that act or omission in Canada.

(4.1) Notwithstanding anything in this Act or any other Act, every one who, outside Canada, commits an act or omission that if committed in Canada would be an offence against section 151, 152, 153 or 155, subsection 160(2) or (3), section 163.1, 170, 171, 171.1, 172.1, 172.2 or 173 or subsection 286.1(2) shall be deemed to commit that act or omission in Canada if the person who commits the act or omission is a Canadian citizen or a "permanent resident" within the meaning of subsection 2(1) of the *Immigration and Refugee Protection Act*.

(4.11) Notwithstanding anything in this Act or any other Act, every one who, outside Canada, commits an act or omission that if committed in Canada would be an offence against section 279.01, 279.011, 279.02 or 279.03 shall be deemed to commit that act or omission in Canada if the person who commits the act or omission is a Canadian citizen or a permanent resident within the meaning of subsection 2(1) of the *Immigration and Refugee Protection Act*.

(4.2) [*Repealed*, 2002, c. 13, s. 3(2).]

(4.3) Proceedings with respect to an act or omission deemed to have been committed in Canada under subsection (4.1) may only be instituted with the consent of the Attorney General.

(5) Where a person is alleged to have committed an act or omission that is an offence by virtue of this section, proceedings in respect of that offence may, whether or not that person is in Canada, be commenced in any territorial division

in Canada and the accused may be tried and punished in respect of that offence in the same manner as if the offence had been committed in that territorial division.

(5.1) For greater certainty, the provisions of this Act relating to

   (*a*) requirements that an accused appear at and be present during proceedings, and

   (*b*) the exceptions to those requirements,

apply to proceedings commenced in any territorial division pursuant to subsection (5).

(6) If a person is alleged to have committed an act or omission that is an offence by virtue of this section and that person has been tried and dealt with outside Canada in respect of the offence in such a manner that, if that person had been tried and dealt with in Canada, they would be able to plead *autrefois acquit, autrefois convict*, pardon or an expungement order under the *Expungement of Historically Unjust Convictions Act*, that person shall be deemed to have been so tried and dealt with in Canada.

(7) If the accused is not a Canadian citizen, no proceedings in respect of which courts have jurisdiction by virtue of this section shall be continued unless the consent of the Attorney General of Canada is obtained not later than eight days after the proceedings are commenced.

(8) For the purposes of this section, of the definition "peace officer" in section 2 and of sections 27.1, 76 and 77, "flight" means the act of flying or moving through the air and an aircraft is deemed to be in flight from the time when all external doors are closed following embarkation until the later of

   (*a*) the time at which any such door is opened for the purpose of disembarkation, and

   (*b*) where the aircraft makes a forced landing in circumstances in which the owner or operator thereof or a person acting on behalf of either of them is not in control of the aircraft, the time at which control of the aircraft is restored to the owner or operator thereof or a person acting on behalf of either of them.

(9) For the purposes of this section and section 77, an aircraft shall be deemed to be in service from the time when pre-flight preparation of the aircraft by ground personnel or the crew thereof begins for a specific flight until

   (*a*) the flight is cancelled before the aircraft is in flight,

   (*b*) twenty-four hours after the aircraft, having commenced the flight, lands, or

   (*c*) the aircraft, having commenced the flight, ceases to be in flight,

whichever is the latest.

(10) In any proceedings under this Act, a certificate purporting to have been issued by or under the authority of the Minister of Foreign Affairs is admissible in evidence without proof of the signature or authority of the person appearing to have signed it and, in the absence of evidence to the contrary, is proof of the facts it states that are relevant to the question of whether any person is a member of United Nations personnel, a member of associated personnel or a person who is entitled under international law to protection from attack or threat of attack against his or her person, freedom or dignity.

(11) A certificate purporting to have been issued by or under the authority of the Minister of Foreign Affairs stating

    (*a*) that at a certain time any state was engaged in an armed conflict against Canada or was allied with Canada in an armed conflict,

    (*b*) that at a certain time any convention, treaty or other international agreement was or was not in force and that Canada was or was not a party thereto, or

    (*c*) that Canada agreed or did not agree to accept and apply the provisions of any convention, treaty or other international agreement in an armed conflict in which Canada was involved,

is admissible in evidence in any proceedings without proof of the signature or authority of the person appearing to have issued it, and is proof of the facts so stated. R.S., c. C-34, s. 6; 1972, c. 13, s. 3; 1974-75-76, c. 93, s. 3; 1980-81-82-83, c. 125, s. 3; R.S.C. 1985, c. 27 (1st Supp.), s. 5; R.S.C. 1985, c. 10 (3rd Supp.), s. 1, c. 30 (3rd Supp.), s. 1; 1992, c. 1, s. 58; 1993, c. 7, s. 1; 1995, c. 5, s. 25; 1997, c. 16, s. 1; 1999, c. 35, s. 11; 2000, c. 24, s. 42; 2001, c. 41, ss. 3, 126(1) and (2); 2002, c. 13, s. 3; 2004, c. 12, s. 1; 2005, c. 40, s. 2; 2012, c. 1, s. 10; 2012, c. 15, s. 1; 2013, c. 9, s. 2; 2013, c. 13, s. 3; 2014, c. 25, s. 3; 2018, c. 11, s. 27; 2019, c. 25, s. 4.

APPLICATION TO TERRITORIES / Application of criminal law of England / Common law principles continued.

8. (1) The provisions of this Act apply throughout Canada except

    (*a*) in Yukon, in so far as they are inconsistent with the *Yukon Act*;

    (*b*) in the Northwest Territories, in so far as they are inconsistent with the *Northwest Territories Act*, and

    (*c*) in Nunavut, in so far as they are inconsistent with the *Nunavut Act*.

(2) The criminal law of England that was in force in a province immediately before April 1, 1955 continues in force in the province except as altered, varied, modified or affected by this Act or any other Act of the Parliament of Canada.

(3) Every rule and principle of the common law that renders any circumstance a justification or excuse for an act or a defence to a charge continues in force and applies in respect of proceedings for an offence under this Act or any other Act of Parliament except in so far as they are altered by or are inconsistent with this Act or any other Act of Parliament. R.S., c. C-34, s. 7; 1993, c. 28, Sch. III, s. 26; 2002, c. 7, s. 138.

CRIMINAL OFFENCES TO BE UNDER LAW OF CANADA.

9. Notwithstanding anything in this Act or any other Act, no person shall be convicted or discharged under section 730

    (*a*) of an offence at common law,

    (*b*) of an offence under an Act of the Parliament of England, or of Great Britain, or of the United Kingdom of Great Britain and Ireland, or

    (*c*) of an offence under an Act or ordinance in force in any province, territory or place before that province, territory or place became a province of Canada, but nothing in this section affects the power, jurisdiction or authority that a court, judge, justice or provincial court judge had, immediately before April 1, 1955, to impose punishment for contempt of court. R.S., c. C-34, s. 8; R.S.C. 1985, c. 27 (1st Supp.), s. 6; 1995, c. 22, s. 10.

APPEAL / Idem / Part XXI applies.

10. (1) Where a court, judge, justice or provincial court judge summarily convicts a person for a contempt of court committed in the face of the court and imposes punishment in respect thereof, that person may appeal

    (a) from the conviction; or

    (b) against the punishment imposed.

(2) Where a court or judge summarily convicts a person for a contempt of court not committed in the face of the court and punishment is imposed in respect thereof, that person may appeal

    (a) from the conviction; or

    (b) against the punishment imposed.

(3) An appeal under this section lies to the court of appeal of the province in which the proceedings take place, and, for the purposes of this section, the provisions of Part XXI apply, with such modifications as the circumstances require. R.S., c. C-34, s. 9; 1972, c. 13, s. 4.

CIVIL REMEDY NOT SUSPENDED.

11. No civil remedy for an act or omission is suspended or affected by reason that the act or omission is a criminal offence. R.S., c. C-34, s. 10.

OFFENCE PUNISHABLE UNDER MORE THAN ONE ACT.

12. Where an act or omission is an offence under more than one Act of Parliament, whether punishable by indictment or on summary conviction, a person who does the act or makes the omission is, unless a contrary intention appears, subject to proceedings under any of those Acts, but is not liable to be punished more than once for the same offence. R.S., c. C-34, s. 11.

CHILD UNDER TWELVE.

13. No person shall be convicted of an offence in respect of an act or omission on his part while that person was under the age of twelve years. R.S., c. C-34, s. 12; 1980-81-82-83, c. 110, s. 72.

CONSENT TO DEATH.

14. No person is entitled to consent to have death inflicted on them, and such consent does not affect the criminal responsibility of any person who inflicts death on the person who gave consent. R.S., c. C-34, s. 14, 2016, c. 3, s. 1.

OBEDIENCE TO *DE FACTO* LAW.

15. No person shall be convicted of an offence in respect of an act or omission in obedience to the laws for the time being made and enforced by persons in *de facto* possession of the sovereign power in and over the place where the act or omission occurs. R.S., c. C-34, s. 15.

DEFENCE OF MENTAL DISORDER / Presumption / Burden of proof.

CODE

16. (1) No person is criminally responsible for an act committed or an omission made while suffering from a mental disorder that rendered the person incapable of appreciating the nature and quality of the act or omission or of knowing that it was wrong.

(2) Every person is presumed not to suffer from a mental disorder so as to be exempt from criminal responsibility by virtue of subsection (1), until the contrary is proved on the balance of probabilities.

(3) The burden of proof that an accused was suffering from a mental disorder so as to be exempt from criminal responsibility is on the party that raises the issue. R.S. c. C-34, s. 16; 1991, c. 43, s. 2.

COMPULSION BY THREATS.

17. A person who commits an offence under compulsion by threats of immediate death or bodily harm from a person who is present when the offence is committed is excused for committing the offence if the person believes that the threats will be carried out and if the person is not a party to a conspiracy or association whereby the person is subject to compulsion, but this section does not apply where the offence that is committed is high treason or treason, murder, piracy, attempted murder, sexual assault, sexual assault with a weapon, threats to a third party or causing bodily harm, aggravated sexual assault, forcible abduction, hostage taking, robbery, assault with a weapon or causing bodily harm, aggravated assault, unlawfully causing bodily harm, arson or an offence under sections 280 to 283 (abduction and detention of young persons). R.S., c. C-34, s. 17; 1974-75-76, c. 105, s. 29; 1980-81-82-83, c. 125, s. 4; R.S.C. 1985, c. 27 (1st Supp.), s. 40(2).

COMPULSION OF SPOUSE.

18. No presumption arises that a married person who commits an offence does so under compulsion by reason only that the offence is committed in the presence of the spouse of that married person. R.S., c. C-34, s. 18; 1980-81-82-83, c. 125, s. 4.

IGNORANCE OF THE LAW.

19. Ignorance of the law by a person who commits an offence is not an excuse for committing that offence. R.S., c. C-34, s. 19.

39

CERTAIN ACTS ON HOLIDAYS VALID.

20. A warrant, summons, appearance notice, undertaking, release order or recognizance that is authorized by this Act may be executed, issued, given or entered into, as the case may be, on a holiday. R.S., c. C-34, s. 20; c. 2 (2nd Supp.), s. 2; 2019, c. 25, s. 5.

Parties to Offences

PARTIES TO OFFENCE / Common intention.

21. (1) Every one is a party to an offence who
   (a)   actually commits it;
   (b)   does or omits to do anything for the purpose of aiding any person to commit it; or
   (c)   abets any person in committing it.

(2) Where two or more persons form an intention in common to carry out an unlawful purpose and to assist each other therein and any one of them, in carrying out the common purpose, commits an offence, each of them who knew or ought to have known that the commission of the offence would be a probable consequence of carrying out the common purpose is a party to that offence. R.S., c. C-34, s. 21.

PERSON COUNSELLING OFFENCE / Idem / Definition of "counsel".

22. (1) Where a person counsels another person to be a party to an offence and that other person is afterwards a party to that offence, the person who counselled is a party to that offence, notwithstanding that the offence was committed in a way different from that which was counselled.

(2) Every one who counsels another person to be a party to an offence is a party to every offence that the other commits in consequence of the counselling that the person who counselled knew or ought to have known was likely to be committed in consequence of the counselling.

(3) For the purposes of this Act, "counsel" includes procure, solicit or incite. R.S., c. C-34, s. 22; R.S.C. 1985, c. 27 (1st Supp.), s. 7(1).

OFFENCES OF NEGLIGENCE / Organizations.

22.1 In respect of an offence that requires the prosecution to prove negligence, an organization is a party to the offence if
   (a)   acting within the scope of their authority
      (i)   one of its representatives is a party to the offence, or
      (ii) two or more of its representatives engage in conduct, whether by act or omission, such that, if it had been the conduct of only one representative, that representative would have been a party to the offence; and
   (b)   the senior officer who is responsible for the aspect of the organization's activities that is relevant to the offence departs — or the senior officers,

collectively, depart — markedly from the standard of care that, in the circumstances, could reasonably be expected to prevent a representative of the organization from being a party to the offence. 2003, c. 21, s. 2.

OTHER OFFENCES / Organizations.

22.2 In respect of an offence that requires the prosecution to prove fault — other than negligence — an organization is a party to the offence if, with the intent at least in part to benefit the organization, one of its senior officers

(a) acting within the scope of their authority, is a party to the offence;

(b) having the mental state required to be a party to the offence and acting within the scope of their authority, directs the work of other representatives of the organization so that they do the act or make the omission specified in the offence; or

(c) knowing that a representative of the organization is or is about to be a party to the offence, does not take all reasonable measures to stop them from being a party to the offence. 2003, c. 21, s. 2.

ACCESSORY AFTER THE FACT.

23. (1) An accessory after the fact to an offence is one who, knowing that a person has been a party to the offence, receives, comforts or assists that person for the purpose of enabling that person to escape. R.S., c. C-34, s. 23; 1974-75-76, c. 66, s. 7; 2000, c. 12, s. 92.

(2) [*Repealed*, 2000, c. 12, s. 92.]

WHERE ONE PARTY CANNOT BE CONVICTED.

23.1 For greater certainty, sections 21 to 23 apply in respect of an accused notwithstanding the fact that the person whom the accused aids or abets, counsels or procures or receives, comforts or assists cannot be convicted of the offence. R.S.C. 1985, c. 24 (2nd Supp.), s. 45.

ATTEMPTS / Question of law.

24. (1) Every one who, having an intent to commit an offence, does or omits to do anything for the purpose of carrying out his intention is guilty of an attempt to commit the offence whether or not it was possible under the circumstances to commit the offence.

(2) The question whether an act or omission by a person who has an intent to commit an offence is or is not mere preparation to commit the offence, and too remote to constitute an attempt to commit the offence, is a question of law. R.S., c. C-34, s. 24.

41

Protection of Persons Administering and Enforcing the Law

PROTECTION OF PERSONS ACTING UNDER AUTHORITY / Idem / When not protected / When protected / Power in case of escape from penitentiary.

25. (1) Every one who is required or authorized by law to do anything in the administration or enforcement of the law

   (a) as a private person,

   (b) as a peace officer or public officer,

   (c) in aid of a peace officer or public officer, or

   (d) by virtue of his office,

is, if he acts on reasonable grounds, justified in doing what he is required or authorized to do and in using as much force as is necessary for that purpose.

(2) Where a person is required or authorized by law to execute a process or to carry out a sentence, that person or any person who assists him is, if that person acts in good faith, justified in executing the process or in carrying out the sentence notwithstanding that the process or sentence is defective or that it was issued or imposed without jurisdiction or in excess of jurisdiction.

(3) Subject to subsections (4) and (5), a person is not justified for the purposes of subsection (1) in using force that is intended or is likely to cause death or grievous bodily harm unless the person believes on reasonable grounds that it is necessary for the self-preservation of the person or the preservation of any one under that person's protection from death or grievous bodily harm.

(4) A peace officer, and every person lawfully assisting the peace officer, is justified in using force that is intended or is likely to cause death or grievous bodily harm to a person to be arrested, if

   (a) the peace officer is proceeding lawfully to arrest, with or without warrant, the person to be arrested;

   (b) the offence for which the person is to be arrested is one for which that person may be arrested without warrant;

   (c) the person to be arrested takes flight to avoid arrest;

   (d) the peace officer or other person using the force believes on reasonable grounds that the force is necessary for the purpose of protecting the peace officer, the person lawfully assisting the peace officer or any other person from imminent or future death or grievous bodily harm; and

   (e) the flight cannot be prevented by reasonable means in a less violent manner.

(5) A peace officer is justified in using force that is intended or is likely to cause death or grievous bodily harm against an inmate who is escaping from a penitentiary within the meaning of subsection 2(1) of the *Corrections and Conditional Release Act*, if

   (a) the peace officer believes on reasonable grounds that any of the inmates of the penitentiary poses a threat of death or grievous bodily harm to the peace officer or any other person; and

(b) the escape cannot be prevented by reasonable means in a less violent manner. R.S., c. C-34, s. 25; 1994, c. 12, s. 1.

DEFINITIONS / "Competent authority" / "Public officer" / "Senior official" / Principle / Designation of public officers / Condition — civilian oversight / Declaration as evidence / Considerations / Designation of senior officials / Emergency designation / Conditions / Justification for acts or omissions / Requirements for certain acts / Person acting at direction of public officer / Limitation / Protection, defences and immunities unaffected / Compliance with requirements / Exception — *Controlled Drugs and Substances Act* and *Cannabis Act*.

25.1 (1) The following definitions apply in this section and sections 25.2 to 25.4.

"competent authority" means, with respect to a public officer or a senior official,
   (a) in the case of a member of the Royal Canadian Mounted Police, the Minister of Public Safety and Emergency Preparedness, personally;
   (b) in the case of a member of a police service constituted under the laws of a province, the Minister responsible for policing in the province, personally; and
   (c) in the case of any other public officer or senior official, the Minister who has responsibility for the Act of Parliament that the officer or official has the power to enforce, personally.

"public officer" means a peace officer, or a public officer who has the powers of a peace officer under an Act of Parliament.

"senior official" means a senior official who is responsible for law enforcement and who is designated under subsection (5).

(2) It is in the public interest to ensure that public officers may effectively carry out their law enforcement duties in accordance with the rule of law and, to that end, to expressly recognize in law a justification for public officers and other persons acting at their direction to commit acts or omissions that would otherwise constitute offences.

(3) A competent authority may designate public officers for the purposes of this section and sections 25.2 to 25.4.

(3.1) A competent authority referred to in paragraph (a) or (b) of the definition of that term in subsection (1) may not designate any public officer under subsection (3) unless there is a public authority composed of persons who are not peace officers that may review the public officer's conduct.

(3.2) The Governor in Council or the lieutenant governor in council of a province, as the case may be, may designate a person or body as a public authority for the purposes of subsection (3.1), and that designation is conclusive evidence that the person or body is a public authority described in that subsection.

(4) The competent authority shall make designations under subsection (3) on the advice of a senior official and shall consider the nature of the duties performed by the public officer in relation to law enforcement generally, rather than in relation to any particular investigation or enforcement activity.

(5) A competent authority may designate senior officials for the purposes of this section and sections 25.2 to 25.4.

(6) A senior official may designate a public officer for the purposes of this section and sections 25.2 to 25.4 for a period of not more than 48 hours if the senior official is of the opinion that

(a) by reason of exigent circumstances, it is not feasible for the competent authority to designate a public officer under subsection (3); and

(b) in the circumstances of the case, the public officer would be justified in committing an act or omission that would otherwise constitute an offence.

The senior official shall without delay notify the competent authority of the designation.

(7) A designation under subsection (3) or (6) may be made subject to conditions, including conditions limiting

(a) the duration of the designation;

(b) the nature of the conduct in the investigation of which a public officer may be justified in committing, or directing another person to commit, acts or omissions that would otherwise constitute an offence; and

(c) the acts or omissions that would otherwise constitute an offence and that a public officer may be justified in committing or directing another person to commit.

(8) A public officer is justified in committing an act or omission — or in directing the commission of an act or omission under subsection (10) — that would otherwise constitute an offence if the public officer

(a) is engaged in the investigation of an offence under, or the enforcement of, an Act of Parliament or in the investigation of criminal activity;

(b) is designated under subsection (3) or (6); and

(c) believes on reasonable grounds that the commission of the act or omission, as compared to the nature of the offence or criminal activity being investigated, is reasonable and proportional in the circumstances, having regard to such matters as the nature of the act or omission, the nature of the investigation and the reasonable availability of other means for carrying out the public officer's law enforcement duties.

(9) No public officer is justified in committing an act or omission that would otherwise constitute an offence and that would be likely to result in loss of or serious damage to property, or in directing the commission of an act or omission under subsection (10), unless, in addition to meeting the conditions set out in paragraphs (8)(a) to (c), he or she

(a) is personally authorized in writing to commit the act or omission — or direct its commission — by a senior official who believes on reasonable grounds that committing the act or omission, as compared to the nature of the offence or criminal activity being investigated, is reasonable and proportional in the circumstances, having regard to such matters as the nature of the act or omission, the nature of the investigation and the reasonable availability of other means for carrying out the public officer's law enforcement duties; or (*b*) believes on reasonable grounds that the grounds for obtaining an authorization under paragraph (*a*) exist but it is not feasible in the circumstances to obtain the authorization and that the act or omission is necessary to

   (i) preserve the life or safety of any person,

   (ii) prevent the compromise of the identity of a public officer acting in an undercover capacity, of a confidential informant or of a person acting covertly under the direction and control of a public officer, or

   (iii) prevent the imminent loss or destruction of evidence of an indictable offence.

(10) A person who commits an act or omission that would otherwise constitute an offence is justified in committing it if

(*a*) a public officer directs him or her to commit that act or omission and the person believes on reasonable grounds that the public officer has the authority to give that direction; and

(*b*) he or she believes on reasonable grounds that the commission of that act or omission is for the purpose of assisting the public officer in the public officer's law enforcement duties.

(11) Nothing in this section justifies

(*a*) the intentional or criminally negligent causing of death or bodily harm to another person;

(*b*) the wilful attempt in any manner to obstruct, pervert or defeat the course of justice; or

(*c*) conduct that would violate the sexual integrity of an individual.

(12) Nothing in this section affects the protection, defences and immunities of peace officers and other persons recognized under the law of Canada.

(13) Nothing in this section relieves a public officer of criminal liability for failing to comply with any other requirements that govern the collection of evidence.

(14) Nothing in this section justifies a public officer or a person acting at his or her direction in committing an act or omission — or a public officer in directing the commission of an act or omission — that constitutes an offence under a provision of Part I of the *Controlled Drugs and Substances Act* or of the regulations made under it or a provision of Division 1 of Part 1 of the *Cannabis Act*. 2001, c. 32, s. 2; 2005, c. 10, s. 34(1)(*f*)(ii); 2018, c. 16, s. 207.

PUBLIC OFFICER TO FILE REPORT.

25.2 Every public officer who commits an act or omission — or directs the commission by another person of an act or omission — under paragraph 25.1(9)(*a*) or (*b*) shall, as soon as is feasible after the commission of the act or omission, file a written report with the appropriate senior official describing the act or omission. 2001, c. 32, s. 2.

ANNUAL REPORT / Limitation.

25.3 (1) Every competent authority shall publish or otherwise make available to the public an annual report for the previous year that includes, in respect of public officers and senior officials designated by the competent authority,

    (*a*) the number of designations made under subsection 25.1(6) by the senior officials;

    (*b*) the number of authorizations made under paragraph 25.1(9)(*a*) by the senior officials;

    (*c*) the number of times that acts and omissions were committed in accordance with paragraph 25.1(9)(*b*) by the public officers;

    (*d*) the nature of the conduct being investigated when the designations referred to in paragraph (*a*) or the authorizations referred to in paragraph (*b*) were made or when the acts or omissions referred to in paragraph (*c*) were committed; and

    (*e*) the nature of the acts or omissions committed under the designations referred to in paragraph (*a*), under the authorizations referred to in paragraph (*b*) and in the manner described in paragraph (*c*).

(2) The annual report shall not contain any information the disclosure of which would

    (*a*) compromise or hinder an ongoing investigation of an offence under an Act of Parliament;

    (*b*) compromise the identity of a public officer acting in an undercover capacity, of a confidential informant or of a person acting covertly under the direction and control of a public officer;

    (*c*) endanger the life or safety of any person;

    (*d*) prejudice a legal proceeding; or

    (*e*) otherwise be contrary to the public interest. 2001, c. 32, s. 2.

WRITTEN NOTIFICATION TO BE GIVEN / Limitation.

25.4 (1) When a public officer commits an act or omission — or directs the commission by another person of an act or omission — under paragraph 25.1(9)(*a*) or (*b*), the senior official with whom the public officer files a written report under section 25.2 shall, as soon as is feasible after the report is filed, and no later than one year after the commission of the act or omission, notify in writing any person whose property was lost or seriously damaged as a result of the act or omission.

(2) The competent authority may authorize the senior official not to notify the person under subsection (1) until the competent authority is of the opinion that notification would not

    (*a*) compromise or hinder an ongoing investigation of an offence under an Act of Parliament;

    (*b*) compromise the identity of a public officer acting in an undercover capacity, of a confidential informant or of a person acting covertly under the direction and control of a public officer;

    (*c*) endanger the life or safety of any person;

    (*d*) prejudice a legal proceeding; or

(e) otherwise be contrary to the public interest. 2001, c. 32, s. 2.

Transitional provision
2001, c. 32, s. 46.1 provides as follows:

46.1 Within three years after this section comes into force, a review of sections 25.1 to 25.4 of the *Criminal Code* and their operation shall be undertaken by any committee of the Senate, of the House of Commons or of both Houses of Parliament that is designated or established for that purpose.

EXCESSIVE FORCE.

26. Every one who is authorized by law to use force is criminally responsible for any excess thereof according to the nature and quality of the act that constitutes the excess. R.S., c. C-34, s. 26.

USE OF FORCE TO PREVENT COMMISSION OF OFFENCE.

27. Every one is justified in using as much force as is reasonably necessary
  (a) to prevent the commission of an offence
    (i) for which, if it were committed, the person who committed it might be arrested without warrant, and
    (ii) that would be likely to cause immediate and serious injury to the person or property of anyone; or
  (b) to prevent anything being done that, on reasonable grounds, he believes would, if it were done, be an offence mentioned in paragraph (a). R.S., c. C-34, s. 27.

USE OF FORCE ON BOARD AN AIRCRAFT / Application of this section.

27.1 (1) Every person on an aircraft in flight is justified in using as much force as is reasonably necessary to prevent the commission of an offence against this Act or another Act of Parliament that the person believes on reasonable grounds, if it were committed, would be likely to cause immediate and serious injury to the aircraft or to any person or property therein.

(2) This section applies in respect of any aircraft in flight in Canadian airspace and in respect of any aircraft registered in Canada in accordance with the regulations made under the *Aeronautics Act* in flight outside Canadian airspace. 2004, c. 12, s. 2.

ARREST OF WRONG PERSON / Person assisting.

28. (1) Where a person who is authorized to execute a warrant to arrest believes, in good faith and on reasonable grounds, that the person whom he arrests is the person named in the warrant, he is protected from criminal responsibility in respect thereof to the same extent as if that person were the person named in the warrant.

(2) Where a person is authorized to execute a warrant to arrest,

    (*a*) every one who, being called on to assist him, believes that the person in whose arrest he is called on to assist is the person named in the warrant, and

    (*b*) every keeper of a prison who is required to receive and detain a person who he believes has been arrested under the warrant,

is protected from criminal responsibility in respect thereof to the same extent as if that person were the person named in the warrant. R.S., c. C-34, s. 28.

DUTY OF PERSON ARRESTING / Notice / Failure to comply.

29. (1) It is the duty of every one who executes a process or warrant to have it with him, where it is feasible to do so, and to produce it when requested to do so.

(2) It is the duty of every one who arrests a person, whether with or without a warrant, to give notice to that person, where it is feasible to do so, of

    (*a*) the process or warrant under which he makes the arrest; or

    (*b*) the reason for the arrest.

(3) Failure to comply with subsection (1) or (2) does not of itself deprive a person who executes a process or warrant, or a person who makes an arrest, or those who assist them, of protection from criminal responsibility. R.S., c. C-34, s. 29.

PREVENTING BREACH OF PEACE.

30. Every one who witnesses a breach of the peace is justified in interfering to prevent the continuance or renewal thereof and may detain any person who commits or is about to join in or to renew the breach of the peace, for the purpose of giving him into the custody of a peace officer, if he uses no more force than is reasonably necessary to prevent the continuance or renewal of the breach of the peace or than is reasonably proportioned to the danger to be apprehended from the continuance or renewal of the breach of the peace. R.S., c. C-34, s. 30.

ARREST FOR BREACH OF PEACE / Giving person in charge.

31. (1) Every peace officer who witnesses a breach of the peace and every one who lawfully assists the peace officer is justified in arresting any person whom he finds committing the breach of the peace or who, on reasonable grounds, he believes is about to join in or renew the breach of the peace.

(2) Every peace officer is justified in receiving into custody any person who is given into his charge as having been a party to a breach of the peace by one who has, or who on reasonable grounds the peace officer believes has, witnessed the breach of the peace. R.S., c. C-34, s. 31.

Suppression of Riots

USE OF FORCE TO SUPPRESS RIOT / Person bound by military law / Obeying order of peace officer / Apprehension of serious mischief / Question of law.

32. (1) Every peace officer is justified in using or in ordering the use of as much force as the peace officer believes, in good faith and on reasonable grounds,

- (*a*) is necessary to suppress a riot; and
- (*b*) is not excessive, having regard to the danger to be apprehended from the continuance of the riot.

(2) Every one who is bound by military law to obey the command of his superior officer is justified in obeying any command given by his superior officer for the suppression of a riot unless the order is manifestly unlawful.

(3) Every one is justified in obeying an order of a peace officer to use force to suppress a riot if

- (*a*) he acts in good faith; and
- (*b*) the order is not manifestly unlawful.

(4) Every one who, in good faith and on reasonable grounds, believes that serious mischief will result from a riot before it is possible to secure the attendance of a peace officer is justified in using as much force as he believes in good faith and on reasonable grounds,

- (*a*) is necessary to suppress the riot; and
- (*b*) is not excessive, having regard to the danger to be apprehended from the continuance of the riot.

(5) For the purposes of this section, the question whether an order is manifestly unlawful or not is a question of law. R.S., c. C-34, s. 32.

DUTY OF OFFICERS IF RIOTERS DO NOT DISPERSE / Protection of officers / Section not restrictive.

33. (1) Where the proclamation referred to in section 67 has been made or an offence against paragraph 68(*a*) or (*b*) has been committed, it is the duty of a peace officer and of a person who is lawfully required by him to assist, to disperse or to arrest persons who do not comply with the proclamation.

(2) No civil or criminal proceedings lie against a peace officer or a person who is lawfully required by a peace officer to assist him in respect of any death or injury that by reason of resistance is caused as a result of the performance by the peace officer or that person of a duty that is imposed by subsection (1).

(3) Nothing in this section limits or affects any powers, duties or functions that are conferred or imposed by this Act with respect to the suppression of riots. R.S., c. C-34, s. 33.

Self-induced Intoxication

WHEN DEFENCE NOT AVAILABLE / Criminal fault by reason of intoxication / Application.

33.1 (1) It is not a defence to an offence referred to in subsection (3) that the accused, by reason of self-induced intoxication, lacked the general intent or the voluntariness required to commit the offence, where the accused departed markedly from the standard of care as described in subsection (2).

(2) For the purposes of this section, a person departs markedly from the standard of reasonable care generally recognized in Canadian society and is thereby criminally at fault where the person, while in a state of self-induced intoxication that renders the person unaware of, or incapable of consciously controlling, their behaviour, voluntarily or involuntarily interferes or threatens to interfere with the bodily integrity of another person.

(3) This section applies in respect of an offence under this Act or any other Act of Parliament that includes as an element an assault or any other interference or threat of interference by a person with the bodily integrity of another person. 1995, c. 32, s. 1.

Defence of Person

DEFENCE — USE OR THREAT OF FORCE / Factors / No defence.

34. (1) A person is not guilty of an offence if

   (*a*) they believe on reasonable grounds that force is being used against them or another person or that a threat of force is being made against them or another person;

   (*b*) the act that constitutes the offence is committed for the purpose of defending or protecting themselves or the other person from that use or threat of force; and

   (*c*) the act committed is reasonable in the circumstances.

(2) In determining whether the act committed is reasonable in the circumstances, the court shall consider the relevant circumstances of the person, the other parties and the act, including, but not limited to, the following factors:

   (*a*) the nature of the force or threat;

   (*b*) the extent to which the use of force was imminent and whether there were other means available to respond to the potential use of force;

   (*c*) the person's role in the incident;

   (*d*) whether any party to the incident used or threatened to use a weapon;

   (*e*) the size, age, gender and physical capabilities of the parties to the incident;

   (*f*) the nature, duration and history of any relationship between the parties to the incident, including any prior use or threat of force and the nature of that force or threat;

   (*f*.1) any history of interaction or communication between the parties to the incident;

   (*g*) the nature and proportionality of the person's response to the use or threat of force; and

   (*h*) whether the act committed was in response to a use or threat of force that the person knew was lawful.

(3) Subsection (1) does not apply if the force is used or threatened by another person for the purpose of doing something that they are required or authorized by law to do in the administration or enforcement of the law, unless the person who commits the act that constitutes the offence believes on reasonable grounds that the other person is acting unlawfully. R.S., c. C-34, s. 34; 2012, c. 9, s. 2.

Defence of Property

DEFENCE — PROPERTY / No defence / No defence.

35. (1) A person is not guilty of an offence if

   (*a*) they either believe on reasonable grounds that they are in peaceable possession of property or are acting under the authority of, or lawfully assisting, a person whom they believe on reasonable grounds is in peaceable possession of property;

   (*b*) they believe on reasonable grounds that another person

      (i) is about to enter, is entering or has entered the property without being entitled by law to do so,

      (ii) is about to take the property, is doing so or has just done so, or

     (iii) is about to damage or destroy the property, or make it inoperative, or is doing so;

   (*c*) the act that constitutes the offence is committed for the purpose of

      (i) preventing the other person from entering the property, or removing that person from the property, or

      (ii) preventing the other person from taking, damaging or destroying the property or from making it inoperative, or retaking the property from that person; and

   (*d*) the act committed is reasonable in the circumstances.

(2) Subsection (1) does not apply if the person who believes on reasonable grounds that they are, or who is believed on reasonable grounds to be, in peaceable possession of the property does not have a claim of right to it and the other person is entitled to its possession by law.

(3) Subsection (1) does not apply if the other person is doing something that they are required or authorized by law to do in the administration or enforcement of the law, unless the person who commits the act that constitutes the offence believes on reasonable grounds that the other person is acting unlawfully. R.S.C. 1970, c. C-34, s. 35; 2012, c. 9, s. 2.

36. [*Repealed*, 2012, c. 9, s. 2.]

37. [*Repealed*, 2012, c. 9, s. 2.]

51

38. [*Repealed*, 2012, c. 9, s. 2.]

39. [*Repealed*, 2012, c. 9, s. 2.]

40. [*Repealed*, 2012, c. 9, s. 2.]

41. [*Repealed*, 2012, c. 9, s. 2.]

42. [*Repealed*, 2012, c. 9, s. 2.]

Protection of Persons in Authority

CORRECTION OF CHILD BY FORCE.

43. Every schoolteacher, parent or person standing in the place of a parent is justified in using force by way of correction toward a pupil or child, as the case may be, who is under his care, if the force does not exceed what is reasonable under the circumstances. R.S., c. C-34, s. 43.

44. [*Repealed*, 2001, c. 26, s. 294.]

SURGICAL OPERATIONS.

45. Every one is protected from criminal responsibility for performing a surgical operation on any person for the benefit of that person if
   (*a*) the operation is performed with reasonable care and skill; and
   (*b*) it is reasonable to perform the operation, having regard to the state of health of the person at the time the operation is performed and to all the circumstances of the case. R.S., c. C-34, s. 45.

Part II / OFFENCES AGAINST PUBLIC ORDER

Treason and other Offences against the Queen's Authority and Person

HIGH TREASON / Treason / Canadian citizen / Overt act.

46. (1) Every one commits high treason who, in Canada,
   (*a*) kills or attempts to kill Her Majesty, or does her any bodily harm tending to death or destruction, maims or wounds her, or imprisons or restrains her;
   (*b*) levies war against Canada or does any act preparatory thereto; or
   (*c*) assists an enemy at war with Canada, or any armed forces against whom Canadian Forces are engaged in hostilities, whether or not a state of war exists between Canada and the country whose forces they are.

(2) Every one commits treason who, in Canada,

(a) uses force or violence for the purpose of overthrowing the government of Canada or a province;

(b) without lawful authority, communicates or makes available to an agent of a state other than Canada, military or scientific information or any sketch, plan, model, article, note or document of a military or scientific character that he knows or ought to know may be used by that state for a purpose prejudicial to the safety or defence of Canada;

(c) conspires with any person to commit high treason or to do anything mentioned in paragraph (a);

(d) forms an intention to do anything that is high treason or that is mentioned in paragraph (a) and manifests that intention by an overt act; or

(e) conspires with any person to do anything mentioned in paragraph (b) or forms an intention to do anything mentioned in paragraph (b) and manifests that intention by an overt act.

(3) Notwithstanding subsection (1) or (2), a Canadian citizen or a person who owes allegiance to Her Majesty in right of Canada,

(a) commits high treason if, while in or out of Canada, he does anything mentioned in subsection (1); or

(b) commits treason if, while in or out of Canada, he does anything mentioned in subsection (2).

(4) Where it is treason to conspire with any person, the act of conspiring is an overt act of treason. R.S., c. C-34, s. 46; 1974-75-76, c. 105, s. 2.

PUNISHMENT FOR HIGH TREASON / Punishment for treason / Corroboration / Minimum punishment.

47. (1) Every one who commits high treason is guilty of an indictable offence and shall be sentenced to imprisonment for life.

(2) Every one who commits treason is guilty of an indictable offence and liable

(a) to be sentenced to imprisonment for life if he is guilty of an offence under paragraph 46(2)(a), (c) or (d);

(b) to be sentenced to imprisonment for life if he is guilty of an offence under paragraph 46(2)(b) or (e) committed while a state of war exists between Canada and another country; or

(c) to be sentenced to imprisonment for a term not exceeding fourteen years if he is guilty of an offence under paragraph 46(2)(b) or (e) committed while no state of war exists between Canada and another country.

(3) No person shall be convicted of high treason or treason on the evidence of only one witness, unless the evidence of that witness is corroborated in a material particular by evidence that implicates the accused.

(4) For the purposes of Part XXIII, the sentence of imprisonment for life prescribed by subsection (1) is a minimum punishment. R.S., c. C-34, s. 47; 1974-75-76, c. 105, s. 2.

LIMITATION / Information for treasonable words.

48. (1) No proceedings for an offence of treason as defined by paragraph 46(2)(*a*) shall be commenced more than three years after the time when the offence is alleged to have been committed.

(2) No proceedings shall be commenced under section 47 in respect of an overt act of treason expressed or declared by open and considered speech unless

   (*a*) an information setting out the overt act and the words by which it was expressed or declared is laid under oath before a justice within six days after the time when the words are alleged to have been spoken; and

   (*b*) a warrant for the arrest of the accused is issued within ten days after the time when the information is laid. R.S., c. C-34, s. 48; 1974-75-76, c. 105, s. 29.

Prohibited Acts

49. [*Repealed*, 2018, c. 29, s. 1.]

ASSISTING ALIEN ENEMY TO LEAVE CANADA, OR OMITTING TO PREVENT
TREASON / Punishment.

50. (1) Every one commits an offence who

   (*a*) incites or wilfully assists a subject of

      (i) a state that is at war with Canada, or

      (ii) a state against whose forces Canadian Forces are engaged in hostilities, whether or not a state of war exists between Canada and the state whose forces they are,

   to leave Canada without the consent of the Crown, unless the accused establishes that assistance to the state referred to in subparagraph (i) or the forces of the state referred to in subparagraph (ii), as the case may be, was not intended thereby; or

   (*b*) knowing that a person is about to commit high treason or treason does not, with all reasonable dispatch, inform a justice of the peace or other peace officer thereof or make other reasonable efforts to prevent that person from committing high treason or treason.

(2) Every one who commits an offence under subsection (1) is guilty of an indictable offence and liable to imprisonment for a term not exceeding fourteen years. R.S., c. C-34, s. 50; 1974-75-76, c. 105, s. 29.

INTIMIDATING PARLIAMENT OR LEGISLATURE.

51. Every one who does an act of violence in order to intimidate Parliament or the legislature of a province is guilty of an indictable offence and liable to imprisonment for a term not exceeding fourteen years. R.S., c. C-34, s. 51.

SABOTAGE / Definition of "prohibited act" / Saving / Idem.

52. (1) Every person is guilty of an indictable offence and liable to imprisonment for a term of not more than 10 years or is guilty of an offence punishable on summary conviction who does a prohibited act for a purpose prejudicial to

(a) the safety, security or defence of Canada, or

(b) the safety or security of the naval, army or air forces of any state other than Canada that are lawfully present in Canada.

(2) In this section, "prohibited act" means an act or omission that

(a) impairs the efficiency or impedes the working of any vessel, vehicle, aircraft, machinery, apparatus or other thing; or

(b) causes property, by whomever it may be owned, to be lost, damaged or destroyed.

(3) No person does a prohibited act within the meaning of this section by reason only that

(a) he stops work as a result of the failure of his employer and himself to agree on any matter relating to his employment;

(b) he stops work as a result of the failure of his employer and a bargaining agent acting on his behalf to agree on any matter relating to his employment; or

(c) he stops work as a result of his taking part in a combination of workmen or employees for their own reasonable protection as workmen or employees.

(4) No person does a prohibited act within the meaning of this section by reason only that he attends at or near or approaches a dwelling-house or place for the purpose only of obtaining or communicating information. R.S., c. C-34, s. 52; 2019, c. 25, s. 6.

INCITING TO MUTINY.

53. Every one who

(a) attempts, for a traitorous or mutinous purpose, to seduce a member of the Canadian Forces from his duty and allegiance to Her Majesty, or

(b) attempts to incite or to induce a member of the Canadian Forces to commit a traitorous or mutinous act,

is guilty of an indictable offence and liable to imprisonment for a term not exceeding fourteen years. R.S., c. C-34, s. 53.

ASSISTING DESERTER.

54. Every one who aids, assists, harbours or conceals a person who he knows is a deserter or absentee without leave from the Canadian Forces is guilty of an offence punishable on summary conviction, but no proceedings shall be instituted under this section without the consent of the Attorney General of Canada. R.S., c. C-34, s. 54.

EVIDENCE OF OVERT ACTS.

55. In proceedings for an offence against any provision in section 47 or sections 50 to 53, evidence of an overt act is not admissible unless that overt act is set out in the indictment or unless the evidence is otherwise relevant as tending to prove an overt act that is set out in the indictment. R.S., c. C-34, s. 55; 2018, c. 29, s. 2.

OFFENCES IN RELATION TO MEMBERS OF R.C.M.P.

56. Every one who wilfully
  (a) persuades or counsels a member of the Royal Canadian Mounted Police to desert or absent himself without leave,
  (b) aids, assists, harbours or conceals a member of the Royal Canadian Mounted Police who he knows is a deserter or absentee without leave, or
  (c) aids or assists a member of the Royal Canadian Mounted Police to desert or absent himself without leave, knowing that the member is about to desert or absent himself without leave,
is guilty of an offence punishable on summary conviction. R.S., c. C-34, s. 57; R.S.C. 1985, c. 27 (1st Supp.), s. 8.

Official Documents

IDENTITY DOCUMENTS / For greater certainty / Definition of "identity document" / Punishment.

56.1 (1) Every person commits an offence who, without lawful excuse, procures to be made, possesses, transfers, sells or offers for sale an identity document that relates or purports to relate, in whole or in part, to another person.

(2) For greater certainty, subsection (1) does not prohibit an act that is carried out
  (a) in good faith, in the ordinary course of the person's business or employment or in the exercise of the duties of their office;
  (b) for genealogical purposes;
  (c) with the consent of the person to whom the identity document relates or of a person authorized to consent on behalf of the person to whom the document relates, or of the entity that issued the identity document; or
  (d) for a legitimate purpose related to the administration of justice.

(3) For the purposes of this section, "identity document" means a Social Insurance Number card, a driver's licence, a health insurance card, a birth certificate, a death certificate, a passport as defined in subsection 57(5), a document that simplifies the process of entry into Canada, a certificate of citizenship, a document indicating immigration status in Canada, a certificate of Indian status or an employee identity card that bears the employee's photograph and signature, or any similar document, issued or purported to be issued by a department or agency of the federal government or of a provincial or foreign government.

(4) Every person who commits an offence under subsection (1)
  (a) is guilty of an indictable offence and liable to imprisonment for a term of not more than five years; or

(b) is guilty of an offence punishable on summary conviction. 2009, c. 28, s. 1.

CODE

FORGERY OF OR UTTERING FORGED PASSPORT / False statement in relation to passport / Possession of forged, etc., passport / Special provisions applicable / Definition of "passport" / Jurisdiction / Appearance of accused at trial.

57. (1) Every one who, while in or out of Canada,

(a) forges a passport, or

(b) knowing that a passport is forged

    (i) uses, deals with or acts on it, or

    (ii) causes or attempts to cause any person to use, deal with, or act on it, as if the passport were genuine,

is guilty of an indictable offence and liable to imprisonment for a term not exceeding fourteen years.

(2) Every one who, while in or out of Canada, for the purpose of procuring a passport for himself or any other person or for the purpose of procuring any material alteration or addition to any such passport, makes a written or an oral statement that he knows is false or misleading

(a) is guilty of an indictable offence and liable to imprisonment for a term not exceeding two years; or

(b) is guilty of an offence punishable on summary conviction.

(3) Every person who, without lawful excuse, has in their possession a forged passport or a passport in respect of which an offence under subsection (2) has been committed is guilty of

(a) an indictable offence and liable to imprisonment for a term of not more than five years; or

(b) an offence punishable on summary conviction.

(4) For the purposes of proceedings under this section,

(a) the place where a passport was forged is not material; and

(b) the definition "false document" in section 321, and section 366, apply with such modifications as the circumstances require.

(5) In this section, "passport" has the same meaning as in section 2 of the *Canadian Passport Order*.

(6) Where a person is alleged to have committed, while out of Canada, an offence under this section, proceedings in respect of that offence may, whether or not that person is in Canada, be commenced in any territorial division in Canada and the accused may be tried and punished in respect of that offence in the same manner as if the offence had been committed in that territorial division.

(7) For greater certainty, the provisions of this Act relating to

(a) requirements that an accused appear at and be present during proceedings, and

(b) the exceptions to those requirements,

apply to proceedings commenced in any territorial division pursuant to subsection (6). R.S., c. C-34, s. 58; R.S.C. 1985, c. 27 (1st Supp.), s. 9; 1994, c. 44, s. 4; 1995, c. 5, s. 25; 2013, c. 19, s. 1; 2018, c. 29, s. 3; 2019, c. 25, s. 7.

FRAUDULENT USE OF CERTIFICATE OF CITIZENSHIP / Definition of "certificate of citizenship" and "certificate of naturalization".

58. (1) Every person is guilty of an indictable offence and liable to imprisonment for a term of not more than two years or is guilty of an offence punishable on summary conviction who, while in or outside Canada,

(*a*) uses a certificate of citizenship or a certificate of naturalization for a fraudulent purpose, or

(*b*) being a person to whom a certificate of citizenship or a certificate of naturalization has been granted, knowingly parts with the possession of that certificate with intent that it should be used for a fraudulent purpose.

(2) In this section, "certificate of citizenship" and "certificate of naturalization", respectively, mean a certificate of citizenship and a certificate of naturalization as defined by the *Citizenship Act*. R.S., c. C-34, s. 59; 1974-75-76, c. 108, s. 41; 2019, c. 25, s. 8.

Sedition

SEDITIOUS WORDS / Seditious libel / Seditious conspiracy / Seditious intention.

59. (1) Seditious words are words that express a seditious intention.

(2) A seditious libel is a libel that expresses a seditious intention.

(3) A seditious conspiracy is an agreement between two or more persons to carry out a seditious intention.

(4) Without limiting the generality of the meaning of the expression "seditious intention", every one shall be presumed to have a seditious intention who

(*a*) teaches or advocates, or

(*b*) publishes or circulates any writing that advocates,

the use, without the authority of law, of force as a means of accomplishing a governmental change within Canada. R.S., c. C-34, s. 60.

EXCEPTION.

60. Notwithstanding subsection 59(4), no person shall be deemed to have a seditious intention by reason only that he intends, in good faith,

(*a*) to show that Her Majesty has been misled or mistaken in her measures;

(*b*) to point out errors or defects in

(i) the government or constitution of Canada or a province,

(ii) Parliament or the legislature of a province, or

(iii) the administration of justice in Canada;

(*c*) to procure, by lawful means, the alteration of any matter of government in Canada; or

(*d*) to point out, for the purpose of removal, matters that produce or tend to produce feelings of hostility and ill-will between different classes of persons in Canada. R.S., c. C-34, s. 61.

PUNISHMENT OF SEDITIOUS OFFENCES.

61. Every one who
  (*a*) speaks seditious words,
  (*b*) publishes a seditious libel, or
  (*c*) is a party to a seditious conspiracy,
is guilty of an indictable offence and liable to imprisonment for a term not exceeding fourteen years. R.S., c. C-34, s. 62.

OFFENCES IN RELATION TO MILITARY FORCES / Definition of "member of a force".

62. (1) Every person is guilty of an indictable offence and liable to imprisonment for a term of not more than five years or is guilty of an offence punishable on summary conviction who intentionally
  (*a*) interferes with, impairs or influences the loyalty or discipline of a member of a force,
  (*b*) publishes, edits, issues, circulates or distributes a writing that advises, counsels or urges insubordination, disloyalty, mutiny or refusal of duty by a member of a force, or
  (*c*) advises, counsels, urges or in any manner causes insubordination, disloyalty, mutiny or refusal of duty by a member of a force.

(2) In this section, "member of a force" means a member of
  (*a*) the Canadian Forces; or
  (*b*) the naval, army or air forces of a state other than Canada that are lawfully present in Canada. R.S., c. C-34, s. 63; 2019, c. 25, s. 9.

Unlawful Assemblies and Riots

UNLAWFUL ASSEMBLY / Lawful assembly becoming unlawful / Exception.

63. (1) An unlawful assembly is an assembly of three or more persons who, with intent to carry out any common purpose, assemble in such a manner or so conduct themselves when they are assembled as to cause persons in the neighbourhood of the assembly to fear, on reasonable grounds, that they
  (*a*) will disturb the peace tumultuously; or
  (*b*) will by that assembly needlessly and without reasonable cause provoke other persons to disturb the peace tumultuously.

(2) Persons who are lawfully assembled may become an unlawful assembly if they conduct themselves with a common purpose in a manner that would have made the assembly unlawful if they had assembled in that manner for that purpose.

(3) Persons are not unlawfully assembled by reason only that they are assembled to protect the dwelling-house of any one of them against persons who are threatening to break and enter it for the purpose of committing an indictable offence therein. R.S., c. C-34, s. 64.

RIOT.

64. A riot is an unlawful assembly that has begun to disturb the peace tumultuously. R.S., c. C-34, s. 65.

PUNISHMENT OF RIOTER / Concealment of identity.

65. (1) Every person who takes part in a riot is guilty of
  (*a*) an indictable offence and liable to imprisonment for a term of not more than two years; or
  (*b*) an offence punishable on summary conviction.

(2) Every person who commits an offence under subsection (1) while wearing a mask or other disguise to conceal their identity without lawful excuse is guilty of
  (*a*) an indictable offence and liable to imprisonment for a term of not more than 10 years; or
  (*b*) an offence punishable on summary conviction. R.S., c. C-34, s. 66; 2013, c. 15, s. 2; 2019, c. 25, s. 10.

PUNISHMENT FOR UNLAWFUL ASSEMBLY / Concealment of identity.

66. Every one who is a member of an unlawful assembly is guilty of an offence punishable on summary conviction.

(2) Every person who commits an offence under subsection (1) while wearing a mask or other disguise to conceal their identity without lawful excuse is guilty of
  (*a*) an indictable offence and liable to imprisonment for a term not exceeding five years; or
  (*b*) an offence punishable on summary conviction. R.S., c. C-34, s. 67; 2013, c. 15, s. 3.

READING PROCLAMATION.

67. A person who is
  (*a*) a justice, mayor or sheriff, or the lawful deputy of a mayor or sheriff,
  (*b*) a warden or deputy warden of a prison, or
  (*c*) the institutional head of a penitentiary, as those expressions are defined in subsection 2(1) of the *Corrections and Conditional Release Act*, or that person's deputy,
who receives notice that, at any place within the jurisdiction of the person, twelve or more persons are unlawfully and riotously assembled together shall go to that place and, after approaching as near as is safe, if the person is satisfied that a riot is in progress, shall command silence and thereupon make or cause to be made in a loud voice a proclamation in the following words or to the like effect:

Her Majesty the Queen charges and commands all persons being assembled immediately to disperse and peaceably to depart to their habitations or to their lawful business on the pain of being guilty of an offence for which, on conviction, they may be sentenced to imprisonment for life. GOD SAVE THE QUEEN. R.S., c. C-34, s. 68; 1994, c. 44, s. 5.

OFFENCES RELATED TO PROCLAMATION.

68. Every one is guilty of an indictable offence and liable to imprisonment for life who

(a) opposes, hinders or assaults, wilfully and with force, a person who begins to make or is about to begin to make or is making the proclamation referred to in section 67 so that it is not made;

(b) does not peaceably disperse and depart from a place where the proclamation referred to in section 67 is made within thirty minutes after it is made; or

(c) does not depart from a place within thirty minutes when he has reasonable grounds to believe that the proclamation referred to in section 67 would have been made in that place if some person had not opposed, hindered or assaulted, wilfully and with force, a person who would have made it. R.S., c. C-34, s. 69.

NEGLECT BY PEACE OFFICER.

69. A peace officer who receives notice that there is a riot within their jurisdiction and, without reasonable excuse, fails to take all reasonable steps to suppress the riot is guilty of

(a) an indictable offence and liable to imprisonment for a term of not more than two years; or

(b) an offence punishable on summary conviction. R.S., c. C-34, s. 70; 2019, c. 25, s. 11.

Unlawful Drilling

ORDERS BY GOVERNOR IN COUNCIL / General or special order / Punishment.

70. (1) The Governor in Council may, by proclamation, make orders

(a) to prohibit assemblies, without lawful authority, of persons for the purpose

   (i) of training or drilling themselves,

   (ii) of being trained or drilled to the use of arms, or

   (iii) of practising military exercises; or

(b) to prohibit persons when assembled for any purpose from training or drilling themselves or from being trained or drilled.

(2) An order that is made under subsection (1) may be general or may be made applicable to particular places, districts or assemblies to be specified in the order.

(3) Every person who contravenes an order made under this section is guilty of

(a) an indictable offence and liable to imprisonment for a term of not more than five years; or

(b) an offence punishable on summary conviction. R.S., c. C-34, s. 71; 2019, c. 25, s. 12.

Duels

71. [*Repealed*, 2018, c. 29, s. 4.]

Forcible Entry and Detainer

FORCIBLE ENTRY / Matters not material / Forcible detainer / Questions of law.

72. (1) A person commits forcible entry when that person enters real property that is in the actual and peaceable possession of another in a manner that is likely to cause a breach of the peace or reasonable apprehension of a breach of the peace.

(1.1) For the purposes of subsection (1), it is immaterial whether or not a person is entitled to enter the real property or whether or not that person has any intention of taking possession of the real property.

(2) A person commits forcible detainer when, being in actual possession of real property without colour of right, he detains it in a manner that is likely to cause a breach of the peace or reasonable apprehension of a breach of the peace, against a person who is entitled by law to possession of it.

(3) The questions whether a person is in actual and peaceable possession or is in actual possession without colour of right are questions of law. R.S., c. C-34, s. 73; R.S.C. 1985, c. 27 (1st Supp.), s. 10.

PUNISHMENT.

73. Every person who commits forcible entry or forcible detainer is guilty of
   (*a*) an indictable offence and liable to imprisonment for a term of not more than two years; or
   (*b*) an offence punishable on summary conviction. R.S., c. C-34, s. 74; R.S.C. 1985, c. 27 (1st Supp.), s. 11; 1992, c. 1, s. 58; 2019, c. 25, s. 13.

Piracy

PIRACY BY LAW OF NATIONS / Punishment.

74. (1) Every one commits piracy who does any act that, by the law of nations, is piracy.

(2) Every one who commits piracy while in or out of Canada is guilty of an indictable offence and liable to imprisonment for life. R.S., c. C-34, s. 75; 1974-75-76, c. 105, s. 3.

PIRATICAL ACTS.

75. Every one who, while in or out of Canada,
   (*a*) steals a Canadian ship,

CODE

(b) steals or without lawful authority throws overboard, damages or destroys anything that is part of the cargo, supplies or fittings in a Canadian ship,

(c) does or attempts to do a mutinous act on a Canadian ship, or

(d) counsels a person to do anything mentioned in paragraph (a), (b) or (c),

is guilty of an indictable offence and liable to imprisonment for a term not exceeding fourteen years. R.S., c. C-34, s. 76; R.S.C. 1985, c. 27 (1st Supp.), s. 7(3).

Offences against Air or Maritime Safety   1993, c. 7, s. 2.

HIJACKING.

76. Every one who, unlawfully, by force or threat thereof, or by any other form of intimidation, seizes or exercises control of an aircraft with intent

(a) to cause any person on board the aircraft to be confined or imprisoned against his will,

(b) to cause any person on board the aircraft to be transported against his will to any place other than the next scheduled place of landing of the aircraft,

(c) to hold any person on board the aircraft for ransom or to service against his will, or

(d) to cause the aircraft to deviate in a material respect from its flight plan, is guilty of an indictable offence and liable to imprisonment for life. 1972, c. 13, s. 6.

ENDANGERING SAFETY OF AIRCRAFT OR AIRPORT.

77. Every one who

(a) on board an aircraft in flight, commits an act of violence against a person that is likely to endanger the safety of the aircraft,

(b) using a weapon, commits an act of violence against a person at an airport serving international civil aviation that causes or is likely to cause serious injury or death and that endangers or is likely to endanger safety at the airport,

(c) causes damage to an aircraft in service that renders the aircraft incapable of flight or that is likely to endanger the safety of the aircraft in flight,

(d) places or causes to be placed on board an aircraft in service anything that is likely to cause damage to the aircraft, that will render it incapable of flight or that is likely to endanger the safety of the aircraft in flight,

(e) causes damage to or interferes with the operation of any air navigation facility where the damage or interference is likely to endanger the safety of an aircraft in flight,

(f) using a weapon, substance or device, destroys or causes serious damage to the facilities of an airport serving international civil aviation or to any aircraft not in service located there, or causes disruption of services of the airport, that endangers or is likely to endanger safety at the airport, or

(g) endangers the safety of an aircraft in flight by communicating to any other person any information that the person knows to be false, is guilty of an indictable offence and liable to imprisonment for life. 1972, c. 13, s. 6; 1993, c. 7, s. 3.

OFFENSIVE WEAPONS AND EXPLOSIVE SUBSTANCES / Definition of "civil aircraft".

78. (1) Every one, other than a peace officer engaged in the execution of his duty, who takes on board a civil aircraft an offensive weapon or any explosive substance

    (*a*) without the consent of the owner or operator of the aircraft or of a person duly authorized by either of them to consent thereto, or

    (*b*) with the consent referred to in paragraph (*a*) but without complying with all terms and conditions on which the consent was given,

is guilty of an indictable offence and liable to imprisonment for a term not exceeding fourteen years.

(2) For the purposes of this section, "civil aircraft" means all aircraft other than aircraft operated by the Canadian Forces, a police force in Canada or persons engaged in the administration or enforcement of the *Customs Act*, the *Excise Act* or the *Excise Act, 2001*. 1972, c. 13, s. 6; R.S.C. 1985, c. 1 (2nd Supp.), s. 213(3); 2002, c. 22, s. 325.

SEIZING CONTROL OF SHIP OR FIXED PLATFORM / Endangering safety of ship or fixed platform / False communication / Threats causing death or injury/ Definitions / "fixed platform" / "ship".

78.1 (1) Every one who seizes or exercises control over a ship or fixed platform by force or threat of force or by any other form of intimidation is guilty of an indictable offence and liable to imprisonment for life.

(2) Every one who

    (*a*) commits an act of violence against a person on board a ship or fixed platform,

    (*b*) destroys or causes damage to a ship or its cargo or to a fixed platform,

    (*c*) destroys or causes serious damage to or interferes with the operation of any maritime navigational facility, or

    (*d*) places or causes to be placed on board a ship or fixed platform anything that is likely to cause damage to the ship or its cargo or to the fixed platform,

where that act is likely to endanger the safe navigation of a ship or the safety of a fixed platform, is guilty of an indictable offence and liable to imprisonment for life.

(3) Every one who communicates information that endangers the safe navigation of a ship, knowing the information to be false, is guilty of an indictable offence and liable to imprisonment for life.

(4) Every one who threatens to commit an offence under paragraph (2)(*a*), (*b*) or (*c*) in order to compel a person to do or refrain from doing any act, where the threat is likely to endanger the safe navigation of a ship or the safety of a fixed platform, is guilty of an indictable offence and liable to imprisonment for life.

(5) In this section,

"fixed platform" means an artificial island or a marine installation or structure that is permanently attached to the seabed for the purpose of exploration or exploitation of resources or for other economic purposes;

"ship" means every description of vessel not permanently attached to the seabed, other than a warship, a ship being used as a naval auxiliary or for customs or police purposes or a ship that has been withdrawn from navigation or is laid up; 1993, c. 7, s. 4.

Dangerous Materials and Devices   2013, c. 13, s. 4.

DUTY OF CARE RE EXPLOSIVE.

79. Every one who has an explosive substance in his possession or under his care or control is under a legal duty to use reasonable care to prevent bodily harm or death to persons or damage to property by that explosive substance. R.S., c. C-34, s. 77.

BREACH OF DUTY.

80. Every one who, being under a legal duty within the meaning of section 79, fails without lawful excuse to perform that duty, is guilty of an indictable offence and, if as a result an explosion of an explosive substance occurs that

- (a) causes death or is likely to cause death to any person, is liable to imprisonment for life; or
- (b) causes bodily harm or damage to property or is likely to cause bodily harm or damage to property, is liable to imprisonment for a term not exceeding fourteen years. R.S., c. C-34, s. 78.

USING EXPLOSIVES / Punishment.

81. (1) Every one commits an offence who

- (a) does anything with intent to cause an explosion of an explosive substance that is likely to cause serious bodily harm or death to persons or is likely to cause serious damage to property;
- (b) with intent to do bodily harm to any person
  - (i) causes an explosive substance to explode,
  - (ii) sends or delivers to a person or causes a person to take or receive an explosive substance or any other dangerous substance or thing, or
  - (iii) places or throws anywhere or at or on a person a corrosive fluid, explosive substance or any other dangerous substance or thing;
- (c) with intent to destroy or damage property without lawful excuse, places or throws an explosive substance anywhere; or
- (d) makes or has in his possession or has under his care or control any explosive substance with intent thereby
  - (i) to endanger life or to cause serious damage to property, or
  - (ii) to enable another person to endanger life or to cause serious damage to property.

(2) Every one who commits an offence under subsection (1) is guilty of an indictable offence and liable

   (*a*) for an offence under paragraph (1)(*a*) or (*b*), to imprisonment for life; or

   (*b*) for an offence under paragraph (1)(*c*) or (*d*), to imprisonment for a term not exceeding fourteen years. R.S., c. C-34, s. 79.

POSSESSION OF EXPLOSIVE / Possession in association with criminal organization.

82. (1) Every person who, without lawful excuse, makes or has in their possession or under their care or control any explosive substance is guilty of

   (*a*) an indictable offence and liable to imprisonment for a term of not more than five years; or

   (*b*) an offence punishable on summary conviction.

(2) Every person who, without lawful excuse, makes or has in their possession or under their care or control any explosive substance for the benefit of, at the direction of or in association with a criminal organization is guilty of an indictable offence and liable to imprisonment for a term of not more than 14 years. R.S., c. C-34, s. 80; R.S.C. 1985, c. 27 (1st Supp.), s. 12; 1997, c. 23, s. 2; 2018, c. 29, s. 5; 2019, c. 25, s. 14.

SENTENCES TO BE SERVED CONSECUTIVELY

82.1 A sentence imposed on a person for an offence under subsection 82(2) shall be served consecutively to any other punishment imposed on the person for an offence arising out of the same event or series of events and to any other sentence to which the person is subject at the time the sentence is imposed on the person for an offence under subsection 82(2). 1997, c. 23, s. 2.

DEFINITION OF "DEVICE".

82.2 For the purposes of sections 82.3 to 82.5, "device" means any of the following:

   (*a*) a nuclear explosive device;

   (*b*) a device that disperses radioactive material;

   (*c*) a device that emits ionizing radiation and that is capable of causing death, serious bodily harm or substantial damage to property or the environment;

   (*d*) a device that emits ionizing radiation and that is capable of causing death, serious bodily harm or substantial damage to property or the environment. 2013, c. 13, s. 5.

POSSESSION, ETC., OF NUCLEAR MATERIAL, RADIOACTIVE MATERIAL OR DEVICE.

82.3 Everyone who, with intent to cause death, serious bodily harm or substantial damage to property or the environment, makes a device or possesses, uses, transfers, exports, imports, alters or disposes of nuclear material, radioactive material or a device or commits an act against a nuclear facility or an act that causes serious interference with or serious disruption of its operations, is guilty of an indictable offence and liable to imprisonment for life. 2013, c. 13, s. 5.

USE OR ALTERATION OF NUCLEAR MATERIAL, RADIOACTIVE MATERIAL OR DEVICE.

82.4 Everyone who, with intent to compel a person, government or international organization to do or refrain from doing any act, uses or alters nuclear material, radioactive material or a device or commits an act against a nuclear facility or an act that causes serious interference with or serious disruption of its operations, is guilty of an indictable offence and liable to imprisonment for life. 2013, c. 13, s. 5.

COMMISSION OF INDICTABLE OFFENCE TO OBTAIN NUCLEAR MATERIAL, ETC.

82.5 Everyone who commits an indictable offence under this or any other Act of Parliament, with intent to obtain nuclear material, radioactive material or a device or to obtain access to a nuclear facility, is guilty of an indictable offence and is liable to imprisonment for life. 2013, c. 13, s. 5.

THREATS.

82.6 Everyone who threatens to commit an offence under any of sections 82.3 to 82.5 is guilty of an indictable offence and is liable to imprisonment for a term of not more than 14 years. 2013, c. 13, s. 5.

ARMED FORCES.

82.7 For greater certainty, sections 82.3 to 82.6 do not apply to an act that is committed during an armed conflict and that, at the time and in the place of its commission, is in accordance with customary international law or conventional international law applicable to the conflict, or to activities undertaken by military forces of a state in the exercise of their official duties, to the extent that those activities are governed by other rules of international law. 2013, c. 13, s. 5.

Prize Fights

ENGAGING IN PRIZE FIGHT / Definition of "prize fight".

83. (1) Every one who
  (a) engages as a principal in a prize fight,
  (b) advises, encourages or promotes a prize fight, or
  (c) is present at a prize fight as an aid, second, surgeon, umpire, backer or reporter,
is guilty of an offence punishable on summary conviction.

(2) In this section, "prize fight" means an encounter or fight with fists, hands or feet between two persons who have met for that purpose by previous arrangement made by or for them, but does not include

    (*a*) a contest between amateur athletes in a combative sport with fists, hands or feet held in a province if the sport is on the programme of the International Olympic Committee or the International Paralympic Committee and, in the case where the province's lieutenant governor in council or any other person or body specified by him or her requires it, the contest is held with their permission;

    (*b*) a contest between amateur athletes in a combative sport with fists, hands or feet held in a province if the sport has been designated by the province's lieutenant governor in council or by any other person or body specified by him or her and, in the case where the lieutenant governor in council or other specified person or body requires it, the contest is held with their permission;

    (*c*) a contest between amateur athletes in a combative sport with fists, hands or feet held in a province with the permission of the province's lieutenant governor in council or any other person or body specified by him or her; and

    (*d*) a boxing contest or mixed martial arts contest held in a province with the permission or under the authority of an athletic board, commission or similar body established by or under the authority of the province's legislature for the control of sport within the province. R.S., c. C-34, s. 81; R.S.C. 1985, c. 27 (1st Supp.), s. 186; 2013, c. 19, s. 1.

Part II.1 / TERRORISM

Note: Part II.1 (ss. 83.01 to 83.33) enacted by 2001, c. 41, s. 4 (in force January 17, 2002).

Interpretation

DEFINITIONS / For greater certainty / For greater certainty / Facilitation.

83.01 (1) The following definitions apply in this Part.

"Canadian" means a Canadian citizen, a permanent resident within the meaning of subsection 2(1) of the *Immigration and Refugee Protection Act* or a body corporate incorporated and continued under the laws of Canada or a province.

"entity" means a person, group, trust, partnership or fund or an unincorporated association or organization.

"listed entity" means an entity on a list established by the Governor in Council under section 83.05.

"terrorist activity" means

    (*a*) an act or omission that is committed in or outside Canada and that, if committed in Canada, is one of the following offences:

        (i) the offences referred to in subsection 7(2) that implement the Convention for the Suppression of Unlawful Seizure of Aircraft, signed at The Hague on December 16, 1970,

(ii) the offences referred to in subsection 7(2) that implement the Convention for the Suppression of Unlawful Acts against the Safety of Civil Aviation, signed at Montreal on September 23, 1971,

(iii) the offences referred to in subsection 7(3) that implement the Convention on the Prevention and Punishment of Crimes against Internationally Protected Persons, including Diplomatic Agents, adopted by the General Assembly of the United Nations on December 14, 1973,

(iv) the offences referred to in subsection 7(3.1) that implement the International Convention against the Taking of Hostages, adopted by the General Assembly of the United Nations on December 17, 1979,

(v) the offences referred to in subsection 7(2.21) that implement the Convention on the Physical Protection of Nuclear Material, done at Vienna and New York on March 3, 1980, as amended by the Amendment to the Convention on the Physical Protection of Nuclear Material, done at Vienna on July 8, 2005 and the International Convention for the Suppression of Acts of Nuclear Terrorism, done at New York on September 14, 2005,

(vi) the offences referred to in subsection 7(2) that implement the Protocol for the Suppression of Unlawful Acts of Violence at Airports Serving International Civil Aviation, supplementary to the Convention for the Suppression of Unlawful Acts against the Safety of Civil Aviation, signed at Montreal on February 24, 1988,

(vii) the offences referred to in subsection 7(2.1) that implement the Convention for the Suppression of Unlawful Acts against the Safety of Maritime Navigation, done at Rome on March 10, 1988,

(viii) the offences referred to in subsection 7(2.1) or (2.2) that implement the Protocol for the Suppression of Unlawful Acts against the Safety of Fixed Platforms Located on the Continental Shelf, done at Rome on March 10, 1988,

(ix) the offences referred to in subsection 7(3.72) that implement the International Convention for the Suppression of Terrorist Bombings, adopted by the General Assembly of the United Nations on December 15, 1997, and

(x) the offences referred to in subsection 7(3.73) that implement the International Convention for the Suppression of the Financing of Terrorism, adopted by the General Assembly of the United Nations on December 9, 1999, or

(b) an act or omission, in or outside Canada,

(i) that is committed

(A) in whole or in part for a political, religious or ideological purpose, objective or cause, and

(B) in whole or in part with the intention of intimidating the public, or a segment of the public, with regard to its security, including its economic security, or compelling a person, a government or a domestic or an international organization to do or to refrain from doing any act, whether the public or the person, government or organization is inside or outside Canada, and

69

(ii) that intentionally

    (A) causes death or serious bodily harm to a person by the use of violence,

    (B) endangers a person's life,

    (C) causes a serious risk to the health or safety of the public or any segment of the public,

    (D) causes substantial property damage, whether to public or private property, if causing such damage is likely to result in the conduct or harm referred to in any of clauses (A) to (C), or

    (E) causes serious interference with or serious disruption of an essential service, facility or system, whether public or private, other than as a result of advocacy, protest, dissent or stoppage of work that is not intended to result in the conduct or harm referred to in any of clauses (A) to (C),

and includes a conspiracy, attempt or threat to commit any such act or omission, or being an accessory after the fact or counselling in relation to any such act or omission, but, for greater certainty, does not include an act or omission that is committed during an armed conflict and that, at the time and in the place of its commission, is in accordance with customary international law or conventional international law applicable to the conflict, or the activities undertaken by military forces of a state in the exercise of their official duties, to the extent that those activities are governed by other rules of international law.

"terrorist group" means

    (*a*) an entity that has as one of its purposes or activities facilitating or carrying out any terrorist activity, or

    (*b*) a listed entity,

and includes an association of such entities.

(1.1) For greater certainty, the expression of a political, religious or ideological thought, belief or opinion does not come within paragraph (*b*) of the definition "terrorist activity" in subsection (1) unless it constitutes an act or omission that satisfies the criteria of that paragraph.

(1.2) For greater certainty, a suicide bombing is an act that comes within paragraph (*a*) or (*b*) of the definition "terrorist activity" in subsection (1) if it satisfies the criteria of that paragraph.

(2) For the purposes of this Part, facilitation shall be construed in accordance with subsection 83.19(2). 2001, c. 41, ss. 4, 126(3); 2010, c. 19, s. 1; 2013, c. 13, s. 6.

Financing of Terrorism

PROVIDING OR COLLECTING PROPERTY FOR CERTAIN ACTIVITIES.

83.02 Every person is guilty of an indictable offence and liable to imprisonment for a term of not more than 10 years who, directly or indirectly, wilfully and without lawful justification or excuse, provides or collects property intending that it be used or knowing that it will be used, in whole or in part, in order to carry out

(a) an act or omission that constitutes an offence referred to in subparagraphs (a)(i) to (ix) of the definition of "terrorist activity" in subsection 83.01(1), or

(b) any other act or omission intended to cause death or serious bodily harm to a civilian or to any other person not taking an active part in the hostilities in a situation of armed conflict, if the purpose of that act or omission, by its nature or context, is to intimidate the public, or to compel a government or an international organization to do or refrain from doing any act. 2001, c. 41, s. 4; 2019, c. 25, s. 15.

CODE

PROVIDING, MAKING AVAILABLE, ETC., PROPERTY OR SERVICES FOR TERRORIST PURPOSES.

83.03 Every person is guilty of an indictable offence and liable to imprisonment for a term of not more than 10 years who, directly or indirectly, collects property, provides or invites a person to provide, or makes available property or financial or other related services

(a) intending that they be used, or knowing that they will be used, in whole or in part, for the purpose of facilitating or carrying out any terrorist activity, or for the purpose of benefiting any person who is facilitating or carrying out such an activity, or

(b) knowing that, in whole or part, they will be used by or will benefit a terrorist group. 2001, c. 41, s. 4; 2019, c. 25, s. 16.

USING OR POSSESSING PROPERTY FOR TERRORIST PURPOSES.

83.04 Every person is guilty of an indictable offence and liable to imprisonment for a term of not more than 10 years who

(a) uses property, directly or indirectly, in whole or in part, for the purpose of facilitating or carrying out a terrorist activity, or

(b) possesses property intending that it be used or knowing that it will be used, directly or indirectly, in whole or in part, for the purpose of facilitating or carrying out a terrorist activity. 2001, c. 41, s. 4; 2019, c. 25, s. 17.

List of Entities

ESTABLISHMENT OF LIST / Recommendation / Amendment to name of listed entity / Application to Minister / Deeming / Notice of the decision to the applicant / Judicial review / Reference / Evidence / Publication / New application / Review — listed entity / Validity / Publication / Definition of "judge".

83.05 (1) The Governor in Council may, by regulation, establish a list on which the Governor in Council may place any entity if, on the recommendation of the Minister of Public Safety and Emergency Preparedness, the Governor in Council is satisfied that there are reasonable grounds to believe that

(a) the entity has knowingly carried out, attempted to carry out, participated in or facilitated a terrorist activity; or

(b) the entity has knowingly acted on behalf of, at the direction of or in association with an entity referred to in paragraph (a).

(1.1) The Minister may make a recommendation referred to in subsection (1) only if he or she has reasonable grounds to believe that the entity to which the recommendation relates is an entity referred to in paragraph (1)(a) or (b).

(1.2) The Minister may, by regulation,
  (a) change the name of a listed entity, or add to the list any other name by which a listed entity may also be or have been known, if the Minister has reasonable grounds to believe that the listed entity is using a name that is not on the list; and
  (b) delete from the list any other name by which a listed entity may also have been known, if the entity is no longer using that name.

(2) On application in writing by a listed entity to be removed from the list, the Minister shall decide whether the applicant should remain a listed entity or whether the Minister should recommend to the Governor in Council that the applicant be removed from the list, taking into account the grounds set out in subsection (1).

(3) If the Minister does not make a decision on the application referred to in subsection (2) within 90 days after receipt of the application, or within any longer period that may be agreed to in writing by the Minister and the applicant, the Minister is deemed to have decided that the applicant should remain a listed entity.

(4) The Minister shall give notice without delay to the applicant of any decision taken or deemed to have been taken respecting the application referred to in subsection (2).

(5) Within 60 days after the receipt of the notice of the decision referred to in subsection (4), the applicant may apply to a judge for judicial review of the decision.

(6) When an application is made under subsection (5), the judge shall, without delay
  (a) examine, in private, any security or criminal intelligence reports considered in the making of the decision on whether the applicant should remain a listed entity and hear any other evidence or information that may be presented by or on behalf of the Minister and may, at his or her request, hear all or part of that evidence or information in the absence of the applicant and any counsel representing the applicant, if the judge is of the opinion that the disclosure of the information would injure national security or endanger the safety of any person;
  (b) provide the applicant with a statement summarizing the information available to the judge so as to enable the applicant to be reasonably informed of the reasons for the decision, without disclosing any information the disclosure of which would, in the judge's opinion, injure national security or endanger the safety of any person;
  (c) provide the applicant with a reasonable opportunity to be heard; and

(*d*) determine whether the decision is reasonable on the basis of the information available to the judge and, if found not to be reasonable, order that the applicant no longer be a listed entity.

(6.1) The judge may receive into evidence anything that, in the opinion of the judge, is reliable and appropriate, even if it would not otherwise be admissible under Canadian law, and may base his or her decision on that evidence.

(7) The Minister shall cause to be published, without delay, in the *Canada Gazette* notice of a final order of a court that the applicant no longer be a listed entity.

(8) A listed entity may not make another application under subsection (2) except if, since the time when the entity made its last application,
    (*a*) there has been a material change in its circumstances; or
    (*b*) the Minister has completed a review under subsection (8.1) with respect to that entity.

(8.1) The Minister shall review whether there are still reasonable grounds, as set out in subsection (1), for an entity to be a listed entity and make a recommendation to the Governor in Council as to whether the entity should remain a listed entity
    (*a*) within five years after
        (i) the day on which this subsection comes into force, if the entity is a listed entity on that day, or
        (ii) the day on which the entity is added to the list, if the entity is added to the list after the day on which this subsection comes into force; and
    (*b*) subsequently, within five years after the most recent recommendation made under this subsection with respect to the entity.

(9) Reviews undertaken under subsection (8.1) do not affect the validity of the list.

(10) The Minister shall cause notice of the results of every review of a listed entity undertaken under subsection (8.1) to be published in the *Canada Gazette* within five years after the review is completed.

(11) In this section, "judge" means the Chief Justice of the Federal Court or a judge of the Trial Division of that Court designated by the Chief Justice. 2001, c. 41, s. 4; 2005, c. 10, ss. 18 and 34(1)(*f*)(iii); 2019, c. 13, s. 141.

**ADMISSION OF FOREIGN INFORMATION OBTAINED IN CONFIDENCE /
Return of information / Use of information.**

83.06 (1) For the purposes of subsection 83.05(6), in private and in the absence of the applicant or any counsel representing it,
    (*a*) the Minister of Public Safety and Emergency Preparedness may make an application to the judge for the admission of information obtained in confidence from a government, an institution or an agency of a foreign state, from an international organization of states or from an institution or an agency of an international organization of states; and
    (*b*) the judge shall examine the information and provide counsel representing the Minister with a reasonable opportunity to be heard as to whether the information is relevant but should not be disclosed to the applicant or any

counsel representing it because the disclosure would injure national security or endanger the safety of any person.

(2) The information shall be returned to counsel representing the Minister and shall not be considered by the judge in making the determination under paragraph 83.05(6)(*d*), if

(*a*) the judge determines that the information is not relevant;

(*b*) the judge determines that the information is relevant but should be summarized in the statement to be provided under paragraph 83.05(6)(*b*); or

(*c*) the Minister withdraws the application.

(3) If the judge decides that the information is relevant but that its disclosure would injure national security or endanger the safety of persons, the information shall not be disclosed in the statement mentioned in paragraph 83.05(6)(*b*), but the judge may base the determination under paragraph 83.05(6)(*d*) on it. 2001, c. 41, s. 4; 2005, c. 10, s. 19.

MISTAKEN IDENTITY / Issuance of certificate.

83.07 (1) An entity whose name is the same as or similar to a name, appearing on the list, of a listed entity and who claims not to be that listed entity may apply in writing to the Minister of Public Safety and Emergency Preparedness for a certificate stating that it is not that listed entity.

(2) The Minister shall, within 30 days after receiving the application, issue a certificate if he or she is satisfied that the applicant is not that listed entity. 2001, c. 41, s. 4; 2005, c. 10, s. 20; 2019, c. 13, s. 142.

Freezing of Property

FREEZING OF PROPERTY / No civil liability.

83.08 (1) No person in Canada and no Canadian outside Canada shall knowingly

(*a*) deal directly or indirectly in any property that is owned or controlled by or on behalf of a terrorist group;

(*b*) enter into or facilitate, directly or indirectly, any transaction in respect of property referred to in paragraph (*a*); or

(*c*) provide any financial or other related services in respect of property referred to in paragraph (*a*) to, for the benefit of or at the direction of a terrorist group.

(2) A person who acts reasonably in taking, or omitting to take, measures to comply with subsection (1) shall not be liable in any civil action arising from having taken or omitted to take the measures, if they took all reasonable steps to satisfy themselves that the relevant property was owned or controlled by or on behalf of a terrorist group. 2001, c. 41, s. 4; 2013, c. 9, s. 3(2).

EXEMPTIONS / Ministerial authorization / Existing equities maintained / Third party involvement.

83.09 (1) The Minister of Public Safety and Emergency Preparedness, or a person designated by him or her, may authorize any person in Canada or any Canadian outside Canada to carry out a specified activity or transaction that is prohibited by section 83.08, or a class of such activities or transactions.

(2) The Minister, or a person designated by him or her, may make the authorization subject to any terms and conditions that are required in their opinion and may amend, suspend, revoke or reinstate it.

(3) All secured and unsecured rights and interests in the frozen property that are held by persons, other than terrorist groups or their agents, are entitled to the same ranking that they would have been entitled to had the property not been frozen.

(4) If a person has obtained an authorization under subsection (1), any other person involved in carrying out the activity or transaction, or class of activities or transactions, to which the authorization relates is not subject to sections 83.08, 83.1 and 83.11 if the terms or conditions of the authorization that are imposed under subsection (2), if any, are met. 2001, c. 41, s. 4; 2005, c. 10, s. 21.

DISCLOSURE / Immunity.

83.1 (1) Every person in Canada and every Canadian outside Canada shall disclose without delay to the Commissioner of the Royal Canadian Mounted Police or to the Director of the Canadian Security Intelligence Service

  (a) the existence of property in their possession or control that they know is owned or controlled by or on behalf of a terrorist group; and

  (b) information about a transaction or proposed transaction in respect of property referred to in paragraph (a).

(2) No criminal or civil proceedings lie against a person for disclosure made in good faith under subsection (1). 2001, c. 41, s. 4; 2013, c. 9, s. 4.

AUDIT / Monthly report / Immunity / Regulations.

83.11 (1) The following entities must determine on a continuing basis whether they are in possession or control of property owned or controlled by or on behalf of a listed entity:

  (a) authorized foreign banks within the meaning of section 2 of the *Bank Act* in respect of their business in Canada, or banks to which that Act applies;

  (b) cooperative credit societies, savings and credit unions and caisses populaires regulated by a provincial Act and associations regulated by the *Cooperative Credit Associations Act*;

  (c) foreign companies within the meaning of subsection 2(1) of the *Insurance Companies Act* in respect of their insurance business in Canada;

  (c.1) companies, provincial companies and societies within the meaning of subsection 2(1) of the *Insurance Companies Act*;

(*c*.2) fraternal benefit societies regulated by a provincial Act in respect of their insurance activities, and insurance companies and other entities engaged in the business of insuring risks that are regulated by a provincial Act;

(*d*) companies to which the *Trust and Loan Companies Act* applies;

(*e*) trust companies regulated by a provincial Act;

(*f*) loan companies regulated by a provincial Act; and

(*g*) entities authorized under provincial legislation to engage in the business of dealing in securities, or to provide portfolio management or investment counselling services.

(2) Subject to the regulations, every entity referred to in paragraphs (1)(*a*) to (*g*) must report, within the period specified by regulation or, if no period is specified, monthly, to the principal agency or body that supervises or regulates it under federal or provincial law either

(*a*) that it is not in possession or control of any property referred to in subsection (1), or

(*b*) that it is in possession or control of such property, in which case it must also report the number of persons, contracts or accounts involved and the total value of the property.

(3) No criminal or civil proceedings lie against a person for making a report in good faith under subsection (2).

(4) The Governor in Council may make regulations

(*a*) excluding any entity or class of entities from the requirement to make a report referred to in subsection (2), and specifying the conditions of exclusion; and

(*b*) specifying a period for the purposes of subsection (2). 2001, c. 41, s. 4.

OFFENCES — FREEZING OF PROPERTY, DISCLOSURE OR AUDIT.

83.12 (1) Every person who contravenes any of sections 83.08, 83.1 and 83.11 is guilty of an offence and liable

(*a*) on conviction on indictment, to imprisonment for a term of not more than 10 years; or

(*b*) on summary conviction, to a fine of not more than $100,000 or to imprisonment for a term of not more than two years less a day, or to both. 2001, c. 41, s. 4; 2013, c. 9, c. 5; 2019, c. 25 s. 18.

(2) [*Repealed*, 2013, c. 9, s. 5.]

Seizure and Restraint of Property

SEIZURE AND RESTRAINT OF ASSETS / Contents of application / Appointment of manager / Appointment of Minister of Public Works and Government Services / Power to manage / Application for destruction order / Notice / Manner of giving notice / Destruction order / Forfeiture order / When management order ceases to have effect / For greater certainty / Application to vary / Procedure / Procedure.

83.13 (1) Where a judge of the Federal Court, on an *ex parte* application by the Attorney General, after examining the application in private, is satisfied that there are reasonable grounds to believe that there is in any building, receptacle or place any property in respect of which an order of forfeiture may be made under subsection 83.14(5), the judge may issue

    (*a*) if the property is situated in Canada, a warrant authorizing a person named therein or a peace officer to search the building, receptacle or place for that property and to seize that property and any other property in respect of which that person or peace officer believes, on reasonable grounds, that an order of forfeiture may be made under that subsection; or

    (*b*) if the property is situated in or outside Canada, a restraint order prohibiting any person from disposing of, or otherwise dealing with any interest in, that property other than as may be specified in the order.

(1.1) An affidavit in support of an application under subsection (1) may be sworn on information and belief, and, notwithstanding the *Federal Court Rules, 1998*, no adverse inference shall be drawn from a failure to provide evidence of persons having personal knowledge of material facts.

(2) On an application under subsection (1), at the request of the Attorney General, if a judge is of the opinion that the circumstances so require, the judge may

    (*a*) appoint a person to take control of, and to manage or otherwise deal with, all or part of the property in accordance with the directions of the judge; and

    (*b*) require any person having possession of that property to give possession of the property to the person appointed under paragraph (*a*).

(3) When the Attorney General of Canada so requests, a judge appointing a person under subsection (2) shall appoint the Minister of Public Works and Government Services.

(4) The power to manage or otherwise deal with property under subsection (2) includes

    (*a*) the power to make an interlocutory sale of perishable or rapidly depreciating property;

    (*b*) the power to destroy, in accordance with subsections (5) to (8), property that has little or no value; and

    (*c*) the power to have property, other than real property or a conveyance, forfeited to Her Majesty in accordance with subsection (8.1).

(5) Before a person who is appointed to manage property destroys property that has little or no value, they shall apply to a judge of the Federal Court for a destruction order.

(6) Before making a destruction order, a judge shall require notice in accordance with subsection (7) to be given to and may hear any person who, in the judge's opinion, appears to have a valid interest in the property.

(7) A notice shall
    (*a*) be given in the manner that the judge directs or that may be specified in the rules of the Federal Court; and
    (*b*) specify the effective period of the notice that the judge considers reasonable or that may be set out in the rules of the Federal Court.

(8) A judge shall order that the property be destroyed if they are satisfied that the property has little or no financial or other value.

(8.1) On application by a person who is appointed to manage the property, a judge of the Federal Court shall order that the property, other than real property or a conveyance, be forfeited to Her Majesty to be disposed of or otherwise dealt with in accordance with the law if
    (*a*) a notice is given or published in the manner that the judge directs or that may be specified in the rules of the Federal Court;
    (*b*) the notice specifies a period of 60 days during which a person may make an application to the judge asserting their interest in the property; and
    (*c*) during that period, no one makes such an application.

(9) A management order ceases to have effect when the property that is the subject of the management order is returned in accordance with the law, destroyed or forfeited to Her Majesty.

(9.1) Before making a destruction order, a judge shall require notice in accordance with subsection (7) to be given to and may hear any person who, in the judge's opinion, appears to have a valid interest in the property.

(10) The Attorney General may at any time apply to a judge of the Federal Court to cancel or vary an order or warrant made under this section, other than an appointment made under subsection (3).

(11) Subsections 462.32(4) and (6), sections 462.34 to 462.35 and 462.4, subsection 487(3) and section 488 apply, with any modifications that the circumstances require, to a warrant issued under paragraph (1)(*a*). Any peace officer who executes the warrant must have authority to act as a peace officer in the place where it is executed.

(12) Subsections 462.33(4) and (6) to (11) and sections 462.34 to 462.35 and 462.4 apply, with such modifications as the circumstances require, to an order issued under paragraph (1)(*b*). 2001, c. 41, s. 4; 2017, c. 7, s. 54; 2019, c. 25, s. 19.

Forfeiture of Property

APPLICATION FOR ORDER OF FORFEITURE / Contents of application / Respondents / Notice / Granting of forfeiture order / Use of proceeds / Regulations / Order refusing forfeiture / Notice / Third party interests / Dwelling-house / Motion to vary or set aside / No extension of time.

83.14 (1) The Attorney General may make an application to a judge of the Federal Court for an order of forfeiture in respect of

   (a) property owned or controlled by or on behalf of a terrorist group; or

   (b) property that has been or will be used, in whole or in part, to facilitate or carry out a terrorist activity.

(2) An affidavit in support of an application by the Attorney General under subsection (1) may be sworn on information and belief, and, notwithstanding the *Federal Court Rules, 1998*, no adverse inference shall be drawn from a failure to provide evidence of persons having personal knowledge of material facts.

(3) The Attorney General is required to name as a respondent to an application under subsection (1) only those persons who are known to own or control the property that is the subject of the application.

(4) The Attorney General shall give notice of an application under subsection (1) to named respondents in such a manner as the judge directs or as provided in the rules of the Federal Court.

(5) If a judge is satisfied on a balance of probabilities that property is property referred to in paragraph (1)(a) or (b), the judge shall order that the property be forfeited to Her Majesty to be disposed of as the Attorney General directs or otherwise dealt with in accordance with the law.

(5.1) Any proceeds that arise from the disposal of property under subsection (5) may be used to compensate victims of terrorist activities and to fund anti-terrorist initiatives in accordance with any regulations made by the Governor in Council under subsection (5.2).

(5.2) The Governor in Council may make regulations for the purposes of specifying how the proceeds referred to in subsection (5.1) are to be distributed.

(6) Where a judge refuses an application under subsection (1) in respect of any property, the judge shall make an order that describes the property and declares that it is not property referred to in that subsection.

(7) On an application under subsection (1), a judge may require notice to be given to any person who, in the opinion of the Court, appears to have an interest in the property, and any such person shall be entitled to be added as a respondent to the application.

(8) If a judge is satisfied that a person referred to in subsection (7) has an interest in property that is subject to an application, has exercised reasonable care to ensure that the property would not be used to facilitate or carry out a terrorist activity, and is not a member of a terrorist group, the judge shall order that the

interest is not affected by the forfeiture. Such an order shall declare the nature and extent of the interest in question.

(9) Where all or part of property that is the subject of an application under subsection (1) is a dwelling-house, the judge shall also consider

    (*a*) the impact of an order of forfeiture on any member of the immediate family of the person who owns or controls the dwelling-house, if the dwelling-house was the member's principal residence at the time the dwelling-house was ordered restrained or at the time the forfeiture application was made and continues to be the member's principal residence; and

    (*b*) whether the member appears innocent of any complicity or collusion in the terrorist activity.

(10) A person who claims an interest in property that was forfeited and who did not receive notice under subsection (7) may bring a motion to the Federal Court to vary or set aside an order made under subsection (5) not later than 60 days after the day on which the forfeiture order was made.

(11) The Court may not extend the period set out in subsection (10). 2001, c. 41, s. 4.

DISPOSITION OF PROPERTY.

83.15 Subsection 462.42(6) and sections 462.43 and 462.46 apply, with such modifications as the circumstances require, to property subject to a warrant or restraint order issued under subsection 83.13(1) or ordered forfeited under subsection 83.14(5). 2001, c. 41, s. 4.

INTERIM PRESERVATION RIGHTS / Appeal of refusal to grant order.

83.16 (1) Pending any appeal of an order made under section 83.14, property restrained under an order issued under section 83.13 shall continue to be restrained, property seized under a warrant issued under that section shall continue to be detained, and any person appointed to manage, control or otherwise deal with that property under that section shall continue in that capacity.

(2) Section 462.34 applies, with such modifications as the circumstances require, to an appeal taken in respect of a refusal to grant an order under subsection 83.14(5). 2001, c. 41, s. 4.

OTHER FORFEITURE PROVISIONS UNAFFECTED / Priority for restitution to victims of crime.

83.17 (1) This Part does not affect the operation of any other provision of this or any other Act of Parliament respecting the forfeiture of property.

(2) Property is subject to forfeiture under subsection 83.14(5) only to the extent that it is not required to satisfy the operation of any other provision of this or any other Act of Parliament respecting restitution to, or compensation of, persons affected by the commission of offences. 2001, c. 41, s. 4.

Participating, Facilitating, Instructing and Harbouring

PARTICIPATION IN ACTIVITY OF TERRORIST GROUP / Prosecution / Meaning of participating or contributing / Factors.

83.18 (1) Every person who knowingly participates in or contributes to, directly or indirectly, any activity of a terrorist group for the purpose of enhancing the ability of any terrorist group to facilitate or carry out a terrorist activity is guilty of an indictable offence and liable to imprisonment for a term of not more than 10 years.

(2) An offence may be committed under subsection (1) whether or not
   (a) a terrorist group actually facilitates or carries out a terrorist activity;
   (b) the participation or contribution of the accused actually enhances the ability of a terrorist group to facilitate or carry out a terrorist activity; or
   (c) the accused knows the specific nature of any terrorist activity that may be facilitated or carried out by a terrorist group.

(3) Participating in or contributing to an activity of a terrorist group includes
   (a) providing, receiving or recruiting a person to receive training;
   (b) providing or offering to provide a skill or an expertise for the benefit of, at the direction of or in association with a terrorist group;
   (c) recruiting a person in order to facilitate or commit
       (i) a terrorism offence, or
       (ii) an act or omission outside Canada that, if committed in Canada, would be a terrorism offence;
   (d) entering or remaining in any country for the benefit of, at the direction of or in association with a terrorist group; and
   (e) making oneself, in response to instructions from any of the persons who constitute a terrorist group, available to facilitate or commit
       (i) a terrorism offence, or
       (ii) an act or omission outside Canada that, if committed in Canada, would be a terrorism offence.

(4) In determining whether an accused participates in or contributes to any activity of a terrorist group, the court may consider, among other factors, whether the accused
   (a) uses a name, word, symbol or other representation that identifies, or is associated with, the terrorist group;
   (b) frequently associates with any of the persons who constitute the terrorist group;
   (c) receives any benefit from the terrorist group; or
   (d) repeatedly engages in activities at the instruction of any of the persons who constitute the terrorist group. 2001, c. 41, s. 4; 2019, c. 25, s. 20.

LEAVING CANADA TO PARTICIPATE IN ACTIVITY OF TERRORIST GROUP.

83.181 Every person who leaves or attempts to leave Canada, or goes or attempts to go on board a conveyance with the intent to leave Canada, for the purpose of committing an act or omission outside Canada that, if committed in Canada, would be an offence under subsection 83.18(1) is guilty of an indictable offence and liable to imprisonment for a term of not more than 10 years. 2013, c. 9, s. 6; 2019, c. 25, s. 21.

FACILITATING TERRORIST ACTIVITY / Facilitation.

83.19 (1) Every one who knowingly facilitates a terrorist activity is guilty of an indictable offence and liable to imprisonment for a term not exceeding fourteen years.

(2) For the purposes of this Part, a terrorist activity is facilitated whether or not
   (a) the facilitator knows that a particular terrorist activity is facilitated;
   (b) any particular terrorist activity was foreseen or planned at the time it was facilitated; or
   (c) any terrorist activity was actually carried out. 2001, c. 41, s. 4.

LEAVING CANADA TO FACILITATE TERRORIST ACTIVITY.

83.191 Everyone who leaves or attempts to leave Canada, or goes or attempts to go on board a conveyance with the intent to leave Canada, for the purpose of committing an act or omission outside Canada that, if committed in Canada, would be an offence under subsection 83.19(1) is guilty of an indictable offence and liable to imprisonment for a term of not more than 14 years. 2013, c. 9, s. 7.

COMMISSION OF OFFENCE FOR TERRORIST GROUP.

83.2 Every one who commits an indictable offence under this or any other Act of Parliament for the benefit of, at the direction of or in association with a terrorist group is guilty of an indictable offence and liable to imprisonment for life. 2001, c. 41, s. 4.

LEAVING CANADA TO COMMIT OFFENCE FOR TERRORIST GROUP.

83.201 Everyone who leaves or attempts to leave Canada, or goes or attempts to go on board a conveyance with the intent to leave Canada, for the purpose of committing an act or omission outside Canada that, if committed in Canada, would be an indictable offence under this or any other Act of Parliament for the benefit of, at the direction of or in association with a terrorist group is guilty of an indictable offence and liable to imprisonment for a term of not more than 14 years. 2013, c. 9, s. 8.

LEAVING CANADA TO COMMIT OFFENCE THAT IS TERRORIST ACTIVITY.

83.202 Everyone who leaves or attempts to leave Canada, or goes or attempts to go on board a conveyance with the intent to leave Canada, for the purpose of committing an act or omission outside Canada that, if committed in Canada, would be an indictable offence under this or any other Act of Parliament if the act or omission constituting the offence also constitutes a terrorist activity is guilty of an indictable offence and liable to imprisonment for a term of not more than 14 years. 2013, c. 9, s. 8.

CODE

INSTRUCTING TO CARRY OUT ACTIVITY FOR TERRORIST GROUP / Prosecution.

83.21 (1) Every person who knowingly instructs, directly or indirectly, any person to carry out any activity for the benefit of, at the direction of or in association with a terrorist group, for the purpose of enhancing the ability of any terrorist group to facilitate or carry out a terrorist activity, is guilty of an indictable offence and liable to imprisonment for life.

(2) An offence may be committed under subsection (1) whether or not
  (a) the activity that the accused instructs to be carried out is actually carried out;
  (b) the accused instructs a particular person to carry out the activity referred to in paragraph (a);
  (c) the accused knows the identity of the person whom the accused instructs to carry out the activity referred to in paragraph (a);
  (d) the person whom the accused instructs to carry out the activity referred to in paragraph (a) knows that it is to be carried out for the benefit of, at the direction of or in association with a terrorist group;
  (e) a terrorist group actually facilitates or carries out a terrorist activity;
  (f) the activity referred to in paragraph (a) actually enhances the ability of a terrorist group to facilitate or carry out a terrorist activity; or
  (g) the accused knows the specific nature of any terrorist activity that may be facilitated or carried out by a terrorist group. 2001, c. 41, s. 4.

INSTRUCTING TO CARRY OUT TERRORIST ACTIVITY / Prosecution.

83.22 (1) Every person who knowingly instructs, directly or indirectly, any person to carry out a terrorist activity is guilty of an indictable offence and liable to imprisonment for life.

(2) An offence may be committed under subsection (1) whether or not
  (a) the terrorist activity is actually carried out;
  (b) the accused instructs a particular person to carry out the terrorist activity;
  (c) the accused knows the identity of the person whom the accused instructs to carry out the terrorist activity; or
  (d) the person whom the accused instructs to carry out the terrorist activity knows that it is a terrorist activity. 2001, c. 41, s. 4.

COUNSELLING COMMISSION OF TERRORISM OFFENCE / Application.

83.221 (1) Every person who counsels another person to commit a terrorism offence without identifying a specific terrorism offence is guilty of an indictable offence and is liable to imprisonment for a term of not more than five years.

(2) An offence may be committed under subsection (1) whether or not a terrorism offence is committed by the person who is counselled. 2015, c. 20, s. 16; 2019, c. 13, s. 143.

WARRANT OF SEIZURE / Summons to occupier / Owner and author may appear / Order of forfeiture / Disposal of matter / Appeal / Consent / Definitions.

83.222 (1) A judge who is satisfied by information on oath that there are reasonable grounds to believe that any publication, copies of which are kept for sale or distribution in premises within the court's jurisdiction, is terrorist propaganda may issue a warrant authorizing seizure of the copies.

(2) Within seven days after the day on which the warrant is issued, the judge shall issue a summons to the premises' occupier requiring the occupier to appear before the court and to show cause why the matter seized should not be forfeited to Her Majesty.

(3) The owner and the author of the matter seized and alleged to be terrorist propaganda may appear and be represented before the court in order to oppose the making of an order for the forfeiture of the matter.

(4) If the court is satisfied, on a balance of probabilities, that the publication is terrorist propaganda, it may make an order declaring that the matter be forfeited to Her Majesty, for disposal as the Attorney General may direct.

(5) If the court is not satisfied that the publication is terrorist propaganda, it may order that the matter be restored to the person from whom it was seized without delay after the time for final appeal has expired.

(6) An appeal lies from an order made under subsection (4) or (5) by any person who appeared before the court, on any ground of appeal that involves a question of law or fact alone, or a question of mixed law and fact, as if it were an appeal against conviction or against a judgment or verdict of acquittal, as the case may be, on a question of law alone under Part XXI, and sections 673 to 696 apply with any modifications that the circumstances require.

(7) No proceeding under this section shall be instituted without the Attorney General's consent.

(8) The following definitions apply in this section.

"court" has the same meaning as in subsection 320(8).

"judge" has the same meaning as in subsection 320(8).

"terrorist propaganda" means any writing, sign, visible representation or audio recording that counsels the commission of a terrorism offence. 2015, c. 20, s. 16; 2019, c. 13, s. 144.

ORDER TO COMPUTER SYSTEM'S CUSTODIAN / Notice to person who posted material / Person who posted material may appear / Non-appearance / Order of deletion / Destruction of electronic copy / Return of material / Appeal / Consent / When order takes effect / Definitions.

83.223 (1) If a judge is satisfied by information on oath that there are reasonable grounds to believe that there is material — that is terrorist propaganda or computer data that makes terrorist propaganda available — stored on and made available to the public through a computer system that is within the court's jurisdiction, the judge may order the computer system's custodian to

(a) give an electronic copy of the material to the court;

(b) ensure that the material is no longer stored on and made available through the computer system; and

(c) provide the information that is necessary to identify and locate the person who posted the material.

(2) Within a reasonable time after receiving the information referred to in paragraph (1)(c), the judge shall cause notice to be given to the person who posted the material, giving that person the opportunity to appear and be represented before the court and to show cause why the material should not be deleted. If the person cannot be identified or located or does not reside in Canada, the judge may order the computer system's custodian to post the text of the notice at the location where the material was previously stored and made available, until the time set for the appearance.

(3) The person who posted the material may appear and be represented before the court in order to oppose the making of an order under subsection (5).

(4) If the person who posted the material does not appear before the court, the court may proceed to hear and determine the proceedings in the absence of the person as fully and effectually as if the person had appeared.

(5) If the court is satisfied, on a balance of probabilities, that the material is available to the public and is terrorist propaganda or computer data that makes terrorist propaganda available, it may order the computer system's custodian to delete the material.

(6) When the court makes the order for the deletion of the material, it may order the destruction of the electronic copy in the court's possession.

(7) If the court is not satisfied that the material is available to the public and is terrorist propaganda or computer data that makes terrorist propaganda available, the court shall order that the electronic copy be returned to the computer system's custodian and terminate the order under paragraph (1)(b).

(8) An appeal lies from an order made under subsection (5) or (6) by any person who appeared before the court, on any ground of appeal that involves a question of law or fact alone, or a question of mixed law and fact, as if it were an appeal against conviction or against a judgment or verdict of acquittal, as the case may be, on a question of law alone under Part XXI, and sections 673 to 696 apply with any modifications that the circumstances require.

(9) No proceeding under this section shall be instituted without the Attorney General's consent.

(10) No order made under any of subsections (5) to (7) takes effect until the time for final appeal has expired.

(11) The following definitions apply in this section.

"computer data" has the same meaning as in subsection 342.1(2).

"computer system" has the same meaning as in subsection 342.1(2).

"court" has the same meaning as in subsection 320(8).

"data" [Repealed 2015, c. 20, s. 35(d).]

"judge" has the same meaning as in subsection 320(8).

"terrorist propaganda" has the same meaning as in subsection 83.222(8). 2015, c. 20, ss. 16, 35.

CONCEALING PERSON WHO CARRIED OUT TERRORIST ACTIVITY / Concealing person who is likely to carry out terrorist activity.

83.23 (1) Every person who knowingly harbours or conceals another person whom they know to be a person who has carried out a terrorist activity, for the purpose of enabling that other person to facilitate or carry out any terrorist activity, is guilty of

(a) an indictable offence and liable to imprisonment for a term of not more than 14 years, if the person who is harboured or concealed carried out a terrorist activity that is a terrorism offence for which that person is liable to imprisonment for life; and

(b) an indictable offence and liable to imprisonment for a term of not more than 10 years, if the person who is harboured or concealed carried out a terrorist activity that is a terrorism offence for which that person is liable to any other punishment.

(2) Every person who knowingly harbours or conceals another person whom they know to be a person who is likely to carry out a terrorist activity, for the purpose of enabling that other person to facilitate or carry out any terrorist activity, is guilty of an indictable offence and liable to imprisonment for a term of not more than 10 years. 2001, c. 41, s. 4; 2013, c. 9, s. 9; 2019, c. 25, s. 22.

Hoax Regarding Terrorist Activity

HOAX — TERRORIST ACTIVITY / Punishment / Causing bodily harm / Causing death.

83.231 (1) Every one commits an offence who, without lawful excuse and with intent to cause any person to fear death, bodily harm, substantial damage to property or serious interference with the lawful use or operation of property,

(a) conveys or causes or procures to be conveyed information that, in all the circumstances, is likely to cause a reasonable apprehension that terrorist activity is occurring or will occur, without believing the information to be true; or

(b) commits an act that, in all the circumstances, is likely to cause a reasonable apprehension that terrorist activity is occurring or will occur, without believing that such activity is occurring or will occur.

(2) Every one who commits an offence under subsection (1) is guilty of
 (a) an indictable offence and liable to imprisonment for a term not exceeding five years; or
 (b) an offence punishable on summary conviction.

(3) Every one who commits an offence under subsection (1) and thereby causes bodily harm to any other person is guilty of
 (a) an indictable offence and liable to imprisonment for a term not exceeding ten years; or
 (b) an offence punishable on summary conviction.

(4) Every one who commits an offence under subsection (1) and thereby causes the death of any other person is guilty of an indictable offence and liable to imprisonment for life. 2004, c. 15, s. 32; 2019, c. 25, s. 23.

Proceedings and Aggravated Punishment

ATTORNEY GENERAL'S CONSENT.

83.24 Proceedings in respect of a terrorism offence or an offence under section 83.12 shall not be commenced without the consent of the Attorney General. 2001, c. 41, s. 4.

JURISDICTION / Trial and punishment.

83.25 (1) Where a person is alleged to have committed a terrorism offence or an offence under section 83.12, proceedings in respect of that offence may, whether or not that person is in Canada, be commenced at the instance of the Government of Canada and conducted by the Attorney General of Canada or counsel acting on his or her behalf in any territorial division in Canada, if the offence is alleged to have occurred outside the province in which the proceedings are commenced, whether or not proceedings have previously been commenced elsewhere in Canada.

(2) An accused may be tried and punished in respect of an offence referred to in subsection (1) in the same manner as if the offence had been committed in the territorial division where the proceeding is conducted. 2001, c. 41, s. 4.

SENTENCES TO BE SERVED CONSECUTIVELY.

83.26 A sentence, other than one of life imprisonment, imposed on a person for an offence under any of sections 83.02 to 83.04 and 83.18 to 83.23 shall be served consecutively to
 (a) any other punishment imposed on the person, other than a sentence of life imprisonment, for an offence arising out of the same event or series of events; and

(b) any other sentence, other than one of life imprisonment, to which the person is subject at the time the sentence is imposed on the person for an offence under any of those sections. 2001, c. 41, s. 4.

PUNISHMENT FOR TERRORIST ACTIVITY / Offender must be notified.

83.27 (1) Notwithstanding anything in this Act, a person convicted of an indictable offence, other than an offence for which a sentence of imprisonment for life is imposed as a minimum punishment, where the act or omission constituting the offence also constitutes a terrorist activity, is liable to imprisonment for life.

(2) Subsection (1) does not apply unless the prosecutor satisfies the court that the offender, before making a plea, was notified that the application of that subsection would be sought. 2001, c. 41, s. 4.

[*Heading repealed*, 2019, c. 13, s. 145.]

83.28 [*Repealed*, 2019, c. 13, s. 145.]

83.29 [*Repealed*, 2019, c. 13, s. 145.]

Recognizance with Conditions

ATTORNEY GENERAL'S CONSENT / Terrorist activity / Appearance / Arrest without warrant / Duty of peace officer / When person to be taken before judge / How person dealt with / Adjournment under subparagraph (7)(b)(ii) / Adjournment under paragraph (7.1)(b) / Hearing before judge / Duration extended / Refusal to enter into recognizance / Conditions — firearms / Surrender, etc. / Condition — passport / Condition — specified geographic area / Reasons / Variance of conditions / Other provisions to apply.

83.3 (1) The Attorney General's consent is required before a peace officer may lay an information under subsection (2).

(2) Subject to subsection (1), a peace officer may lay an information before a provincial court judge if the peace officer
   (a) believes on reasonable grounds that a terrorist activity may be carried out; and
   (b) suspects on reasonable grounds that the imposition of a recognizance with conditions on a person, or the arrest of a person, is necessary to prevent the carrying out of the terrorist activity.

(3) The judge who receives the information may cause the person to appear before any provincial court judge.

(4) Despite subsections (2) and (3), a peace officer may arrest a person without a warrant and cause the person to be detained in custody, in order to bring them before a provincial court judge in accordance with subsection (6), if
   (a) either

    (i) the grounds for laying an information referred to in paragraphs (2)(*a*) and (*b*) exist but, by reason of exigent circumstances, it would be impracticable to lay an information under subsection (2), or

   (ii) an information has been laid under subsection (2) and a summons has been issued; and

  (*b*) the peace officer suspects on reasonable grounds that the detention of the person in custody is necessary to prevent a terrorist activity.

(5) If a peace officer arrests a person without a warrant in the circumstance described in subparagraph (4)(*a*)(i), the peace officer shall, within the time prescribed by paragraph (6)(*a*) or (*b*),

  (*a*) lay an information in accordance with subsection (2); or

  (*b*) release the person.

(6) Unless a peace officer is satisfied that a person should be released from custody without conditions before their appearance before a provincial court judge in accordance with the rules in paragraph (*a*) or (*b*), and so releases the person, the person detained in custody shall be taken before a provincial court judge in accordance with the following rules:

  (*a*) if a provincial court judge is available within 24 hours after the person has been arrested, the person shall be taken before a provincial court judge without unreasonable delay and in any event within that period; and

  (*b*) if a provincial court judge is not available within 24 hours after the person has been arrested, the person shall be taken before a provincial court judge as soon as feasible.

(7) When a person is taken before a provincial court judge under subsection (6),

  (*a*) if an information has not been laid under subsection (2), the judge shall order that the person be released; or

  (*b*) if an information has been laid under subsection (2),

    (i) the judge shall order that the person be released unless the peace officer who laid the information shows cause why the person's detention in custody is justified on one or more of the following grounds:

    (A) the detention is necessary to ensure the person's appearance before a provincial court judge in order to be dealt with in accordance with subsection (8),

    (B) the detention is necessary for the protection or safety of the public, including any witness, having regard to all the circumstances including

      (I) the likelihood that, if the person is released from custody, a terrorist activity will be carried out, and

     (II) any substantial likelihood that the person will, if released from custody, interfere with the administration of justice, and

    (C) the detention is necessary to maintain confidence in the administration of justice, having regard to all the circumstances, including the apparent strength of the peace officer's grounds under subsection (2), and the gravity of any terrorist activity that may be carried out, and

    (ii) the judge may adjourn the matter for a hearing under subsection (8) but, if the person is not released under subparagraph (i), the adjournment may not exceed 48 hours.

(7.1) If a judge has adjourned the matter under subparagraph (7)(*b*)(ii) and the person remains in custody at the end of the period of adjournment, the person shall be taken before a provincial court judge who

   (*a*) shall order that the person be released unless a peace officer shows cause why the person's detention in custody is justified on one or more of the grounds set out in clauses (7)(*b*)(i)(A) to (C) and satisfies the judge that the investigation in relation to which the person is detained is being conducted diligently and expeditiously; and

   (*b*) may adjourn the matter for a hearing under subsection (8) but, if the person is not released under paragraph (*a*), the adjournment may not exceed 48 hours.

(7.2) If a judge has adjourned the matter under paragraph (7.1)(*b*) and the person remains in custody at the end of the period of adjournment, the person shall be taken before a provincial court judge who

   (*a*) shall order that the person be released unless a peace officer shows cause why the person's detention in custody is justified on one or more of the grounds set out in clauses (7)(*b*)(i)(A) to (C) and satisfies the judge that the investigation in relation to which the person is detained is being conducted diligently and expeditiously; and

   (*b*) may adjourn the matter for a hearing under subsection (8) but, if the person is not released under paragraph (*a*), the adjournment may not exceed 48 hours.

(8) The judge before whom the person appears in accordance with subsection (3)

   (*a*) may, if the judge is satisfied by the evidence adduced that the peace officer has reasonable grounds for the suspicion, order that the person enter into a recognizance, with or without sureties, to keep the peace and be of good behaviour for a period of not more than 12 months and to comply with any other reasonable conditions prescribed in the recognizance, including the conditions set out in subsections (10), (11.1) and (11.2), that the judge considers desirable for preventing the carrying out of a terrorist activity; and

   (*b*) if the person was not released under subparagraph (7)(*b*)(i) or paragraph (7.1)(*a*) or (7.2)(*a*), shall order that the person be released, subject to the recognizance, if any, ordered under paragraph (*a*).

(8.1) However, if the judge is also satisfied that the person was convicted previously of a terrorism offence, the judge may order that the person enter into the recognizance for a period of not more than two years.

(9) The judge may commit the person to prison for a term not exceeding 12 months if the person fails or refuses to enter into the recognizance.

(10) Before making an order under paragraph (8)(*a*), the judge shall consider whether it is desirable, in the interests of the safety of the person or of any other person, to include as a condition of the recognizance that the person be prohibited from possessing any firearm, crossbow, prohibited weapon, restricted weapon,

prohibited device, ammunition, prohibited ammunition or explosive substance, or all of those things, for any period specified in the recognizance, and if the judge decides that it is so desirable, they shall add the condition to the recognizance.

(11) If the judge adds the condition described in subsection (10) to a recognizance, they shall specify in it the manner and method by which

(a) the things referred to in that subsection that are in the person's possession shall be surrendered, disposed of, detained, stored or dealt with; and

(b) the authorizations, licences and registration certificates that are held by the person shall be surrendered.

(11.1) The judge shall consider whether it is desirable, to prevent the carrying out of a terrorist activity, to include in the recognizance a condition that the person deposit, in the specified manner, any passport or other travel document issued in their name that is in their possession or control. If the judge decides that it is desirable, the judge shall add the condition to the recognizance and specify the period during which it applies.

(11.2) The judge shall consider whether it is desirable, to prevent the carrying out of a terrorist activity, to include in the recognizance a condition that the person remain within a specified geographic area unless written permission to leave that area is obtained from the judge or any individual designated by the judge. If the judge decides that it is desirable, the judge shall add the condition to the recognizance and specify the period during which it applies.

(12) If the judge does not add a condition described in subsection (10), (11.1) or (11.2) to a recognizance, the judge shall include in the record a statement of the reasons for not adding it.

(13) The judge, or any other judge of the same court, may, on application of the peace officer, the Attorney General or the person, vary the conditions fixed in the recognizance.

(14) Subsections 810(4) and (5) apply, with any necessary modifications, to proceedings under this section. 2001, c. 41, s. 4; 2013, c. 9, s. 10; 2015, c. 20, s. 17; 2019, c. 13, s. 146(1), (3); 2019, c. 25, s. 24.

ANNUAL REPORT (SECTION 83.3) / Annual report (section 83.3) / Opinions / Limitation.

83.31 (1) [*Repealed*, 2019, c. 13, s. 147.]

(1.1) [*Repealed*, 2019, c. 13, s. 147.]

(2) The Attorney General of Canada shall prepare and cause to be laid before Parliament and the Attorney General of every province shall publish or otherwise make available to the public an annual report for the previous year on the operation of section 83.3 that includes

(a) the number of consents to lay an information that were sought, and the number that were obtained, by virtue of subsections 83.3(1) and (2);

(b) the number of cases in which a summons or a warrant of arrest was issued for the purposes of subsection 83.3(3);

   (c) the number of cases in which a person was not released under subsection 83.3(7), (7.1) or (7.2) pending a hearing;

   (d) the number of cases in which an order to enter into a recognizance was made under paragraph 83.3(8)(a), and the types of conditions that were imposed;

   (e) the number of times that a person failed or refused to enter into a recognizance, and the term of imprisonment imposed under subsection 83.3(9) in each case; and

   (f) the number of cases in which the conditions fixed in a recognizance were varied under subsection 83.3(13).

(3) The Minister of Public Safety and Emergency Preparedness shall prepare and cause to be laid before Parliament and the Minister responsible for policing in every province shall publish or otherwise make available to the public an annual report for the previous year on the operation of section 83.3 that includes

   (a) the number of arrests without warrant that were made under subsection 83.3(4) and the period of the arrested person's detention in custody in each case; and

   (b) the number of cases in which a person was arrested without warrant under subsection 83.3(4) and was released

     (i) by a peace officer under paragraph 83.3(5)(b), or

     (ii) by a judge under paragraph 83.3(7)(a), (7.1)(a) or (7.2)(a).

(3.1) The Attorney General of Canada and the Minister of Public Safety and Emergency Preparedness shall include in their annual reports under subsections (2) and (3), respectively, their opinion, supported by reasons, on whether the operation of section 83.3 should be extended.

(4) The annual report shall not contain any information the disclosure of which would

   (a) compromise or hinder an ongoing investigation of an offence under an Act of Parliament;

   (b) endanger the life or safety of any person;

   (c) prejudice a legal proceeding; or

   (d) otherwise be contrary to the public interest. 2001, c. 41, s. 4; 2005, c. 10, s. 35(1)(f)(iv); 2013, c. 9, s. 11; 2015, c. 20, s. 18; 2019, c. 13, s. 147.

SUNSET PROVISION / Review / Report / Order in Council / Rules / Subsequent extensions.

83.32 (1) Section 83.3 ceases to have effect at the end of the fifth anniversary of the day on which the *National Security Act, 2017* receives royal assent unless, before the end of that fifth anniversary, the operation of that section is extended by resolution — whose text is established under subsection (2) — passed by both Houses of Parliament in accordance with the rules set out in subsection (3).

(1.1) A comprehensive review of section 83.3 and its operation shall be undertaken by any committee of the Senate, of the House of Commons or of both Houses of Parliament that may be designated or established by the Senate or the

House of Commons, or by both Houses of Parliament, as the case may be, for that purpose.

(1.2) The committee shall, no later than one year before the fifth anniversary referred to subsection (1), submit a report on the review to the appropriate House of Parliament, or to both Houses, as the case may be, including its recommendation with respect to extending the operation of section 83.3.

(2) The Governor in Council may, by order, establish the text of a resolution that provides for the extension of the operation of section 83.3 and that specifies the period of the extension, which may not exceed five years from the first day on which the resolution has been passed by both Houses of Parliament.

(3) A motion for the adoption of the resolution may be debated in both Houses of Parliament but may not be amended. At the conclusion of the debate, the Speaker of the House of Parliament shall immediately put every question necessary to determine whether or not the motion is concurred in.

(4) The operation of section 83.3 may be further extended in accordance with this section, but

    (*a*) the reference to "at the end of the fifth anniversary of the day on which the *National Security Act, 2017* receives royal assent unless, before the end of that fifth anniversary" in subsection (1) is to be read as a reference to "on the expiry of the most recent extension under this section unless, before that extension expires"; and

    (*b*) the reference to "the fifth anniversary referred to subsection (1)" in subsection (1.2) is to be read as a reference to "the expiry of the most recent extension under this section". 2001, c. 41, s. 4; 2013, c. 9, s. 12; 2019, c. 13, s. 148.

(5) [*Repealed*, 2019, c. 13, s. 148(2).]

TRANSITIONAL PROVISION — SECTION 83.3.

83.33 (1) [*Repealed*, 2019, c. 13, s. 149.]

(2) In the event that section 83.3 ceases to have effect in accordance with section 83.32, a person detained in custody under section 83.3 shall be released when that section ceases to have effect, except that subsections 83.3(7) to (14) continue to apply to a person who was taken before a judge under subsection 83.3(6) before section 83.3 ceased to have effect. 2001, c. 41, s. 4; 2013, c. 9, s. 13; 2019, c. 13, s. 149.

Part III / FIREARMS AND OTHER WEAPONS

Note: Part III (ss. 84, 86 to 96, 98 to 117) replaced 1995, c. 39, s. 139 (brought into force December 1, 1998) (s. 85 in force January 1, 1996) (s. 97 in force January 1, 2003):

Interpretation

DEFINITIONS / "Ammunition" / "Antique firearm" / "Authorization" /
"Automatic firearm" / "Cartridge magazine" / "Chief firearms officer" /
"Commissioner of firearms" / "Cross-bow" / "Export" / "Firearms officer" /
"Handgun" / "Imitation firearm" / "Import" / "Licence" / "Non-restricted
firearm" / "Prescribed" / "Prohibited ammunition" / "Prohibited device" /
"Prohibited firearm" / "Prohibited weapon" / "Prohibition order" /
"Registrar" / "Registration certificate" / "Replica firearm" / "Restricted
firearm" / "Restricted weapon" / "Superior court" / "Transfer" / Barrel
length / Certain weapons deemed not to be firearms / Exception / antique
firearms / Meaning of "holder" / Subsequent offences / Sequence of
convictions only.

84. (1) In this Part,

"ammunition" means a cartridge containing a projectile designed to be discharged
from a firearm and, without restricting the generality of the foregoing, includes a
caseless cartridge and a shot shell;

"antique firearm" means

(a) any firearm manufactured before 1898 that was not designed to discharge
rim-fire or centre-fire ammunition and that has not been redesigned to
discharge such ammunition, or

(b) any firearm that is prescribed to be an antique firearm;

"authorization" means an authorization issued under the *Firearms Act*;

"automatic firearm" means a firearm that is capable of, or assembled or designed
and manufactured with the capability of, discharging projectiles in rapid
succession during one pressure of the trigger;

"cartridge magazine" means a device or container from which ammunition may be
fed into the firing chamber of a firearm;

"chief firearms officer" means a chief firearms officer as defined in subsection
2(1) of the *Firearms Act*;

"Commissioner of Firearms" means the Commissioner of Firearms appointed
under section 81.1 of the *Firearms Act*.

"cross-bow" means a device with a bow and a bowstring mounted on a stock that
is designed to propel an arrow, a bolt, a quarrel or any similar projectile on a
trajectory guided by a barrel or groove and that is capable of causing serious
bodily injury or death to a person;

"export" means export from Canada and, for greater certainty, includes the
exportation of goods from Canada that are imported into Canada and shipped in
transit through Canada;

"firearms officer" means a firearms officer as defined in subsection 2(1) of the
Firearms Act;

"handgun" means a firearm that is designed, altered or intended to be aimed and fired by the action of one hand, whether or not it has been redesigned or subsequently altered to be aimed and fired by the action of both hands;

"imitation firearm" means any thing that imitates a firearm, and includes a replica firearm;

"import" means import into Canada and, for greater certainty, includes the importation of goods into Canada that are shipped in transit through Canada and exported from Canada;

"licence" means a licence issued under the *Firearms Act*;

"non-restricted firearm" means

    (a) a firearm that is neither a prohibited firearm nor a restricted firearm, or

    (b) a firearm that is prescribed to be a non-restricted firearm;

Note: Definition "non-restricted firearm" replaced by 2019, c. 9, s. 16 (to come into force by order of the Governor in Council).

"non-restricted firearm" means a firearm that is neither a prohibited firearm nor a restricted firearm;

"prescribed" means prescribed by the regulations;

"prohibited ammunition" means ammunition, or a projectile of any kind, that is prescribed to be prohibited ammunition;

"prohibited device" means

    (a) any component or part of a weapon, or any accessory for use with a weapon, that is prescribed to be a prohibited device,

    (b) a handgun barrel that is equal to or less than 105 mm in length, but does not include any such handgun barrel that is prescribed, where the handgun barrel is for use in international sporting competitions governed by the rules of the International Shooting Union,

    (c) a device or contrivance designed or intended to muffle or stop the sound or report of a firearm,

    (d) a cartridge magazine that is prescribed to be a prohibited device, or

    (e) a replica firearm;

"prohibited firearm" means

    (a) a handgun that

        (i) has a barrel equal to or less than 105 mm in length, or

        (ii) is designed or adapted to discharge a 25 or 32 calibre cartridge,

    but does not include any such handgun that is prescribed, where the handgun is for use in international sporting competitions governed by the rules of the International Shooting Union,

    (b) a firearm that is adapted from a rifle or shotgun, whether by sawing, cutting or any other alteration, and that, as so adapted,

        (i) is less than 660 mm in length, or

        (ii) is 660 mm or greater in length and has a barrel less than 457 mm in length,

    (c) an automatic firearm, whether or not it has been altered to discharge only one projectile with one pressure of the trigger, or

    (d) any firearm that is prescribed to be a prohibited firearm;

"prohibited weapon" means

   (a) a knife that has a blade that opens automatically by gravity or centrifugal force or by hand pressure applied to a button, spring or other device in or attached to the handle of the knife, or

   (b) any weapon, other than a firearm, that is prescribed to be a prohibited weapon;

"prohibition order" means an order made under this Act or any other Act of Parliament prohibiting a person from possessing any firearm, cross-bow, prohibited weapon, restricted weapon, prohibited device, ammunition, prohibited ammunition or explosive substance, or all such things;

"Registrar" means the Registrar of Firearms appointed under section 82 of the *Firearms Act*;

"registration certificate" means a registration certificate issued under the *Firearms Act*;

"replica firearm" means any device that is designed or intended to exactly resemble, or to resemble with near precision, a firearm, and that itself is not a firearm, but does not include any such device that is designed or intended to exactly resemble, or to resemble with near precision, an antique firearm;

"restricted firearm" means

   (a) a handgun that is not a prohibited firearm,

   (b) a firearm that

      (i) is not a prohibited firearm,

      (ii) has a barrel less than 470 mm in length, and

      (iii) is capable of discharging centre-fire ammunition in a semi-automatic manner,

   (c) a firearm that is designed or adapted to be fired when reduced to a length of less than 660 mm by folding, telescoping or otherwise, or

   (d) a firearm of any other kind that is prescribed to be a restricted firearm;

"restricted weapon" means any weapon, other than a firearm, that is prescribed to be a restricted weapon;

"superior court" means

   (a) in Ontario, the Superior Court of Justice, sitting in the region, district or county or group of counties where the relevant adjudication was made,

   (b) in Quebec, the Superior Court,

   (c) in New Brunswick, Manitoba, Saskatchewan and Alberta, the Court of Queen's Bench,

   (d) in Nova Scotia, British Columbia, Prince Edward Island and a territory, the Supreme Court, and

   (e) in Newfoundland and Labrador, the Trial Division of the Supreme Court;

"transfer" means sell, provide, barter, give, lend, rent, send, transport, ship, distribute or deliver.

(2) For the purposes of this Part, the length of a barrel of a firearm is

   (a) in the case of a revolver, the distance from the muzzle of the barrel to the breach end immediately in front of the cylinder, and (*b*) in any other case, the distance from the muzzle of the barrel to and including the chamber,

but does not include the length of any component, part or accessory including any component, part or accessory designed or intended to suppress the muzzle flash or reduce recoil.

(3) For the purposes of sections 91 to 95, 99 to 101, 103 to 107 and 117.03 of this Act and the provisions of the *Firearms Act*, the following weapons are deemed not to be firearms:

    (*a*) any antique firearm;

    (*b*) any device that is

        (i) designed exclusively for signalling, for notifying of distress, for firing blank cartridges or for firing stud cartridges, explosive-driven rivets or other industrial projectiles, and

        (ii) intended by the person in possession of it to be used exclusively for the purpose for which it is designed;

    (*c*) any shooting device that is

        (i) designed exclusively for the slaughtering of domestic animals, the tranquilizing of animals or the discharging of projectiles with lines attached to them, and

        (ii) intended by the person in possession of it to be used exclusively for the purpose for which it is designed; and

    (*d*) any other barrelled weapon, where it is proved that the weapon is not designed or adapted to discharge

        (i) a shot, bullet or other projectile at a muzzle velocity exceeding 152.4 m per second or at a muzzle energy exceeding 5.7 Joules, or

        (ii) a shot, bullet or other projectile that is designed or adapted to attain a velocity exceeding 152.4 m per second or an energy exceeding 5.7 Joules.

(3.1) Notwithstanding subsection (3), an antique firearm is a firearm for the purposes of regulations made under paragraph 117(*h*) of the *Firearms Act* and subsection 86(2) of this Act.

(4) For the purposes of this Part, a person is the holder of

    (*a*) an authorization or a licence if the authorization or licence has been issued to the person and the person continues to hold it; and

    (*b*) a registration certificate for a firearm if

        (i) the registration certificate has been issued to the person and the person continues to hold it, or

        (ii) the person possesses the registration certificate with the permission of its lawful holder.

(5) In determining, for the purpose of subsection 85(3), 95(2), 99(2), 100(2) or 103(2), whether a convicted person has committed a second or subsequent offence, if the person was earlier convicted of any of the following offences, that offence is to be considered as an earlier offence:

    (*a*) an offence under section 85, 95, 96, 98, 98.1, 99, 100, 102 or 103 or subsection 117.01(1);

    (*b*) an offence under section 244 or 244.2; or

(*c*)   an offence under section 220, 236, 239, 272 or 273, subsection 279(1) or section 279.1, 344 or 346 if a firearm was used in the commission of the offence.

However, an earlier offence shall not be taken into account if 10 years have elapsed between the day on which the person was convicted of the earlier offence and the day on which the person was convicted of the offence for which sentence is being imposed, not taking into account any time in custody.

(6) For the purposes of subsection (5), the only question to be considered is the sequence of convictions and no consideration shall be given to the sequence of commission of offences or whether any offence occurred before or after any conviction. 1995, c. 39, s. 139; 1998, c. 30, s. 16; 2003, c. 8, s. 2; 2008, c. 6, s. 2; 2009, c. 22, s. 2; 2015, c. 3, s. 45; 2015, c. 27, s. 18.

REGULATIONS PRESCRIBING CERTAIN FIREARMS AND OTHER WEAPONS, COMPONENTS AND PARTS OF WEAPONS, ACCESSORIES, CARTRIDGE MAGAZINES, AMMUNITION AND PROJECTILES AS PROHIBITED OR RESTRICTED

Interpretation

1. In these Regulations, "semi-automatic", in respect of a firearm, means a firearm that is equipped with a mechanism that, following the discharge of a cartridge, automatically operates to complete any part of the reloading cycle necessary to prepare for the discharge of the next cartridge.

Prescription

2. The firearms listed in Part 1 of the schedule are prohibited firearms for the purposes of paragraph (*d*) of the definition "prohibited firearm" in subsection 84(1) of the *Criminal Code*.

3. The firearms listed in Part 2 of the schedule are restricted firearms for the purposes of paragraph (*d*) of the definition "restricted firearm" in subsection 84(1) of the *Criminal Code*, except for those firearms that are prohibited firearms within the meaning of paragraph (*b*) or (*c*) of the definition "prohibited firearm" in that subsection.

3.1 [*Repealed*, SOR/2020-96, s. 2.]

3.2 [*Repealed*, SOR/2020-96, s. 2.]

4. The weapons listed in Part 3 of the schedule are prohibited weapons for the purposes of paragraph (*b*) of the definition "prohibited weapon" in subsection 84(1) of the *Criminal Code*.

5. The components and parts of weapons, the accessories and the cartridge magazines listed in Part 4 of the schedule are prohibited devices for the purposes of paragraphs (*a*) and (*d*) of the definition "prohibited device" in subsection 84(1) of the *Criminal Code*.

6. The ammunition and projectiles listed in Part 5 of the schedule are prohibited ammunition for the purposes of the definition "prohibited ammunition" in subsection 84(1) of the *Criminal Code*.

Coming into Force

7. These Regulations come into force on December 1, 1998.

Schedule

(Sections 2 to 6)

PART 1
Prohibited Firearms

Former Prohibited Weapons Order, No. 3

1. Any firearm capable of discharging a dart or other object carrying an electrical current or substance, including the firearm of the design commonly known as the Taser Public Defender and any variant or modified version of it.

Former Prohibited Weapons Order, No. 8

2. The firearm known as the SSS-1 Stinger and any similar firearm designed or of a size to fit in the palm of the hand.

Former Prohibited Weapons Order, No. 11

3. The firearm of the design commonly known as the Franchi SPAS 12 shotgun, and any variant or modified version of it, including the Franchi LAW 12 shotgun.

4. The firearm of the design commonly known as the Striker shotgun, and any variant or modified version of it, including the Striker 12 shotgun and the Streetsweeper shotgun.

5. The firearm of the design commonly known as the USAS-12 Auto Shotgun, and any variant or modified version of it.

6. The firearm of the design commonly known as the Franchi SPAS-15 shotgun, and any variant or modified version of it.

7. The firearms of the designs commonly known as the Benelli M1 Super 90 shotgun and the Benelli M3 Super 90 shotgun, and any variants or modified versions of them, with the exception of the

(a) M1 Super 90 Field;
(b) M1 Super 90 Sporting Special;
(c) Montefeltro Super 90;
(d) Montefeltro Super 90 Standard Hunter;
(e) Montefeltro Super 90 Left Hand;
(f) Montefeltro Super 90 Turkey;
(g) Montefeltro Super 90 Uplander;

(h) Montefeltro Super 90 Slug;

(i) Montefeltro Super 90 20 Gauge;

(j) Black Eagle;

(k) Black Eagle Limited Edition;

(l) Black Eagle Competition;

(m) Black Eagle Slug Gun;

(n) Super Black Eagle; and

(o) Super Black Eagle Custom Slug.

8. The firearms of the designs commonly known as the Bernardelli B4 shotgun and the Bernardelli B4/B shotgun, and any variants or modified versions of them.

9. The firearm of the design commonly known as the American 180 Auto Carbine, and any variant or modified version of it, including the AM-180 Auto Carbine and the Illinois Arms Company Model 180 Auto Carbine.

10. The firearms of the designs commonly known as the Barrett "Light Fifty" Model 82A1 rifle and the Barrett Model 90 rifle, and any variants or modified versions of them.

11. The firearm of the design commonly known as the Calico M-900 rifle, and any variant or modified version of it, including the M-951 carbine, M-100 carbine and M-105 carbine.

12. The firearm of the design commonly known as the Iver Johnson AMAC long-range rifle, and any variant or modified version of it.

13. The firearm of the design commonly known as the McMillan M87 rifle, and any variant or modified version of it, including the McMillan M87R rifle and the McMillan M88 carbine.

14. The firearms of the designs commonly known as the Pauza Specialties P50 rifle and P50 carbine, and any variants or modified versions of them.

15. The firearm of the design commonly known as the Encom MK-IV carbine, and any variant or modified version of it.

16. The firearms of the designs commonly known as the Encore MP-9 and MP-45 carbines, and any variants or modified versions of them.

17. The firearm of the design commonly known as the FAMAS rifle, and any variant or modified version of it, including the MAS 223, FAMAS Export, FAMAS Civil and Mitchell MAS/22.

18. The firearm of the design commonly known as the Feather AT-9 Semi-Auto Carbine, and any variant or modified version of it, including the Feather AT-22 Auto Carbine.

19. The firearm of the design commonly known as the Federal XC-450 Auto Rifle, and any variant or modified version of it, including the Federal XC-900 rifle and Federal XC-220 rifle.

20. The firearm of the design commonly known as the Gepard long-range sniper rifle, and any variant or modified version of it.

21. The firearm of the design commonly known as the Heckler and Koch (HK) Model G11 rifle, and any variant or modified version of it.

22. The firearm of the design commonly known as the Research Armament Industries (RAI) Model 500 rifle, and any variant or modified version of it.

23. The firearm of the design commonly known as the Spectre Auto Carbine, and any variant or modified version of it.

24. The firearm of the design commonly known as the US Arms PMAI "Assault" 22 rifle, and any variant or modified version of it.

25. The firearm of the design commonly known as the Weaver Arms Nighthawk Carbine, and any variant or modified version of it.

26. The firearm of the design commonly known as the A.A. Arms AR9 Semi-Automatic Rifle, and any variant or modified version of it.

27. The firearms of the designs commonly known as the Claridge HI-TEC c. LEC-9 and ZLEC-9 carbines, and any variants or modified versions of them.

28. The firearm of the design commonly known as the Kimel Industries AR-9 rifle or carbine, and any variant or modified version of it.

29. The firearm of the design commonly known as the Grendel R-31 Auto Carbine, and any variant or modified version of it.

30. The firearms of the designs commonly known as the Maadi Griffin Rifle and the Maadi Griffin Carbine, and any variants or modified versions of them.

31. The firearm of the design commonly known as the AA Arms Model AR-9 carbine, and any variant or modified version of it.

32. The firearm of the design commonly known as the Bushmaster Auto Pistol, and any variant or modified version of it.

33. The firearm of the design commonly known as the Calico M-950 Auto Pistol, and any variant or modified version of it, including the M-110 pistol.

34. The firearm of the design commonly known as the Encom MK-IV assault pistol, and any variant or modified version of it.

35. The firearms of the designs commonly known as the Encom MP-9 and MP-45 assault pistols, and any variants or modified versions of them, including the Encom MP-9 and MP-45 mini pistols.

36. The firearm of the design commonly known as the Federal XP-450 Auto Pistol, and any variant or modified version of it, including the XP-900 Auto Pistol.

37. The firearm of the design commonly known as the Heckler and Koch (HK) SP89 Auto Pistol, and any variant or modified version of it.

38. The firearm of the design commonly known as the Intratec Tec-9 Auto Pistol, and any variant or modified version of it, including the Tec-9S, Tec-9M, Tec-9MS, and any semi-automatic variants of them, including the Tec-DC9, Tec-DC9M, Tec-9A, Tec-Scorpion, Tec-22T and Tec-22TN.

39. The firearms of the designs commonly known as the Iver Johnson Enforcer Model 3000 Auto Pistol and the Iver Johnson Plainfield Super Enforcer Carbine, and any variants or modified versions of them.

40. The firearm of the design commonly known as the Skorpion Auto Pistol, and any variant or modified version of it.

41. The firearm of the design commonly known as the Spectre Auto Pistol, and any variant or modified version of it.

42. The firearm of the design commonly known as the Sterling Mk 7 pistol, and any variant or modified version of it, including the Sterling Mk 7 C4 and Sterling Mk 7 C8.

43. The firearm of the design commonly known as the Universal Enforcer Model 3000 Auto Carbine, and any variant or modified version of it, including the Universal Enforcer Model 3010N, Model 3015G, Model 3020TRB and Model 3025TCO Carbines.

44. The firearm of the design commonly known as the US Arms PMAIP "Assault" 22 pistol, and any variant or modified version of it.

45. The firearm of the design commonly known as the Goncz High-Tech Long Pistol, and any variant or modified version of it, including the Claridge Hi-Tec models s. L, T, ZL-9 and ZT-9 pistols.

46. The firearm of the design commonly known as the Leader Mark 5 Auto Pistol, and any variant or modified version of it.

47. The firearm of the design commonly known as the OA-93 assault pistol, and any variant or modified version of it.

48. The firearm of the design commonly known as the A.A. Arms AP9 Auto Pistol, and any variant or modified version of it.

49. The firearm of the design commonly known as the Patriot pistol, and any variant or modified version of it.

50. The firearm of the design commonly known as the XM 231S pistol, and any variant or modified version of it, including the A1, A2 and A3 Flattop pistols.

51. The firearm of the design commonly known as the AA Arms Model AP-9 pistol, and any variant or modified version of it, including the Target AP-9 and the Mini AP-9 pistols.

52. The firearm of the design commonly known as the Kimel Industries AP-9 pistol, and any variant or modified version of it.

53. The firearms of the designs commonly known as the Grendel P-30, P-30 M, P-30 L and P-31 pistols, and any variants or modified versions of them.

54. The firearms of the designs commonly known as the Claridge HI-TEC ZL-9, HI-TEC S. HI-TEC L, HI-TEC T, HI-TEC ZT-9 and HI-TEC ZL-9 pistols, and any variants or modified versions of them.

55. The firearm of the design commonly known as the Steyr SPP Assault Pistol, and any variant or modified version of it.

56. The firearm of the design commonly known as the Maadi Griffin Pistol, and any variant or modified version of it.

57. The firearm of the design commonly known as the Interdynamics KG-99 Assault Pistol, and any variant or modified version of it.

Former Prohibited Weapons Order, No. 12

58. The firearm of the design commonly known as the Sterling Mk 6 Carbine, and any variant or modified version of it.

59. The firearm of the design commonly known as the Steyr AUG rifle, and any variant or modified version of it.

60. The firearm of the design commonly known as the UZI carbine, and any variant or modified version of it, including the UZI Model A carbine and the Mini-UZI carbine.

61. The firearms of the designs commonly known as the Ingram M10 and M11 pistols, and any variants or modified versions of them, including the Cobray M10 and M11 pistols, the RPB M10, M11, SM10 and SM11 pistols and the SWD M10, M11, SM10 and SM11 pistols.

62. The firearm of the design commonly known as the Partisan Avenger Auto Pistol, and any variant or modified version of it.

63. The firearm of the design commonly known as the UZI pistol, and any variant or modified version of it, including the Micro-UZI pistol.

Former Prohibited Weapons Order, No. 13

64. The firearm of the design commonly known as the AK-47 rifle, and any variant or modified version of it except for the Valmet Hunter, the Valmet Hunter Auto and the Valmet M78 rifles, but including the

(a) AK-74;
(b) AK Hunter;
(c) AKM;
(d) AKM-63;
(e) AKS-56S;
(f) AKS-56S-1;
(g) AKS-56S-2;
(h) AKS-74;
(i) AKS-84S-1;
(j) AMD-65;
(k) AR Model .223;
(l) Dragunov;
(m) Galil;
(n) KKMPi69;
(o) M60;
(p) M62;
(q) M70B1;
(r) M70AB2;
(s) M76;
(t) M77B1;
(u) M78;
(v) M80;
(w) M80A;

(x) MAK90;

(y) MPiK;

(z) MPiKM;

(z.1) MPiKMS-72;

(z.2) MPiKS;

(z.3) PKM;

(z.4) PKM-DGN-60;

(z.5) PMKM;

(z.6) RPK;

(z.7) RPK-74;

(z.8) RPK-87S;

(z.9) Type 56;

(z.10) Type 56-1;

(z.11) Type 56-2;

(z.12) Type 56-3;

(z.13) Type 56-4;

(z.14) Type 68;

(z.15) Type 79;

(z.16) American Arms AKY39;

(z.17) American Arms AKF39;

(z.18) American Arms AKC47;

(z.19) American Arms AKF47;

(z.20) MAM70WS762;

(z.21) MAM70FS762;

(z.22) Mitchell AK-22;

(z.23) Mitchell AK-47;

(z.24) Mitchell Heavy Barrel AK-47;

(z.25) Norinco 84S;

(z.26) Norinco 84S AK;

(z.27) Norinco 56;

(z.28) Norinco 56-1;

(z.29) Norinco 56-2;

(z.30) Norinco 56-3;

(z.31) Norinco 56-4;

(z.32) Poly Technologies Inc. AK-47/S;

(z.33) Poly Technologies Inc. AKS-47/S;

(z.34) Poly Technologies Inc. AKS-762;

(z.35) Valmet M76;

(z.36) Valmet M76 carbine;

(z.37) Valmet M78/A2;

(z.38) Valmet M78 (NATO) LMG;

(z.39) Valmet M82; and

(z.40) Valmet M82 Bullpup.

65. The firearm of the design commonly known as the Armalite AR-180 Spotter carbine, and any variant or modified version of it.

66. The firearm of the design commonly known as the Beretta AR70 assault rifle, and any variant or modified version of it.

67. The firearm of the design commonly known as the BM 59 rifle, and any variant or modified version of it, including

(a) the Beretta
(i) BM 59,
(ii) BM 59R,
(iii) BM 59GL,
(iv) BM 59D,
(v) BM 59 Mk E,
(vi) BM 59 Mk I,
(vii) BM 59 Mk Ital,
(viii) BM 59 Mk II,
(ix) BM 59 Mk III,
(x) BM 59 Mk Ital TA,
(xi) BM 59 Mk Ital Para,
(xii) BM 59 Mk Ital TP, and
(xiii) BM 60CB; and
(b) the Springfield Armory
(i) BM 59 Alpine,
(ii) BM 59 Alpine Paratrooper, and
(iii) BM 59 Nigerian Mk IV.

68. The firearm of the design commonly known as the Bushmaster Auto Rifle, and any variant or modified version of it.

69. The firearm of the design commonly known as the Cetme Sport Auto Rifle, and any variant or modified version of it.

70. The firearm of the design commonly known as the Daewoo K1 rifle, and any variant or modified version of it, including the Daewoo K1A1, K2, Max 1, Max 2, AR-100, AR 110C, MAXI-II and KC-20.

71. The firearm of the design commonly known as the Demro TAC-1M carbine, and any variant or modified version of it, including the Demro XF-7 Wasp Carbine.

72. The firearm of the design commonly known as the Eagle Apache Carbine, and any variant or modified version of it.

73. The firearm of the design commonly known as the FN-FNC rifle, and any variant or modified version of it, including the FNC Auto Rifle, FNC Auto Paratrooper, FNC-11, FNC-22 and FNC-33.

74. The firearm of the design commonly known as the FN-FAL (FN-LAR) rifle, and any variant or modified version of it, including the FN 308 Model 44, FN-FAL (FN-LAR) Competition Auto, FN-FAL (FN-LAR) Heavy Barrel 308 Match, FN-FAL (FN-LAR) Paratrooper 308 Match 50-64 and FN 308 Model 50-63.

75. The firearm of the design commonly known as the G3 rifle, and any variant or modified version of it, including the Heckler and Koch

(a) HK 91;
(b) HK 91A2;
(c) HK 91A3;

(d) HK G3 A3;

(e) HK G3 A3 ZF;

(f) HK G3 A4;

(g) HK G3 SG/1; and

(h) HK PSG1.

76. The firearm of the design commonly known as the Galil assault rifle, and any variant or modified version of it, including the AP-84, Galil ARM, Galil AR, Galil SAR, Galil 332 and Mitchell Galil/22 Auto Rifle.

77. The firearm of the design commonly known as the Goncz High-Tech Carbine, and any variant or modified version of it.

78. The firearm of the design commonly known as the Heckler and Koch HK 33 rifle, and any variant or modified version of it, including the

(a) HK 33A2;

(b) HK 33A3;

(c) HK 33KA1;

(d) HK 93;

(e) HK 93A2; and

(f) HK 93A3.

79. The firearm of the design commonly known as the J & R Eng M-68 carbine, and any variant or modified version of it, including the PJK M-68 and the Wilkinson Terry carbine.

80. The firearm of the design commonly known as the Leader Mark Series Auto Rifle, and any variant or modified version of it.

81. The firearms of the designs commonly known as the MP5 submachine gun and MP5 carbine, and any variants or modified versions of them, including the Heckler and Koch

(a) HK MP5;

(b) HK MP5A2;

(c) HK MP5A3;

(d) HK MP5K;

(e) HK MP5SD;

(f) HK MP5SD1;

(g) HK MP5SD2;

(h) HK MP5SD3;

(i) HK 94;

(j) HK 94A2; and

(k) HK 94A3.

82. The firearm of the design commonly known as the PE57 rifle, and any variant or modified version of it.

83. The firearms of the designs commonly known as the SG-550 rifle and SG-551 carbine, and any variants or modified versions of them, including the SAN Swiss Arms

(a) Aestas;

(b) Autumnus;

(c) Black Special;
(d) Black Special Carbine;
(e) Black Special CQB;
(f) Black Special Target;
(g) Blue Star;
(h) Classic Green;
(i) Classic Green Carbine;
(j) Classic Green CQB;
(k) Classic Green Sniper;
(l) Heavy Metal;
(m) Hiemis;
(n) Red Devil;
(o) Swiss Arms Edition; and
(p) Ver.

84. The firearm of the design commonly known as the SIG AMT rifle, and any variant or modified version of it.

85. The firearm of the design commonly known as the Springfield Armory SAR-48 rifle, and any variant or modified version of it, including the SAR-48 Bush, SAR-48 Heavy Barrel, SAR-48 Para and SAR-48 Model 22.

86. The firearm of the design commonly known as the Thompson submachine gun, and any variant or modified version of it, including the

(a) Thompson Model 1921;
(b) Thompson Model 1927;
(c) Thompson Model 1928;
(d) Thompson Model M1;
(e) Auto-Ordnance M27A-1;
(f) Auto-Ordnance M27A-1 Deluxe;
(g) Auto-Ordnance M1927A-3;
(h) Auto-Ordnance M1927A-5;
(i) Auto-Ordnance Thompson M1;
(j) Commando Arms Mk I;
(k) Commando Arms Mk II;
(l) Commando Arms Mk III;
(m) Commando Arms Mk 9; and
(n) Commando Arms Mk 45.

Other

87. The firearms of the designs commonly known as the M16, AR-10 and AR-15 rifles and the M4 carbine, and any variants or modified versions of them — other than one referred to in item 47, 49 or 50 of this Part — including the
(a) 2 Vets Arms 2VA-10;
(b) 2 Vets Arms 2VA-15;
(c) Accuracy Systems A-15 Custom Edition LR Tech Tactical;
(d) Adams Arms AA15;
(e) Adams Arms AASF-308;

(f) Adams Arms Multical;

(g) ADC ADC234;

(h) ADC ADC253;

(i) Adcor Defense A556 Elite GI;

(j) Adcor Defense ADC15;

(k) Adcor Defense B.E.A.R.;

(l) Adcor Defense Elite;

(m) Addax Tactical ADDAX-ZK;

(n) Addax Tactical AT-15;

(o) AdeQ Firearms L-Tac;

(p) AdeQ Firearms Paladin;

(q) AdeQ Firearms Venator;

(r) Advanced Armament Corporation MPW;

(s) Advanced Armaments Incorporated M15;

(t) Aero Precision A15;

(u) Aero Precision AP15;

(v) Aero Precision G15 Ghost Gun;

(w) Aero Precision H15;

(x) Aero Precision M4 Carbine;

(y) Aero Precision M4E1;

(z) Aero Precision M5;

(z.001) Aero Precision M16A4;

(z.002) Aero Precision Pistol;

(z.003) Aero Precision P-15 PEW;

(z.004) Aero Precision STS15;

(z.005) Aero Precision X15;

(z.006) Airtronic DMR;

(z.007) Alamo Tactical AT-15;

(z.008) Alberta Tactical Rifle AT15;

(z.009) Alexander Arms AAR15;

(z.01) Alexander Arms AAR15 Beowulf;

(z.011) Alexander Arms AAR15 Beowulf Overwatch;

(z.012) Alexander Arms AAR15 Genghis;

(z.013) Alexander Arms AAR15 Grendel;

(z.014) Alexander Arms AAR15 Grendel Overwatch;

(z.015) Alexander Arms AAR17;

(z.016) Alien Armory UFO-10;

(z.017) Ambush Firearms A11;

(z.018) Ameetec Arms AM-15 General;

(z.019) Ameetec Arms AM-15 Modular;

(z.02) Ameetec Arms AM-15 M4 Tactical Master;

(z.021) Ameetec Arms AM-15 Standard Tactical;

(z.022) Ameetec Arms AM-15 Standard Varmint;

(z.023) Ameetec Arms AM-15 Tactical Predator;

(z.024) Ameetec Arms AM-15 Varmint Master;

(z.025) Ameetec Arms AM-15 9MM;

(z.026) Ameetec Arms WM-15;

(z.027) America Remembers Colt AR15A2 Match HBar Vietnam Commemorative;
(z.028) American Defense Manufacturing UICH;
(z.029) American Defense Manufacturing UIC 10A;
(z.03) American Historical Foundation Colt AR15A2 Sporter Match HBar Vietnam Tribute Special Edition;
(z.031) American Historical Foundation Colt AR15A2 Sporter Target Operation Desert Storm Commemorative;
(z.032) American Precision Arms A15;
(z.033) American Spirit Arms ASA15;
(z.034) American Spirit Arms ASA15 Pistol;
(z.035) American Spirit Arms ASA308;
(z.036) American Spirit Arms Canadian Carbine;
(z.037) American Tactical Imports AT-15;
(z.038) American Tactical Imports ATI-15;
(z.039) American Tactical Imports MilSport;
(z.04) American Tactical Imports MilSport Canadian;
(z.041) American Tactical Imports Omni;
(z.042) American Tactical Imports Omni Hybrid;
(z.043) American Tactical Imports Omni Hybrid Pistol;
(z.044) American Tactical Imports T14;
(z.045) Anderson Manufacturing AM-10;
(z.046) Anderson Manufacturing AM-15;
(z.047) Angstadt Arms JACK9;
(z.048) Anvil Arms AA15;
(z.049) Area 53 El Capitan;
(z.05) Area 53 El Jefe;
(z.051) Ares Defense Systems Ares-15;
(z.052) Ares Defense Systems Ares-15 MCR;
(z.053) Ares Defense Systems Ares-15 MCR Sub-Carbine;
(z.054) Ares Defense Systems SCR;
(z.055) AR Five Seven AR15;
(z.056) AR Five Seven AR57 LEM;
(z.057) AR Five Seven AR57A1 PDW;
(z.058) Armalite AR-10A;
(z.059) Armalite AR-10A2;
(z.06) Armalite AR-10A4;
(z.061) Armalite AR-10B;
(z.062) Armalite AR-10 KLM;
(z.063) Armalite AR-10 Magnum;
(z.064) Armalite AR-10NM;
(z.065) Armalite AR-10T;
(z.066) Armalite AR-102 Sporter;
(z.067) Armalite M4C Carbine;
(z.068) Armalite M15;
(z.069) Armalite M15A2;
(z.07) Armalite M15A4;
(z.071) Armalite M15A4 T;

(z.072) Armalite M15 Pistol;
(z.073) Armalite SPR Mod 1;
(z.074) Armalite SPR Mod 2;
(z.075) Armalite SPR Mod 2A;
(z.076) Armalite AR-10 Pistol;
(z.077) Armi Jager AP15;
(z.078) Armi Jager AP74;
(z.079) Armitage International BR-15-A6S;
(z.08) Armscorp AC-15;
(z.081) Arms East N8S;
(z.082) Armtech X;
(z.083) Ascend Armory A15;
(z.084) AR15 Chatterbox CB-15;
(z.085) AR15.Com ARFCOM;
(z.086) AR15.Com AR15.Com;
(z.087) AXTS AX556;
(z.088) Badrock Tactical BR10;
(z.089) Badrock Tactical BR15;
(z.09) Bartlett Enterprises 1202009;
(z.091) Barrett Firearms M468;
(z.092) Barrett Firearms REC7;
(z.093) Barrett Firearms REC10;
(z.094) Battle Arms Development BAD-PDW;
(z.095) Battle Arms Development BAD-15;
(z.096) Battle Arms Development BAD556-LW;
(z.097) Battle Rifle Company BR15;
(z.098) Battle Rifle Company BR16;
(z.099) Battle Rifle Company BR308;
(z.1) BCI Defense SQS-15;
(z.101) BCM Rifle Company BCM4;
(z.102) BCM Rifle Company M4A1;
(z.103) Bean Firearms BFC-15A;
(z.104) Bear Creek Arsenal BCA15;
(z.105) Black Creek Labs BCL15;
(z.106) Black Creek Labs BCL102;
(z.107) Black Creek Labs BCL102B;
(z.108) Black Dawn BDR-15;
(z.109) Black Forge BF15;
(z.11) Blackheart International BHI-15;
(z.111) Black Leaf Industries BL10;
(z.112) Black Leaf Industries BL10B Prototype;
(z.113) Black Leaf Industries BL15;
(z.114) Black Rain Ordnance Fallout 10;
(z.115) Black Rain Ordnance Fallout 15;
(z.116) Black Rain Ordnance SPEC15;
(z.117) Black Rifle Company BRC15B;
(z.118) Blackwater BW-15;
(z.119) Black Weapons Armory BWA-15;

(z.12)   Blue Line BL-15LE1;
(z.121) Boberg CDH-15;
(z.122) Bohica M16SA;
(z.123) BPM BP15;
(z.124) BPM CQB-10;
(z.125) BPM LR-10;
(z.126) Breda B4;
(z.127) Brownell's BRN-16A1;
(z.128) Brownell's BRN-601;
(z.129) Brownell's XBRN16E1;
(z.13)   Bushmaster Carbon 15;
(z.131) Bushmaster XM15E2S;
(z.132) Bushmaster XM15E2S Law Enforcement;
(z.133) Bushmaster XM15E2S M4;
(z.134) Bushmaster XM15E2S M4GP;
(z.135) Bushmaster XM15E2S Predator;
(z.136) Bushmaster XM15E2S Varminter;
(z.137) Bushmaster XM15E2S 450 Bushmaster;
(z.138) Bushmaster XM15E2S DCM Competition Rifle;
(z.139) Bushmaster Bushmaster 308;
(z.14)   Bushmaster BAR-10;
(z.141) Bushmaster XM15E2S V Match;
(z.142) Bushmaster BR-308;
(z.143) C3 Defense C3-15;
(z.144) Cadex AR15 Karpat SPVM;
(z.145) Cadex CDX-10;
(z.146) Cadex CDX-15;
(z.147) Calguns AR15;
(z.148) Canstar Arms AR 338 Lapua;
(z.149) Cavalry Arms CAV-15;
(z.15)   Cavalry Arms CAV-15 MARK 2;
(z.151) Cavalry Arms CAV-15 Rifleman;
(z.152) Centurion Arms C4;
(z.153) Centurion Tactical CT-15;
(z.154) Century Arms C15A1 Sporter;
(z.155) Century Arms C15 Sporter;
(z.156) Century International Arms Centurion 15 Sporter;
(z.157) Charles Daly Defense CDD-15;
(z.158) Chiappa Firearms M Four-22;
(z.159) Chiappa Firearms M Four-22 Pistol;
(z.16)   Chirstensen Arms Carbon CA-10 DMR;
(z.161) Christensen Arms Carbon CA-10 G2;
(z.162) Christensen Arms Carbon CA-10 Recon;
(z.163) Christensen Arms Carbon CA-15;
(z.164) Christensen Arms Carbon CA-15 Predator;
(z.165) Christensen Arms Carbon CA-15 Recon;
(z.166) Christensen Arms Carbon CA TAC 10;
(z.167) Clark Custom Guns Gator;

(z.168) CLE MR15;
(z.169) CMMG Mod4SA;
(z.17) CMMG MK3;
(z.171) CMMG MK-4;
(z.172) CMMG MK-5;
(z.173) CMMG MK-8;
(z.174) CMMG MK-9;
(z.175) CMMG MKG-45;
(z.176) CMMG MKW-15;
(z.177) CMT LT-15;
(z.178) Cobalt Kinetics BAMF;
(z.179) Cobalt Kinetics CARS;
(z.18) Cobb MCR;
(z.181) Cobb MCR 30-06 SPRG 100th Anniversary Commemorative;
(z.182) Colt AR15A2 Sporter 2;
(z.183) Colt AR15;
(z.184) Colt AR15 SP1;
(z.185) Colt AR15A2 Match Target Lightweight;
(z.186) Colt AR15A2 Government;
(z.187) Colt AR15A2 Sporter Delta HBar;
(z.188) Colt AR15A2 Government Carbine;
(z.189) Colt AR15A2 Sporter Competition HBar;
(z.19) Colt AR15A2 Match Target HBar;
(z.191) Colt AR15A2;
(z.192) Colt AR15A2 Sporter HBar;
(z.193) Colt AR15 Match HBar;
(z.194) Colt AR15 Sporter;
(z.195) Colt M4 Carbine Match Target;
(z.196) Colt AR15A2 Match Target Target Model;
(z.197) Colt AR15A3 Tactical Carbine;
(z.198) Colt AR15A3 Match Target Competition HBar;
(z.199) Colt AR15A2 Sporter Match Target Competition HBar 2;
(z.2) Colt AR15 Sporter Lightweight;
(z.201) Colt AR15A2 Sporter Match Target Lightweight;
(z.202) Colt AR15A2 Sporter Target;
(z.203) Colt AR15A2 Government Target;
(z.204) Colt AR15A2 Sporter Match Target HBar;
(z.205) Colt AR15A2 Sporter Match Delta HBar;
(z.206) Colt AR15A2 Match Delta HBar;
(z.207) Colt AR15A2 Sporter Match Target Competition HBar;
(z.208) Colt AR15A2 Sporter Competition HBar Range Selected;
(z.209) Colt AR15A2 Match Target Competition HBar 2;
(z.21) Colt CAR15A3 HBar Elite;
(z.211) Colt AR15 9MM Carbine;
(z.212) Colt AR15A2 Carbine;
(z.213) Colt AR15A2 Sporter Match HBar;
(z.214) Colt Colts Law Enforcement Carbine;
(z.215) Colt C7CT;

(z.216) Colt C7A1;
(z.217) Colt C7A2;
(z.218) Colt IUR;
(z.219) Colt M4 Carbine Sporter;
(z.22) Colt Modular Carbine;
(z.221) Colt M4A1 Carbine;
(z.222) Colt M4 Carbine;
(z.223) Colt SA15.7;
(z.224) Colt SA20;
(z.225) Colt AR-15A4;
(z.226) Colt AR15A4 Lightweight LE Carbine;
(z.227) Colt AR15 M16A1;
(z.228) Colt AR15 Target Model;
(z.229) Colt M4LE;
(z.23) Colt M4 Light Carbine;
(z.231) Colt M16 Rifle;
(z.232) Colt M16 SPR;
(z.233) Colt M16A2;
(z.234) Colt AR15A2 Sporter Carbine;
(z.235) Colt M16A2 Carbine;
(z.236) Colt SMG;
(z.237) Colt Competition CCR Competition;
(z.238) Colt Competition CSR Sporting;
(z.239) Combat Shooters BMF;
(z.24) Conquest Arms CA-15;
(z.241) Core Core-15;
(z.242) Cross Machine Tool UHP-15;
(z.243) Cross Machine Tool UHP15A;
(z.244) Cross Machine Tool UHP15H;
(z.245) Cross Machine Tool UHP15-PDW;
(z.246) Cross Machine Tool UHP15SSA;
(z.247) Cross Machine Tool UHP-10;
(z.248) Dalphon BFD;
(z.249) Dane Armory DAR-15;
(z.25) Daniel Defense DD-15;
(z.251) Daniel Defense M4 Carbine;
(z.252) Daniel Defense DD MK762;
(z.253) Daniel Defense DDM4;
(z.254) Daniel Defense DD5;
(z.255) Daniel Defense M4 Carbine Pistol;
(z.256) Dark Storm Industries DS-15;
(z.257) Defiance DMK22;
(z.258) Defiance Machine XG14;
(z.259) Delaware Machinery AR15;
(z.26) Delphi Tactical Delphi-15;
(z.261) Dennys Guns DG-AR16;
(z.262) Desert Ordnance XM4 Rifle;
(z.263) Detroit Gun Works DGW15;

(z.264) Devil Dog Arms DDA-15B;
(z.265) Devil Dog Arms DDA-10B;
(z.266) Dez Arms DTA-10;
(z.267) Diamondback Firearms DB-10;
(z.268) Diamondback Firearms DB-15;
(z.269) Diemaco Rifle C10;
(z.27) Diemaco Rifle Experimental 84;
(z.271) Dlask Arms AR15 Type;
(z.272) Dlask Arms DAR701;
(z.273) Dlask Arms DAR701 Canada 150 Birthday;
(z.274) Dlask Arms PAC-5;
(z.275) Dominion Arms DA556;
(z.276) Double Star Star-15;
(z.277) Double Star Star-15 Carbine;
(z.278) Double Star Star-15 Super Match Rifle;
(z.279) Double Star Star-15 CritterSlayer;
(z.28) Double Star Star-15 Expedition Rifle;
(z.281) Double Star Star-15 Dissipator;
(z.282) Double Star Star-15 Target Rifle;
(z.283) Double Star Star-15 Lightweight Tactical;
(z.284) Double Star Star-15 Pistol;
(z.285) Double Star Star-10B;
(z.286) Dow FAL-15;
(z.287) DPMS A-15;
(z.288) DPMS A-15 Panther Bull;
(z.289) DPMS A-15 Panther Bull Twenty-Four;
(z.29) DPMS A-15 Panther Bull Twenty-Four Special;
(z.291) DPMS A-15 Panther Bull Twenty-Four Super;
(z.292) DPMS A-15 Panther Bulldog;
(z.293) DPMS A-15 Panther Bull Sixteen;
(z.294) DPMS A-15 Panther Bull SST Sixteen;
(z.295) DPMS A-15 Panther Bull Classic;
(z.296) DPMS A-15 Panther Prairie;
(z.297) DPMS A-15 Panther Arctic;
(z.298) DPMS A-15 Panther Classic;
(z.299) DPMS A-15 Panther DCM;
(z.3) DPMS A-15 Panther Southpaw;
(z.301) DPMS A-15 Panther Classic Sixteen;
(z.302) DPMS A-15 Panther Kitty Kat;
(z.303) DPMS A-15 Panther Carbine;
(z.304) DPMS A-15 Panther Race Gun;
(z.305) DPMS A-15 Panther Tactical;
(z.306) DPMS A-15 Panther Classic Lo-Pro;
(z.307) DPMS LR-308 Panther;
(z.308) DPMS A-15 Panther Carbine M-4;
(z.309) DPMS A-15 Panther Lite;
(z.31) DPMS A-15 Panther Tuber;
(z.311) DPMS LR-300 Panther;

(z.312) DPMS A-15 Panther 20th Anniversary;
(z.313) DPMS LR-243 Panther;
(z.314) DPMS LR-260 Panther;
(z.315) DPMS LR-204 Panther;
(z.316) DPMS LR-30S Panther;
(z.317) DPMS A-15 Panther Pardus;
(z.318) DPMS LR-338 Panther;
(z.319) DPMS LR-6.5 Panther;
(z.32) DPMS A-15 Panther Sportical;
(z.321) DPMS A-15 Panther The Agency;
(z.322) DPMS A-15 Panther CSAT;
(z.323) DPMS A-15 Panther LBR Carbine;
(z.324) DPMS A-15 Panther Hunter;
(z.325) DPMS A-15 Panther 300 Blackout;
(z.326) DPMS LR-G2 Panther;
(z.327) DPMS A-15 Panther VRS Single Shot;
(z.328) DPMS A-15 Panther Pump Rifle;
(z.329) DPMS A-15 Panther 22;
(z.33) DPMS A-15 Panther VAS Single Shot;
(z.331) DPMS A-150 Panther;
(z.332) DPMS G2;
(z.333) DRD Paratus;
(z.334) DRD M762;
(z.335) DRD CDR-15;
(z.336) DRD Kivaari;
(z.337) DRD D8;
(z.338) DSA Incorporated ZM4;
(z.339) DTI DTI-15;
(z.34) Dynamic Arms Research (DAR) DAR-10;
(z.341) Dynamic Arms Research (DAR) DAR-15;
(z.342) E3 Arms Omega-15;
(z.343) Eagle Arms Division of Armalite AR-10;
(z.344) Eagle Arms Division of Armalite Eagle-15;
(z.345) Eagle Arms Division of Armalite M15;
(z.346) Eagle Arms Division of Armalite M15A2;
(z.347) Eagle Arms Division of Armalite M15A3;
(z.348) Eagle Arms Division of Armalite M15P;
(z.349) Eagle Arms Incorporated EA-15;
(z.35) EDs Tactical Armory 2A;
(z.351) Elite Machining GRX15;
(z.352) Emtan EM-15;
(z.353) Enfield Rifle Company MERC415;
(z.354) EP Armory AR15/M16 Type;
(z.355) Essential Arms Company J15;
(z.356) Essential Arms Company J15F;
(z.357) Essential Arms Company J15-2;
(z.358) F&D Defense FD308;
(z.359) F-1 Firearms BDR-10 CA;

(z.36) F-1 Firearms BDR-10-3G CA;
(z.361) F-1 Firearms BDR-15 CA;
(z.362) F-1 Firearms BDR-15-3G CA;
(z.363) F-1 Firearms FDR-15 CA;
(z.364) F-1 Firearms UDR-15-3G;
(z.365) Falkor Defense FD-15A;
(z.366) Faxon Firearms ARAK-21 XRS;
(z.367) Ferfrans SOACR;
(z.368) Fightlite Industries MCR;
(z.369) Firebird Precision Firearms FPX-15;
(z.37) FMK AR-1 Patriot;
(z.371) FMK AR1 Extreme;
(z.372) FN FNX-01;
(z.373) FN FN15;
(z.374) FN FN15 Carbine;
(z.375) FN FN15 Rifle;
(z.376) Fortis Manufacturing FM15;
(z.377) Frankford Arsenal XM-177E2;
(z.378) Franklin Armory F17-L;
(z.379) Franklin Armory F17-V4;
(z.38) Franklin Armory HSC-15;
(z.381) Franklin Armory Libertas;
(z.382) Fulton Armory FAR-15;
(z.383) Fulton Armory FAR-308;
(z.384) GA Precision GAP-10;
(z.385) GA Precision GAP-10 G2;
(z.386) Gilboa Shorty 7;
(z.387) Gilboa Commando 11.5;
(z.388) Gilboa SMG;
(z.389) Gilboa M-43;
(z.39) Gilboa Carabine 14.5;
(z.391) Gilboa DMR;
(z.392) Gilboa Snake;
(z.393) GPI Manufacturing SLR15;
(z.394) Grande Armeria Camuna (GAC) GAC-15;
(z.395) Grey Ghost Precision GGP-SBL;
(z.396) Grey Ghost Precision GGP-S Grim;
(z.397) Grey Ghost Precision GGP-S Heavy;
(z.398) Grey Ghost Precision GGP-SLF;
(z.399) Grey Ghost Precision GGP-S Light;
(z.4) Grey Ghost Precision Specter Light;
(z.401) GT Virtual Concepts GT15;
(z.402) GTO Core-15;
(z.403) GTO Hard Core 15;
(z.404) Gun Room Company Noreen Bad News;
(z.405) Gunwerks WY15;
(z.406) Haenel CR223;
(z.407) Haenel CR308;

(z.408) Hayes Custom Guns H15;
(z.409) Head Down HD-15;
(z.41) Heckler & Koch HK416D;
(z.411) Heckler & Koch HK417;
(z.412) Heckler & Koch HKM4C;
(z.413) Heckler & Koch MR;
(z.414) Heckler & Koch MR223;
(z.415) Heckler & Koch MR308;
(z.416) Heckler & Koch MR556A1;
(z.417) Heckler & Koch MR762A1;
(z.418) Hera Arms HLS;
(z.419) Hera Arms HCL;
(z.42) Hera Arms HCL9M;
(z.421) Hesse Arms HAR15A2;
(z.422) Hesse Arms HAR15A2 Bull Gun;
(z.423) Hesse Arms HAR15A2 National Match;
(z.424) Hesse Arms HAR15A2 Standard;
(z.425) Hesse Arms HAR25;
(z.426) Hesse Arms Omega Match;
(z.427) High Standard HSA-15;
(z.428) High Standard HSA-15 Crusader;
(z.429) High Standard HSA-15 Enforcer;
(z.43) High Standard HSA-15 Enforcer 300;
(z.431) Hogan Manufacturing H-308;
(z.432) Hogan Manufacturing H223;
(z.433) Hogan Manufacturing H-415;
(z.434) Hogan Manufacturing H-416;
(z.435) Holland Gunworks HGW15;
(z.436) Hughes Precision HR-15F;
(z.437) Huldra MARK 4;
(z.438) Imperial Defence Services M16A3;
(z.439) Interarms ISA-15;
(z.44) Inter Ordnance IO-G9;
(z.441) Intrepid Tactical Solutions RAS-12;
(z.442) Iron City Rifle Works IC-9;
(z.443) Iron City Rifle Works IC-15;
(z.444) Iron Ridge Arms IRA-10D;
(z.445) Irunguns Anarchy;
(z.446) ISSC PAR223 Delta;
(z.447) Jager AP74;
(z.448) Jard J15;
(z.449) JC Weaponry JC Weaponry;
(z.45) JD Machine PR3;
(z.451) Jesse James Firearms Unlimited M4 Carbine;
(z.452) Joe Firearms JOE-15;
(z.453) JP Enterprises JP-15 Match;
(z.454) JP Enterprises JP-15;
(z.455) JP Enterprises JP-15 IPSC Limited Class;

CODE

(z.456) JP Enterprises JP-15 NRA Match;
(z.457) JP Enterprises JP-15 Tactical/SOF;
(z.458) JP Enterprises AR-10;
(z.459) JP Enterprises Edge Grade 3;
(z.46) JP Enterprises CTR-02;
(z.461) JP Enterprises LRP-07;
(z.462) JP Enterprises SCR-11;
(z.463) JP Enterprises JPE-15;
(z.464) JP Enterprises MBRG-13;
(z.465) JP Enterprises GMR15;
(z.466) Juggernaut Tactical JT-10;
(z.467) Juggernaut Tactical JT-15;
(z.468) Kaiser Defense Calguns.Net;
(z.469) Kaiser Defense KR5;
(z.47) Kaiser Military Technologies KR7;
(z.471) KE Arms KE-15;
(z.472) Kiss Tactical KISS-15;
(z.473) Kiss Tactical K-15SE;
(z.474) Knights Manufacturing Company SR-15;
(z.475) Kodiak Defence JTF2 Silver Edition;
(z.476) Kodiak Defence KD9;
(z.477) Kodiak Defence KD15;
(z.478) Kodiak Defence Kodiak-15;
(z.479) Kodiak Defence Kodiak-39;
(z.48) Lancer Systems LP L15;
(z.481) Lancer Systems LP L30;
(z.482) Lantac LA-N15;
(z.483) Lantac LA-R15;
(z.484) Lantac LA-SF15;
(z.485) Lantac MK-4;
(z.486) LAR Manufacturing Grizzly-15;
(z.487) LAR Manufacturing AA15;
(z.488) LAR Manufacturing SK15;
(z.489) LaRue Tactical LT-15;
(z.49) LaRue Tactical LT-762;
(z.491) Lauer Custom Weaponry LCW15;
(z.492) Lead Star LSA9;
(z.493) LEI LM7;
(z.494) Leitner-Wise Rifle LW15-7.82;
(z.495) Leitner-Wise Rifle LW15-22;
(z.496) Leitner-Wise Rifle LW15-499;
(z.497) Les Baer Custom Ultimate AR;
(z.498) Les Baer Custom Ultimate;
(z.499) Les Baer Custom Match;
(z.5)   Les Baer Custom Match AR;
(z.501) Les Baer Custom Thunder Ranch Special;
(z.502) Les Baer Custom Monolith SWAT;
(z.503) Les Baer Custom AR IPSC Action;

(z.504) Les Baer Custom AR Super Match;
(z.505) LMT Defender 2000;
(z.506) LMT L129A1;
(z.507) LMT LM308MWS;
(z.508) LMT MARS LS;
(z.509) Loki Weapon Systems LWSF;
(z.51) Lone Wolf R & D LWD-AR9G;
(z.511) Lone Wolf R & D LWD-AR9G Pistol;
(z.512) LRB Arms M15SA;
(z.513) Luvo BL-15LE;
(z.514) Luvo BL-15LE1;
(z.515) Luvo LA-15;
(z.516) LWRC SABR;
(z.517) LWRC REPR;
(z.518) LWRC Six8;
(z.519) LWRC CSASS;
(z.52) LWRC REPR MARK 2;
(z.521) LWRC 224 Valkyrie;
(z.522) LWRC M6IC;
(z.523) LWRC M6/M6A2;
(z.524) M2 M16C;
(z.525) M2 M16SP;
(z.526) M2 M16X;
(z.527) M2 M4N;
(z.528) M2 Patrol;
(z.529) M2 M16Z1;
(z.53) MAG Tactical Systems MG-G4;
(z.531) Magpul Armament MPLA;
(z.532) Manta Machining PA15;
(z.533) Manta Machining JH 308-F2;
(z.534) Matrix Aerospace MA-15;
(z.535) Matrix Aerospace M-762;
(z.536) Matrix Aerospace M762-D;
(z.537) Maxim Firearms B7075;
(z.538) McDuffee Arms MAR15;
(z.539) McDuffee Arms MLR308;
(z.54) McKay Enterprises RM16A2;
(z.541) Mega Arms MEGA MA-Ten;
(z.542) Mega Arms GTR-3H;
(z.543) Mega Machine Shop MEGA MMS;
(z.544) Mega Machine Shop MEGA Gator;
(z.545) Mega Machine Shop MEGA GTR-3H;
(z.546) Mega Machine Shop MEGA GTR-3S;
(z.547) Mega Machine Shop MEGA GTR-MA-Ten;
(z.548) Mega Machine Shop MEGA MG-XTR;
(z.549) MG Arms K-Yote;
(z.55) MG Arms Taranis Light;
(z.551) MGI Marck 15;

(z.552) MGO Zombie;
(z.553) Midwest Industries MI-15F;
(z.554) Miller Precision Arms MPA300 Guardian;
(z.555) Miller Precision Arms MPA556;
(z.556) Miller Precision Arms MPA762;
(z.557) Miller Precision Arms MPAR10;
(z.558) Mil-Sport AR15;
(z.559) Mil-Sport AR15 Pistol;
(z.56) Mitchell Arms CAR15/22;
(z.561) Mitchell Arms M16/22;
(z.562) Mitchell Arms M16A1/22;
(z.563) Mitchell Arms M16A3/22;
(z.564) MKE KNT-76;
(z.565) MMC Armory MA-15;
(z.566) MOLOT Vepr-15;
(z.567) Moores Machine Company MMC M4;
(z.568) Mossberg MMR Tactical;
(z.569) Mossberg MMR Hunter;
(z.57) Motiuk Manufacturing MRC-15;
(z.571) MVB Industries MVB-15F;
(z.572) Nemesis Arms 11X10;
(z.573) NEMO Battle Light;
(z.574) NEMO Omen;
(z.575) NEMO Battle Light 1.0;
(z.576) New Frontier Armory C9;
(z.577) New Frontier Armory G-15;
(z.578) New Frontier Armory LW-15;
(z.579) Next Generation Arms MFR;
(z.58) Next Generation Arms MP168 SPC;
(z.581) Next Level Armament NLX556;
(z.582) NoDak Spud NDS-16A1;
(z.583) NoDak Spud NDS-16A2;
(z.584) NoDak Spud NDS-601;
(z.585) NoDak Spud NDS-635;
(z.586) NoDak Spud NDS-XM16E1;
(z.587) Nord Arms NA-308;
(z.588) Nordic Components NC-PCC;
(z.589) Noreen Firearms Noreen Bad News;
(z.59) Noreen Firearms Noreen BN36;
(z.591) Noreen Firearms Noreen BN308;
(z.592) Norinco 311-3;
(z.593) Norinco Type CQ 311;
(z.594) Norinco Type CQ 311-1;
(z.595) Norinco Type CQ Semi-Automatic Rifle;
(z.596) Norinco Type CQ-A Semi-Automatic Rifle;
(z.597) Norinco Type CQ-A-1 Semi-Automatic Rifle;
(z.598) North Eastern Arms NEA-15;
(z.599) North Eastern Arms NEA-15 Pistol;

(z.6)   North Eastern Arms NEA-25;
(z.601) North Eastern Arms NEA102;
(z.602) Northtech Defense NT15S;
(z.603) Noveske N4;
(z.604) Noveske N6;
(z.605) Noveske Varmageddon AR;
(z.606) Oberland Arms OA10;
(z.607) Oberland Arms OA15;
(z.608) Olympic Arms PCR;
(z.609) Olympic Arms MFR;
(z.61) Olympic Arms K3B;
(z.611) Olympic Arms K40GL;
(z.612) Olympic Arms K9GL;
(z.613) Olympic Arms LTF;
(z.614) Olympic Arms Plinker Plus;
(z.615) Olympic Arms UM1P Ultramatch;
(z.616) Olympic Arms UMAR;
(z.617) Olympic Arms MPR 308-15;
(z.618) Olympic Arms CAR15 AR;
(z.619) Olympic Arms CAR97;
(z.62) Olympic Arms UM1 Ultramatch;
(z.621) Olympic Arms ML1 Multimatch;
(z.622) Olympic Arms ML2 Multimatch;
(z.623) Olympic Arms K4B;
(z.624) Olympic Arms Bill of Rights Bicentennial Commemorative;
(z.625) Olympic Arms SM1 Servicematch;
(z.626) Olympic Arms Titanium;
(z.627) Olympic Arms Plinker;
(z.628) Olympic Arms FAR-15;
(z.629) Olympic Arms K8;
(z.63) Olympic Arms MQ356;
(z.631) Olympic Arms Vietnam Limited Edition Commemorative;
(z.632) Olympic Arms SM1P Servicematch;
(z.633) Olympic Arms K22 Rimfire Target Match;
(z.634) Palmetto Armory BH15A1;
(z.635) Palmetto State Armory GX-9;
(z.636) Palmetto State Armory PA-10;
(z.637) Palmetto State Armory PA-15;
(z.638) Palmetto State Armory PX9;
(z.639) Palmetto State Armory PX-10;
(z.64) Patriot Defense Arms PDA-15;
(z.641) Performance Engineering SOT-15;
(z.642) Phase 5 Tactical P5T15;
(z.643) Phase 5 Tactical Atlas One;
(z.644) Plumcrazy Firearms C15;
(z.645) POF CMR;
(z.646) POF P-15;
(z.647) POF P300;

CODE

(z.648) POF P308;
(z.649) POF P415;
(z.65) POF P416;
(z.651) Poly Technologies Type CQ-A Semi-Automatic Rifle;
(z.652) Precision Firearms PF15;
(z.653) Precision Firearms PF-X08;
(z.654) PWA AR15 Commando;
(z.655) PWA Commando;
(z.656) PWS MARK 1;
(z.657) PWS MARK 2;
(z.658) PWS MARK 1 Modern Musket;
(z.659) PWS PCC9;
(z.66) PWS MARK 1 Pistol;
(z.661) PWS MARK 1 Modern Musket Pistol;
(z.662) PWS MARK 1 Mod 2-M;
(z.663) Q Honey Badger;
(z.664) Quartercircle10 GSF Pistol;
(z.665) Quentin Defense QD-15;
(z.666) Quentin Defense SBR;
(z.667) Quentin Defense ZRT;
(z.668) Radian 1;
(z.669) Radical Firearms RF-15;
(z.67) Radical Firearms RM-15;
(z.671) Radical Firearms RMR-10;
(z.672) Rainier Arms Overthrow;
(z.673) Rainier Arms RB-15;
(z.674) Rainier Arms RB308;
(z.675) Rainier Arms RM-15;
(z.676) Rat Worx M-7;
(z.677) Red River Tactical RRT-TAC15;
(z.678) Red Stag Technologies Red Stag;
(z.679) Remington R15 VTR;
(z.68) Remington LRP-07;
(z.681) Remington R4;
(z.682) Remington R25;
(z.683) Remington R25 G2;
(z.684) Revolution Armory AR-410;
(z.685) RGM Incorporated Marksman;
(z.686) RGuns TRR15;
(z.687) Rhino Arms RA-4;
(z.688) Rhino Arms RA-4R;
(z.689) Rise Armament Ripper;
(z.69) RND Edge;
(z.691) Rock Island Armory M15A1;
(z.692) Rock Island Armory XM15;
(z.693) Rock Island Armory XM15E2;
(z.694) Rock River Arms LAR-15;
(z.695) Rock River Arms LAR-15 Law Enforcement;

(z.696) Rock River Arms LAR-15 Varmint;
(z.697) Rock River Arms LAR-15/9MM;
(z.698) Rock River Arms LAR-15 Pistol;
(z.699) Rock River Arms LAR-15 Elite;
(z.7)   Rock River Arms LAR-15 Coyote;
(z.701) Rock River Arms LAR-15 Predator Pursuit;
(z.702) Rock River Arms LAR-458;
(z.703) Rock River Arms LAR-6.8;
(z.704) Rock River Arms LAR-8;
(z.705) Rock River Arms LAR-15 ATH;
(z.706) Rock River Arms LAR-15 Operator;
(z.707) Rock River Arms LAR-8 Operator;
(z.708) Rock River Arms LAR-47;
(z.709) Rock River Arms LAR-15LH;
(z.71) Rock River Arms LAR-15 Hunter;
(z.711) Rock River Arms LAR-15 Fred Eichler Series;
(z.712) Rock River Arms LAR-15 R3 Competition;
(z.713) Rock River Arms LAR-15 Texas;
(z.714) Rock River Arms LAR-15 Tactical;
(z.715) Rock River Arms LAR-15 Government;
(z.716) Rock River Arms LAR-15 TASC;
(z.717) Rock River Arms LAR-15 National Match;
(z.718) Rock River Arms LAR-15 DEA;
(z.719) Rock River Arms LAR-9;
(z.72) Rock River Arms LAR-9 Pistol;
(z.721) Rock River Arms LAR-40;
(z.722) Rock River Arms LAR-PDS;
(z.723) Rock River Arms LAR-40 Pistol;
(z.724) Rock River Arms LAR-6;
(z.725) Rock River Arms LAR-8M;
(z.726) Rock River Arms LAR-10;
(z.727) Rocky Point Guns LE15;
(z.728) Roggio RA15;
(z.729) Royal Arms Rak15;
(z.73) Ruger SR556;
(z.731) Ruger SR556 VT;
(z.732) Ruger AR556;
(z.733) S&J Hardware SJ-15;
(z.734) Sabatti SAR;
(z.735) Sabertooth Defence M4;
(z.736) Sabre Defence Industries SR-15;
(z.737) Sabre Defence Industries XR10;
(z.738) Sabre Defence Industries XR15;
(z.739) Safir T12;
(z.74) Safir T14;
(z.741) Salient Arms International GRY;
(z.742) Salient Arms International SAI-T2;
(z.743) Savage MSR-10;

(z.744) Savage MSR-15;
(z.745) Schmeisser AR15;
(z.746) Schmeisser MR-BA19;
(z.747) Seekins Precision NX15;
(z.748) Seekins Precision SBA15;
(z.749) Seekins Precision SP15;
(z.75) Seekins Precision SP223;
(z.751) Seekins Precision SPX;
(z.752) Sendra Corp M15A1;
(z.753) Sendra Corp XM15E2;
(z.754) SFRC SFRC-15;
(z.755) SGW AR15;
(z.756) SGW AR15A1;
(z.757) SGW AR15A2;
(z.758) SGW CAR15;
(z.759) SGW CAR15 AR;
(z.76) SGW K3B;
(z.761) SGW Ultra Match Rifle;
(z.762) SGW XM15A1;
(z.763) Sharps Bros The Jack;
(z.764) Sharps Bros Warthog;
(z.765) Sharps Rifle Company Sharps 15;
(z.766) ShoeLess Ventures FAB10;
(z.767) Shooting Edge OA15;
(z.768) SI Defense SI AR-15;
(z.769) SI Defense SI-D;
(z.77) SI Defense SI-HK;
(z.771) SI Defense SI-C;
(z.772) SIG Sauer SIG 516;
(z.773) SIG Sauer SIG 716;
(z.774) SIG Sauer SIG M400;
(z.775) SIG Sauer SIG M400 Elite;
(z.776) Six Sigma Arms P18-32;
(z.777) Smith & Wesson M&P 15T;
(z.778) Smith & Wesson M&P 15;
(z.779) Smith & Wesson M&P 15-22;
(z.78) Smith & Wesson M&P 15FT;
(z.781) Smith & Wesson M&P 15-22PC;
(z.782) Smith & Wesson M&P 15 Magpul;
(z.783) Smith & Wesson M&P 10;
(z.784) Smith & Wesson M&P 15A;
(z.785) Smith & Wesson M&P 15PC;
(z.786) Smith & Wesson M&P 15OR;
(z.787) Smith & Wesson M&P 15PS;
(z.788) Smith & Wesson M&P 10 Creedmoor;
(z.789) Smith & Wesson M&P 15i;
(z.79) SMOS SM-15;
(z.791) SMOS Rogue-15;

(z.792) SMOS Rogue-50;
(z.793) Sniper Central SI-C;
(z.794) SNS Industries Max 15;
(z.795) SNS Industries LFT-15;
(z.796) SNS Industries NO-15;
(z.797) SNS Industries Max 15 Pistol;
(z.798) Socom Firearms Corporation Recon AR15;
(z.799) Socom Manufacturing BR-15-A6S;
(z.8)   Spartan Precision SP15;
(z.801) Special Ops Tactical SO15;
(z.802) Spike's Tactical ST-15;
(z.803) Spike's Tactical SL-15;
(z.804) Spike's Tactical ST-22;
(z.805) Spike's Tactical CJ15;
(z.806) Spike's Tactical Hellbreaker;
(z.807) Spike's Tactical Warthog;
(z.808) Spike's Tactical The Jack;
(z.809) Spike's Tactical Spartan;
(z.81) Spike's Tactical Jack 10;
(z.811) Spirit Gun Manufacturing Company SGM9;
(z.812) Springfield Armory Saint;
(z.813) STAG Arms STAG-6L;
(z.814) STAG Arms STAG-6.8;
(z.815) STAG Arms STAG-9;
(z.816) STAG Arms STAG-10;
(z.817) STAG Arms STAG-10S;
(z.818) STAG Arms STAG-15;
(z.819) STAG Arms STAG-223;
(z.82) Sterling Arms SAI 102;
(z.821) STI International AR15 Custom Rifle;
(z.822) Stillers Precision Firearms Predator XT;
(z.823) Stoner SR-25;
(z.824) Stoner SR-15;
(z.825) Stoner MARK 11 Model 0;
(z.826) Stoner M110;
(z.827) Stoner XM110;
(z.828) Stoner MARK 11 Model 1;
(z.829) Sun Devil SD15;
(z.83) Sun Devil SD308;
(z.831) Superior Arms S-15;
(z.832) Surplus Ammo & Arms LOW15;
(z.833) Surplus Ammo & Arms LOW16;
(z.834) Surplus Ammo & Arms SA15;
(z.835) SWAT Firearms SF-15;
(z.836) SWORD International MARK 15 Model 0;
(z.837) SWORD International MARK 16 Model 0;
(z.838) SWORD International MARK 17 Model 0;
(z.839) SWORD International MARK 18 Model 0;

CODE

(z.84) SWORD International MARK 18 Model 0 Mjolnir;
(z.841) Tactical Armz TA-15;
(z.842) Tactical Innovations T-15;
(z.843) Tactical Innovations T-15BDX;
(z.844) Tactical Machining TM-15;
(z.845) Tactical Machining TM308;
(z.846) Tactical Machining TSG-15;
(z.847) Tactical Rifles Government;
(z.848) Tactical Rifles Tactical M4C;
(z.849) Tactical Rifles Tactical SPG;
(z.85) Tactical Rifles Tactical SVR;
(z.851) Talon Arms TA-15;
(z.852) Taran Tactical TR-1;
(z.853) Tech Designs AR-15;
(z.854) Territorial Gunsmiths SLR15;
(z.855) Thor TR15 Carbine;
(z.856) Tippmann Arms M4-22;
(z.857) Titusville Armory TA-15;
(z.858) TKS Engineering AR15HD;
(z.859) TNW SGP15;
(z.86) Tom Sawyer M4-Z1;
(z.861) Tom Sawyer Jolly Roger;
(z.862) Trojan Firearms PRO9V1;
(z.863) Trojan Firearms TFA-PCC9G;
(z.864) Trojan Firearms ULV1;
(z.865) Troy Defense Troy 102;
(z.866) Troy Defense Troy Carbine;
(z.867) Troy Defense Troy M4A1 Carbine;
(z.868) Troy Defense Troy M4A1 SOCC;
(z.869) Troy Defense Troy M7A1 CQB;
(z.87) Troy Defense Troy M7A1 PDW Carbine;
(z.871) Troy Defense Troy M16A2 Mogadishu;
(z.872) Troy Defense Troy Northern Guard;
(z.873) Troy Industries Troy CQB-SPC;
(z.874) True North Arms TNA-15;
(z.875) Turnbull Manufacturing TAR-15;
(z.876) Turnbull Manufacturing TAR-10;
(z.877) Umbrella Corporation AR15;
(z.878) Umlaut Industries U4;
(z.879) Unik Alpha;
(z.88) United Defense S7;
(z.881) US Arms Patriot 15;
(z.882) US Autoweapons USM4;
(z.883) US Firearms Academy BB-16;
(z.884) USA Tactical Firearms USA-15;
(z.885) UT Arms GEN-1AR;
(z.886) Utas XTR-12;
(z.887) V Seven Weapons GI Seven;

(z.888) VC Defense VC-15;
(z.889) Vidalia Police Supply VPS-15;
(z.89) VM Hy-Tech VM15;
(z.891) Vulcan Armament V15;
(z.892) Web Arms WA-15;
(z.893) Wilson Combat AR15 UT;
(z.894) Wilson Combat AR15 TPR;
(z.895) Wilson Combat AR15 M4;
(z.896) Wilson Combat AR15 TL;
(z.897) Wilson Combat AR15 SM;
(z.898) Wilson Combat AR15 SS;
(z.899) Wilson Combat AR15;
(z.9)   Wilson Combat AR-10;
(z.901) Wilson Combat AR9G;
(z.902) Wilson Tactical WT-15;
(z.903) Windham Weaponry MCS;
(z.904) Windham Weaponry WW-15;
(z.905) Windham Weaponry WW-308;
(z.906) Windham Weaponry WW-CF;
(z.907) WMA WMA-15;
(z.908) Wolverine Tactical Firearms WAR-15;
(z.909) Wolverine Tactical Firearms WT-15;
(z.91) Xtreme Gun XG15;
(z.911) Xtreme Machining XR15;
(z.912) YHM 57;
(z.913) YHM YHM-15;
(z.914) ZEV Technologies Mega-LF;
(z.915) ZEV Technologies Mega-TR15;
(z.916) ZEV Technologies ZEV-BL;
(z.917) ZEV Technologies ZEV-FL;
(z.918) ZM Weapons LR300ML;
(z.919) ZM Weapons LR300SR; and
(z.92) Zombie Defense Z-4.

88. The firearm of the design commonly known as the Ruger Mini-14 rifle, and any variant or modified version of it, including the
(a) Clark Custom Guns Ruger Mini-14;
(b) Ruger Mini-14 GB;
(c) Ruger Mini-14 Ranch Rifle;
(d) Ruger Mini-14 Ranch Rifle Deluxe;
(e) Ruger Mini-14 Ranch Rifle LE;
(f) Ruger Mini-14 Ranch Rifle LET;
(g) Ruger Mini-14 Ranch Rifle NRA Edition;
(h) Ruger Mini-14 Ranch Target Rifle; and
(i) Ruger Mini Thirty.

89. The firearm of the design commonly known as the US Rifle, M14, and any variant or modified version of it, including the

127

(a) American Historical Foundation Federal Ordnance M14 US Rifle Vietnam War Commemorative;

(b) Armscorp US Rifle M14;

(c) Armscorp US Rifle M14 National Match;

(d) AR Sales MARK 4;

(e) Bula Defense Systems M14;

(f) Dominion Arms Socom 18;

(g) Entreprise Arms US Rifle M14A2;

(h) Federal Ordnance M14SA US Rifle;

(i) Fulton Armory M14;

(j) Hesse Arms M14H Brush;

(k) Hesse Arms M14H;

(l) James River Armory M14;

(m) La France Specialties M14K;

(n) LRB Arms M14SA US Rifle;

(o) LRB Arms M25;

(p) McMillan M1A;

(q) McMillan M3A;

(r) MK Specialties M14A1 Semi-Automatic;

(s) Norinco M14 Semi-Automatic;

(t) Norinco 305;

(u) Norinco CSLR27;

(v) Norinco CSLR28;

(w) Norinco M305;

(x) Norinco 305A;

(y) Norinco M305C;

(z) Norinco M305D;

(z.01) Poly Technologies M14 Semi-Automatic;

(z.02) Poly Technologies M305;

(z.03) Rockola US Rifle M14F;

(z.04) Smith Enterprises US Rifle M14 National Match;

(z.05) Smith Enterprises US Rifle M14;

(z.06) Springfield Armory US Rifle M1A-A1 Bush Rifle;

(z.07) Springfield Armory US Rifle M1A-A1 Scout Rifle;

(z.08) Springfield Armory US Rifle M21;

(z.09) Springfield Armory US Rifle M1A National Match;

(z.1) Springfield Armory US Rifle M1A Super Match;

(z.11) Springfield Armory US Rifle M1A;

(z.12) Springfield Armory US Rifle M25;

(z.13) Springfield Armory US Rifle M1A SOCOM 16;

(z.14) Springfield Armory US Rifle M1A SOCOM 2;

(z.15) Springfield Armory US Rifle M1A NRA Camp Perry National Matches 100th Anniversary;

(z.16) Springfield Armory US Rifle M1A Loaded; and

(z.17) Springfield Armory US Rifle M1A Scout Squad.

90. The firearm of the design commonly known as the Vz58 rifle, and any variant or modified version of it, including the

(a) Century Arms VZ2008 Sporter;

(b) CZ CZ958 2P;

(c) CZ CZ958 2V;

(d) CZ CZ958 Hunter P;

(e) CZ CZH2003 Sport;

(f) CZ CZ858 Tactical-2 P;

(g) CZ CZ858 Tactical-2 V;

(h) CZ CZ858 Tactical-4 P;

(i) CZ CZ858 Tactical-4 V;

(j) CZ CZ858 Tactical-2 P Spartan Limited Edition;

(k) Czech Small Arms SA VZ58 Canadian Sporter 7.62;

(l) Czech Small Arms SA VZ58 Sporter 5.56;

(m) Czech Small Arms SA VZ58 Sporter 7.62;

(n) Czech Small Arms SA VZ58 Sporter 222 REM;

(o) Czech Small Arms SA VZ58 Sporter 223 REM;

(p) D-Technik SA VZ58 Sporter 7.62;

(q) Gazela Gazela 58;

(r) Grand Power SA VZ58 Sporter 7.62;

(s) Kodiak Defence WR762;

(t) Ohio Ordnance Works VZ2000;

(u) Petr Novohradsky FSN-01;

(v) Petr Novohradsky FSN-01K;

(w) PPK KSK;

(x) PPK KSK Hunter;

(y) Rock Island Armory WR762USA;

(z) West Rifle WR762; and

(z.1) Zelanysport Gazela 58.

91. The firearm of the design commonly known as the Robinson Armament XCR rifle, and any variant or modified version of it, including the Robinson Armament

(a) XCR-L;

(b) XCR-L Micro Pistol;

(c) XCR-M; and

(d) XCR-M Micro Pistol.

92. The firearms of the designs commonly known as the CZ Scorpion EVO 3 carbine and CZ Scorpion EVO 3 pistol, and any variants or modified versions of them, including the CZ

(a) CZ Scorpion EVO 3 S1 Carbine;

(b) CZ Scorpion EVO 3 S1 Pistol; and

(c) CZ Scorpion EVO 3 S2 Pistol Micro.

93. The firearm of the design commonly known as the Beretta Cx4 Storm carbine, and any variant or modified version of it.

94. The firearms of the designs commonly known as the SIG Sauer SIG MCX carbine, SIG Sauer SIG MCX pistol, SIG Sauer SIG MPX carbine and SIG Sauer SIG MPX pistol, and any variants or modified versions of them, including the SIG Sauer

(a) SIG MCX Rattler; and

(b) SIG MCX Rattler Pistol.

95. Any firearm with a bore diameter of 20 mm or greater — other than one designed exclusively for the purpose of neutralizing explosive devices — including the

(a) Aerotek NTW;

(b) Airtronic M203;

(c) Alpimex APK 20;

(d) Amtec Less-Lethal Systems (ALS) 40MM Launcher;

(e) Anzio Ironworks Anzio 20;

(f) Argentine Mortar FMK2 81MM;

(g) Argentine Mortar FMK2 120MM;

(h) Argentine Mortar FMK1 60MM;

(i) Argentine Mortar FMK2 60MM;

(j) Argentine Mortar FMK3 60MM;

(k) Armsan BA 40;

(l) Armscor Stopper;

(m) Arsenal UGGL-M1;

(n) Arsenal UBGL;

(o) Arsenal MSGL;

(p) Astra Arms SL203;

(q) Astra Arms GL203;

(r) Austrian Mortar C6 60MM;

(s) Austrian Mortar M6 60MM;

(t) Austrian Mortar M8 81MM;

(u) Austrian Mortar M12 120MM;

(v) Bates & Dittus UBL-37;

(w) Bates & Dittus ExD-37;

(x) Bates & Dittus TBL-37;

(y) Bates & Dittus SML-37 Pistol;

(z) Beretta GLX160;

(z.001) British Mortar ML-3 Inch;

(z.002) British Mortar ML-4.2 Inch;

(z.003) Brugger & Thomet GL06;

(z.004) Bulgarian Mortar M60 60MM;

(z.005) Bulgarian Mortar M81 81MM;

(z.006) Bulgarian Mortar M82 82MM;

(z.007) Chilean Mortar Commando;

(z.008) Chilean Mortar M57 81MM;

(z.009) China Lake EX-41;

(z.01) Chinese Mortar Type 53;

(z.011) Cobray 37MM Launcher;

(z.012) Colt Eagle;

(z.013) Colt M203;

(z.014) Colt M79;

(z.015) Corner Blast PGL A1;

(z.016) CQ Type CQ 40MM;

(z.017) Croatian Service RT-20;

(z.018) CZ CZ805 G1;
(z.019) Czech Weapons SAG 30;
(z.02) Czech Weapons CZW 40;
(z.021) Czechoslovakian Mortar VZ52;
(z.022) Daewoo K201;
(z.023) Defense Technology L8;
(z.024) Defense Technology 40MM Launcher;
(z.025) Defense Technology 37MM Gas Gun;
(z.026) Defense Technology 37MM Gas Gun Pistol;
(z.027) Defense Technology 1375 Multi-Launcher;
(z.028) Degtyarev ASVK;
(z.029) Denel NTW 20HS;
(z.03) Denel PAW-20;
(z.031) Denel NTW;
(z.032) Dezamet GSBO-40;
(z.033) Dezamet GPBO-40;
(z.034) Diemaco M203A1;
(z.035) Diemaco Eagle;
(z.036) DPMS A-15 37MM Launcher;
(z.037) DSA 40MM Launcher;
(z.038) DSA Incorporated M203;
(z.039) Elite Machining ELM-40;
(z.04) ERE Systems M203 ERE Elite Launcher;
(z.041) Et Cetera 37MM Launcher;
(z.042) Exotic Firearms Nemesis-SL;
(z.043) Federal Laboratories 201Z;
(z.044) Federal Laboratories 203A;
(z.045) Federal Laboratories Federal Gas Riot Gun;
(z.046) Floro International 40MM Launcher;
(z.047) Floro International M400;
(z.048) Floro International M203;
(z.049) FN EGLM;
(z.05) FN MARK 13 Model 0;
(z.051) FN FN40GL;
(z.052) German Anti-Tank Rifle GrB39;
(z.053) German Anti-Tank Rifle M41;
(z.054) German Anti-Tank Rifle PzB38;
(z.055) German Anti-Tank Rifle PzB39;
(z.056) German Anti-Tank Rifle PzB41;
(z.057) German Mortar 1934 Granatwerfer;
(z.058) German Mortar Kurzer Granatewerfer 42;
(z.059) Greek Mortar C6 60MM;
(z.06) Greek Mortar E44 81MM;
(z.061) Greek Mortar E56 120MM;
(z.062) Heckler & Koch HKMZP1;
(z.063) Heckler & Koch HK69A1 Granatpistole;
(z.064) Heckler & Koch HKAG-G36;
(z.065) Heckler & Koch HKAG-C;

(z.066) Heckler & Koch HKXM320;
(z.067) Heckler & Koch HKAG-HK416;
(z.068) Heckler & Koch HKAG 36;
(z.069) Heckler & Koch HKGLM;
(z.07) Heckler & Koch HKAG-M16A4;
(z.071) Heckler & Koch HKAG-M4;
(z.072) Heckler & Koch HKM320;
(z.073) Heckler & Koch HKM320 A1;
(z.074) Heckler & Koch HK168E1;
(z.075) Heckler & Koch HK79;
(z.076) Heckler & Koch HK269;
(z.077) Heckler & Koch HK169;
(z.078) Helenius RK20;
(z.079) Helenius RK99 MARK 2;
(z.08) Hotchkiss 1934 Canon SAH;
(z.081) IOF Ugra;
(z.082) IOF UBGL;
(z.083) IOF Vidhwansak;
(z.084) Israeli Mortar C03;
(z.085) Italian Mortar Otobreda 81MM;
(z.086) IWI UBGL;
(z.087) Japanese Anti-Tank Rifle Type 97;
(z.088) Knights Armament Company M203;
(z.089) Lahti 39;
(z.09) Lake Erie Chemical Company Tru-Flite;
(z.091) Lamperd L40SL;
(z.092) LEI M203-PR;
(z.093) LMT M203;
(z.094) LMT M2032003 FMT;
(z.095) LMT 37MM Launcher;
(z.096) LMT 40MM Launcher;
(z.097) Luvo M203;
(z.098) Maadi UBGL;
(z.099) Manville Manville Gas Gun;
(z.1)   Metallic Limited RBG-1;
(z.101) Metallic Limited RBG-6;
(z.102) Milkor Stopper;
(z.103) Milkor MGL MARK 1;
(z.104) Milkor M79;
(z.105) Milkor MRGL;
(z.106) Milkor USA MGL-140 M32;
(z.107) Milkor USA MGL-140;
(z.108) Milkor USA MGL-105;
(z.109) Milkor USA MGL-AV140;
(z.11) Missile Launcher 9K111 Fagot;
(z.111) Missile Launcher 9K310 Igla-1;
(z.112) Missile Launcher 9K32 Strela-2;
(z.113) Missile Launcher 9K34 Strela-3;

(z.114) Missile Launcher 9K38 Igla;
(z.115) Missile Launcher BGM-71 TOW;
(z.116) Missile Launcher Eryx;
(z.117) Missile Launcher FGM-148 Javelin;
(z.118) Missile Launcher FIM-43 Redeye;
(z.119) Missile Launcher FIM-92 Stinger;
(z.12) Missile Launcher HN-5;
(z.121) Missile Launcher Ingwe;
(z.122) Missile Launcher M47 Dragon;
(z.123) Missile Launcher MILAN;
(z.124) Missile Launcher Saegheh;
(z.125) Missile Launcher Starstreak;
(z.126) Missile Launcher Toophan;
(z.127) Missile Launcher Type 79;
(z.128) MKE T40;
(z.129) MKE Grenade Launcher;
(z.13) Oerlikon SSG 32;
(z.131) Oerlikon SSG 36;
(z.132) Ordnance Group TAC79;
(z.133) Ordnance Group TAC-D;
(z.134) Penn Arms L140;
(z.135) Penn Arms H140;
(z.136) Penn Arms P540;
(z.137) Penn Arms L640;
(z.138) Penn Arms P837;
(z.139) Penn Arms L837;
(z.14) Penn Arms L137;
(z.141) Penn Arms AML1-37;
(z.142) Penn Arms HL;
(z.143) Penn Arms HG;
(z.144) Penn Arms L8;
(z.145) Penn Arms L6;
(z.146) Penn Arms L1;
(z.147) Penn Arms GL1;
(z.148) Penn Arms PGL65;
(z.149) Penn Arms GL6;
(z.15) Penn Arms GL65;
(z.151) Penn Arms PL8;
(z.152) Penn Arms TL1;
(z.153) Penn Arms TL8;
(z.154) Penn Arms TGL1;
(z.155) Penn Arms TGL6;
(z.156) Pindad SPG-1;
(z.157) PMP NTW;
(z.158) Polish Grenade Launcher Wz74;
(z.159) Polish Grenade Launcher Wz83;
(z.16) Portuguese Mortar M965;
(z.161) Portuguese Mortar M937;

CODE

(z.162) Recoilless Rifle AT4;
(z.163) Recoilless Rifle B-10;
(z.164) Recoilless Rifle FMK1 105MM;
(z.165) Recoilless Rifle Folgore;
(z.166) Recoilless Rifle M136 AT4;
(z.167) Recoilless Rifle M18A1;
(z.168) Recoilless Rifle M40A1;
(z.169) Recoilless Rifle M60;
(z.17) Recoilless Rifle M60A;
(z.171) Recoilless Rifle M65;
(z.172) Recoilless Rifle Pansarskott M68 Miniman;
(z.173) Recoilless Rifle RGW 60;
(z.174) Recoilless Rifle RGW 90;
(z.175) Recoilless Rifle SPG-9;
(z.176) Recoilless Rifle Type 36 M18A1 Recoilless Rifle Copy;
(z.177) Recoilless Rifle Type 65;
(z.178) Recoilless Rifle Type 78;
(z.179) Rippel Effect XRGL40;
(z.18) Rippel Effect LL40;
(z.181) RM Equipment M203PI;
(z.182) Rocket Launcher P27;
(z.183) Rocket Launcher RPG-27 Tavolga;
(z.184) Rocket Launcher ALAC;
(z.185) Rocket Launcher MARA;
(z.186) Rocket Launcher Shipon;
(z.187) Rocket Launcher RPG-22 Netto;
(z.188) Rocket Launcher MARK 153 SMAW;
(z.189) Rocket Launcher B-300;
(z.19) Rocket Launcher RPG-26 Aglen;
(z.191) Rocket Launcher RPG-76;
(z.192) Rocket Launcher RPG-7;
(z.193) Rocket Launcher M1;
(z.194) Rocket Launcher M1A1;
(z.195) Rocket Launcher M9;
(z.196) Rocket Launcher RPG-75;
(z.197) Rocket Launcher LRAC89-F1;
(z.198) Rocket Launcher RPG-16 Udar;
(z.199) Rocket Launcher RPG-7B;
(z.2)   Rocket Launcher RL100 Blindicide;
(z.201) Rocket Launcher M141 SMAW-D;
(z.202) Rocket Launcher MARK 777 RPG;
(z.203) Rocket Launcher ATGL RPG;
(z.204) Rocket Launcher Type 69 RPG;
(z.205) Rocket Launcher Type 56 RPG;
(z.206) Rocket Launcher RPG-2;
(z.207) Rocket Launcher Cobra RPG;
(z.208) Rocket Launcher Panzerfaust 3;
(z.209) Rocket Launcher APILAS;

(z.21) Rocket Launcher Wasp;
(z.211) Rocket Launcher Bunkerfaust;
(z.212) Rocket Launcher Type 2004 RPG;
(z.213) Rocket Launcher PF98;
(z.214) Rocket Launcher RPG-28 Klyukva;
(z.215) Rocket Launcher RPG-29 Vampir;
(z.216) Rocket Launcher FT5;
(z.217) Rocket Launcher C90;
(z.218) Rocket Launcher M20B1;
(z.219) Rocket Launcher M72;
(z.22) Romarm AG-40;
(z.221) Russian Artillery M1942 Anti-Tank Gun;
(z.222) Russian Mortar M1937;
(z.223) Russian Service DP-64;
(z.224) Sabre Defence Industries XR40;
(z.225) Sabre Defence Industries XR37;
(z.226) Sage ML40 MARK 1;
(z.227) Sage Ace 37MM Launcher;
(z.228) Sage Ace 40MM Launcher;
(z.229) Sage Deuce 37MM Launcher;
(z.23) Sage Deuce 40MM Launcher;
(z.231) Schermuly 38MM Multi-Purpose Gun;
(z.232) Singapore Technologies Kinetics 40GL;
(z.233) Smith & Wesson 210/276;
(z.234) Smith & Wesson 276;
(z.235) Solothurn S18-100;
(z.236) Solothurn S18-1000;
(z.237) Spike's Tactical 37MM Launcher STZ Havoc;
(z.238) Swiss Anti Tank Rifle Tankbusche 41;
(z.239) Swiss Arms GL5040;
(z.24) Swiss Arms GL5140;
(z.241) Swiss Arms GLG40;
(z.242) Taiwanese Grenade Launcher T85;
(z.243) Tarnow RGP-40;
(z.244) Tarnow GP40;
(z.245) Tarnow GS40;
(z.246) Truvelo SR20;
(z.247) Truvelo HSR 20;
(z.248) Truvelo CMS 20;
(z.249) US Mortar M2;
(z.25) US Mortar M1;
(z.251) US Mortar XM224E3;
(z.252) US Ordnance M6 37MM Gun;
(z.253) US Recoilless M18; and
(z.254) US Recoilless M20.

96. Any firearm capable of discharging a projectile with a muzzle energy greater than 10,000 joules — other than one referred to in item 12, 13, 14, 20, 22 or 30 of

this Part or one designed exclusively for the purpose of neutralizing explosive
devices — including the

(a) AAO 2000;

(b) Accuracy International AW50;

(c) Accuracy International AS50;

(d) Accuracy International AX;

(e) Accuracy International AX50;

(f) Alberta Tactical Rifle Big Bertha;

(g) Alberta Tactical Rifle ATSHL Prototype;

(h) Alberta Tactical Rifle ATSHL;

(i) Alberta Tactical Rifle AT50;

(j) Allied Armament Browning M2 Heavy Barrel;

(k) Allied Armament Browning M3 Aircraft;

(l) Alpimex APK 12.7;

(m) American Tactical Imports Omni Hybrid;

(n) AMP DSR 50;

(o) AMSD OM 50 Nemesis;

(p) Anzio Ironworks Anzio 50 CM1;

(q) Anzio Ironworks Anzio 50 Lightweight;

(r) Anzio Ironworks Anzio SS;

(s) Anzio Ironworks Anzio 50;

(t) Anzio Ironworks Anzio 14.5;

(u) Armalite AR-50;

(v) Armalite AR-50A1;

(w) Armtech BM50;

(x) Azerbaijani Sniper Rifle Istiglal IST 12.7;

(y) Azerbaijani Sniper Rifle Istiglal IST 14.5;

(z) Ballard SB500;

(z.001) Barnard GP;

(z.002) Barrett Firearms 99;

(z.003) BAT Machine EX;

(z.004) BCM Europearms Extreme;

(z.005) BCM Europearms MAAR Extreme;

(z.006) BCM Europearms STD Extreme;

(z.007) Bluegrass Armory Viper XL;

(z.008) Boys MARK 1*;

(z.009) Boys MARK 1;

(z.01) Bushmaster BA50;

(z.011) Cadex CDX-50 Tremor;

(z.012) Canstar Arms CS 50;

(z.013) Canstar Arms CS1 Prototype;

(z.014) Canstar Arms CS2 Prototype;

(z.015) Canstar Arms CS 50-2;

(z.016) Caracal CS50;

(z.017) China South Industries Group AMR-2;

(z.018) China South Industries Group LR2A;

(z.019) Christensen Arms Carbon One Ranger;

(z.02) Christensen Arms Carbon One Conquest;

(z.021) Christensen Arms Carbon Ranger;
(z.022) Cobb FA50;
(z.023) Cobb FA50(T);
(z.024) Cobb BA50;
(z.025) Croatian Service MACS M3;
(z.026) Croatian Service MACS M4;
(z.027) Czech Weapons CZW 127;
(z.028) Defence Industries Organization AM-50;
(z.029) Degtyarev ASVK;
(z.03) Denel NTW;
(z.031) Desert Tactical Arms HTI;
(z.032) Desert Tech HTI;
(z.033) DPMS A-15;
(z.034) DPMS A-15 Panther VRS Single Shot;
(z.035) EAA M93 Black Arrow;
(z.036) East Ridge/State Arms Gun Company Big Bertha;
(z.037) EDM Arms XM-107 Windrunner;
(z.038) EDM Arms SA-01 Windrunner;
(z.039) EDM Arms 96 Windrunner;
(z.04) Elite Machining Elite 50;
(z.041) Essential Arms Company J15;
(z.042) Essential Arms Company J15F;
(z.043) Evolution USA Phantom 3;
(z.044) FN Hecate 2;
(z.045) FN Nemesis;
(z.046) Fortmeier, Heinrich 2001;
(z.047) Fortmeier, Heinrich 2002;
(z.048) Gepard GM6 Lynx;
(z.049) German Anti-Tank Rifle PzB42;
(z.05) Gun Room Company Noreen ULR;
(z.051) Hagelberg FH50;
(z.052) Halo Arms HA50 FTR;
(z.053) Halo Arms HA50 LRR;
(z.054) Helenius RK97;
(z.055) Helenius RK99;
(z.056) Helenius RK99 MARK 1;
(z.057) IOF Vidhwansak;
(z.058) Jard J50;
(z.059) Jard J51;
(z.06) JRS 510;
(z.061) Karta Tool Frenchy 1 Prototype;
(z.062) Kovrov SVN-98;
(z.063) LAR Manufacturing Grizzly Big Boar;
(z.064) LAR Manufacturing Grizzly T-50;
(z.065) McBros 50 BMG Benchrest;
(z.066) McBros 50 BMG Sporter;
(z.067) McBros 50 BMG Tactical;
(z.068) McMillan 50 BMG Benchrest;

CODE

(z.069) McMillan Brothers 50 BMG Benchrest;
(z.07) McMillan Brothers 50 BMG Sporter;
(z.071) McMillan Brothers 50 BMG Tactical;
(z.072) McMillan Brothers TAC-50;
(z.073) McMillan TAC-50;
(z.074) McMillan TAC-416;
(z.075) MG Arms Behemoth;
(z.076) Mitchells Mausers M93 Black Arrow Target;
(z.077) Modulo Masterpiece Wizard Extreme Long Range Match;
(z.078) Noreen Firearms Noreen ULR;
(z.079) Noreen Firearms Noreen ULR Extreme;
(z.08) Norinco JS 05;
(z.081) Norinco CSLR5;
(z.082) Northwest Imports Browning M2 Heavy Barrel;
(z.083) Odessa Patriot 50;
(z.084) Omni Windrunner;
(z.085) PGM Precision Hecate 2;
(z.086) Phase 5 Tactical P5T15;
(z.087) Pietsch P B 50 Canadian;
(z.088) PMP NTW;
(z.089) Poly Technologies M99;
(z.09) Poly Technologies M99B;
(z.091) Prairie Gun Works LRT3REP;
(z.092) Prairie Gun Works LRT3SS;
(z.093) Prairie Gun Works LRT50;
(z.094) RAD M650 SLAMR;
(z.095) RAD M614;
(z.096) Ramo 600;
(z.097) Ramo 650;
(z.098) Rib Mountain Arms 92;
(z.099) Robar RC-50;
(z.1) RPA Quadlock;
(z.101) RPA Rangemaster 50;
(z.102) Russian Anti-Tank Rifle PTRS41;
(z.103) Russian Anti-Tank Rifle PTRD41;
(z.104) Russian Anti-Tank Rifle PTRR39;
(z.105) Russian Anti-Tank Rifle PTRSh;
(z.106) Safety Harbor Firearms SHF/R50;
(z.107) Safety Harbor Firearms Ultra Mag 50;
(z.108) Safety Harbor Firearms SHF/S50;
(z.109) Saxonia Big Valve M2;
(z.11) Semtecx Single Shot Pistol;
(z.111) Serbu BFG-50;
(z.112) Serbu BFG-50A;
(z.113) Serbu RN-50;
(z.114) Sero GM6 Lynx;
(z.115) SIG Sauer SIG 50;
(z.116) SMOS Rogue-50;

(z.117) SMOS Rogue-SS;
(z.118) Spider Firearms Ferret 50;
(z.119) St George Arms Leader 50 A1;
(z.12) State Arms Gun Company Rebel;
(z.121) State Arms Gun Company Mosquito;
(z.122) State Arms Gun Company Shorty;
(z.123) State Arms Gun Company Competitor 2000;
(z.124) Steyr-Mannlicher HS50;
(z.125) Steyr-Mannlicher HS50M1;
(z.126) Steyr-Mannlicher HS460;
(z.127) Stoner SR-50;
(z.128) Swiss Arms SAN511;
(z.129) Tactical Machining TM-SS;
(z.13) Tarnow WKW;
(z.131) Tasko 7ET3;
(z.132) Tech Designs Kodiak;
(z.133) Thompson Machine ARSSL;
(z.134) Thor Global Defense Group M96 Windrunner Series;
(z.135) TNW Browning M2 Heavy Barrel;
(z.136) Triple Action Thunder 50;
(z.137) Truvelo CMS 12.7;
(z.138) Truvelo CMS 14.5;
(z.139) Truvelo SR50;
(z.14) Ursus Firearms Kodiak;
(z.141) Valkyrie Arms Browning M2 Heavy Barrel;
(z.142) VM Hy-Tech VM50;
(z.143) Vulcan Armament V50SS;
(z.144) Watsons Weapons 50;
(z.145) Zastava M93;
(z.146) Zastava Arms M93 Black Arrow;
(z.147) Zastava Europe M93;
(z.148) ZVI OP96; and
(z.149) ZVI OP99.

PART 2
Restricted Firearms

Former Restricted Weapons Order

1. The firearms of the designs commonly known as the High Standard Model 10, Series A shotgun and the High Standard Model 10, Series B shotgun, and any variants or modified versions of them.

2. [*Replaced*, SOR/2020-96, s. 4.]

PART 2.1
[Heading repealed, SOR/2020-96, s. 5.]

1. [*Repealed*, SOR/2020-96, s. 5.]
2. [*Repealed*, SOR/2020-96, s. 5.]
3. [*Repealed*, SOR/2020-96, s. 5.]
4. [*Repealed*, SOR/2020-96, s. 5.]
5. [*Repealed*, SOR/2020-96, s. 5.]
6. [*Repealed*, SOR/2020-96, s. 5.]
7. [*Repealed*, SOR/2020-96, s. 5.]
8. [*Repealed*, SOR/2020-96, s. 5.]
9. [*Repealed*, SOR/2020-96, s. 5.]
10. [*Repealed*, SOR/2020-96, s. 5.]
11. [*Repealed*, SOR/2020-96, s. 5.]
12. [*Repealed*, SOR/2020-96, s. 5.]
13. [*Repealed*, SOR/2020-96, s. 5.]
14. [*Repealed*, SOR/2020-96, s. 5.]
15. [*Repealed*, SOR/2020-96, s. 5.]

PART 3
Prohibited Weapons

Former Prohibited Weapons Order, No. 1

1. Any device designed to be used for the purpose of injuring, immobilizing or otherwise incapacitating any person by the discharge therefrom of

(a) tear gas, Mace or other gas; or
(b) any liquid, spray, powder or other substance that is capable of injuring, immobilizing or otherwise incapacitating any person.

Former Prohibited Weapons Order, No. 2

2. Any instrument or device commonly known as "nunchaku", being hard non-flexible sticks, clubs, pipes, or rods linked by a length or lengths of rope, cord, wire or chain, and any similar instrument or device.

3. Any instrument or device commonly known as "shuriken", being a hard non-flexible plate having three or more radiating points with one or more sharp edges in the shape of a polygon, trefoil, cross, star, diamond or other geometrical shape, and any similar instrument or device.

4. Any instrument or device commonly known as "manrikigusari" or "kusari", being hexagonal or other geometrically shaped hard weights or hand grips linked

by a length or lengths of rope, cord, wire or chain, and any similar instrument or device.

5. Any finger ring that has one or more blades or sharp objects that are capable of being projected from the surface of the ring.

Former Prohibited Weapons Order, No. 3

6. Any device that is designed to be capable of injuring, immobilizing or incapacitating a person or an animal by discharging an electrical charge produced by means of the amplification or accumulation of the electrical current generated by a battery, where the device is designed or altered so that the electrical charge may be discharged when the device is of a length of less than 480 mm, and any similar device.

7. A crossbow or similar device that

(a) is designed or altered to be aimed and fired by the action of one hand, whether or not it has been redesigned or subsequently altered to be aimed and fired by the action of both hands; or
(b) has a length not exceeding 500 mm.

Former Prohibited Weapons Order, No. 4

8. The device known as the "Constant Companion", being a belt containing a blade capable of being withdrawn from the belt, with the buckle of the belt forming a handle for the blade, and any similar device.

9. Any knife commonly known as a "push-dagger" that is designed in such a fashion that the handle is placed perpendicular to the main cutting edge of the blade and any other similar device other than the aboriginal "ulu" knife.

10. Any device having a length of less than 30 cm and resembling an innocuous object but designed to conceal a knife or blade, including the device commonly known as the "knife-comb", being a comb with the handle of the comb forming a handle for the knife, and any similar device.

Former Prohibited Weapons Order, No. 5

11. The device commonly known as a "Spiked Wristband", being a wristband to which a spike or blade is affixed, and any similar device.

Former Prohibited Weapons Order, No. 6

12. The device commonly known as "Yaqua Blowgun", being a tube or pipe designed for the purpose of shooting arrows or darts by the breath, and any similar device.

Former Prohibited Weapons Order, No. 7

13. The device commonly known as a "Kiyoga Baton" or "Steel Cobra" and any similar device consisting of a manually triggered telescoping spring-loaded steel whip terminated in a heavy calibre striking tip.

14. The device commonly known as a "Morning Star" and any similar device consisting of a ball of metal or other heavy material, studded with spikes and connected to a handle by a length of chain, rope or other flexible material.

Former Prohibited Weapons Order, No. 8

15. The device known as "Brass Knuckles" and any similar device consisting of a band of metal with one or more finger holes designed to fit over the fingers of the hand.

PART 4
Prohibited Devices

Former Prohibited Weapons Order, No. 9

1. Any electrical or mechanical device that is designed or adapted to operate the trigger mechanism of a semi-automatic firearm for the purpose of causing the firearm to discharge cartridges in rapid succession.

2. Any rifle, shotgun or carbine stock of the type known as the "bull-pup" design, being a stock that, when combined with a firearm, reduces the overall length of the firearm such that a substantial part of the reloading action or the magazine-well is located behind the trigger of the firearm when it is held in the normal firing position.

Former Cartridge Magazine Control Regulations

3. (1) Any cartridge magazine

(a) that is capable of containing more than five cartridges of the type for which the magazine was originally designed and that is designed or manufactured for use in

(i) a semi-automatic handgun that is not commonly available in Canada,

(ii) a semi-automatic firearm other than a semi-automatic handgun,

(iii) an automatic firearm whether or not it has been altered to discharge only one projectile with one pressure of the trigger,

(iv) the firearms of the designs commonly known as the Ingram M10 and M11 pistols, and any variants or modified versions of them, including the Cobray M10 and M11 pistols, the RPB M10, M11 and SM11 pistols and the SWD M10, M11, SM10 and SM11 pistols,

(v) the firearm of the design commonly known as the Partisan Avenger Auto Pistol, and any variant or modified version of it, or

(vi) the firearm of the design commonly known as the UZI pistol, and any variant or modified version of it, including the Micro-UZI pistol; or

(b) that is capable of containing more than 10 cartridges of the type for which the magazine was originally designed and that is designed or manufactured for use in a semi-automatic handgun that is commonly available in Canada.

(2) Paragraph (1)(*a*) does not include any cartridge magazine that

(a) was originally designed or manufactured for use in a firearm that

(i) is chambered for, or designed to use, rimfire cartridges,

(ii) is a rifle of the type commonly known as the "Lee Enfield" rifle, where the magazine is capable of containing not more than 10 cartridges of the type for which the magazine was originally designed, or

(iii) is commonly known as the U.S. Rifle M1 (Garand) including the Beretta M1 Garand rifle, the Breda M1 Garand rifle and the Springfield Armoury M1 Garand rifle;

(b) is not a reproduction and was originally designed or manufactured for use in a firearm that

(i) is commonly known as the Charlton Rifle,

(ii) is commonly known as the Farquhar-Hill Rifle, or

(iii) is commonly known as the Huot Automatic Rifle;

(c) is of the "drum" type, is not a reproduction and was originally designed or manufactured for use in a firearm commonly known as

(i) the .303 in. Lewis Mark 1 machine-gun, or any variant or modified version of it, including the Lewis Mark ★, Mark 2, Mark 2★, Mark 3, Mark 4, Lewis SS and .30 in. Savage-Lewis,

(ii) the .303 in. Vickers Mark 1 machine-gun, or any variant or modified version of it, including the Mark 1★, Mark 2, Mark 2★, Mark 3, Mark 4, Mark 4B, Mark 5, Mark 6, Mark 6★ and Mark 7, or

(iii) the Bren Light machine-gun, or any variant or modified version of it, including the Mark 1, Mark 2, Mark 2/1, Mark 3 and Mark 4;

(d) is of the "metallic-strip" type, is not a reproduction and was originally designed or manufactured for use in conjunction with the firearm known as the Hotchkiss machine-gun, Model 1895 or Model 1897, or any variant or modified version of it, including the Hotchkiss machine-gun, Model 1900, Model 1909, Model 1914 and Model 1917, and the Hotchkiss machine-gun (Enfield), Number 2, Mark 1 and Mark 1★;

(e) is of the "saddle-drum" type (doppeltrommel or satteltrommel), is not a reproduction and was originally designed or manufactured for use in the automatic firearms known as the MG-13, MG-15, MG-17, MG-34, T6-200 or T6-220, or any variant or modified version of it; or

(f) is of the "belt" type consisting of a fabric or metal belt, is not a reproduction and was originally designed or manufactured for the purpose of feeding cartridges into a automatic firearm of a type that was in existence before 1945.

(3) Paragraph (1)(b) does not include any cartridge magazine that

(a) is of the "snail-drum" type (schneckentrommel) that was originally designed or manufactured for use in a firearm that is a handgun known as the Parabellum-Pistol, System Borchardt-Luger, Model 1900, or "Luger", or any variant or modified version of it, including the Model 1902, Model 1904 (Marine), Model 1904/06 (Marine), Model 1904/08 (Marine), Model 1906, Model 1908 and Model 1908 (Artillery) pistols;

(b) was originally designed or manufactured for use in a firearm that is a semi-automatic handgun, where the magazine was manufactured before 1910;

(c) was originally designed or manufactured as an integral part of the firearm known as the Mauser Selbstladepistole C/96 ("broomhandle"), or any variant or modified version of it, including the Model 1895, Model 1896, Model 1902, Model 1905, Model 1912, Model 1915, Model 1930, Model 1931, M711 and M712; or

(d) was originally designed or manufactured for use in the semi-automatic firearm that is a handgun known as the Webley and Scott Self-Loading Pistol, Model 1912 or Model 1915.

(4) A cartridge magazine described in subsection (1) that has been altered or re-manufactured so that it is not capable of containing more than five or ten cartridges, as the case may be, of the type for which it was originally designed is not a prohibited device as prescribed by that subsection if the modification to the magazine cannot be easily removed and the magazine cannot be easily further altered so that it is so capable of containing more than five or ten cartridges, as the case may be.

(5) For the purposes of subsection (4), altering or re-manufacturing a cartridge magazine includes

(a) the indentation of its casing by forging, casting, swaging or impressing;

(b) in the case of a cartridge magazine with a steel or aluminum casing, the insertion and attachment of a plug, sleeve, rod, pin, flange or similar device, made of steel or aluminum, as the case may be, or of a similar material, to the inner surface of its casing by welding, brazing or any other similar method; or

(c) in the case of a cartridge magazine with a casing made of a material other than steel or aluminum, the attachment of a plug, sleeve, rod, pin, flange or similar device, made of steel or of a material similar to that of the magazine casing, to the inner surface of its casing by welding, brazing or any other similar method or by applying a permanent adhesive substance, such as a cement or an epoxy or other glue.

Other

4. The upper receiver of any firearm referred to in item 87 of Part 1 of this schedule.

PART 5
Prohibited Ammunition

Former Prohibited Weapons Order, No. 10

1. Any cartridge that is capable of being discharged from a commonly available semi-automatic handgun or revolver and that is manufactured or assembled with a projectile that is designed, manufactured or altered so as to be capable of penetrating body armour, including KTW, THV and 5.7 x 28 mm P-90 cartridges.

2. Any projectile that is designed, manufactured or altered to ignite on impact, where the projectile is designed for use in or in conjunction with a cartridge and does not exceed 15 mm in diameter.

3. Any projectile that is designed, manufactured or altered so as to explode on impact, where the projectile is designed for use in or in conjunction with a cartridge and does not exceed 15 mm in diameter.

4. Any cartridge that is capable of being discharged from a shotgun and that contains projectiles known as "fléchettes" or any similar projectiles. **SOR/98-462; SOR/98-472; SOR/2015-213; SOR/2018-254, s. 1; SOR/2020-96, ss. 1-6.**

Use Offences

USING FIREARM IN COMMISSION OF OFFENCE / Using imitation firearm in commission of offence / Punishment / Sentences to be served consecutively.

85. (1) Every person commits an offence who uses a firearm, whether or not the person causes or means to cause bodily harm to any person as a result of using the firearm,

- (*a*) while committing an indictable offence, other than an offence under section 220 (criminal negligence causing death), 236 (manslaughter), 239 (attempted murder), 244 (discharging firearm with intent), 244.2 (discharging firearm — recklessness), 272 (sexual assault with a weapon) or 273 (aggravated sexual assault), subsection 279(1) (kidnapping) or section 279.1 (hostage taking), 344 (robbery) or 346 (extortion);
- (*b*) while attempting to commit an indictable offence; or
- (*c*) during flight after committing or attempting to commit an indictable offence.

(2) Every person commits an offence who uses an imitation firearm

(a) while committing an indictable offence,

(b) while attempting to commit an indictable offence, or

(c) during flight after committing or attempting to commit an indictable offence,

whether or not the person causes or means to cause bodily harm to any person as a result of using the imitation firearm.

(3) Every person who commits an offence under subsection (1) or (2) is guilty of an indictable offence and liable

(a) in the case of a first offence, except as provided in paragraph (b), to imprisonment for a term not exceeding fourteen years and to a minimum punishment of imprisonment for a term of one year; and

(b) in the case of a second or subsequent offence, to imprisonment for a term not exceeding 14 years and to a minimum punishment of imprisonment for a term of three years.

(c) [Repealed, 2008, c. 6, s. 3(2).]

(4) A sentence imposed on a person for an offence under subsection (1) or (2) shall be served consecutively to any other punishment imposed on the person for an offence arising out of the same event or series of events and to any other sentence to which the person is subject at the time the sentence is imposed on the person for an offence under subsection (1) or (2). R.S., c. C-34, s. 83; 1976-77, c. 53, s. 3; 1995, c. 39, s. 139; 2003, c. 8, s. 3; 2008, c. 6, s. 3; 2009, c. 22, s. 3.

CARELESS USE OF FIREARM, ETC. / Contravention of storage regulations, etc. / Punishment.

86. (1) Every person commits an offence who, without lawful excuse, uses, carries, handles, ships, transports or stores a firearm, a prohibited weapon, a restricted weapon, a prohibited device or any ammunition or prohibited ammunition in a careless manner or without reasonable precautions for the safety of other persons.

(2) Every person commits an offence who contravenes a regulation made under paragraph 117(h) of the *Firearms Act* respecting the storage, handling, transportation, shipping, display, advertising and mail-order sales of firearms and restricted weapons.

(3) Every person who commits an offence under subsection (1) or (2)

(a) is guilty of an indictable offence and liable to imprisonment

(i) in the case of a first offence, for a term not exceeding two years, and

(ii) in the case of a second or subsequent offence, for a term not exceeding five years; or

(b) is guilty of an offence punishable on summary conviction. 1995, c. 39, s. 139.

Editor's Note: Regulations respecting the *Storage, Display, Transportation and Handling of Firearms by Individuals Regulations*, SOR/98-209, enacted under the *Firearms Act*, may be found in *Martin's Related Criminal Statutes*.

CODE

POINTING A FIREARM / Punishment.

87. (1) Every person commits an offence who, without lawful excuse, points a firearm at another person, whether the firearm is loaded or unloaded.

(2) Every person who commits an offence under subsection (1)

   (a) is guilty of an indictable offence and liable to imprisonment for a term not exceeding five years; or

   (b) is guilty of an offence punishable on summary conviction. 1995, c. 39, s. 139.

Possession Offences

POSSESSION OF WEAPON FOR DANGEROUS PURPOSE / Punishment.

88. (1) Every person commits an offence who carries or possesses a weapon, an imitation of a weapon, a prohibited device or any ammunition or prohibited ammunition for a purpose dangerous to the public peace or for the purpose of committing an offence.

(2) Every person who commits an offence under subsection (1)

   (a) is guilty of an indictable offence and liable to imprisonment for a term not exceeding ten years; or

   (b) is guilty of an offence punishable on summary conviction. 1995, c. 39, s. 139.

CARRYING WEAPON WHILE ATTENDING PUBLIC MEETING / Punishment.

89. (1) Every person commits an offence who, without lawful excuse, carries a weapon, a prohibited device or any ammunition or prohibited ammunition while the person is attending or is on the way to attend a public meeting.

(2) Every person who commits an offence under subsection (1) is guilty of an offence punishable on summary conviction. 1995, c. 39, s. 139.

CARRYING CONCEALED WEAPON / Punishment.

90. (1) Every person commits an offence who carries a weapon, a prohibited device or any prohibited ammunition concealed, unless the person is authorized under the *Firearms Act* to carry it concealed.

(2) Every person who commits an offence under subsection (1)

   (a) is guilty of an indictable offence and liable to imprisonment for a term not exceeding five years; or

   (b) is guilty of an offence punishable on summary conviction. 1995, c. 39, s. 139.

147

UNAUTHORIZED POSSESSION OF FIREARM / Unauthorized possession of prohibited weapon or restricted weapon / Punishment / Exceptions / Borrowed firearm for sustenance.

91. (1) Subject to subsection (4), every person commits an offence who possesses a prohibited firearm, a restricted firearm or a non-restricted firearm without being the holder of

(a) a licence under which the person may possess it; and

(b) in the case of a prohibited firearm or a restricted firearm, a registration certificate for it.

(2) Subject to subsection (4), every person commits an offence who possesses a prohibited weapon, a restricted weapon, a prohibited device, other than a replica firearm, or any prohibited ammunition, without being the holder of a licence under which the person may possess it.

(3) Every person who commits an offence under subsection (1) or (2)

(a) is guilty of an indictable offence and liable to imprisonment for a term not exceeding five years; or

(b) is guilty of an offence punishable on summary conviction.

(4) Subsections (1) and (2) do not apply to

(a) a person who possesses a prohibited firearm, a restricted firearm, a non-restricted firearm, a prohibited weapon, a restricted weapon, a prohibited device or any prohibited ammunition while the person is under the direct and immediate supervision of a person who may lawfully possess it, for the purpose of using it in a manner in which the supervising person may lawfully use it; or

(b) a person who comes into possession of a prohibited firearm, a restricted firearm, a non-restricted firearm, a prohibited weapon, a restricted weapon, a prohibited device or any prohibited ammunition by the operation of law and who, within a reasonable period after acquiring possession of it,

(i) lawfully disposes of it, or

(ii) obtains a licence under which the person may possess it and, in the case of a prohibited firearm or a restricted firearm, a registration certificate for it. 1995, c. 39, s. 139; 2008, c. 6, s. 4; 2012, c. 6, s. 2; 2015, c. 27, s. 19.

(5) [*Repealed*, 2012, c. 1, s. 2(3).]

POSSESSION OF FIREARM KNOWING ITS POSSESSION IS UNAUTHORIZED / Possession of prohibited weapon, device or ammunition knowing its possession is unauthorized / Punishment / Exceptions / Borrowed firearm for sustenance / Evidence for previous conviction.

92. (1) Subject to subsection (4), every person commits an offence who possesses a prohibited firearm, a restricted firearm or a non-restricted firearm knowing that the person is not the holder of

(a) a licence under which the person may possess it; and

(b) in the case of a prohibited firearm or a restricted firearm, a registration certificate for it.

(2) Subject to subsection (4), every person commits an offence who possesses a prohibited weapon, a restricted weapon, a prohibited device, other than a replica firearm, or any prohibited ammunition knowing that the person is not the holder of a licence under which the person may possess it.

(3) Every person who commits an offence under subsection (1) or (2) is guilty of an indictable offence and liable

- (a) in the case of a first offence, to imprisonment for a term not exceeding ten years;
- (b) in the case of a second offence, to imprisonment for a term not exceeding ten years and to a minimum punishment of imprisonment for a term of one year; and
- (c) in the case of a third or subsequent offence, to imprisonment for a term not exceeding ten years and to a minimum punishment of imprisonment for a term of two years less a day.

(4) Subsections (1) and (2) do not apply to

- (a) a person who possesses a prohibited firearm, a restricted firearm, a non-restricted firearm, a prohibited weapon, a restricted weapon, a prohibited device or any prohibited ammunition while the person is under the direct and immediate supervision of a person who may lawfully possess it, for the purpose of using it in a manner in which the supervising person may lawfully use it; or
- (b) a person who comes into possession of a prohibited firearm, a restricted firearm, a non-restricted firearm, a prohibited weapon, a restricted weapon, a prohibited device or any prohibited ammunition by the operation of law and who, within a reasonable period after acquiring possession of it,
  - (i) lawfully disposes of it, or
  - (ii) obtains a licence under which the person may possess it and, in the case of a prohibited firearm or a restricted firearm, a registration certificate for it. 1995, c. 39, s. 139; 2008, c. 6, s. 5; 2012, c. 6, s. 3; 2015, c. 27, s. 20.

(5) and (6) [*Repealed*, 2012, c. 6, s. 3(3).]

POSSESSION AT UNAUTHORIZED PLACE / Punishment / Exception.

93. (1) Subject to subsection (3), every person commits an offence who, being the holder of an authorization or a licence under which the person may possess a prohibited firearm, a restricted firearm, a non-restricted firearm, a prohibited weapon, a restricted weapon, a prohibited device or prohibited ammunition, possesses them at a place that is

- (a) indicated on the authorization or licence as being a place where the person may not possess it;
- (b) other than a place indicated on the authorization or licence as being a place where the person may possess it; or
- (c) other than a place where it may be possessed under the *Firearms Act*.

(2) Every person who commits an offence under subsection (1)

(a) is guilty of an indictable offence and liable to imprisonment for a term not exceeding five years; or

(b) is guilty of an offence punishable on summary conviction.

(3) Subsection (1) does not apply to a person who possesses a replica firearm. 1995, c. 39, s. 139; 2008, c. 6, s. 6; 2015, c. 27, s. 21.

UNAUTHORIZED POSSESSION IN MOTOR VEHICLE / Punishment / Exception / Exception.

94. (1) Subject to subsections (3) and (4), every person commits an offence who is an occupant of a motor vehicle in which the person knows there is a prohibited firearm, a restricted firearm, a non-restricted firearm, a prohibited weapon, a restricted weapon, a prohibited device, other than a replica firearm, or any prohibited ammunition, unless

  (a) in the case of a prohibited firearm, a restricted firearm or a non-restricted firearm,

    (i) the person or any other occupant of the motor vehicle is the holder of

      (A) a licence under which the person or other occupant may possess the firearm, and

      (B) in the case of a prohibited firearm or a restricted firearm, an authorization and a registration certificate for it,

    (ii) the person had reasonable grounds to believe that any other occupant of the motor vehicle was the holder of

      (A) a licence under which that other occupant may possess the firearm, and

      (B) in the case of a prohibited firearm or a restricted firearm, an authorization and a registration certificate for it, or

    (iii) the person had reasonable grounds to believe that any other occupant of the motor vehicle was a person who could not be convicted of an offence under this Act by reason of sections 117.07 to 117.1 or any other Act of Parliament; and

  (b) in the case of a prohibited weapon, a restricted weapon, a prohibited device or any prohibited ammunition,

    (i) the person or any other occupant of the motor vehicle is the holder of an authorization or a licence under which the person or other occupant may transport the prohibited weapon, restricted weapon, prohibited device or prohibited ammunition, or

    (ii) the person had reasonable grounds to believe that any other occupant of the motor vehicle was

      (A) the holder of an authorization or a licence under which the other occupant may transport the prohibited weapon, restricted weapon, prohibited device or prohibited ammunition, or

      (B) a person who could not be convicted of an offence under this Act by reason of sections 117.07 to 117.1 or any other Act of Parliament.

(2) Every person who commits an offence under subsection (1)

  (a) is guilty of an indictable offence and liable to imprisonment for a term not exceeding ten years; or (*b*) is guilty of an offence punishable on summary conviction.

(3) Subsection (1) does not apply to an occupant of a motor vehicle who, on becoming aware of the presence of the firearm, weapon, device or ammunition in the motor vehicle, attempted to leave the motor vehicle, to the extent that it was feasible to do so, or actually left the motor vehicle.

(4) Subsection (1) does not apply to an occupant of a motor vehicle when the occupant or any other occupant of the motor vehicle is a person who came into possession of the firearm, weapon, device or ammunition by the operation of law. 1995, c. 39, s. 139; 2008, c. 6, s. 7; 2012, c. 6, s. 4; 2015, c. 27, s. 22.

(5) [*Repealed*, 2012, c. 6, s. 4(3).]

POSSESSION OF PROHIBITED OR RESTRICTED FIREARM WITH AMMUNITION / Punishment / Exception.

95. (1) Subject to subsection (3), every person commits an offence who, in any place, possesses a loaded prohibited firearm or restricted firearm, or an unloaded prohibited firearm or restricted firearm together with readily accessible ammunition that is capable of being discharged in the firearm, without being the holder of

(*a*) an authorization or a licence under which the person may possess the firearm in that place; and

(*b*) the registration certificate for the firearm.

(2) Every person who commits an offence under subsection (1)

(*a*) is guilty of an indictable offence and liable to imprisonment for a term not exceeding 10 years and to a minimum punishment of imprisonment for a term of

(i) in the case of a first offence, three years, and

(ii) in the case of a second or subsequent offence, five years; or

(*b*) is guilty of an offence punishable on summary conviction.

(3) Subsection (1) does not apply to a person who is using the firearm under the direct and immediate supervision of another person who is lawfully entitled to possess it and is using the firearm in a manner in which that other person may lawfully use it. 1995, c. 39, s. 139; 2008, c. 6, s. 8; 2012, c. 6, s. 5; 2019, c. 25, s. 25.

POSSESSION OF WEAPON OBTAINED BY COMMISSION OF OFFENCE / Punishment / Exception.

96. (1) Subject to subsection (3), every person commits an offence who possesses a firearm, a prohibited weapon, a restricted weapon, a prohibited device or any prohibited ammunition that the person knows was obtained by the commission in Canada of an offence or by an act or omission anywhere that, if it had occurred in Canada, would have constituted an offence.

(2) Every person who commits an offence under subsection (1)

(*a*) is guilty of an indictable offence and liable to imprisonment for a term not exceeding ten years and to a minimum punishment of imprisonment for a term of one year; or

(b) is guilty of an offence punishable on summary conviction.

(3) Subsection (1) does not apply to a person who comes into possession of anything referred to in that subsection by the operation of law and who lawfully disposes of it within a reasonable period after acquiring possession of it. 1995, c. 39, s. 139; 2019, c. 25, s. 26.

---

97. [Enacted 1995, c. 39, s. 139; however, repealed before coming into force]

BREAKING AND ENTERING TO STEAL FIREARM / Definitions of "break" and "place" / Entrance / Punishment.

98. (1) Every person commits an offence who
   (a) breaks and enters a place with intent to steal a firearm located in it;
   (b) breaks and enters a place and steals a firearm located in it; or
   (c) breaks out of a place after
       (i) stealing a firearm located in it, or
       (ii) entering the place with intent to steal a firearm located in it.

(2) In this section, "break" has the same meaning as in section 321, and "place" means any building or structure — or part of one — and any motor vehicle, vessel, aircraft, railway vehicle, container or trailer.

(3) For the purposes of this section,
   (a) a person enters as soon as any part of his or her body or any part of an instrument that he or she uses is within any thing that is being entered; and
   (b) a person is deemed to have broken and entered if he or she
       (i) obtained entrance by a threat or an artifice or by collusion with a person within, or
       (ii) entered without lawful justification or excuse by a permanent or temporary opening.

(4) Every person who commits an offence under subsection (1) is guilty of an indictable offence and liable to imprisonment for life. 1995, c. 39, s. 139, 2008, c. 6, s. 9.

ROBBERY TO STEAL FIREARM.

98.1 Every person who commits a robbery within the meaning of section 343 with intent to steal a firearm or in the course of which he or she steals a firearm commits an indictable offence and is liable to imprisonment for life. 2008, c. 6, s. 9.

Trafficking Offences

WEAPONS TRAFFICKING / Punishment — firearm / Punishment — other cases.

99. (1) Every person commits an offence who
   (a) manufactures or transfers, whether or not for consideration, or

(b) offers to do anything referred to in paragraph (a) in respect of

a prohibited firearm, a restricted firearm, a non-restricted firearm, a prohibited weapon, a restricted weapon, a prohibited device, any ammunition or any prohibited ammunition knowing that the person is not authorized to do so under the *Firearms Act* or any other Act of Parliament or any regulations made under any Act of Parliament.

(2) Every person who commits an offence under subsection (1) when the object in question is a prohibited firearm, a restricted firearm, a non-restricted firearm, a prohibited device, any ammunition or any prohibited ammunition is guilty of an indictable offence and liable to imprisonment for a term not exceeding 10 years and to a minimum punishment of imprisonment for a term of

   (a) in the case of a first offence, three years; and

   (b) in the case of a second or subsequent offence, five years.

(3) In any other case, a person who commits an offence under subsection (1) is guilty of an indictable offence and liable to imprisonment for a term not exceeding 10 years and to a minimum punishment of imprisonment for a term of one year. 1995, c. 39, s. 139; 2008, c. 6, s. 10; 2015, c. 27, s. 23.

POSSESSION FOR PURPOSE OF WEAPONS TRAFFICKING / Punishment — firearm / Punishment — other cases.

100. (1) Every person commits an offence who possesses a prohibited firearm, a restricted firearm, a non-restricted firearm, a prohibited weapon, a restricted weapon, a prohibited device, any ammunition or any prohibited ammunition for the purpose of

   (a) transferring it, whether or not for consideration, or

   (b) offering to transfer it,

knowing that the person is not authorized to transfer it under the *Firearms Act* or any other Act of Parliament or any regulations made under any Act of Parliament.

(2) Every person who commits an offence under subsection (1) when the object in question is a prohibited firearm, a restricted firearm, a non-restricted firearm, a prohibited device, any ammunition or any prohibited ammunition is guilty of an indictable offence and liable to imprisonment for a term not exceeding 10 years and to a minimum punishment of imprisonment for a term of

   (a) in the case of a first offence, three years; and

   (b) in the case of a second or subsequent offence, five years.

(3) In any other case, a person who commits an offence under subsection (1) is guilty of an indictable offence and liable to imprisonment for a term not exceeding 10 years and to a minimum punishment of imprisonment for a term of one year. 1995, c. 39, s. 139; 2008, c. 6, s. 11; 2015, c. 27, s. 24.

TRANSFER WITHOUT AUTHORITY / Punishment.

101. (1) Every person commits an offence who transfers a prohibited firearm, a restricted firearm, a non-restricted firearm, a prohibited weapon, a restricted weapon, a prohibited device, any ammunition or any prohibited ammunition to any person otherwise than under the authority of the *Firearms Act* or any other Act of Parliament or any regulations made under an Act of Parliament.

(2) Every person who commits an offence under subsection (1)

(a) is guilty of an indictable offence and liable to imprisonment for a term not exceeding five years; or

(b) is guilty of an offence punishable on summary conviction. 1995, c. 39, s. 139; 2015, c. 27, s. 25.

Assembling Offence

MAKING AUTOMATIC FIREARM / Punishment.

102. (1) Every person commits an offence who, without lawful excuse, alters a firearm so that it is capable of, or manufactures or assembles any firearm that is capable of, discharging projectiles in rapid succession during one pressure of the trigger.

(2) Every person who commits an offence under subsection (1)

(a) is guilty of an indictable offence and liable to imprisonment for a term not exceeding ten years and to a minimum punishment of imprisonment for a term of one year; or

(b) is guilty of an offence punishable on summary conviction. 1995, c. 39, s. 139; 2019, c. 25, s. 27.

Export and Import Offences

IMPORTING OR EXPORTING KNOWING IT IS UNAUTHORIZED / Punishment — firearm / Punishment — other cases / Attorney General of Canada may act.

103. (1) Every person commits an offence who imports or exports

(a) a prohibited firearm, a restricted firearm, a non-restricted firearm, a prohibited weapon, a restricted weapon, a prohibited device or any prohibited ammunition, or

(b) any component or part designed exclusively for use in the manufacture of or assembly into an automatic firearm,

knowing that the person is not authorized to do so under the *Firearms Act* or any other Act of Parliament or any regulations made under an Act of Parliament.

(2) Every person who commits an offence under subsection (1) when the object in question is a prohibited firearm, a restricted firearm, a non-restricted firearm, a prohibited device or any prohibited ammunition is guilty of an indictable offence and liable to imprisonment for a term not exceeding 10 years and to a minimum punishment of imprisonment for a term of

(a) in the case of a first offence, three years; and

(b) in the case of a second or subsequent offence, five years.

(2.1) In any other case, a person who commits an offence under subsection (1) is guilty of an indictable offence and liable to imprisonment for a term not exceeding

10 years and to a minimum punishment of imprisonment for a term of one year. 1995, c. 39, s. 139; 2008, c. 6, s. 12; 2015, c. 27, s. 26; 2019, c. 25, s. 28.

(3) [*Repealed*, 2019, c. 25, s. 28.]

UNAUTHORIZED IMPORTING OR EXPORTING / Punishment / Attorney General of Canada may act.

104. (1) Every person commits an offence who imports or exports

    (*a*) a prohibited firearm, a restricted firearm, a non-restricted firearm, a prohibited weapon, a restricted weapon, a prohibited device or any prohibited ammunition, or

    (*b*) any component or part designed exclusively for use in the manufacture of or assembly into an automatice firearm,

otherwise than under the authority of the *Firearms Act* or any other Act of Parliament or any regulations made under an Act of Parliament.

(2) Every person who commits an offence under subsection (1)

    (*a*) is guilty of an indictable offence and liable to imprisonment for a term not exceeding five years; or

    (*b*) is guilty of an offence punishable on summary conviction. 1995, c. 39, s. 139; 2015, c. 27, s. 27; 2019, c. 25, s. 29.

(3) [*Repealed*, 2019, c. 25, s. 29.]

Offences relating to Lost, Destroyed or Defaced Weapons, etc.

LOSING OR FINDING / Punishment.

105. (1) Every person commits an offence who

    (*a*) having lost a prohibited firearm, a restricted firearm, a non-restricted firearm, a prohibited weapon, a restricted weapon, a prohibited device, any prohibited ammunition, an authorization, a licence or a registration certificate, or having had it stolen from the person's possession, does not with reasonable despatch report the loss to a peace officer, to a firearms officer or a chief firearms officer; or

    (*b*) on finding a prohibited firearm, a restricted firearm, a non-restricted firearm, a prohibited weapon, a restricted weapon, a prohibited device or any prohibited ammunition that the person has reasonable grounds to believe has been lost or abandoned, does not with reasonable despatch deliver it to a peace officer, a firearms officer or a chief firearms officer or report the finding to a peace officer, a firearms officer or a chief firearms officer.

(2) Every person who commits an offence under subsection (1)

    (*a*) is guilty of an indictable offence and liable to imprisonment for a term not exceeding five years; or

    (*b*) is guilty of an offence punishable on summary conviction. 1995, c. 39, s. 139; 2015, c. 27, s. 28.

DESTROYING / Punishment.

106. (1) Every person commits an offence who

    (*a*) after destroying any prohibited firearm, restricted firearm, prohibited weapon, restricted weapon, prohibited device or prohibited ammunition, or

    (*b*) on becoming aware of the destruction of any prohibited firearm, restricted firearm, prohibited weapon, restricted weapon, prohibited device or prohibited ammunition that was in the person's possession before its destruction,

does not with reasonable despatch report the destruction to a peace officer, firearms officer or chief firearms officer.

(2) Every person who commits an offence under subsection (1)

    (*a*) is guilty of an indictable offence and liable to imprisonment for a term not exceeding five years; or

    (*b*) is guilty of an offence punishable on summary conviction. 1995, c. 39, s. 139; 2012, c. 6, s. 6.

FALSE STATEMENTS / Punishment / Definition of "report" or "statement".

107. (1) Every person commits an offence who knowingly makes, before a peace officer, firearms officer or chief firearms officer, a false report or statement concerning the loss, theft or destruction of a prohibited firearm, a restricted firearm, a non-restricted firearm, a prohibited weapon, a restricted weapon, a prohibited device, any prohibited ammunition, an authorization, a licence or a registration certificate.

(2) Every person who commits an offence under subsection (1)

    (*a*) is guilty of an indictable offence and liable to imprisonment for a term not exceeding five years; or

    (*b*) is guilty of an offence punishable on summary conviction.

(3) In this section, "report" or "statement" means an assertion of fact, opinion, belief or knowledge, whether material or not and whether admissible or not. 1995, c. 39, s. 139; 2015, c. 27, s. 29.

TAMPERING WITH SERIAL NUMBER / Punishment / Exception / Evidence.

108. (1) Every person commits an offence who, without lawful excuse,

    (*a*) alters, defaces or removes a serial number on a firearm; or

    (*b*) possesses a firearm knowing that the serial number on it has been altered, defaced or removed.

(2) Every person who commits an offence under subsection (1)

    (*a*) is guilty of an indictable offence and liable to imprisonment for a term not exceeding five years; or

    (*b*) is guilty of an offence punishable on summary conviction.

(3) No person is guilty of an offence under paragraph (1)(*b*) by reason only of possessing a prohibited firearm or restricted firearm the serial number on which has been altered, defaced or removed, if that serial number has been replaced and

a registration certificate in respect of the firearm has been issued setting out a new serial number for the firearm.

(4) In proceedings for an offence under subsection (1), evidence that a person possesses a firearm the serial number on which has been wholly or partially obliterated otherwise than through normal use over time is, in the absence of evidence to the contrary, proof that the person possesses the firearm knowing that the serial number on it has been altered, defaced or removed. 1995, c. 39, s. 139; 2012, c. 6, s. 7; 2018, c. 29, s. 6.

Prohibition Orders

MANDATORY PROHIBITION ORDER / Duration of prohibition order — first offence / Duration of prohibition order — subsequent offences / Definition of "release from imprisonment" / Application of ss. 113 to 117.

109. (1) Where a person is convicted, or discharged under section 730, of

- (*a*) an indictable offence in the commission of which violence against a person was used, threatened or attempted and for which the person may be sentenced to imprisonment for ten years or more,

- (*a*.1) an indictable offence in the commission of which violence was used, threatened or attempted against

  - (i) the person's intimate partner,

  - (ii) a child or parent of the person or of anyone referred to in subparagraph (i), or

  - (iii) any person who resides with the person or with anyone referred to in subparagraph (i) or (ii),

- (*b*) an offence under subsection 85(1) (using firearm in commission of offence), subsection 85(2) (using imitation firearm in commission of offence), 95(1) (possession of prohibited or restricted firearm with ammunition), 99(1) (weapons trafficking), 100(1) (possession for purpose of weapons trafficking), 102(1) (making automatic firearm), 103(1) (importing or exporting knowing it is unauthorized) or section 264 (criminal harassment),

- (*c*) an offence relating to the contravention of subsection 5(1) or (2), 6(1) or (2) or 7(1) of the *Controlled Drugs and Substances Act*,

- (*c*.1) an offence relating to the contravention of subsection 9(1) or (2), 10(1) or (2), 11(1) or (2), 12(1), (4), (5), (6) or (7), 13(1) or 14(1) of the *Cannabis Act*, or

- (*d*) an offence that involves, or the subject-matter of which is, a firearm, a cross-bow, a prohibited weapon, a restricted weapon, a prohibited device, any ammunition, any prohibited ammunition or an explosive substance and, at the time of the offence, the person was prohibited by any order made under this Act or any other Act of Parliament from possessing any such thing,

the court that sentences the person or directs that the person be discharged, as the case may be, shall, in addition to any other punishment that may be imposed for that offence or any other condition prescribed in the order of discharge, make an order prohibiting the person from possessing any firearm, cross-bow, prohibited weapon, restricted weapon, prohibited device, ammunition, prohibited ammunition and explosive substance during the period specified in the order as determined in accordance with subsection (2) or (3), as the case may be.

(2) An order made under subsection (1) shall, in the case of a first conviction for or discharge from the offence to which the order relates, prohibit the person from posssessing

   (*a*) any firearm, other than a prohibited firearm or restricted firearm, and any cross-bow, restricted weapon, ammunition and explosive substance during the period that

      (i) begins on the day on which the order is made, and

      (ii) ends not earlier than ten years after the person's release from imprisonment after conviction for the offence or, if the person is not then imprisoned or subject to imprisonment, after the person's conviction for or discharge from the offence; and

   (*b*) any prohibited firearm, restricted firearm, prohibited weapon, prohibited device and prohibited ammunition for life.

(3) An order made under subsection (1) shall, in any case other than a case described in subsection (2), prohibit the person from possessing any firearm, cross-bow, restricted weapon, ammunition and explosive substance for life.

(4) In subparagraph (2)(*a*)(ii), "release from imprisonment" means release from confinement by reason of expiration of sentence, commencement of statutory release or grant of parole.

(5) Sections 113 to 117 apply in respect of every order made under subsection (1). 1995, c. 39, ss. 139, 188(*a*), 190(*d*); 1996, c. 19, s. 65.1; 2003, c. 8, s. 4; 2015, c. 27, s. 30; 2018, c. 16, s. 208; 2019, c. 25, s. 30.

DISCRETIONARY PROHIBITION ORDER / Duration of prohibition order / Exception / Reasons / Definition of "release from imprisonment" / Application of ss. 113 to 117.

110. (1) Where a person is convicted, or discharged under section 730, of

   (*a*) an offence, other than an offence referred to in any of paragraphs 109(1)(*a*) to (*c*.1), in the commission of which violence against a person was used, threatened or attempted, or

   (*b*) an offence that involves, or the subject-matter of which is, a firearm, a cross-bow, a prohibited weapon, a restricted weapon, a prohibited device, ammunition, prohibited ammunition or an explosive substance and, at the time of the offence, the person was not prohibited by any order made under this Act or any other Act of Parliament from possessing any such thing,

the court that sentences the person or directs that the person be discharged, as the case may be, shall, in addition to any other punishment that may be imposed for that offence or any other condition prescribed in the order of discharge, consider whether it is desirable, in the interests of the safety of the person or of any other person, to make an order prohibiting the person from possessing any firearm, cross-bow, prohibited weapon, restricted weapon, prohibited device, ammunition, prohibited ammunition or explosive substance, or all such things, and where the court decides that it is so desirable, the court shall so order.

(2) An order made under subsection (1) against a person begins on the day on which the order is made and ends not later than ten years after the person's release from imprisonment after conviction for the offence to which the order relates or, if the person is not then imprisoned or subject to imprisonment, after the person's conviction for or discharge from the offence.

(2.1) Despite subsection (2), an order made under subsection (1) may be imposed for life or for any shorter duration if, in the commission of the offence, violence was used, threatened or attempted against

    (*a*) the person's intimate partner;

    (*b*) a child or parent of the person or of anyone referred to in paragraph (*a*); or

    (*c*) any person who resides with the person or with anyone referred to in paragraph (*a*) or (*b*).

(3) Where the court does not make an order under subsection (1), or where the court does make such an order but does not prohibit the possession of everything referred to in that subsection, the court shall include in the record a statement of the court's reasons for not doing so.

(4) In subsection (2), "release from imprisonment" means release from confinement by reason of expiration of sentence, commencement of statutory release or grant of parole.

(5) Sections 113 to 117 apply in respect of every order made under subsection (1).
1995, c. 39, ss. 139, 190(*e*); 2015, c. 27, s. 31; 2018, c. 16, s. 209; 2019, c. 25, s. 31.

110.1 [*Repealed*, 2019, c. 25, s. 32.]

APPLICATION FOR PROHIBITION ORDER / Date for hearing and notice / Hearing of application / Where hearing may proceed *ex parte* / Prohibition order / Reasons / Application of ss. 113 to 117 / Appeal by person or Attorney General / Appeal by Attorney General / Application of Part XXVII to appeals / Definition of "provincial court judge".

111. (1) A peace officer, firearms officer or chief firearms officer may apply to a provincial court judge for an order prohibiting a person from possessing any firearm, cross-bow, prohibited weapon, restricted weapon, prohibited device, ammunition, prohibited ammunition or explosive substance, or all such things, where the peace officer, firearms officer or chief firearms officer believes on reasonable grounds that it is not desirable in the interests of the safety of the person against whom the order is sought or of any other person that the person against whom the order is sought should possess any such thing.

(2) On receipt of an application made under subsection (1), the provincial court judge shall fix a date for the hearing of the application and direct that notice of the hearing be given, in such manner as the provincial court judge may specify, to the person against whom the order is sought.

(3) Subject to subsection (4), at the hearing of an application made under subsection (1), the provincial court judge shall hear all relevant evidence presented by or on behalf of the applicant and the person against whom the order is sought.

(4) A provincial court judge may proceed *ex parte* to hear and determine an application made under subsection (1) in the absence of the person against whom the order is sought in the same circumstances as those in which a summary conviction court may, under Part XXVII, proceed with a trial in the absence of the defendant.

(5) Where, at the conclusion of a hearing of an application made under subsection (1), the provincial court judge is satisfied that the circumstances referred to in that subsection exist, the provincial court judge shall make an order prohibiting the person from possessing any firearm, cross-bow, prohibited weapon, restricted weapon, prohibited device, ammunition, prohibited ammunition or explosive substance, or all such things, for such period, not exceeding five years, as is specified in the order, beginning on the day on which the order is made.

(6) Where a provincial court judge does not make an order under subsection (1), or where a provincial court judge does make such an order but does not prohibit the possession of everything referred to in that subsection, the provincial court judge shall include in the record a statement of the court's reasons.

(7) Sections 113 to 117 apply in respect of every order made under subsection (5).

(8) Where a provincial court judge makes an order under subsection (5), the person to whom the order relates, or the Attorney General, may appeal to the superior court against the order.

(9) Where a provincial court judge does not make an order under subsection (5), the Attorney General may appeal to the superior court against the decision not to make an order.

(10) The provisions of Part XXVII, except sections 785 to 812, 816 to 819 and 829 to 838, apply in respect of an appeal made under subsection (8) or (9), with such modifications as the circumstances require and as if each reference in that Part to the appeal court were a reference to the superior court.

(11) In this section and sections 112, 117.011 and 117.012, "provincial court judge" means a provincial court judge having jurisdiction in the territorial division where the person against whom the application for an order was brought resides. 1995, c. 39, s. 139.

REVOCATION OF PROHIBITION ORDER UNDER S. 111(5).

112. A provincial court judge may, on application by the person against whom an order is made under subsection 111(5), revoke the order if satisfied that the circumstances for which it was made have ceased to exist. 1995, c. 39, s. 139.

LIFTING OF PROHIBITION ORDER FOR SUSTENANCE OR EMPLOYMENT / Factors / Effect of order / When order can be made / Meaning of "competent authority".

113. (1) Where a person who is or will be a person against whom a prohibition order is made establishes to the satisfaction of a competent authority that

    (*a*) the person needs a firearm or restricted weapon to hunt or trap in order to sustain the person or the person's family, or

    (*b*) a prohibition order against the person would constitute a virtual prohibition against employment in the only vocation open to the person,

the competent authority may, notwithstanding that the person is or will be subject to a prohibition order, make an order authorizing a chief firearms officer or the Registrar to issue, in accordance with such terms and conditions as the competent authority considers appropriate, an authorization, a licence or a registration certificate, as the case may be, to the person for sustenance or employment purposes.

(2) A competent authority may make an order under subsection (1) only after taking the following factors into account:

    (*a*) the criminal record, if any, of the person;

    (*b*) the nature and circumstances of the offence, if any, in respect of which the prohibition order was or will be made; and

    (*c*) the safety of the person and of other persons.

(3) Where an order is made under subsection (1),

    (*a*) an authorization, a licence or a registration certificate may not be denied to the person in respect of whom the order was made solely on the basis of a prohibition order against the person or the commission of an offence in respect of which a prohibition order was made against the person; and

    (*b*) an authorization and a licence may, for the duration of the order, be issued to the person in respect of whom the order was made only for sustenance or employment purposes and, where the order sets out terms and conditions, only in accordance with those terms and conditions but, for greater certainty, the authorization or licence may also be subject to terms and conditions set by the chief firearms officer that are not inconsistent with the purpose for which it is issued and any terms and conditions set out in the order.

(4) For greater certainty, an order under subsection (1) may be made during proceedings for an order under subsection 109(1), 110(1), 111(5), 117.05(4) or 515(2), paragraph 732.1(3)(*d*) or subsection 810(3).

(5) In this section, "competent authority" means the competent authority that made or has jurisdiction to make the prohibition order. 1995, c. 39, ss. 139, 190(*f*).

REQUIREMENT TO SURRENDER.

114. A competent authority that makes a prohibition order against a person may, in the order, require the person to surrender to a peace officer, a firearms officer or a chief firearms officer

   (a) any thing the possession of which is prohibited by the order that is in the possession of the person on the commencement of the order, and

   (b) every authorization, licence and registration certificate relating to any thing the possession of which is prohibited by the order that is held by the person on the commencement of the order,

and where the competent authority does so, it shall specify in the order a reasonable period for surrendering such things and documents and during which section 117.01 does not apply to that person. 1995, c. 39, s. 139.

FORFEITURE / Exception / Disposal.

115. (1) Unless a prohibition order against a person specifies otherwise, every thing the possession of which is prohibited by the order is forfeited to Her Majesty if, on the commencement of the order, the thing is in the person's possession or has been seized and detained by, or surrendered to, a peace officer.

(1.1) Subsection (1) does not apply in respect of an order made under section 515.

(2) Every thing forfeited to Her Majesty under subsection (1) shall be disposed of or otherwise dealt with as the Attorney General directs. 1995, c. 39, s. 139; 2003, c. 8, s. 5; 2019, c. 9, s. 17.

AUTHORIZATIONS REVOKED OR AMENDED / Duration of revocation or amendment — orders under s. 115.

116. (1) Subject to subsection (2), every authorization, licence and registration certificate relating to any thing the possession of which is prohibited by a prohibition order and issued to a person against whom the prohibition order is made is, on the commencement of the prohibition order, revoked, or amended, as the case may be, to the extent of the prohibitions in the order.

(2) An authorization, a licence and a registration certificate relating to a thing the possession of which is prohibited by an order made under section 515 is revoked, or amended, as the case may be, only in respect of the period during which the order is in force. 1995, c. 39, s. 139; 2003, c. 8, s. 6.

RETURN TO OWNER.

117. Where the competent authority that makes a prohibition order or that would have had jurisdiction to make the order is, on application for an order under this section, satisfied that a person, other than the person against whom a prohibition order was or will be made,

   (a) is the owner of any thing that is or may be forfeited to Her Majesty under subsection 115(1) and is lawfully entitled to possess it, and

   (b) in the case of a prohibition order under subsection 109(1) or 110(1), had no reasonable grounds to believe that the thing would or might be used in the commission of the offence in respect of which the prohibition order was made,

the competent authority shall order that the thing be returned to the owner or the proceeds of any sale of the thing be paid to that owner or, if the thing was destroyed, that an amount equal to the value of the thing be paid to the owner. 1995, c. 39, s. 139.

CODE

POSSESSION CONTRARY TO ORDER / Failure to surrender authorization, etc. / Punishment / Exception.

117.01 (1) Subject to subsection (4), every person commits an offence who possesses a firearm, a cross-bow, a prohibited weapon, a restricted weapon, a prohibited device, any ammunition, any prohibited ammunition or an explosive substance while the person is prohibited from doing so by any order made under this Act or any other Act of Parliament.

(2) Every person commits an offence who wilfully fails to surrender to a peace officer, a firearms officer or a chief firearms officer any authorization, licence or registration certificate held by the person when the person is required to do so by any order made under this Act or any other Act of Parliament.

(3) Every person who commits an offence under subsection (1) or (2)

   (a) is guilty of an indictable offence and liable to imprisonment for a term not exceeding ten years; or

   (b) is guilty of an offence punishable on summary conviction.

(4) Subsection (1) does not apply to a person who possessed a firearm in accordance with an authorization or licence issued to the person as the result of an order made under subsection 113(1). 1995, c. 39, s. 139.

Limitations on Access

APPLICATION FOR ORDER / Date for hearing and notice / Hearing of application / Where hearing may proceed *ex parte* / Order / Terms and conditions / Appeal by person or Attorney General / Appeal by Attorney General / Application of Part XXVII to appeals.

117.011 (1) A peace officer, firearms officer or chief firearms officer may apply to a provincial court judge for an order under this section where the peace officer, firearms officer or chief firearms officer believes on reasonable grounds that

   (a) the person against whom the order is sought cohabits with, or is an associate of, another person who is prohibited by any order made under this Act or any other Act of Parliament from possessing any firearm, cross-bow, prohibited weapon, restricted weapon, prohibited device, ammunition, prohibited ammunition or explosive substance, or all such things; and

   (b) the other person would or might have access to any such thing that is in the possession of the person against whom the order is sought.

(2) On receipt of an application made under subsection (1), the provincial court judge shall fix a date for the hearing of the application and direct that notice of the hearing be given, in such manner as the provincial court judge may specify, to the person against whom the order is sought.

(3) Subject to subsection (4), at the hearing of an application made under subsection (1), the provincial court judge shall hear all relevant evidence

presented by or on behalf of the applicant and the person against whom the order is sought.

(4) A provincial court judge may proceed *ex parte* to hear and determine an application made under subsection (1) in the absence of the person against whom the order is sought in the same circumstances as those in which a summary conviction court may, under Part XXVII, proceed with a trial in the absence of the defendant.

(5) Where, at the conclusion of a hearing of an application made under subsection (1), the provincial court judge is satisfied that the circumstances referred to in that subsection exist, the provincial court judge shall make an order in respect of the person against whom the order was sought imposing such terms and conditions on the person's use and possession of anything referred to in subsection (1) as the provincial court judge considers appropriate.

(6) In determining terms and conditions under subsection (5), the provincial court judge shall impose terms and conditions that are the least intrusive as possible, bearing in mind the purpose of the order.

(7) Where a provincial court judge makes an order under subsection (5), the person to whom the order relates, or the Attorney General, may appeal to the superior court against the order.

(8) Where a provincial court judge does not make an order under subsection (5), the Attorney General may appeal to the superior court against the decision not to make an order.

(9) The provisions of Part XXVII, except sections 785 to 812, 816 to 819 and 829 to 838, apply in respect of an appeal made under subsection (7) or (8), with such modifications as the circumstances require and as if each reference in that Part to the appeal court were a reference to the superior court. 1995, c. 39, s. 139.

REVOCATION OF ORDER UNDER S. 117.011.

117.012 A provincial court judge may, on application by the person against whom an order is made under subsection 117.011(5), revoke the order if satisfied that the circumstances for which it was made have ceased to exist. 1995, c. 39, s. 139.

Search and Seizure

SEARCH AND SEIZURE WITHOUT WARRANT WHERE OFFENCE COMMITTED / Disposition of seized things.

117.02 (1) Where a peace officer believes on reasonable grounds

    (*a*) that a weapon, an imitation firearm, a prohibited device, any ammunition, any prohibited ammunition or an explosive substance was used in the commission of an offence, or

    (*b*) that an offence is being committed, or has been committed, under any provision of this Act that involves, or the subject-matter of which is, a firearm, an imitation firearm, a cross-bow, a prohibited weapon, a restricted weapon, a prohibited device, ammunition, prohibited ammunition or an explosive substance,

and evidence of the offence is likely to be found on a person, in a vehicle or in any place or premises other than a dwelling-house, the peace officer may, where the conditions for obtaining a warrant exist but, by reason of exigent circumstances, it would not be practicable to obtain a warrant, search, without warrant, the person, vehicle, place or premises, and seize any thing by means of or in relation to which that peace officer believes on reasonable grounds the offence is being committed or has been committed.

(2) Any thing seized pursuant to subsection (1) shall be dealt with in accordance with sections 490 and 491. 1995, c. 39, s. 139.

SEIZURE ON FAILURE TO PRODUCE AUTHORIZATION / Return of seized thing on production of authorization / Forfeiture of seized thing.

117.03 (1) Despite section 117.02, a peace officer who finds

(a) a person in possession of a prohibited firearm, a restricted firearm or a non-restricted firearm who fails, on demand, to produce, for inspection by the peace officer, an authorization or a licence under which the person may lawfully possess the firearm and, in the case of a prohibited firearm or a restricted firearm, a registration certificate for it, or

(b) a person in possession of a prohibited weapon, a restricted weapon, a prohibited device or any prohibited ammunition who fails, on demand, to produce, for inspection by the peace officer, an authorization or a licence under which the person may lawfully possess it,

may seize the firearm, prohibited weapon, restricted weapon, prohibited device or prohibited ammunition unless its possession by the person in the circumstances in which it is found is authorized by any provision of this Part, or the person is under the direct and immediate supervision of another person who may lawfully possess it.

(2) If a person from whom any thing is seized under subsection (1) claims the thing within 14 days after the seizure and produces for inspection by the peace officer by whom it was seized, or any other peace officer having custody of it,

(a) a licence under which the person is lawfully entitled to possess it, and

(b) in the case of a prohibited firearm or a restricted firearm, an authorization and registration certificate for it,

the thing shall without delay be returned to that person.

(3) Where any thing seized pursuant to subsection (1) is not claimed and returned as and when provided by subsection (2), a peace officer shall forthwith take the thing before a provincial court judge, who may, after affording the person from whom it was seized or its owner, if known, an opportunity to establish that the person is lawfully entitled to possess it, declare it to be forfeited to Her Majesty, to be disposed of or otherwise dealt with as the Attorney General directs. 1995, c. 39, s. 139; 2012, c. 6, s. 8; 2015, c. 27, s. 33.

APPLICATION FOR WARRANT TO SEARCH AND SEIZE / Search and seizure without warrant / Return to justice / Authorizations, etc., revoked.

117.04 (1) Where, pursuant to an application made by a peace officer with respect to any person, a justice is satisfied by information on oath that there are reasonable grounds to believe that the person possesses a weapon, a prohibited device, ammunition, prohibited ammunition or an explosive substance in a building, receptacle or place and that it is not desirable in the interests of the safety of the person, or of any other person, for the person to possess the weapon, prohibited device, ammunition, prohibited ammunition or explosive substance, the justice may issue a warrant authorizing a peace officer to search the building, receptacle or place and seize any such thing, and any authorization, licence or registration certificate relating to any such thing, that is held by or in the possession of the person.

(2) Where, with respect to any person, a peace officer is satisfied that there are reasonable grounds to believe that it is not desirable, in the interests of the safety of the person or any other person, for the person to possess any weapon, prohibited device, ammunition, prohibited ammunition or explosive substance, the peace officer may, where the grounds for obtaining a warrant under subsection (1) exist but, by reason of a possible danger to the safety of that person or any other person, it would not be practicable to obtain a warrant, search for and seize any such thing, and any authorization, licence or registration certificate relating to any such thing, that is held by or in the possession of the person.

(3) A peace officer who executes a warrant referred to in subsection (1) or who conducts a search without a warrant under subsection (2) shall forthwith make a return to the justice who issued the warrant or, if no warrant was issued, to a justice who might otherwise have issued a warrant, showing

    (*a*) in the case of an execution of a warrant, the things or documents, if any, seized and the date of execution of the warrant; and

    (*b*) in the case of a search conducted without a warrant, the grounds on which it was concluded that the peace officer was entitled to conduct the search, and the things or documents, if any, seized.

(4) Where a peace officer who seizes any thing under subsection (1) or (2) is unable at the time of the seizure to seize an authorization or a licence under which the person from whom the thing was seized may possess the thing and, in the case of a seized firearm, a registration certificate for the firearm, every authorization, licence and registration certificate held by the person is, as at the time of the seizure, revoked. 1995, c. 39, s. 139; 2004, c. 12, s. 3.

APPLICATION FOR DISPOSITION / *Ex parte* hearing / Hearing of application / Forfeiture and prohibition order on finding / Reasons / Application of ss. 113 to 117 / Appeal by person / Appeal by Attorney General / Application of part XXVII to appeals.

117.05 (1) Where any thing or document has been seized under subsection 117.04(1) or (2), the justice who issued the warrant authorizing the seizure or, if no warrant was issued, a justice who might otherwise have issued a warrant, shall, on application for an order for the disposition of the thing or document so seized made by a peace officer within thirty days after the date of execution of the warrant or of the seizure without a warrant, as the case may be, fix a date for the hearing of the application and direct that notice of the hearing be given to such persons or in such manner as the justice may specify.

(2) A justice may proceed *ex parte* to hear and determine an application made under subsection (1) in the absence of the person from whom the thing or document was seized in the same circumstances as those in which a summary conviction court may, under Part XXVII, proceed with a trial in the absence of the defendant.

(3) At the hearing of an application made under subsection (1), the justice shall hear all relevant evidence, including evidence respecting the value of the thing in respect of which the application was made.

(4) Where, following the hearing of an application made under subsection (1), the justice finds that it is not desirable in the interests of the safety of the person from whom the thing was seized or of any other person that the person should possess any weapon, prohibited device, ammunition, prohibited ammunition and explosive substance, or any such thing, the justice shall

   (*a*) order that any thing seized be forfeited to Her Majesty or be otherwise disposed of; and

   (*b*) where the justice is satisfied that the circumstances warrant such an action, order that the possession by that person of any weapon, prohibited device, ammunition, prohibited ammunition and explosive substance, or of any such thing, be prohibited during any period, not exceeding five years, that is specified in the order, beginning on the making of the order.

(5) Where a justice does not make an order under subsection (4), or where a justice does make such an order but does not prohibit the possession of all of the things referred to in that subsection, the justice shall include in the record a statement of the justice's reasons.

(6) Sections 113 to 117 apply in respect of every order made under subsection (4).

(7) Where a justice makes an order under subsection (4) in respect of a person, or in respect of any thing that was seized from a person, the person may appeal to the superior court against the order.

(8) Where a justice does not make a finding as described in subsection (4) following the hearing of an application under subsection (1), or makes the finding but does not make an order to the effect described in paragraph (4)(*b*), the Attorney General may appeal to the superior court against the failure to make the finding or to make an order to the effect so described.

(9) The provisions of Part XXVII, except sections 785 to 812, 816 to 819 and 829 to 838, apply in respect of an appeal made under subsection (7) or (8) with such modifications as the circumstances require and as if each reference in that Part to the appeal court were a reference to the superior court. 1995, c. 39, s. 139.

WHERE NO FINDING OR APPLICATION / Restoration of authorizations.

117.06 (1) Any thing or document seized pursuant to subsection 117.04(1) or (2) shall be returned to the person from whom it was seized if

    (*a*) no application is made under subsection 117.05(1) within thirty days after the date of execution of the warrant or of the seizure without a warrant, as the case may be; or

    (*b*) an application is made under subsection 117.05(1) within the period referred to in paragraph (*a*), and the justice does not make a finding as described in subsection 117.05(4).

(2) Where, pursuant to subsection (1), any thing is returned to the person from whom it was seized and an authorization, a licence or a registration certificate, as the case may be, is revoked pursuant to subsection 117.04(4), the justice referred to in paragraph (1)(*b*) may order that the revocation be reversed and that the authorization, licence or registration certificate be restored. 1995, c. 39, s. 139.

Exempted Persons

PUBLIC OFFICERS / Definition of "public officer".

117.07 (1) Notwithstanding any other provision of this Act, but subject to section 117.1, no public officer is guilty of an offence under this Act or the *Firearms Act* by reason only that the public officer

    (*a*) possesses a firearm, a prohibited weapon, a restricted weapon, a prohibited device, any prohibited ammunition or an explosive substance in the course of or for the purpose of the public officer's duties or employment;

    (*b*) manufactures or transfers, or offers to manufacture or transfer, a firearm, a prohibited weapon, a restricted weapon, a prohibited device, any ammunition or any prohibited ammunition in the course of the public officer's duties or employment;

    (*c*) exports or imports a firearm, a prohibited weapon, a restricted weapon, a prohibited device or any prohibited ammunition in the course of the public officer's duties or employment;

    (*d*) exports or imports a component or part designed exclusively for use in the manufacture of or assembly into an automatic firearm in the course of the public officer's duties or employment;

    (*e*) in the course of the public officer's duties or employment, alters a firearm so that it is capable of, or manufactures or assembles any firearm with intent to produce a firearm that is capable of, discharging projectiles in rapid succession during one pressure of the trigger;

    (*f*) fails to report the loss, theft or finding of any firearm, prohibited weapon, restricted weapon, prohibited device, ammunition, prohibited ammunition or explosive substance that occurs in the course of the public officer's duties or employment or the destruction of any such thing in the course of the public officer's duties or employment; or

    (*g*) alters a serial number on a firearm in the course of the public officer's duties or employment.

(2) In this section, "public officer" means
  (*a*) a peace officer;
  (*b*) a member of the Canadian Forces or of the armed forces of a state other than Canada who is attached or seconded to any of the Canadian forces;
  (*c*) an operator of a museum established by the Chief of the Defence Staff or a person employed in any such museum;
  (*d*) a member of a cadet organization under the control and supervision of the Canadian Forces;
  (*e*) a person training to become a police officer or a peace officer under the control and supervision of
     (i) a police force, or
     (ii) a police academy or similar institution designated by the Attorney General of Canada or the lieutenant governor in council of a province;
  (*f*) a member of a visiting force, within the meaning of section 2 of the *Visiting Forces Act*, who is authorized under paragraph 14(*a*) of that Act to possess and carry explosives, ammunition and firearms;
  (*g*) a person, or member of a class of persons, employed in the federal public administration or by the government of a province or municipality who is prescribed to be a public officer; or
  (*h*) the Commissioner of Firearms, the Registrar, a chief firearms officer, any firearms officer and any person designated under section 100 of the *Firearms Act*. 1995, c. 39, s. 139; 2003, c. 8, s. 7; c. 22, s. 224(*z*.23).

PRECLEARANCE OFFICERS.

117.071 Despite any other provision of this Act, but subject to section 117.1, no "*preclearance officer*", as defined in section 5 of the *Preclearance Act, 2016*, is guilty of an offence under this Act or the *Firearms Act* by reason only that the preclearance officer
  (*a*) possesses a firearm, a prohibited weapon, a restricted weapon, a prohibited device or any prohibited ammunition in the course of or for the purpose of their duties or employment;
  (*b*) transfers or offers to transfer a firearm, a prohibited weapon, a restricted weapon, a prohibited device, any ammunition or any prohibited ammunition in the course of their duties or employment;
  (*c*) exports or imports a firearm, a prohibited weapon, a restricted weapon, a prohibited device or any prohibited ammunition in the course of their duties or employment; or
  (*d*) fails to report the loss, theft or finding of any firearm, prohibited weapon, restricted weapon, prohibited device, ammunition, prohibited ammunition or explosive substance that occurs in the course of their duties or employment or the destruction of any such thing in the course of their duties or employment. 2017, c. 27, s. 61.

REGULATIONS PRESCRIBING PUBLIC OFFICERS

1. (1) A member of any of the following classes of persons, if employed in the public service of Canada or by the government of a province or municipality, is a public officer for the purposes of paragraph 117.07(2)(*g*) of the *Criminal Code*:

   (*a*) employees who are responsible for the examination, inventory, storage, maintenance or transportation of court exhibits and evidence;

   (*b*) employees of police forces or other public service agencies who are responsible for the acquisition, examination, inventory, storage, maintenance, issuance or transportation of firearms, prohibited weapons, restricted weapons, prohibited devices, prohibited ammunition or explosive substances;

   (*c*) technicians, laboratory analysts and scientists who work at forensic or research laboratories;

   (*d*) armourers and firearms instructors who work at police academies or similar institutions designated under subparagraph 117.07(2)(*e*)(ii) of the *Criminal Code*, or are employed by a federal or provincial department of natural resources, fisheries, wildlife, conservation or the environment, or by Revenue Canada;

   (*e*) park wardens and other employees of a federal or provincial department who are responsible for the enforcement of laws and regulations dealing with natural resources, fisheries, wildlife, conservation or the environment;

   (*f*) immigration officers;

   (*g*) security personnel employed by the House of Commons or the Senate or by the Service, as defined in section 79.51 of the *Parliament of Canada Act*; and

   (*h*) aircraft pilots employed by the Department of Transport or other public service agencies.

(2) For the purposes of subsection (1), the expression "public service agencies" has the same meaning as in section 1 of the Public Agents Firearms Regulations.

Coming into Force

2. These Regulations come into force on December 1, 1998. **SOR/98-466; SOR/98-472; SOR/2011-68; SOR/2015-166, s. 1.**

INDIVIDUALS ACTING FOR POLICE FORCE, CANADIAN FORCES AND VISITING FORCES.

117.08 Notwithstanding any other provision of this Act, but subject to section 117.1, no individual is guilty of an offence under this Act or the *Firearms Act* by reason only that the individual

   (*a*) possesses a firearm, a prohibited weapon, a restricted weapon, a prohibited device, any prohibited ammunition or an explosive substance,

   (*b*) manufactures or transfers, or offers to manufacture or transfer, a firearm, a prohibited weapon, a restricted weapon, a prohibited device, any ammunition or any prohibited ammunition,

(c) exports or imports a firearm, a prohibited weapon, a restricted weapon, a prohibited device or any prohibited ammunition,

(d) exports or imports a component or part designed exclusively for use in the manufacture of or assembly into an automatic firearm,

(e) alters a firearm so that it is capable of, or manufactures or assembles any firearm with intent to produce a firearm that is capable of, discharging projectiles in rapid succession during one pressure of the trigger,

(f) fails to report the loss, theft or finding of any firearm, prohibited weapon, restricted weapon, prohibited device, ammunition, prohibited ammunition or explosive substance or the destruction of any such thing, or

(g) alters a serial number on a firearm,

if the individual does so on behalf of, and under the authority of, a police force, the Canadian Forces, a visiting force, within the meaning of section 2 of the *Visiting Forces Act*, or a department of the Government of Canada or of a province. 1995, c. 39, s. 139.

EMPLOYEES OF BUSINESS WITH LICENCE / Employees of business with licence / Employees of carriers / Employees of museums handling functioning imitation antique firearm / Employees of museums handling firearms generally / Public safety / Conditions.

117.09 (1) Notwithstanding any other provision of this Act, but subject to section 117.1, no individual who is the holder of a licence to possess and acquire restricted firearms and who is employed by a business as defined in subsection 2(1) of the *Firearms Act* that itself is the holder of a licence that authorizes the business to carry out specified activities in relation to prohibited firearms, prohibited weapons, prohibited devices or prohibited ammunition is guilty of an offence under this Act or the *Firearms Act* by reason only that the individual, in the course of the individual's duties or employment in relation to those specified activities,

(a) possesses a prohibited firearm, a prohibited weapon, a prohibited device or any prohibited ammunition;

(b) manufactures or transfers, or offers to manufacture or transfer, a prohibited weapon, a prohibited device or any prohibited ammunition;

(c) alters a firearm so that it is capable of, or manufactures or assembles any firearm with intent to produce a firearm that is capable of, discharging projectiles in rapid succession during one pressure of the trigger; or

(d) alters a serial number on a firearm.

(2) Notwithstanding any other provision of this Act, but subject to section 117.1, no individual who is employed by a business as defined in subsection 2(1) of the *Firearms Act* that itself is the holder of a licence is guilty of an offence under this Act or the *Firearms Act* by reason only that the individual, in the course of the individual's duties or employment, possesses, manufactures or transfers, or offers to manufacture or transfer, a partially manufactured barrelled weapon that, in its unfinished state, is not a barrelled weapon from which any shot, bullet or other projectile can be discharged and that is capable of causing serious bodily injury or death to a person.

(3) Notwithstanding any other provision of this Act, but subject to section 117.1, no individual who is employed by a carrier, as defined in subsection 2(1) of the *Firearms Act*, is guilty of an offence under this Act or that Act by reason only that the individual, in the course of the individual's duties or employment, possesses any firearm, cross-bow, prohibited weapon, restricted weapon, prohibited device, ammunition or prohibited ammunition or transfers, or offers to transfer any such thing.

(4) Notwithstanding any other provision of this Act, but subject to section 117.1, no individual who is employed by a museum as defined in subsection 2(1) of the *Firearms Act* that itself is the holder of a licence is guilty of an offence under this Act or the *Firearms Act* by reason only that the individual, in the course of the individual's duties or employment, possesses or transfers a firearm that is designed or intended to exactly resemble, or to resemble with near precision, an antique firearm if the individual has been trained to handle and use such a firearm.

(5) Notwithstanding any other provision of this Act, but subject to section 117.1, no individual who is employed by a museum as defined in subsection 2(1) of the *Firearms Act* that itself is the holder of a licence is guilty of an offence under this Act or the *Firearms Act* by reason only that the individual possesses or transfers a firearm in the course of the individual's duties or employment if the individual is designated, by name, by a provincial minister within the meaning of subsection 2(1) of the *Firearms Act*.

(6) A provincial minister shall not designate an individual for the purpose of subsection (5) where it is not desirable, in the interests of the safety of any person, to designate the individual.

(7) A provincial minister may attach to a designation referred to in subsection (4) any reasonable condition that the provincial minister considers desirable in the particular circumstances and in the itnerests of the safety of any person. 1995, c. 39, s. 139.

RESTRICTION.

117.1 Sections 117.07 to 117.09 do not apply if the public officer or the individual is subject to a prohibition order and acts contrary to that order or to an authorization or a licence issued under the authority of an order made under subsection 113(1). 1995, c. 39, s. 139.

General

ONUS ON THE ACCUSED.

117.11 Where, in any proceedings for an offence under any of sections 89, 90, 91, 93, 97, 101, 104 and 105, any question arises as to whether a person is the holder of an authorization, a licence or a registration certificate, the onus is on the accused to prove that the person is the holder of the authorization, licence or registration certificate. 1995, c. 39, s. 139.

AUTHORIZATIONS, ETC., AS EVIDENCE / Certified copies.

117.12 (1) In any proceedings under this Act or any other Act of Parliament, a document purporting to be an authorization, a licence or a registration certificate is evidence of the statements contained therein.

(2) In any proceedings under this Act or any other Act of Parliament, a copy of any authorization, licence or registration certificate is, if certified as a true copy by the Registrar or a chief firearms officer, admissible in evidence and, in the absence of evidence to the contrary, has the same probative force as the authorization, licence or registration certificate would have had if it had been proved in the ordinary way. 1995, c. 39, s. 139.

CERTIFICATE OF ANALYST / Attendance of analyst / Notice of intention to produce certificate.

117.13 (1) A certificate purporting to be signed by an analyst stating that the analyst has analyzed any weapon, prohibited device, ammunition, prohibited ammunition or explosive substance, or any part or component of such a thing, and stating the results of the analysis is evidence in any proceedings in relation to any of those things under this Act or under section 19 of the *Export and Import Permits Act* in relation to subsection 15(2) of that Act without proof of the signature or official character of the person appearing to have signed the certificate.

(2) The party against whom a certificate of an analyst is produce may, with leave of the court, require the attendance of the analyst for the purposes of cross-examination.

(3) No certificate of an analyst may be admitted in evidence unless the party intending to produce it has, before the trial, given to the party against whom it is intended to be produced reasonable notice of that intention together with a copy of the certificate. 1995, c. 39, s. 139; 2008, c. 18, s. 2.

(4) and (5) [*Repealed*, 2008, c. 18, s. 2.]

AMNESTY PERIOD / Purposes of amnesty period / Reliance on amnesty period / Proceedings are a nullity.

117.14 (1) The Governor in Council may, by order, declare for any purpose referred to in subsection (2) any period as an amnesty period with respect to any weapon, prohibited device, prohibited ammunition, explosive substance or component or part designed exclusively for use in the manufacture of or assembly into an automatic firearm.

(2) An order made under subsection (1) may declare an amnesty period for the purpose of

    (*a*) permitting any person in possession of any thing to which the order relates to do anything provided in the order, including, without restricting the generality of the foregoing, delivering the thing to a peace officer, a firearms officer or a chief firearms officer, registering it, destroying it or otherwise disposing of it; or

(b) permitting alterations to be made to any prohibited firearm, prohibited weapon, prohibited device or prohibited ammunition to which the order relates so that it no longer qualifies as a prohibited firearm, a prohibited weapon, a prohibited device or prohibited ammunition, as the case may be.

(3) No person who, during an amnesty period declared by an order made under subsection (1) and for a purpose described in the order, does anything provided for in the order, is, by reason only of the fact that the person did that thing, guilty of an offence under this Part.

(4) Any proceedings taken under this Part against any person for anything done by the person in reliance of this section are a nullity. 1995, c. 39, s. 139.

ORDER DECLARING AN AMNESTY PERIOD (2018)

Definition of *firearm*

1. In this Order, *firearm* means any of the following prohibited firearms:
    (a) a SAN Swiss Arms Model Classic Green Sniper rifle;
    (b) a SAN Swiss Arms Model Ver rifle;
    (c) a SAN Swiss Arms Model Aestas rifle;
    (d) a SAN Swiss Arms Model Autumnus rifle; and
    (e) a SAN Swiss Arms Model Hiemis rifle.

Amnesty

2. (1) The amnesty period set out in subsection (3) is declared under section 117.14 of the *Criminal Code* for a person who
    (a) on the day before the day on which this Order is registered, possessed a firearm and held a licence that was issued under the *Firearms Act*; and
    (b) during the amnesty period, continues to hold a licence while in possession of the firearm.

Purpose

(2) The purpose of the amnesty period is to permit the person to do any of the following during that period:
    (a) possess the firearm;
    (b) deliver the firearm to a peace officer, firearms officer or chief firearms officer;
    (c) sell or give the firearm to a business — including a museum — authorized to acquire and possess prohibited firearms; and
    (d) transport the firearm for the purposes of paragraph (b) or (c).

Amnesty period

(3) The amnesty period begins on the day on which this Order is registered and ends on February 28, 2021.

Coming into force

3. This Order comes into force on the day on which it is registered. **SOR/2018-46.**

REGULATIONS / Restriction/ Non-restricted firearm / Restricted firearm.

117.15 (1) Subject to subsection (2), the Governor in Council may make regulations prescribing anything that by this Part is to be or may be prescribed.

(2) In making regulations, the Governor in Council may not prescribe any thing to be a prohibited firearm, a restricted firearm, a prohibited weapon, a restricted weapon, a prohibited device or prohibited ammunition if, in the opinion of the Governor in Council, the thing to be prescribed is reasonable for use in Canada for hunting or sporting purposes.

(3) Despite the definitions "prohibited firearm" and "restricted firearm" in subsection 84(1), a firearm that is prescribed to be a non-restricted firearm is deemed not to be a prohibited firearm or a restricted firearm.

Note: Subsection 117.15(3) repealed, 2019, c. 9, s. 18 (to come into force by order of the Governor in Council).

(4) Despite the definition "prohibited firearm" in subsection 84(1), a firearm that is prescribed to be a restricted firearm is deemed not to be a prohibited firearm. 1995, c. 39, s. 139; 2015, c. 27, s. 34.

Note: Subsection 117.15(4) repealed, 2019, c. 9, s. 18 (to come into force by order of the Governor in Council).

Part IV / OFFENCES AGAINST THE ADMINISTRATION OF LAW AND JUSTICE

Interpretation

DEFINITIONS / "Evidence" or "statement" / "Government" / "Judicial proceeding" / "Office" / "Official" / "Witness".

118. In this Part

"evidence" or "statement" means an assertion of fact, opinion, belief or knowledge, whether material or not and whether admissible or not;

"government" means

   (*a*) the Government of Canada,

   (*b*) the government of a province, or

   (*c*) Her Majesty in right of Canada or a province;

"judicial proceeding" means a proceeding

   (*a*) in or under the authority of a court of justice,

   (*b*) before the Senate or House of Commons or a committee of the Senate or House of Commons, or before a legislative council, legislative assembly or house of assembly or a committee thereof that is authorized by law to administer an oath,

   (*c*) before a court, judge, justice, provincial court judge or coroner,

   (*d*) before an arbitrator or umpire, or a person or body of persons authorized by law to make an inquiry and take evidence therein under oath, or

   (*e*) before a tribunal by which a legal right or legal liability may be established, whether or not the proceeding is invalid for want of jurisdiction or for any other reason;

"office" includes

    (a) an office or appointment under the government,

    (b) a civil or military commission, and

    (c) a position or an employment in a public department;

"official" means a person who

    (a) holds an office, or

    (b) is appointed or elected to discharge a public duty;

"witness" means a person who gives evidence orally under oath or by affidavit in a judicial proceeding, whether or not he is competent to be a witness, and includes a child of tender years who gives evidence but does not give it under oath, because, in the opinion of the person presiding, the child does not understand the nature of an oath. R.S., c. C-34, s. 107; R.S.C. 1985, c. 27 (1st Supp.), s. 15; 2007, c. 13, s. 2.

Corruption and Disobedience

BRIBERY OF JUDICIAL OFFICERS, ETC. / Consent of Attorney General.

119. (1) Every one is guilty of an indictable offence and liable to imprisonment for a term not exceeding fourteen years who

    (a) being the holder of a judicial office, or being a member of Parliament or of the legislature of a province, directly or in-directly, corruptly accepts, obtains, agrees to accept or attempts to obtain, for themselves or another person, any money, valuable consideration, office, place or employment in respect of anything done or omitted or to be done or omitted by them in their official capacity, or

    (b) directly or indirectly, corruptly gives or offers to a person mentioned in paragraph (a), or to anyone for the benefit of that person, any money, valuable consideration, office, place or employment in respect of anything done or omitted or to be done or omitted by that person in their official capacity.

(2) No proceedings against a person who holds a judicial office shall be instituted under this section without the consent in writing of the Attorney General of Canada. R.S., c. C-34, s. 108; 2007, c. 13, s. 3.

BRIBERY OF OFFICERS.

120. Every one is guilty of an indictable offence and liable to imprisonment for a term not exceeding fourteen years who

    (a) being a justice, police commissioner, peace officer, public officer or officer of a juvenile court, or being employed in the administration of criminal law, directly or indirectly, corruptly accepts, obtains, agrees to accept or attempts to obtain, for themselves or another person, any money, valuable consideration, office, place or employment with intent

     (i) to interfere with the administration of justice,

    (ii) to procure or facilitate the commission of an offence, or

   (iii) to protect from detection or punishment a person who has committed or who intends to commit an offence; or

  (b) directly or indirectly, corruptly gives or offers to a person mentioned in paragraph (a), or to anyone for the benefit of that person, any money, valuable consideration, office, place or employment with intent that the person should do anything mentioned in subparagraph (a)(i), (ii) or (iii).

     R.S., c. C-34, s. 109; 2007, c. 13, s. 4.

CODE

FRAUDS ON THE GOVERNMENT / Contractor subscribing to election fund / Punishment.

121. (1) Every one commits an offence who

  (a) directly or indirectly

     (i) gives, offers or agrees to give or offer to an official or to any member of his family, or to any one for the benefit of an official, or

    (ii) being an official, demands, accepts or offers or agrees to accept from any person for himself or another person,

    a loan, reward, advantage or benefit of any kind as consideration for cooperation, assistance, exercise of influence or an act or omission in connection with

   (iii) the transaction of business with or any matter of business relating to the government, or

   (iv) a claim against Her Majesty or any benefit that Her Majesty is authorized or is entitled to bestow,

    whether or not, in fact, the official is able to cooperate, render assistance, exercise influence or do or omit to do what is proposed, as the case may be;

  (b) having dealings of any kind with the government, directly or indirectly pays a commission or reward to or confers an advantage or benefit of any kind on an employee or official of the government with which the dealings take place, or to any member of the employee's or official's family, or to anyone for the benefit of the employee or official, with respect to those dealings, unless the person has the consent in writing of the head of the branch of government with which the dealings take place;

  (c) being an official or employee of the government, directly or indirectly demands, accepts or offers or agrees to accept from a person who has dealings with the government a commission, reward, advantage or benefit of any kind for themselves or another person, unless they have the consent in writing of the head of the branch of government that employs them or of which they are an official;

  (d) having or pretending to have influence with the government or with a minister of the government or an official, directly or in-directly demands, accepts or offers or agrees to accept, for themselves or another person, a reward, advantage or benefit of any kind as consideration for cooperation, assistance, exercise of influence or an act or omission in connection with

     (i) anything mentioned in subparagraph (a)(iii) or (iv), or

    (ii) the appointment of any person, including themselves, to an office;

(e) directly or indirectly gives or offers, or agrees to give or offer, to a minister of the government or an official, or to anyone for the benefit of a minister or an official, a reward, advantage or benefit of any kind as consideration for cooperation, assistance, exercise of influence, or an act or omission, by that minister or official, in connection with

    (i) anything mentioned in subparagraph (a)(iii) or (iv), or

    (ii) the appointment of any person, including themselves, to an office; or

(f) having made a tender to obtain a contract with the government,

    (i) directly or indirectly gives or offers, or agrees to give or offer, to another person who has made a tender, to a member of that person's family or to another person for the benefit of that person, a reward, advantage or benefit of any kind as consideration for the withdrawal of the tender of that person, or

    (ii) directly or indirectly demands, accepts or offers or agrees to accept from another person who has made a tender a reward, advantage or benefit of any kind for themselves or another person as consideration for the withdrawal of their own tender.

(2) Every one commits an offence who, in order to obtain or retain a contract with the government, or as a term of any such contract, whether express or implied, directly or indirectly subscribes or gives, or agrees to subscribe or give, to any person any valuable consideration

(a) for the purpose of promoting the election of a candidate or a class or party of candidates to Parliament or the legislature of a province; or

(b) with intent to influence or affect in any way the result of an election conducted for the purpose of electing persons to serve in Parliament or the legislature of a province.

(3) Every person who commits an offence under this section is guilty of

(a) an indictable offence and liable to imprisonment for a term of not more than five years; or

(b) an offence punishable on summary conviction. R.S., c. C-34, s. 110; 2007, c. 13, s. 5; 2019, c. 25, s. 33.

**SELLING ETC., OF TOBACCO PRODUCTS AND RAW LEAF TOBACCO /
Exceptions — subsections 30(2) and 32(2) and (3) of *Excise Act, 2001* /
Exception — section 31 of *Excise Act, 2001* / Punishment / Subsequent
offences.**

121.1 (1) No person shall sell, offer for sale, transport, deliver, distribute or have in their possession for the purpose of sale a tobacco product, or raw leaf tobacco that is not packaged, unless it is stamped. The terms "tobacco product", "raw leaf tobacco", "packaged" and "stamped" have the same meanings as in section 2 of the *Excise Act, 2001*.

(2) Subsection (1) does not apply in any of the circumstances described in any of subsections 30(2) and 32(2) and (3) of the *Excise Act, 2001*.

(3) A tobacco grower does not contravene subsection (1) by reason only that they have in their possession raw leaf tobacco described in paragraph 31(*a*), (*b*) or (*c*) of the *Excise Act, 2001*.

(4) Every person who contravenes subsection (1)

   (*a*) is guilty of an indictable offence and liable to imprisonment for a term of not more than five years and, if the amount of tobacco product is 10,000 cigarettes or more or 10 kg or more of any other tobacco product, or the amount of raw leaf tobacco is 10 kg or more,

      (i) in the case of a second offence, to a minimum punishment of imprisonment for a term of 90 days,

      (ii) in the case of a third offence, to a minimum punishment of imprisonment for a term of 180 days, and

     (iii) in the case of a fourth or subsequent offence, to a minimum punishment of imprisonment for a term of two years less a day; or

   (*b*) is guilty of an offence punishable on summary conviction.

(5) For the purpose of determining whether a convicted person has committed a second or subsequent offence, an offence under this section for which the person was previously convicted is considered to be an earlier offence whether it was prosecuted by indictment or by way of summary conviction proceedings. 2014, c. 23, s. 3; 2019, c. 25, s. 34(2).

BREACH OF TRUST BY PUBLIC OFFICER.

122. Every official who, in connection with the duties of their office, commits fraud or a breach of trust, whether or not the fraud or breach of trust would be an offence if it were committed in relation to a private person, is guilty of

   (*a*) an indictable offence and liable to imprisonment for a term of not more than five years; or

   (*b*) an offence punishable on summary conviction. R.S., c. C-34, s. 111; 2019, c. 25, s. 35.

MUNICIPAL CORRUPTION / Influencing municipal official / Definition of "municipal official".

123. (1) Every person is guilty of an indictable offence and liable to imprisonment for a term of not more than five years or is guilty of an offence punishable on summary conviction who directly or indirectly gives, offers or agrees to give or offer to a municipal official or to anyone for the benefit of a municipal official — or, being a municipal official, directly or indirectly demands, accepts or offers or agrees to accept from any person for themselves or another person — a loan, reward, advantage or benefit of any kind as consideration for the official

   (*a*) to abstain from voting at a meeting of the municipal council or a committee of the council;

   (*b*) to vote in favour of or against a measure, motion or resolution;

   (*c*) to aid in procuring or preventing the adoption of a measure, motion or resolution; or

   (*d*) to perform or fail to perform an official act.

(2) Every person is guilty of an indictable offence and liable to imprisonment for a term of not more than five years or is guilty of an offence punishable on summary conviction who influences or attempts to influence a municipal official to do anything mentioned in paragraphs (1)(*a*) to (*d*) by

(*a*) suppression of the truth, in the case of a person who is under a duty to disclose the truth;

(*b*) threats or deceit; or

(*c*) any unlawful means.

(3) In this section, "municipal official" means a member of a municipal council or a person who holds an office under a municipal government. R.S., c. C-34, s. 112; R.S.C. 1985, c. 27 (1st Supp.), s. 16; 2007, c. 13, s. 6; 2019, c. 25, s. 36.

SELLING OR PURCHASING OFFICE.

124. Every person is guilty of an indictable offence and liable to imprisonment for a term of not more than five years or is guilty of an offence punishable on summary conviction who

(*a*) purports to sell or agrees to sell an appointment to or a resignation from an office, or a consent to any such appointment or resignation, or receives or agrees to receive a reward or profit from the purported sale thereof, or

(*b*) purports to purchase or gives a reward or profit for the purported purchase of any such appointment, resignation or consent, or agrees or promises to do so. R.S., c. C-34, s. 113; 2019, c. 25, s. 37.

INFLUENCING OR NEGOTIATING APPOINTMENTS OR DEALING IN OFFICES.

125. Every person is guilty of an indictable offence and liable to imprisonment for a term of not more than five years or is guilty of an offence punishable on summary conviction who

(*a*) receives, agrees to receive, gives or procures to be given, directly or indirectly, a reward, advantage or benefit of any kind as consideration for cooperation, assistance or exercise of influence to secure the appointment of any person to an office,

(*b*) solicits, recommends or negotiates in any manner with respect to an appointment to or resignation from an office, in expectation of a direct or indirect reward, advantage or benefit, or

(*c*) keeps without lawful authority a place for transacting or negotiating any business relating to

(i) the filling of vacancies in offices,

(ii) the sale or purchase of offices, or

(iii) appointments to or resignations from offices. R.S., c. C-34, s. 114; 2018, c. 29, s. 7; 2019, c. 25, s. 38(1).

DISOBEYING A STATUTE / Attorney General of Canada may act.

126. (1) Every person who, without lawful excuse, contravenes an Act of Parliament by intentionally doing anything that it forbids or by intentionally omitting to do anything that it requires to be done is, unless a punishment is expressly provided by law, guilty of

    (*a*) an indictable offence and liable to imprisonment for a term of not more than two years; or

    (*b*) an offence punishable on summary conviction.

(2) Any proceedings in respect of a contravention of or conspiracy to contravene an Act mentioned in subsection (1), other than this Act, may be instituted at the instance of the Government of Canada and conducted by or on behalf of that Government. R.S., c. C-34, s. 115; 1974-75-76, c. 93, s. 4; 2019, c. 25, s. 39.

CODE

DISOBEYING ORDER OF COURT / Attorney General of Canada may act.

127. (1) Every one who, without lawful excuse, disobeys a lawful order made by a court of justice or by a person or body of persons authorized by any Act to make or give the order, other than an order for the payment of money, is, unless a punishment or other mode of proceeding is expressly provided by law, guilty of

    (*a*) an indictable offence and liable to imprisonment for a term not exceeding two years; or

    (*b*) an offence punishable on summary conviction.

(2) Where the order referred to in subsection (1) was made in proceedings instituted at the instance of the Government of Canada and conducted by or on behalf of that Government, any proceedings in respect of a contravention of or conspiracy to contravene that order may be instituted and conducted in like manner. R.S., c. C-34, s. 116; 1974-75-76, c. 93, s. 5; 2005, c. 32, s. 1.

MISCONDUCT OF OFFICERS EXECUTING PROCESS.

128. Every peace officer or coroner is guilty of an indictable offence and liable to imprisonment for a term of not more than two years or is guilty of an offence punishable on summary conviction who, being entrusted with the execution of a process, intentionally

    (*a*) misconducts himself in the execution of the process, or

    (*b*) makes a false return to the process. R.S., c. C-34, s. 117; 2019, c. 25, s. 40.

OFFENCES RELATING TO PUBLIC OR PEACE OFFICER.

129. Every one who

    (*a*) resists or wilfully obstructs a public officer or peace officer in the execution of his duty or any person lawfully acting in aid of such an officer,

    (*b*) omits, without reasonable excuse, to assist a public officer or peace officer in the execution of his duty in arresting a person or in preserving the peace, after having reasonable notice that he is required to do so, or

    (*c*) resists or wilfully obstructs any person in the lawful execution of a process against lands or goods or in making a lawful distress or seizure,

is guilty of

    (*d*) an indictable offence and is liable to imprisonment for a term not exceeding two years, or (*e*) an offence punishable on summary conviction. R.S., c. C-34, s. 118; 1972, c. 13, s. 7.

PERSONATING PEACE OFFICER / Punishment.

130. (1) Everyone commits an offence who
  (*a*) falsely represents himself to be a peace officer or a public officer; or
  (*b*) not being a peace officer or public officer, uses a badge or article of uniform or equipment in a manner that is likely to cause persons to believe that he is a peace officer or a public officer, as the case may be.

(2) Everyone who commits an offence under subsection (1)
  (*a*) is guilty of an indictable offence and liable to imprisonment for a term of not more than five years; or
  (*b*) is guilty of an offence punishable on summary conviction. R.S., c. C-34, s. 119; 2009, c. 28, s. 2.

AGGRAVATING CIRCUMSTANCE.

130.1 If a person is convicted of an offence under section 130, the court imposing the sentence on the person shall consider as an aggravating circumstance the fact that the accused personated a peace officer or a public officer, as the case may be, for the purpose of facilitating the commission of another offence. 2014, c. 10, s. 1.

Misleading Justice

PERJURY / Video links, etc. / Idem / Application.

131. (1) Subject to subsection (3), every one commits perjury who, with intent to mislead, makes before a person who is authorized by law to permit it to be made before him a false statement under oath or solemn affirmation, by affidavit, solemn declaration or deposition or orally, knowing that the statement is false.

(1.1) Subject to subsection (3), every person who gives evidence under subsection 46(2) of the *Canada Evidence Act*, or gives evidence or a statement pursuant to an order made under section 22.2 of the *Mutual Legal Assistance in Criminal Matters Act*, commits perjury who, with intent to mislead, makes a false statement knowing that it is false, whether or not the false statement was made under oath or solemn affirmation in accordance with subsection (1), so long as the false statement was made in accordance with any formalities required by the law of the place outside Canada in which the person is virtually present or heard.

(2) Subsection (1) applies whether or not a statement referred to in that subsection is made in a judicial proceeding.

(3) Subsections (1) and (1.1) do not apply to a statement referred to in either of those subsections that is made by a person who is not specially permitted, authorized or required by law to make that statement. R.S., c. C-34, s. 120; R.S.C. 1985, c. 27 (1st Supp.), s. 17; 1999, c. 18, s. 92.

PUNISHMENT.

132. Every one who commits perjury is guilty of an indictable offence and liable to imprisonment for a term not exceeding fourteen years. R.S., c. C-34, s. 121; R.S.C. 1985, c. 27 (1st Supp.), s. 17; 1998, c. 35, s. 119.

CORROBORATION.

133. No person shall be convicted of an offence under section 132 on the evidence of only one witness unless the evidence of that witness is corroborated in a material particular by evidence that implicates the accused. R.S., c. C-34, s. 122; R.S.C. 1985, c. 27 (1st Supp.), s. 17.

IDEM / Application.

134. (1) Subject to subsection (2), every one who, not being specially permitted, authorized or required by law to make a statement under oath or solemn affirmation, makes such a statement, by affidavit, solemn declaration or deposition or orally before a person who is authorized by law to permit it to be made before him, knowing that the statement is false, is guilty of an offence punishable on summary conviction.

(2) Subsection (1) does not apply to a statement referred to in that subsection that is made in the course of a criminal investigation. 1974-75-76, c. 93, s. 6; R.S.C. 1985, c. 27 (1st Supp.), s. 17.

135. [*Repealed*, R.S.C. 1985, c. 27 (1st Supp.), s. 17.]

WITNESS GIVING CONTRADICTORY EVIDENCE / Evidence in specific cases / Definition of "evidence" / Proof of former trial / Consent required.

136. (1) Every one who, being a witness in a judicial proceeding, gives evidence with respect to any matter of fact or knowledge and who subsequently, in a judicial proceeding, gives evidence that is contrary to his previous evidence is guilty of an indictable offence and liable to imprisonment for a term not exceeding fourteen years, whether or not the prior or later evidence or either is true, but no person shall be convicted under this section unless the court, judge or provincial court judge, as the case may be, is satisfied beyond a reasonable doubt that the accused, in giving evidence in either of the judicial proceedings, intended to mislead.

(1.1) Evidence given under section 714.1, 714.2 or 714.3 or under subsection 46(2) of the *Canada Evidence Act* or evidence or a statement given under an order made under section 22.2 of the *Mutual Legal Assistance in Criminal Matters Act* is deemed to be evidence given by a witness in a judicial proceeding for the purposes of subsection (1).

(2) Notwithstanding the definition "evidence" in section 118, "evidence", for the purposes of this section, does not include evidence that is not material.

(2.1) Where a person is charged with an offence under this section, a certificate specifying with reasonable particularity the proceeding in which that person is alleged to have given the evidence in respect of which the offence is charged, is evidence that it was given in a judicial proceeding, without proof of the signature or official character of the person by whom the certificate purports to be signed if it purports to be signed by the clerk of the court or other official having the custody of the record of that proceeding or by his lawful deputy.

(3) No proceedings shall be instituted under this section without the consent of the Attorney General. R.S., c. C-34, s. 124; R.S.C. 1985, c. 27 (1st Supp.), s. 18; 1999, c. 18, s. 93; 2019, c. 25, s. 41.

FABRICATING EVIDENCE.

137. Every one who, with intent to mislead, fabricates anything with intent that it shall be used as evidence in a judicial proceeding, existing or proposed, by any means other than perjury or incitement to perjury is guilty of an indictable offence and liable to imprisonment for a term not exceeding fourteen years. R.S., c. C-34, s. 125.

OFFENCES RELATING TO AFFIDAVITS.

138. Every person is guilty of an indictable offence and liable to imprisonment for a term of not more than two years or is guilty of an offence punishable on summary conviction who
    (a) signs a writing that purports to be an affidavit or statutory declaration and to have been sworn or declared before him when the writing was not so sworn or declared or when he knows that he has no authority to administer the oath or declaration,
    (b) uses or offers for use any writing purporting to be an affidavit or statutory declaration that he knows was not sworn or declared, as the case may be, by the affiant or declarant or before a person authorized in that behalf, or
    (c) signs as affiant or declarant a writing that purports to be an affidavit or statutory declaration and to have been sworn or declared by him, as the case may be, when the writing was not so sworn or declared. R.S., c. C-34, s. 126; 2019, c. 25, s. 42.

OBSTRUCTING JUSTICE / Idem / Idem.

139. (1) Every one who wilfully attempts in any manner to obstruct, pervert or defeat the course of justice in a judicial proceeding,
    (a) by indemnifying or agreeing to indemnify a surety, in any way and either in whole or in part, or
    (b) where he is a surety, by accepting or agreeing to accept a fee or any form of indemnity whether in whole or in part from or in respect of a person who is released or is to be released from custody,
is guilty of
    (c) an indictable offence and is liable to imprisonment for a term not exceeding two years, or

    (*d*) an offence punishable on summary conviction.

(2) Every person who intentionally attempts in any manner other than a manner described in subsection (1) to obstruct, pervert or defeat the course of justice is guilty of

    (*a*) an indictable offence and liable to imprisonment for a term of not more than 10 years; or

    (*b*) an offence punishable on summary conviction.

(3) Without restricting the generality of subsection (2), every one shall be deemed wilfully to attempt to obstruct, pervert or defeat the course of justice who in a judicial proceeding, existing or proposed,

    (*a*) dissuades or attempts to dissuade a person by threats, bribes or other corrupt means from giving evidence;

    (*b*) influences or attempts to influence by threats, bribes or other corrupt means a person in his conduct as a juror; or

    (*c*) accepts or obtains, agrees to accept or attempts to obtain a bribe or other corrupt consideration to abstain from giving evidence, or to do or to refrain from doing anything as a juror. R.S., c. C-34, s. 127; R.S., c. 2 (2nd Supp.), s. 3; 1972, c. 13, s. 8; 2019, c. 25, s. 43.

PUBLIC MISCHIEF / Punishment.

140. (1) Every one commits public mischief who, with intent to mislead, causes a peace officer to enter on or continue an investigation by

    (*a*) making a false statement that accuses some other person of having committed an offence;

    (*b*) doing anything intended to cause some other person to be suspected of having committed an offence that the other person has not committed, or to divert suspicion from himself;

    (*c*) reporting that an offence has been committed when it has not been committed; or

    (*d*) reporting or in any other way making it known or causing it to be made known that he or some other person has died when he or that other person has not died.

(2) Every one who commits public mischief

    (*a*) is guilty of an indictable offence and liable to imprisonment for a term not exceeding five years; or

    (*b*) is guilty of an offence punishable on summary conviction. R.S., c. C-34, s. 128; 1972, c. 13, s. 8; R.S.C. 1985, c. 27 (1st Supp.), s. 19.

COMPOUNDING INDICTABLE OFFENCE / Exception for diversion agreements.

141. (1) Every person who asks for or obtains or agrees to receive or obtain any valuable consideration for themselves or any other person by agreeing to compound or conceal an indictable offence is guilty of

    (*a*) an indictable offence and liable to imprisonment for a term of not more than two years; or

(b) an offence punishable on summary conviction.

(2) No offence is committed under subsection (1) where valuable consideration is received or obtained or is to be received or obtained under an agreement for compensation or restitution or personal services that is

(a) entered into with the consent of the Attorney General; or

(b) made as part of a program, approved by the Attorney General, to divert persons charged with indictable offences from criminal proceedings. R.S., c. C-34, s. 129; R.S.C. 1985, c. 27 (1st Supp.), s. 19; 2019, c. 25, s. 44.

CORRUPTLY TAKING REWARD FOR RECOVERY OF GOODS.

142. Every person who corruptly accepts any valuable consideration, directly or indirectly, under pretence or on account of helping any person to recover anything obtained by the commission of an indictable offence is guilty of

(a) an indictable offence and liable to imprisonment for a term of not more than five years; or

(b) an offence punishable on summary conviction. R.S., c. C-34, s. 130; 2019, c. 25, s. 45.

143. [*Repealed*, 2018, c. 29, s. 8.]

Escapes and Rescues

PRISON BREACH.

144. Every person is guilty of an indictable offence and liable to imprisonment for a term of not more than 10 years or is guilty of an offence punishable on summary conviction who

(a) by force or violence breaks a prison with intent to set at liberty himself or any other person confined therein, or

(b) with intent to escape forcibly breaks out of, or makes any breach in, a cell or other place within a prison in which he is confined. R.S., c. C-34, s. 132; 1976-77, c. 53, s. 5; 2019, c. 25, s. 46.

ESCAPE AND BEING AT LARGE WITHOUT EXCUSE / Failure to attend court or surrender / Failure to comply with appearance notice or summons / Failure to comply with undertaking / Failure to comply with order / Not an excuse / Election of Crown under *Contraventions Act* / Proof of certain facts by certificate / Attendance and right to cross-examination / Notice of intention to produce.

145. (1) Every person who escapes from lawful custody or who is, before the expiration of a term of imprisonment to which they were sentenced, at large in or outside Canada without lawful excuse, is guilty of

(a) an indictable offence and liable to imprisonment for a term of not more than two years; or

(b) an offence punishable on summary conviction.

CODE

(2) Every person is guilty of an indictable offence and liable to imprisonment for a term not exceeding two years or is guilty of an offence punishable on summary conviction who,

(a) is at large on a release order and who fails, without lawful excuse, to attend court in accordance with the release order;

(b) having appeared before a court, justice or judge, fails, without lawful excuse, to subsequently attend court as required by the court, justice or judge; or

(c) fails to surrender themselves in accordance with an order of the court, justice or judge, as the case may be.

(3) Every person who is named in an appearance notice that has been confirmed by a justice under section 508 or who is served with a summons and who fails, without lawful excuse, to appear at the time and place stated in the notice or the summons, as the case may be, for the purposes of the *Identification of Criminals Act*, or to attend court in accordance with the notice or the summons, as the case may be, is guilty of

(a) an indictable offence and liable to imprisonment for a term of not more than two years; or

(b) an offence punishable on summary conviction.

(4) Every person is guilty of an indictable offence and liable to imprisonment for a term of not more than two years or an offence punishable on summary conviction who,

(a) is at large on an undertaking and who fails, without lawful excuse, to comply with a condition of that undertaking; or

(b) is at large on an undertaking that has been confirmed by a justice under section 508 and who fails, without lawful excuse, to appear at the time and place stated in the undertaking for the purposes of the *Identification of Criminals Act* or to attend court in accordance with the undertaking.

(5) Every person is guilty of an indictable offence and liable to imprisonment for a term of not more than two years, or is guilty of an offence punishable on summary conviction, who

(a) is at large on a release order and who fails, without lawful excuse, to comply with a condition of that release order other than the condition to attend court; or

(b) is bound to comply with an order under subsection 515(12), 516(2) or 522(2.1) and who fails, without lawful excuse, to comply with that order.

(5.1) [*Repealed*, 2019, c. 25, s. 47(1).]

(6) For the purposes of subsections (3) and (4), it is not a lawful excuse that an appearance notice or undertaking states defectively the substance of the alleged offence.

(7) [*Repealed*, R.S.C. 1985, c. 27 (1st Supp.), s. 20(2).]

(8) For the purposes of paragraph (2)(a) and subsections (3) to (5), it is a lawful excuse to fail to attend court in accordance with a summons, appearance notice, undertaking or release order, to comply with a condition of an undertaking or release order or to fail to appear at the time and place stated in a summons, an

appearance notice or an undertaking for the purposes of the *Identification of Criminals Act* if — before the failure — the "Attorney General", within the meaning of the *Contraventions Act*, makes an election under section 50 of that Act.

(9) In any proceedings under subsections (2) to (4), a certificate of the clerk of the court or a judge of the court before which the accused is alleged to have failed to attend or of the person in charge of the place at which it is alleged the accused failed to attend for the purposes of the *Identification of Criminals Act* is evidence of the statements contained in the certificate without proof of the signature or the official character of the person appearing to have signed the certificate if the certificate states that,

(a) in the case of proceedings under subsection (2), the accused failed to attend court as required by the release order or, having attended court, failed to subsequently attend court as required by the court, judge or justice or failed to surrender in accordance with an order of the court, judge or justice, as the case may be;

(b) in the case of proceedings under subsection (3), the accused was named in an appearance notice that was confirmed by a justice under section 508 and the accused failed to attend court in accordance with the notice or failed to appear at the time and place stated in the notice for the purposes of the *Identification of Criminals Act*, as the case may be;

(c) in the case of proceedings under subsection (3), a summons was issued to and served on the accused and the accused failed to attend court in accordance with the summons or failed to appear at the time and place stated in the summons for the purposes of the *Identification of Criminals Act*, as the case may be; and

(d) in the case of proceedings under subsection (4), the accused was at large on an undertaking that was confirmed by a justice under section 508, and the accused failed to attend court in accordance with the undertaking or failed to appear at the time and place stated in the undertaking for the purposes of the *Identification of Criminals Act*, as the case may be.

(10) An accused against whom a certificate described in subsection (9) is produced may, with leave of the court, require the attendance of the person making the certificate for the purposes of cross-examination.

(11) No certificate shall be received in evidence pursuant to subsection (9) unless the party intending to produce it has, before the trial, given to the accused reasonable notice of his intention together with a copy of the certificate. R.S., c. C-34, s. 133; R.S., c. 2 (2nd Supp.), s. 4; 1974-75-76, c. 93, s. 7; R.S.C. 1985, c. 27 (1st Supp.), s. 20; 1992, c. 47, s. 68; 1994, c. 44, s. 8; 1996, c. 7, s. 38; 1997, c. 18, s. 3; 2008, c. 18, s. 3; 2018, c. 29, s. 9(1)-(8), (10), (12); 2019, c. 25, s. 47.

PERMITTING OR ASSISTING ESCAPE.

146. Every person is guilty of an indictable offence and liable to imprisonment for a term of not more than two years or is guilty of an offence punishable on summary conviction who

(a) permits a person whom he has in lawful custody to escape, by failing to perform a legal duty,

(b) conveys or causes to be conveyed into a prison anything, with intent to facilitate the escape of a person imprisoned therein, or

(c) directs or procures, under colour of pretended authority, the discharge of a prisoner who is not entitled to be discharged. R.S., c. C-34, s. 134; 2019, c. 25, s. 48.

RESCUE OR PERMITTING ESCAPE.

147. Every person is guilty of an indictable offence and liable to imprisonment for a term of not more than five years or is guilty of an offence punishable on summary conviction who

(a) rescues any person from lawful custody or assists any person in escaping or attempting to escape from lawful custody,

(b) being a peace officer, wilfully permits a person in his lawful custody to escape, or

(c) being an officer of or an employee in a prison, wilfully permits a person to escape from lawful custody therein. R.S., c. C-34, s. 135; 2019, c. 25, s. 49.

ASSISTING PRISONER OF WAR TO ESCAPE.

148. Every person is guilty of an indictable offence and liable to imprisonment for a term of not more than five years or is guilty of an offence punishable on summary conviction who knowingly

(a) assists a prisoner of war in Canada to escape from a place where he is detained, or

(b) assists a prisoner of war, who is permitted to be at large on parole in Canada, to escape from the place where he is at large on parole. R.S., c. C-34, s. 136; 2019, c. 25, s. 50.

SERVICE OF TERM FOR ESCAPE / Definition of "escape".

149. (1) Notwithstanding section 743.1, a court that convicts a person for an escape committed while undergoing imprisonment may order that the term of imprisonment be served in a penitentiary, even if the time to be served is less than two years.

(2) In this section, "escape" means breaking prison, escaping from lawful custody or, without lawful excuse, being at large before the expiration of a term of imprisonment to which a person has been sentenced. R.S., c. C-34, s. 137; 1972, c. 13, s. 9; 1976-77, c. 53, s. 6; 1992, c. 20, s. 199; 1995, c. 22, ss. 1 and 10.

Part V / SEXUAL OFFENCES, PUBLIC MORALS AND DISORDERLY CONDUCT

Interpretation

DEFINITIONS / "Guardian" / "Public place" / "Theatre".

150. In this Part

"guardian" includes any person who has in law or in fact the custody or control of another person;

"public place" includes any place to which the public have access as of right or by invitation, express or implied;

"theatre" includes any place that is open to the public where entertainments are given, whether or not any charge is made for admission. R.S., c. C-34, s. 138.

Sexual Offences

CONSENT NO DEFENCE / Exception — complainant aged 12 or 13 / Exception — complainant aged 14 or 15 / Exception for transitional purposes / Exception for transitional purposes / Exemption for accused aged twelve or thirteen / Mistake of age / Idem / Idem.

150.1 (1) Subject to subsections (2) to (2.2), when an accused is charged with an offence under section 151 or 152 or subsection 153(1), 160(3) or 173(2) or is charged with an offence under section 271, 272 or 273 in respect of a complainant under the age of 16 years, it is not a defence that the complainant consented to the activity that forms the subject-matter of the charge.

(2) When an accused is charged with an offence under section 151 or 152, subsection 173(2) or section 271 in respect of a complainant who is 12 years of age or more but under the age of 14 years, it is a defence that the complainant consented to the activity that forms the subject-matter of the charge if the accused

    (*a*) is less than two years older than the complainant; and

    (*b*) is not in a position of trust or authority towards the complainant, is not a person with whom the complainant is in a relationship of dependency and is not in a relationship with the complainant that is exploitative of the complainant.

(2.1) If an accused is charged with an offence under section 151 or 152, subsection 173(2) or section 271 in respect of a complainant who is 14 years of age or more but under the age of 16 years, it is a defence that the complainant consented to the activity that forms the subject-matter of the charge if the accused

    (*a*) is less than five years older than the complainant; and

(b) is not in a position of trust or authority towards the complainant, is not a person with whom the complainant is in a relationship of dependency and is not in a relationship with the complainant that is exploitative of the complainant.

(2.2) When the accused referred to in subsection (2.1) is five or more years older than the complainant, it is a defence that the complainant consented to the activity that forms the subject matter of the charge if, on the day on which this subsection comes into force,

(a) the accused is the common-law partner of the complainant, or has been cohabiting with the complainant in a conjugal relationship for a period of less than one year and they have had or are expecting to have a child as a result of the relationship; and

(b) the accused is not in a position of trust or authority towards the complainant, is not a person with whom the complainant is in a relationship of dependency and is not in a relationship with the complainant that is exploitative of the complainant.

(2.3) If, immediately before the day on which this subsection comes into force, the accused referred to in subsection (2.1) is married to the complainant, it is a defence that the complainant consented to the activity that forms the subject-matter of the charge.

(3) No person aged twelve or thirteen years shall be tried for an offence under section 151 or 152 or subsection 173(2) unless the person is in a position of trust or authority towards the complainant, is a person with whom the complainant is in a relationship of dependency or is in a relationship with the complainant that is exploitative of the complainant.

(4) It is not a defence to a charge under section 151 or 152, subsection 160(3) or 173(2), or section 271, 272 or 273 that the accused believed that the complainant was 16 years of age or more at the time the offence is alleged to have been committed unless the accused took all reasonable steps to ascertain the age of the complainant.

(5) It is not a defence to a charge under section 153, 170, 171 or 172 or subsection 286.1(2), 286.2(2) or 286.3(2) that the accused believed that the complainant was 18 years of age or more at the time the offence is alleged to have been committed unless the accused took all reasonable steps to ascertain the age of the complainant.

(6) An accused cannot raise a mistaken belief in the age of the complainant in order to invoke a defence under subsection (2) or (2.1) unless the accused took all reasonable steps to ascertain the age of the complainant. R.S.C. 1985, c. 19 (3rd Supp.), s. 1; 2005, c. 32, s. 2; 2008, c. 6, ss. 13, 54(a); 2014, c. 25, s. 4; 2015, c. 29, s. 6; 2019, c. 25, s. 51.

SEXUAL INTERFERENCE.

151. Every person who, for a sexual purpose, touches, directly or indirectly, with a part of the body or with an object, any part of the body of a person under the age of 16 years (*a*) is guilty of an indictable offence and is liable to imprisonment for a term of not more than 14 years and to a minimum punishment of imprisonment for a term of one year; or

   (*b*) is guilty of an offence punishable on summary conviction and is liable to imprisonment for a term of not more than two years less a day and to a minimum punishment of imprisonment for a term of 90 days. R.S.C. 1985, c. 19 (3rd Supp.), s. 1; 2005, c. 32, s. 3; 2008, c. 6, s. 54(b); 2012, c. 1, s. 11; 2015, c. 23, s. 2.

INVITATION TO SEXUAL TOUCHING.

152. Every person who, for a sexual purpose, invites, counsels or incites a person under the age of 16 years to touch, directly or indirectly, with a part of the body or with an object, the body of any person, including the body of the person who so invites, counsels or incites and the body of the person under the age of 16 years,

   (*a*) is guilty of an indictable offence and is liable to imprisonment for a term of not more than 14 years and to a minimum punishment of imprisonment for a term of one year; or

   (*b*) is guilty of an offence punishable on summary conviction and is liable to imprisonment for a term of not more than two years less a day and to a minimum punishment of imprisonment for a term of 90 days. R.S.C. 1985, c. 19 (3rd Supp.), s. 1; 2005, c. 32, s. 3; 2008, c. 6, s. 54(*b*); 2012, c. 1, s. 12; 2015, c. 23, s. 3.

SEXUAL EXPLOITATION / Punishment / Inference of sexual exploitation / Definition of "young person".

153. (1) Every person commits an offence who is in a position of trust or authority towards a young person, who is a person with whom the young person is in a relationship of dependency or who is in a relationship with a young person that is exploitative of the young person, and who

   (*a*) for a sexual purpose, touches, directly or indirectly, with a part of the body or with an object, any part of the body of the young person; or

   (*b*) for a sexual purpose, invites, counsels or incites a young person to touch, directly or indirectly, with a part of the body or with an object, the body of any person, including the body of the person who so invites, counsels or incites and the body of the young person.

(1.1) Every person who commits an offence under subsection (1)

   (*a*) is guilty of an indictable offence and is liable to imprisonment for a term of not more than 14 years and to a minimum punishment of imprisonment for a term of one year; or

   (*b*) is guilty of an offence punishable on summary conviction and is liable to imprisonment for a term of not more than two years less a day and to a minimum punishment of imprisonment for a term of 90 days.

(1.2) A judge may infer that a person is in a relationship with a young person that is exploitative of the young person from the nature and circumstances of the relationship, including

(a) the age of the young person;

(b) the age difference between the person and the young person;

(c) the evolution of the relationship; and

(d) the degree of control or influence by the person over the young person.

(2) In this section, "young person" means a person 16 years of age or more but under the age of eighteen years. R.S.C. 1985, c. 19 (3rd Supp.), s. 1; 2005, c. 32, s. 4; 2008, c. 6, s. 54(c); 2012, c. 1, s. 13; 2015, c. 23, s. 4.

SEXUAL EXPLOITATION OF PERSON WITH DISABILITY / Definition of "consent" / Consent / Question of law / When no consent obtained / Subsection (3) not limiting / When belief in consent not a defence / Accused's belief as to consent.

153.1 (1) Every person who is in a position of trust or authority towards a person with a mental or physical disability or who is a person with whom a person with a mental or physical disability is in a relationship of dependency and who, for a sexual purpose, counsels or incites that person to touch, without that person's consent, his or her own body, the body of the person who so counsels or incites, directly or indirectly, with a part of the body or with an object, the body of any person, including the body of the person who so invites, counsels or incites and the body of the person with the disability, is guilty of

(a) an indictable offence and liable to imprisonment for a term not exceeding five years; or

(b) an offence punishable on summary conviction.

(2) Subject to subsection (3), "consent" means, for the purposes of this section, the voluntary agreement of the complainant to engage in the sexual activity in question.

(2.1) Consent must be present at the time the sexual activity in question takes place.

(2.2) The question of whether no consent is obtained under subsection (3) or (4) or 265(3) is a question of law.

(3) For the purposes of this section, no consent is obtained if

(a) the agreement is expressed by the words or conduct of a person other than the complainant;

(a.1) the complainant is unconscious;

(b) the complainant is incapable of consenting to the activity for any reason other than the one referred to in paragraph (a.1);

(c) the accused counsels or incites the complainant to engage in the activity by abusing a position of trust, power or authority;

(d) the complainant expresses, by words or conduct, a lack of agreement to engage in the activity; or

(e) the complainant, having consented to engage in sexual activity, expresses, by words or conduct, a lack of agreement to continue to engage in the activity.

(4) Nothing in subsection (3) shall be construed as limiting the circumstances in which no consent is obtained.

(5) It is not a defence to a charge under this section that the accused believed that the complainant consented to the activity that forms the subject-matter of the charge if

(a) the accused's belief arose from

(i) the accused's self-induced intoxication,

(ii) the accused's recklessness or wilful blindness, or

(iii) any circumstance referred to in subsection (3) or (4) or 265(3) in which no consent is obtained;

(b) the accused did not take reasonable steps, in the circumstances known to the accused at the time, to ascertain that the complainant was consenting.

(c) there is no evidence that the complainant's voluntary agreement to the activity was affirmatively expressed by words or actively expressed by conduct.

(6) If an accused alleges that he or she believed that the complainant consented to the conduct that is the subject-matter of the charge, a judge, if satisfied that there is sufficient evidence and that, if believed by the jury, the evidence would constitute a defence, shall instruct the jury, when reviewing all the evidence relating to the determination of the honesty of the accused's belief, to consider the presence or absence of reasonable grounds for that belief. 1998, c. 9, s. 2; 2018, c. 29, s. 10(1)-(2.1), (4)-(6); 2019, c. 25, s. 52(2).

---

154. [*Repealed*, R.S.C. 1985, c. 19 (3rd Supp.), s. 1.]

INCEST / Punishment / Defence / Definition of "brother" and "sister".

155. (1) Every one commits incest who, knowing that another person is by blood relationship his or her parent, child, brother, sister, grandparent or grandchild, as the case may be, has sexual intercourse with that person.

(2) Everyone who commits incest is guilty of an indictable offence and is liable to imprisonment for a term of not more than 14 years and, if the other person is under the age of 16 years, to a minimum punishment of imprisonment for a term of five years.

(3) No accused shall be determined by a court to be guilty of an offence under this section if the accused was under restraint, duress or fear of the person with whom the accused had the sexual intercourse at the time the sexual intercourse occurred.

(4) In this section, "brother" and "sister", respectively, include half-brother and half-sister. R.S., c. C-34, s. 150; 1972, c. 13, s. 10; R.S.C. 1985, c. 27 (1st Supp.), s. 21; 2012, c. 1, s. 14.

HISTORICAL OFFENCES.

156. No person shall be convicted of any sexual offence under this Act as it read from time to time before January 4, 1983 unless the conduct alleged would be an offence under this Act if it occurred on the day on which the charge was laid. 2019, c. 25, s. 53.

157. [*Repealed*, R.S.C. 1985, c. 19 (3rd Supp.), s. 2.]

158. [*Repealed*, R.S.C. 1985, c. 19 (3rd Supp.), s. 2.]

159. [*Repealed*, 2019, c. 25, s. 54.]

BESTIALITY / Compelling the commission of bestiality / Bestiality in presence of or by child / Order of prohibition or restitution / Breach of order / Application / Definition of "bestiality".

160. (1) Every person who commits bestiality is guilty of an indictable offence and liable to imprisonment for a term not exceeding ten years or is guilty of an offence punishable on summary conviction.

(2) Every person who compels another to commit bestiality is guilty of an indictable offence and liable to imprisonment for a term not exceeding ten years or is guilty of an offence punishable on summary conviction.

(3) Despite subsection (1), every person who commits bestiality in the presence of a person under the age of 16 years, or who incites a person under the age of 16 years to commit bestiality,

- (*a*) is guilty of an indictable offence and is liable to imprisonment for a term of not more than 14 years and to a minimum punishment of imprisonment for a term of one year; or
- (*b*) is guilty of an offence punishable on summary conviction and is liable to imprisonment for a term of not more than two years less a day and to a minimum punishment of imprisonment for a term of six months.

(4) The court may, in addition to any other sentence that it may impose under any of subsections (1) to (3),

- (*a*) make an order prohibiting the accused from owning, having the custody or control of or residing in the same premises as an animal during any period that the court considers appropriate but, in the case of a second or subsequent offence, for a minimum of five years; and
- (*b*) on application of the Attorney General or on its own motion, order that the accused pay to a person or an organization that has taken care of an animal as a result of the commission of the offence the reasonable costs that the person or organization incurred in respect of the animal, if the costs are readily ascertainable.

(5) Every person who contravenes an order made under paragraph (4)(*a*) is guilty of an offence punishable on summary conviction.

(6) Sections 740 to 741.2 apply, with any modifications that the circumstances require, to orders made under paragraph (4)(*b*).

(7) In this section, "bestiality" means any contact, for a sexual purpose, with an animal. R.S.C. 1985, c. 19 (3rd Supp.), s. 3; 2008, c. 6, s. 54(d); 2012, c. 1, s. 15; 2015, c. 23, s. 5; 2019, c. 17, s. 1.

161. (old provision) [*Repealed*, R.S.C. 1985, c. 19 (3rd Supp.), s. 4.]

CODE

ORDER OF PROHIBITION / Offences / Duration of prohibition / Court may vary order / Offence.

161. (1) When an offender is convicted, or is discharged on the conditions prescribed in a probation order under section 730, of an offence referred to in subsection (1.1) in respect of a person who is under the age of 16 years, the court that sentences the offender or directs that the accused be discharged, as the case may be, in addition to any other punishment that may be imposed for that offence or any other condition prescribed in the order of discharge, shall consider making and may make, subject to the conditions or exemptions that the court directs, an order prohibiting the offender from

(*a*) attending a public park or public swimming area where persons under the age of 16 years are present or can reasonably be expected to be present, or a daycare centre, schoolground, playground or community centre;

(*a*.1) being within two kilometres, or any other distance specified in the order, of any dwelling-house where the victim identified in the order ordinarily resides or of any other place specified in the order;

(*b*) seeking, obtaining or continuing any employment, whether or not the employment is remunerated, or becoming or being a volunteer in a capacity, that involves being in a position of trust or authority towards persons under the age of 16 years;

(*c*) having any contact — including communicating by any means — with a person who is under the age of 16 years, unless the offender does so under the supervision of a person whom the court considers appropriate; or

(*d*) using the Internet or other digital network, unless the offender does so in accordance with conditions set by the court.

(1.1) The offences for the purpose of subsection (1) are

(*a*) an offence under section 151, 152 or 155, subsection 160(2) or (3), section 163.1, 170, 171, 171.1, 172.1 or 172.2, subsection 173(2), section 271, 272, 273 or 279.011, subsection 279.02(2) or 279.03(2), section 280 or 281 or subsection 286.1(2), 286.2(2) or 286.3(2);

(*b*) an offence under section 144 (rape), 145 (attempt to commit rape), 149 (indecent assault on female), 156 (indecent assault on male) or 245 (common assault) or subsection 246(1) (assault with intent) of the *Criminal Code*, chapter C-34 of the Revised Statutes of Canada, 1970, as it read immediately before January 4, 1983;

(*c*) an offence under subsection 146(1) (sexual intercourse with a female under 14) or section 153 (sexual intercourse with step-daughter), 155 (buggery or bestiality), 157 (gross indecency), 166 (parent or guardian procuring defilement) or 167 (householder permitting defilement) of the *Criminal Code*, chapter C-34 of the Revised Statutes of Canada, 1970, as it read immediately before January 1, 1988; or

(*d*) an offence under subsection 212(1) (procuring), 212(2) (living on the avails of prostitution of person under 18 years), 212(2.1) (aggravated offence in relation to living on the avails of prostitution of person under 18 years) or 212(4) (prostitution of person under 18 years) of this Act, as it read from time to time before the day on which this paragraph comes into force.

(2) The prohibition may be for life or for any shorter duration that the court considers desirable and, in the case of a prohibition that is not for life, the prohibition begins on the later of

(a) the date on which the order is made; and

(b) where the offender is sentenced to a term of imprisonment, the date on which the offender is released from imprisonment for the offence, including release on parole, mandatory supervision or statutory release.

(3) A court that makes an order of prohibition or, where the court is for any reason unable to act, another court of equivalent jurisdiction in the same province, may, on application of the offender or the prosecutor, require the offender to appear before it at any time and, after hearing the parties, that court may vary the conditions prescribed in the order if, in the opinion of the court, the variation is desirable because of changed circumstances after the conditions were prescribed.

(4) Every person who is bound by an order of prohibition and who does not comply with the order is guilty of

(a) an indictable offence and is liable to imprisonment for a term of not more than four years; or

(b) an offence punishable on summary conviction. 1993, c. 45, s. 1; 1995, c. 22, s. 18 (Sched. IV, item 26); 1997, c. 18, s. 4; 1999, c. 31, s. 67; 2002, c. 13, s. 4; 2005, c. 32, s. 5; 2008, c. 6, s. 54(e); 2012, c. 1, s. 16; 2014, c. 21, s. 1; 2014, c. 25, s. 5; 2015, c. 23, s. 6; 2019, c. 25, s. 55.

---

162. (old provision) [*Repealed*, R.S.C. 1985, c. 19 (3rd Supp.), s. 4.]

VOYEURISM / Definition of "visual recording" / Exemption / Printing, publication, etc., of voyeuristic recordings / Punishment / Defence / Question of law, motives

162. (1) Every one commits an offence who, surreptitiously, observes — including by mechanical or electronic means — or makes a visual recording of a person who is in circumstances that give rise to a reasonable expectation of privacy, if

(a) the person is in a place in which a person can reasonably be expected to be nude, to expose his or her genital organs or anal region or her breasts, or to be engaged in explicit sexual activity;

(b) the person is nude, is exposing his or her genital organs or anal region or her breasts, or is engaged in explicit sexual activity, and the observation or recording is done for the purpose of observing or recording a person in such a state or engaged in such an activity; or

(c) the observation or recording is done for a sexual purpose.

(2) In this section, "visual recording" includes a photographic, film or video recording made by any means.

(3) Paragraphs (1)(a) and (b) do not apply to a peace officer who, under the authority of a warrant issued under section 487.01, is carrying out any activity referred to in those paragraphs.

(4) Every one commits an offence who, knowing that a recording was obtained by the commission of an offence under subsection (1), prints, copies, publishes,

distributes, circulates, sells, advertises or makes available the recording, or has the recording in his or her possession for the purpose of printing, copying, publishing, distributing, circulating, selling or advertising it or making it available.

(5) Every one who commits an offence under subsection (1) or (4)

(a) is guilty of an indictable offence and liable to imprisonment for a term not exceeding five years; or

(b) is guilty of an offence punishable on summary conviction.

(6) No person shall be convicted of an offence under this section if the acts that are alleged to constitute the offence serve the public good and do not extend beyond what serves the public good.

(7) For the purposes of subsection (6),

(a) it is a question of law whether an act serves the public good and whether there is evidence that the act alleged goes beyond what serves the public good, but it is a question of fact whether the act does or does not extend beyond what serves the public good; and

(b) the motives of an accused are irrelevant. 2005, c. 32, s. 6.

PUBLICATION ETC., OF AN INTIMATE IMAGE WITHOUT CONSENT / Definition of "intimate image" / Defence / Question of fact and law, motives.

162.1 (1) Everyone who knowingly publishes, distributes, transmits, sells, makes available or advertises an intimate image of a person knowing that the person depicted in the image did not give their consent to that conduct, or being reckless as to whether or not that person gave their consent to that conduct, is guilty

(a) of an indictable offence and liable to imprisonment for a term of not more than five years; or

(b) of an offence punishable on summary conviction.

(2) In this section, "intimate image" means a visual recording of a person made by any means including a photographic, film or video recording,

(a) in which the person is nude, is exposing his or her genital organs or anal region or her breasts or is engaged in explicit sexual activity;

(b) in respect of which, at the time of the recording, there were circumstances that gave rise to a reasonable expectation of privacy; and

(c) in respect of which the person depicted retains a reasonable expectation of privacy at the time the offence is committed.

(3) No person shall be convicted of an offence under this section if the conduct that forms the subject-matter of the charge serves the public good and does not extend beyond what serves the public good.

(4) For the purposes of subsection (3),

(a) it is a question of law whether the conduct serves the public good and whether there is evidence that the conduct alleged goes beyond what serves the public good, but it is a question of fact whether the conduct does or does not extend beyond what serves the public good; and

(b) the motives of an accused are irrelevant. 2014, c. 31, s. 3.

PROHIBITION ORDER / Duration of prohibition / Court may vary order / Offence.

162.2 (1) When an offender is convicted, or is discharged on the conditions prescribed in a probation order under section 730, of an offence referred to in subsection 162.1(1), the court that sentences or discharges the offender, in addition to any other punishment that may be imposed for that offence or any other condition prescribed in the order of discharge, may make, subject to the conditions or exemptions that the court directs, an order prohibiting the offender from using the Internet or other digital network, unless the offender does so in accordance with conditions set by the court.

(2) The prohibition may be for any period that the court considers appropriate, including any period to which the offender is sentenced to imprisonment.

(3) A court that makes an order of prohibition or, if the court is for any reason unable to act, another court of equivalent jurisdiction in the same province may, on application of the offender or the prosecutor, require the offender to appear before it at any time and, after hearing the parties, that court may vary the conditions prescribed in the order if, in the opinion of the court, the variation is desirable because of changed circumstances after the conditions were prescribed.

(4) Every person who is bound by an order of prohibition and who does not comply with the order is guilty of
- (a) an indictable offence and is liable to imprisonment for a term of not more than four years; or
- (b) an offence punishable on summary conviction. 2014, c. 31, s. 3; 2015, c. 23, s. 33; 2019, c. 25, s. 56.

Offences Tending to Corrupt Morals

OBSCENE MATERIALS / Idem / Defence of public good / Question of law and question of fact / Motives irrelevant / Ignorance of nature no defence / Obscene publication.

163. (1) Every person commits an offence who makes, prints, publishes, distributes, circulates or has in their possession for the purpose of publication, distribution or circulation any obscene written matter, picture, model, phonograph record or any other obscene thing.

(2) Every person commits an offence who knowingly, without lawful justification or excuse,
- (a) sells, exposes to public view or has in their possession for that purpose any obscene written matter, picture, model, phonograph record or any other obscene thing;
- (b) publicly exhibits a disgusting object or an indecent show;
- (c) [Repealed, 2018, c. 29, s. 11(3).]
- (d) [Repealed, 2018, c. 29, s. 11(3).]

199

(3) No person shall be convicted of an offence under this section if the public good was served by the acts that are alleged to constitute the offence and if the acts alleged did not extend beyond what served the public good.

(4) For the purposes of this section, it is a question of law whether an act served the public good and whether there is evidence that the act alleged went beyond what served the public good, but it is a question of fact whether the acts did or did not extend beyond what served the public good.

(5) For the purposes of this section, the motives of an accused are irrelevant.

(6) [Repealed, 1993, c. 46, s. 1.]

(7) [Repealed, 2018, c. 29, s. 11(3).]

(8) For the purposes of this Act, any publication a dominant characteristic of which is the undue exploitation of sex, or of sex and any one or more of the following subjects, namely, crime, horror, cruelty and violence, shall be deemed to be obscene. R.S., c. C-34, s. 159; 1993, c. 46, s. 1; 2018, c. 29, s. 11.

DEFINITION OF "CHILD PORNOGRAPHY" / Making child pornography / Distribution, etc. of child pornography / Possession of child pornography / Accessing child pornography / Interpretation / Aggravating factor / Defence / Defence / Question of law.

163.1 (1) In this section, "child pornography" means

(a) a photographic, film, video or other visual representation, whether or not it was made by electronic or mechanical means,

   (i) that shows a person who is or is depicted as being under the age of eighteen years and is engaged in or is depicted as engaged in explicit sexual activity, or

   (ii) the dominant characteristic of which is the depiction, for a sexual purpose, of a sexual organ or the anal region of a person under the age of eighteen years;

(b) any written material, visual representation or audio recording that advocates or counsels sexual activity with a person under the age of eighteen years that would be an offence under this Act;

(c) any written material whose dominant characteristic is the description, for a sexual purpose, of sexual activity with a person under the age of eighteen years that would be an offence under this Act; or

(d) any audio recording that has as its dominant characteristic the description, presentation or representation, for a sexual purpose, of sexual activity with a person under the age of eighteen years that would be an offence under this Act.

(2) Every person who makes, prints, publishes or possesses for the purpose of publication any child pornography is guilty of an indictable offence and liable to imprisonment for a term of not more than 14 years and to a minimum punishment of imprisonment for a term of one year.

(3) Every person who transmits, makes available, distributes, sells, advertises, imports, exports or possesses for the purpose of transmission, making available,

distribution, sale, advertising or exportation any child pornography is guilty of an indictable offence and liable to imprisonment for a term of not more than 14 years and to a minimum punishment of imprisonment for a term of one year.

(4) Every person who possesses any child pornography is guilty of

    (a) an indictable offence and is liable to imprisonment for a term of not more than 10 years and to a minimum punishment of imprisonment for a term of one year; or

    (b) an offence punishable on summary conviction and is liable to imprisonment for a term of not more than two years less a day and to a minimum punishment of imprisonment for a term of six months.

(4.1) Every person who accesses any child pornography is guilty of

    (a) an indictable offence and is liable to imprisonment for a term of not more than 10 years and to a minimum punishment of imprisonment for a term of one year; or

    (b) an offence punishable on summary conviction and is liable to imprisonment for a term of not more than two years less a day and to a minimum punishment of imprisonment for a term of six months.

(4.2) For the purposes of subsection (4.1), a person accesses child pornography who knowingly causes child pornography to be viewed by, or transmitted to, himself or herself.

(4.3) If a person is convicted of an offence under this section, the court that imposes the sentence shall consider as an aggravating factor the fact that the person committed the offence with intent to make a profit.

(5) It is not a defence to a charge under subsection (2) in respect of a visual representation that the accused believed that a person shown in the representation that is alleged to constitute child pornography was or was depicted as being eighteen years of age or more unless the accused took all reasonable steps to ascertain the age of that person and took all reasonable steps to ensure that, where the person was eighteen years of age or more, the representation did not depict that person as being under the age of eighteen years.

(6) No person shall be convicted of an offence under this section if the act that is alleged to constitute the offence

    (a) has a legitimate purpose related to the administration of justice or to science, medicine, education or art; and

    (b) does not pose an undue risk of harm to persons under the age of eighteen years.

(7) For greater certainty, for the purposes of this section, it is a question of law whether any written material, visual representation or audio recording advocates or counsels sexual activity with a person under the age of eighteen years that would be an offence under this Act. 1993, c. 46. s. 2; 2002, c. 13, s. 5; 2005, c. 32, s. 7; 201, c. 1, s. 17; 2015, c. 23, s. 7.

WARRANT OF SEIZURE / Summons to occupier / Owner and maker may appear / Order of forfeiture / Disposal of matter / Appeal / Consent / Definitions / "Advertisement of sexual services" / "Court" / "Crime comic" / "Judge" / "Voyeuristic recording".

164. (1) A judge may issue a warrant authorizing seizure of copies of a recording, a publication, a representation or any written material, if the judge is satisfied by information on oath that there are reasonable grounds to believe that

- (a) the recording, copies of which are kept for sale or distribution in premises within the jurisdiction of the court, is a voyeuristic recording;
- (b) the recording, copies of which are kept for sale or distribution in premises within the jurisdiction of the court, is an intimate image;
- (c) the publication, copies of which are kept for sale or distribution in premises within the jurisdiction of the court, is *obscene*, within the meaning of subsection 163(8);
- (d) the representation, written material or recording, copies of which are kept in premises within the jurisdiction of the court, is child pornography as defined in section 163.1; or
- (e) the representation, written material or recording, copies of which are kept in premises within the jurisdiction of the court, is an advertisement of sexual services.

(2) Within seven days of the issue of the warrant under subsection (1), the judge shall issue a summons to the occupier of the premises requiring him to appear before the court and show cause why the matter seized should not be forfeited to Her Majesty.

(3) The owner and the maker of the matter seized under subsection (1), and alleged to be obscene, child pornography, a voyeuristic recording, an intimate image or an advertisement of sexual services, may appear and be represented in the proceedings to oppose the making of an order for the forfeiture of the matter.

(4) If the court is satisfied, on a balance of probabilities, that the publication, representation, written material or recording referred to in subsection (1) is obscene, child pornography, a voyeuristic recording, an intimate image or an advertisement of sexual services, it may make an order declaring the matter forfeited to Her Majesty in right of the province in which the proceedings take place, for disposal as the Attorney General may direct.

(5) If the court is not satisfied that the publication, representation, written material or recording referred to in subsection (1) is obscene, child pornography, a voyeuristic recording, an intimate image or an advertisement of sexual services, it shall order that the matter be restored to the person from whom it was seized without delay after the time for final appeal has expired.

(6) An appeal lies from an order made under subsection (4) or (5) by any person who appeared in the proceedings

- (a) on any ground of appeal that involves a question of law alone,
- (b) on any ground of appeal that involves a question of fact alone, or
- (c) on any ground of appeal that involves a question of mixed law and fact,

as if it were an appeal against conviction or against a judgment or verdict of acquittal, as the case may be, on a question of law alone under Part XXI and sections 673 to 696 apply with such modifications as the circumstances require.

(7) If an order is made under this section by a judge in a province with respect to one or more copies of a publication, a representation, written material or a recording, no proceedings shall be instituted or continued in that province under section 162, 162.1, 163, 163.1 or 286.4 with respect to those or other copies of the same publication, representation, written material or recording without the consent of the Attorney General.

CODE

(8) In this section,

"advertisement of sexual services" means any material — including a photographic, film, video, audio or other recording, made by any means, a visual representation or any written material — that is used to advertise sexual services contrary to section 286.4.

"court" means

  (a) in the Province of Quebec, the Court of Quebec, the municipal court of Montreal and the municipal court of Quebec,

(a.1) in the Province of Ontario, the Superior Court of Justice,

  (b) in the Provinces of New Brunswick, Manitoba, Saskatchewan and Alberta, the Court of Queen's Bench,

  (c) in the Province of Newfoundland and Labrador, the Trial Division of the Supreme Court,

(c.1) [Repealed. 1992, c. 51, s. 34.]

  (d) in the Provinces of Nova Scotia, British Columbia and Prince Edward Island, in Yukon and in the Northwest Territories, the Supreme Court, and

  (e) in Nunavut, the Nunavut Court of Justice;

"crime comic" [Repealed, 2018, c. 29, s. 12(3).]

"intimate image" has the same meaning as in subsection 162.1(2).

"judge" means a judge of a court.

"voyeuristic recording" means a visual recording within the meaning of subsection 162(2) that is made as described in subsection 162(1). R.S., c. C-34, s. 160; 1974-75-76, c. 48, s. 25; 1978-79, c. 11, s. 10; R.S.C. 1985, c. 27 (2nd Supp.), s. 10; c. 40 (4th Supp.), s. 2; 1990, c. 16, s. 3; 1990, c. 17, s. 9; 1992, c. 1, s. 58; 1992, c. 51, s. 34; 1993, c. 28, Sch. III, s. 28 (repealed by 1999, c. 3, s. 12); 1993, c. 46, s. 3; 1997, c. 18, s. 5; 1998, c. 30, s. 14(d); 1999, c. 3, ss. 12, 27; 2002, c. 7, s. 139; c. 13, s. 6; 2005, c. 32, s. 8; 2014, c. 25, s. 6; 2014, c. 31, s. 4; 2015, c. 3, s. 46; 2018, c. 29, s. 12.

WARRANT OF SEIZURE / Notice to person who posted the material / Person who posted the material may appear / Non-appearance / Order / Destruction of copy / Return of material / Other provisions to apply / When order takes effect.

164.1 (1) If a judge is satisfied by information on oath that there are reasonable grounds to believe that there is material — namely, child pornography as defined in section 163.1, a voyeuristic recording, an intimate image or an advertisement of sexual services as defined in 164(8) or computer data as defined in subsection 342.1(2) that makes child pornography, a voyeuristic recording, an intimate image or an advertisement of sexual services available — that is stored on and made available through a computer system as defined in subsection 342.1(2) that is within the jurisdiction of the court, the judge may order the custodian of the computer system to

(a) give an electronic copy of the material to the court;

(b) ensure that the material is no longer stored on and made available through the computer system; and

(c) provide the information necessary to identify and locate the person who posted the material.

(2) Within a reasonable time after receiving the information referred to in paragraph (1)(c), the judge shall cause notice to be given to the person who posted the material, giving that person the opportunity to appear and be represented before the court, and show cause why the material should not be deleted. If the person cannot be identified or located or does not reside in Canada, the judge may order the custodian of the computer system to post the text of the notice at the location where the material was previously stored and made available, until the time set for the appearance.

(3) The person who posted the material may appear and be represented in the proceedings in order to oppose the making of an order under subsection (5).

(4) If the person who posted the material does not appear for the proceedings, the court may proceed *ex parte* to hear and determine the proceedings in the absence of the person as fully and effectually as if the person had appeared.

(5) If the court is satisfied, on a balance of probabilities, that the material is child pornography as defined in section 163.1, a voyeuristic recording, an intimate image or an advertisement of sexual services as defined in subsection 164(8) or computer data as defined in subsection 342.1(2) that makes child pornography, the voyeuristic recording, the intimate image or the advertisement of sexual services available, it may order the custodian of the computer system to delete the material.

(6) When the court makes the order for the deletion of the material, it may order the destruction of the electronic copy in the court's possession.

(7) If the court is not satisfied that the material is child pornography as defined in 163.1, a voyeuristic recording, an intimate image or an advertisement of sexual services as defined in subsection 164(8) or computer data as defined in subsection 342.1(2) that makes child pornography, the voyeuristic recording, the intimate image or the advertisement of sexual services available, the court shall order that the electronic copy be returned to the custodian of the computer system and terminate the order under paragraph (1)(b).

(8) Subsections 164(6) to (8) apply, with any modifications that the circumstances require, to this section.

(9) No order made under subsections (5) to (7) takes effect until the time for final appeal has expired. 2002, c. 13, s. 7; 2005, c. 32, s. 9; 2014, c. 25, s. 7; 2014, c. 31, s. 5.

FORFEITURE AFTER CONVICTION / Third party rights / Right of appeal — third party / Right of appeal — Attorney General / Application of Part XXI.

164.2 (1) On application of the Attorney General, a court that convicts a person of an offence under section 162.1, 163.1, 172.1 or 172.2, in addition to any other punishment that it may impose, may order that anything — other than real property — be forfeited to Her Majesty and disposed of as the Attorney General directs if it is satisfied, on a balance of probabilities, that the thing

(*a*) was used in the commission of the offence; and

(*b*) is the property of

(i) the convicted person or another person who was a party to the offence, or

(ii) a person who acquired the thing from a person referred to in subparagraph (i) under circumstances that give rise to a reasonable inference that it was transferred for the purpose of avoiding forfeiture.

(2) Before making an order under subsection (1), the court shall cause notice to be given to, and may hear, any person whom it considers to have an interest in the thing, and may declare the nature and extent of the person's interest in it.

(3) A person who was heard in response to a notice given under subsection (2) may appeal to the court of appeal against an order made under subsection (1).

(4) The Attorney General may appeal to the court of appeal against the refusal of a court to make an order under subsection (1).

(5) Part XXI applies, with any modifications that the circumstances require, with respect to the procedure for an appeal under subsections (3) and (4). 2002, c. 13, s. 7; 2008, c. 18, s. 4; 2012, c. 1, s. 18; 2014, c. 31, s. 6.

RELIEF FROM FORFEITURE / Hearing of application / Notice to Attorney General / Order / Appeal to court of appeal / Powers of Attorney General.

164.3 (1) Within thirty days after an order under subsection 164.2(1) is made, a person who claims an interest in the thing forfeited may apply in writing to a judge for an order under subsection (4).

(2) The judge shall fix a day — not less than thirty days after the application is made — for its hearing.

(3) At least fifteen days before the hearing, the applicant shall cause notice of the application and of the hearing day to be served on the Attorney General.

(4) The judge may make an order declaring that the applicant's interest in the thing is not affected by the forfeiture and declaring the nature and extent of the interest if the judge is satisfied that the applicant

(*a*) was not a party to the offence; and

(*b*) did not acquire the thing from a person who was a party to the offence under circumstances that give rise to a reasonable inference that it was transferred for the purpose of avoiding forfeiture.

(5) A person referred to in subsection (4) or the Attorney General may appeal to the court of appeal against an order made under that subsection. Part XXI applies,

with any modifications that the circumstances require, with respect to the procedure for an appeal under this subsection.

(6) On application by a person who obtained an order under subsection (4), made after the expiration of the time allowed for an appeal against the order and, if an appeal is taken, after it has been finally disposed of, the Attorney General shall direct that

(*a*) the thing be returned to the person; or

(*b*) an amount equal to the value of the extent of the person's interest, as declared in the order, be paid to the person. 2002, c. 13, s. 7.

---

165. [*Repealed*, 2018, c. 29, s. 13.]

---

166. [*Repealed*, 1994, c. 44, s. 9.]

IMMORAL THEATRICAL PERFORMANCE / Person taking part.

167. (1) Every one commits an offence who, being the lessee, manager, agent or person in charge of a theatre, presents or gives or allows to be presented or given therein an immoral, indecent or obscene performance, entertainment or representation.

(2) Every one commits an offence who takes part or appears as an actor, a performer or an assistant in any capacity, in an immoral, indecent or obscene performance, entertainment or representation in a theatre. R.S., c. C-34, s. 163.

MAILING OBSCENE MATTER / Exceptions.

168. (1) Every one commits an offence who makes use of the mails for the purpose of transmitting or delivering anything that is obscene, indecent, immoral or scurrilous.

(2) Subsection (1) does not apply to a person who

(*a*) prints or publishes any matter for use in connection with any judicial proceedings or communicates it to persons who are concerned in the proceedings;

(*b*) prints or publishes a notice or report under the direction of a court; or

(*c*) prints or publishes any matter

(i) in a volume or part of a genuine series of law reports that does not form part of any other publication and consists solely of reports of proceedings in courts of law, or

(ii) in a publication of a technical character that is intended, in good faith, for circulation among members of the legal or medical profession. R.S., c. C-34, s. 164; 1999, c. 5, s. 2.

PUNISHMENT.

169. Every one who commits an offence under section 163, 165, 167 or 168 is guilty of (*a*) an indictable offence and liable to imprisonment for a term not exceeding two years; or

   (*b*) an offence punishable on summary conviction. R.S., c. C-34, s. 165; 1999, c. 5, s. 3.

PARENT OR GUARDIAN PROCURING SEXUAL ACTIVITY.

170. Every parent or guardian of a person under the age of 18 years who procures the person for the purpose of engaging in any sexual activity prohibited by this Act with a person other than the parent or guardian is guilty of an indictable offence and liable to imprisonment for a term of not more than 14 years and to a minimum punishment of imprisonment for a term of one year. R.S.C. 1985, c. 19 (3rd Supp.), s. 5; 2005, c. 32, s. 9.1; 2008, c. 6, s. 54(*f*); 2012, c. 1, s. 19; 2015, c. 23, s. 8.

HOUSEHOLDER PERMITTING PROHIBITED SEXUAL ACTIVITY.

171. Every owner, occupier or manager of premises, or any other person who has control of premises or assists in the management or control of premises, who knowingly permits a person under the age of 18 years to resort to or to be in or on the premises for the purpose of engaging in any sexual activity prohibited by this Act is guilty of an indictable offence and liable to imprisonment for a term of not more than 14 years and to a minimum punishment of imprisonment for a term of one year. R.S.C. 1985, c. 19 (3rd Supp.), s. 5; 2005, c. 32, s. 9.1; 2008, c. 6, s. 54(*g*); 2012, c. 1, s. 20; 2015, c. 23, s. 9.

MAKING SEXUALLY EXPLICIT MATERIAL AVAILABLE TO CHILD / Punishment / Presumption / No defence / Definition of "sexually explicit material".

171.1 (1) Every person commits an offence who transmits, makes available, distributes or sells sexually explicit material to

   (*a*) a person who is, or who the accused believes is, under the age of 18 years, for the purpose of facilitating the commission of an offence with respect to that person under subsection 153(1), section 155, 163.1, 170, 171 or 279.011 or subsection 279.02(2), 279.03(2), 286.1(2), 286.2(2) or 286.3(2);

   (*b*) a person who is, or who the accused believes is, under the age of 16 years, for the purpose of facilitating the commission of an offence under section 151 or 152, subsection 160(3) or 173(2) or section 271, 272, 273 or 280 with respect to that person; or

   (*c*) a person who is, or who the accused believes is, under the age of 14 years, for the purpose of facilitating the commission of an offence under section 281 with respect to that person.

(2) Every person who commits an offence under subsection (1)

   (*a*) is guilty of an indictable offence and is liable to imprisonment for a term of not more than 14 years and to a minimum punishment of imprisonment for a term of six months; or

(b) is guilty of an offence punishable on summary conviction and is liable to imprisonment for a term of not more than two years less a day and to a minimum punishment of imprisonment for a term of 90 days.

(3) Evidence that the person referred to in paragraph (1)(*a*), (*b*) or (*c*) was represented to the accused as being under the age of 18, 16 or 14 years, as the case may be, is, in the absence of evidence to the contrary, proof that the accused believed that the person was under that age.

(4) It is not a defence to a charge under paragraph (1)(*a*), (*b*) or (*c*) that the accused believed that the person referred to in that paragraph was at least 18, 16 or 14 years of age, as the case may be, unless the accused took reasonable steps to ascertain the age of the person.

(5) In subsection (1), "sexually explicit material" means material that is not child pornography, as defined in subsection 163.1(1), and that is

(*a*) a photographic, film, video or other visual representation, whether or not it was made by electronic or mechanical means,

   (i) that shows a person who is engaged in or is depicted as engaged in explicit sexual activity, or

   (ii) the dominant characteristic of which is the depiction, for a sexual purpose, of a person's genital organs or anal region or, if the person is female, her breasts;

(*b*) written material whose dominant characteristic is the description, for a sexual purpose, of explicit sexual activity with a person; or

(*c*) an audio recording whose dominant characteristic is the description, presentation or representation, for a sexual purpose, of explicit sexual activity with a person. 2012, c. 1, s. 21; 2014, c. 25, s. 8; 2015, c. 23, s. 10.

CORRUPTING CHILDREN / Limitation / Definition of "child" / Who may institute prosecutions.

172. (1) Every person who, in the home of a child, participates in adultery or sexual immorality or indulges in habitual drunkenness or any other form of vice, and by doing so endangers the morals of the child or renders the home an unfit place for the child to be in, is guilty of

(*a*) an indictable offence and liable to imprisonment for a term of not more than two years; or

(*b*) an offence punishable on summary conviction.

(2) [*Repealed*, R.S.C. 1985, c. 19 (3rd Supp.), s. 6.]

(3) For the purposes of this section, "child" means a person who is or appears to be under the age of eighteen years.

(4) No proceedings shall be commenced under subsection (1) without the consent of the Attorney General, unless they are instituted by or at the instance of a recognized society for the protection of children or by an officer of a juvenile court. R.S., c. C-34, s. 168; R.S.C. 1985, c. 19 (3rd Supp.), s. 6; 2019, c. 25, s. 57.

LURING A CHILD / Punishment / Presumption re age / No defence.

172.1 (1) Every person commits an offence who, by a means of telecommunication, communicates with

    (*a*) a person who is, or who the accused believes is, under the age of 18 years, for the purpose of facilitating the commission of an offence with respect to that person under subsection 153(1), section 155, 163.1, 170, 171 or 279.011 or subsection 279.02(2), 279.03(2), 286.1(2), 286.2(2) or 286.3(2);

    (*b*) a person who is, or who the accused believes is, under the age of 16 years, for the purpose of facilitating the commission of an offence under section 151 or 152, subsection 160(3) or 173(2) or section 271, 272, 273 or 280 with respect to that person; or

    (*c*) a person who is, or who the accused believes is, under the age of 14 years, for the purpose of facilitating the commission of an offence under section 281 with respect to that person.

(2) Every person who commits an offence under subsection (1)

    (*a*) is guilty of an indictable offence and is liable to imprisonment for a term of not more than 14 years and to a minimum punishment of imprisonment for a term of one year; or

    (*b*) is guilty of an offence punishable on summary conviction and is liable to imprisonment for a term of not more than two years less a day and to a minimum punishment of imprisonment for a term of six months.

(3) Evidence that the person referred to in paragraph (1)(*a*), (*b*) or (*c*) was represented to the accused as being under the age of eighteen years, sixteen years or fourteen years, as the case may be, is, in the absence of evidence to the contrary, proof that the accused believed that the person was under that age.

(4) It is not a defence to a charge under paragraph (1)(*a*), (*b*) or (*c*) that the accused believed that the person referred to in that paragraph was at least eighteen years of age, sixteen years or fourteen years of age, as the case may be, unless the accused took reasonable steps to ascertain the age of the person. 2002, c. 13, s. 8; 2007, c. 20, s. 1; 2008, c. 6, s. 14; 2012, c. 1, s. 22; 2014, c. 25, s. 9; 2015, c. 23, s. 11.

AGREEMENT OR ARRANGEMENT — SEXUAL OFFENCE AGAINST CHILD / Punishment / Presumption / No defence / No defence.

172.2 (1) Every person commits an offence who, by a means of telecommunication, agrees with a person, or makes an arrangement with a person, to commit an offence

    (*a*) under subsection 153(1), section 155, 163.1, 170, 171 or 279.011 or subsection 279.02(2), 279.03(2), 286.1(2), 286.2(2) or 286.3(2) with respect to another person who is, or who the accused believes is, under the age of 18 years;

    (*b*) under section 151 or 152, subsection 160(3) or 173(2) or section 271, 272, 273 or 280 with respect to another person who is, or who the accused believes is, under the age of 16 years; or

    (*c*) under section 281 with respect to another person who is, or who the accused believes is, under the age of 14 years.

(2) Every person who commits an offence under subsection (1)

    (*a*) is guilty of an indictable offence and is liable to imprisonment for a term of not more than 14 years and to a minimum punishment of imprisonment for a term of one year; or

    (*b*) is guilty of an offence punishable on summary conviction and is liable to imprisonment for a term of not more than two years less a day and to a minimum punishment of imprisonment for a term of six months.

(3) Evidence that the person referred to in paragraph (1)(*a*), (*b*) or (*c*) was represented to the accused as being under the age of 18, 16 or 14 years, as the case may be, is, in the absence of evidence to the contrary, proof that the accused believed that the person was under that age.

(4) It is not a defence to a charge under paragraph (1)(*a*), (*b*) or (*c*) that the accused believed that the person referred to in that paragraph was at least 18, 16 or 14 years of age, as the case may be, unless the accused took reasonable steps to ascertain the age of the person.

(5) It is not a defence to a charge under paragraph (1)(*a*), (*b*) or (*c*)

    (*a*) that the person with whom the accused agreed or made an arrangement was a peace officer or a person acting under the direction of a peace officer; or

    (*b*) that, if the person with whom the accused agreed or made an arrangement was a peace officer or a person acting under the direction of a peace officer, the person referred to in paragraph (1)(*a*), (*b*) or (*c*) did not exist. 2012, c. 1, s. 23; 2014, c. 25, s. 10; 2015, c. 23, s. 12.

Disorderly Conduct

INDECENT ACTS / Exposure.

173. (1) Everyone who wilfully does an indecent act in a public place in the presence of one or more persons, or in any place with intent to insult or offend any person,

    (*a*) is guilty of an indictable offence and is liable to imprisonment for a term of not more than two years; or

    (*b*) is guilty of an offence punishable on summary conviction.

(2) Every person who, in any place, for a sexual purpose, exposes his or her genital organs to a person who is under the age of 16 years

    (*a*) is guilty of an indictable offence and is liable to imprisonment for a term of not more than two years and to a minimum punishment of imprisonment for a term of 90 days; or

    (*b*) is guilty of an offence punishable on summary conviction and is liable to imprisonment for a term of not more than six months and to a minimum punishment of imprisonment for a term of 30 days. R.S., c. C-34, s. 169; R.S.C. 1985, c. 19 (3rd Supp.), s. 7; 2008, c. 6, s. 54(*h*); 2010, c. 17, s. 2; 2012, c. 1, s. 23; 2019, c. 25, s. 58.

NUDITY / Nude / Consent of Attorney General.

174. (1) Every one who, without lawful excuse,

    (*a*) is nude in a public place, or

    (*b*) is nude and exposed to public view while on private property, whether or not the property is his own,

is guilty of an offence punishable on summary conviction.

(2) For the purposes of this section, a person is nude who is so clad as to offend against public decency or order.

(3) No proceedings shall be commenced under this section without the consent of the Attorney General. R.S., c. C-34, s. 170.

CAUSING DISTURBANCE, INDECENT EXHIBITION, LOITERING, ETC. / Evidence of peace officer.

175. (1) Every one who

    (*a*) not being in a dwelling-house, causes a disturbance in or near a public place,

        (i) by fighting, screaming, shouting, swearing, singing or using insulting or obscene language,

        (ii) by being drunk, or

       (iii) by impeding or molesting other persons,

    (*b*) openly exposes or exhibits an indecent exhibition in a public place,

    (*c*) loiters in a public place and in any way obstructs persons who are in that place, or

    (*d*) disturbs the peace and quiet of the occupants of a dwelling-house by discharging firearms or by other disorderly conduct in a public place or who, not being an occupant of a dwelling-house comprised in a particular building or structure, disturbs the peace and quiet of the occupants of a dwelling-house comprised in the building or structure by discharging firearms or by other disorderly conduct in any part of a building or structure to which, at the time of such conduct, the occupants of two or more dwelling-houses comprised in the building or structure have access as of right or by invitation, express or implied,

is guilty of an offence punishable on summary conviction.

(2) In the absence of other evidence, or by way of corroboration of other evidence, a summary conviction court may infer from the evidence of a peace officer relating to the conduct of a person or persons, whether ascertained or not, that a disturbance described in paragraph (1)(*a*) or (*d*) or an obstruction described in paragraph (1)(*c*) was caused or occurred. R.S., c. C-34, s. 171; 1972, c. 13, s. 11; 1974-75-76, c. 93, s. 9; 1997, c. 18, s. 6.

OBSTRUCTING OR VIOLENCE TO OR ARREST OF OFFICIATING CLERGYMAN / Disturbing religious worship or certain meetings / Idem.

176. (1) Every person is guilty of an indictable offence and liable to imprisonment for a term of not more than two years or is guilty of an offence punishable on summary conviction who

(a) by threats or force, unlawfully obstructs or prevents or endeavours to obstruct or prevent an officiant from celebrating a religious or spiritual service or performing any other function in connection with their calling, or

(b) knowing that an officiant is about to perform, is on their way to perform or is returning from the performance of any of the duties or functions mentioned in paragraph (a)

  (i) assaults or offers any violence to them, or

  (ii) arrests them on a civil process, or under the pretence of executing a civil process.

(2) Every one who wilfully disturbs or interrupts an assemblage of persons met for religious worship or for a moral, social or benevolent purpose is guilty of an offence punishable on summary conviction.

(3) Every one who, at or near a meeting referred to in subsection (2), wilfully does anything that disturbs the order or solemnity of the meeting is guilty of an offence punishable on summary conviction. R.S., c. C-34, s. 172; 2018, c. 29, s. 13.1; 2019, c. 25, s. 59.

TRESPASSING AT NIGHT.

177. Every person who, without lawful excuse, loiters or prowls at night on the property of another person near a dwelling-house situated on that property is guilty of an offence punishable on summary conviction. R.S., c. C-34, s. 173; 2018, c. 29, s. 14.

---

178. [Repealed, 2018, c. 29, s. 14.]

---

179. [Repealed, 2019, c. 25, s. 60.]

Nuisances

COMMON NUISANCE / Definition.

180. (1) Every person is guilty of an indictable offence and liable to imprisonment for a term of not more than two years or is guilty of an offence punishable on summary conviction who commits a common nuisance and by doing so

(a) endangers the lives, safety or health of the public, or

(b) causes physical injury to any person.

(2) For the purposes of this section, every one commits a common nuisance who does an unlawful act or fails to discharge a legal duty and thereby

(a) endangers the lives, safety, health, property or comfort of the public; or

(b) obstructs the public in the exercise or enjoyment of any right that is common to all the subjects of Her Majesty in Canada. R.S., c. C-34, s. 176; 2019, c. 25, s. 61.

---

181. [Repealed, 2019, c. 25, s. 62.]

DEAD BODY.

182. Every person is guilty of an indictable offence and liable to imprisonment for a term of not more than five years or is guilty of an offence punishable on summary conviction who

(a) neglects, without lawful excuse, to perform any duty that is imposed on him by law or that he undertakes with reference to the burial of a dead human body or human remains, or

(b) improperly or indecently interferes with or offers any indignity to a dead human body or human remains, whether buried or not. R.S., c. C-34, s. 178; 2019, c. 25, s. 63.

Part VI / INVASION OF PRIVACY

Definitions

DEFINITIONS / "authorization" / "electro-magnetic, acoustic, mechanical or other device" / "intercept" / "offence" / "police officer" / "private communication" / "public switched telephone network" / "radio-based telephone communication" / "sell" / "solicitor".

183. In this Part,

"authorization" means an authorization to intercept a private communication given under section 186 or subsection 184.2(3), 184.3(6) or 188(2);

"electro-magnetic, acoustic, mechanical or other device" means any device or apparatus that is used or is capable of being used to intercept a private communication, but does not include a hearing aid used to correct subnormal hearing of the user to not better than normal hearing;

"intercept" includes listen to, record or acquire a communication or acquire the substance, meaning or purport thereof;

"offence" means an offence contrary to, any conspiracy or attempt to commit or being an accessory after the fact in relation to an offence contrary to, or any counselling in relation to an offence contrary to

(a) any of the following provisions of this Act, namely,
  (i) section 47 (high treason),
  (ii) section 51 (intimidating Parliament or a legislature),
  (iii) section 52 (sabotage),
  (iii.1) section 56.1 (identity documents),
  (iv) section 57 (forgery, etc.),
  (v) section 61 (sedition),
  (vi) section 76 (hijacking),
  (vii) section 77 (endangering safety of aircraft or airport),
  (viii) section 78 (offensive weapons, etc., on aircraft),
  (ix) section 78.1 (offences against maritime navigation or fixed platforms),
  (x) section 80 (breach of duty),
  (xi) section 81 (using explosives),

213

(xii)	section 82 (possessing explosives),
(xii.01)	section 82.3 (possession, etc., of nuclear material, radioactive material or device),
(xii.02)	section 82.4 (use or alteration of nuclear material, radioactive material or device),
(xii.03)	section 82.5 (commission of indictable offence to obtain nuclear material, etc.),
(xii.04)	section 82.6 (threats),
(xii.1)	section 83.02 (providing or collecting property for certain activities),
(xii.2)	section 83.03 (providing, making available, etc., property or services for terrorist purposes),
(xii.3)	section 83.04 (using or possessing property for terrorist purposes),
(xii.4)	section 83.18 (participation in activity of terrorist group),
(xii.41)	section 83.181 (leaving Canada to participate in activity of terrorist group),
(xii.5)	section 83.19 (facilitating terrorist activity),
(xii.51)	section 83.191 (leaving Canada to facilitate terrorist activity),
(xii.6)	section 83.2 (commission of offence for terrorist group),
(xii.61)	section 83.201 (leaving Canada to commit offence for terrorist group),
(xii.62)	section 83.202 (leaving Canada to commit offence that is terrorist activity),
(xii.7)	section 83.21 (instructing to carry out activity for terrorist group),
(xii.8)	section 83.22 (instructing to carry out terrorist activity),
(xii.81)	section 83.221 (counselling commission of terrorism offence),
(xii.9)	section 83.23 (harbouring or concealing),
(xii.91)	section 83.231 (hoax — terrorist activity),
(xiii)	section 96 (possession of weapon obtained by commission of offence),
(xiii.1)	section 98 (breaking and entering to steal firearm),
(xiii.2)	section 98.1 (robbery to steal firearm),
(xiv)	section 99 (weapons trafficking),
(xv)	section 100 (possession for purpose of weapons trafficking),
(xvi)	section 102 (making automatic firearm),
(xvii)	section 103 (importing or exporting knowing it is unauthorized),
(xviii)	section 104 (unauthorized importing or exporting),
(xix)	section 119 (bribery, etc.),
(xx)	section 120 (bribery, etc.),
(xxi)	section 121 (fraud on government),
(xxii)	section 122 (breach of trust),
(xxiii)	section 123 (municipal corruption),
(xxiv)	section 132 (perjury),
(xxv)	section 139 (obstructing justice),
(xxvi)	section 144 (prison breach),
(xxvii)	subsection 145(1) (escape, etc.),
(xxvii.1)	section 162 (voyeurism),
(xxvii.2)	section 162.1 (intimate image),
(xxviii)	subsection 163(1) (obscene materials),
(xxix)	section 163.1 (child pornography),
(xxix.1)	section 170 (parent or guardian procuring sexual activity),

(xxix.2) section 171 (householder permitting sexual activity),

(xxix.3) section 171.1 (making sexually explicit material available to child),

(xxix.4) section 172.1 (luring a child),

(xxix.5) section 172.2 (agreement or arrangement — sexual offence against child),

(xxx) section 184 (unlawful interception),

(xxxi) section 191 (possession of intercepting device),

(xxxii) subsection 201(1) (keeping gaming or betting house),

(xxxiii) paragraph 202(1)(e) (pool-selling, etc.),

(xxxiv) [*Repealed*, 2019, c. 25, s. 63.1.]

(xxxv) [*Repealed*, 2014, c. 25, s. 11(1).]

(xxxvi) [*Repealed*, 2014, c. 25, s. 11(1).]

(xxxvii) [*Repealed*, 2014, c. 25, s. 11(1).]

(xxxviii) [*Repealed*, 2014, c. 25, s. 11(1).]

(xxxix) section 235 (murder),

(xxxix.1) section 244 (discharging firearm with intent),

(xxxix.2) section 244.2 (discharging firearm — recklessness),

(xl) section 264.1 (uttering threats),

(xli) section 267 (assault with a weapon or causing bodily harm),

(xlii) section 268 (aggravated assault),

(xliii) section 269 (unlawfully causing bodily harm),

(xliii.1) section 270.01 (assaulting peace officer with weapon or causing bodily harm),

(xliii.2) section 270.02 (aggravated assault of peace officer),

(xliv) section 271 (sexual assault),

(xlv) section 272 (sexual assault with a weapon, threats to a third party or causing bodily harm),

(xlvi) section 273 (aggravated sexual assault),

(xlvii) section 279 (kidnapping),

(xlvii.1) section 279.01 (trafficking in persons),

(xlvii.11) section 279.011 (trafficking of a person under the age of eighteen years),

(xlvii.2) section 279.02 (material benefit),

(xlvii.3) section 279.03 (withholding or destroying documents),

(xlviii) section 279.1 (hostage taking),

(xlix) section 280 (abduction of person under sixteen),

(l) section 281 (abduction of person under fourteen),

(li) section 282 (abduction in contravention of custody order or parenting order),

(lii) section 283 (abduction),

(lii.1) 286.1 (obtaining sexual services for consideration),

(lii.2) 286.2 (material benefit from sexual services),

(lii.3) 286.3 (procuring),

(lii.4) 286.4 (advertising sexual services),

(liii) section 318 (advocating genocide),

(liv) section 327 (possession of device to obtain telecommunication facility or service),

(liv.1) section 333.1 (motor vehicle theft),

215

(lv)	section 334 (theft),
(lvi)	section 342 (theft, forgery, etc., of credit card),
(lvi.1)	section 342.01 (instruments for copying credit card data or forging or falsifying credit cards),
(lvii)	section 342.1 (unauthorized use of computer),
(lviii)	section 342.2 (possession of device to obtain unauthorized use of computer system or to commit mischief),
(lix)	section 344 (robbery),
(lx)	section 346 (extortion),
(lxi)	section 347 (criminal interest rate),
(lxii)	section 348 (breaking and entering),
(lxii.1)	section 353.1 (tampering with vehicle identification number),
(lxiii)	section 354 (possession of property obtained by crime),
(lxiii.1)	section 355.2 (trafficking in property obtained by crime),
(lxiii.2)	section 355.4 (possession of property obtained by crime — trafficking),
(lxiv)	section 356 (theft from mail),
(lxv)	section 367 (forgery),
(lxvi)	section 368 (use, trafficking or possession of forged document),
(lxvi.1)	section 368.1 (forgery instruments),
(lxvii)	section 372 (false information),
(lxviii)	section 380 (fraud),
(lxix)	section 381 (using mails to defraud),
(lxx)	section 382 (fraudulent manipulation of stock exchange transactions),

Note: Paragraph (*a*) of the definition offence in s. 183 amended by adding the following after subpara. (lxx), 2020, c. 1, s. 36 (to come into force by order of the Governor in Council):

(lxx.01)	section 391 (trade secret),
(lxx.1)	subsection 402.2(1) (identity theft),
(lxx.2)	subsection 402.2(2) (trafficking in identity information),
(lxx.3)	section 403 (identity fraud),
(lxxi)	section 423.1 (intimidation of justice system participant or journalist),
(lxxii)	section 424 (threat to commit offences against internationally protected person),
(lxxii.1)	section 424.1 (threat against United Nations or associated personnel),
(lxxiii)	section 426 (secret commissions),
(lxxiv)	section 430 (mischief),
(lxxv)	section 431 (attack on premises, residence or transport of internationally protected person),
(lxxv.1)	section 431.1 (attack on premises, accommodation or transport of United Nations or associated personnel),
(lxxv.2)	subsection 431.2(2) (explosive or other lethal device),
(lxxvi)	section 433 (arson),
(lxxvii)	section 434 (arson),
(lxxviii)	section 434.1 (arson),
(lxxix)	section 435 (arson for fraudulent purpose),
(lxxx)	section 449 (making counterfeit money),
(lxxxi)	section 450 (possession, etc., of counterfeit money),

(lxxxii) section 452 (uttering, etc., counterfeit money),

(lxxxiii) section 462.31 (laundering proceeds of crime),

(lxxxiv) subsection 462.33(11) (acting in contravention of restraint order),

(lxxxv) section 467.11 (participation in criminal organization),

(lxxxv.1) section 467.111 (recruitment of members — criminal organization),

(lxxxvi) section 467.12 (commission of offence for criminal organization), or

(lxxxvii) section 467.13 (instructing commission of offence for criminal organization),

(b) section 198 (fraudulent bankruptcy) of the *Bankruptcy and Insolvency Act*,

(b.1) any of the following provisions of the *Biological and Toxin Weapons Convention Implementation Act*, namely,

   (i) section 6 (production, etc., of biological agents and means of delivery), or

   (ii) section 7 (unauthorized production, etc., of biological agents),

(b.2) any of the following provisions of the *Cannabis Act*, namely,

   (i) section 9 (distribution and possession for purpose of distributing),

   (ii) section 10 (selling and possession for purpose of selling),

   (iii) section 11 (importing and exporting and possession for purpose of exporting),

   (iv) section 12 (production),

   (v) section 13 (possession, etc., for use in production or distribution of illicit cannabis), or

   (vi) section 14 (use of young person),

(c) any of the following provisions of the *Competition Act*, namely,

   (i) section 45 (conspiracies, agreements or arrangements between competitors),

   (ii) section 47 (bid-rigging), or

   (iii) subsection 52.1(3) (deceptive telemarketing),

(d) any of the following provisions of the *Controlled Drugs and Substances Act*, namely,

   (i) section 5 (trafficking),

   (ii) section 6 (importing and exporting);

   (iii) section 7 (production); or

   (iv) section 7.1 (possession, sale, etc., for use in production or trafficking),

(d.1) section 42 (offences related to infringement of copyright) of the *Copyright Act*,

(e) section 3 (bribing a foreign public official) of the *Corruption of Foreign Public Officials Act*,

(e.1) the *Crimes Against Humanity and War Crimes Act*,

(f) either of the following provisions of the *Customs Act*, namely,

   (i) section 153 (false statements), or

   (ii) section 159 (smuggling),

(g) any of the following provisions of the *Excise Act, 2001*, namely,

   (i) section 214 (unlawful production, sale, etc., of tobacco, alcohol or cannabis),

   (ii) section 216 (unlawful possession of tobacco product),

   (iii) section 218 (unlawful possession, sale, etc., of alcohol),

   (iii.1) section 218.1 (unlawful possession, sale, etc., of unstamped cannabis),

(iv)   section 219 (falsifying or destroying records),
(v)   section 230 (possession of property obtained by excise offences), or
(vi)   section 231 (laundering proceeds of excise offences),

(h)   any of the following provisions of the *Export and Import Permits Act*, namely,

(i)   section 13 (export or attempt to export),
(ii)   section 14 (import or attempt to import),
(ii.1)   section 14.2 (broker or attempt to broker),
(iii)   section 15 (diversion, etc.),
(iv)   section 16 (no transfer of permits),
(v)   section 17 (false information), or
(vi)   section 18 (aiding and abetting),

(i)   any of the following provisions of the *Immigration and Refugee Protection Act*, namely,

(i)   section 117 (organizing entry into Canada),
(ii)   section 118 (trafficking in persons),
(iii)   section 119 (disembarking persons at sea),
(iv)   section 122 (offences related to documents),
(v)   section 126 (counselling misrepresentation), or
(vi)   section 129 (offences relating to officers),

(j)   any offence under the *Security of Information Act*, or
(k)   section 51.01 (offences related to goods, labels, packaging or services) of the *Trademarks Act*,

and includes any other offence that there are reasonable grounds to believe is a criminal organization offence or any other offence that there are reasonable grounds to believe is an offence described in paragraph (*b*) or (*c*) of the definition "terrorism offence" in section 2;

Note: Definition "offence" amended by 2001, c. 27, s. 245 (to come into force by order of the Governor in Council; however, repealed before coming into force, 2004, c. 15, s. 110).

"police officer" means any officer, constable or other person employed for the preservation and maintenance of the public peace;

"private communication" means any oral communication, or any telecommunication, that is made by an originator who is in Canada or is intended by the originator to be received by a person who is in Canada and that is made under circumstances in which it is reasonable for the originator to expect that it will not be intercepted by any person other than the person intended by the originator to receive it, and includes any radio-based telephone communication that is treated electronically or otherwise for the purpose of preventing intelligible reception by any person other than the person intended by the originator to receive it;

"public switched telephone network" means a telecommunication facility the primary purpose of which is to provide a land line-based telephone service to the public for compensation;

"radio-based telephone communication" means any radiocommunication within the meaning of the *Radiocommunication Act* that is made over apparatus that is used primarily for connection to a public switched telephone network;

"sell" includes offer for sale, expose for sale, have in possession for sale or distribute or advertise for sale;

"solicitor" means, in the Province of Quebec, an advocate or notary and, in any other province, a barrister or solicitor. 1973-74, c. 50, s. 2; 1976-77, c. 53, s. 7; 1980-81-82-83, c. 125, s. 10; 1984, c. 21, s. 76; 1985, c. 27 (1st Supp.), ss. 7(2)(a), 23; R.S.C. 1985, c. 1 (2nd Supp.), s. 213; R.S.C. 1985, c. 1 (4th Supp.), s. 13; c. 29 (4th Supp.), s. 17; c. 42 (4th Supp.), s. 1; 1991, c. 28, s. 12; 1992, c. 27, s. 90; 1993, c. 7, s. 5; 1993, c. 25, s. 94; 1993, c. 40, s. 1; 1993, c. 46, s. 4; 1995, c. 39, s. 140; 1996, c. 19, s. 66; 1997, c. 18, s. 7; 1997, c. 23, s. 3; 1998, c. 34, s. 8; 1999, c. 2, s. 47; c. 5, s. 4; 2000, c. 24, s. 43; 2001, c. 32, s. 4; 2001, c. 41, ss. 5, 31, 133(2) and (5); 2002, c. 22, s. 409(2)(b); 2004, c. 15, s. 108; 2005, c. 32, s. 10; 2005, 43, s. 1; 2008, c. 6, s. 15; 2009, c. 22, s. 4; 2009, c. 28, s. 3; 2010, c. 3, s. 1; 2010, c. 17, s. 2; 2012, c. 1, s. 24; 2013, c. 8, s. 2; 2013, c. 9, s. 14; 2013, c. 13, s. 7; 2014, c. 17, s. 2; 2014, c. 25, s. 11; 2014, c. 31, s. 7; 2014, c. 32, s. 59; 2015, c. 20, s. 19; 2017, c. 7, s. 56; 2018, c. 12, s. 114; 2018, c. 16, s. 210; 2018, c. 26, s. 23; 2018, c. 29, s. 15; 2019, c. 13, s. 150; 2019, c. 16, s. 122; 2019, c. 25, s. 63.1.

CONSENT TO INTERCEPTION.

183.1 Where a private communication is originated by more than one person or is intended by the originator thereof to be received by more than one person, a consent to the interception thereof by any one of those persons is sufficient consent for the purposes of any provision of this Part. 1993, c. 40, s. 2.

Interception of Communications

INTERCEPTION / Saving provision / Use or retention.

184. (1) Every person who, by means of any electromagnetic, acoustic, mechanical or other device, knowingly intercepts a private communication is guilty of

   (a) an indictable offence and liable to imprisonment for a term of not more than five years; or

   (b) an offence punishable on summary conviction.

(2) Subsection (1) does not apply to

   (a) a person who has the consent to intercept, express or implied, of the originator of the private communication or of the person intended by the originator thereof to receive it;

   (b) a person who intercepts a private communication in accordance with an authorization or pursuant to section 184.4 or any person who in good faith aids in any way another person who the aiding person believes on reasonable grounds is acting with an authorization or pursuant to section 184.4;

   (c) a person engaged in providing a telephone, telegraph or other communication service to the public who intercepts a private communication,

      (i) if the interception is necessary for the purpose of providing the service,

    (ii) in the course of service observing or random monitoring necessary for the purpose of mechanical or service quality control checks, or

    (iii) if the interception is necessary to protect the person's rights or property directly related to providing the service;

  (d) an officer or servant of Her Majesty in right of Canada who engages in radio frequency spectrum management, in respect of a private communication intercepted by that officer or servant for the purpose of identifying, isolating or preventing an unauthorized or interfering use of a frequency or of a transmission; or

  (e) a person, or any person acting on their behalf, in possession or control of a computer system, as defined in subsection 342.1(2), who intercepts a private communication originating from, directed to or transmitting through that computer system, if the interception is reasonably necessary for

    (i) managing the quality of service of the computer system as it relates to performance factors such as the responsiveness and capacity of the system as well as the integrity and availability of the system and data, or

    (ii) protecting the computer system against any act that would be an offence under subsection 342.1(1) or 430(1.1).

(3) A private communication intercepted by a person referred to in paragraph (2)(e) can be used or retained only if

  (a) it is essential to identify, isolate or prevent harm to the computer system; or

  (b) it is to be disclosed in circumstances referred to in subsection 193(2). 1973-74, c. 50, s. 2; 1993, c. 40, s. 3; 2004, c. 12, s. 4; 2019, c. 25, s. 64.

INTERCEPTION TO PREVENT BODILY HARM / Admissibility of intercepted communication / Destruction of recordings and transcripts / Definition of "agent of the state".

184.1 (1) An agent of the state may intercept, by means of any electro-magnetic, acoustic, mechanical or other device, a private communication if

  (a) either the originator of the private communication or the person intended by the originator to receive it has consented to the interception;

  (b) the agent of the state believes on reasonable grounds that there is a risk of bodily harm to the person who consented to the interception; and

  (c) the purpose of the interception is to prevent the bodily harm.

(2) The contents of a private communication that is obtained from an interception pursuant to subsection (1) are inadmissible as evidence except for the purpose of proceedings in which actual, attempted or threatened bodily harm is alleged, including proceedings in respect of an application for an authorization under this Part or in respect of a search warrant or a warrant for the arrest of any person.

(3) The agent of the state who intercepts a private communication pursuant to subsection (1) shall, as soon as is practicable in the circumstances, destroy any recording of the private communication that is obtained from an interception pursuant to subsection (1), any full or partial transcript of the recording and any notes made by that agent of the private communication if nothing in that private

communication suggests that bodily harm, attempted bodily harm or threatened bodily harm has occurred or is likely to occur.

(4) For the purposes of this section, "agent of the state" means
  (a) a peace officer; and
  (b) a person acting under the authority of, or in cooperation with, a peace officer. 1993, c. 40, s. 4.

INTERCEPTION WITH CONSENT / Application for authorization / Judge to be satisfied / Content and limitation of authorization / Related warrant or order.

184.2 (1) A person may intercept, by means of any electro-magnetic, acoustic, mechanical or other device, a private communication where either the originator of the private communication or the person intended by the originator to receive it has consented to the interception and an authorization has been obtained pursuant to subsection (3).

(2) An application for an authorization under this section shall be made by a peace officer, or a public officer who has been appointed or designated to administer or enforce any federal or provincial law and whose duties include the enforcement of this or any other Act of Parliament, *ex parte* and in writing to a provincial court judge, a judge of a superior court of criminal jurisdiction or a judge as defined in section 552, and shall be accompanied by an affidavit, which may be sworn on the information and belief of that peace officer or public officer or of any other peace officer or public officer, deposing to the following matters:
  (a) that there are reasonable grounds to believe that an offence against this or any other Act of Parliament has been or will be committed;
  (b) the particulars of the offence;
  (c) the name of the person who has consented to the interception;
  (d) the period for which the authorization is requested; and
  (e) in the case of an application for an authorization where an authorization has previously been granted under this section or section 186, the particulars of the authorization.

(3) An authorization may be given under this section if the judge to whom the application is made is satisfied that
  (a) there are reasonable grounds to believe that an offence against this or any other Act of Parliament has been or will be committed;
  (b) either the originator of the private communication or the person intended by the originator to receive it has consented to the interception; and
  (c) there are reasonable grounds to believe that information concerning the offence referred to in paragraph (a) will be obtained through the interception sought.

(4) An authorization given under this section shall
  (a) state the offence in respect of which private communications may be intercepted;
  (b) state the type of private communication that may be intercepted;

(*c*) state the identity of the persons, if known, whose private communications are to be intercepted, generally describe the place at which private communications may be intercepted, if a general description of that place can be given, and generally describe the manner of interception that may be used;

(*d*) contain the terms and conditions that the judge considers advisable in the public interest; and

(*e*) be valid for the period, not exceeding sixty days, set out therein.

(5) A judge who gives an authorization under this section may, at the same time, issue a warrant or make an order under any of sections 487, 487.01, 487.014 to 487.018, 487.02, 492.1 and 492.2 if the judge is of the opinion that the requested warrant or order is related to the execution of the authorization. 1993, c. 40, s. 4; 2014, c. 31, s. 8.

APPLICATION BY MEANS OF TELECOMMUNICATION / Application / Recording / Oath / Alternative to oath / Authorization / Giving authorization / Giving authorization where telecommunication produces writing.

184.3 (1) Notwithstanding section 184.2, an application for an authorization under subsection 184.2(2) may be made *ex parte* to a provincial court judge, a judge of a superior court of criminal jurisdiction or a judge as defined in section 552, by telephone or other means of telecommunication, if it would be impracticable in the circumstances for the applicant to appear personally before a judge.

(2) An application for an authorization made under this section shall be on oath and shall be accompanied by a statement that includes the matters referred to in paragraphs 184.2(2)(*a*) to (*e*) and that states the circumstances that make it inpracticable for the applicant to appear personally before a judge.

(3) The judge shall record, in writing or otherwise, the application for an authorization made under this section and, on determination of the application, shall cause the writing or recording to be placed in the packet referred to in subsection 187(1) and sealed in that packet, and a recording sealed in a packet shall be treated as if it were a document for the purposes of section 187.

(4) For the purposes of subsection (2), an oath may be administered by telephone or other means of telecommunication.

(5) An applicant who uses a means of telecommunication that produces a writing may, instead of swearing an oath for the purposes of subsection (2), make a statement in writing stating that all matters contained in the application are true to the knowledge or belief of the applicant and such a statement shall be deemed to be a statement made under oath.

(6) Where the judge to whom an application is made under this section is satisfied that the circumstances referred to in paragraphs 184.2(3)(*a*) to (*c*) exist and that the circumstances referred to in subsection (2) make it impracticable for the applicant to appear personally before a judge, the judge may, on such terms and conditions, if any, as are considered advisable, given an authorization by

telephone or other means of telecommunication for a period of up to thirty-six hours.

(7) Where a judge gives an authorization by telephone or other means of telecommunication, other than a means of telecommunication that produces a writing,

- (a) the judge shall complete and sign the authorization in writing, noting on its face the time, date and place at which it is given;
- (b) the applicant shall, on the direction of the judge, complete a facsimile of the authorization in writing, noting on its face the name of the judge who gave it and the time, date and place at which it was given; and
- (c) the judge shall, as soon as is practicable after the authorization has been given, cause the authorization to be placed in the packet referred to in subsection 187(1) and sealed in that packet.

(8) Where a judge gives an authorization by a means of telecommunication that produces a writing, the judge shall

- (a) complete and sign the authorization in writing, noting on its face the time, date and place at which it is given;
- (b) transmit the authorization by the means of telecommunication to the applicant, and the copy received by the applicant shall be deemed to be a facsimile referred to in paragraph (7)(b); and
- (c) as soon as is practicable after the authorization has been given, cause the authorization to be placed in the packet referred to in subsection 187(1) and sealed in that packet. 1993, c. 40, s. 4.

IMMEDIATE INTERCEPTION — IMMINENT HARM.

184.4 A police officer may intercept, by means of any electro-magnetic, acoustic, mechanical or other device, a private communication if the police officer has reasonable grounds to believe that

- (a) the urgency of the situation is such that an authorization could not, with reasonable diligence, be obtained under any other provision of this Part;
- (b) the interception is immediately necessary to prevent an offence that would cause serious harm to any person or to property; and
- (c) either the originator of the private communication or the person intended by the originator to receive it is the person who would commit the offence that is likely to cause the harm or is the victim, or intended victim, of the harm. 1993, c. 40, s. 4; 2013, c. 8, s. 3

INTERCEPTION OF RADIO-BASED TELEPHONE COMMUNICATIONS / Other provisions to apply.

184.5 (1) Every person who intercepts, by means of any electro-magnetic, acoustic, mechanical or other device, maliciously or for gain, a radio-based telephone communication, if the originator of the communication or the person intended by the originator of the communication to receive it is in Canada, is guilty of

(a) an indictable offence and liable to imprisonment for a term of not more than five years; or

(b) an offence punishable on summary conviction.

(2) Section 183.1, subsection 184(2) and sections 184.1 to 190 and 194 to 196 apply, with such modifications as the circumstances require, to interceptions of radio-based telephone communications referred to in subsection (1). 1993, c. 40, s. 4; 2019, c. 25, s. 65.

ONE APPLICATION FOR AUTHORIZATION SUFFICIENT.

184.6 For greater certainty, an application for an authorization under this Part may be made with respect to both private communications and radio-based telephone communications at the same time. 1993, c. 40, s. 4.

APPLICATION FOR AUTHORIZATION / Exception for criminal organizations and terrorist groups / Extension of period for notification / Where extension to be granted / Where extension not granted.

185. (1) An application for an authorization to be given under section 186 shall be made *ex parte* and in writing to a judge of a superior court of criminal jurisdiction or a judge as defined in section 552 and shall be signed by the Attorney General of the province in which the application is made or the Minister of Public Safety and Emergency Preparedness or an agent specially designated in writing for the purposes of this section by

(a) the Minister personally or the Deputy Minister of Public Safety and Emergency Preparedness personally, if the offence under investigation is one in respect of which proceedings, if any, may be instituted at the instance of the Government of Canada and conducted by or on behalf of the Attorney General of Canada, or

(b) the Attorney General of a province personally or the Deputy Attorney General of a province personally, in any other case,

and shall be accompanied by an affidavit, which may be sworn on the information and belief of a peace officer or public officer deposing to the following matters:

(c) the facts relied on to justify the belief that an authorization should be given together with particulars of the offence,

(d) the type of private communication proposed to be intercepted,

(e) the names, addresses and occupations, if known, of all persons, the interception of whose private communications there are reasonable grounds to believe may assist the investigation of the offence, a general description of the nature and location of the place, if known, at which private communications are proposed to be intercepted and a general description of the manner of interception proposed to be used,

(f) the number of instances, if any, on which an application has been made under this section in relation to the offence and a person named in the affidavit pursuant to paragraph (e) and on which the application was withdrawn or no authorization was given, the date on which each application was made and the name of the judge to whom each application was made,

   (g) the period for which the authorization is requested, and

   (h) whether other investigative procedures have been tried and have failed or why it appears they are unlikely to succeed or that the urgency of the matter is such that it would be impractical to carry out the investigation of the offence using only other investigative procedures.

(1.1) Notwithstanding paragraph (1)(h), that paragraph does not apply where the application for an authorization is in relation to

   (a) an offence under section 467.11, 467.111, 467.12 or 467.13;

   (b) an offence committed for the benefit of, at the direction of or in association with a criminal organization; or

   (c) a terrorism offence.

(2) An application for an authorization may be accompanied by an application, personally signed by the Attorney General of the province in which the application for the authorization is made or the Minister of Public Safety and Emergency Preparedness if the application for the authorization is made by him or on his behalf, to substitute for the period mentioned in subsection 196(1) such longer period not exceeding three years as is set out in the application.

(3) Where an application for an authorization is accompanied by an application referred to in subsection (2), the judge to whom the applications are made shall first consider the application referred to in subsection (2) and where, on the basis of the affidavit in support of the application for the authorization and any other affidavit evidence submitted in support of the application referred to in subsection (2), the judge is of the opinion that the interests of justice warrant the granting of such application, he shall fix a period, not exceeding three years, in substitution for the period mentioned in subsection 196(1).

(4) Where the judge to whom an application for an authorization and an application referred to in subsection (2) are made refuses to fix a period in substitution for the period mentioned in subsection 196(1) or where the judge fixes a period in substitution therefor that is less than the period set out in the application referred to in subsection (2), the person appearing before the judge on the application for the authorization may withdraw the application for the authorization and thereupon the judge shall not proceed to consider the application for the authorization or to give the authorization and shall return to the person appearing before him on the application for the authorization both applications and all other material pertaining thereto. 1973-74, c. 50, s. 2; 1976-77, c. 53, s. 8; 1993, c. 40, s. 5; 1997, c. 18, s. 8; 1997, c. 23, s. 4; 2001, c. 32, s. 5; 2001, c. 41, s. 6 and 133(8); 2005, c. 10, ss. 22 and 34(1)(f)(v); 2014, c. 17, s. 3.

JUDGE TO BE SATISFIED / Exception for criminal organizations and terrorism offences / Where authorization not to be given / Terms and conditions / Content and limitation of authorization / Persons designated / Installation and removal of device / Removal after expiry of authorization / Renewal of authorization / Renewal / Related warrant or order.

186. (1) An authorization under this section may be given if the judge to whom the application is made is satisfied (*a*) that it would be in the best interests of the administration of justice to do so; and

(*b*) that other investigative procedures have been tried and have failed, other investigative procedures are unlikely to succeed or the urgency of the matter is such that it would be impractical to carry out the investigation of the offence using only other investigative procedures.

(1.1) Notwithstanding paragraph (1)(*b*), that paragraph does not apply where the judge is satisfied that the application for an authorization is in relation to

(*a*) an offence under section 467.11, 467.111, 467.12 or 467.13;

(*b*) an offence committed for the benefit of, at the direction of or in association with a criminal organization; or

(*c*) a terrorism offence.

(2) No authorization may be given to intercept a private communication at the office or residence of a solicitor, or at any other place ordinarily used by a solicitor and by other solicitors for the purpose of consultation with clients, unless the judge to whom the application is made is satisfied that there are reasonable grounds to believe that the solicitor, any other solicitor practising with him, any person employed by him or any other such solicitor or a member of the solicitor's household has been or is about to become a party to an offence.

(3) Where an authorization is given in relation to the interception of private communications at a place described in subsection (2), the judge by whom the authorization is given shall include therein such terms and conditions as he considers advisable to protect privileged communications between solicitors and clients.

(4) An authorization shall

(*a*) state the offence in respect of which private communications may be intercepted;

(*b*) state the type of private communication that may be intercepted;

(*c*) state the identity of the persons, if known, whose private communications are to be intercepted, generally describe the place at which private communications may be intercepted, if a general description of that place can be given, and generally describe the manner of interception that may be used;

(*d*) contain such terms and conditions as the judge considers advisable in the public interest; and

(*e*) be valid for the period, not exceeding sixty days, set out therein.

(5) The Minister of Public Safety and Emergency Preparedness or the Attorney General, as the case may be, may designate a person or persons who may intercept private communications under authorizations.

(5.1) For greater certainty, an authorization that permits interception by means of an electro-magnetic, acoustic, mechanical or other device includes the authority to install, maintain or remove the device covertly.

(5.2) On an *ex parte* application, in writing, supported by affidavit, the judge who gave an authorization referred to in subsection (5.1) or any other judge having jurisdiction to give such an authorization may give a further authorization for the covert removal of the electro-magnetic, acoustic, mechanical or other device after the expiry of the original authorization

    (a) under any terms or conditions that the judge considers advisable in the public interest; and

    (b) during any specified period of not more than sixty days.

(6) Renewals of an authorization may be given by a judge of a superior court of criminal jurisdiction or a judge as defined in section 552 on receipt by him or her of an *ex parte* application in writing signed by the Attorney General of the province in which the application is made or the Minister of Public Safety and Emergency Preparedness — or an agent specially designated in writing for the purposes of section 185 by the Minister or the Attorney General, as the case may be — accompanied by an affidavit of a peace officer or public officer deposing to the following matters:

    (a) the reason and period for which the renewal is required,

    (b) full particulars, together with times and dates, when interceptions, if any, were made or attempted under the authorization, and any information that has been obtained by any interception, and

    (c) the number of instances, if any, on which, to the knowledge and belief of the deponent, an application has been made under this subsection in relation to the same authorization and on which the application was withdrawn or no renewal was given, the date on which each application was made and the name of the judge to whom each such application was made,

and supported by such other information as the judge may require.

(7) A renewal of an authorization may be given if the judge to whom the application is made is satisfied that any of the circumstances described in subsection (1) still obtain, but no renewal shall be for a period exceeding sixty days.

(8) A judge who gives an authorization under this section may, at the same time, issue a warrant or make an order under any of sections 487, 487.01, 487.014 to 487.018, 487.02, 492.1 and 492.2 if the judge is of the opinion that the requested warrant or order is related to the execution of the authorization. 1973-74, c. 50, s. 2; 1976-77, c. 53, s. 9; 1993, c. 40, s. 6; 1997, c. 23, s. 5; 1999, c. 5, s. 5; 2001, c. 32, s. 6; 2001, c. 41, s. 6.1 and 133(8.1); 2005, c. 10, ss. 23 and 34(1)(f)(vi); 2014, c. 17, s. 4; 2014, c. 31, s. 9.

TIME LIMITATION IN RELATION TO CRIMINAL ORGANIZATIONS AND TERRORISM OFFENCES.

186.1 Notwithstanding paragraphs 184.2(4)(e) and 186(4)(e) and subsection 186(7), an authorization or any renewal of an authorization may be valid for one or more periods specified in the authorization exceeding sixty days, each not exceeding one year, where the authorization is in relation to

    (a) an offence under section 467.11, 467.111, 467.12 or 467.13;

    (b) an offence committed for the benefit of, at the direction of or in association with a criminal organization; or (*c*) a terrorism offence. 1997, c. 23, s. 6; 2001, c. 32, s. 7; 2001, c. 41, s. 7 and 133(9); 2014, c. 17, s. 5.

MANNER IN WHICH APPLICATION TO BE KEPT SECRET / Exception / Opening for further application / Opening on order of judge / Opening on order of trial judge / Order for destruction of documents / Order of judge / Idem / Editing of copies / Accused to be provided with copies / Original documents to be returned / Deleted parts / Documents to be kept secret — related warrant or order.

187. (1) All documents relating to an application made pursuant to any provision of this Part are confidential and, subject to subsection (1.1), shall be placed in a packet and sealed by the judge to whom the application is made immediately on determination of the application, and that packet shall be kept in the custody of the court in a place to which the public has no access or in such other place as the judge may authorize and shall not be dealt with except in accordance with subsections (1.2) to (1.5).

(1.1) An authorization given under this Part need not be placed in the packet except where, pursuant to subsection 184.3(7) or (8), the original authorization is in the hands of the judge, in which case that judge must place it in the packet and the facsimile remains with the applicant.

(1.2) The sealed packet may be opened and its contents removed for the purpose of dealing with an application for a further authorization or with an application for renewal of an authorization.

(1.3) A provincial court judge, a judge of a superior court of criminal jurisdiction or a judge as defined in section 552 may order that the sealed packet be opened and its contents removed for the purpose of copying and examining the documents contained in the packet.

(1.4) A judge or provincial court judge before whom a trial is to be held and who has jurisdiction in the province in which an authorization was given may order that the sealed packet be opened and its contents removed for the purpose of copying and examining the documents contained in the packet if

(*a*) any matter relevant to the authorization or any evidence obtained pursuant to the authorization is in issue in the trial; and

(*b*) the accused applies for such an order for the purpose of consulting the documents to prepare for trial.

(1.5) Where a sealed packet is opened, its contents shall not be destroyed except pursuant to an order of a judge of the same court as the judge who gave the authorization.

(2) An order under subsection (1.2), (1.3), (1.4) or (1.5) made with respect to documents relating to an application made pursuant to section 185 or subsection 186(6) or 196(2) may only be made after the Attorney General or the Minister of Public Safety and Emergency Preparedness by whom or on whose authority the application for the authorization to which the order relates was made has been given an opportunity to be heard.

(3) An order under subsection (1.2), (1.3), (1.4) or (1.5) made with respect to documents relating to an application made pursuant to subsection 184.2(2) or section 184.3 may only be made after the Attorney General has been given an opportunity to be heard.

(4) Where a prosecution has been commenced and an accused applies for an order for the copying and examination of documents pursuant to subsection (1.3) or (1.4), the judge shall not, notwithstanding those subsections, provide any copy of any document to the accused until the prosecutor has deleted any part of the copy of the document that the prosecutor believes would be prejudicial to the public interest, including any part that the prosecutor believes could

    (*a*) compromise the identity of any confidential informant;

    (*b*) compromise the nature and extent of ongoing investigations;

    (*c*) endanger persons engaged in particular intelligence-gathering techniques and thereby prejudice future investigations in which similar techniques would be used; or

    (*d*) prejudice the interests of innocent persons.

(5) After the prosecutor has deleted the parts of the copy of the document to be given to the accused under subsection (4), the accused shall be provided with an edited copy of the document.

(6) After the accused has received an edited copy of a document, the prosecutor shall keep a copy of the original document, and an edited copy of the document and the original document shall be returned to the packet and the packet resealed.

(7) An accused to whom an edited copy of a document has been provided pursuant to subsection (5) may request that the judge before whom the trial is to be held order that any part of the document deleted by the prosecutor be made available to the accused, and the judge shall order that a copy of any part that, in the opinion of the judge, is required in order for the accused to make full answer and defence and for which the provision of a judicial summary would not be sufficient, be made available to the accused.

(8) The rules provided for in this section apply to all documents relating to a request for a related warrant or order referred to in subsection 184.2(5), 186(8) or 188(6) with any necessary modifications. 1973-74, c. 50, s. 2, R.S.C. 1985, c. 27 (1st Supp.), s. 24; 1993, c. 40, s. 7; 2005, c. 10, s. 24; 2014, c. 31, s. 10.

APPLICATIONS TO SPECIALLY APPOINTED JUDGES / Authorizations in emergency / Certain interceptions deemed not lawful / Definition of "Chief Justice" / Inadmissibility of evidence / Related warrant or order.

188. (1) Notwithstanding section 185, an application made under that section for an authorization may be made *ex parte* to a judge of a superior court of criminal jurisdiction, or a judge as defined in section 552, designated from time to time by the Chief Justice, by a peace officer specially designated in writing, by name or otherwise, for the purposes of this section by

    (*a*) the Minister of Public Safety and Emergency Preparedness, if the offence is one in respect of which proceedings, if any, may be instituted by the

Government of Canada and conducted by or on behalf of the Attorney General of Canada, or

(b) the Attorney General of a province, in respect of any other offence in the province,

if the urgency of the situation requires interception of private communications to commence before an authorization could, with reasonable diligence, be obtained under section 186.

(2) Where the judge to whom an application is made pursuant to subsection (1) is satisfied that the urgency of the situation requires that interception of private communications commence before an authorization could, with reasonable diligence, be obtained under section 186, he may, on such terms and conditions, if any, as he considers advisable, give an authorization in writing for a period of up to thirty-six hours.

(3) [*Repealed*, 1993, c. 40, s. 8.]

(4) In this section, "Chief Justice" means

(a) in the Province of Ontario, the Chief Justice of the Ontario Court;

(b) in the Province of Quebec, the Chief Justice of the Superior Court;

(c) in the Provinces of Nova Scotia, British Columbia and Prince Edward Island, and in the Yukon and the Northwest Territories, the Chief Justice of the Supreme Court;

(d) in the Provinces of New Brunswick, Manitoba, Saskatchewan and Alberta, the Chief Justice of the Court of Queen's Bench;

(e) in the Province of Newfoundland and Labrador, the Chief Justice of the Supreme Court, Trial Division; and

(f) in Nunavut, the Chief Justice of the Nunavut Court of Justice.

(5) The trial judge may deem inadmissible the evidence obtained by means of an interception of a private communication pursuant to a subsequent authorization given under this section, where he finds that the application for the subsequent authorization was based on the same facts, and involved the interception of the private communications of the same person or persons, or related to the same offence, on which the application for the original authorization was based.

(6) A judge who gives an authorization under this section may, at the same time, issue a warrant or make an order under any of sections 487, 487.01, 487.014 to 487.018, 487.02, 492.1 and 492.2 if the judge is of the opinion that the requested warrant or order is related to the execution of the authorization, that the urgency of the situation requires the warrant or the order and that it can be reasonably executed or complied with within 36 hours. 1973-74, c. 50, s. 2; 1974-75-76, c. 19, s. 1; 1978-79, c. 11, s. 10; R.S.C. 1985, c. 27 (1st Supp.), s. 25; c. 27 (2nd Supp.), s. 10; 1990, c. 17, s. 10; 1992, c. 1, s. 58; 1992, c. 51, s. 35; 1993, c. 28, Sch. III, s. 29 (repealed by 1999, c. 3, s. 12); 1993, c. 40, s. 8; 1999, c. 3, ss. 12, 28; 2002, c. 7, s. 140; 2005, c. 10, s. 34(1)(*f*)(vii); 2014, c. 31, s. 11; 2015, c. 3, s. 47; 2017, c. 33, s. 255.

EXECUTION IN CANADA.

188.1 An authorization given under section 184.2, 184.3, 186 or 188 may be executed at any place in Canada. Any peace officer who executes the authorization must have authority to act as a peace officer in the place where it is executed. 1993, c. 40, s. 9; 2019, c. 25, s. 66.

NO CIVIL OR CRIMINAL LIABILITY.

188.2 No person who acts in accordance with an authorization or under section 184.1 or 184.4 or who aids, in good faith, a person who he or she believes on reasonable grounds is acting in accordance with an authorization or under one of those sections incurs any criminal or civil liability for anything reasonably done further to the authorization or to that section. 1993, c. 40, s. 9.

NOTICE OF INTENTION TO PRODUCE EVIDENCE / Privileged evidence.

189. (1) to (4) [*Repealed*, 1993, c. 40, s. 10.]

(5) The contents of a private communication that is obtained from an interception of the private communication pursuant to any provision of, or pursuant to an authorization given under, this Part shall not be received in evidence unless the party intending to adduce it has given to the accused reasonable notice of the intention together with

   (*a*) a transcript of the private communication, where it will be adduced in the form of a recording, or a statement setting out full particulars of the private communication, where evidence of the private communication will be given *viva voce*; and

   (*b*) a statement respecting the time, place and date of the private communication and the parties thereto, if known.

(6) Any information obtained by an interception that, but for the interception, would have been privileged remains privileged and inadmissible as evidence without the consent of the person enjoying the privilege. 1973-74, c. 50, s. 2; 1976-77, c. 53, s. 10; 1993, c. 40, s. 10.

FURTHER PARTICULARS.

190. Where an accused has been given notice pursuant to subsection 189(5), any judge of the court in which the trial of the accused is being or is to be held may at any time order that further particulars be given of the private communication that is intended to be adduced in evidence. 1973-74, c. 50, s. 2.

POSSESSION, ETC. / Exemptions / Terms and conditions of licence.

191. (1) Every person who possesses, sells or purchases any electro-magnetic, acoustic, mechanical or other device or any component of it knowing that its design renders it primarily useful for surreptitious interception of private communications is guilty of

   (*a*) an indictable offence and liable to imprisonment for a term of not more than two years; or

(b) an offence punishable on summary conviction.

(2) Subsection (1) does not apply to

   (a) a police officer in possession of a device or component described in subsection (1) in the course of his employment;

   (b) a person in possession of such a device or component for the purpose of using it in an interception made or to be made in accordance with an authorization;

  (b.1) a person in possession of such a device or component under the direction of a police officer in order to assist that officer in the course of his duties as a police officer;

   (c) an officer or a servant of Her Majesty in right of Canada or a member of the Canadian Forces in possession of such a device or component in the course of his duties as such an officer, servant or member, as the case may be; and

   (d) any other person in possession of such a device or component under the authority of a licence issued by the Minister of Public Safety and Emergency Preparedness.

(3) A licence issued for the purpose of paragraph (2)(d) may contain such terms and conditions relating to the possession, sale or purchase of a device or component described in subsection (1) as the Minister of Public Safety and Emergency Preparedness may prescribe. 1973-74, c. 50, s. 2; R.S.C. 1985, c. 27 (1st Supp.), s. 26; 2005, c. 10, s. 34(1)(f)(viii); 2013, c. 8, s. 4; 2019, c. 25, s. 67.

FORFEITURE / Limitation.

192. (1) Where a person is convicted of an offence under section 184 or 191, any electro-magnetic, acoustic, mechanical or other device by means of which the offence was committed or the possession of which constituted the offence, on the conviction, in addition to any punishment that is imposed, may be ordered forfeited to Her Majesty whereupon it may be disposed of as the Attorney General directs.

(2) No order for forfeiture shall be made under subsection (1) in respect of telephone, telegraph or other communication facilities or equipment owned by a person engaged in providing telephone, telegraph or other communication service to the public or forming part of the telephone, telegraph or other communication service or system of that person by means of which an offence under section 184 has been committed if that person was not a party to the offence. 1973-74, c. 50, s. 2.

DISCLOSURE OF INFORMATION / Punishment / Exemptions / Publishing of prior lawful disclosure.

193. (1) If a private communication has been intercepted by means of an electro-magnetic, acoustic, mechanical or other device without the consent, express or implied, of the originator of that communication or of the person intended by the originator to receive it, every person commits an offence who, without the express consent of the originator of that communication or of the person intended to receive it, knowingly

- (a) uses or discloses the private communication or any part of it or the substance, meaning or purpose of it or of any part of it, or
- (b) discloses the existence of the private communication.

(1.1) Every person who commits an offence under subsection (1) is guilty of

- (a) an indictable offence and liable to imprisonment for a term of not more than two years; or
- (b) an offence punishable on summary conviction.

(2) Subsection (1) does not apply to a person who discloses a private communication or any part thereof or the substance, meaning or purport thereof or of any part thereof or who discloses the existence of a private communication

- (a) in the course of or for the purpose of giving evidence in any civil or criminal proceedings or in any other proceedings in which the person may be required to give evidence on oath;
- (b) in the course of or for the purpose of any criminal investigation if the private communication was lawfully intercepted;
- (c) in giving notice under section 189 or furnishing further particulars pursuant to an order under section 190;
- (d) in the course of the operation of
  - (i) a telephone, telegraph or other communication service to the public,
  - (ii) a department or an agency of the Government of Canada, or
  - (iii) services relating to the management or protection of a computer system, as defined in subsection 342.1(2),

  if the disclosure is necessarily incidental to an interception described in paragraph 184(2)(c), (d) or (e);
- (e) where disclosure is made to a peace officer or prosecutor in Canada or to a person or authority with responsibility in a foreign state for the investigation or prosecution of offences and is intended to be in the interests of the administration of justice in Canada or elsewhere; or
- (f) where the disclosure is made to the Director of the Canadian Security Intelligence Service or to an employee of the Service for the purpose of enabling the Service to perform its duties and functions under section 12 of the *Canadian Security Intelligence Service Act*.

(3) Subsection (1) does not apply to a person who discloses a private communication or any part thereof or the substance, meaning or purport thereof or of any part thereof or who discloses the existence of a private communication where that which is disclosed by him was, prior to the disclosure, lawfully disclosed in the course of or for the purpose of giving evidence in proceedings referred to in paragraph (2)(a). 1973-74, c. 50, s. 2; 1976-77, c. 53, s. 11; 1984, c. 21, s. 77; R.S.C. 1985, c. 30 (4th Supp.), s. 45; 1993, c. 40, s. 11; 2004, c. 12, s. 5; 2019, c. 25, s. 68.

DISCLOSURE OF INFORMATION RECEIVED FROM INTERCEPTION OF RADIO-BASED TELEPHONE COMMUNICATIONS / Other provisions to apply.

193.1 (1) Every person who knowingly uses or discloses a radio-based telephone communication or who knowingly discloses the existence of such a communication is guilty of an indictable offence and liable to imprisonment for a term of not more than two years or is guilty of an offence punishable on summary conviction, if

(a) the originator of the communication or the person intended by the originator of the communication to receive it was in Canada when the communication was made;

(b) the communciation was intercepted by means of an electromagnetic, acoustic, mechanical or other device without the consent, express or implied, of the originator of the communication or of the person intended by the originator to receive the communication; and

(c) the person does not have the express or implied consent of the originator of the communication or of the person intended by the originator to receive the communication.

(2) Subsections 193(2) and (3) apply, with such modifications as the circumstances require, to disclosures of radio-based telephone communications. 1993, c. 40, s. 12; 2019, c. 25, s. 69.

DAMAGES / No damages where civil proceedings commenced / Judgment may be registered / Moneys in possession of accused may be taken.

194. (1) Subject to subsection (2), a court that convicts an accused of an offence under section 184, 184.5, 193 or 193.1 may, on the application of a person aggrieved, at the time sentence is imposed, order the accused to pay to that person an amount not exceeding five thousand dollars as punitive damages.

(2) No amount shall be ordered to be paid under subsection (1) to a person who has commenced an action under Part II of the *Crown Liability Act*.

(3) Where an amount that is ordered to be paid under subsection (1) is not paid forthwith, the applicant may, by filing the order, enter as a judgment, in the superior court of the province in which the trial was held, the amount ordered to be paid, and that judgment is enforceable against the accused in the same manner as if it were a judgment rendered against the accused in that court in civil proceedings.

(4) All or any part of an amount that is ordered to be paid under subsection (1) may be taken out of moneys found in the possession of the accused at the time of his arrest, except where there is a dispute respecting ownership of or right of possession to those moneys by claimants other than the accused. 1973-74, c. 50, s. 2; 1993, c. 40, s. 13.

ANNUAL REPORT / Information respecting authorizations — sections 185 and 188 / Information respecting interceptions — section 184.4 / Other information / Report to be laid before Parliament / Report by Attorneys General.

195. (1) The Minister of Public Safety and Emergency Preparedness shall, as soon as possible after the end of each year, prepare a report relating to

(a) authorizations for which that Minister and agents specially designated in writing by that Minister for the purposes of section 185 applied and the interceptions made under those authorizations in the immediately preceding year;

(b) authorizations given under section 188 for which peace officers specially designated by that Minister for the purposes of that section applied and the interceptions made under those authorizations in the immediately preceding year; and

(c) interceptions made under section 184.4 in the immediately preceding year if the interceptions relate to an offence for which proceedings may be commenced by the Attorney General of Canada.

(2) The report shall, in relation to the authorizations and interceptions referred to in paragraphs (1)(a) and (b), set out

(a) the number of applications made for authorizations;

(b) the number of applications made for renewal of authorizations;

(c) the number of applications referred to in paragraphs (a) and (b) that were granted, the number of those applications that were refused and the number of applications referred to in paragraph (a) that were granted subject to terms and conditions;

(d) the number of persons identified in an authorization against whom proceedings were commenced at the instance of the Attorney General of Canada in respect of

(i) an offence specified in the authorization,

(ii) an offence other than an offence specified in the authorization but in respect of which an authorization may be given, and

(iii) an offence in respect of which an authorization may not be given;

(e) the number of persons not identified in an authorization against whom proceedings were commenced at the instance of the Attorney General of Canada in respect of

(i) an offence specified in such an authorization,

(ii) an offence other than an offence specified in such an authorization but in respect of which an authorization may be given, and

(iii) an offence other than an offence specified in such an authorization and for which no such authorization may be given,

and whose commission or alleged commission of the offence became known to a peace officer as a result of an interception of a private communication under an authorization;

(f) the average period for which authorizations were given and for which renewals thereof were granted;

(*g*) the number of authorizations that, by virtue of one or more renewals thereof, were valid for more than sixty days, for more than one hundred and twenty days, for more than one hundred and eighty days and for more than two hundred and forty days;

(*h*) the number of notifications given pursuant to section 196;

(*i*) the offences in respect of which authorizations were given, specifying the number of authorizations given in respect of each of those offences;

(*j*) a description of all classes of places specified in authorizations and the number of authorizations in which each of those classes of places was specified;

(*k*) a general description of the methods of interception involved in each interception under an authorization;

(*l*) the number of persons arrested whose identity became known to a peace officer as a result of an interception under an authorization;

(*m*) the number of criminal proceedings commenced at the instance of the Attorney General of Canada in which private communications obtained by interception under an authorization were adduced in evidence and the number of those proceedings that resulted in a conviction; and

(*n*) the number of criminal investigations in which information obtained as a result of the interception of a private communication under an authorization was used although the private communication was not adduced in evidence in criminal proceedings commenced at the instance of the Attorney General of Canada as a result of the investigations.

(2.1) The report shall, in relation to the interceptions referred to in paragraph (1)(*c*), set out

(*a*) the number of interceptions made;

(*b*) the number of parties to each intercepted private communication against whom proceedings were commenced in respect of the offence that the police officer sought to prevent in intercepting the private communication or in respect of any other offence that was detected as a result of the interception;

(*c*) the number of persons who were not parties to an intercepted private communication but whose commission or alleged commission of an offence became known to a police officer as a result of the interception of a private communication, and against whom proceedings were commenced in respect of the offence that the police officer sought to prevent in intercepting the private communication or in respect of any other offence that was detected as a result of the interception;

(*d*) the number of notifications given under section 196.1;

(*e*) the offences in respect of which interceptions were made and any other offences for which proceedings were commenced as a result of an interception, as well as the number of interceptions made with respect to each offence;

(*f*) a general description of the methods of interception used for each interception;

(*g*) the number of persons arrested whose identity became known to a police officer as a result of an interception;

CODE

(*h*) the number of criminal proceedings commenced in which private communications obtained by interception were adduced in evidence and the number of those proceedings that resulted in a conviction;

(*i*) the number of criminal investigations in which information obtained as a result of the interception of a private communication was used even though the private communication was not adduced in evidence in criminal proceedings commenced as a result of the investigations; and

(*j*) the duration of each interception and the aggregate duration of all the interceptions related to the investigation of the offence that the police officer sought to prevent in intercepting the private communication.

(3) The report shall, in addition to the information referred to in subsections (2) and (2.1), set out

(*a*) the number of prosecutions commenced against officers or servants of Her Majesty in right of Canada or members of the Canadian Forces for offences under section 184 or 193; and

(*b*) a general assessment of the importance of interception of private communications for the investigation, detection, prevention and prosecution of offences in Canada.

(4) The Minister of Public Safety and Emergency Preparedness shall cause a copy of each report prepared by him under subsection (1) to be laid before Parliament forthwith on completion thereof, or if Parliament is not then sitting, on any of the first fifteen days next thereafter that Parliament is sitting.

(5) The Attorney General of each province shall, as soon as possible after the end of each year, prepare and publish or otherwise make available to the public a report relating to

(*a*) authorizations for which the Attorney General and agents specially designated in writing by the Attorney General for the purposes of section 185 applied and to the interceptions made under those authorizations in the immediately preceding year;

(*b*) authorizations given under section 188 for which peace officers specially designated by the Attorney General for the purposes of that section applied and to the interceptions made under those authorizations in the immediately preceding year; and

(*c*) interceptions made under section 184.4 in the immediately preceding year, if the interceptions relate to an offence not referred to in paragraph (1)(*c*).

The report must set out, with any modifications that the circumstances require, the information described in subsections (2) to (3). 1973-74, c. 50, s. 2; 1976-77, c. 53, s. 11.1; R.S.C. 1985, c. 27 (1st Supp.), s. 27; 2005, c. 10, s. 34(1)(*f*)(ix) and (x); 2013, c. 8, s. 5; 2015, c. 20, s. 20.

WRITTEN NOTIFICATION TO BE GIVEN / Extension of period for notification / Where extension to be granted / Application to be accompanied by affidavit / Exception for criminal organization and terrorist groups.

196. (1) The Attorney General of the province in which an application under subsection 185(1) was made or the Minister of Public Safety and Emergency

Preparedness if the application was made by or on behalf of that Minister shall, within 90 days after the period for which the authorization was given or renewed or within such other period as is fixed pursuant to subsection 185(3) or subsection (3) of this section, notify in writing the person who was the object of the interception pursuant to the authorization and shall, in a manner prescribed by regulations made by the Governor in Council, certify to the court that gave the authorization that the person has been so notified.

(2) The running of the 90 days referred to in subsection (1), or of any other period fixed pursuant to subsection 185(3) or subsection (3) of this section, is suspended until any application made by the Attorney General or the Minister to a judge of a superior court of criminal jurisdiction or a judge as defined in section 552 for an extension or a subsequent extension of the period for which the authorization was given or renewed has been heard and disposed of.

(3) Where the judge to whom an application referred to in subsection (2) is made, on the basis of an affidavit submitted in support of the application, is satisfied that

- (a) the investigation of the offence to which the authorization relates, or
- (b) a subsequent investigation of an offence listed in section 183 commenced as a result of information obtained from the investigation referred to in paragraph (a),

is continuing and is of the opinion that the interests of justice warrant the granting of the application, the judge shall grant an extension, or a subsequent extension, of the period, each extension not to exceed three years.

(4) An application pursuant to subsection (2) shall be accompanied by an affidavit deposing to

- (a) the facts known or believed by the deponent and relied on to justify the belief that an extension should be granted; and
- (b) the number of instances, if any, on which an application has, to the knowledge or belief of the deponent, been made under that subsection in relation to the particular authorization and on which the application was withdrawn or the application was not granted, the date on which each application was made and the judge to whom each application was made.

(5) Notwithstanding subsections (3) and 185(3), where the judge to whom an application referred to in subsection (2) or 185(2) is made, on the basis of an affidavit submitted in support of the application, is satisfied that the investigation is in relation to

- (a) an offence under section 467.11, 467.111, 467.12 or 467.13,
- (b) an offence committed for the benefit of, at the direction of, or in association with, a criminal organization, or
- (c) a terrorism offence.

and is of the opinion that the interests of justice warrant the granting of the application, the judge shall grant an extension, or a subsequent extension, of the period, but no extension may exceed three years. 1973-74, c. 50, s. 2; 1976-77, c. 53, s. 12; R.S.C. 1985, c. 27 (1st Supp.), s. 28; 1993, c. 40, s. 14; 1997, c. 23, s. 7; 2001, c. 32, s. 8; 2001, c. 41, s. 8 and 133(10); 2005, c. 10, s. 25; 2014, c. 17, s. 6.

CODE

REGULATIONS: PROTECTION OF PRIVACY REGULATIONS

2. For the purposes of subsection [196(1)] of the *Criminal Code*, the Attorney General of a province who gave a notice required to be given by that subsection, or the Solicitor General of Canada where the notice was given by him, shall certify to the court that issued the authorization that such notice was given by filing with a judge of the court a certificate signed by the person who gave the notice specifying

(*a*) the name and address of the person who was the object of the interception;

(*b*) the date on which the authorization and any renewal thereof expired;

(*c*) if any delay for the giving of notice was granted under section [196] or subsection [185(3)] of the *Criminal Code*, the period of such delay; and

(*d*) the date, place and method of the giving of the notice.

3. [*Revoked.* SOR/81-859, s. 2.]

4. A certificate filed pursuant to section 2 shall be treated as a confidential document, shall be placed in a packet, sealed by the judge with whom it is filed and kept with the packet sealed pursuant to section [187] of the *Criminal Code* that relates to the authorization to which the certificate relates. **C.R.C. 1978, c. 440; SOR/81-859, *Can. Gaz., Part II,* 26/10/81, p. 3153.**

WRITTEN NOTICE — INTERCEPTION IN ACCORDANCE WITH SECTION 184.4 / Extension of period for notification / Where extension to be granted / Application to be accompanied by affidavit / Exception — criminal organization or terrorism offence.

196.1 (1) Subject to subsections (3) and (5), the Attorney General of the province in which a police officer intercepts a private communication under section 184.4 or, if the interception relates to an offence for which proceedings may be commenced by the Attorney General of Canada, the Minister of Public Safety and Emergency Preparedness shall give notice in writing of the interception to any person who was the object of the interception within 90 days after the day on which it occurred.

(2) The running of the 90-day period or of any extension granted under subsection (3) or (5) is suspended until any application made by the Attorney General of the province or the Minister to a judge of a superior court of criminal jurisdiction or a judge as defined in section 552 for an extension or a subsequent extension of the period has been heard and disposed of.

(3) The judge to whom an application under subsection (2) is made shall grant an extension or a subsequent extension of the 90-day period — each extension not to exceed three years — if the judge is of the opinion that the interests of justice warrant granting the application and is satisfied, on the basis of an affidavit submitted in support of the application, that one of the following investigations is continuing:

(*a*) the investigation of the offence to which the interception relates; or

(*b*) a subsequent investigation of an offence commenced as a result of information obtained from the investigation referred to in paragraph (*a*).

(4) An application shall be accompanied by an affidavit deposing to
  (*a*) the facts known or believed by the deponent and relied on to justify the belief that an extension should be granted; and
  (*b*) the number of instances, if any, on which an application has, to the knowledge or belief of the deponent, been made under subsection (2) in relation to the particular interception and on which the application was withdrawn or the application was not granted, the date on which each application was made and the judge to whom each application was made.

(5) Despite subsection (3), the judge to whom an application under subsection (2) is made shall grant an extension or a subsequent extension of the 90-day period — each extension not to exceed three years — if the judge is of the opinion that the interests of justice warrant granting the application and is satisfied, on the basis of an affidavit submitted in support of the application, that the interception of the communication relates to an investigation of
  (*a*) an offence under section 467.11, 467.12 or 467.13;
  (*b*) an offence committed for the benefit of, at the direction of or in association with a criminal organization; or
  (*c*) a terrorism offence. 2013, c. 8, s. 6.

Part VII / DISORDERLY HOUSES, GAMING AND BETTING

Interpretation

DEFINITIONS / "bet" / "common bawdy-house" / "common betting house" / "common gaming house" / "disorderly house" / "game" / "gaming equipment" / "keeper" / "place" / "public place" / Exception / Onus / Effect when game partly played on premises.

197. (1) In this Part

"bet" means a bet that is placed on any contingency or event that is to take place in or out of Canada, and without restricting the generality of the foregoing, includes a bet that is placed on any contingency relating to a horse-race, fight, match or sporting event that is to take place in or out of Canada;

"common bawdy-house" [*Repealed*, 2019, c. 25, s. 69.1(1).]

"common betting house" means a place that is opened, kept or used for the purpose of
  (*a*) enabling, encouraging or assisting persons who resort thereto to bet between themselves or with the keeper, or
  (*b*) enabling any person to receive, record, register, transmit or pay bets or to announce the results of betting;

"common gaming house" means a place that is
  (*a*) kept for gain to which persons resort for the purpose of playing games, or
  (*b*) kept or used for the purpose of playing games
      (i) in which a bank is kept by one or more but not all of the players,

(ii) in which all or any portion of the bets on or proceeds from a game is paid, directly or indirectly, to the keeper of the place,

(iii) in which, directly or indirectly, a fee is charged to or paid by the players for the privilege of playing or participating in a game or using gaming equipment, or

(iv) in which the chances of winning are not equally favourable to all persons who play the game, including the person, if any, who conducts the game;

"disorderly house" means a common betting house or a common gaming house;

"game" means a game of chance or mixed chance and skill;

"gaming equipment" means anything that is or may be used for the purpose of playing games or for betting;

"keeper" includes a person who
(*a*) is an owner or occupier of a place,
(*b*) assists or acts on behalf of an owner or occupier of a place,
(*c*) appears to be, or to assist or act on behalf of an owner or occupier of a place,
(*d*) has the care or management of a place, or
(*e*) uses a place permanently or temporarily, with or without the consent of the owner or occupier thereof;

"place" includes any place, whether or not
(*a*) it is covered or enclosed,
(*b*) it is used permanently or temporarily, or
(*c*) any person has an exclusive right of user with respect to it;

"prostitute" [*Repealed*, 2014, c. 25, s. 12(1).]

"public place" includes any place to which the public have access as of right or by invitation, express or implied.

(2) A place is not a common gaming house within the meaning of paragraph (*a*) or subparagraph (*b*)(ii) or (iii) of the definition "common gaming house" in subsection (1) while it is occupied and used by an incorporated genuine social club or branch thereof, if
(*a*) the whole or any portion of the bets on or proceeds from games played therein is not directly or indirectly paid to the keeper thereof; and
(*b*) no fee is charged to persons for the right or privilege of participating in the games played therein other than under the authority of and in accordance with the terms of a licence issued by the Attorney General of the province in which the place is situated or by such other person or authority in the province as may be specified by the Attorney General thereof.

(3) The onus of proving that, by virtue of subsection (2), a place is not a common gaming house is on the accused.

(4) A place may be a common gaming house notwithstanding that
(*a*) it is used for the purpose of playing part of a game and another part of the game is played elsewhere;
(*b*) the stake that is played for is in some other place; or

(c) it is used on only one occasion in the manner described in paragraph (b) of the definition "common gaming house" in subsection (1), if the keeper or any person acting on behalf of or in concert with the keeper has used another place on another occasion in the manner described in that paragraph. R.S., c. C-34, s. 179; 1972, c. 13, s. 13; 1980-81-82-83, c. 125, s. 11; R.S.C. 1985, c. 27 (1st Supp.), s. 29; 2014, c. 25, s. 12; 2019, c. 25, s. 69.1.

Presumptions

198. [*Repealed*, 2018, c. 29, s. 16.]

Search

WARRANT TO SEARCH / Search without warrant, seizure and arrest / Disposal of property seized / When declaration or direction may be made / Conversion into money / Telephones exempt from seizure / Exception.

199. (1) A justice who is satisfied by information on oath that there are reasonable grounds to believe that an offence under section 201, 202, 203, 206 or 207 is being committed at any place within the jurisdiction of the justice may issue a warrant authorizing a peace officer to enter and search the place by day or night and seize anything found in that place that may be evidence that an offence under section 201, 202, 203, 206 or 207, as the case may be, is being committed at that place, and to take into custody all persons who are found in or at that place and requiring those persons and things to be brought before that justice or before another justice having jurisdiction, to be dealt with according to law.

(2) A peace officer may, whether or not he is acting under a warrant issued pursuant to this section, take into custody any person whom he finds keeping a common gaming house and any person whom he finds therein, and may seize anything that may be evidence that such an offence is being committed and shall bring those persons and things before a justice having jurisdiction, to be dealt with according to law.

(3) Except where otherwise expressly provided by law, a court, judge, justice or provincial court judge before whom anything that is seized under this section is brought may declare that the thing is forfeited, in which case it shall be disposed of or dealt with as the Attorney General may direct if no person shows sufficient cause why it should not be forfeited.

(4) No declaration or direction shall be made pursuant to subsection (3) in respect of anything seized under this section until
   (a) it is no longer required as evidence in any proceedings that are instituted pursuant to the seizure; or
   (b) the expiration of thirty days from the time of seizure where it is not required as evidence in any proceedings.

(5) The Attorney General may, for the purpose of converting anything forfeited under this section into money, deal with it in all respects as if he were the owner thereof.

(6) Nothing in this section or in section 489 authorizes the seizure, forfeiture or destruction of telephone, telegraph or other communication facilities or equipment that may be evidence of or that may have been used in the commission of an offence under section 201, 202, 203, 206 or 207 and that is owned by a person engaged in providing telephone, telegraph or other communication service to the public or forming part of the telephone, telegraph or other communication service or system of that person.

(7) Subsection (6) does not apply to prohibit the seizure, for use as evidence, of any facility or equipment described in that subsection that is designed or adapted to record a communication. R.S., c. C-34, s. 181; 1994, c. 44, s. 10; 2019, c. 25, s. 69.2.

200. [*Repealed*, R.S.C. 1985, c. 27 (1st Supp.), s. 30.]

Gaming and Betting

KEEPING GAMING OR BETTING HOUSE / Person found in or owner permitting use.

201. (1) Every person who keeps a common gaming house or common betting house is guilty of

    (*a*) an indictable offence and liable to imprisonment for a term of not more than two years; or

    (*b*) an offence punishable on summary conviction.

(2) Every one who

    (*a*) is found, without lawful excuse, in a common gaming house or common betting house, or

    (*b*) as owner, landlord, lessor, tenant, occupier or agent, knowingly permits a place to be let or used for the purposes of a common gaming house or common betting house,

is guilty of an offence punishable on summary conviction. R.S., c. C-34, s. 185; 2019, c. 25, s. 70.

BETTING, POOL-SELLING, BOOK-MAKING, ETC. / Punishment.

202. (1) Every one commits an offence who

    (*a*) uses or knowingly allows a place under his control to be used for the purpose of recording or registering bets or selling a pool;

    (*b*) imports, makes, buys, sells, rents, leases, hires or keeps, exhibits, employs or knowingly allows to be kept, exhibited or employed in any place under his control any device or apparatus for the purpose of recording or registering bets or selling a pool, or any machine or device for gambling or betting;

  (*c*) has under his control any money or other property relating to a transaction that is an offence under this section;

  (*d*) records or registers bets or sells a pool;

  (*e*) engages in book-making or pool-selling, or in the business or occupation of betting, or makes any agreement for the purchase or sale of betting or gaming privileges, or for the purchase or sale of information that is intended to assist in book-making, pool-selling or betting;

  (*f*) prints, provides or offers to print or provide information intended for use in connection with book-making, pool-selling or betting on any horse-race, fight, game or sport, whether or not it takes place in or outside of Canada or has or has not taken place;

  (*g*) imports or brings into Canada any information or writing that is intended or is likely to promote or be of use in gambling, book-making, pool-selling or betting on a horse-race, fight, game or sport, and where this paragraph applies it is immaterial

    (i) whether the information is published before, during or after the race, fight, game or sport, or

    (ii) whether the race, fight, game or sport takes place in Canada or elsewhere,

but this paragraph does not apply to a newspaper, magazine or other periodical published in good faith primarily for a purpose other than the publication of such information;

  (*h*) advertises, prints, publishes, exhibits, posts up, or otherwise gives notice of any offer, invitation or inducement to bet on, to guess or to foretell the result of a contest, or a result of or contingency relating to any contest;

  (*i*) wilfully and knowingly sends, transmits, delivers or receives any message that conveys any information relating to book-making, pool-selling, betting or wagering, or that is intended to assist in book-making, poolselling, betting or wagering; or

  (*j*) aids or assists in any manner in anything that is an offence under this section.

(2) Every one who commits an offence under this section is guilty of an indictable offence and liable

  (*a*) for a first offence, to imprisonment for not more than two years;

  (*b*) for a second offence, to imprisonment for a term not more than two years and not less than fourteen days; and

  (*c*) for each subsequent offence, to imprisonment for not more than two years and not less than three months. R.S., c. C-34, s. 186; 1974-75-76, c. 93, s. 11; 2008, c. 18, s. 5.

PLACING BETS ON BEHALF OF OTHERS.

203. Every one who

  (*a*) places or offers or agrees to place a bet on behalf of another person for a consideration paid or to be paid by or on behalf of that other person,

  (*b*) engages in the business or practice of placing or agreeing to place bets on behalf of other persons, whether for a consideration or otherwise, or (*c*) holds himself out or allows himself to be held out as engaging in the business or practice of placing or agreeing to place bets on behalf of other persons, whether for a consideration or otherwise,

is guilty of an indictable offence and liable

(*d*) for a first offence, to imprisonment for not more than two years,

(*e*) for a second offence, to imprisonment for not more than two years and not less than fourteen days, and

(*f*) for each subsequent offence, to imprisonment for not more than two years and not less than three months. R.S., c. C-34, s. 187; 1974-75-76, c. 93, s. 11.

CODE

EXEMPTION / Exception / Presumption / Operation of pari-mutuel system / Supervision of pari-mutuel system / Percentage that may be deducted and retained / Percentage that may be deducted and retained / Stopping of betting / Regulations / Approvals / Idem / 900 metre zone / Contravention / Definition of "association".

204. (1) Sections 201 and 202 do not apply to

(*a*) any person or association by reason of his or their becoming the custodian or depository of any money, property or valuable thing staked, to be paid to

  (i) the winner of a lawful race, sport, game or exercise,

  (ii) the owner of a horse engaged in a lawful race, or

  (iii) the winner of any bets between not more than ten individuals;

(*b*) a private bet between individuals not engaged in any way in the business of betting;

(*c*) bets made or records of bets made through the agency of a pari-mutuel system on running, trotting or pacing horse-races if

  (i) the bets or records of bets are made on the race-course of an association in respect of races conducted at that race-course or another race-course in or out of Canada, and, in the case of a race conducted on a race-course situated outside Canada, the governing body that regulates the race has been certified as acceptable by the Minister of Agriculture and Agri-Food or a person designated by that Minister pursuant to subsection (8.1) and that Minister or person has permitted pari-mutuel betting in Canada on the race pursuant to that subsection, and

  (ii) the provisions of this section and the regulations are complied with.

(1.1) For greater certainty, a person may, in accordance with the regulations, do anything described in section 201 or 202, if that person does it for the purposes of legal pari-mutuel betting.

(2) For the purposes of paragraph (1)(*c*), bets made, in accordance with the regulations, in a betting theatre referred to in paragraph (8)(*e*), or by any means of telecommunication to the racecourse of an association or to such a betting theatre, are deemed to be made on the racecourse of the association.

(3) No person or association shall use a pari-mutuel system of betting in respect of a horse-race unless the system has been approved by and its operation is carried on under the supervision of an officer appointed by the Minister of Agriculture and Agri-Food.

(4) Every person or association operating a pari-mutuel system of betting in accordance with this section in respect of a horse-race, whether or not the person or association is conducting the race-meeting at which the race is run, shall pay to the Receiver General in respect of each individual pool of the race and each individual feature pool one-half of one per cent, or such greater fraction not exceeding one per cent as may be fixed by the Governor in Council, of the total amount of money that is bet through the agency of the pari-mutuel system of betting.

(5) Where any person or association becomes a custodian or depository of any money, bet or stakes under a pari-mutuel system in respect of a horse-race, that person or association shall not deduct or retain any amount from the total amount of money, bets or stakes unless it does so pursuant to subsection (6).

(6) An association operating a pari-mutuel system of betting in accordance with this section in respect of a horse-race, or any other association or person acting on its behalf, may deduct and retain from the total amount of money that is bet through the agency of the pari-mutuel system, in respect of each individual pool of each race or each individual feature pool, a percentage not exceeding the percentage prescribed by the regulations plus any odd cents over any multiple of five cents in the amount calculated in accordance with the regulations to be payable in respect of each dollar bet.

(7) Where an officer appointed by the Minister of Agriculture and Agri-Food is not satisfied that the provisions of this section and the regulations are being carried out in good faith by any person or association in relation to a race-meeting, he may, at any time, order any betting in relation to the race-meeting to be stopped for any period that he considers proper.

(8) The Minister of Agriculture and Agri-Food may make regulations

   (a) prescribing the maximum number of races for each race-course on which a race meeting is conducted, in respect of which a pari-mutuel system of betting may be used for the race meeting or on any one calendar day during the race meeting, and the circumstances in which the Minister of Agriculture and Agri-Food or a person designated by him for that purpose may approve of the use of that system in respect of additional races on any race-course for a particular race meeting or on a particular day during the race meeting;

   (b) prohibiting any person or association from using a pari-mutuel system of betting for any race-course on which a race meeting is conducted in respect of more than the maximum number of races prescribed pursuant to paragraph (a) and the additional races, if any, in respect of which the use of a pari-mutuel system of betting has been approved pursuant to that paragraph;

   (c) prescribing the maximum percentage that may be deducted and retained pursuant to subsection (6) by or on behalf of a person or association operating a pari-mutuel system of betting in respect of a horse-race in accordance with this section and providing for the determination of the percentage that each such person or association may deduct and retain;

    (*d*) respecting pari-mutuel betting in Canada on horse-races conducted on a race-course situated outside Canada; and

    (*e*) authorizing pari-mutuel betting and governing the conditions for pari-mutuel betting, including the granting of licences therefor, that is conducted by an association in a betting theatre owned or leased by the association in a province in which the Lieutenant Governor in Council, or such other person or authority in the province as may be specified by the Lieutenant Governor in Council thereof, has issued a licence to that association for the betting theatre.

(8.1) The Minister of Agriculture and Agri-Food or a person designated by that Minister may, with respect to a horse-race conducted on a race-course situated outside Canada,

    (*a*) certify as acceptable, for the purposes of this section, the governing body that regulates the race; and

    (*b*) permit pari-mutuel betting in Canada on the race.

(9) The Minister of Agriculture and Agri-Food may make regulations respecting

    (*a*) the supervision and operation of pari-mutuel systems related to race meetings, and the fixing of the dates on which and the places at which an association may conduct such meetings;

    (*b*) the method of calculating the amount payable in respect of each dollar bet;

    (*c*) the conduct of race-meetings in relation to the supervision and operation of pari-mutuel systems, including photo-finishes, video patrol and the testing of bodily substances taken from horses entered in a race at such meetings, including, in the case of a horse that dies while engaged in racing or immediately before or after the race, the testing of any tissue taken from its body;

    (*d*) the prohibition, restriction or regulation of

        (i) the possession of drugs or medicaments or of equipment used in the administering of drugs or medicaments at or near race-courses, or

        (ii) the administering of drugs or medicaments to horses participating in races run at a race meeting during which a pari-mutuel system of betting is used; and

    (*e*) the provision, equipment and maintenance of accommodation, services or other facilities for the proper supervision and operation of pari-mutuel systems related to race meetings, by associations conducting those meetings or by other associations.

(9.1) For the purposes of this section, the Minister of Agriculture and Agri-Food may designate, with respect to any race-course, a zone that shall be deemed to be part of the race-course, if

    (*a*) the zone is immediately adjacent to the race-course;

    (*b*) the farthest point of that zone is not more than 900 metres from the nearest point on the race track of the race-course; and

    (*c*) all real property situated in that zone is owned or leased by the person or association who owns or leases the race-course.

(10) Every person who contravenes or fails to comply with any of the provisions of this section or of any regulations made under this section is guilty of

(a) an indictable offence and liable to imprisonment for a term not exceeding two years; or

(b) an offence punishable on summary conviction.

(11) For the purposes of this section, "association" means an association incorporated by or pursuant to an Act of Parliament or of the legislature of a province that owns or leases a race-course and conducts horse-races in the ordinary course of its business and, to the extent that the applicable legislation requires that the purposes of the association be expressly stated in its constating instrument, having as one of its purposes the conduct of horse-races. R.S., c. C-34, s. 188; 1980-81-82-83, c. 99, s. 1; R.S.C. 1985, c. 47 (1st Supp.), s. 1; 1989, c. 2, s. 1; 1994, c. 38, ss. 14, 25; 2008, c. 18, s. 6.

---

205. [*Repealed*, R.S.C. 1985, c. 52 (1st Supp.), s. 1.]

**OFFENCE IN RELATION TO LOTTERIES AND GAMES OF CHANCE /
Definition of "three-card monte" / Exemption for fairs / Definition of "fair
or exhibition" / Offence / Lottery sale void /** *Bona fide* **exception / Foreign
lottery included / Saving.**

206. (1) Every person is guilty of an indictable offence and liable to imprisonment for a term of not more than two years or is guilty of an offence punishable on summary conviction who

(a) makes, prints, advertises or publishes, or causes or procures to be made, printed, advertised or published, any proposal, scheme or plan for advancing, lending, giving, selling or in any way disposing of any property by lots, cards, tickets or any mode of chance whatever;

(b) sells, barters, exchanges or otherwise disposes of, or causes or procures, or aids or assists in, the sale, barter, exchange or other disposal of, or offers for sale, barter or exchange, any lot, card, ticket or other means or device for advancing, lending, giving, selling or otherwise disposing of any property by lots, tickets or any mode of chance whatever;

(c) knowingly sends, transmits, mails, ships, delivers or allows to be sent, transmitted, mailed, shipped or delivered, or knowingly accepts for carriage or transport or conveys any article that is used or intended for use in carrying out any device, proposal, scheme or plan for advancing, lending, giving, selling or otherwise disposing of any property by any mode of chance whatever;

(d) conducts or manages any scheme, contrivance or operation of any kind for the purpose of determining who, or the holders of what lots, tickets, numbers or chances, are the winners of any property so proposed to be advanced, lent, given, sold or disposed of;

(e) conducts, manages or is a party to any scheme, contrivance or operation of any kind by which any person, on payment of any sum of money, or the giving of any valuable security, or by obligating himself to pay any sum of money or give any valuable security, shall become entitled under the scheme, contrivance or operation to receive from the person conducting or managing the scheme, contrivance or operation, or any other person, a larger sum of money or amount of valuable security than the sum or amount paid or given, or to be paid or given, by reason of the fact that other persons have paid or given, or obligated themselves to pay or give any sum of money or valuable security under the scheme, contrivance or operation;

(f) disposes of any goods, wares or merchandise by any game of chance or any game of mixed chance and skill in which the contestant or competitor pays money or other valuable consideration;

(g) induces any person to stake or hazard any money or other valuable property or thing on the result of any dice game, three-card monte, punch board, coin table or on the operation of a wheel of fortune;

(h) for valuable consideration carries on or plays or offers to carry on or to play, or employs any person to carry on or play in a public place or a place to which the public have access, the game of three-card monte;

(i) receives bets of any kind on the outcome of a game of three-card monte; or

(j) being the owner of a place, permits any person to play the game of three-card monte therein.

(2) In this section "three-card monte" means the game commonly known as three-card monte and includes any other game that is similar to it, whether or not the game is played with cards and notwithstanding the number of cards or other things that are used for the purpose of playing.

(3) Paragraphs (1)(f) and (g), in so far as they do not relate to a dice game, three-card monte, punch board or coin table, do not apply to the board of an annual fair or exhibition, or to any operator of a concession leased by that board within its own grounds and operated during the fair or exhibition on those grounds.

(3.1) For the purposes of this section, "fair or exhibition" means an event where agricultural or fishing products are presented or where activities relating to agriculture or fishing take place.

(4) Every one who buys, takes or receives a lot, ticket or other device mentioned in subsection (1) is guilty of an offence punishable on summary conviction.

(5) Every sale, loan, gift, barter or exchange of any property, by any lottery, ticket, card or other mode of chance depending on or to be determined by chance or lot, is void, and all property so sold, lent, given, bartered or exchanged is forfeited to Her Majesty.

(6) Subsection (5) does not affect any right or title to property acquired by any *bona fide* purchaser for valuable consideration without notice.

(7) This section applies to the printing or publishing, or causing to be printed or published, of any advertisement, scheme, proposal or plan of any foreign lottery, and the sale or offer for sale of any ticket, chance or share, in any such lottery, or the advertisement for sale of such ticket, chance or share, and the conducting or managing of any such scheme, contrivance or operation for determining the winners in any such lottery.

(8) This section does not apply to

(a) the division by lot or chance of any property by joint tenants or tenants in common, or persons having joint interests in any such property; or

(b) [*Repealed*, 1999, c. 28, s. 156.]

(c) bonds, debentures, debenture stock or other securities recallable by drawing of lots and redeemable with interest and providing for payment of premiums on redemption or otherwise. R.S., c. C-34, s. 189; R.S.C. 1985, c. 52 (1st Supp.), s. 2; 1999, c. 28, s. 156; 2019, c. 25, s. 71.

PERMITTED LOTTERIES / Terms and conditions of licence / Offence / Definition of "lottery scheme" / Exception — charitable or religious organization / Definition of "slot machine" / Exception re: pari-mutuel betting.

207. (1) Notwithstanding any of the provisions of this Part relating to gaming and betting, it is lawful

(a) for the government of a province, either alone or in conjunction with the government of another province, to conduct and manage a lottery scheme in that province, or in that and the other province, in accordance with any law enacted by the legislature of that province;

(b) for a charitable or religious organization, pursuant to a licence issued by the Lieutenant Governor in Council of a province or by such other person or authority in the province as may be specified by the Lieutenant Governor in Council thereof, to conduct and manage a lottery scheme in that province if the proceeds from the lottery scheme are used for a charitable or religious object or purpose;

(c) for the board of a fair or of an exhibition or an operator of a concession leased by that board, to conduct and manage a lottery scheme in a province where the Lieutenant Governor in Council of the province or such other person or authority in the province as may be specified by the Lieutenant Governor in Council thereof has

  (i) designated that fair or exhibition as a fair or exhibition where a lottery scheme may be conducted and managed, and

  (ii) issued a licence for the conduct and management of a lottery scheme to that board or operator;

(d) for any person, pursuant to a licence issued by the Lieutenant Governor in Council of a province or by such other person or authority in the province as may be specified by the Lieutenant Governor in Council thereof, to conduct and manage a lottery scheme at a public place of amusement in that province if

  (i) the amount or value of each prize awarded does not exceed five hundred dollars, and

  (ii) the money or other valuable consideration paid to secure a chance to win a prize does not exceed two dollars;

(e) for the government of a province to agree with the government of another province that lots, cards or tickets in relation to a lottery scheme that is by any of paragraphs (a) to (d) authorized to be conducted and managed in that other province may be sold in the province;

(f) for any person, pursuant to a licence issued by the Lieutenant Governor in Council of a province or such other person or authority in the province as may be designated by the Lieutenant Governor in Council thereof, to conduct and manage in the province a lottery scheme that is authorized to be conducted and managed in one or more other provinces where the authority by which the lottery scheme was first authorized to be conducted and managed consents thereto;

(g) for any person, for the purpose of a lottery scheme that is lawful in a province under any of paragraphs (a) to (f), to do anything in the province, in accordance with the applicable law or licence, that is required for the conduct, management or operation of the lottery scheme or for the person to participate in the scheme; and

(h) for any person to make or print anywhere in Canada or to cause to be made or printed anywhere in Canada anything relating to gaming and betting that is to be used in a place where it is or would, if certain conditions provided by law are met, be lawful to use such a thing, or to send, transmit, mail, ship, deliver or allow to be sent, transmitted, mailed, shipped or delivered or to accept for carriage or transport or convey any such thing where the destination thereof is such a place.

(2) Subject to this Act, a licence issued by or under the authority of the Lieutenant Governor in Council of a province as described in paragraph (1)(b), (c), (d) or (f) may contain such terms and conditions relating to the conduct, management and operation of or participation in the lottery scheme to which the licence relates as the Lieutenant Governor in Council of that province, the person or authority in the province designated by the Lieutenant Governor in Council thereof or any law enacted by the legislature of that province may prescribe.

(3) Every one who, for the purposes of a lottery scheme, does anything that is not authorized by or pursuant to a provision of this section

(a) in the case of the conduct, management or operation of that lottery scheme,

(i) is guilty of an indictable offence and liable to imprisonment for a term not exceeding two years, or

(ii) is guilty of an offence punishable on summary conviction; or

(b) in the case of participating in that lottery scheme, is guilty of an offence punishable on summary conviction.

(4) In this section, "lottery scheme" means a game or any proposal, scheme, plan, means, device, contrivance or operation described in any of paragraphs 206(1)(a) to (g), whether or not it involves betting, pool selling or a pool system of betting other than

(a) three-card monte, punch board or coin table;

(b) bookmaking, pool selling or the making or recording of bets, including bets made through the agency of a pool or pari-mutuel system, on any race or fight, or on a single sport event or athletic contest; or

(c) for the purposes of paragraphs (1)(b) to (f), a game or proposal, scheme, plan, means, device, contrivance or operation described in any of paragraphs 206(1)(a) to (g) that is operated on or through a computer, video device, slot machine or a dice game.

(4.01) In paragraph 4(c), "slot machine" means any automatic machine or slot machine, other than any automatic machine or slot machine that dispenses as prizes only one or more free games on that machine, that (*a*) is used or intended to be used for any purpose other than selling merchandise or services; or

(*b*) is used or intended to be used for the purpose of selling merchandise or services if

   (i) the result of one of any number of operations of the machine is a matter of chance or uncertainty to the operator,

   (ii) as a result of a given number of successive operations by the operator, the machine produces different results, or

   (iii) on any operation of the machine, it discharges or emits a slug or token.

(4.1) The use of a computer for the sale of a ticket, selection of a winner or the distribution of a prize in a raffle, including a 50/50 draw, is excluded from paragraph (4)(*c*) in so far as the raffle is authorized under paragraph (1)(*b*) and the proceeds are used for a charitable or religious object or purpose.

(5) For greater certainty, nothing in this section shall be construed as authorizing the making or recording of bets on horse-races through the agency of a pari-mutuel system other than in accordance with section 204. R.S., c. C-34, s. 190; 1974-75-76, c. 93, s. 12; R.S.C. 1985, c. 27 (1st Supp.), s. 31, c. 52 (1st Supp.), s. 3; 1999, c. 5, s. 6; 2014, c. 39, s. 171; 2018, c. 29, s. 17.

EXEMPTION — LOTTERY SCHEME ON AN INTERNATIONAL CRUISE SHIP / Paragraph 207(1)(*h*) and subsection 207(5) apply / Offence / Definitions.

207.1 (1) Despite any of the provisions of this Part relating to gaming and betting, it is lawful for the owner or operator of an international cruise ship, or their agent, to conduct, manage or operate and for any person to participate in a lottery scheme during a voyage on an international cruise ship when all of the following conditions are satisfied:

(*a*) all the people participating in the lottery scheme are located on the ship;

(*b*) the lottery scheme is not linked, by any means of communication, with any lottery scheme, betting, pool selling or pool system of betting located off the ship;

(*c*) the lottery scheme is not operated within five nautical miles of a Canadian port at which the ship calls or is scheduled to call; and

(*d*) the ship is registered

   (i) in Canada and its entire voyage is scheduled to be outside Canada, or

   (ii) anywhere, including Canada, and its voyage includes some scheduled voyaging within Canada and the voyage

     (A) is of at least forty-eight hours duration and includes some voyaging in international waters and at least one non-Canadian port of call including the port at which the voyage begins or ends, and

     (B) is not scheduled to disembark any passengers at a Canadian port who have embarked at another Canadian port, without calling on at least one non-Canadian port between the two Canadian ports.

(2) For greater certainty, paragraph 207(1)(*h*) and subsection 207(5) apply for the purposes of this section.

(3) Every one who, for the purpose of a lottery scheme, does anything that is not authorized by this section

(a) in the case of the conduct, management or operation of the lottery scheme,

   (i) is guilty of an indictable offence and liable to imprisonment for a term of not more than two years, or

   (ii) is guilty of an offence punishable on summary conviction; and

(b) in the case of participating in the lottery scheme, is guilty of an offence punishable on summary conviction.

(4) The definitions in this subsection apply in this section.

"international cruise ship" means a passenger ship that is suitable for continuous ocean voyages of at least forty-eight hours duration, but does not include such a ship that is used or fitted for the primary purpose of transporting cargo or vehicles.

"lottery scheme" means a game or any proposal, scheme, plan, means, device, contrivance or operation described in any of paragraphs 206(1)(a) to (g), whether or not it involves betting, pool selling or a pool system of betting. It does not include

(a) three-card monte, punch board or coin table; or

(b) bookmaking, pool selling or the making or recording of bets, including bets made through the agency of a pool or pari-mutuel system, on any race or fight, or on a single sporting event or athletic contest. 1999, c. 5, s. 7.

---

208. [*Repealed*, R.S.C. 1985, c. 27 (1st Supp.), s. 32.]

CHEATING AT PLAY.

209. Every person who, with intent to defraud any person, cheats while playing a game or in holding the stakes for a game or in betting is guilty of

(a) an indictable offence and liable to imprisonment for a term of not more than two years; or

(b) an offence punishable on summary conviction. R.S., c. C-34, s. 192; 2019, c. 25, s. 72.

[*Heading repealed*, 2019, c. 25, s. 73.]

---

210. [*Repealed*, 2019, c. 25, s. 73.]

---

211. [*Repealed*, 2019, c. 25, s. 73.]

[*Heading repealed*, 2014, c. 25, s. 13.]

---

212. [*Repealed*, 2014, c. 25, s. 13.]

Offences in Relation to Offering, Providing or Obtaining Sexual Services for Consideration   2014, c. 25, s. 14.

STOPPING OR IMPEDING TRAFFIC / Communicating to provide sexual services for consideration / Definition of "public place".

213. (1) Everyone is guilty of an offence punishable on summary conviction who, in a public place or in any place open to public view, for the purpose of offering, providing or obtaining sexual services for consideration,

   (a) stops or attempts to stop any motor vehicle, or

   (b) impedes the free flow of pedestrian or vehicular traffic or ingress to or egress from premises adjacent to that place.

   (c) [*Repealed*, 2014, c. 25, s. 15(2).]

(1.1) Everyone is guilty of an offence punishable on summary conviction who communicates with any person — for the purpose of offering or providing sexual services for consideration — in a public place, or in any place open to public view, that is or is next to a school ground, playground or daycare centre.

(2) In this section, "public place" includes any place to which the public have access as of right or by invitation, express or implied, and any motor vehicle located in a public place or in any place open to public view. 1972, c. 13, s. 15; R.S.C. 1985, c. 50 (1st Supp.), s. 1; 2014, c. 25, s. 15.

Part VIII / OFFENCES AGAINST THE PERSON AND REPUTATION

Interpretation

DEFINITIONS / "abandon" or "expose" / "aircraft" / "child" / "form of marriage" / "guardian" / "operate" / "vessel".

214. In this Part

"abandon" or "expose" includes

   (a) a wilful omission to take charge of a child by a person who is under a legal duty to do so, and

   (b) dealing with a child in a manner that is likely to leave that child exposed to risk without protection;

"aircraft" [*Repealed*, 2018, c. 21, s. 13.]

"child" [*Repealed*, 2002, c. 13, s. 9.]

"form of marriage" includes a ceremony of marriage that is recognized as valid

   (a) by the law of the place where it was celebrated, or

   (b) by the law of the place where an accused is tried, notwithstanding that it is not recognized as valid by the law of the place where it was celebrated;

"guardian" includes a person who has in law or in fact the custody or control of a child. R.S., c. C-34, s. 196; R.S.C. 1985, c. 27 (1st Supp.), s. 33; c. 32 (4th Supp.), s. 56; 2018, c. 21, s. 13.

"operate" [*Repealed*, 2018, c. 21, s. 13.]

"vessel" [*Repealed*, 2018, c. 21, s. 13.]

Duties Tending to Preservation of Life

CODE

DUTY OF PERSONS TO PROVIDE NECESSARIES / Offence / Punishment / Presumptions.

215. (1) Every one is under a legal duty

- (*a*) as a parent, foster parent, guardian or head of a family, to provide necessaries of life for a child under the age of sixteen years;
- (*b*) to provide necessaries of life to their spouse or common-law partner; and
- (*c*) to provide necessaries of life to a person under his charge if that person
  - (i) is unable, by reason of detention, age, illness, mental disorder or other cause, to withdraw himself from that charge, and
  - (ii) is unable to provide himself with necessaries of life.

(2) Every person commits an offence who, being under a legal duty within the meaning of subsection (1), fails without lawful excuse to perform that duty, if

- (*a*) with respect to a duty imposed by paragraph (1)(*a*) or (*b*),
  - (i) the person to whom the duty is owed is in destitute or necessitous circumstances, or
  - (ii) the failure to perform the duty endangers the life of the person to whom the duty is owed, or causes or is likely to cause the health of that person to be endangered permanently; or
- (*b*) with respect to a duty imposed by paragraph (1)(*c*), the failure to perform the duty endangers the life of the person to whom the duty is owed or causes or is likely to cause the health of that person to be injured permanently.

(3) Every one who commits an offence under subsection (2)

- (*a*) is guilty of an indictable offence and liable to imprisonment for a term not exceeding five years; or
- (*b*) is guilty of an offence punishable on summary conviction.

(4) For the purpose of proceedings under this section,

- (*a*) [*Repealed*, 2000, c. 12, s. 93(2).];
- (*b*) evidence that a person has in any way recognized a child as being his child is, in the absence of any evidence to the contrary, proof that the child is his child;
- (*c*) evidence that a person has failed for a period of one month to make provision for the maintenance of any child of theirs under the age of sixteen years is, in the absence of any evidence to the contrary, proof that the person has failed without lawful excuse to provide necessaries of life for the child; and

(*d*) the fact that a spouse or common-law partner or child is receiving or has received necessaries of life from another person who is not under a legal duty to provide them is not a defence. R.S., c. C-34, s. 197; 1974-75-76, c. 66, s. 8; 1991, c. 43, s. 9; 2000, c. 12, ss. 93, 95(*a*); 2005, c. 32, s. 11; 2018, c. 29, s. 18; 2019, c. 25, s. 74.

DUTY OF PERSONS UNDERTAKING ACTS DANGEROUS TO LIFE.

216. Every one who undertakes to administer surgical or medical treatment to another person or to do any other lawful act that may endanger the life of another person is, except in cases of necessity, under a legal duty to have and to use reasonable knowledge, skill and care in so doing. R.S., c. C-34, s. 198.

DUTY OF PERSONS UNDERTAKING ACTS.

217. Every one who undertakes to do an act is under a legal duty to do it if an omission to do the act is or may be dangerous to life. R.S., c. C-34, s. 199.

DUTY OF PERSONS DIRECTING WORK.

217.1 Every one who undertakes, or has the authority, to direct how another person does work or performs a task is under a legal duty to take reasonable steps to prevent bodily harm to that person, or any other person, arising from that work or task. 2003, c. 21, s. 3.

ABANDONING CHILD.

218. Every one who unlawfully abandons or exposes a child who is under the age of ten years, so that its life is or is likely to be endangered or its health is or is likely to be permanently injured,

(*a*) is guilty of an indictable offence and liable to imprisonment for a term not exceeding five years; or

(*b*) is guilty of an offence punishable on summary conviction. R.S., c. C-34, s. 200; 2005, c. 32, s. 12; 2019, c. 25, s. 75.

Criminal Negligence

CRIMINAL NEGLIGENCE / Definition of "duty".

219. (1) Every one is criminally negligent who

(*a*) in doing anything, or

(*b*) in omitting to do anything that it is his duty to do,

shows wanton or reckless disregard for the lives or safety of other persons.

(2) For the purposes of this section, "duty" means a duty imposed by law. R.S., c. C-34, s. 202.

CAUSING DEATH BY CRIMINAL NEGLIGENCE.

220. Every person who by criminal negligence causes death to another person is guilty of an indictable offence and liable
- (a) where a firearm is used in the commission of the offence, to imprisonment for life and to a minimum punishment of imprisonment for a term of four years; and
- (b) in any other case, to imprisonment for life. R.S., c. C-34, s. 203; 1995, c. 39, s. 141.

CAUSING BODILY HARM BY CRIMINAL NEGLIGENCE.

221. Every person who by criminal negligence causes bodily harm to another person is guilty of
- (a) an indictable offence and liable to imprisonment for a term of not more than 10 years; or
- (b) an offence punishable on summary conviction. R.S., c. C-34, s. 204; 2019, c. 25, s. 76.

Homicide

HOMICIDE / Kinds of homicide / Non culpable homicide / Culpable homicide / Idem / Exception.

222. (1) A person commits homicide when, directly or indirectly, by any means, he causes the death of a human being.

(2) Homicide is culpable or not culpable.

(3) Homicide that is not culpable is not an offence.

(4) Culpable homicide is murder or manslaughter or infanticide.

(5) A person commits culpable homicide when he causes the death of a human being,
- (a) by means of an unlawful act,
- (b) by criminal negligence,
- (c) by causing that human being, by threats or fear of violence or by deception, to do anything that causes his death, or
- (d) by wilfully frightening that human being, in the case of a child or sick person.

(6) Notwithstanding anything in this section, a person does not commit homicide within the meaning of this Act by reason only that he causes the death of a human being by procuring, by false evidence, the conviction and death of that human being by sentence of the law. R.S., c. C-34, s. 205.

WHEN CHILD BECOMES HUMAN BEING / Killing child.

223. (1) A child becomes a human being within the meaning of this Act when it has completely proceeded, in a living state, from the body of its mother whether or not (*a*) it has breathed,

    (*b*) it has an independent circulation, or

    (*c*) the navel string is severed.

(2) A person commits homicide when he causes injury to a child before or during its birth as a result of which the child dies after becoming a human being. R.S., c. C-34, s. 206.

DEATH THAT MIGHT HAVE BEEN PREVENTED.

224. Where a person, by an act or omission, does any thing that results in the death of a human being, he causes the death of that human being notwithstanding that death from that cause might have been prevented by resorting to proper means. R.S., c. C-34, s. 207.

DEATH FROM TREATMENT OF INJURY.

225. Where a person causes to a human being a bodily injury that is of itself of a dangerous nature and from which death results, he causes the death of that human being notwithstanding that the immediate cause of death is proper or improper treatment that is applied in good faith. R.S., c. C-34, s. 208.

ACCELERATION OF DEATH.

226. Where a person causes to a human being a bodily injury that results in death, he causes the death of that human being notwithstanding that the effect of the bodily injury is only to accelerate his death from a disease or disorder arising from some other cause. R.S., c. C-34, s. 209.

EXEMPTION FOR MEDICAL ASSISTANCE IN DYING / Exemption for person aiding practitioner / Reasonable but mistaken belief / Non-application of section 14 / Definitions.

227. (1) No medical practitioner or nurse practitioner commits culpable homicide if they provide a person with medical assistance in dying in accordance with section 241.2.

(2) No person is a party to culpable homicide if they do anything for the purpose of aiding a medical practitioner or nurse practitioner to provide a person with medical assistance in dying in accordance with section 241.2.

(3) For greater certainty, the exemption set out in subsection (1) or (2) applies even if the person invoking it has a reasonable but mistaken belief about any fact that is an element of the exemption.

(4) Section 14 does not apply with respect to a person who consents to have death inflicted on them by means of medical assistance in dying provided in accordance with section 241.2.

(5) In this section, *medical assistance in dying*, *medical practitioner* and *nurse practitioner* have the same meanings as in section 241.1. 2016, c. 3, s. 2.

KILLING BY INFLUENCE ON THE MIND.

228. No person commits culpable homicide where he causes the death of a human being

    (*a*) by any influence on the mind alone, or

    (*b*) by any disorder or disease resulting from influence on the mind alone,

but this section does not apply where a person causes the death of a child or sick person by wilfully frightening him. R.S., c. C-34, s. 211.

Murder, Manslaughter and Infanticide

MURDER.

229. Culpable homicide is murder

    (*a*) where the person who causes the death of a human being

        (i) means to cause his death, or

        (ii) means to cause him bodily harm that he knows is likely to cause his death, and is reckless whether death ensues or not;

    (*b*) where a person, meaning to cause death to a human being or meaning to cause him bodily harm that he knows is likely to cause his death, and being reckless whether death ensues or not, by accident or mistake causes death to another human being, notwithstanding that he does not mean to cause death or bodily harm to that human being; or

    (*c*) if a person, for an unlawful object, does anything that they know is likely to cause death, and by doing so causes the death of a human being, even if they desire to effect their object without causing death or bodily harm to any human being. R.S., c. C-34, s. 212; 2019, c. 25, s. 77.

---

230. [*Repealed*, 2019, c. 25, s. 78.]

CLASSIFICATION OF MURDER / Planned and deliberate murder / Contracted murder / Murder of peace officer, etc. / Hijacking, sexual assault or kidnapping / Criminal harassment / Murder — terrorist activity / Murder — criminal organization / Intimidation / Second degree murder.

231. (1) Murder is first degree murder or second degree murder.

(2) Murder is first degree murder when it is planned and deliberate.

(3) Without limiting the generality of subsection (2), murder is planned and deliberate when it is committed pursuant to an arrangement under which money or anything of value passes or is intended to pass from one person to another, or is promised by one person to another, as consideration for that other's causing or assisting in causing the death of anyone or counselling another person to do any act causing or assisting in causing that death.

(4) Irrespective of whether a murder is planned and deliberate on the part of any person, murder is first degree murder when the victim is

(a) a police officer, police constable, constable, sheriff, deputy sheriff, sheriff's officer or other person employed for the preservation and maintenance of the public peace, acting in the course of his duties;

(b) a warden, deputy warden, instructor, keeper, jailer, guard or other officer or a permanent employee of a prison, acting in the course of his duties; or

(c) a person working in a prison with the permission of the prison authorities and acting in the course of his work therein.

(5) Irrespective of whether a murder is planned and deliberate on the part of any person, murder is first degree murder in respect of a person when the death is caused by that person while committing or attempting to commit an offence under one of the following sections:

(a) section 76 (hijacking an aircraft);

(b) section 271 (sexual assault);

(c) section 272 (sexual assault with a weapon, threats to a third party or causing bodily harm);

(d) section 273 (aggravated sexual assault);

(e) section 279 (kidnapping and forcible confinement); or

(f) section 279.1 (hostage taking).

(6) [*Repealed*, R.S.C. 1985, c. 27 (1st Supp.), s. 35.]

(6) Irrespective of whether a murder is planned and deliberate on the part of any person, murder is first degree murder when the death is caused by that person while committing or attempting to commit an offence under section 264 and the person committing that offence intended to cause the person murdered to fear for the safety of the person murdered or the safety of anyone known to the person murdered.

(6.01) Irrespective of whether a murder is planned and deliberate on the part of a person, murder is first degree murder when the death is caused by that person while committing or attempting to commit an indictable offence under this or any other Act of Parliament if the act or omission constituting the offence also constitutes a terrorist activity.

(6.1) Irrespective of whether a murder is planned and deliberate on the part of a person, murder is first degree murder when

(a) the death is caused by that person for the benefit of, at the direction of or in association with a criminal organization; or

(b) the death is caused by that person while committing or attempting to commit an indictable offence under this or any other Act of Parliament for the benefit of, at the direction of or in association with a criminal organization.

(6.2) Irrespective of whether a murder is planned and deliberate on the part of a person, murder is first degree murder when the death is caused by that person while committing or attempting to commit an offence under section 423.1.

(7) All murder that is not first degree murder is second degree murder. R.S., c. C-34, s. 214; R.S. c. C-35, s. 4; 1973-74, c. 38, s. 2; 1974-75-76, c. 105, s. 4; 1980-81-82-83, c. 125, s. 16; R.S.C. 1985, c. 27 (1st Supp.), ss. 7(2)(*b*), 35, 40(2); 1997, c. 16, s. 3; 1997, c. 23, s. 8; 2001, c. 32, s. 9(2); 2001, c. 41, s. 9; 2009, c. 22, s. 5.

MURDER REDUCED TO MANSLAUGHTER / What is provocation / Questions of fact / Death during illegal arrest.

232. (1) Culpable homicide that otherwise would be murder may be reduced to manslaughter if the person who committed it did so in the heat of passion caused by sudden provocation.

(2) Conduct of the victim that would constitute an indictable offence under this Act that is punishable by five or more years of imprisonment and that is of such a nature as to be sufficient to deprive an ordinary person of the power of self-control is provocation for the purposes of this section, if the accused acted on it on the sudden and before there was time for their passion to cool.

(3) For the purposes of this section, the questions
- (*a*) whether the conduct of the victim amounted to provocation under subsection (2), and
- (*b*) whether the accused was deprived of the power of self-control by the provocation that he alleges he received,

are questions of fact, but no one shall be deemed to have given provocation to another by doing anything that he had a legal right to do, or by doing anything that the accused incited him to do in order to provide the accused with an excuse for causing death or bodily harm to any human being.

(4) Culpable homicide that otherwise would be murder is not necessarily manslaughter by reason only that it was committed by a person who was being arrested illegally, but the fact that the illegality of the arrest was known to the accused may be evidence of provocation for the purpose of this section. R.S., c. C-34, s. 215; 2015, c. 29, s. 7.

INFANTICIDE.

233. A female person commits infanticide when by a wilful act or omission she causes the death of her newly-born child, if at the time of the act or omission she is not fully recovered from the effects of giving birth to the child and by reason thereof or of the effect of lactation consequent on the birth of the child her mind is then disturbed. R.S., c. C-34, s. 216.

MANSLAUGHTER.

234. Culpable homicide that is not murder or infanticide is manslaughter. R.S., c. C-34, s. 217.

PUNISHMENT FOR MURDER / Minimum punishment.

235. (1) Every one who commits first degree murder or second degree murder is guilty of an indictable offence and shall be sentenced to imprisonment for life.

(2) For the purposes of Part XXIII, the sentence of imprisonment for life prescribed by this section is a minimum punishment. R.S., c. C-34, s. 218; 1973-74, c. 38, s. 3; 1974-75-76, c. 105, s. 5.

MANSLAUGHTER.

236. Every person who commits manslaughter is guilty of an indictable offence and liable

- (*a*) where a firearm is used in the commission of the offence, to imprisonment for life and to a minimum punishment of imprisonment for a term of four years; and
- (*b*) in any other case, to imprisonment for life. R.S., c. C-34, s. 219; 1995, c. 39, s. 142.

PUNISHMENT FOR INFANTICIDE.

237. Every female person who commits infanticide is guilty of

- (*a*) an indictable offence and liable to imprisonment for a term of not more than five years; or
- (*b*) an offence punishable on summary conviction. R.S., c. C-34, s. 220; 2019, c. 25, s. 79.

KILLING UNBORN CHILD IN ACT OF BIRTH / Saving.

238. (1) Every one who causes the death, in the act of birth, of any child that has not become a human being, in such a manner that, if the child were a human being, he would be guilty of murder, is guilty of an indictable offence and liable to imprisonment for life.

(2) This section does not apply to a person who, by means that, in good faith, he considers necessary to preserve the life of the mother of a child, causes the death of that child. R.S., c. C-34, s. 221.

ATTEMPT TO COMMIT MURDER / Subsequent offences / Sequence of convictions only.

239. (1) Every person who attempts by any means to commit murder is guilty of an indictable offence and liable

- (*a*) if a restricted firearm or prohibited firearm is used in the commission of the offence or if any firearm is used in the commission of the offence and the offence is committed for the benefit of, at the direction of, or in association with, a criminal organization, to imprisonment for life and to a minimum punishment of imprisonment for a term of
  - (i) in the case of a first offence, five years, and
  - (ii) in the case of a second or subsequent offence, seven years;
- (*a*.1) in any other case where a firearm is used in the commission of the offence, to imprisonment for life and to a minimum punishment of imprisonment for a term of four years; and
- (*b*) in any other case, to imprisonment for life.

(2) In determining, for the purpose of paragraph (1)(*a*), whether a convicted person has committed a second or subsequent offence, if the person was earlier convicted of any of the following offences, that offence is to be considered as an earlier offence:

(*a*) an offence under this section;

(*b*) an offence under subsection 85(1) or (2) or section 244 or 244.2; or

(*c*) an offence under section 220, 236, 272 or 273, subsection 279(1) or section 279.1, 344 or 346 if a firearm was used in the commission of the offence.

However, an earlier offence shall not be taken into account if 10 years have elapsed between the day on which the person was convicted of the earlier offence and the day on which the person was convicted of the offence for which sentence is being imposed, not taking into account any time in custody.

(3) For the purposes of subsection (2), the only question to be considered is the sequence of convictions and no consideration shall be given to the sequence of commission of offences or whether any offence occurred before or after any conviction. R.S., c. C-34, s. 222; 1995, c. 39, s. 143; 2008, c. 6, s. 16; 2009, c. 22, s. 6.

ACCESSORY AFTER FACT TO MURDER.

240. Every one who is an accessory after the fact to murder is guilty of an indictable offence and liable to imprisonment for life. R.S., c. C-34, s. 223.

Suicide

COUNSELLING OR AIDING SUICIDE / Exemption for medical assistance in dying / Exemption for person aiding practitioner / Exemption for pharmacist / Exemption for person aiding patient / Clarification / Reasonable but mistaken belief / Definitions.

241. (1) Everyone is guilty of an indictable offence and liable to imprisonment for a term of not more than 14 years who, whether suicide ensues or not,

(*a*) counsels a person to die by suicide or abets a person in dying by suicide; or

(*b*) aids a person to die by suicide.

(2) No medical practitioner or nurse practitioner commits an offence under paragraph (1)(*b*) if they provide a person with medical assistance in dying in accordance with section 241.2.

(3) No person is a party to an offence under paragraph (1)(*b*) if they do anything for the purpose of aiding a medical practitioner or nurse practitioner to provide a person with medical assistance in dying in accordance with section 241.2.

(4) No pharmacist who dispenses a substance to a person other than a medical practitioner or nurse practitioner commits an offence under paragraph (1)(*b*) if the pharmacist dispenses the substance further to a prescription that is written by such a practitioner in providing medical assistance in dying in accordance with section 241.2.

(5) No person commits an offence under paragraph (1)(*b*) if they do anything, at another person's explicit request, for the purpose of aiding that other person to self-administer a substance that has been prescribed for that other person as part of the provision of medical assistance in dying in accordance with section 241.2.

(5.1) For greater certainty, no social worker, psychologist, psychiatrist, therapist, medical practitioner, nurse practitioner or other health care professional commits an offence if they provide information to a person on the lawful provision of medical assistance in dying.

(6) For greater certainty, the exemption set out in any of subsections (2) to (5) applies even if the person invoking the exemption has a reasonable but mistaken belief about any fact that is an element of the exemption.

(7) In this section, *medical assistance in dying*, *medical practitioner*, *nurse practitioner* and *pharmacist* have the same meanings as in section 241.1. R.S., c. C-34, s. 224; R.S.C. 1985, c. 27 (1st Supp.), s. 7(3); 2016, c. 3, s. 3.

Medical Assistance in Dying   2016, c. 3, s. 3.

DEFINITIONS.

241.1 The following definitions apply in this section and in sections 241.2 to 241.4.

medical assistance in dying means
  (a) the administering by a medical practitioner or nurse practitioner of a substance to a person, at their request, that causes their death; or
  (b) the prescribing or providing by a medical practitioner or nurse practitioner of a substance to a person, at their request, so that they may self-administer the substance and in doing so cause their own death.

medical practitioner means a person who is entitled to practise medicine under the laws of a province.

nurse practitioner means a registered nurse who, under the laws of a province, is entitled to practise as a nurse practitioner — or under an equivalent designation — and to autonomously make diagnoses, order and interpret diagnostic tests, prescribe substances and treat patients.

pharmacist means a person who is entitled to practice pharmacy under the laws of a province. 2016, c. 3, s. 3.

ELIGIBILITY FOR MEDICAL ASSISTANCE IN DYING / Grievous and irremediable medical condition / Safeguards / Unable to sign / Independent witness / Independence — medical practitioners and nurse practitioners / Reasonable knowledge, care and skill / Informing pharmacist / Clarification.

241.2 (1) A person may receive medical assistance in dying only if they meet all of the following criteria:
  (a) they are eligible — or, but for any applicable minimum period of residence or waiting period, would be eligible — for health services funded by a government in Canada;
  (b) they are at least 18 years of age and capable of making decisions with respect to their health;
  (c) they have a grievous and irremediable medical condition;

(*d*) they have made a voluntary request for medical assistance in dying that, in particular, was not made as a result of external pressure; and

(*e*) they give informed consent to receive medical assistance in dying after having been informed of the means that are available to relieve their suffering, including palliative care.

(2) A person has a grievous and irremediable medical condition only if they meet all of the following criteria:

(*a*) they have a serious and incurable illness, disease or disability;

(*b*) they are in an advanced state of irreversible decline in capability;

(*c*) that illness, disease or disability or that state of decline causes them enduring physical or psychological suffering that is intolerable to them and that cannot be relieved under conditions that they consider acceptable; and

(*d*) their natural death has become reasonably foreseeable, taking into account all of their medical circumstances, without a prognosis necessarily having been made as to the specific length of time that they have remaining.

(3) Before a medical practitioner or nurse practitioner provides a person with medical assistance in dying, the medical practitioner or nurse practitioner must

(*a*) be of the opinion that the person meets all of the criteria set out in subsection (1);

(*b*) ensure that the person's request for medical assistance in dying was

　(i) made in writing and signed and dated by the person or by another person under subsection (4), and

　(ii) signed and dated after the person was informed by a medical practitioner or nurse practitioner that the person has a grievous and irremediable medical condition;

(*c*) be satisfied that the request was signed and dated by the person — or by another person under subsection (4) — before two independent witnesses who then also signed and dated the request;

(*d*) ensure that the person has been informed that they may, at any time and in any manner, withdraw their request;

(*e*) ensure that another medical practitioner or nurse practitioner has provided a written opinion confirming that the person meets all of the criteria set out in subsection (1);

(*f*) be satisfied that they and the other medical practitioner or nurse practitioner referred to in paragraph (*e*) are independent;

(*g*) ensure that there are at least 10 clear days between the day on which the request was signed by or on behalf of the person and the day on which the medical assistance in dying is provided or — if they and the other medical practitioner or nurse practitioner referred to in paragraph (*e*) are both of the opinion that the person's death, or the loss of their capacity to provide informed consent, is imminent — any shorter period that the first medical practitioner or nurse practitioner considers appropriate in the circumstances;

(*h*) immediately before providing the medical assistance in dying, give the person an opportunity to withdraw their request and ensure that the person gives express consent to receive medical assistance in dying; and (*i*) if the person has difficulty communicating, take all necessary measures to provide a reliable means by which the person may understand the information that is provided to them and communicate their decision.

(4) If the person requesting medical assistance in dying is unable to sign and date the request, another person — who is at least 18 years of age, who understands the nature of the request for medical assistance in dying and who does not know or believe that they are a beneficiary under the will of the person making the request, or a recipient, in any other way, of a financial or other material benefit resulting from that person's death — may do so in the person's presence, on the person's behalf and under the person's express direction.

(5) Any person who is at least 18 years of age and who understands the nature of the request for medical assistance in dying may act as an independent witness, except if they

(*a*) know or believe that they are a beneficiary under the will of the person making the request, or a recipient, in any other way, of a financial or other material benefit resulting from that person's death;

(*b*) are an owner or operator of any health care facility at which the person making the request is being treated or any facility in which that person resides;

(*c*) are directly involved in providing health care services to the person making the request; or

(*d*) directly provide personal care to the person making the request.

(6) The medical practitioner or nurse practitioner providing medical assistance in dying and the medical practitioner or nurse practitioner who provides the opinion referred to in paragraph (3)(*e*) are independent if they

(*a*) are not a mentor to the other practitioner or responsible for supervising their work;

(*b*) do not know or believe that they are a beneficiary under the will of the person making the request, or a recipient, in any other way, of a financial or other material benefit resulting from that person's death, other than standard compensation for their services relating to the request; or

(*c*) do not know or believe that they are connected to the other practitioner or to the person making the request in any other way that would affect their objectivity.

(7) Medical assistance in dying must be provided with reasonable knowledge, care and skill and in accordance with any applicable provincial laws, rules or standards.

(8) The medical practitioner or nurse practitioner who, in providing medical assistance in dying, prescribes or obtains a substance for that purpose must, before any pharmacist dispenses the substance, inform the pharmacist that the substance is intended for that purpose.

(9) For greater certainty, nothing in this section compels an individual to provide or assist in providing medical assistance in dying. 2016, c. 3, s. 3.

FAILURE TO COMPLY WITH SAFEGUARDS.

241.3 A medical practitioner or nurse practitioner who, in providing medical assistance in dying, knowingly fails to comply with all of the requirements set out in paragraphs 241.2(3)(*b*) to (*i*) and subsection 241.2(8) is guilty of

(*a*) an indictable offence and liable to imprisonment for a term of not more than five years; or

(*b*) an offence punishable on summary conviction. 2016, c. 3, s. 3; 2019, c. 25, s. 80.

CODE

FILING INFORMATION — MEDICAL PRACTITIONER OR NURSE PRACTITIONER / Filing information — pharmacist / Regulations / Guidelines — information on death certificates / Offence and punishment / Offence and punishment.

241.31 (1) Unless they are exempted under regulations made under subsection (3), a medical practitioner or nurse practitioner who receives a written request for medical assistance in dying must, in accordance with those regulations, provide the information required by those regulations to the recipient designated in those regulations.

(2) Unless they are exempted under regulations made under subsection (3), a pharmacist who dispenses a substance in connection with the provision of medical assistance in dying must, in accordance with those regulations, provide the information required by those regulations to the recipient designated in those regulations.

(3) The Minister of Health must make regulations that he or she considers necessary

(*a*) respecting the provision and collection, for the purpose of monitoring medical assistance in dying, of information relating to requests for, and the provision of, medical assistance in dying, including

(i) the information to be provided, at various stages, by medical practitioners or nurse practitioners and by pharmacists, or by a class of any of them,

(ii) the form, manner and time in which the information must be provided,

(iii) the designation of a person as the recipient of the information, and

(iv) the collection of information from coroners and medical examiners;

(*b*) respecting the use of that information, including its analysis and interpretation, its protection and its publication and other disclosure;

(*c*) respecting the disposal of that information; and

(*d*) exempting, on any terms that may be specified, a class of persons from the requirement set out in subsection or (2).

(3.1) The Minister of Health, after consultation with representatives of the provincial governments responsible for health, must establish guidelines on the information to be included on death certificates in cases where medical assistance in dying has been provided, which may include the way in which to clearly identify medical assistance in dying as the manner of death, as well as the illness, disease or disability that prompted the request for medical assistance in dying.

(4) A medical practitioner or nurse practitioner who knowingly fails to comply with subsection (1), or a pharmacist who knowingly fails to comply with subsection (2),

    (*a*) is guilty of an indictable offence and liable to a term of imprisonment of not more than two years; or

    (*b*) is guilty of an offence punishable on summary conviction.

(5) Everyone who knowingly contravenes the regulations made under subsection (3)

    (*a*) is guilty of an indictable offence and liable to a term of imprisonment of not more than two years; or

    (*b*) is guilty of an offence punishable on summary conviction. 2016, c. 3, s. 4.

FORGERY / Destruction of documents / Punishment / Definition of "document".

241.4 (1) Everyone commits an offence who commits forgery in relation to a request for medical assistance in dying.

(2) Everyone commits an offence who destroys a document that relates to a request for medical assistance in dying with intent to interfere with

    (*a*) another person's access to medical assistance in dying;

    (*b*) the lawful assessment of a request for medical assistance in dying; or

    (*c*) another person invoking an exemption under any of subsections 227(1) or (2), 241(2) to (5) or 245(2); or

    (*d*) the provision by a person of information under section 241.31.

(3) Everyone who commits an offence under subsection (1) or (2) is guilty of

    (*a*) an indictable offence and liable to imprisonment for a term of not more than five years; or

    (*b*) an offence punishable on summary conviction.

(4) In subsection (2), *document* has the same meaning as in section 321. 2016, c. 3, ss. 3, 5; 2019, c. 25, s. 81.

Neglect in Child-birth and Concealing Dead Body

NEGLECT TO OBTAIN ASSISTANCE IN CHILDBIRTH.

242. A female person who, being pregnant and about to be delivered, with intent that the child shall not live or with intent to conceal the birth of the child, fails to make provision for reasonable assistance in respect of her delivery is, if the child is permanently injured as a result of the failure or dies immediately before, during or in a short time after birth, as a result of the failure, guilty of

    (*a*) an indictable offence and liable to imprisonment for a term of not more than five years; or

    (*b*) an offence punishable on summary conviction. R.S., c. C-34, s. 226; 2019, c. 25, s. 82.

CONCEALING BODY OF CHILD.

243. Every person who in any manner disposes of the dead body of a child, with intent to conceal the fact that its mother has been delivered of it, whether the child died before, during or after birth, is guilty of

(*a*) an indictable offence and liable to imprisonment for a term of not more than two years; or

(*b*) an offence punishable on summary conviction. R.S., c. C-34, s. 227; 2019, c. 25, s. 82.

CODE

Bodily Harm and Acts and Omissions Causing Danger to the Person

DISCHARGING FIREARM WITH INTENT / Punishment / Subsequent offences / Sequence of convictions only.

244. (1) Every person commits an offence who discharges a firearm at a person with intent to wound, maim or disfigure, to endanger the life of or to prevent the arrest or detention of any person — whether or not that person is the one at whom the firearm is discharged.

(2) Every person who commits an offence under subsection (1) is guilty of an indictable offence and liable

(*a*) if a restricted firearm or prohibited firearm is used in the commission of the offence or if the offence is committed for the benefit of, at the direction of, or in association with, a criminal organization, to imprisonment for a term not exceeding 14 years and to a minimum punishment of imprisonment for a term of

(i) in the case of a first offence, five years, and

(ii) in the case of a second or subsequent offence, seven years; and

(*b*) in any other case, to imprisonment for a term not exceeding 14 years and to a minimum punishment of imprisonment for a term of four years.

(3) In determining, for the purpose of paragraph (2)(*a*), whether a convicted person has committed a second or subsequent offence, if the person was earlier convicted of any of the following offences, that offence is to be considered as an earlier offence:

(*a*) an offence under this section;

(*b*) an offence under subsection 85(1) or (2) or section 244.2; or

(*c*) an offence under section 220, 236, 239, 272 or 273, subsection 279(1) or section 279.1, 344 or 346 if a firearm was used in the commission of the offence.

However, an earlier offence shall not be taken into account if 10 years have elapsed between the day on which the person was convicted of the earlier offence and the day on which the person was convicted of the offence for which sentence is being imposed, not taking into account any time in custody.

(4) For the purposes of subsection (3), the only question to be considered is the sequence of convictions and no consideration shall be given to the sequence of commission of offences or whether any offence occurred before or after any

conviction. R.S., c. C-34, s. 228; 1980-81-82-83, c. 125, s. 17; 1995, c. 39, s. 144; 2008, c. 6, s. 17; 2009, c. 22, s. 7.

CAUSING BODILY HARM WITH INTENT — AIR GUN OR PISTOL.

244.1 Every person who, with intent

    (a) to wound, maim or disfigure any person,

    (b) to endanger the life of any person, or

    (c) to prevent the arrest or detention of any person,

discharges an air or compressed gas gun or pistol at any person, whether or not that person is the person mentioned in paragraph (a), (b) or (c), is guilty of an indictable offence and liable to imprisonment for a term not exceeding fourteen years. 1995, c. 39, s. 144.

DISCHARGING FIREARM — RECKLESSNESS / Definition of "place" / Punishment / Subsequent offences / Sequence of convictions only.

244.2 (1) Every person commits an offence

    (a) who intentionally discharges a firearm into or at a place, knowing that or being reckless as to whether another person is present in the place; or

    (b) who intentionally discharges a firearm while being reckless as to the life or safety of another person.

(2) For the purpose of paragraph (1)(a), "place" means any building or structure — or part of one — or any motor vehicle, vessel, aircraft, railway vehicle, container or trailer.

(3) Every person who commits an offence under subsection (1) is guilty of an indictable offence and

    (a) if a restricted firearm or prohibited firearm is used in the commission of the offence or if the offence is committed for the benefit of, at the direction of or in association with a criminal organization, is liable to imprisonment for a term of not more than 14 years and to a minimum punishment of imprisonment for a term of

        (i) five years, in the case of a first offence, and

        (ii) seven years, in the case of a second or subsequent offence; and

    (b) in any other case, is liable to imprisonment for a term of not more than 14 years and to a minimum punishment of imprisonment for a term of four years.

(4) In determining, for the purpose of paragraph (3)(a), whether a convicted person has committed a second or subsequent offence, if the person was earlier convicted of any of the following offences, that offence is to be considered as an earlier offence:

    (a) an offence under this section;

    (b) an offence under subsection 85(1) or (2) or section 244; or

    (c) an offence under section 220, 236, 239, 272 or 273, subsection 279(1) or section 279.1, 344 or 346 if a firearm was used in the commission of the offence.

However, an earlier offence shall not be taken into account if 10 years have elapsed between the day on which the person was convicted of the earlier offence and the day on which the person was convicted of the offence for which sentence is being imposed, not taking into account any time in custody.

(5) For the purpose of subsection (4), the only question to be considered is the sequence of convictions and no consideration shall be given to the sequence of commission of offences or whether any offence occurred before or after any conviction. 2009; c. 22, s. 8.

ADMINISTERING NOXIOUS THING / Exemption / Definitions.

245. (1) Every person who administers or causes to be administered to any other person or causes any other person to take poison or any other destructive or noxious thing is guilty

    (*a*) of an indictable offence and liable to imprisonment for a term of not more than 14 years, if they did so with intent to endanger the life of or to cause bodily harm to that person; or

    (*b*) of an indictable offence and liable to imprisonment for a term of not more than two years or of an offence punishable on summary conviction, if they did so with intent to aggrieve or annoy that person.

(2) Subsection (1) does not apply to

    (*a*) a medical practitioner or nurse practitioner who provides medical assistance in dying in accordance with section 241.2; and

    (*b*) a person who does anything for the purpose of aiding a medical practitioner or nurse practitioner to provide medical assistance in dying in accordance with section 241.2.

(3) In subsection (2), *medical assistance in dying*, *medical practitioner* and *nurse practitioner* have the same meanings as in section 241.1. R.S., c. C-34, s. 229; 2016, c. 3, s. 6; 2019, c. 25, s. 83.

OVERCOMING RESISTANCE TO COMMISSION OF OFFENCE.

246. Every one who, with intent to enable or assist himself or another person to commit an indictable offence,

    (*a*) attempts, by any means, to choke, suffocate or strangle another person, or by any means calculated to choke, suffocate or strangle, attempts to render another person insensible, unconscious or incapable of resistance, or

    (*b*) administers or causes to be administered to any person, or attempts to administer to any person, or causes or attempts to cause any person to take a stupefying or overpowering drug, matter or thing,

is guilty of an indictable offence and liable to imprisonment for life. R.S., c. C-34, s. 230; 1972, c. 13, s. 70.

TRAPS LIKELY TO CAUSE BODILY HARM / Bodily harm / Offence-related place / Offence-related place — bodily harm / Death.

247. (1) Every person is guilty of an indictable offence and liable to imprisonment for a term of not more than five years or is guilty of an offence punishable on summary conviction who with intent to cause death or bodily harm to a person, whether ascertained or not,

(a) sets or places a trap, device or other thing that is likely to cause death or bodily harm to a person; or

(b) being in occupation or possession of a place, knowingly permits such a trap, device or other thing to remain in that place.

(2) Every person who commits an offence under subsection (1), and by doing so causes bodily harm to any other person, is guilty of

(a) an indictable offence and liable to imprisonment for a term of not more than 10 years; or

(b) an offence punishable on summary conviction.

(3) Every person who commits an offence under subsection (1), in a place kept or used for the purpose of committing another indictable offence, is guilty of

(a) an indictable offence and liable to imprisonment for a term of not more than 10 years; or

(b) an offence punishable on summary conviction.

(4) Every one who commits an offence under subsection (1), in a place kept or used for the purpose of committing another indictable offence, and thereby causes bodily harm to a person is guilty of an indictable offence and liable to a term of imprisonment not exceeding fourteen years.

(5) Every one who commits an offence under subsection (1) and thereby causes the death of any other person is guilty of an indictable offence and liable to imprisonment for life. R.S., c. C-34, s. 231; 2004, c. 12, s. 6; 2019, c. 25, s. 84.

INTERFERING WITH TRANSPORTATION FACILITIES.

248. Every one who, with intent to endanger the safety of any person, places anything on or does anything to any property that is used for or in connection with the transportation of persons or goods by land, water or air that is likely to cause death or bodily harm to persons is guilty of an indictable offence and liable to imprisonment for life. R.S., c. C-34, s. 232.

[*Heading repealed*, 2018, c. 21, s. 14.]

---

249. [*Repealed*, 2018, c. 21, s. 14.]

249.1 [*Repealed*, 2018, c. 21, s. 14.]

249.2 [*Repealed*, 2018, c. 21, s. 14.]

249.3 [*Repealed*, 2018, c. 21, s. 14.]

249.4 [*Repealed*, 2018, c. 21, s. 14.]

250. [*Repealed*, 2018, c. 21, s. 14.]

251. [*Repealed*, 2018, c. 21, s. 14.]

252. [*Repealed*, 2018, c. 21, s. 14.]

253. [*Repealed*, 2018, c. 21, s. 14.]

253.1 [*Repealed*, 2018, c. 21, s. 14.]

254. [*Repealed*, 2018, c. 21, s. 14.]

254.01 [*Repealed*, 2018, c. 21, s. 14.]

254.1 [*Repealed*, 2018, c. 21, s. 14.]

255. [*Repealed*, 2018, c. 21, s. 14.]

255.1 [*Repealed*, 2018, c. 21, s. 14.]

256. [*Repealed*, 2018, c. 21, s. 14.]

257. [*Repealed*, 2018, c. 21, s. 14.]

258. [*Repealed*, 2018, c. 21, s. 14.]

258.1 [*Repealed*, 2018, c. 21, s. 14.]

259. [*Repealed*, 2018, c. 21, s. 14.]

260. [*Repealed*, 2018, c. 21, s. 14.]

261. [*Repealed*, 2018, c. 21, s. 14.]

IMPEDING ATTEMPT TO SAVE LIFE.

262. Every person is guilty of an indictable offence and liable to imprisonment for a term of not more than 10 years or is guilty of an offence punishable on summary conviction who

(*a*) prevents or impedes or attempts to prevent or impede any person who is attempting to save his own life, or

(b) without reasonable cause prevents or impedes or attempts to prevent or impede any person who is attempting to save the life of another person. R.S., c. C-34, s. 241; 2019, c. 25, s. 90.

DUTY TO SAFEGUARD OPENING IN ICE / Excavation on land / Offences.

263. (1) Every one who makes or causes to be made an opening in ice that is open to or frequented by the public is under a legal duty to guard it in a manner that is adequate to prevent persons from falling in by accident and is adequate to warn them that the opening exists.

(2) Every one who leaves an excavation on land that he owns or of which he has charge or supervision is under a legal duty to guard it in a manner that is adequate to prevent persons from falling in by accident and is adequate to warn them that the excavation exists.

(3) Every one who fails to perform a duty imposed by subsection (1) or (2) is guilty of

(a) manslaughter, if the death of any person results therefrom;

(b) an offence under section 269, if bodily harm to any person results therefrom; or

(c) an offence punishable on summary conviction. R.S., c. C-34, s. 242; 1980-81-82-83, c. 125, s. 18.

264. [*Repealed* (old provision), R.S.C. 1985, c. 27 (1st Supp.), s. 37.]

CRIMINAL HARASSMENT / Prohibited conduct / Punishment / Factors to be considered / Reasons.

264. (1) No person shall, without lawful authority and knowing that another person is harassed or recklessly as to whether the other person is harassed, engage in conduct referred to in subsection (2) that causes that other person reasonably, in all the circumstances, to fear for their safety or the safety of anyone known to them.

(2) The conduct mentioned in subsection (1) consists of

(a) repeatedly following from place to place the other person or anyone known to them;

(b) repeatedly communicating with, either directly or indirectly, the other person or anyone known to them;

(c) besetting or watching the dwelling-house, or place where the other person, or anyone known to them, resides, works, carries on business or happens to be; or

(d) engaging in threatening conduct directed at the other person or any member of their family.

(3) Every person who contravenes this section is guilty of

(a) an indictable offence and is liable to imprisonment for a term not exceeding ten years; or

(b) an offence punishable on summary conviction.

(4) Where a person is convicted of an offence under this section, the court imposing the sentence on the person shall consider as an aggravating factor that, at the time the offence was committed, the person contravened

- (a) the terms or conditions of an order made pursuant to section 161 or a recognizance entered into pursuant to section 810, 810.1 or 810.2; or
- (b) the terms or conditions of any other order or recognizance, or of an undertaking, made or entered into under the common law, this Act or any other Act of Parliament or of a provincial legislature that is similar in effect to an order or recognizance referred to in paragraph (a).

(5) Where the court is satisfied of the existence of an aggravating factor referred to in subsection (4), but decides not to give effect to it for sentencing purposes, the court shall give reasons for its decision. 1993, c. 45, s. 2; 1997, c. 16. s. 4; 1997, c. 17, s. 9; 2002, c. 13, s. 10; 2019, c. 25, s. 91.

Assaults

UTTERING THREATS / Punishment / Idem.

264.1 (1) Every one commits an offence who, in any manner, knowingly utters, conveys or causes any person to receive a threat

- (a) to cause death or bodily harm to any person;
- (b) to burn, destroy or damage real or personal property; or
- (c) to kill, poison or injure an animal or bird that is the property of any person.

(2) Every one who commits an offence under paragraph (1)(a) is guilty of

- (a) an indictable offence and liable to imprisonment for a term not exceeding five years; or
- (b) an offence punishable on summary conviction.

(3) Every one who commits an offence under paragraph (1)(b) or (c)

- (a) is guilty of an indictable offence and liable to imprisonment for a term not exceeding two years; or
- (b) is guilty of an offence punishable on summary conviction. R.S.C. 1985, c. 27 (1st Supp.), s. 38; 1994, c. 44, s. 16; 2019, c. 25, s. 92.

ASSAULT / Application / Consent / Accused's belief as to consent.

265. (1) A person commits an assault when

- (a) without the consent of another person, he applies force intentionally to that other person, directly or indirectly;
- (b) he attempts or threatens, by an act or a gesture, to apply force to another person, if he has, or causes that other person to believe upon reasonable grounds that he has, present ability to effect his purpose; or
- (c) while openly wearing or carrying a weapon or an imitation thereof, he accosts or impedes another person or begs.

(2) This section applies to all forms of assault, including sexual assault, sexual assault with a weapon, threats to a third party or causing bodily harm and aggravated sexual assault.

(3) For the purposes of this section, no consent is obtained where the complainant submits or does not resist by reason of

(a) the application of force to the complainant or to a person other than the complainant;

(b) threats or fear of the application of force to the complainant or to a person other than the complainant;

(c) fraud; or

(d) the exercise of authority.

(4) Where an accused alleges that he believed that the complainant consented to the conduct that is the subject-matter of the charge, a judge, if satisfied that there is sufficient evidence and that, if believed by the jury, the evidence would constitute a defence, shall instruct the jury, when reviewing all the evidence relating to the determination of the honesty of the accused's belief, to consider the presence or absence of reasonable grounds for that belief. R.S., c. C-34, s. 244; 1974-75-76, c. 93, s. 21; 1980-81-82-83, c. 125, s. 19.

ASSAULT.

266. Every one who commits an assault is guilty of

(a) an indictable offence and liable to imprisonment for a term not exceeding five years; or

(b) an offence punishable on summary conviction. R.S., c. C-34, s. 245; 1972, c. 13, s. 21; 1974-75-76, c. 93, s. 22; 1980-81-82-83, c. 125, s. 19.

ASSAULT WITH A WEAPON OR CAUSING BODILY HARM.

267. Every person is guilty of an indictable offence and liable to imprisonment for a term of not more than 10 years or is guilty of an offence punishable on summary conviction who, in committing an assault,

(a) carries, uses or threatens to use a weapon or an imitation thereof,

(b) causes bodily harm to the complainant, or

(c) chokes, suffocates or strangles the complainant. 1980-81-82-83, c. 125, s. 19; 1994, c. 44, s. 17; 2019, c. 25, s. 93.

AGGRAVATED ASSAULT / Punishment / Excision / Consent.

268. (1) Every one commits an aggravated assault who wounds, maims, disfigures or endangers the life of the complainant.

(2) Every one who commits an aggravated assault is guilty of an indictable offence and liable to imprisonment for a term not exceeding fourteen years.

(3) For greater certainty, in this section, "wounds" or "maims" includes to excise, infibulate or mutilate, in whole or in part, the labia majora, labia minora or clitoris of a person, except where

(a) a surgical procedure is performed, by a person duly qualified by provincial law to practise medicine, for the benefit of the physical health of the person or for the purpose of that person having normal reproductive functions or normal sexual appearance or function; or

(b)   the person is at least eighteen years of age and there is no resulting bodily harm.

(4) For the purposes of this section and section 265, no consent to the excision, infibulation or mutilation, in whole or in part, of the labia majora, labia minora or clitoris of a person is valid, except in the cases described in paragraphs (3)(*a*) and (*b*). 1980-81-82-83, c. 125, s. 19; 1997, c. 16, s. 5.

CODE

UNLAWFULLY CAUSING BODILY HARM.

269. Every one who unlawfully causes bodily harm to any person is guilty of
   (*a*)   an indictable offence and liable to imprisonment for a term not exceeding ten years; or
   (*b*)   an offence punishable on summary conviction. 1980-81-82-83, c. 125, s. 19; 1994, c. 44, s. 18; 2019, c. 25, s. 94.

AGGRAVAGING CIRCUMSTANCE — ASSAULT AGAINST A PUBLIC TRANSIT OPERATOR / Definitions.

269.01 (1) When a court imposes a sentence for an offence referred to in paragraph 264.1(1)(*a*) or any of sections 266 to 269, it shall consider as an aggravating circumstance the fact that the victim of the offence was, at the time of the commission of the offence, a public transit operator engaged in the performance of his or her duty.

(2) The following definitions apply in this section.

"public transit operator" means an individual who operates a vehicle used in the provision of passenger transportation services to the public, and includes an individual who operates a school bus.

"vehicle" includes a bus, paratransit vehicle, licensed taxi cab, train, subway, tram and ferry. 2015, c. 1, s. 1.

TORTURE / definitions / "official" / "torture" / no defence / evidence.

269.1 (1) Every official, or every person acting at the instigation of or with the consent or acquiescence of an official, who inflicts torture on any other person is guilty of an indictable offence and liable to imprisonment for a term not exceeding fourteen years.

(2) For the purposes of this section,
"official" means
   (*a*)   a peace officer,
   (*b*)   a public officer,
   (*c*)   a member of the Canadian Forces, or
   (*d*)   any person who may exercise powers, pursuant to a law in force in a foreign state, that would, in Canada, be exercised by a person referred to in paragraph (*a*), (*b*), or (*c*),
whether the person exercises powers in Canada or outside Canada;
"torture" means any act or omission by which severe pain or suffering, whether physical or mental, is intentionally inflicted on a person

277

   (a) for a purpose including
       (i) obtaining from the person or from a third person information or a statement,
      (ii) punishing the person for an act that the person or a third person has committed or is suspected of having committed, and
     (iii) intimidating or coercing the person or a third person, or
   (b) for any reason based on discrimination of any kind,

but does not include any act or omission arising only from, inherent in or incidental to lawful sanctions.

(3) It is no defence to a charge under this section that the accused was ordered by a superior or a public authority to perform the act or omission that forms the subject-matter of the charge or that the act or omission is alleged to have been justified by exceptional circumstances, including a state of war, a threat of war, internal political instability or any other public emergency.

(4) In any proceedings over which Parliament has jurisdiction, any statement obtained as a result of the commission of an offence under this section is inadmissible in evidence, except as evidence that the statement was so obtained. R.S.C. 1985, c. 10 (3rd Supp.), s. 2.

ASSAULTING A PEACE OFFICER / Punishment.

270. (1) Every one commits an offence who
   (a) assaults a public officer or peace officer engaged in the execution of his duty or a person acting in aid of such an officer;
   (b) assaults a person with intent to resist or prevent the lawful arrest or detention of himself or another person; or
   (c) assaults a person
       (i) who is engaged in the lawful execution of a process against lands or goods or in making a lawful distress or seizure, or
      (ii) with intent to rescue anything taken under lawful process, distress or seizure.

(2) Every one who commits an offence under subsection (1) is guilty of
   (a) an indictable offence and liable to imprisonment for a term not exceeding five years; or
   (b) an offence punishable on summary conviction. R.S., c. C-34, s. 246; 1972, c. 13, s. 22; 1980-81-82-83, c. 125, s. 19.

ASSAULTING PEACE OFFICER WITH WEAPON OR CAUSING BODILY HARM / Punishment.

270.01 (1) Everyone commits an offence who, in committing an assault referred to in section 270,
   (a) carries, uses or threatens to use a weapon or an imitation of one; or
   (b) causes bodily harm to the complainant.

(2) Everyone who commits an offence under subsection (1) is guilty of
   (a) an indictable offence and liable to imprisonment for a term of not more than 10 years; or

(*b*) an offence punishable on summary conviction. 2009, c. 22, s. 9; 2019, c. 25, s. 95.

AGGRAVATED ASSAULT OF PEACE OFFICER.

270.02 Everyone who, in committing an assault referred to in section 270, wounds, maims, disfigures or endangers the life of the complainant is guilty of an indictable offence and liable to imprisonment for a term of not more than 14 years. 2009, c. 22, s. 9.

SENTENCES TO BE SERVED CONSECUTIVELY.

270.03 A sentence imposed on a person for an offence under subsection 270(1) or 270.01(1) or section 270.02 committed against a law enforcement officer, as defined in subsection 445.01(4), shall be served consecutively to any other punishment imposed on the person for an offence arising out of the same event or series of events. 2015, c. 34, s. 2.

DISARMING A PEACE OFFICER / Definition of "weapon" / Punishment.

270.1 (1) Every one commits an offence who, without the consent of a peace officer, takes or attempts to take a weapon that is in the possession of the peace officer when the peace officer is engaged in the execution of his or her duty.

(2) For the purpose of subsection (1), "weapon" means any thing that is designed to be used to cause injury or death to, or to temporarily incapacitate, a person.

(3) Every one who commits an offence under subsection (1) is guilty of
(*a*) an indictable offence and liable to imprisonment for a term of not more than five years; or
(*b*) an offence punishable on summary conviction. 2002, c. 13, s. 11; 2019, c. 25, s. 96.

SEXUAL ASSAULT.

271. Everyone who commits a sexual assault is guilty of
(*a*) an indictable offence and is liable to imprisonment for a term of not more than 10 years or, if the complainant is under the age of 16 years, to imprisonment for a term of not more than 14 years and to a minimum punishment of imprisonment for a term of one year; or
(*b*) an offence punishable on summary conviction and is liable to imprisonment for a term of not more than 18 months or, if the complainant is under the age of 16 years, to imprisonment for a term of not more than two years less a day and to a minimum punishment of imprisonment for a term of six months. 1980-81-82-83, c. 125, c. 19; R.S.C. 1985, c. 19 (3rd Supp.), s. 10; 1994, c. 44, s. 19; 2012, c. 1, s. 25; 2015, c. 23, s. 14.

SEXUAL ASSAULT WITH A WEAPON, THREATS TO A THIRD PARTY OR CAUSING BODILY HARM / Punishment / Subsequent offences / Sequence of convictions only.

272. (1) Every person commits an offence who, in committing a sexual assault,

   (*a*) carries, uses or threatens to use a weapon or an imitation of a weapon;

   (*b*) threatens to cause bodily harm to a person other than the complainant;

   (*c*) causes bodily harm to the complainant;

 (*c*.1) chokes, suffocates or strangles the complainant; or

   (*d*) is a party to the offence with any other person.

(2) Every person who commits an offence under subsection (1) is guilty of an indictable offence and liable

   (*a*) if a restricted firearm or prohibited firearm is used in the commission of the offence or if any firearm is used in the commission of the offence and the offence is committed for the benefit of, at the direction of, or in association with, a criminal organization, to imprisonment for a term not exceeding 14 years and to a minimum punishment of imprisonment for a term of

     (i) in the case of a first offence, five years, and

     (ii) in the case of a second or subsequent offence, seven years;

 (*a*.1) in any other case where a firearm is used in the commission of the offence, to imprisonment for a term not exceeding 14 years and to a minimum punishment of imprisonment for a term of four years;

 (*a*.2) if the complainant is under the age of 16 years, to imprisonment for life and to a minimum punishment of imprisonment for a term of five years; and

   (*b*) in any other case, to imprisonment for a term not exceeding fourteen years.

(3) In determining, for the purpose of paragraph (2)(*a*), whether a convicted person has committed a second or subsequent offence, if the person was earlier convicted of any of the following offences, that offence is to be considered as an earlier offence:

   (*a*) an offence under this section;

   (*b*) an offence under subsection 85(1) or (2) or section 244 or 244.2; or

   (*c*) an offence under section 220, 236, 239 or 273, subsection 279(1) or section 279.1, 344 or 346 if a firearm was used in the commission of the offence.

However, an earlier offence shall not be taken into account if 10 years have elapsed between the day on which the person was convicted of the earlier offence and the day on which the person was convicted of the offence for which sentence is being imposed, not taking into account any time in custody.

(4) For the purposes of subsection (3), the only question to be considered is the sequence of convictions and no consideration shall be given to the sequence of commission of offences or whether any offence occurred before or after any conviction. 1980-81-82-83, c. 125, s. 19; 1995, c. 39, s. 145; 2008, c. 6, s. 28; 2009, c. 22, s. 10; 2012, c. 1, s. 26; 2015, c. 23, s. 15; 2019, c. 25, s. 97.

AGGRAVATED SEXUAL ASSAULT / Punishment / Subsequent offences / Sequence of convictions only.

273. (1) Every one commits an aggravated sexual assault who, in committing a sexual assault, wounds, maims, disfigures or endangers the life of the complainant.

(2) Every person who commits an aggravated sexual assault is guilty of an indictable offence and liable

  (a) if a restricted firearm or prohibited firearm is used in the commission of the offence or if any firearm is used in the commission of the offence and the offence is committed for the benefit of, at the direction of, or in association with, a criminal organization, to imprisonment for life and to a minimum punishment of imprisonment for a term of

  (i) in the case of a first offence, five years, and

  (ii) in the case of a second or subsequent offence, seven years;

  (a.1) in any other case where a firearm is used in the commission of the offence, to imprisonment for life and to a minimum punishment of imprisonment for a term of four years;

  (a.2) if the complainant is under the age of 16 years, to imprisonment for life and to a minimum punishment of imprisonment for a term of five years; and

  (b) in any other case, to imprisonment for life.

(3) In determining, for the purpose of paragraph (2)(a), whether a convicted person has committed a second or subsequent offence, if the person was earlier convicted of any of the following offences, that offence is to be considered as an earlier offence:

  (a) an offence under this section;

  (b) an offence under subsection 85(1) or (2) or section 244 or 244.2; or

  (c) an offence under section 220, 236, 239 or 272, subsection 279(1) or section 279.1, 344 or 346 if a firearm was used in the commission of the offence.

However, an earlier offence shall not be taken into account if 10 years have elapsed between the day on which the person was convicted of the earlier offence and the day on which the person was convicted of the offence for which sentence is being imposed, not taking into account any time in custody.

(4) For the purposes of subsection (3), the only question to be considered is the sequence of convictions and no consideration shall be given to the sequence of commission of offences or whether any offence occurred before or after any conviction. 1980-81-82-83, c. 125, s. 19; 1995, c. 39, s. 146; 2008, c. 6, s. 29; 2009, c. 22, s. 11; 2012, c. 1, s. 27.

MEANING OF "CONSENT" / Consent / Question of law / No consent obtained / Subsection (2) not limiting.

273.1 (1) Subject to subsection (2) and subsection 265(3), "consent" means, for the purposes of sections 271, 272 and 273, the voluntary agreement of the complainant to engage in the sexual activity in question.

(1.1) Consent must be present at the time the sexual activity in question takes place.

(1.2) The question of whether no consent is obtained under subsection 265(3) or subsection (2) or (3) is a question of law.

(2) For the purpose of subsection (1), no consent is obtained if

   (a) the agreement is expressed by the words or conduct of a person other than the complainant;

(a.1) the complainant is unconscious;

   (b) the complainant is incapable of consenting to the activity for any reason other than the one referred to in paragraph (a.1);

   (c) the accused induces the complainant to engage in the activity by abusing a position of trust, power or authority;

   (d) the complainant expresses, by words or conduct, a lack of agreement to engage in the activity; or

   (e) the complainant, having consented to engage in sexual activity, expresses, by words or conduct, a lack of agreement to continue to engage in the activity.

(3) Nothing in subsection (2) shall be construed as limiting the circumstance in which no consent is obtained. 1992, c. 38, s. 1; 2018, c. 29, s. 19(1)-(2.1).

WHERE BELIEF IN CONSENT NOT A DEFENCE.

273.2 It is not a defence to a charge under section 271, 272 or 273 that the accused believed that the complainant consented to the activity that forms the subject-matter of the charge, where

   (a) the accused's belief arose from

      (i) the accused's self-induced intoxication,

      (ii) the accused's recklessness or wilful blindness, or

      (iii) any circumstance referred to in subsection 265(3) or 273.1(2) or (3) in which no consent is obtained;

   (b) the accused did not take reasonable steps, in the circumstances known to the accused at the time, to ascertain that the complainant was consenting.

   (c) there is no evidence that the complainant's voluntary agreement to the activity was affirmatively expressed by words or actively expressed by conduct. 1992, c. 38, s. 1; 2018, c. 29, s. 20.

REMOVAL OF CHILD FROM CANADA / Punishment.

273.3 (1) No person shall do anything for the purpose of removing from Canada a person who is ordinarily resident in Canada and who is

   (a) under the age of 16 years, with the intention that an act be committed outside Canada that if it were committed in Canada would be an offence against section 151 or 152 or subsection 160(3) or 173(2) in respect of that person;

   (b) 16 years of age or more but under the age of eighteen years, with the intention that an act be committed outside Canada that if it were committed in Canada would be an offence against section 153 in respect of that person; or

(c) under the age of eighteen years, with the intention that an act be committed outside Canada that if it were committed in Canada would be an offence against section 155, subsection 160(2) or section 170, 171, 267, 268, 269, 271, 272 or 273 in respect of that person; or

(d) under the age of 18 years, with the intention that an act be committed outside Canada that, if it were committed in Canada, would be an offence against section 293.1 in respect of that person or under the age of 16 years, with the intention that an act be committed outside Canada that, if it were committed in Canada, would be an offence against section 293.2 in respect of that person.

(2) Every person who contravenes this section is guilty of

(a) an indictable offence and is liable to imprisonment for a term not exceeding five years; or

(b) an offence punishable on summary conviction. 1993, c. 45, s. 3; 1997, c. 18, s. 13; 2008, c. 6, s. 54(i); 2015, c. 29, s. 8; 2019, c. 25, s. 98.

CORROBORATION NOT REQUIRED.

274. If an accused is charged with an offence under section 151, 152, 153, 153.1, 155, 160, 170, 171, 172, 173, 271, 272, 273, 286.1, 286.2 or 286.3, no corroboration is required for a conviction and the judge shall not instruct the jury that it is unsafe to find the accused guilty in the absence of corroboration. 1980-81-82-83, c. 125, s. 19; R.S.C. 1985, c. 19 (3rd Supp.), s. 11; 2002, c. 13, s. 12; 2014, c. 25, s. 16; 2019, c. 25, s. 99.

RULES RESPECTING RECENT COMPLAINT ABROGATED.

275. The rules relating to evidence of recent complaint are hereby abrogated with respect to offences under sections 151, 152, 153, 153.1 and 155, subsections 160(2) and (3) and sections 170, 171, 172, 173, 271, 272 and 273. 1980-81-82-83, c. 125, s. 19; R.S.C. 1985, c. 19 (3rd Supp.), s. 11; 2002, c. 13, s. 12; 2019, c. 25, s. 99.

EVIDENCE OF COMPLAINANT'S SEXUAL ACTIVITY / Conditions for admissibility / Factors that judge must consider / Interpretation.

276. (1) In proceedings in respect of an offence under section 151, 152, 153, 153.1 or 155, subsection 160(2) or (3) or section 170, 171, 172, 173, 271, 272 or 273, evidence that the complainant has engaged in sexual activity, whether with the accused or with any other person, is not admissible to support an inference that, by reason of the sexual nature of that activity, the complainant

(a) is more likely to have consented to the sexual activity that forms the subject-matter of the charge; or

(b) is less worthy of belief.

(2) In proceedings in respect of an offence referred to in subsection (1), evidence shall not be adduced by or on behalf of the accused that the complainant has engaged in sexual activity other than the sexual activity that forms the subject-matter of the charge, whether with the accused or with any other person, unless the

judge, provincial court judge or justice determines, in accordance with the procedures set out in sections 278.93 and 278.94, that the evidence

- (a) is not being adduced for the purpose of supporting an inference described in subsection (1);
- (b) is relevant to an issue at trial; and
- (c) is of specific instances of sexual activity; and
- (d) has significant probative value that is not substantially outweighed by the danger of prejudice to the proper administration of justice.

(3) In determining whether evidence is admissible under subsection (2), the judge, provincial court judge or justice shall take into account

- (a) the interests of justice, including the right of the accused to make a full answer and defence;
- (b) society's interest in encouraging the reporting of sexual assault offences;
- (c) whether there is a reasonable prospect that the evidence will assist in arriving at a just determination in the case;
- (d) the need to remove from the fact-finding process any discriminatory belief or bias;
- (e) the risk that the evidence may unduly arouse sentiments of prejudice, sympathy or hostility in the jury;
- (f) the potential prejudice to the complainant's personal dignity and right of privacy;
- (g) the right of the complainant and of every individual to personal security and to the full protection and benefit of the law; and
- (h) any other factor that the judge, provincial court judge or justice considers relevant.

(4) For the purpose of this section, "sexual activity" includes any communication made for a sexual purpose or whose content is of a sexual nature. 1980-81-82-83, c. 125, s. 19; R.S.C. 1985, c. 19 (3rd Supp.), s. 12; c. 27 (1st Supp.), s. 203; 1992, c. 38, s. 2; 2002, c. 13, s. 13; 2018, c. 29, s. 21; 2019, c. 25, s. 100.

276.1 [*Repealed*, 2018, c. 29, s. 22.]

276.2 [*Repealed*, 2018, c. 29, s. 22.]

276.3 [*Repealed*, 2018, c. 29, s. 22.]

276.4 [*Repealed*, 2018, c. 29, s. 22.]

276.5 [*Repealed*, 2018, c. 29, s. 22.]

REPUTATION EVIDENCE.

277. In proceedings in respect of an offence under section 151, 152, 153, 153.1 or 155, subsection 160(2) or (3) or section 170, 171, 172, 173, 271, 272 or 273, evidence of sexual reputation, whether general or specific, is not admissible for the purpose of challenging or supporting the credibility of the complainant. 1980-

81-82-83, c. 125, s. 19; R.S.C. 1985, c. 19 (3rd Supp.), s. 13; 2002, c. 13, s. 14; 2019, c. 25, s. 101.

SPOUSE MAY BE CHARGED.

278. A husband or wife may be charged with an offence under section 271, 272 or 273 in respect of his or her spouse, whether or not the spouses were living together at the time the activity that forms the subject-matter of the charge occurred. 1980-81-82-83, c. 125, s. 19.

Editor's Note: PERSONAL INFORMATION RECORDS

The following ss. 278.1 to 278.91 were enacted in response to the decision of the Supreme Court of Canada in *R. v. O'Connor*, [1995] 4 S.C.R. 411, 103 C.C.C. (3d) 1, 44 C.R. (4th) 1, which mandated the disclosure of therapeutic records in the possession of the Crown and set out a common law procedure for production and disclosure of records in the possession of third parties. *O'Connor* and related cases are noted under s. 650.

These provisions are triggered by an application by the accused charged with any of the sexual offences, enumerated in s. 278.2, for disclosure or production of records as defined in s. 278.1. That section contains a wide definition to include any record that contains personal information for which there is a reasonable expectation of privacy. Certain types of documents are listed and, as well, the definition includes documents protected under provincial or other federal legislation. Hospital records would be an obvious example of such documents. The only exception is a record created by a person responsible for the investigation or prosecution of the offence. Further, the procedure set out in these sections applies even to records in the possession of the Crown, thus expressly overruling a part of the holding in *O'Connor*, unless the complainant or the person to whom the records relate expressly waives the application of these sections. The Crown's disclosure obligation with respect to such records is limited to notifying the accused that they are in the possession of the prosecution, but without disclosing the their contents.

Sections 278.3 to 278.7 envisage a careful multi-staged procedure. Under s. 278.3, the accused first makes a written application for production to the trial judge identifying the record, the person in control of the record and the grounds for seeking production. Section 278.3(3) identifies the two purposes for which a record may be produced, *i.e.*, that it is relevant to an issue at trial or to the competence of a witness. A key provision is subsec. (4), which deems certain assertions that, on their own, are not to be sufficient to provide grounds for production of the record. The application must be served on the prosecutor, the person in control of the record and the complainant or witness to whom the records relate. At the same time, the accused must serve a subpoena in Form 16.1 on the person having control of the record. This form of subpoena notifies the person that the record need not be disclosed to any other party nor brought to court until a judge has made an order for their production. A judge presiding at a preliminary inquiry has no jurisdiction to order production of records under these sections.

The next stage in the process requires the judge to conduct an in camera hearing in accordance with s. 278.4 to determine whether to require production of the records to the judge for review. The person in control of the records and the complainant or witness, as the case may be, have standing to make submissions at this hearing. No order for costs may be made against any such person in respect of their participation in the hearing. The basis upon which the judge may decide to require production of the records is set out in s. 278.5. It would seem clear that the judge is to make this determination without necessarily reviewing the documents, on the basis of submissions. It may be that the parties are entitled to call evidence on this hearing, but the person in control of the records, the complainant or the witness to whom the records relate, are not compellable witnesses. Before ordering that the records be produced, the judge must be satisfied that the application is in accordance with s. 278.3, that the accused has established that the record is likely to be relevant to an issue at trial or to the competence of a witness and that production is necessary in the interests of justice. Section 278.5(2) sets out the test the judge must apply. In general terms, the judge is required to consider the accused's right to make full answer and defence as well as the privacy and equality rights of the person to whom the records relate. The judge is also directed in mandatory terms to consider a number of listed factors that focus not only on the probative value of the evidence and the privacy interests of any person, but broader societal concerns such as the interest in encouraging complainants to obtain treatment. Section 278.8 requires the judge to give reason for the decision.

The third stage in the procedure is set out in s. 278.6. If the judge decides that the record should be produced to the judge, the judge must then decide whether to disclose the record to the accused. This determination will ordinarily be made by the judge in private in the absence of the parties. However, the judge may hold an in camera hearing if it will assist in making the determination. The person to whom the records relate or the person in control of the records is not a compellable witness at this hearing. This may pose a difficulty for the judge if, for example, the need for the hearing is the difficulty in deciphering or understanding the documents. The test for determining whether to order disclosure is set out in s. 278.7(1) and (2) and involves application of the same factors that the judge applied under s. 278.5. Section 278.8 requires the judge to give reason for the decision.

The final stage in the procedure is set out in s. 278.7(3) to (6), which applies where the judge decides that a record or part of a record should be produced to the accused. Subsection (3) permits the judge to impose conditions on the disclosure. For example, the judge may require that the record be edited, that copies of the record not be made and that it be examined only at the court offices. The judge will also order a copy of the record be disclosed to the prosecutor unless the judge determines that it is not in the interests of justice to do so. Production of the record is made subject to the condition that it not be used in any other proceeding. If the judge decides not to order production of the record, a copy is to be kept in a sealed packet pending any appeal proceedings.

A decision whether or not to order production of the record to the judge under s. 278.5 or to the accused under s. 278.7 is deemed to be a question of law for the purposes of appeal by the accused or the Crown under s. 675 or s. 676.

It is a summary conviction offence under s. 278.9 to publish, broadcast or transmit in any way the contents of the application or any of the proceedings at the in camera hearings. Moreover, it is also an offence to publish, broadcast or transmit in any way the judge's reasons unless the judge orders that the determination may be published taking into account the interests of justice and privacy interests. The penalty for this offence is as prescribed in s. 787. The limitation period for instituting proceedings for this offence is six months pursuant to s. 786(2).

DEFINITION OF "RECORD".

278.1 For the purposes of sections 278.2 to 278.92, "record" means any form of record that contains personal information for which there is a reasonable expectation of privacy and includes medical, psychiatric, therapeutic, counselling, education, employment, child welfare, adoption and social services records, personal journals and diaries, and records containing personal information the production or disclosure of which is protected by any other Act of Parliament or a provincial legislature, but does not include records made by persons responsible for the investigation or prosecution of the offence. 1997, c. 30, s. 1; 2018, c. 29, s. 23.

PRODUCTION OF RECORD TO ACCUSED / Application of provisions / Duty of prosecutor to give notice.

278.2 (1) Except in accordance with sections 278.3 to 278.91, no record relating to a complainant or a witness shall be produced to an accused in any proceedings in respect of any of the following offences or in any proceedings in respect of two or more offences at least one of which is any of the following offences:

(a) an offence under section 151, 152, 153, 153.1, 155, 160, 170, 171, 172, 173, 213, 271, 272, 273, 279.01, 279.011, 279.02, 279.03, 286.1, 286.2 or 286.3; or

(b) any offence under this Act, as it read from time to time before the day on which this paragraph comes into force, if the conduct alleged would be an offence referred to in paragraph (a) if it occurred on or after that day.

(c) [*Repealed*, 2014, c. 25, s. 17(3).]

(2) Section 278.1, this section and sections 278.3 to 278.91 apply where a record is in the possession or control of any person, including the prosecutor in the proceedings, unless, in the case of a record in the possession or control of the prosecutor, the complainant or witness to whom the record relates has expressly waived the application of those sections.

(3) In the case of a record in respect of which this section applies that is in the possession or control of the prosecutor, the prosecutor shall notify the accused that the record is in the prosecutor's possession but, in doing so, the prosecutor shall not disclose the record's contents. 1997, c. 30, s. 1; 1998, c. 9, s. 3; 2014, c. 25, ss. 17, 48(5); 2015, c. 13, s. 5(2); 2019, c. 25, s. 102.

APPLICATION FOR PRODUCTION / No application in other proceedings / Form and content of application / Insufficient grounds / Service of application and subpoena / Service on other persons.

278.3 (1) An accused who seeks production of a record referred to in subsection 278.2(1) must make an application to the judge before whom the accused is to be, or is being, tried.

(2) For greater certainty, an application under subsection (1) may not be made to a judge or justice presiding at any other proceedings, including a preliminary inquiry.

(3) An application must be made in writing and set out
- (a) particulars identifying the record that the accused seeks to have produced and the name of the person who has possession or control of the record; and
- (b) the grounds on which the accused relies to establish that the record is likely relevant to an issue at trial or to the competence of a witness to testify.

(4) Any one or more of the following assertions by the accused are not sufficient on their own to establish that the record is likely relevant to an issue at trial or to the competence of a witness to testify:
- (a) that the record exists;
- (b) that the record relates to medical or psychiatric treatment, therapy or counselling that the complainant or witness has received or is receiving;
- (c) that the record relates to the incident that is the subject-matter of the proceedings;
- (d) that the record may disclose a prior inconsistent statement of the complainant or witness;
- (e) that the record may relate to the credibility of the complainant or witness;
- (f) that the record may relate to the reliability of the testimony of the complainant or witness merely because the complainant or witness has received or is receiving psychiatric treatment, therapy or counselling;
- (g) that the record may reveal allegations of sexual abuse of the complainant by a person other than the accused;
- (h) that the record relates to the sexual activity of the complainant with any person, including the accused;
- (i) that the record relates to the presence or absence of a recent complaint;
- (j) that the record relates to the complainant's sexual reputation; or
- (k) that the record was made close in time to a complaint or to the activity that forms the subject-matter of the charge against the accused.

(5) The accused shall serve the application on the prosecutor, on the person who has possession or control of the record, on the complainant or witness, as the case may be, and on any other person to whom, to the knowledge of the accused, the record relates, at least 60 days before the hearing referred to in subsection 278.4(1) or any shorter interval that the judge may allow in the interests of justice. The accused shall also serve a subpoena issued under Part XXII in Form 16.1 on the person who has possession or control of the record at the same time as the application is served.

(6) The judge may at any time order that the application be served on any person to whom the judge considers the record may relate. 1997, c. 30, s. 1; 2015, c. 13, s. 6; 2018, c. 29, s. 24.

HEARING *IN CAMERA* / Persons who may appear at hearing / Right to counsel / Costs.

278.4 (1) The judge shall hold a hearing *in camera* to determine whether to order the person who has possession or control of the record to produce it to the court for review by the judge.

(2) The person who has possession or control of the record, the complainant or witness, as the case may be, and any other person to whom the record relates may appear and make submissions at the hearing, but they are not compellable as witnesses at the hearing.

(2.1) The judge shall, as soon as feasible, inform any person referred to in subsection (2) who participates in the hearing of their right to be represented by counsel.

(3) No order for costs may be made against a person referred to in subsection (2) in respect of their participation in the hearing. 1997, c. 30, s. 1; 2015, c. 13, s. 7.

JUDGE MAY ORDER PRODUCTION OF RECORD FOR REVIEW / Factors to be considered.

278.5 (1) The judge may order the person who has possession or control of the record to produce the record or part of the record to the court for review by the judge if, after the hearing referred to in subsection 278.4(1), the judge is satisfied that

(*a*) the application was made in accordance with subsections 278.3(2) to (6);

(*b*) the accused has established that the record is likely relevant to an issue at trial or to the competence of a witness to testify; and

(*c*) the production of the record is necessary in the interests of justice.

(2) In determining whether to order the production of the record or part of the record for review pursuant to subsection (1), the judge shall consider the salutary and deleterious effects of the determination on the accused's right to make a full answer and defence and on the right to privacy, personal security and equality of the complainant or witness, as the case may be, and of any other person to whom the record relates. In particular, the judge shall take the following factors into account:

(*a*) the extent to which the record is necessary for the accused to make a full answer and defence;

(*b*) the probative value of the record;

(*c*) the nature and extent of the reasonable expectation of privacy with respect to the record;

(*d*) whether production of the record is based on a discriminatory belief or bias;

(*e*) the potential prejudice to the personal dignity and right to privacy of any person to whom the record relates;

   (*f*) society's interest in encouraging the reporting of sexual offences;

   (*g*) society's interest in encouraging the obtaining of treatment by complainants of sexual offences; and

   (*h*) the effect of the determination on the integrity of the trial process. 1997, c. 30, s. 1; 2015, c. 13, s. 8.

REVIEW OF RECORD BY JUDGE / Hearing *in camera* / Provision re hearing.

278.6 (1) Where the judge has ordered the production of the record or part of the record for review, the judge shall review it in the absence of the parties in order to determine whether the record or part of the record should be produced to the accused.

(2) The judge may hold a hearing *in camera* if the judge considers that it will assist in making the determination.

(3) Subsections 278.4(2) to (3) apply in the case of a hearing under subsection (2). 1997, c. 30, s. 1; 2015, c. 13, s. 9.

JUDGE MAY ORDER PRODUCTION OF RECORD TO ACCUSED / Factors to be considered / Conditions on production / Copy to prosecutor / Record not to be used in other proceedings / Retention of record by court.

278.7 (1) Where the judge is satisfied that the record or part of the record is likely relevant to an issue at trial or to the competence of a witness to testify and its production is necessary in the interests of justice, the judge may order that the record or part of the record that is likely relevant be produced to the accused, subject to any conditions that may be imposed pursuant to subsection (3).

(2) In determining whether to order the production of the record or part of the record to the accused, the judge shall consider the salutary and deleterious effects of the determination on the accused's right to make a full answer and defence and on the right to privacy, personal security and equality of the complainant or witness, as the case may be, and of any other person to whom the record relates and, in particular, shall take the factors specified in paragraphs 278.5(2)(*a*) to (*h*) into account.

(3) If the judge orders the production of the record or part of the record to the accused, the judge may impose conditions on the production to protect the interests of justice and, to the greatest extent possible, the privacy, personal security and equality interests of the complainant or witness, as the case may be, and of any other person to whom the record relates, including, for example, the following conditions:

   (*a*) that the record be edited as directed by the judge;

   (*b*) that a copy of the record, rather than the original, be produced;

   (*c*) that the accused and counsel for the accused not disclose the contents of the record to any other person, except with the approval of the court;

   (*d*) that the record be viewed only at the offices of the court;

   (*e*) that no copies of the record be made or that restrictions be imposed on the number of copies of the record that may be made; and

(f) that information regarding any person named in the record, such as their address, telephone number and place of employment, be severed from the record.

(4) Where the judge orders the production of the record or part of the record to the accused, the judge shall direct that a copy of the record or part of the record be provided to the prosecutor, unless the judge determines that it is not in the interests of justice to do so.

(5) The record or part of the record that is produced to the accused pursuant to an order under subsection (1) shall not be used in any other proceedings.

(6) Where the judge refuses to order the production of the record or part of the record to the accused, the record or part of the record shall, unless a court orders otherwise, be kept in a sealed package by the court until the later of the expiration of the time for any appeal and the completion of any appeal in the proceedings against the accused, whereupon the record or part of the record shall be returned to the person lawfully entitled to possession or control of it. 1997, c. 30, s. 1; 2015, c. 13, s. 10.

REASONS FOR DECISION / Record of reasons.

278.8 (1) The judge shall provide reasons for ordering or refusing to order the production of the record or part of the record pursuant to subsection 278.5(1) or 278.7(1).

(2) The reasons referred to in subsection (1) shall be entered in the record of the proceedings or, where the proceedings are not recorded, shall be provided in writing. 1997, c. 30, s. 1.

PUBLICATION PROHIBITED / Offence.

278.9 (1) No person shall publish in any document, or broadcast or transmit in any way, any of the following:
  (a) the contents of an application made under section 278.3;
  (b) any evidence taken, information given or submissions made at a hearing under subsection 278.4(1) or 278.6(2); or
  (c) the determination of the judge pursuant to subsection 278.5(1) or 278.7(1) and the reasons provided pursuant to section 278.8, unless the judge, after taking into account the interests of justice and the right to privacy of the person to whom the record relates, orders that the determination may be published.

(2) Every person who contravenes subsection (1) is guilty of an offence punishable on summary conviction. 1997, c. 30, s. 1; 2005, c. 32, s. 14.

APPEAL.

278.91 For the purposes of sections 675 and 676, a determination to make or refuse to make an order pursuant to subsection 278.5(1) or 278.7(1) is deemed to be a question of law. 1997, c. 30, s. 1.

ADMISSIBILITY — ACCUSED IN POSSESSION OF RECORDS RELATING TO COMPLAINANT / Requirements for admissibility / Factors that judge shall consider.

278.92 (1) Except in accordance with this section, no record relating to a complainant that is in the possession or control of the accused — and which the accused intends to adduce — shall be admitted in evidence in any proceedings in respect of any of the following offences or in any proceedings in respect of two or more offences at least one of which is any of the following offences:

    (*a*) an offence under section 151, 152, 153, 153.1, 155, 160, 170, 171, 172, 173, 210, 211, 213, 271, 272, 273, 279.01, 279.011, 279.02, 279.03, 286.1, 286.2 or 286.3; or

    (*b*) any offence under this Act, as it read from time to time before the day on which this paragraph comes into force, if the conduct alleged would be an offence referred to in paragraph (*a*) if it occurred on or after that day.

(2) The evidence is inadmissible unless the judge, provincial court judge or justice determines, in accordance with the procedures set out in sections 278.93 and 278.94,

    (*a*) if the admissibility of the evidence is subject to section 276, that the evidence meets the conditions set out in subsection 276(2) while taking into account the factors set out in subsection (3); or

    (*b*) in any other case, that the evidence is relevant to an issue at trial and has significant probative value that is not substantially outweighed by the danger of prejudice to the proper administration of justice.

(3) In determining whether evidence is admissible under subsection (2), the judge, provincial court judge or justice shall take into account

    (*a*) the interests of justice, including the right of the accused to make a full answer and defence;

    (*b*) society's interest in encouraging the reporting of sexual assault offences;

    (*c*) society's interest in encouraging the obtaining of treatment by complainants of sexual offences;

    (*d*) whether there is a reasonable prospect that the evidence will assist in arriving at a just determination in the case;

    (*e*) the need to remove from the fact-finding process any discriminatory belief or bias;

    (*f*) the risk that the evidence may unduly arouse sentiments of prejudice, sympathy or hostility in the jury;

    (*g*) the potential prejudice to the complainant's personal dignity and right of privacy;

    (*h*) the right of the complainant and of every individual to personal security and to the full protection and benefit of the law; and

    (*i*) any other factor that the judge, provincial court judge or justice considers relevant. 2018, c. 29, s. 25.

APPLICATION FOR HEARING — SECTIONS 276 AND 278.92 / Form and content of application / Jury and public excluded / Judge may decide to hold hearing.

278.93 (1) Application may be made to the judge, provincial court judge or justice by or on behalf of the accused for a hearing under section 278.94 to determine whether evidence is admissible under subsection 276(2) or 278.92(2).

(2) An application referred to in subsection (1) must be made in writing, setting out detailed particulars of the evidence that the accused seeks to adduce and the relevance of that evidence to an issue at trial, and a copy of the application must be given to the prosecutor and to the clerk of the court.

(3) The judge, provincial court judge or justice shall consider the application with the jury and the public excluded.

(4) If the judge, provincial court judge or justice is satisfied that the application was made in accordance with subsection (2), that a copy of the application was given to the prosecutor and to the clerk of the court at least seven days previously, or any shorter interval that the judge, provincial court judge or justice may allow in the interests of justice and that the evidence sought to be adduced is capable of being admissible under subsection 276(2), the judge, provincial court judge or justice shall grant the application and hold a hearing under section 278.94 to determine whether the evidence is admissible under subsection 276(2) or 278.92(2). 2018, c. 29, s. 25.

HEARING — JURY AND PUBLIC EXCLUDED / Complainant not compellable / Right to counsel / Judge's determination and reasons / Record of reasons.

278.94 (1) The jury and the public shall be excluded from a hearing to determine whether evidence is admissible under subsection 276(2) or 278.92(2).

(2) The complainant is not a compellable witness at the hearing but may appear and make submissions.

(3) The judge shall, as soon as feasible, inform the complainant who participates in the hearing of their right to be represented by counsel.

(4) At the conclusion of the hearing, the judge, provincial court judge or justice shall determine whether the evidence, or any part of it, is admissible under subsection 276(2) or 278.92(2) and shall provide reasons for that determination, and

   (a) if not all of the evidence is to be admitted, the reasons must state the part of the evidence that is to be admitted;

   (b) the reasons must state the factors referred to in subsection 276(3) or 278.92(3) that affected the determination; and

   (c) if all or any part of the evidence is to be admitted, the reasons must state the manner in which that evidence is expected to be relevant to an issue at trial.

(5) The reasons provided under subsection (4) shall be entered in the record of the proceedings or, if the proceedings are not recorded, shall be provided in writing. 2018, c. 29, s. 25.

PUBLICATION PROHIBITED / Offence.

278.95 (1) A person shall not publish in any document, or broadcast or transmit in any way, any of the following:

- (a) the contents of an application made under subsection 278.93;
- (b) any evidence taken, the information given and the representations made at an application under section 278.93 or at a hearing under section 278.94;
- (c) the decision of a judge or justice under subsection 278.93(4), unless the judge or justice, after taking into account the complainant's right of privacy and the interests of justice, orders that the decision may be published, broadcast or transmitted; and
- (d) the determination made and the reasons provided under subsection 278.94(4), unless
  - (i) that determination is that evidence is admissible, or
  - (ii) the judge or justice, after taking into account the complainant's right of privacy and the interests of justice, orders that the determination and reasons may be published, broadcast or transmitted.

(2) Every person who contravenes subsection (1) is guilty of an offence punishable on summary conviction. 2018, c. 29, s. 25.

JUDGE TO INSTRUCT JURY — RE USE OF EVIDENCE.

278.96 If evidence is admitted at trial on the basis of a determination made under subsection 278.94(4), the judge shall instruct the jury as to the uses that the jury may and may not make of that evidence. 2018, c. 29, s. 25.

APPEAL.

278.97 For the purposes of sections 675 and 676, a determination made under subsection 278.94(4) shall be deemed to be a question of law. 2018, c. 29, s. 25.

Kidnapping, Trafficking in Persons, Hostage Taking and Abduction
2005, c. 43, s. 2.

KIDNAPPING / Punishment / Subsequent offences / Factors to consider / Sequence of convictions only / Forcible confinement.

279. (1) Every person commits an offence who kidnaps a person with intent

- (a) to cause the person to be confined or imprisoned against the person's will;
- (b) to cause the person to be unlawfully sent or transported out of Canada against the person's will; or
- (c) to hold the person for ransom or to service against the person's will.

CODE

(1.1) Every person who commits an offence under subsection (1) is guilty of an indictable offence and liable

(a) if a restricted firearm or prohibited firearm is used in the commission of the offence or if any firearm is used in the commission of the offence and the offence is committed for the benefit of, at the direction of, or in association with, a criminal organization, to imprisonment for life and to a minimum punishment of imprisonment for a term of

(i) in the case of a first offence, five years, and

(ii) in the case of a second or subsequent offence, seven years;

(a.1) in any other case where a firearm is used in the commission of the offence, to imprisonment for life and to a minimum punishment of imprisonment for a term of four years;

(a.2) if the person referred to in paragraph (1)(a), (b) or (c) is under 16 years of age, to imprisonment for life and, unless the person who commits the offence is a parent, guardian or person having the lawful care or charge of the person referred to in that paragraph, to a minimum punishment of imprisonment for a term of five years; and

(b) in any other case, to imprisonment for life.

(1.2) In determining, for the purpose of paragraph (1.1)(a), whether a convicted person has committed a second or subsequent offence, if the person was earlier convicted of any of the following offences, that offence is to be considered as an earlier offence:

(a) an offence under subsection (1);

(b) an offence under subsection 85(1) or (2) or section 244 or 244.2; or

(c) an offence under section 220, 236, 239, 272, 273, 279.1, 344 or 346 if a firearm was used in the commission of the offence.

However, an earlier offence shall not be taken into account if 10 years have elapsed between the day on which the person was convicted of the earlier offence and the day on which the person was convicted of the offence for which sentence is being imposed, not taking into account any time in custody.

(1.21) In imposing a sentence under paragraph (1.1)(a.2), the court shall take into account the age and vulnerability of the victim.

(1.3) For the purposes of subsection (1.2), the only question to be considered is the sequence of convictions and no consideration shall be given to the sequence of commission of offences or whether any offence occurred before or after any conviction.

(2) Every one who, without lawful authority, confines, imprisons or forcibly seizes another person is guilty of

(a) an indictable offence and liable to imprisonment for a term not exceeding ten years; or

(b) an offence punishable on summary conviction. R.S., c. C-34, s. 247; R.S.C. 1985, c. 27 (1st Supp.), s. 39; 1995, c. 39, s. 147; 1997, c. 18, s. 14; 2008, c. 6, s. 30; 2009, c. 22, s. 12; 2013, c. 32, s. 1; 2018, c. 29, s. 26; 2019, c. 25, s. 103.

(3) [*Repealed*, 2018, c. 29, s. 26.]

TRAFFICKING IN PERSONS / Consent / Presumption.

279.01 (1) Every person who recruits, transports, transfers, receives, holds, conceals or harbours a person, or exercises control, direction or influence over the movements of a person, for the purpose of exploiting them or facilitating their exploitation is guilty of an indictable offence and liable

  (a) to imprisonment for life and to a minimum punishment of imprisonment for a term of five years if they kidnap, commit an aggravated assault or aggravated sexual assault against, or cause death to, the victim during the commission of the offence; or

  (b) to imprisonment for a term of not more than 14 years and to a minimum punishment of imprisonment for a term of four years in any other case.

(2) No consent to the activity that forms the subject-matter of a charge under subsection (1) is valid.

(3) For the purposes of subsections (1) and 279.011(1), evidence that a person who is not exploited lives with or is habitually in the company of a person who is exploited is, in the absence of evidence to the contrary, proof that the person exercises control, direction or influence over the movements of that person for the purpose of exploiting them or facilitating their exploitation. 2005, c. 43, s. 3; 2014, c. 25, s. 18; 2014, c. 25, s. 18; 2015, c. 16, s. 1.

TRAFFICKING OF A PERSON UNDER THE AGE OF EIGHTEEN YEARS / Consent.

279.011 (1) Every person who recruits, transports, transfers, receives, holds, conceals or harbours a person under the age of eighteen years, or exercises control, direction or influence over the movements of a person under the age of eighteen years, for the purpose of exploiting them or facilitating their exploitation is guilty of an indictable offence and liable

  (a) to imprisonment for life and to a minimum punishment of imprisonment for a term of six years if they kidnap, commit an aggravated assault or aggravated sexual assault against, or cause death to, the victim during the commission of the offence; or

  (b) to imprisonment for a term of not more than fourteen years and to a minimum punishment of imprisonment for a term of five years, in any other case.

(2) No consent to the activity that forms the subject-matter of a charge under subsection (1) is valid. 2010, c. 3, s. 2.

MATERIAL BENEFIT — TRAFFICKING / Material benefit — trafficking of person under 18 years.

279.02 (1) Every person who receives a financial or other material benefit, knowing that it is obtained by or derived directly or indirectly from the commission of an offence under subsection 279.01(1), is guilty of

  (a) an indictable offence and liable to imprisonment for a term of not more than 10 years; or

  (b) an offence punishable on summary conviction.

(2) Everyone who receives a financial or other material benefit, knowing that it is obtained by or derived directly or indirectly from the commission of an offence under subsection 279.011(1), is guilty of an indictable offence and liable to imprisonment for a term of not more than 14 years and to a minimum punishment of imprisonment for a term of two years. 2005, c. 43, s. 3; 2010, c. 3, s. 3; 2014, c. 25, s. 19; 2019, c. 25, s. 104.

CODE

WITHHOLDING OR DESTROYING DOCUMENTS — TRAFFICKING / Withholding or destroying documents — trafficking of person under 18 years.

279.03 (1) Every person who, for the purpose of committing or facilitating an offence under subsection 279.01(1), conceals, removes, withholds or destroys any travel document that belongs to another person or any document that establishes or purports to establish another person's identity or immigration status — whether or not the document is of Canadian origin or is authentic — is guilty of

(a) an indictable offence and liable to imprisonment for a term of not more than five years; or

(b) an offence punishable on summary conviction.

(2) Everyone who, for the purpose of committing or facilitating an offence under subsection 279.011(1), conceals, removes, withholds or destroys any travel document that belongs to another person or any document that establishes or purports to establish another person's identity or immigration status — whether or not the document is of Canadian origin or is authentic — is guilty of an indictable offence and liable to imprisonment for a term of not more than 10 years and to a minimum punishment of imprisonment for a term of one year. 2005, c. 43, s. 3; 2010, c. 3, s. 3; 2014, c. 25, s. 19; 2019, c. 25, s. 105.

EXPLOITATION / Factors / Organ or tissue removal.

279.04 (1) For the purposes of sections 279.01 to 279.03, a person exploits another person if they cause them to provide, or offer to provide, labour or a service by engaging in conduct that, in all the circumstances, could reasonably be expected to cause the other person to believe that their safety or the safety of a person known to them would be threatened if they failed to provide, or offer to provide, the labour or service.

(2) In determining whether an accused exploits another person under subsection (1), the Court may consider, among other factors, whether the accused

(a) used or threatened to use force or another form of coercion;

(b) used deception; or

(c) abused a position of trust, power or authority.

(3) For the purposes of sections 279.01 to 279.03, a person exploits another person if they cause them, by means of deception or the use or threat of force or of any other form of coercion, to have an organ or tissue removed. 2005, c. 43, s. 3; 2012, c. 15, s. 2.

Note: Section 279.05 enacted, to come after s. 279.04, 2015, c. 16, s. 3 (to come into force by order of the Governor in Council):

Sentences to be served consecutively

279.05 A sentence imposed on a person for an offence under sections 279.01 to 279.03 shall be served consecutively to any other punishment imposed on the person for an offence arising out of the same event or series of events and to any other sentence to which the person is subject at the time the sentence is imposed on the person for an offence under any of those sections.

HOSTAGE TAKING / Punishment / Subsequent offences / Sequence of convictions only.

279.1 (1) Everyone takes a person hostage who — with intent to induce any person, other than the hostage, or any group of persons or any state or international or intergovernmental organization to commit or cause to be committed any act or omission as a condition, whether express or implied, of the release of the hostage —

    (a) confines, imprisons, forcibly seizes or detains that person; and

    (b) in any manner utters, conveys or causes any person to receive a threat that the death of, or bodily harm to, the hostage will be caused or that the confinement, imprisonment or detention of the hostage will be continued.

(2) Every person who takes a person hostage is guilty of an indictable offence and liable

    (a) if a restricted firearm or prohibited firearm is used in the commission of the offence or if any firearm is used in the commission of the offence and the offence is committed for the benefit of, at the direction of, or in association with, a criminal organization, to imprisonment for life and to a minimum punishment of imprisonment for a term of

        (i) in the case of a first offence, five years, and

        (ii) in the case of a second or subsequent offence, seven years;

  (a.1) in any other case where a firearm is used in the commission of the offence, to imprisonment for life and to a minimum punishment of imprisonment for a term of four years; and

    (b) in any other case, to imprisonment for life.

(2.1) In determining, for the purpose of paragraph (2)(a), whether a convicted person has committed a second or subsequent offence, if the person was earlier convicted of any of the following offences, that offence is to be considered as an earlier offence:

    (a) an offence under this section;

    (b) an offence under subsection 85(1) or (2) or section 244 or 244.2; or

    (c) an offence under section 220, 236, 239, 272 or 273, subsection 279(1) or section 344 or 346 if a firearm was used in the commission of the offence.

However, an earlier offence shall not be taken into account if 10 years have elapsed between the day on which the person was convicted of the earlier offence and the day on which the person was convicted of the offence for which sentence is being imposed, not taking into account any time in custody.

(2.2) For the purposes of subsection (2.1), the only question to be considered is the sequence of convictions and no consideration shall be given to the sequence of commission of offences or whether any offence occurred before or after any conviction. R.S.C. 1985, c. 27 (1st Supp.), s. 40(1); 1995, c. 39, s. 148; 2008, c. 6, s. 31; 2009, c. 22, s. 13; 2018, c. 29, s. 27.

(3) [*Repealed*, 2018, c. 29, s. 27.]

ABDUCTION OF PERSON UNDER AGE OF 16 / Definition of "guardian".

280. (1) Every person who, without lawful authority, takes or causes to be taken a person under the age of 16 years out of the possession of and against the will of the parent or guardian of that person or of any other person who has the lawful care or charge of that person is guilty of

    (*a*) an indictable offence and liable to imprisonment for a term of not more than five years; or

    (*b*) an offence punishable on summary conviction.

(2) In this section and sections 281 to 283, "guardian" includes any person who has in law or in fact the custody or control of another person. R.S., c. C-34, s. 249; 1980-81-82-83, c. 125, s. 20; 2019, c. 25, s. 106.

ABDUCTION OF PERSON UNDER AGE OF 14.

281. Every person who, not being the parent, guardian or person having the lawful care or charge of a person under the age of 14 years, unlawfully takes, entices away, conceals, detains, receives or harbours that person with intent to deprive a parent or guardian, or any other person who has the lawful care or charge of that person, of the possession of that person is guilty of

    (*a*) an indictable offence and liable to imprisonment for a term of not more than 10 years; or

    (*b*) an offence punishable on summary conviction. R.S., c. C-34, s. 250; 1980-81-82-83, c. 125, s. 20; 2019, c. 25, s. 107.

ABDUCTION IN CONTRAVENTION OF CUSTODY OR PARENTING ORDER / If no belief in validity of custody order or parenting order.

282. (1) Every one who, being the parent, guardian or person having the lawful care or charge of a child under the age of 14 years, takes, entices away, conceals, detains, receives or harbours that child, in contravention of a custody order or a parenting order made by a court anywhere in Canada, with intent to deprive a parent or guardian, or any other person who has the lawful care or charge of that child, of the possession of that child is guilty of

    (*a*) an indictable offence and is liable to imprisonment for a term not exceeding ten years; or

    (*b*) an offence punishable on summary conviction.

(2) If a count charges an offence under subsection (1) and the offence is not proven only because the accused did not believe that there was a valid custody order or parenting order but the evidence does prove an offence under section 283,

the accused may be convicted of an offence under that section. 1980-81-82-83, c. 125, s. 20; 1993, c. 45, s. 4; 2019, c. 16, s. 123.

ABDUCTION / Consent required.

283. (1) Everyone who, being the parent, guardian or person having the lawful care or charge of a child under the age of 14 years, takes, entices away, conceals, detains, receives or harbours that child, whether or not there is an order referred to in subsection 282(1) in respect of the child , with intent to deprive a parent, guardian or any other person who has the lawful care or charge of that child, of the possession of that child, is guilty of

- (*a*) an indictable offence and is liable to imprisonment for a term not exceeding ten years; or
- (*b*) an offence punishable on summary conviction.

(2) No proceedings may be commenced under subsection (1) without the consent of the Attorney General or counsel instructed by him for that purpose. 1980-81-82-83, c. 125, s. 20; 1993, c. 45, s. 5; 2019, c. 25, 124.

DEFENCE.

284. No one shall be found guilty of an offence under sections 281 to 283 if he establishes that the taking, enticing away, concealing, detaining, receiving or harbouring of any young person was done with the consent of the parent, guardian or other person having the lawful possession, care or charge of that young person. 1980-81-82-83, c. 125, s. 20.

DEFENCE.

285. No one shall be found guilty of an offence under sections 280 to 283 if the court is satisfied that the taking, enticing away, concealing, detaining, receiving or harbouring of any young person was necessary to protect the young person from danger of imminent harm or if the person charged with the offence was escaping from danger of imminent harm. 1980-81-82-83, c. 125, s. 20; 1993, c. 45, s. 6.

NO DEFENCE.

286. In proceedings in respect of an offence under sections 280 to 283, it is not a defence to any charge that a young person consented to or suggested any conduct of the accused. 1980-81-82-83, c. 125, s. 20.

Commodification of Sexual Activity   2014, c. 25, s. 20.

OBTAINING SEXUAL SERVICES FOR CONSIDERATION / Obtaining sexual services for consideration from person under 18 years / Subsequent offences / Sequence of convictions only / Definitions of "place" and "public place"

286.1 (1) Everyone who, in any place, obtains for consideration, or communicates with anyone for the purpose of obtaining for consideration, the sexual services of a person is guilty of

   (a) an indictable offence and liable to imprisonment for a term of not more than five years and a minimum punishment of,

      (i) in the case where the offence is committed in a public place, or in any place open to public view, that is or is next to a park or the grounds of a school or religious institution or that is or is next to any other place where persons under the age of 18 can reasonably be expected to be present,

        (A) for a first offence, a fine of $2,000, and

        (B) for each subsequent offence, a fine of $4,000, or

      (ii) in any other case,

        (A) for a first offence, a fine of $1,000, and

        (B) for each subsequent offence, a fine of $2,000; or

   (b) an offence punishable on summary conviction and liable to a fine of not more than $5,000 or to imprisonment for a term of not more than two years less a day, or to both, and to a minimum punishment of,

      (i) in the case referred to in subparagraph (a)(i),

        (A) for a first offence, a fine of $1,000, and

        (B) for each subsequent offence, a fine of $2,000, or

      (ii) in any other case,

        (A) for a first offence, a fine of $500, and

        (B) for each subsequent offence, a fine of $1,000.

(2) Everyone who, in any place, obtains for consideration, or communicates with anyone for the purpose of obtaining for consideration, the sexual services of a person under the age of 18 years is guilty of an indictable offence and liable to imprisonment for a term of not more than 10 years and to a minimum punishment of imprisonment for a term of

   (a) for a first offence, six months; and

   (b) for each subsequent offence, one year.

(3) In determining, for the purpose of subsection (2), whether a convicted person has committed a subsequent offence, if the person was earlier convicted of any of the following offences, that offence is to be considered as an earlier offence:

   (a) an offence under that subsection; or

   (b) an offence under subsection 212(4) of this Act, as it read from time to time before the day on which this subsection comes into force.

(4) In determining, for the purposes of this section, whether a convicted person has committed a subsequent offence, the only question to be considered is the sequence of convictions and no consideration shall be given to the sequence of

commission of offences, whether any offence occurred before or after any conviction or whether offences were prosecuted by indictment or by way of summary conviction proceedings.

(5) For the purposes of this section, "place" and "public place" have the same meaning as in subsection 197(1). 2014, c. 25, s. 20; 2019, c. 25, s. 108.

MATERIAL BENEFIT FROM SEXUAL SERVICES / Material benefit from sexual services provided by person under 18 years / Presumption / Exception / No exception / Aggravating factor

286.2 (1) Every person who receives a financial or other material benefit, knowing that it is obtained by or derived directly or indirectly from the commission of an offence under subsection 286.1(1), is guilty of

(*a*) an indictable offence and liable to imprisonment for a term of not more than 10 years; or

(*b*) an offence punishable on summary conviction.

(2) Everyone who receives a financial or other material benefit, knowing that it is obtained by or derived directly or indirectly from the commission of an offence under subsection 286.1(2), is guilty of an indictable offence and liable to imprisonment for a term of not more than 14 years and to a minimum punishment of imprisonment for a term of two years.

(3) For the purposes of subsections (1) and (2), evidence that a person lives with or is habitually in the company of a person who offers or provides sexual services for consideration is, in the absence of evidence to the contrary, proof that the person received a financial or other material benefit from those services.

(4) Subject to subsection (5), subsections (1) and (2) do not apply to a person who receives the benefit

(*a*) in the context of a legitimate living arrangement with the person from whose sexual services the benefit is derived;

(*b*) as a result of a legal or moral obligation of the person from whose sexual services the benefit is derived;

(*c*) in consideration for a service or good that they offer, on the same terms and conditions, to the general public; or

(*d*) in consideration for a service or good that they do not offer to the general public but that they offered or provided to the person from whose sexual services the benefit is derived, if they did not counsel or encourage that person to provide sexual services and the benefit is proportionate to the value of the service or good.

(5) Subsection (4) does not apply to a person who commits an offence under subsection (1) or (2) if that person

(*a*) used, threatened to use or attempted to use violence, intimidation or coercion in relation to the person from whose sexual services the benefit is derived;

(*b*) abused a position of trust, power or authority in relation to the person from whose sexual services the benefit is derived;

    (*c*) provided a drug, alcohol or any other intoxicating substance to the person from whose sexual services the benefit is derived for the purpose of aiding or abetting that person to offer or provide sexual services for consideration;

    (*d*) engaged in conduct, in relation to any person, that would constitute an offence under section 286.3; or

    (*e*) received the benefit in the context of a commercial enterprise that offers sexual services for consideration.

(6) If a person is convicted of an offence under this section, the court that imposes the sentence shall consider as an aggravating factor the fact that that person received the benefit in the context of a commercial enterprise that offers sexual services for consideration. 2014, c. 25, s. 20; 2019, c. 25, s. 109.

CODE

PROCURING / Procuring — person under 18 years

286.3 (1) Everyone who procures a person to offer or provide sexual services for consideration or, for the purpose of facilitating an offence under subsection 286.1(1), recruits, holds, conceals or harbours a person who offers or provides sexual services for consideration, or exercises control, direction or influence over the movements of that person, is guilty of an indictable offence and liable to imprisonment for a term of not more than 14 years.

(2) Everyone who procures a person under the age of 18 years to offer or provide sexual services for consideration or, for the purpose of facilitating an offence under subsection 286.1(2), recruits, holds, conceals or harbours a person under the age of 18 who offers or provides sexual services for consideration, or exercises control, direction or influence over the movements of that person, is guilty of an indictable offence and liable to imprisonment for a term of not more than 14 years and to a minimum punishment of imprisonment for a term of five years. 2014, c. 25, s. 20.

ADVERTISING SEXUAL SERVICES.

286.4 Everyone who knowingly advertises an offer to provide sexual services for consideration is guilty of

    (*a*) an indictable offence and liable to imprisonment for a term of not more than five years; or

    (*b*) an offence punishable on summary conviction. 2014, c. 25, s. 20; 2019, c. 25, s. 110.

IMMUNITY — MATERIAL BENEFIT AND ADVERTISING / Immunity — aiding, abetting, etc.

286.5 (1) No person shall be prosecuted for

    (*a*) an offence under section 286.2 if the benefit is derived from the provision of their own sexual services; or

    (*b*) an offence under section 286.4 in relation to the advertisement of their own sexual services.

(2) No person shall be prosecuted for aiding, abetting, conspiring or attempting to commit an offence under any of sections 286.1 to 286.4 or being an accessory after the fact or counselling a person to be a party to such an offence, if the offence relates to the offering or provision of their own sexual services. 2014, c. 25, s. 20.

Abortion

287. [*Repealed*, 2019, c. 25, s. 111.]

288. [*Repealed*, 2018, c. 29, s. 28.]

Venereal Diseases

289. [*Repealed*, R.S.C. 1985, c. 27 (1st Supp.), s. 41.]

Offences Against Conjugal Rights

BIGAMY / Matters of defence / Incompetency no defence / Validity presumed / Act or omission by accused.

290. (1) Every one commits bigamy who

- (*a*) in Canada,
  - (i) being married, goes through a form of marriage with another person,
  - (ii) knowing that another person is married, goes through a form of marriage with that person, or
  - (iii) on the same day or simultaneously, goes through a form of marriage with more than one person; or
- (*b*) being a Canadian citizen resident in Canada leaves Canada with intent to do anything mentioned in subparagraphs (*a*)(i) to (iii) and, pursuant thereto, does
  outside Canada anything mentioned in those subparagraphs in circumstances mentioned therein.

(2) No person commits bigamy by going through a form of marriage if

- (*a*) that person in good faith and on reasonable grounds believes that his spouse is dead,
- (*b*) the spouse of that person has been continuously absent from him for seven years immediately preceding the time when he goes through the form of marriage, unless he knew that his spouse was alive at any time during those seven years,
- (*c*) that person has been divorced from the bond of the first marriage, or
- (*d*) the former marriage has been declared void by a court of competent jurisdiction.

(3) Where a person is alleged to have committed bigamy, it is not a defence that the parties would, if unmarried, have been incompetent to contract marriage under the law of the place where the offence is alleged to have been committed.

(4) Every marriage or form of marriage shall, for the purpose of this section, be deemed to be valid unless the accused establishes that it was invalid.

(5) No act or omission on the part of an accused who is charged with bigamy invalidates a marriage or form of marriage that is otherwise valid. R.S., c. C-34, s. 254.

PUNISHMENT / Certificate of marriage.

291. (1) Every person who commits bigamy is guilty of
- (a) an indictable offence and liable to imprisonment for a term of not more than five years; or
- (b) an offence punishable on summary conviction.

(2) For the purposes of this section a certificate of marriage issued under the authority of law is evidence of the marriage or form of marriage to which it relates without proof of the signature or official character of the person by whom it purports to be signed. R.S., c. C-34, s. 255; 2019, c. 25, s. 112.

PROCURING FEIGNED MARRIAGE / Corroboration.

292. (1) Every person who procures or knowingly aids in procuring a feigned marriage between themselves and another person is guilty of
- (a) an indictable offence and liable to imprisonment for a term of not more than five years; or
- (b) an offence punishable on summary conviction.

(2) No person shall be convicted of an offence under this section on the evidence of only one witness unless the evidence of that witness is corroborated in a material particular by evidence that implicates the accused. R.S., c. C-34, s. 256; 1980-81-82-83, c. 125, s. 21; 2019, c. 25, s. 113.

POLYGAMY / Evidence in case of polygamy.

293. (1) Every person is guilty of an indictable offence and liable to imprisonment for a term of not more than five years or is guilty of an offence punishable on summary conviction who
- (a) practises or enters into or in any manner agrees or consents to practise or enter into any form of polygamy or any kind of conjugal union with more than one person at the same time, whether or not it is by law recognized as a binding form of marriage; or
- (b) celebrates, assists or is a party to a rite, ceremony, contract or consent that purports to sanction a relationship mentioned in paragraph (a).

(2) Where an accused is charged with an offence under this section, no averment or proof of the method by which the alleged relationship was entered into, agreed to or consented to is necessary in the indictment or upon the trial of the accused, nor is it necessary on the trial to prove that the persons who are alleged to have entered into the relationship had or intended to have sexual intercourse. R.S., c. C-34, s. 257; 2019, c. 25, s. 114.

FORCED MARRIAGE.

293.1 Every person who celebrates, aids or participates in a marriage rite or ceremony knowing that one of the persons being married is marrying against their will is guilty of

(a) an indictable offence and liable to imprisonment for a term of not more than five years; or

(b) an offence punishable on summary conviction. 2015, c. 29, s. 9; 2019, c. 25, s. 115.

MARRIAGE UNDER AGE OF 16 YEARS.

293.2 Every person who celebrates, aids or participates in a marriage rite or ceremony knowing that one of the persons being married is under the age of 16 years is guilty of

(a) an indictable offence and liable to imprisonment for a term of not more than five years; or

(b) an offence punishable on summary conviction. 2015, c. 29, s. 9; 2019, c. 25, s. 115.

Unlawful Solemnization of Marriage

PRETENDING TO SOLEMNIZE MARRIAGE.

294. Every person is guilty of an indictable offence and liable to imprisonment for a term of not more than two years or is guilty of an offence punishable on summary conviction who

(a) solemnizes or pretends to solemnize a marriage without lawful authority; or

(b) procures a person to solemnize a marriage knowing that he is not lawfully authorized to solemnize the marriage. R.S., c. C-34, s. 258; 2018, c. 29, s. 29; 2019, c. 25, s. 116(1).

MARRIAGE CONTRARY TO LAW.

295. Every person who, being lawfully authorized to solemnize marriage, knowingly solemnizes a marriage in contravention of federal law or the laws of the province in which the marriage is solemnized is guilty of

(a) an indictable offence and liable to imprisonment for a term of not more than two years; or

(b) an offence punishable on summary conviction. R.S., c. C-34, s. 259; 2015, c. 29, s. 10; 2019, c. 25, s. 117.

[*Heading repealed*, 2018, c. 29, s. 30.]

296. [*Repealed*, 2018, c. 29, s. 30.]

Defamatory Libel

DEFINITION OF "NEWSPAPER".

297. In sections 303, 304 and 308, "newspaper" means any paper, magazine or periodical containing public news, intelligence or reports of events, or any remarks or observations thereon, printed for sale and published periodically or in parts or numbers, at intervals not exceeding thirty-one days between the publication of any two such papers, parts or numbers, and any paper, magazine or periodical printed in order to be dispersed and made public, weekly or more often, or at intervals not exceeding thirty-one days, that contains advertisements, exclusively or principally. R.S., c. C-34, s. 261.

DEFINITION / Mode of expression.

298. (1) A defamatory libel is matter published, without lawful justification or excuse, that is likely to injure the reputation of any person by exposing him to hatred, contempt or ridicule, or that is designed to insult the person of or concerning whom it is published.

(2) A defamatory libel may be expressed directly or by insinuation or irony
  (*a*) in words legibly marked on any substance; or
  (*b*) by any object signifying a defamatory libel otherwise than by words. R.S., c. C-34, s. 262.

PUBLISHING.

299. A person publishes a libel when he
  (*a*) exhibits it in public;
  (*b*) causes it to be read or seen; or
  (*c*) shows or delivers it, or causes it to be shown or delivered, with intent that it should be read or seen by any person other than the person whom it defames. R.S., c. C-34, s. 263; 2018, c. 29, s. 31.

PUNISHMENT OF LIBEL KNOWN TO BE FALSE.

300. Every person who publishes a defamatory libel that they know is false is guilty of
  (*a*) an indictable offence and liable to imprisonment for a term of not more than five years; or
  (*b*) an offence punishable on summary conviction. R.S., c. C-34, s. 264; 2019, c. 25, s. 118.

PUNISHMENT FOR DEFAMATORY LIBEL.

301. Every person who publishes a defamatory libel is guilty of
  (*a*) an indictable offence and liable to imprisonment for a term of not more than two years; or

(b) an offence punishable on summary conviction. R.S., c. C-34, s. 265; 2019, c. 25, s. 118.

EXTORTION BY LIBEL / Idem / Punishment.

302. (1) Every one commits an offence who, with intent

(a) to extort money from any person, or

(b) to induce a person to confer on or procure for another person an appointment or office of profit or trust,

publishes or threatens to publish or offers to abstain from publishing or to prevent the publication of a defamatory libel.

(2) Every one commits an offence who, as the result of the refusal of any person to permit money to be extorted or to confer or procure an appointment or office of profit or trust, publishes or threatens to publish a defamatory libel.

(3) Every person who commits an offence under this section is guilty of

(a) an indictable offence and liable to imprisonment for a term of not more than five years; or

(b) an offence punishable on summary conviction. R.S., c. C-34, s. 266; 2019, c. 25, s. 119.

PROPRIETOR OF NEWSPAPER PRESUMED RESPONSIBLE / General authority to manager when negligence / Selling newspapers.

303. (1) The proprietor of a newspaper shall be deemed to publish defamatory matter that is inserted and published therein, unless he proves that the defamatory matter was inserted in the newspaper without his knowledge and without negligence on his part.

(2) Where the proprietor of a newspaper gives to a person general authority to manage or conduct the newspaper as editor or otherwise, the insertion by that person of defamatory matter in the newspaper shall, for the purposes of subsection (1), be deemed not to be negligence on the part of the proprietor unless it is proved that

(a) he intended the general authority to include authority to insert defamatory matter in the newspaper; or

(b) he continued to confer general authority after he knew that it had been exercised by the insertion of defamatory matter in the newspaper.

(3) No person shall be deemed to publish a defamatory libel by reason only that he sells a number or part of a newspaper that contains a defamatory libel, unless he knows that the number or part contains defamatory matter or that defamatory matter is habitually contained in the newspaper. R.S., c. C-34, s. 267.

SELLING BOOK CONTAINING DEFAMATORY LIBEL / Sale by servant.

304. (1) No person shall be deemed to publish a defamatory libel by reason only that he sells a book, magazine, pamphlet or other thing, other than a newspaper that contains a defamatory matter if, at the time of the sale, he does not know that it contains the defamatory matter.

(2) Where a servant, in the course of his employment, sells a book, magazine, pamphlet or other thing, other than a newspaper, the employer shall be deemed not to publish any defamatory matter contained therein unless it is proved that the employer authorized the sale knowing that

    (*a*) defamatory matter was contained therein; or

    (*b*) defamatory matter was habitually contained therein, in the case of a periodical. R.S., c. C-34, s. 268.

PUBLISHING PROCEEDINGS OF COURTS OF JUSTICE.

305. No person shall be deemed to publish a defamatory libel by reason only that he publishes defamatory matter

    (*a*) in a proceeding held before or under the authority of a court exercising judicial authority; or

    (*b*) in an inquiry made under the authority of an Act or by order of Her Majesty, or under the authority of a public department or a department of the government of a province. R.S., c. C-34, s. 269.

PARLIAMENTARY PAPERS.

306. No person shall be deemed to publish a defamatory libel by reason only that he

    (*a*) publishes to the Senate or House of Commons or to a legislature of a province, defamatory matter contained in a petition to the Senate or House of Commons or to the legislature of a province, as the case may be;

    (*b*) publishes by order or under the authority of the Senate or House of Commons or of a legislature of a province, a paper containing defamatory matter; or

    (*c*) publishes, in good faith and without ill-will to the person defamed, an extract from or abstract of a petition or paper mentioned in paragraph (*a*) or (*b*). R.S., c. C-34, s. 270.

FAIR REPORTS OF PARLIAMENTARY OR JUDICIAL PROCEEDINGS / Divorce proceedings an exception.

307. (1) No person shall be deemed to publish a defamatory libel by reason only that he publishes in good faith, for the information of the public, a fair report of the proceedings of the Senate or House of Commons or the legislature of a province, or a committee thereof, or of the public proceedings before a court exercising judicial authority, or publishes, in good faith, any fair comment on any such proceedings.

(2) This section does not apply to a person who publishes a report of evidence taken or offered in any proceeding before the Senate or House of Commons or any committee thereof, on a petition or bill relating to any matter of marriage or divorce, if the report is published without authority from or leave of the House in which the proceeding is held or is contrary to any rule, order or practice of that House. R.S., c. C-34, s. 271.

FAIR REPORT OF PUBLIC MEETING.

308. No person shall be deemed to publish a defamatory libel by reason only that he publishes in good faith, in a newspaper, a fair report of the proceedings of any public meeting if

    (*a*) the meeting is lawfully convened for a lawful purpose and is open to the public;

    (*b*) the report is fair and accurate;

    (*c*) the publication of the matter complained of is for the public benefit; and

    (*d*) he does not refuse to publish in a conspicuous place in the newspaper a reasonable explanation or contradiction by the person defamed in respect of the defamatory matter. R.S., c. C-34, s. 272.

PUBLIC BENEFIT.

309. No person shall be deemed to publish a defamatory libel by reason only that he publishes defamatory matter that, on reasonable grounds, he believes is true, and that is relevant to any subject of public interest, the public discussion of which is for the public benefit. R.S., c. C-34, s. 273.

FAIR COMMENT ON PUBLIC PERSON OR WORK OF ART.

310. No person shall be deemed to publish a defamatory libel by reason only that he publishes fair comments

    (*a*) on the public conduct of a person who takes part in public affairs; or

    (*b*) on a published book or other literary production, or on any composition or work of art or performance publicly exhibited, or on any other communication made to the public on any subject, if the comments are confined to criticism thereof. R.S., c. C-34, s. 274.

WHEN TRUTH A DEFENCE.

311. No person shall be deemed to publish a defamatory libel where he proves that the publication of the defamatory matter in the manner in which it was published was for the public benefit at the time when it was published and that the matter itself was true. R.S., c. C-34, s. 275.

PUBLICATION INVITED OR NECESSARY.

312. No person shall be deemed to publish a defamatory libel by reason only that he publishes defamatory matter

    (*a*) on the invitation or challenge of the person in respect of whom it is published, or

    (*b*) that it is necessary to publish in order to refute defamatory matter published in respect of him by another person,

if he believes that the defamatory matter is true and it is relevant to the invitation, challenge or necessary refutation, as the case may be, and does not in any respect exceed what is reasonably sufficient in the circumstances. R.S., c. C-34, s. 276.

ANSWERS TO INQUIRIES.

313. No person shall be deemed to publish a defamatory libel by reason only that he publishes, in answer to inquiries made to him, defamatory matter relating to a subject-matter in respect of which the person by whom or on whose behalf the inquiries are made has an interest in knowing the truth or who, on reasonable grounds, the person who publishes the defamatory matter believes has such an interest, if

(a) the matter is published, in good faith, for the purpose of giving information in answer to the inquiries;

(b) the person who publishes the defamatory matter believes that it is true;

(c) the defamatory matter is relevant to the inquiries; and

(d) the defamatory matter does not in any respect exceed what is reasonably sufficient in the circumstances. R.S., c. C-34, s. 277.

GIVING INFORMATION TO PERSON INTERESTED.

314. No person shall be deemed to publish a defamatory libel by reason only that he publishes to another person defamatory matter for the purpose of giving information to that person with respect to a subject-matter in which the person to whom the information is given has, or is believed on reasonable grounds by the person who gives it to have, an interest in knowing the truth with respect to that subject-matter if

(a) the conduct of the person who gives the information is reasonable in the circumstances;

(b) the defamatory matter is relevant to the subject-matter; and

(c) the defamatory matter is true, or if it is not true, is made without ill-will toward the person who is defamed and is made in the belief, on reasonable grounds, that it is true. R.S., c. C-34, s. 278.

PUBLICATION IN GOOD FAITH FOR REDRESS OF WRONG.

315. No person shall be deemed to publish a defamatory libel by reason only that he publishes defamatory matter in good faith for the purpose of seeking remedy or redress for a private or public wrong or grievance from a person who has, or who on reasonable grounds he believes has, the right or is under an obligation to remedy or redress the wrong or grievance, if

(a) he believes that the defamatory matter is true;

(b) the defamatory matter is relevant to the remedy or redress that is sought; and

(c) the defamatory matter does not in any respect exceed what is reasonably sufficient in the circumstances. R.S., c. C-34, s. 279.

PROVING PUBLICATION BY ORDER OF LEGISLATURE / Directing verdict / Certificate of order.

316. (1) An accused who is alleged to have published a defamatory libel may, at any stage of the proceedings, adduce evidence to prove that the matter that is alleged to be defamatory was contained in a paper published by order or under the authority of the Senate or House of Commons or a legislature of a province.

(2) Where at any stage in proceedings referred to in subsection (1) the court, judge, justice or provincial court judge is satisfied that the matter alleged to be defamatory was contained in a paper published by order or under the authority of the Senate or House of Commons or a legislature of a province, he shall direct a verdict of not guilty to be entered and shall discharge the accused.

(3) For the purposes of this section, a certificate under the hand of the Speaker or clerk of the Senate or House of Commons or a legislature of a province to the effect that the matter that is alleged to be defamatory was contained in a paper published by order or under the authority of the Senate, House of Commons or legislature of a province, as the case may be, is conclusive evidence thereof. R.S., c. C-34, s. 280.

Verdicts

VERDICTS IN CASES OF DEFAMATORY LIBEL.

317. Where, on the trial of an indictment for publishing a defamatory libel, a plea of not guilty is pleaded, the jury that is sworn to try the issue may give a general verdict of guilty or not guilty on the whole matter put in issue on the indictment, and shall not be required or directed by the judge to find the defendant guilty merely on proof of publication by the defendant of the alleged defamatory libel, and of the sense ascribed thereto in the indictment, but the judge may, in his discretion, give a direction or opinion to the jury on the matter in issue as in other criminal proceedings, and the jury may, on the issue, find a special verdict. R.S., c. C-34, s. 281.

Hate Propaganda

ADVOCATING GENOCIDE / Definition of "genocide" / Consent / Definition of "identifiable group".

318. (1) Every person who advocates or promotes genocide is guilty of an indictable offence and liable to imprisonment for a term of not more than five years.

(2) In this section, "genocide" means any of the following acts committed with intent to destroy in whole or in part any identifiable group, namely,

    (*a*) killing members of the group; or

    (*b*) deliberately inflicting on the group conditions of life calculated to bring about its physical destruction.

(3) No proceeding for an offence under this section shall be instituted without the consent of the Attorney General.

(4) In this section, "identifiable group" means any section of the public distinguished by colour, race, religion, national or ethnic origin, age, sex, sexual orientation, gender identity or expression, or mental or physical disability. R.S., c.

11 (1st Supp.), s. 1; 2004, c. 14, s. 1; 2014, c. 31, s. 12; 2017, c. 13, s. 3; 2019, c. 25, s. 120.

PUBLIC INCITEMENT OF HATRED / Wilful promotion of hatred / Defences / Forfeiture / Exemption from seizure of communication facilities / Consent / Definitions / "communicating" / "identifiable group" / "public place" / "statements".

319. (1) Every one who, by communicating statements in any public place, incites hatred against any identifiable group where such incitement is likely to lead to a breach of the peace is guilty of

    (*a*) an indictable offence and is liable to imprisonment for a term not exceeding two years; or

    (*b*) an offence punishable on summary conviction.

(2) Every one who, by communicating statements, other than in private conversation, wilfully promotes hatred against any identifiable group is guilty of

    (*a*) an indictable offence and is liable to imprisonment for a term not exceeding two years; or

    (*b*) an offence punishable on summary conviction.

(3) No person shall be convicted of an offence under subsection (2)

    (*a*) if he establishes that the statements communicated were true;

    (*b*) if, in good faith, the person expressed or attempted to establish by an argument an opinion on a religious subject or an opinion based on a belief in a religious text;

    (*c*) if the statements were relevant to any subject of public interest, the discussion of which was for the public benefit, and if on reasonable grounds he believed them to be true; or

    (*d*) if, in good faith, he intended to point out, for the purpose of removal, matters producing or tending to produce feelings of hatred toward an identifiable group in Canada.

(4) Where a person is convicted of an offence under section 318 or subsection (1) or (2) of this section, anything by means of or in relation to which the offence was committed, on such conviction, may, in addition to any other punishment imposed, be ordered by the presiding provincial court judge or judge to be forfeited to Her Majesty in right of the province in which that person is convicted, for disposal as the Attorney General may direct.

(5) Subsections 199(6) and (7) apply with such modifications as the circumstances require to section 318 or subsection (1) or (2) of this section.

(6) No proceeding for an offence under subsection (2) shall be instituted without the consent of the Attorney General.

(7) In this section,

"communicating" includes communicating by telephone, broadcasting or other audible or visible means;

"identifiable group" has the same meaning as in section 318;

"public place" includes any place to which the public have access as of right or by invitation, express or implied;

"statements" includes words spoken or written or recorded electronically or electro-magnetically or otherwise, and gestures, signs or other visible representations. R.S., c. 11 (1st Supp.), s. 1; 2004, c. 14, s. 2.

WARRANT OF SEIZURE / Summons to occupier / Owner and author may appear / Order of forfeiture / Disposal of matter / Appeal / Consent / Definitions / "court" / "genocide" / "hate propaganda" / "judge".

320. (1) A judge who is satisfied by information on oath that there are reasonable grounds for believing that any publication, copies of which are kept for sale or distribution in premises within the jurisdiction of the court, is hate propaganda, shall issue a warrant under his hand authorizing seizure of the copies.

(2) Within seven days of the issue of the warrant under subsection (1), the judge shall issue a summons to the occupier of the premises requiring him to appear before the court and show cause why the matter seized should not be forfeited to Her Majesty.

(3) The owner and the author of the matter seized under subsection (1) and alleged to be hate propaganda may appear and be represented in the proceedings in order to oppose the making of an order for the forfeiture of the matter.

(4) If the court is satisfied that the publication referred to in subsection (1) is hate propaganda, it shall make an order declaring the matter forfeited to Her Majesty in right of the province in which the proceedings take place, for disposal as the Attorney General may direct.

(5) If the court is not satisfied that the publication referred to in subsection (1) is hate propaganda, it shall order that the matter be restored to the person from whom it was seized forthwith after the time for final appeal has expired.

(6) An appeal lies from an order made under subsection (4) or (5) by any person who appeared in the proceedings

    (a) on any ground of appeal that involves a question of law alone,

    (b) on any ground of appeal that involves a question of fact alone, or

    (c) on any ground of appeal that involves a question of mixed law and fact,

as if it were an appeal against conviction or against a judgment or verdict of acquittal, as the case may be, on a question of law alone under Part XXI, and sections 673 to 696 apply with such modifications as the circumstances require.

(7) No proceeding under this section shall be instituted without the consent of the Attorney General.

(8) In this section,

"court" means

    (a) in the Province of Quebec, the Court of Quebec,

  (a.1) in the Province of Ontario, the Superior Court of Justice,

    (b) in the Provinces of New Brunswick, Manitoba, Saskatchewan and Alberta, the Court of Queen's Bench,

(c) in the Province of Newfoundland and Labrador, the Supreme Court, Trial Division,

(c.1) [*Repealed*. 1992, c. 51, s. 36.]

(d) in the Provinces of Nova Scotia, British Columbia and Prince Edward Island, in Yukon and in the Northwest Territories, the Supreme Court, and

(e) in Nunavut, the Nunavut Court of Justice;

"genocide" has the same meaning as in section 318;

"hate propaganda" means any writing, sign or visible representation that advocates or promotes genocide or the communication of which by any person would constitute an offence under section 319;

"judge" means a judge of a court. R.S., c. 11 (1st Supp.), s. 1; 1974-75, c. 48, s. 25; 1978-79, c. 11, s. 10; R.S.C. 1985, c. 27 (2nd Supp.), s. 10; c. 40 (4th Supp.), s. 2; 1990, c. 16, s. 4; 1990, c. 17, s. 11; 1992, c. 1, s. 58; 1993, c. 28, Sch. III, s. 31 (repealed 1999, c. 3, s. 12); 1998, c. 30, s. 14(d); 1999, c. 3, ss. 12, 29; 2002, c. 7, s. 142; 2015, c. 3, s. 49.

WARRANT OF SEIZURE / Notice to person who posted the material / Person who posted the material may appear / Non-appearance / Order / Destruction of copy / Return of material / Other provisions to apply / When order takes effect.

320.1 (1) If a judge is satisfied by information on oath that there are reasonable grounds to believe that there is material that is hate propaganda within the meaning of subsection 320(8) or computer data within the meaning of subsection 342.1(2) that makes hate propaganda available, that is stored on and made available to the public through a computer system within the meaning of subsection 342.1(2) that is within the jurisdiction of the court, the judge may order the custodian of the computer system to

(a) give an electronic copy of the material to the court;

(b) ensure that the material is no longer stored on and made available through the computer system; and

(c) provide the information necessary to identify and locate the person who posted the material.

(2) Within a reasonable time after receiving the information referred to in paragraph (1)(c), the judge shall cause notice to be given to the person who posted the material, giving that person the opportunity to appear and be represented before the court and show cause why the material should not be deleted. If the person cannot be identified or located or does not reside in Canada, the judge may order the custodian of the computer system to post the text of the notice at the location where the material was previously stored and made available, until the time set for the appearance.

(3) The person who posted the material may appear and be represented in the proceedings in order to oppose the making of an order under subsection (5).

(4) If the person who posted the material does not appear for the proceedings, the court may proceed *ex parte* to hear and determine the proceedings in the absence of the person as fully and effectually as if the person had appeared.

(5) If the court is satisfied, on a balance of probabilities, that the material is available to the public and is hate propaganda within the meaning of subsection 320(8) or computer data within the meaning of subsection 342.1(2) that makes hate propaganda available, it may order the custodian of the computer system to delete the material.

(6) When the court makes the order for the deletion of the material, it may order the destruction of the electronic copy in the court's possession.

(7) If the court is not satisfied that the material is available to the public and is hate propaganda within the meaning of subsection 320(8) or computer data within the meaning of subsection 342.1(2) that makes hate propaganda available, the court shall order that the electronic copy be returned to the custodian and terminate the order under paragraph (1)(*b*).

(8) Subsections 320(6) to (8) apply, with any modifications that the circumstances require, to this section.

(9) No order made under subsections (5) to (7) takes effect until the time for final appeal has expired. 2001, c. 41, s. 10; 2014, c. 31, s. 13.

PART VIII.1 / OFFENCES RELATING TO CONVEYANCES

Interpretation

DEFINITIONS.

320.11 The following definitions apply in this Part.

"analyst" means a person who is, or a person who is a member of a class of persons that is, designated by the Attorney General under subparagraph 320.4(*b*)(ii) or paragraph 320.4(*c*).

"approved container" means a container that is designed to receive a sample of a person's blood for analysis and that is approved by the Attorney General of Canada under paragraph 320.39(*d*).

"approved drug screening equipment" means equipment that is designed to ascertain the presence of a drug in a person's body and that is approved by the Attorney General of Canada under paragraph 320.39(*b*).

"approved instrument" means an instrument that is designed to receive and make an analysis of a sample of a person's breath to determine their blood alcohol concentration and that is approved by the Attorney General of Canada under paragraph 320.39(*c*).

"approved screening device" means a device that is designed to ascertain the presence of alcohol in a person's blood and that is approved by the Attorney General of Canada under paragraph 320.39(*a*).

"conveyance" means a motor vehicle, a vessel, an aircraft or railway equipment.

"evaluating officer" means a peace officer who has the qualifications prescribed by regulation that are required in order to act as an evaluating officer.

"operate" means

    (a) in respect of a motor vehicle, to drive it or to have care or control of it;

    (b) in respect of a vessel or aircraft, to navigate it, to assist in its navigation or to have care or control of it; and

    (c) in respect of railway equipment, to participate in the direct control of its motion, or to have care or control of it as a member of the equipment's crew, as a person who acts in lieu of a member of the equipment's crew by remote control, or otherwise.

"qualified medical practitioner" means a person who is qualified under provincial law to practise medicine.

"qualified technician" means

    (a) in respect of breath samples, a person who is designated by the Attorney General under paragraph 320.4(a); and

    (b) in respect of blood samples, a person who is, or a person who is a member of a class of persons that is, designated by the Attorney General under subparagraph 320.4(b)(i).

"vessel" includes a hovercraft. 2018, c. 21, s. 15.

Recognition and Declaration

RECOGNITION AND DECLARATION.

320.12 It is recognized and declared that

    (a) operating a conveyance is a privilege that is subject to certain limits in the interests of public safety that include licensing, the observance of rules and sobriety;

    (b) the protection of society is well served by deterring persons from operating conveyances dangerously or while their ability to operate them is impaired by alcohol or a drug, because that conduct poses a threat to the life, health and safety of Canadians;

    (c) the analysis of a sample of a person's breath by means of an approved instrument produces reliable and accurate readings of blood alcohol concentration; and

    (d) an evaluation conducted by an evaluating officer is a reliable method of determining whether a person's ability to operate a conveyance is impaired by a drug or by a combination of alcohol and a drug. 2018, c. 21, s. 15.

Offences and Punishment

DANGEROUS OPERATION / Operation causing bodily harm / Operation causing death.

320.13 (1) Everyone commits an offence who operates a conveyance in a manner that, having regard to all of the circumstances, is dangerous to the public.

(2) Everyone commits an offence who operates a conveyance in a manner that, having regard to all of the circumstances, is dangerous to the public and, as a result, causes bodily harm to another person.

(3) Everyone commits an offence who operates a conveyance in a manner that, having regard to all of the circumstances, is dangerous to the public and, as a result, causes the death of another person. 2018, c. 21, s. 15.

OPERATION WHILE IMPAIRED / Operation causing bodily harm / Operation causing death / Operation — low blood drug concentration / Exception — alcohol / Exception — drugs / Exception — combination of alcohol and drug.

320.14 (1) Everyone commits an offence who

(a) operates a conveyance while the person's ability to operate it is impaired to any degree by alcohol or a drug or by a combination of alcohol and a drug;

(b) subject to subsection (5), has, within two hours after ceasing to operate a conveyance, a blood alcohol concentration that is equal to or exceeds 80 mg of alcohol in 100 mL of blood;

(c) subject to subsection (6), has, within two hours after ceasing to operate a conveyance, a blood drug concentration that is equal to or exceeds the blood drug concentration for the drug that is prescribed by regulation; or

(d) subject to subsection (7), has, within two hours after ceasing to operate a conveyance, a blood alcohol concentration and a blood drug concentration that is equal to or exceeds the blood alcohol concentration and the blood drug concentration for the drug that are prescribed by regulation for instances where alcohol and that drug are combined.

(2) Everyone commits an offence who commits an offence under subsection (1) and who, while operating the conveyance, causes bodily harm to another person.

(3) Everyone commits an offence who commits an offence under subsection (1) and who, while operating the conveyance, causes the death of another person.

(4) Subject to subsection (6), everyone commits an offence who has, within two hours after ceasing to operate a conveyance, a blood drug concentration that is equal to or exceeds the blood drug concentration for the drug that is prescribed by regulation and that is less than the concentration prescribed for the purposes of paragraph (1)(c).

(5) No person commits an offence under paragraph (1)(b) if

(a) they consumed alcohol after ceasing to operate the conveyance;

(b) after ceasing to operate the conveyance, they had no reasonable expectation that they would be required to provide a sample of breath or blood; and

(c) their alcohol consumption is consistent with their blood alcohol concentration as determined in accordance with subsection 320.31(1) or (2) and with their having had, at the time when they were operating the conveyance, a blood alcohol concentration that was less than 80 mg of alcohol in 100 mL of blood.

(6) No person commits an offence under paragraph (1)(c) or subsection (4) if

(a) they consumed the drug after ceasing to operate the conveyance; and

(b) after ceasing to operate the conveyance, they had no reasonable expectation that they would be required to provide a sample of a bodily substance.

(7) No person commits an offence under paragraph (1)(d) if

(a) they consumed the drug or the alcohol or both after ceasing to operate the conveyance;

(b) after ceasing to operate the conveyance, they had no reasonable expectation that they would be required to provide a sample of a bodily substance; and

(c) their alcohol consumption is consistent with their blood alcohol concentration as determined in accordance with subsection 320.31(1) or (2) and with their having had, at the time when they were operating the conveyance, a blood alcohol concentration less than the blood alcohol concentration established under paragraph 320.38(c). 2018, c. 21, s. 15.

FAILURE OR REFUSAL TO COMPLY WITH DEMAND / Accident resulting in bodily harm / Accident resulting in death / Only one conviction.

320.15 (1) Everyone commits an offence who, knowing that a demand has been made, fails or refuses to comply, without reasonable excuse, with a demand made under section 320.27 or 320.28.

(2) Everyone commits an offence who commits an offence under subsection (1) and who, at the time of the failure or refusal, knows that, or is reckless as to whether, they were involved in an accident that resulted in bodily harm to another person.

(3) Everyone commits an offence who commits an offence under subsection (1) and who, at the time of the failure or refusal, knows that, or is reckless as to whether, they were involved in an accident that resulted in the death of another person or in bodily harm to another person whose death ensues.

(4) A person who is convicted of an offence under this section is not to be convicted of another offence under this section with respect to the same transaction. 2018, c. 21, s. 15.

FAILURE TO STOP AFTER ACCIDENT / Accident resulting in bodily harm / Accident resulting in death.

320.16 (1) Everyone commits an offence who operates a conveyance and who at the time of operating the conveyance knows that, or is reckless as to whether, the conveyance has been involved in an accident with a person or another conveyance and who fails, without reasonable excuse, to stop the conveyance, give their name and address and, if any person has been injured or appears to require assistance, offer assistance.

(2) Everyone commits an offence who commits an offence under subsection (1) and who at the time of committing the offence knows that, or is reckless as to whether, the accident resulted in bodily harm to another person.

(3) Everyone commits an offence who commits an offence under subsection (1) and who, at the time of committing the offence, knows that, or is reckless as to whether, the accident resulted in the death of another person or in bodily harm to another person whose death ensues. 2018, c. 21, s. 15.

FLIGHT FROM PEACE OFFICER.

320.17 Everyone commits an offence who operates a motor vehicle or vessel while being pursued by a peace officer and who fails, without reasonable excuse, to stop the motor vehicle or vessel as soon as is reasonable in the circumstances. 2018, c. 21, s. 15.

OPERATION WHILE PROHIBITED / Exception.

320.18 (1) Everyone commits an offence who operates a conveyance while prohibited from doing so
- (*a*) by an order made under this Act; or
- (*b*) by any other form of legal restriction imposed under any other Act of Parliament or under provincial law in respect of a conviction under this Act or a discharge under section 730.

(2) No person commits an offence under subsection (1) arising out of the operation of a motor vehicle if they are registered in an alcohol ignition interlock device program established under the law of the province in which they reside and they comply with the conditions of the program. 2018, c. 21, s. 15.

PUNISHMENT / Summary conviction / Minimum fines for high blood alcohol concentrations / Minimum fine — subsection 320.15(1) / Punishment — dangerous operation and other offences.

320.19 (1) Everyone who commits an offence under subsection 320.14(1) or 320.15(1) is liable on conviction on indictment or on summary conviction
- (*a*) to the following minimum punishment, namely,
  - (i) for a first offence, a fine of $1,000,
  - (ii) for a second offence, imprisonment for a term of 30 days, and
  - (iii) for each subsequent offence, imprisonment for a term of 120 days;
- (*b*) if the offence is prosecuted by indictment, to imprisonment for a term of not more than 10 years; and
- (*c*) if the offence is punishable on summary conviction, to imprisonment for a term of not more than two years less a day.

(2) Everyone who commits an offence under subsection 320.14(4) is liable on summary conviction to a fine of not more than $1,000.

(3) Despite subparagraph (1)(*a*)(i), everyone who commits an offence under paragraph 320.14(1)(*b*) is liable, for a first offence, to
- (*a*) a fine of not less than $1,500, if the person's blood alcohol concentration is equal to or exceeds 120 mg of alcohol in 100 mL of blood but is less than 160 mg of alcohol in 100 mL of blood; and

(b) a fine of not less than $2,000, if the person's blood alcohol concentration is equal to or exceeds 160 mg of alcohol in 100 mL of blood.

(4) Despite subparagraph (1)(a)(i), everyone who commits an offence under subsection 320.15(1) is liable, for a first offence, to a fine of not less than $2,000.

(5) Everyone who commits an offence under subsection 320.13(1) or 320.16(1), section 320.17 or subsection 320.18(1) is liable

(a) on conviction on indictment, to imprisonment for a term of not more than 10 years; or

(b) on summary conviction, to imprisonment for a term of not more than two years less a day. 2018, c. 21, s. 15.

PUNISHMENT IN CASE OF BODILY HARM.

320.2 Everyone who commits an offence under subsection 320.13(2), 320.14(2), 320.15(2) or 320.16(2) is liable on conviction on indictment or on summary conviction

(a) to the following minimum punishment, namely,

(i) for a first offence, a fine of $1,000,

(ii) for a second offence, imprisonment for a term of 30 days, and

(iii) for each subsequent offence, imprisonment for a term of 120 days;

(b) if the offence is prosecuted by indictment, to imprisonment for a term of not more than 14 years; and

(c) if the offence is punishable on summary conviction, to imprisonment for a term of not more than two years less a day. 2018, c. 21, s. 15.

PUNISHMENT IN CASE OF DEATH.

320.21 Everyone who commits an offence under subsection 320.13(3), 320.14(3), 320.15(3) or 320.16(3) is liable on conviction on indictment to imprisonment for life and to a minimum punishment of,

(a) for a first offence, a fine of $1,000;

(b) for a second offence, imprisonment for a term of 30 days; and

(c) for each subsequent offence, imprisonment for a term of 120 days. 2018, c. 21, s. 15.

AGGRAVATING CIRCUMSTANCES FOR SENTENCING PURPOSES.

320.22 A court imposing a sentence for an offence under any of sections 320.13 to 320.18 shall consider, in addition to any other aggravating circumstances, the following:

(a) the commission of the offence resulted in bodily harm to, or the death of, more than one person;

(b) the offender was operating a motor vehicle in a race with at least one other motor vehicle or in a contest of speed, on a street, road or highway or in another public place;

(c) a person under the age of 16 years was a passenger in the conveyance operated by the offender;

(d) the offender was being remunerated for operating the conveyance;

(e) the offender's blood alcohol concentration at the time of committing the offence was equal to or exceeded 120 mg of alcohol in 100 mL of blood;

(f) the offender was operating a large motor vehicle; and

(g) the offender was not permitted, under a federal or provincial Act, to operate the conveyance. 2018, c. 21, s. 15.

DELAY OF SENTENCING / Exception to minimum punishment.

320.23 (1) The court may, with the consent of the prosecutor and the offender, and after considering the interests of justice, delay sentencing of an offender who has been found guilty of an offence under subsection 320.14(1) or 320.15(1) to allow the offender to attend a treatment program approved by the province in which the offender resides. If the court delays sentencing, it shall make an order prohibiting the offender from operating, before sentencing, the type of conveyance in question, in which case subsections 320.24(6) to (9) apply.

(2) If the offender successfully completes the treatment program, the court is not required to impose the minimum punishment under section 320.19 or to make a prohibition order under section 320.24, but it shall not direct a discharge under section 730. 2018, c. 21, s. 15.

MANDATORY PROHIBITION ORDER / Prohibition period / Discretionary order of prohibition — low blood drug concentration / Discretionary order of prohibition — other offences / Prohibition period / Effect of order / Obligation of court / Validity of prohibition order not affected / Application — public place / Consecutive prohibition periods / Minimum absolute prohibition period.

320.24 (1) If an offender is found guilty of an offence under subsection 320.14(1) or 320.15(1), the court that sentences the offender shall, in addition to any other punishment that may be imposed for that offence, make an order prohibiting the offender from operating the type of conveyance in question during a period to be determined in accordance with subsection (2).

(2) The prohibition period is

(a) for a first offence, not less than one year and not more than three years, plus the entire period to which the offender is sentenced to imprisonment;

(b) for a second offence, not less than two years and not more than 10 years, plus the entire period to which the offender is sentenced to imprisonment; and

(c) for each subsequent offence, not less than three years, plus the entire period to which the offender is sentenced to imprisonment.

(3) If an offender is found guilty of an offence under subsection 320.14(4), the court that sentences the offender may, in addition to any other punishment that may be imposed for that offence, make an order prohibiting the offender from operating the type of conveyance in question during a period of not more than one year.

(4) If an offender is found guilty of an offence under section 320.13, subsection 320.14(2) or (3), 320.15(2) or (3) or under any of sections 320.16 to 320.18, the

court that sentences the offender may, in addition to any other punishment that may be imposed for that offence, make an order prohibiting the offender from operating the type of conveyance in question during a period to be determined in accordance with subsection (5).

(5) The prohibition period is

(a) if the offender is liable to imprisonment for life in respect of that offence, of any duration that the court considers appropriate, plus the entire period to which the offender is sentenced to imprisonment;

(b) if the offender is liable to imprisonment for more than five years but less than life in respect of that offence, not more than 10 years, plus the entire period to which the offender is sentenced to imprisonment; and

(c) in any other case, not more than three years, plus the entire period to which the offender is sentenced to imprisonment.

(5.1) Subject to subsection (9), a prohibition order takes effect on the day that it is made.

(6) A court that makes a prohibition order under this section shall cause the order to be read by or to the offender or a copy of the order to be given to the offender.

(7) A failure to comply with subsection (6) does not affect the validity of the prohibition order.

(8) A prohibition order in respect of a motor vehicle applies only to its operation on a street, road or highway or in any other public place.

(9) If the offender is, at the time of the commission of the offence, subject to an order made under this Act prohibiting the offender from operating a conveyance, a court that makes a prohibition order under this section that prohibits the offender from operating the same type of conveyance may order that the prohibition order be served consecutively to that order.

(10) A person may not be registered in an alcohol ignition interlock device program referred to in subsection 320.18(2) until the expiry of

(a) in the case of a first offence, a period, if any, that may be fixed by order of the court;

(b) in the case of a second offence, a period of three months after the day on which the sentence is imposed or any longer period that may be fixed by order of the court; and

(c) in the case of a subsequent offence, a period of six months after the day on which the sentence is imposed or any longer period that may be fixed by order of the court. 2018, c. 21, s. 15.

STAY OF ORDER PENDING APPEAL / Appeals to Supreme Court of Canada / Effect of conditions.

320.25 (1) Subject to subsection (2), if an appeal is taken against a conviction or sentence for an offence under any of sections 320.13 to 320.18, a judge of the court to which the appeal is taken may direct that the prohibition order under section 320.24 arising out of the conviction shall, on any conditions that the judge imposes, be stayed pending the final disposition of the appeal or until otherwise ordered by that court.

(2) In the case of an appeal to the Supreme Court of Canada, a direction may be made only by a judge of the court from which the appeal was taken.

(3) The imposition of conditions on a stay of a prohibition order does not operate to decrease the prohibition period provided in the prohibition order. 2018, c. 21, s. 15.

EARLIER AND SUBSEQUENT OFFENCES.

320.26 In determining, for the purpose of imposing a sentence for an offence under subsection 320.14(1) or 320.15(1), whether the offence is a second, third or subsequent offence, any of the following offences for which the offender was previously convicted is considered to be an earlier offence:

    (*a*) an offence under any of subsections 320.14(1) to (3) or section 320.15; or

    (*b*) an offence under any of sections 253, 254 and 255, as those sections read from time to time before the day on which this section comes into force. 2018, c. 21, s. 15.

Investigative Matters

TESTING FOR PRESENCE OF ALCOHOL OR DRUG / Mandatory alcohol screening.

320.27 (1) If a peace officer has reasonable grounds to suspect that a person has alcohol or a drug in their body and that the person has, within the preceding three hours, operated a conveyance, the peace officer may, by demand, require the person to comply with the requirements of either or both of paragraphs (*a*) and (*b*) in the case of alcohol or with the requirements of either or both of paragraphs (*a*) and (*c*) in the case of a drug:

    (*a*) to immediately perform the physical coordination tests prescribed by regulation and to accompany the peace officer for that purpose;

    (*b*) to immediately provide the samples of breath that, in the peace officer's opinion, are necessary to enable a proper analysis to be made by means of an approved screening device and to accompany the peace officer for that purpose;

    (*c*) to immediately provide the samples of a bodily substance that, in the peace officer's opinion, are necessary to enable a proper analysis to be made by means of approved drug screening equipment and to accompany the peace officer for that purpose.

(2) If a peace officer has in his or her possession an approved screening device, the peace officer may, in the course of the lawful exercise of powers under an Act of Parliament or an Act of a provincial legislature or arising at common law, by demand, require the person who is operating a motor vehicle to immediately

provide the samples of breath that, in the peace officer's opinion, are necessary to enable a proper analysis to be made by means of that device and to accompany the peace officer for that purpose. 2018, c. 21, s. 15.

SAMPLES OF BREATH OR BLOOD — ALCOHOL / Evaluation and samples of blood — drugs / Samples of breath — alcohol / Samples of bodily substances / Types of drugs / Condition / Approved containers / Retained sample / Validity of analysis not affected / Release of retained sample.

CODE

320.28 (1) If a peace officer has reasonable grounds to believe that a person has operated a conveyance while the person's ability to operate it was impaired to any degree by alcohol or has committed an offence under paragraph 320.14(1)(*b*), the peace officer may, by demand made as soon as practicable,

(*a*) require the person to provide, as soon as practicable,

(i) the samples of breath that, in a qualified technician's opinion, are necessary to enable a proper analysis to be made by means of an approved instrument, or

(ii) if the peace officer has reasonable grounds to believe that, because of their physical condition, the person may be incapable of providing a sample of breath or it would be impracticable to take one, the samples of blood that, in the opinion of the qualified medical practitioner or qualified technician taking the samples, are necessary to enable a proper analysis to be made to determine the person's blood alcohol concentration; and

(*b*) require the person to accompany the peace officer for the purpose of taking samples of that person's breath or blood.

(2) If a peace officer has reasonable grounds to believe that a person has operated a conveyance while the person's ability to operate it was impaired to any degree by a drug or by a combination of alcohol and a drug, or has committed an offence under paragraph 320.14(1)(*c*) or (*d*) or subsection 320.14(4), the peace officer may, by demand, made as soon as practicable, require the person to comply with the requirements of either or both of paragraphs (*a*) and (*b*):

(*a*) to submit, as soon as practicable, to an evaluation conducted by an evaluating officer to determine whether the person's ability to operate a conveyance is impaired by a drug or by a combination of alcohol and a drug, and to accompany the peace officer for that purpose; or

(*b*) to provide, as soon as practicable, the samples of blood that, in the opinion of the qualified medical practitioner or qualified technician taking the samples, are necessary to enable a proper analysis to be made to determine the person's blood drug concentration, or the person's blood drug concentration and blood alcohol concentration, as the case may be, and to accompany the peace officer for that purpose.

(3) An evaluating officer who has reasonable grounds to suspect that a person has alcohol in their body may, if a demand was not made under subsection (1), by demand made as soon as practicable, require the person to provide, as soon as practicable, the samples of breath that, in a qualified technician's opinion, are

necessary to enable a proper analysis to be made by means of an approved instrument.

(4) If, on completion of the evaluation, the evaluating officer has reasonable grounds to believe that one or more of the types of drugs set out in subsection (5) — or that a combination of alcohol and one or more of those types of drugs — is impairing the person's ability to operate a conveyance, the evaluating officer shall identify the type or types of drugs in question and may, by demand made as soon as practicable, require the person to provide, as soon as practicable,

   (*a*) a sample of oral fluid or urine that, in the evaluating officer's opinion, is necessary to enable a proper analysis to be made to ascertain the presence in the person's body of one or more of the types of drugs set out in subsection (5); or

   (*b*) the samples of blood that, in the opinion of the qualified medical practitioner or qualified technician taking the samples, are necessary to enable a proper analysis to be made to ascertain the presence in the person's body of one or more of the types of drugs set out in subsection (5) or to determine the person's blood drug concentration for one or more of those types of drugs.

(5) For the purpose of subsection (4), the types of drugs are the following:

   (*a*) a depressant;

   (*b*) an inhalant;

   (*c*) a dissociative anaesthetic;

   (*d*) cannabis;

   (*e*) a stimulant;

   (*f*) a hallucinogen; or

   (*g*) a narcotic analgesic.

(6) A sample of blood may be taken from a person under this section only by a qualified medical practitioner or a qualified technician, and only if they are satisfied that taking the sample would not endanger the person's health.

(7) A sample of blood shall be received into an approved container that shall be subsequently sealed.

(8) A person who takes samples of blood under this section shall cause one of the samples to be retained for the purpose of analysis by or on behalf of the person from whom the blood samples were taken.

(9) A failure to comply with subsection (7) or (8) does not by itself affect the validity of the taking of the sample or of an analysis made of the sample.

(10) A judge of a superior court of criminal jurisdiction or a court of criminal jurisdiction shall, on the summary application of the person from whom samples of blood were taken under this section, made within six months after the day on which the samples were taken, order the release of any sample that was retained to the person for the purpose of examination or analysis, subject to any terms that the judge considers appropriate to ensure that the sample is safeguarded and preserved for use in any proceedings in respect of which it was taken. 2018, c. 21, s. 15.

WARRANTS TO OBTAIN BLOOD SAMPLES / Form / Procedure — telephone or other means of telecommunication / Duration of warrant / Copy or facsimile to person / Taking of samples.

320.29 (1) A justice may issue a warrant authorizing a peace officer to require a qualified medical practitioner or a qualified technician to take the samples of a person's blood that, in the opinion of the practitioner or technician taking the samples, are necessary to enable a proper analysis to be made to determine the person's blood alcohol concentration or blood drug concentration, or both, if the justice is satisfied, on an information on oath in Form 1 or on an information on oath submitted to the justice by telephone or other means of telecommunication, that

    (*a*) there are reasonable grounds to believe that the person has, within the preceding eight hours, operated a conveyance that was involved in an accident that resulted in bodily harm to themselves or another person or in the death of another person;

    (*b*) there are reasonable grounds to suspect that the person has alcohol or a drug in their body; and

    (*c*) a qualified medical practitioner is of the opinion that

        (i) by reason of any physical or mental condition of the person, the person is unable to consent to the taking of samples of their blood, and

        (ii) the taking of samples of the person's blood will not endanger their health.

(2) A warrant issued under subsection (1) may be in Form 5 or 5.1, varied to suit the case.

(3) Section 487.1 applies, with any modifications that the circumstances require, in respect of an application for a warrant that is submitted by telephone or other means of telecommunication.

(4) Samples of blood may be taken from a person under a warrant issued under subsection (1) only during the time that a qualified medical practitioner is satisfied that the conditions referred to in subparagraphs (1)(*c*)(i) and (ii) continue to exist.

(5) If a warrant issued under subsection (1) is executed, the peace officer shall, as soon as practicable, give a copy of it — or, in the case of a warrant issued by telephone or other means of telecommunication, a facsimile — to the person from whom the samples of blood are taken.

(6) Subsections 320.28(7) to (10) apply with respect to the taking of samples of blood under this section. 2018, c. 21, s. 15.

TESTING BLOOD — DRUG OR ALCOHOL.

320.3 Samples of a person's blood that are taken for the purposes of this Part may be analyzed to determine the person's blood alcohol concentration or blood drug concentration, or both. 2018, c. 21, s. 15.

Evidentiary Matters

BREATH SAMPLES / Blood samples — concentration when sample taken / Evidence not included / Presumption — blood alcohol concentration / Admissibility of evaluating officer's opinion / Presumption — drug / Admissibility of result of analysis / Evidence of failure to provide sample / Admissibility of statement / Evidence of failure to comply with demand.

320.31 (1) If samples of a person's breath have been received into an approved instrument operated by a qualified technician, the results of the analyses of the samples are conclusive proof of the person's blood alcohol concentration at the time when the analyses were made if the results of the analyses are the same — or, if the results of the analyses are different, the lowest of the results is conclusive proof of the person's blood alcohol concentration at the time when the analyses were made — if

    (*a*) before each sample was taken, the qualified technician conducted a system blank test the result of which is not more than 10 mg of alcohol in 100 mL of blood and a system calibration check the result of which is within 10% of the target value of an alcohol standard that is certified by an analyst;

    (*b*) there was an interval of at least 15 minutes between the times when the samples were taken; and

    (*c*) the results of the analyses, rounded down to the nearest multiple of 10 mg, did not differ by more than 20 mg of alcohol in 100 mL of blood.

(2) The result of an analysis made by an analyst of a sample of a person's blood is proof of their blood alcohol concentration or their blood drug concentration, as the case may be, at the time when the sample was taken in the absence of evidence tending to show that the analysis was performed improperly.

(3) Evidence of the following does not constitute evidence tending to show that an analysis of a sample of a person's blood was performed improperly:

    (*a*) the amount of alcohol or a drug that they consumed;

    (*b*) the rate at which the alcohol or the drug would have been absorbed or eliminated by their body; or

    (*c*) a calculation based on the evidence referred to in paragraphs (*a*) and (*b*) of what their blood alcohol concentration or blood drug concentration would have been at the time the sample was taken.

(4) For the purpose of paragraphs 320.14(1)(*b*) and (*d*), if the first of the samples of breath was taken, or the sample of blood was taken, more than two hours after the person ceased to operate the conveyance and the person's blood alcohol concentration was equal to or exceeded 20 mg of alcohol in 100 mL of blood, the person's blood alcohol concentration within those two hours is conclusively presumed to be the concentration established in accordance with subsection (1) or (2), as the case may be, plus an additional 5 mg of alcohol in 100 mL of blood for every interval of 30 minutes in excess of those two hours.

(5) An evaluating officer's opinion relating to the impairment, by a type of drug that they identified, or by a combination of alcohol and that type of drug, of a

person's ability to operate a conveyance is admissible in evidence without qualifying the evaluating officer as an expert.

(6) If the analysis of a sample provided under subsection 320.28(4) demonstrates that the person has a drug in their body that is of a type that the evaluating officer has identified as impairing the person's ability to operate a conveyance, that drug — or, if the person has also consumed alcohol, the combination of alcohol and that drug — is presumed, in the absence of evidence to the contrary, to be the drug, or the combination of alcohol and that drug, that was present in the person's body at the time when the person operated the conveyance and, on proof of the person's impairment, to have been the cause of that impairment.

(7) The result of an analysis of a sample of a person's breath, blood, urine, sweat or other bodily substance that they were not required to provide under this Part may be admitted in evidence even if the person was not warned before they provided the sample that they were not required to do so or that the result of the analysis of the sample might be used in evidence.

(8) Unless a person is required to provide a sample of a bodily substance under this Part, evidence that they failed or refused to provide a sample for analysis or that a sample was not taken is not admissible and the failure, refusal or fact that a sample was not taken shall not be the subject of comment by any person in any proceedings under this Part.

(9) A statement made by a person to a peace officer, including a statement compelled under a provincial Act, is admissible in evidence for the purpose of justifying a demand made under section 320.27 or 320.28.

(10) In any proceedings in respect of an offence under section 320.14, evidence that the accused, without reasonable excuse, failed or refused to comply with a demand made under section 320.27 or 320.28 is admissible and the court may draw an inference adverse to the accused from that evidence. 2018, c. 21, s. 15.

CERTIFICATES / Notice of intention to produce certificate / Attendance and cross-examination / Form and content of application / Time of hearing / Certificate admissible in evidence / Onus.

320.32 (1) A certificate of an analyst, qualified medical practitioner or qualified technician made under this Part is evidence of the facts alleged in the certificate without proof of the signature or the official character of the person who signed the certificate.

(2) No certificate shall be received in evidence unless the party intending to produce it has, before the trial, given to the other party reasonable notice of their intention to produce it and a copy of the certificate.

(3) A party against whom the certificate is produced may apply to the court for an order requiring the attendance of the person who signed the certificate for the purposes of cross-examination.

(4) The application shall be made in writing and set out the likely relevance of the proposed cross-examination with respect to the facts alleged in the certificate. A

copy of the application shall be given to the prosecutor at least 30 days before the day on which the application is to be heard.

(5) The hearing of the application shall be held at least 30 days before the day on which the trial is to be held.

(6) In proceedings in respect of an offence under subsection 320.18(1), the following certificates are evidence of the facts alleged in them without proof of the signature or official character of the person who signed them:

(*a*) a certificate setting out with reasonable particularity that the person named in it is prohibited from operating a motor vehicle in the province specified in the certificate, signed by the person who is responsible for the registration of motor vehicles in that province or any person authorized by the responsible person to sign it; and

(*b*) a certificate setting out with reasonable particularity that the person named in it is prohibited from operating a conveyance other than a motor vehicle, signed by the Minister of Transport or any person authorized by him or her to sign it.

(7) If it is proved that a prohibition under paragraph 320.18(1)(*b*) has been imposed on a person and that notice of the prohibition has been mailed to them at their last known address, that person is, beginning on the tenth day after the day on which the notice is mailed, in the absence of evidence to the contrary, presumed to have received the notice and to have knowledge of the prohibition, of the date of its commencement and of its duration. 2018, c. 21, s. 15.

PRINTOUT FROM APPROVED INSTRUMENT.

320.33 A document that is printed out from an approved instrument and signed by a qualified technician who certifies it to be the printout produced by the approved instrument when it made an analysis of a sample of a person's breath is evidence of the facts alleged in the document without proof of the signature or official character of the person who signed it. 2018, c. 21, s. 15.

DISCLOSURE OF INFORMATION / Application for further disclosure / Form and content of application / Time of hearing / For greater certainty.

320.34 (1) In proceedings in respect of an offence under section 320.14, the prosecutor shall disclose to the accused, with respect to any samples of breath that the accused provided under section 320.28, information sufficient to determine whether the conditions set out in paragraphs 320.31(1)(*a*) to (*c*) have been met, namely:

(*a*) the results of the system blank tests;

(*b*) the results of the system calibration checks;

(*c*) any error or exception messages produced by the approved instrument at the time the samples were taken;

(*d*) the results of the analysis of the accused's breath samples; and

(*e*) a certificate of an analyst stating that the sample of an alcohol standard that is identified in the certificate is suitable for use with an approved instrument.

(2) The accused may apply to the court for a hearing to determine whether further information should be disclosed.

(3) The application shall be in writing and set out detailed particulars of the information that the accused seeks to have disclosed and the likely relevance of that information to determining whether the approved instrument was in proper working order. A copy of the application shall be given to the prosecutor at least 30 days before the day on which the application is to be heard.

(4) The hearing of the application shall be held at least 30 days before the day on which the trial is to be held.

(5) For greater certainty, nothing in this section limits the disclosure to which the accused may otherwise be entitled. 2018, c. 21, s. 15.

PRESUMPTION OF OPERATION.

320.35 In proceedings in respect of an offence under section 320.14 or 320.15, if it is proved that the accused occupied the seat or position ordinarily occupied by a person who operates a conveyance, the accused is presumed to have been operating the conveyance unless they establish that they did not occupy that seat or position for the purpose of setting the conveyance in motion. 2018, c. 21, s. 15.

General Provisions

UNAUTHORIZED USE OF BODILY SUBSTANCE / Unauthorized use or disclosure of results / Exception / Offence.

320.36 (1) No person shall use a bodily substance obtained under this Part for any purpose other than for an analysis under this Part.

(2) No person shall use, disclose or allow the disclosure of the results obtained under this Part of any evaluation, physical coordination test or analysis of a bodily substance, except for the purpose of the administration or enforcement of a federal or provincial Act related to drugs and/or alcohol and/or to the operation of a motor vehicle, vessel, aircraft or railway equipment.

(3) The results of an evaluation, test or analysis referred to in subsection (2) may be disclosed to the person to whom they relate, and may be disclosed to any other person if the results are made anonymous and the disclosure is made for statistical or research purposes.

(4) Everyone who contravenes subsection (1) or (2) commits an offence punishable on summary conviction. 2018, c. 21, s. 15.

REFUSAL TO TAKE SAMPLE / No liability.

320.37 (1) No qualified medical practitioner or qualified technician shall be found guilty of an offence by reason only of their refusal to take a sample of blood from a person for the purposes of this Part if they have a reasonable excuse for refusing to do so.

(2) No qualified medical practitioner, and no qualified technician, who takes a sample of blood from a person under this Part incurs any liability for doing anything necessary to take the sample that was done with reasonable care and skill. 2018, c. 21, s. 15.

REGULATIONS.

320.38 The Governor in Council may make regulations

- (a) prescribing the qualifications required for a peace officer to act as an evaluating officer and respecting the training of evaluating officers;
- (b) prescribing the blood drug concentration for a drug for the purpose of paragraph 320.14(1)(c);
- (c) prescribing a blood alcohol concentration and a blood drug concentration for a drug for the purposes of paragraph 320.14(1)(d);
- (d) prescribing the blood drug concentration for a drug for the purpose of subsection 320.14(4);
- (e) prescribing the physical coordination tests to be conducted under paragraph 320.27(1)(a); and
- (f) prescribing the tests to be conducted and procedures to be followed during an evaluation under paragraph 320.28(2)(a) and the forms to be used in recording the results of the evaluation. 2018, c. 21, s. 15.

APPROVAL — ATTORNEY GENERAL OF CANADA.

320.39 The Attorney General of Canada may, by order, approve

- (a) a device that is designed to ascertain the presence of alcohol in a person's blood;
- (b) equipment that is designed to ascertain the presence of a drug in a person's body;
- (c) an instrument that is designed to receive and make an analysis of a sample of a person's breath to determine their blood alcohol concentration; and
- (d) a container that is designed to receive a sample of a person's blood for analysis. 2018, c. 21, s. 15.

DESIGNATION — ATTORNEY GENERAL.

320.4 The Attorney General may designate

- (a) a person as qualified, for the purposes of this Part, to operate an approved instrument;
- (b) a person or class of persons as qualified, for the purposes of this Part,
  - (i) to take samples of blood, or
  - (ii) to analyze samples of bodily substances; and
- (c) a person or class of persons as qualified, for the purposes of this Part, to certify that an alcohol standard is suitable for use with an approved instrument. 2018, c. 21, s. 15.

REGULATIONS: ORDER APPROVING BLOOD SAMPLE CONTAINERS
Approved Containers

1. The following containers, being containers of a kind that is designed to receive a sample of blood of a person for analysis, are hereby approved as suitable, in respect of blood samples, for the purposes of section 258 of the *Criminal Code*:

   (a) Vacutainer® XF947;

   (b) BD Vacutainer TM 367001;

   (c) Vacutainer® 367001;

   (d) Tri-Tech Inc. TUG10;

   (e) BD Vacutainer® REF 367001; and

   (f) TRITECHFORENSICS TUG10.

Repeal

2. The Approved Blood Sample Container Order is repealed.
Coming into force

3. This Order comes into force on the day on which it is registered. **SOR/2005-37; SOR/2010-64, s. 1**; **SOR/2012-60, s. 1**.

REGULATIONS: APPROVED BREATH ANALYSIS INSTRUMENTS ORDER
Approved Instruments

2. The following instruments, each being an instrument of a kind that is designed to receive and make an analysis of a sample of the breath of a person in order to measure the concentration of alcohol in the blood of that person, are hereby approved as suitable for the purposes of section 258 of the *Criminal Code*:

   (a) [*Repealed*, SOR/2012-237, s. 1(1).]

   (b) [*Repealed*, SOR/2012-237, s. 1(1).]

   (c) [*Repealed*, SOR/2012-237, s. 1(1).]

   (d) [*Repealed*, SOR/2013-107, s. 1(1).]

   (e) [*Repealed*, SOR/2013-107, s. 1(1).]

   (f) [*Repealed*, SOR/2013-107, s. 1(1).]

   (g) [*Repealed*, SOR/2013-107, s. 1(1).]

   (h) Intoxilyzer® 5000C;

   (i) [*Repealed*, SOR/2012-237, s. 1(2).]

   (j) [*Repealed*, SOR/2013-107, s. 1(2).]

   (k) BAC Datamaster C;

   (l) Alco-Sensor IV-RBT IV;

   (m) [*Repealed*, SOR/2013-107, s. 1(3).]

   (n) Alco-Sensor IV/RBT IV-K;

   (o) Alcotest 7110 MKIII Dual C;

   (p) Intoxilyzer® 8000 C;

   (q) DataMaster DMT-C;

   (r) Intox EC/IR II; and

   (s) Intoxilyzer® 9000.

SI/85-201, *Can. Gaz. Part II*, 27/11/85, p. 4692; SI/92-105, *Can. Gaz. Part II*, 17/6/92, p. 2577; SI/92-167, *Can. Gaz. Part II*, 23/9/92, p. 3807; SI/93-61, *Can. Gaz., Part II*, 5/5/93, p. 2198; SI/93-175, *Can. Gaz., Part II*, 8/9/93, p. 3714; SOR/94-422, *Can. Gaz., Part II*, 15/6/94, p. 2451; SOR/94-572, *Can. Gaz., Part II*, 7/9/94, p. 3132; SOR/95-312, *Can. Gaz., Part II*, 12/7/95, p. 1885; SOR/2000-200, *Can. Gaz., Part II*, s. 1; SOR/2002-99, *Can. Gaz., Part II*, s. 1; SOR/2007-197, s. 1; SOR/2008-106, s. 1; SOR/2009-205, s. 1; SOR/2012-237, s. 1; SOR/2013-107, s. 1; SOR/2019-26, s. 1.

REGULATIONS: APPROVED SCREENING DEVICES ORDER
Approved Screening Devices

2. The following devices, each being a device of a kind that is designed to ascertain the presence of alcohol in the blood of a person, are hereby approved for the purposes of section 254 of the *Criminal Code*:

    (*a*)   Alcolmeter S-L2;

    (*b*)   Alco-Sûr;

    (*c*)   Alcotest® 7410 PA3;

    (*d*)   Alcotest® 7410 GLC;

    (*e*)   Alco-Sensor IV DWF;

    (*f*)   Alco-Sensor IV PWF;

    (*g*)   Intoxilyzer 400D;

    (*h*)   Alco-Sensor FST;

    (*i*)   Dräger Alcotest 6810; and

    (*j*)   Dräger Alcotest® 6820.

SI/85-200, *Can. Gaz. Part II*, 27/11/85, p. 4691; SI/88-136, *Can. Gaz. Part II*, 28/9/88, p. 4074; SOR/93-263, *Can. Gaz., Part II*, 2/6/93, p. 2403; SOR/94-193, *Can. Gaz., Part II*, 9/3/94, p. 1232; SOR/94-423, *Can. Gaz., Part II*, 15/6/94, p. 2453; SOR/96-81, *Can. Gaz., Part II*, 24/1/96, p. 609; SOR/97-116, *Can. Gaz., Part II*, 53/97, p. 649; SOR/2009-239, s. 1; SOR/2011-313, s. 1; SOR/2012-61, s. 1; SOR/2019-25, s. 1.

Part IX / OFFENCES AGAINST RIGHTS OF PROPERTY

Interpretation

DEFINITIONS / "break" / "credit card" / "document" / "exchequer bill" / "exchequer bill paper" / "false document" / "revenue paper".

321. In this Part

"break" means

    (*a*)   to break any part, internal or external, or

    (*b*)   to open any thing that is used or intended to be used to close or to cover an internal or external opening;

"Credit card" means any card, plate, coupon book or other device issued or otherwise distributed for the purpose of being used

(a) on presentation to obtain, on credit, money, goods, services or any other thing of value, or

(b) in an automated teller machine, a remote service unit or a similar automated banking device to obtain any of the services offered through the machine, unit or device;

"document" means any paper, parchment or other material on which is recorded or marked anything that is capable of being read or understood by a person, computer system or other device, and includes a credit card, but does not include trademarks on articles of commerce or inscriptions on stone or metal or other like material;

"exchequer bill" means a bank-note, bond, note, debenture or security that is issued or guaranteed by Her Majesty under the authority of Parliament or the legislature of a province;

"exchequer bill paper" means paper that is used to manufacture exchequer bills;

"false document" means a document

(a) the whole or a material part of which purports to be made by or on behalf of a person
    (i) who did not make it or authorize it to be made, or
    (ii) who did not in fact exist,

(b) that is made by or on behalf of the person who purports to make it but is false in some material particular,

(c) that is made in the name of an existing person, by him or under his authority, with a fraudulent intention that it should pass as being made by a person, real or fictitious, other than the person who makes it or under whose authority it is made;

"revenue paper" means paper that is used to make stamps, licences or permits or for any purpose connected with the public revenue. R.S., c. C-34, s. 282; R.S.C. 1985, c. 27 (1st Supp.), s. 42; 2014, c. 20, s. 366(1).

Theft

THEFT / Time when theft completed / Secrecy / Purpose of taking / Wild living creature.

322. (1) Every one commits theft who fraudulently and without colour of right takes, or fraudulently and without colour of right converts to his use or to the use of another person, anything whether animate or inanimate, with intent,

(a) to deprive, temporarily or absolutely, the owner of it, or a person who has a special property or interest in it, of the thing or of his property or interest in it;

(b) to pledge it or deposit it as security;

(c) to part with it under a condition with respect to its return that the person who parts with it may be unable to perform; or

(d) to deal with it in such a manner that it cannot be restored in the condition in which it was at the time it was taken or converted.

335

(2) A person commits theft when, with intent to steal anything, he moves it or causes it to move or to be moved, or begins to cause it to become movable.

(3) A taking or conversion of anything may be fraudulent notwithstanding that it is effected without secrecy or attempt at concealment.

(4) For the purposes of this Act, the question whether anything that is converted is taken for the purpose of conversion, or whether it is, at the time it is converted, in the lawful possession of the person who converts it is not material.

(5) For the purposes of this section, a person who has a wild living creature in captivity shall be deemed to have a special property or interest in it while it is in captivity and after it has escaped from captivity. R.S., c. C-34, s. 283.

OYSTERS / Oyster bed.

323. (1) Where oysters and oyster brood are in oyster beds, layings or fisheries that are the property of any person and are sufficiently marked out or known as the property of that person, that person shall be deemed to have a special property or interest in them.

(2) An indictment is sufficient if it describes an oyster bed, laying or fishery by name or in any other way, without stating that it is situated in a particular territorial division. R.S., c. C-34, s. 284.

THEFT BY BAILEE OF THINGS UNDER SEIZURE.

324. Every one who is a bailee of anything that is under lawful seizure by a peace officer or public officer in the execution of the duties of his office, and who is obliged by law or agreement to produce and deliver it to that officer or to another person entitled thereto at a certain time and place, or on demand, steals it if he does not produce and deliver it in accordance with his obligation, but he does not steal it if his failure to produce and deliver it is not the result of a wilful act or omission by him. R.S., c. C-34, s. 285.

AGENT PLEDGING GOODS, WHEN NOT THEFT.

325. A factor or an agent does not commit theft by pledging or giving a lien on goods or documents of title to goods that are entrusted to him for the purpose of sale or for any other purpose, if the pledge or lien is for an amount that does not exceed the sum of

   (*a*) the amount due to him from his principal at the time the goods or documents are pledged or the lien is given; and

   (*b*) the amount of any bill of exchange that he has accepted for or on account of his principal. R.S., c. C-34, s. 286.

THEFT OF TELECOMMUNICATION SERVICE / Definition of "telecommunication".

326. (1) Every one commits theft who fraudulently, maliciously, or without colour of right,

    (a) abstracts, consumes or uses electricity or gas or causes it to be wasted or diverted; or

    (b) uses any telecommunication facility or obtains any telecommunication service. R.S., c. C-34, s. 287; 1974-75-76, c. 93, s. 23; 2014, c. 31, s. 14(2).

(2) [*Repealed*. 2014, c. 31, s. 14(2).]

POSSESSION OF DEVICE TO OBTAIN USE OF TELECOMMUNICATION FACILITY OR SERVICE / Forfeiture / Limitation / Definition of "device".

327. (1) Every person who, without lawful excuse, makes, possesses, sells, offers for sale, imports, obtains for use, distributes or makes available a device that is designed or adapted primarily to use a telecommunication facility or obtain a telecommunication service without payment of a lawful charge, knowing that the device has been used or is intended to be used for that purpose, is

    (a) guilty of an indictable offence and liable to imprisonment for a term of not more than two years; or

    (b) guilty of an offence punishable on summary conviction.

(2) If a person is convicted of an offence under subsection (1) or paragraph 326(1)(*b*), in addition to any punishment that is imposed, any device in relation to which the offence was committed or the possession of which constituted the offence may be ordered forfeited to Her Majesty and may be disposed of as the Attorney General directs.

(3) No order for forfeiture is to be made in respect of telecommunication facilities or equipment by means of which an offence under subsection (1) is committed if they are owned by a person engaged in providing a telecommunication service to the public or form part of such a person's telecommunication service or system and that person is not a party to the offence.

(4) In this section, "device" includes

    (a) a component of a device; and

    (b) a computer program within the meaning of subsection 342.1(2). 1974-75-76, c. 93, s. 24; 2014, c. 31, s. 15; 2018, c. 29, s. 32.

THEFT BY OR FROM PERSON HAVING SPECIAL PROPERTY OR INTEREST.

328. A person may be convicted of theft notwithstanding that anything that is alleged to have been stolen was stolen

    (a) by the owner of it from a person who has a special property or interest in it;

    (b) by a person who has a special property or interest in it from the owner of it;

    (c) by a lessee of it from his reversioner;

    (d) by one of several joint owners, tenants in common or partners of or in it from the other persons who have an interest in it; or

    (e) by the representatives of an organization from the organization. R.S., c. C-34, s. 288; 2003, c. 21, s. 4.

329. [*Repealed*, 2000, c. 12, s. 94.]

THEFT BY PERSON REQUIRED TO ACCOUNT / Effect of entry in account.

330. (1) Every one commits theft who, having received anything from any person on terms that require him to account for or pay it or the proceeds of it or a part of the proceeds to that person or another person, fraudulently fails to account for or pay it or the proceeds of it or the part of the proceeds of it accordingly.

(2) Where subsection (1) otherwise applies, but one of the terms is that the thing received or the proceeds or part of the proceeds of it shall be an item in a debtor and creditor account between the person who receives the thing and the person to whom he is to account for or to pay it, and that the latter shall rely only on the liability of the other as his debtor in respect thereof, a proper entry in that account of the thing received or the proceeds or part of the proceeds of it, as the case may be, is a sufficient accounting therefor, and no fraudulent conversion of the thing or the proceeds or part of the proceeds of it thereby accounted for shall be deemed to have taken place. R.S., c. C-34, s. 290.

THEFT BY PERSON HOLDING POWER OF ATTORNEY.

331. Every one commits theft who, being entrusted, whether solely or jointly with another person, with a power of attorney for the sale, mortgage, pledge or other disposition of real or personal property, fraudulently sells, mortgages, pledges or otherwise disposes of the property or any part of it, or fraudulently converts the proceeds of a sale, mortgage, pledge or other disposition of the property, or any part of the proceeds, to a purpose other than that for which he was entrusted by the power of attorney. R.S., c. C-34, s. 291.

MISAPPROPRIATION OF MONEY HELD UNDER DIRECTION / Effect of entry in account.

332. (1) Every one commits theft who, having received, either solely or jointly with another person, money or valuable security or a power of attorney for the sale of real or personal property, with a direction that the money or a part of it, or the proceeds or a part of the proceeds of the security or the property shall be applied to a purpose or paid to a person specified in the direction, fraudulently and contrary to the direction applies to any other purpose or pays to any other person the money or proceeds or any part of it.

(2) This section does not apply where a person who receives anything mentioned in subsection (1) and the person from whom he receives it deal with each other on such terms that all money paid to the former would, in the absence of any such direction, be properly treated as an item in a debtor and creditor account between them, unless the direction is in writing. R.S., c. C-34, s. 292.

TAKING ORE FOR SCIENTIFIC PURPOSE.

333. No person commits theft by reason only that he takes, for the purpose of exploration or scientific investigation, a specimen of ore or mineral from land that is not enclosed and is not occupied or worked as a mine, quarry or digging. R.S., c. C-34, s. 293.

MOTOR VEHICLE THEFT / Subsequent offences.

333.1 (1) Everyone who commits theft is, if the property stolen is a motor vehicle, guilty of an offence and liable

    (*a*) on proceedings by way of indictment, to imprisonment for a term of not more than 10 years, and to a minimum punishment of imprisonment for a term of six months in the case of a third or subsequent offence under this subsection; or

    (*b*) on summary conviction, to imprisonment for a term of not more than two years less a day.

(2) For the purpose of determining whether a convicted person has committed a third or subsequent offence, an offence for which the person was previously convicted is considered to be an earlier offence whether it was prosecuted by indictment or by way of summary conviction proceedings. 2010, c. 14, s. 3; 2019, c. 25, s. 121.

PUNISHMENT FOR THEFT.

334. Except where otherwise provided by law, every one who commits theft

    (*a*) if the property stolen is a testamentary instrument or the value of what is stolen is more than $5,000, is guilty of

        (i) an indictable offence and liable to imprisonment for a term of not more than 10 years, or

        (ii) an offence punishable on summary conviction; or

    (*b*) if the value of what is stolen is not more than $5,000, is guilty

        (i) of an indictable offence and is liable to imprisonment for a term not exceeding two years, or

        (ii) of an offence punishable on summary conviction. R.S., c. C-34, s. 294; 1972, c. 13, s. 23; 1974-75-76, c. 93, s. 25; R.S.C. 1985, c. 27 (1st Supp.), s. 43; 1994, c. 44, s. 20; 2019, c. 25, s. 122.

Offences Resembling Theft

TAKING MOTOR VEHICLE OR VESSEL OR FOUND THEREIN WITHOUT CONSENT / Exception / Definition of "vessel".

335. (1) Subject to subsection (1.1), every one who, without the consent of the owner, takes a motor vehicle or vessel with intent to drive, use, navigate or operate it or cause it to be driven, used, navigated or operated, or is an occupant of a motor vehicle or vessel knowing that it was taken without the consent of the owner, is guilty of an offence punishable on summary conviction.

(1.1) Subsection (1) does not apply to an occupant of a motor vehicle or vessel who, on becoming aware that it was taken without the consent of the owner, attempted to leave the motor vehicle or vessel, to the extent that it was feasible to do so, or actually left the motor vehicle or vessel.

(2) For the purposes of subsection (1), "vessel" has the same meaning as in section 320.11. R.S., c. C-34, s. 296; 1972, c. 13, s. 23; R.S.C. 1985, c. 1 (4th Supp.), s. 15; 1997, c. 18, s. 15; 2018, c. 21, s. 16.

CRIMINAL BREACH OF TRUST.

336. Every one who, being a trustee of anything for the use or benefit, whether in whole or in part, of another person, or for a public or charitable purpose, converts, with intent to defraud and in contravention of his trust, that thing or any part of it to a use that is not authorized by the trust is guilty of an indictable offence and liable to imprisonment for a term not exceeding fourteen years. R.S., c. C-34, s. 296.

337. [*Repealed*, 2018, c. 29, s. 33.]

FRAUDULENTLY TAKING CATTLE OR DEFACING BRAND / Punishment for theft of cattle / Evidence of property in cattle / Presumption from possession.

338. (1) Every person is guilty of an indictable offence and liable to imprisonment for a term of not more than five years or is guilty of an offence punishable on summary conviction who, without the consent of the owner,

- (*a*) fraudulently takes, holds, keeps in his possession, conceals, receives, appropriates, purchases or sells cattle that are found astray, or
- (*b*) fraudulently, in whole or in part,
  - (i) obliterates, alters or defaces a brand or mark on cattle, or
  - (ii) makes a false or counterfeit brand or mark on cattle.

(2) Every person who commits theft of cattle is guilty of

- (*a*) an indictable offence and liable to imprisonment for a term of not more than 10 years; or
- (*b*) an offence punishable on summary conviction.

(3) In any proceedings under this Act, evidence that cattle are marked with a brand or mark that is recorded or registered in accordance with any Act is, in the absence of any evidence to the contrary, proof that the cattle are owned by the registered owner of that brand or mark.

(4) Where an accused is charged with an offence under subsection (1) or (2), the burden of proving that the cattle came lawfully into the possession of the accused or his employee or into the possession of another person on behalf of the accused is on the accused, if the accused is not the registered owner of the brand or mark with which the cattle are marked, unless that it appears that possession of the cattle by an employee of the accused or by another person on behalf of the accused was without the knowledge and authority, sanction or approval of the accused. R.S., c. C-34, s. 298; 1974-75-76, c. 93, s. 26; 2019, c. 25, s. 123.

TAKING POSSESSION, ETC., OF DRIFT TIMBER / Dealer in second-hand goods / Search for timber unlawfully detained / Evidence of property in timber / Presumption from possession / Definitions / "coastal waters of Canada" / "lumber" / "lumbering equipment".

339. (1) Every person is guilty of an indictable offence and liable to imprisonment for a term of not more than five years or is guilty of an offence punishable on summary conviction who, without the consent of the owner,

   (*a*) fraudulently takes, holds, keeps in their possession, conceals, receives, appropriates, purchases or sells any lumber or lumbering equipment that is found adrift, cast ashore or lying on or embedded in the bed or bottom, or on the bank or beach, of a river, stream or lake in Canada, or in the harbours or any of the coastal waters of Canada;

   (*b*) removes, alters, obliterates or defaces a mark or number on such lumber or lumbering equipment; or

   (*c*) refuses to deliver such lumber or lumbering equipment up to the owner or to the person in charge of it on behalf of the owner or to a person authorized by the owner to receive it.

(2) Every one who, being a dealer in second-hand goods of any kind, trades or traffics in or has in his possession for sale or traffic any lumbering equipment that is marked with the mark, brand, registered timber mark, name or initials of a person, without the written consent of that person, is guilty of an offence punishable on summary conviction.

(3) A peace officer who suspects, on reasonable grounds, that any lumber owned by any person and bearing the registered timber mark of that person is kept or detained in or on any place without the knowledge or consent of that person, may enter into or on that place to ascertain whether or not it is detained there without the knowledge or consent of that person.

(4) Where any lumber or lumbering equipment is marked with a timber mark or a boom chain brand registered under any Act, the mark or brand is, in proceedings under subsection (1), and, in the absence of any evidence to the contrary, proof that it is the property of the registered owner of the mark or brand.

(5) Where an accused or his servants or agents are in possession of lumber or lumbering equipment marked with the mark, brand, registered timber mark, name or initials of another person, the burden of proving that it came lawfully into his possession or into possession of his servants or agents is, in proceedings under subsection (1), on the accused.

(6) In this section,

"coastal waters of Canada" includes all of Queen Charlotte Sound, all of the Strait of Georgia and the Canadian waters of the Strait of Juan de Fuca;

"lumber" means timber, mast, spar, shingle bolt, sawlog or lumber of any description;

"lumbering equipment" includes a boom chain, chain, line and shackle. R.S., c. C-34, s. 299; 2019, c. 25, s. 124.

DESTROYING DOCUMENTS OF TITLE.

340. Every person is guilty of an indictable offence and liable to imprisonment for a term of not more than 10 years or is guilty of an offence punishable on summary conviction who, for a fraudulent purpose, destroys, cancels, conceals or obliterates

 (a) a document of title to goods or lands,

 (b) a valuable security or testamentary instrument, or

 (c) a judicial or official document. R.S., c. C-34, s. 300; 2019, c. 25, s. 125.

FRAUDULENT CONCEALMENT.

341. Every person who, for a fraudulent purpose, takes, obtains, removes or conceals anything is guilty of

 (a) an indictable offence and liable to imprisonment for a term of not more than two years; or

 (b) an offence punishable on summary conviction. R.S., c. C-34, s. 301; 2019, c. 25, s. 126.

THEFT, FORGERY, ETC., OF CREDIT CARD / Jurisdiction / Unauthorized use of credit card data / Definitions.

342. (1) Every person who

 (a) steals a credit card,

 (b) forges or falsifies a credit card,

 (c) possesses, uses or traffics in a credit card or a forged or falsified credit card, knowing that it was obtained, made or altered

   (i) by the commission in Canada of an offence, or

   (ii) by an act or omission anywhere that, if it had occurred in Canada, would have constituted an offence, or

 (d) uses a credit card knowing that it has been revoked or cancelled,

is guilty of

 (e) an indictable offence and is liable to imprisonment for a term not exceeding ten years, or

 (f) an offence punishable on summary conviction.

(2) An accused who is charged with an offence under subsection (1) may be tried and punished by any court having jurisdiction to try that offence in the place where the offence is alleged to have been committed or in the place where the accused is found, is arrested or is in custody, but where the place where the accused is found, is arrested or is in custody is outside the province in which the offence is alleged to have been committed, no proceedings in respect of that offence shall be commenced in that place without the consent of the Attorney General of that province.

(3) [*Repealed* (old provision), R.S.C. 1985, c. 27 (1st Supp.), s. 44.]

(3) Every person who, fraudulently and without colour of right, possesses, uses, traffics in or permits another person to use credit card data, including personal authentication information, whether or not the data is authentic, that would enable a person to use a credit card or to obtain the services that are provided by the issuer of a credit card to credit card holders is guilty of

    (*a*) an indictable offence and is liable to imprisonment for a term not exceeding ten years; or

    (*b*) an offence punishable on summary conviction.

(4) In this section,

"personal authentication information" means a personal identification number or any other password or information that a credit card holder creates or adopts to be used to authenticate his or her identity in relation to the credit card;

"traffic" means, in relation to a credit card or credit card data, to sell, export from or import into Canada, distribute or deal with in any other way. 1974-75-76, c. 93, s. 27; R.S.C. 1985, c. 27 (1st Supp.), s. 44; 1997, c. 18, s. 16; 2009, c. 28, s. 4.

INSTRUMENTS FOR COPYING CREDIT CARD DATA OR FORGING OR FALSIFYING CREDIT CARDS / Forfeiture / Limitation.

342.01 (1) Every person is guilty of an indictable offence and liable to imprisonment for a term of not more than 10 years, or is guilty of an offence punishable on summary conviction, who, without lawful justification or excuse, makes, repairs, buys, sells, exports from Canada, imports into Canada or possesses any instrument, device, apparatus, material or thing that they know has been used or know is adapted or intended for use

    (*a*) in the copying of credit card data for use in the commission of an offence under subsection 342(3); or

    (*b*) in the forging or falsifying of credit cards.

(2) Where a person is convicted of an offence under subsection (1), any instrument, device, apparatus, material or thing in relation to which the offence was committed or the possession of which constituted the offence may, in addition to any other punishment that may be imposed, be ordered forfeited to Her Majesty, whereupon it may be disposed of as the Attorney General directs.

(3) No order of forfeiture may be made under subsection (2) in respect of any thing that is the property of a person who was not a party to the offence under subsection (1). 1997, c. 18, s. 17; 2009, c. 28, s. 5.

UNAUTHORIZED USE OF COMPUTER / Definitions / "computer password" / "computer program" / "computer service" / "computer system" / "data" / "electro-magnetic, acoustic, mechanical or other device" / "function" / "intercept" / "traffic".

342.1 (1) Everyone is guilty of an indictable offence and liable to imprisonment for a term of not more than 10 years, or is guilty of an offence punishable on summary conviction who, fraudulently and without colour of right,

    (*a*) obtains, directly or indirectly, any computer service;

    (*b*) by means of an electro-magnetic, acoustic, mechanical or other device, intercepts or causes to be intercepted, directly or indirectly, any function of a computer system;

    (*c*) uses or causes to be used, directly or indirectly, a computer system with intent to commit an offence under paragraph (*a*) or (*b*) or under section 430 in relation to computer data or a computer system; or

    (*d*) uses, possesses, traffics in or permits another person to have access to a computer password that would enable a person to commit an offence under paragraph (*a*), (*b*) or (*c*).

(2) In this section,

"computer data" means representations, including signs, signals or symbols, that are in a form suitable for processing in a computer system;

"computer password" means any computer data by which a computer service or computer system is capable of being obtained or used;

"computer program" means computer data representing instructions or statements that, when executed in a computer system, causes the computer system to perform a function;

"computer service" includes data processing and the storage or retrieval of computer data;

"computer system" means a device that, or a group of interconnected or related devices one or more of which,

    (*a*) contains computer programs or other computer data, and

    (*b*) by means of computer programs,

        (i) performs logic and control, and

        (ii) may perform any other function;

"data" [*Repealed.* 2014, c. 31, s. 16(2).]

"electro-magnetic, acoustic, mechanical or other device" means any device or apparatus that is used or is capable of being used to intercept any function of a computer system, but does not include a hearing aid used to correct subnormal hearing of the user to not better than normal hearing;

"function" includes logic, control, arithmetic, deletion, storage and retrieval and communication or telecommunication to, from or within a computer system;

"intercept" includes listen to or record a function of a computer system, or acquire the substance, meaning or purport thereof.

"traffic" means, in respect of a computer password, to sell, export from or import into Canada, distribute or deal with in any other way. R.S.C. 1985, c. 27 (1st Supp.), s. 45; 1997, c. 18, s. 18; 2014, c. 31, s. 16.

POSSESSION OF DEVICE TO OBTAIN UNAUTHORIZED USE OF COMPUTER SYSTEM OR TO COMMIT MISCHIEF / Forfeiture / Limitation / Definition of "device".

342.2 (1) Every person who, without lawful excuse, makes, possesses, sells, offers for sale, imports, obtains for use, distributes or makes available a device that is designed or adapted primarily to commit an offence under section 342.1 or 430, knowing that the device has been or is intended to be used to commit such an offence, is

(a) guilty of an indictable offence and liable to imprisonment for a term of not more than two years; or

(b) guilty of an offence punishable on summary conviction.

(2) If a person is convicted of an offence under subsection (1), in addition to any punishment that is imposed, any device in relation to which the offence was committed or the possession of which constituted the offence may be ordered forfeited to Her Majesty and may be disposed of as the Attorney General directs.

(3) No order of forfeiture may be made under subsection (2) in respect of any thing that is the property of a person who was not a party to the offence under subsection (1).

(4) In this section, "device" includes

(a) a component of a device; and

(b) a computer program within the meaning of subsection 342.1(2). 1997, c. 18, s. 19; 2014, c. 31, s. 17; 2018, c. 29, s. 34.

Robbery and Extortion

ROBBERY.

343. Every one commits robbery who

(a) steals, and for the purpose of extorting whatever is stolen or to prevent or overcome resistance to the stealing, uses violence or threats of violence to a person or property;

(b) steals from any person and, at the time he steals or immediately before or immediately thereafter, wounds, beats, strikes or uses any personal violence to that person;

(c) assaults any person with intent to steal from him; or

(d) steals from any person while armed with an offensive weapon or imitation thereof. R.S., c. C-34, s. 302.

ROBBERY / Subsequent offences / Sequence of convictions only.

344. (1) Every person who commits robbery is guilty of an indictable offence and liable

(a) if a restricted firearm or prohibited firearm is used in the commission of the offence or if any firearm is used in the commission of the offence and the offence is committed for the benefit of, at the direction of, or in association with, a criminal organization, to imprisonment for life and to a minimum punishment of imprisonment for a term of

(i) in the case of a first offence, five years, and

(ii) in the case of a second or subsequent offence, seven years;

(a.1) in any other case where a firearm is used in the commission of the offence, to imprisonment for life and to a minimum punishment of imprisonment for a term of four years; and

(b) in any other case, to imprisonment for life.

CODE

(2) In determining, for the purpose of paragraph (1)(*a*), whether a convicted person has committed a second or subsequent offence, if the person was earlier convicted of any of the following offences, that offence is to be considered as an earlier offence:

(*a*) an offence under this section;

(*b*) an offence under subsection 85(1) or (2) or section 244 or 244.2; or

(*c*) an offence under section 220, 236, 239, 272 or 273, subsection 279(1) or section 279.1 or 346 if a firearm was used in the commission of the offence.

However, an earlier offence shall not be taken into account if 10 years have elapsed between the day on which the person was convicted of the earlier offence and the day on which the person was convicted of the offence for which sentence is being imposed, not taking into account any time in custody.

(3) For the purposes of subsection (2), the only question to be considered is the sequence of convictions and no consideration shall be given to the sequence of commission of offences or whether any offence occurred before or after any conviction. R.S., c. C-34, s. 303; 1972, c. 13, s. 70; 1995, c. 39, s. 149; 2008, c. 6, s. 32; 2009, c. 22, s. 14.

STOPPING MAIL WITH INTENT.

345. Every one who stops a mail conveyance with intent to rob or search it is guilty of an indictable offence and liable to imprisonment for life. R.S., c. C-34, s. 304.

EXTORTION / Punishment / Subsequent offences / Sequence of convictions only / Saving.

346. (1) Every one commits extortion who, without reasonable justification or excuse and with intent to obtain anything, by threats, accusations, menaces or violence induces or attempts to induce any person, whether or not he is the person threatened, accused or menaced or to whom violence is shown, to do anything or cause anything to be done.

(1.1) Every person who commits extortion is guilty of an indictable offence and liable

(*a*) if a restricted firearm or prohibited firearm is used in the commission of the offence or if any firearm is used in the commission of the offence and the offence is committed for the benefit of, at the direction of, or in association with, a criminal organization, to imprisonment for life and to a minimum punishment of imprisonment for a term of

(i) in the case of a first offence, five years, and

(ii) in the case of a second or subsequent offence, seven years;

(*a*.1) in any other case where a firearm is used in the commission of the offence, to imprisonment for life and to a minimum punishment of imprisonment for a term of four years; and

(*b*) in any other case, to imprisonment for life.

(1.2) In determining, for the purpose of paragraph (1.1)(*a*), whether a convicted person has committed a second or subsequent offence, if the person was earlier convicted of any of the following offences, that offence is to be considered as an earlier offence:

(*a*) an offence under this section;

(*b*) an offence under subsection 85(1) or (2) or section 244 or 244.2; or

(*c*) an offence under section 220, 236, 239, 272 or 273, subsection 279(1) or section 279.1 or 344 if a firearm was used in the commission of the offence.

However, an earlier offence shall not be taken into account if 10 years have elapsed between the day on which the person was convicted of the earlier offence and the day on which the person was convicted of the offence for which sentence is being imposed, not taking into account any time in custody.

(1.3) For the purposes of subsection (1.2), the only question to be considered is the sequence of convictions and no consideration shall be given to the sequence of commission of offences or whether any offence occurred before or after any conviction.

(2) A threat to institute civil proceedings is not a threat for the purposes of this section. R.S., c. C-34, s. 305; R.S.C. 1985, c. 27 (1st Supp.), s. 46; 1995, c. 39, s. 150; 2008, c. 6, s. 33; 2009, c. 22, s. 15.

Criminal Interest Rate

CRIMINAL INTEREST RATE / Definitions / "credit advanced" / "criminal rate" / "insurance charge" / "interest" / "official fee" / "overdraft charge" / "required deposit balance" / Presumption / Proof of effective annual rate / Notice / Cross-examination with leave / Consent required for proceedings / Application.

347. (1) Despite any other Act of Parliament, every one who enters into an agreement or arrangement to receive interest at a criminal rate, or receives a payment or partial payment of interest at a criminal rate, is

(*a*) guilty of an indictable offence and liable to imprisonment for a term not exceeding five years; or

(*b*) guilty of an offence punishable on summary conviction and liable to a fine of not more than $25,000 or to imprisonment for a term of not more than two years less a day, or to both.

(*c*) [*Repealed*, 2007, c. 9, s. 1.]

(*d*) [*Repealed*, 2007, c. 9, s. 1.]

(2) In this section,

"credit advanced" means the aggregate of the money and the monetary value of any goods, services or benefits actually advanced or to be advanced under an agreement or arrangement minus the aggregate of any required deposit balance and any fee, fine, penalty, commission and other similar charge or expense directly or indirectly incurred under the original or any collateral agreement or arrangement;

"criminal rate" means an effective annual rate of interest calculated in accordance with generally accepted actuarial practices and principles that exceeds sixty per cent on the credit advanced under an agreement or arrangement;

"insurance charge" means the cost of insuring the risk assumed by the person who advances or is to advance credit under an agreement or arrangement, where the face amount of the insurance does not exceed the credit advanced;

"interest" means the aggregate of all charges and expenses, whether in the form of a fee, fine, penalty, commission or other similar charge or expense or in any other form, paid or payable for the advancing of credit under an agreement or arrangement, by or on behalf of the person to whom the credit is or is to be advanced, irrespective of the person to whom any such charges and expenses are or are to be paid or payable, but does not include any repayment of credit advanced or any insurance charge, official fee, overdraft charge, required deposit balance or, in the case of a mortgage transaction, any amount required to be paid on account of property taxes;

"official fee" means a fee required by law to be paid to any governmental authority in connection with perfecting any security under an agreement or arrangement for the advancing of credit;

"overdraft charge" means a charge not exceeding five dollars for the creation of or increase in an overdraft, imposed by a credit union or caisse populaire the membership of which is wholly or substantially comprised of natural persons or a deposit taking institution the deposits in which are insured, in whole or in part, by the Canada Deposit Insurance Corporation or guaranteed, in whole or in part, by the Quebec Deposit Insurance Board;

"required deposit balance" means a fixed or an ascertainable amount of the money actually advanced or to be advanced under an agreement or arrangement that is required, as a condition of the agreement or arrangement, to be deposited or invested by or on behalf of the person to whom the advance is or is to be made and that may be available, in the event of his defaulting in any payment, to or for the benefit of the person who advances or is to advance the money.

(3) Where a person receives a payment or partial payment of interest at a criminal rate, he shall, in the absence of evidence to the contrary, be deemed to have knowledge of the nature of the payment and that it was received at a criminal rate.

(4) In any proceedings under this section, a certificate of a Fellow of the Canadian Institute of Actuaries stating that he has calculated the effective annual rate of interest on any credit advanced under an agreement or arrangement and setting out the calculations and the information on which they are based is, in the absence of evidence to the contrary, proof of the effective annual rate without proof of the signature or official character of the person appearing to have signed the certificate.

(5) A certificate referred to in subsection (4) shall not be received in evidence unless the party intending to produce it has given to the accused or defendant reasonable notice of that intention together with a copy of the certificate.

(6) An accused or a defendant against whom a certificate referred to in subsection (4) is produced may, with leave of the court, require the attendance of the actuary for the purposes of cross-examination.

(7) No proceedings shall be commenced under this section without the consent of the Attorney General.

(8) This section does not apply to any transaction to which the *Tax Rebate Discounting Act* applies. 1980-81-82-83, c. 43, s. 9; 2007, c. 9, s. 1; 2019, c. 25, s. 127.

DEFINITIONS / "interest" / "payday loan" / Non-application / Designation of province / Revocation.

347.1 (1) The following definitions apply in subsection (2).

"interest" has the same meaning as in subsection 347(2).

"payday loan" means an advancement of money in exchange for a post-dated cheque, a pre-authorized debit or a future payment of a similar nature but not for any guarantee, suretyship, overdraft protection or security on property and not through a margin loan, pawnbroking, a line of credit or a credit card.

(2) Section 347 and section 2 of the *Interest Act* do not apply to a person, other than a financial institution within the meaning of paragraphs (*a*) to (*d*) of the definition "financial institution" in section 2 of the *Bank Act*, in respect of a payday loan agreement entered into by the person to receive interest, or in respect of interest received by that person under the agreement, if

    (*a*) the amount of money advanced under the agreement is $1,500 or less and the term of the agreement is 62 days or less;

    (*b*) the person is licensed or otherwise specifically authorized under the laws of a province to enter into the agreement; and

    (*c*) the province is designated under subsection (3).

(3) The Governor in Council shall, by order and at the request of the lieutenant governor in council of a province, designate the province for the purposes of this section if the province has legislative measures that protect recipients of payday loans and that provide for limits on the total cost of borrowing under the agreements.

(4) The Governor in Council shall, by order, revoke the designation made under subsection (3) if requested to do so by the lieutenant governor in council of the province or if the legislative measures described in that subsection are no longer in force in that province. 2007, c. 9, s. 2.

Breaking and Entering

BREAKING AND ENTERING WITH INTENT, COMMITTING OFFENCE OR BREAKING OUT / Presumptions / Definition of "place".

348. (1) Every one who

(a) breaks and enters a place with intent to commit an indictable offence therein,

(b) breaks and enters a place and commits an indictable offence therein, or

(c) breaks out of a place after

    (i) committing an indictable offence therein, or

    (ii) entering the place with intent to commit an indictable offence therein,

is guilty

(d) if the offence is committed in relation to a dwelling-house, of an indictable offence and liable to imprisonment for life, and

(e) if the offence is committed in relation to a place other than a dwelling-house, of an indictable offence and liable to imprisonment for a term not exceeding ten years or of an offence punishable on summary conviction.

(2) For the purposes of proceedings under this section, evidence that an accused

(a) broke and entered a place or attempted to break and enter a place is, in the absence of evidence to the contrary, proof that he broke and entered the place or attempted to do so, as the case may be, with intent to commit an indictable offence therein; or

(b) broke out of a place is, in the absence of any evidence to the contrary, proof that he broke out after

    (i) committing an indictable offence therein, or

    (ii) entering with intent to commit an indictable offence therein.

(3) For the purposes of this section and section 351, "place" means

(a) a dwelling-house;

(b) a building or structure or any part thereof, other than a dwelling-house;

(c) a railway vehicle, a vessel, an aircraft or a trailer; or

(d) a pen or an enclosure in which fur-bearing animals are kept in captivity for breeding or commercial purposes. R.S., c. C-34, s. 306; 1972, c. 13, s. 24; R.S.C. 1985, c. 27 (1st Supp.), s. 47; 1997, c. 18, s. 20.

AGGRAVATING CIRCUMSTANCE — HOME INVASION.

348.1 If a person is convicted of an offence under section 98 or 98.1, subsection 279(2) or section 343, 346 or 348 in relation to a dwelling-house, the court imposing the sentence on the person shall consider as an aggravating circumstance the fact that the dwelling-house was occupied at the time of the commission of the offence and that the person, in committing the offence,

(a) knew that or was reckless as to whether the dwelling-house was occupied; and

(b) used violence or threats of violence to a person or property. 2002, c. 13, s. 15; 2008, c. 6, s. 34.

BEING UNLAWFULLY IN DWELLING-HOUSE / Presumption.

349. (1) Every person who, without lawful excuse, enters or is in a dwelling-house with intent to commit an indictable offence in it is guilty of an indictable offence and liable to imprisonment for a term of not more than 10 years or of an offence punishable on summary conviction.

(2) For the purposes of proceedings under this section, evidence that an accused, without lawful excuse, entered or was in a dwelling-house is, in the absence of any evidence to the contrary, proof that he entered or was in the dwelling-house with intent to commit an indictable offence therein. R.S., c. C-34, s. 307; 1997, c. 18, s. 21; 2018, c. 29, s. 35.

ENTRANCE.

350. For the purposes of sections 348 and 349,

    (a) a person enters as soon as any part of his body or any part of an instrument that he uses is within any thing that is being entered; and

    (b) a person shall be deemed to have broken and entered if

        (i) he obtained entrance by a threat or artifice or by collusion with a person within, or

        (ii) he entered without lawful justification or excuse by a permanent or temporary opening. R.S., c. C-34, s. 308; 2018, c. 29, s. 36.

POSSESSION OF BREAK-IN INSTRUMENT / Disguise with intent.

351. (1) Every person who, without lawful excuse, has in their possession any instrument suitable for the purpose of breaking into any place, motor vehicle, vault or safe knowing that the instrument has been used or is intended to be used for that purpose,

    (a) is guilty of an indictable offence and liable to imprisonment for a term not exceeding ten years; or

    (b) is guilty of an offence punishable on summary conviction.

(2) Every person who, with intent to commit an indictable offence, has their face masked or coloured or is otherwise disguised is guilty of

    (a) an indictable offence and liable to imprisonment for a term of not more than 10 years; or

    (b) an offence punishable on summary conviction. R.S., c. C-34, s. 309; 1972, c. 13, s. 25; R.S.C. 1985, c. 27 (1st Supp.), s. 48; 2008, c. 18, s. 9; 2018, c. 29, s. 37; 2019, c. 25, s. 128.

POSSESSION OF INSTRUMENTS FOR BREAKING INTO COIN-OPERATED OR CURRENCY EXCHANGE DEVICES.

352. Every person who, without lawful excuse, has in their possession any instrument suitable for the purpose of breaking into a coin-operated device or a currency exchange device, knowing that the instrument has been used or is or was intended to be used for that purpose, is guilty of

    (a) an indictable offence and liable to imprisonment for a term of not more than two years; or

    (b) an offence punishable on summary conviction. R.S., c. C-34, s. 310; 1972, c. 13, s. 26; 1974-75-76, c. 93, s. 28; 2018, c. 29, s. 38; 2019, c. 25, s. 129.

SELLING, ETC., AUTOMOBILE MASTER KEY / Exception / Terms and conditions of licence / Fees / Record to be kept / Failure to comply with subsection (3) / Definitions / "automobile master key" / "licence".

353. (1) Every person is guilty of an indictable offence and liable to imprisonment for a term of not more than two years or is guilty of an offence punishable on summary conviction who

(a) sells, offers for sale or advertises in a province an automobile master key otherwise than under the authority of a licence issued by the Attorney General of that province, or

(b) purchases or has in his possession in a province an automobile master key otherwise than under the authority of a licence issued by the Attorney General of that province.

(1.1) A police officer specially authorized by the chief of the police force to possess an automobile master key is not guilty of an offence under subsection (1) by reason only that the police officer possesses an automobile master key for the purposes of the execution of the police officer's duties.

(2) A licence issued by the Attorney General of a province as described in paragraph (1)(a) or (b) may contain such terms and conditions relating to the sale, offering for sale, advertising, purchasing, having in possession or use of an automobile master key as the Attorney General of that province may prescribe.

(2.1) The Attorney General of a province may prescribe fees for the issue or renewal of licences as described in paragraph (1)(a) or (b).

(3) Every one who sells an automobile master key

(a) shall keep a record of the transaction showing the name and address of the purchaser and particulars of the licence issued to the purchaser as described in paragraph (1)(b); and

(b) shall produce the record for inspection at the request of a peace officer.

(4) Every one who fails to comply with subsection (3) is guilty of an offence punishable on summary conviction.

(5) The definitions in this subsection apply in this section.

"automobile master key" includes a key, pick, rocker key or other instrument designed or adapted to operate the ignition or other switches or locks of a series of motor vehicles.

"licence" includes any authorization.R.S., c. C-34, s. 311; 1997, c. 18, s. 22; 2019, c. 25, s. 130.

TAMPERING WITH VEHICLE IDENTIFICATION NUMBER / Definition of "vehicle identification number" / Exception / Punishment.

353.1 (1) Every person commits an offence who, without lawful excuse, wholly or partially alters, removes or obliterates a vehicle identification number on a motor vehicle.

(2) For the purpose of this section, "vehicle identification number" means any number or other mark placed on a motor vehicle for the purpose of distinguishing it from other similar motor vehicles.

(3) Despite subsection (1), it is not an offence to wholly or partially alter, remove or obliterate a vehicle identification number on a motor vehicle during regular maintenance or any repair or other work done on the vehicle for a legitimate purpose, including a modification of the vehicle.

(4) Every person who commits an offence under subsection (1)
- (*a*) is guilty of an indictable offence and liable to imprisonment for a term of not more than five years; or
- (*b*) is guilty of an offence punishable on summary conviction. 2010, c. 14, s. 4.

CODE

Possession and Trafficking   2010, c. 14, s. 5.

POSSESSION OF PROPERTY OBTAINED BY CRIME / Obliterated vehicle identification number / Definition of "vehicle identification number" / Exception.

354. (1) Every one commits an offence who has in his possession any property or thing or any proceeds of any property or thing knowing that all or part of the property or thing or of the proceeds was obtained by or derived directly or indirectly from
- (*a*) the commission in Canada of an offence punishable by indictment; or
- (*b*) an act or omission anywhere that, if it had occurred in Canada, would have constituted an offence punishable by indictment.

(2) In proceedings in respect of an offence under subsection (1), evidence that a person has in their possession a motor vehicle the vehicle identification number of which has been wholly or partially removed or obliterated or a part of a motor vehicle being a part bearing a vehicle identification number that has been wholly or partially removed or obliterated is, in the absence of any evidence to the contrary, proof that the motor vehicle or part, as the case may be, was obtained,
- (*a*) by the commission in Canada of an offence punishable by indictment; or
- (*b*) by an act or omission anywhere that, if it had occurred in Canada, would have constituted an offence punishable by indictment.

(3) For the purposes of subsection (2), "vehicle identification number" means any number or other mark placed on a motor vehicle for the purpose of distinguishing the motor vehicle from other similar motor vehicles.

(4) A peace officer or a person acting under the direction of a peace officer is not guilty of an offence under this section by reason only that the peace officer or person possesses property or a thing or the proceeds of property or a thing mentioned in subsection (1) for the purposes of an investigation or otherwise in the execution of the peace officer's duties. R.S., c. C-34, s. 312; 1972, c. 13, s. 27; 1974-75-76, c. 93, s. 29; 1997, c. 18, s. 23; 2018, c. 29, s. 39.

PUNISHMENT.

355. Every one who commits an offence under section 354

    (a) if the subject matter of the offence is a testamentary instrument or the value of the subject matter of the offence is more than $5,000, is guilty of

        (i) an indictable offence and liable to imprisonment for a term of not more than 10 years, or

        (ii) an offence punishable on summary conviction; or

    (b) if the value of the subject matter of the offence is not more than $5,000, is guilty

        (i) of an indictable offence and liable to imprisonment for a term not exceeding two years, or

        (ii) of an offence punishable on summary conviction. R.S., c. C-34, s. 313; 1972, c. 13, s. 28; 1974-75-76, c. 93, s. 30; R.S.C. 1985, c. 27 (1st Supp.), s. 49; 1994, c. 44, s. 21; 2019, c. 25, s. 131.

DEFINITION OF "TRAFFIC".

355.1 For the purposes of sections 355.2 and 355.4, "traffic" means to sell, give, transfer, transport, export from Canada, import into Canada, send, deliver or deal with in any other way, or to offer to do any of those acts. 2010, c. 14, s. 6.

TRAFFICKING IN PROPERTY OBTAINED BY CRIME.

355.2 Everyone commits an offence who traffics in any property or thing or any proceeds of any property or thing knowing that all or part of the property, thing or proceeds was obtained by or derived directly or indirectly from

    (a) the commission in Canada of an offence punishable by indictment; or

    (b) an act or omission anywhere that, if it had occurred in Canada, would have constituted an offence punishable by indictment. 2010, c. 14, s. 6.

IN REM PROHIBITION.

355.3 The importation into Canada or exportation from Canada of any property or thing or any proceeds of any property or thing is prohibited if all or part of the property, thing or proceeds was obtained by or derived directly or indirectly from

    (a) the commission in Canada of an offence punishable by indictment; or

    (b) an act or omission anywhere that, if it had occurred in Canada, would have constituted an offence punishable by indictment. 2010, c. 14, s. 6.

POSSESSION OF PROPERTY OBTAINED BY CRIME — TRAFFICKING.

355.4 Everyone commits an offence who has in their possession, for the purpose of trafficking, any property or thing or any proceeds of any property or thing knowing that all or part of the property, thing or proceeds was obtained by or derived directly or indirectly from

    (a) the commission in Canada of an offence punishable by indictment; or

    (b) an act or omission anywhere that, if it had occurred in Canada, would have constituted an offence punishable by indictment. 2010, c. 14, s. 6.

PUNISHMENT.

355.5 Everyone who commits an offence under section 355.2 or 355.4

(a) is, if the value of the subject matter of the offence is more than $5,000, guilty of an indictable offence and liable to imprisonment for a term of not more than 14 years; or

(b) is, if the value of the subject matter of the offence is not more than $5,000,

(i) guilty of an indictable offence and liable to imprisonment for a term of not more than five years, or

(ii) guilty of an offence punishable on summary conviction. 2010, c. 14, s. 6.

CODE

THEFT FROM MAIL / Allegation of value not necessary / Punishment.

356. (1) Everyone commits an offence who

(a) steals

(i) anything sent by post, after it is deposited at a post office and before it is delivered, or after it is delivered but before it is in the possession of the addressee or of a person who may reasonably be considered to be authorized by the addressee to receive mail,

(ii) a bag, sack or other container or covering in which mail is conveyed, whether or not it contains mail, or

(iii) a key suited to a lock adopted for use by the Canada Post Corporation;

(a.1) with intent to commit an offence under paragraph (a), makes, possesses or uses a copy of a key suited to a lock adopted for use by the Canada Post Corporation, or a key suited to obtaining access to a receptacle or device provided for the receipt of mail;

(b) has in their possession anything that they know has been used to commit an offence under paragraph (a) or (a.1) or anything in respect of which they know that such an offence has been committed; or

(c) fraudulently redirects, or causes to be redirected, anything sent by post.

(2) In proceedings for an offence under this section it is not necessary to allege in the indictment or to prove on the trial that anything in respect of which the offence was committed had any value.

(3) Everyone who commits an offence under subsection (1)

(a) is guilty of an indictable offence and liable to imprisonment for a term of not more than 10 years; or

(b) is guilty of an offence punishable on summary conviction. R.S., c. C-34, s. 314; 1980-81-82-83, c. 54, s. 56; 2009, c. 28, s. 6.

BRINGING INTO CANADA PROPERTY OBTAINED BY CRIME.

357. Every person who brings into or has in Canada anything that they have obtained outside Canada by an act that, if it had been committed in Canada, would have been the offence of theft or an offence under section 342 or 354 is guilty of

(a) an indictable offence and liable to imprisonment for a term of not more than 10 years; or

(b)   an offence punishable on summary conviction. R.S., c. C-34, s. 315; R.S.C. 1985, c. 27 (1st Supp.), s. 50; 2019, c. 25, s. 132.

HAVING IN POSSESSION WHEN COMPLETE.

358. For the purposes of sections 342 and 354 and paragraph 356(1)(b), the offence of having in possession is complete when a person has, alone or jointly with another person, possession of or control over anything mentioned in those sections or when he aids in concealing or disposing of it, as the case may be. R.S., c. C-34, s. 316; R.S.C. 1985, c. 27 (1st Supp.), s. 50.

359. [*Repealed*, 2018, c. 29, s. 40.]

360. [*Repealed*, 2018, c. 29, s. 40.]

False Pretences

FALSE PRETENCE / Exaggeration / Question of fact.

361. (1) A false pretence is a representation of a matter of fact either present or past, made by words or otherwise, that is known by the person who makes it to be false and that is made with a fraudulent intent to induce the person to whom it is made to act on it.

(2) Exaggerated commendation or depreciation of the quality of anything is not a false pretence unless it is carried to such an extent that it amounts to a fraudulent misrepresentation of fact.

(3) For the purposes of subsection (2) it is a question of fact whether commendation or depreciation amounts to a fraudulent misrepresentation of fact. R.S., c. C-34, s. 319.

FALSE PRETENCE OR FALSE STATEMENT / Punishment / Idem / Presumption from cheque issued without funds / Definition of "cheque".

362. (1) Every one commits an offence who
  (a)   by a false pretence, whether directly or through the medium of a contract obtained by a false pretence, obtains anything in respect of which the offence of theft may be committed or causes it to be delivered to another person;
  (b)   obtains credit by a false pretence or by fraud;
  (c)   knowingly makes or causes to be made, directly or indirectly, a false statement in writing with intent that it should be relied on, with respect to the financial condition or means or ability to pay of himself or herself or any person or organization that he or she is interested in or that he or she acts for, for the purpose of procuring, in any form whatever, whether for his or her benefit or the benefit of that person or organization,
      (i)   the delivery of personal property,
      (ii)   the payment of money,

    (iii) the making of a loan,

    (iv) the grant or extension of credit,

    (v) the discount of an account receivable, or

    (vi) the making, accepting, discounting or endorsing of a bill of exchange, cheque, draft, or promissory note; or

  (*d*) knowing that a false statement in writing has been made with respect to the financial condition or means or ability to pay of himself or herself or another person or organization that he or she is interested in or that he or she acts for, procures on the faith of that statement, whether for his or her benefit or for the benefit of that person or organization, anything mentioned in subparagraphs (*c*)(i) to (vi).

(2) Every one who commits an offence under paragraph (1)(*a*)

  (*a*) if the property obtained is a testamentary instrument or the value of what is obtained is more than $5,000, is guilty of

    (i) an indictable offence and liable to imprisonment for a term of not more than 10 years, or

    (ii) an offence punishable on summary conviction; or

  (*b*) if the value of what is obtained is not more than $5,000, is guilty

    (i) of an indictable offence and liable to imprisonment for a term not exceeding two years, or

    (ii) of an offence punishable on summary conviction.

(3) Every person who commits an offence under paragraph (1)(*b*), (*c*) or (*d*) is guilty of

  (*a*) an indictable offence and liable to imprisonment for a term of not more than 10 years; or

  (*b*) an offence punishable on summary conviction.

(4) Where, in proceedings under paragraph (1)(*a*), it is shown that anything was obtained by the accused by means of a cheque that, when presented for payment within a reasonable time, was dishonoured on the ground that no funds or insufficient funds were on deposit to the credit of the accused in the bank or other institution on which the cheque was drawn, it shall be presumed to have been obtained by a false pretence, unless the court is satisfied by evidence that when the accused issued the cheque he believed on reasonable grounds that it would be honoured if presented for payment within a reasonable time after it was issued.

(5) In this section, "cheque" includes, in addition to its ordinary meaning, a bill of exchange drawn on any institution that makes it a business practice to honour bills of exchange or any particular kind thereof drawn on it by depositors. R.S., c. C-34, s. 320; 1972, c. 13, s. 29; 1974-75-76, c. 93, s. 31; R.S.C. 1985, c. 27 (1st Supp.), s. 52; 1994, c. 44, s. 22; 2003, c. 21, s. 5; 2019, c. 25, s. 133.

OBTAINING EXECUTION OF VALUABLE SECURITY BY FRAUD.

363. Every person is guilty of an indictable offence and liable to imprisonment for a term of not more than five years or is guilty of an offence punishable on summary conviction who, with intent to defraud or injure another person, by a false pretence causes or induces any person (*a*) to execute, make, accept, endorse or destroy the whole or any part of a valuable security, or

   (*b*) to write, impress or affix a name or seal on any paper or parchment in order that it may afterwards be made or converted into or used or dealt with as a valuable security. R.S., c. C-34, s. 321; 2019, c. 25, s. 134.

FRAUDULENTLY OBTAINING FOOD, BEVERAGE OR ACCOMMODATION / Presumption / Definition of "cheque".

364. (1) Every one who fraudulently obtains food, a beverage or accommodation at any place that is in the business of providing those things is guilty of an offence punishable on summary conviction

(2) In proceedings under this section, evidence that the accused obtained food, a beverage or accommodation at a place that is in the business of providing those things and did not pay for it and

   (*a*) made a false or fictitious show or pretence of having baggage,

   (*b*) had any false or pretended baggage,

   (*c*) surreptitiously removed or attempted to remove his baggage or any material part of it,

   (*d*) absconded or surreptitiously left the premises,

   (*e*) knowingly made a false statement to obtain credit or time for payment, or

   (*f*) offered a worthless cheque, draft or security in payment for the food, beverage or accommodation,

is, in the absence of any evidence to the contrary, proof of fraud.

(3) In this section, "cheque" includes, in addition to its ordinary meaning, a bill of exchange drawn on any institution that makes it a business practice to honour bills of exchange or any particular kind thereof drawn on it by depositors. R.S., c. C-34, s. 322; 1994, c. 44, s. 23.

---

365. [*Repealed*, 2018, c. 29, s. 41.]

Forgery and Offences Resembling Forgery

FORGERY / Making false document / When forgery complete / Forgery complete though document incomplete / Exception.

366. (1) Every one commits forgery who makes a false document, knowing it to be false, with intent

   (*a*) that it should in any way be used or acted on as genuine, to the prejudice of any one whether within Canada or not; or

   (*b*) that a person should be induced, by the belief that it is genuine, to do or to refrain from doing anything, whether within Canada or not.

(2) Making a false document includes

   (*a*) altering a genuine document in any material part;

   (*b*) making a material addition to a genuine document or adding to it a false date, attestation, seal or other thing that is material; or

(c) making a material alteration in a genuine document by erasure, obliteration, removal or in any other way.

(3) Forgery is complete as soon as a document is made with the knowledge and intent referred to in subsection (1), notwithstanding that the person who makes it does not intend that any particular person should use or act on it as genuine or be induced, by the belief that it is genuine, to do or refrain from doing anything.

(4) Forgery is complete notwithstanding that the false document is incomplete or does not purport to be a document that is binding in law, if it is such as to indicate that it was intended to be acted on as genuine.

(5) No person commits forgery by reason only that the person, in good faith, makes a false document at the request of a police force, the Canadian Forces or a department or agency of the federal government or of a provincial government. R.S., c. C-34, s. 324; 2009, c. 28, s. 7.

CODE

PUNISHMENT FOR FORGERY.

367. Every one who commits forgery

    (a) is guilty of an indictable offence and liable to imprisonment for a term not exceeding ten years; or

    (b) is guilty of an offence punishable on summary conviction. R.S.C., c. C-34, s. 325; 1994, c. 44, s. 24; 1997, c. 18, s. 24.

USE, TRAFFICKING OR POSSESSION OF FORGED DOCUMENT / Punishment / Wherever forged.

368. (1) Everyone commits an offence who, knowing or believing that a document is forged,

    (a) uses, deals with or acts on it as if it were genuine;

    (b) causes or attempts to cause any person to use, deal with or act on it as if it were genuine;

    (c) transfers, sells or offers to sell it or makes it available, to any person, knowing that or being reckless as to whether an offence will be committed under paragraph (a) or (b); or

    (d) possesses it with intent to commit an offence under any of paragraphs (a) to (c).

(1.1) Everyone who commits an offence under subsection (1)

    (a) is guilty of an indictable offence and liable to imprisonment for a term of not more than 10 years; or

    (b) is guilty of an offence punishable on summary conviction.

(2) For the purposes of proceedings under this section, the place where a document was forged is not material. R.S., c. C-34, s. 326; 1997, c. 18, s. 25; 2009, c. 28, s. 8.

FORGERY.

368.1 Everyone is guilty of an indictable offence and liable to imprisonment for a term of not more than 14 years, or is guilty of an offence punishable on summary conviction, who, without lawful authority or excuse, makes, repairs, buys, sells, exports from Canada, imports into Canada or possesses any instrument, device, apparatus, material or thing that they know has been used or know is adapted or intended for use by any person to commit forgery. 2009, c. 28, s. 9.

PUBLIC OFFICERS ACTING IN THE COURSE OF THEIR DUTIES OR EMPLOYMENT.

368.2 No public officer, as defined in subsection 25.1(1), is guilty of an offence under any of sections 366 to 368.1 if the acts alleged to constitute the offence were committed by the public officer for the sole purpose of establishing or maintaining a covert identity for use in the course of the public officer's duties or employment. 2009, c. 28, s. 9.

EXCHEQUER BILL PAPER, PUBLIC SEALS, ETC.

369. Everyone is guilty of an indictable offence and liable to imprisonment for a term of not more than 14 years who, without lawful authority or excuse,

   (a) makes, uses or possesses

      (i) any exchequer bill paper, revenue paper or paper that is used to make bank-notes, or

      (ii) any paper that is intended to resemble paper mentioned in subparagraph (i); or

   (b) makes, reproduces or uses a public seal of Canada or of a province, or the seal of a public body or authority in Canada or of a court of law. R.S., c. C-34, s. 327; 2009, c. 28, s. 9.

370. [*Repealed*, 2018, c. 29, s. 42.]

371. [*Repealed*, 2018, c. 29, s. 42.]

FALSE INFORMATION / Indecent communications / Harassing communications / Punishment.

372. (1) Everyone commits an offence who, with intent to injure or alarm a person, conveys information that they know is false, or causes such information to be conveyed by letter or any means of telecommunication.

(2) Everyone commits an offence who, with intent to alarm or annoy a person, makes an indecent communication to that person or to any other person by a means of telecommunication.

(3) Everyone commits an offence who, without lawful excuse and with intent to harass a person, repeatedly communicates, or causes repeated communications to be made, with them by a means of telecommunication.

(4) Everyone who commits an offence under this section is

   (a) guilty of an indictable offence and liable to imprisonment for a term of not more than two years; or

   (b) guilty of an offence punishable on summary conviction. R.S., c. C-34, s. 330; 2014, c. 31, s. 18.

373. [*Repealed*, R.S.C. 1985, c. 27 (1st Supp.), s. 53.]

DRAWING DOCUMENT WITHOUT AUTHORITY, ETC.

374. Every one who

   (*a*) with intent to defraud and without lawful authority makes, executes, draws, signs, accepts or endorses a document in the name or on the account of another person by procuration or otherwise, or

   (*b*) makes use of or utters a document knowing that it has been made, executed, signed, accepted or endorsed with intent to defraud and without lawful authority, in the name or on the account of another person, by procuration or otherwise,

is guilty of an indictable offence and liable to imprisonment for a term not exceeding fourteen years. R.S., c. C-34, s. 332.

OBTAINING, ETC., BY INSTRUMENT BASED ON FORGED DOCUMENT.

375. Every one who demands, receives or obtains anything, or causes or procures anything to be delivered or paid to any person under, on, or by virtue of any instrument issued under the authority of law, knowing that it is based on a forged document, is guilty of an indictable offence and liable to imprisonment for a term not exceeding fourteen years. R.S., c. C-34, s. 333.

COUNTERFEITING STAMP, ETC. / Counterfeiting mark / Definitions / "mark" / "stamp".

376. (1) Every person is guilty of an indictable offence and liable to imprisonment for a term of not more thatn 14 years who

   (*a*) fraudulently uses, mutilates, affixes, removes or counterfeits a stamp or part thereof,

   (*b*) knowingly and without lawful excuse has in their possession

      (i) a counterfeit stamp or a stamp that has been fraudulently mutilated, or

      (ii) anything bearing a stamp of which a part has been fraudulently erased, removed or concealed, or

   (*c*) without lawful excuse makes or knowingly has in their possession a die or instrument that is capable of making the impression of a stamp or part of a stamp.

(2) Every one who, without lawful authority,

   (*a*) makes a mark,

   (*b*) sells, or exposes for sale, or has in his possession a counterfeit mark,

   (*c*) affixes a mark to anything that is required by law to be marked, branded, sealed or wrapped other than the thing to which the mark was originally affixed or was intended to be affixed, or

   (*d*) affixes a counterfeit mark to anything that is required by law to be marked, branded, sealed or wrapped,

is guilty of an indictable offence and liable to imprisonment for a term not exceeding fourteen years.

(3) In this section

"mark" means a mark, brand, seal, wrapper or design used by or on behalf of
- (a) the government of Canada or of a province,
- (b) the government of a state other than Canada, or
- (c) a department, board, commission or agent established by a government mentioned in paragraph (a) or (b) in connection with the service or business of that government;

"stamp" means an impressed or adhesive stamp used for the purpose of revenue by the government of Canada or a province or by the government of a state other than Canada. R.S., c. C-34, s. 334; 2018, c. 29, s. 43.

DAMAGING DOCUMENTS / Definition of "election document".

377. (1) Every person is guilty of an indictable offence and liable to imprisonment for a term of not more than five years or is guilty of an offence punishable on summary conviction who unlawfully
- (a) destroys, defaces or injures a register, or any part of a register, of births, baptisms, marriages, deaths or burials that is required or authorized by law to be kept in Canada, or a copy or any part of a copy of such a register that is required by law to be transmitted to a registrar or other officer,
- (b) inserts or causes to be inserted in a register or copy referred to in paragraph (a) an entry, that he knows is false, of any matter relating to a birth, baptism, marriage, death or burial, or erases any material part from that register or copy,
- (c) destroys, damages or obliterates an election document or causes an election document to be destroyed, damaged or obliterated, or
- (d) makes or causes to be made an erasure, alteration or interlineation in or on an election document.

(2) In this section, "election document" means any document or writing issued under the authority of an Act of Parliament or the legislature of a province with respect to an election held pursuant to the authority of that Act. R.S., c. C-34, s. 335; 2019, c. 25, s. 135.

OFFENCES IN RELATION TO REGISTERS.

378. Every person is guilty of an indictable offence and liable to imprisonment for a term of not more than five years or is guilty of an offence punishable on summary conviction who
- (a) being authorized or required by law to make or issue a certified copy of, extract from or certificate in respect of a register, record or document, knowingly makes or issues a false certified copy, extract or certificate,
- (b) not being authorized or required by law to make or issue a certified copy of, extract from or certificate in respect of a register, record or document, fraudulently makes or issues a copy, extract or certificate that purports to be certified as authorized or required by law, or
- (c) being authorized or required by law to make a certificate or declaration concerning any particular required for the purpose of making entries in a

register, record or document, knowingly and falsely makes the certificate or declaration. R.S., c. C-34, s. 336; 2019, c. 25, s. 136.

Part X / FRAUDULENT TRANSACTIONS RELATING TO CONTRACTS AND TRADE

Interpretation

DEFINITIONS OF GOODS.

379. In this Part, "goods" means anything that is the subject of trade or commerce. R.S., c. C-34, s. 337; 2018, c. 29, s. 43.1.

Fraud

FRAUD / Minimum punishment / Affecting public market.

380. (1) Every one who, by deceit, falsehood or other fraudulent means, whether or not it is a false pretence within the meaning of this Act, defrauds the public or any person, whether ascertained or not, of any property, money or valuable security or any service,

(a) is guilty of an indictable offence and liable to a term of imprisonment not exceeding fourteen years, where the subject-matter of the offence is a testamentary instrument or the value of the subject-matter of the offence exceeds five thousand dollars; or

(b) is guilty

(i) of an indictable offence and liable to imprisonment for a term not exceeding two years, or

(ii) of an offence punishable on summary conviction,

where the value of the subject-matter of the offence does not exceed five thousand dollars.

(1.1) When a person is prosecuted on indictment and convicted of one or more offences referred to in subsection (1), the court that imposes the sentence shall impose a minimum punishment of imprisonment for a term of two years if the total value of the subject-matter of the offences exceeds one million dollars.

(2) Every one who, by deceit, falsehood or other fraudulent means, whether or not it is a false pretence within the meaning of this Act, with intent to defraud, affects the public market price of stocks, shares, merchandise or anything that is offered for sale to the public is guilty of an indictable offence and liable to imprisonment for a term not exceeding fourteen years. R.S., c. C-34, s. 338; 1974-75-76, c. 93, s. 32; R.S.C. 1985, c. 27 (1st Supp.), s. 54; 1994, c. 44, s. 25; 1997, c. 18, s. 26; 2004, c. 3, s. 2; 2011, c. 6, s. 2.

SENTENCING — AGGRAVATING CIRCUMSTANCES / Aggravating circumstance — value of the fraud / Non-mitigating factors / Record of proceedings.

380.1 (1) Without limiting the generality of section 718.2, where a court imposes a sentence for an offence referred to in section 380, 382, 382.1 or 400, it shall consider the following as aggravating circumstances:

  (*a*) the magnitude, complexity, duration or degree of planning of the fraud committed was significant;

  (*b*) the offence adversely affected, or had the potential to adversely affect, the stability of the Canadian economy or financial system or any financial market in Canada or investor confidence in such a financial market;

  (*c*) the offence involved a large number of victims;

  (*c*.1) the offence had a significant impact on the victims given their personal circumstances including their age, health and financial situation;

  (*d*) in committing the offence, the offender took advantage of the high regard in which the offender was held in the community;

  (*e*) the offender did not comply with a licensing requirement, or professional standard, that is normally applicable to the activity or conduct that forms the subject-matter of the offence; and

  (*f*) the offender concealed or destroyed records related to the fraud or to the disbursement of the proceeds of the fraud.

(1.1) Without limiting the generality of section 718.2, when a court imposes a sentence for an offence referred to in section 382, 382.1 or 400, it shall also consider as an aggravating circumstance the fact that the value of the fraud committed exceeded one million dollars.

(2) When a court imposes a sentence for an offence referred to in section 380, 382, 382.1 or 400, it shall not consider as mitigating circumstances the offender's employment, employment skills or status or reputation in the community if those circumstances were relevant to, contributed to, or were used in the commission of the offence.

(3) The court shall cause to be stated in the record the aggravating and mitigating circumstances it took into account when determining the sentence. 2004, c. 3, s. 2; 2011, c. 6, s. 3.

PROHIBITION ORDER / Duration / Court may vary order / Offence.

380.2 (1) When an offender is convicted, or is discharged on the conditions prescribed in a probation order under section 730, of an offence referred to in subsection 380(1), the court that sentences or discharges the offender, in addition to any other punishment that may be imposed for that offence or any other condition prescribed in the order of discharge, may make, subject to the conditions or exemptions that the court directs, an order prohibiting the offender from seeking, obtaining or continuing any employment, or becoming or being a volunteer in any capacity, that involves having authority over the real property, money or valuable security of another person.

CODE

(2) The prohibition may be for any period that the court considers appropriate, including any period to which the offender is sentenced to imprisonment.

(3) A court that makes an order of prohibition or, if the court is for any reason unable to act, another court of equivalent jurisdiction in the same province, may, on application of the offender or the prosecutor, require the offender to appear before it at any time and, after hearing the parties, that court may vary the conditions prescribed in the order if, in the opinion of the court, the variation is desirable because of changed circumstances.

(4) Every person who is bound by an order of prohibition and who does not comply with the order is guilty of

    (a) an indictable offence and is liable to imprisonment for a term not exceeding two years; or

    (b) an offence punishable on summary conviction. 2011, c. 6, s. 4.

380.3 [*Repealed*, 2015, c. 13, s. 11.]

380.4 [*Repealed*, 2015, c. 13, s. 11.]

USING MAILS TO DEFRAUD.

381. Every person who makes use of the mails for the purpose of transmitting or delivering letters or circulars concerning schemes devised or intended to deceive or defraud the public, or for the purpose of obtaining money under false pretences, is guilty of

    (a) an indictable offence and liable to imprisonment for a term of not more than two years; or

    (b) an offence punishable on summary conviction. R.S., c. C-34, s. 339; 2019, c. 25, s. 137.

FRAUDULENT MANIPULATION OF STOCK EXCHANGE TRANSACTIONS.

382. Every person is guilty of an indictable offence and liable to imprisonment for a term of not more than 10 years or is guilty of an offence punishable on summary conviction who, through the facility of a stock exchange, curb market or other market, with intent to create a false or misleading appearance of active public trading in a security or with intent to create a false or misleading appearance with respect to the market price of a security,

    (a) effects a transaction in the security that involves no change in the beneficial ownership thereof,

    (b) enters an order for the purchase of the security, knowing that an order of substantially the same size at substantially the same time and at substantially the same price for the sale of the security has been or will be entered by or for the same or different persons, or

    (c) enters an order for the sale of the security, knowing that an order of substantially the same size at substantially the same time and at substantially the same price for the purchase of the security has been or will be entered by or for the same or different persons. R.S., c. C-34, s. 340; 2004, c. 3, s. 4; 2019, c. 25, s. 138.

PROHIBITED INSIDER TRADING / Tipping / Saving / Definition of "inside information".

382.1 (1) Every person is guilty of an indictable offence and liable to imprisonment for a term of not more than 10 years or is guilty of an offence punishable on summary conviction who, directly or indirectly, buys or sells a security, knowingly using inside information that they

(a) possess by virtue of being a shareholder of the issuer of that security;

(b) possess by virtue of, or obtained in the course of, their business or professional relationship with that issuer;

(c) possess by virtue of, or obtained in the course of, a proposed takeover or reorganization of, or amalgamation, merger or similar business combination with, that issuer;

(d) possess by virtue of, or obtained in the course of, their employment, office, duties or occupation with that issuer or with a person referred to in paragraphs (a) to (c); or

(e) obtained from a person who possesses or obtained the information in a manner referred to in paragraphs (a) to (d).

(2) Except when necessary in the course of business, a person who knowingly conveys inside information that they possess or obtained in a manner referred to in subsection (1) to another person, knowing that there is a risk that the person will use the information to buy or sell, directly or indirectly, a security to which the information relates, or that they may convey the information to another person who may buy or sell such a security, is guilty of

(a) an indictable offence and liable to imprisonment for a term not exceeding five years; or

(b) an offence punishable on summary conviction.

(3) For greater certainty, an act is not an offence under this section if it is authorized or required, or is not prohibited, by any federal or provincial Act or regulation applicable to it.

(4) In this section, "inside information" means information relating to or affecting the issuer of a security or a security that they have issued, or are about to issue, that

(a) has not been generally disclosed; and

(b) could reasonably be expected to significantly affect the market price or value of a security of the issuer. 2004, c. 3, s. 5; 2019, c. 25, s. 139.

GAMING IN STOCKS OR MERCHANDISE / Onus.

383. (1) Every person is guilty of an indictable offence and liable to imprisonment for a term of not more than five years or is guilty of an offence punishable on summary conviction who, with intent to make gain or profit by the rise or fall in price of the stock of an incorporated or unincorporated company or undertaking, whether in or outside Canada, or of any goods, wares or merchandise, (*a*) makes or signs, or authorizes to be made or signed, any contract or agreement, oral or written, purporting to be for the purchase or sale of shares of stock or goods, wares or merchandise, without the *bona fide* intention of acquiring the shares, goods, wares or merchandise or of selling them, as the case may be, or

(*b*) makes or signs, or authorizes to be made or signed, any contract or agreement, oral or written, purporting to be for the sale or purchase of shares of stock or goods, wares or merchandise in respect of which no delivery of the thing sold or purchased is made or received, and without the *bona fide* intention of making or receiving delivery thereof, as the case may be,

This section does not apply if a broker, on behalf of a purchaser, receives delivery, even if the broker retains or pledges what is delivered as security for the advance of the purchase money or any part of it.

(2) Where, in proceedings under this section, it is established that the accused made or signed a contract or agreement for the sale or purchase of shares of stock or goods, wares or merchandise, or acted, aided or abetted in the making or signing thereof, the burden of proof of a *bona fide* intention to acquire or to sell the shares, goods, wares or merchandise or to deliver or to receive delivery thereof, as the case may be, lies on the accused. R.S., C. C-34, s. 341; 2019, c. 25, s. 140.

BROKER REDUCING STOCK BY SELLING FOR THEIR OWN ACCOUNT / Punishment.

384. (1) Every person commits an offence who, being an individual, or a member or employee of a partnership, or a director, officer or employee of a corporation, if they or the partnership or corporation is employed as a broker by any customer to buy and carry on margin any shares of an incorporated or unincorporated company or undertaking, whether in or outside Canada, later sells or causes to be sold shares of the company or undertaking for any account in which they or their firm or a partner of the firm or the corporation or a director of the corporation has a direct or indirect interest, if the effect of the sale is, otherwise than unintentionally, to reduce the amount of those shares in the hands of the broker or under their control in the ordinary course of business below the amount of those shares that the broker should be carrying for all customers.

(2) Every person who commits an offence under subsection (1) is guilty of

(*a*) an indictable offence and liable to imprisonment for a term of not more than five years; or

(*b*) an offence punishable on summary conviction. R.S., c. C-34, s. 342; 2019, c. 25, s. 141.

FRAUDULENT CONCEALMENT OF TITLE DOCUMENTS / Consent required.

385. (1) Every person is guilty of an indictable offence and liable to imprisonment for a term of not more than two years or is guilty of an offence punishable on summary conviction who, being a vendor, mortgagor or hypothecary debtor of property or a chose in action or an incorporeal right or being a lawyer or notary for or agent or mandatary of a vendor, mortgagor or hypothecary debtor of property, a chose in action or incorporeal right, is served with a written demand for an abstract of title by or on behalf of the purchaser, mortgagee or hypothecary creditor before the completion of the purchase, mortgage or hypothec, and who

(a) with intent to defraud and for the purpose of inducing the purchaser, mortgagee or hypothecary creditor to accept the title offered or produced to them, conceals from them any settlement, deed, will or other instrument or act material to the title, or any encumbrance on the title, or

(b) falsifies any pedigree on which the title depends.

(2) No proceedings shall be instituted under this section without the consent of the Attorney General. R.S., c. C-34, s. 343; 2019, c. 25, s. 142.

FRAUDULENT REGISTRATION OF TITLE.

386. Every person is guilty of an indictable offence and liable to imprisonment for a term of not more than five years or is guilty of an offence punishable on summary conviction who, as principal, agent or mandatary in a proceeding to register title to real property or immovable property, or in a transaction relating to real property or immovable property that is or is proposed to be registered, knowingly and with intent to deceive,

(a) makes a material false statement or representation,

(b) suppresses or conceals from a judge or registrar, or any person employed by or assisting the registrar, any material document, fact, matter or information, or

(c) is privy to anything mentioned in paragraph (a) or (b). R.S., c. C-34, s. 344; 2019, c. 25, s. 143.

FRAUDULENT SALE OF REAL PROPERTY.

387. Every person who, knowing of an unregistered prior sale or of an existing unregistered grant, mortgage, hypothec, lien or encumbrance of or on real property, fraudulently sells the property or any part of it is guilty of

(a) an indictable offence and liable to imprisonment for a term of not more than two years; or

(b) an offence punishable on summary conviction. R.S., c. C-34, s. 345; 2019, c. 25, s. 144.

MISLEADING RECEIPT.

388. Every person is guilty of an indictable offence and liable to imprisonment for a term of not more than two years or is guilty of an offence punishable on summary conviction who knowingly,

(a) with intent to mislead, injure or defraud any person, whether or not that person is known to him, gives to a person anything in writing that purports to be a receipt for or an acknowledgment of property that has been delivered to or received by him, before the property referred to in the

CODE

purported receipt or acknowledgment has been delivered to or received by him, or

(b) accepts, transmits or uses a purported receipt or acknowledgment to which paragraph (a) applies. R.S., c. C-34, s. 346; 2019, c. 25, s. 145.

FRAUDULENT DISPOSAL OF GOODS ON WHICH MONEY ADVANCED / Saving.

389. (1) Every person is guilty of an indictable offence and liable to imprisonment for a term of not more than two years or is guilty of an offence punishable on summary conviction who

(a) having shipped or delivered to the keeper of a warehouse or to a factor, an agent or a carrier, anything on which the consignee thereof has advanced money or has given valuable security, thereafter, with intent to deceive, defraud or injure the consignee, disposes of it in a manner that is different from and inconsistent with any agreement that has been made in that behalf between him and the consignee, or

(b) knowingly and wilfully aids or assists any person to make a disposition of anything to which paragraph (a) applies for the purpose of deceiving, defrauding or injuring the consignee.

(2) No person is guilty of an offence under this section where, before disposing of anything in a manner that is different from and inconsistent with any agreement that has been made in that behalf between him and the consignee, he pays or tenders to the consignee the full amount of money or valuable security that the consignee has advanced. R.S., c. C-34, s. 347; 2019, c. 25, s. 146.

FRAUDULENT RECEIPTS UNDER *BANK ACT*.

390. Every person is guilty of an indictable offence and liable to imprisonment for a term of not more than two years or is guilty of an offence punishable on summary conviction who

(a) knowingly makes a false statement in any receipt, certificate or acknowledgment for anything that may be used for a purpose mentioned in the *Bank Act*; or

(b) knowingly, after either giving to another person or after a person employed by them has, to their knowledge, given to another person, or after obtaining and endorsing or assigning to another person, any receipt, certificate or acknowledgment for anything that may be used for a purpose mentioned in the *Bank Act*, without the consent in writing of the holder or endorsee or the production and delivery of the receipt, certificate or acknowledgment, alienates or parts with, or does not deliver to the holder or owner the property mentioned in the receipt, certificate or acknowledgment. R.S., c. C-34, s. 348; 2019, c. 25, s. 147.

391. [*Repealed*, 2003, c. 21, s. 6.]

Note: Section 391 enacted, 2020, c. 1, s. 37 (to come into force by order of the Governor in Council):

Trade secret

391. (1) Everyone commits an offence who, by deceit, falsehood or other fraudulent means, knowingly obtains a trade secret or communicates or makes available a trade secret.

Trade secret — prior knowledge

(2) Everyone commits an offence who knowingly obtains a trade secret or communicates or makes available a trade secret knowing that it was obtained by the commission of an offence under subsection (1).

Punishment

(3) Everyone who commits an offence referred to in subsection (1) or (2) is guilty
  (a) of an indictable offence and is liable to imprisonment for a term not exceeding 14 years; or
  (b) of an offence punishable on summary conviction.

For greater certainty

(4) For greater certainty, no person commits an offence under subsection (1) or (2) if the trade secret was obtained by independent development or by reason only of reverse engineering.

Definition of *trade secret*

(5) For the purpose of this section, *trade secret* means any information that
  (a) is not generally known in the trade or business that uses or may use that information;
  (b) has economic value from not being generally known; and
  (c) is the subject of efforts that are reasonable under the circumstances to maintain its secrecy.

DISPOSAL OF PROPERTY TO DEFRAUD CREDITORS.

392. Every person is guilty of an indictable offence and liable to imprisonment for a term of not more than two years or is guilty of an offence punishable on summary conviction who,
  (a) with intent to defraud his creditors,
    (i) makes or causes to be made a gift, conveyance, assignment, sale, transfer or delivery of his property, or
    (ii) removes, conceals or disposes of any of his property, or
  (b) with intent that any one should defraud his creditors, receives any property by means of or in relation to which an offence has been committed under paragraph (a). R.S., c. C-34, s. 350; 2019, c. 25, s. 148.

FRAUD IN RELATION TO FARES, ETC. / Idem / Fraudulently obtaining transportation.

393. (1) Every person whose duty it is to collect a fare, toll, ticket or admission and who intentionally does any of the following is guilty of an indictable offence and liable to imprisonment for a term of not more than two years or is guilty of an offence punishable on summary conviction:

    (*a*) fails to collect it,

    (*b*) collects less than the proper amount payable in respect thereof, or

    (*c*) accepts any valuable consideration for failing to collect it or for collecting less than the proper amount payable in respect thereof.

(2) Every person is guilty of an indictable offence and liable to imprisonment for a term of not more than two years or is guilty of an offence punishable on summary conviction who gives or offers to a person whose duty it is to collect a fare, toll, ticket or admission fee any valuable consideration

    (*a*) for failing to collect it, or

    (*b*) for collecting an amount less than the amount payable in respect thereof.

(3) Every one who, by any false pretence or fraud, unlawfully obtains transportation by land, water or air is guilty of an offence punishable on summary conviction. R.S., c. C-34, s. 351; 2019, c. 25, s. 149.

FRAUD IN RELATION TO VALUABLE MINERALS / Sale of valuable minerals / Purchase of valuable minerals / Presumption / Offence / Forfeiture / Exception.

394. (1) No person who is the holder of a lease or licence issued under an Act relating to the mining of valuable minerals, or by the owner of land that is supposed to contain valuable minerals, shall

    (*a*) by a fraudulent device or contrivance, defraud or attempt to defraud any person of

        (i) any valuable minerals obtained under or reserved by the lease or licence, or

        (ii) any money or valuable interest or thing payable in respect of valuable minerals obtained or rights reserved by the lease or licence; or

    (*b*) fraudulently conceal or make a false statement with respect to the amount of valuable minerals obtained under the lease or licence.

(2) No person, other than the owner or the owner's agent or someone otherwise acting under lawful authority, shall sell any valuable mineral that is unrefined, partly refined, uncut or otherwise unprocessed.

(3) No person shall buy any valuable mineral that is unrefined, partly refined, uncut or otherwise unprocessed from anyone who the person has reason to believe is not the owner or the owner's agent or someone otherwise acting under lawful authority.

(4) In any proceeding in relation to subsection (2) or (3), in the absence of evidence raising a reasonable doubt to the contrary, it is presumed that

    (*a*) in the case of a sale, the seller is not the owner of the valuable mineral or the owner's agent or someone otherwise acting under lawful authority; and

(b) in the case of a purchase, the purchaser, when buying the valuable mineral, had reason to believe that the seller was not the owner of the mineral or the owner's agent or someone otherwise acting under lawful authority.

(5) A person who contravenes subsection (1), (2) or (3) is guilty of

(a) an indictable offence and liable to imprisonment for a term of not more than five years; or

(b) an offence punishable on summary conviction.

(6) If a person is convicted of an offence under this section, the court may order anything by means of or in relation to which the offence was committed, on such conviction, to be forfeited to Her Majesty.

(7) Subsection (6) does not apply to real property other than real property built or significantly modified for the purpose of facilitating the commission of an offence under this section. R.S., c. C-34, s. 352; R.S.C. 1985, c. 27 (1st Supp.), s. 186; 1999, c. 5, s. 10; 2019, c. 25, s. 150.

POSSESSION OF STOLEN OR FRAUDULENTLY OBTAINED VALUABLE MINERALS / Evidence / Offence / Forfeiture / Exception.

394.1 (1) No person shall possess any valuable mineral that is unrefined, partly refined, uncut or otherwise unprocessed that has been stolen or dealt with contrary to section 394.

(2) Reasonable grounds to believe that the valuable mineral has been stolen or dealt with contrary to section 394 are, in the absence of evidence raising a reasonable doubt to the contrary, proof that the valuable mineral has been stolen or dealt with contrary to section 394.

(3) A person who contravenes subsection (1) is guilty of

(a) an indictable offence and liable to imprisonment for a term of not more than five years; or

(b) an offence punishable on summary conviction.

(4) If a person is convicted of an offence under this section, the court may, on that conviction, order that anything by means of or in relation to which the offence was committed be forfeited to Her Majesty.

(5) Subsection (4) does not apply to real property, other than real property built or significantly modified for the purpose of facilitating the commission of an offence under subsection (3). 1999, c. 5, s. 10; 2019, c. 25, s. 151.

SEARCH FOR VALUABLE MINERALS / Execution in Canada / Power to seize / Appeal.

395. (1) If an information in writing is laid under oath before a justice by a peace officer or by a public officer who has been appointed or designated to administer or enforce a federal or provincial law and whose duties include the enforcement of this Act or any other Act of Parliament and the justice is satisfied that there are reasonable grounds to believe that, contrary to this Act or any other Act of Parliament, any valuable mineral is deposited in a place or held by a person, the justice may issue a warrant authorizing a peace officer or a public officer, if the public officer is named in it, to search any of the places or persons mentioned in the information.

(1.1) A warrant issued under subsection (1) may be executed at any place in Canada. A public officer named in the warrant, or any peace officer, who executes the warrant must have authority to act in that capacity in the place where the warrant is executed.

(2) Where, on search, anything mentioned in subsection (1) is found, it shall be seized and carried before the justice who shall order

(*a*) that it be detained for the purposes of an inquiry or a trial; or
(*b*) if it is not detained for the purposes of an inquiry or a trial,
  (i) that it be restored to the owner, or
  (ii) that it be forfeited to Her Majesty in right of the province in which the proceedings take place if the owner cannot be ascertained.

(3) An appeal lies from an order made under paragraph (2)(*b*) in the manner in which an appeal lies in summary conviction proceedings under Part XXVII and the provisions of that Part relating to appeals apply to appeals under this subsection. R.S., c. C-34, s. 353; 1999, c. 5, s. 11; 2019, c. 25, s. 152.

OFFENCES IN RELATION TO MINES / Presumption.

396. (1) Every person is guilty of an indictable offence and liable to imprisonment for a term of not more than 10 years or is guilty of an offence punishable on summary conviction who

(*a*) adds anything to or removes anything from any existing or prospective mine, mining claim or oil well with a fraudulent intent to affect the result of an assay, a test or a valuation that has been made or is to be made with respect to the mine, mining claim or oil well, or
(*b*) adds anything to, removes anything from or tampers with a sample or material that has been taken or is being or is about to be taken from any existing or prospective mine, mining claim or oil well for the purpose of being assayed, tested or otherwise valued, with a fraudulent intent to affect the result of the assay, test or valuation.

(2) For the purposes of proceedings under subsection (1), evidence that

(*a*) something has been added to or removed from anything to which subsection (1) applies, or
(*b*) anything to which subsection (1) applies has been tampered with,

is, in the absence of any evidence to the contrary, proof of a fraudulent intent to affect the result of an assay, a test or a valuation. R.S., c. C-34, s. 354; 2019, c. 25, s. 153.

Falsification of Books and Documents

BOOKS AND DOCUMENTS / Privy.

397. (1) Every person is guilty of an indictable offence and liable to imprisonment for a term of not more than five years or is guilty of an offence punishable on summary conviction who, with intent to defraud,

- (*a*) destroys, mutilates, alters, falsifies or makes a false entry in a book, paper, writing, valuable security or document, or
- (*b*) omits a material particular from, or alters a material particular in, a book, paper, writing, valuable security or document.

(2) Every person who, with intent to defraud their creditors, is privy to the commission of an offence under subsection (1) is guilty of

- (*a*) an indictable offence and liable to imprisonment for a term of not more than five years; or
- (*b*) an offence punishable on summary conviction. R.S., c. C-34, s. 355; 2019, c. 25, s. 154.

FALSIFYING EMPLOYMENT RECORD.

398. Every one who, with intent to deceive, falsifies an employment record by any means, including the punching of a time clock, is guilty of an offence punishable on summary conviction. R.S., c. C-34, s. 356.

FALSE RETURN BY PUBLIC OFFICER.

399. Every person is guilty of an indictable offence and liable to imprisonment for a term of not more than five years or is guilty of an offence punishable on summary conviction who, being entrusted with the receipt, custody or management of any part of the public revenues, knowingly furnishes a false statement or return of

- (*a*) any sum of money collected by him or entrusted to his care, or
- (*b*) any balance of money in his hands or under his control. R.S., c. C-34, s. 357; 2019, c. 25, s. 155.

FALSE PROSPECTUS, ETC. / Definition of "company".

400. (1) Every person is guilty of an indictable offence and liable to imprisonment for a term of not more than 10 years or is guilty of an offence punishable on summary conviction who makes, circulates or publishes a prospectus, a statement or an account, whether written or oral, that they know is false in a material particular, with intent

- (*a*) to induce persons, whether ascertained or not, to become shareholders or partners in a company,
- (*b*) to deceive or defraud the members, shareholders or creditors, whether ascertained or not, of a company, or

(c) to induce any person to
    (i) entrust or advance anything to a company, or
    (ii) enter into any security for the benefit of a company.

(2) In this section, "company" means a syndicate, body corporate or company, whether existing or proposed to be created. R.S., c. C-34, s. 358; 1994, c. 44, s. 26; 2019, c. 25, s. 156.

OBTAINING CARRIAGE BY FALSE BILLING / Forfeiture.

401. (1) Every one who, by means of a false or misleading representation, knowingly obtains or attempts to obtain the carriage of anything by any person into a country, province, district or other place, whether or not within Canada, where the importation or transportation of it is, in the circumstances of the case, unlawful is guilty of an offence punishable on summary conviction.

(2) Where a person is convicted of an offence under subsection (1), anything by means of or in relation to which the offence was committed, on such conviction, in addition to any punishment that is imposed, is forfeited to Her Majesty and shall be disposed of as the court may direct. R.S., c. C-34, s. 359.

402. [*Repealed*, 2018, c. 29, s. 44.]

Identity Theft and Identity Fraud

DEFINITION OF "IDENTITY INFORMATION".

402.1 For the purposes of sections 402.2 and 403, "identity information" means any information — including biological or physiological information — of a type that is commonly used alone or in combination with other information to identify or purport to identify an individual, including a fingerprint, voice print, retina image, iris image, DNA profile, name, address, date of birth, written signature, electronic signature, digital signature, user name, credit card number, debit card number, financial institution account number, passport number, Social Insurance Number, health insurance number, driver's licence number or password. 2009, c. 28, s. 10.

IDENTITY THEFT / Trafficking in identity information / Clarification / Jurisdiction / Punishment.

402.2 (1) Every person commits an offence who obtains or possesses another person's identity information with intent to use it to commit an indictable offence that includes fraud, deceit or falsehood as an element of the offence.

(2) Everyone commits an offence who transmits, makes available, distributes, sells or offers for sale another person's identity information, or has it in their possession for any of those purposes, knowing that or being reckless as to whether the information will be used to commit an indictable offence that includes fraud, deceit or falsehood as an element of the offence.

(3) For the purposes of subsections (1) and (2), an indictable offence referred to in either of those subsections includes an offence under any of the following sections:

    (*a*) section 57 (forgery of or uttering forged passport);
    (*b*) section 58 (fraudulent use of certificate of citizenship);
    (*c*) section 130 (personating peace officer);
    (*d*) section 131 (perjury);
    (*e*) section 342 (theft, forgery, etc., of credit card);
    (*f*) section 362 (false pretence or false statement);
    (*g*) section 366 (forgery);
    (*h*) section 368 (use, trafficking or possession of forged document);
    (*i*) section 380 (fraud); and
    (*j*) section 403 (identity fraud).

(4) An accused who is charged with an offence under subsection (1) or (2) may be tried and punished by any court having jurisdiction to try that offence in the place where the offence is alleged to have been committed or in the place where the accused is found, is arrested or is in custody. However, no proceeding in respect of the offence shall be commenced in a province without the consent of the Attorney General of that province if the offence is alleged to have been committed outside that province.

(5) Everyone who commits an offence under subsection (1) or (2)

    (*a*) is guilty of an indictable offence and liable to imprisonment for a term of not more than five years; or
    (*b*) is guilty of an offence punishable on summary conviction. 2009, c. 28, s. 10; 2018, c. 29, s. 45.

IDENTITY FRAUD / Clarification / Punishment.

403. (1) Everyone commits an offence who fraudulently personates another person, living or dead,

    (*a*) with intent to gain advantage for themselves or another person;
    (*b*) with intent to obtain any property or an interest in any property;
    (*c*) with intent to cause disadvantage to the person being personated or another person; or
    (*d*) with intent to avoid arrest or prosecution or to obstruct, pervert or defeat the course of justice.

(2) For the purposes of subsection (1), personating a person includes pretending to be the person or using the person's identity information — whether by itself or in combination with identity information pertaining to any person — as if it pertains to the person using it.

(3) Everyone who commits an offence under subsection (1)

    (*a*) is guilty of an indictable offence and liable to imprisonment for a term of not more than 10 years; or
    (*b*) is guilty of an offence punishable on summary conviction. R.S., c. C-34, s. 361; 1994, c. 44, s. 27; 2009, c. 28, s. 10.

404. [*Repealed*, 2018, c. 29, s. 46.]

ACKNOWLEDGING INSTRUMENT IN FALSE NAME.

405. Every person who, without lawful authority or excuse, acknowledges, in the name of another person before a court or a judge or other person authorized to receive the acknowledgment, a recognizance, undertaking, release order, confession of judgment, consent to judgment or judgment, deed or other instrument or act is guilty of

(*a*) an indictable offence and liable to imprisonment for a term of not more than five years; or

(*b*) an offence punishable on summary conviction. R.S., c. C-34, s. 363; 2018, c. 29, s. 46; 2019, c. 25, s. 157.

Forgery of Trademarks and Trade Descriptions

2014, c. 20, s. 366(1).

FORGING TRADEMARK.

406. For the purposes of this Part, every one forges a trademark who

(*a*) without the consent of the proprietor of the trademark, makes or reproduces in any manner that trademark or a mark so nearly resembling it as to be calculated to deceive; or

(*b*) falsifies, in any manner, a genuine trademark. R.S., c. C-34, s. 364; 2014, c. 20, s. 366(1).

OFFENCE.

407. Every one commits an offence who, with intent to deceive or defraud the public or any person, whether ascertained or not, forges a trademark. R.S., c. C-34, s. 365; 2014, c. 20, s. 366(1).

PASSING OFF.

408. Every one commits an offence who, with intent to deceive or defraud the public or any person, whether ascertained or not,

(*a*) passes off other wares or services as and for those ordered or required; or

(*b*) makes use, in association with wares or services, of any description that is false in a material respect regarding

(i) the kind, quality, quantity or composition,

(ii) the geographical origin, or

(iii) the mode of the manufacture, production or performance

of those wares or services. R.S., c. C-34, s. 366.

CODE

INSTRUMENTS FOR FORGING TRADEMARK / Saving.

409. (1) Every one commits an offence who makes, has in his possession or disposes of a die, block, machine or other instrument, designed or intended to be used in forging a trademark.

(2) No person shall be convicted of an offence under this section where he proves that he acted in good faith in the ordinary course of his business or employment. R.S., c. C-34, s. 367; 2014, c. 20, s. 366(1).

OTHER OFFENCES IN RELATION TO TRADEMARKS.

410. Every one commits an offence who, with intent to deceive or defraud,
- (a) defaces, conceals or removes a trademark or the name of another person from anything without the consent of that other person; or
- (b) being a manufacturer, dealer, trader or bottler, fills any bottle or siphon that bears the trademark or name of another person, without the consent of that other person, with a beverage, milk, by-product of milk or other liquid commodity for the purpose of sale or traffic. R.S., c. C-34, s. 368; 2014, c. 20, s. 366(1).

USED GOODS SOLD WITHOUT DISCLOSURE.

411. Every one commits an offence who sells, exposes or has in his possession for sale, or advertises for sale, goods that have been used, reconditioned or remade and that bear the trademark or the trade-name of another person, without making full disclosure that the goods have been reconditioned, rebuilt or remade for sale and that they are not then in the condition in which they were originally made or produced. R.S., c. C-34, s. 369; 2014, c. 20, s. 366(1).

PUNISHMENT / Forfeiture.

412. (1) Every one who commits an offence under section 407, 408, 409, 410 or 411 is guilty of
- (a) an indictable offence and liable to imprisonment for a term not exceeding two years; or
- (b) an offence punishable on summary conviction.

(2) Anything by means of or in relation to which a person commits an offence under section 407, 408, 409, 410 or 411 is, unless the court otherwise orders, forfeited on the conviction of that person for that offence. R.S., c. C-34, s. 370.

413. [*Repealed*, 2018, c. 29, s. 47.]

PRESUMPTION FROM PORT OF SHIPMENT.

414. Where, in proceedings under this Part, the alleged offence relates to imported goods, evidence that the goods were shipped to Canada from a place outside Canada is, in the absence of any evidence to the contrary, proof that the goods were made or produced in the country from which they were shipped. R.S., c. C-34, s. 372.

Wreck

OFFENCES IN RELATION TO WRECK.

415. Every one who

- (*a*) secretes wreck, defaces or obliterates the marks on wreck or uses any means to disguise or conceal the fact that anything is wreck, or in any manner conceals the character of wreck, from a person who is entitled to inquire into the wreck,
- (*b*) receives wreck, knowing that it is wreck, from a person other than the owner thereof or a receiver of wreck, and does not within forty-eight hours thereafter inform the receiver of wreck thereof,
- (*c*) offers wreck for sale or otherwise deals with it, knowing that it is wreck, and not having a lawful authority to sell or deal with it,
- (*d*) keeps wreck in his possession knowing that it is wreck, without lawful authority to keep it, for any time longer than the time reasonably necessary to deliver it to the receiver of wreck, or
- (*e*) boards, against the will of the master, a vessel that is wrecked, stranded or in distress unless he is a receiver of wreck or a person acting under orders of a receiver of wreck,

is guilty of

- (*f*) an indictable offence and liable to imprisonment for a term not exceeding two years, or
- (*g*) an offence punishable on summary conviction. R.S., c. C-34, s. 373.

Public Stores

DISTINGUISHING MARK ON PUBLIC STORES.

416. The Governor in Council may, by notice to be published in the *Canada Gazette*, prescribe distinguishing marks that are appropriated for use on public stores to denote the property of Her Majesty therein, whether the stores belong to Her Majesty in right of Canada or to Her Majesty in any other right. R.S., c. C-34, s. 374.

APPLYING OR REMOVING MARKS WITHOUT AUTHORITY / Unlawful transactions in public stores / Definition of "distinguishing mark".

417. (1) Every person is guilty of an indictable offence and liable to imprisonment for a term of not more than two years or is guilty of an offence punishable on summary conviction who,

- (*a*) without lawful authority applies a distinguishing mark to anything, or
- (*b*) with intent to conceal the property of Her Majesty in public stores, removes, destroys or obliterates, in whole or in part, a distinguishing mark.

(2) Every person who, without lawful authority, receives, possesses, keeps, sells or delivers public stores that they know bear a distinguishing mark is guilty of

- (a) an indictable offence and liable to imprisonment for a term not exceeding two years; or
- (b) an offence punishable on summary conviction.

(3) For the purposes of this section, "distinguishing mark" means a distinguishing mark that is appropriated for use on public stores pursuant to section 416. R.S., c. C-34, s. 375; 2018, c. 29, s. 48; 2019, c. 25, s. 158(1).

SELLING DEFECTIVE STORES TO HER MAJESTY / Offences by representatives.

418. (1) Every one who knowingly sells or delivers defective stores to Her Majesty or commits fraud in connection with the sale, lease or delivery of stores to Her Majesty or the manufacture of stores for Her Majesty is guilty of an indictable offence and liable to imprisonment for a term not exceeding fourteen years.

(2) Every one who, being a representative of an organization that commits, by fraud, an offence under subsection (1),

- (a) knowingly takes part in the fraud, or
- (b) knows or has reason to suspect that the fraud is being committed or has been or is about it be committed and does not inform the responsible government, or a department thereof, of Her Majesty,

is guilty of an indictable offence and liable to imprisonment for a term not exceeding fourteen years. R.S., c. C-34, s. 376; 2003, c. 21, s. 6.1.

UNLAWFUL USE OF MILITARY UNIFORMS OR CERTIFICATES.

419. Every person is guilty of an offence punishable on summary conviction who, without lawful authority,

- (a) wears a uniform of the Canadian Forces or any other naval, army or air force or a uniform that is so similar to the uniform of any of those forces that it is likely to be mistaken therefor,
- (b) wears a distinctive mark relating to wounds received or service performed in war, or a military medal, ribbon, badge, chevron or any decoration or order that is awarded for war services, or any imitation thereof, or any mark or device or thing that is likely to be mistaken for any such mark, medal, ribbon, badge, chevron, decoration or order,
- (c) has in his possession a certificate of discharge, certificate of release, statement of service or identity card from the Canadian Forces or any other naval, army or air force that has not been issued to and does not belong to him, or
- (d) has in his possession a commission or warrant or a certificate of discharge, certificate of release, statement of service or identity card, issued to an officer or person in or who has been in the Canadian Forces or any other naval, army or air force, that contains any alteration that is not verified by the initials of the officer who issued it, or by the initials of some officer thereto lawfully authorized. R.S., c. C-34, s. 377; 2018, c. 29, s. 49.

MILITARY STORES / Exception.

420. (1) Every one who buys, receives or detains from a member of the Canadian Forces or a deserter or an absentee without leave therefrom any military stores that are owned by Her Majesty or for which the member, deserter or absentee without leave is accountable to Her Majesty is guilty of

- (*a*) an indictable offence and liable to imprisonment for a term not exceeding five years; or
- (*b*) an offence punishable on summary conviction.

(2) No person shall be convicted of an offence under this section where he establishes that he did not know and had no reason to suspect that the military stores in respect of which the offence was committed were owned by Her Majesty or were military stores for which the member, deserter or absentee without leave was accountable to Her Majesty. R.S., c. C-34, s. 378.

EVIDENCE OF ENLISTMENT / Presumption when accused a dealer in stores.

421. (1) In proceedings under sections 417 to 420, evidence that a person was at any time performing duties in the Canadian Forces is, in the absence of any evidence to the contrary, proof that his enrolment in the Canadian Forces prior to that time was regular.

(2) An accused who is charged with an offence under subsection 417(2) shall be presumed to have known that the stores in respect of which the offence is alleged to have been committed bore a distinguishing mark within the meaning of that subsection at the time the offence is alleged to have been committed if he was, at that time, in the service or employment of Her Majesty or was a dealer in marine stores or in old metals. R.S., c. C-34, s. 379.

Breach of Contract, Intimidation and Discrimination Against Trade Unionists

CRIMINAL BREACH OF CONTRACT / Saving / Consent required.

422. (1) Every one who wilfully breaks a contract, knowing or having reasonable cause to believe that the probable consequences of doing so, whether alone or in combination with others, will be

- (*a*) to endanger human life,
- (*b*) to cause serious bodily injury,
- (*c*) to expose valuable property, real or personal, to destruction or serious injury,
- (*d*) to deprive the inhabitants of a city or place, or part thereof, wholly or to a great extent, of their supply of light, power, gas or water, or
- (*e*) to delay or prevent the running of any locomotive engine, tender, freight or passenger train or car, on a railway that is a common carrier,

is guilty of

- (*f*) an indictable offence and liable to imprisonment for a term not exceeding five years, or

   (g) an offence punishable on summary conviction.

(2) No person wilfully breaks a contract within the meaning of subsection (1) by reason only that

   (a) being the employee of an employer, he stops work as a result of the failure of his employer and himself to agree on any matter relating to his employment, or,

   (b) being a member of an organization of employees formed for the purpose of regulating relations between employers and employees, he stops work as a result of the failure of the employer and a bargaining agent acting on behalf of the organization to agree on any matter relating to the employment of members of the organization,

if, before the stoppage of work occurs, all steps provided by law with respect to the settlement of industrial disputes are taken and any provision for the final settlement of differences, without stoppage of work, contained in or by law deemed to be contained in a collective agreement is complied with and effect given thereto.

(3) No proceedings shall be instituted under this section without the consent of the Attorney General. R.S., c. C-34, s. 380.

INTIMIDATION / Exception.

423. (1) Every one is guilty of an indictable offence and liable to imprisonment for a term of not more than five years or is guilty of an offence punishable on summary conviction who, wrongfully and without lawful authority, for the purpose of compelling another person to abstain from doing anything that he or she has a lawful right to do, or to do anything that he or she has a lawful right to abstain from doing,

   (a) uses violence or threats of violence to that person or their intimate partner or children, or injures the person's property;

   (b) intimidates or attempts to intimidate that person or a relative of that person by threats that, in Canada or elsewhere, violence or other injury will be done to or punishment inflicted on him or her or a relative of his or hers, or that the property of any of them will be damaged;

   (c) persistently follows that person;

   (d) hides any tools, clothes or other property owned or used by that person, or deprives him or her of them or hinders him or her in the use of them;

   (e) with one or more other persons, follows that person, in a disorderly manner, on a highway;

   (f) besets or watches the place where that person resides, works, carries on business or happens to be; or

   (g) blocks or obstructs a highway.

(2) A person who attends at or near or approaches a dwelling-house or place, for the purpose only of obtaining or communicating information, does not watch or beset within the meaning of this section. R.S., c. C-34, s. 381; 1980-81-82-83, c. 125, s. 22; 2000, c. 12, s. 95(b); 2001, c. 32, s. 10; 2019, c. 25, s. 159.

INTIMIDATION OF A JUSTICE SYSTEM PARTICIPANT OR A JOURNALIST / Prohibited conduct / Punishment.

423.1 (1) No person shall, without lawful authority, engage in any conduct with the intent to provoke a state of fear in

   (*a*) a group of persons or the general public in order to impede the administration of criminal justice;

   (*b*) a justice system participant in order to impede him or her in the performance of his or her duties; or

Note: Paragraph 423.1(1)(*b*) replaced, 2019, c. 15, s. 47(1) (to come into force by order of the Governor in Council):

   (*b*) a justice system participant or military justice system participant in order to impede him or her in the performance of his or her duties; or

   (*c*) a journalist in order to impede him or her in the transmission to the public of information in relation to a criminal organization.

(2) [*Repealed*, 2015, c. 13, s. 12(2).]

(3) Every person who contravenes this section is guilty of an indictable offence and is liable to imprisonment for a term of not more than fourteen years. 2001, c. 32, s. 11; 2015, c. 13, s. 12.

Note: Section 423.1 amended by enacting subsec. (4), 2019, c. 15, s. 47(2) (to come into force by order of the Governor in Council):

Definition of "military justice system participant"

(4) In this section, "military justice system participant" has the same meaning as in subsection 2(1) of the *National Defence Act*.

THREAT AGAINST INTERNATIONALLY PROTECTED PERSON.

424. Every person who threatens to commit an offence under section 235, 236, 266, 267, 268, 269, 269.1, 271, 272, 273, 279 or 279.1 against an internationally protected person or who threatens to commit an offence under section 431 is guilty of

   (*a*) an indictable offence and liable to imprisonment for a term of not more than five years; or

   (*b*) an offence punishable on summary conviction. 1974-75-76, c. 93, s. 33; R.S.C. 1985, c. 27 (1st Supp.), s. 55; 2001, c. 41, s. 11; 2019, c. 25, s. 160.

THREAT AGAINST UNITED NATIONS OR ASSOCIATED PERSONNEL.

424.1 Every person who, with intent to compel any person, group of persons, state or any international or intergovernmental organization to do or refrain from doing any act, threatens to commit an offence under section 235, 236, 266, 267, 268, 269, 269.1, 271, 272, 273, 279 or 279.1 against a member of United Nations personnel or associated personnel or threatens to commit an offence under section 431.1 is guilty of

   (*a*) an indictable offence and liable to imprisonment for a term of not more than 10 years; or *(b)* an offence punishable on summary conviction. 2001, c. 41, s. 11; 2019, c. 25, s. 160.

OFFENCES BY EMPLOYERS.

425. Every one who, being an employer or the agent of an employer, wrongfully and without lawful authority

   (a) refuses to employ or dismisses from his employment any person for the reason only that the person is a member of a lawful trade union or of a lawful association or combination of workmen or employees formed for the purpose of
advancing, in a lawful manner, their interests and organized for their protection in the regulation of wages and conditions of work,

   (b) seeks by intimidation, threat of loss of position or employment, or by causing actual loss of position or employment, or by threatening or imposing any pecuniary penalty, to compel workmen or employees to abstain from belonging to a trade union, association or combination to which they have a lawful right to belong, or

   (c) conspires, combines, agrees or arranges with any other employer or his agent to do anything mentioned in paragraph *(a)* or *(b)*,

is guilty of an offence punishable on summary conviction. R.S., c. C-34, s. 382.

THREATS AND RETALIATION AGAINST EMPLOYEES / Punishment.

425.1 (1) No employer or person acting on behalf of an employer or in a position of authority in respect of an employee of the employer shall take a disciplinary measure against, demote, terminate or otherwise adversely affect the employment of such an employee, or threaten to do so,

   (a) with the intent to compel the employee to abstain from providing information to a person whose duties include the enforcement of federal or provincial law, respecting an offence that the employee believes has been or is being committed contrary to this or any other federal or provincial Act or regulation by the employer or an officer or employee of the employer or, if the employer is a corporation, by one or more of its directors; or

   (b) with the intent to retaliate against the employee because the employee has provided information referred to in paragraph *(a)* to a person whose duties include the enforcement of federal or provincial law.

(2) Any one who contravenes subsection (1) is guilty of

   (a) an indictable offence and liable to imprisonment for a term not exceeding five years; or

   (b) an offence punishable on summary conviction. 2004, c. 3, s. 6.

Secret Commissions

SECRET COMMISSIONS / Privity to offence / Punishment / Definition of "agent" and "principal".

426. (1) Every one commits an offence who

(a) directly or indirectly, corruptly gives, offers or agrees to give or offer to an agent or to anyone for the benefit of the agent — or, being an agent, directly or indirectly, corruptly demands, accepts or offers or agrees to accept from any person, for themselves or another person — any reward, advantage or benefit of any kind as consideration for doing or not doing, or for having done or not done, any act relating to the affairs or business of the agent's principal, or for showing or not showing favour or disfavour to any person with relation to the affairs or business of the agent's principal; or

(b) with intent to deceive a principal, gives to an agent of that principal, or, being an agent, uses with intent to deceive his principal, a receipt, an account, or other writing
  (i) in which the principal has an interest,
  (ii) that contains any statement that is false or erroneous or defective in any material particular, and
  (iii) that is intended to mislead the principal.

(2) Every one commits an offence who is knowingly privy to the commission of an offence under subsection (1).

(3) A person who commits an offence under this section is guilty of
  (a) an indictable offence and liable to imprisonment for a term of not more than five years; or
  (b) an offence punishable on summary conviction.

(4) In this section "agent" includes an employee, and "principal" includes an employer. R.S., c. C-34, s. 383; R.S.C. 1985, c. 27 (1st Supp.), s. 56; 2007, c. 13, s. 7; 2019, c. 25, s. 161.

[*Heading repealed*, 2018, c. 29, s. 50.]

---

427. [*Repealed*, 2018, c. 29, s. 50.]

Part XI / WILFUL AND FORBIDDEN ACTS IN RESPECT OF CERTAIN PROPERTY

Interpretation

DEFINITION OF "PROPERTY"

428. In this Part, "property" means real or personal corporeal property. R.S., c. C-34, s. 385.

WILFULLY CAUSING EVENT TO OCCUR / Colour of right / Interest.

429. (1) Every one who causes the occurrence of an event by doing an act or by omitting to do an act that it is his duty to do, knowing that the act or omission will probably cause the occurrence of the event and being reckless whether the event occurs or not, shall be deemed, for the purposes of this Part, wilfully to have caused the occurrence of the event.

(2) A person shall not be convicted of an offence under sections 430 to 446 if they act with legal justification or excuse or colour of right.

(3) Where it is an offence to destroy or to damage anything,

    (*a*) the fact that a person has a partial interest in what is destroyed or damaged does not prevent him from being guilty of the offence if he caused the destruction or damage; and

    (*b*) the fact that a person has a total interest in what is destroyed or damaged does not prevent him from being guilty of the offence if he caused the destruction or damage with intent to defraud. R.S., c. C-34, s. 386; 2018, c. 29, s. 51.

Mischief

MISCHIEF / Mischief in relation to computer data / Punishment / Punishment / Idem / Mischief relating to religious property, educational institutions, etc. / Definition of "property" / Mischief relating to war memorials / Mischief in relation to cultural property / Mischief in relation to computer data / Offence / Saving / Idem / Definition of "computer data".

430. (1) Every one commits mischief who wilfully

    (*a*) destroys or damages property;

    (*b*) renders property dangerous, useless, inoperative or ineffective;

    (*c*) obstructs, interrupts or interferes with the lawful use, enjoyment or operation of property; or

    (*d*) obstructs, interrupts or interferes with any person in the lawful use, enjoyment or operation of property.

(1.1) Everyone commits mischief who wilfully

    (*a*) destroys or alters computer data;

    (*b*) renders computer data meaningless, useless or ineffective;

    (*c*) obstructs, interrupts or interferes with the lawful use of computer data; or

    (*d*) obstructs, interrupts or interferes with a person in the lawful use of computer data or denies access to computer data to a person who is entitled to access to it.

(2) Every one who commits mischief that causes actual danger to life is guilty of an indictable offence and liable to imprisonment for life.

(3) Every one who commits mischief in relation to property that is a testamentary instrument or the value of which exceeds five thousand dollars

    (*a*) is guilty of an indictable offence and liable to imprisonment for a term not exceeding ten years; or

    (*b*) is guilty of an offence punishable on summary conviction.

(4) Every one who commits mischief in relation to property, other than property described in subsection (3),

(a) is guilty of an indictable offence and liable to imprisonment for a term not exceeding two years; or

(b) is guilty of an offence punishable on summary conviction.

(4.1) Everyone who commits mischief in relation to property described in any of paragraphs (4.101)(a) to (d), if the commission of the mischief is motivated by bias, prejudice or hate based on colour, race, religion, national or ethnic origin, age, sex, sexual orientation, gender identity or expression or mental or physical disability,

(a) is guilty of an indictable offence and liable to imprisonment for a term not exceeding ten years; or

(b) is guilty of an offence punishable on summary conviction.

(4.101) For the purposes of subsection (4.1), "property" means

(a) a building or structure, or part of a building or structure, that is primarily used for religious worship — including a church, mosque, synagogue or temple — , an object associated with religious worship located in or on the grounds of such a building or structure, or a cemetery;

(b) a building or structure, or part of a building or structure, that is primarily used by an "identifiable group" as defined in subsection 318(4) as an educational institution — including a school, daycare centre, college or university — , or an object associated with that institution located in or on the grounds of such a building or structure;

(c) a building or structure, or part of a building or structure, that is primarily used by an "identifiable group" as defined in subsection 318(4) for administrative, social, cultural or sports activities or events — including a town hall, community centre, playground or arena — , or an object associated with such an activity or event located in or on the grounds of such a building or structure; or

(d) a building or structure, or part of a building or structure, that is primarily used by an "identifiable group" as defined in subsection 318(4) as a residence for seniors or an object associated with that residence located in or on the grounds of such a building or structure.

(4.11) Everyone who commits mischief in relation to property that is a building, structure or part thereof that primarily serves as a monument to honour persons who were killed or died as a consequence of a war, including a war memorial or cenotaph, or an object associated with honouring or remembering those persons that is located in or on the grounds of such a building or structure, or a cemetery is guilty of an indictable offence or an offence punishable on summary conviction and is liable,

(a) whether the offence is prosecuted by indictment or punishable on summary conviction, to the following minimum punishment, namely,
(i) for a first offence, to a fine of not less than $1,000,
(ii) for a second offence, to imprisonment for not less than 14 days, and
(iii) for each subsequent offence, to imprisonment for not less than 30 days;

(b) if the offence is prosecuted by indictment, to imprisonment for a term not exceeding 10 years; and

(c) if the offence is punishable on summary conviction, to imprisonment for a term of not more than two years less a day.

(4.2) Every one who commits mischief in relation to cultural property as defined in Article 1 of the Convention for the Protection of Cultural Property in the Event of Armed Conflict, done at The Hague on May 14, 1954, as set out in the schedule to the *Cultural Property Export and Import Act,*

- (*a*) is guilty of an indictable offence and liable to imprisonment for a term not exceeding ten years; or
- (*b*) is guilty of an offence punishable on summary conviction.

(5) Everyone who commits mischief in relation to computer data

- (*a*) is guilty of an indictable offence and liable to imprisonment for a term not exceeding ten years; or
- (*b*) is guilty of an offence punishable on summary conviction.

(5.1) Everyone who wilfully does an act or wilfully omits to do an act that it is their duty to do, if that act or omission is likely to constitute mischief causing actual danger to life, or to constitute mischief in relation to property or computer data,

- (*a*) is guilty of an indictable offence and liable to imprisonment for a term not exceeding five years; or
- (*b*) is guilty of an offence punishable on summary conviction.

(6) No person commits mischief within the meaning of this section by reason only that

- (*a*) he stops work as a result of the failure of his employer and himself to agree on any matter relating to his employment; or
- (*b*) he stops work as a result of the failure of his employer and a bargaining agent acting on his behalf to agree on any matter relating to his employment; or
- (*c*) he stops work as a result of his taking part in a combination of workmen or employees for their own reasonable protection as workmen or employees.

(7) No person commits mischief within the meaning of this section by reason only that he attends at or near or approaches a dwelling-house or place for the purpose only of obtaining or communicating information.

(8) In this section, "computer data" has the same meaning as in subsection 342.1(2). R.S., c. C-34, s. 387; 1972, c. 13, s. 30; R.S.C. 1985, c. 27 (1st Supp.), s. 57; 1994, c. 44, s. 28; 2001, c. 41, s. 12; 2005, c. 40, s. 3; 2014, c. 9, s. 1; 2014, c. 31, s. 19; 2017, c. 23, ss. 1, 2; 2019, c. 25, s. 162.

ATTACK ON PREMISES, RESIDENCE OR TRANSPORT OF INTERNATIONALLY PROTECTED PERSON.

431. Every one who commits a violent attack on the official premises, private accommodation or means of transport of an internationally protected person that is likely to endanger the life or liberty of such a person is guilty of an indictable offence and liable to imprisonment for a term of not more than fourteen years. 1974-75-76, c. 93, s. 34; R.S.C. 1985, c. 27 (1st Supp.), s. 58; 2001, c. 41, s. 13.

ATTACK ON PREMISES, ACCOMMODATION OR TRANSPORT OF UNITED NATIONS OR ASSOCIATED PERSONNEL.

431.1 Every one who commits a violent attack on the official premises, private accommodation or means of transport of a member of United Nations personnel or associated personnel that is likely to endanger the life or liberty of such a person is guilty of an indictable offence and liable to imprisonment for a term of not more than fourteen years. 2001, c. 41, s. 13.

CODE

DEFINITIONS / Explosive or other lethal device / Armed forces.

431.2 (1) The following definitions apply in this section.

"explosive or other lethal device" means

    (*a*) an explosive or incendiary weapon or device that is designed to cause, or is capable of causing, death, serious bodily injury or substantial material damage; or

    (*b*) a weapon or device that is designed to cause, or is capable of causing, death, serious bodily injury or substantial material damage through the release, dissemination or impact of toxic chemicals, biological agents or toxins or similar substances, or radiation or radioactive material.

"infrastructure facility" means a publicly or privately owned facility that provides or distributes services for the benefit of the public, including services relating to water, sewage, energy, fuel and communications.

"military forces of a state" means the armed forces that a state organizes, trains and equips in accordance with the law of the state for the primary purpose of national defence or national security, and every person acting in support of those armed forces who is under their formal command, control and responsibility.

"place of public use" means those parts of land, a building, street, waterway or other location that are accessible or open to members of the public, whether on a continuous, periodic or occasional basis, and includes any commercial, business, cultural, historical, educational, religious, governmental, entertainment, recreational or other place that is accessible or open to the public on such a basis.

"public transportation system" means a publicly or privately owned facility, conveyance or other thing that is used in connection with publicly available services for the transportation of persons or cargo.

(2) Every one who delivers, places, discharges or detonates an explosive or other lethal device to, into, in or against a place of public use, a government or public facility, a public transportation system or an infrastructure facility, either with intent to cause death or serious bodily injury or with intent to cause extensive destruction of such a place, system or facility that results in or is likely to result in major economic loss, is guilty of an indictable offence and liable to imprisonment for life.

(3) For greater certainty, subsection (2) does not apply to an act or omission that is committed during an armed conflict and that, at the time and in the place of its commission, is in accordance with customary international law or conventional international law applicable to the conflict, or to activities undertaken by military

forces of a state in the exercise of their official duties, to the extent that those activities are governed by other rules of international law. 2001, c. 41, s. 13.

432. [*Repealed*, R.S.C. 1985, c. 27 (1st Supp.), s. 58 (old provision).]

UNAUTHORIZED RECORDING OF A MOVIE / Unauthorized recording for purpose of sale, etc. / Forfeiture / Forfeiture — limitation.

432. (1) A person who, without the consent of the theatre manager, records in a movie theatre a performance of a cinematographic work within the meaning of section 2 of the *Copyright Act* or its soundtrack

  (a) is guilty of an indictable offence and liable to imprisonment for a term of not more than two years; or

  (b) is guilty of an offence punishable on summary conviction.

(2) A person who, without the consent of the theatre manager, records in a movie theatre a performance of a cinematographic work within the meaning of section 2 of the *Copyright Act* or its soundtrack for the purpose of the sale, rental or other commercial distribution of a copy of the cinematographic work

  (a) is guilty of an indictable offence and liable to imprisonment for a term of not more than five years; or

  (b) is guilty of an offence punishable on summary conviction.

(3) In addition to any punishment that is imposed on a person who is convicted of an offence under this section, the court may order that anything that is used in the commission of the offence be forfeited to Her Majesty in right of the province in which the proceedings are taken. Anything that is forfeited may be disposed of as the Attorney General directs.

(4) No order may be made under subsection (3) in respect of anything that is the property of a person who is not a party to the offence. 2007, c. 28, s. 1.

Arson and Other Fires

ARSON / Disregard for human life.

433. Every person who intentionally or recklessly causes damage by fire or explosion to property, whether or not that person owns the property, is guilty of an indictable offence and liable to imprisonment for life where

  (a) the person knows that or is reckless with respect to whether the property is inhabited or occupied; or

  (b) the fire or explosion causes bodily harm to another person. R.S., c. C-34, s. 389; 1990, c. 15, s. 1.

ARSON / Damage to property.

434. Every person who intentionally or recklessly causes damage by fire or explosion to property that is not wholly owned by that person is guilty of an indictable offence and liable to imprisonment for a term not exceeding fourteen years. R.S., c. C-34, s. 390; 1990, c. 15, s. 1.

ARSON / Own property.

434.1 Every person who intentionally or recklessly causes damage by fire or explosion to property that is owned, in whole or in part, by that person is guilty of an indictable offence and liable to imprisonment for a term not exceeding fourteen years, where the fire or explosion seriously threatens the health, safety or property of another person. 1990, c. 15, s. 1.

ARSON FOR FRAUDULENT PURPOSE / Holder or beneficiary of fire insurance policy.

435. (1) Every person who, with intent to defraud any other person, causes damage by fire or explosion to property, whether or not that person owns, in whole or in part, the property, is guilty of

   (*a*) an indictable offence and liable to imprisonment for a term of not more than 10 years; or

   (*b*) an offence punishable on summary conviction.

(2) Where a person is charged with an offence under subsection (1), the fact that the person was the holder of or was named as a beneficiary under a policy of fire insurance relating to the property in respect of which the offence is alleged to have been committed is a fact from which intent to defraud may be inferred by the court. R.S., c. C-34, s. 391; 1990, c. 15, s. 1; 2019, c. 25, s. 163.

ARSON BY NEGLIGENCE / Non-compliance with prevention laws.

436. (1) Every person who owns, in whole or in part, or controls property and who, as a result of a marked departure from the standard of care that a reasonably prudent person would use to prevent or control the spread of fires or to prevent explosions, is a cause of a fire or explosion in that property that causes bodily harm to another person or damage to property is guilty of

   (*a*) an indictable offence and liable to imprisonment for a term of not more than five years; or

   (*b*) an offence punishable on summary conviction.

(2) Where a person is charged with an offence under subsection (1), the fact that the person has failed to comply with any law respecting the prevention or control of fires or explosions in the property is a fact from which a marked departure from the standard of care referred to in that subsection may be inferred by the court. R.S., c. C-34, s. 392; 1990, c. 15, s. 1; 2019, c. 25, s. 164.

POSSESSION OF INCENDIARY MATERIAL.

436.1 Every person who possesses any incendiary material, incendiary device or explosive substance for the purpose of committing an offence under any of sections 433 to 436 is guilty of

   (*a*) an indictable offence and liable to imprisonment for a term of not more than five years; or

   (*b*) an offence punishable on summary conviction. 1990, c. 15, s. 1; 2019, c. 25, s. 165.

Other Interference with Property

FALSE ALARM OF FIRE.

437. Every one who wilfully, without reasonable cause, by outcry, ringing bells, using a fire alarm, telephone or telegraph, or in any other manner, makes or circulates or causes to be made or circulated an alarm of fire is guilty of

    (*a*) an indictable offence and liable to imprisonment for a term not exceeding two years; or

    (*b*) an offence punishable on summary conviction. R.S., c. C-34, s. 393; 1972, c. 13, s. 31.

INTERFERING WITH SAVING OF WRECKED VESSEL / Interfering with saving of wreck.

438. (1) Every person is guilty of an indictable offence and liable to imprisonment for a term of not more than five years or is guilty of an offence punishable on summary conviction who intentionally prevents or impedes, or who intentionally endeavours to prevent or impede,

    (*a*) the saving of a vessel that is wrecked, stranded, abandoned or in distress, or

    (*b*) a person who attempts to save a vessel that is wrecked, stranded, abandoned or in distress.

(2) Every one who wilfully prevents or impedes or wilfully endeavours to prevent or impede the saving of wreck is guilty of an offence punishable on summary conviction. R.S., c. C-34, s. 394; 2019, c. 25, s. 166.

INTERFERING WITH MARINE SIGNAL, ETC. / Idem.

439. (1) Every one who makes fast a vessel or boat to a signal, buoy or other sea-mark that is used for purposes of navigation is guilty of an offence punishable on summary conviction.

(2) Every person who intentionally alters, removes or conceals a signal, buoy or other sea-mark that is used for purposes of navigation is guilty of

    (*a*) an indictable offence and liable to imprisonment for a term of not more than 10 years; or

    (*b*) an offence punishable on summary conviction. R.S., c. C-34, s. 395; 2019, c. 25, s. 167.

REMOVING NATURAL BAR WITHOUT PERMISSION.

440. Every person who knowingly and without the written permission of the Minister of Transport removes any stone, wood, earth or other material that forms a natural bar necessary to the existence of a public harbour, or that forms a natural protection to such a bar, is guilty of

    (*a*) an indictable offence and liable to imprisonment for a term of not more than two years; or

    (*b*) an offence punishable on summary conviction. R.S., c. C-34, s. 396; 2019, c. 25, s. 168.

OCCUPANT INJURING BUILDING.

441. Every person who, intentionally and to the prejudice of a mortgagee, a hypothecary creditor or an owner, pulls down, demolishes or removes all or any part of a dwelling-house or other building of which they are in possession or occupation, or severs from the freehold any fixture fixed to it or from the immovable property any movable property permanently attached or joined to the immovable property, is guilty of

    (*a*) an indictable offence and liable to imprisonment for a term of not more than five years; or

    (*b*) an offence punishable on summary conviction. R.S., c. C-34, s. 397; 2019, c. 25, s. 168.

INTERFERING WITH BOUNDARY LINES.

442. Every one who wilfully pulls down, defaces, alters or removes anything planted or set up as the boundary line or part of the boundary line of land is guilty of an offence punishable on summary conviction. R.S., c. C-34, s. 398.

INTERFERING WITH INTERNATIONAL BOUNDARY MARKS, ETC. / Saving provision.

443. (1) Every person is guilty of an indictable offence and liable to imprisonment for a term of not more than five years or is guilty of an offence punishable on summary conviction who intentionally pulls down, defaces, alters or removes

    (*a*) a boundary mark lawfully placed to mark any international, provincial, county or municipal boundary, or

    (*b*) a boundary mark lawfully placed by a land surveyor to mark a limit, boundary or angle of a concession, range, lot or parcel of land.

(2) A land surveyor does not commit an offence under subsection (1) where, in his operations as a land surveyor,

    (*a*) he takes up, when necessary, a boundary mark mentioned in paragraph (1)(*b*) and carefully replaces it as it was before he took it up; or

    (*b*) he takes up a boundary mark mentioned in paragraph (1)(*b*) in the course of surveying for a highway or other work that, when completed, will make it impossible or impracticable for that boundary mark to occupy its original position, and he establishes a permanent record of the original position sufficient to permit such position to be ascertained. R.S., c. C-34, s. 399; 2019, c. 25, s. 169.

Animals   2018, c. 29, s. 52.

444. [*Repealed*, 2018, c. 29, s. 52.]

INJURING OR ENDANGERING OTHER ANIMALS / Punishment.

445. (1) Every one commits an offence who, wilfully and without lawful excuse,

(a) kills, maims, wounds, poisons or injures dogs, birds or animals that are kept for a lawful purpose; or

(b) places poison in such a position that it may easily be consumed by dogs, birds or animals that are kept for a lawful purpose.

(2) Every one who commits an offence under subsection (1) is guilty of

(a) an indictable offence and liable to imprisonment for a term of not more than five years; or

(b) an offence punishable on summary conviction and liable to a fine of not more than $10,000 or to imprisonment for a term of not more than two years less a day, or to both. R.S., c. C-34, s. 401, 2008, c. 12, s. 1; 2018, c. 29, s. 53; 2019, c. 25, s. 170.

KILLING OR INJURING CERTAIN ANIMALS / Punishment / Sentences to be served consecutively / Definitions.

445.01 (1) Every one commits an offence who, wilfully and without lawful excuse, kills, maims, wounds, poisons or injures a law enforcement animal while it is aiding a law enforcement officer in carrying out that officer's duties, a military animal while it is aiding a member of the Canadian Forces in carrying out that member's duties or a service animal.

(2) Every one who commits an offence under subsection (1) is guilty of

(a) an indictable offence and liable to imprisonment for a term of not more than five years and, if a law enforcement animal is killed in the commission of the offence, to a minimum punishment of imprisonment for a term of six months; or

(b) an offence punishable on summary conviction and liable to a fine of not more than $10,000 or to imprisonment for a term of not more than two years less a day, or to both.

(3) A sentence imposed on a person for an offence under subsection (1) committed against a law enforcement animal shall be served consecutively to any other punishment imposed on the person for an offence arising out of the same event or series of events.

(4) The following definitions apply in this section.

"law enforcement animal" means a dog or horse that is trained to aid a law enforcement officer in carrying out that officer's duties.

"law enforcement officer" means a police officer, a police constable or any person referred to in paragraph (b), (c.1), (d), (d.1), (e) or (g) of the definition "peace officer" in section 2.

"military animal" means an animal that is trained to aid a member of the Canadian Forces in carrying out that member's duties.

"service animal" means an animal that is required by a person with a disability for assistance and is certified, in writing, as having been trained by a professional service animal institution to assist a person with a disability. 2015, c. 34, s. 3; 2019, c. 25, s. 171.

Cruelty to Animals

CAUSING UNNECESSARY SUFFERING / Punishment / Failure to exercise reasonable care as evidence / Presence at baiting as evidence.

445.1 (1) Every one commits an offence who

(a) wilfully causes or, being the owner, wilfully permits to be caused unnecessary pain, suffering or injury to an animal or a bird;

(b) in any manner encourages, aids, promotes, arranges, assists at, receives money for or takes part in

(i) the fighting or baiting of animals or birds, or

(ii) the training, transporting or breeding of animals or birds for the purposes of subparagraph (i);

(c) wilfully, without reasonable excuse, administers a poisonous or an injurious drug or substance to a domestic animal or bird or an animal or a bird wild by nature that is kept in captivity or, being the owner of such an animal or a bird, wilfully permits a poisonous or an injurious drug or substance to be administered to it;

(d) promotes, arranges, conducts, assists in, receives money for or takes part in any meeting, competition, exhibition, pastime, practice, display or event at or in the course of which captive birds are liberated by hand, trap, contrivance or any other means for the purpose of being shot when they are liberated; or

(e) being the owner, occupier or person in charge of any premises, permits the premises or any part thereof to be used for a purpose mentioned in paragraph (d).

(2) Every one who commits an offence under subsection (1) is guilty of

(a) an indictable offence and liable to imprisonment for a term of not more than five years; or

(b) an offence punishable on summary conviction and liable to a fine of not more than $10,000 or to imprisonment for a term of not more than two years less a day, or to both.

(3) For the purposes of proceedings under paragraph (1)(a), evidence that a person failed to exercise reasonable care or supervision of an animal or a bird thereby causing it pain, suffering or injury is, in the absence of any evidence to the contrary, proof that the pain, suffering or injury was caused or was permitted to be caused wilfully, as the case may be.

(4) For the purpose of proceedings under paragraph (1)(b), evidence that an accused was present at the fighting or baiting of animals or birds is, in the absence of any evidence to the contrary, proof that he or she encouraged, aided or assisted at the fighting or baiting. 2008, c. 12, s. 1; 2019, c. 17, s. 2; 2019, c. 25, s. 172.

DEFINITION OF "cetacean" / Offence / Exception — gestation / Exception — offspring / Exception / Exception / Exception — authorization / Punishment.

445.2 (1) In this section, "cetacean" includes any member of the cetacean order, including a whale, dolphin or porpoise.

(2) Subject to subsections (2.1) to (3.1), every person commits an offence who
  (*a*) owns, has the custody of or controls a cetacean that is kept in captivity;
  (*b*) breeds or impregnates a cetacean; or
  (*c*) possesses or seeks to obtain reproductive materials of cetaceans, including sperm or an embryo.

(2.1) If a cetacean is gestating on the day on which this subsection comes into force, paragraphs (2)(*b*) and (*c*) do not apply in respect of that cetacean for the period in which it gestates that includes the day on which this subsection comes into force.

(2.2) Paragraph (2)(*a*) does not apply to the offspring of a cetacean if that offspring was born immediately after a gestational period that included the day on which this subsection came into force.

(3) Paragraph (2)(*a*) does not apply to a person who
  (*a*) owns, has the custody of or controls a cetacean that is kept in captivity at the coming into force of this section and remains continuously in captivity thereafter;
  (*b*) has the custody of or controls a cetacean that is kept in captivity for the purpose of providing it with assistance or care or to rehabilitate it following an injury or another state of distress; or
  (*c*) is authorized to keep a cetacean in captivity in the best interests of the cetacean's welfare pursuant to a licence issued by the Lieutenant Governor in Council of a province or by such other person or authority in the province as may be specified by the Lieutenant Governor in Council.

(3.1) Subsection (2) does not apply to a person who is conducting scientific research pursuant to a licence issued by the Lieutenant Governor in Council of a province or by such other person or authority in the province as may be specified by the Lieutenant Governor in Council.

(4) Every person commits an offence who promotes, arranges, conducts, assists in, receives money for or takes part in any meeting, competition, exhibition, pastime, practice, display or event at or in the course of which captive cetaceans are used, in Canada, for performance for entertainment purposes, unless the performance is authorized under a licence issued by the Lieutenant Governor in Council of a province or by an authority in the province as may be specified by the Lieutenant Governor in Council.

(5) Every one who commits an offence under subsection (2) or (4) is guilty of an offence punishable on summary conviction and liable to a fine not exceeding $200,000. 2019, c. 11, s. 2; 2019, c. 14, s. 58.3.

CAUSING DAMAGE OR INJURY / Punishment / Failure to exercise reasonable care as evidence.

446. (1) Every one commits an offence who
- (a) by wilful neglect causes damage or injury to animals or birds while they are being driven or conveyed; or
- (b) being the owner or the person having the custody or control of a domestic animal or a bird or an animal or a bird wild by nature that is in captivity, abandons it in distress or wilfully neglects or fails to provide suitable and adequate food, water, shelter and care for it.

(2) Every one who commits an offence under subsection (1) is guilty of
- (a) an indictable offence and liable to imprisonment for a term of not more than two years; or
- (b) an offence punishable on summary conviction.

(3) For the purposes of proceedings under paragraph (1)(a), evidence that a person failed to exercise reasonable care or supervision of an animal or a bird thereby causing it damage or injury is, in the absence of any evidence to the contrary, proof that the damage or injury was caused by willful neglect. R.S., c. C-34, s. 402; 1974-75-76, c. 93, s. 35; 2008, c. 12, s. 1; 2019, c. 25, s. 173.

ARENA FOR ANIMAL FIGHTING / Punishment.

447. (1) Everyone commits an offence who builds, makes, maintains or keeps an arena for animal fighting on premises that he or she owns or occupies, or allows such an arena to be built, made, maintained or kept on such premises.

(2) Every one who commits an offence under subsection (1) is guilty of
- (a) an indictable offence and liable to imprisonment for a term of not more than five years; or
- (b) an offence punishable on summary conviction and liable to a fine of not more than $10,000 or to imprisonment for a term of not more than two years less a day, or to both. R.S., c. C-34, s. 403; 2008, c. 12, s. 1; 2019, c. 17, s. 3(2); 2019, c. 25, s. 174.

(3) [*Repealed*, 2019, c. 17, s. 3(2).]

ORDER OF PROHIBITION OR RESTITUTION / Breach of order / Application.

447.1 (1) The court may, in addition to any other sentence that it may impose under subsection 445(2), 445.1(2), 446(2) or 447(2),
- (a) make an order prohibiting the accused from owning, having the custody or control of or residing in the same premises as an animal or a bird during any period that the court considers appropriate but, in the case of a second or subsequent offence, for a minimum of five years; and
- (b) on application of the Attorney General or on its own motion, order that the accused pay to a person or an organization that has taken care of an animal or a bird as a result of the commission of the offence the reasonable costs

that the person or organization incurred in respect of the animal or bird, if the costs are readily ascertainable.

(2) Every one who contravenes an order made under paragraph (1)(*a*) is guilty of an offence punishable on summary conviction.

(3) Sections 740 to 741.2 apply, with any modifications that the circumstances require, to orders made under paragraph (1)(*b*). 2008, c. 12, s. 1; 2018, c. 29, s. 54.

Part XII / OFFENCES RELATING TO CURRENCY

Interpretation

DEFINITIONS / "counterfeit money" / "counterfeit token of value" / "current" / "utter".

448. In this Part,

"counterfeit money" includes

    (*a*) a false coin or false paper money that resembles or is apparently intended to resemble or pass for a current coin or current paper money,

    (*b*) a forged bank-note or forged blank bank-note, whether complete or incomplete,

    (*c*) a genuine coin or genuine paper money that is prepared or altered to resemble or pass for a current coin or current paper money of a higher denomination,

    (*d*) a current coin from which the milling is removed by filing or cutting the edges and on which new milling is made to restore its appearance,

    (*e*) a coin cased with gold, silver, or nickel, as the case may be, that is intended to resemble or pass for a current gold, silver or nickel coin, and

    (*f*) a coin or a piece of metal or mixed metals that is washed or coloured by any means with a wash or material capable of producing the appearance of gold, silver or nickel and that is intended to resemble or pass for a current gold, silver or nickel coin;

"counterfeit token of value" means a counterfeit excise stamp, postage stamp or other evidence of value, by whatever technical, trivial or deceptive designation it may be described, and includes genuine coin or paper money that has no value as money;

"current" means lawfully current in Canada or elsewhere by virtue of a law, proclamation or regulation in force in Canada or elsewhere as the case may be;

"utter" includes sell, pay, tender and put off. R.S., c. C-34, s. 406.

Making

MAKING.

449. Every one who makes or begins to make counterfeit money is guilty of an indictable offence and liable to imprisonment for a term not exceeding fourteen years. R.S., c. C-34, s. 407.

Possession

POSSESSION, ETC., OF COUNTERFEIT MONEY.

450. Every person is guilty of an indictable offence and liable to imprisonment for a term of not more than 14 years who, without lawful justification or excuse,
  (*a*) buys, receives or offers to buy or receive counterfeit money;
  (*b*) has in their custody or possession counterfeit money; or
  (*c*) introduces counterfeit money into Canada. R.S., c. C-34, s. 408; 2018, c. 29, s. 55.

HAVING CLIPPINGS, ETC.

451. Every person who, without lawful justification or excuse, has in their custody or possession gold or silver filings, clippings or bullion or gold or silver in dust, solution or otherwise, produced or obtained by impairing, diminishing or lightening a current gold or silver coin, knowing that it has been so produced or obtained, is guilty of
  (*a*) an indictable offence and liable to imprisonment for a term of not more than five years; or
  (*b*) an offence punishable on summary conviction. R.S., c. C-34, s. 409; 2018, c. 29, s. 56; 2019, c. 25, s. 175.

Uttering

UTTERING, ETC., COUNTERFEIT MONEY

452. Every person is guilty of an indictable offence and liable to imprisonment for a term of not more than 14 years who, without lawful justification or excuse,
  (*a*) utters or offers to utter counterfeit money or uses counterfeit money as if it were genuine, or
  (*b*) exports, sends or takes counterfeit money out of Canada. R.S., c. C-34, s. 410; 2018, c. 29, s. 57.

UTTERING COIN.

453. Every person is guilty of an indictable offence and liable to imprisonment for a term of not more than two years or is guilty of an offence punishable on summary conviction who, with intent to defraud, knowingly utters

(a) a coin that is not current, or
(b) a piece of metal or mixed metals that resembles in size, figure or colour a current coin for which it is uttered. R.S., c. C-34, s. 411; 2019, c. 25, s. 176.

SLUGS AND TOKENS.

454. Every person is guilty of an offence punishable on summary conviction who, without lawful excuse, manufactures, produces, sells or has in their possession anyting that is intended to be fraudulently used in substitution for a coin or token of value that any coin or token-operated device is designed to receive,
(a) manufactures, produces or sells, or
(b) has in his possession. R.S., c. C-34, s. 412; 1972, c. 13, s. 32; 2018, c. 29, s. 58.

Defacing or Impairing

CLIPPING AND UTTERING CLIPPED COIN.

455. Every one who
(a) impairs, diminishes or lightens a current gold or silver coin with intent that it should pass for a current gold or silver coin, or
(b) utters a coin knowing that it has been impaired, diminished or lightened contrary to paragraph (a),
is guilty of an indictable offence and liable to imprisonment for a term not exceeding fourteen years. R.S., c. C-34, s. 413.

DEFACING CURRENT COINS.

456. Every one who
(a) defaces a current coin, or
(b) utters a current coin that has been defaced,
is guilty of an offence punishable on summary conviction. R.S., c. C-34, s. 414.

LIKENESS OF BANK-NOTES / Exception / Offence / Defence.

457. (1) No person shall make, publish, print, execute, issue, distribute or circulate, including by electronic or computer-assisted means, anything in the likeness of
(a) a current bank-note; or
(b) an obligation or a security of a government or bank.

(2) Subsection (1) does not apply to
(a) the Bank of Canada or its employees when they are carrying out their duties;
(b) the Royal Canadian Mounted Police or its members or employees when they are carrying out their duties; or
(c) any person acting under a contract or licence from the Bank of Canada or Royal Canadian Mounted Police.

(3) A person who contravenes subsection (1) is guilty of an offence punishable on summary conviction.

(4) No person shall be convicted of an offence under subsection (3) in relation to the printed likeness of a Canadian bank-note if it is established that the length or width of the likeness is less than three-fourths or greater than one-and-one-half times the length or width, as the case may be, of the bank-note and

   (a) the likeness is in black-and-white only; or

   (b) the likeness of the bank-note appears on only one side of the likeness. R.S., c. C-34, s. 415; 1999, c. 5, s. 12.

Instruments or Materials

MAKING, HAVING OR DEALING IN INSTRUMENTS FOR COUNTERFEITING.

458. Every person who, without lawful justification or excuse, makes, repairs, buys, sells or has in their custody or possession any machine, engine, tool, instrument, material or other thing that they know has been used or is adapted and intended for use in making counterfeit money or counterfeit tokens of value, is guilty of an indictable offence and liable to imprisonment for a term of not more than 14 years. R.S., c. C-34, s. 416; 2018, c. 29, s. 59.

CONVEYING INSTRUMENTS FOR COINING OUT OF MINT.

459. Every person is guilty of an indictable offence and liable to imprisonment for a term of not more than 14 years who, without lawful justification or excuse, knowingly conveys out of any of Her Majesty's mints in Canada,

   (a) any machine, engine, tool, instrument, material or thing used or employed in connection with the manufacture of coins,

   (b) a useful part of anything mentioned in paragraph (a), or

   (c) coin, bullion, metal or a mixture of metals. R.S., c. C-34, s. 417; 2018, c. 29, s. 60.

Advertising and Trafficking in Counterfeit Money or Counterfeit Tokens of Value

ADVERTISING AND DEALING IN COUNTERFEIT MONEY, ETC. / Fraudulent use of money genuine but valueless.

460. (1) Every person is guilty of an indictable offence and liable to imprisonment for a term of not more than five years or is guilty of an offence punishable on summary conviction who

   (a) by an advertisement or any other writing, offers to sell, procure or dispose of counterfeit money or counterfeit tokens of value or to give information with respect to the manner in which or the means by which counterfeit money or counterfeit tokens of value may be sold, procured or disposed of, or

    (b) purchases, obtains, negotiates or otherwise deals with counterfeit tokens of value, or offers to negotiate with a view to purchasing or obtaining them.

(2) No person shall be convicted of an offence under subsection (1) in respect of genuine coin or genuine paper money that has no value as money unless, at the time when the offence is alleged to have been committed, he knew that the coin or paper money had no value as money and he had a fraudulent intent in his dealings with or with respect to the coin or paper money. R.S., c. C-34, s. 418; 2019, c. 25, s. 177.

Special Provisions as to Proof

WHEN COUNTERFEIT COMPLETE / Certificate of examiner of counterfeit / Notice of intention to produce certificate / Attendance and cross-examination.

461. (1) Every offence relating to counterfeit money or counterfeit tokens of value shall be deemed to be complete notwithstanding that the money or tokens of value in respect of which the proceedings are taken are not finished or perfected or do not copy exactly the money or tokens of value that they are apparently intended to resemble or for which they are apparently intended to pass.

(2) In any proceedings under this Part, a certificate signed by a person designated as an examiner of counterfeit by the Minister of Public Safety and Emergency Preparedness, stating that any coin, paper money or bank-note described therein is counterfeit money or that any coin, paper money or bank-note described therein is genuine and is or is not, as the case may be, current in Canada or elsewhere, is evidence of the statements contained in the certificate without proof of the signature or official character of the person appearing to have signed the certificate.

(3) No certificate shall be received in evidence unless the party intending to produce it has, before the trial, given to the other party reasonable notice of their intention and a copy of the certificate.

(4) A party against whom the certificate is produced may, with leave of the court, require the attendance of the person who signed the certificate for the purposes of cross-examination. R.S., c. C-34, s. 419; 1992, c. 1, s. 58; 2005, c. 10, s. 34(1)(f)(xi); 2018, c. 21, s. 17.

Forfeiture

OWNERSHIP / Seizure.

462. (1) Counterfeit money, counterfeit tokens of value and anything that is used or is intended to be used to make counterfeit money or counterfeit tokens of value belong to Her Majesty.

(2) A peace officer may seize and detain
    (a) counterfeit money,
    (b) counterfeit tokens of value, and

(c) machines, engines, tools, instruments, materials or things that have been
     used or that have been adapted and are intended for use in making
     counterfeit money or counterfeit tokens of value,

and anything seized shall be sent to the Minister of Finance to be disposed of or
dealt with as he may direct, but anything that is required as evidence in any
proceedings shall not be sent to the Minister until it is no longer required in those
proceedings. R.S., c. C-34, s. 420.

Part XII.1   [*Heading repealed*, 2018, c. 16, s. 211.]

[*Heading repealed*, 2018, c. 16, s. 211.]

462.1 [*Repealed*, 2018, c. 16, s. 211.]

[*Heading repealed*, 2018, c. 16, s. 211.]

462.2 [*Repealed*, 2018, c. 16, s. 211.]

Part XII.2 / PROCEEDS OF CRIME

Interpretation

**DEFINITIONS / "designated drug offence" / "designated offence" /
"enterprise crime offence" / "judge" / "proceeds of crime" / Regulations.**

462.3 (1) In this Part,

"designated drug offence" [*Repealed*, 1996, c. 19, s. 68(1).]

"designated offence" means

  (a) any offence that may be prosecuted as an indictable offence under this or
       any other Act of Parliament, other than an indictable offence prescribed by
       regulation, or

  (b) a conspiracy or an attempt to commit, being an accessory after the fact in
       relation to, or any counselling in relation to, an offence referred to in
       paragraph (a);

"designated substance offence" [*Repealed*, 2001, c. 32, s. 12(3).]

"enterprise crime offence" [*Repealed*, 2001, c. 32, s. 12(2).]

Note: Definition "enterprise crime offence" amended 2001, c. 27, s. 246; however
definition repealed by 2001, c. 32, s. 12(2).

"judge" means a judge as defined in section 552 or a judge of a superior court of
criminal jurisdiction;

"proceeds of crime" means any property, benefit or advantage, within or outside
Canada, obtained or derived directly or indirectly as a result of

  (a) the commission in Canada of a designated offence, or

403

(b)   an act or omission anywhere that, if it had occurred in Canada, would have constituted a designated offence.

(2) The Governor in Council may make regulations prescribing indictable offences that are excluded from the definition "designated offence" in subsection (1). R.S.C. 1985, c. 42 (4th Supp.), s. 2; 1993, c. 25, s. 95; 1993, c. 37, s. 32; 1993, c. 46, s. 5; 1994, c. 44, s. 29; 1995, c. 39, s. 151; 1996, c. 19, ss. 68, 70(a); 1997, c. 18, s. 27; 1997, c. 23, s. 9; 1998, c. 34, ss. 9, 11; 1999, c. 5, s. 52; 2001, c. 32, s. 12; 2001, c. 41, ss. 14, 33; 2005, c. 44, s. 1; 2010, c. 14, s. 7; 2019, c. 25, s. 179.

(3) [*Repealed*, 2019, c. 25, s. 179.]

(4) [*Repealed*, 2019, c. 25, s. 179.]

Offence

LAUNDERING PROCEEDS OF CRIME / Punishment / Exception.

462.31 (1) Every one commits an offence who uses, transfers the possession of, sends or delivers to any person or place, transports, transmits, alters, disposes of or otherwise deals with, in any manner and by any means, any property or any proceeds of any property with intent to conceal or convert that property or those proceeds, knowing or believing that, or being reckless as to whether, all or a part of that property or of those proceeds was obtained or derived directly or indirectly as a result of

(a)   the commission in Canada of a designated offence; or

(b)   an act or omission anywhere that, if it had occurred in Canada, would have constituted a designated offence.

(2) Every one who commits an offence under subsection (1)

(a)   is guilty of an indictable offence and is liable to imprisonment for a term not exceeding ten years; or

(b)   is guilty of an offence punishable on summary conviction.

(3) A peace officer or a person acting under the direction of a peace officer is not guilty of an offence under subsection (1) if the peace officer or person does any of the things mentioned in that subsection for the purposes of an investigation or otherwise in the execution of the peace officer's duties. R.S.C. 1985, c. 42 (4th Supp.), s. 2; 1996, c. 19, s. 70; 1997, c. 18, s. 28; 2001, c. 32, s. 13; 2019, c. 29, s. 103.

Search, Seizure and Detention of Proceeds of Crime

SPECIAL SEARCH WARRANT / Procedure / Execution in Canada / Other provisions to apply / Detention and record of property seized / Return of proceeds / Notice / Undertakings by Attorney General.

462.32 (1) Subject to subsection (3), if a judge, on application of the Attorney General, is satisfied by information on oath in Form 1 that there are reasonable grounds to believe that there is in any building, receptacle or place, within the province in which the judge has jurisdiction or any other province, any property in respect of which an order of forfeiture may be made under subsection 462.37(1) or

(2.01) or 462.38(2), in respect of a designated offence alleged to have been committed within the province in which the judge has jurisdiction, the judge may issue a warrant authorizing a person named in the warrant or a peace officer to search the building, receptacle or place for that property and to seize that property and any other property in respect of which that person or peace officer believes, on reasonable grounds, that an order of forfeiture may be made under that subsection.

(2) An application for a warrant under subsection (1) may be made *ex parte*, shall be made in writing and shall include a statement as to whether any previous applications have been made under subsection (1) with respect to the property that is the subject of the application.

(2.1) A warrant issued under subsection (1) may be executed at any place in Canada. Any peace officer who executes the warrant must have authority to act as a peace officer in the place where it is executed.

(2.2) [*Repealed*, 2019, c. 25, s. 180.]

(3) Subsections 487(2.1) to (3) and section 488 apply, with any modifications that the circumstances require, to a warrant issued under this section.

(4) Every person who executes a warrant issued by a judge under this section shall
- (a) detain or cause to be detained the property seized, taking reasonable care to ensure that the property is preserved so that it may be dealt with in accordance with the law;
- (b) as soon as practicable after the execution of the warrant but within a period not exceeding seven days thereafter, prepare a report in Form 5.3, identifying the property seized and the location where the property is being detained, and cause the report to be filed with the clerk of the court; and
- (c) cause a copy of the report to be provided, on request, to the person from whom the property was seized and to any other person who, in the opinion of the judge, appears to have a valid interest in the property.

(4.1) Subject to this or any other Act of Parliament, a peace officer who has seized anything under a warrant issued by a judge under this section may, with the written consent of the Attorney General, on being issued a receipt for it, return the thing seized to the person lawfully entitled to its possession, if
- (a) the peace officer is satisfied that there is no dispute as to who is lawfully entitled to possession of the thing seized;
- (b) the peace officer is satisfied that the continued detention of the thing seized is not required for the purpose of forfeiture; and
- (c) the thing seized is returned before a report is filed with the clerk of the court under paragraph (4)(b).

(5) Before issuing a warrant under this section in relation to any property, a judge, may require notice to be given to and may hear any person who, in the opinion of the judge, appears to have a valid interest in the property unless the judge is of the opinion that giving such notice before the issuance of the warrant would result in the disappearance, dissipation or reduction in value of the property or otherwise affect the property so that all or a part thereof could not be seized pursuant to the warrant.

(6) Before issuing a warrant under this section, a judge shall require the Attorney General to give such undertakings as the judge considers appropriate with respect to the payment of damages or costs, or both, in relation to the issuance and execution of the warrant. R.S.C. 1985, c. 42 (4th Supp.), s. 2; 1997, c. 18, s. 29; 2001, c. 32, s. 14; 2005, c. 44, s. 3; 2019, c. 25, s. 180.

APPLICATION FOR RESTRAINT ORDER / Procedure / Restraint order / Effect of order / Property outside Canada / Idem / Notice / Order in writing / Undertakings by Attorney General / Service of order / Registration of order / Continues in force / Offence.

462.33 (1) The Attorney General may make an application in accordance with subsection (2) for a restraint order under subsection (3) in respect of any property.

(2) An application made under subsection (1) for a restraint order under subsection (3) in respect of any property may be made *ex parte* and shall be made in writing to a judge and be accompanied by an affidavit sworn on the information and belief of the Attorney General or any other person deposing to the following matters, namely,

    (a) the offence or matter under investigation;

    (b) the person who is believed to be in possession of the property;

    (c) the grounds for the belief that an order of forfeiture may be made under subsection 462.37(1) or (2.01) or 462.38(2) in respect of the property;

    (d) a description of the property; and

    (e) whether any previous applications have been made under this section with respect to the property.

(3) A judge who hears an application for a restraint order made under subsection (1) may — if the judge is satisfied that there are reasonable grounds to believe that there exists, within the province in which the judge has jurisdiction or any other province, any property in respect of which an order of forfeiture may be made under subsection 462.37(1) or (2.01) or 462.38(2), in respect of a designated offence alleged to have been committed within the province in which the judge has jurisdiction — make an order prohibiting any person from disposing of, or otherwise dealing with any interest in, the property specified in the order otherwise than in the manner that may be specified in the order.

(3.01) A restraint order issued under subsection (1) has effect throughout Canada.

(3.1) A restraint order may be issued under this section in respect of property situated outside Canada, with any modifications that the circumstances require.

(4) An order made by a judge under subsection (3) may be subject to such reasonable conditions as the judge thinks fit.

(5) Before making an order under subsection (3) in relation to any property, a judge may require notice to be given to and may hear any person who, in the opinion of the judge, appears to have a valid interest in the property unless the judge is of the opinion that giving such notice before making the order would result in the disappearance, dissipation or reduction in value of the property or otherwise affect the property so that all or a part thereof could not be subject to an order of forfeiture under subsection 462.37(1) or (2.01) or 462.38(2).

(6) An order made under subsection (3) shall be made in writing.

(7) Before making an order under subsection (3), a judge shall require the Attorney General to give such undertakings as the judge considers appropriate with respect to the payment of damages or costs, or both, in relation to

    (*a*) the making of an order in respect of property situated within or outside Canada; and

    (*b*) the execution of an order in respect of property situated within Canada.

(8) A copy of an order made by a judge under subsection (3) shall be served on the person to whom the order is addressed in such manner as the judge directs or as may be prescribed by rules of court.

(9) A copy of an order made under subsection (3), shall be registered against any property in accordance with the laws of the province in which the property is situated.

(10) An order made under subsection (3) remains in effect until

    (*a*) it is revoked or varied under subsection 462.34(4) or revoked under paragraph 462.43(*a*);

    (*b*) it ceases to be in force under section 462.35; or

    (*c*) an order of forfeiture or restoration of the property is made under subsection 462.37(1) or (2.01), 462.38(2) or 462.41(3) or any other provision of this or any other Act of Parliament.

(11) Any person on whom an order made under subsection (3) is served in accordance with this section and who, while the order is in force, acts in contravention of or fails to comply with the order is guilty of an indictable offence or an offence punishable on summary conviction. R.S.C. 1985, c. 42 (4th Supp.), s. 2; 1993, c. 37, s. 21; 1996, c. 16, s. 60(1)(*d*); 1997, c. 18, s. 30; 2001, c. 32, s. 15; 2005, c. 44, s. 4; 2019, c. 25, s. 181.

MANAGEMENT ORDER / Appointment of Minister of Public Works and Government Services / Power to manage / Application for destruction order / Notice / Manner of giving notice / Destruction order / Forfeiture order / When management order ceases to have effect / For greater certainty / Application to vary conditions.

462.331 (1) With respect to property seized under section 462.32 or restrained under section 462.33, other than a "controlled substance", within the meaning of the *Controlled Drugs and Substances Act*, or "cannabis", as defined in subsection 2(1) of the *Cannabis Act*, on application of the Attorney General or of any other person with the written consent of the Attorney General, if a judge is of the opinion that the circumstances so require, the judge may

    (*a*) appoint a person to take control of and to manage or otherwise deal with all or part of the property in accordance with the directions of the judge; and

    (*b*) require any person having possession of that property to give possession of the property to the person appointed under paragraph (*a*).

(2) When the Attorney General of Canada so requests, a judge appointing a person under subsection (1) shall appoint the Minister of Public Works and Government Services.

(3) The power to manage or otherwise deal with property under subsection (1) includes

(a) the power to make an interlocutory sale of perishable or rapidly depreciating property;

(b) the power to destroy, in accordance with subsections (4) to (7), property that has little or no value; and

(c) the power to have property, other than real property or a conveyance, forfeited to Her Majesty in accordance with subsection (7.1).

(4) Before a person who is appointed to manage property destroys property that has little or no value, they shall apply to a court for a destruction order.

(5) Before making a destruction order, a court shall require notice in accordance with subsection (6) to be given to and may hear any person who, in the court's opinion, appears to have a valid interest in the property.

(6) A notice shall

(a) be given in the manner that the court directs or that may be specified in the rules of the court; and

(b) specify the effective period of the notice that the court considers reasonable or that may be set out in the rules of the court.

(7) A court shall order that the property be destroyed if it is satisfied that the property has little or no financial or other value.

(7.1) On application by a person who is appointed to manage the property, a court shall order that the property, other than real property or a conveyance, be forfeited to Her Majesty to be disposed of or otherwise dealt with in accordance with the law if

(a) a notice is given or published in the manner that the court directs or that may be specified in the rules of the court;

(b) the notice specifies a period of 60 days during which a person may make an application to the court asserting their interest in the property; and

(c) during that period, no one makes such an application.

(8) A management order ceases to have effect when the property that is the subject of the management order is returned in accordance with the law, destroyed or forfeited to Her Majesty.

(8.1) For greater certainty, if property that is the subject of a management order is sold, the management order applies to the net proceeds of the sale.

(9) The Attorney General may at any time apply to the judge to cancel or vary any condition to which a management order is subject but may not apply to vary an appointment made under subsection (2). 2001, c. 32, s. 16; 2017, c. 7, s. 58; 2018, c. 16, s. 212.

APPLICATION FOR REVIEW OF SPECIAL WARRANTS AND RESTRAINT ORDERS / Notice to Attorney General / Terms of examination order / Order of restoration of property or revocation or variation of order / Hearing / Expenses / Taxing legal fees / Conditions to be satisfied / Saving provision / Form of recognizance.

462.34 (1) Any person who has an interest in property that was seized under a warrant issued pursuant to section 462.32 or in respect of which a restraint order was made under subsection 462.33(3) may, at any time, apply to a judge

    (a) for an order under subsection (4); or

    (b) for permission to examine the property.

(2) Where an application is made under paragraph (1)(a),

    (a) the application shall not, without the consent of the Attorney General, be heard by a judge unless the applicant has given to the Attorney General at least two clear days notice in writing of the application; and

    (b) the judge may require notice of the application to be given to and may hear any person who, in the opinion of the judge, appears to have a valid interest in the property.

(3) A judge may, on an application made to the judge under paragraph (1)(b), order that the applicant be permitted to examine property subject to such terms as appear to the judge to be necessary or desirable to ensure that the property is safeguarded and preserved for any purpose for which it may subsequently be required.

(4) On an application made to a judge under paragraph (1)(a) in respect of any property and after hearing the applicant and the Attorney General and any other person to whom notice was given pursuant to paragraph (2)(b), the judge may order that the property or a part thereof be returned to the applicant or, in the case of a restraint order made under subsection 462.33(3), revoke the order, vary the order to exclude the property or any interest in the property or part thereof from the application of the order or make the order subject to such reasonable conditions as the judge thinks fit,

    (a) if the applicant enters into a recognizance before the judge, with or without sureties, in such amount and with such conditions, if any, as the judge directs and, where the judge considers it appropriate, deposits with the judge such sum of money or other valuable security as the judge directs;

    (b) if the conditions referred to in subsection (6) are satisfied; or

    (c) for the purpose of

        (i) meeting the reasonable living expenses of the person who was in possession of the property at the time the warrant was executed or the order was made or any person who, in the opinion of the judge, has a valid interest in the property and of the dependants of that person,

        (ii) meeting the reasonable business and legal expenses of a person referred to in subparagraph (i), or

        (iii) permitting the use of the property in relation to an undertaking or release order, if the judge is satisfied that the applicant has no other assets or means available for the purposes set out in this paragraph and that no other person appears to be the lawful owner of or lawfully entitled to possession of the property.

(5) For the purpose of determining the reasonableness of legal expenses referred to in subparagraph (4)(*c*)(ii), a judge shall hold an in camera hearing, without the presence of the Attorney General, and shall take into account the legal aid tariff of the province.

(5.1) For the purpose of determining the reasonableness of expenses referred to in paragraph (4)(*c*), the Attorney General may

    (*a*) at the hearing of the application, make representations as to what would constitute the reasonableness of the expenses, other than legal expenses; and

    (*b*) before or after the hearing of the application held in camera pursuant to subsection (5), make representations as to what would constitute reasonable legal expenses referred to in subparagraph (4)(*c*)(ii).

(5.2) The judge who made an order under paragraph (4)(*c*) may, and on the application of the Attorney General shall, tax the legal fees forming part of the legal expenses referred to in subparagraph (4)(*c*)(ii) and, in so doing, shall take into account

    (*a*) the value of property in respect of which an order of forfeiture may be made;

    (*b*) the complexity of the proceedings giving rise to those legal expenses;

    (*c*) the importance of the issues involved in those proceedings;

    (*d*) the duration of any hearings held in respect of those proceedings;

    (*e*) whether any stage of those proceedings was improper or vexatious;

    (*f*) any representations made by the Attorney General; and

    (*g*) any other relevant matter.

(6) An order under paragraph (4)(*b*) in respect of property may be made by a judge if the judge is satisfied

    (*a*) where the application is made by

        (i) a person charged with a designated offence, or

        (ii) any person who acquired title to or a right of possession of that property from a person referred to in subparagraph (i) under circumstances that give rise to a reasonable inference that the title or right was transferred from that person for the purpose of avoiding the forfeiture of the property,

    that a warrant should not have been issued pursuant to section 462.32 or a restraint order under subsection 462.33(3) should not have been made in respect of that property, or

    (*b*) in any other case, that the applicant is the lawful owner of or lawfully entitled to possession of the property and appears innocent of any complicity in a designated offence or of any collusion in relation to such an offence, and that no other person appears to be the lawful owner of or lawfully entitled to possession of the property, and that the property will no longer be required for the purpose of any investigation or as evidence in any proceeding.

(7) Sections 354, 355.2 and 355.4 do not apply to a person who comes into possession of any property that, by virtue of an order made under paragraph (4)(*c*), was returned to any person after having been seized or was excluded from the application of a restraint order made under subsection 462.33(3). R.S.C. 1985, c. 42 (4th Supp.), s. 2; 1996, c. 19, ss. 69 and 70; 1997, c. 18, ss. 31, 140; 2001, c. 32, s. 17; 2010, c. 14, s. 8; 2019, c. 25, s. 182.

(8) [*Repealed*, 2019, c. 9, s. 182(2).]

APPLICATION OF PROPERTY RESTITUTION PROVISIONS.

462.341 Subsection 462.34(2), paragraph 462.34(4)(*c*) and subsections 462.34(5), (5.1) and (5.2) apply, with any modifications that the circumstances require, to a person who has an interest in money or bank-notes that are seized under this Act, the *Controlled Drugs and Substances Act* or the *Cannabis Act* and in respect of which proceedings may be taken under subsection 462.37(1) or (2.01) or 462.38(2). 1997, c. 18, ss. 32, 140; 1999, c. 5, s. 14; 2005, c. 44, s. 5; 2018, c. 16, s. 213.

EXPIRATION OF SPECIAL WARRANTS AND RESTRAINT ORDERS/Where proceedings instituted/Where application made.

462.35 (1) Subject to this section, where property has been seized under a warrant issued pursuant to section 462.32 or a restraint order has been made under section 462.33 in relation to property, the property may be detained or the order may continue in force, as the case may be, for a period not exceeding six months from the seizure or the making of the order, as the case may be.

(2) The property may continue to be detained, or the order may continue in force, for a period that exceeds six months if proceedings are instituted in respect of which the thing detained may be forfeited.

(3) The property may continue to be detained or the order may continue in force for a period or periods that exceed six months if the continuation is, on application made by the Attorney General, ordered by a judge, where the judge is satisfied that the property is required, after the expiration of the period or periods, for the purpose of section 462.37 or 462.38 or any other provision of this or any other Act of Parliament respecting forfeiture or for the purpose of any investigation or as evidence in any proceeding. R.S.C. 1985, c. 42 (4th Supp.), s. 2; 1997, c. 18, s. 33.

FORWARDING TO CLERK WHERE ACCUSED TO STAND TRIAL.

462.36 Where a judge issues a warrant under section 462.32 or makes a restraint order under section 462.33 in respect of any property, the clerk of the court shall, when an accused is ordered to stand trial for a designated offence, cause to be forwarded to the clerk of the court to which the accused has been ordered to stand trial a copy of the report filed pursuant to paragraph 462.32(4)(*b*) or of the restraint order in respect of the property. R.S.C. 1985, c. 42 (4th Supp.), s. 2; 2001, c. 32, s. 18.

Forfeiture of Proceeds of Crime

ORDER OF FORFEITURE OF PROPERTY / Proceeds of crime — other offences / Order of forfeiture — particular circumstances / Offences / Offender may establish that property is not proceeds of crime / Pattern of criminal activity / Conditions — pattern of criminal activity / Application under subsection (1) not prevented / Exception / Property outside Canada / Fine instead of forfeiture / Imprisonment in default of payment of fine / Fine option program not available to offender.

462.37 (1) Subject to this section and sections 462.39 to 462.41, if an offender is convicted, or discharged under section 730, of a designated offence and the court imposing sentence on or discharging the offender, on application of the Attorney General, is satisfied, on a balance of probabilities, that any property is proceeds of crime obtained through the commission of the designated offence, the court shall order that the property be forfeited to Her Majesty to be disposed of as the Attorney General directs or otherwise dealt with in accordance with the law.

(2) If the evidence does not establish to the satisfaction of the court that property in respect of which an order of forfeiture would otherwise be made under subsection (1) was obtained through the commission of the designated offence of which the offender is convicted or discharged, but the court is satisfied, beyond a reasonable doubt, that the property is proceeds of crime, the court may make an order of forfeiture under subsection (1) in relation to that property.

(2.01) A court imposing sentence on an offender convicted of an offence described in subsection (2.02) shall, on application of the Attorney General and subject to this section and sections 462.4 and 462.41, order that any property of the offender that is identified by the Attorney General in the application be forfeited to Her Majesty to be disposed of as the Attorney General directs or otherwise dealt with in accordance with the law if the court is satisfied, on a balance of probabilities, that

    (*a*) within 10 years before the proceedings were commenced in respect of the offence for which the offender is being sentenced, the offender engaged in a pattern of criminal activity for the purpose of directly or indirectly receiving a material benefit, including a financial benefit; or

    (*b*) the income of the offender from sources unrelated to designated offences cannot reasonably account for the value of all the property of the offender.

(2.02) The offences are the following:

    (*a*) a criminal organization offence punishable by five or more years of imprisonment;

    (*b*) an offence under section 5, 6 or 7 of the *Controlled Drugs and Substances Act* — or a conspiracy or an attempt to commit, being an accessory after the fact in relation to, or any counselling in relation to an offence under any of those sections — prosecuted by indictment;

(c) an offence under subsection 9(1) or (2), 10(1) or (2), 11(1) or (2), 12(1), (4), (5), (6) or (7), 13(1) or 14(1) of the *Cannabis Act* — or a conspiracy or an attempt to commit, being an accessory after the fact in relation to, or any counselling in relation to an offence under any of those subsections — prosecuted by indictment; and

(d) an offence under any of sections 279.01 to 279.03.

(2.03) A court shall not make an order of forfeiture under subsection (2.01) in respect of any property that the offender establishes, on a balance of probabilities, is not proceeds of crime.

(2.04) In determining whether the offender has engaged in a pattern of criminal activity described in paragraph (2.01)(a), the court shall consider

(a) the circumstances of the offence for which the offender is being sentenced;

(b) any act or omission — other than an act or omission that constitutes the offence for which the offender is being sentenced — that the court is satisfied, on a balance of probabilities, was committed by the offender and constitutes an offence punishable by indictment under any Act of Parliament;

(c) any act or omission that the court is satisfied, on a balance of probabilities, was committed by the offender and is an offence in the place where it was committed and, if committed in Canada, would constitute an offence punishable by indictment under any Act of Parliament; and

(d) any other factor that the court considers relevant.

(2.05) A court shall not determine that an offender has engaged in a pattern of criminal activity unless the court is satisfied, on a balance of probabilities, that the offender committed, within the period referred to in paragraph (2.01)(a),

(a) acts or omissions — other than an act or omission that constitutes the offence for which the offender is being sentenced — that constitute at least two serious offences or one criminal organization offence;

(b) acts or omissions that are offences in the place where they were committed and, if committed in Canada, would constitute at least two serious offences or one criminal organization offence; or

(c) an act or omission described in paragraph (a) that constitutes a serious offence and an act or omission described in paragraph (b) that, if committed in Canada, would constitute a serious offence.

(2.06) Nothing in subsection (2.01) shall be interpreted as preventing the Attorney General from making an application under subsection (1) in respect of any property.

(2.07) A court may, if it considers it in the interests of justice, decline to make an order of forfeiture against any property that would otherwise be subject to forfeiture under subsection (2.01). The court shall give reasons for its decision.

(2.1) An order may be issued under this section in respect of property situated outside Canada, with any modifications that the circumstances require.

(3) If a court is satisfied that an order of forfeiture under subsection (1) or (2.01) should be made in respect of any property of an offender but that the property or any part of or interest in the property cannot be made subject to an order, the court

may, instead of ordering the property or any part of or interest in the property to be forfeited, order the offender to pay a fine in an amount equal to the value of the property or the part of or interest in the property. In particular, a court may order the offender to pay a fine if the property or any part of or interest in the property

- (a) cannot, on the exercise of due diligence, be located;
- (b) has been transferred to a third party;
- (c) is located outside Canada;
- (d) has been substantially diminished in value or rendered worthless; or
- (e) has been commingled with other property that cannot be divided without difficulty.

(4) Where a court orders an offender to pay a fine pursuant to subsection (3), the court shall

- (a) impose, in default of payment of that fine, a term of imprisonment
  - (i) not exceeding six months, where the amount of the fine does not exceed ten thousand dollars,
  - (ii) of not less than six months and not exceeding twelve months, where the amount of the fine exceeds ten thousand dollars but does not exceed twenty thousand dollars,
  - (iii) of not less than twelve months and not exceeding eighteen months, where the amount of the fine exceeds twenty thousand dollars but does not exceed fifty thousand dollars,
  - (iv) of not less than eighteen months and not exceeding two years, where the amount of the fine exceeds fifty thousand dollars but does not exceed one hundred thousand dollars,
  - (v) of not less than two years and not exceeding three years, where the amount of the fine exceeds one hundred thousand dollars but does not exceed two hundred and fifty thousand dollars,
  - (vi) of not less than three years and not exceeding five years, where the amount of the fine exceeds two hundred and fifty thousand dollars but does not exceed one million dollars, or
  - (vii) of not less than five years and not exceeding ten years, where the amount of the fine exceeds one million dollars; and
- (b) direct that the term of imprisonment imposed pursuant to paragraph (a) be served consecutively to any other term of imprisonment imposed on the offender or that the offender is then serving.

(5) Section 736 does not apply to an offender against whom a fine is imposed pursuant to subsection (3). R.S.C. 1985, c. 42 (4th Supp.), s. 2; 1995, c. 22, s. 10; 2001, c. 32, s. 19; 2005, c. 44, s. 6; 2015, c. 16, s. 4; 2017, c. 7, s. 59(1); 2018, c. 16, ss. 214, 225.

DEFINITION OF "ORDER" / Execution / Filing of order from another province / Attorney General of Canada / Effect of registered order / Notice / Application of section 462.42 / Application under section 462.42 to be made in one province / Finding in one court binding

462.371 (1) In this section, "order" means an order made under section 462.37 or 462.38.

(2) An order may be executed anywhere in Canada.

(3) Where the Attorney General of a province in which property that is the subject of an order made in another province is situated receives a certified copy of the order and files it with the superior court of criminal jurisdiction of the province in which the property is situated, the order shall be entered as a judgment of that court.

(4) Where the Attorney General of Canada receives a certified copy of an order made in a province in respect of property situated in another province and files the order with the superior court of criminal jurisdiction of the province in which the property is situated, the order shall be entered as a judgment of that court.

(5) An order has, from the date it is filed in a court of a province under subsection (3) or (4), the same effect as if it had been an order originally made by that court.

(6) Where an order has been filed in a court under subsection (3) or (4), it shall not be executed before notice in accordance with subsection 462.41(2) is given to every person who, in the opinion of the court, appears to have a valid interest in the property.

(7) Section 462.42 applies, with such modifications as the circumstances require, in respect of a person who claims an interest in property that is the subject of an order filed under subsection (3) or (4).

(8) No person may make an application under section section 462.42 in relation to property that is the subject of an order filed under subsection (3) or (4) if that person has previously made an application in respect of the same property in another province.

(9) The finding by a court of a province in relation to property that is the subject of an order filed under subsection (3) or (4) as to whether or not an applicant referred to in subsection 462.42(4) is affected by the forfeiture referred to in that subsection or declaring the nature and extent of the interest of the applicant under that subsection is binding on the superior court of criminal jurisdiction of the province where the order is entered as a judgment. 1997, c. 18, s. 34.

APPLICATION FOR FORFEITURE / Order of forfeiture of property / Property outside Canada / Person deemed absconded.

462.38 (1) Where an information has been laid in respect of a designated offence, the Attorney General may make an application to a judge for an order of forfeiture under subsection (2) in respect of any property.

(2) Subject to sections 462.39 to 462.41, where an application is made to a judge under subsection (1), the judge shall, if the judge is satisfied that
    (*a*) any property is, beyond a reasonable doubt, proceeds of crime,
    (*b*) that property was obtained through the commission of a designated offence in respect of which proceedings were commenced, and
    (*c*) the accused charged with the offence referred to in paragraph (*b*) has died or absconded,
order that the property be forfeited to Her Majesty to be disposed of as the Attorney General directs or otherwise dealt with in accordance with the law.

(2.1) An order may be issued under this section in respect of property situated outside Canada, with any modifications that the circumstances require.

(3) For the purposes of this section, a person shall be deemed to have absconded in connection with a designated offence if

   (a) an information has been laid alleging the commission of the offence by the person,

   (b) a warrant for the arrest of the person or a summons in respect of an organization has been issued in relation to that information, and

   (c) reasonable attempts to arrest the person pursuant to the warrant or to serve the summons have been unsuccessful during the period of six months commencing on the day the warrant or summons was issued, or, in the case of a person who is not or never was in Canada, the person cannot be brought within that period to the jurisdiction in which the warrant or summons was issued,

and the person shall be deemed to have so absconded on the last day of that period of six months. R.S.C. 1985, c. 42 (4th Supp.), s. 2; 1997, c. 18, s. 35(2); 2001, c. 32, s. 20; 2003, c. 21, s. 7; 2017, c. 7, s. 60(1).

INFERENCE.

462.39 For the purpose of subsection 462.37(1) or 462.38(2), the court may infer that property was obtained or derived as a result of the commission of a designated offence where evidence establishes that the value, after the commission of that offence, of all the property of the person alleged to have committed the offence exceeds the value of all the property of that person before the commission of that offence and the court is satisfied that the income of that person from sources unrelated to designated offences committed by that person cannot reasonably account for such an increase in value. R.S.C. 1985, c. 42 (4th Supp.), s. 2; 1996, c. 19, s. 70; 2001, c. 32, s. 21.

VOIDABLE TRANSFERS.

462.4 A court may,

   (a) prior to ordering property to be forfeited under subsection 462.37(1) or (2.01) or 462.38(2), and

   (b) in the case of property in respect of which a restraint order was made under section 462.33, where the order was served in accordance with subsection 462.33(8),

set aside any conveyance or transfer of the property that occurred after the seizure of the property or the service of the order under section 462.33, unless the conveyance or transfer was for valuable consideration to a person acting in good faith. R.S. 1985, c. 42 (4th Supp.) s. 2; 1997, c. 18, s. 36; 2005, c. 44, s. 7.

NOTICE / Manner of giving notice / Order of restoration of property.

462.41 (1) Before making an order under subsection 462.37(1) or (2.01) or 462.38(2) in relation to any property, a court shall require notice in accordance with subsection (2) to be given to and may hear any person who, in the opinion of the court, appears to have a valid interest in the property.

(2) A notice shall

   (a) be given in the manner that the court directs or that may be specified in the rules of the court;

   (b) specify the period that the court considers reasonable or that may be set out in the rules of the court during which a person may make an application to the court asserting their interest in the property; and

   (c) set out the designated offence charged and a description of the property.

(3) Where a court is satisfied that any person, other than

   (a) a person who is charged with, or was convicted of, a designated offence, or

   (b) a person who acquired title to or a right of possession of that property from a person referred to in paragraph (a) under circumstances that give rise to a reasonable inference that the title or right was transferred for the purpose of avoiding the forfeiture of the property,

is the lawful owner or is lawfully entitled to possession of any property or any part thereof that would otherwise be forfeited pursuant to subsection 462.37(1) or (2.01) or 462.38(2) and that the person appears innocent of any complicity in an offence referred to in paragraph (a) or of any collusion in relation to such an offence, the court may order that the property or part thereof be returned to that person. R.S.C. 1985, c. 42 (4th Supp.), s. 2; 1996, c. 19, s. 70; 1997, c. 18, ss. 37, 140; 2001, c. 32, s. 22; 2005, c. 44, s. 8; 2017, c. 7, s. 61.

APPLICATION BY PERSON CLAIMING INTEREST FOR RELIEF FROM FORFEITURE / Fixing day for hearing / Notice / Order declaring interest not subject to forfeiture / Appeal from order under subsection (4) / Return of property.

462.42 (1) Any person who claims an interest in property that is forfeited to Her Majesty under subsection 462.37(1) or (2.01) or 462.38(2) may, within thirty days after the forfeiture, apply by notice in writing to a judge for an order under subsection (4) unless the person is

   (a) a person who is charged with, or was convicted of, a designated offence that resulted in the forfeiture; or

   (b) a person who acquired title to or a right of possession of the property from a person referred to in paragraph (a) under circumstances that give rise to a reasonable inference that the title or right was transferred from that person for the purpose of avoiding the forfeiture of the property.

(2) The judge to whom an application is made under subsection (1) shall fix a day not less than thirty days after the date of filing of the application for the hearing thereof.

(3) An applicant shall serve a notice of the application made under subsection (1) and of the hearing thereof on the Attorney General at least fifteen days before the day fixed for the hearing.

(4) Where, on the hearing of an application made under subsection (1), the judge is satisfied that the applicant is not a person referred to in paragraph (1)(a) or (b) and

appears innocent of any complicity in any designated offence that resulted in the forfeiture or of any collusion in relation to any such offence, the judge may make an order declaring that the interest of the applicant is not affected by the forfeiture and declaring the nature and extent of the interest.

(5) An applicant or the Attorney General may appeal to the court of appeal from an order under subsection (4) and the provisions of Part XXI with respect to procedure on appeals apply, with such modifications as the circumstances require, to appeals under this subsection.

(6) The Attorney General shall, on application made to the Attorney General by any person who has obtained an order under subsection (4) and where the periods with respect to the taking of appeals from that order have expired and any appeal from that order taken under subsection (5) has been determined,

(a) direct that the property or the part thereof to which the interest of the applicant relates be returned to the applicant; or

(b) direct that an amount equal to the value of the interest of the applicant, as declared in the order, be paid to the applicant. R.S.C. 1985, c. 42 (4th Supp.), s. 2; 1996, c. 19, s. 70; 1997, c. 18, ss. 38, 140; 2001, c. 32, s. 23; 2005, c. 44, s. 9.

RESIDUAL DISPOSAL OF PROPERTY SEIZED OR DEALT WITH PURSUANT TO SPECIAL WARRANTS OR RESTRAINT ORDERS / Property outside Canada.

462.43 (1) Where property has been seized under a warrant issued pursuant to section 462.32, a restraint order has been made under section 462.33 in relation to any property or a recognizance has been entered into pursuant to paragraph 462.34(4)(a) in relation to any property and a judge, on application made to the judge by the Attorney General or any person having an interest in the property or on the judge's own motion, after notice given to the Attorney General and any other person having an interest in the property, is satisfied that the property will no longer be required for the purpose of section 462.37, 462.38 or any other provision of this or any other Act of Parliament respecting forfeiture or for the purpose of any investigation or as evidence in any proceeding, the judge

(a) in the case of a restraint order, shall revoke the order;

(b) in the case of a recognizance, shall cancel the recognizance; and

(c) in the case of property seized under a warrant issued pursuant to section 462.32 or property under the control of a person appointed pursuant to paragraph 462.331(1)(a),

(i) if possession of it by the person from whom it was taken is lawful, shall order that it be returned to that person,

(ii) if possession of it by the person from whom it was taken is unlawful and the lawful owner or person who is lawfully entitled to its possession is known, shall order that it be returned to the lawful owner or the person who is lawfully entitled to its possession, or

(iii) if possession of it by the person from whom it was taken is unlawful and the lawful owner or person who is lawfully entitled to its possession is not known, may order that it be forfeited to Her Majesty, to be disposed of as the Attorney General directs, or otherwise dealt with in accordance with the law.

(2) An order may be issued under this section in respect of property situated outside Canada, with any modifications that the circumstances require. R.S.C. 1985, c. 42 (4th Supp.), s. 2; 2001, c. 32, s. 24; 2004, c. 12, s. 7.

APPEALS FROM CERTAIN ORDERS

462.44 Any person who considers that they are aggrieved by an order made under subsection 462.38(2) or 462.41(3) or section 462.43 may appeal from the order as if the order were an appeal against conviction or against a judgment or verdict of acquittal, as the case may be, under Part XXI, and that Part applies, with such modifications as the circumstances require, to such an appeal. R.S.C. 1985, c. 42 (4th Supp.), s. 2; 1997, c. 18, s. 39.

SUSPENSION OF FORFEITURE PENDING APPEAL.

462.45 Despite anything in this Part, the operation of an order of forfeiture or restoration of property under subsection 462.34(4), 462.37(1) or (2.01), 462.38(2) or 462.41(3) or section 462.43 is suspended pending

(a) any application made in respect of the property under any of those provisions or any other provision of this or any other Act of Parliament that provides for the restoration or forfeiture of such property,

(b) any appeal taken from an order of forfeiture or restoration in respect of the property, or

(c) any other proceeding in which the right of seizure of the property is questioned,

and property shall not be disposed of within thirty days after an order of forfeiture is made under any of those provisions. R.S.C. 1985, c. 42 (4th Supp.), s. 2; 2005, c. 44, s. 10.

COPIES OF DOCUMENTS RETURNED OR FORFEITED / Probative force.

462.46 (1) If any document is returned or ordered to be returned, forfeited or otherwise dealt with under subsection 462.34(3) or (4), 462.37(1) or (2.01), 462.38(2) or 462.41(3) or section 462.43, the Attorney General may, before returning the document or complying with the order, cause a copy of the document to be made and retained.

(2) Every copy made under subsection (1) shall, if certified as a true copy by the Attorney General, be admissible in evidence and, in the absence of evidence to the contrary, shall have the same probative force as the original document would have had if it had been proved in the ordinary way. R.S.C. 1985, c. 42 (4th Supp.), s. 2; 2005, c. 44, s. 11.

Disclosure Provisions

NO CIVIL OR CRIMINAL LIABILITY INCURRED BY INFORMANTS.

462.47 For greater certainty but subject to section 241 of the *Income Tax Act*, a person is justified in disclosing to a peace officer or the Attorney General any facts on the basis of which that person reasonably suspects that any property is proceeds of crime or that any person has committed or is about to commit a designated offence. R.S.C. 1985, c. 42 (4th Supp.), s. 2; 1996, c. 19, s. 70; 2001, c. 32, s. 25.

DEFINITION OF "DESIGNATED SUBSTANCE OFFENCE" / Disclosure of income tax information / Application / Order for disclosure of information / Service of order / Extension of period for compliance with order / Objection to disclosure of information / Determination of objection / Judge may examine information / Limitation period / Appeal to Federal Court of Appeal / Limitation period for appeal / Special rules for hearings / *Ex parte* representations / Copies / Further disclosure / Form / Definitions of "police officer".

462.48 (1) In this section, "designated substance offence" means

   (*a*) an offence under Part I of the *Controlled Drugs and Substances Act*, except subsection 4(1) of that Act;

  (*a*.1) an offence under Division 1 of Part 1 of the *Cannabis Act*, except subsection 8(1) of that Act; or

   (*b*) a conspiracy or an attempt to commit, being an accessory after the fact in relation to, or any counselling in relation to, an offence referred to in paragraph (*a*) or (*a*.1).

(1.1) The Attorney General may make an application in accordance with subsection (2) for an order for disclosure of information under subsection (3), for the purposes of an investigation in relation to

   (*a*) a designated substance offence;

   (*b*) an offence against section 354, 355.2, 355.4 or 462.31 if the offence is alleged to have been committed in relation to any property, thing or proceeds obtained or derived directly or indirectly as a result of

      (i) the commission in Canada of a designated substance offence, or

     (ii) an act or omission anywhere that, if it had occurred in Canada, would have constituted a designated substance offence;

   (*c*) an offence against section 467.11, 467.111, 467.12 or 467.13 or a conspiracy or an attempt to commit, or being an accessory after the fact in relation to, such an offence; or

   (*d*) a terrorism offence.

(2) An application under subsection (1.1) shall be made *ex parte* in writing to a judge and be accompanied by an affidavit sworn on the information and belief of the Attorney General or a person specially designated by the Attorney General for that purpose deposing to the following matters, namely,

   (*a*) the offence or matter under investigation;

(b) the person in relation to whom the information or documents referred to in paragraph (c) are required;

(c) the type of information or book, record, writing, return or other document obtained by or on behalf of the Minister of National Revenue for the purposes of the *Income Tax Act*, Part IX of the *Excise Tax Act* or the *Excise Act, 2001* to which access is sought or that is proposed to be examined or communicated; and

(d) the facts relied on to justify the belief, on reasonable grounds, that the person referred to in paragraph (b) has committed or benefited from the commission of any of the offences referred to in subsection (1.1) and that the information or documents referred to in paragraph (c) are likely to be of substantial value, whether alone or together with other material, to the investigation for the purposes of which the application is made.

(3) Where the judge to whom an application under subsection (1.1) is made is satisfied

(a) of the matters referred to in paragraph (2)(d), and

(b) that there are reasonable grounds for believing that it is in the public interest to allow access to the information or documents to which the application relates, having regard to the benefit likely to accrue to the investigation if the access is obtained,

the judge may, subject to any conditions that the judge considers advisable in the public interest, order the Commissioner of Revenue or any person specially designated in writing by the Commissioner for the purposes of this section

(c) to allow a police officer named in the order access to all such information and documents and to examine them, or

(d) where the judge considers it necessary in the circumstances, to produce all such information and documents to the police officer and allow the police officer to remove the information and documents from the possession of that person,

within such period as the judge may specify after the expiration of seven clear days following the service of the order pursuant to subsection (4).

(4) A copy of an order made by a judge under subsection (3) shall be served on the person to whom the order is addressed in such manner as the judge directs or as may be prescribed by rules of court.

(5) A judge who makes an order under subsection (3) may, on application of the Minister of National Revenue, extend the period within which the order is to be complied with.

(6) The Minister of National Revenue or any person specially designated in writing by that Minister for the purposes of this section may object to the disclosure of any information or document in respect of which an order under subsection (3) has been made by certifying orally or in writing that the information or document should not be disclosed on the ground that

(a) the Minister of National Revenue is prohibited from disclosing the information or document by any bilateral or international treaty, convention or other agreement respecting taxation to which the Government of Canada is a signatory;

    (b) a privilege is attached by law to the information or document;

    (c) the information or document has been placed in a sealed package pursuant to law or an order of a court of competent jurisdiction; or

    (d) disclosure of the information or document would not, for any other reason, be in the public interest.

(7) Where an objection to the disclosure of information or a document is made under subsection (6), the objection may be determined, on application, in accordance with subsection (8), by the Chief Justice of the Federal Court, or by such other judge of that court as the Chief Justice may designate to hear such applications.

(8) A judge who is to determine an objection pursuant to subsection (7) may, if the judge considers it necessary to determine the objection, examine the information or document in relation to which the objection is made and shall grant the objection and order that disclosure of the information or document be refused where the judge is satisfied of any of the grounds mentioned in subsection (6).

(9) An application under subsection (7) shall be made within ten days after the objection is made or within such greater or lesser period as the Chief Justice of the Federal Court, or such other judge of that court as the Chief Justice may designate to hear such applications, considers appropriate.

(10) An appeal lies from a determination under subsection (7) to the Federal Court of Appeal.

(11) An appeal under subsection (10) shall be brought within ten days from the date of the determination appealed from or within such further time as the Federal Court of Appeal considers appropriate in the circumstances.

(12) An application under subsection (7) or an appeal brought in respect of that application shall

    (a) be heard in camera; and

    (b) on the request of the person objecting to the disclosure of information, be heard and determined in the National Capital Region described in the schedule to the *National Capital Act*.

(13) During the hearing of an application under subsection (7) or an appeal brought in respect of that application, the person who made the objection in respect of which the application was made or the appeal was brought shall, on the request of that person, be given the opportunity to make representations *ex parte*.

(14) When any information or document is examined or provided under subsection (3), the person by whom it is examined or to whom it is provided or any officer of the Canada Revenue Agency may make, or cause to be made, one or more copies of it, and any copy purporting to be certified by the Minister of National Revenue or an authorized person to be a copy made under this subsection is evidence of the nature and content of the original information or document and has the same probative force as the original information or document would have had if it had been proved in the ordinary way.

(15) No person to whom information or documents have been disclosed or provided pursuant to this subsection or pursuant to an order made under subsection

(3) shall further disclose the information or documents except for the purposes of the investigation in relation to which the order was made.

(16) An order made under subsection (3) may be in Form 47.

(17) In this section, "police officer" means any officer, constable or other person employed for the preservation and maintenance of the public peace. R.S.C. 1985, c. 42 (4th Supp.), s. 2; 1994, c. 13, s. 7; 1996, c. 19, s. 70; 1997, c. 23, s. 10; 1999, c. 17, s. 120; 2001, c. 32, s. 26; 2001, c. 41, s. 133(11); 2005, c. 38, ss. 138(*e*), 140(*b*); 2010, c. 14, s. 9; 2013, c. 9, s. 15; 2014, c. 17, s. 7; 2018, c. 16, s. 215; 2018, c. 27, s. 28.

Specific Rules of Forfeiture

SPECIFIC FORFEITURE PROVISIONS UNAFFECTED BY THIS PART / Priority for restitution to victims of crime.

462.49 (1) This Part does not affect the operation of any other provision of this or any other Act of Parliament respecting the forfeiture of property.

(2) The property of an offender may be used to satisfy the operation of a provision of this or any other Act of Parliament respecting the forfeiture of property only to the extent that is is not required to satisfy the operation of any other provision of this or any other Act of Parliament respecting the restitution or compensation of persons affected by the commission of offences. R.S.C. 1985, c. 42 (4th Supp.), s. 2.

Regulations

REGULATIONS.

462.5 The Attorney General may make regulations governing the manner of disposing of or otherwise dealing with, in accordance with the law, property forfeited under this Part. R.S.C. 1985, c. 42 (4th Supp.), s. 2.

Part XIII / ATTEMPTS – CONSPIRACIES – ACCESSORIES

ATTEMPTS, ACCESSORIES.

463. Except where otherwise expressly provided by law, the following provisions apply in respect of persons who attempt to commit or are accessories after the fact to the commission of offences:

    (*a*) every one who attempts to commit or is an accessory after the fact to the commission of an indictable offence for which, on conviction, an accused is liable to be sentenced to imprisonment for life is guilty of an indictable offence and liable to imprisonment for a term not exceeding fourteen years;

    (*b*) every one who attempts to commit or is an accessory after the fact to the commission of an indictable offence for which, on conviction, an accused is liable to imprisonment for fourteen years or less is guilty of an indictable offence and liable to imprisonment for a term that is one-half of the longest term to which a person who is guilty of that offence is liable;

(c) every one who attempts to commit or is an accessory after the fact to the commission of an offence punishable on summary conviction is guilty of an offence punishable on summary conviction; and

(d) every one who attempts to commit or is an accessory after the fact to the commission of an offence for which the offender may be prosecuted by indictment or for which he is punishable on summary conviction

  (i) is guilty of an indictable offence and liable to imprisonment for a term not exceeding a term that is one-half of the longest term to which a person who is guilty of that offence is liable, or

  (ii) is guilty of an offence punishable on summary conviction. R.S., c. C-34, s. 421; R.S.C. 1985, c. 27 (1st Supp.), s. 59; 1998, c. 35, s. 120.

COUNSELLING OFFENCE THAT IS NOT COMMITTED.

464. Except where otherwise expressly provided by law, the following provisions apply in respect of persons who counsel other persons to commit offences, namely,

(a) every one who counsels another person to commit an indictable offence is, if the offence is not committed, guilty of an indictable offence and liable to the same punishment to which a person who attempts to commit that offence is liable; and

(b) every one who counsels another person to commit an offence punishable on summary conviction is, if the offence is not committed, guilty of an offence punishable on summary conviction. R.S., c. C-34, s. 422; R.S.C. 1985, c. 27 (1st Supp.), s. 60.

CONSPIRACY / Conspiracy to commit offences / Idem / Jurisdiction / Appearance of accused at trial / If previously tried outside Canada.

465. (1) Except where otherwise expressly provided by law, the following provisions apply in respect of conspiracy:

(a) every one who conspires with any one to commit murder or to cause another person to be murdered, whether in Canada or not, is guilty of an indictable offence and liable to a maximum term of imprisonment for life;

(b) every one who conspires with any one to prosecute a person for an alleged offence, knowing that they did not commit that offence, is guilty of

  (i) an indictable offence and liable to imprisonment for a term of not more than 10 years or an offence punishable on summary conviction, if the alleged offence is one for which, on conviction, that person would be liable to be sentenced to imprisonment for life or for a term of not more than 14 years, or

  (ii) an indictable offence and liable to imprisonment for a term of not more than five years or an offence punishable on summary conviction, if the alleged offence is one for which, on conviction, that person would be liable to imprisonment for less than 14 years;

(c)   every one who conspires with any one to commit an indictable offence not provided for in paragraph (a) or (b) is guilty of an indictable offence and liable to the same punishment as that to which an accused who is guilty of that offence would, on conviction, be liable; and

(d)   every one who conspires with any one to commit an offence punishable on summary conviction is guilty of an offence punishable on summary conviction.

(2) [*Repealed*, R.S.C. 1985, c. 27 (1st Supp.), s. 61(3).]

(3) Every one who, while in Canada, conspires with any one to do anything referred to in subsection (1) in a place outside Canada that is an offence under the laws of that place shall be deemed to have conspired to do that thing in Canada.

(4) Every one who, while in a place outside Canada, conspires with any one to do anything referred to in subsection (1) in Canada shall be deemed to have conspired in Canada to do that thing.

(5) Where a person is alleged to have conspired to do anything that is an offence by virtue of subsection (3) or (4), proceedings in respect of that offence may, whether or not that person is in Canada, be commenced in any territorial division in Canada, and the accused may be tried and punished in respect of that offence in the same manner as if the offence had been committed in that territorial division.

(6) For greater certainty, the provisions of this Act relating to

(a)   requirements that an accused appear at and be present during proceedings, and

(b)   the exceptions to those requirements,

apply to proceedings commenced in any territorial division pursuant to subsection (5).

(7) If a person is alleged to have conspired to do anything that is an offence by virtue of subsection (3) or (4) and that person has been tried and dealt with outside Canada in respect of the offence in such a manner that, if the person had been tried and dealt with in Canada, they would be able to plead *autrefois acquit*, *autrefois convict*, pardon or an expungement order under the *Expungement of Historically Unjust Convictions Act*, the person shall be deemed to have been so tried and dealt with in Canada. R.S., c. C-34, s. 423; 1974-75-76, c. 93, s. 36; 1980-81-82-83, c. 125, s. 23; R.S.C. 1985, c. 27 (1st Supp.), s. 61; 1998, c. 35, s. 121; 2018, c. 11, s. 28; 2019, c. 25, s. 183.

CONSPIRACY IN RESTRAINT OF TRADE / Trade union, exception.

466. (1) A conspiracy in restraint of trade is an agreement between two or more persons to do or to procure to be done any unlawful act in restraint of trade.

(2) The purposes of a trade union are not, by reason only that they are in restraint of trade, unlawful within the meaning of subsection (1). R.S., c. C-34, s. 424.

SAVING / Definition of "trade combination".

467. (1) No person shall be convicted of the offence of conspiracy by reason only that he (*a*) refuses to work with a workman or for an employer; or

   (*b*) does any act or causes any act to be done for the purpose of a trade combination, unless that act is an offence expressly punishable by law.

(2) In this section, "trade combination" means any combination between masters or workmen or other persons for the purpose of regulating or altering the relations between masters or workmen, or the conduct of a master or workman in or in respect of his business, employment or contract of employment or service. R.S., c. C-34, s. 425.

DEFINITIONS / "Criminal organization" / "Serious offence" / Facilitation / Commission of offence / Regulations.

467.1 (1) The following definitions apply in this Act.

"criminal organization" means a group, however organized, that

   (*a*) is composed of three or more persons in or outside Canada; and

   (*b*) has as one of its main purposes or main activities the facilitation or commission of one or more serious offences that, if committed, would likely result in the direct or indirect receipt of a material benefit, including a financial benefit, by the group or by any of the persons who constitute the group.

It does not include a group of persons that forms randomly for the immediate commission of a single offence.

"serious offence" means an indictable offence under this or any other Act of Parliament for which the maximum punishment is imprisonment for five years or more, or another offence that is prescribed by regulation.

(2) For the purposes of this section, section 467.11 and 467.111, facilitation of an offence does not require knowledge of a particular offence the commission of which is facilitated, or that an offence actually be committed.

(3) In this section and in sections 467.11 to 467.13, committing an offence means being a party to it or counselling any person to be a party to it.

(4) The Governor in Council may make regulations prescribing offences that are included in the definition "serious offence" in subsection (1). 1997, c. 23, s. 11; 2001, c. 32, s. 27; 2014, c. 17, s. 8.

PARTICIPATION IN ACTIVITIES OF CRIMINAL ORGANIZATION / Prosecution / Factors.

467.11 (1) Every person who, for the purpose of enhancing the ability of a criminal organization to facilitate or commit an indictable offence under this or any other Act of Parliament, knowingly, by act or omission, participates in or contributes to any activity of the criminal organization is guilty of

   (*a*) an indictable offence and liable to imprisonment for a term of not more than five years; or

   (*b*) an offence punishable on summary conviction.

(2) In a prosecution for an offence under subsection (1), it is not necessary for the prosecutor to prove that

(a) the criminal organization actually facilitated or committed an indictable offence;

(b) the participation or contribution of the accused actually enhanced the ability of the criminal organization to facilitate or commit an indictable offence;

(c) the accused knew the specific nature of any indictable offence that may have been facilitated or committed by the criminal organization; or

(d) the accused knew the identity of any of the persons who constitute the criminal organization.

(3) In determining whether an accused participates in or contributes to any activity of a criminal organization, the Court may consider, among other factors, whether the accused

(a) uses a name, word, symbol or other representation that identifies, or is associated with, the criminal organization;

(b) frequently associates with any of the persons who constitute the criminal organization;

(c) receives any benefit from the criminal organization; or

(d) repeatedly engages in activities at the instruction of any of the persons who constitute the criminal organization. 2001, c. 32, s. 27; 2019, c. 25, s. 184.

RECRUITMENT OF MEMBERS BY A CRIMINAL ORGANIZATION.

467.111 Every person who, for the purpose of enhancing the ability of a criminal organization to facilitate or commit an indictable offence under this Act or any other Act of Parliament, recruits, solicits, encourages, coerces or invites a person to join the criminal organization, is guilty of an indictable offence and liable,

(a) in the case where the person recruited, solicited, encouraged or invited is under 18 years of age, to imprisonment for a term not exceeding five years, and to a minimum punishment of imprisonment for a term of six months; and

(b) in any other case, to imprisonment for a term not exceeding five years. 2014, c. 17, s. 9.

COMMISSION OF OFFENCE FOR CRIMINAL ORGANIZATION / Prosecution.

467.12 (1) Every person who commits an indictable offence under this or any other Act of Parliament for the benefit of, at the direction of, or in association with, a criminal organization is guilty of an indictable offence and liable to imprisonment for a term not exceeding fourteen years.

(2) In a prosecution for an offence under subsection (1), it is not necessary for the prosecutor to prove that the accused knew the identity of any of the persons who constitute the criminal organization. 2001, c. 32, s. 27.

INSTRUCTING COMMISSION OF OFFENCE FOR CRIMINAL ORGANIZATION / Prosecution.

467.13 (1) Every person who is one of the persons who constitute a criminal organization and who knowingly instructs, directly or indirectly, any person to commit an offence under this or any other Act of Parliament for the benefit of, at the direction of, or in association with, the criminal organization is guilty of an indictable offence and liable to imprisonment for life.

(2) In a prosecution for an offence under subsection (1), it is not necessary for the prosecutor to prove that

  (a) an offence other than the offence under subsection (1) was actually committed;

  (b) the accused instructed a particular person to commit an offence; or

  (c) the accused knew the identity of all of the persons who constitute the criminal organization. 2001, c. 32, s. 27.

SENTENCES TO BE SERVED CONSECUTIVELY.

467.14 A sentence imposed on a person for an offence under section 467.11, 467.111, 467.12 or 467.13 shall be served consecutively to any other punishment imposed on the person for an offence arising out of the same event or series of events and to any other sentence to which the person is subject at the time the sentence is imposed on the person for an offence under any of those sections. 2001, c. 32, s. 27; 2014, c. 17, s. 10.

467.2 [*Repealed*, 2019, c. 25, s. 185.]

Part XIV / JURISDICTION

General

SUPERIOR COURT OF CRIMINAL JURISDICTION.

468. Every superior court of criminal jurisdiction has jurisdiction to try any indictable offence. R.S., c. C-34, s. 426.

COURT OF CRIMINAL JURISDICTION / Accessories / Corrupting justice / Attempts / Conspiracy.

469. Every court of criminal jurisdiction has jurisdiction to try an indictable offence other than

  (a) an offence under any of the following sections:

    (i) section 47 (treason),

    (ii) [*Repealed*, 2018, c. 29, s. 61.]

    (iii) section 51 (intimidating Parliament or a legislature),

(iv) section 53 (inciting to mutiny),
(v) section 61 (seditious offences),
(vi) section 74 (piracy),
(vii) section 75 (piratical acts), or
(viii) section 235 (murder);

(b) the offence of being an accessory after the fact to high treason or treason or murder;

(c) an offence under section 119 (bribery) by the holder of a judicial office;

(c.1) an offence under any of sections 4 to 7 of the *Crimes Against Humanity and War Crimes Act*;

(d) the offence of attempting to commit any offence mentioned in subparagraphs (a)(i) to (vii); or

(e) the offence of conspiring to commit any offence mentioned in paragraph (a). R.S., c. C-34, s. 427; 1972, c. 13, s. 33; 1974-75-76, c. 93, s. 37, c. 105, s. 29; R.S.C. 1985, c. 27 (1st Supp.), s. 62; 2000, c. 24, s. 44; 2018, c. 29, s. 61.

JURISDICTION OVER PERSON.

470. Subject to this Act, every superior court of criminal jurisdiction and every court of criminal jurisdiction that has power to try an indictable offence is competent to try an accused for that offence

(a) if the accused is found, is arrested or is in custody within the territorial jurisdiction of the court; or

(b) if the accused has been ordered to be tried by
(i) that court, or
(ii) any other court, the jurisdiction of which has by lawful authority been transferred to that court. R.S., c. C-34, s. 428; R.S.C. 1985, c. 27 (1st Supp.), s. 101(3).

TRIAL BY JURY COMPULSORY.

471. Except where otherwise expressly provided by law, every accused who is charged with an indictable offence shall be tried by a court composed of a judge and jury. R.S., c. C-34, s. 429.

---

472. [*Repealed*, R.S.C. 1985, c. 27 (1st Supp.), s. 63.]

TRIAL WITHOUT JURY / Joinder of other offences / Withdrawal of consent.

473. (1) Notwithstanding anything in this Act, an accused charged with an offence listed in section 469 may, with the consent of the accused and the Attorney General, be tried without a jury by a judge of a superior court of criminal jurisdiction.

(1.1) Where the consent of the accused and the Attorney General is given in accordance with subsection (1), the judge of the superior court of criminal jurisdiction may order that any offence be tried by that judge in conjunction with the offence listed in section 469.

(2) Notwithstanding anything in this Act, where the consent of an accused and the Attorney General is given in accordance with subsection (1), that consent shall not be withdrawn unless both the accused and the Attorney General agree to the withdrawal. R.S., c. C-34, s. 430; R.S.C. 1985, c. 27 (1st Supp.), s. 63; 1994, c. 44, s. 30.

ADJOURNMENT WHEN NO JURY SUMMONED / Adjournment on instruction of judge.

474. (1) Where the competent authority has determined that a panel of jurors is not to be summoned for a term or sittings of the court for the trial of criminal cases in any territorial division, the clerk of the court may, on the day of the opening of the term or sittings, if a judge is not present to preside over the court, adjourn the court and the business of the court to a subsequent day. R.S., c. C-34, s. 431.

(2) A clerk of the court for the trial of criminal cases in any territorial division may, at any time, on the instructions of the presiding judge or another judge of the court, adjourn the court and the business of the court to a subsequent day. R.S., c. C-34, s. 431; 1994, c. 44, s. 31.

ACCUSED ABSCONDING DURING TRIAL / Adverse inference / Accused not entitled to re-opening / Counsel for accused may continue to act.

475. (1) Notwithstanding any other provision of this Act, where an accused, whether or not he is charged jointly with another, absconds during the course of his trial,

    (*a*) he shall be deemed to have waived his right to be present at his trial, and

    (*b*) the court may

        (i) continue the trial and proceed to a judgment or verdict and, if it finds the accused guilty, impose a sentence on him in his absence, or

        (ii) if a warrant in Form 7 is issued for the arrest of the accused, adjourn the trial to await his appearance,

but where the trial is adjourned pursuant to subparagraph (*b*)(ii), the court may, at any time, continue the trial if it is satisfied that it is no longer in the interests of justice to await the appearance of the accused.

(2) Where a court continues a trial pursuant to subsection (1), it may draw an inference adverse to the accused from the fact that he has absconded.

(3) Where an accused reappears at his trial that is continuing pursuant to subsection (1), he is not entitled to have any part of the proceedings that was conducted in his absence re-opened unless the court is satisfied that because of exceptional circumstances it is in the interests of justice to re-open the proceedings.

(4) Where an accused has absconded during the course of his trial and the court continues the trial, counsel for the accused is not thereby deprived of any authority he may have to continue to act for the accused in the proceedings. 1974-75-76, c. 93, s. 39.

Special Jurisdiction

SPECIAL JURISDICTIONS.

476. For the purposes of this Act,

   (a) where an offence is committed in or on any water or on a bridge between two or more territorial divisions, the offence shall be deemed to have been committed in any of the territorial divisions;

   (b) where an offence is committed on the boundary of two or more territorial divisions or within five hundred metres of any such boundary, or the offence was commenced within one territorial division and completed within another, the offence shall be deemed to have been committed in any of the territorial divisions;

   (c) where an offence is committed in or on a vehicle employed in a journey, or on board a vessel employed on a navigable river, canal or inland water, the offence shall be deemed to have been committed in any territorial division through which the vehicle or vessel passed in the course of the journey or voyage on which the offence was committed, and where the center or other part of the road, or navigable river, canal or inland water on which the vehicle or vessel passed in the course of the journey or voyage is the boundary of two or more territorial divisions, the offence shall be deemed to have been committed in any of the territorial divisions;

   (d) where an offence is committed in an aircraft in the course of a flight of that aircraft, it shall be deemed to have been committed

   (i) in the territorial division in which the flight commenced,

   (ii) in any territorial division over which the aircraft passed in the course of the flight, or

   (iii) in the territorial division in which the flight ended; and

   (e) where an offence is committed in respect of the mail in the course of its door-to-door delivery, the offence shall be deemed to have been committed in any territorial division through which the mail was carried on that delivery. R.S., c. C-34, s. 432; R.S.C. 1985, c. 27 (1st Supp.), s. 186; 1992, c. 1, s. 58.

WORDS AND EXPRESSIONS / Saving.

477. (1) In sections 477.1 to 477.4, "ship" includes any description of vessel, boat or craft designed, used or capable of being used solely or partly for marine navigation, without regard to method or lack of propulsion.

(2) Nothing in sections 477.1 to 477.4 limits the operation of any other Act of Parliament or the jurisdiction that a court may exercise apart from those sections. 1990, c. 44, s. 15; 1996, c. 31, s. 67.

OFFENCES IN, ABOVE OR BEYOND CONTINENTAL SHELF.

477.1 Every person who commits an act or omission that, if it occurred in Canada, would be an offence under a federal law, within the meaning of section 2 of the

Oceans Act, is deemed to have committed that act or omission in Canada if it is an act or omission

 (*a*) in the exclusive economic zone of Canada that

  (i) is committed by a person who is in the exclusive economic zone of Canada in connection with exploring or exploiting, conserving or managing the natural resources, whether living or non-living, of the exclusive economic zone of Canada, and

  (ii) is committed by or in relation to a person who is a Canadian citizen or a permanent resident within the meaning of subsection 2(1) of the *Immigration and Refugee Protection Act*.

 (*b*) that is committed in a place in or above the continental shelf of Canada and that is an offence in that place by virtue of section 20 of the *Oceans Act*;

 (*c*) that is committed outside Canada on board or by means of a ship registered or licensed, or for which an identification number has been issued, pursuant to any Act of Parliament:

 (*d*) that is committed outside Canada in the course of hot pursuit; or

 (*e*) that is committed outside the territory of any state by a Canadian citizen. 1990, c. 44, s. 15; 1996, c. 31, s. 68; 2001, c. 27, s. 247.

CONSENT OF ATTORNEY GENERAL / Exception / Consent of Attorney General / Idem / Consent to be filed.

477.2 (1) No proceedings in respect of an offence committed in or on the territorial sea of Canada shall be continued unless the consent of the Attorney General of Canada is obtained not later than eight days after the proceedings are commenced, if the accused is not a Canadian citizen and the offence is alleged to have been committed on board any ship registered outside Canada.

(1.1) Subsection (1) does not apply to proceedings by way of summary conviction.

(2) No proceedings in respect of which courts have jurisdiction by virtue only of paragraph 477.1(*a*) or (*b*) shall be continued unless the consent of the Attorney General of Canada is obtained not later than eight days after the proceedings are commenced, if the accused is not a Canadian citizen and the offence is alleged to have been committed on board any ship registered outside Canada.

(3) No proceedings in respect of which courts have jurisdiction by virtue only of paragraph 477.1(*d*) or (*e*) shall be continued unless the consent of the Attorney General of Canada is obtained not later than eight days after the proceedings are commenced.

(4) The consent of the Attorney General required by subsection (1), (2) or (3) must be filed with the clerk of the court in which the proceedings have been instituted. 1990, c. 44, s. 15; 1994, c. 44, s. 32; 1996, c. 31, s. 69.

EXERCISING POWERS OF ARREST, ENTRY, ETC. / Arrest, search, seizure, etc. / Limitation.

477.3 (1) Every power of arrest, entry, search or seizure or other power that could be exercised in Canada in respect of an act or omission referred to in section 477.1 may be exercised, in the circumstances referred to in that section.

(a) at the place or on board the ship or marine installation or structure, within the meaning of section 2 of the *Oceans Act*, where the act or omission occurred; or

(b) where hot pursuit has been commenced, at any place on the seas, other than a place that is part of the territorial sea of any other state.

(2) A justice or judge in any territorial division in Canada has jurisdiction to authorize an arrest, entry, search or seizure or an investigation or other ancillary matter related to an offence

(a) committed in or on the territorial sea of Canada or any area of the sea that forms part of the internal waters of Canada, or

(b) referred to in section 477.1 in the same manner as if the offence had been committed in that territorial division.

(3) Where an act or omission that is an offence by virtue only of section 477.1 is alleged to have been committed on board any ship registered outside Canada, the powers referred to in subsection (1) shall not be exercised outside Canada with respect to that act or omission without the consent of the Attorney General of Canada. 1990, c. 44, s. 15; 1996, c. 31, s. 70.

TERRITORIAL DIVISION FOR PROSECUTION / Evidence / Certificate cannot be compelled.

477.4 (1) [*Repealed*, 1996, c. 31, s. 71.]

(2) [*Repealed*, 1996, c. 31, s. 71.]

(3) In proceedings in respect of an offence,

(a) a certificate referred to in subsection 23(1) of the *Oceans Act*, or

(b) a certificate issued by or under the authority of the Minister of Foreign Affairs containing a statement that any geographical location specified in the certificate was, at any time material to the proceedings, in an area of a fishing zone of Canada that is not within the internal waters of Canada or the territorial sea of Canada or outside the territory of any state,

is conclusive proof of the truth of the statement without proof of the signature or official character of the person appearing to have issued the certificate.

(4) A certificate referred to in subsection (3) is admissible in evidence in proceedings referred to in that subsection but its production cannot be compelled. 1990, c. 44, s. 15; 1995, c. 5, s. 25; 1996, c. 31, s. 71.

OFFENCE COMMITTED ENTIRELY IN ONE PROVINCE / Exception / Idem / Where accused committed to stand trial / Definition of "newspaper".

478. (1) Subject to this Act, a court in a province shall not try an offence committed entirely in another province.

(2) Every proprietor, publisher, editor or other person charged with the publication of a defamatory libel in a newspaper or with conspiracy to publish a defamatory libel in a newspaper shall be dealt with, indicted, tried and punished in the province where he resides or in which the newspaper is printed.

(3) An accused who is charged with an offence that is alleged to have been committed in Canada outside the province in which the accused is, may, if the offence is not an offence mentioned in section 469 and

(*a*) in the case of proceedings instituted at the instance of the Government of Canada and conducted by or on behalf of that Government, if the Attorney General of Canada consents, or

(*b*) in any other case, if the Attorney General of the province where the offence is alleged to have been committed consents,

appear before a court or judge that would have had jurisdiction to try that offence if it had been committed in the province where the accused is, and where the accused consents to plead guilty and pleads guilty to that offence, the court or judge shall determine the accused to be guilty of the offence and impose the punishment warranted by law, but where the accused does not consent to plead guilty and does not plead guilty, the accused shall, if the accused was in custody prior to appearance, be returned to custody and shall be dealt with according to law.

(4) Notwithstanding that an accused described in subsection (3) has been ordered to stand trial or that an indictment has been preferred against the accused in respect of the offence to which he desires to plead guilty, the accused shall be deemed simply to stand charged of that offence without a preliminary inquiry having been conducted or an indictment having been preferred with respect thereto.

(5) In this section, "newspaper" has the same meaning as in section 297. R.S., c. C-34, s. 434; 1974-75-76, c. 93, s. 40; R.S.C. 1985, c. 27 (1st Suppl.), ss. 64, 101(3); 1994, c. 44, s. 33.

OFFENCE OUTSTANDING IN SAME PROVINCE.

479. Where an accused is charged with an offence that is alleged to have been committed in the province in which he is, he may, if the offence is not an offence mentioned in section 469, and

(*a*) in the case of proceedings instituted at the instance of the Government of Canada and conducted by or on behalf of that Government, the Attorney General of Canada consents, or

(*b*) in any other case, the Attorney General of the province where the offence is alleged to have been committed consents,

appear before a court or judge that would have had jurisdiction to try that offence if it had been committed in the place where the accused is, and where the accused consents to plead guilty and pleads guilty to that offence, the court or judge shall determine the accused to be guilty of the offence and impose the punishment warranted by law, but where the accused does not consent to plead guilty and does not plead guilty, the accused shall, if the accused was in custody prior to his appearance, be returned to custody and shall be dealt with according to law. R.S., c. C-34, s. 435; 1974-75-76, c. 93, s. 41; R.S.C. 1985, c. 27 (1st Suppl.), s. 65; 1994, c. 44, s. 34.

OFFENCE IN UNORGANIZED TERRITORY / New territorial division.

480. (1) Where an offence is committed in an unorganized tract of country in any province or on a lake, river or other water therein, not included in a territorial division or in a provisional judicial district, proceedings in respect thereof may be commenced and an accused may be charged, tried and punished in respect thereof within any territorial division or provisional judicial district of the province in the same manner as if the offence had been committed within that territorial division or provisional judicial district.

(2) Where a provisional judicial district or a new territorial division is constituted in an unorganized tract referred to in subsection (1), the jurisdiction conferred by that subsection continues until appropriate provision is made by law for the administration of criminal justice within the provisional judicial district or new territorial division. R.S., c. C-34, s. 436.

OFFENCE NOT IN A PROVINCE.

481. Where an offence is committed in a part of Canada not in a province, proceedings in respect thereof may be commenced and the accused may be charged, tried and punished within any territorial division in any province in the same manner as if that offence had been committed in that territorial division. R.S., c. C-34, s. 437.

OFFENCE IN CANADIAN WATERS.

481.1 Where an offence is committed in or on the territorial sea of Canada or any area of the sea that forms part of the internal waters of Canada, proceedings in respect thereof may, whether or not the accused is in Canada, be commenced and an accused may be charged, tried and punished within any territorial division in Canada in the same manner as if the offence had been committed in that territorial division. 1996, c. 31, s. 72.

OFFENCE OUTSIDE CANADA.

481.2 Subject to this or any other Act of Parliament, where an act or omission is committed outside Canada and the act or omission is an offence when committed outside Canada under this or any other Act of Parliament, proceedings in respect of the offence may, whether or not the accused is in Canada, be commenced, and an accused may be charged, tried and punished within any territorial division in Canada in the same manner as if the offence had been committed in that territorial division. 1996, c. 31, s. 72; 2008, c. 18, s. 10.

APPEARANCE OF ACCUSED AT TRIAL.

481.3 For greater certainty, the provisions of this Act relating to

(a) the requirement of the appearance of an accused at proceedings, and

(b) the exceptions to that requirement

apply to proceedings commenced in any territorial division pursuant to section 481, 481.1 or 481.2. 1996, c. 31, s. 72.

Rules of Court

POWER TO MAKE RULES / Power to make rules / Purpose of rules / Publication / Regulations to secure uniformity.

482. (1) Every superior court of criminal jurisdiction and every court of appeal may make rules of court not inconsistent with this or any other Act of Parliament, and any rules so made apply to any prosecution, proceeding, action or appeal, as the case may be, within the jurisdiction of that court, instituted in relation to any matter of a criminal nature or arising from or incidental to any such prosecution, proceeding, action or appeal.

(2) The following courts may make rules of court not inconsistent with this Act or any other Act of Parliament that are applicable to any prosecution, proceeding, including a preliminary inquiry or proceedings within the meaning of Part XXVII, action or appeal, as the case may be, within the jurisdiction of that court, instituted in relation to any matter of a criminal nature or arising from or incidental to the prosecution, proceeding, action or appeal:

- (*a*) every court of criminal jurisdiction for a province;
- (*b*) every appeal court within the meaning of section 812 that is not a court referred to in subsection (1);
- (*c*) the Ontario Court of Justice;
- (*d*) the Court of Quebec and every municipal court in the Province of Quebec;
- (*e*) the Provincial Court of Nova Scotia;
- (*f*) the Provincial Court of New Brunswick;
- (*g*) the Provincial Court of Manitoba;
- (*h*) the Provincial Court of British Columbia;
- (*i*) the Provincial Court of Prince Edward Island;
- (*j*) the Provincial Court of Saskatchewan;
- (*k*) the Provincial Court of Alberta;
- (*l*) the Provincial Court of Newfoundland and Labrador;
- (*m*) the Territorial Court of Yukon;
- (*n*) the Territorial Court of the Northwest Territories; and
- (*o*) the Nunavut Court of Justice.

(3) Rules under subsection (1) or (2) may be made

- (*a*) generally to regulate the duties of the officers of the court and any other matter considered expedient to attain the ends of justice and carry into effect the provisions of the law;
- (*b*) to regulate the sittings of the court or any division thereof, or of any judge of the court sitting in chambers, except in so far as they are regulated by law;
- (*c*) to regulate the pleading, practice and procedure in criminal matters, including pre-hearing conferences held under section 625.1, proceedings with respect to judicial interim release and preliminary inquiries and, in the case of rules under subsection (1), proceedings with respect to mandamus, certiorari, habeas corpus, prohibition and procedendo and proceedings on an appeal under section 830; and

(*d*) to carry out the provisions of this Act relating to appeals from conviction, acquittal or sentence and, without restricting the generality of this paragraph,

    (i) for furnishing necessary forms and instructions in relation to notices of appeal or applications for leave to appeal to officials or other persons requiring or demanding them,

    (ii) for ensuring the accuracy of notes taken at a trial and the verification of any copy or transcript,

    (iii) for keeping writings, exhibits or other things connected with the proceedings on the trial,

    (iv) for securing the safe custody of property during the period in which the operation of an order with respect to that property is suspended under subsection 689(1), and

    (v) for providing that the Attorney General and counsel who acted for the Attorney General at the trial be supplied with certified copies of writings, exhibits and things connected with the proceedings that are required for the purposes of their duties.

(4) Rules of court that are made under this section must be published or otherwise made available to the public.

(5) Notwithstanding anything in this section, the Governor in Council may make such provision as he considers proper to secure uniformity in the rules of court in criminal matters, and all uniform rules made under the authority of this subsection prevail and have effect as if enacted by this Act. R.S., c. C-34, s. 438; 1974-75-76, c. 93, s. 42; R.S.C. 1985, c. 27 (1st Supp.), s. 66; 1994, c. 44, s. 35; 2002, c. 13, s. 17; 2015, c. 3, s. 50; 2019, c. 25, s. 186.

POWER TO MAKE RULES RESPECTING CASE MANAGEMENT / Compliance with directions / Summons or warrant / Provisions to apply / Subsections 482(4) and (5) to apply.

482.1 (1) A court referred to in subsection 482(1) or (2) may make rules for case management, including rules

(*a*) for the determination of any matter that would assist the court in effective and efficient case management;

(*b*) permitting personnel of the court to deal with administrative matters relating to proceedings out of court if the accused is represented by counsel; and

(*c*) establishing case management schedules.

(2) The parties to a case shall comply with any direction made in accordance with a rule made under subsection (1).

(3) If rules are made under subsection (1), a court, justice or judge may issue a summons or warrant to compel the presence of the accused at case management proceedings.

(4) Sections 512 and 512.3 apply, with any modifications that the circumstances require, to the issuance of a summons or a warrant under subsection (3).

(5) Subsections 482(4) and (5) apply, with any modifications that the circumstances require, to rules made under subsection (1). 2002, c. 13, s. 18; 2019, c. 25, s. 187.

(6) [*Repealed*, 2019, c. 25, s. 187(2).]

Part XV / SPECIAL PROCEDURE AND POWERS

General Powers of Certain Officials

OFFICIALS WITH POWERS OF TWO JUSTICES.

483. Every judge or provincial court judge authorized by the law of the province in which he is appointed to do anything that is required to be done by two or more justices may do alone anything that this Act or any other Act of Parliament authorizes two or more justices to do. R.S., c. C-34, s. 439.

PRESERVING ORDER IN COURT.

484. Every judge or provincial court judge has the same power and authority to preserve order in a court over which he presides as may be exercised by the superior court of criminal jurisdiction of the province during the sittings thereof. R.S., c. C-34, s. 440.

PROCEDURAL IRREGULARITIES / When accused not appearing personally / Summons or warrant / Dismissal for want of prosecution / Adjournment and order / Part XVI to apply.

485. (1) Jurisdiction over an offence is not lost by reason of the failure of any court, judge, provincial court judge or justice to act in the exercise of that jurisdiction at any particular time, or by reason of a failure to comply with any of the provisions of this Act respecting adjournments or remands.

(1.1) Jurisdiction over an accused is not lost by reason of the failure of the accused to appear personally, so long as the provisions of this Act or a rule made under section 482 or 482.1 permitting the accused not to appear personally apply.

(2) Where jurisdiction over an accused or a defendant is lost and has not been regained, a court, judge, provincial court judge or justice may, within three months after the loss of jurisdiction, issue a summons, or if it or he considers it necessary in the public interest, a warrant for the arrest of the accused or defendant.

(3) Where no summons or warrant is issued under subsection (2) within the period provided therein, the proceedings shall be deemed to be dismissed for want of prosecution and shall not be recommenced except in accordance with section 485.1.

(4) Where, in the opinion of the court, judge, provincial court judge or justice, an accused or a defendant who appears at a proceeding has been misled or prejudiced by reason of any matter referred to in subsection (1), the court, judge, provincial

court judge or justice may adjourn the proceeding and may make such order as it or he considers appropriate.

(5) The provisions of Part XVI apply with such modifications as the circumstances require where a summons or warrant is issued under subsection (2). 1974-75-76, c. 93, s. 43; R.S.C. 1985, c. 27 (1st Supp.), s. 67; 1997, c. 18, s. 40; 2002, c. 13, s. 19; 2019, c. 25, s. 188.

RECOMMENCEMENT WHERE DISMISSAL FOR WANT OF PROSECUTION.

485.1 Where an indictment in respect of a transaction is dismissed or deemed by any provision of this Act to be dismissed for want of prosecution, a new information shall not be laid and a new indictment shall not be preferred before any court in respect of the same transaction without

    (*a*) the personal consent in writing of the Attorney General or Deputy Attorney General, in any prosecution conducted by the Attorney General or in which the Attorney General intervenes; or

    (*b*) the written order of a judge of that court, in any prosecution conducted by a prosecutor other than the Attorney General and in which the Attorney General does not intervene. R.S.C. 1985, c. 27 (1st Supp.), s. 67.

EXCLUSION OF PUBLIC / Application / Factors to be considered / Reasons to be stated / No adverse inference.

486. (1) Any proceedings against an accused shall be held in open court, but the presiding judge or justice may, on application of the prosecutor or a witness or on his or her own motion, order the exclusion of all or any members of the public from the court room for all or part of the proceedings, or order that the witness testify behind a screen or other device that would allow the witness not to be seen by members of the public, if the judge or justice is of the opinion that such an order is in the interest of public morals, the maintenance of order or the proper administration of justice or is necessary to prevent injury to international relations or national defence or national security.

(1.1) The application may be made, during the proceedings, to the presiding judge or justice or, before the proceedings begin, to the judge or justice who will preside at the proceedings or, if that judge or justice has not been determined, to any judge or justice having jurisdiction in the judicial district where the proceedings will take place.

(2) In determining whether the order is in the interest of the proper administration of justice, the judge or justice shall consider

    (*a*) society's interest in encouraging the reporting of offences and the participation of victims and witnesses in the criminal justice process;

    (*b*) the safeguarding of the interests of witnesses under the age of 18 years in all proceedings;

    (*c*) the ability of the witness to give a full and candid account of the acts complained of if the order were not made;

    (*d*) whether the witness needs the order for their security or to protect them from intimidation or retaliation;

(*e*) the protection of justice system participants who are involved in the proceedings;

(*f*) whether effective alternatives to the making of the proposed order are available in the circumstances;

(*g*) the salutary and deleterious effects of the proposed order; and

(*h*) any other factor that the judge or justice considers relevant.

(3) If an accused is charged with an offence under section 151, 152, 153, 153.1 or 155, subsection 160(2) or (3) or section 163.1, 170, 171, 171.1, 172, 172.1, 172.2, 173, 271, 272, 273, 279.01, 279.011, 279.02, 279.03, 286.1, 286.2 or 286.3 and the prosecutor or the accused applies for an order under subsection (1), the judge or justice shall, if no such order is made, state, by reference to the circumstances of the case, the reason for not making an order.

(4) No adverse inference may be drawn from the fact that an order is, or is not, made under this section. R.S., c. C-34, s. 442; 1974-75-76, c. 93, s. 44; 1980-81-82-83, c. 110, s. 74, c. 125, s. 25; R.S.C. 1985, c. 19 (3rd Supp.), s. 14; c. 23 (4th Supp.), s. 1; 1992, c. 21, s. 9; 1993, c. 45, s. 7; 1997, c. 16, s. 6; 1999, c. 25, s. 2; 2001, c. 32, s. 29; 2001, c. 41, s. 16, 34 and 133(13), (14); 2002, c. 13, s. 20; 2005, c. 32, s. 15; 2005, c. 43, ss. 4 and 8(3)(*a*); 2010, c. 3, s. 4; 2012, c. 1, s. 28; 2014, c. 25, s. 21; 2015, c. 13, s. 13; c. 20, s. 21; 2019, c. 25, s. 189.

SUPPORT PERSON — WITNESSES UNDER 18 OR WHO HAVE A DISABILITY / Other witnesses / Application / Factors to be considered / Witness not to be a support person / No communication while testifying / No adverse inference.

486.1 (1) In any proceedings against an accused, the judge or justice shall, on application of the prosecutor in respect of a witness who is under the age of 18 years or who has a mental or physical disability, or on application of such a witness, order that a support person of the witness' choice be permitted to be present and to be close to the witness while the witness testifies, unless the judge or justice is of the opinion that the order would interfere with the proper administration of justice.

(2) In any proceedings against an accused, the judge or justice may, on application of the prosecutor in respect of a witness, or on application of a witness, order that a support person of the witness' choice be permitted to be present and to be close to the witness while the witness testifies if the judge or justice is of the opinion that the order would facilitate the giving of a full and candid account by the witness of the acts complained of or would otherwise be in the interest of the proper administration of justice.

(2.1) An application referred to in subsection (1) or (2) may be made, during the proceedings, to the presiding judge or justice or, before the proceedings begin, to the judge or justice who will preside at the proceedings or, if that judge or justice has not been determined, to any judge or justice having jurisdiction in the judicial district where the proceedings will take place.

(3) In determining whether to make an order under subsection (2), the judge or justice shall consider

(a) the age of the witness;
(b) the witness' mental or physical disabilities, if any;
(c) the nature of the offence;
(d) the nature of any relationship between the witness and the accused;
(e) whether the witness needs the order for their security or to protect them from intimidation or retaliation;
(f) society's interest in encouraging the reporting of offences and the participation of victims and witnesses in the criminal justice process; and
(g) any other factor that the judge or justice considers relevant.

(4) The judge or justice shall not permit a witness to be a support person unless the judge or justice is of the opinion that doing so is necessary for the proper administration of justice.

(5) The judge or justice may order that the support person and the witness not communicate with each other while the witness testifies.

(6) No adverse inference may be drawn from the fact that an order is, or is not, made under this section. 2005, c. 32, s. 15; 2015, c. 13, s. 14.

TESTIMONY OUTSIDE COURT ROOM — WITNESSES UNDER 18 OR WHO HAVE A DISABILITY / Other witnesses / Application / Factors to be considered / Same procedure for determination / Conditions of exclusion / No adverse inference.

486.2 (1) Despite section 650, in any proceedings against an accused, the judge or justice shall, on application of the prosecutor in respect of a witness who is under the age of 18 years or who is able to communicate evidence but may have difficulty doing so by reason of a mental or physical disability, or on application of such a witness, order that the witness testify outside the court room or behind a screen or other device that would allow the witness not to see the accused, unless the judge or justice is of the opinion that the order would interfere with the proper administration of justice.

(2) Despite section 650, in any proceedings against an accused, the judge or justice may, on application of the prosecutor in respect of a witness, or on application of a witness, order that the witness testify outside the court room or behind a screen or other device that would allow the witness not to see the accused if the judge or justice is of the opinion that the order would facilitate the giving of a full and candid account by the witness of the acts complained of or would otherwise be in the interest of the proper administration of justice.

(2.1) An application referred to in subsection (1) or (2) may be made, during the proceedings, to the presiding judge or justice or, before the proceedings begin, to the judge or justice who will preside at the proceedings or, if that judge or justice has not been determined, to any judge or justice having jurisdiction in the judicial district where the proceedings will take place.

(3) In determining whether to make an order under subsection (2), the judge or justice shall consider
(a) the age of the witness;
(b) the witness' mental or physical disabilities, if any;

(c) the nature of the offence;

(d) the nature of any relationship between the witness and the accused;

(e) whether the witness needs the order for their security or to protect them from intimidation or retaliation;

(f) whether the order is needed to protect the identity of a peace officer who has acted, is acting or will be acting in an undercover capacity, or of a person who has acted, is acting or will be acting covertly under the direction of a peace officer;

(f.1) whether the order is needed to protect the witness's identity if they have had, have or will have responsibilities relating to national security or intelligence;

(g) society's interest in encouraging the reporting of offences and the participation of victims and witnesses in the criminal justice process; and

(h) any other factor that the judge or justice considers relevant.

(4) If the judge or justice is of the opinion that it is necessary for a witness to testify in order to determine whether an order under subsection (2) should be made in respect of that witness, the judge or justice shall order that the witness testify in accordance with that subsection.

(5) A witness shall not testify outside the court room in accordance with an order made under subsection (1) or (2) unless arrangements are made for the accused, the judge or justice and the jury to watch the testimony of the witness by means of closed-circuit television or otherwise and the accused is permitted to communicate with counsel while watching the testimony.

(6) No adverse inference may be drawn from the fact that an order is, or is not, made under subsection (1) or (2). 2005, c. 32, s. 15; 2014, c. 17, s. 12; 2015, c. 13, s. 15; 2015, c. 20, s. 38(2).

(7) [*Repealed*, 2015, c. 13, s. 15.]

(8) [*Repealed*, 2015, c. 13, s. 15.]

ACCUSED NOT TO CROSS-EXAMINE WITNESSES UNDER 18 / Accused not to cross-examine complainant — certain offences / Other witnesses / Factors to be considered / Application / No adverse inference.

486.3 (1) In any proceedings against an accused, the judge or justice shall, on application of the prosecutor in respect of a witness who is under the age of 18 years, or on application of such a witness, order that the accused not personally cross-examine the witness, unless the judge or justice is of the opinion that the proper administration of justice requires the accused to personally conduct the cross-examination. If such an order is made, the judge or justice shall appoint counsel to conduct the cross-examination.

(2) In any proceedings against an accused in respect of an offence under any of sections 264, 271, 272 and 273, the judge or justice shall, on application of the prosecutor in respect of a witness who is a victim, or on application of such a witness, order that the accused not personally cross-examine the witness, unless the judge or justice is of the opinion that the proper administration of justice requires the accused to personally conduct the cross-examination. If such an order

is made, the judge or justice shall appoint counsel to conduct the cross-examination.

(3) In any proceedings against an accused, the judge or justice may, on application of the prosecutor in respect of a witness who is not entitled to make an application under subsection (1) or (2), or on application of such a witness, order that the accused not personally cross-examine the witness if the judge or justice is of the opinion that the order would allow the giving of a full and candid account from the witness of the acts complained of or would otherwise be in the interest of the proper administration of justice. If the order is made, the judge or justice shall appoint counsel to conduct the cross-examination.

(4) In determining whether to make an order under subsection (3), the judge or justice shall consider
- (a) the age of the witness;
- (b) the witness' mental or physical disabilities, if any;
- (c) the nature of the offence;
- (d) whether the witness needs the order for their security or to protect them from intimidation or retaliation;
- (e) the nature of any relationship between the witness and the accused;
- (f) society's interest in encouraging the reporting of offences and the participation of victims and witnesses in the criminal justice process; and
- (g) any other factor that the judge or justice considers relevant.

(4.1) An application referred to in any of subsections (1) to (3) may be made during the proceedings to the presiding judge or justice or, before the proceedings begin, to the judge or justice who will preside at the proceedings or, if that judge or justice has not been determined, to any judge or justice having jurisdiction in the judicial district where the proceedings will take place.

(5) No adverse inference may be drawn from the fact that counsel is, or is not, appointed under this section. 2005, c. 32, s. 15; 2015, c. 13, s. 16.

NON-DISCLOSURE OF WITNESS' IDENTITY / Hearing may be held / Factors to be considered / No adverse inference.

486.31 (1) In any proceedings against an accused, the judge or justice may, on application of the prosecutor in respect of a witness, or on application of a witness, make an order directing that any information that could identify the witness not be disclosed in the course of the proceedings if the judge or justice is of the opinion that the order is in the interest of the proper administration of justice.

(2) The judge or justice may hold a hearing to determine whether the order should be made, and the hearing may be in private.

(3) In determining whether to make the order, the judge or justice shall consider
- (a) the right to a fair and public hearing;
- (b) the nature of the offence;
- (c) whether the witness needs the order for their security or to protect them from intimidation or retaliation;
- (d) whether the order is needed to protect the security of anyone known to the witness;

    (*e*) whether the order is needed to protect the identity of a peace officer who has acted, is acting or will be acting in an undercover capacity, or of a person who has acted, is acting or will be acting covertly under the direction of a peace officer;

(*e*.1) whether the order is needed to protect the witness's identity if they have had, have or will have responsibilities relating to national security or intelligence;

    (*f*) society's interest in encouraging the reporting of offences and the participation of victims and witnesses in the criminal justice process;

    (*g*) the importance of the witness' testimony to the case;

    (*h*) whether effective alternatives to the making of the proposed order are available in the circumstances;

    (*i*) the salutary and deleterious effects of the proposed order; and

    (*j*) any other factor that the judge or justice considers relevant.

(4) No adverse inference may be drawn from the fact that an order is, or is not, made under this section. 2015, c. 13, s. 17; c. 20, s. 38(3).

ORDER RESTRICTING PUBLICATION — SEXUAL OFFENCES / Mandatory order on application / Victim under 18 — other offences / Mandatory order on application / Child pornography / Limitation.

486.4 (1) Subject to subsection (2), the presiding judge or justice may make an order directing that any information that could identify the victim or a witness shall not be published in any document or broadcast or transmitted in any way, in proceedings in respect of

    (*a*) any of the following offences:

        (i) an offence under section 151, 152, 153, 153.1, 155, 160, 162, 163.1, 170, 171, 171.1, 172, 172.1, 172.2, 173, 213, 271, 272, 273, 279.01, 279.011, 279.02, 279.03, 280, 281, 286.1, 286.2, 286.3, 346 or 347, or

        (ii) any offence under this Act, as it read from time to time before the day on which this subparagraph comes into force, if the conduct alleged would be an offence referred to in subparagraph (i) if it occurred on or after that day; or

        (iii) [*Repealed*, 2014, c. 25, s. 22(2).]

    (*b*) two or more offences being dealt with in the same proceeding, at least one of which is an offence referred to in paragraph (*a*).

(2) In proceedings in respect of the offences referred to in paragraph (1)(*a*) or (*b*), the presiding judge or justice shall

    (*a*) at the first reasonable opportunity, inform any witness under the age of eighteen years and the victim of the right to make an application for the order; and

    (*b*) on application made by the victim, the prosecutor or any such witness, make the order.

(2.1) Subject to subsection (2.2), in proceedings in respect of an offence other than an offence referred to in subsection (1), if the victim is under the age of 18 years, the presiding judge or justice may make an order directing that any information that could identify the victim shall not be published in any document or broadcast or transmitted in any way.

(2.2) In proceedings in respect of an offence other than an offence referred to in subsection (1), if the victim is under the age of 18 years, the presiding judge or justice shall

    (*a*) as soon as feasible, inform the victim of their right to make an application for the order; and

    (*b*) on application of the victim or the prosecutor, make the order.

(3) In proceedings in respect of an offence under section 163.1, a judge or justice shall make an order directing that any information that could identify a witness who is under the age of eighteen years, or any person who is the subject of a representation, written material or a recording that constitutes child pornography within the meaning of that section, shall not be published in any document or broadcast or transmitted in any way.

(4) An order made under this section does not apply in respect of the disclosure of information in the course of the administration of justice when it is not the purpose of the disclosure to make the information known in the community. 2005, c. 32, s. 15; c. 43, s. 8(3)(*b*); 2010, c. 3, s. 5; 2012, c. 1, s. 29; 2014, c. 25, ss. 22, 48(6); 2015, c. 13, s. 18(1), (2), (4); 2019, c. 25, s. 190.

ORDER RESTRICTING PUBLICATION — VICTIMS AND WITNESSES / Justice system participants / Offences / Limitation / Application and notice / Grounds / Hearing may be held / Factors to be considered / Conditions / Publication prohibited.

486.5 (1) Unless an order is made under section 486.4, on application of the prosecutor in respect of a victim or a witness, or on application of a victim or a witness, a judge or justice may make an order directing that any information that could identify the victim or witness shall not be published in any document or broadcast or transmitted in any way if the judge or justice is of the opinion that the order is in the interest of the proper administration of justice.

(2) On application of the prosecutor in respect of a justice system participant who is involved in proceedings in respect of an offence referred to in subsection (2.1), or on application of such a justice system participant, a judge or justice may make an order directing that any information that could identify the justice system participant shall not be published in any document or broadcast or transmitted in any way if the judge or justice is of the opinion that the order is in the interest of the proper administration of justice.

(2.1) The offences for the purposes of subsection (2) are

    (*a*) an offence under section 423.1, 467.11, 467.111, 467.12 or 467.13, or a serious offence committed for the benefit of, at the direction of, or in association with, a criminal organization;

    (*b*) a terrorism offence;

    (*c*) an offence under subsection 16(1) or (2), 17(1), 19(1), 20(1) or 22(1) of the *Security of Information Act*; or (*d*) an offence under subsection 21(1) or section 23 of the *Security of Information Act* that is committed in relation to an offence referred to in paragraph (*c*).

(3) An order made under this section does not apply in respect of the disclosure of information in the course of the administration of justice if it is not the purpose of the disclosure to make the information known in the community.

(4) An applicant for an order shall

(*a*) apply in writing to the presiding judge or justice or, if the judge or justice has not been determined, to a judge of a superior court of criminal jurisdiction in the judicial district where the proceedings will take place; and

(*b*) provide notice of the application to the prosecutor, the accused and any other person affected by the order that the judge or justice specifies.

(5) An applicant for an order shall set out the grounds on which the applicant relies to establish that the order is necessary for the proper administration of justice.

(6) The judge or justice may hold a hearing to determine whether an order should be made, and the hearing may be in private.

(7) In determining whether to make an order, the judge or justice shall consider

(*a*) the right to a fair and public hearing;

(*b*) whether there is a real and substantial risk that the victim, witness or justice system participant would suffer harm if their identity were disclosed;

(*c*) whether the victim, witness or justice system participant needs the order for their security or to protect them from intimidation or retaliation;

(*d*) society's interest in encouraging the reporting of offences and the participation of victims, witnesses and justice system participants in the criminal justice process;

(*e*) whether effective alternatives are available to protect the identity of the victim, witness or justice system participant;

(*f*) the salutary and deleterious effects of the proposed order;

(*g*) the impact of the proposed order on the freedom of expression of those affected by it; and

(*h*) any other factor that the judge or justice considers relevant.

(8) An order may be subject to any conditions that the judge or justice thinks fit.

(9) Unless the judge or justice refuses to make an order, no person shall publish in any document or broadcast or transmit in any way

(*a*) the contents of an application;

(*b*) any evidence taken, information given or submissions made at a hearing under subsection (6); or

(*c*) any other information that could identify the person to whom the application relates as a victim, witness or justice system participant in the proceedings. 2005, c. 32, s. 15; 2015, c. 13, s. 19.

OFFENCE / Application of order.

486.6 (1) Every person who fails to comply with an order made under any of subsections 486.4(1) to (3) or subsection 486.5(1) or (2) is guilty of an offence punishable on summary conviction.

(2) For greater certainty, an order referred to in subsection (1) applies to prohibit, in relation to proceedings taken against any person who fails to comply with the order, the publication in any document or the broadcasting or transmission in any way of information that could identify a victim, witness or justice system participant whose identity is protected by the order. 2005, c. 32, s. 15; 2019, c. 13, s. 151.

CODE

SECURITY OF WITNESSES / Application / Factors to be considered / No adverse inference.

486.7 (1) In any proceedings against an accused, the presiding judge or justice may, on application of the prosecutor or a witness or on his or her own motion, make any order, other than one that may be made under any of sections 486 to 486.5, if the judge or justice is of the opinion that the order is necessary to protect the security of any witness and is otherwise in the interest of the proper administration of justice.

(2) The application may be made, during the proceedings, to the presiding judge or justice or, before the proceedings begin, to the judge or justice who will preside at the proceedings or, if that judge or justice has not been determined, to any judge or justice having jurisdiction in the judicial district where the proceedings will take place.

(3) In determining whether to make the order, the judge or justice shall consider

    (*a*) the age of the witness;

    (*b*) the witness's mental or physical disabilities, if any;

    (*c*) the right to a fair and public hearing;

    (*d*) the nature of the offence;

    (*e*) whether the witness needs the order to protect them from intimidation or retaliation;

    (*f*) whether the order is needed to protect the security of anyone known to the witness;

    (*g*) society's interest in encouraging the reporting of offences and the participation of victims and witnesses in the criminal justice process;

    (*h*) the importance of the witness's testimony to the case;

    (*i*) whether effective alternatives to the making of the proposed order are available in the circumstances;

    (*j*) the salutary and deleterious effects of the proposed order; and

    (*k*) any other factor that the judge or justice considers relevant.

(4) No adverse inference may be drawn from the fact that an order is, or is not, made under this section. 2015, c. 20, s. 22.

INFORMATION FOR SEARCH WARRANT / Execution in Canada / Operation of computer system and copying equipment / Duty of person in possession or control / Form / Effect of endorsement.

487. (1) A justice who is satisfied by information on oath in Form 1 that there are reasonable grounds to believe that there is in a building, receptacle or place

- (a) anything on or in respect of which any offence against this Act or any other Act of Parliament has been or is suspected to have been committed,
- (b) anything that there are reasonable grounds to believe will afford evidence with respect to the commission of an offence, or will reveal the whereabouts of a person who is believed to have committed an offence, against this Act or any other Act of Parliament,
- (c) anything that there are reasonable grounds to believe is intended to be used for the purpose of committing any offence against the person for which a person may be arrested without warrant, or
- (c.1) any offence-related property,

may at any time issue a warrant authorizing a peace officer or a public officer who has been appointed or designated to administer or enforce a federal or provincial law and whose duties include the enforcement of this Act or any other Act of Parliament and who is named in the warrant

- (d) to search the building, receptacle or place for any such thing and to seize it, and
- (e) subject to any other Act of Parliament, to, as soon as practicable, bring the thing seized before, or make a report in respect thereof to, the justice or some other justice for the same territorial division in accordance with section 489.1.

(2) A warrant issued under subsection (1) may be executed at any place in Canada. A public officer named in the warrant, or any peace officer, who executes the warrant must have authority to act in that capacity in the place where the warrant is executed.

(2.1) A person authorized under this section to search a computer system in a building or place for data may

- (a) use or cause to be used any computer system at the building or place to search any data contained in or available to the computer system;
- (b) reproduce or cause to be reproduced any data in the form of a print-out or other intelligible output;
- (c) seize the print-out or other output for examination or copying; and
- (d) use or cause to be used any copying equipment at the place to make copies of the data.

(2.2) Every person who is in possession or control of any building or place in respect of which a search is carried out under this section shall, on presentation of the warrant, permit the person carrying out the search

- (a) to use or cause to be used any computer system at the building or place in order to search any data contained in or available to the computer system for data that the person is authorized by this section to search for;
- (b) to obtain a hard copy of the data and to seize it; and

   (*c*) to use or cause to be used any copying equipment at the place to make copies of the data.

(3) A search warrant issued under this section may be in the form set out as Form 5 in Part XXVIII, varied to suit the case. R.S., c. C-34, s. 443; R.S.C. 1985, c. 27 (1st Supp.), s. 68; 1994, c. 44, s. 36; 1997, c. 18, s. 41; 1997, c. 23, s. 12; 1999, c. 5, s. 16; 2008, c. 18, s. 11; 2019, c. 25, s. 191.

(4) [*Repealed*, 2019, c. 25, s. 191(2).]

INFORMATION FOR GENERAL WARRANT / Limitation / Search or seizure to be reasonable / Video surveillance / Other provisions to apply / Notice after covert entry / Extension of period for giving notice / Execution in Canada / Telewarrant provisions to apply.

487.01 (1) A provincial court judge, a judge of a superior court of criminal jurisdiction or a judge as defined in section 552 may issue a warrant in writing authorizing a peace officer to, subject to this section, use any device or investigative technique or procedure or do any thing described in the warrant that would, if not authorized, constitute an unreasonable search or seizure in respect of a person or a person's property if

   (*a*) the judge is satisfied by information on oath in writing that there are reasonable grounds to believe that an offence against this or any other Act of Parliament has been or will be committed and that information concerning the offence will be obtained through the use of the technique, procedure or device or the doing of the thing;

   (*b*) the judge is satisfied that it is in the best interests of the administration of justice to issue the warrant; and

   (*c*) there is no other provision in this or any other Act of Parliament that would provide for a warrant, authorization or order permitting the technique, procedure or device to be used or the thing to be done.

(2) Nothing in subsection (1) shall be construed as to permit interference with the bodily integrity of any person.

(3) A warrant issued under subsection (1) shall contain such terms and conditions as the judge considers advisable to ensure that any search or seizure authorized by the warrant is reasonable in the circumstances.

(4) A warrant issued under subsection (1) that authorizes a peace officer to observe, by means of a television camera or other similar electronic device, any person who is engaged in activity in circumstances in which the person has a reasonable expectation of privacy shall contain such terms and conditions as the judge considers advisable to ensure that the privacy of the person or of any other person is respected as much as possible.

(5) The definition "offence" in section 183 and sections 183.1, 184.2, 184.3 and 185 to 188.2, subsection 189(5), and sections 190, 193 and 194 to 196 apply, with such modifications as the circumstances require, to a warrant referred to in subsection (4) as though references in those provisions to interceptions of private communications were read as references to observations by peace officers by

means of television cameras or similar electronic devices of activities in circumstances in which persons had reasonable expectations of privacy.

(5.1) A warrant issued under subsection (1) that authorizes a peace officer to enter and search a place covertly shall require, as part of the terms and conditions referred to in subsection (3), that notice of the entry and search be given within any time after the execution of the warrant that the judge considers reasonable in the circumstances.

(5.2) Where the judge who issues a warrant under subsection (1) or any other judge having jurisdiction to issue such a warrant is, on the basis of an affidavit submitted in support of an application to vary the period within which the notice referred to in subsection (5.1) is to be given, is satisfied that the interests of justice warrant the granting of the application, the judge may grant an extension, or a subsequent extension, of the period, but no extension may exceed three years.

(6) A warrant issued under subsection (1) may be executed at any place in Canada. Any peace officer who executes the warrant must have authority to act as a peace officer in the place where it is executed.

(7) Where a peace officer believes that it would be impracticable to appear personally before a judge to make an application for a warrant under this section, a warrant may be issued under this section on an information submitted by telephone or other means of telecommunication and, for that purpose, section 487.1 applies, with such modifications as the circumstances require, to the warrant. 1993, c. 40, s. 15; 1997, c. 18, s. 42; 1997, c. 23, s. 13; 2019, c. 25, s. 192.

DEFINITIONS.

487.011 The following definitions apply in this section and in sections 487.012 to 487.0199.

"computer data" has the same meaning as in subsection 342.1(2).

"data" means representations, including signs, signals or symbols, that are capable of being understood by an individual or processed by a computer system or other device.

"document" means a medium on which data is registered or marked.

"judge" means a judge of a superior court of criminal jurisdiction or a judge of the Court of Quebec.

"public officer" means a public officer who is appointed or designated to administer or enforce a federal or provincial law and whose duties include the enforcement of this Act or any other Act of Parliament.

"tracking data" means data that relates to the location of a transaction, individual or thing.

"transmission data" means data that

  (a) relates to the telecommunication functions of dialling, routing, addressing or signalling;

(b) is transmitted to identify, activate or configure a device, including a computer program as defined in subsection 342.1(2), in order to establish or maintain access to a telecommunication service for the purpose of enabling a communication, or is generated during the creation, transmission or reception of a communication and identifies or purports to identify the type, direction, date, time, duration, size, origin, destination or termination of the communication; and

(c) does not reveal the substance, meaning or purpose of the communication.
2004, c. 3, s. 7; 2014, c. 31, s. 20.

PRESERVATION DEMAND / Conditions for making demand / Limitation / Expiry and revocation of demand / Conditions in demand / No further demand.

487.012 (1) A peace officer or public officer may make a demand to a person in Form 5.001 requiring them to preserve computer data that is in their possession or control when the demand is made.

(2) The peace officer or public officer may make the demand only if they have reasonable grounds to suspect that

(a) an offence has been or will be committed under this or any other Act of Parliament or has been committed under a law of a foreign state;

(b) in the case of an offence committed under a law of a foreign state, an investigation is being conducted by a person or authority with responsibility in that state for the investigation of such offences; and

(c) the computer data is in the person's possession or control and will assist in the investigation of the offence.

(3) A demand may not be made to a person who is under investigation for the offence referred to in paragraph (2)(a).

(4) A peace officer or public officer may revoke the demand by notice given to the person at any time. Unless the demand is revoked earlier, the demand expires

(a) in the case of an offence that has been or will be committed under this or any other Act of Parliament, 21 days after the day on which it is made; and

(b) in the case of an offence committed under a law of a foreign state, 90 days after the day on which it is made.

(5) The peace officer or public officer who makes the demand may impose any conditions in the demand that they consider appropriate — including conditions prohibiting the disclosure of its existence or some or all of its contents — and may revoke a condition at any time by notice given to the person.

(6) A peace officer or public officer may not make another demand requiring the person to preserve the same computer data in connection with the investigation.
2004, c. 3, s. 7; 2014, c. 31, s. 20.

(7) [*Repealed*, 2014, c. 31, s. 20.]

(8) [*Repealed*, 2014, c. 31, s. 20.]

PRESERVATION ORDER — COMPUTER DATA / Conditions for making order / Offence against law of foreign state / Form / Limitation / Expiry of order.

487.013 (1) On *ex parte* application made by a peace officer or public officer, a justice or judge may order a person to preserve computer data that is in their possession or control when they receive the order.

(2) Before making the order, the justice or judge must be satisfied by information on oath in Form 5.002

   (a) that there are reasonable grounds to suspect that an offence has been or will be committed under this or any other Act of Parliament or has been committed under a law of a foreign state, that the computer data is in the person's possession or control and that it will assist in the investigation of the offence; and

   (b) that a peace officer or public officer intends to apply or has applied for a warrant or an order in connection with the investigation to obtain a document that contains the computer data.

(3) If an offence has been committed under a law of a foreign state, the justice or judge must also be satisfied that a person or authority with responsibility in that state for the investigation of such offences is conducting the investigation.

(4) The order is to be in Form 5.003.

(5) A person who is under investigation for an offence referred to in paragraph (2)(a) may not be made subject to an order.

(6) Unless the order is revoked earlier, it expires 90 days after the day on which it is made. 2004, c. 3. s. 7; 2014, c. 31, s. 20.

GENERAL PRODUCTION ORDER / Conditions for making order / Form / Limitation.

487.014 (1) Subject to sections 487.015 to 487.018, on *ex parte* application made by a peace officer or public officer, a justice or judge may order a person to produce a document that is a copy of a document that is in their possession or control when they receive the order, or to prepare and produce a document containing data that is in their possession or control at that time.

(2) Before making the order, the justice or judge must be satisfied by information on oath in Form 5.004 that there are reasonable grounds to believe that

   (a) an offence has been or will be committed under this or any other Act of Parliament; and

   (b) the document or data is in the person's possession or control and will afford evidence respecting the commission of the offence.

(3) The order is to be in Form 5.005.

(4) A person who is under investigation for the offence referred to in subsection (2) may not be made subject to an order. 2004, c. 3, s. 7; 2014, c. 31, s. 20.

PRODUCTION ORDER TO TRACE SPECIFIED COMMUNICATION / Conditions for making order / Form / Service / Limitation / Report.

487.015 (1) On *ex parte* application made by a peace officer or public officer for the purpose of identifying a device or person involved in the transmission of a communication, a justice or judge may order a person to prepare and produce a document containing transmission data that is related to that purpose and that is, when they are served with the order, in their possession or control.

(2) Before making the order, the justice or judge must be satisfied by information on oath in Form 5.004 that there are reasonable grounds to suspect that

    (*a*) an offence has been or will be committed under this or any other Act of Parliament;

    (*b*) the identification of a device or person involved in the transmission of a communication will assist in the investigation of the offence; and

    (*c*) transmission data that is in the possession or control of one or more persons whose identity is unknown when the application is made will enable that identification.

(3) The order is to be in Form 5.006.

(4) A peace officer or public officer may serve the order on any person who was involved in the transmission of the communication and whose identity was unknown when the application was made

    (*a*) within 60 days after the day on which the order is made; or

    (*b*) within one year after the day on which the order is made, in the case of an offence under section 467.11, 467.12 or 467.13, an offence committed for the benefit of, at the direction of or in association with a criminal organization, or a terrorism offence.

(5) A person who is under investigation for the offence referred to in subsection (2) may not be made subject to an order.

(6) A peace officer or public officer named in the order must provide a written report to the justice or judge who made the order as soon as feasible after the person from whom the communication originated is identified or after the expiry of the period referred to in subsection (4), whichever occurs first. The report must state the name and address of each person on whom the order was served, and the date of service. 2004, c. 3, s. 7; 2014, c. 31, s. 20.

PRODUCTION ORDER — TRANSMISSION DATA / Conditions for making order / Form / Limitation.

487.016 (1) On *ex parte* application made by a peace officer or public officer, a justice or judge may order a person to prepare and produce a document containing transmission data that is in their possession or control when they receive the order.

(2) Before making the order, the justice or judge must be satisfied by information on oath in Form 5.004 that there are reasonable grounds to suspect that

    (*a*) an offence has been or will be committed under this or any other Act of Parliament; and

(b) the transmission data is in the person's possession or control and will assist in the investigation of the offence.

(3) The order is to be in Form 5.007.

(4) A person who is under investigation for the offence referred to in subsection (2) may not be made subject to an order. 2004, c. 3, s. 7; 2014, c. 31, s. 20.

PRODUCTION ORDER — TRACKING DATA / Conditions for making order / Form / Limitation.

487.017 (1) On *ex parte* application made by a peace officer or public officer, a justice or judge may order a person to prepare and produce a document containing tracking data that is in their possession or control when they receive the order.

(2) Before making the order, the justice or judge must be satisfied by information on oath in Form 5.004 that there are reasonable grounds to suspect that

(a) an offence has been or will be committed under this or any other Act of Parliament; and

(b) the tracking data is in the person's possession or control and will assist in the investigation of the offence.

(3) The order is to be in Form 5.007.

(4) A person who is under investigation for the offence referred to in subsection (2) may not be made subject to an order. 2004, c. 7, s. 7; 2014, c. 31, s. 20.

PRODUCTION ORDER — FINANCIAL DATA / Identification of person / Conditions for making order / Form / Limitation.

487.018 (1) On *ex parte* application made by a peace officer or public officer, a justice or judge may order a financial institution, as defined in section 2 of the *Bank Act*, or a person or entity referred to in section 5 of the *Proceeds of Crime (Money Laundering) and Terrorist Financing Act*, to prepare and produce a document setting out the following data that is in their possession or control when they receive the order:

(a) either the account number of a person named in the order or the name of a person whose account number is specified in the order;

(b) the type of account;

(c) the status of the account; and

(d) the date on which it was opened or closed.

(2) For the purpose of confirming the identity of a person who is named or whose account number is specified in the order, the order may also require the institution, person or entity to prepare and produce a document setting out the following data that is in their possession or control:

(a) the date of birth of a person who is named or whose account number is specified in the order;

(b) that person's current address; and

(c) any previous addresses of that person.

(3) Before making the order, the justice or judge must be satisfied by information on oath in Form 5.004 that there are reasonable grounds to suspect that

(*a*) an offence has been or will be committed under this or any other Act of Parliament; and

(*b*) the data is in the possession or control of the institution, person or entity and will assist in the investigation of the offence.

(4) The order is to be in Form 5.008.

(5) A financial institution, person or entity that is under investigation for the offence referred to in subsection (3) may not be made subject to an order. 2014, c. 31, s. 20.

CONDITIONS IN PRESERVATION AND PRODUCTION ORDERS / Effect of order / Power to revoke or vary order.

487.019 (1) An order made under any of sections 487.013 to 487.018 may contain any conditions that the justice or judge considers appropriate including, in the case of an order made under section 487.014, conditions to protect a privileged communication between a person who is qualified to give legal advice and their client.

(2) The order has effect throughout Canada.

(3) On *ex parte* application made by a peace officer or public officer, the justice or judge who made the order — or a judge in the judicial district where the order was made — may, on the basis of an information on oath in Form 5.0081, revoke or vary the order. The peace officer or public officer must give notice of the revocation or variation to the person who is subject to the order as soon as feasible. 2014, c. 31, s. 20; 2019, c. 25, s. 193.

ORDER PROHIBITING DISCLOSURE / Conditions for making order / Form / Application to revoke or vary order.

487.0191 (1) On *ex parte* application made by a peace officer or public officer, a justice or judge may make an order prohibiting a person from disclosing the existence or some or all of the contents of a preservation demand made under section 487.012 or a preservation or production order made under any of sections 487.013 to 487.018 during the period set out in the order.

(2) Before making the order, the justice or judge must be satisfied by information on oath in Form 5.009 that there are reasonable grounds to believe that the disclosure during that period would jeopardize the conduct of the investigation of the offence to which the preservation demand or the preservation or production order relates.

(3) The order is to be in Form 5.0091.

(4) A peace officer or a public officer or a person, financial institution or entity that is subject to an order made under subsection (1) may apply in writing to the justice or judge who made the order — or to a judge in the judicial district where the order was made — to revoke or vary the order. 2014, c. 31, s. 20.

PARTICULARS — PRODUCTION ORDERS / Particulars — production order to trace specified communication / Form of production / Non-application / Probative force of copies / *Canada Evidence Act.*

487.0192 (1) An order made under any of sections 487.014 and 487.016 to 487.018 must require a person, financial institution or entity to produce the document to a peace officer or public officer named in the order within the time, at the place and in the form specified in the order.

(2) An order made under section 487.015 must require a person to produce the document to a peace officer or public officer named in the order as soon as feasible after they are served with the order at the place and in the form specified in the order.

(3) For greater certainty, an order under any of sections 487.014 to 487.018 may specify that a document may be produced on or through an electro-magnetic medium.

(4) For greater certainty, sections 489.1 and 490 do not apply to a document that is produced under an order under any of sections 487.014 to 487.018.

(5) Every copy of a document produced under section 487.014 is admissible in evidence in proceedings under this or any other Act of Parliament on proof by affidavit that it is a true copy and has the same probative force as the document would have if it were proved in the ordinary way.

(6) A document that is prepared for the purpose of production is considered to be original for the purposes of the *Canada Evidence Act*. 2014, c. 31, s. 20.

APPLICATION FOR REVIEW OF PRODUCTION ORDER / Notice required / No obligation to produce / Revocation or variation of order.

487.0193 (1) Before they are required by an order made under any of sections 487.014 to 487.018 to produce a document, a person, financial institution or entity may apply in writing to the justice or judge who made the order — or to a judge in the judicial district where the order was made — to revoke or vary the order.

(2) The person, institution or entity may make the application only if they give notice of their intention to do so to a peace officer or public officer named in the order within 30 days after the day on which the order is made.

(3) The person, institution or entity is not required to prepare or produce the document until a final decision is made with respect to the application.

(4) The justice or judge may revoke or vary the order if satisfied that
   (*a*) it is unreasonable in the circumstances to require the applicant to prepare or produce the document; or
   (*b*) production of the document would disclose information that is privileged or otherwise protected from disclosure by law. 2014, c. 31, s. 20.

**DESTRUCTION OF PRESERVED COMPUTER DATA AND DOCUMENTS —
PRESERVATION DEMAND / Destruction of preserved computer data and
documents — preservation order / Destruction of preserved computer
data and documents — production order / Destruction of preserved computer
data and documents — warrant.**

487.0194 (1) A person to whom a preservation demand is made under section
487.012 shall destroy the computer data that would not be retained in the ordinary
course of business and any document that is prepared for the purpose of preserving
computer data under that section as soon as feasible after the demand expires or is
revoked, unless they are subject to an order made under any of sections 487.013 to
487.017 with respect to the computer data.

(2) A person who is subject to a preservation order made under section 487.013
shall destroy the computer data that would not be retained in the ordinary course
of business and any document that is prepared for the purpose of preserving
computer data under that section as soon as feasible after the order expires or is
revoked, unless they are subject to a new preservation order or to a production
order made under any of sections 487.014 to 487.017 with respect to the computer
data.

(3) A person who is subject to a production order made under any of sections
487.014 to 487.017 with respect to computer data that they preserved under a
preservation demand or order made under section 487.012 or 487.013 shall
destroy the computer data that would not be retained in the ordinary course of
business and any document that is prepared for the purpose of preserving
computer data under that section as soon as feasible after the earlier of
  (*a*) the day on which the production order is revoked, and
  (*b*) the day on which a document that contains the computer data is produced
         under the production order.

(4) Despite subsections (1) to (3), a person who preserved computer data under a
preservation demand or order made under section 487.012 or 487.013 shall
destroy the computer data that would not be retained in the ordinary course of
business and any document that is prepared for the purpose of preserving
computer data under that section when a document that contains the computer data
is obtained under a warrant. 2014, c. 31, s. 20.

FOR GREATER CERTAINTY / No civil or criminal liability.

487.0195 (1) For greater certainty, no preservation demand, preservation order or
production order is necessary for a peace officer or public officer to ask a person
to voluntarily preserve data that the person is not prohibited by law from
preserving or to voluntarily provide a document to the officer that the person is not
prohibited by law from disclosing.

(2) A person who preserves data or provides a document in those circumstances
does not incur any criminal or civil liability for doing so. 2014, c. 31, s. 20.

SELF-INCRIMINATION.

487.0196 No one is excused from complying with an order made under any of sections 487.014 to 487.018 on the ground that the document that they are required to produce may tend to incriminate them or subject them to a proceeding or penalty. However, no document that an individual is required to prepare may be used or received in evidence against them in a criminal proceeding that is subsequently instituted against them, other than a prosecution for an offence under section 132, 136 or 137. 2014, c. 31, s. 20.

OFFENCE — PRESERVATION DEMAND.

487.0197 A person who contravenes a preservation demand made under section 487.012 without lawful excuse is guilty of an offence punishable on summary conviction and is liable to a fine of not more than $5,000. 2014, c. 31, s. 20.

OFFENCE — PRESERVATION OR PRODUCTION ORDER.

487.0198 A person, financial institution or entity that contravenes an order made under any of sections 487.013 to 487.018 without lawful excuse is guilty of an offence punishable on summary conviction and liable to a fine of not more than $250,000 or to imprisonment for a term of not more than two years less a day, or to both. 2014, c. 31, s. 20; 2019, c. 25, s. 194.

OFFENCE — DESTRUCTION OF PRESERVED DATA.

487.0199 A person who contravenes section 487.0194 without lawful excuse is guilty of an offence punishable on summary conviction. 2014, c. 31, s. 20.

ASSISTANCE ORDER.

487.02 If an authorization is given under section 184.2, 184.3, 186 or 188 or a warrant is issued under this Act, the judge or justice who gives the authorization or issues the warrant may order a person to provide assistance, if the person's assistance may reasonably be considered to be required to give effect to the authorization or warrant. The order has effect throughout Canada. 1993, c. 40, s. 15; 1997, c. 18, s. 43; 2014, c. 31, s. 20; 2019, c. 25, s. 195.

REVIEW / Report.

487.021 (1) Within seven years after the coming into force of this section, a comprehensive review of the provisions and operation of sections 487.011 to 487.02 shall be undertaken by such committee of the House of Commons as may be designated or established by the House for that purpose.

(2) The committee referred to in subsection (1) shall, within a year after a review is undertaken pursuant to that subsection or within such further time as the House may authorize, submit a report on the review to the Speaker of the House, including a statement of any changes the committee recommends. 2014, c. 31, s. 20.

487.03 [*Repealed*, 2019, c. 25, s. 196.]

Forensic DNA Analysis

DEFINITIONS / **"Adult"** / **"Designated offence"** / **"DNA"** / **"Forensic DNA analysis"** / **"Primary designated offence"** / **"Provincial court judge"** / **"Secondary designated offence"** / **"Young Offenders Act"** / **"Young person".**

487.04 In this section and in sections 487.05 to 487.0911,

"adult" has the meaning assigned by subsection 2(1) of the *Youth Criminal Justice Act*;

"designated offence" means a primary designated offence or a secondary designated offence;

"DNA" means deoxyribonucleic acid;

"forensic DNA analysis"

   (*a*) in relation to a bodily substance that is taken from a person in execution of a warrant under section 487.05, means forensic DNA analysis of the bodily substance and the comparison of the results of that analysis with the results of the analysis of the DNA in the bodily substance referred to in paragraph 487.05(1)(*b*), and includes any incidental tests associated with that analysis, and

   (*b*) in relation to a bodily substance that is provided voluntarily in the course of an investigation of a designated offence or is taken from a person under an order made under section 487.051 or an authorization granted under section 487.055 or 487.091, or to a bodily substance referred to in paragraph 487.05(1)(*b*), means forensic DNA analysis of the bodily substance;

"primary designated offence" means

   (*a*) an offence under any of the following provisions, namely,

      (i) subsection 7(4.1) (offence in relation to sexual offences against children),

    (i.1) section 151 (sexual interference),

    (i.2) section 152 (invitation to sexual touching),

    (i.3) section 153 (sexual exploitation),

    (i.4) section 153.1 (sexual exploitation of person with disability),

    (i.5) section 155 (incest),

    (i.6) subsection 160(2) (compelling the commission of bestiality),

    (i.7) subsection 160(3) (bestiality in presence of or by a child),

    (i.8) section 163.1 (child pornography),

    (i.9) section 170 (parent or guardian procuring sexual activity),

  (i.901) section 171.1 (making sexually explicit material available to child),

   (i.91) section 172.1 (luring a child),

  (i.911) section 172.2 (agreement or arrangement — sexual offence against child),

   (i.92) subsection 173(2) (exposure),

   (i.93) [*Repealed*, 2014, c. 25, s. 23(1).]

   (i.94) [*Repealed*, 2014, c. 25, s. 23(1).]

459

(i.95) [*Repealed*, 2014, c. 25, s. 23(1).]

(i.96) [*Repealed*, 2014, c. 25, s. 23(1).]

(ii) section 235 (murder),

(iii) section 236 (manslaughter),

(iv) section 239 (attempt to commit murder),

(v) section 244 (discharging firearm with intent),

(vi) section 244.1 (causing bodily harm with intent — air gun or pistol),

(vi.1) section 244.2 (discharging firearm — recklessness),

(vii) paragraph 245(a) (administering noxious thing with intent to endanger life or cause bodily harm),

(viii) section 246 (overcoming resistance to commission of offence),

(ix) section 267 (assault with a weapon or causing bodily harm),

(x) section 268 (aggravated assault),

(xi) section 269 (unlawfully causing bodily harm),

(xi.1) section 270.01 (assaulting peace officer with weapon or causing bodily harm),

(xi.2) section 270.02 (aggravated assault of peace officer),

(xi.3) section 271 (sexual assault),

(xii) section 272 (sexual assault with a weapon, threats to a third party or causing bodily harm),

(xiii) section 273 (aggravated sexual assault),

(xiii.1) subsection 273.3(2) (removal of a child from Canada),

(xiv) section 279 (kidnapping),

(xiv.1) section 279.011 (trafficking — person under 18 years),

(xiv.2) subsection 279.02(2) (material benefit — trafficking of person under 18 years),

(xiv.3) subsection 279.03(2) (withholding or destroying documents — trafficking of person under 18 years),

(xiv.4) subsection 286.1(2) (obtaining sexual services for consideration from person under 18 years),

(xiv.5) subsection 286.2(2) (material benefit from sexual services provided by person under 18 years),

(xiv.6) subsection 286.3(2) (procuring — person under 18 years),

(xv) section 344 (robbery), and

(xvi) section 346 (extortion),

(*a*.1) an offence under any of the following provisions, namely,

(i) section 75 (piratical acts),

(i.01) section 76 (hijacking),

(i.02) section 77 (endangering safety of aircraft or airport),

(i.03) section 78.1 (seizing control of ship or fixed platform),

(i.04) subsection 81(1) (using explosives),

(i.041) section 82.3 (possession, etc., of nuclear material, radioactive material or device),

(i.042) section 82.4 (use or alteration of nuclear material, radioactive material or device),

(i.043) section 82.5 (commission of indictable offence to obtain nuclear material, etc.),

(i.044) section 82.6 (threats),

(i.05) section 83.18 (participation in activity of terrorist group),
(i.051) section 83.181 (leaving Canada to participate in activity of terrorist group),
(i.06) section 83.19 (facilitating terrorist activity),
(i.061) section 83.191 (leaving Canada to facilitate terrorist activity),
(i.07) section 83.2 (commission of offence for terrorist group),
(i.071) section 83.201 (leaving Canada to commit offence for terrorist group),
(i.072) section 83.202 (leaving Canada to commit offence that is terrorist activity),
(i.08) section 83.21 (instructing to carry out activity for terrorist group),
(i.09) section 83.22 (instructing to carry out terrorist activity),
(i.091) section 83.221 (counselling commission of terrorism offence),
(i.1) section 83.23 (harbouring or concealing),
(i.11) [*Repealed*, 2010, c. 17, s. 3(4).]
(ii) [*Repealed*, 2010, c. 17, s. 3(4).]
(iii) [*Repealed*, 2010, c. 17, s. 3(4).]
(iii.1) [*Repealed*, 2010, c. 17, s. 3(4).]
(iv) [*Repealed*, 2014, c. 25, s. 23(3).]
(iv.1) [*Repealed*, 2010, c. 17, s. 3(4).]
(iv.2) [*Repealed*, 2010, c. 17, s. 3(4).]
(iv.3) [*Repealed*, 2010, c. 17, s. 3(4).]
(iv.4) [*Repealed*, 2010, c. 17, s. 3(4).]
(iv.5) [*Repealed*, 2010, c. 17, s. 3(4).]
(v) [*Repealed*, 2014, c. 25, s. 23(3).]
(v.1) [*Repealed*, 2010, c. 17, s. 3(4).]
(v.2) [*Repealed*, 2010, c. 17, s. 3(4).]
(vi) section 233 (infanticide),
(vii) [*Repealed*, 2010, c. 17, s. 3(5).]
(vii.1) section 279.01 (trafficking in persons),
(vii.11) subsection 279.02(1) (material benefit — trafficking),
(vii.12) subsection 279.03(1) (withholding or destroying documents — trafficking),
(viii) section 279.1 (hostage taking),
(viii.1) subsection 286.2(1) (material benefit from sexual services),
(viii.2) subsection 286.3(1) (procuring),
(ix) paragraph 348(1)(*d*) (breaking and entering a dwelling-house),
(x) section 423.1 (intimidation of a justice system participant or journalist),
(xi) section 431 (attack on premises, residence or transport of internationally protected person),
(xii) section 431.1 (attack on premises, accommodation or transport of United Nations or associated personnel),
(xiii) subsection 431.2(2) (explosive or other lethal device),
(xiv) section 467.11 (participation in activities of criminal organization),
(xiv.1) section 467.111 (recruitment of members — criminal organization),
(xv) section 467.12 (commission of offence for criminal organization), and
(xvi) section 467.13 (instructing commission of offence for criminal organization),

(xvi.1) [*Repealed*, 2005, c. 25, s. 1(4).]
(xvii) [*Repealed*, 2005, c. 25, s. 1(4).]
(xviii) [*Repealed*, 2005, c. 25, s. 1(4).]
(xix) [*Repealed*, 2005, c. 25, s. 1(4).]
(xx) [*Repealed*, 2005, c. 25, s. 1(4).]

(b) an offence under any of the following provisions of the *Criminal Code*, chapter C-34 of the Revised Statutes of Canada, 1970, as they read from time to time before January 4, 1983, namely,

(i) section 144 (rape),
(i.1) section 145 (attempt to commit rape),
(ii) section 146 (sexual intercourse with female under fourteen and between fourteen and sixteen),
(iii) section 148 (sexual intercourse with feeble-minded, etc.),
(iv) section 149 (indecent assault on female),
(v) section 156 (indecent assault on male),
(vi) section 157 (acts of gross indecency), and
(vii) subsection 246(1) (assault with intent) if the intent is to commit an offence referred to in subparagraphs (i) to (vi),

(c) an offence under any of the following provisions of the *Criminal Code*, chapter C-34 of the Revised Statutes of Canada, 1970, as they read from time to time before January 1, 1988:

(i) subsection 146(1) (sexual intercourse with a female under age of 14),
(ii) subsection 146(2) (sexual intercourse with a female between ages of 14 and 16),
(iii) section 153 (sexual intercourse with step-daughter),
(iv) section 157 (gross indecency),
(v) section 166 (parent or guardian procuring defilement), and
(vi) section 167 (householder permitting defilement),

(c.01) an offence under any of the following provisions of the *Criminal Code*, chapter C-34 of the Revised Statutes of Canada, 1970, as enacted by section 19 of *An Act to amend the Criminal Code in relation to sexual offences and other offences against the person and to amend certain other Acts in relation thereto or in consequence thereof*, chapter 125 of the Statutes of Canada, 1980-81-82-83:

(i) section 246.1 (sexual assault),
(ii) section 246.2 (sexual assault with a weapon, threats to a third party or causing bodily harm), and
(iii) section 246.3 (aggravated sexual assault),

(c.02) an offence under any of the following provisions of this Act, as they read from time to time before the day on which this paragraph comes into force:

(i) paragraph 212(1)(i) (stupefying or overpowering for the purpose of sexual intercourse),
(ii) subsection 212(2) (living on the avails of prostitution of person under 18 years),
(iii) subsection 212(2.1) (aggravated offence in relation to living on the avails of prostitution of person under 18 years), and
(iv) subsection 212(4) (prostitution of person under 18 years),

(c.03) an offence under any of paragraphs 212(1)(*a*) to (*h*) (procuring) of this Act, as they read from time to time before the day on which this paragraph comes into force,

(c.1) an offence under any of the following provisions of the *Security of Information Act*, namely,

   (i) section 6 (approaching, entering, etc., a prohibited place),

   (ii) subsection 20(1) (threats or violence), and

   (iii) subsection 21(1) (harbouring or concealing), and

(d) an attempt to commit or, other than for the purposes of subsection 487.05(1), a conspiracy to commit an offence referred to in any of paragraphs (*a*) to (*c*.03);

"provincial court judge", in relation to a young person, includes a youth court judge within the meaning of subsection 2(1) of the *Youth Criminal Justice Act*;

"secondary designated offence" means an offence, other than a primary designated offence, that is

(a) an offence under this Act that may be prosecuted by indictment — or, for section 487.051 to apply, is prosecuted by indictment — for which the maximum punishment is imprisonment for five years or more,

(a.1) an offence under any of the following provisions of the *Cannabis Act* that may be prosecuted by indictment — or, for section 487.051 to apply, is prosecuted by indictment — for which the maximum punishment is imprisonment for five years or more:

   (i) section 9 (distribution and possession for purpose of distributing)

   (ii) section 10 (selling and possession for purpose of selling),

   (iii) section 11 (importing and exporting and possession for purpose of exporting),

   (iv) section 12 (production),

   (v) section 13 (possession, etc., for use in production or distribution of illicit cannabis), and

   (vi) section 14 (use of young person),

(b) an offence under any of the following provisions of the *Controlled Drugs and Substances Act* that may be prosecuted by indictment — or, for section 487.051 to apply, is prosecuted by indictment — for which the maximum punishment is imprisonment for five years or more

   (i) section 5 (trafficking in substance and possession for purpose of trafficking),

   (ii) section 6 (importing and exporting), and

   (iii) section 7 (production of substance),

(c) an offence under any of the following provisions of this Act:

   (i) subsection 52(1) (sabotage),

(i.001) subsection 57(3) (possession of a forged passport),

(i.002) section 62 (offences in relation to military forces),

(i.003) subsection 65(2) (riot — concealing identity),

(i.004) subsection 70(3) (contravening order made by governor in council),

(i.005) subsection 82(1) (explosives, possession without lawful excuse),

(i.006) subsection 121(1) (frauds on the government),

(i.007) subsection 121(2) (contractor subscribing to election fund),

(i.008)   section 122 (breach of trust by public officer),
(i.009)   subsection 123(1) (municipal corruption),
(i.01)   subsection 123(2) (influencing municipal official),
(i.011)   section 124 (selling or purchasing office),
(i.012)   section 125 (influencing or negotiating appointments or dealings in offices),
(i.013)   subsection 139(2) (obstructing justice),
(i.014)   section 142 (corruptly taking reward for recovery of goods),
(i.015)   section 144 (prison breach),
(i.016)   section 145 (escape and being at large without excuse),
(i.1)   section 146 (permitting or assisting escape),
(i.2)   section 147 (rescue or permitting escape),
(i.3)   section 148 (assisting prisoner of war to escape),
(i.4)   and (ii) [*Repealed*, 2010, c. 17, s. 3(10).]
(iii)   subsection 173(1) (indecent acts),
(iv)   section 182 (dead body — neglect to perform duty, improper or indecent interference with),
(iv.1)   section 184 (interception of private communication),
(iv.2)   section 184.5 (interception of radio-based telephone communications),
(iv.3)   section 221 (cause bodily harm by criminal negligence),
(iv.4)   section 237 (infanticide),
(iv.5)   section 242 (neglect to obtain assistance in child-birth),
(iv.6)   subsection 247(1) (traps likely to cause bodily harm),
(iv.7)   subsection 247(2) (traps — causing bodily harm),
(iv.8)   subsection 247(3) (traps — in a place kept or used for committing other indictable offence),
(iv.9)   section 262 (impeding attempt to save life),
(v)   section 264 (criminal harassment),
(vi)   section 264.1 (uttering threats),
(vii)   section 266 (assault),
(viii)   section 270 (assaulting a peace officer),
(viii.01)   section 280 (abduction of person under 16),
(viii.02)   section 281 (abduction of person under 14),
(viii.1)   subsection 286.1(1) (obtaining sexual services for consideration),
(viii.11)   section 291 (bigamy),
(viii.12)   section 292 (procuring feigned marriage),
(viii.13)   section 293 (polygamy),
(viii.14)   section 293.1 (forced marriage),
(viii.15)   section 293.2 (marriage under age of 16 years),
(viii.16)   section 300 (publishing defamatory libel known to be false),
(viii.17)   section 302 (extortion by libel),
(viii.2)   subsection 320.16(1) (failure to stop after accident),
(viii.21)   paragraph 334(a) (theft over $5,000 or testamentary instrument),
(viii.22)   section 338 (fraudulently taking cattle or defacing brand),
(viii.23)   subsection 339(1) (take possession of drift timber, etc.),
(viii.24)   section 340 (destroying documents of title),
(ix)   paragraph 348(1)(*e*) (breaking and entering a place other than a dwelling-house),

- (x) section 349 (being unlawfully in dwelling-house),
- (x.1) subsection 351(2) (disguise with intent),
- (x.11) paragraph 355(a) (possession of property over \$5,000 or testamentary instrument),
- (x.12) section 357 (bring into Canada property obtained by crime),
- (x.13) paragraph 362(2)(a) (false pretence, property over \$5,000 or testamentary instrument),
- (x.14) subsection 362(3) (obtain credit, etc. by false pretence),
- (x.15) section 363 (obtain execution of valuable security by fraud),
- (x.16) subsection 377(1) (damaging documents),
- (x.17) section 378 (offences in relation to registers),
- (x.18) section 382 (manipulation of stock exchange),
- (x.19) subsection 382.1(1) (prohibited insider trading),
- (x.2) section 383 (gaming in stocks or merchandise),
- (x.21) section 384 (broker reducing stock by selling his own account),
- (x.22) section 386 (fraudulent registration of title),
- (x.23) section 394 (fraud in relation to minerals),
- (x.24) section 394.1 (possession of stolen minerals),
- (x.25) section 396 (offences in relation to mines),
- (x.26) section 397 (falsification of books and documents),
- (x.27) section 399 (false return by public officer),
- (x.28) section 400 (false prospectus),
- (x.29) section 405 (acknowledging instrument in false name),
- (xi) section 423 (intimidation),
- (xi.1) section 424 (threat against an internationally protected person),
- (xi.11) section 424.1 (threat against United Nations or associated personnel),
- (xi.12) section 426 (secret commissions),
- (xi.13) section 435 (arson for fraudulent purpose),
- (xi.14) section 436 (arson by negligence),
- (xi.15) section 436.1 (possession incendiary material),
- (xi.16) subsection 438(1) (interfering with saving of a wrecked vessel),
- (xi.17) subsection 439(2) (interfering with a marine signal),
- (xi.18) section 441 (occupant injuring building),
- (xi.19) section 443 (interfering with international boundary marks, etc.),
- (xi.2) section 451 (having clippings, etc.),
- (xi.21) section 460 (advertising and dealing in counterfeit money),
- (xi.22) subparagraphs 465(1)(b)(i) and (ii) (conspiracy to prosecute),
- (xi.23) section 753.3 (breach of long-term supervision).
- (d) an offence under any of the following provisions of the *Criminal Code*, as they read from time to time before July 1, 1990:
    - (i) section 433 (arson), and
    - (ii) section 434 (setting fire to other substance),
- (d.1) an offence under section 252, as it read from time to time before the day on which section 14 of *An Act to amend the Criminal Code (offences relating to conveyances) and to make consequential amendments to other Acts* comes into force;
- (d.2) an offence under any of sections 249, 249.1, 249.2, 249.3, 249.4, 253, 254 and 255, as they read from time to time before the day on which section 14

of *An Act to amend the Criminal Code (offences relating to conveyances) and to make consequential amendments to other Acts* comes into force, that may be prosecuted by indictment or, for section 487.051 to apply, is prosecuted by indictment; and

(*e*) an attempt to commit or, other than for the purposes of subsection 487.05(1), a conspiracy to commit

    (i) an offence referred to in paragraph (*a*) or (*b*) — which, for section 487.051 to apply, is prosecuted by indictment, or

    (ii) an offence referred to in any of paragraphs (*c*) to (*d*.2);

"Young Offenders Act" means chapter Y-1 of the Revised Statutes of Canada, 1985.

"young person" has the meaning assigned by subsection 2(1) of the *Youth Criminal Justice Act* or subsection 2(1) of the *Young Offenders Act*, as the case may be. 1995, c. 27, s. 1; 1998, c. 37, s. 15; 2001, c. 41, s. 17; 2002, c. 1, s. 175; 2005, c. 25, s. 1; 2005, c. 43, ss. 5, 9(2); 2007, c. 22, ss. 2, 8; 2008, c. 6, s. 35, 63(2); 2009, c. 22, s. 16; 2010, c. 3, s. 6; 2010, c. 17, s. 3; 2012, c. 1, s. 30; 2013, c. 9, s. 16; 2013, c. 13, s. 8; 2014, c. 17, s. 13; 2014, c. 25, s. 23; 2015, c. 20, s. 23; 2018, c. 16, s. 216; 2018, c. 21, s. 18; 2019, c. 13, s. 152; 2019, c. 25, s. 196.1.

INFORMATION FOR WARRANT TO TAKE BODILY SUBSTANCES FOR DNA ANALYSIS / Criteria / Telewarrant / Execution in Canada.

487.05 (1) A provincial court judge who on *ex parte* application made in Form 5.01 is satisfied by information on oath that there are reasonable grounds to believe

(*a*) that a designated offence has been committed,

(*b*) that a bodily substance has been found or obtained

    (i) at the place where the offence was committed,

    (ii) on or within the body of the victim of the offence,

    (iii) on anything worn or carried by the victim at the time when the offence was committed, or

    (iv) on or within the body of any person or thing or at any place associated with the commission of the offence,

(*c*) that a person was a party to the offence, and

(*d*) that forensic DNA analysis of a bodily substance from the person will provide evidence about whether the bodily substance referred to in paragraph (*b*) was from that person

and who is satisfied that it is in the best interests of the administration of justice to do so may issue a warrant in Form 5.02 authorizing the taking, from that person, for the purpose of forensic DNA analysis, of any number of samples of one or more bodily substances that is reasonably required for that purpose, by means of the investigative procedures described in subsection 487.06(1).

(2) In considering whether to issue the warrant, the provincial court judge shall have regard to all relevant matters, including

(*a*) the nature of the designated offence and the circumstances of its commission; and

(b) whether there is

    (i) a peace officer who is able, by virtue of training or experience, to take samples of bodily substances from the person, by means of the investigative procedures described in subsection 487.06(1), or

    (ii) another person who is able, by virtue of training or experience, to take, under the direction of a peace officer, samples of bodily substances from the person, by means of those investigative procedures.

(3) Where a peace officer believes that it would be impracticable to appear personally before a judge to make an application for a warrant under this section, a warrant may be issued under this section on an information submitted by telephone or other means of telecommunication and, for that purpose, section 487.1 applies, with such modifications as the circumstances require, to the warrant.

(4) A warrant issued under subsection (1) may be executed at any place in Canada. Any peace officer who executes the warrant must have authority to act as a peace officer in the place where it is executed. 1995, c. 27, s. 1; 1997, c. 18, s. 44; 1998, c. 37, s. 16; 2019, c. 25, s. 197.

ORDER — PRIMARY DESIGNATED OFFENCES / Order — primary designated offences / Order — persons found not criminally responsible and secondary designated offences / Order to offender

487.051 (1) The court shall make an order in Form 5.03 authorizing the taking of the number of samples of bodily substances that is reasonably required for the purpose of forensic DNA analysis from a person who is convicted, discharged under section 730 or found guilty under the *Youth Criminal Justice Act* or the *Young Offenders Act*, of an offence committed at any time, including before June 30, 2000, if that offence is a primary designated offence within the meaning of paragraphs (a) and (c.02) of the definition "primary designated offence" in section 487.04 when the person is sentenced or discharged.

(2) The court shall make such an order in Form 5.03 in relation to a person who is convicted, discharged under section 730 or found guilty under the *Youth Criminal Justice Act* or the *Young Offenders Act*, of an offence committed at any time, including before June 30, 2000, if that offence is a primary designated offence within the meaning of any of paragraphs (a.1) to (c.01) and (c.03) to (d) of the definition "primary designated offence" in section 487.04 when the person is sentenced or discharged. However, the court is not required to make the order if it is satisfied that the person has established that the impact of such an order on their privacy and security of the person would be grossly disproportionate to the public interest in the protection of society and the proper administration of justice, to be achieved through the early detection, arrest and conviction of offenders.

(3) The court may, on application by the prosecutor and if it is satisfied that it is in the best interests of the administration of justice to do so, make such an order in Form 5.04 in relation to

  (a) a person who is found not criminally responsible on account of mental disorder for an offence committed at any time, including before June 30, 2000, if that offence is a designated offence when the finding is made; or

  (b) a person who is convicted, discharged under section 730 or found guilty under the *Youth Criminal Justice Act* or the *Young Offenders Act*, of an offence committed at any time, including before June 30, 2000, if that offence is a secondary designated offence when the person is sentenced or discharged.

In deciding whether to make the order, the court shall consider the person's criminal record, whether they were previously found not criminally responsible on account of mental disorder for a designated offence, the nature of the offence, the circumstances surrounding its commission and the impact such an order would have on the person's privacy and security of the person and shall give reasons for its decision.

(4) When the court makes an order authorizing the taking of samples of bodily substances, it may make an order in Form 5.041 to require the person to report at the place, day and time set out in the order and submit to the taking of the samples. 1998, c. 37, s. 17; 2002, c. 1, s. 176; 2005, c. 25, s. 3; 2007, c. 22, s. 9; 2014, c. 25, s. 24.

487.052 [*Repealed*, 2005, c. 25, s. 4; 2007, c. 22, s. 3.]

TIMING OF ORDER / Hearing.

487.053 (1) The court may make an order under section 487.051 authorizing the taking of samples of bodily substances when it imposes a sentence on a person, finds the person not criminally responsible on account of mental disorder or directs that they be discharged under section 730.

(2) If the court does not consider the matter at that time, it

  (a) shall, within 90 days after the day on which it imposes the sentence, makes the finding or directs that the person be discharged, set a date for a hearing to do so;

  (b) retains jurisdiction over the matter; and

  (c) may require the person to appear by closed-circuit television or videoconference, as long as the person is given the opportunity to communicate privately with counsel if they are represented by counsel. 1998, c. 37, s. 17; 2000, c. 10, s. 14; 2005, c. 25, s. 4; 2007, c. 22, s. 3; 2019, c. 25, s. 198.

APPEAL.

487.054 The offender or the prosecutor may appeal from a decision of the court under any of subsections 487.051(1) to (3). 1998, c. 37, s. 17; 2007, c. 22, s. 10.

OFFENDERS SERVING SENTENCES / Certificate / Definition of "sexual offence" / Manner of appearance / Criteria / Order / Summons / Service on individual.

487.055 (1) A provincial court judge may, on *ex parte* application made in Form 5.05, authorize in Form 5.06 the taking, for the purpose of forensic DNA analysis, of any number of samples of bodily substances that is reasonably required for that purpose, by means of the investigative procedures described in subsection 487.06(1), from a person who, before June 30, 2000,

- (a) had been declared a dangerous offender under Part XXIV;
- (b) had been declared a dangerous offender or a dangerous sexual offender under Part XXI of the *Criminal Code*, being chapter C-34 of the Revised Statutes of Canada, 1970, as it read from time to time before January 1, 1988;
- (c) had been convicted of murder;
- (c.1) had been convicted of attempted murder or conspiracy to commit murder or to cause another person to be murdered and, on the date of the application, is serving a sentence of imprisonment for that offence;
- (d) had been convicted of a sexual offence within the meaning of subsection (3) and, on the date of the application, is serving a sentence of imprisonment for that offence; or
- (e) had been convicted of manslaughter and, on the date of the application, is serving a sentence of imprisonment for that offence.

(2) The application shall be accompanied by a certificate referred to in paragraph 667(1)(a) that establishes that the person is a person referred to in subsection (1). The certificate may be received in evidence without giving the notice referred to in subsection 667(4).

(3) For the purposes of subsection (1), "sexual offence" means

- (a) an offence under any of the following provisions, namely,
    - (i) section 151 (sexual interference),
    - (ii) section 152 (invitation to sexual touching),
    - (iii) section 153 (sexual exploitation),
    - (iv) section 155 (incest),
    - (v) subsection 212(4) (offence in relation to juvenile prostitution),
    - (vi) section 271 (sexual assault),
    - (vii) section 272 (sexual assault with a weapon, threats to a third party or causing bodily harm), and
    - (viii) section 273 (aggravated sexual assault);
- (a.1) an offence under subsection 348(1) if the indictable offence referred to in that subsection is a sexual offence within the meaning of paragraph (a), (b), (c) or (d);
- (b) an offence under any of the following provisions of the *Criminal Code*, chapter C-34 of the Revised Statutes of Canada, 1970, as they read from time to time before January 4, 1983, namely,
    - (i) section 144 (rape),
    - (ii) section 146 (sexual intercourse with female under fourteen or between fourteen and sixteen),
    - (iii) section 148 (sexual intercourse with feeble-minded, etc.),

      (iv) section 149 (indecent assault on female),

      (v) section 156 (indecent assault on male), or

      (vi) section 157 (acts of gross indecency);

  (c) an offence under paragraph 153(1)(*a*) (sexual intercourse with step-daughter, etc.) of the *Criminal Code*, chapter C-34 of the Revised Statutes of Canada, 1970, as it read from time to time before January 1, 1988; and

  (d) an attempt to commit an offence referred to in any of paragraphs (*a*) to (*c*).

(3.01) The court may require a person who is given notice of an application under subsection (1) and who wishes to appear at the hearing to appear by closed-circuit television or videoconference, as long as the person is given the opportunity to communicate privately with counsel if they are represented by counsel.

(3.1) In deciding whether to grant an authorization under subsection (1), the court shall consider the person's criminal record, the nature of the offence and the circumstances surrounding its commission and the impact such an authorization would have on the privacy and security of the person and shall give reasons for its decision.

(3.11) If the court authorizes the taking of samples of bodily substances from a person who is on conditional release and who has appeared at the hearing, it shall make an order in Form 5.041 to require the person to report at the place, day and time set out in the order and submit to the taking of the samples.

(4) However, if a person who is on conditional release has not appeared at the hearing, a summons in Form 5.061 setting out the information referred to in paragraphs 487.07(1)(*b*) to (*d*) shall be directed to them requiring them to report at the place, day and time set out in the summons and submit to the taking of the samples.

(5) The summons shall be accompanied by a copy of the authorization referred to in subsection (1) and be served by a peace officer who shall either deliver it personally to the person to whom it is directed or, if that person cannot conveniently be found, leave it for the person at their latest or usual place of residence with any person found there who appears to be at least sixteen years of age. 1998, c. 37, s. 17; 2000, c. 10, s. 15; 2005, c. 25, s. 5; 2007, c. 22, s. 11; 2008, c. 18, s. 13; 2019, c. 25, s. 199.

(6) [*Repealed*, 2008, c. 18, s. 13.]

(7) to (10) [*Repealed*, 2007, c. 22, s. 11(4).]

FAILURE TO APPEAR / Execution of warrant.

487.0551 (1) If a person fails to appear at the place, day and time set out in an order made under subsection 487.051(4) or 487.055(3.11) or in a summons referred to in subsection 487.055(4) or 487.091(3), a justice of the peace may issue a warrant for their arrest in Form 5.062 to allow samples of bodily substances to be taken.

(2) The warrant may be executed anywhere in Canada by a peace officer who has jurisdiction in that place or over the person. The warrant remains in force until it is executed. 2007, c. 22, s. 12.

FAILURE TO COMPLY WITH ORDER OR SUMMONS / For greater certainty

487.0552 (1) Every person who, without reasonable excuse, fails to comply with an order made under subsection 487.051(4) or 487.055(3.11) of this Act or under subsection 196.14(4) or 196.24(4) of the *National Defence Act*, or with a summons referred to in subsection 487.055(4) or 487.091(3) of this Act, is guilty of

- (a) an indictable offence and liable to imprisonment for a term of not more than two years; or
- (b) an offence punishable on summary conviction.

(2) For greater certainty, a lawful command that prevents a person from complying with an order or summons is a reasonable excuse if, at the time, the person is subject to the Code of Service Discipline within the meaning of subsection 2(1) of the *National Defence Act*. 2007, c. 22, s. 12.

WHEN COLLECTION TO TAKE PLACE / When collection to take place / When collection to take place / Appeal / Collection of samples / Who collects samples.

487.056 (1) Samples of bodily substances shall be taken as authorized under section 487.051

- (a) at the place, day and time set out in an order made under subsection 487.051(4) or as soon as feasible afterwards; or
- (b) in any other case, on the day on which the order authorizing the taking of the samples is made or as soon as feasible afterwards.

(2) Samples of bodily substances shall be taken as authorized under section 487.055 or 487.091

- (a) at the place, day and time set out in an order made under subsection 487.055(3.11) or a summons referred to in subsection 487.055(4) or 487.091(3) or as soon as feasible afterwards; or
- (b) in any other case, as soon as feasible after the authorization is granted.

(3) If a person fails to appear as required by an order made under subsection 487.051(4) or 487.055(3.11) or a summons referred to in subsection 487.055(4) or 487.091(3), samples of bodily substances shall be taken

- (a) when the person is arrested under a warrant issued under subsection 487.0551(1) or as soon as feasible afterwards; or
- (b) as soon as feasible after the person appears at the place set out in the order or summons if no warrant is issued.

(4) Subsections (1) to (3) apply even if the order or authorization to take the samples of bodily substances is appealed.

(5) A peace officer who is authorized under section 487.051, 487.055 or 487.091 to take samples of bodily substances may cause the samples to be taken in any place in Canada in which the person who is subject to the order or authorization is located.

(6) The samples shall be taken by a peace officer who has jurisdiction over the person or in the place in which the samples are taken — or a person acting under

their direction — who is able, by virtue of training or experience, to take them. 1998, c. 37, s. 17; 2000, c. 10, s. 16; 2002, c. 1, s. 179; 2005, c. 25, s. 6; 2007, c. 22, s. 13.

REPORT OF PEACE OFFICER / Contents of report / Copy of report.

487.057 (1) A peace officer who takes samples of bodily substances from a person or who causes a person who is not a peace officer to take samples under their direction shall, as soon as feasible after the samples are taken, make a written report in Form 5.07 and cause the report to be filed with

- (a) the provincial court judge who issued the warrant under section 487.05 or granted the authorization under section 487.055 or 487.091 or another judge of that provincial court; or
- (b) the court that made the order under section 487.051.

(2) The report shall include

- (a) a statement of the time and date the samples were taken; and
- (b) a description of the bodily substances that were taken.

(3) A peace officer who takes the samples or causes the samples to be taken under their direction at the request of another peace officer shall send a copy of the report to the other peace officer unless that other peace officer had jurisdiction to take the samples. 1998, c. 37, s. 17; 2000, c. 10, s. 17; 2007, c. 22, s. 14.

NO CRIMINAL OR CIVIL LIABILITY.

487.058 No peace officer, and no person acting under a peace officer's direction, incurs any criminal or civil liability for anything necessarily done with reasonable care and skill in the taking of samples of bodily substances from a person under a warrant issued under section 487.05, an order made under section 487.051 or an authorization granted under section 487.055 or 487.091. 1998, c. 37, s. 17; 2000; c. 10, s. 18; 2007, c. 22, s. 15.

INVESTIGATIVE PROCEDURES / Terms and conditions / Fingerprints.

487.06 (1) A peace officer or a person acting under a peace officer's direction is authorized by a warrant issued under section 487.05, an order made under section 487.051 or an authorization granted under section 487.055 or 487.091 to take samples of bodily substances by any of the following means:

- (a) the plucking of individual hairs from the person, including the root sheath;
- (b) the taking of buccal swabs by swabbing the lips, tongue and inside cheeks of the mouth to collect epithelial cells; or
- (c) the taking of blood by pricking the skin surface with a sterile lancet.

(2) The warrant, order or authorization shall include any terms and conditions that the provincial court judge or court, as the case may be, considers advisable to ensure that the taking of the samples authorized by the warrant, order or authorization is reasonable in the circumstances.

(3) A peace officer who is authorized to take samples of bodily substances from a person by an order made under section 487.051 or an authorization granted under

section 487.055 or 487.091, or a person acting under their direction, may take fingerprints from the person for the purpose of the *DNA Identification Act*. 1995, c. 27, s. 1; 1998, c. 37, s. 18; 2000, c. 10, s. 19; 2007, c. 22, s. 16.

DUTY TO INFORM / Detention of person / Respect of privacy / Execution of warrant against young person / Waiver of rights of young person.

487.07 (1) Before taking samples of bodily substances from a person, or causing samples to be taken under their direction, in execution of a warrant issued under section 487.05 or an order made under section 487.051 or under an authorization granted under section 487.055 or 487.091, a peace officer shall inform the person of

- (*a*) the contents of the warrant, order or authorization;
- (*b*) the nature of the investigative procedures by means of which the samples are to be taken;
- (*c*) the purpose of taking the samples;
- (*d*) the authority of the peace officer and any other person under the direction of the peace officer to use as much force as is necessary for the purpose of taking the samples; and
- (*d*.1) [*Repealed*, 2000, c. 10, s. 20(2).]
- (*e*) in the case of samples of bodily substances taken in execution of a warrant,
  - (i) the possibility that the results of forensic DNA analysis may be used in evidence, and
  - (ii) if the sample is taken from a young person, the rights of the young person under subsection (4).

(2) A person from whom samples of bodily substances are to be taken may
- (*a*) be detained for that purpose for a period that is reasonable in the circumstances; and
- (*b*) be required to accompany a peace officer for that purpose.

(3) A peace officer who takes samples of bodily substances from a person, or a person who takes such samples under the direction of a peace officer, shall ensure that the person's privacy is respected in a manner that is reasonable in the circumstances.

(4) A young person against whom a warrant is executed has, in addition to any other rights arising from his or her detention under the warrant,
- (*a*) the right to a reasonable opportunity to consult with, and
- (*b*) the right to have the warrant executed in the presence of

counsel and a parent or, in the absence of a parent, an adult relative or, in the absence of a parent and an adult relative, any other appropriate adult chosen by the young person.

(5) A young person may waive his or her rights under subsection (4) but any such waiver
- (*a*) must be recorded on audio tape or video tape or otherwise; or
- (*b*) must be made in writing and contain a statement signed by the young person that he or she has been informed of the right being waived. 1995, c. 27, ss. 1 and 3; 1998, c. 37, s. 19; 2000, c. 10, s. 20; 2007, c. 22, s. 17.

VERIFICATION / DNA profile in data bank / DNA profile not in data bank.

487.071 (1) Before taking samples of bodily substances from a person under an order made under section 487.051 or an authorization granted under section 487.055 or 487.091, a peace officer, or a person acting under their direction, shall verify whether the convicted offenders index of the national DNA data bank, established under the *DNA Identification Act*, contains the person's DNA profile.

(2) If the person's DNA profile is in the convicted offenders index of the national DNA data bank, the peace officer or person acting under their direction shall not take any bodily substances from the person but shall

- (*a*) confirm in writing on the order or authorization that he or she has been advised that the person's DNA profile is in the DNA data bank; and
- (*b*) transmit a copy of the order or authorization containing that confirmation and any other information prescribed by regulations made under the *DNA Identification Act* to the Commissioner of the Royal Canadian Mounted Police.

(3) If the person's DNA profile is not in the convicted offenders index of the national DNA data bank, the peace officer or person acting under their direction shall execute the order or authorization and transmit to the Commissioner of the Royal Canadian Mounted Police

- (*a*) any bodily substances taken; and
- (*b*) a copy of the order or authorization and any other information prescribed by regulations made under the *DNA Identification Act*. 1998, c. 37, s. 20; 2000, c. 10, s. 21; 2005, c. 25, s. 8; 2007, c. 22, s. 18.

USE OF BODILY SUBSTANCES — WARRANT / Use of bodily substances — order, authorization / Use of results — warrant / Offence / Offence.

487.08 (1) No person shall use bodily substances that are taken in execution of a warrant under section 487.05 or under section 196.12 of the *National Defence Act* except to use them for the purpose of forensic DNA analysis in the course of an investigation of a designated offence.

(1.1) No person shall use bodily substances that are taken in execution of an order made under section 487.051 of this Act or section 196.14 of the *National Defence Act*, or under an authorization granted under section 487.055 or 487.091 of this Act or section 196.24 of the *National Defence Act*, except to transmit them to the Commissioner of the Royal Canadian Mounted Police for the purpose of forensic DNA analysis in accordance with the *DNA Identification Act*.

(2) No person shall use the results of forensic DNA analysis of bodily substances that are taken in execution of a warrant under section 487.05 or under section 196.12 of the *National Defence Act* except

- (*a*) in the course of an investigation of the designated offence or any other designated offence in respect of which a warrant was issued or a bodily substance was found in the circumstances described in paragraph 487.05(1)(*b*) or in paragraph 196.12(1)(*b*) of the *National Defence Act*; or
- (*b*) in any proceeding for such an offence.

(2.1) [*Repealed*, 2005, c. 25, s. 9(2).]

(3) Every person who contravenes subsection (1) or (2) is guilty of an offence punishable on summary conviction.

(4) Every person who contravenes subsection (1.1)

- (a) is guilty of an indictable offence and liable to imprisonment for a term not exceeding two years; or
- (b) is guilty of an offence punishable on summary conviction. 1995, c. 27, s. 1; 1998, c. 37, s. 21; 2000, c. 10, s. 22; 2005, c. 25, s. 9; 2007, c. 22, s. 19; 2019, c. 25, s. 200.

CODE

DESTRUCTION OF BODILY SUBSTANCES, etc. — WARRANT / Exception / Destruction of bodily substances, etc., voluntarily given.

487.09 (1) Subject to subsection (2), bodily substances that are taken from a person in execution of a warrant under section 487.05 and the results of forensic DNA analysis shall be destroyed or, in the case of results in electronic form, access to those results shall be permanently removed, without delay after

- (a) the results of that analysis establish that the bodily substance referred to in paragraph 487.05(1)(b) was not from that person;
- (b) the person is finally acquitted of the designated offence and any other offence in respect of the same transaction; or
- (c) the expiration of one year after
  - (i) the person is discharged after a preliminary inquiry into the designated offence or any other offence in respect of the same transaction,
  - (ii) the dismissal, for any reason other than acquittal, or the withdrawal of any information charging the person with the designated offence or any other offence in respect of the same transaction, or
  - (iii) any proceeding against the person for the offence or any other offence in respect of the same transaction is stayed under section 579 or under that section as applied by section 572 or 795,

unless during that year a new information is laid or an indictment is preferred charging the person with the designated offence or any other offence in respect of the same transaction or the proceeding is recommenced.

(2) A provincial court judge may order that the bodily substances that are taken from a person and the results of forensic DNA analysis not be destroyed during any period that the provincial court judge considers appropriate if the provincial court judge is satisfied that the bodily substances or results might reasonably be required in an investigation or prosecution of the person for another designated offence or of another person for the designated offence or any other offence in respect of the same transaction.

(3) Bodily substances that are provided voluntarily by a person and the results of forensic DNA analysis shall be destroyed or, in the case of results in electronic form, access to those results shall be permanently removed, without delay after the results of that analysis establish that the bodily substance referred to in paragraph 487.05(1)(b) was not from that person. 1995, c. 27, s. 1; 1998, c. 37, s. 22.

COLLECTION OF ADDITIONAL BODILY SUBSTANCES / Reasons / Persons not in custody.

487.091 (1) A provincial court judge may, on *ex parte* application made in Form 5.08, authorize in Form 5.09 the taking from a person, for the purpose of forensic DNA analysis, of any number of additional samples of bodily substances that is reasonably required for that purpose, by means of the investigative procedures described in subsection 487.06(1), if

(*a*) a DNA profile cannot be derived from the bodily substances that were taken from that person under an order made under section 487.051 or an authorization granted under section 487.055; or

(*b*) the information or bodily substances required by regulations made under the *DNA Identification Act* were not transmitted in accordance with the requirements of the regulations or were lost.

(2) The application shall state the reasons why a DNA profile cannot be derived from the bodily substances or why the information or bodily substances were not transmitted in accordance with the regulations or were lost.

(3) If the court authorizes the taking of samples of bodily substances from a person who is not in custody, a summons in Form 5.061 setting out the information referred to in paragraphs 487.07(1)(*b*) to (*d*) shall be directed to the person requiring them to report at the place, day and time set out in the summons and submit to the taking of the samples. Subsections 487.055(5) and (6) apply, with any modifications that the circumstances require. 1998, c. 37, s. 23; 2000, c. 10, s. 23; 2005, c. 25, s. 10; 2007, c. 22, s. 20.

REVIEW BY ATTORNEY GENERAL / Clerical error / Substantive defect / No defect.

487.0911 (1) On receipt of a notice from the Commissioner of the Royal Canadian Mounted Police under subsection 5.2(1) of the *DNA Identification Act* that an order made under section 487.051 or an authorization granted under section 487.091 appears to be defective, the Attorney General shall review the order or authorization and the court record.

(2) If the Attorney General is of the opinion that the defect is due to a clerical error, the Attorney General shall

(*a*) apply, *ex parte*, to the judge who made the order or authorization, or to a judge of the same court, to have it corrected; and

(*b*) transmit a copy of the corrected order or authorization, if any, to the Commissioner.

(3) If the Attorney General is of the opinion that the offence referred to in the order or authorization is not a designated offence, the Attorney General shall inform the Commissioner of that opinion.

(4) If the Attorney General is of the opinion that the offence referred to in the order or authorization is a designated offence, the Attorney General shall transmit that opinion, with written reasons, to the Commissioner. 2005, c. 25, s. 11; 2007, c. 22, s. 21.

INFORMATION FOR IMPRESSION WARRANT / Search or seizure to be reasonable / Execution in Canada / Telewarrant

487.092 (1) A justice may issue a warrant in writing authorizing a peace officer to do any thing, or cause any thing to be done under the direction of the peace officer, described in the warrant in order to obtain any handprint, fingerprint, footprint, foot impression, teeth impression or other print or impression of the body or any part of the body in respect of a person if the justice is satisfied

(a) by information on oath in writing that there are reasonable grounds to believe that an offence against this or any other Act of Parliament has been committed and that information concerning the offence will be obtained by the print or impression; and

(b) that it is in the best interests of the administration of justice to issue the warrant.

(2) A warrant issued under subsection (1) shall contain such terms and conditions as the justice considers advisable to ensure that any search or seizure authorized by the warrant is reasonable in the circumstances.

(3) A warrant issued under subsection (1) may be executed at any place in Canada. Any peace officer who executes the warrant must have authority to act as a peace officer in the place where it is executed.

(4) Where a peace officer believes that it would be impracticable to appear personally before a justice to make an application for a warrant under this section, a warrant may be issued under this section on an information submitted by telephone or other means of telecommunication and, for that purpose, section 487.1 applies, with such modifications as the circumstances require, to the warrant. 1997, c. 18, s. 45; 1998, c. 37, s. 23; 2019, c. 25, s. 201.

Other Provisions Respecting Search Warrants, Preservation Orders and Production Orders 2014, c. 31, s. 21.

TELEWARRANTS / Information submitted by telephone / Information submitted by other means of telecommunication / Administration of oath / Alternative to oath / Contents of information / Issuing warrant / Formalities respecting warrant and facsimiles / Issuance of warrant where telecommunication produces writing / Providing facsimile / Affixing fascimile / Report of peace officer / Bringing before justice / Proof of authorization / Duplicates and facsimiles acceptable.

487.1 (1) If a peace officer believes that an indictable offence has been committed and that it would be impracticable to appear personally before a justice to make an application for a warrant in accordance with section 487, the peace officer may submit an information on oath by telephone or other means of telecommunication to a justice designated for the purpose by the chief judge of the provincial court having jurisdiction in the matter.

(2) An information submitted by telephone or other means of telecommunication, other than a means of telecommunication that produces a writing, shall be on oath

and shall be recorded verbatim by the justice, who shall, as soon as practicable, cause to be filed, with the clerk of the court for the territorial division in which the warrant is intended for execution, the record or a transcription of it, certified by the justice as to time, date and contents.

(2.1) The justice who receives an information submitted by a means of telecommunication that produces a writing shall, as soon as practicable, cause to be filed, with the clerk of the court for the territorial division in which the warrant is intended for execution, the information certified by the justice as to time and date of receipt.

(3) For the purposes of subsection (2), an oath may be administered by telephone or other means of telecommunication.

(3.1) A peace officer who uses a means of telecommunication referred to in subsection (2.1) may, instead of swearing an oath, make a statement in writing stating that all matters contained in the information are true to his or her knowledge and belief and such a statement is deemed to be a statement made under oath.

(4) An information submitted by telephone or other means of telecommunication shall include

    (*a*) a statement of the circumstances that make it impracticable for the peace officer to appear personally before a justice;

    (*b*) a statement of the indictable offence alleged, the place or premises to be searched and the items alleged to be liable to seizure;

    (*c*) a statement of the peace officer's grounds for believing that items liable to seizure in respect of the offence alleged will be found in the place of premises to be searched; and

    (*d*) a statement as to any prior application for a warrant under this section or any other search warrant, in respect of the same matter, of which the peace officer has knowledge.

(5) A justice referred to in subsection (1) may issue a warrant to a peace officer conferring the same authority respecting search and seizure as may be conferred by a warrant issued under subsection 487(1) if the justice is satisfied that an information submitted by telephone or other means of telecommunication

    (*a*) is in respect of an indictable offence and conforms to the requirements of subsection (4);

    (*b*) discloses reasonable grounds for dispensing with an information presented personally and in writing; and

    (*c*) discloses reasonable grounds in accordance with paragraph 487(1)(*a*), (*b*) or (*c*), as the case may be, for the issuance of a warrant in respect of an indictable offence.

The justice may require that the warrant be executed within the period that he or she may order.

(6) Where a justice issues a warrant by telephone or other means of telecommunication, other than a means of telecommunication that produces a writing,

    (*a*) the justice shall complete and sign the warrant in Form 5.1, noting on its face the time, date and place of issuance;

(b) the peace officer, on the direction of the justice, shall complete, in duplicate, a facsimile of the warrant in Form 5.1, noting on its face the name of the issuing justice and the time, date and place of issuance; and

(c) the justice shall, as soon as practicable after the warrant has been issued, cause the warrant to be filed with the clerk of the court for the territorial division in which the warrant is intended for execution.

(6.1) Where a justice issues a warrant by a means of telecommunication that produces a writing,

(a) the justice shall complete and sign the warrant in Form 5.1, noting on its face the time, date and place of issuance;

(b) the justice shall transmit the warrant by the means of telecommunication to the peace officer who submitted the information and the copy of the warrant received by the peace officer is deemed to be a facsimile within the meaning of paragraph (6)(b);

(c) the peace officer shall procure another facsimile of the warrant; and

(d) the justice shall, as soon as practicable after the warrant has been issued, cause the warrant to be filed with the clerk of the court for the territorial division in which the warrant is intended for execution.

(7) A peace officer who executes a warrant issued by telephone or other means of telecommunication shall, before or as soon as practicable after entering the place or premises to be searched, give a facsimile of the warrant to any person who is present and ostensibly in control of the place or premises.

(8) A peace officer who, in any unoccupied place or premises, executes a warrant issued by telephone or other means of telecommunication shall, on entering or as soon as practicable after entering the place or premises, cause a facsimile of the warrant to be suitably affixed in a prominent place within the place or premises.

(9) A peace officer to whom a warrant is issued by telephone or other means of telecommunication shall file a written report with the clerk of the court for the territorial division in which the warrant was intended for execution as soon as practicable but within a period not exceeding seven days after the warrant has been executed, which report shall include

(a) a statement of the time and date the warrant was executed or, if the warrant was not executed, a statement of the reasons why it was not executed;

(b) a statement of the things, if any, that were seized pursuant to the warrant and the location where they are being held; and

(c) a statement of the things, if any, that were seized in addition to the things mentioned in the warrant and the location where they are being held, together with a statement of the peace officer's grounds for believing that those additional things had been obtained by, or used in, the commission of an offence.

(10) The clerk of the court shall, as soon as practicable, cause the report, together with the information and the warrant to which it pertains, to be brought before a justice to be dealt with, in respect of the things seized referred to in the report, in the same manner as if the things were seized pursuant to a warrant issued, on an information presented personally by a peace officer, by that justice or another justice for the same territorial division.

(11) In any proceeding in which it is material for a court to be satisfied that a search or seizure was authorized by a warrant issued by telephone or other means of telecommunication, the absence of the information or warrant, signed by the justice and carrying on its face a notation of the time, date and place of issuance, is, in the absence of evidence to the contrary, proof that the search or seizure was not authorized by a warrant issued by telephone or other means of telecommunication.

(12) A duplicate or a facsimile of an information or a warrant has the same probative force as the original for the purposes of subsection (11). R.S.C. 1985, c. 27 (1st Supp.), s. 69; 1992, c. 1, ss. 58, 59; 1994, c. 44, s. 37; 2018, c. 21, s. 19.

WHERE WARRANT NOT NECESSARY.

487.11 A peace officer, or a public officer who has been appointed or designated to administer or enforce any federal or provincial law and whose duties include the enforcement of this or any other Act of Parliament, may, in the course of his or her duties, exercise any of the powers described in subsection 487(1) or 492.1(1) without a warrant if the conditions for obtaining a warrant exist but by reason of exigent circumstances it would be impracticable to obtain a warrant. 1997, c. 18, s. 46.

RESTRICTION ON PUBLICATION.

487.2 If a search warrant is issued under section 487 or 487.1 or a search is made under such a warrant, every one who publishes in any document, or broadcasts or transmits in any way, any information with respect to
  (*a*) the location of the place searched or to be searched, or
  (*b*) the identity of any person who is or appears to occupy or be in possession or control of that place or who is suspected of being involved in any offence in relation to which the warrant was issued,
without the consent of every person referred to in paragraph (*b*) is, unless a charge has been laid in respect of any offence in relation to which the warrant was issued, guilty of an offence punishable on summary conviction. R.S.C. 1985, c. 27 (1st Supp.), s. 69; 2005, c. 32, s. 16.

(2) [*Repealed*, 2005, c. 32, s. 16(2).]

ORDER DENYING ACCESS TO INFORMATION / Reasons / Procedure / Application for variance of order.

487.3 (1) On application made at the time an application is made for a warrant under this or any other Act of Parliament, an order under any of sections 487.013 to 487.018 or an authorization under section 529 or 529.4, or at a later time, a justice, a judge of a superior court of criminal jurisdiction or a judge of the Court of Quebec may make an order prohibiting access to, and the disclosure of, any information relating to the warrant, order or authorization on the ground that
  (*a*) the ends of justice would be subverted by the disclosure for one of the reasons referred to in subsection (2) or the information might be used for an improper purpose; and

(*b*) the reason referred to in paragraph (*a*) outweighs in importance the access to the information.

(2) For the purposes of paragraph (1)(*a*), an order may be made under subsection (1) on the ground that the ends of justice would be subverted by the disclosure

(*a*) if disclosure of the information would

(i) compromise the identity of a confidential informant,

(ii) compromise the nature and extent of an ongoing investigation

(iii) endanger a person engaged in particular intelligence-gathering techniques and thereby prejudice future investigations in which similar techniques would be used, or

(iv) prejudice the interests of an innocent person; and

(*b*) for any other sufficient reason

(3) Where an order is made under subsection (1), all documents relating to the application shall, subject to any terms and conditions that the justice or judge considers desirable in the circumstances, including, without limiting the generality of the foregoing, any term or condition concerning the duration of the prohibition, partial disclosure of a document, deletion of any information or the occurrence of a condition, be placed in a packet and sealed by the justice or judge immediately on determination of the application, and that packet shall be kept in the custody of the court in a place to which the public has no access or in any other place that the justice or judge may authorize and shall not be dealt with except in accordance with the terms and conditions specified in the order or as varied under subsection (4).

(4) An application to terminate the order or vary any of its terms and conditions may be made to the justice or judge who made the order or a judge of the court before which any proceedings arising out of the investigation in relation to which the warrant or production order was obtained may be held. 1997, c. 23, s. 14; 1997, c. 39, s. 1; 2004, c. 3, s. 8; 2014, c. 31, s. 22.

EXECUTION OF SEARCH WARRANT.

488. A warrant issued under section 487 or 487.1 shall be executed by day, unless

(*a*) the justice is satisfied that there are reasonable grounds for it to be executed by night;

(*b*) the reasonable grounds are included in the information; and

(*c*) the warrant authorizes that it be executed by night. R.S., c. C-34, s. 444; R.S.C. 1985, c. 27, (1st. Supp.), s. 70; 1997, c. 18, s. 47.

DEFINITIONS / "data" / "document" / "journalist" / "journalistic source" / "officer" / Warrant, Authorization and Order / Warrant, Authorization and Order / Special Advocate / Offence by Journalist — Exception / Offence by Journalist — Order / Conditions / Powers / Discovery of Relation to Journalist / Powers of Judge.

488.01 (1) The following definitions apply in this section and in section 488.02.

"data" has the same meaning as in section 487.011.

"document" has the same meaning as in section 487.011.

"journalist" has the same meaning as in subsection 39.1(1) of the *Canada Evidence Act*.

"journalistic source" has the same meaning as in subsection 39.1(1) of the *Canada Evidence Act*.

"officer" means a peace officer or public officer.

(2) Despite any other provision of this Act, if an applicant for a warrant under section 487.01, 487.1, 492.1 or 492.2, a search warrant under this Act, notably under section 487, an authorization under section 184.2, 184.3, 186 or 188, or an order under any of sections 487.014 to 487.017 knows that the application relates to a journalist's communications or an object, document or data relating to or in the possession of a journalist, they shall make an application to a judge of a superior court of criminal jurisdiction or to a judge as defined in section 552. That judge has exclusive jurisdiction to dispose of the application.

(3) A judge may issue a warrant, authorization or order under subsection (2) only if, in addition to the conditions required for the issue of the warrant, authorization or order, he or she is satisfied that

   (*a*) there is no other way by which the information can reasonably be obtained; and

   (*b*) the public interest in the investigation and prosecution of a criminal offence outweighs the journalist's right to privacy in gathering and disseminating information.

(4) The judge to whom the application for the warrant, authorization or order is made may, in his or her discretion, request that a special advocate present observations in the interests of freedom of the press concerning the conditions set out in subsection (3).

(5) Subsections (3) and (4) do not apply in respect of an application for a warrant, authorization or order that is made in relation to the commission of an offence by a journalist.

(6) If a warrant, authorization or order referred to in subsection (2) is sought in relation to the commission of an offence by a journalist and the judge considers it necessary to protect the confidentiality of journalistic sources, the judge may order that some or all documents obtained pursuant to the warrant, authorization or order are to be dealt with in accordance with section 488.02.

(7) The warrant, authorization or order referred to in subsection (2) may contain any conditions that the judge considers appropriate to protect the confidentiality of journalistic sources and to limit the disruption of journalistic activities.

(8) The judge who rules on the application for the warrant, authorization or order referred to in subsection (2) has the same powers, with the necessary adaptations, as the authority who may issue the warrant, authorization or order.

(9) If an officer, acting under a warrant, authorization or order referred to in subsection (2) for which an application was not made in accordance with that subsection, becomes aware that the warrant, authorization or order relates to a journalist's communications or an object, document or data relating to or in the

possession of a journalist, the officer shall, as soon as possible, make an *ex parte* application to a judge of a superior court of criminal jurisdiction or a judge as defined in section 552 and, until the judge disposes of the application,

(*a*) refrain from examining or reproducing, in whole or in part, any document obtained pursuant to the warrant, authorization or order; and

(*b*) place any document obtained pursuant to the warrant, authorization or order in a sealed packet and keep it in a place to which the public has no access.

(10) On an application under subsection (9), the judge may

(*a*) confirm the warrant, authorization or order if the judge is of the opinion that no additional conditions to protect the confidentiality of journalistic sources and to limit the disruption of journalistic activities should be imposed;

(*b*) vary the warrant, authorization or order to impose any conditions that the judge considers appropriate to protect the confidentiality of journalistic sources and to limit the disruption of journalistic activities;

(*c*) if the judge considers it necessary to protect the confidentiality of journalistic sources, order that some or all documents that were or will be obtained pursuant to the warrant, authorization or order are to be dealt with in accordance with section 488.02; or

(*d*) revoke the warrant, authorization or order if the judge is of the opinion that the applicant knew or ought reasonably to have known that the application for the warrant, authorization or order related to a journalist's communications or an object, document or data relating to or in the possession of a journalist. 2017, c. 22, s. 3.

DOCUMENTS / Notice / Application / Disclosure: Prohibition / Disclosure Order / Examination / Order.

488.02 (1) Any document obtained pursuant to a warrant, authorization or order issued in accordance with subsection 488.01(3), or that is the subject of an order made under subsection 488.01(6) or paragraph 488.01(10)(*c*), is to be placed in a packet and sealed by the court that issued the warrant, authorization or order and is to be kept in the custody of the court in a place to which the public has no access or in such other place as the judge may authorize and is not to be dealt with except in accordance with this section.

(2) No officer is to examine or reproduce, in whole or in part, a document referred to in subsection (1) without giving the journalist and relevant media outlet notice of his or her intention to examine or reproduce the document.

(3) The journalist or relevant media outlet may, within 10 days of receiving the notice referred to in subsection (2), apply to a judge of the court that issued the warrant, authorization or order to issue an order that the document is not to be disclosed to an officer on the grounds that the document identifies or is likely to identity a journalistic source.

(4) A document that is subject to an application under subsection (3) is to be disclosed to an officer only following a disclosure order in accordance with paragraph (7)(*b*).

(5) The judge may order the disclosure of a document only if he or she is satisfied that

(*a*) there is no other way by which the information can reasonably be obtained; and

(*b*) the public interest in the investigation and prosecution of a criminal offence outweighs the journalist's right to privacy in gathering and disseminating information.

(6) The judge may, if he or she considers it necessary, examine a document to determine whether it should be disclosed.

(7) The judge must,

(*a*) if he or she is of the opinion that the document should not be disclosed, order that it be returned to the journalist or the media outlet, as the case may be; or

(*b*) if he or she is of the opinion that the document should be disclosed, order that it be delivered to the officer who gave the notice under subsection (2), subject to such restrictions and conditions as the judge deems appropriate. 2017, c. 22, s. 3.

DEFINITIONS / "custodian" / "document" / "judge" / "lawyer" / "officer" / Examination or seizure of certain documents where privilege claimed / Application to judge / Disposition of application / Privilege continues / Order to custodian to deliver / Application to another judge / Prohibition / Authority to make copies / Hearing in private / Exception.

488.1 (1) In this section,

"custodian" means a person in whose custody a package is placed pursuant to subsection (2);

"document", for the purposes of this section, has the same meaning as in section 321;

"judge" means a judge of a superior court of criminal jurisdiction of the province where the seizure was made;

"lawyer" means, in the Province of Quebec, an advocate, lawyer or notary and, in any other province, a barrister or solicitor;

"officer" means a peace officer or public officer.

(2) Where an officer acting under the authority of this or any other Act of Parliament is about to examine, copy or seize a document in the possession of a lawyer who claims that a named client of his has a solicitor-client privilege in respect of that document, the officer shall, without examining or making copies of the document,

(*a*) seize the document and place it in a package and suitably seal and identify the package; and

(b) place the package in the custody of the sheriff of the district or county in which the seizure was made or, if there is agreement in writing that a specified person act as custodian, in the custody of that person.

(3) Where a document has been seized and placed in custody under subsection (2), the Attorney General or the client or the lawyer on behalf of the client, may

(a) within fourteen days from the day the document was so placed in custody, apply, on two days notice of motion to all other persons entitled to make application, to a judge for an order

(i) appointing a place and a day, not later than twenty-one days after the date of the order, for the determination of the question whether the document should be disclosed, and

(ii) requiring the custodian to produce the document to the judge at that time and place;

(b) serve a copy of the order on all other persons entitled to make application and on the custodian within six days of the date on which it was made; and

(c) if he has proceeded as authorized by paragraph (b), apply, at the appointed time and place, for an order determining the question.

(4) On an application under paragraph (3)(c), the judge

(a) may, if the judge considers it necessary to determine the question whether the document should be disclosed, inspect the document;

(b) where the judge is of the opinion that it would materially assist him in deciding whether or not the document is privileged, may allow the Attorney General to inspect the document;

(c) shall allow the Attorney General and the person who objects to the disclosure of the document to make representations; and

(d) shall determine the question summarily and,

(i) if the judge is of the opinion that the document should not be disclosed, ensure that it is repackaged and resealed and order the custodian to deliver the document to the lawyer who claimed the solicitor-client privilege or to the client, or

(ii) if the judge is of the opinion that the document should be disclosed, order the custodian to deliver the document to the officer who seized the document or some other person designated by the Attorney General, subject to such restrictions or conditions as the judge deems appropriate,

and shall, at the same time, deliver concise reasons for the determination in which the nature of the document is described without divulging the details thereof.

(5) Where the judge determines pursuant to paragraph (4)(d) that a solicitor-client privilege exists in respect of a document, whether or not the judge has, pursuant to paragraph (4)(b), allowed the Attorney General to inspect the document, the document remains privileged and inadmissible as evidence unless the client consents to its admission in evidence or the privilege is otherwise lost.

(6) Where a document has been seized and placed in custody under subsection (2) and a judge, on the application of the Attorney General, is satisfied that no application has been made under paragraph (3)(*a*) or that following such an application no further application has been made under paragraph (3)(*c*), the judge shall order the custodian to deliver the document to the officer who seized the document or to some other person designated by the Attorney General.

(7) Where the judge to whom an application has been made under paragraph (3)(*c*) cannot act or continue to act under this section for any reason, subsequent applications under that paragraph may be made to another judge.

(8) No officer shall examine, make copies of or seize any document without affording a reasonable opportunity for a claim of solicitor-client privilege to be made under subsection (2).

(9) At any time while a document is in the custody of a custodian under this section, a judge may, on an *ex parte* application of a person claiming a solicitor-client privilege under this section, authorize that person to examine the document or make a copy of it in the presence of the custodian or the judge, but any such authorization shall contain provisions to ensure that the document is repackaged and that the package is resealed without alteration or damage.

(10) An application under paragraph (3)(*c*) shall be heard in private.

(11) This section does not apply in circumstances where a claim of solicitor-client privilege may be made under the *Income Tax Act* or under the *Proceeds of Crime (Money Laundering) and Terrorist Financing Act*. R.S.C. 1985, c. 27 (1st Supp.), s. 71; 2000, c. 17, s. 89; 2001, c. 41, s. 80.

SEIZURE OF THINGS NOT SPECIFIED / Seizure without warrant

489. (1) Every person who executes a warrant may seize, in addition to the things mentioned in the warrant, any thing that the person believes on reasonable grounds

(*a*) has been obtained by the commission of an offence against this or any other Act of Parliament;

(*b*) has been used in the commission of an offence against this or any other Act of Parliament; or

(*c*) will afford evidence in respect of an offence against this or any other Act of Parliament.

(2) Every peace officer, and every public officer who has been appointed or designated to administer or enforce any federal or provincial law and whose duties include the enforcement of this or any other Act of Parliament, who is lawfully present in a place pursuant to a warrant or otherwise in the execution of duties may, without a warrant, seize any thing that the officer believes on reasonable grounds

(*a*) has been obtained by the commission of an offence against this or any other Act of Parliament;

(*b*) has been used in the commission of an offence against this or any other Act of Parliament; or (*c*) will afford evidence in respect of an offence against this or any other Act of Parliament. R.S. c. C-34, s. 445; R.S.C 1985, c. 27 (1st. Supp.), s. 72; c. 42 (4th Supp.), s. 3; 1993, 40, s. 16; 1997, c. 18, s. 48.

CODE

RESTITUTION OF PROPERTY OR REPORT BY PEACE OFFICER / Idem / Form.

489.1 (1) Subject to this or any other Act of Parliament, where a peace officer has seized anything under a warrant issued under this Act or under section 487.11 or 489 or otherwise in the execution of duties under this or any other Act of Parliament, the peace officer shall, as soon as is practicable,

(*a*) where the peace officer is satisfied,

    (i)   that there is no dispute as to who is lawfully entitled to possession of the thing seized, and

    (ii) that the continued detention of the thing seized is not required for the purposes of any investigation or a preliminary inquiry, trial or other proceeding,

return the thing seized, on being issued a receipt therefor, to the person lawfully entitled to its possession and report to the justice who issued the warrant or some other justice for the same territorial division or, if no warrant was issued, a justice having jurisdiction in respect of the matter, that he has done so; or

(*b*) where the peace officer is not satisfied as described in subparagraphs (*a*)(i) and (ii),

    (i)   bring the thing seized before the justice referred to in paragraph (*a*), or

    (ii) report to the justice that he has seized the thing and is detaining it or causing it to be detained

to be dealt with by the justice in accordance with subsection 490(1).

(2) Subject to this or any other Act of Parliament, where a person, other than a peace officer, has seized anything under a warrant issued under this Act or under section 487.11 or 489 or otherwise in the execution of duties under this or any other Act of Parliament, that person shall, as soon as is practicable,

(*a*) bring the thing seized before the justice who issued the warrant or some other justice for the same territorial division or, if no warrant was issued, before a justice having jurisdiction in respect of the matter, or

(*a*) report to the justice referred to in paragraph (*a*) that he has seized the thing and is detaining it or causing it to be detained,

to be dealt with by the justice in accordance with subsection 490(1).

(3) A report to a justice under this section shall be in the form set out as Form 5.2 in Part XXVIII, varied to suit the case and shall include, in the case of a report in respect of a warrant issued by telephone or other means of telecommunication, the statements referred to in subsection 487.1(9). R.S.C. 1985, c. 27 (1st Supp.), s. 72; 1993, c. 40, s. 17; 1997, c. 18, s. 49.

DETENTION OF THINGS SEIZED / Further detention / Idem / Detention without application where consent / When accused ordered to stand trial / Where continued detention no longer required / Idem / Application for order of return / Exception / Disposal of things seized / Exception / Application by lawful owner / Order / Detention pending appeal, etc. / Copies of documents returned / Probative force / Access to things seized / Conditions / Appeal / Waiver of notice.

490. (1) Subject to this or any other Act of Parliament, where, pursuant to paragraph 489.1(1)(b) or subsection 489.1(2), anything that has been seized is brought before a justice or a report in respect of anything seized is made to a justice, the justice shall,

(a) where the lawful owner or person who is lawfully entitled to possession of the thing seized is known, order it to be returned to that owner or person, unless the prosecutor, or the peace officer or other person having custody of the thing seized, satisfies the justice that the detention of the thing seized is required for the purposes of any investigation or a preliminary inquiry, trial or other proceeding; or

(b) where the prosecutor, or the peace officer or other person having custody of the thing seized, satisfies the justice that the thing seized should be detained for a reason set out in paragraph (a), detain the thing seized or order that it be detained, taking reasonable care to ensure that it is preserved until the conclusion of any investigation or until it is required to be produced for the purposes of a preliminary inquiry, trial or other proceeding.

(2) Nothing shall be detained under the authority of paragraph (1)(b) for a period of more than three months after the day of the seizure, or any longer period that ends when an application made under paragraph (a) is decided, unless

(a) a justice, on the making of a summary application to him after three clear days' notice thereof to the person from whom the thing detained was seized, is satisfied that, having regard to the nature of the investigation, its further detention for a specified period is warranted and the justice so orders; or

(b) proceedings are instituted in which the thing detained may be required.

(3) More than one order for further detention may be made under paragraph (2)(a) but the cumulative period of detention shall not exceed one year from the day of the seizure, or any longer period that ends when an application made under paragraph (a) is decided, unless

(a) a judge of a superior court of criminal jurisdiction or a judge as defined in section 552, on the making of a summary application to him after three clear days notice thereof to the person from whom the thing detained was seized, is satisfied, having regard to the complex nature of the investigation, that the further detention of the thing seized is warranted for a specified period and subject to such other conditions as the judge considers just, and he so orders; or

(b) proceedings are instituted in which the thing detained may be required.

(3.1) A thing may be detained under paragraph (1)(*b*) for any period, whether or not an application for an order under subsection (2) or (3) is made, if the lawful owner or person who is lawfully entitled to possession of the thing seized consents in writing to its detention for that period.

(4) When an accused has been ordered to stand trial, the justice shall forward anything detained pursuant to subsections (1) to (3) to the clerk of the court to which the accused has been ordered to stand trial to be detained by the clerk of the court and disposed of as the court directs.

(5) Where at any time before the expiration of the periods of detention provided for or ordered under subsections (1) to (3) in respect of anything seized, the prosecutor, or the peace officer or other person having custody of the thing seized, determines that the continued detention of the thing seized is no longer required for any purpose mentioned in subsection (1) or (4), the prosecutor, peace officer or other person shall apply to

  (*a*) a judge of a superior court of criminal jurisdiction or a judge as defined in section 552, where a judge ordered its detention under subsection (3), or

  (*b*) a justice, in any other case,

who shall, after affording the person from whom the thing was seized or the person who claims to be the lawful owner thereof or person entitled to its possession, if known, an opportunity to establish that he is lawfully entitled to the possession thereof, make an order in respect of the property under subsection (9).

(6) Where the periods of detention provided for or ordered under subsections (1) to (3) in respect of anything seized have expired and proceedings have not been instituted in which the thing detained may be required, the prosecutor, peace officer or other person shall apply to a judge or justice referred to in paragraph 5(*a*) or (*b*) in the circumstances set out in that paragraph, for an order in respect of the property under subsection (9) or (9.1).

(7) A person from whom anything has been seized may, after the expiration of the periods of detention provided for or ordered under subsections (1) to (3) and on three clear days notice to the Attorney General, apply summarily to

  (*a*) a judge of a superior court of criminal jurisdiction or a judge as defined in section 552, where a judge ordered the detention of the thing seized under subsection (3), or

  (*b*) a justice, in any other case,

for an order under paragraph (9)(*c*) that the thing seized be returned to the applicant.

(8) A judge of a superior court of criminal jurisdiction or a judge as defined in section 552, where a judge ordered the detention of the thing seized under subsection (3), or a justice, in any other case, may allow an application to be made under subsection (7) prior to the expiration of the periods referred to therein where he is satisfied that hardship will result unless the application is so allowed.

(9) Subject to this or any other Act of Parliament, if

  (*a*) a judge referred to in subsection (7), where a judge ordered the detention of anything seized under subsection (3), or

  (*b*) a justice, in any other case,

is satisfied that the periods of detention provided for or ordered under subsections (1) to (3) in respect of anything seized have expired and proceedings have not been instituted in which the thing detained may be required or, where those periods have not expired, that the continued detention of the thing seized will not be required for any purpose mentioned in subsection (1) or (4), he shall

    (c) if possession of it by the person from whom it was seized is lawful, order it to be returned to that person; or

    (d) if possession of it by the person from whom it was seized is unlawful and the lawful owner or person who is lawfully entitled to its possession is known, order it to be returned to the lawful owner or to the person who is lawfully entitled to its possession,

and may, if possession of it by the person from whom it was seized is unlawful, or if it was seized when it was not in the possession of any person, and the lawful owner or person who is lawfully entitled to its possession is not known, order it to be forfeited to Her Majesty, to be disposed of as the Attorney General directs, or otherwise dealt with in accordance with the law.

(9.1) Notwithstanding subsection (9), a judge or justice referred to in paragraph (9)(a) or (b) may, if the periods of detention provided for or ordered under subsections (1) to (3) in respect of a thing seized have expired but proceedings have not been instituted in which the thing may be required, order that the thing continue to be detained for such period as the judge or justice considers necessary if the judge or justice is satisfied

    (a) that the continued detention of the thing might reasonably be required for a purpose mentioned in subsection (1) or (4); and

    (b) that it is in the interests of justice to do so.

(10) Subject to this or any other Act of Parliament, a person, other than a person who may make an application under subsection (7), who claims to be the lawful owner or person lawfully entitled to possession of anything seized and brought before or reported to a justice under section 489.1 may, at any time, on three clear days notice to the Attorney General and the person from whom the thing was seized, apply summarily to

    (a) a judge referred to in subsection (7), where a judge ordered the detention of the thing seized under subsection (3), or

    (b) a justice, in any other case,

for an order that the thing detained be returned to the applicant.

(11) Subject to this or any other Act of Parliament, on an application under subsection (10), where a judge or justice is satisfied that

    (a) the applicant is the lawful owner or lawfully entitled to possession of the thing seized, and

    (b) the periods of detention provided for or ordered under subsections (1) to (3) in respect of the thing seized have expired and proceedings have not been instituted in which the thing detained may be required or, where such periods have not expired, that the continued detention of the thing seized will not be required for any purpose mentioned in subsection (1) or (4),

the judge or justice shall order that

    (c) the thing seized be returned to the applicant; or

(*d*) except as otherwise provided by law, where, pursuant to subsection (9), the thing seized was forfeited, sold or otherwise dealt with in such a manner that it cannot be returned to the applicant, the applicant be paid the proceeds of sale or the value of the thing seized.

(12) Notwithstanding anything in this section, nothing shall be returned, forfeited or disposed of under this section pending any application made, or appeal taken, thereunder in respect of the thing or proceeding in which the right of seizure thereof is questioned or within thirty days after an order in respect of the thing is made under this section.

CODE

(13) The Attorney General, the prosecutor or the peace officer or other person having custody of a document seized may, before bringing it before a justice or complying with an order that the document be returned, forfeited or otherwise dealt with under subsection (1), (9) or (11), make or cause to be made, and may retain, a copy of the document.

(14) Every copy made under subsection (13) that is certified as a true copy by the Attorney General, the person who made the copy or the person in whose presence the copy was made is admissible in evidence and, in the absence of evidence to the contrary, has the same probative force as the original document would have if it had been proved in the ordinary way.

(15) Where anything is detained pursuant to subsections (1) to (3.1), a judge of a superior court of criminal jurisdiction, a judge as defined in section 552 or a provincial court judge may, on summary application on behalf of a person who has an interest in what is detained, after three clear days notice to the Attorney General, order that the person by or on whose behalf the application is made be permitted to examine anything so detained.

(16) An order that is made under subsection (15) shall be made on such terms as appear to the judge to be necessary or desirable to ensure that anything in respect of which the order is made is safeguarded and preserved for any purpose for which it may subsequently be required.

(17) A person who feels aggrieved by an order made under subsection (8), (9), (9.1) or (11) may appeal from the order

(*a*) to the court of appeal as defined in section 673 if the order was made by a judge of a superior court of criminal jurisdiction, in which case sections 678 to 689 apply with any modifications that the circumstances require; or

(*b*) to the appeal court as defined in section 812 in any other case, in which case sections 813 to 828 apply with any modifications that the circumstances require.

(18) Any person to whom three days notice must be given under paragraph (2)(*a*) or (3)(*a*) or subsection (7), (10) or (15) may agree that the application for which the notice is given be made before the expiration of the three days. R.S., c. C-34, s. 446; R.S.C. 1985, c. 27 (1st Supp.), s. 73; 1994, c. 44, s. 38; 1997, c. 18, s. 50; 2008, c. 18, s. 14.

PERISHABLE THINGS.

490.01 Where any thing seized pursuant to this Act is perishable or likely to depreciate rapidly, the person who seized the thing or any other person having custody of the thing

- (*a*) may return it to its lawful owner or the person who is lawfully entitled to possession of it; or
- (*b*) where, on *ex parte* application to a justice, the justice so authorizes, may
  - (i) dispose of it and give the proceeds of disposition to the lawful owner of the thing seized, if the lawful owner was not a party to an offence in relation to the thing or, if the identity of that lawful owner cannot be reasonably ascertained, the proceeds of disposition are forfeited to Her Majesty, or
  - (ii) destroy it. 1997, c. 18, s. 51; 1999, c. 5, s. 17.

SEX OFFENDER INFORMATION

Interpretation

DEFINITIONS / Interpretation.

490.011 (1) The following definitions apply in this section and in sections 490.012 to 490.032.

"crime of a sexual nature" means a crime referred to in subsection 3(2) of the *Sex Offender Information Registration Act*.

"database" has the same meaning as in subsection 3(1) of the *Sex Offender Information Registration Act*.

"designated offence" means

- (*a*) an offence under any of the following provisions:
  - (i) subsection 7(4.1) (offence in relation to sexual offences against children),
  - (ii) section 151 (sexual interference),
  - (iii) section 152 (invitation to sexual touching),
  - (iv) section 153 (sexual exploitation),
  - (v) section 153.1 (sexual exploitation of person with disability),
  - (vi) section 155 (incest),
  - (vi.01) subsection 160(1) (bestiality),
  - (vi.1) subsection 160(2) (compelling the commission of bestiality),
  - (vii) subsection 160(3) (bestiality in presence of or by a child),
  - (viii) section 163.1 (child pornography),
  - (ix) section 170 (parent or guardian procuring sexual activity),
  - (ix.1) section 171.1 (making sexually explicit material available to child),
  - (x) section 172.1 (luring a child),
  - (x.1) section 172.2 (agreement or arrangement — sexual offence against child),
  - (xi) subsection 173(2) (exposure),

(xii)   [*Repealed*, 2014, c. 25, s. 25(1).]
(xiii) [*Repealed*, 2014, c. 25, s. 25(1).]
(xiv)   [*Repealed*, 2014, c. 25, s. 25(1).]
(xv)   [*Repealed*, 2014, c. 25, s. 25(1).]
(xvi)   section 271 (sexual assault),
(xvii) section 272 (sexual assault with a weapon, threats to a third party or causing bodily harm),
(xviii) paragraph 273(2)(*a*) (aggravated sexual assault — use of a restricted firearm or prohibited firearm or any firearm in connection with criminal organization),
(xviii.1) paragraph 273(2)(*a*.1) (aggravated sexual assault — use of a firearm),
(xix)   paragraph 273(2)(*b*) (aggravated sexual assault),
(xx)   subsection 273.3(2) (removal of a child from Canada),
(xxi)   section 279.011 (trafficking — person under 18 years),
(xxii) subsection 279.02(2) (material benefit — trafficking of person under 18 years),
(xxiii) subsection 279.03(2) (withholding or destroying documents — trafficking of person under 18 years),
(xxiv) subsection 286.1(2) (obtaining sexual services for consideration from person under 18 years),
(xxv)   subsection 286.2(2) (material benefit from sexual services provided by person under 18 years), and
(xxvi) subsection 286.3(2) (procuring — person under 18 years);
(*b*) an offence under any of the following provisions:
(i)   section 162 (voyeurism),
(i.1)   subsection 173(1) (indecent acts),
(ii)   section 177 (trespassing at night),
(iii)   [*Repealed*, 2019, c. 25, s. 202.]
(iii.1) section 231 (murder),
(iv)   section 234 (manslaughter),
(v)   paragraph 246(*b*) (overcoming resistance to commission of offence),
(vi)   section 264 (criminal harassment),
(vii)   section 279 (kidnapping),
(vii.1) section 279.01 (trafficking in persons),
(vii.11) subsection 279.02(1) (material benefit — trafficking),
(vii.12) subsection 279.03(1) (withholding or destroying documents — trafficking),
(viii) section 280 (abduction of a person under age of sixteen),
(ix)   section 281 (abduction of a person under age of fourteen),
(ix.1) subsection 286.1(1) (obtaining sexual services for consideration),
(ix.2) subsection 286.2(1) (material benefit from sexual services),
(ix.3) subsection 286.3(1) (procuring),
(x)   paragraph 348(1)(*d*) (breaking and entering a dwelling house with intent to commit an indictable offence),
(xi)   paragraph 348(1)(*d*) (breaking and entering a dwelling house and committing an indictable offence),
(xii)   paragraph 348(1)(*e*) (breaking and entering a place other than a dwelling house with intent to commit an indictable offence), and

(xiii) paragraph 348(1)(*e*) (breaking and entering a place other than a dwelling house and committing an indictable offence);

(*c*) an offence under any of the following provisions of the *Criminal Code*, chapter C-34 of the Revised Statutes of Canada, 1970, as they read from time to time before January 4, 1983:

(i) section 144 (rape),

(ii) section 145 (attempt to commit rape),

(iii) section 149 (indecent assault on female),

(iv) section 156 (indecent assault on male),

(v) subsection 246(1) (assault with intent) if the intent is to commit an offence referred to in any of subparagraphs (i) to (iv);

(*c*.1) an offence under any of the following provisions of the *Criminal Code*, chapter C-34 of the Revised Statutes of Canada, 1970, as enacted by section 19 of *An Act to amend the Criminal Code in relation to sexual offences and other offences against the person and to amend certain other Acts in relation thereto or in consequence thereof*, chapter 125 of the Statutes of Canada, 1980-81-82-83:

(i) section 246.1 (sexual assault),

(ii) section 246.2 (sexual assault with a weapon, threats to a third party or causing bodily harm), and

(iii) section 246.3 (aggravated sexual assault);

(*d*) an offence under any of the following provisions of the *Criminal Code*, chapter C-34 of the Revised Statutes of Canada, 1970, as they read from time to time before January 1, 1988:

(i) subsection 146(1) (sexual intercourse with a female under age of fourteen),

(ii) subsection 146(2) (sexual intercourse with a female between ages of fourteen and sixteen),

(iii) section 153 (sexual intercourse with step-daughter),

(iv) section 157 (gross indecency),

(v) section 166 (parent or guardian procuring defilement), and

(vi) section 167 (householder permitting defilement);

(*d*.1) an offence under any of the following provisions of this Act, as they read from time to time before the day on which this paragraph comes into force:

(i) paragraph 212(1)(i) (stupefying or overpowering for the purpose of sexual intercourse),

(ii) subsection 212(2) (living on the avails of prostitution of person under 18 years),

(iii) subsection 212(2.1) (aggravated offence in relation to living on the avails of prostitution of person under 18 years), and

(iv) subsection 212(4) (prostitution of person under 18 years);

(*e*) an attempt or conspiracy to commit an offence referred to in any of paragraphs (*a*), (*c*), (*c*.1), (*d*) and (*d*.1); or

(*f*) an attempt or conspiracy to commit an offence referred to in paragraph (*b*).

"Ontario Act" means *Christopher's Law (Sex Offender Registry), 2000*, S.O. 2000, c. 1.

"pardon" means a conditional pardon granted under Her Majesty's royal prerogative of mercy or under section 748 that has not been revoked.

"record suspension" means a record suspension, as defined in subsection 2(1) of the *Criminal Records Act*, that has not been revoked or ceased to have effect.

"registration centre" has the same meaning as in subsection 3(1) of the *Sex Offender Information Registration Act*.

"Review Board" means the Review Board established or designated for a province under subsection 672.38(1).

"verdict of not criminally responsible on account of mental disorder" means a verdict of not criminally responsible on account of mental disorder within the meaning of subsection 672.1(1) or a finding of not responsible on account of mental disorder within the meaning of subsection 2(1) of the *National Defence Act*, as the case may be.

(2) For the purpose of this section and sections 490.012 to 490.032, a person who is convicted of, or found not criminally responsible on account of mental disorder for, a designated offence does not include a young person

   (*a*)   within the meaning of subsection 2(1) of the *Youth Criminal Justice Act* unless they are given an adult sentence within the meaning of that subsection for the offence; or

   (*b*)   within the meaning of subsection 2(1) of the *Young Offenders Act*, chapter Y-1 of the Revised Statutes of Canada, 1985, unless they are convicted of the offence in ordinary court within the meaning of that subsection. 2004, c. 10, s. 20; 2005, c. 43, s. 6; 2007, c. 5, s. 11; 2008, c. 6, s. 36; 2010, c. 3, s. 7; 2010, c. 17, s. 4; 2012, c. 1, s. 141(2) and (3); 2012, c. 1, s. 31; 2014, c. 25, s. 25; 2019, c. 17, s. 4; 2019, c. 25, s. 202.

Order to Comply with the *Sex Offender Information Registration Act*

2007, c. 5, s. 12.

ORDER / Order — if intent established / Order — if previous offence established / Failure to make order.

490.012 (1) When a court imposes a sentence on a person for an offence referred to in paragraph (*a*), (*c*), (*c*.1), (*d*), (*d*.1) or (*e*) of the definition "designated offence" in subsection 490.011(1) or renders a verdict of not criminally responsible on account of mental disorder for such an offence, it shall make an order in Form 52 requiring the person to comply with the *Sex Offender Information Registration Act* for the applicable period specified in section 490.013.

(2) When a court imposes a sentence on a person for an offence referred to in paragraph (*b*) or (*f*) of the definition "designated offence" in subsection 490.011(1), it shall, on application of the prosecutor, make an order in Form 52 requiring the person to comply with the *Sex Offender Information Registration Act* for the applicable period specified in section 490.013 if the prosecutor establishes beyond a reasonable doubt that the person committed the offence with the intent to

commit an offence referred to in paragraph (*a*), (*c*), (*c*.1), (*d*), (*d*.1) or (*e*) of that definition.

(3) When a court imposes a sentence on a person for a designated offence in connection with which an order may be made under subsection (1) or (2) or renders a verdict of not criminally responsible on account of mental disorder for such an offence, it shall, on application of the prosecutor, make an order in Form 52 requiring the person to comply with the *Sex Offender Information Registration Act* for the applicable period specified in section 490.013 if the prosecutor establishes that

- (*a*) the person was, before or after the coming into force of this paragraph, previously convicted of, or found not criminally responsible on account of mental disorder for, an offence referred to in paragraph (*a*), (*c*), (*c*.1), (*d*), (*d*.1) or (*e*) of the definition "designated offence" in subsection 490.011(1) or in paragraph (*a*) or (*c*) of the definition "designated offence" in section 227 of the *National Defence Act*;

- (*b*) the person was not served with a notice under section 490.021 or 490.02903 or under section 227.08 of the *National Defence Act* in connection with that offence; and

- (*c*) no order was made under subsection (1) or under subsection 227.01(1) of the *National Defence Act* in connection with that offence.

(4) If the court does not consider the matter under subsection (1) or (3) at that time, the court

- (*a*) shall, within 90 days after the day on which it imposes the sentence or renders the verdict, set a date for a hearing to do so;

- (*b*) retains jurisdiction over the matter; and

- (*c*) may require the person to appear at the hearing by closed-circuit television or videoconference, as long as the person is given the opportunity to communicate privately with counsel if they are represented by counsel. 2004, c. 10, s. 20; 2007, c. 5, s. 13; 2010, c. 17, s. 5; 2014, c. 25, s. 26; 2019, c. 25, s. 203.

DATE ORDER BEGINS / Duration of order / Duration of order / Duration of order / Duration of order / Duration of order.

490.013 (1) An order made under section 490.012 begins on the day on which it is made.

(2) An order made under subsection 490.012(1) or (2)

- (*a*) ends 10 years after it was made if the offence in connection with which it was made was prosecuted summarily or if the maximum term of imprisonment for the offence is two or five years;

- (*b*) ends 20 years after it was made if the maximum term of imprisonment for the offence is 10 or 14 years; and

- (*c*) applies for life if the maximum term of imprisonment for the offence is life.

(2.1) An order made under subsection 490.012(1) applies for life if the person is convicted of, or found not criminally responsible on account of mental disorder for, more than one offence referred to in paragraph (*a*), (*c*), (*c*.1), (*d*), (*d*.1) or (*e*) of the definition "designated offence" in subsection 490.011(1).

(3) An order made under subsection 490.012(1) or (2) applies for life if the person is, or was at any time, subject to an obligation under section 490.019 or 490.02901, under section 227.06 of the *National Defence Act* or under section 36.1 of the *International Transfer of Offenders Act*.

(4) An order made under subsection 490.012(1) or (2) applies for life if the person is, or was at any time, subject to an order made previously under section 490.012 of this Act or section 227.01 of the *National Defence Act*.

(5) An order made under subsection 490.012(3) applies for life. 2004, c. 10, s. 20; 2007, c. 5, s. 14; 2010, c. 17, s. 6; 2014, c. 25, s. 27.

APPEAL.

490.014 The prosecutor, or a person who is subject to an order under subsection 490.012(2), may appeal from a decision of the court under that subsection on any ground of appeal that raises a question of law or of mixed law and fact. The appeal court may dismiss the appeal, or allow it and order a new hearing, quash the order or make an order that may be made under that subsection. 2004, c. 10, s. 20; 2010, c. 17, s. 7.

APPLICATION FOR TERMINATION ORDER / Multiple orders / Pardon or record suspension / Scope of application / Re-application / Jurisdiction.

490.015 (1) A person who is subject to an order may apply for a termination order
  (*a*) if five years have elapsed since the order was made, in the case of an order referred to in paragraph 490.013(2)(*a*);
  (*b*) if 10 years have elapsed since the order was made, in the case of an order referred to in paragraph 490.013(2)(*b*); or
  (*c*) if 20 years have elapsed since the order was made, in the case of an order referred to in paragraph 490.013(2)(*c*) or subsection 490.013(2.1), (3) or (5).

(2) A person who is subject to more than one order made under section 490.012 of this Act, or under that section and section 227.01 of the *National Defence Act*, may apply for a termination order if 20 years have elapsed since the most recent order was made.

(3) Despite subsections (1) and (2), a person may apply for a termination order once they receive a pardon or once a record suspension is ordered.

(4) The application shall be in relation to every order that is in effect. If a person is subject to an obligation under section 490.019 or 490.02901, under section 227.06 of the *National Defence Act* or under section 36.1 of the *International Transfer of Offenders Act*, the application shall also be in relation to that obligation.

(5) A person whose application is refused may re-apply if five years have elapsed since they made the previous application. They may also re-apply once they receive a pardon or once a record suspension is ordered. However, they may not re-apply under this subsection if an order is made with respect to them under

section 490.012 of this Act or section 227.01 of the *National Defence Act* after the previous application was made.

(6) The application shall be made to

(*a*) a superior court of criminal jurisdiction if

(i) one or more of the orders to which it relates were made by such a court under section 490.012, or

(ii) one or more of the orders to which it relates were made under section 227.01 of the *National Defence Act* and the Chief Military Judge does not have jurisdiction to receive the application under subsection 227.03(6) of that Act; or

(*b*) a court of criminal jurisdiction, in any other case in which the application relates to one or more orders made under section 490.012. 2004, c. 10, s. 20; 2007, c. 5, s. 15; 2010, c. 17, s. 8; 2012, c. 1, s. 142.

TERMINATION ORDER / Reasons for decision / Requirements relating to notice.

490.016 (1) The court shall make a termination order if it is satisfied that the person has established that the impact on them of continuing an order or an obligation, including on their privacy or liberty, would be grossly disproportionate to the public interest in protecting society through the effective prevention or investigation of crimes of a sexual nature, to be achieved by the registration of information relating to sex offenders under the *Sex Offender Information Registration Act*.

(2) The court shall give reasons for its decision.

(3) If the court makes a termination order, it shall cause the Commissioner of the Royal Canadian Mounted Police and the Attorney General of the province, or the minister of justice of the territory, to be notified of the decision. 2004, c. 10, s. 20; 2007, c. 15, s. 16; 2010, c. 17, s. 9.

APPEAL / Requirements relating to notice.

490.017 (1) The prosecutor or the person who applied for a termination order may appeal from a decision made under subsection 490.016(1) on any ground of appeal that raises a question of law or of mixed law and fact. The appeal court may dismiss the appeal, or allow it and order a new hearing, quash the termination order or make an order that may be made under that subsection.

(2) If the appeal court makes an order that may be made under subsection 490.016(1), it shall cause the Commissioner of the Royal Canadian Mounted Police and the Attorney General of the province, or the minister of justice of the territory, in which the application for the order was made to be notified of the decision. 2004, c. 10, s. 20; 2007, c. 5, s. 17; 2010, c. 17, s. 10.

REQUIREMENTS RELATING TO NOTICE / Endorsement / Notice on disposition by Review Board / Notice before release.

490.018 (1) When a court or appeal court makes an order under section 490.012, it shall cause

   (a) the order to be read by or to the person who is subject to it;

   (b) a copy of the order to be given to that person;

   (c) that person to be informed of sections 4 to 7.1 of the *Sex Offender Information Registration Act*, sections 490.031 and 490.0311 of this Act and section 119.1 of the *National Defence Act*; and

   (d) a copy of the order to be sent to

     (i) the Review Board that is responsible for making a disposition with respect to that person, if applicable,

     (ii) the person in charge of the place in which that person is to serve the custodial portion of a sentence or is to be detained in custody as part of a disposition under Part XX.1, if applicable,

     (iii) the police service whose member charged that person with the offence in connection with which the order is made, and

     (iv) the Commissioner of the Royal Canadian Mounted Police.

(2) After paragraphs (1)(a) to (c) have been complied with, the person who is subject to the order shall endorse the order.

(3) A Review Board shall cause a copy of the order to be given to the person who is subject to it when it directs

   (a) under paragraph 672.54(a), that the person be discharged absolutely; or

   (b) under paragraph 672.54(b), that the person be discharged subject to conditions, unless the conditions restrict the person's liberty in a manner and to an extent that prevent them from complying with sections 4, 4.1, 4.3 and 6 of the *Sex Offender Information Registration Act*.

(4) The person in charge of the place in which the person is serving the custodial portion of a sentence, or is detained in custody, before their release or discharge shall give the person a copy of the order not earlier than 10 days before their release or discharge. 2004, c. 10, s. 20; 2007, c. 5, s. 18; 2010, c. 17, s. 11.

Notice and Obligation to Comply with the *Sex Offender Information Registration Act* — Convictions Before December 15, 2004
2010, c. 17, s. 12.

OBLIGATION TO COMPLY.

490.019 A person who is served with a notice in Form 53 shall comply with the *Sex Offender Information Registration Act* for the applicable period specified in section 490.022 unless a court makes an exemption order under subsection 490.023(2). 2004, c. 10, s. 20.

PERSONS WHO MAY BE SERVED / Exception.

490.02 (1) The Attorney General of a province or minister of justice of a territory may serve a person with a notice only if the person was convicted of, or found not criminally responsible on account of mental disorder for, an offence referred to in paragraph (*a*), (*c*), (*c*.1), (*d*) or (*e*) of the definition "designated offence" in subsection 490.011(1) and

- (*a*) on the day on which the *Sex Offender Information Registration Act* comes into force, they are subject to a sentence for, or have not received an absolute discharge under Part XX.1 from, the offence; or
- (*b*) in any other case,
  - (i) their name appears in connection with the offence, immediately before the *Sex Offender Information Registration Act* comes into force, in the sex offender registry established under the Ontario Act, and
  - (ii) they either were a resident of Ontario at any time between April 23, 2001 and the day on which the *Sex Offender Information Registration Act* comes into force or committed the offence in Ontario.

(2) A notice shall not be served on a person

- (*a*) if they have been finally acquitted of, or have received a free pardon granted under Her Majesty's royal prerogative of mercy or under section 748 for, every offence in connection with which a notice may be served on them under section 490.021 of this Act or section 227.08 of the *National Defence Act*;
- (*b*) if an application has been made for an order under subsection 490.012(3) of this Act or subsection 227.01(3) of the *National Defence Act* in relation to any offence in connection with which a notice may be served on them under section 490.021 of this Act or section 227.08 of the *National Defence Act*; or
- (*c*) who is referred to in paragraph (1)(*b*) if they have provided proof of a pardon in accordance with subsection 9(1) of the Ontario Act. 2004, c. 10, s. 20; 2007, c. 5, s. 20.

PERIOD FOR AND METHOD OF SERVICE / Exception / Exception / Exception / Proof of Service / Requirements relating to notice.

490.021 (1) The notice shall be personally served within one year after the day on which the *Sex Offender Information Registration Act* comes into force.

(2) If a person referred to in paragraph 490.02(1)(*a*) is unlawfully at large or is in breach of any terms of their sentence or discharge, or of any conditions set under this Act or under Part III of the *National Defence Act*, that relate to residence, the notice may be served by registered mail at their last known address.

(3) If a person referred to in paragraph 490.02(1)(*b*) is not in compliance with section 3 of the Ontario Act on the day on which the *Sex Offender Information Registration Act* comes into force, the notice may be served by registered mail at their last known address.

(4) If a person referred to in paragraph 490.02(1)(*b*) is in compliance with section 3 and subsection 7(2) of the Ontario Act on the day on which the *Sex Offender*

Information Registration Act comes into force but fails to comply with subsection 3(1) or 7(2) of the Ontario Act within one year after that day, the notice shall be served within one year after the day on which they failed to comply and may be served by registered mail at their last known address.

(5) An affidavit of the person who served the notice, sworn before a commissioner or other person authorized to take affidavits, is evidence of the service and the notice if it sets out that

- (a) the person who served the notice has charge of the appropriate records and has knowledge of the facts in the particular case;
- (b) the notice was personally served on, or mailed to, the person to whom it was directed on a named day; and
- (c) the person who served the notice identifies a true copy of the notice as an exhibit attached to the affidavit.

(6) The person who served the notice shall, without delay, send a copy of the affidavit and the notice to the Attorney General of the province, or the minister of justice of the territory, in which the person was served. 2004, c. 10, s. 20; 2007, c. 5, s. 21(2).

DATE OBLIGATION BEGINS / Date obligation ends / Duration of obligation.

490.022 (1) The obligation under section 490.019 begins

- (a) either one year after the day on which the person is served with the notice or when an exemption order is refused under subsection 490.023(2), whichever is later; or
- (b) when an exemption order is quashed.

(2) The obligation ends on the earliest of

- (a) the day on which an exemption order is made on an appeal from a decision made under subsection 490.023(2),
- (b) the day on which the obligation of a person referred to in paragraph 490.02(1)(b) to comply with section 3 of the Ontario Act ends under paragraph 7(1)(a) of that Act, or
- (c) the day on which a person referred to in paragraph 490.02(1)(b) provides satisfactory proof of a pardon or record suspension to a person who collects information, as defined in subsection 3(1) of the *Sex Offender Information Registration Act*, at a registration centre.

(3) If none of paragraphs (2)(a) to (c) applies earlier, the obligation

- (a) ends 10 years after the person was sentenced, or found not criminally responsible on account of mental disorder, for the offence listed in the notice if the offence was prosecuted summarily or if the maximum term of imprisonment for the offence is two or five years;
- (b) ends 20 years after the person was sentenced, or found not criminally responsible on account of mental disorder, for the offence listed in the notice if the maximum term of imprisonment for the offence is 10 or 14 years;

    (*c*) applies for life if the maximum term of imprisonment for the offence listed in the notice is life; or

    (*d*) applies for life if, at any time, the person was convicted of, or found not criminally responsible on account of mental disorder for, more than one offence that is referred to in paragraph (*a*), (*c*), (*c*.1), (*d*) or (*e*) of the definition "designated offence" in subsection 490.011(1) of this Act or in paragraph (*a*) or (*c*) of the definition "designated offence" in section 227 of the *National Defence Act* and if more than one of those offences is listed in the notice. 2004, c. 10, s. 20; 2007, c. 5, s. 22; 2012, c. 1, s. 143.

APPLICATION FOR EXEMPTION ORDER / Jurisdiction / Exemption order / Reasons for decision / Removal of information from database.

490.023 (1) A person who is not subject to an order under section 490.012 of this Act or section 227.01 of the *National Defence Act* may apply for an order exempting them from the obligation within one year after they are served with a notice under section 490.021 of this Act or section 227.08 of the *National Defence Act*.

(1.1) The application shall be made to a court of criminal jurisdiction if

    (*a*) it relates to an obligation under section 490.019 of this Act; or

    (*b*) it relates to an obligation under section 227.06 of the *National Defence Act* and the Chief Military Judge does not have jurisdiction to receive the application under subsection 227.1(2) of that Act.

(2) The court shall make an exemption order if it is satisfied that the person has established that the impact of the obligation on them, including on their privacy or liberty, would be grossly disproportionate to the public interest in protecting society through the effective prevention or investigation of crimes of a sexual nature, to be achieved by the registration of information relating to sex offenders under the *Sex Offender Information Registration Act*.

(3) The court shall give reasons for its decision.

(4) If the court makes an exemption order, it shall also make an order requiring the Royal Canadian Mounted Police to permanently remove from the database all information that relates to the person that was registered in the database on receipt of the copy of the notice. 2004, c. 10, s. 20; 2007, c. 5, s. 23; 2010, c. 17, s. 13.

APPEAL / Removal of information from database.

490.024 (1) The Attorney General or the person who applied for an exemption order may appeal from a decision of the court under subsection 490.023(2) on any ground of appeal that raises a question of law or of mixed law and fact. The appeal court may dismiss the appeal, or allow it and order a new hearing, quash the exemption order or make an order that may be made under that subsection.

(2) If the appeal court makes an exemption order, it shall also make an order requiring the Royal Canadian Mounted Police to permanently remove from the database all information that relates to the person that was registered in the database on receipt of the copy of the notice. 2004, c. 10, s. 20; 2010, c. 17, s. 14.

REQUIREMENTS RELATING TO NOTICE.

490.025 If a court refuses to make an exemption order or an appeal court dismisses an appeal from such a decision or quashes an exemption order, it shall cause the Commissioner of the Royal Canadian Mounted Police and the Attorney General of the province, or the minister of justice of the territory, in which the application for the order was made to be notified of the decision and shall cause the person who applied for the order to be informed of sections 4 to 7.1 of the *Sex Offender Information Registration Act*, sections 490.031 and 490.0311 of this Act and section 119.1 of the *National Defence Act.* 2004, c. 10, s. 20; 2007, c. 5, s. 24; 2010, c. 17, s. 15.

APPLICATION FOR TERMINATION ORDER / Time for application / More than one offence / Pardon or record suspension / Re-application / Jurisdiction.

490.026 (1) A person who is subject to an obligation under section 490.019 may apply for a termination order unless they are also subject to an obligation under section 490.02901, under section 227.06 of the *National Defence Act* or under section 36.1 of the *International Transfer of Offenders Act* — or an order under section 490.012 or under section 227.01 of the *National Defence Act* — that began later.

(2) A person may apply for a termination order if the following period has elapsed since they were sentenced, or found not criminally responsible on account of mental disorder, for an offence referred to in paragraph (*a*), (*c*), (*c*.1), (*d*) or (*e*) of the definition "designated offence" in subsection 490.011(1) of this Act or in paragraph (*a*) or (*c*) of the definition "designated offence" in section 227 of the *National Defence Act*:

(*a*) five years if the offence was prosecuted summarily or if the maximum term of imprisonment for the offence is two or five years;

(*b*) 10 years if the maximum term of imprisonment for the offence is 10 or 14 years; or

(*c*) 20 years if the maximum term of imprisonment for the offence is life.

(3) If more than one offence is listed in the notice served under section 490.021, the person may apply for a termination order if 20 years have elapsed since they were sentenced, or found not criminally responsible on account of mental disorder, for the most recent offence referred to in paragraph (*a*), (*c*), (*c*.1), (*d*) or (*e*) of the definition "designated offence" in subsection 490.011(1) of this Act or in paragraph (*a*) or (*c*) of the definition "designated offence" in section 227 of the *National Defence Act*.

(4) Despite subsections (2) and (3), a person may apply for a termination order once they receive a pardon or once a record suspension is ordered.

(5) A person whose application is refused may apply again if five years have elapsed since they made the previous application. They may also apply again once they receive a pardon or once a record suspension is ordered. However, they may not apply again if, after the previous application was made, they become subject to an obligation under section 490.02901, under section 227.06 of the *National*

Defence Act or under section 36.1 of the *International Transfer of Offenders Act* or to an order under section 490.012 or under section 227.01 of the *National Defence Act*.

(6) The application shall be made to a court of criminal jurisdiction if
- (a) it relates to an obligation under section 490.019 of this Act; or
- (b) it relates to an obligation under section 227.06 of the *National Defence Act* and the Chief Military Judge does not have jurisdiction to receive the application under subsection 227.12(6) of that Act. 2004, c. 10, s. 20; 2007, c. 5, s. 24; 2010, c. 17, s. 16; 2012, c. 1, s. 144.

TERMINATION ORDER / Reasons for decision / Requirements relating to notice.

490.027 (1) The court shall make an order terminating the obligation if it is satisfied that the person has established that the impact on them of continuing the obligation, including on their privacy or liberty, would be grossly disproportionate to the public interest in protecting society through the effective prevention or investigation of crimes of a sexual nature, to be achieved by the registration of information relating to sex offenders under the *Sex Offender Information Registration Act*.

(2) The court shall give reasons for its decision.

(3) If the court makes a termination order, it shall cause the Commissioner of the Royal Canadian Mounted Police and the Attorney General of the province, or the minister of justice of the territory, to be notified of the decision. 2004, c. 10, s. 20; 2007, c. 5, s. 25; 2010, c. 17, s. 17.

DEEMED APPLICATION.

490.028 If a person is eligible to apply for both an exemption order under section 490.023 and a termination order under section 490.026 within one year after they are served with a notice under section 490.021 of this Act or section 227.08 of the *National Defence Act*, an application within that period for one order is deemed to be an application for both. 2004, c. 10, s. 20; 2007, c. 5, s. 26.

APPEAL / Requirements relating to notice.

490.029 (1) The Attorney General or the person who applied for a termination order may appeal from a decision of the court made under subsection 490.027(1) on any ground of appeal that raises a question of law or of mixed law and fact. The appeal court may dismiss the appeal, or allow it and order a new hearing, quash the termination order or make an order that may be made under that subsection.

(2) If the appeal court makes an order that may be made under subsection 490.027(1), it shall cause the Commissioner of the Royal Canadian Mounted Police and the Attorney General of the province, or the minister of justice of the territory, in which the application for the order was made to be notified of the decision. 2004, c. 10, s. 20; 2007, c. 5, s. 26; 2010, c. 17, s. 18.

Notice and Obligation to Comply with the *Sex Offender Information Registration Act* — Convictions Outside Canada

OBLIGATION.

490.02901 A person who is served with a notice in Form 54 shall comply with the *Sex Offender Information Registration Act* for the applicable period specified in section 490.02904 unless a court makes an exemption order under subsection 490.02905(2). 2010, c. 17, s. 19.

PERSONS WHO MAY BE SERVED / Exception.

490.02902 (1) The Attorney General of a province, or the minister of justice of a territory, may serve a person with a notice in Form 54 only if the person arrived in Canada after the coming into force of this subsection and they were convicted of or found not criminally responsible on account of mental disorder for an offence outside Canada — other than a service offence as defined in subsection 2(1) of the *National Defence Act* — that is, in the opinion of the Attorney General or minister of justice, equivalent to an offence referred to in paragraph (*a*) of the definition "designated offence" in subsection 490.011(1).

(2) The notice shall not be served on a person who has been acquitted of every offence in connection with which a notice may be served on them under section 490.02903. 2010, c. 17, s. 19.

PERIOD FOR AND METHOD OF SERVICE / Proof of service / Requirements relating to notice.

490.02903 (1) A notice in Form 54 shall be personally served.

(2) An affidavit of the person who served the notice, sworn before a commissioner or other person authorized to take affidavits, is evidence of the service and the notice if it sets out that
   (*a*) the person who served the notice has charge of the appropriate records and has knowledge of the facts in the particular case;
   (*b*) the notice was personally served on the person to whom it was directed on a named day; and
   (*c*) the person who served the notice identifies a true copy of the notice as an exhibit attached to the affidavit.

(3) The person who served the notice shall, without delay, send a copy of the affidavit and the notice to the Attorney General of the province, or the minister of justice of the territory, in which the person was served. 2010, c. 17, s. 19.

WHEN OBLIGATION BEGINS / When obligation ends / Duration of obligation.

490.02904 (1) The obligation under section 490.02901 begins on the day on which the person is served with the notice.

505

(2) The obligation ends on the day on which an exemption order is made.

(3) If subsection (2) does not apply, the obligation

    (*a*) ends 10 years after the person was sentenced or found not criminally responsible on account of mental disorder if the maximum term of imprisonment provided for in Canadian law for the equivalent offence is two or five years;

    (*b*) ends 20 years after the person was sentenced or found not criminally responsible on account of mental disorder if the maximum term of imprisonment provided for in Canadian law for the equivalent offence is 10 or 14 years;

    (*c*) applies for life if the maximum term of imprisonment provided for in Canadian law for the equivalent offence is life; or

    (*d*) applies for life if, before or after the coming into force of this paragraph, the person was convicted of, or found not criminally responsible on account of mental disorder for, more than one offence referred to in paragraph (*a*), (*c*), (*c*.1), (*d*), (*d*.1) or (*e*) of the definition "designated offence" in subsection 490.011(1) or referred to in paragraph (*a*) or (*c*) of the definition "designated offence" in section 227 of the *National Defence Act* and if more than one of those offences is listed in the notice. 2010, c. 17, s. 19; 2014, c. 25, s. 28.

APPLICATION FOR EXEMPTION ORDER / Exemption order / Reasons for decision / Removal of information from database / Notification.

490.02905 (1) A person who is served with a notice in Form 54 under section 490.02903 may apply to a court of criminal jurisdiction for an order exempting them from the obligation within one year after they are served.

(2) The court

    (*a*) shall make an exemption order if it is satisfied that the person has established that

        (i) they were not convicted of or found not criminally responsible on account of mental disorder for or were acquitted of the offence in question, or

        (ii) the offence in question is not equivalent to an offence referred to in paragraph (*a*) of the definition "designated offence" in subsection 490.011(1); and

    (*b*) shall order that the notice be corrected if it is satisfied that the offence in question is not equivalent to the offence referred to in the notice but is equivalent to another offence referred to in paragraph (*a*) of the definition "designated offence" in subsection 490.011(1).

(3) The court shall give reasons for its decision.

(4) If the court makes an exemption order, it shall also make an order requiring the Royal Canadian Mounted Police to permanently remove from the database all information that relates to the person that was registered in the database on receipt of the copy of the notice.

(5) If the court makes an order referred to in paragraph (2)(*b*), it shall cause the Commissioner of the Royal Canadian Mounted Police and the Attorney General of the province, or the minister of justice of the territory, in which the application for the order was made to be notified of the decision. 2010, c. 17, s. 19.

APPEAL / Removal of information from database.

490.02906 (1) The Attorney General or the person who applied for an exemption order may appeal from a decision under subsection 490.02905(2) on any ground of appeal that raises a question of law or of mixed law and fact. The appeal court may

    (*a*) dismiss the appeal;

    (*b*) allow the appeal and order a new hearing;

    (*c*) quash the exemption order; or

    (*d*) make an order that may be made under that subsection.

(2) If an appeal court makes an exemption order, it shall also make an order requiring the Royal Canadian Mounted Police to permanently remove from the database all information that relates to the person that was registered in the database on receipt of the copy of the notice. 2010, c. 17, s. 19.

REQUIREMENTS RELATING TO NOTICE.

490.02907 If an appeal court quashes an exemption order, it shall cause the Commissioner of the Royal Canadian Mounted Police and the Attorney General of the province, or the minister of justice of the territory, in which the application for the order was made to be notified of the decision and shall cause the person who applied for the order to be informed of sections 4 to 7.1 of the *Sex Offender Information Registration Act*, sections 490.031 and 490.0311 of this Act and section 119.1 of the *National Defence Act*. 2010, c. 17, s. 19.

APPLICATION FOR TERMINATION ORDER / Time for application — one offence / Time for application — more than one offence / Re-application.

490.02908 (1) A person who is subject to an obligation under section 490.02901 may apply to a court of criminal jurisdiction for a termination order unless they are also subject to another obligation under that section — or to an obligation under section 490.019, under section 227.06 of the *National Defence Act* or under section 36.1 of the *International Transfer of Offenders Act* or an order under section 490.012 or under section 227.01 of the *National Defence Act* — that began later.

(2) The person may apply for a termination order if the following period has elapsed since the sentence was imposed or the verdict of not criminally responsible on account of mental disorder was rendered:

    (*a*) five years if the maximum term of imprisonment provided for in Canadian law for the equivalent offence is two or five years;

    (*b*) 10 years if the maximum term of imprisonment provided for in Canadian law for the equivalent offence is 10 or 14 years; or (*c*) 20 years if the maximum term of imprisonment provided for in Canadian law for the equivalent offence is life.

(3) If more than one offence is listed in the notice served under section 490.02903, the person may apply for a termination order if 20 years have elapsed since the sentence was imposed, or the verdict of not criminally responsible on account of mental disorder was rendered, for the most recent offence.

(4) A person whose application is refused may apply again if five years have elapsed since the application was made. 2010, c. 17, s. 19.

TERMINATION ORDER / Reasons for decision / Requirements relating to notice.

490.02909 (1) The court shall make an order terminating the obligation if it is satisfied that the person has established that the impact on them of continuing the obligation, including on their privacy or liberty, would be grossly disproportionate to the public interest in protecting society through the effective prevention or investigation of crimes of a sexual nature to be achieved by the registration of information relating to sex offenders under the *Sex Offender Information Registration Act*.

(2) The court shall give reasons for its decision.

(3) If the court makes a termination order, it shall cause the Commissioner of the Royal Canadian Mounted Police and the Attorney General of the province, or the minister of justice of the territory, to be notified of the decision. 2010, c. 17, s. 19.

APPEAL / Requirements relating to notice.

490.0291 (1) The Attorney General or the person who applied for a termination order may appeal from a decision under subsection 490.02909(1) on any ground of appeal that raises a question of law or of mixed law and fact. The appeal court may dismiss the appeal, allow the appeal and order a new hearing, quash the termination order or make an order that may be made under that subsection.

(2) If the appeal court makes an order that may be made under subsection 490.02909(1), it shall cause the Commissioner of the Royal Canadian Mounted Police and the Attorney General of the province, or the minister of justice of the territory, in which the application for the order was made to be notified of the decision. 2010, c. 17, s. 19.

OBLIGATION TO ADVISE POLICE SERVICE / Change in address / Information to be provided to Attorney General / Obligation ends.

490.02911 (1) A person who was convicted of or found not criminally responsible on account of mental disorder for an offence outside Canada shall, if the offence is equivalent to one referred to in paragraph (*a*) of the definition "designated offence" in subsection 490.011(1), advise a police service within seven days after the day on which they arrive in Canada of that fact and of their name, date of birth, gender and address. They are not required to so advise the police service again unless they are later convicted of or found not criminally responsible on account of mental disorder for another such offence.

(2) The person shall, if they are in Canada, advise a police service of a change in address within seven days after the day on which the change is made.

(3) The police service shall cause the Attorney General of the province, or the minister of justice of the territory, in which it is located to be provided with the information.

(4) A person's obligation under subsection (2) ends when they are served under section 490.02902 or, if it is earlier, one year after the day on which they advise the police service under subsection (1). 2010, c. 17, s. 19.

International Transfer of Offenders Act

APPLICATION FOR TERMINATION ORDER / Time for application — one offence / More than one offence / Re-application.

490.02912 (1) A person who is subject to an obligation under section 36.1 of the *International Transfer of Offenders Act* may apply to a court of criminal jurisdiction for a termination order unless they are also subject to an obligation under section 490.019 or 490.02901 or under section 227.06 of the *National Defence Act* — or to an order under section 490.012 or under section 227.01 of the *National Defence Act* — that began later.

(2) The person may apply for a termination order if the following period has elapsed since the sentence was imposed or the verdict of not criminally responsible on account of mental disorder was rendered:

   (a) five years if the maximum term of imprisonment provided for in Canadian law for the equivalent offence is two or five years;

   (b) 10 years if the maximum term of imprisonment provided for in Canadian law for the equivalent offence is 10 or 14 years; or

   (c) 20 years if the maximum term of imprisonment provided for in Canadian law for the equivalent offence is life.

(3) If more than one offence is listed in the copy of the Form 1 that was delivered under subparagraph 8(4)(a)(ii) of the *International Transfer of Offenders Act*, the person may apply for a termination order if 20 years have elapsed since the sentence was imposed, or the verdict of not criminally responsible on account of mental disorder was rendered, for the most recent offence.

(4) A person whose application is refused may apply again if five years have elapsed since the application was made. 2010, c. 17, s. 19.

TERMINATION ORDER / Reasons for decision / Requirements relating to notice.

490.02913 (1) The court shall make an order terminating the obligation if it is satisfied that the person has established that the impact on them of continuing the obligation, including on their privacy or liberty, would be grossly disproportionate to the public interest in protecting society through the effective prevention or investigation of crimes of a sexual nature to be achieved by the registration of information relating to sex offenders under the *Sex Offender Information Registration Act*.

(2) The court shall give reasons for its decision.

(3) If the court makes a termination order, it shall cause the Commissioner of the Royal Canadian Mounted Police and the Attorney General of the province, or the minister of justice of the territory, to be notified of the decision. 2010, c. 17, s. 19.

APPEAL / Requirements relating to notice.

490.02914 (1) The Attorney General or the person who applied for a termination order may appeal from a decision under subsection 490.02913(1) on any ground of appeal that raises a question of law or of mixed law and fact. The appeal court may dismiss the appeal, allow the appeal and order a new hearing, quash the termination order or make an order that may be made under that subsection.

(2) If the appeal court makes an order that may be made under subsection 490.02913(1), it shall cause the Commissioner of the Royal Canadian Mounted Police and the Attorney General of the province, or the minister of justice of the territory, in which the application for the order was made to be notified of the decision. 2010, c. 17, s. 19.

NOTICE BEFORE RELEASE / Notice on disposition by Review Board.

490.02915 (1) The person in charge of the place in which a person who is subject to an obligation under section 36.1 of the *International Transfer of Offenders Act* is serving the custodial portion of a sentence, or is detained in custody before their release or discharge, shall give the person a copy of the Form 1 referred to in subsection 490.02912(3) not earlier than 10 days before their release or discharge.

(2) A Review Board shall cause a copy of the Form 1 to be given to the person when it directs

   (a) under paragraph 672.54(a), that the person be discharged absolutely; or
   (b) under paragraph 672.54(b), that the person be discharged subject to conditions unless the conditions restrict the person's liberty in a manner and to an extent that prevent them from complying with sections 4, 4.1, 4.3 and 6 of the *Sex Offender Information Registration Act*. 2010, c. 17, s. 19.

Disclosure of Information

DISCLOSURE BY COMMISSIONER / Disclosure in connection with proceedings / Disclosure in proceedings.

490.03 (1) The Commissioner of the Royal Canadian Mounted Police or a person authorized by the Commissioner shall, on request, disclose information that is registered in the database or the fact that such information is registered in the database (*a*) to the prosecutor if the disclosure is necessary for the purpose of a proceeding under section 490.012; or

(*b*) to the Attorney General if the disclosure is necessary for the purpose of a proceeding under subsection 490.016(1), 490.023(2), 490.027(1), 490.02905(2), 490.02909(1) or 490.02913(1) or for the purpose of an appeal from a decision made in any of those proceedings or in a proceeding under subsection 490.012(2).

(2) The Commissioner or that person shall, on request, disclose to the prosecutor or Attorney General the information that is registered in the database relating to a person if the person discloses, in connection with a proceeding or appeal other than one referred to in subsection (1), the fact that information relating to them is registered in the database.

(3) The prosecutor or the Attorney General may, if the information is relevant to the proceeding, appeal or any subsequent appeal, disclose it to the presiding court. 2004, c. 10, s. 20; 2007, c. 5, s. 27; 2010, c. 17, s. 20.

Offences

OFFENCE / Reasonable excuse / Proof of certain facts by certificate / Attendance and cross-examination / Notice of intention to produce.

490.031 (1) Every person who, without reasonable excuse, fails to comply with an order made under section 490.012 or under section 227.01 of the *National Defence Act* or with an obligation under section 490.019 or 490.02901, under section 227.06 of the *National Defence Act* or under section 36.1 of the *International Transfer of Offenders Act* is guilty of an offence and liable

(*a*) on conviction on indictment, to a fine of not more than $10,000 or to imprisonment for a term of not more than two years, or to both; or

(*b*) on summary conviction, to a fine of not more than $10,000 or to imprisonment for a term of not more than two years less a day, or to both.

(2) For greater certainty, a lawful command that prevents a person from complying with an order or obligation is a reasonable excuse if, at the time, the person is subject to the Code of Service Discipline within the meaning of subsection 2(1) of the *National Defence Act*.

(3) In proceedings under subsection (1), a certificate of a person referred to in paragraph 16(2)(*b*) of the *Sex Offender Information Registration Act* stating that the sex offender failed to report under section 4, 4.1, 4.2 or 4.3 — or provide information under section 5 or notify a person under subsection 6(1) — of that Act is evidence of the statements contained in it without proof of the signature or official character of the person appearing to have signed it.

Note: Subsection 490.031(3) replaced, 2015, c. 23, s. 30 (to come into force by order of the Governor in Council):

Proof of certain facts by certificate

(3) In proceedings under subsection (1), a certificate of a person referred to in paragraph 16(2)(*b*) of the *Sex Offender Information Registration Act* stating that

the sex offender failed to report under section 4, 4.1, 4.2 or 4.3 — or provide information under section 5 or notify a person under subsection 6(1) or (1.01) — of that Act is evidence of the statements contained in it without proof of the signature or official character of the person appearing to have signed it.

(4) The sex offender named in the certificate may, with the leave of the court, require the attendance of the person who signed it for the purpose of cross-examination.

(5) A certificate is not to be received in evidence unless, before the commencement of the trial, the party who intends to produce it gives the sex offender a copy of it and reasonable notice of their intention to produce it. 2004, c. 10, s. 20; 2007, c. 5, s. 28; 2010, c. 17, s. 21; 2019, c. 25, s. 204.

OFFENCE.

490.0311 Every person who knowingly provides false or misleading information under subsection 5(1) or 6(1) of the *Sex Offender Information Registration Act* is guilty of an offence and liable

Note: The portion of section 490.0311 before para. (*a*) replaced, 2015, c. 23, s. 31 (to come into force by order of the Governor in Council):

Offence

490.0311 Every person who knowingly provides false or misleading information under subsection 5(1) or 6(1) or (1.01) of the *Sex Offender Information Registration Act* is guilty of an offence and liable

- (*a*) on conviction on indictment, to a fine of not more than $10,000 or to imprisonment for a term of not more than two years, or to both; or
- (*b*) on summary conviction, to a fine of not more than $10,000 or to imprisonment for a term of not more than two years less a day, or to both. 2007, c. 5, s. 29; 2010, c. 17, s. 22; 2019, c. 25, s. 205.

OFFENCE.

490.0312 Every person who, without reasonable excuse, fails to comply with an obligation under subsection 490.02911(1) or (2) is guilty of an offence punishable on summary conviction. 2010, c. 17, s. 23.

Regulations

REGULATIONS.

490.032 The Governor in Council may make regulations

- (*a*) requiring that additional information be contained in a notice under Form 53 or Form 54; and
- (*b*) prescribing, for one or more provinces, the form and content of that information. 2004, c. 10, s. 20; 2010, c. 17, s. 24.

Forfeiture of Offence-related Property

ORDER OF FORFEITURE OF PROPERTY ON CONVICTION / Property related to other offences / Property outside Canada / Appeal.

490.1 (1) Subject to sections 490.3 to 490.41, if a person is convicted, or discharged under section 730, of an indictable offence under this Act or the *Corruption of Foreign Public Officials Act* and, on application of the Attorney General, the court is satisfied, on a balance of probabilities, that offence-related property is related to the commission of the offence, the court shall

(a) if the prosecution of the offence was commenced at the instance of the government of a province and conducted by or on behalf of that government, order that the property be forfeited to Her Majesty in right of that province to be disposed of or otherwise dealt with in accordance with the law by the Attorney General or Solicitor General of that province; and

(b) in any other case, order that the property be forfeited to Her Majesty in right of Canada to be disposed of or otherwise dealt with in accordance with the law by the member of the Queen's Privy Council for Canada that is designated by the Governor in Council for the purpose of this paragraph.

(1.1) [*Repealed*, 2001, c. 41, s. 130(7.1).]

(2) Subject to sections 490.3 to 490.41, if the evidence does not establish to the satisfaction of the court that property in respect of which an order of forfeiture would otherwise be made under subsection (1) is related to the commission of the indictable offence under this Act or the *Corruption of Foreign Public Officials Act* of which a person is convicted or discharged, but the court is satisfied, beyond a reasonable doubt, that the property is offence-related property, the court may make an order of forfeiture under subsection (1) in relation to that property.

(2.1) An order may be issued under this section in respect of property situated outside Canada, with any modifications that the circumstances require.

(3) A person who has been convicted of an indictable offence under this Act or the *Corruption of Foreign Public Officials Act*, or the Attorney General, may appeal to the court of appeal from an order or a failure to make an order under subsection (1) as if the appeal were an appeal against the sentence imposed on the person in respect of the offence. 1997, c. 23, s. 15; 2001, c. 32, s. 30(2); 2001, c. 41, s. 18, 130(7.1); 2007, c. 13, s. 8; 2017, c. 7, s. 64.

APPLICATION FOR *IN REM* FORFEITURE / Order of forfeiture of property / Accused deemed absconded / Who may dispose of property / Property outside Canada / Definition of "judge".

490.2 (1) If an information has been laid in respect of an indictable offence under this Act or the *Corruption of Foreign Public Officials Act*, the Attorney General may make an application to a judge for an order of forfeiture under subsection (2).

(2) Subject to sections 490.3 to 490.41, the judge to whom an application is made under subsection (1) shall order that the property that is subject to the application

513

be forfeited and disposed of in accordance with subsection (4) if the judge is satisfied

(a) beyond a reasonable doubt that the property is offence-related property;

(b) that proceedings in respect of an indictable offence under this Act or the *Corruption of Foreign Public Officials Act* in relation to the property were commenced; and

(c) that the accused charged with the offence has died or absconded.

(3) For the purpose of subsection (2), an accused is deemed to have absconded in connection with the indictable offence if

(a) an information has been laid alleging the commission of the offence by the accused,

(b) a warrant for the arrest of the accused has been issued in relation to that information, and

(c) reasonable attempts to arrest the accused under the warrant have been unsuccessful during a period of six months beginning on the day on which the warrant was issued,

and the accused is deemed to have so absconded on the last day of that six month period.

(4) For the purpose of subsection (2), the judge shall

(a) if the prosecution of the offence was commenced at the instance of the government of a province and conducted by or on behalf of that government, order that the property be forfeited to Her Majesty in right of that province to be disposed of or otherwise dealt with in accordance with the law by the Attorney General or Solicitor General of that province; and

(b) in any other case, order that the property be forfeited to Her Majesty in right of Canada to be disposed of or otherwise dealt with in accordance with the law by the member of the Queen's Privy Council for Canada that is designated by the Governor in Council for the purpose of this paragraph.

(4.1) An order may be issued under this section in respect of property situated outside Canada, with any modifications that the circumstances require.

(5) In this section and sections 490.5 and 490.8, "judge" means a judge as defined in section 552 or a judge of a superior court of criminal jurisdiction. 1997, c. 23, s. 15; 2001, c. 32, s. 31; 2007, c. 13, s. 9; 2017, c. 7, s. 65.

VOIDABLE TRANSFERS.

490.3 A court may, before ordering that offence-related property be forfeited under subsection 490.1(1) or 490.2(2), set aside any conveyance or transfer of the property that occurred after the seizure of the property, or the making of a restraint order in respect of the property, unless the conveyance or transfer was for valuable consideration to a person acting in good faith. 1997, c. 23, s. 15.

NOTICE / Manner of giving notice / Order of restoration of property.

490.4 (1) Before making an order under subsection 490.1(1) or 490.2(2) in relation to any property, a court shall require notice in accordance with subsection (2) to be given to, and may hear, any person who, in the opinion of the court, appears to have a valid interest in the property.

(2) A notice shall

    (*a*) be given in the manner that the court directs or that may be specified in the rules of the court;

    (*b*) specify the period that the court considers reasonable or that may be set out in the rules of the court during which a person may make an application to the court asserting their interest in the property; and

    (*c*) set out the offence charged and a description of the property.

(3) A court may order that all or part of the property that would otherwise be forfeited under subsection 490.1(1) or 490.2(2) be returned to a person — other than a person who was charged with an indictable offence under this Act or the *Corruption of Foreign Public Officials Act* or a person who acquired title to or a right of possession of the property from such a person under circumstances that give rise to a reasonable inference that the title or right was transferred for the purpose of avoiding the forfeiture of the property — if the court is satisfied that the person is the lawful owner or is lawfully entitled to possession of all or part of that property, and that the person appears innocent of any complicity in, or collusion in relation to, the offence. 1997, c. 23, s. 15; 2001, c. 32, s. 32; 2007, c. 13, s. 10; 2017, c. 7, s. 66.

NOTICE / Manner of giving notice / Non-forfeiture of property / Factors in relation to dwelling-house.

490.41 (1) If all or part of offence-related property that would otherwise be forfeited under subsection 490.1(1) or 490.2(2) is a dwelling-house, before making an order of forfeiture, a court shall require that notice in accordance with subsection (2) be given to, and may hear, any person who resides in the dwelling-house and is a member of the immediate family of the person charged with or convicted of the indictable offence under this Act or the *Corruption of Foreign Public Officials Act* in relation to which the property would be forfeited.

(2) A notice shall

    (*a*) be given in the manner that the court directs or that may be specified in the rules of the court;

    (*b*) specify the period that the court considers reasonable or that may be set out in the rules of the court during which a member of the immediate family who resides in the dwelling-house may make themselves known to the court; and

    (*c*) set out the offence charged and a description of the property.

(3) Subject to an order made under subsection 490.4(3), if a court is satisfied that the impact of an order of forfeiture made under subsection 490.1(1) or 490.2(2) would be disproportionate to the nature and gravity of the offence, the circumstances surrounding the commission of the offence and the criminal record, if any, of the person charged with or convicted of the offence, as the case may be, it may decide not to order the forfeiture of the property or part of the

property and may revoke any restraint order made in respect of that property or part.

(4) Where all or part of the property that would otherwise be forfeited under subsection 490.1(1) or 490.2(2) is a dwelling-house, when making a decision under subsection (3), the court shall also consider

- (*a*) the impact of an order of forfeiture on any member of the immediate family of the person charged with or convicted of the offence, if the dwelling-house was the member's principal residence at the time the charge was laid and continues to be the member's principal residence; and
- (*b*) whether the member referred to in paragraph (*a*) appears innocent of any complicity in the offence or of any collusion in relation to the offence. 2001, c. 32, s. 33; 2007, c. 13, s. 11; 2017, c. 7, s. 67.

APPLICATION / Fixing day for hearing / Notice / Order declaring interest not affected by forfeiture / Appeal from order made under subsection (4) / Return of property.

490.5 (1) Where any offence-related property is forfeited to Her Majesty pursuant to an order made under subsection 490.1(1) or 490.2(2), any person who claims an interest in the property, other than

- (*a*) in the case of property forfeited pursuant to an order made under subsection 490.1(1), a person who was convicted of the indictable offence in relation to which the property was forfeited,
- (*b*) in the case of property forfeited pursuant to an order made under subsection 490.2(2), a person who was charged with the indictable offence in relation to which the property was forfeited, or
- (*c*) a person who acquired title to or a right of possession of the property from a person referred to in paragraph (*a*) or (*b*) under circumstances that give rise to a reasonable inference that the title or right was transferred from that person for the purpose of avoiding the forfeiture of the property,

may, within thirty days after the forfeiture, apply by notice in writing to a judge for an order under subsection (4).

(2) The judge to whom an application is made under subsection (1) shall fix a day not less than thirty days after the date of the filing of the application for the hearing of the application.

(3) An applicant shall serve a notice of the application made under subsection (1) and of the hearing of it on the Attorney General at least fifteen days before the day fixed for the hearing.

(4) Where, on the hearing of an application made under subsection (1), the judge is satisfied that the applicant

- (*a*) is not a person referred to in paragraph (1)(*a*), (*b*) or (*c*) and appears innocent of any complicity in any indictable offence that resulted in the forfeiture of the property or of any collusion in relation to such an offence, and (*b*) exercised all reasonable care to be satisfied that the property was not likely to have been used in connection with the commission of an unlawful act by the person who was permitted by the applicant to obtain possession of the property or from whom the applicant obtained possession or, where the applicant is a mortgagee or lienholder, by the mortgagor or lien-giver,

the judge may make an order declaring that the interest of the applicant is not affected by the forfeiture and declaring the nature and the extent or value of the interest.

(5) An applicant or the Attorney General may appeal to the court of appeal from an order made under subsection (4), and the provisions of Part XXI with respect to procedure on appeals apply, with any modifications that the circumstances require, in respect of appeals under this subsection.

(6) The Attorney General shall, on application made to the Attorney General by any person in respect of whom a judge has made an order under subsection (4), and where the periods with respect to the taking of appeals from that order have expired and any appeal from that order taken under subsection (5) has been determined, direct that

(*a*) the property, or the part of it to which the interest of the applicant relates, be returned to the applicant; or

(*b*) an amount equal to the value of the interest of the applicant, as declared in the order, be paid to the applicant. 1997, c. 23, s. 15; 2001, c. 32, s. 34.

APPEALS FROM ORDERS UNDER SUBSECTION 490.2(2).

490.6 Any person who, in their opinion, is aggrieved by an order made under subsection 490.2(2) may appeal from the order as if the order were an appeal against conviction or against a judgment or verdict of acquittal, as the case may be, under Part XXI, and that Part applies, with any modifications that the circumstances require, in respect of such an appeal. 1997, c. 23, s. 15.

SUSPENSION OF ORDER PENDING APPEAL.

490.7 Notwithstanding anything in this Act, the operation of an order made in respect of property under subsection 490.1(1), 490.2(2) or 490.5(4) is suspended pending

(*a*) any application made in respect of the property under any of those provisions or any other provision of this or any other Act of Parliament that provides for restoration or forfeiture of the property, or

(*b*) any appeal taken from an order of forfeiture or restoration in respect of the property,

and the property shall not be disposed of or otherwise dealt with until thirty days have expired after an order is made under any of those provisions. 1997, c. 23, s. 15.

APPLICATION FOR RESTRAINT ORDER / Procedure / Restraint order / Property outside Canada / Conditions / Order in writing / Service of order / Registration of order / Order continues in force / Offence.

490.8 (1) The Attorney General may make an application in accordance with this section for a restraint order under this section in respect of any offence-related property.

(2) An application made under subsection (1) for a restraint order in respect of any offence-related property may be made *ex parte* and shall be made in writing to a judge and be accompanied by an affidavit sworn on the information and belief of the Attorney General or any other person deposing to the following matters:

    (*a*) the indictable offence to which the offence-related property relates;

    (*b*) the person who is believed to be in possession of the offence-related property; and

    (*c*) a description of the offence-related property.

(3) Where an application for a restraint order is made to a judge under subsection (1), the judge may, if satisfied that there are reasonable grounds to believe that the property is offence-related property, make a restraint order prohibiting any person from disposing of, or otherwise dealing with any interest in, the offence-related property specified in the order otherwise than in the manner that may be specified in the order.

(3.1) A restraint order may be issued under this section in respect of property situated outside Canada, with any modifications that the circumstances require.

(4) A restraint order made by a judge under this section may be subject to any reasonable conditions that the judge thinks fit.

(5) A restraint order made under this section shall be made in writing.

(6) A copy of a restraint order made under this section shall be served on the person to whom the order is addressed in any manner that the judge making the order directs or in accordance with the rules of the court.

(7) A copy of a restraint order made under this section shall be registered against any property in accordance with the laws of the province in which the property is situated.

(8) A restraint order made under this section remains in effect until

    (*a*) an order is made under subsection 490(9) or (11), 490.4(3) or 490.41(3) in relation to the property; or

    (*b*) an order of forfeiture of the property is made under section 490 or subsection 490.1(1) or 490.2(2).

(9) Any person on whom a restraint order made under this section is served in accordance with this section and who, while the order is in force, acts in contravention of or fails to comply with the order is guilty of

    (*a*) an indictable offence and liable to imprisonment for a term of not more than five years; or

    (*b*) an offence punishable on summary conviction. 1997, c. 23, s. 15; 2001, c. 32, s. 35; 2019, c. 25, s. 206.

MANAGEMENT ORDER / Appointment of Minister of Public Works and Government Services / Power to manage / Application for destruction order / Notice / Manner of giving notice / Destruction order / Forfeiture order / When management order ceases to have effect / For greater certainty / Application to vary conditions.

490.81 (1) With respect to offence-related property other than a "controlled substance" within the meaning of the *Controlled Drugs and Substances Act* or cannabis as defined in subsection 2(1) of the *Cannabis Act*, on application of the Attorney General or of any other person with the written consent of the Attorney General, a judge or justice in the case of offence-related property seized under section 487, or a judge in the case of offence-related property restrained under section 490.8, may, if he or she is of the opinion that the circumstances so require,

    (*a*) appoint a person to take control of and to manage or otherwise deal with all or part of the property in accordance with the directions of the judge or justice; and

    (*b*) require any person having possession of that property to give possession of the property to the person appointed under paragraph (*a*).

(2) When the Attorney General of Canada so requests, a judge or justice appointing a person under subsection (1) shall appoint the Minister of Public Works and Government Services.

(3) The power to manage or otherwise deal with property under subsection (1) includes

    (*a*) the power to make an interlocutory sale of perishable or rapidly depreciating property;

    (*b*) the power to destroy, in accordance with subsections (4) to (7), property that has little or no value; and

    (*c*) the power to have property, other than real property or a conveyance, forfeited to Her Majesty in accordance with subsection (7.1).

(4) Before a person who is appointed to manage property destroys property that has little or no value, they shall apply to a court for a destruction order.

(5) Before making a destruction order, a court shall require notice in accordance with subsection (6) to be given to and may hear any person who, in the court's opinion, appears to have a valid interest in the property.

(6) A notice shall

    (*a*) be given in the manner that the court directs or that may be specified in the rules of the court; and

    (*b*) specify the effective period of the notice that the court considers reasonable or that may be set out in the rules of the court.

(7) A court shall order that the property be destroyed if it is satisfied that the property has little or no financial or other value.

(7.1) On application by a person who is appointed to manage the property, a court shall order that the property, other than real property or a conveyance, be forfeited to Her Majesty to be disposed of or otherwise dealt with in accordance with the law if

(a) a notice is given or published in the manner that the court directs or that may be specified in the rules of the court;

(b) the notice specifies a period of 60 days during which a person may make an application to the court asserting their interest in the property; and

(c) during that period, no one makes such an application.

(8) A management order ceases to have effect when the property that is the subject of the management order is returned in accordance with the law, destroyed or forfeited to Her Majesty.

(8.1) For greater certainty, if property that is the subject of a management order is sold, the management order applies to the net proceeds of the sale.

(9) The Attorney General may at any time apply to the judge or justice to cancel or vary any condition to which a management order is subject, but may not apply to vary an appointment made under subsection (2). 2001, c. 32, s. 36; 2017, c. 7, s. 68; 2018, c. 16, s. 217.

SECTIONS 489.1 AND 490 APPLICABLE / Recognizance.

490.9 (1) Subject to sections 490.1 to 490.7, sections 489.1 and 490 apply, with any modifications that the circumstances require, to any offence-related property that is the subject of a restraint order made under section 490.8.

(2) Where, pursuant to subsection (1), an order is made under paragraph 490(9)(c) for the return of any offence-related property that is the subject of a restraint order under section 490.8, the judge or justice making the order may require the applicant for the order to enter into a recognizance before the judge or justice, with or without sureties, in any amount and with any conditions that the judge or justice directs and, where the judge or justice considers it appropriate, require the applicant to deposit with the judge or justice any sum of money or other valuable security that the judge or justice directs. 1997, c. 23, s. 15.

FORFEITURE OF WEAPONS AND AMMUNITION / Return to lawful owner / Application of proceeds.

491. (1) Subject to subsection (2), where it is determined by a court that

(a) a weapon, an imitation firearm, a prohibited device, any ammunition, any prohibited ammunition or an explosive substance was used in the commission of an offence and that thing has been seized and detained, or

(b) that a person has committed an offence that involves, or the subject-matter of which is, a firearm, a cross-bow, a prohibited weapon, a restricted weapon, a prohibited device, ammunition, prohibited ammunition or an explosive substance and any such thing has been seized and detained,

the thing so seized and detained is forfeited to Her Majesty and shall be disposed of as the Attorney General directs.

(2) If the court by which a determination referred to in subsection (1) is made is satisfied that the lawful owner of any thing that is or may be forfeited to Her Majesty under subsection (1) was not a party to the offence and had no reasonable grounds to believe that the thing would or might be used in the commission of an

offence, the court shall order that the thing be returned to that lawful owner, that the proceeds of any sale of the thing be paid to that lawful owner or, if the thing was destroyed, that an amount equal to the value of the thing be paid to the owner.

(3) Where any thing in respect of which this section applies is sold, the proceeds of the sale shall be paid to the Attorney General or, where an order is made under subsection (2), to the person who was, immediately prior to the sale, the lawful owner of the thing. 1972, c. 13, s. 37; 1991, c. 40, s. 30; 1995, c. 39, s. 152.

ORDER FOR RESTITUTION OR FORFEITURE OF PROPERTY OBTAINED BY CRIME / Idem / When certain orders not to be made / By whom order executed.

491.1 (1) Where an accused or defendant is tried for an offence and the court determines that an offence has been committed, whether or not the accused has been convicted or discharged under section 730 of the offence, and at the time of the trial any property obtained by the commission of the offence

(*a*) is before the court or has been detained so that it can be immediately dealt with, and

(*b*) will not be required as evidence in any other proceedings,

section 490 does not apply in respect of the property and the court shall make an order under subsection (2) in respect of the property.

(2) In the circumstances referred to in subsection (1), the court shall order, in respect of any property,

(*a*) if the lawful owner or person lawfully entitled to possession of the property is known, that it be returned to that person; and

(*b*) if the lawful owner or person lawfully entitled to possession of the property is not known, that it be forfeited to Her Majesty, to be disposed of as the Attorney General directs or otherwise dealt with in accordance with the law.

(3) An order shall not be made under subsection (2)

(*a*) in the case of proceedings against a trustee, banker, merchant, attorney, factor, broker or other agent entrusted with the possession of goods or documents of title to goods, for an offence under section 330, 331, 332 or 336; or

(*b*) in respect of

(i) property to which a person acting in good faith and without notice has acquired lawful title for valuable consideration,

(ii) a valuable security that has been paid or discharged in good faith by a person who was liable to pay or discharge it,

(iii) a negotiable instrument that has, in good faith, been taken or received by transfer or delivery for valuable consideration by a person who had no notice and no reasonable cause to suspect that an offence had been committed, or

(iv) property in respect of which there is a dispute as to ownership or right of possession by claimants other than the accused or defendant.

(4) An order made under this section shall, on the direction of the court, be executed by the peace officers by whom the process of the court is ordinarily executed. R.S.C. 1985, c. 27 (1st Supp.), s. 74.

PHOTOGRAPHIC EVIDENCE / Certified photograph admissible in evidence / Statements made in certificate / Secondary evidence of peace officer / Notice of intention to produce certified photograph / Attendance for examination / Production of property in court / Definition of "photograph".

491.2 (1) Before any property that would otherwise be required to be produced for the purposes of a preliminary inquiry, trial or other proceeding in respect of an offence under section 334, 344, 348, 354, 355.2, 355.4, 362 or 380 is returned or ordered to be returned, forfeited or otherwise dealt with under section 489.1 or 490 or is otherwise returned, a peace officer or any person under the direction of a peace officer may take and retain a photograph of the property.

(2) Every photograph of property taken under subsection (1), accompanied by a certificate of a person containing the statements referred to in subsection (3), shall be admissible in evidence and, in the absence of evidence to the contrary, shall have the same probative force as the property would have had if it had been proved in the ordinary way.

(3) For the purposes of subsection (2), a certificate of a person stating that
   (a) the person took the photograph under the authority of subsection (1),
   (b) the person is a peace officer or took the photograph under the direction of a peace officer, and
   (c) the photograph is a true photograph
shall be admissible in evidence and, in the absence of evidence to the contrary, is evidence of the statements contained in the certificate without proof of the signature of the person appearing to have signed the certificate.

(4) An affidavit or solemn declaration of a peace officer or other person stating that the person has seized property and detained it or caused it to be detained from the time that person took possession of the property until a photograph of the property was taken under subsection (1) and that the property was not altered in any manner before the photograph was taken shall be admissible in evidence and, in the absence of evidence to the contrary, is evidence of the statements contained in the affidavit or solemn declaration without proof of the signature or official character of the person appearing to have signed the affidavit or solemn declaration.

(5) Unless the court orders otherwise, no photograph, certificate, affidavit or solemn declaration shall be received in evidence at a trial or other proceeding pursuant to subsection (2), (3) or (4) unless the prosecutor has, before the trial or other proceeding, given to the accused a copy thereof and reasonable notice of intention to produce it in evidence.

(6) Notwithstanding subsection (3) or (4), the court may require the person who appears to have signed a certificate, an affidavit or a solemn declaration referred to in that subsection to appear before it for examination or cross-examination in

respect of the issue of proof of any of the facts contained in the certificate, affidavit or solemn declaration.

(7) A court may order any property seized and returned pursuant to section 489.1 or 490 to be produced in court or made available for examination by all parties to a proceeding at a reasonable time and place, notwithstanding that a photograph of the property has been received in evidence pursuant to subsection (2), where the court is satisfied that the interests of justice so require and that it is possible and practicable to do so in the circumstances.

(8) In this section, "photograph" includes a still photograph, a photographic film or plate, a microphotographic film, a photostatic negative, an X-ray film, a motion picture and a videotape. R.S.C. 1985, c. 23 (4th Supp.), s. 2; 1992, c. 1, s. 58; 2010, c. 14, s. 10.

CODE

SEIZURE OF EXPLOSIVES / Forfeiture / Application of proceeds.

492. (1) Every person who executes a warrant issued under section 487 or 487.1 may seize any explosive substance that he suspects is intended to be used for an unlawful purpose, and shall, as soon as possible, remove to a place of safety anything that he seizes by virtue of this section and detain it until he is ordered by a judge of a superior court to deliver it to some other person or an order is made pursuant to subsection (2).

(2) Where an accused is convicted of an offence in respect of anything seized by virtue of subsection (1), it is forfeited and shall be dealt with as the court that makes the conviction may direct.

(3) Where anything to which this section applies is sold, the proceeds of the sale shall be paid to the Attorney General. R.S., c. C-34, s. 447; R.S.C. 1985, c. 27 (1st Supp.), s. 70.

WARRANT FOR TRACKING DEVICE — TRANSACTIONS AND THINGS / Warrant for tracking device — individuals / Scope of warrant / Conditions / Period of validity / Period of validity — organized crime and terrorism offence / Execution in Canada / Removal after expiry of warrant / Definitions.

492.1 (1) A justice or judge who is satisfied by information on oath that there are reasonable grounds to suspect that an offence has been or will be committed under this or any other Act of Parliament and that tracking the location of one or more transactions or the location or movement of a thing, including a vehicle, will assist in the investigation of the offence may issue a warrant authorizing a peace officer or a public officer to obtain that tracking data by means of a tracking device.

(2) A justice or judge who is satisfied by information on oath that there are reasonable grounds to believe that an offence has been or will be committed under this or any other Act of Parliament and that tracking an individual's movement by identifying the location of a thing that is usually carried or worn by the individual will assist in the investigation of the offence may issue a warrant authorizing a

peace officer or a public officer to obtain that tracking data by means of a tracking device.

(3) The warrant authorizes the peace officer or public officer, or a person acting under their direction, to install, activate, use, maintain, monitor and remove the tracking device, including covertly.

(4) A warrant may contain any conditions that the justice or judge considers appropriate, including conditions to protect a person's interests.

(5) Subject to subsection (6), a warrant is valid for the period specified in it as long as that period ends no more than 60 days after the day on which the warrant is issued.

(6) A warrant is valid for the period specified in it as long as that period ends no more than one year after the day on which the warrant is issued, if the warrant relates to

- (*a*) an offence under any of sections 467.11 to 467.13;
- (*b*) an offence committed for the benefit of, at the direction of, or in association with a criminal organization; or
- (*c*) a terrorism offence.

(6.1) A warrant issued under this section may be executed at any place in Canada. Any public officer or peace officer who executes the warrant must have authority to act in that capacity in the place where the warrant is executed.

(7) On *ex parte* application supported by an affidavit, the justice or judge who issued a warrant or another justice or judge who has jurisdiction to issue such warrants may authorize the covert removal of the tracking device after the expiry of the warrant under any conditions that the justice or judge considers advisable in the public interest. The authorization is valid for the period specified in it as long as that period is not more than 90 days.

(8) The following definitions apply in this section.

"data" means representations, including signs, signals or symbols, that are capable of being understood by an individual or processed by a computer system or other device.

"judge" means a judge of a superior court of criminal jurisdiction or a judge of the Court of Quebec.

"public officer" means a public officer who is appointed or designated to administer or enforce a federal or provincial law and whose duties include the enforcement of this or any other Act of Parliament.

"tracking data" means data that relates to the location of a transaction, individual or thing.

"tracking device" means a device, including a computer program within the meaning of subsection 342.1(2), that may be used to obtain or record tracking data or to transmit it by a means of telecommunication. 1993, c. 40, s. 18; 1999, c. 5, s. 18; 2014, c. 31, s. 23; 2019, c. 25, s. 207.

WARRANT FOR TRANSMISSION DATA RECORDER / Scope of warrant / Limitation / Period of validity / Period of validity — organized crime or terrorism offence / Execution in Canada / Definitions.

492.2 (1) A justice or judge who is satisfied by information on oath that there are reasonable grounds to suspect that an offence has been or will be committed against this or any other Act of Parliament and that transmission data will assist in the investigation of the offence may issue a warrant authorizing a peace officer or a public officer to obtain the transmission data by means of a transmission data recorder.

(2) The warrant authorizes the peace officer or public officer, or a person acting under their direction, to install, activate, use, maintain, monitor and remove the transmission data recorder, including covertly.

(3) No warrant shall be issued under this section for the purpose of obtaining tracking data.

(4) Subject to subsection (5), a warrant is valid for the period specified in it as long as that period ends no more than 60 days after the day on which the warrant is issued.

(5) The warrant is valid for the period specified in it as long as that period ends no more than one year after the day on which the warrant is issued, if the warrant relates to

   (*a*) an offence under any of sections 467.11 to 467.13;

   (*b*) an offence committed for the benefit of, at the direction of, or in association with a criminal organization; or

   (*c*) a terrorism offence.

(5.1) A warrant issued under subsection (1) may be executed at any place in Canada. Any public officer or peace officer who executes the warrant must have authority to act in that capacity in the place where the warrant is executed.

(6) The following definitions apply in this section.

"data" means representations, including signs, signals or symbols, that are capable of being understood by an individual or processed by a computer system or other device.

"judge" means a judge of a superior court of criminal jurisdiction or a judge of the Court of Quebec.

"public officer" means a public officer who is appointed or designated to administer or enforce a federal or provincial law and whose duties include the enforcement of this or any other Act of Parliament.

"transmission data" means data that

   (*a*) relates to the telecommunication functions of dialling, routing, addressing or signalling;

   (*b*) is transmitted to identify, activate or configure a device, including a computer program as defined in subsection 342.1(2), in order to establish or maintain access to a telecommunication service for the purpose of enabling a communication, or is generated during the creation, transmission or reception of a communication and identifies or purports to identify

525

the type, direction, date, time, duration, size, origin, destination or termination of the communication; and

(c) does not reveal the substance, meaning or purpose of the communication.

"transmission data recorder" means a device, including a computer program within the meaning of subsection 342.1(2), that may be used to obtain or record transmission data or to transmit it by a means of telecommunication. 1993, c. 40, s. 18; 1999, c. 5, s. 19; 2014, c. 31, s. 23; 2019, c. 25, s. 208.

Part XVI / COMPELLING APPEARANCE OF ACCUSED BEFORE A JUSTICE AND INTERIM RELEASE

Interpretation

DEFINITIONS / "accused" / "appearance notice" / "judge" / "officer in charge" / "promise to appear" / "recognizance" / "summons" / "undertaking" / "warrant".

493. In this Part,

"accused" includes

(a) a person to whom a peace officer has issued an appearance notice under section 497, and

(b) a person arrested for a criminal offence;

"appearance notice" [*Repealed*, 2019, c. 25, s. 209(1).]

"judge" means

(a) in the Province of Ontario, a judge of the superior court of criminal jurisdiction of the Province,

(b) in the Province of Quebec, a judge of the superior court of criminal jurisdiction of the province or three judges of the Court of Quebec,

(c) [*Repealed*, 1992, c. 51, s. 37.]

(d) in the Provinces of Nova Scotia, New Brunswick, Manitoba, British Columbia, Prince Edward Island, Saskatchewan, Alberta and Newfoundland and Labrador, a judge of the superior court of criminal jurisdiction of the Province,

(e) in Yukon and the Northwest Territories, a judge of the Supreme Court, and

(f) in Nunavut, a judge of the Nunavut Court of Justice;

"officer in charge" [*Repealed*, 2019, c. 25, s. 209(1).]

"promise to appear" [*Repealed*, 2019, c. 25, s. 209(1).]

"recognizance" [*Repealed*, 2019, c. 25, s. 209(1).]

"summons" [*Repealed*, 2019, c. 25, s. 209(1).]

"undertaking" [*Repealed*, 2019, c. 25, s. 209(1).]

"warrant", when used in relation to a warrant for the arrest of a person, means a warrant in Form 7 and, when used in relation to a warrant for the committal of a person, means a warrant in Form 8. R.S., c. C-34, s. 448; R.S., c. 2 (2nd Supp.), s.

5; 1972, c. 17, s. 3; 1974-75-76, c. 48, s. 25(1); 1978-79, c. 11, s. 10; R.S.C. 1985, c. 11 (1st Supp.), s. 2; c. 27 (2nd Supp.), s. 10; c. 40 (4th Supp.), s. 2; 1990, c. 16, s. 5; 1990, c. 17, s. 12; 1992, c. 51, s. 37; 1993, c. 28, Sch. III., s. 32 (repealed 1999, c. 3, s. 12); 1994, c. 44, s. 39; 1999, c. 3, ss. 12, 30; 2002, c. 7, s. 143; 2015, c. 3, s. 51; 2019, c. 25, s. 209.

Principle and Considerations   2019, c. 25, s. 210.

PRINCIPLE OF RESTRAINT.

493.1 In making a decision under this Part, a peace officer, justice or judge shall give primary consideration to the release of the accused at the earliest reasonable opportunity and on the least onerous conditions that are appropriate in the circumstances, including conditions that are reasonably practicable for the accused to comply with, while taking into account the grounds referred to in subsection 498(1.1) or 515(10), as the case may be. 2019, c. 25, s. 210.

ABORIGINAL ACCUSED OR VULNERABLE POPULATIONS.

493.2 In making a decision under this Part, a peace officer, justice or judge shall give particular attention to the circumstances of
   (*a*) Aboriginal accused; and
   (*b*) accused who belong to a vulnerable population that is overrepresented in the criminal justice system and that is disadvantaged in obtaining release under this Part. 2019, c. 25, s. 210.

Arrest Without Warrant and Release from Custody

ARREST WITHOUT WARRANT BY ANY PERSON / Arrest by owner, etc. of property / Delivery to peace officer / For greater certainty.

494. (1) Any one may arrest without warrant
   (*a*) a person whom he finds committing an indictable offence; or
   (*b*) a person who, on reasonable grounds, he believes
      (i) has committed a criminal offence, and
      (ii) is escaping from and freshly pursued by persons who have lawful authority to arrest that person.

(2) The owner or a person in lawful possession of property, or a person authorized by the owner or by a person in lawful possession of property, may arrest a person without a warrant if they find them committing a criminal offence on or in relation to that property and
   (*a*) they make the arrest at that time; or
   (*b*) they make the arrest within a reasonable time after the offence is committed and they believe on reasonable grounds that it is not feasible in the circumstances for a peace officer to make the arrest.

(3) Any one other than a peace officer who arrests a person without warrant shall forthwith deliver the person to a peace officer.

(4) For greater certainty, a person who is authorized to make an arrest under this section is a person who is authorized by law to do so for the purposes of section 25. R.S., c. C-34, s. 449; R.S., c. 2 (2nd Supp.), s. 5; 2012, c. 9, s. 3.

ARREST WITHOUT WARRANT BY PEACE OFFICER / Limitation / Consequences of arrest without warrant.

495. (1) A peace officer may arrest without warrant

- (a) a person who has committed an indictable offence or who, on reasonable grounds, he believes has committed or is about to commit an indictable offence;
- (b) a person whom he finds committing a criminal offence; or
- (c) a person in respect of whom he has reasonable grounds to believe that a warrant of arrest or committal, in any form set out in Part XXVIII in relation thereto, is in force within the territorial jurisdiction in which the person is found.

(2) A peace officer shall not arrest a person without warrant for

- (a) an indictable offence mentioned in section 553,
- (b) an offence for which the person may be prosecuted by indictment or for which he is punishable on summary conviction, or
- (c) an offence punishable on summary conviction,

in any case where

- (d) he believes on reasonable grounds that the public interest, having regard to all the circumstances including the need to
  - (i) establish the identity of the person,
  - (ii) secure or preserve evidence of or relating to the offence, or
  - (iii) prevent the continuation or repetition of the offence or the commission of another offence,

may be satisfied without so arresting the person, and

- (e) he has no reasonable grounds to believe that, if he does not so arrest the person, the person will fail to attend court in order to be dealt with according to law.

(3) Notwithstanding subsection (2), a peace officer acting under subsection (1) is deemed to be acting lawfully and in the execution of his duty for the purposes of

- (a) any proceedings under this or any other Act of Parliament; and
- (b) any other proceedings, unless in any such proceedings it is alleged and established by the person making the allegation that the peace officer did not comply with the requirements of subsection (2). R.S., c. C-34, s. 450; R.S., c. 2 (2nd Supp.), s. 5; R.S.C. 1985, c. 27 (1st Supp.), s. 75.

ARREST WITHOUT WARRANT — APPLICATION OF SECTION 524.

495.1 Despite any other provision in this Act, if a peace officer has reasonable grounds to believe that an accused has contravened or is about to contravene a summons, appearance notice, undertaking or release order that was issued or given to the accused or entered into by the accused, or has committed an indictable offence while being subject to a summons, appearance notice, undertaking or release order, the peace officer may arrest the accused without a warrant for the purpose of taking them before a judge or justice to be dealt with under section 524. 2019, c. 25, s. 211.

APPEARANCE NOTICE FOR JUDICIAL REFERRAL HEARING.

496. If a peace officer has reasonable grounds to believe that a person has failed to comply with a summons, appearance notice, undertaking or release order or to attend court as required and that the failure did not cause a victim physical or emotional harm, property damage or economic loss, the peace officer may, without laying a charge, issue an appearance notice to the person to appear at a judicial referral hearing under section 523.1. R.S., c. C-34, s. 451; R.S., c. 2 (2nd Supp.), s. 5; 2019, c. 25, s. 212.

ISSUE OF APPEARANCE NOTICE BY PEACE OFFICER.

497. If, by virtue of subsection 495(2), a peace officer does not arrest a person, they may issue an appearance notice to the person if the offence is

(a) an indictable offence mentioned in section 553;

(b) an offence for which the person may be prosecuted by indictment or for which they are punishable on summary conviction; or

(c) an offence punishable on summary conviction. R.S., c. C-34, s. 452; R.S., c. 2 (2nd Supp.), s. 5; 1999, c. 25, s. 3; 2019, c. 25, s. 212.

RELEASE FROM CUSTODY — ARREST WITHOUT WARRANT / Person delivered or detained / Exception / When subsections (1) and (1.01) do not apply / Consequences of non-release.

498. (1) Subject to subsection (1.1), if a person has been arrested without warrant for an offence, other than one listed in section 469, and has not been taken before a justice or released from custody under any other provision of this Part, a peace officer shall, as soon as practicable, release the person, if

(a) the peace officer intends to compel the person's appearance by way of summons;

(b) the peace officer issues an appearance notice to the person; or

(c) the person gives an undertaking to the peace officer.

(1.01) Subsection (1) also applies in respect of a person who has been arrested without warrant and delivered to a peace officer under subsection 494(3) or placed in the custody of a peace officer under subsection 163.5(3) of the *Customs Act* and who is detained in custody for an offence other than one listed in section 469 and who has not been taken before a justice or released from custody under any other provision of this Part.

(1.1) The peace officer shall not release the person if the peace officer believes, on reasonable grounds,

(a) that it is necessary in the public interest that the person be detained in custody or that the matter of their release from custody be dealt with under another provision of this Part, having regard to all the circumstances including the need to

(i) establish the identity of the person,

(ii) secure or preserve evidence of or relating to the offence,

(iii) prevent the continuation or repetition of the offence or the commission of another offence, or

(iv) ensure the safety and security of any victim of or witness to the offence; or

(*b*) that, if the person is released from custody, the person will fail to attend court in order to be dealt with according to law.

(2) Subsections (1) and (1.01) do not apply in respect of a person who has been arrested without warrant by a peace officer for an offence described in subsection 503(3).

(3) A peace officer who has arrested a person without a warrant, or who has been given the custody of a person arrested without a warrant, for an offence described in subsection (1), and who does not release the person from custody as soon as practicable in the manner described in that subsection shall be deemed to be acting lawfully and in the execution of the officer's duty for the purposes of

(*a*) any proceedings under this or any other Act of Parliament; or

(*b*) any other proceedings, unless in any such proceedings it is alleged and established by the person making the allegation that the peace officer did not comply with the requirements of subsection (1). R.S., c. C-34, s. 453; R.S., c. 2 (2nd Supp.), s. 5; R.S.C. 1985, c. 27 (1st Supp.), s. 186; 1997, c. 18, s. 52; 1998, c. 7, s. 2; 1999, c. 25, ss. 4, 30; 2019, c. 25, s. 213.

RELEASE FROM CUSTODY — ARREST WITH WARRANT.

499. If a person who has been arrested with a warrant by a peace officer is taken into custody for an offence other than one listed in section 469 and the warrant has been endorsed by a justice under subsection 507(6), a peace officer may release the person, if

(*a*) the peace officer issues an appearance notice to the person; or

(*b*) the person gives an undertaking to the peace officer. S.S., c. 2 (2nd Supp.), s. 5; R.S.C. 1985, c. 27 (1st Supp.), s. 186; 1994, c. 44, s. 40; 1997, c. 18, s. 53; 1999, c. 25, s. 5; 2019, c. 25, s. 214.

CONTENTS OF APPEARANCE NOTICE / Summary of consequences — failure to appear / Attendance for purposes of *Identification of Criminals Act* / Signature of accused.

500. (1) An appearance notice shall

(*a*) set out the name, date of birth and contact information of the accused;

(*b*) set out the substance of the offence that the accused is alleged to have committed;

(*c*) require the accused to attend court at a time and place to be stated in the notice and to attend afterwards as required by the court; and

(*d*) indicate if the accused is required to appear at a judicial referral hearing under section 523.1 for a failure under section 496.

(2) An appearance notice shall set out a summary of subsections 145(3) and (6), section 512.2 and subsection 524(4) and the possible consequences of a failure to appear at a judicial referral hearing under section 523.1.

(3) An appearance notice may require the accused to appear at the time and place stated in it for the purposes of the *Identification of Criminals Act*, if the accused is alleged to have committed an indictable offence and, in the case of an offence designated as a contravention under the *Contraventions Act*, the "Attorney General", within the meaning of that Act, has not made an election under section 50 of that Act.

(4) An accused shall be requested to sign in duplicate their appearance notice and, whether or not they comply with that request, one of the duplicates shall be given to the accused. If the accused fails or refuses to sign, the lack of their signature does not invalidate the appearance notice. R.S., c. 2 (2nd Supp.), s. 5; 1999, c. 5, s. 20; c. 25, s. 6; 2019, c. 25, s. 215.

CONTENTS OF UNDERTAKING / Mandatory conditions / Additional conditions / Attendance for purposes of *Identification of Criminals Act* / Money or other valuable security to be deposited with justice / Signature of accused.

501. (1) An undertaking under paragraph 498(1)(*c*), 499(*b*) or 503(1.1)(*b*) must set out

   (*a*) the name, date of birth and contact information of the accused;

   (*b*) the substance of the offence that the accused is alleged to have committed; and

   (*c*) a summary of subsections 145(4) and (6), sections 512 and 512.2 and subsection 524(4).

(2) The undertaking must contain a condition that the accused attend court at the time and place stated in the undertaking and to attend afterwards as required by the court.

(3) The undertaking may contain one or more of the following conditions, if the condition is reasonable in the circumstances of the offence and necessary, to ensure the accused's attendance in court or the safety and security of any victim of or witness to the offence, or to prevent the continuation or repetition of the offence or the commission of another offence:

   (*a*) report at specified times to the peace officer or other specified person;

   (*b*) remain within a specified territorial jurisdiction;

   (*c*) notify the peace officer or other specified person of any change in their address, employment or occupation;

   (*d*) abstain from communicating, directly or indirectly, with any victim, witness or other person identified in the undertaking, except in accordance with any specified conditions;

   (*e*) abstain from going to any specified place or entering any geographic area related to any person referred to in paragraph (*d*), except in accordance with any specified conditions;

(f) deposit all their passports with the peace officer or other specified person;

(g) reside at a specified address, be at that address at specified hours and present themselves at the entrance of that residence to a peace officer or other specified person, at the officer's or specified person's request during those hours;

(h) abstain from possessing a firearm, cross-bow, prohibited weapon, restricted weapon, prohibited device, ammunition, prohibited ammunition or explosive substance, and surrender those that are in their possession to the peace officer or other specified person and also any authorization, licence or registration certificate or other document enabling them to acquire or possess them;

(i) promise to pay an amount specified in the undertaking, which shall not be more than $500, if they fail to comply with any condition of the undertaking;

(j) deposit, with the peace officer specified in the undertaking, money or other valuable security whose value does not exceed $500 if, at the time of giving the undertaking, the accused is not ordinarily resident in the province or does not ordinarily reside within 200 kilometres of the place in which they are in custody; and

(k) comply with any other specified condition for ensuring the safety and security of any victim of or witness to the offence.

(4) The undertaking may require the accused to appear at the time and place stated in it for the purposes of the *Identification of Criminals Act* if the accused is alleged to have committed an indictable offence and, in the case of an offence designated as a contravention under the *Contraventions Act*, the "Attorney General", within the meaning of that Act, has not made an election under section 50 of that Act.

(5) If the accused has deposited an amount of money or other valuable security with a peace officer, the officer shall, without delay after the deposit, cause the money or valuable security to be delivered to a justice for deposit with the justice.

(6) The accused shall be requested to sign in duplicate their undertaking and, whether or not they comply with that request, one of the duplicates shall be given to them. If they fail or refuse to sign, the lack of their signature does not invalidate the undertaking. R.S., c. 2 (2nd Supp.), s. 5; R.S.C. 1985, c. 27 (1st Supp.), s. 76; 1992, c. 47, s. 69; 1994, c. 44, s. 41; 1996, c. 7, s. 38; 2008, c. 18, s. 15; 2019, c. 25, s. 215.

VARIATION OF UNDERTAKING ON CONSENT / Replacement by justice of undertaking with order.

502. (1) The undertaking in respect of which an accused has been released under section 498, 499 or 503 may, with the written consent of the accused and the prosecutor, be varied and the undertaking so varied is deemed to be an undertaking given under section 498, 499 or 503, as the case may be.

(2) The accused or the prosecutor may, in the absence of consent between them, apply to a justice for a release order under subsection 515(1) or (2) to replace an undertaking given by the accused under paragraph 498(1)(c), 499(b) or

503(1.1)(*b*) with the order. If the prosecutor applies for the order, the prosecutor must provide three days notice to the accused. R.S., c. 2 (2nd Supp.), s. 5; 1992, c. 47, s. 70; 1996, c. 7, s. 38; 1997, c. 18, s. 54; 2019, c. 25, s. 215.

Appearance of Accused Before Justice

APPEARANCE OF THE ACCUSED / Witness in Canada / Witness outside Canada / Participants / Justice.

502.1 (1) Except as otherwise provided in this Part, an accused who is required to appear in a proceeding under this Part shall appear personally but may appear by audioconference or videoconference, if arrangements are made with the court in advance and those arrangements are satisfactory to the justice.

(2) Despite section 714.1, a witness in Canada who is required to give evidence in a proceeding under this Part may do so by audioconference or videoconference, if it is satisfactory to the justice.

(3) For greater certainty, sections 714.2 to 714.8 apply when a witness outside Canada gives evidence in a proceeding under this Part.

(4) A "participant", as defined in subsection 715.25(1), who is to participate in a proceeding under this Part shall participate personally but may participate by audioconference or videoconference, if it is satisfactory to the justice.

(5) The justice who is to preside at a proceeding under this Part shall preside personally but may preside by audioconference or videoconference, if the justice considers it necessary in the circumstances. 2019, c. 25, s. 216.

TAKING BEFORE JUSTICE / Re-evaluation of detention / Person delivered or in custody / Remand to custody for return to jurisdiction where offence alleged to have been committed / Interim release / Release of person about to commit indictable offence / Consequences of non-release.

503. (1) Subject to the other provisions of this section, a peace officer who arrests a person with or without warrant and who has not released the person under any other provision under this Part shall, in accordance with the following paragraphs, cause the person to be taken before a justice to be dealt with according to law:

   (*a*) if a justice is available within a period of 24 hours after the person has been arrested by the peace officer, the person shall be taken before a justice without unreasonable delay and in any event within that period; and

   (*b*) if a justice is not available within a period of 24 hours after the person has been arrested by the peace officer, the person shall be taken before a justice as soon as possible.

(1.1) At any time before the expiry of the time referred to in paragraph (1)(*a*) or (*b*), a peace officer who is satisfied that the continued detention of the person in custody for an offence that is not listed in section 469 is no longer necessary shall release the person, if

   (*a*) the peace officer issues an appearance notice to the person; or

   (*b*) the person gives an undertaking to the peace officer.

(2) Subsections (1) and (1.1) also apply to a peace officer to whom a person is delivered under subsection 494(3) or into whose custody a person is placed under subsection 163.5(3) of the *Customs Act*, except that the 24-hour period referred to in paragraphs (1)(*a*) and (*b*) begins after the person is delivered to the officer.

(2.1) [*Repealed*, 2019, c. 25, s. 217(1).]

(2.2) [*Repealed*, 2019, c. 25, s. 217(1).]

(2.3) [*Repealed*, 2019, c. 25, s. 217(1).]

(3) Where a person has been arrested without warrant for an indictable offence alleged to have been committed in Canada outside the territorial division to where the arrest took place, the person shall, within the time prescribed in paragraph (1)(*a*) or (*b*), be taken before a justice within whose jurisdiction the person was arrested unless, where the offence was alleged to have been committed within the province in which the person was arrested, the person was taken before a justice within whose jurisdiction the offence was alleged to have been committed, and the justice within whose jurisdiction the person was arrested

    (*a*) if the justice is not satisfied that there are reasonable grounds to believe that the person arrested is the person alleged to have committed the offence, shall release that person; or

    (*b*) if the justice is satisfied that there are reasonable grounds to believe that the person arrested is the person alleged to have committed the offence, may

        (i) remand the person to the custody of a peace officer to await execution of a warrant for his or her arrest in accordance with section 528, but if no warrant is so executed within a period of six days after the time he or she is remanded to such custody, the person in whose custody he or she then is shall release him or her, or

        (ii) where the offence was alleged to have been committed within the province in which the person was arrested, order the person to be taken before a justice having jurisdiction with respect to the offence.

(3.1) Notwithstanding paragraph (3)(*b*), a justice may, with the consent of the prosecutor, order that the person referred to in subsection (3), pending the execution of a warrant for the arrest of that person, be released

    (*a*) without conditions; or

    (*b*) on the terms of a release order containing any conditions referred to in paragraphs 515(2)(*a*) to (*e*) that the justice considers desirable and to which the prosecutor consents.

(4) A peace officer having the custody of a person who has been arrested without warrant as a person about to commit an indictable offence shall release that person as soon as practicable after the officer is satisfied that the continued detention of that person is no longer necessary in order to prevent that person from committing an indictable offence.

(5) Despite subsection (4), a peace officer having the custody of a person referred to in that subsection who does not release the person before the expiry of the time

prescribed in paragraph (1)(*a*) or (*b*) for taking the person before the justice shall be deemed to be acting lawfully and in the execution of the peace officer's duty for the purposes of

    (*a*) any proceedings under this or any other Act of Parliament; or

    (*b*) any other proceedings, unless in those proceedings it is alleged and established by the person making the allegation that the peace officer did not comply with the requirements of subsection (4). R.S., c. C-34, s. 454; R.S., c. 2 (2nd Supp.), s. 5; 1974-75-76, c. 93, s. 46; R.S.C. 1985, c. 27 (1st Supp.), s. 77; 1994, c. 44, s. 42; 1997, c. 18, s. 55; 1998, c. 7, s. 3; 1999, c. 25, s. 7; 2019, c. 25, s. 217.

CODE

Information, Summons and Warrant

IN WHAT CASES JUSTICE MAY RECEIVE INFORMATION.

504. Any one who, on reasonable grounds, believes that a person has committed an indictable offence may lay an information in writing and under oath before a justice, and the justice shall receive the information, where it is alleged

    (*a*) that the person has committed, anywhere, an indictable offence that may be tried in the province in which the justice resides, and that the person

        (i) is or is believed to be, or

        (ii) resides or is believed to reside,

    within the territorial jurisdiction of the justice;

    (*b*) that the person, wherever he may be, has committed an indictable offence within the territorial jurisdiction of the justice;

    (*c*) that the person has, anywhere, unlawfully received property that was unlawfully obtained within the territorial jurisdiction of the justice; or

    (*d*) that the person has in his possession stolen property within the territorial jurisdiction of the justice. R.S., c. C-34, s. 455; R.S., c. 2 (2nd Supp.), s. 5.

TIME WITHIN WHICH INFORMATION TO BE LAID IN CERTAIN CASES.

505. If an appearance notice has been issued to an accused under section 497, or if an accused has been released from custody under section 498 or 503, an information relating to the offence alleged to have been committed by the accused or relating to an included or other offence alleged to have been committed by them shall be laid before a justice as soon as practicable after the issuance or release, and in any event before the time stated in the appearance notice or undertaking for their attendance in court. R.S., c. 2 (2nd Supp.), s. 5; 2019, c. 25, s. 218.

FORM

506. An information laid under section 504 or 505 may be in Form 2. R.S., c. 2 (2nd Supp.), s. 5.

JUSTICE TO HEAR INFORMANT AND WITNESSES — PUBLIC PROSECUTIONS / Process compulsory / Procedure when witnesses attend / Summons to be issued except in certain cases / No process in blank / Endorsement of warrant by justice / Undertaking or appearance notice deemed confirmed / Issue of summons or warrant.

507. (1) Subject to subsection 523(1.1), a justice who receives an information laid under section 504 by a peace officer, a public officer, the Attorney General or the Attorney General's agent, other than an information laid before the justice under section 505, shall, except if an accused has already been arrested with or without a warrant,

   (*a*) hear and consider, *ex parte*,
      (i) the allegations of the informant, and
      (ii) the evidence of witnesses, where he considers it desirable or necessary to do so; and
   (*b*) where he considers that a case for so doing is made out, issue, in accordance with this section, either a summons or a warrant for the arrest of the accused to compel the accused to attend before him or some other justice for the same territorial division to answer to a charge of an offence.

(2) No justice shall refuse to issue a summons or warrant by reason only that the alleged offence is one for which a person may be arrested without warrant.

(3) A justice who hears the evidence of a witness pursuant to subsection (1) shall
   (*a*) take the evidence on oath; and
   (*b*) cause the evidence to be taken in accordance with section 540 in so far as that section is capable of being applied.

(4) Where a justice considers that a case is made out for compelling an accused to attend before him to answer to a charge of an offence, he shall issue a summons to the accused unless the allegations of the informant or the evidence of any witness or witnesses taken in accordance with subsection (3) discloses reasonable grounds to believe that it is necessary in the public interest to issue a warrant for the arrest of the accused.

(5) A justice shall not sign a summons or warrant in blank.

(6) A justice who issues a warrant under this section or section 508, 512, 512.1 or 512.2 may, unless the offence is one listed in section 469, authorize the release of the accused under section 499 by making an endorsement on the warrant in Form 29.

(7) If, under subsection (6), a justice authorizes the release of an accused under section 499, an appearance notice or undertaking referred to in that section shall be deemed, for the purposes of subsection 145(3) or (4), as the case may be, to have been confirmed by a justice under section 508.

(8) Where, on an appeal from or review of any decision or matter of jurisdiction, a new trial or hearing or a continuance or renewal of a trial or hearing is ordered, a justice may issue either a summons or a warrant for the arrest of the accused in order to compel the accused to attend at the new or continued or renewed trial or hearing. R.S., c. 2 (2nd Supp.), s. 5; 1972, c. 13, s. 35; R.S.C. 1985, c. 27 (1st Supp.), s. 78; 1994, c. 44, s. 43; 2002, c. 13, s. 21; 2019, c. 25, s. 219.

REFERRAL WHEN PRIVATE PROSECUTION / Summons or warrant / Conditions for issuance / Appearance of Attorney General / Information deemed not to have been laid / Information deemed not to have been laid — proceedings commenced / New evidence required for new hearing / Subsections 507(2) to (8) to apply / Non-application — informations laid under sections 810 and 810.1 / Definition of "designated justice" / Meaning of "Attorney General".

507.1 (1) A justice who receives an information laid under section 504, other than an information referred to in subsection 507(1), shall refer it to a provincial court judge or, in Quebec, a judge of the Court of Quebec, or to a designated justice, to consider whether to compel the appearance of the accused on the information.

(2) A judge or designated justice to whom an information is referred under subsection (1) and who considers that a case for doing so is made out shall issue either a summons or warrant for the arrest of the accused to compel him or her to attend before a justice to answer to a charge of the offence charged in the information.

(3) The judge or designated justice may issue a summons or warrant only if he or she

  (*a*) has heard and considered the allegations of the informant and the evidence of witnesses;
  (*b*) is satisfied that the Attorney General has received a copy of the information;
  (*c*) is satisfied that the Attorney General has received reasonable notice of the hearing under paragraph (*a*); and
  (*d*) has given the Attorney General an opportunity to attend the hearing under paragraph (*a*) and to cross-examine and call witnesses and to present any relevant evidence at the hearing.

(4) The Attorney General may appear at the hearing held under paragraph (3)(*a*) without being deemed to intervene in the proceeding.

(5) If the judge or designated justice does not issue a summons or warrant under subsection (2), he or she shall endorse the information with a statement to that effect. Unless the informant, not later than six months after the endorsement, commences proceedings to compel the judge or designated justice to issue a summons or warrant, the information is deemed never to have been laid.

(6) If proceedings are commenced under subsection (5) and a summons or warrant is not issued as a result of those proceedings, the information is deemed never to have been laid.

(7) If a hearing in respect of an offence has been held under paragraph (3)(*a*) and the judge or designated justice has not issued a summons or a warrant, no other hearings may be held under that paragraph with respect to the offence or an included offence unless there is new evidence in support of the allegation in respect of which the hearing is sought to be held.

(8) Subsections 507(2) to (8) apply to proceedings under this section.

(9) Subsections (1) to (8) do not apply in respect of an information laid under section 810 or 810.1.

(10) In this section, "designated justice" means a justice designated for the purpose by the chief judge of the provincial court having jurisdiction in the matter or, in Quebec, a justice designated by the chief judge of the Court of Quebec.

(11) In this section, "Attorney General" includes the Attorney General of Canada and his or her lawful deputy in respect of proceedings that could have been commenced at the instance of the Government of Canada and conducted by or on behalf of that Government. 2002, c. 13, s. 22; 2008, c. 18, s. 16.

JUSTICE TO HEAR INFORMANT AND WITNESSES / Procedure when witnesses attend.

508. (1) A justice who receives an information laid before him under section 505 shall

(a) hear and consider, *ex parte*,

　(i) the allegations of the informant, and

　(ii) the evidence of witnesses, where he considers it desirable or necessary to do so;

(b) if the justice considers that a case for so doing is made out, whether the information relates to the offence alleged in the appearance notice or undertaking or to an included or other offence,

　(i) confirm the appearance notice or undertaking and endorse the information accordingly, or

　(ii) cancel the appearance notice or undertaking and issue, in accordance with section 507, either a summons or a warrant for the arrest of the accused to compel the accused to attend before the justice or some other justice for the same territorial division to answer to a charge of an offence and endorse on the summons or warrant that the appearance notice or undertaking has been cancelled; and

(c) if the justice considers that a case is not made out for the purposes of paragraph (b), cancel the appearance notice or undertaking and cause the accused to be immediately notified of the cancellation.

(2) A justice who hears the evidence of a witness pursuant to subsection (1) shall

(a) take the evidence on oath; and

(b) cause the evidence to be taken in accordance with section 540 in so far as that section is capable of being applied. R.S., c. 2 (2nd Supp.), s. 5; R.S.C. 1985, c. 27 (1st Supp.), s. 79; 2019, c. 25, s. 220.

INFORMATION LAID OTHERWISE THAN IN PERSON / Alternative to oath.

508.1 (1) For the purposes of sections 504 to 508, a peace officer may lay an information by any means of telecommunication that produces a writing.

(2) A peace officer who uses a means of telecommunication referred to in subsection (1) shall, instead of swearing an oath, make a statement in writing stating that all matters contained in the information are true to the officer's knowledge and belief, and such a statement is deemed to be a statement made under oath. 1997, c. 18, s. 56.

SUMMONS / Service on individual / Summary of certain provisions / Attendance for purposes of *Identification of Criminals Act*.

509. (1) A summons issued under this Part shall

    (*a*) be directed to the accused;

    (*b*) set out briefly the offence in respect of which the accused is charged; and

    (*c*) require the accused to attend court at a time and place to be stated therein and to attend thereafter as required by the court in order to be dealt with according to law.

(2) A summons shall be served by a peace officer who shall deliver it personally to the person to whom it is directed or, if that person cannot conveniently be found, shall leave it for him at his last or usual place of abode with some inmate thereof who appears to be at least sixteen years of age.

(3) [*Repealed*, 2008, c. 18, s. 17.]

(4) The summons must set out a summary of subsection 145(3), section 512.1 and subsection 524(4).

(5) A summons may require the accused to appear at a time and place stated in it for the purposes of the *Identification of Criminals Act*, where the accused is alleged to have committed an indictable offence and, in the case of an offence designated as a contravention under the *Contraventions Act*, the Attorney General, within the meaning of that Act, has not made an election under section 50 of that Act. R.S., c. 2 (2nd Supp.), s. 5; R.S.C. 1985, c. 27 (1st Supp.), s. 80; 1992, c. 47, s. 71; 1996, c. 7, s. 38; 2008, c. 18, s. 17; 2019, c. 25, s. 221.

510. [*Repealed*, 2019, c. 25, s. 222.]

CONTENTS OF WARRANT TO ARREST / No return day / Discretion to postpone execution / Deemed execution of warrant.

511. (1) A warrant issued under this Part shall

    (*a*) name or describe the accused;

    (*b*) set out briefly the offence in respect of which the accused is charged; and

    (*c*) order that the accused be forthwith arrested and brought before the judge or justice who issued the warrant or before some other judge or justice having jurisdiction in the same territorial division, to be dealt with according to law.

(2) A warrant issued under this Part remains in force until it is executed and need not be made returnable at any particular time.

(3) Notwithstanding paragraph (1)(*c*), a judge or justice who issues a warrant may specify in the warrant the period before which the warrant shall not be executed, to allow the accused to appear voluntarily before a judge or justice having jurisdiction in the territorial division in which the warrant was issued.

(4) Where the accused appears voluntarily for the offence in respect of which the accused is charged, the warrant is deemed to be executed. R.S., c. C-34, s. 456; R.S., c. 2 (2nd Supp.), s. 5; R.S.C. 1985, c. 27 (1st. Supp.), s. 81; 1997, c. 18, s. 57.

CERTAIN ACTIONS NOT TO PRECLUDE ISSUE OF WARRANT / Warrant in default of appearance.

512. (1) A justice may, where the justice has reasonable and probable grounds to believe that it is necessary in the public interest to issue a summons or a warrant for the arrest of the accused, issue a summons or warrant notwithstanding that

    (*a*) an appearance notice or undertaking has been confirmed or cancelled under subsection 508(1);

    (*b*) a summons has previously been issued under subsection 507(4); or

    (*c*) the accused has been released without conditions or with the intention of compelling their appearance by way of summons.

(2) Where

    (*a*) service of a summons is proved and the accused fails to attend court in accordance with the summons,

    (*b*) an appearance notice or undertaking has been confirmed under subsection 508(1) and the accused fails to attend court in accordance with it in order to be dealt with according to law, or

    (*c*) it appears that a summons cannot be served because the accused is evading service,

a justice may issue a warrant for the arrest of the accused. R.S., c. 2 (2nd Supp.), s. 5; R.S.C. 1985, c. 27 (1st Supp.), s. 82; 1997, c. 18, s. 58; 2019, c. 25, s. 223.

ARREST WARRANT — FAILURE TO APPEAR UNDER SUMMONS.

512.1 If an accused who is required by a summons to appear at the time and place stated in it for the purposes of the *Identification of Criminals Act* does not appear at that time and place and, in the case of an offence designated as a contravention under the *Contraventions Act*, the "Attorney General", within the meaning of that Act, has not made an election under section 50 of that Act, a justice may issue a warrant for the arrest of the accused for the offence with which the accused is charged. 2019, c. 25, s. 224.

ARREST WARRANT — FAILURE TO APPEAR UNDER APPEARANCE NOTICE OR UNDERTAKING.

512.2 If an accused who is required by an appearance notice or undertaking to appear at the time and place stated in it for the purposes of the *Identification of Criminals Act* does not appear at that time and place, a justice may, if the appearance notice or undertaking has been confirmed by a justice under section 508, issue a warrant for the arrest of the accused for the offence with which the accused is charged. 2019, c. 25, s. 224.

WARRANT TO APPEAR UNDER SECTION 524.

512.3 If a justice is satisfied that there are reasonable grounds to believe that an accused has contravened or is about to contravene any summons, appearance notice, undertaking or release order that was issued or given to the accused or entered into by the accused or has committed an indictable offence while being subject to any summons, appearance notice, undertaking or release order, the justice may issue a warrant for the purpose of taking them before a justice under section 524. 2019, c. 25, s. 224.

FORMALITIES OF WARRANT.

513. A warrant in accordance with this Part shall be directed to the peace officers within the territorial jurisdiction of the justice, judge or court by whom or by which it is issued. R.S., c. 2 (2nd Supp.), s. 5.

EXECUTION OF WARRANT / By whom warrant may be executed.

514. (1) A warrant in accordance with this Part may be executed by arresting the accused

- (a) wherever he is found within the territorial jurisdiction of the justice, judge or court by whom or by which the warrant was issued; or
- (b) wherever he is found in Canada, in the case of fresh pursuit.

(2) A warrant in accordance with this Part may be executed by a person who is one of the peace officers to whom it is directed, whether or not the place in which the warrant is to be executed is within the territory for which the person is a peace officer. R.S., c. 2 (2nd Supp.), s. 5.

Judicial Interim Release

RELEASE ORDER WITHOUT CONDITIONS / Release order with conditions / Imposition of least onerous form of release / Promise to pay favoured over deposit / Restraint in use of surety / Power of justice — sureties / Appearance of the accused / When consent required for audioconference / Factors to consider / Conditions authorized / Condition prohibiting possession of firearms, etc. / Surrender, etc. / Reasons / Additional conditions / Offences / Detention in custody / Order of detention / Reasons / Release order / Sufficiency of record / Written reasons / Justification for detention in custody / Detention in custody for offence mentioned in s. 469 / Order re no communication / Consideration of victim's safety and security / Copy to victim.

515. (1) Subject to this section, when an accused who is charged with an offence other than an offence listed in section 469 is taken before a justice, the justice shall, unless a plea of guilty by the accused is accepted, make a release order in respect of that offence, without conditions, unless the prosecutor, having been given a reasonable opportunity to do so, shows cause, in respect of that offence, why the detention of the accused in custody is justified or why an order under any other provision of this section should be made.

(2) If the justice does not make an order under subsection (1), the justice shall, unless the prosecutor shows cause why the detention of the accused is justified, make a release order that sets out the conditions directed by the justice under subsection (4) and, as the case may be,

(a) an indication that the release order does not include any financial obligations;

(b) the accused's promise to pay a specified amount if they fail to comply with a condition of the order;

(c) the obligation to have one or more sureties, with or without the accused's promise to pay a specified amount if they fail to comply with a condition of the order;

(d) the obligation to deposit money or other valuable security in a specified amount or value, with or without the accused's promise to pay a specified amount if they fail to comply with a condition of the order; or

(e) if the accused is not ordinarily resident in the province in which they are in custody or does not ordinarily reside within 200 kilometres of the place in which they are in custody, the obligation to deposit money or other valuable security in a specified amount or value, with or without the accused's promise to pay a specified amount by the justice if they fail to comply with a condition of the order and with or without sureties.

(2.01) The justice shall not make an order containing the conditions referred to in one of the paragraphs (2)(b) to (e) unless the prosecution shows cause why an order containing the conditions referred to in the preceding paragraphs for any less onerous form of release would be inadequate.

(2.02) The justice shall favour a promise to pay an amount over the deposit of an amount of money if the accused or the surety, if applicable, has reasonably recoverable assets.

(2.03) For greater certainty, before making an order requiring that the accused have a surety, the justice shall be satisfied that this requirement is the least onerous form of release possible for the accused in the circumstances.

(2.1) If, under subsection (2) or any other provision of this Act, a judge, justice or court makes a release order with a requirement for sureties, the judge, justice or court may name particular persons as sureties.

(2.2) If, by this Act, the appearance of an accused is required for the purposes of judicial interim release, the accused shall appear personally but the justice may allow the accused to appear by videoconference or, subject to subsection (2.3), by audioconference, if the technological means is satisfactory to the justice.

(2.3) If the accused cannot appear by closed-circuit television or videoconference and the evidence of a witness is to be taken at the appearance, the consent of the prosecutor and the accused is required for the appearance of the accused by audioconference.

(3) In making an order under this section, the justice shall consider any relevant factors, including,

(a) whether the accused is charged with an offence in the commission of which violence was used, threatened or attempted against their intimate partner; or

(b) whether the accused has been previously convicted of a criminal offence.

(4) When making an order under subsection (2), the justice may direct the accused to comply with one or more of the following conditions specified in the order:

(a) report at specified times to a peace officer, or other person, designated in the order;

(b) remain within a specified territorial jurisdiction;

(c) notify a peace officer or other person designated in the order of any change in their address, employment or occupation;

(d) abstain from communicating, directly or indirectly, with any victim, witness or other person identified in the order, except in accordance with any specified conditions that the justice considers necessary;

(e) abstain from going to any place or entering any geographic area specified in the order, except in accordance with any specified conditions that the justice considers necessary;

(f) deposit all their passports as specified in the order;

(g) comply with any other specified condition that the justice considers necessary to ensure the safety and security of any victim of or witness to the offence; and

(h) comply with any other reasonable conditions specified in the order that the justice considers desirable.

(4.1) When making an order under subsection (2), in the case of an accused who is charged with

(a) an offence in the commission of which violence against a person was used, threatened or attempted,

(a.1) a terrorism offence,

(b) an offence under section 264 (criminal harassment),

(b.1) an offence under section 423.1 (intimidation of a justice system participant),

(b.2) an offence relating to the contravention of any of sections 9 to 14 of the *Cannabis Act*,

(c) an offence relating to the contravention of any of sections 5 to 7 of the *Controlled Drugs and Substances Act*,

(d) an offence that involves, or the subject-matter of which is, a firearm, a cross-bow, a prohibited weapon, a restricted weapon, a prohibited device, ammunition, prohibited ammunition or an explosive substance, or

(e) an offence under subsection 20(1) of the *Security of Information Act*, or an offence under subsection 21(1) or 22(1) or section 23 of that Act that is committed in relation to an offence under subsection 20(1) of that Act,

the justice shall add to the order a condition prohibiting the accused from possessing a firearm, cross-bow, prohibited weapon, restricted weapon, prohibited device, ammunition, prohibited ammunition or explosive substance, or all those things, until the accused is dealt with according to law unless the justice considers that such a condition is not required in the interests of the safety of the accused or the safety and security of a victim of the offence or of any other person.

(4.11) Where the justice adds a condition described in subsection (4.1) to an order made under subsection (2), the justice shall specify in the order the manner and method by which

(a) the things referred to in subsection (4.1) that are in the possession of the accused shall be surrendered, disposed of, detained, stored or dealt with; and (*b*) the authorizations, licences and registration certificates held by the person shall be surrendered.

(4.12) Where the justice does not add a condition described in subsection (4.1) to an order made under subsection (2), the justice shall include in the record a statement of the reasons for not adding the condition.

(4.2) Before making an order under subsection (2), in the case of an accused who is charged with an offence referred to in subsection (4.3), the justice shall consider whether it is desirable, in the interests of the safety and security of any person, particularly a victim of or witness to the offence or a justice system participant, to include as a condition of the order

    (*a*) that the accused abstain from communicating, directly or indirectly, with any victim, witness or other person identified in the order, except in accordance with any specified conditions that the justice considers necessary;

   (*a*.1) that the accused abstain from going to any place or entering any geographic area specified in the order, except in accordance with any specified conditions that the justice considers necessary; or

    (*b*) that the accused comply with any other condition specified in the order that the justice considers necessary to ensure the safety and security of those persons.

(4.3) The offences for the purposes of subsection (4.2) are

    (*a*) a terrorism offence;

    (*b*) an offence described in section 264 or 423.1

    (*c*) an offence in the commission of which violence against a person was used, threatened or attempted; and

    (*d*) an offence under subsection 20(1) of the *Security of Information Act*, or an offence under subsection 21(1) or 22(1) or section 23 of that Act that is committed in relation to an offence under subsection 20(1) of that Act.

(5) Where the prosecutor shows cause why the detention of the accused in custody is justified, the justice shall order that the accused be detained in custody until he is dealt with according to law and shall include in the record a statement of his reasons for making the order.

(6) Unless the accused, having been given a reasonable opportunity to do so, shows cause why the accused's detention in custody is not justified, the justice shall order, despite any provision of this section, that the accused be detained in custody until the accused is dealt with according to law, if the accused is charged

    (*a*) with an indictable offence, other than an offence listed in section 469,

      (i) that is alleged to have been committed while at large after being released in respect of another indictable offence pursuant to the provisions of this Part or section 679 or 680,

     (ii) that is an offence under section 467.11, 467.111, 467.12 or 467.13, or a serious offence alleged to have been committed for the benefit of, at the direction of, or in association with, a criminal organization,

    (iii) that is an offence under any of sections 83.02 to 83.04 and 83.18 to 83.23 or otherwise is alleged to be a terrorism offence,

    (iv) that is an offence under subsection 16(1) or (2), 17(1), 19(1), 20(1) or 22(1) of the *Security of Information Act*,

    (v) that is an offence under subsection 21(1) or 22(1) or section 23 of the *Security of Information Act* committed in relation to an offence referred to in subparagraph (iv),

    (vi) that is an offence under section 99, 100 or 103,

    (vii) that is an offence under section 244 or 244.2, or an offence under section 239, 272 or 273, subsection 279(1) or section 279.1, 344 or 346 that is alleged to have been committed with a firearm, or

    (viii) that is alleged to involve, or whose subject-matter is alleged to be, a firearm, a cross-bow, a prohibited weapon, a restricted weapon, a prohibited device, any ammunition or prohibited ammunition or an explosive substance, and that is alleged to have been committed while the accused was under a prohibition order within the meaning of subsection 84(1);

  (b) with an indictable offence, other than an offence listed in section 469 and is not ordinarily resident in Canada,

  (b.1) with an offence in the commission of which violence was allegedly used, threatened or attempted against their intimate partner, and the accused has been previously convicted of an offence in the commission of which violence was used, threatened or attempted against any intimate partner of theirs;

  (c) with an offence under any of subsections 145(2) to (5) that is alleged to have been committed while they were at large after being released in respect of another offence under the provisions of this Part or section 679, 680 or 816; or

  (d) with having committed an offence punishable by imprisonment for life under any of sections 5 to 7 of the *Controlled Drugs and Substances Act* or the offence of conspiring to commit such an offence.

(6.1) If the justice orders that an accused to whom subsection (6) applies be released, the justice shall include in the record a statement of the justice's reasons for making the order.

(7) If an accused to whom subsection (6) applies shows cause why their detention in custody is not justified, the justice shall make a release order under this section. If the accused was already at large on a release order, the new release order may include any additional conditions described in subsections (4) to (4.2) that the justice considers desirable.

(8) [*Repealed*, 2019, c. 24, s. 225(7).]

(9) For the purposes of subsections (5) and (6), it is sufficient if a record is made of the reasons in accordance with the provisions of Part XVIII relating to the taking of evidence at preliminary inquiries.

(9.1) Despite subsection (9), if the justice orders that the accused be detained in custody primarily because of a previous conviction of the accused, the justice shall state that reason, in writing, in the record.

(10) For the purposes of this section, the detention of an accused in custody is justified only on one or more of the following grounds:

(a) where the detention is necessary to ensure his or her attendance in court in order to be dealt with according to law;

(b) where the detention is necessary for the protection or safety of the public, including any victim of or witness to the offence, or any person under the age of 18 years, having regard to all the circumstances including any substantial likelihood that the accused will, if released from custody, commit a criminal offence or interfere with the administration of justice; and

(c) if the detention is necessary to maintain confidence in the administration of justice, having regard to all the circumstances, including

(i) the apparent strength of the prosecution's case,

(ii) the gravity of the offence,

(iii) the circumstances surrounding the commission of the offence, including whether a firearm was used, and

(iv) the fact that the accused is liable, on conviction, for a potentially lengthy term of imprisonment or, in the case of an offence that involves, or whose subject-matter is, a firearm, a minimum punishment of imprisonment for a term of three years or more.

(11) Where an accused who is charged with an offence mentioned in section 469 is taken before a justice, the justice shall order that the accused be detained in custody until he is dealt with according to law and shall issue a warrant in Form 8 for the committal of the accused.

(12) A justice who orders that an accused be detained in custody under this section may include in the order a direction that the accused abstain from communicating, directly or indirectly, with any victim, witness or other person identified in the order, except in accordance with such conditions specified in the order as the justice considers necessary.

(13) A justice who makes an order under this section shall include in the record of the proceedings a statement that he or she considered the safety and security of every victim of the offence when making the order.

(14) If an order is made under this section, the justice shall, on request by a victim of the offence, cause a copy of the order to be given to the victim. R.S., c. C-34, s. 457; R.S., c. 2 (2nd Supp.), s. 5; 1974-75-76, c. 93, s. 47; R.S.C. 1985, c. 27 (1st Supp.), ss. 83, 186 (Sched. IV, item 7); 1991, c. 40, s. 31; 1993, c. 45, s. 8; 1994, c. 44, s. 44; 1995, c. 39, ss. 153, 188(b); 1996, c. 19, ss. 71, 93.3; 1997, c. 18, s. 59; c. 23, s. 16; 1999, c. 5, s. 21; c. 25, s. 8; 2001, c. 32, s. 37; c. 41, ss. 19, 133(15)-(17); 2008, c. 6, s. 37; 2009, c. 22, s. 17; c. 29, s. 2; 2010, c. 20, s. 1; 2012, c. 1, s. 32; 2014, c. 17, s. 14; 2015, c. 13, s. 20; 2018, c. 16, s. 218; 2019, c. 25, s. 225.

DECLARATION OF SURETY / Exception / Means of telecommunication.

515.1 (1) Before a judge, justice or court names a particular person as a surety, the person shall provide the judge, justice or court with a signed declaration under oath, solemn declaration or solemn affirmation in Form 12 that sets out

(a) their name, date of birth and contact information;

(b) information demonstrating that they are suitable to act as a surety for the accused, including financial information;

(c) their relationship to the accused;

(d) the name and date of birth of any other accused for whom they act as a surety;

(e) their acknowledgment of the charge, and of any other outstanding charges against the accused and the contents of the accused's criminal record, if any;

(f) their acknowledgment of the amount that they are willing to promise to pay or deposit to the court and that may be forfeited if the accused fails to comply with any condition of the release order;

(g) their acknowledgment that they understand the role and responsibilities of a surety and that they assume these voluntarily; and

(h) a description of the contents of their criminal record and any outstanding charges against them, if any.

(2) Despite subsection (1), a judge, justice or court may name a person as a surety without a declaration if

(a) the prosecutor consents to it; or

(b) the judge, justice or court is satisfied that

    (i) the person cannot reasonably provide a declaration in the circumstances,

    (ii) the judge, justice or court has received sufficient information of the kind that would be set out in a declaration to evaluate whether the person is suitable to act as a surety for the accused, and

    (iii) the person has acknowleged that they have received sufficient information with respect to the matters referred to in paragraphs (1)(e) to (g) to accept the role and responsibilities of a surety.

(3) A person may provide the judge, justice or court with the declaration referred to in subsection (1) by a means of telecommunication that produces a writing. 1997, c. 18, s. 60; 2019, c. 25, s. 226.

REMAND IN CUSTODY / Detention pending bail hearing / Duration of order.

516. (1) A justice may, before or at any time during the course of any proceedings under section 515, on application by the prosecutor or the accused, adjourn the proceedings and remand the accused to custody in prison by warrant in Form 19, but no adjournment shall be for more than three clear days except with the consent of the accused.

(2) A justice who remands an accused to custody under subsection (1) or subsection 515(11) may order that the accused abstain from communicating directly or indirectly, with any victim, witness or other person identified in the order, except in accordance with any conditions specified in the order that the justice considers necessary.

(3) An order made under subsection (2) remains in force,

(a) until it is varied or revoked;

   (*b*) until an order in respect of the accused is made under section 515;
   (*c*) until the accused is acquitted of the offence, if applicable; or
   (*d*) until the time the accused is sentenced, if applicable. R.S., c. 2 (2nd Supp.),
      s. 5; 1999, c. 5, s. 22; c. 25, s. 31(3); 2019, c. 25, s. 227.

ORDER DIRECTING MATTERS NOT TO BE PUBLISHED FOR SPECIFIED PERIOD / Failure to comply / Definition of "newspaper".

517. (1) If the prosecutor or the accused intends to show cause under section 515, he or she shall so state to the justice and the justice may, and shall on application by the accused, before or at any time during the course of the proceedings under that section, make an order directing that the evidence taken, the information given or the representations made and the reasons, if any, given or to be given by the justice shall not be published in any document, or broadcast or transmitted in any way before such time as

   (*a*) if a preliminary inquiry is held, the accused in respect of whom the proceedings are held is discharged; or
   (*b*) if the accused in respect of whom the proceedings are held is tried or ordered to stand trial, the trial is ended.

(2) Every person who fails, without lawful excuse, to comply with an order made under subsection (1) is guilty of an offence punishable on summary conviction. R.S., c. 2 (2nd Supp.), s. 5; 1974-75-76, c. 93, s. 48; R.S.C. 1985, c. 27 (1st Supp.), s. 101(2)(*a*); 2005, c. 32, s. 17; 2018, c. 29, s. 62.

(3) [*Repealed*, 2005, c. 32, s. 17(2).]

INQUIRIES TO BE MADE BY JUSTICE AND EVIDENCE / Release pending sentence.

518. (1) In any proceedings under section 515,

   (*a*) the justice may, subject to paragraph (*b*), make such inquiries, on oath or otherwise, of and concerning the accused as he considers desirable;
   (*b*) the accused shall not be examined by the justice or any other person except counsel for the accused respecting the offence with which the accused is charged, and no inquiry shall be made of the accused respecting that offence by way of cross-examination unless the accused has testified respecting the offence;
   (*c*) the prosecutor may, in addition to any other relevant evidence, lead evidence
      (i) to prove that the accused has previously been convicted of a criminal offence,
      (ii) to prove that the accused has been charged with and is awaiting trial for another criminal offence,
      (iii) to prove that the accused has previously committed an offence under section 145, or
      (iv) to show the circumstances of the alleged offence, particularly as they relate to the probability of conviction of the accused;

(*d*) the justice may take into consideration any relevant matters agreed on by the prosecutor and the accused or his counsel;

(*d*.1) the justice may receive evidence obtained as a result of an interception of a private communication under and within the meaning of Part VI, in writing, orally or in the form of a recording and, for the purposes of this section, subsection 189(5) does not apply to that evidence;

(*d*.2) the justice shall take into consideration any evidence submitted regarding the need to ensure the safety or security of any victim of or witness to an offence; and

(*e*) the justice may receive and base his decision on evidence considered credible or trustworthy by him in the circumstances of each case.

(2) Where, before or at any time during the course of any proceedings under section 515, the accused pleads guilty and that plea is accepted, the justice may make any order provided for in this Part for the release of the accused until the accused is sentenced. R.S., c. 2 (2nd Supp.), s. 5; 1974-75-76, c. 93, s. 49; R.S.C. 1985, c. 27 (1st Supp.), s. 84; 1994, c. 44, s. 45; 1999, c. 25, s. 9.

RELEASE OF ACCUSED / Discharge from custody / Warrant for committal.

519. (1) If a justice makes a release order under section 515,

(*a*) if the accused thereupon complies with the order, the justice shall direct that the accused be released
  (i) forthwith, if the accused is not required to be detained in custody in respect of any other matter, or
  (ii) as soon thereafter as the accused is no longer required to be detained in custody in respect of any other matter;

(*b*) if the accused does not thereupon comply with the order, the justice who made the order or another justice having jurisdiction shall issue a warrant for the committal of the accused and may endorse thereon an authorization to the person having the custody of the accused to release the accused when the accused complies with the order
  (i) forthwith after the compliance, if the accused is not required to be detained in custody in respect of any other matter, or
  (ii) as soon thereafter as the accused is no longer required to be detained in custody in respect of any other matter

and if the justice so endorses the warrant, he shall attach to it a copy of the order; and

(*c*) any condition in the order that an accused abstain from communicating, directly or indirectly, with any victim, witness or other person identified in the order, except in accordance with any specified conditions, is effective from the moment it is made, whether or not the accused has been released from custody.

(2) Where the accused complies with an order referred to in paragraph (1)(*b*) and is not required to be detained in custody in respect of any other matter, the justice who made the order or another justice having jurisdiction shall, unless the accused has been or will be released pursuant to an authorization referred to in that paragraph, issue an order for discharge in Form 39.

(3) Where the justice makes an order under subsection 515(5) or (6) for the detention of the accused, he shall issue a warrant for the committal of the accused. R.S., c. 2 (2nd Supp.), s. 5; 1974-75-76, c. 93, s. 50; R.S.C. 1985, c. 27 (1st Supp.), s. 85; 2019, c. 25, s. 228.

VARIATION OF RELEASE ORDER WITH CONSENT.

519.1 A release order under which an accused has been released under section 515 may be varied with the written consent of the accused, prosecutor and any sureties. The order so varied is considered to be a release order under section 515. 2019, c. 25, s. 229.

REVIEW OF ORDER / Notice to prosecutor / Accused to be present / Adjournment of proceedings / Failure of accused to attend / Execution / Evidence and powers of judge on review / Limitation of further applications / Application of ss. 517, 518 and 519.

520. (1) If a justice, or a judge of the Nunavut Court of Justice, makes an order under subsection 515(2), (5), (6), (7), or (12) or makes or vacates any order under paragraph 523(2)(b), the accused may, at any time before the trial of the charge, apply to a judge for a review of the order.

(2) An application under this section shall not, unless the prosecutor otherwise consents, be heard by a judge unless the accused has given to the prosecutor at least two clear days notice in writing of the application.

(3) If the judge so orders or the prosecutor or the accused or his counsel so requests, the accused shall be present at the hearing of an application under this section and, where the accused is in custody, the judge may order, in writing, the person having the custody of the accused to bring him before the court.

(4) A judge may, before or at any time during the hearing of an application under this section, on application by the prosecutor or the accused, adjourn the proceedings, but if the accused is in custody no adjournment shall be for more than three clear days except with the consent of the accused.

(5) Where an accused, other than an accused who is in custody, has been ordered by a judge to be present at the hearing of an application under this section and does not attend the hearing, the judge may issue a warrant for the arrest of the accused.

(6) A warrant issued under subsection (5) may be executed anywhere in Canada.

(7) On the hearing of an application under this section, the judge may consider
   (a) the transcript, if any, of the proceedings heard by the justice and by any judge who previously reviewed the order made by the justice,
   (b) the exhibits, if any, filed in the proceedings before the justice, and
   (c) such additional evidence or exhibits as may be tendered by the accused or the prosecutor,
and shall either
   (d) dismiss the application, or

(e) if the accused shows cause, allow the application, vacate the order previously made by the justice and make any other order provided for in section 515 that he considers is warranted.

(8) Where an application under this section or section 521 has been heard, a further or other application under this section or section 521 shall not be made with respect to that same accused, except with leave of a judge, prior to the expiration of thirty days from the date of the decision of the judge who heard the previous application.

(9) The provisions of section 517, 518 and 519 apply with such modifications as the circumstances require in respect of an application under this section. R.S., c. 2 (2nd Supp.), s. 5; 1974-75-76, c. 93, s. 51; R.S.C. 1985, c. 27 (1st Supp.), s. 86; 1994, c. 44, s. 46; 1999, c. 3, s. 31; 2019, c. 25, s. 230.

REVIEW OF ORDER / Notice to accused / Accused to be present / Adjournment of proceedings / Failure of accused to attend / Warrant for detention / Execution / Evidence and powers of judge on review / Limitation of further applications / Application of ss. 517, 518 and 519.

521. (1) If a justice, or a judge of the Nunavut Court of Justice, makes an order under subsection 515(1), (2), (7) or (12) or makes or vacates any order under paragraph 523(2)(b), the prosecutor may, at any time before the trial of the charge, apply to a judge for a review of the order.

(2) An application under this section shall not be heard by a judge unless the prosecutor has given to the accused at least two clear days notice in writing of the application.

(3) If the judge so orders or the prosecutor or the accused or his counsel so requests, the accused shall be present at the hearing of an application under this section and, where the accused is in custody, the judge may order, in writing, the person having the custody of the accused to bring him before the court.

(4) A judge may, before or at any time during the hearing of an application under this section, on application of the prosecutor or the accused, adjourn the proceedings, but if the accused is in custody no adjournment shall be for more than three clear days except with the consent of the accused.

(5) Where an accused, other than an accused who is in custody, has been ordered by a judge to be present at the hearing of an application under this section and does not attend the hearing, the judge may issue a warrant for the arrest of the accused.

(6) Where, pursuant to paragraph (8)(e), the judge makes an order that the accused be detained in custody until he is dealt with according to law, he shall, if the accused is not in custody, issue a warrant for the committal of the accused.

(7) A warrant issued under subsection (5) or (6) may be executed anywhere in Canada.

(8) On the hearing of an application under this section, the judge may consider
(a) the transcript, if any, of the proceedings heard by the justice and by any judge who previously reviewed the order made by the justice,

(*b*) the exhibits, if any, filed in the proceedings before the justice, and

(*c*) such additional evidence or exhibits as may be tendered by the prosecutor or the accused,

and shall either

(*d*) dismiss the application, or

(*e*) if the prosecutor shows cause, allow the application, vacate the order previously made by the justice and make any other order provided for in section 515 that he considers to be warranted.

(9) Where an application under this section or section 520 has been heard, a further or other application under this section or section 520 shall not be made with respect to the same accused, except with leave of a judge, prior to the expiration of thirty days from the date of the decision of the judge who heard the previous application.

(10) The provisions of sections 517, 518 and 519 apply with such modifications as the circumstances require in respect of an application under this section. R.S., c. 2 (2nd Supp.), s. 5; 1974-75-76, c. 93, s. 52; R.S.C. 1985, c. 27 (1st Supp.), s. 87; 1994, c. 44, s. 47; 1999, c. 3, s. 32; 2019, c. 25, s. 231.

INTERIM RELEASE BY JUDGE ONLY / Idem / Order re no communication / Release of accused / Order not reviewable except under s. 680 / Application of sections 517, 518 and 519 / Other offences.

522. (1) Where an accused is charged with an offence listed in section 469, no court, judge or justice, other than a judge of or a judge presiding in a superior court of criminal jurisdiction for the province in which the accused is so charged, may release the accused before or after the accused has been ordered to stand trial.

(2) Where an accused is charged with an offence listed in section 469, a judge of or a judge presiding in a superior court of criminal jurisdiction for the province in which the accused is charged shall order that the accused be detained in custody unless the accused, having been given a reasonable opportunity to do so, shows cause why his detention in custody is not justified within the meaning of subsection 515(10).

(2.1) A judge referred to in subsection (2) who orders that an accused be detained in custody under this section may include in the order a direction that the accused abstain from communicating, directly or indirectly, with any victim, witness or other person identified in the order except in accordance with such conditions specified in the order as the judge considers necessary.

(3) If the judge does not order that the accused be detained in custody under subsection (2), the judge may make a release order referred to in section 515.

(4) An order made under this section is not subject to review, except as provided in section 680.

(5) The provisions of sections 517, 518 except subsection (2) thereof, and 519 apply with such modifications as the circumstances require in respect of an application for an order under subsection (2).

(6) Where an accused is charged with an offence mentioned in section 469 and with any other offence, a judge acting under this section may apply the provisions of this Part respecting judicial interim release to that other offence. R.S., c. 2 (2nd Supp.), s. 5; 1972, c. 13, s. 36; 1974-75-76, c. 93, s. 53; R.S.C. 1985, c. 27 (1st Supp.), s. 88; 1991, c. 40, s. 32; 1994, c. 44, s. 48; 1999, c. 25, s. 10; 2019, c. 25, s. 232.

PERIOD FOR WHICH APPEARANCE NOTICE, ETC., CONTINUES IN FORCE / When new information is received / When direct indictment preferred / Order vacating previous order for release or detention / Provisions applicable to proceedings under subsection (2).

523. (1) If an accused, in respect of an offence with which they are charged, has not been taken into custody or has been released from custody under any provision of this Part, the appearance notice, summons, undertaking or release order issued to, given or entered into by the accused continues in force, subject to its terms, and applies in respect of any new information charging the same offence or an included offence that was received after the appearance notice, summons, undertaking or release order was issued, given or entered into,

- (a) where the accused was released from custody pursuant to an order of a judge made under subsection 522(3), until his trial is completed; or
- (b) in any other case,
  - (i) until his trial is completed, and
  - (ii) where the accused is, at his trial, determined to be guilty of the offence, until a sentence within the meaning of section 673 is imposed on the accused unless, at the time the accused is determined to be guilty, the court, judge or justice orders that the accused be taken into custody pending such sentence.

(1.1) If an accused is charged with an offence and a new information, charging the same offence or an included offence, is received while the accused is subject to an order for detention, release order, appearance notice, summons or undertaking, section 507 or 508, as the case may be, does not apply in respect of the new information and the order for detention, release order, appearance notice, summons or undertaking applies in respect of the new information.

(1.2) If an accused is charged with an offence, and an indictment is preferred under section 577 charging the same offence or an included offence while the accused is subject to an order for detention, release order, appearance notice, summons or undertaking, the order for detention, release order, appearance notice, summons or undertaking applies in respect of the indictment.

(2) Despite subsections (1) to (1.2),

- (a) the court, judge or justice before whom an accused is being tried, at any time,
- (b) the justice, on completion of the preliminary inquiry in relation to an offence for which an accused is ordered to stand trial, other than an offence listed in section 469, or

    (*c*) with the consent of the prosecutor and the accused or, where the accused or the prosecutor applies to vacate an order that would otherwise apply pursuant to subsection (1.1), without such consent, at any time

        (i) where the accused is charged with an offence other than an offence listed in section 469, the justice by whom an order was made under this Part or any other justice,

        (ii) where the accused is charged with an offence listed in section 469, a judge of or a judge presiding in a superior court of criminal jurisdiction for the province, or

        (iii) the court, judge or justice before which or whom an accused is to be tried,

may, on cause being shown, vacate any order previously made under this Part for the interim release or detention of the accused and make any other order provided for in this Part for the detention or release of the accused until his trial is completed that the court, judge or justice considers to be warranted.

(3) The provisions of sections 517, 518 and 519 apply, with such modifications as the circumstances require, in respect of any proceedings under subsection (2), except that subsection 518(2) does not apply in respect of an accused who is charged with an offence listed in section 469. R.S., c. 2 (2nd Supp.), s. 5; 1974-75-76, c. 93, s. 54; R.S.C. 1985, c. 27 (1st Supp.), s. 89; 2011, c. 16, s. 2; 2019, c. 25, s. 233.

Proceedings Respecting Failure to Comply with Release Conditions
2019, c. 25, s. 234.

JUDICIAL REFERRAL HEARING / Circumstances / Powers — Judge or Justice / Dismissal of charge / No information or indictment.

523.1 (1) When an accused appears before a justice in any of the circumstances described in subsection (2), the justice shall

    (*a*) if the accused was released from custody under an order made under subsection 522(3) by a judge of the superior court of criminal jurisdiction of any province, order that the accused appear before a judge of that court so that the judge may hear the matter; or

    (*b*) in any other case, hear the matter.

(2) The circumstances referred to in subsection (1) are the following:

    (*a*) an appearance notice has been issued to the accused for failing to comply with a summons, appearance notice, undertaking or release order or to attend court as required and the prosecutor seeks a decision under this section; or

    (*b*) a charge has been laid against the accused for the contravention referred to in paragraph (*a*) and the prosecutor seeks a decision under this section.

(3) If the judge or justice who hears the matter is satisfied that the accused failed to comply with a summons, appearance notice, undertaking or release order or to attend court as required and that the failure did not cause a victim physical or emotional harm, property damage or economic loss, the judge or justice shall

review any conditions of release that have been imposed on the accused and may, as the case may be,

    (a) take no action;

    (b) cancel any other summons, appearance notice, undertaking or release order in respect of the accused and, as the case may be,

        (i) make a release order under section 515, or

        (ii) if the prosecutor shows cause why the detention of the accused in custody is justified under subsection 515(10), make an order that the accused be detained in custody until the accused is dealt with according to law and if so detained, the judge or justice shall include in the record a statement of the judge's or justice's reasons for making the order; or

    (c) remand the accused to custody for the purposes of the *Identification of Criminals Act*.

(4) If a charge has been laid against the accused for the failure referred to in paragraph (2)(a) and the judge or justice, as the case may be, makes a decision under subsection (3), the judge or justice shall also dismiss that charge.

(5) If the judge or justice makes a decision under subsection (3), no information may be laid nor indictment be preferred against the accused for the failure referred to in paragraph (2)(a). 2019, c. 25, s. 234.

HEARING / Circumstances / Cancellation / Detention / Release order / Reasons / Release / Provisions applicable to proceedings under this section / Review — order by judge / Review — order of justice.

524. (1) When an accused is taken before a justice in any of the circumstances described in subsection (2), the justice shall

    (a) if the accused was released from custody under an order made under subsection 522(3) by a judge of the superior court of criminal jurisdiction of any province, order that the accused be taken before a judge of that court so that the judge may hear the matter; or

    (b) in any other case, hear the matter.

(2) The circumstances referred to in subsection (1) are the following:

    (a) the accused has been arrested for the contravention of or having been about to contravene, a summons, appearance notice, undertaking or release order and the prosecutor seeks to have it cancelled under this section; or

    (b) the accused has been arrested for having committed an indictable offence while being subject to a summons, appearance notice, undertaking or release order and the prosecutor seeks to have it cancelled under this section.

(3) The judge or justice who hears the matter shall cancel a summons, appearance notice, undertaking or release order in respect of the accused if the judge or justice finds that

    (a) the accused has contravened or had been about to contravene the summons, appearance notice, undertaking or release order; or (*b*) there are reasonable grounds to believe that the accused has committed an indictable offence while being subject to the summons, appearance notice, undertaking or release order.

(4) If the judge or justice cancels the summons, appearance notice, undertaking or release order, the judge or justice shall order that the accused be detained in custody unless the accused, having been given a reasonable opportunity to do so, shows cause why their detention in custody is not justified under subsection 515(10).

(5) If the judge or justice does not order that the accused be detained in custody under subsection (4), the judge or justice shall make a release order referred to in section 515.

(6) If the judge or justice makes a release order under subsection (5), the judge or justice shall include in the record a statement of the reasons for making the order, and subsection 515(9) applies with any modifications that the circumstances require.

(7) If the judge or justice does not cancel the summons, appearance notice, undertaking or release order under subsection (3), the judge or justice shall order that the accused be released from custody.

(8) The provisions of sections 516 to 519 apply with any modifications that the circumstances require in respect of any proceedings under this section, except that subsection 518(2) does not apply in respect of an accused who is charged with an offence mentioned in section 469.

(9) An order made under subsection (4) or (5) respecting an accused referred to in paragraph (1)(*a*) is not subject to review except as provided in section 680.

(10) An order made under subsection (4) or (5) respecting an accused other than the accused referred to in paragraph (1)(*a*), is subject to review under sections 520 and 521 as if the order were made under section 515. R.S., c. C-34, s. 458; R.S., c. 2 (2nd Supp.), s. 5; 1974-75-76, c. 93, s. 55; 1999, c. 3, s. 33; 2019, c. 25, s. 234.

(11) [*Repealed*, 2019, c. 25, s. 234.]

(12) [*Repealed*, 2019, c. 25, s. 234.]

(13) [*Repealed*, 2019, c. 25, s. 234.]

Review of Detention Where Trial Delayed

TIME FOR APPLICATION TO JUDGE / Waiver of right to hearing / Notice of hearing / Cancellation of hearing / Consideration of proceeding's progression / Release order / Provisions applicable to proceedings / Definition of "judge" in the Province of Quebec.

525. (1) The person having the custody of an accused — who has been charged with an offence other than an offence listed in section 469, who is being detained in custody pending their trial for that offence and who is not required to be detained in custody in respect of any other matter — shall apply to a judge having jurisdiction in the place in which the accused is in custody to fix a date for a hearing to determine whether or not the accused should be released from custody, if the trial has not commenced within 90 days from

    (a) the day on which the accused was taken before a justice under section 503; or

    (b) in the case where an order that the accused be detained in custody has been made under section 521, paragraph 523.1(3)(b)(ii) or section 524, or a decision has been made with respect to a review under section 520, the later of the day on which the accused was taken into custody under that order and the day of the decision.

The person shall make the application immediately after the expiry of those 90 days.

(1.1) However, the person having the custody of the accused is not required to make the application if the accused has waived in writing their right to a hearing and the judge has received the waiver before the expiry of the 90-day period referred to in subsection (1).

(2) On receiving an application under subsection (1), the judge shall

    (a) fix a date for the hearing described in subsection (1) to be held in the jurisdiction

        (i) where the accused is in custody, or

        (ii) where the trial is to take place; and

    (b) direct that notice of the hearing be given to such persons, including the prosecutor and the accused, and in such manner, as the judge may specify.

(3) The judge may cancel the hearing if the judge receives the accused's waiver before the hearing.

(4) On the hearing described in subsection (1), the judge shall consider whether the prosecutor or the accused has been responsible for any delay and, if the judge is concerned that the proceedings are progressing slowly and that an unreasonable delay may result, the judge may

    (a) give directions for expediting the proceedings; or

    (b) require a further hearing under this section within 90 days or any other period that the judge considers appropriate in the circumstances.

(5) If, following the hearing, the judge is not satisfied that the continued detention of the accused in custody is justified within the meaning of subsection 515(10), the judge shall make a release order referred to in section 515.

(6) Sections 495.1, 512.3, 517 to 519 and 524 apply, with any modifications that the circumstances require, in respect of any proceedings under this section.

(7) In this section, "judge", in the Province of Quebec,

    (a) in the case where the order that the accused be detained in custody has been made by a judge of the superior court of criminal jurisdiction of the Province of Quebec, has the same meaning as in paragraph (b) of the definition "judge" in section 493; and

    (b) in any other case, means a judge of the superior court of criminal jurisdiction of the province, a judge of the Court of Quebec or three judges of the Court of Quebec. R.S., c. C-34, s. 459; R.S., c. 2 (2nd Supp.), s. 5;

1974-75-76, c. 93, s. 56; R.S.C. 1985, c. 27 (1st Supp.), s. 90; 1994, c. 44, s. 49; 1997, c. 18, s. 61; 2019, c. 25, s. 235.

(8) [*Repealed*, 2019, c. 25, s. 235(2).]

(9) [*Repealed*, 2019, c. 25, s. 235(2).]

DIRECTIONS FOR EXPEDITING PROCEEDINGS.

526. Subject to subsection 525(4), a court, judge or justice before which or whom an accused appears under this Part may give directions for expediting any proceedings in respect of the accused. R.S., c. 2 (2nd Supp.), s. 5; R.S.C. 1985, c. 27 (1st Supp.), s. 91; 2019, c. 25, s. 236.

Procedure to Procure Attendance of a Prisoner

PROCURING ATTENDANCE / Provincial court judge's order / Conveyance of prisoner / Detention of prisoner required as witness / Detention in other cases / Application of sections respecting sentence / Transfer of prisoner / Conveyance of prisoner / Return.

527. (1) A judge of a superior court of criminal jurisdiction may order in writing that a person who is confined in a prison be brought before the court, judge, justice or provincial court judge before whom the prisoner is required to attend, from day to day as may be necessary, if

    (*a*) the applicant for the order sets out the facts of the case in an affidavit and produces the warrant, if any; and

    (*b*) the judge is satisfied that the ends of justice require that an order be made.

(2) A provincial court judge has the same powers for the purposes of subsection (1) or (7) as a judge has under that subsection where the person whose attendance is required is within the province in which the provincial court judge has jurisdiction.

(3) An order that is made under subsection (1) or (2) shall be addressed to the person who has custody of the prisoner, and on receipt thereof that person shall

    (*a*) deliver the prisoner to any person who is named in the order to receive him; or

    (*b*) bring the prisoner before the court, judge, justice or provincial court judge, as the case may be, on payment of his reasonable charges in respect thereof.

(4) Where a prisoner is required as a witness, the judge or provincial court judge shall direct, in the order, the manner in which the prisoner shall be kept in custody and returned to the prison from which he is brought.

(5) Where the appearance of a prisoner is required for the purposes of paragraph (1)(*a*) or (*b*), the judge or provincial court judge shall give appropriate directions in the order with respect to the manner in which the prisoner is

    (*a*) to be kept in custody, if he is ordered to stand trial; or

(b) to be returned, if he is discharged on a preliminary inquiry or if he is acquitted of the charge against him.

(6) Sections 718.3 and 743.1 apply where a prisoner to whom this section applies is convicted and sentenced to imprisonment by the court, judge, justice or provincial court judge.

(7) On application by the prosecutor, a judge of a superior court of criminal jurisdiction may, if a prisoner or a person in the custody of a peace officer consents in writing, order the transfer of the prisoner or other person to the custody of a peace officer named in the order for a period specified in the order, where the judge is satisfied that the transfer is required for the purpose of assisting a peace officer acting in the execution of his or her duties.

(8) An order under subsection (7) shall be addressed to the person who has custody of the prisoner and on receipt thereof that person shall deliver the prisoner to the peace officer who is named in the order to receive him.

(9) When the purposes of any order made under this section have been carried out, the prisoner shall be returned to the place where he was confined at the time the order was made. R.S., c. C-34, s. 460; R.S.C. 1985, c. 27 (1st Supp.), ss. 92, 101(2)(b); 1994, c. 44, s. 50; 1995, c. 22, s. 10; 1997, c. 18, s. 62.

Endorsement of Warrant

ENDORSING WARRANT / Copy of affidavit or warrant / Effect of endorsement.

528. (1) Where a warrant for the arrest or committal of an accused, in any form set out in Part XXVIII in relation thereto, cannot be executed in accordance with section 514 or 703, a justice within whose jurisdiction the accused is or is believed to be shall, on application and proof on oath or by affidavit of the signature of the justice who issued the warrant, authorize the arrest of the accused within his jurisdiction by making an endorsement, which may be in Form 28, on the warrant.

(1.1) A copy of an affidavit or warrant submitted by a means of telecommunication that produces a writing has the same probative force as the original for the purposes of subsection (1).

(2) An endorsement that is made on a warrant pursuant to subsection (1) is sufficient authority to the peace officers to whom it was originally directed, and to all peace officers within the territorial jurisdiction of the justice by whom it is endorsed, to execute the warrant and to take the accused before the justice who issued the warrant or before any other justice for the same territorial division. R.S., c. C-34, s. 461; 1974-75-76, c. 93, s. 57; R.S.C. 1985, c. 27 (1st Supp.), s. 93; 1994, c. 44, s. 51.

529. [*Repealed* (old provision, with heading), 1994, c. 44, s. 52.]

Powers to Enter Dwelling-houses to Carry out Arrests

INCLUDING AUTHORIZATION TO ENTER IN WARRANT OF ARREST / Execution

529. (1) A warrant to arrest or apprehend a person issued by a judge or justice under this or any other Act of Parliament may authorize a peace officer, subject to subsection (2), to enter a dwelling-house described in the warrant for the purpose of arresting or apprehending the person if the judge or justice is satisfied by information on oath in writing that there are reasonable grounds to believe that the person is or will be present in the dwelling-house.

(2) An authorization to enter a dwelling-house granted under subsection (1) is subject to the condition that the peace officer may not enter the dwelling-house unless the peace officer has, immediately before entering the dwelling-house, reasonable grounds to believe that the person to be arrested or apprehended is present in the dwelling-house. 1994, c. 44, s. 52; 1997, c. 39, s. 2.

WARRANT TO ENTER DWELLING-HOUSE

529.1 A judge or justice may issue a warrant in Form 7.1 authorizing a peace officer to enter a dwelling-house described in the warrant for the purpose of arresting or apprehending a person identified or identifiable by the warrant if the judge or justice is satisfied by information on oath that there are reasonable grounds to believe that the person is or will be present in the dwelling-house and that

(a) a warrant referred to in this or any other Act of Parliament to arrest or apprehend the person is in force anywhere in Canada;

(b) grounds exist to arrest the person without warrant under paragraph 495(1)(a) or (b) or section 672.91; or

(c) grounds exist to arrest or apprehend without warrant the person under an Act of Parliament, other than this Act. 1997, c. 39, s. 2; 2002, c. 13, s. 23.

REASONABLE TERMS AND CONDITIONS

529.2 Subject to section 529.4, the judge or justice shall include in a warrant referred to in section 529 or 529.1 any terms and conditions that the judge or justice considers advisable to ensure that the entry into the dwelling-house is reasonable in the circumstances. 1997, c. 39, s. 2.

AUTHORITY TO ENTER DWELLING WITHOUT WARRANT / Exigent circumstances

529.3 (1) Without limiting or restricting any power a peace officer may have to enter a dwelling-house under this or any other Act or law, the peace officer may enter the dwelling-house for the purpose of arresting or apprehending a person, without a warrant referred to in section 529 or 529.1 authorizing the entry, if the peace officer has reasonable grounds to believe that the person is present in the dwelling-house, and the conditions for obtaining a warrant under section 529.1

exist but by reason of exigent circumstances it would be impracticable to obtain a warrant.

(2) For the purposes of subsection (1), exigent circumstances include circumstances in which the peace officer

   (*a*) has reasonable grounds to suspect that entry into the dwelling-house is necessary to prevent imminent bodily harm or death to any person; or

   (*b*) has reasonable grounds to believe that evidence relating to the commission of an indictable offence is present in the dwelling-house and that entry into the dwelling-house is necessary to prevent the imminent loss or imminent destruction of the evidence. 1997, c. 39, s. 2.

CODE

OMITTING ANNOUNCEMENT BEFORE ENTRY / Execution of authorization / Exception.

529.4 (1) A judge or justice who authorizes a peace officer to enter a dwelling-house under section 529 or 529.1, or any other judge or justice, may authorize the peace officer to enter the dwelling-house without prior announcement if the judge or justice is satisfied by information on oath that there are reasonable grounds to believe that prior announcement of the entry would

   (*a*) expose the peace officer or any other person to imminent bodily harm or death; or

   (*b*) result in the imminent loss or imminent destruction of evidence relating to the commission of an indictable offence.

(2) An authorization under this section is subject to the condition that the peace officer may not enter the dwelling-house without prior announcement despite being authorized to do so unless the peace officer has, immediately before entering the dwelling-house,

   (*a*) reasonable grounds to suspect that prior announcement of the entry would expose the peace officer or any other person to imminent bodily harm or death; or

   (*b*) reasonable grounds to believe that prior announcement of the entry would result in the imminent loss or imminent destruction of evidence relating to the commission of an indictable offence.

(3) A peace officer who enters a dwelling-house without a warrant under section 529.3 may not enter the dwelling-house without prior announcement unless the peace officer has, immediately before entering the dwelling-house,

   (*a*) reasonable grounds to suspect that prior announcement of the entry would expose the peace officer or any other person to imminent bodily harm or death; or

   (*b*) reasonable grounds to believe that prior announcement of the entry would result in the imminent loss or imminent destruction of evidence relating to the commission of an indictable offence. R.S. 1985, c. 27 (1st Supp.), s. 203; 1997, c. 39, s. 2.

TELEWARRANT

529.5 If a peace officer believes that it would be impracticable in the circumstances to appear personally before a judge or justice to make an application for a warrant under section 529.1 or an authorization under section 529 or 529.4, the warrant or authorization may be issued on an information submitted by telephone or other means of telecommunication and, for that purpose, section 487.1 applies, with any modifications that the circumstances require, to the warrant or authorization. 1997, c. 39, s. 2.

Part XVII / LANGUAGE OF ACCUSED

LANGUAGE OF ACCUSED / Idem / Accused to be advised of right / Remand / Variation of order / Circumstances warranting order directing trial in both official languages.

530. (1) On application by an accused whose language is one of the official languages of Canada, made not later than the time of the appearance of the accused at which their trial date is set, a judge, provincial court judge, judge of the Nunavut Court of Justice or justice of the peace shall grant an order directing that the accused be tried before a justice of the peace, provincial court judge, judge or judge and jury, as the case may be, who speak the official language of Canada that is the language of the accused or, if the circumstances warrant, who speak both official languages of Canada.

(2) On application by an accused whose language is not one of the official languages of Canada, made not later than the time of the appearance of the accused at which their trial date is set, a judge, provincial court judge, judge of the Nunavut Court of Justice or justice of the peace may grant an order directing that the accused be tried before a justice of the peace, provincial court judge, judge or judge and jury, as the case may be, who speak the official language of Canada in which the accused, in the opinion of the judge, provincial court judge, judge of the Nunavut Court of Justice or justice of the peace, can best give testimony or, if the circumstances warrant, who speak both official languages of Canada.

(3) The judge, provincial court judge, judge of the Nunavut Court of Justice or justice of the peace before whom an accused first appears shall ensure that they are advised of their right to apply for an order under subsection (1) or (2) and of the time before which such an application must be made.

(4) If an accused fails to apply for an order under subsection (1) or (2) and the judge, provincial court judge, judge of the Nunavut Court of Justice or justice of the peace before whom the accused is to be tried, in this Part referred to as "the court", is satisfied that it is in the best interests of justice that the accused be tried before a justice of the peace, provincial court judge, judge or judge and jury who speak the official language of Canada that is the language of the accused or, if the language of the accused is not one of the official languages of Canada, the official language of Canada in which the accused, in the opinion of the court, can best give testimony, the court may, if it does not speak that language, by order remand the accused to be tried by a justice of the peace, provincial court judge, judge or judge

and jury, as the case may be, who speak that language or, if the circumstances warrant, who speak both official languages of Canada.

(5) An order under this section that a trial be held in one of the official languages of Canada may, if the circumstances warrant, be varied by the court to require that it be held in both official languages of Canada, and vice versa.

(6) The facts that two or more accused who are to be tried together are each entitled to be tried before a justice of the peace, provincial court judge, judge or judge and jury who speak one of the official languages of Canada and that those official languages are different may constitute circumstances that warrant that an order be granted directing that they be tried before a justice of the peace, provincial court judge, judge or judge and jury who speak both official languages of Canada. 1977-78, c. 36, s. 1; R.S.C. 1985, c. 27 (1st Supp.), s. 94; 1999, c. 3, s. 34; 2008, c. 18, s. 18; 2019, c. 25, s. 237.

TRANSLATION OF DOCUMENTS / Original version prevails.

530.01 (1) If an order is granted under section 530, a prosecutor — other than a private prosecutor — shall, on application by the accused,

(a) cause any portion of an information or indictment against the accused that is in an official language that is not that of the accused or that in which the accused can best give testimony to be translated into the other official language; and

(b) provide the accused with a written copy of the translated text at the earliest possible time.

(2) In the case of a discrepancy between the original version of a document and the translated text, the original version shall prevail. 2008, c. 18, s. 19.

IF ORDER GRANTED.

530.1 If an order is granted under section 530,

(a) the accused and his counsel have the right to use either official language for all purposes during the preliminary inquiry and trial of the accused;

(b) the accused and his counsel may use either official language in written pleadings or other documents used in any proceedings relating to the preliminary inquiry or trial of the accused;

(c) any witness may give evidence in either official language during the preliminary inquiry or trial;

(c.1) the presiding justice or judge may, if the circumstances warrant, authorize the prosecutor to examine or cross-examine a witness in the official language of the witness even though it is not that of the accused or that in which the accused can best give testimony;

(d) the accused has a right to have a justice presiding over the preliminary inquiry who speaks the official language of the accused or both official languages, as the case may be;

(e) the accused has a right to have a prosecutor — other than a private prosecutor — who speaks the official language of the accused or both official languages, as the case may be;

(f) the court shall make interpreters available to assist the accused, his counsel or any witness during the preliminary inquiry or trial;

(g) the record of proceedings during the preliminary inquiry or trial shall include

(i) a transcript of everything that was said during those proceedings in the official language in which it was said,

(ii) a transcript of any interpretation into the other official language of what was said, and

(iii) any documentary evidence that was tendered during those proceedings in the official language in which it was tendered; and

(h) any trial judgment, including any reasons given therefor, issued in writing in either official language, shall be made available by the court in the official language that is the language of the accused. R.S.C. 1985, c. 31 (4th Supp.), s. 94; 2008, c. 18, s. 20.

LANGUAGE USED IN PROCEEDING / Right of the accused.

530.2 (1) If an order is granted directing that an accused be tried before a justice of the peace, provincial court judge, judge or judge and jury who speak both official languages, the justice or judge presiding over a preliminary inquiry or trial may, at the start of the proceeding, make an order setting out the circumstances in which, and the extent to which, the prosecutor and the justice or judge may use each official language.

(2) Any order granted under this section shall, to the extent possible, respect the right of the accused to be tried in his or her official language. 2008, c. 18, s. 21.

CHANGE OF VENUE.

531. Despite any other provision of this Act but subject to any regulations made under section 533, if an order made under section 530 cannot be conveniently complied with in the territorial division in which the offence would otherwise be tried, the court shall, except if that territorial division is in the Province of New Brunswick, order that the trial of the accused be held in another territorial division in the same province. 1977-78, c. 36, s. 1; R.S. 1985, c. 27 (1st Supp.), s. 203; 2008, c. 18, s. 21.

SAVING.

532. Nothing in this Part or the *Official Languages Act* derogates from or otherwise adversely affects any right afforded by a law of a province in force on the coming into force of this Part in that province or thereafter coming into force relating to the language of proceedings or testimony in criminal matters that is not inconsistent with this Part or that Act. 1977-78, c. 36, s. 1.

REGULATIONS.

533. The Lieutenant Governor in Council of a province may make regulations generally for carrying into effect the purposes and provisions of this Part in the province and the Commissioner of Yukon, the Commissioner of the Northwest Territories and the Commissioner of Nunavut may make regulations generally for carrying into effect the purposes and provisions of this Part in Yukon, the Northwest Territories and Nunavut, respectively. 1977-78, c. 36, s. 1; 1993, c. 28, Sch. III, s. 33; 2002, c. 7, s. 144.

534. [*Repealed*, 1997, c. 18, s. 63.]

Part XVIII / PROCEDURE ON PRELIMINARY INQUIRY

Jurisdiction

INQUIRY BY JUSTICE.

535. If an accused who is charged with an indictable offence that is punishable by 14 years or more of imprisonment is before a justice and a request has been made for a preliminary inquiry under subsection 536(4) or 536.1(3), the justice shall, in accordance with this Part, inquire into the charge and any other indictable offence, in respect of the same transaction, founded on the facts that are disclosed by the evidence taken in accordance with this Part. R.S., c. C-34, s. 463; R.S.C. 1985, c. 27 (1st Supp.), s. 96; 2002, c. 13, s. 24; 2019, c. 25, s. 238.

REMAND BY JUSTICE TO PROVINCIAL COURT JUDGE IN CERTAIN CASES / Election before justice — 14 years or more of imprisonment / Election before justice — other indictable offences / Procedure where accused elects trial by provincial court judge / Request for preliminary inquiry / Endorsement on the information — accused referred to in subsection (2) / Endorsement on the information — other accused charged with an offence punishable by 14 years or more of imprisonment / Endorsement on the information — accused referred to in subsection (2.1) / Preliminary inquiry if two or more accused / When no request for preliminary inquiry / Jurisdiction

536. (1) Where an accused is before a justice other than a provincial court judge charged with an offence over which a provincial court judge has absolute jurisdiction under section 553, the justice shall remand the accused to appear before a provincial court judge having jurisdiction in the territorial division in which the offence is alleged to have been committed.

(2) If an accused is before a justice, charged with an indictable offence that is punishable by 14 years or more of imprisonment, other than an offence listed in section 469, the justice shall, after the information has been read to the accused, put the accused to an election in the following words:

> You have the option to elect to be tried by a provincial court judge without a jury and without having had a preliminary inquiry; or you may elect to be tried by a judge without a jury; or you may elect to be tried by a court composed of a judge and jury. If you do not elect now, you are deemed to

have elected to be tried by a court composed of a judge and jury. If you elect to be tried by a judge without a jury or by a court composed of a judge and jury or if you are deemed to have elected to be tried by a court composed of a judge and jury, you will have a preliminary inquiry only if you or the prosecutor requests one. How do you elect to be tried?

(2.1) If an accused is before a justice, charged with an indictable offence — other than an offence that is punishable by 14 years or more of imprisonment, an offence listed in section 469 that is not punishable by 14 years or more of imprisonment or an offence over which a provincial court judge has absolute jurisdiction under section 553 —, the justice shall, after the information has been read to the accused, put the accused to an election in the following words:

You have the option to elect to be tried by a provincial court judge without a jury; or you may elect to be tried by a judge without a jury; or you may elect to be tried by a court composed of a judge and jury. If you do not elect now, you are deemed to have elected to be tried by a court composed of a judge and jury. How do you elect to be tried?

(3) Where an accused elects to be tried by a provincial court judge, the justice shall endorse on the information a record of the election and shall

   (a) where the justice is not a provincial court judge, remand the accused to appear and plead to the charge before a provincial court judge having jurisdiction in the territorial division in which the offence is alleged to have been committed; or

   (b) where the justice is a provincial court judge, call on the accused to plead to the charge and if the accused does not plead guilty, proceed with the trial or fix a time for the trial.

(4) If an accused referred to in subsection (2) elects to be tried by a judge without a jury or by a court composed of a judge and jury or does not elect when put to the election or is deemed under paragraph 565(1)(a) to have elected to be tried by a court composed of a judge and jury, or if an accused is charged with an offence listed in section 469 that is punishable by 14 years or more of imprisonment, the justice shall, subject to section 577, on the request of the accused or the prosecutor made at that time or within the period fixed by rules of court made under section 482 or 482.1 or, if there are no such rules, by the justice, hold a preliminary inquiry into the charge.

(4.1) If an accused referred to in subsection (2) elects to be tried by a judge without a jury or by a court composed of a judge and jury or does not elect when put to the election or is deemed under paragraph 565(1)(a) to have elected to be tried by a court composed of a judge and jury, the justice shall endorse on the information and, if the accused is in custody, on the warrant of remand, a statement showing

   (a) the nature of the election or deemed election of the accused or that the accused did not elect, as the case may be; and

   (b) whether the accused or the prosecutor has requested that a preliminary inquiry be held.

(4.11) If an accused is before a justice, charged with an offence listed in section 469 that is punishable by 14 years or more of imprisonment, the justice shall endorse on the information and, if the accused is in custody, on the warrant of remand, a statement showing whether the accused or the prosecutor has requested that a preliminary inquiry be held.

(4.12) If an accused referred to in subsection (2.1) elects to be tried by a judge without a jury or by a court composed of a judge and jury or does not elect when put to the election or is deemed under paragraph 565(1)(a) to have elected to be tried by a court composed of a judge and jury, the justice shall endorse on the information and, if the accused is in custody, on the warrant of remand, a statement showing the nature of the election or deemed election of the accused or that the accused did not elect, as the case may be.

(4.2) If two or more persons are jointly charged in an information and one or more of them make a request for a preliminary inquiry under subsection (4), a preliminary inquiry must be held with respect to all of them.

(4.3) If no request for a preliminary inquiry is made under subsection (4), the justice shall fix the date for the trial or the date on which the accused must appear in the trial court to have the date fixed.

(5) Where a justice before whom a preliminary inquiry is being or is to be held has not commenced to take evidence, any justice having jurisdiction in the province where the offence with which the accused is charged is alleged to have been committed has jurisdiction for the purposes of subsection (4). R.S., c. C-34, s. 464; R.S.C. 1985, c. 27 (1st Supp.), s. 96; 2002, c. 13, s. 25; 2004, c. 12, s. 9; 2019, c. 25, s. 239(1), (3)-(5).

REMAND BY JUSTICE — NUNAVUT / Election before judge or justice of the peace in Nunavut — 14 years or more of imprisonment / Election before judge or justice of the peace in Nunavut — other indictable offences / Request for preliminary inquiry — Nunavut / Endorsement on the information — accused referred to in subsection (2) / Endorsement on the information — other accused charged with an offence punishable by 14 years or more of imprisonment / Endorsement on the information — accused referred to in subsection (2.1) / Preliminary inquiry if two or more accused / Procedure if accused elects trial by judge — Nunavut / Jurisdiction — Nunavut / Application to Nunavut.

536.1 (1) If an accused is before a justice of the peace charged with an indictable offence mentioned in section 553, the justice of the peace shall remand the accused to appear before a judge.

(2) If an accused is before a judge or justice of the peace, charged with an indictable offence that is punishable by 14 years or more of imprisonment, other than an offence mentioned in section 469, the judge or justice of the peace shall, after the information has been read to the accused, put the accused to an election in the following words:

> You have the option to elect to be tried by a judge without a jury or to be tried by a court composed of a judge and jury. If you do not elect now, you are deemed to have elected to be tried by a court composed of a judge and jury. If you elect to be tried by a judge without a jury or by a court

composed of a judge and jury or if you are deemed to have elected to be tried by a court composed of a judge and jury, you will have a preliminary inquiry only if you or the prosecutor requests one. How do you elect to be tried?

(2.1) If an accused is before a judge or justice of the peace, charged with an indictable offence – other than an offence that is punishable by 14 years or more of imprisonment, an offence listed in section 469 that is not punishable by 14 years or more of imprisonment or an offence mentioned in section 553 –, the judge or justice of the peace shall, after the information has been read to the accused, put the accused to an election in the following words:

You have the option to elect to be tried by a judge without a jury or to be tried by a court composed of a judge and jury. If you do not elect now, you are deemed to have elected to be tried by a court composed of a judge and jury. How do you elect to be tried?

(3) If an accused referred to in subsection (2) elects to be tried by a judge without a jury or by a court composed of a judge and jury or does not elect when put to the election or is deemed under paragraph 565(1)(*a*) to have elected to be tried by a court composed of a judge and jury or if an accused is charged with an offence listed in section 469 that is punishable by 14 years or more of imprisonment, the justice or judge shall, subject to section 577, on the request of the accused or the prosecutor made at that time or within the period fixed by rules of court made under section 482 or 482.1 or, if there are no such rules, by the judge or justice, hold a preliminary inquiry into the charge.

(4) If an accused referred to in subsection (2) elects to be tried by a judge without a jury or by a court composed of a judge and jury or does not elect when put to the election or is deemed under paragraph 565(1)(*a*) to have elected to be tried by a court composed of a judge and jury, the justice or judge shall endorse on the information and, if the accused is in custody, on the warrant of remand, a statement showing

(*a*) the nature of the election or deemed election of the accused or that the accused did not elect, as the case may be; and

(*b*) whether the accused or the prosecutor has requested that a preliminary inquiry be held.

(4.01) If an accused is before a judge or justice of the peace, charged with an offence listed in section 469 that is punishable by 14 years or more of imprisonment, the justice or judge shall endorse on the information and, if the accused is in custody, on the warrant of remand, a statement showing whether the accused or the prosecutor has requested that a preliminary inquiry be held.

(4.02) If an accused referred to in subsection (2.1) elects to be tried by a judge without a jury or by a court composed of a judge and jury or does not elect when put to the election or is deemed under paragraph 565(1)(*a*) to have elected to be tried by a court composed of a judge and jury, the justice shall endorse on the information and, if the accused is in custody, on the warrant of remand, a statement showing the nature of the election or deemed election of the accused or that the accused did not elect, as the case may be.

(4.1) If two or more persons are jointly charged in an information and one or more of them make a request for a preliminary inquiry under subsection (3), a preliminary inquiry must be held with respect to all of them.

(4.2) If no request for a preliminary inquiry is made under subsection (3),

   (a) if the accused is before a justice of the peace, the justice of the peace shall remand the accused to appear and plead to the charge before a judge; or

   (b) if the accused is before a judge, the judge shall

     (i) if the accused elects to be tried by a judge without a jury, call on the accused to plead to the charge and if the accused does not plead guilty, proceed with the trial or fix a time for the trial, or

     (ii) if the accused elects or is deemed to have elected to be tried by a court composed of a judge and jury, fix a time for the trial.

(5) If a justice of the peace before whom a preliminary inquiry is being or is to be held has not commenced to take evidence, any justice of the peace having jurisdiction in Nunavut has jurisdiction for the purpose of subsection (3).

(6) This section, and not section 536, applies in respect of criminal proceedings in Nunavut. 1999, c. 3, s. 35; 2002, c. 13, s. 26; 2004, c. 12, s. 10; 2019, c. 25, s. 240.

ELECTIONS AND RE-ELECTIONS IN WRITING.

536.2 An election or a re-election by an accused in respect of a mode of trial may be made by submission of a document in writing without the personal appearance of the accused. 2002, c. 13, s. 27.

Procedures before Preliminary Inquiry

STATEMENT OF ISSUES AND WITNESSES.

536.3 If a request for a preliminary inquiry is made, the prosecutor or, if the request was made by the accused, counsel for the accused shall, within the period fixed by rules of court made under section 482 or 482.1 or, if there are no such rules, by the justice, provide the court and the other party with a statement that identifies

   (a) the issues on which the requesting party wants evidence to be given at the inquiry; and

   (b) the witnesses that the requesting party wants to hear at the inquiry. 2002, c. 13, s. 27.

ORDER FOR HEARING / Agreement to be recorded.

536.4 (1) The justice before whom a preliminary inquiry is to be held may order, on application of the prosecutor or the accused or on the justice's own motion, that a hearing be held, within the period fixed by rules of court made under section 482 or 482.1 or, if there are no such rules, by the justice, to

   (a) assist the parties to identify the issues on which evidence will be given at the inquiry;

   (b) assist the parties to identify the witnesses to be heard at the inquiry, taking into account the witnesses' needs and circumstances; and

   (c) encourage the parties to consider any other matters that would promote a fair and expeditious inquiry.

(2) When the hearing is completed, the justice shall record any admissions of fact agreed to by the parties and any agreement reached by the parties. 2002, c. 13, s. 27.

AGREEMENT TO LIMIT SCOPE OF PRELIMINARY INQUIRY.

536.5 Whether or not a hearing is held under section 536.4, the prosecutor and the accused may agree to limit the scope of the preliminary inquiry to specific issues. An agreement shall be filed with the court or recorded under subsection 536.4(2), as the case may be. 2002, c. 13, s. 27; 2019, c. 25, s. 241.

Powers of Justice

POWERS OF JUSTICE / Power provided under paragraph (1)(i) / Section 715 or 715.01 / Inappropriate questioning / Change of venue.

537. (1) A justice acting under this Part may

   (a) adjourn an inquiry from time to time and change the place of hearing, where it appears to be desirable to do so by reason of the absence of a witness who is ill to attend at the place where the justice usually sits or for any other sufficient reason;

   (b) remand the accused to custody for the purposes of the *Identification of Criminals Act;*

   (b) [*Repealed* (old provision). 1991, c. 43, s. 9.]

   (c) except where the accused is authorized pursuant to Part XVI to be at large, remand the accused to custody in a prison by warrant in Form 19;

   (d) resume an inquiry before the expiration of a period for which it has been adjourned with the consent of the prosecutor and the accused or his counsel;

   (e) order in writing, in Form 30, that the accused be brought before him, or any other justice for the same territorial division, at any time before the expiration of the time for which the accused has been remanded;

   (f) grant or refuse permission to the prosecutor or his counsel to address him in support of the charge, by way of opening or summing up or by way of reply on any evidence that is given on behalf of the accused;

   (g) receive evidence on the part of the prosecutor or the accused, as the case may be, after hearing any evidence that has been given on behalf of either of them;

   (h) order that no person other than the prosecutor, the accused and their counsel shall have access to or remain in the room in which the inquiry is held, where it appears to him that the ends of justice will be best served by so doing;

(*i*) regulate the course of the inquiry in any way that appears to the justice to be desirable, including to promote a fair and expeditious inquiry, that is consistent with this Act and that, unless the justice is satisfied that to do so would be contrary to the best interests of the administration of justice, is in accordance with any admission of fact or agreement recorded under subsection 536.4(2) or agreement made under section 536.5;

(*j*) if the prosecutor and the accused so agree, permit the accused to appear by counsel or by closed-circuit television or videoconference, for any part of the inquiry other than a part in which the evidence of a witness is taken;

(*j*.1) permit, on the request of the accused, that the accused be out of court during the whole or any part of the inquiry on any conditions that the justice considers appropriate; and

(*k*) require an accused who is confined in prison to appear by closed-circuit television or videoconference, for any part of the inquiry other than a part in which the evidence of a witness is taken, as long as the accused is given the opportunity to communicate privately with counsel if they are represented by counsel.

(1.01) For the purpose of paragraph (1)(*i*), the justice may, among other things, limit the scope of the preliminary inquiry to specific issues and limit the witnesses to be heard on these issues.

(1.02) If a justice grants a request under paragraph (1)(*j*.1), the Court must inform the accused that the evidence taken during their absence could still be admissible under section 715 or 715.01.

(1.1) A justice acting under this Part shall order the immediate cessation of any part of an examination or cross-examination of a witness that is, in the opinion of the justice, abusive, too repetitive or otherwise inappropriate.

(2) [*Repealed* [old provision], 1991, c. 43, s. 9.]

(2) Where a justice changes the place of hearing under paragraph (1)(*a*) to a place in the same province, other than a place in a territorial division in which the justice has jurisdiction, any justice who has jurisdiction in the place to which the hearing is changed may continue the hearing. R.S., c. C-34, s. 465; R.S.,. c. 2 (2nd Supp.), s. 6; 1972, c. 13, s. 38; 1974-75-76, c. 93, s. 58; 1991, c. 43, s. 9; 1994, c. 44, s. 53; 1997, c. 18, s. 64; 2002, c. 13, s. 28; 2008, c. 18, s. 22; 2019, c. 25, s. 242.

(3) and (4) [*Repealed*, 1991, c. 43, s. 9.].

ORGANIZATION.

538. Where an accused is an organization, subsections 556(1) and (2) apply with such modifications as the circumstances require. R.S., c. C-34, s. 466; 2003, c. 21, s. 8

Taking Evidence of Witnesses

ORDER RESTRICTING PUBLICATION OF EVIDENCE TAKEN AT PRELIMINARY INQUIRY / Accused to be informed of right to apply for order / Failure to comply with order / Definition of "newspaper".

539. (1) Prior to the commencement of the taking of evidence at a preliminary inquiry, the justice holding the inquiry

    (*a*) may, if application therefor is made by the prosecutor, and

    (*b*) shall, if application therefor is made by any of the accused,

make an order directing that the evidence taken at the inquiry shall not be published in any document or broadcast or transmitted in any way before such time as, in respect of each of the accused,

    (*c*) he or she is discharged, or

    (*d*) if he or she is ordered to stand trial, the trial is ended.

(2) Where an accused is not represented by counsel at a preliminary inquiry, the justice holding the inquiry shall, prior to the commencement of the taking of evidence at the inquiry, inform the accused of his right to make application under subsection (1).

(3) Everyone who fails to comply with an order made pursuant to subsection (1) is guilty of an offence punishable on summary conviction. R.S., c. C-34, s. 467; R.S.C. 1985, c. 27 (1st Supp.), s. 97; 2005, c. 32, s. 18.

(4) [*Repealed*, 2005, c. 32, s. 18(2).]

TAKING EVIDENCE / Reading and signing depositions / Authentication by justice / Stenographer to be sworn / Authentication of transcript / Transcription of record taken by sound recording apparatus / Evidence / Notice of intention to tender / Appearance for examination.

540. (1) Where an accused is before a justice holding a preliminary inquiry, the justice shall

    (*a*) take the evidence under oath of the witnesses called on the part of the prosecution, subject to subsection 537(1.01), and allow the accused or counsel for the accused to cross-examine them; and

    (*b*) cause a record of the evidence of each witness to be taken

        (i) in legible writing in the form of a deposition, in Form 31, or by a stenographer appointed by him or pursuant to law, or

        (ii) in a province where a sound recording apparatus is authorized by or under provincial legislation for use in civil cases, by the type of apparatus so authorized and in accordance with the requirements of the provincial legislation.

(2) Where a deposition is taken down in writing, the justice shall, in the presence of the accused, before asking the accused if he wishes to call witnesses,

    (*a*) cause the deposition to be read to the witness;

    (*b*) cause the deposition to be signed by the witness; and

    (*c*) sign the deposition himself.

(3) Where depositions are taken down in writing, the justice may sign
  (*a*) at the end of each deposition; or
  (*b*) at the end of several or of all the depositions in a manner that will indicate that his signature is intended to authenticate each deposition.

(4) Where a stenographer appointed to take down the evidence is not a duly sworn court stenographer, he shall make oath that he will truly and faithfully report the evidence.

(5) Where the evidence is taken down by a stenographer appointed by the justice or pursuant to law, it need not be read to or signed by the witnesses, but, on request of the justice or of one of the parties, shall be transcribed, in whole or in part, by the stenographer and the transcript shall be accompanied by
  (*a*) an affidavit of the stenographer that it is a true report of the evidence; or
  (*b*) a certificate that it is a true report of the evidence if the stenographer is a duly sworn court stenographer.

(6) Where, in accordance with this Act, a record is record taken in any proceedings under this Act by a sound recording apparatus, the record so taken shall, on request of the justice or of one of the parties, be dealt with and transcribed, in whole or in part, and the transcription certified and used in accordance with the provincial legislation, with such modifications as the circumstances require mentioned in subsection (1).

(7) A justice acting under this Part may receive as evidence any information that would not otherwise be admissible but that the justice considers credible or trustworthy in the circumstances of the case, including a statement that is made by a witness in writing or otherwise recorded.

(8) Unless the justice orders otherwise, no information may be received as evidence under subsection (7) unless the party has given to each of the other parties reasonable notice of his or her intention to tender it, together with a copy of the statement, if any, referred to in that subsection.

(9) The justice shall, on application of a party, require any person whom the justice considers appropriate to appear for examination or cross-examination with respect to information intended to be tendered as evidence under subsection (7). R.S., c. C-34, s. 468; R.S.C. 1985, c. 27 (1st Supp.), s. 98; 1997, c. 18, s. 65; 2002, c. 13, s. 29; 2019, c. 25, s. 243.

HEARING OF WITNESSES / Contents of address to accused / Statement of accused / Witnesses for accused / Depositions of witnesses.

541. (1) When the evidence of the witnesses called on the part of the prosecution has been taken down and, if required by this Part, has been read, the justice shall, subject to this section and subsection 537(1.01), hear the witnesses called by the accused.

(2) Before hearing any witness called by an accused who is not represented by counsel, the justice shall address the accused as follows or to the like effect:

"Do you wish to say anything in answer to these charges or to any other charges which might have arisen from the evidence led by the prosecution? You are not obliged to say anything, but whatever you do say may be given in evidence against you at your trial. You should not make any confession or admission of guilt because of any promise or threat made to you but if you do make any statement it may be given in evidence against you at your trial in spite of the promise or threat."

(3) Where the accused who is not represented by counsel says anything in answer to the address made by the justice pursuant to subsection (2), the answer shall be taken down in writing and shall be signed by the justice and kept with the evidence of the witnesses and dealt with in accordance with this Part.

(4) Where an accused is not represented by counsel, the justice shall ask the accused if he or she wishes to call any witnesses after subsections (2) and (3) have been complied with.

(5) Subject to subsection 537(1.01), the justice shall hear each witness called by the accused who testifies to any matter relevant to the inquiry, and for the purposes of this subsection, section 540 applies with any modifications that the circumstances require. R.S., c. C-34, s. 469; R.S.C. 1985, c. 27 (1st Supp.), s. 99; 1994, c. 44, s. 54; 2019, c. 25, s. 244.

CONFESSION OR ADMISSION OF ACCUSED / Restriction of publication of reports of preliminary inquiry / Definition of "newspaper".

542. (1) Nothing in this Act prevents a prosecutor giving in evidence at a preliminary inquiry any admission, confession or statement made at any time by the accused that by law is admissible against him.

(2) Every one who publishes in any document, or broadcasts or transmits in any way, a report that any admission or confession was tendered in evidence at a preliminary inquiry or a report of the nature of such admission or confession so tendered in evidence unless

    (*a*) the accused has been discharged, or

    (*b*) if the accused has been ordered to stand trial, the trial has ended,

is guilty of an offence punishable on summary conviction. R.S., c. C-34, s. 470; R.S.C. 1985, c. 27 (1st Supp.), s. 101(2)(*c*); 2005, c. 32, s. 19.

(3) [*Repealed*, 2005, c. 32, s. 19(2).]

Remand Where Offence Committed in Another Jurisdiction

ORDER THAT ACCUSED APPEAR OR BE TAKEN BEFORE JUSTICE WHERE OFFENCE ALLEGED TO HAVE BEEN COMMITTED / Transmission of transcript and documents and effect of order or warrant.

543. (1) If an accused is charged with an offence alleged to have been committed out of the limits of the jurisdiction in which they have been charged, the justice before whom they appear or are brought may, at any stage of the inquiry after hearing both parties, order the accused to appear or, if the accused is in custody, issue a warrant in Form 15 to convey the accused before a justice who, having jurisdiction in the place where the offence is alleged to have been committed, shall continue and complete the inquiry.

(2) Where a justice makes an order or issues a warrant pursuant to subsection (1), he shall cause the transcript of any evidence given before him in the inquiry and all documents that were then before him and that are relevant to the inquiry to be transmitted to a justice having jurisdiction in the place where the offence is alleged to have been committed and

 (a) any evidence the transcript of which is so transmitted shall be deemed to have been taken by the justice to whom it is transmitted; and

 (b) any appearance notice, undertaking or release order issued to or given or entered into by the accused shall be deemed to have been issued, given or entered into in the jurisdiction where the offence is alleged to have been committed and to require the accused to appear before the justice to whom the transcript and documents are transmitted at the time provided in the order made in respect of the accused under paragraph (1)(a). R.S., c. C-34, s. 471; R.S., c. 2 (2nd Supp.), s. 7; 2019, c. 25, s. 245.

Absconding Accused

ACCUSED ABSCONDING DURING INQUIRY / Adverse inference / Accused not entitled to re-opening / Counsel for accused may continue to act / Accused calling witnesses.

544. (1) Notwithstanding any other provision of this Act, where an accused, whether or not he is charged jointly with another, absconds during the course of a preliminary inquiry into an offence with which he is charged,

 (a) he shall be deemed to have waived his right to be present at the inquiry, and

 (b) the justice

 (i) may continue the inquiry and, when all the evidence has been taken, shall dispose of the inquiry in accordance with section 548, or

 (ii) if a warrant is issued for the arrest of the accused, may adjourn the inquiry to await his appearance,

but where the inquiry is adjourned pursuant to subparagraph (b)(ii), the justice may continue it at any time pursuant to subparagraph (b)(i) if he is satisfied that it would no longer be in the interests of justice to await the appearance of the accused.

(2) Where the justice continues a preliminary inquiry pursuant to subsection (1), he may draw an inference adverse to the accused from the fact that he has absconded.

(3) Where an accused reappears at a preliminary inquiry that is continuing pursuant to subsection (1), he is not entitled to have any part of the proceedings that was conducted in his absence re-opened unless the justice is satisfied that because of exceptional circumstances it is in the interests of justice to re-open the inquiry.

(4) Where the accused has absconded during the course of a preliminary inquiry and the justice continues the inquiry, counsel for the accused is not thereby

deprived of any authority he may have to continue to act for the accused in the proceedings.

(5) If, at the conclusion of the evidence on the part of the prosecution at a preliminary inquiry that has been continued under subsection (1), the accused is absent but their counsel is present, the counsel shall be given an opportunity to call witnesses on behalf of the accused, subject to subsection 537(1.01), and subsection 541(5) applies with any modifications that the circumstances require. 1974-75-76, c. 93, s. 59; 1994, c. 44, s. 55; 2019, c. 25, s. 246.

Procedure Where Witness Refuses to Testify

WITNESS REFUSING TO BE EXAMINED / Further commitment / Saving.

545. (1) Where a person, being present at a preliminary inquiry and being required by the justice to give evidence,

    (*a*) refuses to be sworn,

    (*b*) having been sworn, refuses to answer the questions that are put to him,

    (*c*) fails to produce any writings that he is required to produce, or

    (*d*) refuses to sign his deposition,

without offering a reasonable excuse for his failure or refusal, the justice may adjourn the inquiry and may, by warrant in Form 20, commit the person to prison for a period not exceeding eight clear days or for the period during which the inquiry is adjourned, whichever is the lesser period.

(2) Where a person to whom subsection (1) applies is brought before the justice upon the resumption of the adjourned inquiry and again refuses to do what is required of him, the justice may again adjourn the inquiry for a period not exceeding eight clear days and commit him to prison for the period of adjournment or any part thereof, and may adjourn the inquiry and commit the person to prison from time to time until the person consents to do what is required of him.

(3) Nothing in this section shall be deemed to prevent the justice from sending the case for trial on any other sufficient evidence taken by him. R.S., c. C-34, s. 472.

Remedial Provisions

IRREGULARITY OR VARIANCE NOT TO AFFECT VALIDITY.

546. The validity of any proceeding at or subsequent to a preliminary inquiry is not affected by

    (*a*) any irregularity or defect in the substance or form of the summons or warrant;

    (*b*) any variance between the charge set out in the summons or warrant and the charge set out in the information; or

    (*c*) any variance between the charge set out in the summons, warrant or information and the evidence adduced by the prosecution at the inquiry. R.S., c. C-34, s. 473.

ADJOURNMENT IF ACCUSED MISLED.

547. Where it appears to the justice that the accused has been deceived or misled by any irregularity, defect or variance mentioned in section 546, he may adjourn the inquiry and may remand the accused or grant him interim release in accordance with Part XVI. R.S., c. C-34, s. 474; 1974-75-76, c. 93, s. 59.1.

INABILITY OF JUSTICE TO CONTINUE.

547.1 Where a justice acting under this Part has commenced to take evidence and dies or is unable to continue for any reason, another justice may

    (*a*) continue taking the evidence at the point at which the interruption in the taking of the evidence occurred, where the evidence was recorded pursuant to section 540 and is available; or

    (*b*) commence taking the evidence as if no evidence had been taken, where no evidence was recorded pursuant to section 540 or where the evidence is not available. R.S.C. 1985, c. 27 (1st Supp.), s. 100.

Adjudication and Recognizances

ORDER TO STAND TRIAL OR DISCHARGE / Endorsing charge / Where accused ordered to stand trial / Defect not to affect validity.

548. (1) When all the evidence has been taken by the justice, he shall

    (*a*) if in his opinion there is sufficient evidence to put the accused on trial for the offence charged or any other indictable offence in respect of the same transaction, order the accused to stand trial; or

    (*b*) discharge the accused, if in his opinion on the whole of the evidence no sufficient case is made out to put the accused on trial for the offence charged or any other indictable offence in respect of the same transaction.

(2) Where the justice orders the accused to stand trial for an indictable offence, other than or in addition to the one with which the accused was charged, the justice shall endorse on the information the charges on which he orders the accused to stand trial.

(2.1) A justice who orders that an accused is to stand trial has the power to fix the date for the trial or the date on which the accused must appear in the trial court to have that date fixed.

(3) The validity of an order to stand trial is not affected by any defect apparent on the face of the information in respect of which the preliminary inquiry is held or in respect of any charge on which the accused is ordered to stand trial unless, in the opinion of the court before which an objection to the information or charge is taken, the accused has been misled or prejudiced in his defence by reason of that defect. R.S., c. C-34, s. 475; R.S., c. 2 (2nd Supp.), s. 8; R.S.C. 1985, c. 27 (1st Supp.), s. 101(1); 1994, c. 44, s. 56.

ORDER TO STAND TRIAL AT ANY STAGE OF INQUIRY WITH CONSENT / Limited preliminary inquiry / Procedure.

549. (1) Notwithstanding any other provision of this Act, the justice may, at any stage of a preliminary inquiry, with the consent of the accused and the prosecutor, order the accused to stand trial in the court having criminal jurisdiction, without taking or recording any evidence or further evidence.

(1.1) If the prosecutor and the accused agree under section 536.5 to limit the scope of a preliminary inquiry to specific issues, the justice, without taking or recording evidence on any other issues, may order the accused to stand trial in the court having criminal jurisdiction.

(2) If an accused is ordered to stand trial under this section, the justice shall endorse on the information a statement of the consent of the accused and the prosecutor, and the accused shall after that be dealt with in all respects as if ordered to stand trial under section 548. R.S., c. C-34, s. 476; R.S.C. 1985, c. 27 (1st Supp.), s. 101(3); 2002, c. 13, s. 30; 2019, c. 25, s. 247.

RECOGNIZANCE OF WITNESS / Clarification / Sureties or deposit for appearance of witness / Witness refusing to be bound / Discharge.

550. (1) Where an accused is ordered to stand trial, the justice who held the preliminary inquiry may require any witness whose evidence is, in his opinion, material to enter into a recognizance to give evidence at the trial of the accused and to comply with such reasonable conditions prescribed in the recognizance as the justice considers desirable for securing the attendance of the witness to give evidence at the trial of the accused.

(2) A recognizance entered into under this section may be set out at the end of a deposition or be separate from it.

(3) A justice may, for any reason satisfactory to him, require any witness entering into a recognizance pursuant to this section

    (a) to produce one or more sureties in such amount as he may direct; or

    (b) to deposit with him a sum of money sufficient in his opinion to ensure that the witness will appear and give evidence.

(4) Where a witness does not comply with subsection (1) or (3) when required to do so by a justice, he may be committed by the justice, by warrant in Form 24, to a prison in the territorial division where the trial is to be held, there to be kept until he does what is required of him or until the trial is concluded.

(5) Where a witness has been committed to prison pursuant to subsection (4), the court before which the witness appears or a justice having jurisdiction in the territorial division where the prison is situated may, by order in Form 39, discharge the witness from custody when the trial is concluded. R.S., c. C-34, s. 477; 1974-75-76, c. 39, s. 60; R.S.C. 1985, c. 27 (1st Supp.), s. 101(3); 2019, c. 25, s. 248.

Transmission of Record

TRANSMISSION OF RECORD BY JUSTICE.

551. If a justice orders an accused to stand trial, the justice shall immediately send to the clerk or other proper officer of the court by which the accused is to be tried, any information, evidence, exhibits, or statement of the accused taken down in writing in accordance with section 541, any appearance notice, undertaking or release order given by or issued to the accused and any evidence taken before a coroner that is in the possession of the justice. R.S., c. C-34, s. 478; R.S., c. 2 (2nd Supp.), s. 9; R.S.C. 1985, c. 27 (1st Supp.), s. 102; 2019, c. 25, s. 249.

PART XVIII.1 / CASE MANAGEMENT JUDGE

APPOINTMENT / Conference or hearing / Same judge.

551.1 (1) On application by the prosecutor or the accused or on his or her own motion, the Chief Justice or the Chief Judge of the court before which a trial is to be or is being held or the judge that the Chief Justice or the Chief Judge designates may, if he or she is of the opinion that it is necessary for the proper administration of justice, appoint a judge as the case management judge for that trial at any time before the jury selection, if the trial is before a judge and jury, or before the stage at which the evidence on the merits is presented, if the trial is being heard by a judge without a jury or a provincial court judge.

(2) The Chief Justice or the Chief Judge or his or her designate may order that a conference between the prosecutor and the accused or counsel for the accused or a hearing be held for the purpose of deciding if it is necessary for the proper administration of justice to proceed with the appointment.

(3) [*Repealed*, 2019, c. 25, s. 250.]

(4) The appointment of a judge as the case management judge does not prevent him or her from becoming the judge who hears the evidence on the merits. 2011, c. 16, s. 4; 2019, c. 25, s. 250.

ROLE.

551.2 The case management judge shall assist in promoting a fair and efficient trial, including by ensuring that the evidence on the merits is presented, to the extent possible, without interruption. 2011, c. 16, s. 4.

POWERS BEFORE EVIDENCE ON MERITS PRESENTED / Hearing / Power exercised at trial / Decision binding.

551.3 (1) In performing their duties before the stage of the presentation of the evidence on the merits, the case management judge, as a trial judge, exercises the powers that a trial judge has before that stage in order to assist in promoting a fair and efficient trial, including by

(a) assisting the parties to identify the witnesses to be heard, taking into account the witnesses' needs and circumstances;

(b) encouraging the parties to make admissions and reach agreements;

(c) encouraging the parties to consider any other matters that would promote a fair and efficient trial;

(d) establishing schedules and imposing deadlines on the parties;

(e) hearing guilty pleas and imposing sentences;

(f) assisting the parties to identify the issues that are to be dealt with at the stage at which the evidence on the merits is presented;

(g) subject to section 551.7, adjudicating any issues that can be decided before that stage, including those related to

   (i) the disclosure of evidence,

   (ii) the admissibility of evidence,

   (iii) the *Canadian Charter of Rights and Freedoms*,

   (iv) expert witnesses,

   (v) the severance of counts, and

   (vi) the separation of trials on one or more counts when there is more than one accused; and

(h) ordering, in each case set out in subsection 599(1), that the trial be held in a territorial division in the same province other than that in which the offence would otherwise be tried.

(2) The case management judge shall order that a hearing be held for the purpose of exercising the power referred to in paragraph (1)(g).

(3) When the case management judge exercises the power referred to in paragraph (1)(g), he or she is doing so at trial.

(4) A decision that results from the exercise of the power referred to in paragraph (1)(g) is binding on the parties for the remainder of the trial — even if the judge who hears the evidence on the merits is not the same as the case management judge — unless the court is satisfied that it would not be in the interests of justice because, among other considerations, fresh evidence has been adduced. 2011, c. 16, s. 4; 2019, c. 25, s. 251.

INFORMATION RELEVANT TO PRESENTATION OF EVIDENCE ON MERITS TO BE PART OF COURT RECORD / Exception.

551.4 (1) When the case management judge is of the opinion that the measures to promote a fair and efficient trial that can be taken before the stage of the presentation of the evidence on the merits have been taken — including adjudicating the issues that can be decided — he or she shall ensure that the court record includes information that, in his or her opinion, may be relevant at the stage of the presentation of the evidence on the merits, including

(a) the names of the witnesses to be heard that have been identified by the parties;

(b) any admissions made and agreements reached by the parties;

(c) the estimated time required to conclude the trial;

(d) any orders and decisions; and

(*e*) any issues identified by the parties that are to be dealt with at the stage of the presentation of the evidence on the merits.

(2) This section does not apply to a case management judge who also hears the evidence on the merits. 2011, c. 16, s. 4.

TRIAL CONTINUOUS.

551.5 Even if the judge who hears the evidence on the merits is not the same as the case management judge, the trial of an accused shall proceed continuously, subject to adjournment by the court. 2011, c. 16, s. 4.

ISSUES REFERRED TO CASE MANAGEMENT JUDGE / Powers at stage of presentation of evidence on merits.

551.6 (1) During the presentation of the evidence on the merits, the case management judge shall adjudicate any issue referred to him or her by the judge hearing the evidence on the merits.

(2) For the purposes of adjudicating an issue, the case management judge may exercise the powers of a trial judge. 2011, c. 16, s. 4.

DECISION WHETHER TO HOLD JOINT HEARING / Considerations / Order for joint hearing / Limitation — indictable offence / Order in court record and transmission to parties / Transmission of court record / Order to appear at joint hearing / Removal of prisoner / Powers of judge / Adjudication at trial / Decision in court records and return of documents.

551.7 (1) If an issue referred to in any of subparagraphs 551.3(1)(*g*)(i) to (iii) is to be adjudicated in related trials that are to be or are being held in the same province before a court of the same jurisdiction, the Chief Justice or the Chief Judge of that court or his or her designate may, on application by the prosecutor or the accused or on his or her own motion, determine if it is in the interests of justice, including ensuring consistent decisions, to adjudicate that issue at a joint hearing for some or all of those trials.

(2) To make the determination, the Chief Justice or the Chief Judge or his or her designate
   (*a*) shall take into account, among other considerations, the degree to which the evidence relating to the issue is similar in the related trials; and
   (*b*) may order that a conference between the prosecutor and the accused or counsel for the accused or a hearing be held.

(3) If the Chief Justice or the Chief Judge or his or her designate determines that it is in the interests of justice to adjudicate the issue at a joint hearing for some or all of the related trials, he or she shall issue an order
   (*a*) declaring that a joint hearing be held to adjudicate the issue in the related trials that he or she specifies;
   (*b*) naming the parties who are to appear at the hearing;
   (*c*) appointing a judge to adjudicate the issue; and

(d) designating the territorial division in which the hearing is to be held, if the trials are being held in different territorial divisions.

(4) However, the order may only be made in respect of a trial for an indictable offence, other than a trial before a provincial court judge, if the indictment has been preferred.

(5) The Chief Justice or the Chief Judge or his or her designate shall cause a copy of the order to be included in the court record of each of the trials specified in the order and to be provided to each of the parties named in it.

(6) If one of the specified trials is being held in a territorial division other than the one in which the joint hearing will be held, the officer in that territorial division who has custody of the indictment or information and the writings relating to the trial shall, when he or she receives the order, transmit the indictment or information and the writings without delay to the clerk of the court before which the joint hearing is to be held.

(7) The judge appointed under the order shall require the parties who are named in it to appear at the joint hearing.

(8) The order made under subsection (2) or (3) is sufficient warrant, justification and authority to all sheriffs, keepers of prisons and peace officers for an accused's removal, disposal and reception in accordance with the terms of the order, and the sheriff may appoint and authorize any peace officer to convey the accused to a prison for the territorial division in which the hearing, as the case may be, is to be held.

(9) The judge appointed under the order may, as a trial judge and for the purpose of adjudicating the issue at the joint hearing, exercise the powers of a trial judge.

(10) When the judge adjudicates the issue, he or she is doing so at trial.

(11) Once the judge has adjudicated the issue, he or she shall cause his or her decision, with reasons, to be included in the court record of each of the related trials in respect of which the joint hearing was held and, in the case of a trial for which an indictment, information or writings were transmitted by an officer under subsection (6), the judge shall have the documents returned to the officer. 2011, c. 16, s. 4.

Part XIX / INDICTABLE OFFENCES — TRIAL WITHOUT JURY

Interpretation

DEFINITIONS / "Judge".

552. In this Part,

"judge" means,

    (a) in the Province of Ontario, a judge of the superior court of criminal jurisdiction of the Province,

(b) in the Province of Quebec, a judge of the Court of Quebec,

(c) in the Province of Nova Scotia, a judge of the superior court of criminal jurisdiction of the Province,

(d) in the Province of New Brunswick, a judge of the Court of Queen's Bench,

(e) in the Province of British Columbia, the Chief Justice or a puisne judge of the Supreme Court,

(f) in the Province of Prince Edward Island, a judge of the Supreme Court,

(g) in the Province of Manitoba, the Chief Justice or a puisne judge of the Court of Queen's Bench,

(h) in the Provinces of Saskatchewan and Alberta, a judge of the superior court of criminal jurisdiction of the province,

(h.1) in the Province of Newfoundland and Labrador, a judge of the Trial Division of the Supreme Court,

(i) in Yukon and the Northwest Territories, a judge of the Supreme Court, and

(j) in Nunavut, a judge of the Nunavut Court of Justice. R.S., c. C-34, s. 482; 1972, c. 13, s. 39, c. 17, s. 2; 1974-75-76, c. 48, s. 25, c. 93, s. 61; 1978-79, c. 11, s. 10; R.S.C. 1985, c. 11 (1st Supp.), s. 2, c. 27 (1st Supp.), s. 103(1); c. 27 (2nd Supp.), s. 10; c. 40 (4th Supp.), s. 2; 1990, c. 16, s. 6; 1990, c. 17, s. 13; 1992, c. 51, s. 38; 1993, c. 28, Sch. III, s. 34 (repealed 1999, c. 3, s. 12); 1999, c. 3, ss. 12, 36; 2002, c. 7, s. 145; 2015, c. 3, s. 53.

"magistrate". [*Repealed*, R.S.C. 1985, c. 27 (1st Supp.), s. 103(2).]

JURISDICTION OF PROVINCIAL COURT JUDGES

Absolute Jurisdiction

ABSOLUTE JURISDICTION.

553. The jurisdiction of a provincial court judge, or in Nunavut, of a judge of the Nunavut Court of Justice, to try an accused is absolute and does not depend on the consent of the accused where the accused is charged in an information

(a) with

(i) theft, other than theft of cattle,

(ii) obtaining money or property by false pretences,

(iii) unlawfully having in his possession any property or thing or any proceeds of any property or thing knowing that all or a part of the property or thing or of the proceeds was obtained by or derived directly or indirectly from the commission in Canada of an offence punishable by indictment or an act or omission anywhere that, if it had occurred in Canada, would have constituted an offence punishable by indictment,

(iv) having, by deceit, falsehood or other fraudulent means, defrauded the public or any person, whether ascertained or not, of any property, money or valuable security, or

(v) mischief under subsection 430(4),

where the subject-matter of the offence is not a testamentary instrument and the alleged value of the subject-matter of the offence does not exceed five thousand dollars;

(b) with counselling or with a conspiracy or attempt to commit or with being an accessory after the fact to the commission of

   (i) any offence referred to in paragraph (a) in respect of the subject-matter and value thereof referred to in that paragraph, or

   (ii) any offence referred to in paragraph (c); or

(c) with an offence under

   (i) section 201 (keeping gaming or betting house),

   (ii) section 202 (betting, pool-selling, book-making, etc.),

   (iii) section 203 (placing bets),

   (iv) section 206 (lotteries and games of chance),

   (v) section 209 (cheating at play),

   (vi) [*Repealed*, 2019, c. 25, s. 251.1.]

   (vii) [*Repealed*, 2000, c. 25, s. 4.]

   (viii) section 393 (fraud in relation to fares),

   (viii.01) section 490.031 (failure to comply with order or obligation),

   (viii.02) section 490.0311 (providing false or misleading information),

   (viii.1) section 811 (breach of recognizance),

   (ix) subsection 733.1(1) (failure to comply with probation order), or

   (x) paragraph 4(4)(a) of the *Controlled Drugs and Substances Act*. R.S., c. C-34, s. 483; 1972, c. 13, s. 40; 1974-75-76, c. 93, s. 62; R.S.C. 1985, c. 27 (1st Supp.), s. 104; 1992, c. 1, s. 58; 1994, c. 44, s. 57; 1995, c. 22, s. 2; 1996, c. 19, s. 72; 1997, c. 18, s. 66; 1999, c. 3, s. 37; 2000, c. 25, s. 4; 2010, c. 17, s. 25; 2012, c. 1, s. 33, 2018, c. 16, s. 219; 2019, c. 25, s. 251.1.

   (xi) [*Repealed*, 2018, c. 16, s. 219.]

Provincial Court Judge's Jurisdiction with Consent

TRIAL BY PROVINCIAL COURT JUDGE WITH CONSENT / Nunavut.

554. (1) Subject to subsection (2), if an accused is charged in an information with an indictable offence other than an offence that is mentioned in section 469, and the offence is not one over which a provincial court judge has absolute jurisdiction under section 553, a provincial court judge may try the accused if the accused elects to be tried by a provincial court judge.

(2) With respect to criminal proceedings in Nunavut, if an accused is charged in an information with an indictable offence other than an offence that is mentioned in section 469 and the offence is not one over which a judge of the Nunavut Court of Justice has absolute jurisdiction under section 553, a judge of the Nunavut Court of Justice may try the accused if the accused elects to be tried by a judge without a jury. R.S., c. C-34, s. 484; R.S.C. 1985, c. 27 (1st Supp.), s. 105; 1999, c. 3, s. 38; 2002, c 13, s. 31.

IF CHARGE SHOULD BE PROSECUTED BY INDICTMENT / Election before justice / Continuing proceedings / If subject matter is testamentary instrument or exceeds $5,000 in value / Continuing proceedings.

555. (1) If in any proceedings under this Part an accused is before a provincial court judge and it appears to the provincial court judge that for any reason the charge should be prosecuted in superior court, the provincial court judge may, at any time before the accused has entered a defence, decide not to adjudicate and shall then inform the accused of the decision.

(1.1) If the provincial court judge has decided not to adjudicate, the judge shall put the accused to an election in the following words:

You have the option to elect to be tried by a superior court judge without a jury or you may elect to be tried by a court composed of a judge and jury. If you do not elect now, you are deemed to have elected to be tried by a court composed of a judge and jury. If you elect to be tried by a judge without a jury or by a court composed of a judge and jury or if you are deemed to have elected to be tried by a court composed of a judge and jury, you will have a preliminary inquiry only if you are entitled to one and you or the prosecutor requests one. How do you elect to be tried?

(1.2) If the accused is entitled to a preliminary inquiry and they or the prosecutor requests one, the provincial court judge shall continue the proceedings as a preliminary inquiry.

(2) If an accused is before a provincial court judge, charged with an offence prosecuted by indictment mentioned in paragraph 553(*a*) or subparagraph 553(*b*)(i), and, at any time before the provincial court judge makes an adjudication, the evidence establishes that the subject matter of the offence is a testamentary instrument or that its value exceeds $5,000, the provincial court judge shall put the accused to their election in accordance with subsection 536(2.1).

(3) If an accused is put to their election under subsection (1.1) or (2), the following provisions apply:
- (*a*) if the accused elects to be tried by a superior court judge without a jury or a court composed of a judge and jury or does not elect when put to their election, the provincial court judge shall endorse on the information a record of the nature of the election or deemed election; and
- (*b*) if the accused elects to be tried by a provincial court judge, the provincial court judge shall endorse on the information a record of the election and continue with the trial. R.S., c. C-34, s. 485; 1972, c. 13, s. 41; R.S.C. 1985, c. 27 (1st Supp.), s. 106; 1994, c. 44, s. 58; 2002, c. 13, s. 32; 2019, c. 25, s. 252.

IF CHARGE SHOULD BE PROSECUTED BY INDICTMENT — NUNAVUT / Election before justice / Continuing proceedings / If subject-matter is testamentary instrument or exceeds $5,000 in value — Nunavut / Continuing proceedings — Nunavut / Application to Nunavut.

555.1 (1) If in any criminal proceedings under this Part an accused is before a judge of the Nunavut Court of Justice and it appears to the judge that for any reason the charge should be prosecuted by indictment, the judge may, at any time before the accused has entered a defence, decide not to adjudicate and shall then inform the accused of the decision.

(1.1) If the judge has decided not to adjudicate, the judge shall put the accused to an election in the following words:

> You have the option to elect to be tried by a judge without a jury or to be tried by a court composed of a judge and jury. If you do not elect now, you are deemed to have elected to be tried by a court composed of a judge and jury. If you elect to be tried by a judge without a jury or by a court composed of a judge and jury or if you are deemed to have elected to be tried by a court composed of a judge and jury, you will have a preliminary inquiry only if you are entitled to one and you or the prosecutor requests one. How do you elect to be tried?

(1.2) If the accused is entitled to a preliminary inquiry and they or the prosecutor requests one, the judge shall endorse on the information a record of the nature of the election or deemed election and continue the proceedings as a preliminary inquiry.

(2) If an accused is before a judge of the Nunavut Court of Justice, charged with an offence prosecuted by indictment mentioned in paragraph 553(*a*) or subparagraph 553(*b*)(i), and, at any time before the judge makes an adjudication, the evidence establishes that the subject matter of the offence is a testamentary instrument or that its value exceeds $5,000, the judge shall put the accused to their election in accordance with subsection 536.1(2.1).

(3) If an accused is put to their election under subsection (1.1) and no preliminary inquiry is requested, or is put to an election under subsection (2), and elects to be tried by a judge without a jury or a court composed of a judge and jury or does not elect when put to the election, the judge shall endorse on the information a record of the nature of the election or deemed election and continue with the trial.

(4) This section, and not section 555, applies in respect of criminal proceedings in Nunavut. 1999, c. 3, s. 39; 2002, c. 13, s. 33; 2019, c. 25, s. 253.

(5) [*Repealed*, 2019, c. 25, s. 253.]

ORGANIZATION / Non-appearance / Preliminary inquiry not requested / Preliminary inquiry not requested — Nunavut.

556. (1) An accused organization shall appear by counsel or agent.

(2) Where an accused organization does not appear pursuant to a summons and service of the summons on the organization is proved, the provincial court judge or, in Nunavut, the judge of the Nunavut Court of Justice

   (*a*) may, if the charge is one over which the judge has absolute jurisdiction, proceed with the trial of the charge in the absence of the accused organization; and

   (*b*) shall, if the charge is not one over which the judge has absolute jurisdiction, fix the date for the trial or the date on which the accused organization must appear in the trial court to have that date fixed.

(3) If an accused organization appears and a preliminary inquiry is not requested under subsection 536(4), the provincial court judge shall fix the date for the trial or the date on which the organization must appear in the trial court to have that date fixed.

(4) If an accused organization appears and a preliminary inquiry is not requested under subsection 536.1(3), the justice of the peace or the judge of the Nunavut Court of Justice shall fix the date for the trial or the date on which the organization must appear in the trial court to have that date fixed. R.S., c. C-34, s. 486; R.S.C. 1985, c. 27 (1st Supp.), s. 107; 1999, c. 3, s. 40; 2002, c. 13, s. 34; 2003, c. 21, ss. 9, 22.

CODE

TAKING EVIDENCE.

557. If an accused is tried by a provincial court judge or a judge of the Nunavut Court of Justice in accordance with this Part, the evidence of witnesses for the prosecutor and the accused must be taken in accordance with the provisions of Part XVIII, other than subsections 540(7) to (9), relating to preliminary inquiries. R.S., c. C-34, s. 487; 1999, c. 30, s. 41; 2002, c. 13, s. 35.

JURISDICTION OF JUDGES

Judge's Jurisdiction with Consent

TRIAL BY JUDGE WITHOUT A JURY.

558. If an accused who is charged with an indictable offence, other than an offence mentioned in section 469, elects under section 536 or 536.1 or re-elects under section 561 or 561.1 to be tried by a judge without a jury, the accused shall, subject to this Part, be tried by a judge without a jury. R.S., c. C-34, s. 488; R.S.C. 1985, c. 27 (1st Supp.), s. 108; 1999, c. 3, s. 41.

COURT OF RECORD / Custody of records.

559. (1) A judge who holds a trial under this Part shall, for all purposes thereof and proceedings connected therewith or relating thereto, be a court of record.

(2) The record of a trial that a judge holds under this Part shall be kept in the court over which the judge presides. R.S., c. C-34, s. 489.

Election

DUTY OF JUDGE / Notice by sheriff, when given / Duty of sheriff when date set for trial / Duty of accused when not in custody.

560. (1) If an accused elects, under section 536 or 536.1, to be tried by a judge without a jury, a judge having jurisdiction shall (*a*) on receiving a written notice from the sheriff or other person having custody of the accused stating that the accused is in custody and setting out the nature of the charge against him, or

    (*b*) on being notified by the clerk of the court that the accused is not in custody and of the nature of the charge against him,

fix a time and place for the trial of the accused.

(2) The sheriff or other person having custody of the accused shall give the notice mentioned in paragraph (1)(*a*) within twenty-four hours after the accused is ordered to stand trial, if the accused is in custody pursuant to that order or if, at the time of the order, he is in custody for any other reason.

(3) Where, pursuant to subsection (1), a time and place is fixed for the trial of an accused who is in custody, the accused

    (*a*) shall be notified forthwith by the sheriff or other person having custody of the accused of the time and place so fixed, and

    (*b*) shall be produced at the time and place so fixed.

(4) Where an accused is not in custody, the duty of ascertaining from the clerk of the court the time and place fixed for the trial, pursuant to subsection (1), is on the accused, and he shall attend for his trial at the time and place so fixed. R.S., c. C-34, s. 490; R.S.C. 1985, c. 27 (1st Supp.), ss. 101(3), 109(1); 1999, c. 3, s. 42; 2002, c. 13, s. 36.

(5) [*Repealed.* R.S.C. 1985, *c*.27 (1st Supp.), *s*. 109(2).]

RIGHT TO RE-ELECT / Right to re-elect / Notice of re-election under paragraph (1)(*a*) / Notice of re-election under paragraph (1)(*b*) or subsection (2) / Notice and transmitting record / Time and place for re-election / Proceedings on re-election.

561. (1) An accused who elects or is deemed to have elected a mode of trial other than trial by a provincial court judge may re-elect,

    (*a*) if the accused is charged with an offence for which a preliminary inquiry has been requested under subsection 536(4),

        (i) at any time before or after the completion of the preliminary inquiry, with the written consent of the prosecutor, to be tried by a provincial court judge,

        (ii) at any time before the completion of the preliminary inquiry or before the 60th day following the completion of the preliminary inquiry, as of right, another mode of trial other than trial by a provincial court judge, and

        (iii) on or after the 60th day following the completion of the preliminary inquiry, any mode of trial with the written consent of the prosecutor; or

    (*b*) if the accused is charged with an offence for which they are not entitled to request a preliminary inquiry or if they did not request a preliminary inquiry under subsection 536(4),

        (i) as of right, not later than 60 days before the day first appointed for the trial, another mode of trial other than trial by a provincial court judge, or

(ii) any mode of trial with the written consent of the prosecutor.

(2) An accused who elects to be tried by a provincial court judge may, not later than 60 days before the day first appointed for the trial, re-elect as of right another mode of trial, and may do so after that time with the written consent of the prosecutor.

(3) If an accused intends to re-elect under paragraph (1)(a) before the completion of the preliminary inquiry, they shall give notice in writing of their intention to re-elect, together with the written consent of the prosecutor, if that consent is required, to the justice presiding at the preliminary inquiry who shall on receipt of the notice,

CODE

(a) in the case of a re-election under subparagraph (1)(a)(ii), put the accused to their re-election in the manner set out in subsection (7); or

(b) if the accused intends to re-elect under subparagraph (1)(a)(i) and the justice is not a provincial court judge, notify a provincial court judge or clerk of the court of the accused's intention to re-elect and send to the provincial court judge or clerk any information, appearance notice, undertaking or release order given by or issued to the accused and any evidence taken before a coroner that is in the possession of the justice.

(4) If an accused intends to re-elect under paragraph (1)(b) or subsection (2), they shall give notice in writing that they intend to re-elect together with the written consent of the prosecutor, if that consent is required, to the provincial court judge before whom the accused appeared and pleaded or to a clerk of the court.

(5) If an accused intends to re-elect under paragraph (1)(a) after the completion of the preliminary inquiry, they shall give notice in writing, together with the written consent of the prosecutor, if that consent is required, to a judge or clerk of the court of the accused's original election. The judge or clerk shall, on receipt of the notice,

(a) notify the judge or provincial court judge or clerk of the court by which the accused wishes to be tried of the accused's intention to re-elect; and

(b) send to that judge or provincial court judge or clerk any information, evidence, exhibits and statement of the accused taken down in writing in accordance with section 541, any appearance notice, undertaking or release order given by or issued to the accused and any evidence taken before a coroner that is in the possession of the first-mentioned judge or clerk.

(6) Where a provincial court judge or judge or clerk of the court is notified under paragraph (3)(b) or subsection (4) or (5) that the accused wishes to re-elect, the provincial court judge or judge shall forthwith appoint a time and place for the accused to re-elect and shall cause notice thereof to be given to the accused and the prosecutor.

(7) The accused shall attend or, if in custody, shall be produced at the time and place appointed under subsection (6) and shall be put to a re-election after

(a) the charge on which the accused has been ordered to stand trial or the indictment, if an indictment has been preferred under section 566, 574 or 577 or is filed with the court before which the indictment is to be preferred under section 577, has been read to the accused; or

(b)   the information, in the case of a re-election under paragraph (1)(*a*), before the completion of the preliminary inquiry, or under paragraph (1)(*b*) or subsection (2), has been read to the accused.

The accused shall be put to their re-election in the following words or in words to the like effect:

> You have given notice of your intention to re-elect the mode of your trial. You now have the option to do so. How do you intend to reelect? R.S., c. C-34, s. 491; R.S.C. 1985, c. 27 (1st Supp.), s. 110; 2002, c. 13, s. 37; 2019, c. 25, s. 254(1), (2), (3), (5).

RIGHT TO RE-ELECT WITH CONSENT — NUNAVUT / Right to re-elect before trial — Nunavut / Right to re-elect at preliminary inquiry — Nunavut / Notice of re-election under subsection (1) or (3) — Nunavut / Notice at preliminary inquiry — Nunavut / Notice when no preliminary inquiry or preliminary inquiry completed — Nunavut / Time and place for re-election — Nunavut / Proceedings on re-election — Nunavut / Application to Nunavut.

561.1 (1) An accused who has elected or is deemed to have elected a mode of trial may re-elect any other mode of trial at any time with the written consent of the prosecutor.

(2) An accused who has elected or is deemed to have elected a mode of trial but has not requested a preliminary inquiry under subsection 536.1(3) or is not entitled to make such a request under that subsection may, as of right, re-elect to be tried by any other mode of trial at any time up to 60 days before the day first appointed for the trial.

(3) An accused who has elected or is deemed to have elected a mode of trial and has requested a preliminary inquiry under subsection 536.1(3) may, as of right, reelect to be tried by the other mode of trial at any time before the completion of the preliminary inquiry or before the 60th day after its completion.

(4) If an accused wishes to re-elect under subsection (1) or (3), before the completion of the preliminary inquiry, the accused shall give notice in writing of the wish to re-elect, together with the written consent of the prosecutor, if that consent is required, to the justice of the peace or judge presiding at the preliminary inquiry who shall on receipt of the notice put the accused to a re-election in the manner set out in subsection (9).

(5) If at a preliminary inquiry an accused intends to reelect under subsection (1) or (3) to be tried by a judge without a jury but does not intend to request a preliminary inquiry under subsection 536.1(3), the presiding justice of the peace shall notify a judge or a clerk of the Nunavut Court of Justice of the accused's intention to reelect and send to the judge or clerk any information, appearance notice, undertaking or release order given by or issued to the accused and any evidence taken before a coroner that is in the possession of the justice of the peace.

(6) If an accused who has not requested a preliminary inquiry under subsection 536.1(3), who has had one or who was not entitled to make such a request under that subsection intends to re-elect under this section, the accused shall give notice

in writing of the intention to re-elect together with the written consent of the prosecutor, if that consent is required, to the judge before whom the accused appeared and pleaded or to a clerk of the Nunavut Court of Justice.

(7) [*Repealed*, 2002, c. 13, s. 38.]

(8) On receipt of a notice given under any of subsections (4) to (7) that the accused wishes to re-elect, a judge shall immediately appoint a time and place for the accused to re-elect and shall cause notice of the time and place to be given to the accused and the prosecutor.

(9) The accused shall attend or, if in custody, shall be produced at the time and place appointed under subsection (8) and shall be put to a re-election after

(a) the charge on which the accused has been ordered to stand trial has been read to the accused or, if an indictment has been preferred under section 566, 574 or 577 or is filed with the court before which the indictment is to be preferred under section 577, the indictment has been read to the accused; or

(b) the information — in the case of a re-election under subsection (1) or (3), before the completion of the preliminary inquiry, or under subsection (2) — has been read to the accused.

The accused shall be put to their re-election in the following words or in words to the like effect:

You have given notice of your intention to re-elect the mode of your trial. You now have the option to do so. How do you intend to reelect?

(10) This section, and not section 561, applies in respect of criminal proceedings in Nunavut. 1999, c. 3, s. 43; 2002, c. 13, s. 38; 2019, c. 25, s. 255(1), (3), (4), (5).

PROCEEDINGS FOLLOWING RE-ELECTION / Proceedings following re-election.

562. (1) If the accused re-elects under subparagraph 561(1)(a)(i) before the completion of the preliminary inquiry, under paragraph 561(1)(a) after the completion of the preliminary inquiry or under paragraph 561(1)(b), the provincial court judge or judge, as the case may be, shall proceed with the trial or appoint a time and place for the trial.

(2) If the accused re-elects under subparagraph 561(1)(a)(ii) before the completion of the preliminary inquiry, or under subsection 561(2), and requests a preliminary inquiry under subsection 536(4), the justice shall proceed with the preliminary inquiry. R.S., c. C-34, s. 492; R.S.C. 1985, c. 27 (1st Supp.), s. 110; 2019, c. 25, s. 256.

PROCEEDINGS FOLLOWING RE-ELECTION — NUNAVUT / Proceedings following re-election — Nunavut / Application to Nunavut.

562.1 (1) If the accused re-elects under subsection 561.1(1) to be tried by a judge without a jury and does not request a preliminary inquiry under subsection 536.1(3), or if the accused re-elects any other mode of trial under subsection 561.1(2) but is not entitled to make a request for a preliminary inquiry under subsection 536.1(3), the judge shall proceed with the trial or appoint a time and place for the trial.

(2) If the accused re-elects under section 561.1 before the completion of the preliminary inquiry to be tried by a judge without a jury or by a court composed of a judge and jury, and requests a preliminary inquiry under subsection 536.1(3), the justice of the peace or judge shall proceed with the preliminary inquiry.

(3) This section, and not section 562, applies in respect of criminal proceedings in Nunavut. 1999, c. 3, s. 44; 2002, c. 13, s. 39; 2019, c. 25, s. 257.

PROCEEDINGS ON RE-ELECTION TO BE TRIED BY PROVINCIAL COURT JUDGE WITHOUT JURY.

563. Where an accused re-elects under section 561 to be tried by a provincial court judge,

   (a) the accused shall be tried on the information that was before the justice at the preliminary inquiry, if applicable, subject to any amendments to the information that may be allowed by the provincial court judge by whom the accused is tried; and

   (b) the provincial court judge before whom the re-election is made shall endorse on the information a record of the re-election. R.S., c. C-34, s. 493; R.S.C. 1985, c. 27 (1st Supp.), s. 110; 2019, c. 25, s. 258.

PROCEEDINGS ON RE-ELECTION TO BE TRIED BY JUDGE WITHOUT JURY — NUNAVUT / Application to Nunavut.

563.1 (1) If an accused re-elects under section 561.1 to be tried by a judge without a jury and does not request a preliminary inquiry under subsection 536.1(3) or is not entitled to make such a request under that subsection,

   (a) the accused shall be tried on the information that was before the justice of the peace or judge at the preliminary inquiry, if applicable, subject to any amendments that may be allowed by the judge by whom the accused is tried; and

   (b) the judge before whom the re-election is made shall endorse on the information a record of the re-election.

(2) This section, and not section 563, applies in respect of criminal proceedings in Nunavut. 1999, c. 3, s. 45; 2002, c. 13, s. 40; 2019, c. 25, s. 259.

564. [*Repealed*, R.S.C. 1985, c. 27 (1st Supp.), s. 110.]

ELECTION DEEMED TO HAVE BEEN MADE / When direct indictment preferred / Notice of re-election / Application.

565. (1) If an accused is ordered to stand trial for an offence that, under this Part, may be tried by a judge without a jury, the accused shall, for the purposes of the provisions of this Part relating to election and re-election, be deemed to have elected to be tried by a court composed of a judge and jury if

(a) the justice of the peace, provincial court judge or judge, as the case may be, declined to record the election or re-election of the accused under section 567 or subsection 567.1(1); or

(b) the accused does not elect when put to an election under section 536 or 536.1.

(1.1) [*Repealed*, 2019, c. 25, s. 260(1).]

(2) If an accused is to be tried after an indictment has been preferred against the accused on the basis of a consent or order given under section 577, the accused is, for the purposes of the provisions of this Part relating to election and re-election, deemed to have elected to be tried by a court composed of a judge and jury and not to have requested a preliminary inquiry under subsection 536(4) or 536.1(3), if they were entitled to make such a request, and may re-elect to be tried by a judge without a jury without a preliminary inquiry.

(3) If an accused intends to re-elect under subsection (2), the accused shall give notice in writing to a judge or clerk of the court where the indictment has been filed or preferred. The judge or clerk shall, on receipt of the notice, notify a judge having jurisdiction or clerk of the court by which the accused wishes to be tried of the accused's intention to re-elect and send to that judge or clerk any indictment, appearance notice, undertaking or release order given by or issued to the accused, any summons or warrant issued under section 578 and any evidence taken before a coroner that is in the possession of the first-mentioned judge or clerk.

(4) Subsections 561(6) and (7), or subsections 561.1(8) and (9), as the case may be, apply to a re-election made under subsection (3). R.S., c. C-34, s. 495; R.S.C. 1985, c. 27 (1st Supp.), s. 111; 1999, c. 3, s. 46; 2002, c. 13, s. 41; 2008; c. 18, s. 23; 2019, c. 25, s. 260.

Trial

INDICTMENT / Preferring indictment / What counts may be included and who may prefer indictment.

566. (1) The trial of an accused for an indictable offence, other than a trial before a provincial court judge, shall be on an indictment in writing setting forth the offence with which he is charged.

(2) Where an accused elects under section 536 or re-elects under section 561 to be tried by a judge without a jury, an indictment in Form 4 may be preferred.

(3) Section 574 and subsection 576(1) apply, with such modifications as the circumstances require, to the preferring of an indictment pursuant to indictment subsection (2). R.S., c. C-34, s. 496; R.S.C. 1985, c. 27 (1st Supp.), s. 111; 1997, c. 18, s. 67.

INDICTMENT — NUNAVUT / Preferring indictment — Nunavut / What counts may be included and who may prefer indictment — Nunavut / Application to Nunavut.

566.1 (1) The trial of an accused for an indictable offence, other than an indictable offence referred to in section 553 or an offence in respect of which the accused has elected or re-elected to be tried by a judge without a jury and in respect of which no party has requested a preliminary inquiry under subsection 536.1(3) or was not entitled to make such a request under that subsection, must be on an indictment in writing setting out the offence with which the accused is charged.

(2) If an accused elects under section 536.1 or re-elects under section 561.1 to be tried by a judge without a jury and one of the parties requests a preliminary inquiry under subsection 536.1(3), an indictment in Form 4 may be preferred.

(3) Section 574 and subsection 576(1) apply, with any modifications that the circumstances require, to the preferring of an indictment under subsection (2).

(4) This section, and not section 566, applies in respect of criminal proceedings in Nunavut. 1999, c. 3, s. 47; 2002, c. 13, s. 42; 2019, c. 25, s. 261.

General

MODE OF TRIAL WHEN TWO OR MORE ACCUSED.

567. Despite any other provision of this Part, if two or more persons are jointly charged in an information, unless all of them elect or re-elect or are deemed to have elected the same mode of trial, the justice, provincial court judge or judge may decline to record any election, re-election or deemed election for trial by a provincial court judge or a judge without a jury. R.S., c. C-34, s. 497; R.S.C. 1985, c. 27 (1st Supp.), s. 111; 2002, c. 13, s. 43.

MODE OF TRIAL IF TWO OR MORE ACCUSED — NUNAVUT / Application to Nunavut.

567.1 (1) Despite any other provision of this Part, if two or more persons are jointly charged in an information, unless all of them elect or re-elect or are deemed to have elected the same mode of trial, the justice of the peace or judge may decline to record any election, re-election or deemed election for trial by a judge without a jury.

(2) This section, and not section 567, applies in respect of criminal proceedings in Nunavut. 1999, c. 3, s. 48; 2002, c. 13, s. 43.

ATTORNEY GENERAL MAY REQUIRE TRIAL BY JURY.

568. Even if an accused elects under section 536 or re-elects under section 561 or subsection 565(2) to be tried by a judge or provincial court judge, as the case may be, the Attorney General may require the accused to be tried by a court composed of a judge and jury unless the alleged offence is one that is punishable with imprisonment for five years or less. If the Attorney General so requires, a judge or provincial court judge has no jurisdiction to try the accused under this Part and a preliminary inquiry must be held if requested under subsection 536(4), unless one has already been held or the reelection was made under subsection 565(2). R.S., c. C-34, s. 498; R.S.C. 1985, c. 27 (1st Supp.), s. 111; 2002, c. 13, s. 43; 2008, c. 18, s. 24.

569. [*Repealed*, R.S.C. 1985, c. 27 (1st Supp.), s. 111 (old provision).]

CODE

ATTORNEY GENERAL MAY REQUIRE TRIAL BY JURY — NUNAVUT / Application to Nunavut.

569. (1) Even if an accused elects under section 536.1 or re-elects under section 561.1 or subsection 565(2) to be tried by a judge without a jury, the Attorney General may require the accused to be tried by a court composed of a judge and jury unless the alleged offence is one that is punishable with imprisonment for five years or less. If the Attorney General so requires, a judge has no jurisdiction to try the accused under this Part and a preliminary inquiry must be held if requested under subsection 536.1(3), unless one has already been held or the re-election was made under subsection 565(2).

(2) This section, and not section 568, applies in respect of criminal proceedings in Nunavut. 1999, c. 3, s. 49; 2002, c. 13, s. 44; 2008, c. 18, s. 24.1.

RECORD OF CONVICTION OR ORDER / Acquittal and record of acquittal / Transmission of record / Proof of conviction, order or acquittal / Warrant of committal / Admissibility of certified copy.

570. (1) If an accused who is tried under this Part is determined by a judge or provincial court judge to be guilty of an offence on acceptance of a plea of guilty or on a finding of guilt, the judge or provincial court judge, as the case may be, shall endorse the information accordingly and shall sentence the accused or otherwise deal with the accused in the manner authorized by law and, on request by the accused, the prosecutor, a peace officer or any other person, a conviction in Form 35 and a certified copy of it, or an order in Form 36 and a certified copy of it, shall be drawn up and the certified copy shall be delivered to the person making the request.

(2) If an accused who is tried under this Part is found not guilty of an offence with which the accused is charged, the judge or provincial court judge, as the case may be, shall immediately acquit the accused in respect of that offence, an order in Form 37 shall be drawn up and, on request, a certified copy shall be drawn up and delivered to the accused.

(3) Where an accused elects to be tried by a provincial court judge under this Part, the provincial court judge shall transmit the written charge, the memorandum of adjudication and the conviction, if any, into such custody as the Attorney General may direct.

(4) A copy of a conviction in Form 35 or of an order in Form 36 or 37, certified by the judge or by the clerk or other proper officer of the court, or by the provincial

court judge, as the case may be, or proved to be a true copy, is, on proof of the identity of the person to whom the conviction or order relates, sufficient evidence in any legal proceedings to prove the conviction of that person or the making of the order against him or his acquittal, as the case may be, for the offence mentioned in the copy of the conviction or order.

(5) If an accused other than an organization is convicted, the judge or provincial court judge, as the case may be, shall issue a warrant of committal in Form 21, and section 528 applies in respect of a warrant of committal issued under this subsection.

(6) If a warrant of committal is signed by a clerk of a court, a copy of the warrant of committal, certified by the clerk, is admissible in evidence in any proceeding. R.S., c. C-34, s. 500; R.S.C. 1985, c. 27 (1st Supp.), s. 112; 1994, c. 44, s. 59; 2003, c. 21, s. 10; 2019, c. 25, s. 262.

ADJOURNMENT.

571. A judge or provincial court judge acting under this Part may from time to time adjourn a trial until it is finally terminated. R.S., c. C-34, s. 501.

APPLICATION OF PARTS XVI, XVIII, XX and XXIII.

572. The provisions of Part XVI, the provisions of Part XVIII relating to transmission of the record by a provincial court judge where he holds a preliminary inquiry, and the provisions of Parts XX and XXIII, in so far as they are not inconsistent with this Part, apply, with such modifications as the circumstances require, to proceedings under this Part. R.S., c. C-34, s. 502; R.S., c. 2 (2nd Supp.), s. 10.

---

573. [*Repealed*, R.S.C. 1985, c. 27 (1st Supp.), s. 113 (old provision).]

Part XIX.1 / NUNAVUT COURT OF JUSTICE

NUNAVUT COURT OF JUSTICE / Status when exercising power / Interpretation.

573. (1) The powers to be exercised and the duties and functions to be performed under this Act by a court of criminal jurisdiction, a summary conviction court, a judge, a provincial court judge, a justice or a justice of the peace may be exercised or performed by a judge of the Nunavut Court of Justice.

(2) A power exercised or a duty or function performed by a judge of the Nunavut Court of Justice under subsection (1) is exercised or performed by that judge as a judge of a superior court.

(3) Subsection (2) does not authorize a judge of the Nunavut Court of Justice who is presiding at a preliminary inquiry to grant a remedy under section 24 of the *Canadian Charter of Rights and Freedoms*. 1999, c. 3, s. 50.

APPLICATION FOR REVIEW — NUNAVUT / Limitation / Grounds of review / Powers of judge / Interim orders / Rules / Appeal.

573.1 (1) An application for review may be made by the Attorney General or the accused, or by any person directly affected by the decision or order, to a judge of the Court of Appeal of Nunavut in respect of a decision or order of a judge of the Nunavut Court of Justice

- (a) relating to a warrant or summons;
- (b) relating to the conduct of a preliminary inquiry, including an order under subsection 548(1);
- (c) relating to a subpoena;
- (d) relating to the publication or broadcasting of information or access to the court room for all or part of the proceedings;
- (e) to refuse to quash an information or indictment; or
- (f) relating to the detention, disposal or forfeiture of any thing seized under a warrant or order.

(2) A decision or order may not be reviewed under this section if

- (a) the decision or order is of a kind that could only be made in a province or a territory other than Nunavut by a superior court of criminal jurisdiction or a judge as defined in section 552; or
- (b) another statutory right of review is available.

(3) The judge of the Court of Appeal of Nunavut may grant relief under subsection (4) only if the judge is satisfied that

- (a) in the case of any decision or order mentioned in subsection (1),
    - (i) the judge of the Nunavut Court of Justice failed to observe a principle of natural justice or failed or refused to exercise the judge's jurisdiction, or
    - (ii) the decision or order was made as a result of an irrelevant consideration or for an improper purpose;
- (b) in the case of a decision or order mentioned in paragraph (1)(a), that
    - (i) the judge failed to comply with a statutory requirement for the making of the decision or order,
    - (ii) the decision or order was made in the absence of any evidence that a statutory requirement for the making of the decision or order was met,
    - (iii) the decision or order was made as a result of reckless disregard for the truth, fraud, intentional misrepresentation of material facts or intentional omission to state material facts,
    - (iv) the warrant is so vague or lacking in particularity that it authorizes an unreasonable search, or
    - (v) the warrant lacks a material term or condition that is required by law;
- (c) in the case of a decision or order mentioned in paragraph (1)(b), that the judge of the Nunavut Court of Justice
    - (i) failed to follow a mandatory provision of this Act relating to the conduct of a preliminary inquiry,
    - (ii) ordered the accused to stand trial when there was no evidence adduced on which a properly instructed jury acting reasonably could convict, or
    - (iii) discharged the accused when there was some evidence adduced on which a properly instructed jury acting reasonably could convict;

597

    (*d*) in the case of a decision or order mentioned in paragraph (1)(*c*) or (*d*), that the judge of the Nunavut Court of Justice erred in law;

    (*e*) in the case of a decision or order mentioned in paragraph (1)(*e*), that

        (i) the information or indictment failed to give the accused notice of the charge,

        (ii) the judge of the Nunavut Court of Justice did not have jurisdiction to try the offence, or

        (iii) the provision creating the offence alleged to have been committed by the accused is unconstitutional; or

    (*f*) in the case of a decision or order mentioned in paragraph (1)(*f*), that

        (i) the judge failed to comply with a statutory requirement for the making of the decision or order,

        (ii) the decision or order was made in the absence of any evidence that a statutory requirement for the making of the decision or order was met, or

        (iii) the decision or order was made as a result of reckless disregard for the truth, fraud, intentional misrepresentation of material facts or intentional omission to state material facts.

(4) On the hearing of the application for review, the judge of the Court of Appeal of Nunavut may do one or more of the following:

    (*a*) order a judge of the Nunavut Court of Justice to do any act or thing that the judge or any other judge of that court failed or refused to do or has delayed in doing;

    (*b*) prohibit or restrain a decision, order or proceeding of a judge of the Nunavut Court of Justice;

    (*c*) declare invalid or unlawful, quash or set aside, in whole or in part, a decision, order or proceeding of a judge of the Nunavut Court of Justice;

    (*d*) refer back for determination in accordance with any directions that the judge considers to be appropriate, a decision, order or proceeding of a judge of the Nunavut Court of Justice;

    (*e*) grant any remedy under subsection 24(1) of the *Canadian Charter of Rights and Freedoms*;

    (*f*) refuse to grant any relief if the judge is of the opinion that no substantial wrong or miscarriage of justice has occurred or that the subject-matter of the application should be determined at trial or on appeal; and

    (*g*) dismiss the application.

(5) If an application for review is made, a judge of the Court of Appeal of Nunavut may make any interim order that the judge considers appropriate pending the final disposition of the application for review.

(6) A person who proposes to make an application for review shall do so in the manner and within the period that may be directed by rules of court, except that a judge of the Court of Appeal of Nunavut may at any time extend any period specified in the rules.

(7) An appeal lies to the Court of Appeal of Nunavut against a decision or order made under subsection (4). The provisions of Part XXI apply, with any modifications that the circumstances require, to the appeal. 1999, c. 3, s. 50.

HABEAS CORPUS / Exception / Provisions apply.

573.2 (1) *Habeas corpus* proceedings may be brought before a judge of the Court of Appeal of Nunavut in respect of an order made or warrant issued by a judge of the Nunavut Court of Justice, except where

   (a) the order or warrant is of a kind that could only be made or issued in a province or a territory other than Nunavut by a superior court of criminal jurisdiction or a judge as defined in section 552; or

   (b) another statutory right of review or appeal is available.

(2) Despite subsection (1), *habeas corpus* proceedings may be brought before a judge of the Court of Appeal of Nunavut with respect to an order or warrant of a judge of the Nunavut Court of Justice if the proceedings are brought to challenge the constitutionality of a person's detention or confinement.

(3) Subsections 784(2) to (6) apply in respect of any proceedings brought under subsection (1) or (2). 1999, c. 3, s. 50.

Part XX / PROCEDURE IN JURY TRIALS AND GENERAL PROVISIONS

Preferring Indictment

PROSECUTOR MAY PREFER INDICTMENT / Preferring indictment when no preliminary inquiry / Preferring single indictment / Consent to inclusion of other charges / Private prosecutor requires consent.

574. (1) Subject to subsection (3), the prosecutor may, whether the charges were included in one information or not, prefer an indictment against any person who has been ordered to stand trial in respect of

   (a) any charge on which that person was ordered to stand trial; or

   (b) any charge founded on the facts disclosed by the evidence taken on the preliminary inquiry, in addition to or in substitution for any charge on which that person was ordered to stand trial.

(1.1) If a person has not requested a preliminary inquiry under subsection 536(4) or 536.1(3) into the charge or was not entitled to make such a request, the prosecutor may, subject to subsection (3), prefer an indictment against a person in respect of a charge set out in an information or informations, or any included charge, at any time after the person has made an election, re-election or deemed election on the information or informations.

(1.2) If indictments may be preferred under both subsections (1) and (1.1), the prosecutor may prefer a single indictment in respect of one or more charges referred to in subsection (1) combined with one or more charges or included charges referred to in subsection (1.1).

(2) An indictment preferred under any of subsections (1) to (1.2) may, if the accused consents, include a charge that is not referred to in those subsections, and the offence charged may be dealt with, tried and determined and punished in all

599

respects as if it were an offence in respect of which the accused had been ordered to stand trial. However, if the offence was committed wholly in a province other than that in which the accused is before the court, subsection 478(3) applies.

(3) In a prosecution conducted by a prosecutor other than the Attorney General and in which the Attorney General does not intervene, an indictment may not be preferred under any of subsections (1) to (1.2) before a court without the written order of a judge of that court. R.S., c. C-34, s. 504; R.S.C. 1985, c. 27 (1st Supp.), s. 113; 2002, c. 13, s. 45; 2019, c. 25, s. 263.

---

575. [*Repealed*, R.S.C. 1985, c. 27 (1st Supp.), s. 113.]

INDICTMENT / Criminal information and bill of indictment / Coroner's inquisition.

576. (1) Except as provided in this Act, no indictment shall be preferred.

(2) No criminal information shall be laid or granted and no bill of indictment shall be preferred before a grand jury.

(3) No person shall be tried on a coroner's inquisition. R.S., c. C-34, s. 506; R.S.C. 1985, c. 27 (1st Supp.), s. 114.

DIRECT INDICTMENTS.

577. Despite section 574, an indictment may be preferred even if the accused has not been given the opportunity to request a preliminary inquiry, a preliminary inquiry has been commenced but not concluded or a preliminary inquiry has been held and the accused has been discharged, if

    (*a*) in the case of a prosecution conducted by the Attorney General or one in which the Attorney General intervenes, the personal consent in writing of the Attorney General or Deputy Attorney General is filed in court; or

    (*b*) in any other case, a judge of the court so orders. R.S., c. C-34, s. 507; 1974-75-76, c. 93, s. 63; 1984, c. 40, s. 20(2); R.S.C. 1985, c. 27 (1st Supp.), s. 115; 2002, c. 13, s. 46.

SUMMONS OR WARRANT / Part XVI to apply.

578. (1) Where notice of the recommencement of proceedings has been given pursuant to subsection 579(2) or an indictment has been filed with the court before which the proceedings are to commence or recommence, the court, if it considers it necessary, may issue

    (*a*) a summons addressed to, or

    (*b*) a warrant for the arrest of,

the accused or defendant, as the case may be, to compel him to attend before the court to answer the charge described in the indictment.

(2) The provisions of Part XVI apply with such modifications as the circumstances require where a summons or warrant is issued under subsection (1). 1974-75-76, c. 93, s. 64; R.S.C. 1985, c. 27 (1st Supp.), s. 116.

ATTORNEY GENERAL MAY DIRECT STAY / Recommencement of proceedings.

579. (1) The Attorney General or counsel instructed by the Attorney General for that purpose may, at any time after any proceedings in relation to an accused or a defendant are commenced and before judgment, direct the clerk or other proper officer of the court to make an entry on the record that the proceedings are stayed by the Attorney General's or counsel's direction, as the case may be, and the entry shall then be made, at which time the proceedings shall be stayed accordingly and any undertaking or release order relating to the proceedings is vacated.

(2) Proceedings stayed in accordance with subsection (1) may be recommenced, without laying a new information or preferring a new indictment, as the case may be, by the Attorney General or counsel instructed by him for that purpose giving notice of the recommencement to the clerk of the court in which the stay of the proceedings was entered, but where no such notice is given within one year after the entry of the stay of proceedings, or before the expiration of the time within which the proceedings could have been commenced, whichever is the earlier, the proceedings shall be deemed never to have been commenced. R.S., c. C-34, s. 508; 1972, c. 13, s. 43; R.S.C. 1985, c. 27 (1st Supp.), s. 117; 2019, c. 25, s. 264.

INSTRUCTION TO STAY / Stay / Recommencement / Proceedings deemed never commenced / Definition of "Agreement".

579.001 (1) The Attorney General or counsel instructed by him or her for that purpose shall, at any time after proceedings in relation to an act or omission of a "*preclearance officer*", as defined in section 5 of the *Preclearance Act, 2016*, are commenced and before judgment, direct the clerk or other proper officer of the court to make an entry on the record that the proceedings are stayed by direction of the Attorney General if the Government of the United States has provided notice of the exercise of primary criminal jurisdiction under paragraph 14 of Article X of the Agreement.

(2) The clerk or other officer of the court shall make the entry immediately after being so directed, and on the entry being made the proceedings are stayed and any recognizance relating to the proceedings is vacated.

(3) The proceedings may be recommenced without laying a new information or preferring a new indictment, if the Attorney General or counsel instructed by him or her gives notice to the clerk or other officer of the court that
   (a) the Government of the United States has provided notice of waiver under paragraph 15 of Article X of the Agreement; or
   (b) the Government of the United States has declined, or is unable, to prosecute the accused and the accused has returned to Canada.

(4) However, if the Attorney General or counsel does not give notice under subsection (3) on or before the first anniversary of the day on which the stay of proceedings was entered, the proceedings are deemed never to have been commenced.

(5) In this section, "*Agreement*" means the Agreement on Land, Rail, Marine, and Air Transport Preclearance between the Government of Canada and the

Government of the United States of America, done at Washington on March 16, 2015. 2017, c. 27, s. 62.

WHEN ATTORNEY GENERAL DOES NOT STAY PROCEEDINGS.

579.01 If the Attorney General intervenes in proceedings and does not stay them under section 579, he or she may, without conducting the proceedings, call witnesses, examine and cross-examine witnesses, present evidence and make submissions. 2002, c. 13, s. 47.

INTERVENTION BY ATTORNEY GENERAL OF CANADA OR DIRECTOR OF PUBLIC PROSECUTIONS / Sections 579 and 579.01 to apply.

579.1 (1) The Attorney General of Canada or the Director of Public Prosecutions appointed under subsection 3(1) of the *Director of Public Prosecutions Act*, or counsel instructed by him or her for that purpose, may intervene in proceedings in the following circumstances:

(*a*) the proceedings are in respect of an offence for which he or she has the power to commence or to conduct a proceeding;

(*b*) the proceedings have not been instituted by an Attorney General;

(*c*) judgment has not been rendered; and

(*d*) the Attorney General of the province in which the proceedings are taken has not intervened.

(2) Sections 579 and 579.01 apply, with any modifications that the circumstances require, to proceedings in which the Attorney General of Canada or the Director of Public Prosecutions intervenes under this section. 1994, c. 44, s. 60; 2019, c. 25, s. 265(1), (3).

FORM OF INDICTMENT.

580. An indictment is sufficient if it is on paper and is in Form 4. R.S., c. C-34, s. 509; R.S.C. 1985, c. 27 (1st Suppl.), s. 117.

General Provisions Respecting Counts

SUBSTANCE OF OFFENCE / Form of statement / Details of circumstances / Indictment for treason / Reference to section / General provisions not restricted.

581. (1) Each count in an indictment shall in general apply to a single transaction and shall contain in substance a statement that the accused or defendant committed an offence therein specified.

(2) The statement referred to in subsection (1) may be

(*a*) in popular language without technical averments or allegations of matters that are not essential to be proved;

(*b*) in the words of the enactment that describes the offence or declares the matters charged to be an indictable offence; or (*c*) in words that are sufficient to give to the accused notice of the offence with which he is charged.

(3) A count shall contain sufficient detail of the circumstances of the alleged offence to give to the accused reasonable information with respect to the act or omission to be proved against him and to identify the transaction referred to, but otherwise the absence or insufficiency of details does not vitiate the count.

(4) If an accused is charged with an offence under section 47 or sections 50 to 53, every overt act that is to be relied on shall be stated in the indictment.

(5) A count may refer to any section, subsection, paragraph or subparagraph of the enactment that creates the offence charged, and for the purpose of determining whether a count is sufficient, consideration shall be given to any such reference.

(6) Nothing in this Part relating to matters that do not render a count insufficient shall be deemed to restrict or limit the application of this section. R.S., c. C-34, s. 510; R.S.C. 1985, c. 27 (1st Supp.), s. 118; 2018, c. 29, s. 63.

HIGH TREASON AND FIRST DEGREE MURDER.

582. No person shall be convicted for the offence of high treason or first degree murder unless in the indictment charging the offence he is specifically charged with that offence. R.S., c. C-34, s. 511; 1973-74, c. 38, s. 4; 1974-75-76, c. 105, s. 6.

CERTAIN OMISSIONS NOT GROUNDS FOR OBJECTION.

583. No count in an indictment is insufficient by reason of the absence of details where, in the opinion of the court, the count otherwise fulfils the requirements of section 581 and, without restricting the generality of the foregoing, no count in an indictment is insufficient by reason only that

(*a*) it does not name the person injured or intended or attempted to be injured;

(*b*) it does not name the person who owns or has a special property or interest in property mentioned in the count;

(*c*) it charges an intent to defraud without naming or describing the person whom it was intended to defraud;

(*d*) it does not set out any writing that is the subject of the charge;

(*e*) it does not set out the words used where words that are alleged to have been used are the subject of the charge;

(*f*) it does not specify the means by which the alleged offence was committed;

(*g*) it does not name or describe with precision any person, place or thing; or

(*h*) it does not, where the consent of a person, official or authority is required before proceedings may be instituted for an offence, state that the consent has been obtained. R.S., c. C-34, s. 512.

Special Provisions Respecting Counts

SUFFICIENCY OF COUNT CHARGING LIBEL / Specifying sense / Proof.

584. (1) No count for publishing a seditious or defamatory libel, or for selling or exhibiting an obscene book, pamphlet, newspaper or other written matter, is insufficient by reason only that it does not set out the words that are alleged to be libellous or the writing that is alleged to be obscene.

(2) A count for publishing a libel may charge that the published matter was written in a sense that by innuendo made the publication thereof criminal, and may specify that sense without any introduction assertion to show how the matter was written in that sense.

(3) It is sufficient, on the trial of a count for publishing a libel, to prove that the matter published was libellous, with or without innuendo. R.S., c. C-34, s. 513; 2018, c. 29, s. 64.

SUFFICIENCY OF COUNT CHARGING PERJURY, ETC.

585. No count that charges
- (a) perjury,
- (b) the making of a false oath or a false statement,
- (c) fabricating evidence, or
- (d) procuring the commission of an offence mentioned in paragraph (a), (b) or (c),

is insufficient by reason only that it does not state the nature of the authority of the tribunal before which the oath or statement was taken or made, or the subject of the inquiry, or the words used or the evidence fabricated, or that it does not expressly negative the truth of the words used. R.S., c. C-34, s. 514.

SUFFICIENCY OF COUNT RELATING TO FRAUD.

586. No count that alleges false pretences, fraud or an attempt or conspiracy by fraudulent means is insufficient by reason only that it does not set out in detail the nature of the false pretence, fraud or fraudulent means. R.S., c. C-34, s. 515.

Particulars

WHAT MAY BE ORDERED / Regard to evidence / Particular.

587. (1) A court may, where it is satisfied that it is necessary for a fair trial, order the prosecutor to furnish particulars and, without restricting the generality of the foregoing, may order the prosecutor to furnish particulars
- (a) of what is relied on in support of a charge of perjury, the making of a false oath or of a false statement, fabricating evidence or counselling the commission of any of those offences;
- (b) of any false pretence or fraud that is alleged;

    (c) of any alleged attempt or conspiracy by fraudulent means;

    (d) setting out the passages in a book, pamphlet, newspaper or other printing or writing that are relied on in support of a charge of selling or exhibiting an obscene book, pamphlet, newspaper, printing or writing;

    (e) further describing any writing or words that are the subject of a charge;

    (f) further describing the means by which an offence is alleged to have been committed; or

    (g) further describing a person, place or thing referred to in an indictment.

(2) For the purpose of determining whether or not a particular is required, the court may give consideration to any evidence that has been taken.

(3) Where a particular is delivered pursuant to this section,

    (a) a copy shall be given without charge to the accused or his counsel;

    (b) the particular shall be entered in the record; and

    (c) the trial shall proceed in all respects as if the indictment had been amended to conform with the particular. R.S., c. C-34, s. 516; R.S.C. 1985, c. 27 (1st Supp.), s. 7(2)(c).

Ownership of Property

OWNERSHIP.

588. The real and personal property of which a person has, by law, the management, control or custody shall, for the purposes of an indictment or proceeding against any other person for an offence committed on or in respect of the property, be deemed to be the property of the person who has the management, control or custody of it. R.S., c. C-34, s. 517.

Joinder or Severance of Counts

COUNT FOR MURDER.

589. No count that charges an indictable offence other than murder shall be joined in an indictment to a count that charges murder unless

    (a) the count that charges the offence other than murder arises out of the same transaction as a count that charges murder; or

    (b) the accused signifies consent to the joinder of the counts. R.S., c. C-34, s. 518; 1991, c. 4, s. 2.

OFFENCES MAY BE CHARGED IN THE ALTERNATIVE / Application to amend or divide counts / Order.

590. (1) A count is not objectionable by reason only that

    (a) it charges in the alternative several different matters, acts or omissions that are stated in the alternative in an enactment that describes as an indictable offence the matters, acts or omissions charged in the count; or

    (b) it is double or multifarious.

(2) An accused may at any stage of his trial apply to the court to amend or to divide a count that

    (a) charges in the alternative different matters, acts or omissions that are stated in the alternative in the enactment that describes the offence or declares that the matters, acts or omissions charged are an indictable offence, or

    (b) is double or multifarious,

on the ground that, as framed, it embarrasses him in his defence.

(3) The court may, where it is satisfied that the ends of justice require it, order that a count be amended or divided into two or more counts, and thereupon a formal commencement may be inserted before each of the counts into which it is divided. R.S., c. C-34, s. 519.

JOINDER OF COUNTS / Each count separate / Severance of accused and counts / Order for severance / Delayed enforcement / Decisions binding on parties / Subsequent procedure / Idem.

591. (1) Subject to section 589, any number of counts for any number of offences may be joined in the same indictment, but the counts shall be distinguished in the manner shown in Form 4.

(2) Where there is more than one count in an indictment, each count may be treated as a separate indictment.

(3) The court may, where it is satisfied that the interests of justice so require, order

    (a) that the accused or defendant be tried separately on one or more of the counts;

and

    (b) where there is more than one accused or defendant, that one or more of them be tried separately on one or more of the counts.

(4) An order under subsection (3) may be made before or during the trial but, if the order is made during the trial, the jury shall be discharged from giving a verdict on the counts

    (a) on which the trial does not proceed; or

    (b) in respect of the accused or defendant who has been granted as separate trial.

(4.1) The court may make an order under subsection (3) that takes effect either at a specified later date or on the occurrence of a specified event if, taking into account, among other considerations, the need to ensure consistent decisions, it is satisfied that it is in the interests of justice to do so.

(4.2) Unless the court is satisfied that it would not be in the interests of justice, the decisions relating to the disclosure or admissibility of evidence or the *Canadian Charter of Rights and Freedoms* that are made before any order issued under subsection (3) takes effect continue to bind the parties if the decisions are made — or could have been made — before the stage at which the evidence on the merits is presented.

(5) The counts in respect of which a jury is discharged pursuant to paragraph (4)(*a*) may subsequently be proceeded on in all respects as if they were contained in a separate indictment.

(6) Where an order is made in respect of an accused or defendant under paragraph (3)(*b*), the accused or defendant may be tried separately on the counts in relation to which the order was made as if they were contained in a separate indictment. R.S., c. C-34, s. 520; R.S.C. 1985, c. 27 (1st Supp.), s. 119; 2011, c. 16, s. 5.

CODE

Joinder of Accused in Certain Cases

ACCESSORIES AFTER THE FACT.

592. Any one who is charged with being an accessory after the fact to any offence may be indicted, whether or not the principal or any other party to the offence has been indicted or convicted or is or is not amenable to justice. R.S., c. C-34, s. 521.

TRIAL OF PERSONS JOINTLY / Conviction of one or more.

593. (1) Any number of persons may be charged in the same indictment with an offence under section 354 or 355.4 or paragraph 356(1)(*b*), even though

   (*a*) the property was had in possession at different times; or

   (*b*) the person by whom the property was obtained

       (i) is not indicted with them, or

       (ii) is not in custody or is not amenable to justice.

(2) Where, pursuant to subsection (1), two or more persons are charged in the same indictment with an offence referred to in that subsection, any one or more of those persons who separately committed the offence in respect of the property or any part of it may be convicted. R.S., c. C-34, s. 522; 2010, c. 14, s. 11.

594-596. [*Repealed*, R.S.C. 1985, c. 27 (1st Supp.), s. 120.]

Proceedings when Person Indicted is at Large

BENCH WARRANT / Execution / Interim release / Discretion to postpone execution / Deemed execution of warrant.

597. (1) Where an indictment has been preferred against a person who is at large, and that person does not appear or remain in attendance for his trial, the court before which the accused should have appeared or remained in attendance may issue a warrant in Form 7 for his arrest.

(2) A warrant issued under subsection (1) may be executed anywhere in Canada.

(3) If an accused is arrested under a warrant issued under subsection (1), a judge of the court that issued the warrant may make a release order referred to in section 515.

(4) A judge who issues a warrant may specify in the warrant the period before which the warrant shall not be executed, to allow the accused to appear voluntarily

before a judge having jurisdiction in the territorial division in which the warrant was issued.

(5) Where the accused appears voluntarily for the offence in respect of which the accused is charged, the warrant is deemed to be executed. R.S., c. C-34, s. 526; R.S., c. 2 (2nd Supp.), s. 11; 1974-75-76, c. 93, s. 64.1; R.S.C. 1985, c. 27 (1st Supp.), s. 121; 1997, c. 18, s. 68; 2019, c. 25, s. 266.

ELECTION DEEMED TO BE WAIVED / Idem.

598. (1) Notwithstanding anything in this Act, where a person to whom subsection 597(1) applies has elected or is deemed to have elected to be tried by a court composed of a judge and jury and, at the time he failed to appear or to remain in attendance for his trial, he had not re-elected to be tried by a court composed of a judge without a jury or provincial court judge without a jury, he shall not be tried by a court composed of a judge and jury unless

- (*a*) he establishes to the satisfaction of a judge of the court in which he is indicted that there was a legitimate excuse for his failure to appear or remain in attendance for his trial; or
- (*b*) the Attorney General requires pursuant to section 568 or 569 that the accused be tried by a court composed of a judge and jury.

(2) An accused who, under subsection (1), may not be tried by a court composed of a judge and jury is deemed to have elected under section 536 or 536.1 to be tried without a jury by a judge of the court where the accused was indicted and section 561 or 561.1, as the case may be, does not apply in respect of the accused. 1974-75-76, c. 93, s. 65; R.S.C. 1985, c. 27 (1st Supp.), s. 122; 1999, c. 3, s. 51; 2002, c. 13, s. 48.

Change of Venue

REASONS FOR CHANGE OF VENUE / Reasons to be stated / Conditions as to expense / Transmission of record / Idem.

599. (1) A court before which an accused is or may be indicted, at any term or sittings thereof, or a judge who may hold or sit in that court, may at any time before or after an indictment is found, on the application of the prosecutor or the accused, order the trial to be held in a territorial division in the same province other than that in which the offence would otherwise be tried if

- (*a*) it appears expedient to the ends of justice, including
  - (i) to promote a fair and efficient trial, and
  - (ii) to ensure the safety and security of a victim or witness or to protect their interests and those of society; or
- (*b*) a competent authority has directed that a jury is not to be summoned at the time appointed in a territorial division where the trial would otherwise by law be held.

(2) [*Repealed*, R.S.C. 1985, c. 1 (4th Supp.), s. 16.]

(3) The court or judge may, in an order made on an application by the prosecutor under subsection (1), prescribe conditions that he thinks proper with respect to the payment of additional expenses caused to the accused as a result of the change of venue.

(4) Where an order is made under subsection (1), the officer who has custody of the indictment, if any, and the writings and exhibits relating to the prosecution, shall transmit them forthwith to the clerk of the court before which the trial is ordered to be held, and all proceedings in the case shall be held or, if previously commenced, shall be continued in that court.

(5) Where the writings and exhibits referred to in subsection (4) have not been returned to the court in which the trial was to be held at the time an order is made to change the place of trial, the person who obtains the order shall serve a true copy thereof on the person in whose custody they are and that person shall thereupon transmit them to the clerk of the court before which the trial is to be held. R.S., c. C-34, s. 527; 1974-75-76, c. 93, s. 66; R.S.C. 1985, c. 1 (4th Supp.), s. 16; 2019, c. 25, s. 267.

ORDER IS AUTHORITY TO REMOVE PRISONER.

600. An order that is made under section 599 is sufficient warrant, justification and authority to all sheriffs, keepers of prisons and peace officers for the removal, disposal and reception of an accused in accordance with the terms of the order, and the sheriff may appoint and authorize any peace officer to convey the accused to a prison in the territorial division in which the trial is ordered to be held. R.S., c. C-34, s. 528.

Amendment

AMENDING DEFECTIVE INDICTMENT OR COUNT / Amendment where variance / Amending indictment / Matters to be considered by the court / Variance not material / Adjournment if accused prejudiced / Question of law / Endorsing indictment / Mistakes not material / Limitation / Definition of "court" / Application.

601. (1) An objection to an indictment preferred under this Part or to a count in an indictment, for a defect apparent on its face, shall be taken by motion to quash the indictment or count before the accused enters a plea, and, after the accused has entered a plea, only by leave of the court before which the proceedings take place. The court before which an objection is taken under this section may, if it considers it necessary, order the indictment or count to be amended to cure the defect.

(2) Subject to this section, a court may, on the trial of an indictment, amend the indictment or a count therein or a particular that is furnished under section 587, to make the indictment, count or particular conform to the evidence, where there is a variance between the evidence and

   (*a*) a count in the indictment as preferred; or

   (*b*) a count in the indictment

     (i) as amended, or

(ii) as it would have been if it had been amended in conformity with any particular that has been furnished pursuant to section 587.

(3) Subject to this section, a court shall, at any stage of the proceedings, amend the indictment or a count therein as may be necessary where it appears

(a) that the indictment has been preferred under a particular Act of Parliament instead of another Act of Parliament;

(b) that the indictment or a count thereof

(i) fails to state or states defectively anything that is requisite to constitute the offence,

(ii) does not negative an exception that should be negatived,

(iii) is in any way defective in substance,

and the matters to be alleged in the proposed amendment are disclosed by the evidence taken on the preliminary inquiry or on the trial; or

(c) that the indictment or a count thereof is in any way defective in form.

(4) The court shall, in considering whether or not an amendment should be made to the indictment or a count in it, consider

(a) the matters disclosed by the evidence taken on the preliminary inquiry;

(b) the evidence taken on the trial, if any;

(c) the circumstances of the case;

(d) whether the accused has been misled or prejudiced in his defence by any variance, error or omission mentioned in subsection (2) or (3); and

(e) whether, having regard to the merits of the case, the proposed amendment can be made without injustice being done.

(4.1) A variance between the indictment or a count therein and the evidence taken is not material with respect to

(a) the time when the offence is alleged to have been committed, if it is proved that the indictment was preferred within the prescribed period of limitation, if any; or

(b) the place where the subject-matter of the proceedings is alleged to have arisen, if it is proved that it arose within the territorial jurisdiction of the court.

(5) Where, in the opinion of the court, the accused has been misled or prejudiced in his defence by a variance, error or omission in an indictment or a count therein, the court may, if it is of the opinion that the misleading or prejudice may be removed by an adjournment, adjourn the proceedings to a specified day or sittings of the court and may make such an order with respect to the payment of costs resulting from the necessity for amendment as it considers desirable.

(6) The question whether an order to amend an indictment or a count thereof should be granted or refused is a question of law.

(7) An order to amend an indictment or a count therein shall be endorsed on the indictment as part of the record and the proceedings shall continue as if the indictment or count had been originally preferred as amended.

(8) A mistake in the heading of an indictment shall be corrected as soon as it is discovered but, whether corrected or not, is not material.

(9) The authority of a court to amend indictments does not authorize the court to add to the overt acts stated in an indictment for high treason or treason or for an offence against any provision in sections 50, 51 and 53.

(10) In this section, "court" means a court, judge, justice or provincial court judge acting in summary conviction proceedings or in proceedings on indictment.

(11) This section applies to all proceedings, including preliminary inquiries, with such modifications as the circumstances require. R.S., c. C-34, s. 529; 1974-75-76, c. 105, s. 29; R.S.C. 1985, c. 27 (1st Supp.), s. 123; 1999, c. 5, s. 23; 2011, c. 16, s. 6; 2018, c. 29, s. 65.

602. [*Repealed*, R.S.C. 1985, c. 27 (1st Supp.), s. 124.]

Inspection and Copies of Documents

RIGHT OF ACCUSED.

603. An accused is entitled, after he has been ordered to stand trial or at his trial,
  (*a*) to inspect without charge the indictment, his own statement, the evidence and the exhibits, if any; and
  (*b*) to receive, on payment of a reasonable fee determined in accordance with a tariff of fees fixed or approved by the Attorney General of the province, a copy
      (i) of the evidence,
      (ii) of his own statement, if any, and
      (iii) of the indictment;
but the trial shall not be postponed to enable the accused to secure copies unless the court is satisfied that the failure of the accused to secure them before the trial is not attributable to lack of diligence on the part of the accused. R.S., c. C-34, s. 531; 1974-75-76, c. 93, s. 67; R.S.C. 1985, c. 27 (1st Supp.), s. 101(2)(*d*).

604. [*Repealed*, 1997, c. 18, s. 69.]

RELEASE OF EXHIBITS FOR TESTING / Disobeying orders.

605. (1) A judge of a superior court of criminal jurisdiction or a court of criminal jurisdiction may, on summary application on behalf of the accused or the prosecutor, after three days notice to the accused or prosecutor, as the case may be, order the release of any exhibit for the purpose of a scientific or other test or examination, subject to such terms as appear to be necessary or desirable to ensure the safeguarding of the exhibit and its preservation for use at the trial.

(2) Every one who fails to comply with the terms of an order made under subsection (1) is guilty of contempt of court and may be dealt with summarily by the judge or provincial court judge who made the order or before whom the trial of the accused takes place. R.S., c. C-34, s. 533; R.S.C. 1985, c. 27 (1st Supp.), s. 203.

Pleas

PLEAS PERMITTED / Conditions for accepting guilty plea / Validity of plea / Refusal to plead / Allowing time / Included or other offence / Inquiry of court — murder and serious personal injury offences / Inquiry of court — certain indictable offences / Duty to inform / Validity of plea / Video links.

606. (1) An accused who is called on to plead may plead guilty or not guilty, or the special pleas authorized by this Part and no others.

(1.1) A court may accept a plea of guilty only if it is satisfied that
 (*a*) the accused is making the plea voluntarily;
 (*b*) the accused understands
  (i) that the plea is an admission of the essential elements of the offence,
  (ii) the nature and consequences of the plea, and
  (iii) that the court is not bound by any agreement made between the accused and the prosecutor; and
 (*c*) the facts support the charge.

(1.2) The failure of the court to fully inquire whether the conditions set out in subsection (1.1) are met does not affect the validity of the plea.

(2) Where an accused refuses to plead or does not answer directly, the court shall order the clerk of the court to enter a plea of not guilty.

(3) An accused is not entitled as of right to have his trial postponed but the court may, if it considers that the accused should be allowed further time to plead, move to quash, or prepare for his defence or for any other reason, adjourn the trial to a later time in the session or sittings of the court, or to the next of any subsequent session or sittings of the court, on such terms as the court considers proper.

(4) Notwithstanding any other provision of this Act, where an accused or defendant pleads not guilty of the offence charged but guilty of any other offence arising out of the same transaction, whether or not it is an included offence, the court may, with the consent of the prosecutor, accept that plea of guilty and, if such plea is accepted, the court shall find the accused or defendant not guilty of the offence charged and find him guilty of the offence in respect of which the plea of guilty was accepted and enter those findings in the record of the court.

(4.1) If the accused is charged with a serious personal injury offence, as that expression is defined in section 752, or with the offence of murder, and the accused and the prosecutor have entered into an agreement under which the accused will enter a plea of guilty of the offence charged — or a plea of not guilty of the offence charged but guilty of any other offence arising out of the same transaction, whether or not it is an included offence — the court shall, after accepting the plea of guilty, inquire of the prosecutor if reasonable steps were taken to inform the victims of the agreement.

(4.2) If the accused is charged with an offence, as defined in section 2 of the *Canadian Victims Bill of Rights*, that is an indictable offence for which the maximum punishment is imprisonment for five years or more, and that is not an offence referred to in subsection (4.1), and the accused and the prosecutor have entered into an agreement referred to in subsection (4.1), the court shall, after accepting the plea of guilty, inquire of the prosecutor whether any of the victims had advised the prosecutor of their desire to be informed if such an agreement were entered into, and, if so, whether reasonable steps were taken to inform that victim of the agreement.

(4.3) If subsection (4.1) or (4.2) applies, and any victim was not informed of the agreement before the plea of guilty was accepted, the prosecutor shall, as soon as feasible, take reasonable steps to inform the victim of the agreement and the acceptance of the plea.

(4.4) Neither the failure of the court to inquire of the prosecutor, nor the failure of the prosecutor to take reasonable steps to inform the victims of the agreement, affects the validity of the plea.

(5) For greater certainty, subsections 650(1.1) and (1.2) apply, with any modifications that the circumstances require, to pleas under this section if the accused has agreed to use a means referred to in those subsections. R.S., c. C-34, s. 534; 1974-75-76, c. 105, s. 7; R.S.C. 1985, c. 27 (1st Supp.), s. 125; 2002, c. 13, s. 49; 2015, c. 13, s. 21; 2019, c. 25, s. 268.

SPECIAL PLEAS / In case of libel / Disposal / Pleading over / Statement sufficient / Exception: foreign trials *in absentia*.

607. (1) An accused may plead the special pleas of
- (a) *autrefois acquit,*
- (b) *autrefois convict,*
- (c) pardon; and
- (d) an expungement order under the *Expungement of Historically Unjust Convictions Act.*

(2) An accused who is charged with defamatory libel may plead in accordance with sections 611 and 612.

(3) The pleas of *autrefois acquit, autrefois convict*, pardon and an expungement order under the *Expungement of Historically Unjust Convictions Act* shall be disposed of by the judge without a jury before the accused is called on to plead further.

(4) When the pleas referred to in subsection (3) are disposed of against the accused, he may plead guilty or not guilty.

(5) Where an accused pleads *autrefois acquit* or *autrefois convict*, it is sufficient if he
- (a) states that he has been lawfully acquitted, convicted or discharged under subsection 730(1), as the case may be, of the offence charged in the count to which the plea relates; and
- (b) indicates the time and place of the acquittal, conviction or discharge under subsection 730(1).

(6) A person who is alleged to have committed an act or omission outside Canada that is an offence in Canada by virtue of any of subsections 7(2) to (3.1) or (3.7),

or an offence under the *Crimes Against Humanity and War Crimes Act*, and in respect of which the person has been tried and convicted outside Canada, may not plead *autrefois convict* with respect to a count that charges that offence if

   (a) at the trial outside Canada the person was not present and was not represented by counsel acting under the person's instructions, and

   (b) the person was not punished in accordance with the sentence imposed on conviction in respect of the act or omission.

notwithstanding that the person is deemed by virtue of subsection 7(6), or subsection 12(1) of the *Crimes Against Humanity and War Crimes Act*, as the case may be, to have been tried and convicted in Canada in respect of the act or omission. R.S., c. C-34, s. 535; 1974-75-76, c. 105, s. 8; R.S.C. 1985, c. 27 (1st Supp.), s. 126, c. 30 (3rd Supp.), s. 2; 1995, c. 22, s. 10; 2000, c. 24, s. 45; 2013, c. 13, s. 9; 2018, c. 11, s. 29.

EVIDENCE OF IDENTITY OF CHARGES.

608. Where an issue on a plea of *autrefois acquit* or *autrefois convict* is tried, the evidence and adjudication and the notes of the judge and official stenographer on the former trial and the record transmitted to the court pursuant to section 551 on the charge that is pending before that court are admissible in evidence to prove or to disprove the identity of the charges. R.S., c. C-34, s. 536.

WHAT DETERMINES IDENTITY / Allowance of special plea in part.

609. (1) Where an issue on a plea of *autrefois acquit* or *autrefois convict* to a count is tried and it appears

   (a) that the matter on which the accused was given in charge on the former trial is the same in whole or in part as that on which it is proposed to give him in charge, and

   (b) that on the former trial, if all proper amendments had been made that might then have been made, he might have been convicted of all the offences of which he may be convicted on the count to which the plea of *autrefois acquit* or *autrefois convict* is pleaded,

the judge shall give judgment discharging the accused in respect of that count.

(2) The following provisions apply where an issue on a plea of *autrefois acquit* or *autrefois convict* is tried:

   (a) where it appears that the accused might on the former trial have been convicted of an offence of which he may be convicted on the count in issue, the judge shall direct that the accused shall not be found guilty of any offence of which he might have been convicted on the former trial, and

   (b) where it appears that the accused may be convicted on the count in issue of an offence of which he could not have been convicted on the former trial, the accused shall plead guilty or not guilty with respect to that offence. R.S., c. C-34, s. 537.

CIRCUMSTANCES OF AGGRAVATION / Effect of previous charge of murder or manslaughter / Previous charges of first degree murder / Effect of previous charge of infanticide or manslaughter.

610. (1) Where an indictment charges substantially the same offence as that charged in an indictment on which an accused was previously convicted or acquitted, but adds a statement of intention or circumstances of aggravation tending, if proved, to increase the punishment, the previous conviction or acquittal bars the subsequent indictment.

(2) A conviction or an acquittal on an indictment for murder bars a subsequent indictment for the same homicide charging it as manslaughter or infanticide, and a conviction or acquittal on an indictment for manslaughter or infanticide bars a subsequent indictment for the same homicide charging it as murder.

(3) A conviction or an acquittal on an indictment for first degree murder bars a subsequent indictment for the same homicide charging it as second degree murder, and a conviction or acquittal on an indictment for second degree murder bars a subsequent indictment for the same homicide charging it as first degree murder.

(4) A conviction or an acquittal on an indictment for infanticide bars a subsequent indictment for the same homicide charging it as manslaughter, and a conviction or acquittal on an indictment for manslaughter bars a subsequent indictment for the same homicide charging it as infanticide. R.S., c. C-34, s. 538; 1973-74, c. 38, s. 5; 1974-75-76, c. 105, s. 9.

LIBEL, PLEA OF JUSTIFICATION / Where more than one sense alleged / Plea in writing / Reply.

611. (1) An accused who is charged with publishing a defamatory libel may plead that the defamatory matter published by him was true, and that it was for the public benefit that the matter should have been published in the manner in which and at the time when it was published.

(2) A plea that is made under subsection (1) may justify the defamatory matter in any sense in which it is specified in the count, or in the sense that the defamatory matter bears without being specified, or separate pleas justifying the defamatory matter in each sense may be pleaded separately to each count as if two libels had been charged in separate counts.

(3) A plea that is made under subsection (1) shall be in writing, and shall set out the particular facts by reason of which it is alleged to have been for the public good that the matter should have been published.

(4) The prosecutor may in his reply deny generally the truth of a plea that is made under this section. R.S., c. C-34, s. 539.

PLEA OF JUSTIFICATION NECESSARY / Not guilty, in addition / Effect of plea on punishment.

612. (1) The truth of the matters charged in an alleged libel shall not be inquired into in the absence of a plea of justification under section 611 unless the accused is charged with publishing the libel knowing it to be false, in which case evidence of the truth may be given to negative the allegation that the accused knew that the libel was false.

(2) The accused may, in addition to a plea that is made under section 611, plead not guilty and the pleas shall be inquired into together.

(3) Where a plea of justification is pleaded and the accused is convicted, the court may, in pronouncing sentence, consider whether the guilt of the accused is aggravated or mitigated by the plea. R.S., c. C-34, s. 540.

PLEA OF NOT GUILTY.

613. Any ground of defence for which a special plea is not provided by this Act may be relied on under the plea of not guilty. R.S., c. C-34, s. 541.

---

614. [*Repealed* (with heading), 1991, c. 43, s. 3.]

Transitional provision
1991, c. 43, s. 10 provides as follows:

10. (1) Any order for the detention of an accused or accused person made under section 614, 615 or 617 of the *Criminal Code* or section 200 or 201 of the *National Defence Act*, as those sections read immediately before the coming into force of section 3 or 18 of this Act, shall continue in force until the coming into force of section 672.64 of the *Criminal Code*, subject to any order made by a court or Review Board under section 672.54 of the *Criminal Code*.

(2) The Review Board of a province shall, within twelve months after the coming into force of this section, review the case of every person detained in custody in the province by virtue of an order of detention referred to in subsection (1).

---

615. [*Repealed*, 1991, c. 43, s. 3.]

Transitional provision
1991, c. 43, s. 10 provides as follows:

10. (1) Any order for the detention of an accused or accused person made under section 614, 615 or 617 of the *Criminal Code* or section 200 or 201 of the *National Defence Act*, as those sections read immediately before the coming into force of section 3 or 18 of this Act, shall continue in force until the coming into force of section 672.64 of the *Criminal Code*, subject to any order made by a court or Review Board under section 672.54 of the *Criminal Code*.

(2) The Review Board of a province shall, within twelve months after the coming into force of this section, review the case of every person detained in custody in the province by virtue of an order of detention referred to in subsection (1).

---

616. [*Repealed*, 1991, c. 43, s. 3.]

---

617. [*Repealed*, 1991, c. 43, s. 3.]

Transitional provision
1991, c. 43, s. 10 provides as follows:

10. (1) Any order for the detention of an accused or accused person made under section 614, 615 or 617 of the *Criminal Code* or section 200 or 201 of the *National Defence Act*, as those sections read immediately before the coming into force of section 3 or 18 of this Act, shall continue in force until the coming into force of section 672.64 of the *Criminal Code*, subject to any order made by a court or Review Board under section 672.54 of the *Criminal Code*.

(2) The Review Board of a province shall, within twelve months after the coming into force of this section, review the case of every person detained in custody in the province by virtue of an order of detention referred to in subsection (1).

---

618. [*Repealed*, 1991, c. 43, s. 3.]

---

619. [*Repealed*, 1991, c. 43, s. 3.]

Organizations

APPEARANCE BY ATTORNEY.

620. Every organization against which an indictment is filed shall appear and plead by counsel or agent. R.S., c. C-34, s. 548; 1997, c. 18, s. 70; 2003, c. 21, s. 11.

NOTICE TO ORGANIZATION / Contents of notice.

621. (1) The clerk of the court or the prosecutor may, where an indictment is filed against an organization, cause a notice of the indictment to be served on the organization.

(2) A notice of an indictment referred to in subsection (1) shall set out the nature and purport of the indictment and advise that, unless the organization appears on the date set out in the notice or the date fixed under subsection 548(2.1), and enters a plea, a plea of not guilty will be entered for the accused by the court, and that the trial of the indictment will be proceeded with as though the organization had appeared and pleaded. R.S., c. C-34, s. 549; 1997, c. 18, s. 71; 2003, c. 21, s. 11.

PROCEDURE ON DEFAULT OF APPEARANCE.

622. Where an organization does not appear in accordance with the notice referred to in section 621, the presiding judge may, on proof of service of the notice, order the clerk of the court to enter a plea of not guilty on behalf of the organization, and the plea has the same force and effect as if the organization had appeared by its counsel or agent and pleaded that plea. R.S., c. C-34, s. 550; 1997, c. 18, s. 72; 2003, c. 21, s. 11.

TRIAL OF ORGANIZATION.

623. Where an organization appears and pleads to an indictment or a plea of not guilty is entered by order of the court under section 622, the court shall proceed with the trial of the indictment and, where the organization is convicted, section 735 applies. R.S., c. C-34, s. 551; 1995, c. 22, s. 10; 2003, c. 21, s. 11.

Record of Proceedings

HOW RECORDED / Record of proceedings.

624. (1) It is sufficient, in making up the record of a conviction or acquittal on an indictment, to copy the indictment and the plea that was pleaded, without a formal caption or heading.

(2) The court shall keep a record of every arraignment and of proceedings subsequent to arraignment. R.S., c. C-34, s. 552.

FORM OF RECORD IN CASE OF AMENDMENT.

625. Where it is necessary to draw up a formal record in proceedings in which the indictment has been amended, the record shall be drawn up in the form in which the indictment remained after the amendment, without reference to the fact that the indictment was amended. R.S., c. C-34, s. 553.

Pre-hearing Conference

PRE-HEARING CONFERENCE / Mandatory pre-trial hearing for jury trials.

625.1 (1) Subject to subsection (2), on application by the prosecutor or the accused or on its own motion, the court, or a judge of the court, before which, or the judge, provincial court judge or justice before whom, any proceedings are to be held may order that a conference between the prosecutor and the accused or counsel for the accused, to be presided over by the court, judge, provincial court judge or justice, be held prior to the proceedings to consider the matters that, to promote a fair and expeditious hearing, would be better decided before the start of the proceedings, and other similar matters, and to make arrangements for decisions on those matters.

(2) In any case to be tried with a jury, a judge of the court before which the accused is to be tried shall, before the trial, order that a conference between the prosecutor and the accused or counsel for the accused, to be presided over by a judge of that court, be held in accordance with the rules of court made under sections 482 and 482.1 to consider any matters that would promote a fair and expeditious trial. R.S.C. 1985, c. 27 (1st Supp.), s. 127; 1997, c. 18, s. 73; 2002, c. 13, s. 50.

Juries

QUALIFICATION OF JURORS / No disqualification based on sex.

626. (1) A person who is qualified as a juror according to, and summoned as a juror in accordance with, the laws of a province is qualified to serve as a juror in criminal proceedings in that province.

(2) Notwithstanding any law of a province referred to in subsection (1), no person may be disqualified, exempted or excused from serving as a juror in criminal proceedings on the grounds of his or her sex. R.S., c. C-34, s. 554; 1972, c. 13, s. 46; R.S.C. 1985, c. 27 (1st Supp.), s. 128.

PRESIDING JUDGE.

626.1 The judge before whom an accused is tried may be either the judge who presided over matters pertaining to the selection of a jury before the commencement of a trial or another judge of the same court. 2002, c. 13, s. 51.

627. [*Repealed*, R.S.C. 1985, c. 2 (1st Supp.), s. 1.]

SUPPORT FOR JUROR WITH PHYSICAL DISABILITY.

627. The judge may permit a juror with a physical disability who is otherwise qualified to serve as a juror to have technical, personal, interpretative or other support services. 1998, c. 9, s. 4.

628. [*Repealed*, R.S.C. 1985, c. 27 (1st Supp.), s. 129.]

CHALLENGING THE JURY PANEL / In writing / Form.

629. (1) The accused or the prosecutor may challenge the jury panel only on the ground of partiality, fraud or wilful misconduct on the part of the sheriff or other officer by whom the panel was returned.

(2) A challenge under subsection (1) shall be in writing and shall state that the person who returned the panel was partial or fraudulent or that he wilfully misconducted himself, as the case may be.

(3) A challenge under this section may be in Form 40. R.S., c. C-34, s. 558; R.S.C. 1985, c. 27 (1st Supp.), s. 130.

TRYING GROUND OF CHALLENGE.

630. Where a challenge is made under section 629, the judge shall determine whether the alleged ground of challenge is true or not, and where he is satisfied that the alleged ground of challenge is true, he shall direct a new panel to be returned. R.S., c. C-34, s. 559.

Empanelling Jury

NAMES OF JURORS ON CARDS / To be placed in box / Additional jurors / Alternate jurors / Cards to be drawn by clerk of court / Exception / Juror and other persons to be sworn / Drawing additional cards if necessary / Ban on publication, limitation to access or use of information.

631. (1) The name of each juror on a panel of jurors that has been returned, his number on the panel and his address shall be written on a separate card, and all the cards shall, as far as possible, be of equal size.

(2) The sheriff or other officer who returns the panel shall deliver the cards referred to in subsection (1) to the clerk of the court who shall cause them to be placed together in a box to be provided for the purpose and to be thoroughly shaken together.

(2.1) If the judge considers it advisable in the interests of justice to have one or two alternate jurors, the judge shall so order before the clerk of the court draws out the cards under subsection (3).

(2.2) If the judge considers it advisable in the interests of justice, he or she may order that 13 or 14 jurors, instead of 12, be sworn in accordance with this Part before the clerk of the court draws out the cards under subsection (3) or (3.1).

(3) If the array of jurors is not challenged or the array of jurors is challenged but the judge does not direct a new panel to be returned, the clerk of the court shall, in open court, draw out one after another the cards referred to in subsection (1), call out the number on each card as it is drawn and confirm with the person who responds that he or she is the person whose name appears on the card drawn, until the number of persons who have answered is, in the opinion of the judge, sufficient to provide a full jury and any alternate jurors ordered by the judge after allowing for orders to excuse, challenges and directions to stand by.

(3.1) The court, or a judge of the court, before which the jury trial is to be held may, if the court or judge is satisfied that it is necessary for the proper administration of justice, order the clerk of the court to call out the name and the number on each card.

(4) The clerk of the court shall swear each member of the jury, and any alternate jurors, in the order in which the names of the jurors were drawn and shall swear any other person providing technical, personal, interpretative or other support services to a juror with a physical disability.

(5) If the number of persons who answer under subsection (3) or (3.1) is not sufficient to provide a full jury and the number of alternate jurors ordered by the judge, the clerk of the court shall proceed in accordance with subsections (3), (3.1) and (4) until 12 jurors — or 13 or 14 jurors, as the case may be, if the judge makes an order under subsection (2.2) — and any alternate jurors are sworn.

(6) On application by the prosecutor or on its own motion, the court or judge before which a jury trial is to be held may, if the court or judge is satisfied that such an order is necessary for the proper administration of justice, make an order

(a) directing that the identity of a juror or any information that could disclose their identity shall not be published in any document or broadcast or transmitted in any way; or

(b) limiting access to or the use of that information. R.S. c. C-34, s. 560; R.S.C. 1985, c. 27 (1st Supp.), s. 131; 1992, c. 41, s. 1; 1998, c. 9, s. 5; 2001, c. 32, s. 38; 2002, c. 13, s. 52; 2005, c. 32, s. 20; 2011, c. 16, s. 7.

Note: S.C. 2002, c. 13, s. 52(2) replaced the portion of 631(3) after paragraph (b); however subsection 631(3) was previously amended by 2001, c. 32, s. 38 which re-enacted the subsection so that it read as it does above, without the portion following paragraph (b). This inconsistency will be corrected at a later date by the Legislature.

CODE

EXCUSING JURORS.

632. The judge may, at any time before the commencement of a trial, order that any juror be excused from jury service, whether or not the juror has been called pursuant to subsection 631(3) or (3.1) or any challenge has been made in relation to the juror, for reasons of

(a) personal interest in the matter to be tried;

(b) relationship with the judge presiding over the jury selection process, the judge before whom the accused is to be tried, the prosecutor, the accused, the counsel for the accused or a prospective witness; or

(c) personal hardship or any other reasonable cause that, in the opinion of the judge, warrants that the juror be excused. R.S., c. C-34, s. 561; 1992, c. 41, s. 2; 2001, c. 32, s. 39; 2002, c. 13, s. 53.

STAND BY.

633. The judge may direct a juror who has been called under subsection 631(3) or (3.1) to stand by for reasons of personal hardship, maintaining public confidence in the administration of justice or any other reasonable cause. R.S., c. C-34, s. 562; 1974-75-76, c. 105, s. 10; 1992, c. 41, s. 2; 2001, c. 32, s. 40; 2019, c. 25, s. 269.

634. [*Repealed*, 2019, c. 25, s. 269.]

635. [*Repealed* (old provision), R.S.C. 1985, c. 2 (1st Supp.), s. 2.]

ORDER OF CHALLENGES / Where there are joint trials.

635. (1) The accused shall be called on before the prosecutor is called on to declare whether the accused challenges the first juror for cause, and after that the prosecutor and the accused shall be called on alternately, in respect of each of the remaining jurors, to first make such a declaration.

(2) Subsection (1) applies where two or more accused are to be tried together, but all of the accused shall exercise the challenges of the defence in turn, in the order in which their names appear in the indictment or in any other order agreed on by them,

- (a) in respect of the first juror, before the prosecutor; and
- (b) in respect of each of the remaining jurors, either before or after the prosecutor, in accordance with subsection (1). 1992, c. 41, s. 2; 2019, c. 25, s. 270.

---

636. [*Repealed*, 1992, c. 41, s. 2.]

---

637. [*Repealed*, 1992, c. 41, s. 2.]

CHALLENGE FOR CAUSE / No other ground.

638. (1) A prosecutor or an accused is entitled to any number of challenges on the ground that

- (a) the name of a juror does not appear on the panel, but no misnomer or misdescription is a ground of challenge where it appears to the court that the description given on the panel sufficiently designates the person referred to;
- (b) a juror is not impartial;
- (c) a juror has been convicted of an offence for which they were sentenced to a term of imprisonment of two years or more and for which no pardon or record suspension is in effect;
- (d) a juror is not a Canadian citizen;
- (e) a juror, even with the aid of technical, personal, interpretative or other support services provided to the juror under section 627, is physically unable to perform properly the duties of a juror; or
- (f) a juror does not speak the official language of Canada that is the language of the accused or the official language of Canada in which the accused can best give testimony or both official languages of Canada, where the accused is required by reason of an order under section 530 to be tried before a judge and jury who speak the official language of Canada that is the language of the accused or the official language of Canada in which the accused can best give testimony or who speak both official languages of Canada, as the case may be.

(2) No challenge for cause shall be allowed on a ground not mentioned in subsection (1). R.S., c. C-34, s. 567; 1977-78, c. 36, ss. 5, 6; R.S.C. 1985, c. 27 (1st Supp.), s. 132; c. 31 (4th Supp.), s. 96; 1997, c. 18, s. 74; 1998, c. 9, s. 6; 2019, c. 25, s. 271.

(3) [*Repealed*, 1997, c. 18, s. 74.]

(4) [*Repealed*, 1997, c. 18, s. 74.]

CHALLENGE IN WRITING / Form / Denial.

639. (1) Where a challenge is made on a ground mentioned in section 638, the court may, in its discretion, require the party that challenges to put the challenge in writing.

(2) A challenge may be in Form 41.

(3) A challenge may be denied by the other party to the proceedings on the ground that it is not true. R.S., c. C-34, s. 568.

DETERMINATION OF CHALLENGE FOR CAUSE / Exclusion order.

640. (1) If a challenge is made on a ground mentioned in section 638, the judge shall determine whether the alleged ground is true or not and, if the judge is satisfied that it is true, the juror shall not be sworn.

(2) On the application of the accused or prosecutor or on the judge's own motion, the judge may order the exclusion of all jurors, sworn and unsworn, from the court room until it is determined whether the ground of challenge is true if the judge is of the opinion that the order is necessary to preserve the impartiality of the jurors. R.S., c. C-34, s. 569; 2008, c. 18, s. 26; 2011, c. 16, s. 9; 2019, c. 25, s. 272.

(2.1) [*Repealed*, 2019, c. 25, s. 272.]

(2.2) [*Repealed*, 2019, c. 25, s. 272.]

(3) [*Repealed*, 2019, c. 25, s. 272.]

(4) [*Repealed*, 2019, c. 25, s. 272.]

CALLING PERSONS WHO HAVE STOOD BY / Other persons becoming available.

641. (1) If a full jury and any alternate jurors have not been sworn and no cards remain to be drawn, the persons who have been directed to stand by shall be called again in the order in which their cards were drawn and shall be sworn, unless excused by the judge or challenged by the accused or the prosecutor.

(2) If, before a person is sworn as a juror under subsection (1), other persons in the panel become available, the prosecutor may require the cards of those persons to be put into and drawn from the box in accordance with section 631, and those persons shall be challenged, directed to stand by, excused or sworn, as the case may be, before the persons who were originally directed to stand by are called again. R.S., c. C-34, s. 570; 1992, c. 41, s. 3; 2001, c. 32, s. 41; 2002, c. 13, s. 55; 2011, c. 16, s. 10.

SUMMONING OTHER JURORS WHEN PANEL EXHAUSTED / Orally / Adding names to panel.

642. (1) If a full jury and any alternate jurors considered advisable cannot be provided notwithstanding that the relevant provisions of this Part have been complied with, the court may, at the request of the prosecutor, order the sheriff or other proper officer to summon without delay as many persons, whether qualified jurors or not, as the court directs for the purpose of providing a full jury and alternate jurors.

(2) Jurors may be summoned under subsection (1) by word of mouth, if necessary.

(3) The names of the persons who are summoned under this section shall be added to the general panel for the purposes of the trial, and the same proceedings shall be taken with respect to calling and challenging those persons, excusing them and

directing them to stand by as are provided in this Part with respect to the persons named in the original panel. R.S., c. C-34, s. 571; 1992, c. 41, s. 4; 2002, c. 13, s. 56.

SUBSTITUTION OF ALTERNATE JURORS / Excusing of alternate jurors.

642.1 (1) Alternate jurors shall attend at the commencement of the presentation of the evidence on the merits and, if there is not a full jury present, shall replace any absent juror, in the order in which their cards were drawn under subsection 631(3).

(2) An alternate juror who is not required as a substitute shall be excused. 2002, c. 13, s. 57; 2011, c. 16, s. 11.

WHO SHALL BE THE JURY / Names of jurors / Same jury may try another issue by consent / Sections directory.

643. (1) The 12, 13 or 14 jurors who are sworn in accordance with this Part and present at the commencement of the presentation of the evidence on the merits shall be the jury to hear the evidence on the merits.

(1.1) The name of each juror, including alternate jurors, who is sworn shall be kept apart until the juror is excused or the jury gives its verdict or is discharged, at which time the name shall be returned to the box as often as occasion arises, as long as an issue remains to be tried before a jury.

(2) The court may try an issue with the same jury in whole or in part that previously tried or was drawn to try another issue, without the jurors being sworn again, but if the prosecutor or the accused objects to any of the jurors or the court excuses any of the jurors, the court shall order those persons to withdraw and shall direct that the required number of cards to make up a full jury be drawn and, subject to the provisions of this Part relating to challenges, orders to excuse and directions to stand by, the persons whose cards are drawn shall be sworn.

(3) Failure to comply with the directions of this section or section 631, 635 or 641 does not affect the validity of a proceeding. R.S., c. C-34, s. 572; 1992, c. 41, s. 5; 2001, c. 32, s. 42; 2002, c. 13, s. 58; 2011, c. 16, s. 12.

DISCHARGE OF JUROR / Replacement of juror / Trial may continue without jury.

644. (1) Where in the course of a trial the judge is satisfied that a juror should not, by reason of illness or other reasonable cause, continue to act, the judge may discharge the juror.

(1.1) A judge may select another juror to take the place of a juror who by reason of illness or other reasonable cause cannot continue to act, if the jury has not yet begun to hear evidence, either by drawing a name from a panel of persons who were summoned to act as jurors and who are available at the court at the time of replacing the juror or by using the procedure referred to in section 642.

(2) Where in the course of a trial a member of the jury dies or is discharged pursuant to subsection (1), the jury shall, unless the judge otherwise directs and if

the number of jurors is not reduced below ten, be deemed to remain properly constituted for all purposes of the trial and the trial shall proceed and a verdict may be given accordingly.

(3) If in the course of a trial the number of jurors is reduced below 10, the judge may, with the consent of the parties, discharge the jurors, continue the trial without a jury and render a verdict. R.S., c. C-34, s. 573; 1972, c. 13, s. 47; 1980-81-82-83, c. 47, s. 53; 1992, c. 41, s. 6; 1997, c. 18, s. 75; 2019, c. 25, s. 273.

Trial

TRIAL CONTINUOUS / Adjournment / Formal adjournment unnecessary / Questions reserved for decision / Questions reserved for decision in a trial with a jury.

645. (1) The trial of an accused shall proceed continuously subject to adjournment by the court.

(2) The judge may adjourn the trial from time to time in the same sittings.

(3) No formal adjournment of trial or entry thereof is required.

(4) A judge, in any case tried without a jury, may reserve final decision on any question raised at the trial, or any matter raised further to a pre-hearing conference, and the decision, when given, shall be deemed to have been given at the trial.

(5) In any case to be tried with a jury, the judge before whom an accused is or is to be tried has jurisdiction, before any juror on a panel of jurors is called pursuant to subsection 631(3) or (3.1) and in the absence of any such juror, to deal with any matter that would ordinarily or necessarily be dealt with in the absence of the jury after it has been sworn. R.S., c. C-34, s. 574; R.S.C. 1985, c. 27 (1st Supp.), s. 133; 1997, c. 18, s. 76; 2001, c. 32, s. 43.

TAKING EVIDENCE.

646. On the trial of an accused for an indictable offence, the evidence of the witnesses for the prosecutor and the accused and the addresses of the prosecutor and the accused or counsel for the accused by way of summing up shall be taken in accordance with the provisions of Part XVIII, other than subsections 540(7) to (9), relating to the taking of evidence at preliminary inquiries. R.S., c. C-34, s. 575; 2002, c. 13, s. 59.

SEPARATION OF JURORS / Keeping in charge / Non-compliance with subsection (2) / Empanelling new jury in certain cases / Refreshment and accommodation.

647. (1) The judge may, at any time before the jury retires to consider its verdict, permit the members of the jury to separate.

(2) Where permission to separate under subsection (1) cannot be given or is not given, the jury shall be kept under the charge of an officer of the court as the judge

directs, and that officer shall prevent the jurors from communicating with anyone other than himself or another member of the jury without leave of the judge.

(3) Failure to comply with subsection (2) does not affect the validity of the proceedings.

(4) Where the fact that there has been a failure to comply with this section or section 648 is discovered before the verdict of the jury is returned, the judge may, if he considers that the failure to comply might lead to a miscarriage of justice, discharge the jury and

(a) direct that the accused be tried with a new jury during the same session or sittings of the court; or

(b) postpone the trial on such terms as justice may require.

(5) The judge shall direct the sheriff to provide the jurors who are sworn with suitable and sufficient refreshment, food and lodging while they are together until they have given their verdict. R.S., c. C-34, s. 576; 1972, c. 13, s. 48.

RESTRICTION ON PUBLICATION / Offence / Definition of "newspaper".

648. (1) After permission to separate is given to members of a jury under subsection 647(1), no information regarding any portion of the trial at which the jury is not present shall be published in any document or broadcast or transmitted in any way before the jury retires to consider its verdict.

(2) Every one who fails to comply with subsection (1) is guilty of an offence punishable on summary conviction. 1972, c. 13, s. 49; 2005, c. 32, s. 21.

(3) [*Repealed*, 2005, c. 32, s. 21(2).]

DISCLOSURE OF JURY PROCEEDINGS.

649. Every member of a jury, and every person providing technical, personal, interpretative or other support services to a juror with a physical disability, who, except for the purposes of

(a) an investigation of an alleged offence under subsection 139(2) in relation to a juror, or

(b) giving evidence in criminal proceedings in relation to such an offence,

discloses any information relating to the proceedings of the jury when it was absent from the courtroom that was not subsequently disclosed in open court is guilty of an offence punishable on summary conviction. 1972, c. 13, s. 49; 1998, c. 9, s. 7.

ACCUSED TO BE PRESENT / Video links / Video links / Exceptions / To make defence.

650. (1) Subject to subsections (1.1) to (2) and section 650.01, an accused, other than an organization, shall be present in court during the whole of his or her trial.

(1.1) If the court so orders, and if the prosecutor and the accused so agree, the accused may appear by counsel or by closed-circuit television or videoconference, for any part of the trial other than a part in which the evidence of a witness is taken.

(1.2) If the court so orders, an accused who is confined in prison may appear by closed-circuit television or videoconference, for any part of the trial other than a part in which the evidence of a witness is taken, as long as the accused is given the opportunity to communicate privately with counsel if they are represented by counsel.

(2) The court may

    (a) cause the accused to be removed and to be kept out of court, where he misconducts himself by interrupting the proceedings so that to continue the proceedings in his presence would not be feasible;

    (b) permit the accused to be out of court during the whole or any part of his trial on such conditions as the court considers proper; or

    (c) cause the accused to be removed and to be kept out of court during the trial of an issue as to whether the accused is unfit to stand trial, where it is satisfied that failure to do so might have an adverse effect on the mental condition of the accused.

(3) An accused is entitled, after the close of the case for the prosecution, to make full answer and defence personally or by counsel. R.S., c. C-34, s. 577; 1972, c. 13, s. 50; 1991, c. 43, s. 9; 1994, c. 44, s. 61; 1997, c. 18, s. 77; 2002, c. 13, s. 60; 2003, c. 21, s. 12; 2019, c. 25, s. 274.

DESIGNATION OF COUNSEL OF RECORD / Contents of designation / Effect of designation / When court orders presence of accused.

650.01 (1) An accused may appoint counsel to represent the accused for any proceedings under this Act by filing a designation with the court.

(2) The designation must contain the name and address of the counsel and be signed by the accused and the designated counsel.

(3) If a designation is filed,

    (a) the accused may appear by the designated counsel without being present for any part of the proceedings, other than

      (i) a part during which oral evidence of a witness is taken,

      (ii) a part during which jurors are being selected, and

      (iii) an application for a writ of habeas corpus;

    (b) an appearance by the designated counsel is equivalent to the accused's being present, unless the court orders otherwise; and

    (c) a plea of guilty may be made, and a sentence may be pronounced, only if the accused is present, unless the court orders otherwise.

(4) If the court orders the accused to be present otherwise than by appearance by the designated counsel, the court may

    (a) issue a summons to compel the presence of the accused and order that it be served by leaving a copy at the address contained in the designation; or

    (b) issue a warrant to compel the presence of the accused. 2002, c. 13, s. 61.

REMOTE APPEARANCE.

650.02 The prosecutor or the counsel designated under section 650.01 may appear before the court by audioconference or videoconference, if the technological means is satisfactory to the court. 2002, c. 13, s. 61; 2019, c. 25, s. 275.

PRE-CHARGE CONFERENCE.

650.1 A judge in a jury trial may, before the charge to the jury, confer with the accused or counsel for the accused and the prosecutor with respect to the matters that should be explained to the jury and with respect to the choice of instructions to the jury. 1997, c. 18, s. 78.

SUMMING UP BY PROSECUTOR / Summing up by accused / Accused's right of reply / Prosecutor's right of reply where more than one accused.

651. (1) Where an accused, or any one of several accused being tried together, is defended by counsel, the counsel shall, at the end of the case for the prosecution, declare whether or not he intends to adduce evidence on behalf of the accused for whom he appears and if he does not announce his intention to adduce evidence, the prosecutor may address the jury by way of summing up.

(2) Counsel for the accused or the accused, where he is not defended by counsel, is entitled, if he thinks fit, to open the case for the defence, and after the conclusion of that opening to examine such witnesses as he thinks fit, and when all the evidence is concluded to sum up the evidence.

(3) Where no witnesses are examined for an accused, he or his counsel is entitled to address the jury last, but otherwise counsel for the prosecution is entitled to address the jury last.

(4) Where two or more accused are tried jointly and witnesses are examined for any of them, all the accused or their respective counsel are required to address the jury before it is addressed by the prosecutor. R.S., c. C-34, s. 578.

VIEW / Directions to prevent communication / Who shall attend.

652. (1) The judge may, where it appears to be in the interests of justice, at any time after the jury has been sworn and before it gives its verdict, direct the jury to have a view of any place, thing or person, and shall give directions respecting the manner in which, and the persons by whom, the place, thing or person shall be shown to the jury, and may for that purpose adjourn the trial.

(2) Where a view is ordered under subsection (1), the judge shall give any directions that he considers necessary for the purpose of preventing undue communication by any person with members of the jury, but failure to comply with any directions given under this subsection does not affect the validity of the proceedings.

(3) Where a view is ordered under subsection (1) the accused and the judge shall attend. R.S., c. C-34, s. 579.

TRYING OF ISSUES OF INDICTMENT BY JURY / Reduction of number of jurors to 12.

652.1 (1) After the charge to the jury, the jury shall retire to try the issues of the indictment.

(2) However, if there are more than 12 jurors remaining, the judge shall identify the 12 jurors who are to retire to consider the verdict by having the number of each juror written on a card that is of equal size, by causing the cards to be placed together in a box that is to be thoroughly shaken together and by drawing one card if 13 jurors remain or two cards if 14 jurors remain. The judge shall then discharge any juror whose number is drawn. 2011, c. 16, s. 13.

DISAGREEMENT OF JURY / Discretion not reviewable.

653. (1) Where the judge is satisfied that the jury is unable to agree on its verdict and that further detention of the jury would be useless, he may in his discretion discharge that jury and direct a new jury to be empanelled during the sittings of the court, or may adjourn the trial on such terms as justice may require.

(2) A discretion that is exercised under subsection (1) by a judge is not reviewable. R.S., c. C-34, s. 580.

MISTRIAL — RULINGS BINDING AT NEW TRIAL.

653.1 In the case of a mistrial, unless the court is satisfied that it would not be in the interests of justice, rulings relating to the disclosure or admissibility of evidence or the *Canadian Charter of Rights and Freedoms* that were made during the trial are binding on the parties in any new trial if the rulings are made — or could have been made — before the stage at which the evidence on the merits is presented. 2011, c. 16, s. 14.

PROCEEDING ON SUNDAY, ETC., NOT INVALID.

654. The taking of the verdict of a jury and any proceeding incidental thereto is not invalid by reason only that it is done on Sunday or on a holiday. R.S., c. C-34, s. 581.

Evidence on Trial

ADMISSIONS AT TRIAL.

655. Where an accused is on trial for an indictable offence, he or his counsel may admit any fact alleged against him for the purpose of dispensing with proof thereof. R.S., c. C-34, s. 582.

PRESUMPTION — VALUABLE MINERALS.

656. In any proceeding in relation to theft or possession of a valuable mineral that is unrefined, partly refined, uncut or otherwise unprocessed by any person actively engaged in or on a mine, if it is established that the person possesses the valuable mineral, the person is presumed, in the absence of evidence raising a reasonable doubt to the contrary, to have stolen or unlawfully possessed the valuable mineral. R.S., c. C-34, s. 583; 1999, c. 5, s. 24.

USE IN EVIDENCE OF STATEMENT BY ACCUSED.

657. A statement made by an accused under subsection 541(3) and purporting to be signed by the justice before whom it was made may be given in evidence against the accused at his or her trial without proof of the signature of the justice, unless it is proved that the justice by whom the statement purports to be signed did not sign it. R.S., c. C-34, s. 584; 1994, c. 44, s. 62.

PROOF OF OWNERSHIP AND VALUE OF PROPERTY / Statements to be made / Notice of intention to produce affidavit or solemn declaration / Attendance for examination.

657.1 (1) In any proceedings, an affidavit or a solemn declaration of a person who claims to be the lawful owner of, or the person lawfully entitled to possession of, property that was the subject-matter of the offence, or any other person who has specialized knowledge of the property or of that type of property, containing the statements referred to in subsection (2), shall be admissible in evidence and, in the absence of evidence to the contrary, is evidence of the statements contained in the affidavit or solemn declaration without proof of the signature of the person appearing to have signed the affidavit or solemn declaration.

(2) For the purposes of subsection (1), a person shall state in an affidavit or a solemn declaration

- (*a*) that the person is the lawful owner of, or is lawfully entitled to possession of, the property, or otherwise has specialized knowledge of the property or of property of the same type as the property;
- (*b*) the value of the property;
- (*c*) in the case of a person who is the lawful owner of or is lawfully entitled to possession of the property, that the person has been deprived of the property by fraudulent means or otherwise without the lawful consent of the person;
- (*c*.1) in the case of proceedings in respect of an offence under section 342, that the credit card had been revoked or cancelled, is a false document within the meaning of section 321 or that no credit card that meets the exact description of that credit card was ever issued; and
- (*d*) any facts within the personal knowledge of the person relied on to justify the statements referred to in paragraphs (*a*) to (*c*.1).

(3) Unless the court orders otherwise, no affidavit or solemn declaration shall be received in evidence pursuant to subsection (1) unless the prosecutor has, before the trial or other proceeding, given to the accused a copy of the affidavit or solemn declaration and reasonable notice of intention to produce it in evidence.

(4) Notwithstanding subsection (1), the court may require the person who appears to have signed an affidavit or solemn declaration referred to in that subsection to

appear before it for examination or cross-examination in respect of the issue of proof of any of the statements contained in the affidavit or solemn declaration. R.S.C. 1985, c. 23 (4th Supp.), s. 3; 1997, c. 18, s. 79.

THEFT AND POSSESSION / Accessory after the fact.

657.2 (1) Where an accused is charged with possession of any property obtained by the commission of an offence, evidence of the conviction or discharge of another person of theft of the property is admissible against the accused, and in the absence of evidence to the contrary is proof that the property was stolen.

(2) Where an accused is charged with being an accessory after the fact to the commission of an offence, evidence of the conviction or discharge of another person of the offence is admissible against the accused, and in the absence of evidence to the contrary is proof that the offence was committed. 1997, c. 18, s. 80.

EXPERT TESTIMONY / Attendance for examination / Notice for expert testimony / If notices not given / Additional court orders / Use of material by prosecution / No further disclosure.

657.3 (1) In any proceedings, the evidence of a person as an expert may be given by means of a report accompanied by the affidavit or solemn declaration of the person, setting out, in particular, the qualifications of the person as an expert if

    (*a*) the court recognizes that person as an expert; and

    (*b*) the party intending to produce the report in evidence has, before the proceeding, given to the other party a copy of the affidavit or solemn declaration and the report and reasonable notice of the intention to produce it in evidence.

(2) Notwithstanding subsection (1), the court may require the person who appears to have signed an affidavit or solemn declaration referred to in that subsection to appear before it for examination or cross-examination in respect of the issue of proof of any of the statements contained in the affidavit or solemn declaration or report.

(3) For the purpose of promoting the fair, orderly and efficient presentation of the testimony of witnesses,

    (*a*) a party who intends to call a person as an expert witness shall, at least thirty days before the commencement of the trial or within any other period fixed by the justice or judge, give notice to the other party or parties of his or her intention to do so, accompanied by

        (i) the name of the proposed witness,

        (ii) a description of the area of expertise of the proposed witness that is sufficient to permit the other parties to inform themselves about that area of expertise, and

        (iii) a statement of the qualifications of the proposed witness as an expert;

    (*b*) in addition to complying with paragraph (*a*), a prosecutor who intends to call a person as an expert witness shall, within a reasonable period before trial, provide to the other party or parties

631

      (i) a copy of the report, if any, prepared by the proposed witness for the case, and

      (ii) if no report is prepared, a summary of the opinion anticipated to be given by the proposed witness and the grounds on which it is based; and

  (c) in addition to complying with paragraph (*a*), an accused, or his or her counsel, who intends to call a person as an expert witness shall, not later than the close of the case for the prosecution, provide to the other party or parties the material referred to in paragraph (*b*).

(4) If a party calls a person as an expert witness without complying with subsection (3), the court shall, at the request of any other party,

  (a) grant an adjournment of the proceedings to the party who requests it to allow him or her to prepare for cross-examination of the expert witness;

  (b) order the party who called the expert witness to provide that other party and any other party with the material referred to in paragraph (3)(*b*); and

  (c) order the calling or recalling of any witness for the purpose of giving testimony on matters related to those raised in the expert witness's testimony, unless the court considers it inappropriate to do so.

(5) If, in the opinion of the court, a party who has received the notice and material referred to in subsection (3) has not been able to prepare for the evidence of the proposed witness, the court may do one or more of the following:

  (a) adjourn the proceedings;

  (b) order that further particulars be given of the evidence of the proposed witness; and

  (c) order the calling or recalling of any witness for the purpose of giving testimony on matters related to those raised in the expert witness's testimony.

(6) If the proposed witness does not testify, the prosecutor may not produce material provided to him or her under paragraph (3)(*c*) in evidence without the consent of the accused.

(7) Unless otherwise ordered by a court, information disclosed under this section in relation to a proceeding may only be used for the purpose of that proceeding. 1997, c. 18, s. 80; 2002, c. 13, s. 62.

Children and Young Persons

TESTIMONY AS TO DATE OF BIRTH / Testimony of a parent / Proof of age / Other evidence / Inference from appearance.

658. (1) In any proceedings to which this Act applies, the testimony of a person as to the date of his or her birth is admissible as evidence of that date.

(2) In any proceedings to which this Act applies, the testimony of a parent as to the age of a person of whom he or she is a parent is admissible as evidence of the age of that person.

(3) In any proceedings to which this Act applies,

(a) a birth or baptismal certificate or a copy of such a certificate purporting to be certified under the hand of the person in whose custody the certificate is held is evidence of the age of that person; and

(b) an entry or record of an incorporated society or its officers who have had the control or care of a child or young person at or about the time the child or young person was brought to Canada is evidence of the age of the child or young person if the entry or record was made before the time when the offence is alleged to have been committed.

(4) In the absence of any certificate, copy, entry or record mentioned in subsection (3), or in corroboration of any such certificate, copy, entry or record, a jury, judge, justice or provincial court judge, as the case may be, may receive and act on any other information relating to age that they consider reliable.

(5) In the absence of other evidence, or by way of corroboration of other evidence, a jury, judge, justice or provincial court judge, as the case may be, may infer the age of a child or young person from his or her appearance. R.S., c. C-34, s. 585; 1994, c. 44, s. 64.

659. [*Repealed* (old provision), R.S.C. 1985, c. 19 (3rd Supp.), s. 15.]

Corroboration

CHILDREN'S EVIDENCE.

659. Any requirement whereby it is mandatory for a court to give the jury a warning about convicting an accused on the evidence of a child is abrogated. 1993, c. 45, s. 9.

Verdicts

FULL OFFENCE CHARGED, ATTEMPT PROVED.

660. Where the complete commission of an offence charged is not proved but the evidence establishes an attempt to commit the offence, the accused may be convicted of the attempt. R.S., c. C-34, s. 587.

ATTEMPT CHARGED, FULL OFFENCE PROVED / Conviction a bar.

661. (1) Where an attempt to commit an offence is charged but the evidence establishes the commission of the complete offence, the accused is not entitled to be acquitted, but the jury may convict him of the attempt unless the judge presiding at the trial, in his discretion, discharges the jury from giving a verdict and directs that the accused be indicted for the complete offence.

(2) An accused who is convicted under this section is not liable to be tried again for the offence that he was charged with attempting to commit. R.S., c. C-34, s. 588.

OFFENCE CHARGED, PART ONLY PROVED / First degree murder charged / Conviction for infanticide or manslaughter on charge of murder / Conviction for concealing body of child where murder or infanticide charged / Conviction for dangerous operation when another offence charged / Conviction for break and enter with intent.

662. (1) A count in an indictment is divisible and where the commission of the offence charged, as described in the enactment creating it or as charged in the count, includes the commission of another offence, whether punishable by indictment or on summary conviction, the accused may be convicted

- (a) of an offence so included that is proved, notwithstanding that the whole offence that is charged is not proved; or
- (b) of an attempt to commit an offence so included.

(2) For greater certainty and without limiting the generality of subsection (1), where a count charges first degree murder and the evidence does not prove first degree murder but proves second degree murder or an attempt to commit second degree murder, the jury may find the accused not guilty of first degree murder but guilty of second degree murder or an attempt to commit second degree murder, as the case may be.

(3) Subject to subsection (4), where a count charges murder and the evidence proves manslaughter or infanticide but does not prove murder, the jury may find the accused not guilty of murder but guilty of manslaughter or infanticide, but shall not on that count find the accused guilty of any other offence.

(4) Where a count charges the murder of a child or infanticide and the evidence proves the commission of an offence under section 243 but does not prove murder or infanticide, the jury may find the accused not guilty of murder or infanticide, as the case may be, but guilty of an offence under section 243.

(5) For greater certainty, when a count charges an offence under section 220, 221 or 236 arising out of the operation of a conveyance, and the evidence does not prove that offence but proves an offence under section 320.13, the accused may be convicted of an offence under that section.

(6) Where a count charges an offence under paragraph 98(1)(b) or 348(1)(b) and the evidence does not prove that offence but does prove an offence under, respectively, paragraph 98(1)(a) or 348(1)(a), the accused may be convicted of an offence under that latter paragraph. R.S., c. C-34, s. 589; 1973-74, c. 38, s. 6; 1974-75-76, c. 105, s. 11; R.S.C. 1985, c. 27 (1st Supp.), s. 134; 2000, c. 2, s. 3; 2008, c. 6, s. 38; 2018, c. 21, s. 20.

NO ACQUITTAL UNLESS ACT OR OMISSION NOT WILFUL.

663. Where a female person is charged with infanticide and the evidence establishes that she caused the death of her child but does not establish that, at the time of the act or omission by which she caused the death of the child,

- (a) she was not fully recovered from the effects of giving birth to the child or from the effect of lactation consequent on the birth of the child, and

(b) the balance of her mind was, at that time, disturbed by reason of the effect of giving birth to the child or of the effect of lactation consequent on the birth of the child,

she may be convicted unless the evidence establishes that the act or omission was not wilful. R.S., c. C-34, s. 590.

Previous Convictions

NO REFERENCE TO PREVIOUS CONVICTION.

664. No indictment in respect of an offence for which, by reason of previous convictions, a greater punishment may be imposed shall contain any reference to previous convictions. R.S., c. C-34, s. 591.

665. [*Repealed*, 1995, c. 22, s. 3.]

EVIDENCE OF CHARACTER.

666. Where, at a trial, the accused adduces evidence of his good character, the prosecutor may, in answer thereto, before a verdict is returned, adduce evidence of the previous conviction of the accused for any offences, including any previous conviction by reason of which a greater punishment may be imposed. R.S., c. C-34, s. 593.

PROOF OF PREVIOUS CONVICTION / Idem / Proof of identity / Attendance and right to cross-examine / Notice of intention to produce certificate / Definition of "fingerprint examiner".

667. (1) In any proceedings,

(a) a certificate setting out with reasonable particularity the conviction or discharge under section 730, the finding of guilt under the *Young Offenders Act*, chapter Y-1 of the Revised Statutes of Canada, 1985, the finding of guilt under the *Youth Criminal Justice Act* or the conviction and sentence or finding of guilt and sentence in Canada of an offender is, on proof that the accused or defendant is the offender referred to in the certificate, evidence that the accused or defendant was so convicted, so discharged or so convicted and sentenced or found guilty and sentenced, without proof of the signature or the official character of the person appearing to have signed the certificate, if it is signed by

  (i) the person who made the conviction, order for the discharge or finding of guilt,

  (ii) the clerk of the court in which the conviction, order for the discharge or finding of guilt was made, or

  (iii) a fingerprint examiner;

is, on proof that the accused or defendant is the offender referred to in the certificate, evidence that the accused or defendant was so convicted, so discharged or so convicted and sentenced or found guilty and sentenced, or that a judicial determination was made against the accused or defendant, without proof of the signature or the official character of the person appearing to have signed the certificate;

(b) evidence that the fingerprints of the accused or defendant are the same as the fingerprints of the offender whose fingerprints are reproduced in or attached to a certificate issued under subparagraph (a)(iii) is, in the absence of evidence to the contrary, proof that the accused or defendant is the offender referred to in that certificate;

(c) a certificate of a fingerprint examiner stating that he has compared the fingerprints reproduced in or attached to that certificate with the fingerprints reproduced in or attached to a certificate issued under subparagraph (a)(iii) and that they are those of the same person is evidence of the statements contained in the certificate without proof of the signature or the official character of the person appearing to have signed the certificate; and

(d) a certificate under subparagraph (a)(iii) may be in Form 44, and a certificate under paragraph (c) may be in Form 45.

(2) In any proceedings, a copy of the summary conviction or discharge under section 730 in Canada of an offender, signed by the person who made the conviction or order for the discharge or by the clerk of the court in which the conviction or order for the discharge was made, is, on proof that the accused or defendant is the offender referred to in the copy of the summary conviction, evidence of the conviction or discharge under section 730 of the accused or defendant, without proof of the signature or the official character of the person appearing to have signed it.

(2.1) In any summary conviction proceedings, where the name of a defendant is similar to the name of an offender referred to in a certificate made under subparagraph (1)(a)(i) or (ii) in respect of a summary conviction or referred to in a copy of a summary conviction mentioned in subsection (2), that similarity of name is, in the absence of evidence to the contrary, evidence that the defendant is the offender referred to in the certificate or the copy of the summary conviction.

(3) An accused against whom a certificate issued under subparagraph (1)(a)(iii) or paragraph (1)(c) is produced may, with leave of the court, require the attendance of the person who signed the certificate for the purposes of cross-examination.

(4) No certificate issued under subparagraph (1)(a)(iii) or paragraph (1)(c) shall be received in evidence unless the party intending to produce it has given to the accused reasonable notice of his intention together with a copy of the certificate.

(5) In this section, "fingerprint examiner" means a person designated as such for the purposes of this section by the Minister of Public Safety and Emergency Preparedness. R.S., c. C-34, s. 594; 1972, c. 13, s. 51; R.S.C. 1985, c. 27 (1st Supp.), s. 136; 1995, c. 22, s. 10; 2002, c. 1, s. 181; 2005, c. 10, s. 34(1)(f)(xii); 2012, c. 1, s. 200.

---

668. [*Repealed*, R.S.C. 1985, c. C-34; 1995, c. 22, s. 4.]

669. [*Repealed*, R.S.C. 1985, c. C-34; 1995, c. 22, s. 4.]

Jurisdiction

JURISDICTION / Adjournment.

669.1 (1) Where any judge, court or provincial court judge by whom or which the plea of the accused or defendant to an offence was taken has not commenced to hear evidence, any judge, court or provincial court judge having jurisdiction to try the accused or defendant has jurisdiction for the purpose of the hearing and adjudication.

(2) Any court, judge or provincial court judge having jurisdiction to try an accused or a defendant, or any clerk or other proper officer of the court, or in the case of an offence punishable on summary conviction, any justice, may, at any time before or after the plea of the accused or defendant is taken, adjourn the proceedings. R.S.C. 1985, c. 27 (1st Supp.), s. 137.

CONTINUATION OF PROCEEDINGS / Where adjudication is made / If no adjudication made / If no adjudication made — jury trials / Where trial continued.

669.2 (1) Subject to this section, where an accused or a defendant is being tried by
- (*a*) a judge or provincial court judge,
- (*b*) a justice or other person who is, or is a member of, a summary conviction court, or
- (*c*) a court composed of a judge and jury,

as the case may be, and the judge, provincial court judge, justice or other person dies or is for any reason unable to continue, the proceedings may be continued before another judge, provincial court judge, justice or other person, as the case may be, who has jurisdiction to try the accused or defendant.

(2) Where a verdict was rendered by a jury or an adjudication was made by a judge, provincial court judge, justice or other person before whom the trial was commenced, the judge, provincial court judge, justice or other person before whom the proceedings are continued shall, without further election by an accused, impose the punishment or make the order that is authorized by law in the circumstances.

(3) Subject to subsections (4) and (5), if the trial was commenced but no adjudication was made or verdict rendered, the judge, provincial court judge, justice or other person before whom the proceedings are continued shall, without further election by an accused, commence the trial again as if no evidence on the merits had been taken.

(4) If a trial that is before a court composed of a judge and a jury was commenced but no adjudication was made or verdict rendered, the judge before whom the proceedings are continued may, without further election by an accused, continue the trial or commence the trial again as if no evidence on the merits had been taken.

(5) Where a trial is continued under paragraph (4)(*a*), any evidence that was adduced before a judge referred to in paragraph (1)(*c*) is deemed to have been adduced before the judge before whom the trial is continued but, where the prosecutor and the accused so agree, any part of that evidence may be adduced again before the judge before whom the trial is continued. R.S.C. 1985, c. 27 (1st Supp.), s. 137; 1994, c. 44, s. 65; 2011, c. 16, s. 15.

JURISDICTION WHEN APPOINTMENT TO ANOTHER COURT.

669.3 Where a court composed of a judge and a jury, a judge or a provincial court judge is conducting a trial and the judge or provincial court judge is appointed to another court, he or she continues to have jurisdiction in respect of the trial until its completion. 1994, c. 44, s. 66.

Formal Defects in Jury Process

JUDGMENT NOT TO BE STAYED ON CERTAIN GROUNDS.

670. Judgment shall not be stayed or reversed after verdict on an indictment
  (*a*) by reason of any irregularity in the summoning or empanelling of the jury; or
  (*b*) for the reason that a person who served on the jury was not returned as a juror by a sheriff or other officer. R.S., c. C-34, s. 598.

DIRECTIONS RESPECTING JURY OR JURORS DIRECTORY.

671. No omission to observe the directions contained in any Act with respect to the qualification, selection, balloting or distribution of jurors, the preparation of the jurors' book, the selecting of jury lists, or the drafting of panels from the jury lists, is a ground for impeaching or quashing a verdict rendered in criminal proceedings. R.S., c. C-34, s. 599.

SAVING POWERS OF COURT.

672. Nothing in this Act alters, abridges or affects any power or authority that a court or judge had immediately before April 1, 1955, or any practice or form that existed immediately before April 1, 1955, with respect to trials by jury, jury process, juries or jurors, except where the power or authority, practice or form is expressly altered by or is inconsistent with this Act. R.S., c. C-34, s. 600.

Part XX.1 / MENTAL DISORDER

Transitional provision

Note: 1991, c. 43, s. 10 (in force except subsec. (8)) provides as follows:
10. (1) Any order for the detention of an accused or accused person made under section 614, 615 or 617 of the *Criminal Code* or section 200 or 201 of the *National Defence Act*, as those sections read immediately before the coming into force of

section 3 or 18 of this Act, shall continue in force until the coming into force of section 672.64 of the *Criminal Code*, subject to any order made by a court or Review Board under section 672.54 of the *Criminal Code*.

(2) The Review Board of a province shall, within twelve months after the coming into force of this section, review the case of every person detained in custody in the province by virtue of an order of detention referred to in subsection (1).

(3) Sections 672.5 to 672.85 of the *Criminal Code* apply, with such modifications as the circumstances require, to a review under subsection (2) as if

(a) the review were a review of a disposition conducted pursuant to section 672.81 of that Act;

(b) the warrant issued by the lieutenant governor pursuant to which the person is being detained in custody were a disposition made under section 672.54 of that Act;

(c) there were included in the definition "designated offence" in subsection 672.64(1) of that Act a reference to any offence under any Act of Parliament, as that Act read at the time of the commission of the alleged offence for which the person is in custody, involving violence or a threat of violence to a person or danger to the safety or security of the public, including, without limiting the generality of the foregoing, a reference to the following sections of the *Criminal Code*, as those sections read immediately before January 4, 1983, namely,

　(i) section 144 (rape),

　(ii) section 145 (attempt to commit rape),

　(iii) section 149 (indecent assault on female),

　(iv) section 156 (indecent assault on male),

　(v) section 245 (common assault),

　(vi) section 246 (assault with intent); and

(d) there were included in the offences mentioned in paragraph 672.64(3)(a) a reference to any of the following offences under any Act of Parliament, as that Act read at the time of the commission of the alleged offence for which the person is in custody, namely,

　(i) murder punishable by death or punishable by imprisonment for life, capital murder, non-capital murder and any offence of murder, however it had been described or classified by the provisions of the *Criminal Code* that were in force at that time, and

　(ii) any other offence under any Act of Parliament for which a minimum punishment of imprisonment for life had been prescribed by law.

(4) The Attorney General of Canada shall appoint a Commissioner from among the judges of superior courts of criminal jurisdiction to review and determine, before the coming into force of section 672.64 of the *Criminal Code*, whether any person detained in custody by virtue of an order of detention described in subsection (1) would have been a dangerous mentally disordered accused under section 672.65 of the *Criminal Code*, if that section were in force at the time the order of detention was made.

(5) Where an order of detention referred to in subsection (1) was issued against a person found not guilty by reason of insanity of an offence that is a designated offence as defined in subsection 672.64(1) of the *Criminal Code* or that is included as a designated offence under paragraph (3)(c), the Attorney General of the

province where the order was made, or of the province where the person is detained in custody, may apply to the Commissioner for review and determination of whether the person would be a dangerous mentally disordered accused.

(6) Sections 672.65 and 672.66 of the *Criminal Code* apply to an application made under subsection (5) with such modifications as the circumstances require, and

(a) in addition to the evidence described in paragraph 672.65(3)(*a*), the Commissioner shall consider any relevant evidence subsequent to the detention of the person in respect of whom the application is made; and

(b) where the Commissioner determines that the person would be a dangerous mentally disordered accused, the Commissioner may make an order that the person be detained in custody for a maximum of life.

(7) An order made by the Commissioner in respect of an application under this section shall have effect on the coming into force of section 672.64 of the *Criminal Code* and be subject to the rights of appeal described in sections 672.79 and 672.8 as if the order were an order of a court under section 672.65 of that Act.

(8) Where, before the coming into force of section 5 of this Act, a person has committed an offence but a sentence has not been imposed on that person for that offence, that person may be detained in accordance with section 736.11 of the *Criminal Code*, as enacted by section 6 of this Act.

Interpretation

DEFINITIONS / "Accused" / "Assessment" / "Chairperson" / "Court" / "Disposition" / "Dual status offender" / "Hospital" / "Medical practitioner" / "Party" / "Placement decision" / "Prescribed" / "Review Board" / "Verdict of not criminally responsible on account of mental disorder".

672.1 (1) In this Part,

"accused" includes a defendant in summary conviction proceedings and an accused in respect of whom a verdict of not criminally responsible on account of mental disorder has been rendered;

"assessment" means an assessment by a medical practitioner or any other person who has been designated by the Attorney General as being qualified to conduct an assessment of the mental condition of the accused under an assessment order made under section 672.11 or 672.121, and any incidental observation or examination of the accused;

"chairperson" includes any alternate that the chairperson of a Review Board may designate to act on the chairperson's behalf;

"court" includes a summary conviction court as defined in section 785, a judge, a justice and a judge of the court of appeal as defined in section 673;

"disposition" means an order made by a court or Review Board under section 672.54, an order made by a court under section 672.58 or a finding made by a court under subsection 672.64(1);

"dual status offender" means an offender who is subject to a sentence of imprisonment in respect of one offence and a custodial disposition under paragraph 672.54(*c*) in respect of another offence;

"high-risk accused" means an accused who is found to be a high-risk accused by a court under subsection 672.64(1);

"hospital" means a place in a province that is designated by the Minister of Health for the province for the custody, treatment or assessment of an accused in respect of whom an assessment order, a disposition or a placement decision is made.

"medical practitioner" means a person who is entitled to practise medicine by the laws of a province;

"party" in relation to proceedings of a court or Review Board to make or review a disposition, means

    (*a*) the accused,

    (*b*) the person in charge of the hospital where the accused is detained or is to attend pursuant to an assessment order or a disposition,

    (*c*) an Attorney General designated by the court or Review Board under subsection 672.5(3),

    (*d*) any interested person designated by the court or Review Board under subsection 672.5(4), or

    (*e*) where the disposition is to be made by a court, the prosecutor of the charge against the accused;

"placement decision" means a decision by a Review Board under subsection 672.68(2) as to the place of custody of a dual status offender;

"prescribed" means prescribed by regulations made by the Governor in Council under section 672.95;

"Review Board" means the Review Board established or designated for a province pursuant to subsection 672.38(1);

"verdict of not criminally responsible on account of mental disorder" means a verdict that the accused committed the act or made the omission that formed the basis of the offence with which the accused is charged but is not criminally responsible on account of mental disorder.

(2) For the purposes of subsections 672.5(3) and (5), paragraph 672.86(1)(*b*) and subsections 672.86(2) and (2.1), 672.88(2) and 672.89(2), in respect of a territory or proceedings commenced at the instance of the Government of Canada and conducted by or on behalf of that Government, a reference to the Attorney General of a province shall be read as a reference to the Attorney General of Canada. 1991, c. 43, s. 4; 2005, c. 22, s. 1; 2014, c. 6, s. 2.

Assessment Orders

ASSESSMENT ORDER.

672.11 A court having jurisdiction over an accused in respect of an offence may order an assessment of the mental condition of the accused, if it has reasonable grounds to believe that such evidence is necessary to determine

   (*a*) whether the accused is unfit to stand trial;

   (*b*) whether the accused was, at the time of the commission of the alleged offence, suffering from a mental disorder so as to be exempt from criminal responsibility by virtue of subsection 16(1);

   (*c*) whether the balance of the mind of the accused was disturbed at the time of commission of the alleged offence, where the accused is a female person charged with an offence arising out of the death of her newly-born child;

   (*d*) the appropriate disposition to be made, where a verdict of not criminally responsible on account of mental disorder or unfit to stand trial has been rendered in respect of the accused;

  (*d*.1) whether a finding that the accused is a high-risk accused should be revoked under subsection 672.84(3); or

   (*e*) whether an order should be made under section 672.851 for a stay of proceedings, where a verdict of unfit to stand trial has been rendered against the accused. 1991, c. 43, s. 4; 1995, c. 22, s. 10; 2005, c. 22, s. 2; 2014, c. 6, s. 3.

WHERE COURT MAY ORDER ASSESSMENT / Limitation on prosecutor's application for assessment fitness / Limitation on prosecutor's application for assessment.

672.12 (1) The court may make an assessment order at any stage of proceedings against the accused of its own motion, on application of the accused or, subject to subsections (2) and (3), on application of the prosecutor.

(2) Where the prosecutor applies for an assessment in order to determine whether the accused is unfit to stand trial for an offence that is prosecuted by way of summary conviction, the court may only order the assessment if

   (*a*) the accused raised the issue of fitness; or

   (*b*) the prosecutor satisfies the court that there are reasonable grounds to doubt that the accused is fit to stand trial.

(3) Where the prosecutor applies for an assessment in order to determine whether the accused was suffering from a mental disorder at the time of the offence so as to be exempt from criminal responsibility, the court may only order the assessment if

   (*a*) the accused puts his or her mental capacity for criminal intent into issue; or

   (*b*) the prosecutor satisfies the court that there are reasonable grounds to doubt that the accused is criminally responsible for the alleged offence, on account of mental disorder. 1991, c. 43, s. 4.

REVIEW BOARD MAY ORDER ASSESSMENT.

672.121 The Review Board that has jurisdiction over an accused found not criminally responsible on account of mental disorder or unfit to stand trial may order an assessment of the mental condition of the accused of its own motion or on application of the prosecutor or the accused, if it has reasonable grounds to believe that such evidence is necessary to

(a) make a recommendation to the court under subsection 672.851(1);

(b) make a disposition under section 672.54 in one of the following circumstances:

  (i) no assessment report on the mental condition of the accused is available,

  (ii) no assessment of the mental condition of the accused has been conducted in the last twelve months, or

  (iii) the accused has been transferred from another province under section 672.86; or

(c) determine whether to refer to the court for review under subsection 672.84(1) a finding that an accused is a high-risk accused. 2005, c. 22, s. 3; 2014, c. 6, s. 4.

CONTENTS OF ASSESSMENT ORDER / Form.

672.13 (1) An assessment order must specify

(a) the service that or the person who is to make the assessment, or the hospital where it is to be made;

(b) whether the accused is to be detained in custody while the order is in force; and

(c) the period that the order is to be in force, including the time required for the assessment and for the accused to travel to and from the place where the assessment is to be made.

(2) An assessment order may be in Form 48 or 48.1. 1991, c. 43, s. 4; 2005, c. 22, s. 4.

GENERAL RULE FOR PERIOD / Exception in fitness cases / Exception for compelling circumstances.

672.14 (1) An assessment order shall not be in force for more than thirty days.

(2) No assessment order to determine whether the accused is unfit to stand trial shall be in force for more than five days, excluding holidays and the time required for the accused to travel to and from the place where the assessment is to be made, unless the accused and the prosecutor agree to a longer period not exceeding thirty days.

(3) Despite subsections (1) and (2), a court or Review Board may make an assessment order that remains in force for sixty days if the court or Review Board is satisfied that compelling circumstances exist that warrant it. 1991, c. 43, s. 4; 2005, c. 22, s. 5.

EXTENSION / Maximum duration of extensions.

672.15 (1) Subject to subsection (2), a court or Review Board may extend an assessment order, of its own motion or on the application of the accused or the prosecutor made during or at the end of the period during which the order is in force, for any further period that is required, in its opinion, to complete the assessment of the accused.

(2) No extension of an assessment order shall exceed thirty days, and the period of the initial order together with all extensions shall not exceed sixty days. 1991, c. 43. s. 4; 2005, c. 22, s. 6.

PRESUMPTION AGAINST CUSTODY / Presumption against custody — Review Board / Residency as a condition of disposition / Report of medical practitioner / Presumption of custody in certain circumstances.

672.16 (1) Subject to subsection (3), an accused shall not be detained in custody under an assessment order of a court unless

  (*a*) the court is satisfied that on the evidence custody is necessary to assess the accused, or that on the evidence of a medical practitioner custody is desirable to assess the accused and the accused consents to custody;

  (*b*) custody of the accused is required in respect of any other matter or by virtue of any other provision of this Act; or

  (*c*) the prosecutor, having been given a reasonable opportunity to do so, shows that detention of the accused in custody is justified on either of the grounds set out in subsection 515(10).

(1.1) If the Review Board makes an order for an assessment of an accused under section 672.121, the accused shall not be detained in custody under the order unless

  (*a*) the accused is currently subject to a disposition made under paragraph 672.54(*c*);

  (*b*) the Review Board is satisfied on the evidence that custody is necessary to assess the accused, or that on the evidence of a medical practitioner custody is desirable to assess the accused and the accused consents to custody; or

  (*c*) custody of the accused is required in respect of any other matter or by virtue of any other provision of this Act.

(1.2) Subject to paragraphs (1.1)(*b*) and (*c*), if the accused is subject to a disposition made under paragraph 672.54(*b*) that requires the accused to reside at a specified place, an assessment ordered under section 672.121 shall require the accused to reside at the same place.

(2) For the purposes of paragraphs (1)(*a*) and (1.1)(*b*), if the prosecutor and the accused agree, the evidence of a medical practitioner may be received in the form of a report in writing.

(3) An assessment order made in respect of an accused who is detained under subsection 515(6) or 522(2) shall order that the accused be detained in custody under the same circumstances referred to in that subsection, unless the accused

shows that custody is not justified under the terms of that subsection. 1991, c. 43, s. 4; 2005, c. 22, s. 7.

ASSESSMENT ORDER TAKES PRECEDENCE OVER BAIL HEARING.

672.17 During the period that an assessment order made by a court in respect of an accused charged with an offence is in force, no order for the interim release or detention of the accused may be made by virtue of Part XVI or section 679 in respect of that offence or an included offence. 1991, c. 43, s. 4; 2005, c. 22, s. 8.

APPLICATION TO VARY ASSESSMENT ORDER.

672.18 Where at any time while an assessment order made by a court is in force the prosecutor or an accused shows cause, the court may vary the terms of the order respecting the interim release or detention of the accused in such manner as it considers appropriate in the circumstances. 1991, c. 43, s. 4.

NO TREATMENT ORDER ON ASSESSMENT.

672.19 No assessment order may direct that psychiatric or any other treatment of the accused be carried out, or direct the accused to submit to such treatment. 1991, c. 43, s. 4.

WHEN ASSESSMENT COMPLETED.

672.191 An accused in respect of whom an assessment order is made shall appear before the court or Review Board that made the order as soon as practicable after the assessment is completed and not later than the last day of the period that the order is to be in force. 1997, c. 18, s. 81; 2005, c. 22, s. 10.

Assessment Reports

ASSESSMENT REPORT / Assessment report to be filed / Court to send assessment report to Review Board / Copies of reports to accused and prosecutor.

672.2 (1) An assessment order may require the person who makes the assessment to submit in writing an assessment report on the mental condition of the accused.

(2) An assessment report shall be filed with the court or Review Board that ordered it, within the period fixed by the court or Review Board, as the case may be.

(3) The court shall send to the Review Board without delay a copy of any report filed with it pursuant to subsection (2), to assist in determining the appropriate disposition to be made in respect of the accused.

(4) Subject to subsection 672.51(3), copies of any report filed with a court or Review Board under subsection (2) shall be provided without delay to the

prosecutor, the accused and any counsel representing the accused. 1991, c. 43, s. 4; 2005, c. 22, s. 11.

Protected Statements

DEFINITION OF "PROTECTED STATEMENT" / Protected statements not admissible against accused / Exceptions.

672.21 (1) In this section, "protected statement" means a statement made by the accused during the course and for the purposes of an assessment or treatment directed by a disposition, to the person specified in the assessment order or the disposition, or to anyone acting under that person's direction.

(2) No protected statement or reference to a protected statement made by an accused is admissible in evidence, without the consent of the accused, in any proceeding before a court, tribunal, body or person with jurisdiction to compel the production of evidence.

(3) Notwithstanding subsection (2), evidence of a protected statement is admissible for the purpose of

   (*a*) determining whether the accused is unfit to stand trial;
   (*b*) making a disposition or placement decision respecting the accused;
   (*c*) determining, under section 672.84, whether to refer to the court for review a finding that an accused is a high-risk accused or whether to revoke such a finding;
   (*d*) determining whether the balance of the mind of the accused was disturbed at the time of commission of the alleged offence, where the accused is a female person charged with an offence arising out of the death of her newly-born child;
   (*e*) determining whether the accused was, at the time of the commission of an alleged offence, suffering from automatism or a mental disorder so as to be exempt from criminal responsibility by virtue of subsection 16(1), if the accused puts his or her mental capacity for criminal intent into issue, or if the prosecutor raises the issue after verdict;
   (*f*) challenging the credibility of an accused in any proceeding where the testimony of the accused is inconsistent in a material particular with a protected statement that the accused made previously; or
   (*g*) establishing the perjury of an accused who is charged with perjury in respect of a statement made in any proceeding. 1991, c. 43, s. 4; 2005, c. 22, s. 12; 2014, c. 6, s. 5.

Fitness to Stand Trial

PRESUMPTION OF FITNESS.

672.22 An accused is presumed fit to stand trial unless the court is satisfied on the balance of probabilities that the accused is unfit to stand trial. 1991, c. 43, s. 4.

COURT MAY DIRECT ISSUE TO BE TRIED / Burden of proof.

672.23 (1) Where the court has reasonable grounds, at any stage of the proceedings before a verdict is rendered, to believe that the accused is unfit to stand trial, the court may direct, of its own motion or on application of the accused or the prosecutor, that the issue of fitness of the accused be tried.

(2) An accused or a prosecutor who makes an application under subsection (1) has the burden of proof that the accused is unfit to stand trial. 1991, c. 43, s. 4.

COUNSEL / Counsel fees and disbursements / Taxation of fees and disbursements.

672.24 (1) Where the court has reasonable grounds to believe that an accused is unfit to stand trial and the accused is not represented by counsel, the court shall order that the accused be represented by counsel.

(2) Where counsel is assigned pursuant to subsection (1) and legal aid is not granted to the accused pursuant to a provincial legal aid program, the fees and disbursements of counsel shall be paid by the Attorney General to the extent that the accused is unable to pay them.

(3) Where counsel and the Attorney General cannot agree on the fees or disbursements of counsel, the Attorney General or the counsel may apply to the registrar of the court and the registrar may tax the disputed fees and disbursements. 1991, c. 43, s. 4; 1997, c. 18, s. 82.

POSTPONING TRIAL OF ISSUE / Idem.

672.25 (1) The court shall postpone directing the trial of the issue of fitness of an accused in proceedings for an offence for which the accused may be prosecuted by indictment or that is punishable on summary conviction, until the prosecutor has elected to proceed by way of indictment or summary conviction.

(2) The court may postpone directing the trial of the issue of fitness of an accused
  (a) where the issue arises before the close of the case for the prosecution at a preliminary inquiry, until a time that is not later than the time the accused is called on to answer to the charge; or
  (b) where the issue arises before the close of the case for the prosecution at trial, until a time not later than the opening of the case for the defence or, on motion of the accused, any later time that the court may direct. 1991, c. 43, s. 4.

TRIAL OF ISSUE BY JUDGE AND JURY.

672.26 Where an accused is tried or is to be tried before a court composed of a judge and jury,
  (a) if the judge directs that the issue of fitness of the accused be tried before the accused is given in charge to a jury for trial on the indictment, a jury composed of the number of jurors required in respect of the indictment in the province where the trial is to be held shall be sworn to try that issue

and, with the consent of the accused, the issues to be tried on the indictment; and

(b) if the judge directs that the issue of fitness of the accused be tried after the accused has been given in charge to a jury for trial on the indictment, the jury

shall be sworn to try that issue in addition to the issues in respect of which it is already sworn. 1991, c. 43, s. 4.

TRIAL OF ISSUE BY COURT.

672.27 The court shall try the issue of fitness of an accused and render a verdict where the issue arises

(a) in respect of an accused who is tried or is to be tried before a court other than a court composed of a judge and jury; or

(b) before a court at a preliminary inquiry or at any other stage of the proceedings. 1991, c. 43, s. 4.

PROCEEDING CONTINUES WHERE ACCUSED IS FIT.

672.28 Where the verdict on trial of the issue is that an accused is fit to stand trial, the arraignment, preliminary inquiry, trial or other stage of the proceeding shall continue as if the issue of fitness of the accused had never arisen. 1991, c. 43, s. 4.

WHERE CONTINUED DETENTION IN CUSTODY.

672.29 Where an accused is detained in custody on delivery of a verdict that the accused is fit to stand trial, the court may order the accused to be detained in a hospital until the completion of the trial, if the court has reasonable grounds to believe that the accused would become unfit to stand trial if released. 1991, c. 43, s. 4.

ACQUITTAL.

672.3 Where the court has postponed directing the trial of the issue of fitness of an accused pursuant to subsection 672.25(2) and the accused is discharged or acquitted before the issue is tried, it shall not be tried. 1991, c. 43, s. 4.

VERDICT OF UNFIT TO STAND TRIAL.

672.31 Where the verdict on trial of the issue is that an accused is unfit to stand trial, any plea that has been made shall be set aside and any jury shall be discharged. 1991, c. 43, s. 4.

SUBSEQUENT PROCEEDINGS / Burden of proof.

672.32 (1) A verdict of unfit to stand trial shall not prevent the accused from being tried subsequently where the accused becomes fit to stand trial.

(2) The burden of proof that the accused has subsequently become fit to stand trial is on the party who asserts it, and is discharged by proof on the balance of probabilities. 1991, c. 43, s. 4.

PRIMA FACIE **CASE TO BE MADE EVERY TWO YEARS / Extension of time for holding inquiry / Court may order inquiry to be held / Burden of proof / Admissible evidence at an inquiry / Conduct of inquiry / Where *prima facie* case not made.**

672.33 (1) The court that has jurisdiction in respect of the offence charged against an accused who is found unfit to stand trial shall hold an inquiry, not later than two years after the verdict is rendered and every two years thereafter until the accused is acquitted pursuant to subsection (6) or tried, to decide whether sufficient evidence can be adduced at that time to put the accused on trial.

(1.1) Despite subsection (1), the court may extend the period for holding an inquiry where it is satisfied on the basis of an application by the prosecutor or the accused that the extension is necessary for the proper administration of justice.

(2) On application of the accused, the court may order an inquiry under this section to be held at any time if it is satisfied, on the basis of the application and any written material submitted by the accused, that there is reason to doubt that there is a *prima facie* case against the accused.

(3) At an inquiry under this section, the burden of proof that sufficient evidence can be adduced to put the accused on trial is on the prosecutor.

(4) In an inquiry under this section, the court shall admit as evidence
  (a) any affidavit containing evidence that would be admissible if given by the person making the affidavit as a witness in court; or
  (b) any certified copy of the oral testimony given at a previous inquiry or hearing held before a court in respect of the offence with which the accused is charged.

(5) The court may determine the manner in which an inquiry under this section is conducted and may follow the practices and procedures in respect of a preliminary inquiry under Part XVIII where it concludes that the interests of justice so require.

(6) Where, on the completion of an inquiry under this section, the court is satisfied that sufficient evidence cannot be adduced to put the accused on trial, the court shall acquit the accused. 1991, c. 43, s. 4; 2005, c. 22, s. 13.

Verdict of Not Criminally Responsible on Account of Mental Disorder

---

VERDICT OF NOT CRIMINALLY RESPONSIBLE ON ACCOUNT OF MENTAL DISORDER.

672.34 Where the jury, or the judge or provincial court judge where there is no jury, finds that an accused committed the act or made the omission that formed the basis of the offence charged, but was at the time suffering from mental disorder so as to be exempt from criminal responsibility by virtue of subsection 16(1), the jury or the judge shall render a verdict that the accused committed the act or made the omission but is not criminally responsible on account of mental disorder. 1991, c. 43, s. 4.

EFFECT OF VERDICT OF NOT CRIMINALLY RESPONSIBLE ON ACCOUNT OF MENTAL DISORDER.

672.35 Where a verdict of not criminally responsible on account of mental disorder is rendered, the accused shall not be found guilty or convicted of the offence, but

- (a) the accused may plead *autrefois acquit* in respect of any subsequent charge relating to that offence;
- (b) any court may take the verdict into account in considering an application for judicial interim release or in considering what dispositions to make or sentence to impose for any other offence; and
- (c) the Parole Board of Canada or any provincial parole board may take the verdict into account in considering an application by the accused for parole or for a record suspension under the *Criminal Records Act* in respect of any other offence. 1991, c. 43, s. 4; 2012, c. 1, s. 145; 2012, c. 1, s. 160(c)(ii).

VERDICT NOT A PREVIOUS CONVICTION.

672.36 A verdict of not criminally responsible on account of mental disorder is not a previous conviction for the purposes of any offence under any Act of Parliament for which a greater punishment is provided by reason of previous convictions. 1991, c. 43, s. 4.

DEFINITION OF "APPLICATION FOR FEDERAL EMPLOYMENT" / Application for federal employment / Punishment.

672.37 (1) In this section, "application for federal employment" means an application form relating to

- (a) employment in any department, as defined in section 2 of the *Financial Administration Act*;
- (b) employment by any Crown corporation as defined in subsection 83(1) of the *Financial Administration Act*;
- (c) enrollment in the Canadian Forces; or
- (d) employment in connection with the operation of any work, undertaking or business that is within the legislative authority of Parliament.

(2) No application for federal employment shall contain any question that requires the applicant to disclose any charge or finding that the applicant committed an offence that resulted in a finding or a verdict of not criminally responsible on account of mental disorder if the applicant was discharged absolutely or is no longer subject to any disposition in respect of that offence.

(3) Any person who uses or authorizes the use of an application for federal employment that contravenes subsection (2) is guilty of an offence punishable on summary conviction. 1991, c. 43, s. 4.

Review Boards

REVIEW BOARDS TO BE ESTABLISHED / Treated as provincial Board / Personal liability.

672.38 (1) A Review Board shall be established or designated for each province to make or review dispositions concerning any accused in respect of whom a verdict of not criminally responsible by reason of mental disorder or unfit to stand trial is rendered, and shall consist of not fewer than five members appointed by the lieutenant governor in council of the province.

(2) A Review Board shall be treated as having been established under the laws of the province.

(3) No member of a Review Board is personally liable for any act done in good faith in the exercise of the member's powers or the performance of the member's duties and functions or for any default or neglect in good faith in the exercise of those powers or the performance of those duties and functions. 1991, c. 43, s. 4; 1997, c. 18, s. 83.

MEMBERS OF REVIEW BOARD.

672.39 A Review Board must have at least one member who is entitled under the laws of a province to practise psychiatry and, where only one member is so entitled at least one other member must have training and experience in the field of mental health, and be entitled under the laws of a province to practise medicine or psychology. 1991, c. 43, s. 4.

CHAIRPERSON OF A REVIEW BOARD / Transitional.

672.4 (1) Subject to subsection (2), the chairperson of a Review Board shall be a judge of the Federal Court or of a superior, district or county court of a province, or a person who is qualified for appointment to, or has retired from, such a judicial office.

(2) Where the chairperson of a Review Board that was established before the coming into force of subsection (1) is not a judge or other person referred to therein, the chairperson may continue to act until the expiration of his or her term of office if at least one other member of the Review Board is a judge or other person referred to in subsection (1) or is a member of the bar of the province. 1991, c. 43, s. 4.

QUORUM OF REVIEW BOARD / Transitional.

672.41 (1) Subject to subsection (2), the quorum of a Review Board is constituted by the chairperson, a member who is entitled under the laws of a province to practise psychiatry, and any other member.

(2) Where the chairperson of a Review Board that was established before the coming into force of this section is not a judge or other person referred to in subsection 672.4(1), the quorum of the Review Board is constituted by the

chairperson, a member who is entitled under the laws of a province to practise psychiatry, and a member who is a person referred to in that subsection or a member of the bar of the province. 1991, c. 43, s. 4.

MAJORITY VOTE.

672.42 A decision of a majority of the members present and voting is a decision of a Review Board. 1991, c. 43, s. 4.

POWERS OF REVIEW BOARDS.

672.43 At a hearing held by a Review Board to make a disposition or review a disposition in respect of an accused, the chairperson has all the powers that are conferred by sections 4 and 5 of the *Inquiries Act* on persons appointed as commissioners under Part I of that Act. 1991, c. 43, s. 4.

RULES OF REVIEW BOARD / Application and publication of rules / Regulations.

672.44 (1) A Review Board may, subject to the approval of the lieutenant governor in council of the province, make rules providing for the practice and procedure before the Review Board.

(2) The rules made by a Review Board under subsection (1) apply to any proceeding within its jurisdiction, and shall be published in the *Canada Gazette*.

(3) Notwithstanding anything in this section, the Governor in Council may make regulations to provide for the practice and procedure before Review Boards, in particular to make the rules of Review Boards uniform, and all regulations made under this subsection prevail over any rules made under subsection (1). 1991, c. 43, s. 4.

Disposition Hearings

HEARING TO BE HELD BY A COURT / Transmittal of transcript to Review Board / Disposition to be made.

672.45 (1) Where a verdict of not criminally responsible on account of mental disorder or unfit to stand trial is rendered in respect of an accused, the court may of its own motion, and shall on application by the accused or the prosecutor, hold a disposition hearing.

(1.1) If the court does not hold a hearing under subsection (1), it shall send without delay, following the verdict, in original or copied form, any transcript of the court proceedings in respect of the accused, any other document or information related to the proceedings, and all exhibits filed with it, to the Review Board that has jurisdiction in respect of the matter, if the transcript, document, information or exhibits are in its possession.

(2) At a disposition hearing, the court shall make a disposition in respect of the accused, if it is satisfied that it can readily do so and that a disposition should be made without delay. 1991, c. 43, s. 4; 2005, c. 22, s. 14.

STATUS QUO PENDING REVIEW BOARD HEARING / Variation.

672.46 (1) If the court does not make a disposition in respect of the accused at a disposition hearing, any order for the detention of the accused or any release order, appearance notice, summons or undertaking in respect of the accused that is in force at the time the verdict of not criminally responsible on account of mental disorder or unfit to stand trial is rendered continues in force, subject to its terms, until the Review Board makes a disposition.

(2) Despite subsection (1), a court may, pending a disposition by the Review Board in respect of the accused, on cause being shown, vacate the detention order, release order, appearance notice, summons or undertaking referred to in that subsection, and make any other order for the detention of the accused or any other release order that the court considers to be appropriate in the circumstances, including an order directing that the accused be detained in custody in a hospital. 1991, c. 43, s. 4; 2019, c. 25, s. 276.

REVIEW BOARD TO MAKE DISPOSITION WHERE COURT DOES NOT / Extension of time for hearing / Disposition made by court / Exception — high-risk accused / Extension of time for hearing.

672.47 (1) Where a verdict of not criminally responsible on account of mental disorder or unfit to stand trial is rendered and the court makes no disposition in respect of an accused, the Review Board shall, as soon as is practicable but not later than forty-five days after the verdict was rendered, hold a hearing and make a disposition.

(2) Where the court is satisfied that there are exceptional circumstances that warrant it, the court may extend the time for holding a hearing under subsection (1) to a maximum of ninety days after the verdict was rendered.

(3) Where a court makes a disposition under section 672.54 other than an absolute discharge in respect of an accused, the Review Board shall, not later than ninety days after the disposition was made, hold a hearing and make a disposition in respect of the accused.

(4) Despite subsections (1) to (3), if the court makes a disposition under subsection 672.64(3), the Review Board shall, not later than 45 days after the day on which the disposition is made, hold a hearing and make a disposition under paragraph 672.54(c), subject to the restrictions set out in that subsection.

(5) If the court is satisfied that there are exceptional circumstances that warrant it, the court may extend the time for holding a hearing under subsection (4) to a maximum of 90 days after the day on which the disposition is made. 1991, c. 43, s. 4; 2005, c. 22, s. 15; 2014, c. 6, s. 6(2).

REVIEW BOARD TO DETERMINE FITNESS / Review Board shall send accused to court / Chairperson may send accused to court.

672.48 (1) Where a Review Board holds a hearing to make or review a disposition in respect of an accused who has been found unfit to stand trial, it shall determine whether in its opinion the accused is fit to stand trial at the time of the hearing.

(2) If a Review Board determines that the accused is fit to stand trial, it shall order that the accused be sent back to court, and the court shall try the issue and render a verdict.

(3) The chairperson of a Review Board may, with the consent of the accused and the person in charge of the hospital where an accused is being detained, order that the accused be sent back to court for trial of the issue of whether the accused is unfit to stand trial, where the chairperson is of the opinion that

    (*a*) the accused is fit to stand trial; and

    (*b*) the Review Board will not hold a hearing to make or review a disposition
        in respect of the accused within a reasonable period. 1991, c. 43, s. 4.

CONTINUED DETENTION IN HOSPITAL / Copy of disposition to be sent to court.

672.49 (1) In a disposition made pursuant to section 672.47 the Review Board or chairperson may require the accused to continue to be detained in a hospital until the court determines whether the accused is fit to stand trial, if the Review Board or chairperson has reasonable grounds to believe that the accused would become unfit to stand trial if released.

(2) The Review Board or chairperson shall send a copy of a disposition made pursuant to section 672.47 without delay to the court having jurisdiction over the accused and to the Attorney General of the province where the accused is to be tried. 1991, c. 43, s. 4.

PROCEDURE AT DISPOSITION HEARING / Hearing to be informal / Attorneys General may be parties / Interested person may be a party / Notice of hearing / Notice / Notice of discharge and intended place of residence / Order excluding the public / Right to counsel / Assigning counsel / Counsel fees and disbursements / Taxation of fees and disbursements / Right of accused to be present / Removal or absence of accused / Rights of parties at hearing / Request to compel attendance of witnesses / Video links / Adjournment / Determination of mental condition of the accused / Notice to victims — referral of finding to court / Victim impact statement / Copy of statement / Presentation of victim statement / Inquiry by court or Review Board / Adjournment / Definition of "victim".

672.5 (1) A hearing held by a court or Review Board to make or review a disposition in respect of an accuse, including a hearing referred to in subsection 672.84(1) or (3), shall be held in accordance with this section.

(2) The hearing may be conducted in as informal a manner as is appropriate in the circumstances.

(3) On application, the court or Review Board shall designate as a party the Attorney General of the province where the disposition is to be made and, where an accused is transferred from another province, the Attorney General of the province from which the accused is transferred.

(4) The court or Review Board may designate as a party any person who has a substantial interest in protecting the interests of the accused, if the court or Review Board is of the opinion that it is just to do so.

(5) Notice of the hearing shall be given to the parties, the Attorney General of the province where the disposition is to be made and, where the accused is transferred to another province, the Attorney General of the province from which the accused is transferred, within the time and in the manner prescribed, or within the time and in the manner fixed by the rules of the court or Review Board.

(5.1) At the victim's request, notice of the hearing and of the relevant provisions of the Act shall be given to the victim within the time and in the manner fixed by the rules of the court or Review Board.

(5.2) If the accused is discharged absolutely under paragraph 672.54(*a*) or conditionally under paragraph 672.54(*b*), a notice of the discharge and accused's intended place of residence shall, at the victim's request, be given to the victim within the time and in the manner fixed by the rules of the court or Review Board.

(6) Where the court or Review Board considers it to be in the best interests of the accused and not contrary to the public interest, the court or Review Board may order the public or any members of the public to be excluded from the hearing or any part of the hearing.

(7) The accused or any other party has the right to be represented by counsel.

(8) If an accused is not represented by counsel, the court or Review Board shall, either before or at the time of the hearing, assign counsel to act for any accused
- (*a*) who has been found unfit to stand trial; or
- (*b*) wherever the interests of justice so require.

(8.1) Where counsel is assigned pursuant to subsection (8) and legal aid is not granted to the accused pursuant to a provincial legal aid program, the fees and disbursements of counsel shall be paid by the Attorney General to the extent that the accused is unable to pay them.

(8.2) Where counsel and the Attorney General cannot agree on the fees or disbursements of counsel, the Attorney General or the counsel may apply to the registrar of the court and the registrar may tax the disputed fees and disbursements.

(9) Subject to subsection (10), the accused has the right to be present during the whole of the hearing.

(10) The court or the chairperson of the Review Board may
- (*a*) permit the accused to be absent during the whole or any part of the hearing on such conditions as the court or chairperson considers proper; or
- (*b*) cause the accused to be removed and barred from re-entry for the whole or any part of the hearing

   (i) where the accused interrupts the hearing so that to continue in the presence of the accused would not be feasible,

   (ii) on being satisfied that failure to do so would likely endanger the life or safety of another person or would seriously impair the treatment or recovery of the accused, or

   (iii) in order to hear, in the absence of the accused, evidence, oral or written submissions, or the cross-examination of any witness concerning whether grounds exist for removing the accused pursuant to subparagraph (ii).

(11) Any party may adduce evidence, make oral or written submissions, call witnesses and cross-examine any witness called by any other party and, on application, cross-examine any person who made an assessment report that was submitted to the court or Review Board in writing.

(12) A party may not compel the attendance of witnesses, but may request the court or the chairperson of the Review Board to do so.

(13) If the accused so agrees, the court or the chairperson of the Review Board may permit the accused to appear by closed-circuit television or videoconference for any part of the hearing.

(13.1) The Review Board may adjourn the hearing for a period not exceeding thirty days if necessary for the purpose of ensuring that relevant information is available to permit it to make or review a disposition or for any other sufficient reason.

(13.2) On receiving an assessment report, the court or Review Board shall determine whether, since the last time the disposition in respect of the accused was made or reviewed there has been any change in the mental condition of the accused that may provide grounds for the discharge of the accused under paragraph 672.54(a) or (b) and, if there has been such a change, the court or Review Board shall notify every victim of the offence that they are entitled to file a statement in accordance with subsection (14).

(13.3) If the Review Board refers to the court for review under subsection 672.84(1) a finding that an accused is a high-risk accused, it shall notify every victim of the offence that they are entitled to file a statement with the court in accordance with subsection (14).

(14) A victim of the offence may prepare and file with the court or Review Board a written statement describing the physical or emotional harm, property damage or economic loss suffered by the victim as the result of the commission of the offence and the impact of the offence on the victim. Form 48.2 in Part XXVIII, or a form approved by the lieutenant governor in council of the province in which the court or Review Board is exercising its jurisdiction, must be used for this purpose.

(15) The court or Review Board shall ensure that a copy of any statement filed in accordance with subsection (14) is provided to the accused or counsel for the accused, and the prosecutor, as soon as practicable after a verdict of not criminally responsible on account of mental disorder is rendered in respect of the offence.

(15.1) The court or Review Board shall, at the request of a victim, permit the victim to read a statement prepared and filed in accordance with subsection (14), or to present the statement in any other manner that the court or Review Board considers appropriate, unless the court or Review Board is of the opinion that the reading or presentation of the statement would interfere with the proper administration of justice.

(15.2) The court or Review Board shall, as soon as practicable after a verdict of not criminally responsible on account of mental disorder is rendered in respect of an offence and before making a disposition under section 672.45, 672.47 or 672.64, inquire of the prosecutor or a victim of the offence, or any person representing a victim of the offence, whether the victim has been advised of the opportunity to prepare a statement referred to in subsection (14).

(15.3) On application of the prosecutor or a victim or of its own motion, the court or Review Board may adjourn the hearing held under section 672.45, 672.47 or 672.64 to permit the victim to prepare a statement referred to in subsection (14) if the court or Review Board is satisfied that the adjournment would not interfere with the proper administration of justice. 1991, c. 43, s. 4; 1997, c. 18, s. 84; 1999, c. 25, s. 11; 2005, c. 22, s. 16; 2014, c. 6, s. 7(1)-(3), (5); 2015, c. 13, s. 22; 2019, c. 25, s. 277.

(16) [*Repealed*, 2015, c. 13, s. 22(2).]

ORDER RESTRICTING PUBLICATION — SEXUAL OFFENCES / Order restricting publication — child pornography / Order restricting publication — other offences / Order restricting publication / Application and notice / Grounds / Hearing may be held / Factors to be considered / Conditions / Publication of application prohibited / Offence / Application of order.

672.501 (1) Where a Review Board holds a hearing referred to in section 672.5 in respect of an accused who has been declared not criminally responsible on account of mental disorder or unfit to stand trial for an offence referred to in subsection 486.4(1), the Review Board shall make an order directing that any information that could identify a victim, or a witness who is under the age of eighteen years, shall not be published in any document or broadcast or transmitted in any way.

(2) Where a Review Board holds a hearing referred to in section 672.5 in respect of an accused who has been declared not criminally responsible on account of mental disorder or unfit to stand trial for an offence referred to in section 163.1, a Review Board shall make an order directing that any information that could identify a witness who is under the age of eighteen years, or any person who is the subject of a representation, written material or a recording that constitutes child pornography within the meaning of section 163.1, shall not be published in any document or broadcast or transmitted in any way.

(3) Where a Review Board holds a hearing referred to in section 672.5 in respect of an accused who has been declared not criminally responsible on account of mental disorder or unfit to stand trial for an offence other than the offences referred to in subsection (1) or (2), on application of the prosecutor, a victim or a witness, the Review Board may make an order directing that any information that could identify the victim or witness shall not be published in any document or

broadcast or transmitted in any way if the Review Board is satisfied that the order is necessary for the proper administration of justice.

(4) An order made under any of subsections (1) to (3) does not apply in respect of the disclosure of information in the course of the administration of justice if it is not the purpose of the disclosure to make the information known in the community.

(5) An applicant for an order under subsection (3) shall
  (a) apply in writing to the Review Board; and
  (b) provide notice of the application to the prosecutor, the accused and any other person affected by the order that the Review Board specifies.

(6) An applicant for an order under subsection (3) shall set out the grounds on which the applicant relies to establish that the order is necessary for the proper administration of justice.

(7) The Review Board may hold a hearing to determine whether an order under subsection (3) should be made, and the hearing may be in private.

(8) In determining whether to make an order under subsection (3), the Review Board shall consider
  (a) the right to a fair and public hearing;
  (b) whether there is a real and substantial risk that the victim or witness would suffer significant harm if their identity were disclosed;
  (c) whether the victim or witness needs the order for their security or to protect them from intimidation or retaliation;
  (d) society's interest in encouraging the reporting of offences and the participation of victims and witnesses in the criminal justice process;
  (e) whether effective alternatives are available to protect the identity of the victim or witness;
  (f) the salutary and deleterious effects of the proposed order;
  (g) the impact of the proposed order on the freedom of expression of those affected by it; and
  (h) any other factor that the Review Board considers relevant.

(9) An order made under subsection (3) may be subject to any conditions that the Review Board thinks fit.

(10) Unless the Review Board refuses to make an order under subsection (3), no person shall publish in any document or broadcast or transmit in any way
  (a) the contents of an application;
  (b) any evidence taken, information given or submissions made at a hearing under subsection (7); or
  (c) any other information that could identify the person to whom the application relates as a victim or witness in the proceedings.

(11) Every person who fails to comply with an order made under any of subsections (1) to (3) is guilty of an offence punishable on summary conviction.

(12) For greater certainty, an order referred to in subsection (11) also prohibits, in relation to proceedings taken against any person who fails to comply with the order, the publication in any document or the broadcasting or transmission in any

way of information that could identify a victim or witness whose identity is protected by the order. 2005, c. 22, ss. 17 and 64(2).

DEFINITION OF "DISPOSITION INFORMATION" / Disposition information to be made available to parties / Exception where disclosure dangerous to any person / Idem / Exception where disclosure unnecessary or prejudicial / Exclusion of certain persons from hearing / Prohibition of disclosure in certain cases / Idem / Information to be made available to specified persons / Disclosure for research or statistical purposes / Prohibition on publication / Powers of courts not limited.

672.51 (1) In this section, "disposition information" means all or part of an assessment report submitted to the court or Review Board and any other written information before the court or Review Board about the accused that is relevant to making or reviewing a disposition.

(2) Subject to this section, all disposition information shall be made available for inspection by, and the court or Review Board shall provide a copy of it to, each party and any counsel representing the accused.

(3) The court or Review Board shall withhold some or all of the disposition information from an accused where it is satisfied, on the basis of that information and the evidence or report of the medical practitioner responsible for the assessment or treatment of the accused, that disclosure of the information would be likely to endanger the life or safety of another person or would seriously impair the treatment or recovery of the accused.

(4) Notwithstanding subsection (3), the court or Review Board may release some or all of the disposition information to an accused where the interests of justice make disclosure essential in its opinion.

(5) The court or Review Board shall withhold disposition information from a party other than the accused or an Attorney General, where disclosure to that party, in the opinion of the court or Review Board, is not necessary to the proceeding and may be prejudicial to the accused.

(6) A court or Review Board that withholds disposition information from the accused or any other party pursuant to subsection (3) or (5) shall exclude the accused or the other party, as the case may be, from the hearing during
  (a) the oral presentation of that disposition information; or
  (b) the questioning by the court or Review Board or the cross-examination of any person concerning that disposition information.

(7) No disposition information shall be made available for inspection or disclosed to any person who is not a party to the proceedings
  (a) where the disposition information has been withheld from the accused or any other party pursuant to subsection (3) or (5); or
  (b) where the court or Review Board is of the opinion that disclosure of the disposition information would be seriously prejudicial to the accused and that, in the circumstances, protection of the accused takes precedence over the public interest in disclosure.

(8) No part of the record of the proceedings in respect of which the accused was excluded pursuant to subparagraph 672.5(10)(*b*)(ii) or (iii) shall be made available for inspection to the accused or to any person who is not a party to the proceedings.

(9) Notwithstanding subsections (7) and (8), the court or Review Board may make any disposition information, or a copy of it, available on request to any person or member of a class of persons

    (*a*) that has a valid interest in the information for research or statistical purposes, where the court or Review Board is satisfied that disclosure is in the public interest;

    (*b*) that has a valid interest in the information for the purposes of the proper administration of justice; or

    (*c*) that the accused requests or authorizes in writing to inspect it, where the court or Review Board is satisfied that the person will not disclose or give to the accused a copy of any disposition information withheld from the accused pursuant to subsection (3), or of any part of the record of proceedings referred to in subsection (8), or that the reasons for withholding that information from the accused no longer exist.

(10) A person to whom the court or Review Board makes disposition information available under paragraph (9)(*a*) may disclose it for research or statistical purposes, but not in any form or manner that could reasonably be expected to identify any person to whom it relates.

(11) No person shall publish in any document or broadcast or transmit in any way

    (*a*) any disposition information that is prohibited from being disclosed pursuant to subsection (7); or

    (*b*) any part of the record of the proceedings in respect of which the accused was excluded pursuant to subparagraph 672.5(10)(*b*)(ii) or (iii).

(12) Except as otherwise provided in this section, nothing in this section limits the powers that a court may exercise apart from this section. 1991, c. 43, s. 4; 1997, c. 18, s. 85; 2005, c. 22, s. 18; 2005, c. 32, s. 22; 2014, c. 6, s. 8.

RECORD OF PROCEEDINGS / Transmittal of transcript to Review Board / Reasons for disposition and copies to be provided.

672.52 (1) The court or Review Board shall cause a record of the proceedings of its disposition hearings to be kept, and include in the record any assessment report submitted.

(2) If a court holds a disposition hearing under subsection 672.45(1), whether or not it makes a disposition, it shall send without delay to the Review Board that has jurisdiction in respect of the matter, in original or copied form, a transcript of the hearing, any other document or information related to the hearing, and all exhibits filed with it, if the transcript, document, information or exhibits are in its possession.

(3) The court or Review Board shall state its reasons for making a disposition in the record of the proceedings, and shall provide every party with a copy of the disposition and those reasons. 1991, c. 43, s. 4; 2005, c. 22, s. 19.

PROCEEDINGS NOT INVALID.

672.53 Any procedural irregularity in relation to a disposition hearing does not affect the validity of the hearing unless it causes the accused substantial prejudice. 1991, c. 43, s. 4.

DISPOSITIONS BY A COURT OR REVIEW BOARD

Terms of Dispositions

DISPOSITIONS THAT MAY BE MADE.

672.54 When a court or Review Board makes a disposition under subsection 672.45(2), section 672.47, subsection 672.64(3) or section 672.83 or 672.84, it shall, taking into account the safety of the public, which is the paramount consideration, the mental condition of the accused, the reintegration of the accused into society and the other needs of the accused, make one of the following dispositions that is necessary and appropriate in the circumstances:

(*a*) where a verdict of not criminally responsible on account of mental disorder has been rendered in respect of the accused and, in the opinion of the court or Review Board, the accused is not a significant threat to the safety of the public, by order, direct that the accused be discharged absolutely;

(*b*) by order, direct that the accused be discharged subject to such conditions as the court or Review Board considers appropriate; or

(*c*) by order, direct that the accused be detained in custody in a hospital, subject to such conditions as the court or Review Board considers appropriate. 1991, c. 43, s. 4; 2005, c. 22, s. 20; 2014, c. 6, s. 9.

SIGNIFICANT THREAT TO SAFETY OF PUBLIC.

672.5401 For the purposes of section 672.54, a significant threat to the safety of the public means a risk of serious physical or psychological harm to members of the public — including any victim of or witness to the offence, or any person under the age of 18 years — resulting from conduct that is criminal in nature but not necessarily violent. 2014, c. 6, s. 10.

VICTIM IMPACT STATEMENT.

672.541 If a verdict of not criminally responsible on account of mental disorder has been rendered in respect of an accused, the court or Review Board shall

(*a*) at a hearing held under section 672.45, 672.47, 672.64, 672.81 or 672.82 or subsection 672.84(5), take into consideration any statement filed by a victim in accordance with subsection 672.5(14) in determining the appropriate disposition or conditions under section 672.54, to the extent that the statement is relevant to its consideration of the criteria set out in section 672.54;

(*b*) at a hearing held under section 672.64 or subsection 672.84(3), take into consideration any statement filed by a victim in accordance with subsection

672.5(14), to the extent that the statement is relevant to its consideration of the criteria set out in subsection 672.64(1) or 672.84(3), as the case may be, in deciding whether to find that the accused is a high-risk accused, or to revoke such a finding; and

(c) at a hearing held under section 672.81 or 672.82 in respect of a high-risk accused, take into consideration any statement filed by a victim in accordance with subsection 672.5(14) in determining whether to refer to the court for review the finding that the accused is a high-risk accused, to the extent that the statement is relevant to its consideration of the criteria set out in subsection 672.84(1). 1999, c. 25, s. 12; 2005, c. 22, s. 21; 2014, c. 6, s. 10.

ADDITIONAL CONDITIONS — SAFETY AND SECURITY.

672.542 When a court or Review Board holds a hearing referred to in section 672.5, the court or Review Board shall consider whether it is desirable, in the interests of the safety and security of any person, particularly a victim of or witness to the offence or a justice system participant, to include as a condition of the disposition that the accused

(a) abstain from communicating, directly or indirectly, with any victim, witness or other person identified in the disposition, or refrain from going to any place specified in the disposition; or

(b) comply with any other condition specified in the disposition that the court or Review Board considers necessary to ensure the safety and security of those persons. 2014, c. 6, s. 10.

TREATMENT NOT A CONDITION.

672.55 (1) No disposition made under section 672.54 shall direct that any psychiatric or other treatment of the accused be carried out or that the accused submit to such treatment except that the disposition may include a condition regarding psychiatric or other treatment where the accused has consented to the condition and the court or Review Board considers the condition to be reasonable and necessary in the interests of the accused. 1991, c. 43, s. 4; 1997, c. 18, s. 86; 2005, c. 22, s. 22.

(2) [*Repealed*, 2005, c. 22, s. 22.]

DELEGATED AUTHORITY TO VARY RESTRICTIONS ON LIBERTY OF ACCUSED / Exception — high-risk accused / Notice to accused and Review Board of increase in restrictions.

672.56 (1) A Review Board that makes a disposition in respect of an accused under paragraph 672.54(b) or (c) may delegate to the person in charge of the hospital authority to direct that the restrictions on the liberty of the accused be increased or decreased within any limits and subject to any conditions set out in that disposition, and any direction so made is deemed for the purposes of this Act to be a disposition made by the Review Board.

(1.1) If the accused is a high-risk accused, any direction is subject to the restrictions set out in subsection 672.64(3).

(2) A person who increases the restrictions on the liberty of the accused significantly pursuant to authority delegated to the person by a Review Board shall

(a) make a record of the increased restrictions on the file of the accused; and

(b) give notice of the increase as soon as is practicable to the accused and, if the increased restrictions remain in force for a period exceeding seven days, to the Review Board. 1991, c. 43, s. 4; 2014, c. 6, s. 11(2).

WARRANT OF COMMITTAL.

672.57 Where the court or Review Board makes a disposition under paragraph 672.54(c), it shall issue a warrant of committal of the accused, which may be in Form 49. 1991, c. 43, s. 4.

TREATMENT DISPOSITION.

672.58 Where a verdict of unfit to stand trial is rendered and the court has not made a disposition under section 672.54 in respect of an accused, the court may, on application by the prosecutor, by order, direct that treatment of the accused be carried out for a specified period not exceeding sixty days, subject to such conditions as the court considers appropriate and, where the accused is not detained in custody, direct that the accused submit to that treatment by the person or at the hospital specified. 1991, c. 43, s. 4.

CRITERIA FOR DISPOSITION / Evidence required.

672.59 (1) No disposition may be made under section 672.58 unless the court is satisfied, on the basis of the testimony of a medical practitioner, that a specific treatment should be administered to the accused for the purpose of making the accused fit to stand trial.

(2) The testimony required by the court for the purposes of subsection (1) shall include a statement that the medical practitioner has made an assessment of the accused and is of the opinion, based on the grounds specified, that

(a) the accused, at the time of the assessment, was unfit to stand trial;

(b) the psychiatric treatment and any other related medical treatment specified by the medical practitioner will likely make the accused fit to stand trial within a period not exceeding sixty days and that without that treatment the accused is likely to remain unfit to stand trial;

(c) the risk of harm to the accused from the psychiatric and other related medical treatment specified is not disproportionate to the benefit anticipated to be derived from it; and

(d) the psychiatric and other related medical treatment specified is the least restrictive and least intrusive treatment that could, in the circumstances, be specified for the purpose referred to in subsection (1), considering the opinions referred to in paragraphs (b) and (c). 1991, c. 43, s. 4.

NOTICE REQUIRED / Challenge by accused.

672.6 (1) The court shall not make a disposition under section 672.58 unless the prosecutor notifies the accused, in writing and as soon as practicable, of the application.

(2) On receiving the notice referred to in subsection (1), the accused may challenge the application and adduce evidence for that purpose. 1991, c. 43, s. 4; 1997, c. 18, s. 87.

EXCEPTION / Definitions / "electro-convulsive therapy" / "psychosurgery".

672.61 (1) The court shall not direct, and no disposition made under section 672.58 shall include, the performance of psychosurgery or electro-convulsive therapy or any other prohibited treatment that is prescribed.

(2) In this section,

"electro-convulsive therapy" means a procedure for the treatment of certain mental disorders that induces, by electrical stimulation of the brain, a series of generalized convulsions;

"psychosurgery" means any procedure that by direct or indirect access to the brain removes, destroys or interrupts the continuity of histologically normal brain tissue, or inserts indwelling electrodes for pulsed electrical stimulation for the purpose of altering behaviour or treating psychiatric illness, but does not include neurological procedures used to diagnose or treat intractable physical pain, organic brain conditions, or epilepsy, where any of those conditions is clearly demonstrable. 1991, c. 43, s. 4.

CONSENT OF HOSPITAL REQUIRED FOR TREATMENT / Consent of accused not required for treatment.

672.62 (1) No court shall make a disposition under section 672.58 without the consent of
  (a) the person in charge of the hospital where the accused is to be treated; or
  (b) the person to whom responsibility for the treatment of the accused is assigned by the court.

(2) The court may direct that treatment of an accused be carried out pursuant to a disposition made under section 672.58 without the consent of the accused or a person who, according to the laws of the province where the disposition is made, is authorized to consent for the accused. 1991, c. 43, s. 4.

EFFECTIVE DATE OF DISPOSITION.

672.63 A disposition shall come into force on the day on which it is made or on any later day that the court or Review Board specifies in it, and shall remain in force until the Review Board holds a hearing to review the disposition and makes another disposition. 1991, c. 43, s. 4; 2005, c. 22, s. 23.

High-Risk Accused

FINDING / Factors to consider / Detention of high-risk accused / Appeal / For greater certainty.

672.64 (1) On application made by the prosecutor before any disposition to discharge an accused absolutely, the court may, at the conclusion of a hearing, find the accused to be a high-risk accused if the accused has been found not criminally responsible on account of mental disorder for a serious personal injury offence, as defined in subsection 672.81(1.3), the accused was 18 years of age or more at the time of the commission of the offence and

- (a) the court is satisfied that there is a substantial likelihood that the accused will use violence that could endanger the life or safety of another person; or
- (b) the court is of the opinion that the acts that constitute the offence were of such a brutal nature as to indicate a risk of grave physical or psychological harm to another person.

(2) In deciding whether to find that the accused is a high-risk accused, the court shall consider all relevant evidence, including

- (a) the nature and circumstances of the offence;
- (b) any pattern of repetitive behaviour of which the offence forms a part;
- (c) the accused's current mental condition;
- (d) the past and expected course of the accused's treatment, including the accused's willingness to follow treatment; and
- (e) the opinions of experts who have examined the accused.

(3) If the court finds the accused to be a high-risk accused, the court shall make a disposition under paragraph 672.54(c), but the accused's detention must not be subject to any condition that would permit the accused to be absent from the hospital unless

- (a) it is appropriate, in the opinion of the person in charge of the hospital, for the accused to be absent from the hospital for medical reasons or for any purpose that is necessary for the accused's treatment, if the accused is escorted by a person who is authorized by the person in charge of the hospital; and
- (b) a structured plan has been prepared to address any risk related to the accused's absence and, as a result, that absence will not present an undue risk to the public.

(4) A decision not to find an accused to be a high-risk accused is deemed to be a disposition for the purpose of sections 672.72 to 672.78.

(5) For greater certainty, a finding that an accused is a high-risk accused is a disposition and sections 672.72 to 672.78 apply to it. 2014, c. 6, s. 12.

Note: Sections 672.65 and 672.66 and their headings, as enacted by 1991, c. 43, s. 4, have never been brought into force and have since been repealed by 2005, c. 22, s. 24.

Dual Status Offenders

WHERE COURT IMPOSES A SENTENCE / Custodial disposition by court.

672.67 (1) Where a court imposes a sentence of imprisonment on an offender who is, or thereby becomes, a dual status offender, that sentence takes precedence over any prior custodial disposition, pending any placement decision by the Review Board.

(2) Where a court imposes a custodial disposition on an accused who is, or thereby becomes, a dual status offender, the disposition takes precedence over any prior sentence of imprisonment pending any placement decision by the Review Board. 1991, c. 43, s. 4; 1995, c. 22, s. 10; 2005, c. 22, s. 25.

DEFINITION OF "MINISTER" / Placement decision by Review Board / Idem / Time for making placement decision / Effects of placement decision.

672.68 (1) In this section and in sections 672.69 and 672.7, "Minister" means the Minister of Public Safety and Emergency Preparedness or the Minister responsible for correctional services of the province to which a dual status offender may be sent pursuant to a sentence of imprisonment.

(2) On application by the Minister or of its own motion, where the Review Board is of the opinion that the place of custody of a dual status offender pursuant to a sentence or custodial disposition made by the court is inappropriate to meet the mental health needs of the offender or to safeguard the well-being of other persons, the Review Board shall, after giving the offender and the Minister reasonable notice, decide whether to place the offender in custody in a hospital or in a prison.

(3) In making a placement decision, the Review Board shall take into consideration

    (*a*) the need to protect the public from dangerous persons;

    (*b*) the treatment needs of the offender and the availability of suitable treatment resources to address those needs;

    (*c*) whether the offender would consent to or is a suitable candidate for treatment;

    (*d*) any submissions made to the Review Board by the offender or any other party to the proceedings and any assessment report submitted in writing to the Review Board; and

    (*e*) any other factors that the Review Board considers relevant.

(4) The Review Board shall make its placement decision as soon as practicable but not later than thirty days after receiving an application from, or giving notice to, the Minister under subsection (2), unless the Review Board and the Minister agree to a longer period not exceeding sixty days.

(5) Where the offender is detained in a prison pursuant to the placement decision of the Review Board, the Minister is responsible for the supervision and control of the offender. 1991, c. 43, s. 4; 2005, c. 10, s. 34(1)(*f*)(xiii).

MINISTER AND REVIEW BOARD ENTITLED TO ACCESS / Review of placement decisions / Idem / Minister shall be a party.

672.69 (1) The Minister and the Review Board are entitled to have access to any dual status offender in respect of whom a placement decision has been made, for the purpose of conducting a review of the sentence or disposition imposed.

(2) The Review Board shall hold a hearing as soon as is practicable to review a placement decision, on application by the Minister or the dual status offender who is the subject of the decision, where the Review Board is satisfied that a significant change in circumstances requires it.

(3) The Review Board may of its own motion hold a hearing to review a placement decision after giving the Minister and the dual status offender who is subject to it reasonable notice.

(4) The Minister shall be a party in any proceedings relating to the placement of a dual status offender. 1991, c. 43, s. 4.

NOTICE OF DISCHARGE / Warrant of committal.

672.7 (1) Where the Minister or the Review Board intends to discharge a dual status offender from custody, each shall give written notice to the other indicating the time, place and conditions of the discharge.

(2) A Review Board that makes a placement decision shall issue a warrant of committal of the accused, which may be in Form 50. 1991, c. 43, s. 4.

DETENTION TO COUNT AS SERVICE OF TERM / Disposition takes precedence over probation orders.

672.71 (1) Each day of detention of a dual status offender pursuant to a placement decision or a custodial disposition shall be treated as a day of service of the term of imprisonment, and the accused shall be deemed, for all purposes, to be lawfully confined in a prison.

(2) When a dual status offender is convicted or discharged on the conditions set out in a probation order made under section 730 in respect of an offence but is not sentenced to a term of imprisonment, the custodial disposition in respect of the accused comes into force and, notwithstanding subsection 732.2(1), takes precedence over any probation order made in respect of the offence. 1991, c. 43, s. 4; 1995, c. 22, s. 10.

Appeals

GROUNDS FOR APPEAL / Limitation period for appeal / Appeal to be heard expeditiously.

672.72 (1) Any party may appeal against a disposition made by a court or a Review Board, or a placement decision made by a Review Board, to the court of appeal of the province where the disposition or placement decision was made on any ground of appeal that raises a question of law or fact alone or of mixed law and fact.

(2) An appellant shall give notice of an appeal against a disposition or placement decision in the manner directed by the applicable rules of court within fifteen days after the day on which the appellant receives a copy of the placement decision or disposition and the reasons for it or within any further time that the court of appeal, or a judge of that court, may direct.

(3) The court of appeal shall hear an appeal against a disposition or placement decision in or out of the regular sessions of the court, as soon as practicable after the day on which the notice of appeal is given, within any period that may be fixed by the court of appeal, a judge of the court of appeal, or the rules of that court. 1991, c. 43, s. 4; 1997, c. 18, s. 88.

APPEAL ON THE TRANSCRIPT / Additional evidence.

672.73 (1) An appeal against a disposition by a court or Review Board or placement decision by a Review Board shall be based on a transcript of the proceedings and any other evidence that the court of appeal finds necessary to admit in the interests of justice.

(2) For the purpose of admitting additional evidence under this section, subsections 683(1) and (2) apply, with such modifications as the circumstances require. 1991, c. 43, s. 4.

NOTICE OF APPEAL TO BE GIVEN TO COURT OR REVIEW BOARD / Transmission of records to court of appeal / Record to be kept by court of appeal / Appellant to provide transcript of evidence / Saving.

672.74 (1) The clerk of the court of appeal, on receiving notice of an appeal against a disposition or placement decision, shall notify the court or Review Board that made the disposition.

(2) On receipt of notification under subsection (1), the court or Review Board shall transmit to the court of appeal, before the time that the appeal is to be heard or within any time that the court of appeal or a judge of that court may direct,

   (*a*) a copy of the disposition or placement decision;

   (*b*) all exhibits filed with the court or Review Board or a copy of them; and

   (*c*) all other material in its possession respecting the hearing.

(3) The clerk of the court of appeal shall keep the material referred to in subsection (2) with the records of the court of appeal.

(4) Unless it is contrary to an order of the court of appeal or any applicable rules of court, the appellant shall provide the court of appeal and the respondent with a transcript of any evidence taken before a court or Review Board by a stenographer or a sound recording apparatus, certified by the stenographer or in accordance with subsection 540(6), as the case may be.

(5) An appeal shall not be dismissed by the court of appeal by reasons only that a person other than the appellant failed to comply with this section. 1991, c. 43, s. 4.

AUTOMATIC SUSPENSION OF CERTAIN DISPOSITIONS.

672.75 The filing of a notice of appeal against a disposition made under section 672.58 suspends the application of the disposition pending the determination of the appeal. 1991, c. 43, s. 4; 2014, c. 6, s. 13.

APPLICATION RESPECTING DISPOSITIONS UNDER APPEAL / Discretionary powers respecting suspension of dispositions / Copy of order to parties.

672.76 (1) Any party who gives notice to each of the other parties, within the time and in the manner prescribed, may apply to a judge of the court of appeal for an order under this section respecting a disposition or placement decision that is under appeal.

(2) On receipt of an application made pursuant to subsection (1) a judge of the court of appeal may, if satisfied that the mental condition of the accused justifies it,

- (a) by order, direct that a disposition made under section 672.58 be carried out pending the determination of the appeal, notwithstanding section 672.75;
- (a.1) by order, direct that a disposition made under paragraph 672.54(a) be suspended pending the determination of the appeal;
- (b) by order, direct that the application of a placement decision or a disposition made under paragraph 672.54(b) or (c) be suspended pending the determination of the appeal;
- (c) where the application of a disposition is suspended pursuant to section 672.75 or paragraph (b), make any other disposition in respect of the accused that is appropriate in the circumstances, other than a disposition under paragraph 672.54(a) or section 672.58, pending the determination of the appeal;
- (d) where the application of a placement decision is suspended pursuant to an order made under paragraph (b), make any other placement decision that is appropriate in the circumstances, pending the determination of the appeal; and
- (e) give any directions that the judge considers necessary for expediting the appeal.

(3) A judge of the court of appeal who makes an order under this section shall send a copy of the order to each of the parties without delay. 1991, c. 43, s. 4; 2014, c. 6, s. 14.

EFFECT OF SUSPENSION OF DISPOSITION.

672.77 Where the application of a disposition or placement decision appealed from is suspended, a disposition, or in the absence of a disposition any order for the interim release or detention of the accused, that was in effect immediately before the disposition or placement decision appealed from took effect, shall be in force pending the determination of the appeal, subject to any disposition made under paragraph 672.76(2)(c). 1991, c. 43, s. 4.

POWERS OF COURT OF APPEAL / Idem / Orders that the court may make.

672.78 (1) The court of appeal may allow an appeal against a disposition or placement decision and set aside an order made by the court or Review Board, where the court of appeal is of the opinion that

- (a) it is unreasonable or cannot be supported by the evidence;
- (b) it is based on a wrong decision on a question of law; or
- (c) there was a miscarriage of justice.

(2) The court of appeal may dismiss an appeal against a disposition or placement decision where the court is of the opinion

- (a) that paragraphs (1)(a), (b) and (c) do not apply; or
- (b) that paragraph (1)(b) may apply, but the court finds that no substantial wrong or miscarriage of justice has occurred.

(3) Where the court of appeal allows an appeal against a disposition or placement decision, it may

- (a) make any disposition under section 672.54 or any placement decision that the Review Board could have made;
- (b) refer the matter back to the court or Review Board for rehearing, in whole or in part, in accordance with any directions that the court of appeal considers appropriate; or
- (c) make any other order that justice requires. 1991, c. 43, s. 4; 1997, c. 18, s. 89.

672.79 [*Repealed*, 2005, c. 22, s. 26].

672.8 [*Repealed*, 2005, c. 22, s. 26.]

Review of Dispositions

MANDATORY REVIEW OF DISPOSITIONS / Extension on consent / Extension for serious personal violence offence / Definition of "serious personal injury offence" / Extension on consent — high-risk accused / Extension — no likely improvement / Notice / Appeal / Additional mandatory reviews in custody cases / Review in case of increase on restrictions on liberty / Idem.

672.81 (1) A Review Board shall hold a hearing not later than twelve months after making a disposition and every twelve months thereafter for as long as the disposition remains in force, to review any disposition that it has made in respect of an accused, other than an absolute discharge under paragraph 672.54(a).

(1.1) Despite subsection (1), the Review Board may extend the time for holding a hearing to a maximum of twenty-four months after the making or reviewing of a disposition if the accused is represented by counsel and the accused and the Attorney General consent to the extension.

(1.2) Despite subsection (1), at the conclusion of a hearing under this section the Review Board may, after making a disposition, extend the time for holding a subsequent hearing under this section to a maximum of twenty-four months if

(a) the accused has been found not criminally responsible for a serious personal injury offence;

(b) the accused is subject to a disposition made under paragraph 672.54(c); and

(c) the Review Board is satisfied on the basis of any relevant information, including disposition information within the meaning of subsection 672.51(1) and an assessment report made under an assessment ordered under paragraph 672.121(a), that the condition of the accused is not likely to improve and that detention remains necessary for the period of the extension.

(1.3) For the purposes of subsection (1.2), "serious personal injury offence" means

(a) an indictable offence involving

(i) the use or attempted use of violence against another person, or

(ii) conduct endangering or likely to endanger the life or safety of another person or inflicting or likely to inflict severe psychological damage upon another person; or

(b) an indictable offence referred to in section 151, 152, 153, 153.1, 155, 160, 170, 171, 172, 271, 272 or 273 or an attempt to commit such an offence.

(1.31) Despite subsections (1) to (1.2), the Review Board may extend the time for holding a hearing in respect of a high-risk accused to a maximum of 36 months after making or reviewing a disposition if the accused is represented by counsel and the accused and the Attorney General consent to the extension.

(1.32) Despite subsections (1) to (1.2), at the conclusion of a hearing under subsection 672.47(4) or this section in respect of a high-risk accused, the Review Board may, after making a disposition, extend the time for holding a subsequent hearing under this section to a maximum of 36 months if the Review Board is satisfied on the basis of any relevant information, including disposition information as defined in subsection 672.51(1) and an assessment report made under an assessment ordered under paragraph 672.121(c), that the accused's condition is not likely to improve and that detention remains necessary for the period of the extension.

(1.4) If the Review Board extends the time for holding a hearing under subsection (1.2) or (1.32), it shall provide notice of the extension to the accused, the prosecutor and the person in charge of the hospital where the accused is detained.

(1.5) A decision by the Review Board to extend the time for holding a hearing under subsection (1.2) or (1.32) is deemed to be a disposition for the purpose of sections 672.72 to 672.78.

(2) The Review Board shall hold a hearing to review any disposition made under paragraph 672.54(b) or (c) as soon as practicable after receiving notice that the person in charge of the place where the accused is detained or directed to attend requests the review.

(2.1) The Review Board shall hold a hearing to review a decision to significantly increase the restrictions on the liberty of the accused, as soon as practicable after receiving the notice referred to in subsection 672.56(2).

(3) Where an accused is detained in custody pursuant to a disposition made under paragraph 672.54(c) and a sentence of imprisonment is subsequently imposed on the accused in respect of another offence, the Review Board shall hold a hearing to review the disposition as soon as is practicable after receiving notice of that sentence. 1991, c. 43, s. 4; 2005, c. 22, s. 27(2); 2014, c. 6, s. 15.

DISCRETIONARY REVIEW / Review Board to provide notice / Review cancels appeal.

672.82 (1) A Review Board may hold a hearing to review any of its dispositions at any time, of its own motion or at the request of the accused or any other party.

(1.1) Where a Review Board holds a hearing under subsection (1) of its own motion, it shall provide notice to the prosecutor, the accused and any other party.

(2) Where a party requests a review of a disposition under this section, the party is deemed to abandon any appeal against the disposition taken under section 672.72. 1991, c. 43, s. 4; 2005, c. 22, s. 28.

DISPOSITION BY REVIEW BOARD.

672.83 (1) At a hearing held pursuant to section 672.81 or 672.82, the Review Board shall, except where a determination is made under subsection 672.48(1) that the accused is fit to stand trial, review the disposition made in respect of the accused and make any other disposition that the Review Board considers to be appropriate in the circumstances. 1991, c. 43, s. 4; 1997, c. 18, s. 90; 2005, c. 43, s. 29.

(2) [*Repealed*, 2005, c. 22, s. 29.]

REVIEW OF FINDING — HIGH-RISK ACCUSED / Review of finding — high-risk accused / Review of finding by court / Hearing and disposition / Review of conditions / Appeal.

672.84 (1) If a Review Board holds a hearing under section 672.81 or 672.82 in respect of a high-risk accused, it shall, on the basis of any relevant information, including disposition information as defined in subsection 672.51(1) and an assessment report made under an assessment ordered under paragraph 672.121(c), if it is satisfied that there is not a substantial likelihood that the accused — whether found to be a high-risk accused under paragraph 672.64(1)(a) or (b) — will use violence that could endanger the life or safety of another person, refer the finding for review to the superior court of criminal jurisdiction.

(2) If the Review Board is not so satisfied, it shall review the conditions of detention imposed under paragraph 672.54(c), subject to the restrictions set out in subsection 672.64(3).

(3) If the Review Board refers the finding to the superior court of criminal jurisdiction for review, the court shall, at the conclusion of a hearing, revoke the finding if the court is satisfied that there is not a substantial likelihood that the accused will use violence that could endanger the life or safety of another person, in which case the court or the Review Board shall make a disposition under any of paragraphs 672.54(a) to (c).

(4) Any disposition referred to in subsection (3) is subject to sections 672.45 to 672.47 as if the revocation is a verdict.

(5) If the court does not revoke the finding, it shall immediately send to the Review Board, in original or copied form, a transcript of the hearing, any other document or information related to the hearing, and all exhibits filed with it, if the transcript, document, information or exhibits are in its possession. The Review Board shall, as soon as practicable but not later than 45 days after the day on which the court decides not to revoke the finding, hold a hearing and review the conditions of detention imposed under paragraph 672.54(c), subject to the restrictions set out in subsection 672.64(3).

(6) A decision under subsection (1) about referring the finding to the court for review and a decision under subsection (3) about revoking the finding are deemed to be dispositions for the purpose of sections 672.72 to 672.78. 2014, c. 6, s. 16.

Power to Compel Appearance

BRINGING ACCUSED BEFORE REVIEW BOARD.

672.85 For the purpose of bringing the accused in respect of whom a hearing is to be held before the Review Board, including in circumstances in which the accused did not attend a previous hearing in contravention of a summons or warrant, the chairperson

- (a) shall order the person having custody of the accused to bring the accused to the hearing at the time and place fixed for it; or
- (b) may, if the accused is not in custody, issue a summons or warrant to compel the accused to appear at the hearing at the time and place fixed for it. 1991, c. 43, s. 4; 2005, c. 22, ss. 31 (heading) and 32.

Stay of Proceedings

RECOMMENDATION BY REVIEW BOARD / Notice / Inquiry / Court may act on own motion / Assessment order / Application / Stay / Proper administration of justice / Effect of stay.

672.851 (1) The Review Board may, of its own motion, make a recommendation to the court that has jurisdiction in respect of the offence charged against an accused found unfit to stand trial to hold an inquiry to determine whether a stay of proceedings should be ordered if

(a) the Review Board has held a hearing under section 672.81 or 672.82 in respect of the accused; and

(b) on the basis of any relevant information, including disposition information within the meaning of subsection 672.51(1) and an assessment report made under an assessment ordered under paragraph 672.121(a), the Review Board is of the opinion that

    (i) the accused remains unfit to stand trial and is not likely to ever become fit to stand trial, and

    (ii) the accused does not pose a significant threat to the safety of the public.

(2) If the Review Board makes a recommendation to the court to hold an inquiry, the Review Board shall provide notice to the accused, the prosecutor and any party who, in the opinion of the Review Board, has a substantial interest in protecting the interests of the accused.

(3) As soon as practicable after receiving the recommendation referred to in subsection (1), the court may hold an inquiry to determine whether a stay of proceedings should be ordered.

(4) A court may, of its own motion, conduct an inquiry to determine whether a stay of proceedings should be ordered if the court is of the opinion, on the basis of any relevant information, that

(a) the accused remains unfit to stand trial and is not likely to ever become fit to stand trial; and

(b) the accused does not pose a significant threat to the safety of the public.

(5) If the court holds an inquiry under subsection (3) or (4), it shall order an assessment of the accused.

(6) Section 672.51 applies to an inquiry of the court under this section.

(7) The court may, on completion of an inquiry under this section, order a stay of proceedings if it is satisfied

(a) on the basis of clear information, that the accused remains unfit to stand trial and is not likely to ever become fit to stand trial;

(b) that the accused does not pose a significant threat to the safety of the public; and

(c) that a stay is in the interests of the proper administration of justice.

(8) In order to determine whether a stay of proceedings is in the interests of the proper administration of justice, the court shall consider any submissions of the prosecutor, the accused and all other parties and the following factors:

(a) the nature and seriousness of the alleged offence;

(b) the salutary and deleterious effects of the order for a stay of proceedings, including any effect on public confidence in the administration of justice;

(c) the time that has elapsed since the commission of the alleged offence and whether an inquiry has been held under section 672.33 to decide whether sufficient evidence can be adduced to put the accused on trial; and

(d) any other factor that the court considers relevant.

(9) If a stay of proceedings is ordered by the court, any disposition made in respect of the accused ceases to have effect. If a stay of proceedings is not ordered, the

finding of unfit to stand trial and any disposition made in respect of the accused remain in force, until the Review Board holds a disposition hearing and makes a disposition in respect of the accused under section 672.83. 2005, c. 22, s. 33.

APPEAL / Effect.

672.852 (1) The Court of Appeal may allow an appeal against an order made under subsection 672.851(7) for a stay of proceedings, if the Court of Appeal is of the opinion that the order is unreasonable or cannot be supported by the evidence.

(2) If the Court of Appeal allows the appeal, it may set aside the order for a stay of proceedings and restore the finding that the accused is unfit to stand trial and the disposition made in respect of the accused. 2005, c. 22, s. 33.

Interprovincial Transfers

INTERPROVINCIAL TRANSFERS / Transfer where accused in custody / Transfer if accused not in custody / Order.

672.86 (1) An accused who is detained in custody or directed to attend at a hospital pursuant to a disposition made by a court or Review Board under paragraph 672.54(*c*) or a court under section 672.58 may be transferred to any other place in Canada where

(*a*) the Review Board of the province where the accused is detained or directed to attend recommends a transfer for the purpose of the reintegration of the accused into society or the recovery, treatment or custody of the accused; and

(*b*) the Attorney General of the province to which the accused is being transferred, or an officer authorized by that Attorney General, and the Attorney General of the province from which the accused is being transferred, or an officer authorized by that Attorney General, give their consent.

(2) Where an accused who is detained in custody is to be transferred, an officer authorized by the Attorney General of the province where the accused is being detained shall sign a warrant specifying the place in Canada to which the accused is to be transferred.

(2.1) An accused who is not detained in custody may be transferred to any other place in Canada where

(*a*) the Review Board of the province from which the accused is being transferred recommends a transfer for the purpose of the reintegration of the accused into society or the recovery or treatment of the accused; and

(*b*) the Attorney General of the province to which the accused is being transferred, or an officer authorized by that Attorney General, and the Attorney General of the province from which the accused is being transferred, or an officer authorized by that Attorney General, give their consent.

(3) Where an accused is being transferred in accordance with subsection (2.1), the Review Board of the province from which the accused is being transferred shall, by order,

   (*a*) direct that the accused be taken into custody and transferred pursuant to a warrant under subsection (2); or

   (*b*) direct that the accused attend at a specified place in Canada, subject to any conditions that the Review Board of the province to or from which the accused is being transferred considers appropriate. 1991, c. 43, s. 4; 2005, c. 22, s. 34.

DELIVERY AND DETENTION OF ACCUSED.

672.87 A warrant described in subsection 672.86(2) is sufficient authority

   (*a*) for any person who is responsible for the custody of an accused to have the accused taken into custody and conveyed to the person in charge of the place specified in the warrant; and

   (*b*) for the person specified in the warrant to detain the accused in accordance with any disposition made in respect of the accused under paragraph 672.54(*c*). 1991, c. 43, s. 4.

REVIEW BOARD OF RECEIVING PROVINCE / Agreement.

672.88 (1) The Review Board of the province to which an accused is transferred under section 672.86 has exclusive jurisdiction over the accused, and may exercise the powers and shall perform the duties mentioned in sections 672.5 and 672.81 to 672.84 as if that Review Board had made the disposition in respect of the accused.

(2) Notwithstanding subsection (1), the Attorney General of the province to which an accused is transferred may enter into an agreement subject to this Act with the Attorney General of the province from which the accused is transferred, enabling the Review Board of that province to exercise the powers and perform the duties referred to in subsection (1) in respect of the accused, in the circumstances and subject to the terms and conditions set out in the agreement. 1991, c. 43, s. 4; 2014, c. 6, s. 17.

OTHER INTERPROVINCIAL TRANSFERS / Agreement.

672.89 (1) If an accused who is detained in custody under a disposition made by a Review Board is transferred to another province otherwise than under section 672.86, the Review Board of the province from which the accused is transferred has exclusive jurisdiction over the accused and may continue to exercise the powers and shall continue to perform the duties mentioned in sections 672.5 and 672.81 to 672.84.

(2) Notwithstanding subsection (1), the Attorneys General of the provinces to and from which the accused is to be transferred as described in that subsection may, after the transfer is made, enter into an agreement subject to this Act, enabling the Review Board of the province to which an accused is transferred to exercise the powers and perform the duties referred to in subsection (1) in respect of the

accused, subject to the terms and conditions and in the circumstances set out in the agreement. 1991, c. 43, s. 4; 2014, c. 6, s. 18.

Enforcement of Orders and Regulations

EXECUTION OF WARRANT ANYWHERE IN CANADA.

672.9 Any warrant or process issued in relation to an assessment order or disposition made in respect of an accused may be executed or served in any place in Canada outside the province where the order or disposition was made as if it had been issued in that province. 1991, c. 43, s. 4; 1997, c. 18, s. 91.

ARREST WITHOUT WARRANT FOR CONTRAVENTION OF DISPOSITION.

672.91 A peace officer may arrest an accused without a warrant at any place in Canada if the peace officer has reasonable grounds to believe that the accused has contravened or wilfully failed to comply with the assessment order or disposition or any condition of it, or is about to do so. 1991, c. 43, s. 4; 2005, c. 22, s. 36.

RELEASE OR DELIVERY OF ACCUSED SUBJECT TO PARAGRAPH 672.54(b) DISPOSITION ORDER / No release / Accused to be brought before justice / Accused subject to paragraph 672.54(c) disposition order / Justice not available.

672.92 (1) If a peace officer arrests an accused under section 672.91 who is subject to a disposition made under paragraph 672.54(b) or an assessment order, the peace officer, as soon as practicable, may release the accused from custody and

(a) issue a summons or appearance notice compelling the accused's appearance before a justice; and

(b) deliver the accused to the place specified in the disposition or assessment order.

(2) A peace officer shall not release an accused under subsection (1) if the peace officer believes, on reasonable grounds,

(a) that it is necessary in the public interest that the accused be detained in custody having regard to all the circumstances, including the need to
   (i) establish the identity of the accused,
   (ii) establish the terms and conditions of a disposition made under section 672.54 or of an assessment order,
   (iii) prevent the commission of an offence, or
   (iv) prevent the accused from contravening or failing to comply with the disposition or assessment order;

(b) that the accused is subject to a disposition or an assessment order of a court, or Review Board, of another province; or

(c) that, if the accused is released from custody, the accused will fail to attend, as required, before a justice.

677

(3) If a peace officer does not release the accused, the accused shall be taken before a justice having jurisdiction in the territorial division in which the accused is arrested, without unreasonable delay and in any event within twenty-four hours after the arrest.

(4) If a peace officer arrests an accused under section 672.91 who is subject to a disposition under paragraph 672.54(*c*), the accused shall be taken before a justice having jurisdiction in the territorial division in which the accused is arrested without unreasonable delay and, in any event, within twenty-four hours.

(5) If a justice described in subsection (3) or (4) is not available within twenty-four hours after the arrest, the accused shall be taken before a justice as soon as practicable. 1991, c. 43, s. 4; 2005, c. 22, s. 36.

WHERE JUSTICE TO RELEASE ACCUSED / Notice / Order of justice pending decision of Review Board.

672.93 (1) A justice shall release an accused who is brought before the justice under section 672.92 unless the justice is satisfied that there are reasonable grounds to believe that the accused has contravened or failed to comply with a disposition or an assessment order.

(1.1) If the justice releases the accused, notice shall be given to the court or Review Board, as the case may be, that made the disposition or assessment order.

(2) If the justice is satisfied that there are reasonable grounds to believe that the accused has contravened or failed to comply with a disposition or an assessment order, the justice, pending a hearing of a Review Board with respect to the disposition or a hearing of a court or Review Board with respect to the assessment order, may make an order that is appropriate in the circumstances in relation to the accused, including an order that the accused be returned to a place that is specified in the disposition or assessment order. If the justice makes an order under this subsection, notice shall be given to the court or Review Board, as the case may be, that made the disposition or assessment order. 1991, c. 43, s. 4; 2005, c. 22, s. 36.

POWERS OF REVIEW BOARD.

672.94 Where a Review Board receives a notice given under subsection 672.93(1.1) or (2), it may exercise the powers and shall perform the duties mentioned in sections 672.5 and 672.81 to 672.83 as if the Review Board were reviewing a disposition. 1991, c. 43, s. 4; 2005, c. 22, s. 36.

REGULATIONS.

672.95 The Governor in Council may make regulations
- (a) prescribing anything that may be prescribed under this Part; and
- (b) generally to carry out the purposes and provisions of this Part. 1991, c. 43, s. 4.

Part XXI / APPEALS – INDICTABLE OFFENCES

Interpretation

DEFINITIONS / "court of appeal" / "indictment" / "registrar" / "sentence" / "trial court".

673. In this Part

"court of appeal" means the court of appeal, as defined by the definition "court of appeal" in section 2, for the province or territory in which the trial of a person by indictment is held;

"indictment" includes an information or charge in respect of which a person has been tried for an indictable offence under Part XIX;

"registrar" means the registrar or clerk of the court of appeal;

"sentence" includes

(a) a declaration made under subsection 199(3),

(b) an order made under subsection 109(1) or 110(1), section 161, subsection 164.2(1) or 194(1), section 259, 261 or 462.37, subsection 491.1(2), 730(1) or 737(2.1) or (3) or section 738, 739, 742.1, 742.3, 743.6, 745.4 or 745.5,

(c) a disposition made under section 731 or 732 or subsection 732.2(3) or (5), 742.4(3) or 742.6(9),

(d) an order made under subsection 16(1) of the *Controlled Drugs and Substances Act*, and

(e) an order made under subsection 94(1) of the *Cannabis Act*;

"trial court" means the court by which an accused was tried and includes a judge or a provincial court judge acting under Part XIX. R.S., c. C-34, s. 601; 1972, c. 13, s. 52; 1973-74, c. 38, s. 6.1, c. 50, s. 3; 1974-75-76, c. 93, s. 72; 1976-77, c. 53, s. 4; R.S.C. 1985, c. 27 (1st Supp.), s. 138; c. 23 (4th Supp.), s. 4; c. 42 (4th Supp.), s. 4; 1991, c. 43, s. 5; 1992, c. 1, s. 58; 1993, c. 45, s. 10, 16 and 19; 1995, c. 22, s. 5, c. 39, ss. 155, 190(a), (b); 1996, c. 19, s. 74(1); 1999, c. 5, ss. 25, 51 (s. 51 replaced by 2005, c. 22, s. 45; c. 25, ss. 13, 31(5); 2002, c. 13, s. 63; 2005, c. 22, s. 38; 2006, c. 14, s. 6; 2013, c. 11, s. 2; 2018, c. 16, s. 220; 2018, c. 21, s. 21; 2019, c. 25, s. 278.

Right of Appeal

PROCEDURE ABOLISHED.

674. No proceedings other than those authorized by this Part and Part XXVI shall be taken by way of appeal in proceedings in respect of indictable offences. R.S., c. C-34, s. 602.

RIGHT OF APPEAL OF PERSON CONVICTED / Summary conviction appeals / Appeal against absolute term in excess of ten years / Appeal against s. 743.6 order / Persons under 18 / Appeal against s. 745.51(1) order / Appeals against verdicts based on mental disorder / Where application for leave to appeal refused by judge.

675. (1) A person who is convicted by a trial court in proceedings by indictment may appeal to the court of appeal

   (*a*) against his conviction

      (i) on any ground of appeal that involves a question of law alone,

      (ii) on any ground of appeal that involves a question of fact or a question of mixed law and fact, with leave of the court of appeal or a judge thereof or on the certificate of the trial judge that the case is a proper case for appeal, or

      (iii) on any ground of appeal not mentioned in subparagraph (i) or (ii) that appears to the court of appeal to be a sufficient ground of appeal, with leave of the court of appeal; or

   (*b*) against the sentence passed by the trial court, with leave of the court of appeal or a judge thereof unless that sentence is one fixed by law.

(1.1) A person may appeal, pursuant to subsection (1), with leave of the court of appeal or a judge of that court, to that court in respect of a summary conviction or a sentence passed with respect to a summary conviction as if the summary conviction had been a conviction in proceedings by indictment if

   (*a*) there has not been an appeal with respect to the summary conviction;

   (*b*) the summary conviction offence was tried with an indictable offence; and

   (*c*) there is an appeal in respect of the indictable offence.

(2) A person who has been convicted of second degree murder and sentenced to imprisonment for life without eligibility for parole for a specified number of years in excess of ten may appeal to the court of appeal against the number of years in excess of ten of his imprisonment without eligibility for parole.

(2.1) A person against whom an order under section 743.6 has been made may appeal to the court of appeal against the order.

(2.2) A person who was under the age of eighteen at the time of the commission of the offence for which the person was convicted of first degree murder or second degree murder and sentenced to imprisonment for life without eligibility for parole until the person has served the period specified by the judge presiding at the trial may appeal to the court of appeal against the number of years in excess of the minimum number of years of imprisonment without eligibility for parole that are required to be served in respect of that person's case. [as enacted by 1997, c. 18, s. 92]

(2.3) A person against whom an order under subsection 745.51(1) has been made may appeal to the court of appeal against the order.

(3) Where a verdict of not criminally responsible on account of mental disorder or unfit to stand trial is rendered in respect of a person, that person may appeal to the

court of appeal against that verdict on any ground of appeal, mentioned in subparagraph (1)(*a*)(i), (ii) or (iii) and subject to the conditions described therein.

(4) Where a judge of the court of appeal refuses leave to appeal under this section otherwise than under paragraph (1)(*b*), the appellant may, by filing notice in writing with the court of appeal within seven days after the refusal, have the application for leave to appeal determined by the court of appeal. R.S., c. C-34, s. 603; 1974-75-76, c. 105, s. 13; 1991, c. 43, s. 9; 1995, c. 42, s. 73; 1997, c. 18, s. 92; 1999, c. 31, s. 68; 2002, c. 13, s. 64; 2011, c. 5, s. 2.

CODE

RIGHT OF ATTORNEY GENERAL TO APPEAL / Summary conviction appeals / Acquittal / Appeal against verdict of unfit to stand trial / Appeal against ineligible parole period / Appeal against decision not to make s. 743.6 order / Appeal against decision not to make s. 745.51(1) order.

676. (1) The Attorney General or counsel instructed by him for the purpose may appeal to the court of appeal

    (*a*) against a judgment or verdict of acquittal or a verdict of not criminally responsible on account of mental disorder of a trial court in proceedings by indictment on any ground of appeal that involves a question of law alone;

    (*b*) against an order of a superior court of criminal jurisdiction that quashes an indictment or in any manner refuses or fails to exercise jurisdiction on an indictment;

    (*c*) against an order of a trial court that stays proceedings on an indictment or quashes an indictment; or

    (*d*) with leave of the court of appeal or a judge thereof, against the sentence passed by a trial court in proceedings by indictment, unless that sentence is one fixed by law.

(1.1) The Attorney General or counsel instructed by the Attorney General may appeal, pursuant to subsection (1), with leave of the court of appeal or a judge of that court, to that court in respect of a verdict of acquittal in a summary offence proceeding or a sentence passed with respect to a summary conviction as if the summary offence proceeding was a proceeding by indictment if

    (*a*) there has not been an appeal with respect to the summary conviction;

    (*b*) the summary conviction offence was tried with an indictable offence; and

    (*c*) there is an appeal in respect of the indictable offence.

(2) For the purposes of this section, a judgment or verdict of acquittal includes an acquittal in respect of an offence specifically charged where the accused has, on the trial thereof, been convicted or discharged under section 730 of any other offence.

(3) The Attorney General or counsel instructed by the Attorney General for the purpose may appeal to the court of appeal against a verdict that an accused is unfit to stand trial, on any ground of appeal that involves a question of law alone.

(4) The Attorney General or counsel instructed by him for the purpose may appeal to the court of appeal in respect of a conviction for second degree murder, against

the number of years of imprisonment without eligibility for parole, being less than twenty-five, that has been imposed as a result of that conviction.

(5) The Attorney General or counsel instructed by the Attorney General for the purpose may appeal to the court of appeal against the decision of the court not to make an order under section 743.6.

(6) The Attorney General or counsel instructed by the Attorney General for the purpose may appeal to the court of appeal against the decision of the court not to make an order under subsection 745.51(1). R.S., c. C-34, s. 605; 1974-75-76, c. 105, s. 15; R.S.C. 1985, c. 27 (1st Supp.), s. 139; 1991, c. 43, s. 9; 1995, c. 22, s. 10; 1995, c. 42, s. 74; 1997, c. 18, s. 93; 2002, c. 13, s. 65; 2008, c. 18, s. 28; 2011, c. 5, s. 3.

APPEAL RE COSTS.

676.1 A party who is ordered to pay costs may, with leave of the court of appeal or a judge of a court of appeal, appeal the order or the amount of costs ordered. 1997, c. 18, s. 94.

SPECIFYING GROUNDS OF DISSENT.

677. Where a judge of the court of appeal expresses an opinion dissenting from the judgment of the court, the judgment of the court shall specify any grounds in law on which the dissent, in whole or in part, is based. R.S., c. C-34, s. 606; 1994, c. 44, s. 67.

Procedure on Appeals

NOTICE OF APPEAL / Extension of time.

678. (1) An appellant who proposes to appeal to the court of appeal or to obtain the leave of that court to appeal shall give notice of appeal or notice of his application for leave to appeal in such manner and within such period as may be directed by rules of court.

(2) The court of appeal or a judge thereof may at any time extend the time within which notice of appeal or notice of an application for leave to appeal may be given. R.S., c. C-34, s. 607; 1972, c. 13, s. 53; 1974-75-76, c. 105, s. 16.

SERVICE WHERE RESPONDENT CANNOT BE FOUND.

678.1 Where a respondent cannot be found after reasonable efforts have been made to serve the respondent with a notice of appeal or notice of an application for leave to appeal, service of the notice of appeal or the notice of the application for leave to appeal may be effected substitutionally in the manner and within the period directed by a judge of the court of appeal. R.S.C. 1985, c. 27 (1st Supp.), s. 140.

RELEASE PENDING DETERMINATION OF APPEAL / Notice of application for release / Circumstances in which appellant may be released / Idem / Conditions of release order / Immediate release of appellant / Applicable provisions / Release or detention pending hearing of reference / Release or detention pending new trial or new hearing / Application to appeals on summary conviction proceedings / Form of undertaking or recognizance / Directions for expediting appeal, new trial, etc.

CODE

679. (1) A judge of the court of appeal may, in accordance with this section, release an appellant from custody pending the determination of his appeal if,

(a) in the case of an appeal to the court of appeal against conviction, the appellant has given notice of appeal or, where leave is required, notice of his application for leave to appeal pursuant to section 678;

(b) in the case of an appeal to the court of appeal against sentence only, the appellant has been granted leave to appeal; or

(c) in the case of an appeal or an application for leave to appeal to the Supreme Court of Canada, the appellant has filed and served his notice of appeal or, where leave is required, his application for leave to appeal.

(2) Where an appellant applies to a judge of the court of appeal to be released pending the determination of his appeal, he shall give written notice of the application to the prosecutor or to such other person as a judge of the court of appeal directs.

(3) In the case of an appeal referred to in paragraph (1)(a) or (c), the judge of the court of appeal may order that the appellant be released pending the determination of his appeal if the appellant establishes that

(a) the appeal or application for leave to appeal is not frivolous;

(b) he will surrender himself into custody in accordance with the terms of the order; and

(c) his detention is not necessary in the public interest.

(4) In the case of an appeal referred to in paragraph (1)(b), the judge of the court of appeal may order that the appellant be released pending the determination of his appeal or until otherwise ordered by a judge of the court of appeal if the appellant establishes that

(a) the appeal has sufficient merit that, in the circumstances, it would cause unnecessary hardship if he were detained in custody;

(b) he will surrender himself into custody in accordance with the terms of the order; and

(c) his detention is not necessary in the public interest.

(5) If the judge of the court of appeal does not refuse the appellant's application, the judge shall make a release order referred to in section 515, the form of which may be adapted to suit the circumstances, which must include a condition that the accused surrender themselves into custody in accordance with the order.

(5.1) The person having the custody of the appellant shall, if the appellant complies with the release order, immediately release the appellant.

(6) Sections 495.1, 512.3 and 524 apply, with any modifications that the circumstances require, in respect of any proceedings under this section.

(7) If, with respect to any person, the Minister of Justice gives a direction or makes a reference under section 696.3, this section applies to the release or detention of that person pending the hearing and determination of the reference as though that person were an appellant in an appeal described in paragraph (1)(a).

(7.1) Where, with respect to any person, the court of appeal or the Supreme Court of Canada orders a new trial, section 515 or 522, as the case may be, applies to the release or detention of that person pending the new trial or new hearing as though that person were charged with the offence for the first time, except that the powers of a justice under section 515 or of a judge under section 522 are exercised by a judge of the court of appeal.

(8) This section applies to applications for leave to appeal and appeals to the Supreme Court of Canada in summary conviction proceedings.

(9) [*Repealed*, 2019, c. 25, s. 279(2).]

(10) A judge of the court of appeal, where on the application of an appellant he does not make an order under subsection (5) or where he cancels an order previously made under this section, or a judge of the Supreme Court of Canada on application by an appellant in the case of an appeal to that Court, may give such directions as he thinks necessary for expediting the hearing of the appellant's appeal or for expediting the new trial or new hearing or the hearing of the reference, as the case may be. R.S., c. C-34, s. 608; R.S., c. 2 (2nd Supp.), s. 12; R.S.C. 1985, c. 27 (1st Supp.), s. 141; 1997, c. 18, s. 95; 1999, c. 25, s. 14; 2002, c. 13, s. 66; 2019, c. 25, s. 279.

REVIEW BY COURT OF APPEAL / Single judge acting / Enforcement of decision.

680. (1) A decision made by a judge under section 522, a decision made under subsections 524(3) to (5) with respect to an accused referred to in paragraph 524(1)(a) or a decision made by a judge of the court of appeal under section 261 or 679 may, on the direction of the chief justice or acting chief justice of the court of appeal, be reviewed by that court and that court may, if it does not confirm the decision,

    (a) vary the decision; or

    (b) substitute such other decision as, in its opinion, should have been made.

(2) On consent of the parties, the powers of the court of appeal under subsection (1) may be exercised by a judge of that court.

(3) A decision as varied or substituted under this section shall have effect and may be enforced in all respects as though it were the decision originally made. R.S., c. 2 (2nd Supp.), s. 12; 1974-75-76, c. 93, s. 73; R.S.C. 1985, c. 27 (1st Supp.), s. 142; 1994, c. 44, s. 68; 2018, c. 21, s. 22; 2019, c. 25, s. 280.

---

681. [*Repealed*, 1991, c. 43, s. 9.]

REPORT BY JUDGE / Transcript of evidence / Notes of proceedings / Copies to interested parties / Copy for Minister of Justice.

682. (1) Where, under this Part, an appeal is taken or an application for leave to appeal is made, the judge or provincial court judge who presided at the trial shall, at the request of the court of appeal or a judge thereof, in accordance with rules of court, furnish it or him with a report on the case or on any matter relating to the case that is specified in the request.

(2) A copy or transcript of
  (*a*) the evidence taken at the trial,
  (*b*) any charge to the jury and any objections that were made to a charge to the jury,
  (*c*) the reasons for judgment, if any, and
  (*d*) the addresses of the prosecutor and the accused, if a ground for the appeal is based on either of the addresses,

shall be furnished to the court of appeal, except in so far as it is dispensed with by order of a judge of that court.

(3) [*Repealed*, 1997, c. 18, s. 96(2).]

(4) A party to an appeal is entitled to receive, on payment of any charges that are fixed by rules of court, a copy or transcript of any material that is prepared under subsections (1) and (2).

(5) The Minister of Justice is entitled, on request, to receive a copy or transcript of any material that is prepared under subsections (1) and (2). R.S., c. C-34, s. 609; 1972, c. 13, s. 55; 1974-75-76, 105, s. 17; R.S.C. 1985, c. 27 (1st Supp.), s. 143; 1997, c. 18, s. 96.

POWERS OF COURT OF APPEAL / Parties entitled to adduce evidence and be heard / Remote appearance / Virtual presence of witnesses / Application of sections 715.25 and 715.26 / Other powers / Execution of process / Power to order suspension / Release order or recognizance / Revocation of suspension order / Release order to be taken into account.

683. (1) For the purposes of an appeal under this Part, the court of appeal may, where it considers it in the interests of justice,
  (*a*) order the production of any writing, exhibit, or other thing connected with the proceedings;
  (*b*) order any witness who would have been a compellable witness at the trial, whether or not he was called at the trial,
    (i) to attend and be examined before the court of appeal, or
    (ii) to be examined in the manner provided by rules of court before a judge of the court of appeal, or before any officer of the court of appeal or justice of the peace or other person appointed by the court of appeal for the purpose;
  (*c*) admit, as evidence, an examination that is taken under subparagraph (*b*)(ii);
  (*d*) receive the evidence, if tendered, of any witness, including the appellant, who is a competent but not compellable witness;

   (*e*) order that any question arising on the appeal that
      (i) involves prolonged examination of writings or accounts, or scientific or local investigation, and
      (ii) cannot in the opinion of the court of appeal conveniently be inquired into before the court of appeal,

   be referred for inquiry and report, in the manner provided by rules of court, to a special commissioner appointed by the court of appeal;

   (*f*) act on the report of a commissioner who is appointed under paragraph (*e*) in so far as the court of appeal thinks fit to do so, and

   (*g*) amend the indictment, unless it is of the opinion that the accused has been misled or prejudiced in his defence or appeal.

(2) In proceedings under this section, the parties or their counsel are entitled to examine or cross-examine witnesses and, in an inquiry under paragraph (1)(*e*), are entitled to be present during the inquiry, and to adduce evidence and to be heard.

(2.1) In proceedings under this section, the court of appeal may order that a party appear by audioconference or videoconference, if the technological means is satisfactory to the court.

(2.2) Sections 714.1 to 714.8 apply, with any modifications that the circumstances require, to examinations and cross-examinations of witnesses under this section.

(2.3) Sections 715.25 and 715.26 apply, with any modifications that the circumstances require, to proceedings under this section.

(3) A court of appeal may exercise, in relation to proceedings in the court, any powers not mentioned in subsection (1) that may be exercised by the court on appeals in civil matters, and may issue any process that is necessary to enforce the orders or sentences of the court, but no costs shall be allowed to the appellant or respondent on the hearing and determination of an appeal or on any proceedings preliminary or incidental thereto.

(4) Any process that is issued by the court of appeal under this section may be executed anywhere in Canada.

(5) If an appeal or an application for leave to appeal has been filed in the court of appeal, that court, or a judge of that court, may, when the court, or the judge, considers it to be in the interests of justice, order that any of the following be suspended until the appeal has been determined:

   (*a*) an obligation to pay a fine;

   (*b*) an order of forfeiture or disposition of forfeited property;

   (*c*) an order to make restitution under section 738 or 739;

   (*d*) an obligation to pay a victim surcharge under section 737;

   (*e*) a probation order under section 731; and

   (*f*) a conditional sentence order under section 742.1.

(5.1) Before making an order under paragraph (5)(*e*) or (*f*), the court of appeal, or a judge of that court, may make a release order or order the offender to enter into a recognizance.

(6) The court of appeal may revoke any order it makes under subsection (5) where it considers such revocation to be in the interests of justice.

(7) If the offender is subject to a release order under subsection (5.1), the court of appeal shall, in determining whether to vary the sentence of the offender, take into account the conditions of that order and the period for which they were imposed on the offender. R.S., c. C-34, s. 610; R.S.C. 1985, c. 27 (1st Supp.), s. 144; c. 23 (4th Supp.), s. 5; 1995, c. 22, s. 10; 1997, c. 18, ss. 97, 141; 1999, c. 25, s. 15; 2002, c. 13, s. 67; 2008, c. 18, s. 29; 2019, c. 25, s. 281.

CODE

LEGAL ASSISTANCE FOR APPELLANT / Counsel fees and disbursements / Taxation of fees and disbursements.

684. (1) A court of appeal or a judge of that court may, at any time, assign counsel to act on behalf of an accused who is a party to an appeal or to proceedings preliminary or incidental to an appeal where, in the opinion of the court or judge, it appears desirable in the interests of justice that the accused should have legal assistance and where it appears that the accused has not sufficient means to obtain that assistance.

(2) Where counsel is assigned pursuant to subsection (1) and legal aid is not granted to the accused pursuant to a provincial legal aid program, the fees and disbursements of counsel shall be paid by the Attorney General who is the appellant or respondent, as the case may be, in the appeal.

(3) Where subsection (2) applies and counsel and the Attorney General cannot agree on fees or disbursements of counsel, the Attorney General or the counsel may apply to the registrar of the court of appeal and the registrar may tax the disputed fees and disbursements. R.S., c. C-34, s. 611; R.S.C. 1985, c. 34 (3rd Supp.), s. 9.

SUMMARY DETERMINATION OF FRIVOLOUS APPEALS / Summary determination of appeals filed in error.

685. (1) Where it appears to the registrar that a notice of appeal, which purports to be on a ground of appeal that involves a question of law alone, does not show a substantial ground of appeal, the registrar may refer the appeal to the court of appeal for summary determination, and, where an appeal is referred under this section, the court of appeal may, if it considers that the appeal is frivolous or vexatious and can be determined without being adjourned for a full hearing, dismiss the appeal summarily, without calling on any person to attend the hearing or to appear for the respondent on the hearing.

(2) If it appears to the registrar that a notice of appeal should have been filed with another court, the registrar may refer the appeal to a judge of the court of appeal for summary determination, and the judge may dismiss the appeal summarily without calling on any person to attend the hearing or to appear for the respondent on the hearing. R.S., c. C-34, s. 612; 2008, c. 18, s. 30.

Powers of the Court of Appeal

POWERS / Order to be made / Substituting verdict / Appeal from acquittal / New trial under Part XIX / New trial under Part XIX — Nunavut / Election where new trial a jury trial / Election if new trial a jury trial — Nunavut / Where appeal allowed against verdict of unfit to stand trial / Appeal court may set aside verdict of unfit to stand trial / Additional powers.

686. (1) On the hearing of an appeal against a conviction or against a verdict that the appellant is unfit to stand trial or not criminally responsible on account of mental disorder, the court of appeal

(a) may allow the appeal where it is of the opinion that

   (i) the verdict should be set aside on the ground that it is unreasonable or cannot be supported by the evidence,

   (ii) the judgment of the trial court should be set aside on the ground of a wrong decision on a question of law, or

   (iii) on any ground there was a miscarriage of justice;

(b) may dismiss the appeal where

   (i) the court is of the opinion that the appellant, although he was not properly convicted on a count or part of the indictment, was properly convicted on another count or part of the indictment,

   (ii) the appeal is not decided in favour of the appellant on any ground mentioned in paragraph (a),

   (iii) notwithstanding that the court is of the opinion that on any ground mentioned in subparagraph (a)(ii) the appeal might be decided in favour of the appellant, it is of the opinion that no substantial wrong or miscarriage of justice has occurred, or

   (iv) notwithstanding any procedural irregularity at trial, the trial court had jurisdiction over the class of offence of which the appellant was convicted and the court of appeal is of the opinion that the appellant suffered no prejudice thereby;

(c) may refuse to allow the appeal where it is of the opinion that the trial court arrived at a wrong conclusion respecting the effect of a special verdict, may order the conclusion to be recorded that appears to the court to be required by the verdict and may pass a sentence that is warranted in law in substitution for the sentence passed by the trial court, or

(d) may set aside a conviction and find the appellant unfit to stand trial or not criminally responsible on account of mental disorder and may exercise any of the powers of the trial court conferred by or referred to in section 672.45 in any manner deemed appropriate to the court of appeal in the circumstances.

(2) Where a court of appeal allows an appeal under paragraph (1)(a), it shall quash the conviction and

(a) direct a judgment or verdict of acquittal to be entered; or

(b) order a new trial.

(3) Where a court of appeal dismisses an appeal under subparagraph (1)(b)(i), it may substitute the verdict that in its opinion should have been found and

    (*a*) affirm the sentence passed by the trial court; or

    (*b*) impose a sentence that is warranted in law or remit the matter to the trial court and direct the trial court to impose a sentence that is warranted in law.

(4) If an appeal is from an acquittal or verdict that the appellant or respondent was unfit to stand trial or not criminally responsible on account of mental disorder, the court of appeal may

    (*a*) dismiss the appeal; or

    (*b*) allow the appeal, set aside the verdict and

        (i) order a new trial, or

        (ii) except where the verdict is that of a court composed of a judge and jury, enter a verdict of guilty with respect to the offence of which, in its opinion, the accused should have been found guilty but for the error in law, and pass a sentence that is warranted in law, or remit the matter to the trial court and direct the trial court to impose a sentence that is warranted in law.

(5) Subject to subsection (5.01), if an appeal is taken in respect of proceedings under Part XIX and the court of appeal orders a new trial under this Part, the following provisions apply:

    (*a*) if the accused, in his notice of appeal or notice of application for leave to appeal, requested that the new trial, if ordered, should be held before a court composed of a judge and jury, the new trial shall be held accordingly;

    (*b*) if the accused, in his notice of appeal or notice of application for leave to appeal, did not request that the new trial, if ordered, should be held before a court composed of a judge and jury, the new trial shall, without further election by the accused, be held before a judge or provincial court judge, as the case may be, acting under Part XIX, other than a judge or provincial court judge who tried the accused in the first instance, unless the court of appeal directs that the new trial be held before the judge or provincial court judge who tried the accused in the first instance;

    (*c*) if the court of appeal orders that the new trial shall be held before a court composed of a judge and jury, the new trial shall be commenced by an indictment in writing setting forth the offence in respect of which the new trial was ordered; and

    (*d*) notwithstanding paragraph (*a*), if the conviction against which the accused appealed was for an offence mentioned in section 553 and was made by a provincial court judge, the new trial shall be held before a provincial court judge acting under Part XIX, other than the provincial court judge who tried the accused in the first instance, unless the court of appeal directs that the new trial be held before the provincial court judge who tried the accused in the first instance.

(5.01) If an appeal is taken in respect of proceedings under Part XIX and the Court of Appeal of Nunavut orders a new trial under Part XXI, the following provisions apply:

    (*a*) if the accused, in the notice of appeal or notice of application for leave to appeal, requested that the new trial, if ordered, should be held before a court composed of a judge and jury, the new trial shall be held accordingly;

(b) if the accused, in the notice of appeal or notice of application for leave to appeal, did not request that the new trial, if ordered, should be held before a court composed of a judge and jury, the new trial shall, without further election by the accused, and without a preliminary inquiry, be held before a judge, acting under Part XIX, other than a judge who tried the accused in the first instance, unless the Court of Appeal of Nunavut directs that the new trial be held before the judge who tried the accused in the first instance;

(c) if the Court of Appeal of Nunavut orders that the new trial shall be held before a court composed of a judge and jury, the new trial shall be commenced by an indictment in writing setting forth the offence in respect of which the new trial was ordered; and

(d) despite paragraph (a), if the conviction against which the accused appealed was for an indictable offence mentioned in section 553, the new trial shall be held before a judge acting under Part XIX, other than the judge who tried the accused in the first instance, unless the Court of Appeal of Nunavut directs that the new trial be held before the judge who tried the accused in the first instance.

(5.1) Subject to subsection (5.2), if a new trial ordered by the court of appeal is to be held before a court composed of a judge and jury,

(a) the accused may, with the consent of the prosecutor, elect to have the trial heard before a judge without a jury or a provincial court judge;

(b) the election shall be deemed to be a re-election within the meaning of subsection 561(5); and

(c) subsection 561(5) applies, with such modifications as the circumstances require, to the election.

(5.2) If a new trial ordered by the Court of Appeal of Nunavut is to be held before a court composed of a judge and jury, the accused may, with the consent of the prosecutor, elect to have the trial heard before a judge without a jury. The election shall be deemed to be a re-election within the meaning of subsection 561.1(1), and subsection 561.1(6) applies, with any modifications that the circumstances require, to the election.

(6) Where a court of appeal allows an appeal against a verdict that the accused is unfit to stand trial, it shall, subject to subsection (7), order a new trial.

(7) Where the verdict that the accused is unfit to stand trial was returned after the close of the case for the prosecution, the court of appeal may, notwithstanding that the verdict is proper, if it is of the opinion that the accused should have been acquitted at the close of the case for the prosecution, allow the appeal, set aside the verdict and direct a judgment or verdict of acquittal to be entered.

(8) Where a court of appeal exercises any of the powers conferred by subsection (2), (4), (6) or (7), it may make any order, in addition, that justice requires. R.S., c. C-34, s. 613; 1974-75-76, c. 93, s. 75; R.S.C. 1985, c. 27 (1st Supp.), s. 145; 1991, c. 43, s. 9; 1997, c. 18, s. 98; 1999, c. 3, s. 52; c. 5, s. 26; 2019, c. 25, s. 282.

POWERS OF COURT ON APPEAL AGAINST SENTENCE / Effect of judgment.

687. (1) Where an appeal is taken against sentence, the court of appeal shall, unless the sentence is one fixed by law, consider the fitness of the sentence appealed against, and may on such evidence, if any, as it thinks fit to require or to receive,

- (*a*) vary the sentence within the limits prescribed by law for the offence of which the accused was convicted; or
- (*b*) dismiss the appeal.

(2) A judgment of a court of appeal that varies the sentence of an accused who was convicted has the same force and effect as if it were a sentence passed by the trial court. R.S., c. C-34, s. 614.

CODE

RIGHT OF APPELLANT TO ATTEND / Appellant represented by counsel / Manner of appearance / Argument may be oral or in writing / Sentence in absence of appellant.

688. (1) Subject to subsection (2), an appellant who is in custody is entitled, if he desires, to be present at the hearing of the appeal.

(2) An appellant who is in custody and who is represented by counsel is not entitled to be present

- (*a*) at the hearing of the appeal, where the appeal is on a ground involving a question of law alone,
- (*b*) on an application for leave to appeal, or
- (*c*) on any proceedings that are preliminary or incidental to an appeal,

unless rules of court provide that he is entitled to be present or the court of appeal or a judge thereof gives him leave to be present.

(2.1) In the case of an appellant who is in custody and who is entitled to be present at any proceedings on an appeal, the court may order that, instead of the appellant personally appearing,

- (*a*) at an application for leave to appeal or at any proceedings that are preliminary or incidental to an appeal, the appellant appear by audioconference or videoconference, if the technological means is satisfactory to the court; and
- (*b*) at the hearing of the appeal, if the appellant has access to legal advice, they appear by closed-circuit television or videoconference.

(3) An appellant may present his case on appeal and his argument in writing instead of orally, and the court of appeal shall consider any case of argument so presented.

(4) A court of appeal may exercise its power to impose sentence notwithstanding that the appellant is not present. R.S., c. C-34, s. 615; 2002, c. 13, s. 68; 2019, c. 25, s. 283.

RESTITUTION OR FORFEITURE OF PROPERTY / Annulling or varying order.

689. (1) If the trial court makes an order for compensation or for the restitution of property under section 738 or 739 or an order of forfeiture of property under subsection 164.2(1) or 462.37(1) or (2.01), the operation of the order is suspended

- (a) until the expiration of the period prescribed by rules of court for the giving of notice of appeal or of notice of application for leave to appeal, unless the accused waives an appeal; and
- (b) until the appeal or application for leave to appeal has been determined, where an appeal is taken or application for leave to appeal is made.

(2) The court of appeal may by order annul or vary an order made by the trial court with respect to compensation or the restitution of property within the limits prescribed by the provision under which the order was made by the trial court, whether or not the conviction is quashed. R.S., c. C-34, s. 616; R.S.C. 1985, c. 42 (4th Supp.), s. 5; 1995, c. 22, s. 10; 2002, c. 13, s. 69; 2005, c. 44, s. 12.

Powers of Minister of Justice

690. [*Repealed*, 2002, c. 13, s. 70.]

Appeals to the Supreme Court of Canada

APPEAL FROM CONVICTION / Appeal where acquittal set aside.

691. (1) A person who is convicted of an indictable offence and whose conviction is affirmed by the court of appeal may appeal to the Supreme Court of Canada

- (a) on any question of law on which a judge of the court of appeal dissents; or
- (b) on any question of law, if leave to appeal is granted by the Supreme Court of Canada.

(2) A person who is acquitted of an indictable offence other than by reason of a verdict of not criminally responsible on account of mental disorder and whose acquittal is set aside by the court of appeal may appeal to the Supreme Court of Canada

- (a) on any question of law on which a judge of the court of appeal dissents;
- (b) on any question of law, if the Court of Appeal enters a verdict of guilty against the person; or
- (c) on any question of law, if leave to appeal is granted by the Supreme Court of Canada. R.S., c. C-34, s. 618; 1974-75-76, c. 105, s. 18; R.S.C. 1985, c. 34 (3rd Supp.), s. 10; 1991, c. 43, s. 9; 1997, c. 18, s. 99.

CODE

APPEAL AGAINST AFFIRMATION OF VERDICT OF NOT CRIMINALLY RESPONSIBLE ON ACCOUNT OF MENTAL DISORDER / Appeal against affirmation of verdict of unfit to stand trial / Grounds of appeal.

692. (1) A person who has been found not criminally responsible on account of mental disorder and
  (a) whose verdict is affirmed on that ground by the court of appeal, or
  (b) against whom a verdict of guilty is entered by the court of appeal under subparagraph 686(4)(b)(ii),
may appeal to the Supreme Court of Canada.

(2) A person who is found unfit to stand trial and against whom that verdict is affirmed by the court of appeal may appeal to the Supreme Court of Canada.

(3) An appeal under subsection (1) or (2) may be
  (a) on any question of law on which a judge of the court of appeal dissents, or
  (b) on any question of law, if leave to appeal is granted by the Supreme Court of Canada. R.S., c. C-34, s. 620; R.S.C. 1985, c. 34 (3rd Supp.), s. 11; 1991, c. 43, s. 9.

APPEAL BY ATTORNEY GENERAL / Terms.

693. (1) Where a judgment of a court of appeal sets aside a conviction pursuant to an appeal taken under section 675 or dismisses an appeal taken pursuant to paragraph 676(1)(a), (b) or (c) or subsection 676(3), the Attorney General may appeal to the Supreme Court of Canada
  (a) on any question of law on which a judge of the court of appeal dissents; or
  (b) on any question of law, if leave to appeal is granted by the Supreme Court of Canada.

(2) Where leave to appeal is granted under paragraph (1)(b), the Supreme Court of Canada may impose such terms as it sees fit. R.S., c. C-34, s. 621; R.S.C. 1985, c. 27 (1st Supp.), s. 146, c. 34 (3rd Supp.), s. 12.

NOTICE OF APPEAL.

694. No appeal lies to the Supreme Court of Canada unless notice of appeal in writing is served by the appellant on the respondent in accordance with the *Supreme Court Act.* R.S., c. C-34, s. 622; R.S.C. 1985, c. 34 (3rd Supp.), s. 13.

LEGAL ASSISTANCE FOR ACCUSED / Counsel fees and disbursements / Taxation of fees and disbursements.

694.1 (1) The Supreme Court of Canada or a judge thereof may, at any time, assign counsel to act on behalf of an accused who is a party to an appeal to the Court or to proceedings preliminary or incidental to an appeal to the Court where, in the opinion of the Court or judge, it appears desirable in the interests of justice that the accused should have legal assistance and where it appears that the accused has not sufficient means to obtain that assistance.

(2) Where counsel is assigned pursuant to subsection (1) and legal aid is not granted to the accused pursuant to a provincial legal aid program, the fees and

disbursements of counsel shall be paid by the Attorney General who is the appellant or respondent, as the case may be, in the appeal.

(3) Where subsection (2) applies and where counsel and the Attorney General cannot agree on fees or disbursements of counsel, the Attorney General or the counsel may apply to the Registrar of the Supreme Court of Canada, and the Registrar may tax the disputed fees and disbursements. R.S.C. 1985, c. 34 (3rd Supp.), s. 13.

RIGHT OF APPELLANT TO ATTEND / Appellant represented by counsel.

694.2 (1) Subject to subsection (2), an appellant who is in custody and who desires to be present at the hearing of the appeal before the Supreme Court of Canada is entitled to be present at it.

(2) An appellant who is in custody and who is represented by counsel is not entitled to be present before the Supreme Court of Canada

    (*a*) on an application for leave to appeal,

    (*b*) on any proceedings that are preliminary or incidental to an appeal, or

    (*c*) at the hearing of the appeal,

unless rules of court provide that entitlement or the Supreme Court of Canada or a judge thereof gives the appellant leave to be present. R.S.C. 1985, c. 34 (3rd Supp.), s. 13.

ORDER OF SUPREME COURT OF CANADA / Election if new trial / Nunavut.

695. (1) The Supreme Court of Canada may, on an appeal under this Part, make any order that the court of appeal might have made and may make any rule or order that is necessary to give effect to its judgment.

(2) Subject to subsection (3), if a new trial ordered by the Supreme Court of Canada is to be held before a court composed of a judge and jury, the accused may, with the consent of the prosecutor, elect to have the trial heard before a judge without a jury or a provincial court judge. The election is deemed to be a re-election within the meaning of subsection 561(5) and subsections 561(5) to (7) apply to it with any modifications that the circumstances require.

(3) If a new trial ordered by the Supreme Court of Canada is to be held before a court composed of a judge and jury in Nunavut, the accused may, with the consent of the prosecutor, elect to have the trial heard before a judge without a jury. The election is deemed to be a re-election within the meaning of subsection 561.1(6) and subsections 561.1(6) to (9) apply to it with any modifications that the circumstances require. R.S., c. C-34, s. 623; 1999, c. 5, s. 27; 2008, c. 18, s. 31.

Appeals by Attorney General of Canada

RIGHT OF ATTORNEY GENERAL OF CANADA TO APPEAL.

696. The Attorney General of Canada has the same rights of appeal in proceedings instituted at the instance of the Government of Canada and conducted by or on behalf of that Government as the Attorney General of a province has under this Part. R.S., c. C-34, s. 624.

Part XXI.1 / APPLICATIONS FOR MINISTERIAL REVIEW — MISCARRIAGES OF JUSTICE

APPLICATION / Form of application.

696.1 (1) An application for ministerial review on the grounds of miscarriage of justice may be made to the Minister of Justice by or on behalf of a person who has been convicted of an offence under an Act of Parliament or a regulation made under an Act of Parliament or has been found to be a dangerous offender or a long-term offender under Part XXIV and whose rights of judicial review or appeal with respect to the conviction or finding have been exhausted.

(2) The application must be in the form, contain the information and be accompanied by any documents prescribed by the regulations. 2002, c. 13, s. 71.

REVIEW OF APPLICATIONS / Powers of investigation / Delegation.

696.2 (1) On receipt of an application under this Part, the Minister of Justice shall review it in accordance with the regulations.

(2) For the purpose of any investigation in relation to an application under this Part, the Minister of Justice has and may exercise the powers of a commissioner under Part I of the Inquiries Act and the powers that may be conferred on a commissioner under section 11 of that Act.

(3) Despite subsection 11(3) of the Inquiries Act, the Minister of Justice may delegate in writing to any member in good standing of the bar of a province, retired judge or any other individual who, in the opinion of the Minister, has similar background or experience the powers of the Minister to take evidence, issue subpoenas, enforce the attendance of witnesses, compel them to give evidence and otherwise conduct an investigation under subsection (2). 2002, c. 13, s. 71.

DEFINITION OF "COURT OF APPEAL" / Power to refer / Powers of Minister of Justice / No appeal.

696.3 (1) In this section, "the court of appeal" means the court of appeal, as defined by the definition "court of appeal" in section 2, for the province in which the person to whom an application under this Part relates was tried.

(2) The Minister of Justice may, at any time, refer to the court of appeal, for its opinion, any question in relation to an application under this Part on which the Minister desires the assistance of that court, and the court shall furnish its opinion accordingly.

(3) On an application under this Part, the Minister of Justice may
  (a) if the Minister is satisfied that there is a reasonable basis to conclude that a miscarriage of justice likely occurred,

     (i)   direct, by order in writing, a new trial before any court that the Minister thinks proper or, in the case of a person found to be a dangerous offender or a long-term offender under Part XXIV, a new hearing under that Part, or

     (ii) refer the matter at any time to the court of appeal for hearing and determination by that court as if it were an appeal by the convicted person or the person found to be a dangerous offender or a long-term offender under Part XXIV, as the case may be; or

  (b) dismiss the application.

(4) A decision of the Minister of Justice made under subsection (3) is final and is not subject to appeal. 2002, c. 13, s. 71.

CONSIDERATIONS

696.4 In making a decision under subsection 696.3(3), the Minister of Justice shall take into account all matters that the Minister considers relevant, including

  (a) whether the application is supported by new matters of significance that were not considered by the courts or previously considered by the Minister in an application in relation to the same conviction or finding under Part XXIV;

  (b) the relevance and reliability of information that is presented in connection with the application; and

  (c) the fact that an application under this Part is not intended to serve as a further appeal and any remedy available on such an application is an extraordinary remedy. 2002, c. 13, s. 71.

ANNUAL REPORT.

696.5 The Minister of Justice shall within six months after the end of each financial year submit an annual report to Parliament in relation to applications under this Part. 2002, c. 13, s. 71.

REGULATIONS.

696.6 The Governor in Council may make regulations

  (a) prescribing the form of, the information required to be contained in and any documents that must accompany an application under this Part;

  (b) prescribing the process of review in relation to applications under this Part, which may include the following stages, namely, preliminary assessment, investigation, reporting on investigation and decision; and

  (c) respecting the form and content of the annual report under section 696.5. 2002, c. 13, s. 71.

Part XXII / PROCURING ATTENDANCE

Application

APPLICATION.

697. Except where section 527 applies, this Part applies where a person is required to attend to give evidence in a proceeding to which this Act applies. R.S., c. C-34, s. 625; R.S.C. 1985, c. 27 (1st Supp.), s. 147.

Process

SUBPOENA / Warrant in Form 17 / Subpoena issued first.

698. (1) Where a person is likely to give material evidence in a proceeding to which this Act applies, a subpoena may be issued in accordance with this Part requiring that person to attend to give evidence.

(2) Where it is made to appear that a person who is likely to give material evidence

(a) will not attend in response to a subpoena if a subpoena is issued, or

(b) is evading service of a subpoena,

a court, justice or provincial court judge having power to issue a subpoena to require the attendance of that person to give evidence may issue a warrant in Form 17 to cause that person to be arrested and to be brought to give evidence.

(3) Except where paragraph (2)(a) applies, a warrant in Form 17 shall not be issued unless a subpoena has first been issued. R.S., c. C-34, s. 626.

WHO MAY ISSUE / Order of judge / Order of judge / Seal / Signature / Sexual offences / Form of subpoena / Form of subpoena in sexual offences.

699. (1) If a person is required to attend to give evidence before a superior court of criminal jurisdiction, a court of appeal, an appeal court or a court of criminal jurisdiction other than a provincial court judge acting under Part XIX, a subpoena directed to that person shall be issued out of the court before which the attendance of that person is required.

(2) If a person is required to attend to give evidence before a provincial court judge acting under Part XIX or a summary conviction court under Part XXVII or in proceedings over which a justice has jurisdiction, a subpoena directed to the person shall be issued

(a) by a provincial court judge or a justice, where the person whose attendance is required is within the province in which the proceedings were instituted; or

(b) by a provincial court judge or out of a superior court of criminal jurisdiction of the province in which the proceedings were instituted, where the person whose attendance is required is not within the province.

697

(3) A subpoena shall not be issued out of a superior court of criminal jurisdiction pursuant to paragraph (2)(*b*), except pursuant to an order of a judge of the court made on application by a party to the proceedings.

(4) A subpoena or warrant that is issued by a court under this Part shall be under the seal of the court and shall be signed by a judge of the court or by the clerk of the court.

(5) A subpoena or warrant that is issued by a justice or provincial court judge under this Part must be signed by the justice, provincial court judge or the clerk of the court.

(5.1) Despite anything in subsections (1) to (5), in the case of an offence referred to in subsection 278.2(1), a subpoena requiring a witness to bring to the court a record, the production of which is governed by sections 278.1 to 278.91, must be issued by a judge and signed by the judge or the clerk of the court.

(6) Subject to subsection (7), a subpoena issued under this Part may be in Form 16.

(7) In the case of an offence referred to in subsection 278.2(1), a subpoena requiring a witness to bring anything to the court shall be in Form 16.1. R.S., c. C-34, s. 627; 1994, c. 44, s. 69; 1997, c. 30, s. 2; 1999, c. 5, s. 28; 2019, c. 25, s. 284.

CONTENTS OF SUBPOENA / Witness to appear and remain.

700. (1) A subpoena shall require the person to whom it is directed to attend, at a time and place to be stated in the subpoena, to give evidence and, if required, to bring with him anything that he has in his possession or under his control relating to the subject-matter of the proceedings.

(2) A person who is served with a subpoena issued under this Part shall attend and shall remain in attendance throughout the proceedings unless he is excused by the presiding judge, justice or provincial court judge. R.S., c. C-34, s. 628; R.S.C. 1985, c. 27 (1st Supp.), s. 148.

VIDEO LINKS / Sections of *Criminal Code.*

700.1 (1) If a person is to give evidence under section 714.1 or under subsection 46(2) of the *Canada Evidence Act* — or is to give evidence or a statement under an order made under section 22.2 of the *Mutual Legal Assistance in Criminal Matters Act* — at a place within the jurisdiction of a court referred to in subsection 699(1) or (2) where the technology is available, a subpoena shall be issued out of the court to order the person to give that evidence at that place.

(2) Sections 699, 700 and 701 to 703.2 apply, with any modifications that the circumstances require, to a subpoena issued under this section. 1999, c. 18, s. 94; 2019, c. 25, s. 285.

Execution or Service of Process

SERVICE / Personal service.

701. (1) Subject to subsection (2), a subpoena shall be served in a province by a peace officer or any other person who is qualified in that province to serve civil process, in accordance with subsection 509(2), with such modifications as the circumstances require.

(2) A subpoena that is issued pursuant to paragraph 699(2)(*b*) shall be served personally on the person to whom it is directed. R.S., c. C-34, s. 629; 1972, c. 13, s. 56; 1994, c. 44, s. 70; 2008, c. 18, s. 32.

(3) [*Repealed.* 2008, c. 18, s. 32.]

SERVICE IN ACCORDANCE WITH PROVINCIAL LAWS.

701.1 Despite section 701, in any province, service of a document may be made in accordance with the laws of the province relating to offences created by the laws of that province. 1997, c. 18, s. 100; 2008, c. 18, s. 33.

SUBPOENA EFFECTIVE THROUGHOUT CANADA / Subpoena effective throughout province.

702. (1) A subpoena that is issued by a provincial court judge or out of a superior court of criminal jurisdiction, a court of appeal, an appeal court or a court of criminal jurisdiction has effect anywhere in Canada according to its terms.

(2) A subpoena that is issued by a justice has effect anywhere in the province in which it is issued. R.S., c. C-34, s. 630; 1994, c. 44, s. 71.

WARRANT EFFECTIVE THROUGHOUT CANADA / Warrant effective in a province.

703. (1) Notwithstanding any other provision of this Act, a warrant of arrest or committal that is issued out of a superior court of criminal jurisdiction, a court of appeal, an appeal court within the meaning of section 812 or a court of criminal jurisdiction other than a provincial court judge acting under Part XIX may be executed anywhere in Canada.

(2) Despite any other provision of this Act but subject to subsections 487.0551(2) and 705(3), a warrant of arrest or committal that is issued by a justice or provincial court judge may be executed anywhere in the province in which it is issued. R.S., c. C-34, s. 631; R.S.C. 1985, c. 27 (1st Supp.), s. 149; 2007, c. 22, s. 22.

SUMMONS EFFECTIVE THROUGHOUT CANADA.

703.1 A summons may be served anywhere in Canada and, if served, is effective notwithstanding the territorial jurisdiction of the authority that issued the summons. R.S.C. 1985, c. 27 (1st Supp.), s. 149.

SERVICE OF PROCESS ON AN ORGANIZATION.

703.2 Where any summons, notice or other process is required to be or may be served on an organization, and no other method of service is provided, service may be effected by delivery

(a) in the case of a municipality, to the mayor, warden, reeve or other chief officer of the municipality, or to the secretary, treasurer or clerk of the municipality; and

(b) in the case of any other organization, to the manager, secretary or other senior officer of the organization or one of its branches. R.S.C. 1985, c. 27 (1st Supp.), s. 149; 2003, c. 21, s. 13.

Defaulting or Absconding Witness

WARRANT FOR ABSCONDING WITNESS / Endorsement of warrant / Copy of information.

704. (1) Where a person is bound by recognizance to give evidence in any proceedings, a justice who is satisfied on information being made before him in writing and under oath that the person is about to abscond or has absconded may issue his warrant in Form 18 directing a peace officer to arrest that person and to bring him before the court, judge, justice or provincial court judge before whom he is bound to appear.

(2) Section 528 applies, with such modifications as the circumstances require, to a warrant issued under this section.

(3) A person who is arrested under this section is entitled, on request, to receive a copy of the information on which the warrant for his arrest was issued. R.S., c. C-34, s. 632.

WARRANT IF WITNESS DOES NOT ATTEND / Warrant if witness bound by recognizance / Warrant effective throughout Canada.

705. (1) If a person who has been served with a subpoena to give evidence in a proceeding does not attend or remain in attendance, the court, judge, justice or provincial court judge before whom that person was required to attend may issue a warrant in Form 17 for the arrest of that person if it is established

(a) that the subpoena has been served in accordance with this Part, and

(b) that the person is likely to give material evidence.

(2) If a person who has been bound by a recognizance to attend to give evidence in any proceeding does not attend or does not remain in attendance, the court, judge, justice or provincial court judge before whom that person was bound to attend may issue a warrant in Form 17 for the arrest of that person.

(3) A warrant that is issued by a justice or provincial court judge pursuant to subsection (1) or (2) may be executed anywhere in Canada. R.S., c. C-34, s. 633; 2019, c. 25, s. 286(1)-(3).

IF WITNESS ARRESTED UNDER WARRANT.

706. If a person is brought before a court, judge, provincial court judge or justice under a warrant issued under subsection 698(2) or section 704 or 705, the court, judge, provincial court judge or justice may, so that the person will appear and give evidence when required, order that the person be detained in custody or be released on recognizance, with or without sureties. R.S., c. C-34, s. 634; 2019, c. 25, s. 287.

MAXIMUM PERIOD FOR DETENTION OF WITNESS / Application by witness to judge / Review of detention.

707. (1) No person shall be detained in custody under the authority of any provision of this Act, for the purpose only of appearing and giving evidence when required as a witness, for any period exceeding thirty days unless prior to the expiration of those thirty days he has been brought before a judge of a superior court of criminal jurisdiction in the province in which he is being detained.

(2) Where at any time prior to the expiration of the thirty days referred to in subsection (1), a witness being detained in custody as described in that subsection applies to be brought before a judge of a court described therein, the judge before whom the application is brought shall fix a time prior to the expiration of those thirty days for the hearing of the application and shall cause notice of the time so fixed to be given to the witness, the person having custody of the witness and such other persons as the judge may specify, and at the time so fixed for the hearing of the application the person having custody of the witness shall cause the witness to be brought before a judge of the court for that purpose.

(3) If the judge before whom a witness is brought under this section is not satisfied that the continued detention of the witness is justified, the judge shall order them to be discharged or to be released on recognizance, with or without sureties, so that the witness will appear and give evidence when required. However, if the judge is satisfied that the continued detention of the witness is justified, the judge may order their continued detention until they do what is required of them under section 550 or the trial is concluded, or until they appear and give evidence when required, except that the total period of detention of the witness from the time they were first detained in custody shall not in any case exceed 90 days. R.S., c. C-34, s. 635; 2019, c. 25, s. 288.

CONTEMPT / Punishment / Form.

708. (1) A person who, being required by law to attend or remain in attendance for the purpose of giving evidence, fails, without lawful excuse, to attend or remain in attendance accordingly is guilty of contempt of court.

(2) A court, judge, justice or provincial court judge may deal summarily with a person who is guilty of contempt of court under this section and that person is liable to a fine not exceeding one hundred dollars or to imprisonment for a term not exceeding ninety days or to both, and may be ordered to pay the costs that are incident to the service of any process under this Part and to his detention, if any.

(3) A conviction under this section may be in Form 38 and a warrant of committal in respect of a conviction under this section may be in Form 25. R.S., c. C-34, s. 636.

Electronically Transmitted Copies

ELECTRONICALLY TRANSMITTED COPIES.

708.1 A copy of a summons, warrant or subpoena transmitted by a means of telecommunication that produces a writing has the same probative force as the original for the purposes of this Act. 1997, c. 18, s. 101.

Evidence on Commission

ORDER APPOINTING COMMISSIONER / Idem.

709. (1) A party to proceedings by way of indictment or summary conviction may apply for an order appointing a commissioner to take the evidence of a witness who

  (a) is, by reason of
    (i) physical disability arising out of illness, or
    (ii) some other good and sufficient cause,
      not likely to be able to attend at the time the trial is held; or
  (b) is out of Canada.

(2) A decision under subsection (1) is deemed to have been made at the trial held in relation to the proceedings mentioned in that subsection. R.S., c. C-34, s. 637; R.S.C. 1985, c. 27 (1st Supp.), s. 150; 1994, c. 44, s. 72.

APPLICATION WHERE WITNESS IS ILL / Evidence of medical practitioner.

710. (1) An application under paragraph 709(1)(a) shall be made
  (a) to a judge of a superior court of the province in which the proceedings are taken; or
  (b) to a judge of a county or district court in the territorial division in which the proceedings are taken; or
  (c) to a provincial court judge, where
    (i) at the time the application is made, the accused is before a provincial court judge presiding over a preliminary inquiry under Part XXVIII, or
    (ii) the accused or defendant is to be tried by a provincial court judge acting under Part XIX or XXVII.

(2) An application under subparagraph 709(1)(a)(i) may be granted on the evidence of a registered medical practitioner. R.S., c. C-34, s. 638; R.S.C. 1985, c. 27 (1st Supp.), s. 151; 1994, c. 44, s. 73.

READING EVIDENCE OF WITNESS WHO IS ILL.

711. Where the evidence of a witness mentioned in paragraph 709(1)(*a*) is taken by a commissioner appointed under section 710, it may be admitted in evidence in the proceedings if

   (*a*) it is proved by oral evidence or by affidavit that the witness is unable to attend by reason of death or physical disability arising out of illness or some other good and sufficient cause;

   (*b*) the transcript of the evidence is signed by the commissioner by or before whom it purports to have been taken; and

   (*c*) it is proved to the satisfaction of the court that reasonable notice of the time for taking the evidence was given to the other party, and that the accused or his counsel, or the prosecutor or his counsel, as the case may be, had or might have had full opportunity to cross-examine the witness. R.S., c. C-34, s. 639; R.S.C. 1985, c. 27 (1st Supp.), s. 152; 1994, c. 44, s. 74; 1997, c. 18, s. 102.

APPLICATION FOR ORDER WHEN WITNESS OUT OF CANADA / Admitting evidence of witness out of Canada.

712. (1) An application that is made under paragraph 709(1)(*b*) shall be made

   (*a*) to a judge of a superior court of criminal jurisdiction or of a court of criminal jurisdiction before which the accused is to be tried; or

   (*b*) to a provincial court judge, where the accused or defendant is to be tried by a provincial court judge acting under Part XIX or XXVII.

(2) Where the evidence of a witness is taken by a commissioner appointed under this section, it may be admitted in evidence in the proceedings. R.S., c. C-34, s. 640; R.S.C. 1985, c. 27 (1st Supp.), s. 153(1); 1994, c. 44, s. 75; 1997, c. 18, s. 103; 1997, c. 23, s. 17.

(3) [*Repealed*, R.S.C. 1985, c. 27 (1st Supp.), s. 153(2).]

PROVIDING FOR PRESENCE OF ACCUSED COUNSEL / Return of evidence.

713. (1) A judge or provincial court judge who appoints a commissioner may make provision in the order to enable an accused to be present or represented by counsel when the evidence is taken, but failure of the accused to be present or to be represented by counsel in accordance with the order does not prevent the admission of the evidence in the proceedings if the evidence has otherwise been taken in accordance with the order and with this Part.

(2) An order for the taking of evidence by commission shall indicate the officer of the court to whom the evidence that is taken under the order shall be returned. R.S., c. C-34, s. 641; 1997, c. 18, s. 104.

EVIDENCE NOT EXCLUDED.

713.1 Evidence taken by a commissioner appointed under section 712 shall not be excluded by reason only that it would have been taken differently in Canada, provided that the process used to take the evidence is consistent with the law of the country where it was taken and that the process used to take the evidence was not contrary to the principles of fundamental justice. 1994, c. 44, s. 76.

RULES AND PRACTICE SAME AS IN CIVIL CASES.

714. Except where otherwise provided by this Part or by rules of court, the practice and procedure in connection with the appointment of commissioners under this Part, the taking of evidence by commissioners, the certifying and return thereof and the use of the evidence in the proceedings shall, as far as possible, be the same as those that govern like matters in civil proceedings in the superior court of the province in which the proceedings are taken. R.S., c. C-34, s. 642.

Video and Audio Evidence

AUDIOCONFERENCE AND VIDEOCONFERENCE — WITNESS IN CANADA.

714.1 A court may order that a witness in Canada give evidence by audioconference or videoconference, if the court is of the opinion that it would be appropriate having regard to all the circumstances, including
- (a) the location and personal circumstances of the witness;
- (b) the costs that would be incurred if the witness were to appear personally;
- (c) the nature of the witness' anticipated evidence;
- (d) the suitability of the location from where the witness will give evidence;
- (e) the accused's right to a fair and public hearing;
- (f) the nature and seriousness of the offence; and
- (g) any potential prejudice to the parties caused by the fact that the witness would not be seen by them, if the court were to order the evidence to be given by audioconference. 1999, c. 18, s. 95; 2019, c. 25, s. 290.

VIDEOCONFERENCE — WITNESS OUTSIDE CANADA / Notice.

714.2 (1) A court shall receive evidence given by a witness outside Canada by videoconference, unless one of the parties satisfies the court that the reception of such testimony would be contrary to the principles of fundamental justice.

(2) A party who wishes to call a witness to give evidence under subsection (1) shall give notice to the court before which the evidence is to be given and the other parties of their intention to do so not less than 10 days before the witness is scheduled to testify. 1999, c. 18, s. 95; 2019, c. 25, s. 290.

AUDIOCONFERENCE — WITNESS OUTSIDE CANADA.

714.3 The court may receive evidence given by a witness outside Canada by audioconference, if the court is of the opinion that it would be appropriate having regard to all the circumstances, including those set out in paragraphs 714.1(a) to (g). 1999, c. 18, s. 95; 2019, c. 25, s. 290.

REASONS.

714.4 If the court does not make an order under section 714.1 or does not receive evidence under section 714.2 or 714.3, it shall include in the record a statement of the reasons for not doing so. 1999, c. 18, s. 95; 2019, c. 25, s. 290.

CESSATION.

714.41 The court may, at any time, cease the use of the technological means referred to in section 714.1, 714.2 or 714.3 and take any measure that the court considers appropriate in the circumstances to have the witness give evidence. 2019, c. 25, s. 290.

OATH OR AFFIRMATION.

714.5 The evidence referred to in section 714.2 or 714.3, that is given by a witness who is outside of Canada, shall be given
  (a) under oath or affirmation in accordance with Canadian law;
  (b) under oath or affirmation in accordance with the law in the place where the witness is physically present; or
  (c) in any other manner that demonstrates that the witness understands that they must tell the truth. 1999, c. 18, s. 95; 2019, c. 25, s. 290.

OTHER LAWS ABOUT WITNESSES TO APPLY.

714.6 When a witness who is outside Canada gives evidence under section 714.2 or 714.3, the evidence is deemed to be given in Canada, and given under oath or affirmation in accordance with Canadian law, for the purposes of the laws relating to evidence, procedure, perjury and contempt of court. 1999, c. 18, s. 95; 2019, c. 25, s. 290.

COSTS OF TECHNOLOGY.

714.7 Unless the court orders otherwise, a party who calls a witness to give evidence by means of the technology referred to in section 714.1, 714.2 or 714.3 shall pay any costs associated with the use of the technology. 1999, c. 18, s. 95; 2019, c. 25, s. 290.

CONSENT.

714.8 Nothing in sections 714.1 to 714.7 is to be construed as preventing a court from receiving evidence by audioconference or videoconference, if the parties so consent. 1999, c. 18, s. 95; 2019, c. 25, s. 290.

Evidence Previously Taken

EVIDENCE AT PRELIMINARY INQUIRY MAY BE READ AT TRIAL IN CERTAIN CASES / Admission of evidence / Admission of evidence / Absconding accused deemed present / Exception.

715. (1) Where, at the trial of an accused, a person whose evidence was given at a previous trial on the same charge, or whose evidence was taken in the investigation of the charge against the accused or on the preliminary inquiry into the charge, refuses to be sworn or to give evidence, or if facts are proved on oath from which it can be inferred reasonably that the person

   (*a*) is dead,

   (*b*) has since become and is insane,

   (*c*) is so ill that he is unable to travel or testify, or

   (*d*) is absent from Canada,

and where it is proved that the evidence was taken in the presence of the accused, it may be admitted as evidence in the proceedings without further proof, unless the accused proves that the accused did not have full opportunity to cross-examine the witness.

(2) Evidence that has been taken on the preliminary inquiry or other investigation of a charge against an accused may be admitted as evidence in the prosecution of the accused for any other offence on the same proof and in the same manner in all respects, as it might, according to law, be admitted as evidence in the prosecution of the offence with which the accused was charged when the evidence was taken.

(2.1) Despite subsections (1) and (2), evidence that has been taken at a preliminary inquiry in the absence of the accused may be admitted as evidence for the purposes referred to in those subsections if the accused was absent further to the permission of a justice granted under paragraph 537(1)(*j*.1).

(3) For the purposes of this section, where evidence was taken at a previous trial or preliminary hearing or other proceeding in respect of an accused in the absence of the accused, who was absent by reason of having absconded, the accused is deemed to have been present during the taking of the evidence and to have had full opportunity to cross-examine the witness.

(4) Subsections (1) to (3) do not apply in respect of evidence received under subsection 540(7). R.S., c. C-34, s. 643; 1974-75-76, c. 93, s. 76; 1994, c. 44, s. 77; 1997, c. 18, s. 105; 2002, c. 13, s. 72; 2008, c. 18, s. 34.

TRANSCRIPT OF EVIDENCE / Notice of intention to produce evidence / Attendance of police officer / Admission of evidence / Absconding accused deemed present / Exception.

715.01 (1) Despite section 715, the transcript of testimony given by a "police officer", as defined in section 183, in the presence of an accused during a *voir dire* or preliminary inquiry held in relation to the accused's trial may be received in evidence at that trial.

(2) No transcript is to be received in evidence unless the party intending to produce it has given to the party against whom it is intended to be produced reasonable notice of that intention together with a copy of the transcript.

(3) The court may require the attendance of the police officer for the purposes of examination or cross-examination, as the case may be.

(4) Despite subsection (1), evidence that has been taken at a preliminary inquiry in the absence of an accused may be received in evidence for the purposes referred to in that subsection if the accused's absence was authorized by a justice under paragraph 537(1)(*j*.1).

(5) For the purposes of this section, if evidence was taken during a *voir dire* or preliminary inquiry in the absence of an accused, who was absent by reason of having absconded, the accused is deemed to have been present during the taking of the evidence and to have had full opportunity to cross-examine the witness.

(6) This section does not apply to any evidence received under subsection 540(7). 2019, c. 25, s. 291.

Video-recorded Evidence

EVIDENCE OF VICTIM OR WITNESS UNDER 18 / Order prohibiting use.

715.1 (1) In any proceeding against an accused in which a victim or other witness was under the age of eighteen years at the time the offence is alleged to have been committed, a video recording made within a reasonable time after the alleged offence, in which the victim or witness describes the acts complained of, is admissible in evidence if the victim or witness, while testifying, adopts the contents of the video recording, unless the presiding judge or justice is of the opinion that admission of the video recording in evidence would interfere with the proper administration of justice.

(2) The presiding judge or justice may prohibit any other use of a video recording referred to in subsection (1). R.S.C. 1985, c. 19, (3rd supp.), s. 16; 1997, c. 16, s. 7; 2005, c. 32, s. 23.

EVIDENCE OF VICTIM OR WITNESS WHO HAS A DISABILITY / Order prohibiting use.

715.2 (1) In any proceeding against an accused in which a victim or other witness is able to communicate evidence but may have difficulty doing so by reason of a mental or physical disability, a video recording made within a reasonable time after the alleged offence, in which the victim or witness describes the acts complained of, is admissible in evidence if the victim or witness, while testifying, adopts the contents of the video recording, unless the presiding judge or justice is of the opinion that admission of the video recording in evidence would interfere with the proper administration of justice.

(2) The presiding judge or justice may prohibit any other use of a video recording referred to in subsection (1). 1998, c. 9, s. 8; 2005, c. 32, s. 23.

PART XXII.01 / REMOTE ATTENDANCE BY CERTAIN PERSONS

2019, c. 25, s. 292.

Editors' note: The purpose of this part of the Code, enacted in 2019, is to expand and standardize the availability of videoconference and audioconference technology in the court process. It aims to ensure fair and efficient proceedings while enhancing access to justice. It begins by reiterating the general rule that in criminal matters individuals are to appear in person (s. 715.21), then sets out a series of provisions allowing for the use of videoconferences and audioconferences by all participants in the system. When deciding to allow the use of videoconference or audioconference, the judge must consider a list of factors (see ss. 715.23, 715.25 and 715.26), perhaps most significantly "the accused's right to a fair and public hearing".

Principles

ATTENDANCE.

715.21 Except as otherwise provided in this Act, a person who appears at, participates in or presides at a proceeding shall do so personally. 2019, c. 25, s. 292.

PROVISIONS PROVIDING FOR AUDIOCONFERENCE OR VIDEOCONFERENCE.

715.22 The purpose of the provisions of this Act that allow a person to appear at, participate in or preside at a proceeding by audioconference or videoconference, in accordance with the rules of court, is to serve the proper administration of justice, including by ensuring fair and efficient proceedings and enhancing access to justice. 2019, c. 25, s. 292.

Accused

APPEARANCE BY AUDIOCONFERENCE OR VIDEOCONFERENCE / Reasons / Cessation.

715.23 (1) Except as otherwise provided in this Act, the court may order an accused to appear by audioconference or videoconference, if the court is of the opinion that it would be appropriate having regard to all the circumstances, including

- (*a*) the location and personal circumstances of the accused;
- (*b*) the costs that would be incurred if the accused were to appear personally;
- (*c*) the suitability of the location from where the accused will appear;
- (*d*) the accused's right to a fair and public hearing; and
- (*e*) the nature and seriousness of the offence.

(2) If the court does not make an order under subsection (1) it shall include in the record a statement of the reasons for not doing so.

(3) The court may, at any time, cease the use of the technological means referred to in subsection (1) and take any measure that the court considers appropriate in the circumstances to have the accused appear at the proceeding. 2019, c. 25, s. 292.

CODE

ACCUSED IN PRISON.

715.24 Despite anything in this Act, if an accused who is in prison does not have access to legal advice during the proceedings, the court shall, before permitting the accused to appear by videoconference, be satisfied that the accused will be able to understand the proceedings and that any decisions made by the accused during the proceedings will be voluntary. 2019, c. 25, s. 292.

Participants

DEFINITION OF "PARTICIPANT" / Participation by audioconference or videoconference / Reasons / Cessation / Costs.

715.25 (1) In this section, "participant" means any person, other than an accused, a witness, a juror, a judge or a justice, who may participate in a proceeding.

(2) Except as otherwise provided in this Act, the court may order a participant to participate in a proceeding by audioconference or videoconference, if the court is of the opinion that it would be appropriate having regard to all the circumstances, including

- (*a*) the location and personal circumstances of the participant;
- (*b*) the costs that would be incurred if the participant were to participate personally;
- (*c*) the nature of the participation;
- (*d*) the suitability of the location from where the participant will participate;
- (*e*) the accused's right to a fair and public hearing; and
- (*f*) the nature and seriousness of the offence.

(3) If the court does not make an order under subsection (2) it shall include in the record a statement of the reasons for not doing so.

(4) The court may, at any time, cease the use of the technological means referred to in subsection (2) and take any measure that the court considers appropriate in the circumstances to have the participant participate in the proceeding.

(5) Unless the court orders otherwise, a party who has a participant participate by audioconference or videoconference shall pay any costs associated with the use of that technology. 2019, c. 25, s. 292.

Judge or Justice

PRESIDING BY AUDIOCONFERENCE OR VIDEOCONFERENCE / Reasons / Cessation.

715.26 (1) Except as otherwise provided in this Act, the judge or justice may preside at the proceeding by audioconference or videoconference, if the judge or justice considers it necessary having regard to all the circumstances, including

    (a) the accused's right to a fair and public hearing;

    (b) the nature of the witness' anticipated evidence;

    (c) the nature and seriousness of the offence; and

    (d) the suitability of the location from where the judge or justice will preside.

(2) The judge or justice shall include in the record a statement of the judge or justice's reasons for the decision to preside at the proceeding by audioconference or videoconference.

(3) The judge or justice may, at any time, cease the use of the technological means referred to in subsection (1) and take any measure that the judge or justice considers appropriate in the circumstances to preside at the proceeding. 2019, c. 25, s. 292.

PART XXII.1 / REMEDIATION AGREEMENTS 2018, c. 12, s. 404.

DEFINITIONS / Acting on victim's behalf.

715.3 (1) The following definitions apply in this Part.

"court" means a superior court of criminal jurisdiction but does not include a court of appeal.

"offence" means any offence listed in the schedule to this Part.

"organization" has the same meaning as in section 2 but does not include a public body, trade union or municipality.

"remediation agreement" means an agreement, between an organization accused of having committed an offence and a prosecutor, to stay any proceedings related to that offence if the organization complies with the terms of the agreement.

"victim" has the same meaning as in section 2 but, with respect to an offence under section 3 or 4 of the *Corruption of Foreign Public Officials Act*, it includes any person outside Canada.

(2) For the purposes of this Part, a third party not referred to in section 2.2 may also act on a victim's behalf when authorized to do so by the court, if the victim requests it or the prosecutor deems it appropriate. 2018, c. 12, s. 404.

PURPOSE.

715.31 The purpose of this Part is to establish a remediation agreement regime that is applicable to organizations alleged to have committed an offence and that has the following objectives:

- (*a*) to denounce an organization's wrongdoing and the harm that the wrongdoing has caused to victims or to the community;
- (*b*) to hold the organization accountable for its wrongdoing through effective, proportionate and dissuasive penalties;
- (*c*) to contribute to respect for the law by imposing an obligation on the organization to put in place corrective measures and promote a compliance culture;
- (*d*) to encourage voluntary disclosure of the wrongdoing;
- (*e*) to provide reparations for harm done to victims or to the community; and
- (*f*) to reduce the negative consequences of the wrongdoing for persons — employees, customers, pensioners and others — who did not engage in the wrongdoing, while holding responsible those individuals who did engage in that wrongdoing. 2018, c. 12, s. 404.

CONDITIONS FOR REMEDIATION AGREEMENT / Factors to consider / Factors not to consider.

715.32 (1) The prosecutor may enter into negotiations for a remediation agreement with an organization alleged to have committed an offence if the following conditions are met:

- (*a*) the prosecutor is of the opinion that there is a reasonable prospect of conviction with respect to the offence;
- (*b*) the prosecutor is of the opinion that the act or omission that forms the basis of the offence did not cause and was not likely to have caused serious bodily harm or death, or injury to national defence or national security, and was not committed for the benefit of, at the direction of, or in association with, a criminal organization or terrorist group;
- (*c*) the prosecutor is of the opinion that negotiating the agreement is in the public interest and appropriate in the circumstances; and
- (*d*) the Attorney General has consented to the negotiation of the agreement.

(2) For the purposes of paragraph (1)(*c*), the prosecutor must consider the following factors:

- (*a*) the circumstances in which the act or omission that forms the basis of the offence was brought to the attention of investigative authorities;
- (*b*) the nature and gravity of the act or omission and its impact on any victim;
- (*c*) the degree of involvement of senior officers of the organization in the act or omission;
- (*d*) whether the organization has taken disciplinary action, including termination of employment, against any person who was involved in the act or omission;
- (*e*) whether the organization has made reparations or taken other measures to remedy the harm caused by the act or omission and to prevent the commission of similar acts or omissions;

(f) whether the organization has identified or expressed a willingness to identify any person involved in wrongdoing related to the act or omission;

(g) whether the organization — or any of its representatives — was convicted of an offence or sanctioned by a regulatory body, or whether it entered into a previous remediation agreement or other settlement, in Canada or elsewhere, for similar acts or omissions;

(h) whether the organization — or any of its representatives — is alleged to have committed any other offences, including those not listed in the schedule to this Part; and

(i) any other factor that the prosecutor considers relevant.

(3) Despite paragraph (2)(i), if the organization is alleged to have committed an offence under section 3 or 4 of the *Corruption of Foreign Public Officials Act*, the prosecutor must not consider the national economic interest, the potential effect on relations with a state other than Canada or the identity of the organization or individual involved. 2018, c. 12, s. 404.

NOTICE TO ORGANIZATION — INVITATION TO NEGOTIATE /
Admissions not admissible in evidence.

715.33 (1) If the prosecutor wishes to negotiate a remediation agreement, they must give the organization written notice of the offer to enter into negotiations and the notice must include

(a) a summary description of the offence to which the agreement would apply;

(b) an indication of the voluntary nature of the negotiation process;

(c) an indication of the legal effects of the agreement;

(d) an indication that, by agreeing to the terms of this notice, the organization explicitly waives the inclusion of the negotiation period and the period during which the agreement is in force in any assessment of the reasonableness of the delay between the day on which the charge is laid and the end of trial;

(e) an indication that negotiations must be carried out in good faith and that the organization must provide all information requested by the prosecutor that the organization is aware of or can obtain through reasonable efforts, including information enabling the identification of any person involved in the act or omission that forms the basis of the offence or any wrongdoing related to that act or omission;

(f) an indication of how the information disclosed by the organization during the negotiations may be used, subject to subsection (2);

(g) a warning that knowingly making false or misleading statements or knowingly providing false or misleading information during the negotiations may lead to the recommencement of proceedings or prosecution for obstruction of justice;

(h) an indication that either party may withdraw from the negotiations by providing written notice to the other party;

(i) an indication that reasonable efforts must be made by both parties to identify any victim as soon as practicable; and (*j*) a deadline to accept the offer to negotiate according to the terms of the notice.

(2) No admission, confession or statement accepting responsibility for a given act or omission made by the organization during the negotiations is admissible in evidence against that organization in any civil or criminal proceedings related to that act or omission, except those contained in the statement of facts or admission of responsibility referred to in paragraphs 715.34(1)(*a*) and (*b*), if the parties reach an agreement and it is approved by the court. 2018, c. 12, s. 404.

CODE

MANDATORY CONTENTS OF AGREEMENT / Admissions not admissible in evidence / Optional content of agreement.

715.34 (1) A remediation agreement must include

(*a*) a statement of facts related to the offence that the organization is alleged to have committed and an undertaking by the organization not to make or condone any public statement that contradicts those facts;

(*b*) the organization's admission of responsibility for the act or omission that forms the basis of the offence;

(*c*) an indication of the obligation for the organization to provide any other information that will assist in identifying any person involved in the act or omission, or any wrongdoing related to that act or omission, that the organization becomes aware of, or can obtain through reasonable efforts, after the agreement has been entered into;

(*d*) an indication of the obligation for the organization to cooperate in any investigation, prosecution or other proceeding in Canada — or elsewhere if the prosecutor considers it appropriate — resulting from the act or omission, including by providing information or testimony;

(*e*) with respect to any property, benefit or advantage identified in the agreement that was obtained or derived directly or indirectly from the act or omission, an obligation for the organization to

(i) forfeit it to Her Majesty in right of Canada, to be disposed of in accordance with paragraph 4(1)(*b*.2) of the *Seized Property Management Act*,

(ii) forfeit it to Her Majesty in right of a province, to be disposed of as the Attorney General directs, or

(iii) otherwise deal with it, as the prosecutor directs;

(*f*) an indication of the obligation for the organization to pay a penalty to the Receiver General or to the treasurer of a province, as the case may be, for each offence to which the agreement applies, the amount to be paid and any other terms respecting payment;

(*g*) an indication of any reparations, including restitution consistent with paragraph 738(1)(*a*) or (*b*), that the organization is required to make to a victim or a statement by the prosecutor of the reasons why reparations to a victim are not appropriate in the circumstances and an indication of any measure required in lieu of reparations to a victim;

(*h*) an indication of the obligation for the organization to pay a victim surcharge for each offence to which the agreement applies, other than an offence under section 3 or 4 of the *Corruption of Foreign Public Officials Act*, the amount to be paid and any other terms respecting payment;

    (i)   an indication of the obligation for the organization to report to the prosecutor on the implementation of the agreement and an indication of the manner in which the report is to be made and any other terms respecting reporting;

    (j)   an indication of the legal effects of the agreement;

    (k)   an acknowledgement by the organization that the agreement has been made in good faith and that the information it has provided during the negotiation is accurate and complete and a commitment that it will continue to provide accurate and complete information while the agreement is in force;

    (l)   an indication of the use that can be made of information obtained as a result of the agreement, subject to subsection (2);

    (m)   a warning that the breach of any term of the agreement may lead to an application by the prosecutor for termination of the agreement and a recommencement of proceedings;

    (n)   an indication of the obligation for the organization not to deduct, for income tax purposes, the costs of any reparations or other measures referred to in paragraph *(g)* or any other costs incurred to fulfil the terms of the agreement;

    (o)   a notice of the prosecutor's right to vary or terminate the agreement with the approval of the court; and

    (p)   an indication of the deadline by which the organization must meet the terms of the agreement.

(2) No admission, confession or statement accepting responsibility for a given act or omission made by the organization as a result of the agreement is admissible in evidence against that organization in any civil or criminal proceedings related to that act or omission, except those contained in the statement of facts and admission of responsibility referred to in paragraphs (1)*(a)* and *(b)*, if the agreement is approved by the court.

(3) A remediation agreement may include, among other things,

    (a)   an indication of the obligation for the organization to establish, implement or enhance compliance measures to address any deficiencies in the organization's policies, standards or procedures — including those related to internal control procedures and employee training — that may have allowed the act or omission;

    (b)   an indication of the obligation for the organization to reimburse the prosecutor for any costs identified in the agreement that are related to its administration and that have or will be incurred by the prosecutor; and

    (c)   an indication of the fact that an independent monitor has been appointed, as selected with the prosecutor's approval, to verify and report to the prosecutor on the organization's compliance with the obligation referred to in paragraph *(a)*, or any other obligation in the agreement identified by the prosecutor, as well as an indication of the organization's obligations with respect to that monitor, including the obligations to cooperate with the monitor and pay the monitor's costs. 2018, c. 12, s. 404.

INDEPENDENT MONITOR — CONFLICT OF INTEREST.

715.35 A candidate for appointment as an independent monitor must notify the prosecutor in writing of any previous or ongoing relationship, in particular with the organization or any of its representatives, that may have a real or perceived impact on the candidate's ability to provide an independent verification. 2018, c. 12, s. 404.

DUTY TO INFORM VICTIMS / Interpretation / Reasons.

715.36 (1) After an organization has accepted the offer to negotiate according to the terms of the notice referred to in section 715.33, the prosecutor must take reasonable steps to inform any victim, or any third party that is acting on the victim's behalf, that a remediation agreement may be entered into.

(2) The duty to inform any victim is to be construed and applied in a manner that is reasonable in the circumstances and not likely to interfere with the proper administration of justice, including by causing interference with prosecutorial discretion or compromising, hindering or causing excessive delay to the negotiation of an agreement or its conclusion.

(3) If the prosecutor elects not to inform a victim or third party under subsection (1), they must provide the court, when applying for approval of the agreement, with a statement of the reasons why it was not appropriate to do so in the circumstances. 2018, c. 12, s. 404.

APPLICATION FOR COURT APPROVAL / Coming into force / Consideration of victims / Victim or community impact statement / Victim surcharge / Approval order / Stay of proceedings / Other proceedings / Limitation period.

715.37 (1) When the prosecutor and the organization have agreed to the terms of a remediation agreement, the prosecutor must apply to the court in writing for an order approving the agreement.

(2) The coming into force of the agreement is subject to the approval of the court.

(3) To determine whether to approve the agreement, the court hearing an application must consider
  (*a*) any reparations, statement and other measure referred to in paragraph 715.34(1)(*g*);
  (*b*) any statement made by the prosecutor under subsection 715.36(3);
  (*c*) any victim or community impact statement presented to the court; and
  (*d*) any victim surcharge referred to in paragraph 715.34(1)(*h*).

(4) For the purpose of paragraph (3)(*c*), the rules provided for in sections 722 to 722.2 apply, other than subsection 722(6), with any necessary modifications and, in particular,
  (*a*) a victim or community impact statement, or any other evidence concerning any victim, must be considered when determining whether to approve the agreement under subsection (6);

(*b*) the inquiry referred to in subsection 722(2) must be made at the hearing of the application; and

(*c*) the duty of the clerk under section 722.1 or subsection 722.2(5) is deemed to be the duty of the prosecutor to make reasonable efforts to provide a copy of the statement to the organization or counsel for the organization as soon as feasible after the prosecutor obtains it.

(5) For the purpose of paragraph 715.34(1)(*h*), the amount of the victim surcharge is 30% of any penalty referred to in paragraph 715.34(1)(*f*), or any other percentage that the prosecutor deems appropriate in the circumstances, and is payable to the treasurer of the province in which the application for approval referred to in section 715.37 is made.

(6) The court must, by order, approve the agreement if it is satisfied that

(*a*) the organization is charged with an offence to which the agreement applies;

(*b*) the agreement is in the public interest; and

(*c*) the terms of the agreement are fair, reasonable and proportionate to the gravity of the offence.

(7) As soon as practicable after the court approves the agreement, the prosecutor must direct the clerk or other proper officer of the court to make an entry on the record that the proceedings against the organization in respect of any offence to which the agreement applies are stayed by that direction and that entry must be made immediately, after which time the proceedings shall be stayed accordingly.

(8) No other proceedings may be initiated against the organization for the same offence while the agreement is in force.

(9) The running of a limitation period in respect of any offence to which the agreement applies is suspended while the agreement is in force. 2018, c. 12, s. 404.

VARIATION ORDER.

715.38 On application by the prosecutor, the court must, by order, approve any modification to a remediation agreement if the court is satisfied that the agreement continues to meet the conditions set out in subsection 715.37(6). On approval, the modification is deemed to form part of the agreement. 2018, c. 12, s. 404.

TERMINATION ORDER / Recommencement of proceedings / Stay of proceedings.

715.39 (1) On application by the prosecutor, the court must, by order, terminate the agreement if it is satisfied that the organization has breached a term of the agreement.

(2) As soon as the order is made, proceedings stayed in accordance with subsection 715.37(7) may be recommenced, without a new information or a new indictment, as the case may be, by the prosecutor giving notice of the recommencement to the clerk of the court in which the stay of the proceedings was entered.

(3) If no notice is given within one year after the order is made under subsection (1), or before the expiry of the time within which the proceedings could have been commenced, whichever is earlier, the proceedings are deemed never to have been commenced. 2018, c. 12, s. 404.

ORDER DECLARING SUCCESSFUL COMPLETION / Stay of proceedings.

715.4 (1) On application by the prosecutor, the court must, by order, declare that the terms of the agreement were met if it is satisfied that the organization has complied with the agreement.

(2) The order stays the proceedings against the organization for any offence to which the agreement applies, the proceedings are deemed never to have been commenced and no other proceedings may be initiated against the organization for the same offence. 2018, c. 12, s. 404.

DEADLINE / Deeming.

715.41 (1) The prosecutor must, as soon as practicable after the deadline referred to in paragraph 715.34(1)(*p*), apply to the court in writing for a variation order under section 715.38, including to extend the deadline, an order terminating the agreement under section 715.39 or an order under section 715.4 declaring that its terms were met and the court may issue any of these orders as it deems appropriate.

(2) The agreement is deemed to remain in force until a court issues an order terminating it or declaring that its terms were met. 2018, c. 12, s. 404.

PUBLICATION / Decision not to publish / Factors to be considered / Conditions / Review of decision.

715.42 (1) Subject to subsection (2), the following must be published by the court as soon as practicable:

   (*a*) the remediation agreement approved by the court;

   (*b*) an order made under any of sections 715.37 to 715.41 and the reasons for that order or the reasons for the decision not to make that order; and

   (*c*) a decision made under subsection (2) or (5) and the reasons for that decision.

(2) The court may decide not to publish the agreement or any order or reasons referred to in paragraph (1)(*b*), in whole or in part, if it is satisfied that the non-publication is necessary for the proper administration of justice.

(3) To decide whether the proper administration of justice requires making the decision referred to in subsection (2), the court must consider

   (*a*) society's interest in encouraging the reporting of offences and the participation of victims in the criminal justice process;

   (*b*) whether it is necessary to protect the identity of any victims, any person not engaged in the wrongdoing and any person who brought the wrongdoing to the attention of investigative authorities;

   (*c*) the prevention of any adverse effect to any ongoing investigation or prosecution;

   (*d*) whether effective alternatives to the decision referred to in subsection (2) are available in the circumstances;

   (*e*) the salutary and deleterious effects of making the decision referred to in subsection (2); and

   (*f*) any other factor that the court considers relevant.

(4) The court may make its decision subject to any conditions that it considers appropriate, including a condition related to the duration of non-publication.

(5) On application by any person, the court must review the decision made under subsection (2) to determine whether the non-publication continues to be necessary for the proper administration of justice. If the court is satisfied that the non-publication is

no longer necessary, it must publish the agreement, order or reasons, as the case may be, in whole or in part, as soon as practicable. 2018, c. 12, s. 404; 2018, c. 27, s. 686.

REGULATIONS / Amendment of schedule / Deleting offence.

715.43 (1) On the recommendation of the Minister of Justice, the Governor in Council may make regulations generally for the purposes of carrying out this Part, including regulations respecting

   (*a*) the form of the remediation agreement; and

   (*b*) the verification of compliance by an independent monitor, including

      (i)   the qualifications for monitors,

      (ii) the process to select a monitor,

      (iii) the form and content of a conflict of interest notification, and

      (iv) reporting requirements.

(2) On the recommendation of the Minister of Justice, the Governor in Council may, by order, amend the schedule by adding or deleting any offence to which a remediation agreement may apply.

(3) If the Governor in Council orders the deletion of an offence from the schedule to this Part, this Part continues to apply to an organization alleged to have committed that offence if a notice referred to in section 715.33 respecting that offence was sent to the organization before the day on which the order comes into force. 2018, c. 12, s. 404.

PART XXIII / PUNISHMENT (old provision)

Repealed 1995, c. 22, s. 6 (in force Sept. 3, 1996).

PART XXIII / SENTENCING

Interpretation

DEFINITIONS / "Accused" / "Alternative measures" / "Court" / "Fine".

716. In this Part,

"accused" includes a defendant;

"alternative measures" means measures other than judicial proceedings under this Act used to deal with a person who is eighteen years of age or over and alleged to have committed an offence;

"court" means

(a) a superior court of criminal jurisdiction,

(b) a court of criminal jurisdiction,

(c) a justice or provincial court judge acting as a summary conviction court under Part XXVII, or

(d) a court that hears an appeal;

"fine" includes a pecuniary penalty or other sum of money, but does not include restitution. 1999, c. 5, s. 29.

Alternative Measures

WHEN ALTERNATIVE MEASURES MAY BE USED / Restriction on use / Admissions not admissible in evidence / No bar to proceedings / Laying of information, etc.

717. (1) Alternative measures may be used to deal with a person alleged to have committed an offence only if it is not inconsistent with the protection of society and the following conditions are met:

(a) the measures are part of a program of alternative measures authorized by the Attorney General or the Attorney General's delegate or authorized by a person, or a person within a class of persons, designated by the lieutenant governor in council of a province;

(b) the person who is considering whether to use the measures is satisfied that they would be appropriate, having regard to the needs of the person alleged to have committed the offence and the interests of society and of the victim;

(c) the person, having been informed of the alternative measures, fully and freely consents to participate therein;

(d) the person has, before consenting to participate in the alternative measures, been advised of the right to be represented by counsel;

(e) the person accepts responsibility for the act or omission that forms the basis of the offence that the person is alleged to have committed;

(f) there is, in the opinion of the Attorney General or the Attorney General's agent, sufficient evidence to proceed with the prosecution of the offence; and (*g*) the prosecution of the offence is not in any way barred at law.

(2) Alternative measures shall not be used to deal with a person alleged to have committed an offence if the person

   (*a*) denies participation or involvement in the commission of the offence; or

   (*b*) expresses the wish to have any charge against the person dealt with by the court.

(3) No admission, confession or statement accepting responsibility for a given act or omission made by a person alleged to have committed an offence as a condition of the person being dealt with by alternative measures is admissible in evidence against that person in any civil or criminal proceedings.

(4) The use of alternative measures in respect of a person alleged to have committed an offence is not a bar to proceedings against the person under this Act, but, if a charge is laid against that person in respect of that offence,

   (*a*) where the court is satisfied on a balance of probabilities that the person has totally complied with the terms and conditions of the alternative measures, the court shall dismiss the charge; and

   (*b*) where the court is satisfied on a balance of probabilities that the person has partially complied with the terms and conditions of the alternative measures, the court may dismiss the charge if, in the opinion of the court, the prosecution of the charge would be unfair, having regard to the circumstances and that person's performance with respect to the alternative measures.

(5) Subject to subsection (4), nothing in this section shall be construed as preventing any person from laying an information, obtaining the issue or confirmation of any process, or proceeding with the prosecution of any offence, in accordance with law. 1995, c. 22, s. 6.

RECORDS OF PERSONS DEALT WITH.

717.1 Sections 717.2 to 717.4 apply only in respect of persons who have been dealt with by alternative measures, regardless of the degree of their compliance with the terms and conditions of the alternative measures. 1995, c. 22, s. 6.

POLICE RECORDS / Disclosure by peace officer / Idem.

717.2 (1) A record relating to any offence alleged to have been committed by a person, including the original or a copy of any fingerprints or photographs of the person, may be kept by any police force responsible for, or participating in, the investigation of the offence.

(2) A peace officer may disclose to any person any information in a record kept pursuant to this section that it is necessary to disclose in the conduct of the investigation of an offence.

(3) A peace officer may disclose to an insurance company any information in a record kept pursuant to this section for the purpose of investigating any claim arising out of an offence committed or alleged to have been committed by the person to whom the record relates. 1995, c. 22, s. 6.

GOVERNMENT RECORDS / Private records.

717.3 (1) A department or agency of any government in Canada may keep records containing information obtained by the department or agency

  (a) for the purposes of an investigation of an offence alleged to have been committed by a person;

  (b) for use in proceedings against a person under this Act; or

  (c) as a result of the use of alternative measures to deal with a person.

(2) Any person or organization may keep records containing information obtained by the person or organization as a result of the use of alternative measures to deal with a person alleged to have committed an offence. 1995, c. 22, s. 6.

DISCLOSURE OF RECORDS / Subsequent disclosure / Information, copies / Evidence / Idem.

717.4 (1) Any record that is kept pursuant to section 717.2 or 717.3 may be made available to

  (a) any judge or court for any purpose relating to proceedings relating to offences committed or alleged to have been committed by the person to whom the record relates;

  (b) any peace officer

   (i) for the purpose of investigating any offence that the person is suspected on reasonable grounds of having committed, or in respect of which the person has been arrested or charged, or

   (ii) for any purpose related to the administration of the case to which the record relates;

  (c) any member of a department or agency of a government in Canada, or any agent thereof, that is

   (i) engaged in the administration of alternative measures in respect of the person, or

   (ii) preparing a report in respect of the person pursuant to this Act; or

  (d) any other person who is deemed, or any person within a class of persons that is deemed, by a judge of a court to have a valid interest in the record, to the extent directed by the judge, if the judge is satisfied that the disclosure is

   (i) desirable in the public interest for research or statistical purposes, or

   (ii) desirable in the interest of the proper administration of justice.

(2) Where a record is made available for inspection to any person under subparagraph (1)(d)(i), that person may subsequently disclose information contained in the record, but may not disclose the information in any form that would reasonably be expected to identify the person to whom it relates.

(3) Any person to whom a record is authorized to be made available under this section may be given any information contained in the record and may be given a copy of any part of the record.

(4) Nothing in this section authorizes the introduction into evidence of any part of a record that would not otherwise be admissible in evidence.

(5) A record kept pursuant to section 717.2 or 717.3 may not be introduced into evidence, except for the purposes set out in paragraph 721(3)(*c*), more than two years after the end of the period for which the person agreed to participate in the alternative measures. 1995, c. 22, s. 6.

Purpose and Principles of Sentencing

PURPOSE.

718. The fundamental purpose of sentencing is to protect society and to contribute, along with crime prevention initiatives, to respect for the law and the maintenance of a just, peaceful and safe society by imposing just sanctions that have one or more of the following objectives:

(*a*) to denounce unlawful conduct and the harm done to victims or to the community that is caused by unlawful conduct;

(*b*) to deter the offender and other persons from committing offences;

(*c*) to separate offenders from society, where necessary;

(*d*) to assist in rehabilitating offenders;

(*e*) to provide reparations for harm done to victims or to the community; and

(*f*) to promote a sense of responsibility in offenders, and acknowledgment of the harm done to victims or to the community. 1995, c. 22, s. 6; 2015, c. 13, s. 23.

OBJECTIVES — OFFENCES AGAINST CHILDREN.

718.01 When a court imposes a sentence for an offence that involved the abuse of a person under the age of eighteen years, it shall give primary consideration to the objectives of denunciation and deterrence of such conduct. 2005, c. 32, s. 24.

OBJECTIVES — OFFENCE AGAINST PEACE OFFICER OR OTHER JUSTICE SYSTEM PARTICIPANT.

718.02 When a court imposes a sentence for an offence under subsection 270(1), section 270.01 or 270.02 or paragraph 423.1(1)(*b*), the court shall give primary consideration to the objectives of denunciation and deterrence of the conduct that forms the basis of the offence. 2009, c. 22, s. 18.

OBJECTIVES — OFFENCE AGAINST CERTAIN ANIMALS.

718.03 When a court imposes a sentence for an offence under subsection 445.01(1), the court shall give primary consideration to the objectives of denunciation and deterrence of the conduct that forms the basis of the offence. 2015, c. 34, s. 4.

OBJECTIVES — OFFENCE AGAINST VULNERABLE PERSON.

718.04 When a court imposes a sentence for an offence that involved the abuse of a person who is vulnerable because of personal circumstances — including because the person is Aboriginal and female — the court shall give primary consideration to the objectives of denunciation and deterrence of the conduct that forms the basis of the offence. 2019, c. 25, s. 292.1.

FUNDAMENTAL PRINCIPLE.

718.1 A sentence must be proportionate to the gravity of the offence and the degree of responsibility of the offender. 1995, c. 22, s. 6.

OTHER SENTENCING PRINCIPLES.

718.2 A court that imposes a sentence shall also take into consideration the following principles:

(a) a sentence should be increased or reduced to account for any relevant aggravating or mitigating circumstances relating to the offence or the offender, and, without limiting the generality of the foregoing,

　(i) evidence that the offence was motivated by bias, prejudice or hate based on race, national or ethnic origin, language, colour, religion, sex, age, mental or physical disability, sexual orientation, or gender orientation or expression, or on any other similar factor,

　(ii) evidence that the offender, in committing the offence, abused the offender's intimate partner or a member of the victim or the offender's family,

　(ii.1) evidence that the offender, in committing the offence, abused a person under the age of eighteen years,

　(iii) evidence that the offender, in committing the offence, abused a position of trust or authority in relation to the victim,

　(iii.1) evidence that the offence had a significant impact on the victim, considering their age and other personal circumstances, including their health and financial situation,

　(iv) evidence that the offence was committed for the benefit of, at the direction of or in association with a criminal organization,

　(v) evidence that the offence was a terrorism offence; or

　(vi) evidence that the offence was committed while the offender was subject to a conditional sentence order made under section 742.1 or released on parole, statutory release or unescorted temporary absence under the *Corrections and Conditional Release Act*;

shall be deemed to be aggravating circumstances;

(b) a sentence should be similar to sentences imposed on similar offenders for similar offences committed in similar circumstances;

(c) where consecutive sentences are imposed, the combined sentence should not be unduly long or harsh;

(d) an offender should not be deprived of liberty, if less restrictive sanctions may be appropriate in the circumstances; and (*e*) all available sanctions, other than imprisonment, that are reasonable in the circumstances and consistent with the harm done to victims or to the community should be considered for all offenders, with particular attention to the circumstances of Aboriginal offenders. 1995, c. 22, s. 6; 1997, c. 23, s. 17; 2000, c. 12, s. 95(*c*); 2001, c. 41, s. 20; 2005, c. 32, s. 25; 2012, c. 29, s. 2; 2015, c. 13, s. 24; c. 23, s. 16; 2017, c. 13, s. 4; 2019, c. 25, s. 293.

ADDITIONAL CONSIDERATION — INCREASED VULNERABILITY.

718.201 A court that imposes a sentence in respect of an offence that involved the abuse of an intimate partner shall consider the increased vulnerability of female persons who are victims, giving particular attention to the circumstances of Aboriginal female victims. 2019, c. 25, s. 293.1.

Organizations

ADDITIONAL FACTORS.

718.21 A court that imposes a sentence on an organization shall also take into consideration the following factors:

(*a*) any advantage realized by the organization as a result of the offence;

(*b*) the degree of planning involved in carrying out the offence and the duration and complexity of the offence;

(*c*) whether the organization has attempted to conceal its assets, or convert them, in order to show that it is not able to pay a fine or make restitution;

(*d*) the impact that the sentence would have on the economic viability of the organization and the continued employment of its employees;

(*e*) the cost to public authorities of the investigation and prosecution of the offence;

(*f*) any regulatory penalty imposed on the organization or one of its representatives in respect of the conduct that formed the basis of the offence;

(*g*) whether the organization was — or any of its representatives who were involved in the commission of the offence were — convicted of a similar offence or sanctioned by a regulatory body for similar conduct;

(*h*) any penalty imposed by the organization on a representative for their role in the commission of the offence;

(*i*) any restitution that the organization is ordered to make or any amount that the organization has paid to a victim of the offence; and

(*j*) any measures that the organization has taken to reduce the likelihood of it committing a subsequent offence. 2003, c. 21, s. 14.

Punishment Generally

DEGREES OF PUNISHMENT / Discretion respecting punishment / Imprisonment in default where term not specified / Cumulative punishments / Cumulative punishments — fines / Cumulative punishments — youth / Cumulative punishments — sexual offences against children / Maximum penalty — intimate partner.

718.3 (1) Where an enactment prescribes different degrees or kinds of punishment in respect of an offence, the punishment to be imposed is, subject to the limitations prescribed in the enactment, in the discretion of the court that convicts a person who commits the offence.

(2) Where an enactment prescribes a punishment in respect of an offence, the punishment to be imposed is, subject to the limitations prescribed in the enactment, in the discretion of the court that convicts a person who commits the offence, but no punishment is a minimum punishment unless it is declared to be a minimum punishment.

(3) Where an accused is convicted of an offence punishable with both fine and imprisonment and a term of imprisonment in default of payment of the fine is not specified in the enactment that prescribes the punishment to be imposed, the imprisonment that may be imposed in default of payment shall not exceed the term of imprisonment that is prescribed in respect of the offence.

(4) The court that sentences an accused shall consider directing

   (a) that the term of imprisonment that it imposes be served consecutively to a sentence of imprisonment to which the accused is subject at the time of sentencing; and

   (b) that the terms of imprisonment that it imposes at the same time for more than one offence be served consecutively, including when

      (i) the offences do not arise out of the same event or series of events,

      (ii) one of the offences was committed while the accused was on judicial interim release, including pending the determination of an appeal, or

     (iii) one of the offences was committed while the accused was fleeing from a peace officer.

(5) For the purposes of subsection (4), a term of imprisonment includes imprisonment that results from the operation of subsection 734(4).

(6) For the purposes of subsection (4), a sentence of imprisonment includes

   (a) a disposition made under paragraph 20(1)(k) or (k.1) of the *Young Offenders Act*, chapter Y-1 of the Revised Statutes of Canada, 1985;

   (b) a youth sentence imposed under paragraph 42(2)(n), (o), (q) or (r) of the *Youth Criminal Justice Act*; and

   (c) a sentence that results from the operation of subsection 743.5(1) or (2).

(7) When a court sentences an accused at the same time for more than one sexual offence committed against a child, the court shall direct

   (a) that a sentence of imprisonment it imposes for an offence under section 163.1 be served consecutively to a sentence of imprisonment it imposes for a sexual offence under another section of this Act committed against a child; and

(b) that a sentence of imprisonment it imposes for a sexual offence committed against a child, other than an offence under section 163.1, be served consecutively to a sentence of imprisonment it imposes for a sexual offence committed against another child other than an offence under section 163.1.

(8) If an accused is convicted of an indictable offence in the commission of which violence was used, threatened or attempted against an intimate partner and the accused has been previously convicted of an offence in the commission of which violence was used, threatened or attempted against an intimate partner, the court may impose a term of imprisonment that is more than the maximum term of imprisonment provided for that offence but not more than

(a) five years, if the maximum term of imprisonment for the offence is two years or more but less than five years;

(b) 10 years, if the maximum term of imprisonment for the offence is five years or more but less than 10 years;

(c) 14 years, if the maximum term of imprisonment for the offence is 10 years or more but less than 14 years; or

(d) life, if the maximum term of imprisonment for the offence is 14 years or more and up to imprisonment for life. 1995, c. 22, s. 6; 1997, c. 18, s. 141(c); 1999, c. 5, s. 30; 2002, c. 1, s. 182; 2015, c. 23, s. 17; 2019, c. 25, s. 294.

COMMENCEMENT OF SENTENCE / Time at large excluded from term of imprisonment / Determination of sentence / Exception / Reasons / Record of proceedings / Validity not affected / When time begins to run / When fine imposed / Application for leave to appeal.

719. (1) A sentence commences when it is imposed, except where a relevant enactment otherwise provides.

(2) Any time during which a convicted person is unlawfully at large or is lawfully at large on interim release granted pursuant to any provision of this Act does not count as part of any term of imprisonment imposed on the person.

(3) In determining the sentence to be imposed on a person convicted of an offence, a court may take into account any time spent in custody by the person as a result of the offence but the court shall limit any credit for that time to a maximum of one day for each day spent in custody.

(3.1) Despite subsection (3), if the circumstances justify it, the maximum is one and one-half days for each day spent in custody.

(3.2) The court shall give reasons for any credit granted and shall cause those reasons to be stated in the record.

(3.3) The court shall cause to be stated in the record and on the warrant of committal the offence, the amount of time spent in custody, the term of imprisonment that would have been imposed before any credit was granted, the amount of time credited, if any, and the sentence imposed.

(3.4) Failure to comply with subsection (3.2) or (3.3) does not affect the validity of the sentence imposed by the court.

(4) Notwithstanding subsection (1), a term of imprisonment, whether imposed by a trial court or the court appealed to, commences or shall be deemed to be resumed, as the case may be, on the day on which the convicted person is arrested and taken into custody under the sentence.

(5) Notwithstanding subsection (1), where the sentence that is imposed is a fine with a term of imprisonment in default of payment, no time prior to the day of execution of the warrant of committal counts as part of the term of imprisonment.

(6) An application for leave to appeal is an appeal for the purposes of this section. 1995, c. 22, s. 6; 2009, c. 29, s. 3; 2018, c. 29, s. 66.

Procedure and Evidence

SENTENCING PROCEEDINGS / Court-supervised programs.

720. (1) A court shall, as soon as practicable after an offender has been found guilty, conduct proceedings to determine the appropriate sentence to be imposed.

(2) The court may, with the consent of the Attorney General and the offender and after considering the interests of justice and of any victim of the offence, delay sentencing to enable the offender to attend a treatment program approved by the province under the supervision of the court, such as an addiction treatment program or a domestic violence counseling program. 1995, c. 22, s. 6; 2008, c. 18, s. 35.

REPORT BY PROBATION OFFICER / Provincial regulations / Content of report / Idem / Copy of report.

721. (1) Subject to regulations made under subsection (2), where an accused, other than an organization, pleads guilty to or is found guilty of an offence, a probation officer shall, if required to do so by a court, prepare and file with the court a report in writing relating to the accused for the purpose of assisting the court in imposing a sentence or in determining whether the accused should be discharged under section 730.

(2) The lieutenant governor in council of a province may make regulations respecting the types of offences for which a court may require a report, and respecting the content and form of the report.

(3) Unless otherwise specified by the court, the report must, wherever possible, contain information on the following matters:

    (*a*) the offender's age, maturity, character, behaviour, attitude and willingness to make amends;

    (*b*) subject to subsection 119(2) of the *Youth Criminal Justice Act*, the history of previous dispositions under the *Young Offenders Act*, chapter Y-1 of the Revised Statutes of Canada, 1985, the history of previous sentences under the *Youth Criminal Justice Act*, and of previous findings of guilt under this Act and any other Act of Parliament;

(*c*)   the history of any alternative measures used to deal with the offender, and the offender's response to those measures; and

(*d*)   any matter required, by any regulation made under subsection (2), to be included in the report.

(4) The report must also contain information on any other matter required by the court, after hearing argument from the prosecutor and the offender, to be included in the report, subject to any contrary regulation made under subsection (2).

(5) The clerk of the court shall provide a copy of the report, as soon as practicable after filing, to the offender or counsel for the offender, as directed by the court, and to the prosecutor. 1995, c. 22, s. 6; 1999, c. 25, s. 16; 2002, c. 1, s. 183; 2003, c. 21, s. 15.

VICTIM IMPACT STATEMENT / Inquiry by court / Adjournment / Form / Presentation of statement / Photograph / Conditions of exclusion / Consideration of statement / Evidence concerning victim admissible.

722. (1) When determining the sentence to be imposed on an offender or determining whether the offender should be discharged under section 730 in respect of any offence, the court shall consider any statement of a victim prepared in accordance with this section and filed with the court describing the physical or emotional harm, property damage or economic loss suffered by the victim as the result of the commission of the offence and the impact of the offence on the victim.

(2) As soon as feasible after a finding of guilt and in any event before imposing sentence, the court shall inquire of the prosecutor if reasonable steps have been taken to provide the victim with an opportunity to prepare a statement referred to in subsection (1).

(3) On application of the prosecutor or a victim or on its own motion, the court may adjourn the proceedings to permit the victim to prepare a statement referred to in subsection (1) or to present evidence in accordance with subsection (9), if the court is satisfied that the adjournment would not interfere with the proper administration of justice.

(4) The statement must be prepared in writing, using Form 34.2 in Part XXVIII, in accordance with the procedures established by a program designated for that purpose by the lieutenant governor in council of the province in which the court is exercising its jurisdiction.

(5) The court shall, on the request of a victim, permit the victim to present the statement by

(*a*)   reading it;

(*b*)   reading it in the presence and close proximity of any support person of the victim's choice;

(*c*)   reading it outside the court room or behind a screen or other device that would allow the victim not to see the offender; or

(*d*)   presenting it in any other manner that the court considers appropriate.

(6) During the presentation

(*a*) the victim may have with them a photograph of themselves taken before the commission of the offence if it would not, in the opinion of the court, disrupt the proceedings; or

(*b*) if the statement is presented by someone acting on the victim's behalf, that individual may have with them a photograph of the victim taken before the commission of the offence if it would not, in the opinion of the court, disrupt the proceedings.

(7) The victim shall not present the statement outside the court room unless arrangements are made for the offender and the judge or justice to watch the presentation by means of closed-circuit television or otherwise and the offender is permitted to communicate with counsel while watching the presentation.

(8) In considering the statement, the court shall take into account the portions of the statement that it considers relevant to the determination referred to in subsection (1) and disregard any other portion.

(9) Whether or not a statement has been prepared and filed in accordance with this section, the court may consider any other evidence concerning any victim of the offence for the purpose of determining the sentence to be imposed on the offender or whether the offender should be discharged under section 730. 1995, c. 22, s. 6; 1999, c. 25, s. 17; 2000, c. 12, s. 95(*d*); 2015, c. 13, s. 25.

COPY OF STATEMENT.

722.1 The clerk of the court shall provide a copy of a statement referred to in subsection 722(1), as soon as practicable after a finding of guilt, to the offender or counsel for the offender, and to the prosecutor. 1995, c. 22, s. 6; 1999, c. 25, s. 18.

COMMUNITY IMPACT STATEMENT / Form / Presentation of statement / Conditions of exclusion / Copy of statement.

722.2 (1) When determining the sentence to be imposed on an offender or determining whether the offender should be discharged under section 730 in respect of any offence, the court shall consider any statement made by an individual on a community's behalf that was prepared in accordance with this section and filed with the court describing the harm or loss suffered by the community as the result of the commission of the offence and the impact of the offence on the community.

(2) The statement must be prepared in writing, using Form 34.3 in Part XXVIII, in accordance with the procedures established by a program designated for that purpose by the lieutenant governor in council of the province in which the court is exercising its jurisdiction.

(3) The court shall, on the request of the individual making the statement, permit the individual to present the statement by

(*a*) reading it;

(*b*) reading it in the presence and close proximity of any support person of the individual's choice;

   (c) reading it outside the court room or behind a screen or other device that would allow the individual not to see the offender; or

   (d) presenting it in any other manner that the court considers appropriate.

(4) The individual making the statement shall not present it outside the court room unless arrangements are made for the offender and the judge or justice to watch the presentation by means of closed-circuit television or otherwise and the offender is permitted to communicate with counsel while watching the presentation.

(5) The clerk of the court shall, as soon as feasible after a finding of guilt, provide a copy of the statement to the offender or counsel for the offender, and to the prosecutor. 1999, c. 25, s. 18; 2015, c. 13, s. 26.

SUBMISSIONS ON FACTS / Submission of evidence / Production of evidence / Compel appearance / Hearsay evidence.

723. (1) Before determining the sentence, a court shall give the prosecutor and the offender an opportunity to make submissions with respect to any facts relevant to the sentence to be imposed.

(2) The court shall hear any relevant evidence presented by the prosecutor or the offender.

(3) The court may, on its own motion, after hearing argument from the prosecutor and the offender, require the production of evidence that would assist it in determining the appropriate sentence.

(4) Where it is necessary in the interests of justice, the court may, after consulting the parties, compel the appearance of any person who is a compellable witness to assist the court in determining the appropriate sentence.

(5) Hearsay evidence is admissible at sentencing proceedings, but the court may, if the court considers it to be in the interests of justice, compel a person to testify where the person

   (a) has personal knowledge of the matter;

   (b) is reasonably available; and

   (c) is a compellable witness. 1995, c. 22, s. 6.

INFORMATION ACCEPTED / Jury / Disputed facts.

724. (1) In determining a sentence, a court may accept as proved any information disclosed at the trial or at the sentence proceedings and any facts agreed on by the prosecutor and the offender.

(2) Where the court is composed of a judge and jury, the court

   (a) shall accept as proven all facts, express or implied, that are essential to the jury's verdict of guilty; and

   (b) may find any other relevant fact that was disclosed by evidence at the trial to be proven, or hear evidence presented by either party with respect to that fact.

(3) Where there is a dispute with respect to any fact that is relevant to the determination of a sentence,

    (a) the court shall request that evidence be adduced as to the existence of the fact unless the court is satisfied that sufficient evidence was adduced at the trial;

    (b) the party wishing to rely on a relevant fact, including a fact contained in a presentence report, has the burden of proving it;

    (c) either party may cross-examine any witness called by the other party;

    (d) subject to paragraph (e), the court must be satisfied on a balance of probabilities of the existence of the disputed fact before relying on it in determining the sentence; and

    (e) the prosecutor must establish, by proof beyond a reasonable doubt, the existence of any aggravating fact or any previous conviction by the offender. 1995, c. 22, s. 6.

OTHER OFFENCES / Attorney General's consent / No further proceedings.

725. (1) In determining the sentence, a court

    (a) shall consider, if it is possible and appropriate to do so, any other offences of which the offender was found guilty by the same court, and shall determine the sentence to be imposed for each of those offences;

    (b) shall consider, if the Attorney General and the offender consent, any outstanding charges against the offender to which the offender consents to plead guilty and pleads guilty, if the court has jurisdiction to try those charges, and shall determine the sentence to be imposed for each charge unless the court is of the opinion that a separate prosecution for the other offence is necessary in the public interest;

    (b.1) shall consider any outstanding charges against the offender, unless the court is of the opinion that a separate prosecution for one or more of the other offences is necessary in the public interest, subject to the following conditions:

        (i) the Attorney General and the offender consent,

        (ii) the court has jurisdiction to try each charge,

        (iii) each charge has been described in open court,

        (iv) the offender has agreed with the facts asserted in the description of each charge, and

        (v) the offender has acknowledged having committed the offence described in each charge; and

    (c) may consider any facts forming part of the circumstances of the offence that could constitute the basis for a separate charge.

(1.1) For the purpose of paragraphs (1)(b) and (b.1), the Attorney General shall take the public interest into account before consenting.

(2) The court shall, on the information or indictment, note

    (a) any outstanding charges considered in determining the sentence under paragraph (1)(b.1), and

    (b) any facts considered in determining the sentence under paragraph (1)(c), and no further proceedings may be taken with respect to any offence described in those charges or disclosed by those facts unless the conviction for the offence of which the offender has been found guilty is set aside or quashed on appeal. 1995, c. 22, s. 6; 1999, c. 5, s. 31.

OFFENDERS MAY SPEAK TO SENTENCE.

726. Before determining the sentence to be imposed, the court shall ask whether the offender, if present, has anything to say. 1995, c. 22, s. 6.

RELEVANT INFORMATION.

726.1 In determining the sentence, a court shall consider any relevant information placed before it, including any representations or submissions made by or on behalf of the prosecutor or the offender. 1995, c. 22, s. 6.

REASONS FOR SENTENCE.

726.2 When imposing a sentence, a court shall state the terms of the sentence imposed, and the reasons for it, and enter those terms and reasons into the record of the proceedings. 1995, c. 22, s. 6.

PREVIOUS CONVICTION / Procedure / Where hearing *ex parte* / Organizations / Section does not apply.

727. (1) Subject to subsections (3) and (4), where an offender is convicted of an offence for which a greater punishment may be imposed by reason of previous convictions, no greater punishment shall be imposed on the offender by reason thereof unless the prosecutor satisfies the court that the offender, before making a plea, was notified that a greater punishment would be sought by reason thereof.

(2) Where an offender is convicted of an offence for which a greater punishment may be imposed by reason of previous convictions, the court shall, on application by the prosecutor and on being satisfied that the offender was notified in accordance with subsection (1), ask whether the offender was previously convicted and, if the offender does not admit to any previous convictions, evidence of previous convictions may be adduced.

(3) Where a summary conviction court holds a trial pursuant to subsection 803(2) and convicts the offender, the court may, whether or not the offender was notified that a greater punishment would be sought by reason of a previous conviction, make inquiries and hear evidence with respect to previous convictions of the offender and, if any such conviction is proved, may impose a greater punishment by reason thereof.

(4) If, under section 623, the court proceeds with the trial of an organization that has not appeared and pleaded and convicts the organization, the court may, whether or not the organization was notified that a greater punishment would be sought by reason of a previous conviction, make inquiries and hear evidence with respect to previous convictions of the organization and, if any such conviction is proved, may impose a greater punishment by reason of that conviction.

(5) This section does not apply to a person referred to in paragraph 745(*b*). 1995, c. 22, s. 6; 2003, c. 21, s. 16.

SENTENCE JUSTIFIED BY ANY COUNT.

728. Where one sentence is passed on a verdict of guilty on two or more counts of an indictment, the sentence is good if any of the counts would have justified the sentence. 1995, c. 22, s. 6.

PROOF OF CERTIFICATE OF ANALYST / Definition of "analyst" / Notice of intention to produce certificate / Requiring attendance of analyst.

729. (1) In
- (*a*) a prosecution for failure to comply with a condition in a probation order that the accused not have in possession or use drugs, or
- (*b*) a hearing to determine whether the offender breached a condition of a conditional sentence order that the offender not have in possession or use drugs,

a certificate purporting to be signed by an analyst stating that the analyst has analyzed or examined a substance and stating the result of the analysis or examination is admissible in evidence and, in the absence of evidence to the contrary, is proof of the statements contained in the certificate without proof of the signature or official character of the person appearing to have signed the certificate.

(2) In this section, "analyst" means a person designated as an analyst under the *Controlled Drugs and Substances Act* or the *Cannabis Act*.

(3) No certificate shall be admitted in evidence unless the party intending to produce it has, before the trial or hearing, as the case may be, given reasonable notice and a copy of the certificate to the party against whom it is to be produced.

(4) and (5) [*Repealed*, 2008, c. 18, s. 36.]

(6) The party against whom a certificate of an analyst is produced may, with leave of the court, require the attendance of the analyst for cross-examination. 1995, c. 22, s. 6; 1999, c. 31, s. 69; 2004, c. 12, s. 11; 2008, c. 18, s. 36; 2018, c. 16, s. 221.

PROOF OF CERTIFICATE OF ANALYST — BODILY SUBSTANCE / Definition of "analyst" / Notice of intention to produce certificate / Requiring attendance of analyst.

729.1 (1) In a prosecution for failure to comply with a condition in a probation order that the accused not consume drugs, alcohol or any other intoxicating substance, or in a hearing to determine whether the offender breached such a condition of a conditional sentence order, a certificate purporting to be signed by an analyst that states that the analyst has analyzed a sample of a bodily substance and that states the result of the analysis is admissible in evidence and, in the absence of evidence to the contrary, is proof of the statements contained in the certificate without proof of the signature or official character of the person who appears to have signed the certificate.

(2) In this section, "analyst" has the same meaning as in section 320.11.

(3) No certificate shall be admitted in evidence unless the party intending to produce it has, before the trial or hearing, as the case may be, given reasonable notice and a copy of the certificate to the party against whom it is to be produced.

(4) The party against whom a certificate of an analyst is produced may, with leave of the court, require the attendance of the analyst for cross-examination. 2011, c. 7, s. 2; 2018, c. 21, s. 23.

Absolute and Conditional Discharges

CONDITIONAL AND ABSOLUTE DISCHARGE / Period for which appearance notice, etc., continues in force / Effect of discharge / Where person bound by probation order convicted of offence.

730. (1) Where an accused, other than an organization, pleads guilty to or is found guilty of an offence, other than an offence for which a minimum punishment is prescribed by law or an offence punishable by imprisonment for fourteen years or for life, the court before which the accused appears may, if it considers it to be in the best interests of the accused and not contrary to the public interest, instead of convicting the accused, by order direct that the accused be discharged absolutely or on the conditions prescribed in a probation order made under subsection 731(2).

(2) Subject to Part XVI, if an accused who has not been taken into custody or who has been released from custody under any provision of that Part pleads guilty to or is found guilty of an offence but is not convicted, the appearance notice, summons, undertaking or release order issued to, given or entered into by the accused continues in force, subject to its terms, until a disposition in respect of the accused is made under subsection (1) unless, at the time the accused pleads guilty or is found guilty, the court, judge or justice orders that the accused be taken into custody pending such a disposition.

(3) Where a court directs under subsection (1) that an offender be discharged of an offence, the offender shall be deemed not to have been convicted of the offence except that

    (a) the offender may appeal from the determination of guilt as if it were a conviction in respect of the offence;

    (b) the Attorney General and, in the case of summary conviction proceedings, the informant or the informant's agent may appeal from the decision of the court not to convict the offender of the offence as if that decision were a judgment or verdict of acquittal of the offence or a dismissal of the information against the offender; and

    (c) the offender may plead autrefois convict in respect of any subsequent charge relating to the offence.

(4) Where an offender who is bound by the conditions of a probation order made at a time when the offender was directed to be discharged under this section is convicted of an offence, including an offence under section 733.1, the court that made the probation order may, in addition to or in lieu of exercising its authority under subsection 732.2(5), at any time when it may take action under that

subsection, revoke the discharge, convict the offender of the offence to which the discharge relates and impose any sentence that could have been imposed if the offender had been convicted at the time of discharge, and no appeal lies from a conviction under this subsection where an appeal was taken from the order directing that the offender be discharged. 1995, c. 22, s. 6; 1997, c. 18, s. 141; 2003, c. 21, s. 17; 2019, c. 25, s. 296.

Probation

MAKING OF PROBATION ORDER / Idem.

731. (1) Where a person is convicted of an offence, a court may, having regard to the age and character of the offender, the nature of the offence and the circumstances surrounding its commission,

  (a) if no minimum punishment is prescribed by law, suspend the passing of sentence and direct that the offender be released on the conditions prescribed in a probation order; or

  (b) in addition to fining or sentencing the offender to imprisonment for a term not exceeding two years, direct that the offender comply with the conditions prescribed in a probation order.

(2) A court may also make a probation order where it discharges an accused under subsection 730(1). 1995, c. 22, s. 6.

FIREARM, ETC., PROHIBITIONS / Application of s. 109 or 110.

731.1 (1) Before making a probation order, the court shall consider whether section 109 or 110 is applicable.

(2) For greater certainty, a condition of a probation order referred to in paragraph 732.1(3)(d) does not affect the operation of section 109 or 110. 1995, c. 22, s. 6; 2002, c. 13, s. 73.

INTERMITTENT SENTENCE / Application to vary intermittent sentence / Court may vary intermittent sentence if subsequent offence.

732. (1) Where the court imposes a sentence of imprisonment of ninety days or less on an offender convicted of an offence, whether in default of payment of a fine or otherwise, the court may, having regard to the age and character of the offender, the nature of the offence and the circumstances surrounding its commission, and the availability of appropriate accommodation to ensure compliance with the sentence, order

  (a) that the sentence be served intermittently at such times as are specified in the order; and

  (b) that the offender comply with the conditions prescribed in a probation order when not in confinement during the period that the sentence is being served and, if the court so orders, on release from prison after completing the intermittent sentence.

(2) An offender who is ordered to serve a sentence of imprisonment intermittently may, on giving notice to the prosecutor, apply to the court that imposed the sentence to allow it to be served on consecutive days.

(3) Where a court imposes a sentence of imprisonment on a person who is subject to an intermittent sentence in respect of another offence, the unexpired portion of the intermittent sentence shall be served on consecutive days unless the court otherwise orders. 1995, c. 22, s. 6.

DEFINITIONS / "Change" / "Optional conditions" / Compulsory conditions of probation order / Optional conditions of probation order / Optional conditions — organization / Consideration — organizations / Form and period of order / Obligations of court / For greater certainty / Notice — samples at regular intervals / Designations and specifications / Further designations / Restriction / Destruction of samples / Regulations.

732.1 (1) In this section and section 732.2,

"change", in relation to optional conditions, includes deletions and additions;

"optional conditions" means the conditions referred to in subsection (3) or (3.1).

(2) The court shall prescribe, as conditions of a probation order, that the offender do all of the following:

(*a*) keep the peace and be of good behaviour;

(*a*.1) [*Repealed*, 2019, c. 25, s. 297(1).]

(*b*) appear before the court when required to do so by the court; and

(*c*) notify the court or the probation officer in advance of any change of name or address, and promptly notify the court or the probation officer of any change of employment or occupation.

(2.1) [*Repealed*, 2019, c. 25, s. 297(2).]

(2.2) [*Repealed*, 2019, c. 25, s. 297(2).]

(3) The court may prescribe, as additional conditions of a probation order, that the offender do one or more of the following:

(*a*) report to a probation officer;

    (i) within two working days, or such longer period as the court directs, after the making of the probation order, and

    (ii) thereafter, when required by the probation officer and in the manner directed by the probation officer;

(*a*.1) abstain from communicating, directly or indirectly, with any victim, witness or other person identified in the order or from going to any place or geographic

area specified in the order, except in accordance with any specified conditions that the court considers necessary;

(*b*) remain within the jurisdiction of the court unless written permission to go outside that jurisdiction is obtained from the court or the probation officer;

(*c*) abstain from the consumption of drugs except in accordance with a medical prescription, of alcohol or of any other intoxicating substance;

(*c*.1) provide, for the purpose of analysis, a sample of a bodily substance prescribed by regulation on the demand of a peace officer, a probation officer or someone designated under subsection (9) to make a demand, at the place and time and on the day specified by the person making the demand, if that person has reasonable grounds to believe that the offender has breached a condition of the order that requires them to abstain from the consumption of drugs, alcohol or any other intoxicating substance;

(*c*.2) provide, for the purpose of analysis, a sample of a bodily substance prescribed by regulation at regular intervals that are specified by a probation officer in a notice in Form 51 served on the offender, if a condition of the order requires the offender to abstain from the consumption of drugs, alcohol or any other intoxicating substance;

(*d*) abstain from owning, possessing or carrying a weapon;

(*e*) provide for the support or care of dependants;

(*f*) perform up to 240 hours of community service over a period not exceeding eighteen months;

(*g*) if the offender agrees, and subject to the program director's acceptance of the offender, participate actively in a treatment program approved by the province;

(*g*.1) where the lieutenant governor in council of the province in which the probation order is made has established a program for curative treatment in relation to the consumption of alcohol or drugs, attend at a treatment facility, designated by the lieutenant governor in council of the province, for assessment and curative treatment in relation to the consumption by the offender of alcohol or drugs that is recommended pursuant to the program;

(*g*.2) where the lieutenant governor in council of the province in which the probation order is made has established a program governing the use of an alcohol ignition interlock device by an offender and if the offender agrees to participate in the program, comply with the program; and

(*h*) comply with such other reasonable conditions as the court considers desirable, subject to any regulations made under subsection 738(2), for protecting society and for facilitating the offender's successful reintegration into the community.

(3.1) The court may prescribe, as additional conditions of a probation order made in respect of an organization, that the offender do one or more of the following:

(*a*) make restitution to a person for any loss or damage that they suffered as a result of the offence;

(*b*) establish policies, standards and procedures to reduce the likelihood of the organization committing a subsequent offence;

(*c*) communicate those policies, standards and procedures to its representatives;

(*d*) report to the court on the implementation of those policies, standards and procedures;

(*e*) identify the senior officer who is responsible for compliance with those policies, standards and procedures;

(*f*) provide, in the manner specified by the court, the following information to the public, namely,

(i) the offence of which the organization was convicted,

(ii) the sentence imposed by the court, and

(iii) any measures that the organization is taking — including any policies, standards and procedures established under paragraph (*b*) — to reduce the likelihood of it committing a subsequent offence; and

(*g*) comply with any other reasonable conditions that the court considers desirable to prevent the organization from committing subsequent offences or to remedy the harm caused by the offence.

(3.2) Before making an order under paragraph (3.1)(*b*), a court shall consider whether it would be more appropriate for another regulatory body to supervise the development or implementation of the policies, standards and procedures referred to in that paragraph.

(4) A probation order may be in Form 46, and the court that makes the probation order shall specify therein the period for which it is to remain in force.

(5) The court that makes a probation order shall

(*a*) cause a copy of the order to be given to the offender and, on request, to the victim;

(*b*) explain the conditions of the order set under subsections (2) to (3.1) and the substance of section 733.1 to the offender;

(*c*) cause an explanation to be given to the offender of the procedure for applying under subsection 732.2(3) for a change to the optional conditions and of the substance of subsections 732.2(3) and (5); and

(*d*) take reasonable measures to ensure that the offender understands the order and the explanations.

(6) For greater certainty, a failure to comply with subsection (5) does not affect the validity of the probation order.

(7) The notice referred to in paragraph (3)(*c*.2) must specify the places and times at which and the days on which the offender must provide samples of a bodily substance under a condition described in that paragraph. The first sample may not be taken earlier than 24 hours after the offender is served with the notice, and subsequent samples must be taken at regular intervals of at least seven days.

(8) For the purposes of paragraphs (3)(*c*.1) and (*c*.2) and subject to the regulations, the Attorney General of a province or the minister of justice of a territory shall, with respect to the province or territory,

(*a*) designate the persons or classes of persons that may take samples of bodily substances;

(*b*) designate the places or classes of places at which the samples are to be taken;

(*c*) specify the manner in which the samples are to be taken;

(*d*) specify the manner in which the samples are to be analyzed;

(*e*) specify the manner in which the samples are to be stored, handled and destroyed;

(*f*) specify the manner in which the records of the results of the analysis of the samples are to be protected and destroyed;

(*g*) designate the persons or classes of persons that may destroy the samples; and (*h*) designate the persons or classes of persons that may destroy the records of the results of the analysis of the samples.

(9) For the purpose of paragraph (3)(*c*.1) and subject to the regulations, the Attorney General of a province or the minister of justice of a territory may, with respect to the province or territory, designate persons or classes of persons to make a demand for a sample of a bodily substance.

(10) Samples of bodily substances referred to in paragraphs (3)(*c*.1) and (*c*.2) may not be taken, analyzed, stored, handled or destroyed, and the records of the results of the analysis of the samples may not be protected or destroyed, except in accordance with the designations and specifications made under subsection (8).

(11) The Attorney General of a province or the minister of justice of a territory, or a person authorized by the Attorney General or minister, shall cause all samples of bodily substances provided under a probation order to be destroyed within the periods prescribed by regulation unless the samples are reasonably expected to be used as evidence in a proceeding for an offence under section 733.1.

(12) The Governor in Council may make regulations

(*a*) prescribing bodily substances for the purposes of paragraphs (3)(*c*.1) and (*c*.2);

(*b*) respecting the designations and specifications referred to in subsections (8) and (9);

(*c*) prescribing the periods within which samples of bodily substances are to be destroyed under subsection (11); and

(*d*) respecting any other matters relating to the samples of bodily substances. 1995, c. 22, s. 6; 1999, c. 32, s. 6; 2003, c. 21, s. 18; 2008, c. 18, s. 37; 2011, c. 7, s. 3; 2014, c. 21, s. 2; 2015, c. 13, s. 27; 2019, c. 25, s. 297.

PROHIBITION ON USE OF BODILY SUBSTANCE / Prohibition on use or disclosure of result / Exception / Offence.

732.11 (1) No person shall use a bodily substance provided under a probation order except for the purpose of determining whether an offender is complying with a condition of the order that they abstain from the consumption of drugs, alcohol or any other intoxicating substance.

(2) Subject to subsection (3), no person shall use, disclose or allow the disclosure of the results of the analysis of a bodily substance provided under a probation order.

(3) The results of the analysis of a bodily substance provided under a probation order may be disclosed to the offender to whom they relate, and may also be used or disclosed in the course of an investigation of, or in a proceeding for, an offence under section 733.1 or, if the results are made anonymous, for statistical or other research purposes.

(4) Every person who contravenes subsection (1) or (2) is guilty of an offence punishable on summary conviction. 2011, c. 7, s. 4.

COMING INTO FORCE OF ORDER / Duration of order and limit on term of order / Changes to probation order / Judge may act in chambers / Where person convicted of offence / Compelling appearance of person bound.

732.2 (1) A probation order comes into force

(a) on the date on which the order is made;

(b) where the offender is sentenced to imprisonment under paragraph 731(1)(b) or was previously sentenced to imprisonment for another offence, as soon as the offender is released from prison or, if released from prison on conditional release, at the expiration of the sentence of imprisonment; or

(c) where the offender is under a conditional sentence order, at the expiration of the conditional sentence order.

(2) Subject to subsection (5),

(a) where an offender who is bound by a probation order is convicted of an offence, including an offence under section 733.1, or is imprisoned under paragraph 731(1)(b) in default of payment of a fine, the order continues in force except in so far as the sentence renders it impossible for the offender for the time being to comply with the order; and

(b) no probation order shall continue in force for more than three years after the date on which the order came into force.

(3) A court that makes a probation order may at any time, on application by the offender, the probation officer or the prosecutor, require the offender to appear before it and, after hearing the offender and one or both of the probation officer and the prosecutor,

(a) make any changes to the optional conditions that in the opinion of the court are rendered desirable by a change in the circumstances since those conditions were prescribed,

(b) relieve the offender, either absolutely or on such terms or for such period as the court deems desirable, of compliance with any optional condition, or

(c) decrease the period for which the probation order is to remain in force,

and the court shall thereupon endorse the probation order accordingly and, if it changes the optional conditions, inform the offender of its action and give the offender a copy of the order so endorsed.

(4) All the functions of the court under subsection (3) may be exercised in chambers.

(5) Where an offender who is bound by a probation order is convicted of an offence, including an offence under section 733.1, and

(a) the time within which an appeal may be taken against that conviction has expired and the offender has not taken an appeal,

(b) the offender has taken an appeal against that conviction and the appeal has been dismissed, or

(c) the offender has given written notice to the court that convicted the offender that the offender elects not to appeal the conviction or has abandoned the appeal, as the case may be, in addition to any punishment that may be imposed for that offence, the court that made the probation order may, on application by the prosecutor, require the offender to appear before it and, after hearing the prosecutor and the offender,

   (d) where the probation order was made under paragraph 731(1)(a), revoke the order and impose any sentence that could have been imposed if the passing of sentence had not been suspended, or

   (e) make such changes to the optional conditions as the court deems desirable, or extend the period for which the order is to remain in force for such period, not exceeding one year, as the court deems desirable,

and the court shall thereupon endorse the probation order accordingly and, if it changes the optional conditions or extends the period for which the order is to remain in force, inform the offender of its action and give the offender a copy of the order so endorsed.

(6) The provisions of Parts XVI and XVIII with respect to compelling the appearance of an accused before a justice apply, with such modifications as the circumstances require, to proceedings under subsections (3) and (5). 1995, c. 22, s. 6; 2004, c. 12, s. 12.

CODE

TRANSFER OF ORDER / Attorney General's consent / Where court unable to act.

733. (1) Where an offender who is bound by a probation order becomes a resident of, or is convicted or discharged under section 730 of an offence including an offence under section 733.1 in, a territorial division other than the territorial division where the order was made, on the application of a probation officer, the court that made the order may, subject to subsection (1.1), transfer the order to a court in that other territorial division that would, having regard to the mode of trial of the offender, have had jurisdiction to make the order in that other territorial division if the offender had been tried and convicted there of the offence in respect of which the order was made, and the order may thereafter be dealt with and enforced by the court to which it is so transferred in all respects as if that court had made the order.

(1.1) The transfer may be granted only with

   (a) the consent of the Attorney General of the province in which the probation order was made, if the two territorial divisions are not in the same province; or

   (b) the consent of the Attorney General of Canada, if the proceedings that led to the issuance of the probation order were instituted by or on behalf of the Attorney General of Canada.

(2) Where a court that has made a probation order or to which a probation order has been transferred pursuant to subsection (1) is for any reason unable to act, the powers of that court in relation to the probation order may be exercised by any other court that has equivalent jurisdiction in the same province. 1995, c. 22, s. 6; 1999, c. 5, s. 32.

FAILURE TO COMPLY WITH PROBATION ORDER / Where accused may be tried and punished.

733.1 (1) An offender who is bound by a probation order and who, without reasonable excuse, fails or refuses to comply with that order is guilty of

- (a) an indictable offence and is liable to imprisonment for a term of not more than four years; or
- (b) an offence punishable on summary conviction.

(2) An accused who is charged with an offence under subsection (1) may be tried and punished by any court having jurisdiction to try that offence in the place where the offence is alleged to have been committed or in the place where the accused is found, is arrested or is in custody, but where the place where the accused is found, is arrested or is in custody is outside the province in which the offence is alleged to have been committed, no proceedings in respect of that offence shall be instituted in that place without the consent of the Attorney General of that province. 1995, c. 22, s. 6; 2015, c. 23, s. 18; 2019, c. 25, s. 298.

Fines and Forfeiture

POWER OF COURT TO IMPOSE FINE / Offender's ability to pay / Meaning of default of payment / Imprisonment in default of payment / Determination of term / Moneys found on offender / Provincial regulations / Application to other law.

734. (1) Subject to subsection (2), a court that convicts a person, other than an organization, of an offence may fine the offender by making an order under section 734.1

- (a) if the punishment for the offence does not include a minimum term of imprisonment, in addition to or in lieu of any other sanction that the court is authorized to impose; or
- (b) if the punishment for the offence includes a minimum term of imprisonment, in addition to any other sanction that the court is required or authorized to impose.

(2) Except when the punishment for an offence includes a minimum fine or a fine is imposed in lieu of a forfeiture order, a court may fine an offender under this section only if the court is satisfied that the offender is able to pay the fine or discharge it under section 736.

(3) For the purposes of this section and sections 734.1 to 737, a person is in default of payment of a fine if the fine has not been paid in full by the time set out in the order made under section 734.1.

(4) Where an offender is fined under this section, a term of imprisonment, determined in accordance with subsection (5), shall be deemed to be imposed in default of payment of the fine.

(5) The term of imprisonment referred to in subsection (4) is the lesser of

- (a) the number of days that corresponds to a fraction, rounded down to the nearest whole number, of which

LICENCES, PERMITS, ETC.

734.5 If an offender is in default of payment of a fine,

   (*a*) where the proceeds of the fine belong to Her Majesty in right of a province by virtue of subsection 734.4(1), the person responsible, by or under an Act of the legislature of the province, for issuing, renewing or suspending a licence, permit or other similar instrument in relation to the offender may refuse to issue or renew or may suspend the licence, permit or other instrument until the fine is paid in full, proof of which lies on the offender; or

   (*b*) where the proceeds of the fine belong to Her Majesty in right of Canada by virtue of subsection 734.4(2), the person responsible, by or under an Act of Parliament, for issuing or renewing a licence, permit or other similar instrument in relation to the offender may refuse to issue or renew or may suspend the licence, permit or other instrument until the fine is paid in full, proof of which lies on the offender. 1995, c. 22, s. 6; 1999, c. 5, s. 34.

CODE

CIVIL ENFORCEMENT OF FINES FORFEITURE / Effect of filing order.

734.6 (1) Where

   (*a*) an offender is in default of payment of a fine, or

   (*b*) a forfeiture imposed by law is not paid as required by the order imposing it,

then, in addition to any other method provided by law for recovering the fine or forfeiture,

   (*c*) the Attorney General of the province to whom the proceeds of the fine or forfeiture belong, or

   (*d*) the Attorney General of Canada, where the proceeds of the fine or forfeiture belong to Her Majesty in right of Canada.

may, by filing the order, enter as a judgment the amount of the fine or forfeiture, and costs, if any, in any civil court in Canada that has jurisdiction to enter a judgment for that amount.

(2) An order that is entered as a judgment under this section is enforceable in the same manner as if it were a judgment obtained by the Attorney General of the province or the Attorney General of Canada, as the case may be, in civil proceedings. 1995, c. 22, s. 6.

WARRANT OF COMMITTAL / Reasons for committal / Period of imprisonment / Compelling appearance of person bound / Effect of imprisonment.

734.7 (1) Where time has been allowed for payment of a fine, the court shall not issue a warrant of committal in default of payment of the fine

   (*a*) until the expiration of the time allowed for payment of the fine in full; and

   (*b*) unless the court is satisfied

      (i) that the mechanisms provided by sections 734.5 and 734.6 are not appropriate in the circumstances, or

      (ii) that the offender has, without reasonable excuse, refused to pay the fine or discharge it under section 736.

(2) Where no time has been allowed for payment of a fine and a warrant committing the offender to prison for default of payment of the fine is issued, the court shall state in the warrant the reason for immediate committal.

(2.1) The period of imprisonment in default of payment of the fine shall be specified in a warrant of committal referred to in subsection (1) or (2).

(3) The provisions of Parts XVI and XVIII with respect to compelling the appearance of an accused before a justice apply, with such modifications as the circumstances require, to proceedings under paragraph (1)(*b*).

(4) The imprisonment of an offender for default of payment of a fine terminates the operation of sections 734.5 and 734.6 in relation to that fine. 1995, c. 22, s. 6; 1999, c. 5, s. 35.

DEFINITION OF "PENALTY" / Reduction of imprisonment on part payment / Minimum that can be accepted / To whom payment made / Application of money paid.

734.8 (1) In this section, "penalty" means the aggregate of
  (*a*) the fine, and
  (*b*) the costs and charges of committing and conveying the defaulter to prison, calculated in accordance with regulations made under subsection 734(7).

(2) The term of imprisonment in default of payment of a fine shall, on payment of a part of the penalty, whether the payment was made before or after the execution of a warrant of committal, be reduced by the number of days that bears the same proportion to the number of days in the term as the part paid bears to the total penalty.

(3) No amount offered in part payment of a penalty shall be accepted after the execution of a warrant of committal unless it is sufficient to secure a reduction of sentence of one day, or a whole number multiple of one day, and no part payment shall be accepted until any fee that is payable in respect of the warrant or its execution has been paid.

(4) Payment may be made under this section to the person that the Attorney General directs or, if the offender is imprisoned, to the person who has lawful custody of the prisoner or to any other person that the Attorney General directs.

(5) A payment under this section shall be applied firstly to the payment in full of costs and charges, secondly to the payment in full of any victim surcharge imposed under section 737, and then to payment of any part of the fine that remains unpaid. 1995, c. 22, s. 6; 1999, c. 5, s. 36; c. 25, s. 19.

FINES ON ORGANIZATIONS / Application of certain provisions — fines / Effect of filing order.

735. (1) An organization that is convicted of an offence is liable, in lieu of any imprisonment that is prescribed as punishment for that offence, to be fined in an amount, except where otherwise provided by law,
  (*a*) that is in the discretion of the court, where the offence is an indictable offence; or

(b) not exceeding one hundred thousand dollars, where the offence is a summary conviction offence.

(1.1) A court that imposes a fine under subsection (1) or under any other Act of Parliament shall make an order that clearly sets out

(a) the amount of the fine;

(b) the manner in which the fine is to be paid;

(c) the time or times by which the fine, or any portion of it, must be paid; and

(d) any other terms respecting the payment of the fine that the court deems appropriate.

(2) Section 734.6 applies, with any modifications that are required, when an organization fails to pay the fine in accordance with the terms of the order. 1995, c. 22, s. 6; 1999, c. 5, s. 37; 2003, c. 21, s. 20.

FINE OPTION PROGRAM / Credits and other matters / Deemed payment / Federal-provincial agreement.

736. (1) An offender who is fined under section 734 may, whether or not the offender is serving a term of imprisonment imposed in default of payment of the fine, discharge the fine in whole or in part by earning credits for work performed during a period not greater than two years in a program established for that purpose by the lieutenant governor in council

(a) of the province in which the fine was imposed, or

(b) of the province in which the offender resides, where an appropriate agreement is in effect between the government of that province and the government of the province in which the fine was imposed.

if the offender is admissible to such a program.

(2) A program referred to in subsection (1) shall determine the rate at which credits are earned and may provide for the manner of crediting any amounts earned against the fine and any other matters necessary for or incidental to carrying out the program.

(3) Credits earned for work performed as provided by subsection (1) shall, for the purposes of this Act, be deemed to be payment in respect of a fine.

(4) Where, by virtue of subsection 734.4(2), the proceeds of a fine belong to Her Majesty in right of Canada, an offender may discharge the fine in whole or in part in a fine option program of a province pursuant to subsection (1), where an appropriate agreement is in effect between the government of the province and the Government of Canada. 1995, c. 22, s. 6.

VICTIM SURCHARGE / Amount of surcharge / Exception / Definition of "undue hardship" / For greater certainty / Reasons / Increase in surcharge / Time for payment / Amounts applied to aid victims / Notice / Enforcement / Application — subsections (2.1) to (2.4).

737. (1) An offender who is convicted, or discharged under section 730, of an offence under this Act, the *Controlled Drugs and Substances Act* or the *Cannabis*

Act shall pay a victim surcharge for each offence, in addition to any other punishment imposed on the offender.

(2) Subject to subsections (2.1) and (3), the amount of the victim surcharge in respect of an offence is

   (*a*) 30% of any fine that is imposed on the offender for the offence; or

   (*b*) if no fine is imposed on the offender for the offence,

      (i) $100 in the case of an offence punishable by summary conviction, and

      (ii) $200 in the case of an offence punishable by indictment.

(2.1) Despite subsection (1), the court may, on application of the offender or on its own motion, order an offender to pay no victim surcharge, or to pay a reduced amount, if it is satisfied that the victim surcharge

   (*a*) would cause undue hardship to the offender; or

   (*b*) would not cause undue hardship to the offender but would be disproportionate to the gravity of the offence or the degree of responsibility of the offender.

(2.2) For the purposes of subsection (2.1), "undue hardship" means the offender is unable to pay a victim surcharge on account of the offender's precarious financial circumstances, including because of their unemployment, homelessness, lack of assets or significant financial obligations towards their dependants.

(2.3) For greater certainty, for the purposes of subsection (2.2), the imprisonment of the offender alone does not constitute undue hardship.

(2.4) When the court makes an order under subsection (2.1), the court shall state its reasons in the record of the proceedings.

(3) The court may order an offender to pay a victim surcharge in an amount exceeding that set out in subsection (2) if the court considers it appropriate in the circumstances and is satisfied that the offender is able to pay the higher amount.

(4) The victim surcharge imposed in respect of an offence is payable within the time established by the lieutenant governor in council of the province in which the surcharge is imposed. If no time has been so established, the surcharge is payable within a reasonable time after its imposition.

(5) A victim surcharge shall be applied for the purposes of providing such assistance to victims of offences as the lieutenant governor in council of the province in which the surcharge is imposed may direct from time to time.

(6) The court shall cause to be given to the offender a written notice setting out

   (*a*) the amount of the victim surcharge;

   (*b*) the manner in which the victim surcharge is to be paid;

   (*c*) the time by which the victim surcharge must be paid; and

   (*d*) the procedure for applying for a change in any terms referred to in paragraphs (*b*) and (*c*) in accordance with section 734.3.

(7) Subsections 734(3) to (7) and sections 734.3, 734.5, 734.7, 734.8 and 736 apply, with any modifications that the circumstances require, in respect of a victim surcharge imposed under this section and, in particular,

   (*a*) a reference in any of those provisions to "fine", other than in subsection 734.8(5), must be read as if it were a reference to "victim surcharge"; and (*b*) the notice provided under subsection (6) is deemed to be an order made under section 734.1.

(8) Subsections (2.1) to (2.4) apply to any offender who is sentenced for an offence under this Act, the *Controlled Drugs and Substances Act* or the *Cannabis Act* that was committed after the day on which those subsections come into force.

(9) [*Repealed*, 2019, c. 25, s. 301.] 1995, c. 22, s. 6; 1996, c. 19, s. 75 [amended 1995, c. 22, s. 18 (Sched. IV, item 15]; 1999, c. 5, s. 38; c. 25, s. 20; 2013, c. 11, s. 3; 2015, c. 13, s. 28; 2018, c. 16, s. 222; 2019, c. 25, s. 301.]

(10) [*Repealed*, 2013, c. 11, s. 3(5).]

Note: If Bill C-28, introduced in the 1st session of the 42nd Parliament and entitled *An Act to amend the Criminal Code (victim surcharge)*, receives Royal Assent, then, on the first day on which both subsec. 2(1) of that Act and s. 222 of 2018, c. 16 [in force October 17, 2018] are in force, s. 737 is amended by replacing subsec. (1), 2018, c. 16, s. 190 [Conditions not yet satisfied.]:

Victim surcharge

737 (1) Subject to subsection (1.1), an offender who is convicted, or discharged under section 730, of an offence under this Act, the *Controlled Drugs and Substances Act* or the *Cannabis Act* shall pay a victim surcharge for each offence, in addition to any other punishment imposed on the offender.

Restitution

COURT TO CONSIDER RESTITUTION ORDER / Inquiry by court / Adjournment / Form / Reasons.

737.1 (1) If an offender is convicted or is discharged under section 730 of an offence, the court that sentences or discharges the offender, in addition to any other measure imposed on the offender, shall consider making a restitution order under section 738 or 739.

(2) As soon as feasible after a finding of guilt and in any event before imposing the sentence, the court shall inquire of the prosecutor if reasonable steps have been taken to provide the victims with an opportunity to indicate whether they are seeking restitution for their losses and damages, the amount of which must be readily ascertainable.

(3) On application of the prosecutor or on its own motion, the court may adjourn the proceedings to permit the victims to indicate whether they are seeking restitution or to establish their losses and damages, if the court is satisfied that the adjournment would not interfere with the proper administration of justice.

(4) Victims and other persons may indicate whether they are seeking restitution by completing Form 34.1 in Part XXVIII or a form approved for that purpose by the lieutenant governor in council of the province in which the court is exercising its jurisdiction or by using any other method approved by the court, and, if they are seeking restitution, shall establish their losses and damages, the amount of which must be readily ascertainable, in the same manner.

(5) If a victim seeks restitution and the court does not make a restitution order, it shall include in the record a statement of the court's reasons for not doing so. 2015, c. 13, s. 29.

RESTITUTION TO VICTIMS OF OFFENCES / Regulations.

738. (1) Where an offender is convicted or discharged under section 730 of an offence, the court imposing sentence on or discharging the offender may, on application of the Attorney General or on its own motion, in addition to any other measure imposed on the offender, order that the offender make restitution to another person as follows:

(a) in the case of damage to, or the loss or destruction of, the property of any person as a result of the commission of the offence or the arrest or attempted arrest of the offender, by paying to the person an amount not exceeding the replacement value of the property as of the date the order is imposed, less the value of any part of the property that is returned to that person as of the date it is returned, where the amount is readily ascertainable;

(b) in the case of bodily or psychological harm to any person as a result of the commission of the offence or the arrest or attempted arrest of the offender, by paying to the person an amount not exceeding all pecuniary damages incurred as a result of the harm, including loss of income or support, if the amount is readily ascertainable;

(c) in the case of bodily harm or threat of bodily harm to the offender's intimate partner or child, or any other person, as a result of the commission of the offence or the arrest or attempted arrest of the offender, where the intimate partner, child or other person was a member of the offender's household at the relevant time, by paying to the person in question, independently of any amount ordered to be paid under paragraphs (a) and (b), an amount not exceeding actual and reasonable expenses incurred by that person, as a result of moving out of the offender's household, for temporary housing, food, child care and transportation, where the amount is readily ascertainable;

(d) in the case of an offence under section 402.2 or 403, by paying to a person who, as a result of the offence, incurs expenses to reestablish their identity, including expenses to replace their identity documents and to correct their credit history and credit rating, an amount that is not more than the amount of those expenses, to the extent that they are reasonable, if the amount is readily ascertainable; and

(e) in the case of an offence under subsection 162.1(1), by paying to a person who, as a result of the offence, incurs expenses to remove the intimate image from the Internet or other digital network, an amount that is not more than the amount of those expenses, to the extent that they are reasonable, if the amount is readily ascertainable.

(2) The lieutenant governor in council of a province may make regulations precluding the inclusion of provisions on enforcement of restitution orders as an optional condition of a probation order or of a conditional sentence order. 1995, c.

22, s. 6; 2000, c. 12, s. 95(*e*); 2005, c. 43, s. 7; 2009, c. 28, s. 11; 2014, c. 31, s. 24; 2019, c. 25, s. 302.

RESTITUTION TO PERSONS ACTING IN GOOD FAITH.

739. Where an offender is convicted or discharged under section 730 of an offence and

(*a*) any property obtained as a result of the commission of the offence has been conveyed or transferred for valuable consideration to a person acting in good faith and without notice, or

(*b*) the offender has borrowed money on the security of that property from a person acting in good faith and without notice.

the court may, where that property has been returned to the lawful owner or the person who had lawful possession of that property at the time the offence was committed, order the offender to pay as restitution to the person referred to in paragraph (*a*) or (*b*) an amount not exceeding the amount of consideration for that property or the total amount outstanding in respect of the loan, as the case may be. 1995, c. 22, s. 6.

ABILITY TO PAY.

739.1 The offender's financial means or ability to pay does not prevent the court from making an order under section 738 or 739. 2015, c. 13, s. 30.

PAYMENT UNDER ORDER.

739.2 In making an order under section 738 or 739, the court shall require the offender to pay the full amount specified in the order by the day specified in the order, unless the court is of the opinion that the amount should be paid in installments, in which case the court shall set out a periodic payment scheme in the order. 2015, c. 13, s. 30.

MORE THAN ONE PERSON.

739.3 An order under section 738 or 739 may be made in respect of more than one person, in which case the order must specify the amount that is payable to each person. The order may also specify the order of priority in which those persons are to be paid. 2015, c. 13, s. 30.

PUBLIC AUTHORITY / Orders.

739.4 (1) On the request of a person in whose favour an order under section 738 or 739 would be made, the court may make the order in favour of a public authority, designated by the regulations, who is to be responsible for enforcing the order and remitting to the person making the request all amounts received under it.

(2) The lieutenant governor in council of a province may, by order, designate any person or body as a public authority for the purpose of subsection (1). 2015, c. 13, s. 30.

PRIORITY TO RESTITUTION.

740. Where the court finds it applicable and appropriate in the circumstances of a case to make, in relation to an offender, an order of restitution under section 738 or 739, and

(a) an order of forfeiture under this or any other Act of Parliament may be made in respect of property that is the same as property in respect of which the order of restitution may be made, or

(b) the court is considering ordering the offender to pay a fine and it appears to the court that the offender would not have the means or ability to comply with both the order of restitution and the order to pay the fine,

the court shall first make the order of restitution and shall then consider whether and to what extent an order of forfeiture or an order to pay a fine is appropriate in the circumstances. 1995, c. 22, s. 6.

ENFORCING RESTITUTION ORDER / Moneys found on offender.

741. (1) An offender who fails to pay all of the amount that is ordered to be paid under section 732.1, 738, 739 or 742.3 by the day specified in the order or who fails to make a periodic payment required under the order is in default of the order and the person to whom the amount, or the periodic payment, as the case may be, was to be paid may, by filing the order, enter as a judgment any amount ordered to be paid that remains unpaid under the order in any civil court in Canada that has jurisdiction to enter a judgment for that amount, and that judgment is enforceable against the offender in the same manner as if it were a judgment rendered against the offender in that court in civil proceedings.

(2) All or any part of an amount that is orderd to be paid under section 738 or 739 may be taken out of moneys found in the possession of the offender at the time of the arrest of the offender if the court making the order, on being satisfied that ownership of or right to possession of those moneys is not disputed by claimants other than the offender, so directs. 1995, c. 22, s. 6; 2004, c. 12, s. 13; 2015, c. 13, s. 31.

NOTICE OF ORDERS OF RESTITUTION.

741.1 If a court makes an order of restitution under section 738 or 739, it shall cause notice of the content of the order, or a copy of the order, to be given to the person to whom the restitution is ordered to be paid, and if it is to be paid to a public authority designated by regulations made under subsection 739.4(2), to the public authority and the person to whom the public authority is to remit amounts received under the order. 1995, c. 22, s. 6; 2015, c. 13, s. 32.

CIVIL REMEDY NOT AFFECTED.

741.2 A civil remedy for an act or omission is not affected by reason only that an order for restitution under section 738 or 739 has been made in respect of that act or omission. 1995, c. 22, s. 6.

Conditional Sentence of Imprisonment

DEFINITIONS / "Change" / "Optional conditions" / "Supervisor".

742. In sections 742.1 to 742.7,

"change", in relation to optional conditions, includes deletions and additions;

"optional conditions" means the conditions referred to in subsection 742.3(2);

"supervisor" means a person designated by the Attorney General, either by name or by title of office, as a supervisor for the purposes of sections 742.1 to 742.7. 1995, c. 22, s. 6.

CODE

IMPOSING OF CONDITIONAL SENTENCE.

742.1 If a person is convicted of an offence and the court imposes a sentence of imprisonment of less than two years, the court may, for the purpose of supervising the offender's behaviour in the community, order that the offender serve the sentence in the community, subject to the conditions imposed under section 742.3, if

- (*a*) the court is satisfied that the service of the sentence in the community would not endanger the safety of the community and would be consistent with the fundamental purpose and principles of sentencing set out in sections 718 to 718.2;
- (*b*) the offence is not an offence punishable by a minimum term of imprisonment;
- (*c*) the offence is not an offence, prosecuted by way of indictment, for which the maximum term of imprisonment is 14 years or life;
- (*d*) the offence is not a terrorism offence, or a criminal organization offence, prosecuted by way of indictment, for which the maximum term of imprisonment is 10 years or more;
- (*e*) the offence is not an offence, prosecuted by way of indictment, for which the maximum term of imprisonment is 10 years, that
  - (i) resulted in bodily harm,
  - (ii) involved the import, export, trafficking or production of drugs, or
  - (iii) involved the use of a weapon; and
- (*f*) the offence is not an offence, prosecuted by way of indictment, under any of the following provisions:
  - (i) section 144 (prison breach),
  - (ii) section 264 (criminal harassment),
  - (iii) section 271 (sexual assault),
  - (iv) section 279 (kidnapping),
  - (v) section 279.02 (trafficking in persons — material benefit),
  - (vi) section 281 (abduction of person under fourteen),
  - (vii) section 333.1 (motor vehicle theft),
  - (viii) paragraph 334(*a*) (theft over $5000),
  - (ix) paragraph 348(1)(*e*) (breaking and entering a place other than a dwelling-house),
  - (x) section 349 (being unlawfully in a dwelling-house), and

(xi) section 435 (arson for fraudulent purpose). 1995, c. 22, s. 6; 1997, c. 18, s. 107.1; 2007, c. 12, s. 1; 2012, c. 1, s. 34.

FIREARM, ETC., PROHIBITIONS / Application of s. 109 or 110.

742.2 (1) Before imposing a conditional sentence under section 742.1, the court shall consider whether section 109 or 110 is applicable.

(2) For greater certainty, a condition of a conditional sentence order referred to in paragraph 742.3(2)(*b*) does not affect the operation of section 109 or 110. 1995, c. 22, s. 6; 2002, c. 13, s. 75; 2004, c. 12, s. 14.

COMPULSORY CONDITIONS OF CONDITIONAL SENTENCE ORDER / Optional conditions of conditional sentence order / Obligations of court / For greater certainty / Notice — samples at regular intervals / Designations and specifications / Further designations / Restriction / Destruction of samples / Regulations.

742.3 (1) The court shall prescribe, as conditions of a conditional sentence order, that the offender do all of the following:

(*a*) keep the peace and be of good behaviour;

(*b*) appear before the court when required to do so by the court;

(*c*) report to a supervisor

   (i) within two working days, or such longer period as the court directs, after the making of the conditional sentence order, and

   (ii) thereafter, when required by the supervisor and in the manner directed by the supervisor;

(*d*) remain within the jurisdiction of the court unless written permission to go outside that jurisdiction is obtained from the court or the supervisor; and

(*e*) notify the court or the supervisor in advance of any change of name or address, and promptly notify the court or the supervisor of any change of employment or occupation.

(1.1) [*Repealed*, 2019, c. 25, s. 303(1).]

(1.2) [*Repealed*, 2019, c. 25, s. 303(1).]

(1.3) [*Repealed*, 2019, c. 25, s. 303(1).]

(2) The court may prescribe, as additional conditions of a conditional sentence order, that the offender do one or more of the following:

(*a*) abstain from the consumption of drugs except in accordance with a medical prescription, of alcohol or of any other intoxicating substance;

(*a*.1) provide, for the purpose of analysis, a sample of a bodily substance prescribed by regulation on the demand of a peace officer, the supervisor or someone designated under subsection (7) to make a demand, at the place and time and on the day specified by the person making the demand, if that person has reasonable grounds to suspect that the offender has breached a condition of the order that requires them to abstain from the consumption of drugs, alcohol or any other intoxicating substance;

(a.2) provide, for the purpose of analysis, a sample of a bodily substance prescribed by regulation at regular intervals that are specified by the supervisor in a notice in Form 51 served on the offender, if a condition of the order requires the offender to abstain from the consumption of drugs, alcohol or any other intoxicating substance;

(a.3) abstain from communicating, directly or indirectly, with any victim, witness or other person identified in the order or from going to any place or geographic area specified in the order, except in accordance with any specified conditions that the justice considers necessary;

  (b) abstain from owning, possessing or carrying a weapon;

  (c) provide for the support or care of dependants;

  (d) perform up to 240 hours of community service over a period not exceeding eighteen months;

  (e) attend a treatment program approved by the province; and

  (f) comply with such other reasonable conditions as the court considers desirable, subject to any regulations made under subsection 738(2), for securing the good conduct of the offender and for preventing a repetition by the offender of the same offence or the commission of other offences.

(3) A court that makes an order under this section shall

  (a) cause a copy of the order to be given to the offender and, on request, to the victim;

  (b) explain the substance of subsection (1) and sections 742.4 and 742.6 to the offender;

  (c) cause an explanation to be given to the offender of the procedure for applying under section 742.4 for a change to the optional conditions; and

  (d) take reasonable measures to ensure that the offender understands the order and the explanations.

(4) For greater certainty, a failure to comply with subsection (3) does not affect the validity of the order.

(5) The notice referred to in paragraph (2)(a.2) must specify the places and times at which and the days on which the offender must provide samples of a bodily substance under a condition described in that paragraph. The first sample may not be taken earlier than 24 hours after the offender is served with the notice, and subsequent samples must be taken at regular intervals of at least seven days.

(6) For the purposes of paragraphs (2)(a.1) and (a.2) and subject to the regulations, the Attorney General of a province or the minister of justice of a territory shall, with respect to the province or territory,

  (a) designate the persons or classes of persons that may take samples of bodily substances;

  (b) designate the places or classes of places at which the samples are to be taken;

  (c) specify the manner in which the samples are to be taken;

  (d) specify the manner in which the samples are to be analyzed;

  (e) specify the manner in which the samples are to be stored, handled and destroyed;

(f) specify the manner in which the records of the results of the analysis of the samples are to be protected and destroyed;

(g) designate the persons or classes of persons that may destroy the samples; and

(h) designate the persons or classes of persons that may destroy the records of the results of the analysis of the samples.

(7) For the purpose of paragraph (2)(a.1) and subject to the regulations, the Attorney General of a province or the minister of justice of a territory may, with respect to the province or territory, designate persons or classes of persons to make a demand for a sample of a bodily substance.

(8) Samples of bodily substances referred to in paragraphs (2)(a.1) and (a.2) may not be taken, analyzed, stored, handled or destroyed, and the records of the results of the analysis of the samples may not be protected or destroyed, except in accordance with the designations and specifications made under subsection (6).

(9) The Attorney General of a province or the minister of justice of a territory, or a person authorized by the Attorney General or minister, shall cause all samples of bodily substances provided under a conditional sentence order to be destroyed within the periods prescribed by regulation, unless the samples are reasonably expected to be used as evidence in proceedings under section 742.6.

(10) The Governor in Council may make regulations

(a) prescribing bodily substances for the purposes of paragraphs (2)(a.1) and (a.2);

(b) respecting the designations and specifications referred to in subsections (6) and (7);

(c) prescribing the periods within which samples of bodily substances are to be destroyed under subsection (9); and

(d) respecting any other matters relating to the samples of bodily substances.
1995, c. 22, s. 6; 2008, c. 18, s. 40; 2011, c. 7, s. 5; 2014, c. 21, s. 3; 2015, c. 13, s. 33; 2019, c. 25, s. 303.

PROHIBITION ON USE OF BODILY SUBSTANCE / Prohibition on use or disclosure of result / Exception / Offence.

742.31 (1) No person shall use a bodily substance provided under a conditional sentence order except for the purpose of determining whether an offender is complying with a condition of the order that they abstain from the consumption of drugs, alcohol or any other intoxicating substance.

(2) Subject to subsection (3), no person shall use, disclose or allow the disclosure of the results of the analysis of a bodily substance provided under a conditional sentence order.

(3) The results of the analysis of a bodily substance provided under a conditional sentence order may be disclosed to the offender to whom they relate, and may also be used or disclosed in the course of proceedings under section 742.6 or, if the results are made anonymous, for statistical or other research purposes.

(4) Every person who contravenes subsection (1) or (2) is guilty of an offence punishable on summary conviction. 2011, c. 7, s. 6.

SUPERVISOR MAY PROPOSE CHANGES TO OPTIONAL CONDITIONS / Hearing / Decision at hearing / Where no hearing requested or ordered / Changes proposed by offender or prosecutor / Judge may act in chambers.

742.4 (1) Where an offender's supervisor is of the opinion that a change in circumstances makes a change to the optional conditions desirable, the supervisor shall give written notification of the proposed change, and the reasons for it, to the offender, to the prosecutor and to the court.

(2) Within seven days after receiving a notification referred to in subsection (1),
- (a) the offender or the prosecutor may request the court to hold a hearing to consider the proposed change, or
- (b) the court may, of its own initiative, order that a hearing be held to consider the proposed change,

and a hearing so requested or ordered shall be held within thirty days after the receipt by the court of the notification referred to in subsection (1).

(3) At a hearing held pursuant to subsection (2), the court
- (a) shall approve or refuse to approve the proposed change; and
- (b) may make any other change to the optional conditions that the court deems appropriate.

(4) Where no request or order for a hearing is made within the time period stipulated in subsection (2), the proposed change takes effect fourteen days after the receipt by the court of the notification referred to in subsection (1), and the supervisor shall so notify the offender and file proof of that notification with the court.

(5) Subsections (1) and (3) apply, with such modifications as the circumstances require, in respect of a change proposed by the offender or the prosecutor to the optional conditions, and in all such cases a hearing must be held, and must be held within thirty days after the receipt by the court of the notification referred to in subsection (1).

(6) All the functions of the court under this section may be exercised in chambers. 1995, c. 22, s. 6; 1999, c. 5, s. 39.

TRANSFER OF ORDER / Attorney General's consent / Where court unable to act.

742.5 (1) Where an offender who is bound by a conditional sentence order becomes a resident of a territorial division, other than the territorial division where the order was made, on the application of a supervisor, the court that made the order may, subject to subsection (1.1), transfer the order to a court in that other territorial division that would, having regard to the mode of trial of the offender, have had jurisdiction to make the order in that other territorial division if the offender had been tried and convicted there of the offence in respect of which the order was made, and the order may thereafter be dealt with and enforced by the court to which it is so transferred in all respects as if that court had made the order.

(1.1) The transfer may be granted only with

(a) the consent of the Attorney General of the province in which the conditional sentence order was made, if the two territorial divisions are not in the same province; or

(b) the consent of the Attorney General of Canada, if the proceedings that led to the issuance of the conditional sentence order were instituted by or on behalf of the Attorney General of Canada.

(2) Where a court that has made a conditional sentence order or to which a conditional sentence order has been transferred pursuant to subsection (1) is for any reason unable to act, the powers of that court in relation to the conditional sentence order may be exercised by any other court that has equivalent jurisdiction in the same province. 1995, c. 22, s. 6; 1999, c. 5, s. 40.

PROCEDURE ON BREACH OF CONDITION / Interim release / Hearing / Place / Attorney General's consent / Adjournment / Report of supervisor / Admission of report on notice of intent / Requiring attendance of supervisor or witness / Powers of court / Warrant or arrest — suspension of running of conditional sentence / Conditions continue / Detention under s. 515(6) / Earned remission does not apply / Unreasonable delay in execution / Allegation dismissed or reasonable excuse / Powers of court / Considerations.

742.6 (1) For the purpose of proceedings under this section,

(a) the provisions of Parts XVI and XVIII with respect to compelling the appearance of an accused before a justice apply, with any modifications that the circumstances require, and any reference in those Parts to committing an offence shall be read as a reference to breaching a condition of a conditional sentence order;

(b) the powers of arrest for breach of a condition are those that apply to an indictable offence, with any modifications that the circumstances require, and subsection 495(2) does not apply;

(c) despite paragraph (a), if an allegation of breach of condition is made, the proceeding is commenced by

(i) the issuance of a warrant for the arrest of the offender for the alleged breach,

(ii) the arrest without warrant of the offender for the alleged breach, or

(iii) the compelling of the offender's appearance in accordance with paragraph (d);

(d) if the offender is already detained or before a court, the offender's appearance may be compelled under the provisions referred to in paragraph (a);

(e) if an offender is arrested for the alleged breach, the peace officer who makes the arrest or a judge or justice may release the offender and the offender's appearance may be compelled under the provisions referred to in paragraph (a); and

CODE

(f) any judge of a superior court of criminal jurisdiction or of a court of criminal jurisdiction or any justice of the peace may issue a warrant to arrest no matter which court, judge or justice sentenced the offender, and the provisions that apply to the issuance of telewarrants apply, with any modifications that the circumstances require, as if a breach of condition were an indictable offence.

(2) For the purpose of the application of section 515, the release from custody of an offender who is detained on the basis of an alleged breach of a condition of a conditional sentence order shall be governed by subsection 515(6).

(3) The hearing of an allegation of a breach of condition shall be commenced within thirty days, or as soon thereafter as is practicable, after

(a) the offender's arrest; or

(b) the compelling of the offender's appearance in accordance with paragraph (1)(d).

(3.1) The allegation may be heard by any court having jurisdiction to hear that allegation in the place where the breach is alleged to have been committed or the offender is found, arrested or in custody.

(3.2) If the place where the offender is found, arrested or in custody is outside the province in which the breach is alleged to have been committed, no proceedings in respect of that breach shall be instituted in that place without

(a) the consent of the Attorney General of the province in which the breach is alleged to have been committed; or

(b) the consent of the Attorney General of Canada, if the proceedings that led to the issuance of the conditional sentence order were instituted by or on behalf of the Attorney General of Canada.

(3.3) A judge may, at any time during a hearing of an allegation of breach of condition, adjourn the hearing for a reasonable period.

(4) An allegation of a breach of condition must be supported by a written report of the supervisor, which report must include, where appropriate, signed statements of witnesses.

(5) The report is admissible in evidence if the party intending to produce it has, before the hearing, given the offender reasonable notice and a copy of the report.

(6) and (7) [*Repealed*, 2008, c. 18, s. 41.]

(8) The offender may, with leave of the court, require the attendance, for cross-examination, of the supervisor or of any witness whose signed statement is included in the report.

(9) Where the court is satisfied, on a balance of probabilities, that the offender has without reasonable excuse, the proof of which lies on the offender, breached a condition of the conditional sentence order, the court may

(a) take no action;

(b) change the optional conditions;

(c) suspend the conditional sentence order and direct

(i) that the offender serve in custody a portion of the unexpired sentence, and

    (ii) that the conditional sentence order resume on the offender's release from custody, either with or without changes to the optional conditions; or

  (d) terminate the conditional sentence order and direct that the offender be committed to custody until the expiration of the sentence.

(10) The running of a conditional sentence order imposed on an offender is suspended during the period that ends with the determination of whether a breach of condition had occurred and begins with the earliest of

  (a) the issuance of a warrant for the arrest of the offender for the alleged breach,

  (b) the arrest without warrant of the offender for the alleged breach, and

  (c) the compelling of the offender's appearance in accordance with paragraph (1)(d).

(11) If the offender is not detained in custody during any period referred to in subsection (10), the conditions of the order continue to apply, with any changes made to them under section 742.4, and any subsequent breach of those conditions may be dealt with in accordance with this section.

(12) A conditional sentence order referred to in subsection (10) starts running again on the making of an order to detain the offender in custody under subsection 515(6) and, unless section 742.7 applies, continues running while the offender is detained under the order.

(13) Section 6 of the *Prisons and Reformatories Act* does not apply to the period of detention in custody under subsection 515(6).

(14) Despite subsection (10), if there was unreasonable delay in the execution of a warrant, the court may, at any time, order that any period between the issuance and execution of the warrant that it considers appropriate in the interests of justice is deemed to be time served under the conditional sentence order unless the period has been so deemed under subsection (15).

(15) If the allegation is withdrawn or dismissed or the offender is found to have had a reasonable excuse for the breach, the sum of the following periods is deemed to be time served under the conditional sentence order:

  (a) any period for which the running of the conditional sentence order was suspended; and

  (b) if subsection (12) applies, a period equal to one half of the period that the conditional sentence order runs while the offender is detained under an order referred to in that subsection.

(16) If a court is satisfied, on a balance of probabilities, that the offender has without reasonable excuse, the proof of which lies on the offender, breached a condition of the conditional sentence order, the court may, in exceptional cases and in the interests of justice, order that some or all of the period of suspension referred to in subsection (10) is deemed to be time served under the conditional sentence order.

(17) In exercising its discretion under subsection (16), a court shall consider

  (a) the circumstances and seriousness of the breach;

(*b*) whether not making the order would cause the offender undue hardship based on the offender's individual circumstances; and

(*c*) the period for which the offender was subject to conditions while the running of the conditional sentence order was suspended and whether the offender complied with those conditions during that period. 1995, c. 22, s. 6; 1999, c. 5, s. 41; 2004, c. 12, s. 15; 2008, c. 18, s. 41; 2019, c. 25, s. 304.

IF PERSON IMPRISONED FOR NEW OFFENCE / Breach of condition / Multiple sentences / Conditional sentence order resumes.

742.7 (1) If an offender who is subject to a conditional sentence order is imprisoned as a result of a sentence imposed for another offence, whenever committed, the running of the conditional sentence order is suspended during the period of imprisonment for that other offence.

(2) If an order is made under paragraph 742.6(9)(*c*) or (*d*) to commit an offender to custody, the custodial period ordered shall, unless the court considers that it would not be in the interests of justice, be served consecutively to any other period of imprisonment that the offender is serving when that order is made.

(3) If an offender is serving both a custodial period referred to in subsection (2) and any other period of imprisonment, the periods shall, for the purpose of section 743.1 and section 139 of the *Corrections and Conditional Release Act*, be deemed to constitute one sentence of imprisonment.

(4) The running of any period of the conditional sentence order that is to be served in the community resumes upon the release of the offender from prison on parole, on statutory release, on earned remission, or at the expiration of the sentence. 1995, c. 22, s. 6; 1999, c. 5, s. 42; 2004, c. 12, s. 16.

Imprisonment

IMPRISONMENT WHEN NO OTHER PROVISION.

743. Every one who is convicted of an indictable offence for which no punishment is specially provided is liable to imprisonment for a term not exceeding five years. 1995, c. 22, s. 6.

IMPRISONMENT FOR LIFE OR MORE THAN TWO YEARS / Subsequent term less than two years / Imprisonment for term less than two years / Long-term supervision / Sentence to penitentiary of person serving sentence elsewhere / Transfer to penitentiary / Newfoundland.

743.1 (1) Except where otherwise provided, a person who is sentenced to imprisonment for

(*a*) life,

(*b*) a term of two years or more, or

(*c*) two or more terms of less than two years each that are to be served one after the other and that, in the aggregate, amount to two years or more,

shall be sentenced to imprisonment in a penitentiary.

(2) Where a person who is sentenced to imprisonment in a penitentiary is, before the expiration of that sentence, sentenced to imprisonment for a term of less than two years, the person shall serve that term in a penitentiary, but if the previous sentence of imprisonment in a penitentiary is set aside, that person shall serve that term in accordance with subsection (3).

(3) A person who is sentenced to imprisonment and who is not required to be sentenced as provided in subsection (1) or (2) shall, unless a special prison is prescribed by law, be sentenced to imprisonment in a prison or other place of confinement, other than a penitentiary, within the province in which the person is convicted, in which the sentence of imprisonment may be lawfully executed.

(3.1) Despite subsection (3), an offender who is subject to long-term supervision under Part XXIV and is sentenced for another offence during the period of the supervision shall be sentenced to imprisonment in a penitentiary.

(4) Where a person is sentenced to imprisonment in a penitentiary while the person is lawfully imprisoned in a place other than a penitentiary, that person shall, except where otherwise provided, be sent immediately to the penitentiary, and shall serve in the penitentiary the unexpired portion of the term of imprisonment that that person was serving when sentenced to the penitentiary as well as the term of imprisonment for which that person was sentenced to the penitentiary.

(5) Where, at any time, a person who is imprisoned in a prison or place of confinement other than a penitentiary is subject to two or more terms of imprisonment, each of which is for less than two years, that are to be served one after the other, and the aggregate of the unexpired portions of those terms at that time amounts to two years or more, the person shall be transferred to a penitentiary to serve those terms, but if any one or more of such terms is set aside or reduced and the unexpired portions of the remaining term or terms on the day on which that person was transferred under this section amounted to less than two years, that person shall serve that term or terms in accordance with subsection (3).

(6) For the purposes of subsection (3), "penitentiary" does not, until a day to be fixed by order of the Governor in Council, include the facility mentioned in subsection 15(2) of the *Corrections and Conditional Release Act*. 1995, c. 22, s. 6; 1997, c. 17, s. 1; 2008, c. 6, s. 39.

REPORT BY COURT TO CORRECTIONAL SERVICE.

743.2 A court that sentences or commits a person to penitentiary shall forward to the Correctional Service of Canada its reasons and recommendation relating to the sentence or committal, any relevant reports that were submitted to the court, and any other information relevant to administering the sentence or committal. 1995, c. 22, s. 6.

NON-COMMUNICATION ORDER / Failure to comply with order.

743.21 (1) The sentencing judge may issue an order prohibiting the offender from communicating, directly or indirectly, with any victim, witness or other person identified in the order during the custodial period of the sentence, except in accordance with any conditions specified in the order that the sentencing judge considers necessary.

(2) Every person who fails, without lawful excuse, to comply with the order

    (*a*) is guilty of an indictable offence and liable to imprisonment for a term not exceeding two years; or

    (*b*) is guilty of an offence punishable on summary conviction. 2008, c. 18, s. 42; 2018, c. 29, s. 67; 2019, c. 25, s. 305.

SENTENCE SERVED ACCORDING TO REGULATIONS.

743.3 A sentence of imprisonment shall be served in accordance with the enactments and rules that govern the institution to which the prisoner is sentenced. 1995, c. 22, s. 6.

743.4 [*Repealed*, 2002, c. 1, s. 184.]

TRANSFER OF JURISDICTION WHEN PERSON ALREADY SENTENCED UNDER *YOUTH CRIMINAL JUSTICE ACT* / Transfer of jurisdiction when youth sentence imposed under *Youth Criminal Justice Act* / Sentences deemed to constitute one sentence — section 743.1.

743.5 (1) If a young person or an adult is or has been sentenced to a term of imprisonment for an offence while subject to a disposition made under paragraph 20(1)(*k*) or (*k*.1) of the *Young Offenders Act*, chapter Y-1 of the Revised Statutes of Canada, 1985, or a youth sentence imposed under paragraph 42(2)(*n*), (*o*), (*q*) or (*r*) of the *Youth Criminal Justice Act*, the remaining portion of the disposition or youth sentence shall be dealt with, for all purposes under this Act or any other Act of Parliament, as if it had been a sentence imposed under this Act.

(2) If a disposition is made under paragraph 20(1)(*k*) or (*k*.1) of the *Young Offenders Act*, chapter Y-1 of the Revised Statutes of Canada, 1985, with respect to a person or a youth sentence is imposed on a person under paragraph 42(2)(*n*), (*o*), (*q*) or (*r*) of the *Youth Criminal Justice Act* while the young person or adult is under sentence of imprisonment imposed under an Act of Parliament other than the *Youth Criminal Justice Act*, the disposition or youth sentence shall be dealt with, for all purposes under this Act or any other Act of Parliament, as if it had been a sentence imposed under this Act.

(3) For greater certainty, the following are deemed to constitute one sentence of imprisonment for the purposes of section 139 of the *Corrections and Conditional Release Act*:

    (*a*) for the purposes of subsection (1), the remainder of the youth sentence or disposition and the subsequent term of imprisonment; and

    (*b*) for the purposes of subsection (2), the term of imprisonment and the subsequent youth sentence or disposition. 1995, c. 22, s. 6; 2002, c. 1, s. 184; 2008, c. 18, s. 43.

Eligibility for Parole

POWER OF COURT TO DELAY PAROLE / Principles that are to guide the court.

743.6 (1) Notwithstanding subsection 120(1) of the *Corrections and Conditional Release Act*, where an offender receives, on or after November 1, 1992, a sentence of imprisonment of two years or more, including a sentence of imprisonment for life imposed otherwise than as a minimum punishment, on conviction for an offence set out in Schedules I and II to that Act that was prosecuted by way of indictment, the court may, if satisfied, having regard to the circumstances of the commission of the offence and the character and circumstances of the offender, that the expression of society's denunciation of the offence or the objective of specific or general deterrence so requires, order that the portion of the sentence that must be served before the offender may be released on full parole is one half of the sentence or ten years, whichever is less.

(1.1) Notwithstanding section 120 of the *Corrections and Conditional Release Act*, where an offender receives a sentence of imprisonment of two years or more, including a sentence of imprisonment for life imposed otherwise than as a minimum punishment, on conviction for a criminal organization offence other than an offence under section 467.11, 467.111, 467.12 or 467.13, the court may order that the portion of the sentence that must be served before the offender may be released on full parole is one half of the sentence or ten years, whichever is less.

(1.2) Notwithstanding section 120 of the *Corrections and Conditional Release Act*, where an offender receives a sentence of imprisonment of two years or more, including a sentence of imprisonment for life, on conviction for a terrorism offence or an offence under ss. 467.11, 467.111, 467.12 or 467.13, the court shall order that the portion of the sentence that must be served before the offender may be released on full parole is one half of the sentence or ten years, whichever is less, unless the court is satisfied, having regard to the circumstances of the commission of the offence and the character and circumstances of the offender, that the expression of society's denunciation of the offence and the objectives of specific and general deterrence would be adequately served by a period of parole ineligibility determined in accordance with the *Corrections and Conditional Release Act*.

(2) For greater certainty, the paramount principles which are to guide the court under this section are denunciation and specific or general deterrence, with rehabilitation of the offender, in all cases, being subordinate to those paramount principles. 1995, c. 22, s. 6; 1995, c. 42, s. 86(*b*); 1997, c. 23, s. 18; 2001, c. 32, s. 45; 2001, c. 41, ss. 21, 133(18); 2014, c. 17, ss. 15, 16.

Delivery of Offender to Keeper of Prison

EXECUTION OF WARRANT OF COMMITTAL.

744. A peace officer or other person to whom a warrant of committal authorized by this or any other Act of Parliament is directed shall arrest the person named or described therein, if it is necessary to do so in order to take that person into custody, convey that person to the prison mentioned in the warrant and deliver that person, together with the warrant, to the keeper of the prison who shall thereupon give to the peace officer or other person who delivers the prisoner a receipt in Form 43 setting out the state and condition of the prisoner when delivered into custody. 1995, c. 22, s. 6.

Imprisonment for Life

SENTENCE OF LIFE IMPRISONMENT.

745. Subject to section 745.1, the sentence to be pronounced against a person who is to be sentenced to imprisonment for life shall be

(a) in respect of a person who has been convicted of high treason or first degree murder, that the person be sentenced to imprisonment for life without eligibility for parole until the person has served twenty-five years of the sentence;

(b) in respect of a person who has been convicted of second degree murder where that person has previously been convicted of culpable homicide that is murder, however described in this Act, that that person be sentenced to imprisonment for life without eligibility for parole until the person has served twenty-five years of the sentence;

(b.1) in respect of a person who has been convicted of second degree murder where that person has previously been convicted of an offence under section 4 or 6 of the *Crimes Against Humanity and War Crimes Act* that has as its basis an intentional killing, whether or not it was planned and deliberate, that that person be sentenced to imprisonment for life without eligibility for parole until the person has served twenty-five years of the sentence;

(c) in respect of a person who has been convicted of second degree murder, that the person be sentenced to imprisonment for life without eligibility for parole until the person has served at least ten years of the sentence or such greater number of years, not being more than twenty-five years, as has been substituted therefor pursuant to section 745.4; and

(d) in respect of a person who has been convicted of any other offence, that the person be sentenced to imprisonment for life with normal eligibility for parole. 1995, c. 22, s. 6; 2000, c. 24, s. 46.

INFORMATION IN RESPECT OF PAROLE / Exception.

745.01 (1)Except where subsection 745.6(2) applies, at the time of sentencing under paragraph 745(*a*), (*b*) or (*c*), the judge who presided at the trial of the offender shall state the following, for the record:

The offender has been found guilty of (state offence) and sentenced to imprisonment for life. The offender is not eligible for parole until (state date). However, after serving at least 15 years of the sentence, the offender may apply under section 745.6 of the *Criminal Code* for a reduction in the number of years of imprisonment without eligibility for parole. If the jury hearing the application reduces the period of parole ineligibility, the offender may then make an application for parole under the *Corrections and Conditional Release Act* at the end of that reduced period.

(2) Subsection (1) does not apply if the offender is convicted of an offence committed on or after the day on which this subsection comes into force. 1999, c. 25, s. 21; 2011, c. 2, s. 2.

PERSONS UNDER EIGHTEEN.

745.1 The sentence to be pronounced against a person who was under the age of eighteen at the time of the commission of the offence for which the person was convicted of first degree murder or second degree murder and who is to be sentenced to imprisonment for life shall be that the person be sentenced to imprisonment for life without eligibility for parole until the person has served

- (*a*) such period between five and seven years of the sentence as is specified by the judge presiding at the trial, or if no period is specified by the judge presiding at the trial, five years, in the case of a person who was under the age of sixteen at the time of the commission of the offence;
- (*b*) ten years, in the case of a person convicted of first degree murder who was sixteen or seventeen years of age at the time of the commission of the offence; and
- (*c*) seven years, in the case of a person convicted of second degree murder who was sixteen or seventeen years of age at the time of the commission of the offence. 1995, c. 22, ss. 6, 21.

RECOMMENDATION BY JURY.

745.2 Subject to section 745.3, where a jury finds an accused guilty of second degree murder, the judge presiding at the trial shall, before discharging the jury, put to them the following question:

You have found the accused guilty of second degree murder and the law requires that I now pronounce a sentence of imprisonment for life against the accused. Do you wish to make any recommendation with respect to the number of years that the accused must serve before the accused is eligible for release on parole? You are not required to make any recommendation but if you do, your recommendation will be considered by me when I am determining whether I should substitute for the ten year period, which the law would otherwise require the accused to serve before the accused is eligible to be considered for release on parole, a number of years that is more than ten but not more than twenty-five. 1995, c. 22, s. 6.

RECOMMENDATION BY JURY — MULTIPLE MURDERS / Application.

745.21 (1) Where a jury finds an accused guilty of murder and that accused has previously been convicted of murder, the judge presiding at the trial shall, before discharging the jury, put to them the following question:

> You have found the accused guilty of murder. The law requires that I now pronounce a sentence of imprisonment for life against the accused. Do you wish to make any recommendation with respect to the period without eligibility for parole to be served for this murder consecutively to the period without eligibility for parole imposed for the previous murder? You are not required to make any recommendation, but if you do, your recommendation will be considered by me when I make my determination.

(2) Subsection (1) applies to an offender who is convicted of murders committed on a day after the day on which this section comes into force and for which the offender is sentenced under this Act, the *National Defence Act* or the *Crimes Against Humanity and War Crimes Act.* 2011, c. 5, s. 4.

PERSONS UNDER SIXTEEN.

745.3 Where a jury finds an accused guilty of first degree murder or second degree murder and the accused was under the age of sixteen at the time of the commission of the offence, the judge presiding at the trial shall, before discharging the jury, put to them the following question:

> You have found the accused guilty of first degree murder (or second degree murder) and the law requires that I now pronounce a sentence of imprisonment for life against the accused. Do you wish to make any recommendation with respect to the period of imprisonment that the accused must serve before the accused is eligible for release on parole? You are not required to make any recommendation but if you do, your recommendation will be considered by me when I am determining the period of imprisonment that is between five years and seven years that the law would require the accused to serve before the accused is eligible to be considered for release on parole. 1995, c. 22, ss. 6, 22.

INELIGIBILITY FOR PAROLE.

745.4 Subject to section 745.5, at the time of the sentencing under section 745 of an offender who is convicted of second degree murder, the judge who presided at the trial of the offender or, if that judge is unable to do so, any judge of the same court may, having regard to the character of the offender, the nature of the offence and the circumstances surrounding its commission, and to the recommendation, if any, made pursuant to section 745.2, by order, substitute for ten years a number of years of imprisonment (being more than ten but not more than twenty-five) without eligibility for parole, as the judge deems fit in the circumstances. 1995, c. 22, s. 6.

IDEM.

745.5 At the time of the sentencing under section 745.1 of an offender who is convicted of first degree murder or second degree murder and who was under the age of sixteen at the time of the commission of the offence, the judge who presided at the trial of the offender or, if that judge is unable to do so, any judge of the same court, may, having regard to the age and character of the offender, the nature of the offence and the circumstances surrounding its commission, and to the recommendation, if any, made pursuant to section 745.3, by order, decide the period of imprisonment the offender is to serve that is between five years and seven years without eligibility for parole, as the judge deems fit in the circumstances. 1995, c. 22, s. 6.

INELIGIBILITY FOR PAROLE — MULTIPLE MURDERS / Reasons / Application.

745.51 (1) At the time of the sentencing under section 745 of an offender who is convicted of murder and who has already been convicted of one or more other murders, the judge who presided at the trial of the offender or, if that judge is unable to do so, any judge of the same court may, having regard to the character of the offender, the nature of the offence and the circumstances surrounding its commission, and the recommendation, if any, made pursuant to section 745.21, by order, decide that the periods without eligibility for parole for each murder conviction are to be served consecutively.

(2) The judge shall give, either orally or in writing, reasons for the decision to make or not to make an order under subsection (1).

(3) Subsections (1) and (2) apply to an offender who is convicted of murders committed on a day after the day on which this section comes into force and for which the offender is sentenced under this Act, the *National Defence Act* or the *Crimes Against Humanity and War Crimes Act.* 2011, c. 5, s. 5.

APPLICATION FOR JUDICIAL REVIEW / Exception — multiple murders / Less than 15 years of sentence served / At least 15 years of sentence served / Non-application of subsection (2.2) / Further five-year period if no application made / Subsequent applications / Subsequent applications / Definition of "appropriate Chief Justice".

745.6 (1) Subject to subsections (2) to (2.6), a person may apply, in writing, to the appropriate Chief Justice in the province in which their conviction took place for a reduction in the number of years of imprisonment without eligibility for parole if the person

  (*a*) has been convicted of murder or high treason;

  (*a.*1) committed the murder or high treason before the day on which this paragraph comes into force;

  (*b*) has been sentenced to imprisonment for life without eligibility for parole until more than fifteen years of their sentence has been served; and

  (*c*) has served at least fifteen years of their sentence.

(2) A person who has been convicted of more than one murder may not make an application under subsection (1), whether or not proceedings were commenced in respect of any of the murders before another murder was committed.

(2.1) A person who is convicted of murder or high treason and who has served less than 15 years of their sentence on the day on which this subsection comes into force may, within 90 days after the day on which they have served 15 years of their sentence, make an application under subsection (1).

(2.2) A person who is convicted of murder or high treason and who has served at least 15 years of their sentence on the day on which this subsection comes into force may make an application under subsection (1) within 90 days after

    (*a*) the end of five years after the day on which the person was the subject of a determination made under subsection 745.61(4) or a determination or conclusion to which subsection 745.63(8) applies; or

    (*b*) the day on which this subsection comes into force, if the person has not made an application under subsection (1).

(2.3) Subsection (2.2) has no effect on a determination or decision made under subsection 745.61(3) or (5) or 745.63(3), (5) or (6) as it read immediately before the day on which this subsection comes into force. A person in respect of whom a time is set under paragraph 745.61(3)(*a*) or 745.63(6)(*a*) as it read immediately before that day may make an application under subsection (1) within 90 days after the end of that time.

(2.4) If the person does not make an application in accordance with subsection (2.1), (2.2) or (2.3), as the case may be, they may make an application within 90 days after the day on which they have served a further five years of their sentence following the 90-day period referred to in that subsection, as the case may be.

(2.5) A person who makes an application in accordance with subsection (2.1), (2.2) or (2.3), as the case may be, may make another application under subsection (1) within 90 days after

    (*a*) the end of the time set under paragraph 745.61(3)(*a*) or 745.63(6)(*a*), if a time is set under that paragraph; or

    (*b*) the end of five years after the day on which the person is the subject of a determination made under subsection 745.61(4) or a determination or conclusion to which subsection 745.63(8) applies, if the person is the subject of such a determination or conclusion.

(2.6) A person who had made an application under subsection (1) as it read immediately before the day on which this subsection comes into force, whose application was finally disposed of on or after that day and who has then made a subsequent application may make a further application in accordance with subsection (2.5), if either paragraph (2.5)(*a*) or (*b*) is applicable.

(2.7) The 90-day time limits for the making of any application referred to in subsections (2.1) to (2.5) may be extended by the appropriate Chief Justice, or his or her designate, to a maximum of 180 days if the person, due to circumstances beyond their control, is unable to make an application within the 90-day time limit.

(2.8) If a person convicted of murder does not make an application under subsection (1) within the maximum time period allowed by this section, the Commissioner of Correctional Service Canada, or his or her designate, shall immediately notify in writing a parent, child, spouse or common-law partner of the victim that the convicted person did not make an application. If it is not possible to notify one of the aforementioned relatives, then the notification shall be given to another relative of the victim. The notification shall specify the next date on which the convicted person will be eligible to make an application under subsection (1).

(3) For the purposes of this section and sections 745.61 to 745.64, the "appropriate Chief Justice" is

    (a) in relation to the Province of Ontario, the Chief Justice of the Ontario Court;

    (b) in relation to the Province of Quebec, the Chief Justice of the Superior Court;

    (c) in relation to the Province of Newfoundland and Labrador, the Chief Justice of the Supreme Court, Trial Division;

    (d) in relation to the Provinces of New Brunswick, Manitoba, Saskatchewan and Alberta, the Chief Justice of the Court of Queen's Bench;

    (e) in relation to the Provinces of Nova Scotia, British Columbia and Prince Edward Island, the Chief Justice of the Supreme Court; and

    (f) in relation to Yukon, the Northwest Territories and Nunavut, the Chief Justice of the Court of Appeal. 1993, c. 28, Sch. III, s. 35; 1995, c. 22, s. 6; 1996, c. 34, s. 2(2); 2002, c. 7, s. 146; 2011, c. 2, s. 3; 2015, c. 3, s. 55.

JUDICIAL SCREENING / Criteria / Decision re new application / If no decision re new application / Designation of judge to empanel jury.

745.61 (1) On receipt of an application under subsection 745.6(1), the appropriate Chief Justice shall determine, or shall designate a judge of the superior court of criminal jurisdiction to determine, on the basis of the following written material, whether the applicant has shown, on a balance of probabilities, that there is a substantial likelihood that the application will succeed:

    (a) the application;

    (b) any report provided by the Correctional Service of Canada or other correctional authorities; and

    (c) any other written evidence presented to the Chief Justice or judge by the applicant or the Attorney General.

(2) In determining whether the applicant has shown that there is a substantial likelihood that the application will succeed, the Chief Justice or judge shall consider the criteria set out in paragraphs 745.63(1)(a) to (e), with any modifications that the circumstances require.

(3) If the Chief Justice or judge determines that the applicant has not shown that there is a substantial likelihood that the application will succeed, the Chief Justice or judge may

   (*a*) set a time, no earlier than five years after the date of the determination, at or after which the applicant may make another application under subsection 745.6(1); or

   (*b*) decide that the applicant may not make another application under that subsection.

(4) If the Chief Justice or judge determines that the applicant has not shown that there is a substantial likelihood that the application will succeed but does not set a time for another application or decide that such an application may not be made, the applicant may make another application no earlier than five years after the date of the determination.

(5) If the Chief Justice or judge determines that the applicant has shown that there is a substantial likelihood that the application will succeed, the Chief Justice shall designate a judge of the superior court of criminal jurisdiction to empanel a jury to hear the application. 1995, c. 22, s. 6; 1996, c. 34, s. 2(2); 2011, c. 2, s. 4.

APPEAL / Documents to be considered / Sections to apply.

745.62 (1) The applicant or the Attorney General may appeal to the Court of Appeal from a determination or a decision made under section 745.61 on any question of law or fact or mixed law and fact.

(2) The appeal shall be determined on the basis of the documents presented to the Chief Justice or judge who made the determination or decision, any reasons for the determination or decision and any other documents that the Court of Appeal requires.

(3) Sections 673 to 696 apply, with such modifications as the circumstances require. 1995, c. 22, s. 6; 1996, c. 34, s. 2(2).

HEARING OF APPLICATION / Information provided by victim / Definition of "victim" / Reduction / No reduction / Where determination to reduce number of years / Decision re new application / Two-thirds decision / If no decision re new application.

745.63 (1) The jury empanelled under subsection 745.61(5) to hear the application shall consider the following criteria and determine whether the applicant's number of years of imprisonment without eligibility for parole ought to be reduced:

   (*a*) the character of the applicant;

   (*b*) the applicant's conduct while serving the sentence;

   (*c*) the nature of the offence for which the applicant was convicted;

   (*d*) any information provided by a victim at the time of the imposition of the sentence or at the time of the hearing under this section; and

   (*e*) any other matters that the judge considers relevant in the circumstances.

(1.1) Information provided by a victim referred to in paragraph (1)(*d*) may be provided either orally or in writing, at the discretion of the victim, or in any other manner that the judge considers appropriate.

(2) [*Repealed*, 2015, c. 13, s. 34.]

(3) The jury hearing an application under subsection (1) may determine that the applicant's number of years of imprisonment without eligibility for parole ought to be reduced. The determination to reduce the number of years must be by unanimous vote.

(4) The applicant's number of years of imprisonment without eligibility for parole is not reduced if

- (*a*) the jury hearing an application under subsection (1) determines that the number of years ought not to be reduced;
- (*b*) the jury hearing an application under subsection (1) concludes that it cannot unanimously determine that the number of years ought to be reduced; or
- (*c*) the presiding judge, after the jury has deliberated for a reasonable period, concludes that the jury is unable to unanimously determine that the number of years ought to be reduced.

(5) If the jury determines that the number of years of imprisonment without eligibility for parole ought to be reduced, the jury may, by a vote of not less than two thirds of the members of the jury,

- (*a*) substitute a lesser number of years of imprisonment without eligibility for parole than that then applicable; or
- (*b*) terminate the ineligibility for parole.

(6) If the applicant's number of years of imprisonment without eligibility for parole is not reduced, the jury may

- (*a*) set a time, no earlier than five years after the date of the determination or conclusion under subsection (4), at or after which the applicant may make another application under subsection 745.6(1); or
- (*b*) decide that the applicant may not make another application under that subsection.

(7) The decision of the jury under paragraph (6)(*a*) or (*b*) must be made by not less than two thirds of its members.

(8) If the jury does not set a date on or after which another application may be made or decide that such an application may not be made, the applicant may make another application no earlier than five years after the date of the determination or conclusion under subsection (4). 1996, c. 34, s. 2(2); 1999, c. 25, s. 22; 2011, c. 2, s. 5; 2015, c. 13, s. 34.

RULES / *Statutory Instruments Act* / Territories.

745.64 (1) The appropriate Chief Justice in each province or territory may make such rules as are required for the purposes of sections 745.6 to 745.63.

(1.1) The *Statutory Instruments Act* does not apply to those rules.

(2) When the appropriate Chief Justice is designating a judge of the superior court of criminal jurisdiction, for the purpose of a judicial screening under subsection 745.61(1) or to empanel a jury to hear an application under subsection 745.61(5), in respect of a conviction that took place in Yukon, the Northwest Territories or Nunavut, the appropriate Chief Justice may designate the judge from the Court of

Appeal of Yukon, the Northwest Territories or Nunavut, or the Supreme Court of Yukon or the Northwest Territories or the Nunavut Court of Justice, as the case may be. 1993, c. 28, Sch. III, s. 35.1 (repealed 1999, c. 3, s. 12); 1996, c. 34, s. 2(2); 1999, c. 3, ss. 12, 53; 2002, c. 7, s. 147; 2019, c. 25, s. 306.

TIME SPENT IN CUSTODY.

746. In calculating the period of imprisonment served for the purposes of section 745, 745.1, 745.4, 745.5 or 745.6, there shall be included any time spent in custody between

(a) in the case of a sentence of imprisonment for life after July 25, 1976, the day on which the person was arrested and taken into custody in respect of the offence
for which that person was sentenced to imprisonment for life and the day the sentence was imposed; or

(b) in the case of a sentence of death that has been or is deemed to have been commuted to a sentence of imprisonment for life, the day on which the person was arrested and taken into custody in respect of the offence for which that person was sentenced to death and the day the sentence was commuted or deemed to have been commuted to a sentence of imprisonment for life. 1995, c. 22, s. 6.

PAROLE PROHIBITED / Absence with or without escort and day parole / Young offenders.

746.1 (1) Unless Parliament otherwise provides by an enactment making express reference to this section, a person who has been sentenced to imprisonment for life without eligibility for parole for a specified number of years pursuant to this Act shall not be considered for parole or released pursuant to a grant of parole under the *Corrections and Conditional Release Act* or any other Act of Parliament until the expiration or termination of the specified number of years of imprisonment.

(2) Subject to subsection (3), in respect of a person sentenced to imprisonment for life without eligibility for parole for a specified number of years pursuant to this Act, until the expiration of all but three years of the specified number of years of imprisonment,

(a) no day parole may be granted under the *Corrections and Conditional Release Act*;

(b) no absence without escort may be authorized under that Act or the *Prisons and Reformatories Act*; and

(c) except with the approval of the Parole Board of Canada, no absence with escort otherwise than for medical reasons or in order to attend judicial proceedings or a coroner's inquest may be authorized under either of those Acts.

(3) In the case of any person convicted of first degree murder or second degree murder who was under the age of eighteen at the time of the commission of the offence and who is sentenced to imprisonment for life without eligibility for parole for a specified number of years pursuant to this Act, until the expiration of

all but one fifth of the period of imprisonment the person is to serve without eligibility for parole,

   (*a*) no day parole may be granted under the *Corrections and Conditional Release Act*;

   (*b*) no absence without excort may be authorized under that Act or the *Prisons and Reformatories Act*; and

   (*c*) except with the approval of the Parole Board of Canada, no absence with escort otherwise than for medical reasons or in order to attend judicial proceedings or a coroner's inquest may be authorized under either of those Acts. 1995, c. 22, s. 6; 1995, c. 42, s. 87; 1997 c. 17, s. 2; 2012, c. 1, s. 160(*c*)(iii).

---

747. [*Repealed*, 1995, c. 22, s. 6.]

Note: Sections 747 to 747.8, with heading, as enacted by 1995, c. 22, s. 6, have never been brought into force and have since been repealed by 2005, c. 22, s. 39.

Pardons and Remissions

TO WHOM PARDON MAY BE GRANTED / Free or conditional pardon / Effect of free pardon / Punishment for subsequent offence not affected.

748. (1) Her Majesty may extend the royal mercy to a person who is sentenced to imprisonment under the authority of an Act of Parliament, even if the person is imprisoned for failure to pay money to another person.

(2) The Governor in Council may grant a free pardon or a conditional pardon to any person who has been convicted of an offence.

(3) Where the Governor in Council grants a free pardon to a person, that person shall be deemed thereafter never to have committed the offence in respect of which the pardon is granted.

(4) No free pardon or conditional pardon prevents or mitigates the punishment to which the person might otherwise be lawfully sentenced on a subsequent conviction for an offence other than that for which the pardon was granted. 1995, c. 22, s. 6.

REMISSION BY GOVERNOR IN COUNCIL / Terms of remission.

748.1 (1) The Governor in Council may order the remission, in whole or in part, of a fine or forfeiture imposed under an Act of Parliament, whoever the person may be to whom it is payable or however it may be recoverable.

(2) An order for remission under subsection (1) may include the remission of costs incurred in the proceedings, but no costs to which a private prosecutor is entitled shall be remitted. 1995, c. 22, s. 6.

ROYAL PREROGATIVE.

749. Nothing in this Act in any manner limits or affects Her Majesty's royal prerogative of mercy. 1995, c. 22, s. 6.

Disabilities

PUBLIC OFFICE VACATED FOR CONVICTION / When disability ceases / Disability to contract / Application for restoration of privileges / Order of restoration / Removal of disability.

750. (1) Where a person is convicted of an indictable offence for which the person is sentenced to imprisonment for two years or more and holds, at the time that person is convicted, an office under the Crown or other public employment, the office or employment forthwith becomes vacant.

(2) A person to whom subsection (1) applies is, until undergoing the punishment imposed on the person or the punishment substituted therefor for competent authority or receives a free pardon from Her Majesty, incapable of holding any office under the Crown or other public employment, or of being elected or sitting or voting as a member of Parliament or of a legislature or of exercising any right of suffrage.

(3) No person who is convicted of

    (*a*) an offence under section 121, 124 or 418,

    (*b*) an offence under section 380 committed against Her Majesty, or

    (*c*) an offence under paragraph 80(1)(*d*), subsection 80(2) or section 154.01 of the *Financial Administration Act*,

has, after that conviction, capacity to contract with Her Majesty or to receive any benefit under a contract between Her Majesty and any other person or to hold office under Her Majesty.

(4) A person to whom subsection (3) applies may, at any time before a record suspension for which he or she has applied is ordered under the *Criminal Records Act*, apply to the Governor in Council for the restoration of one or more of the capacities lost by the person by virtue of that subsection.

(5) Where an application is made under subsection (4), the Governor in Council may order that the capacities lost by the applicant by virtue of subsection (3) be restored to that applicant in whole or in part and subject to such conditions as the Governor in Council considers desirable in the public interest.

(6) Where a conviction is set aside by competent authority, any disability imposed by this section is removed. 1995, c. 22, s. 6; 2000, c. 1, s. 9; 2006, c. 9, s. 246; 2012, c. 1, s. 146.

Miscellaneous Provisions

COSTS TO SUCCESSFUL PARTY IN CASE OF LIBEL.

751. The person in whose favour judgment is given in proceedings by indictment for defamatory libel is entitled to recover from the opposite party costs in a reasonable amount to be fixed by order of the court. 1995, c. 22, s. 6.

HOW RECOVERED.

751.1 Where costs that are fixed under section 751 are not paid forthwith, the party in whose favour judgment is given may enter judgment for the amount of the costs by filing the order in any civil court of the province in which the trial was held that has jurisdiction to enter a judgment for that amount, and that judgment is enforceable against the opposite party in the same manner as if it were a judgment rendered against that opposite party in that court in civil proceedings. 1995, c. 22, s. 6.

Part XXIV / DANGEROUS OFFENDERS AND LONG-TERM OFFENDERS
1997, c. 17, s. 3.

Interpretation

DEFINITIONS / "court" / "designated offence" / "long-term supervision" / "primary designated offence" / "serious personal injury offence".

752. In this Part,

"court" means the court by which an offender in relation to whom an application under this Part is made was convicted, or a superior court of criminal jurisdiction;

"designated offence" means

   (a) a primary designated offence,

   (b) an offence under any of the following provisions:

      (i) paragraph 81(1)(*a*) (using explosives),

     (ii) paragraph 81(1)(*b*) (using explosives),

    (iii) section 85 (using firearm or imitation firearm in commission of offence),

     (iv) section 87 (pointing firearm),

   (iv.1) section 98 (breaking and entering to steal firearm),

   (iv.2) section 98.1 (robbery to steal firearm),

     (v) section 153.1 (sexual exploitation of person with disability),

    (vi) section 163.1 (child pornography),

   (vii) section 170 (parent or guardian procuring sexual activity),

  (viii) section 171 (householder permitting sexual activity by or in presence of child),

   (ix) section 172.1 (luring child),

CODE

(ix.1) section 172.2 (agreement or arrangement — sexual offence against child),

(x) [*Repealed*, 2014, c. 25, s. 29(1).]

(x.1) [*Repealed*, 2014, c. 25, s. 29(1).]

(xi) [*Repealed*, 2014, c. 25, s. 29(1).]

(xii) [*Repealed*, 2014, c. 25, s. 29(1).]

(xiii) section 245 (administering noxious thing),

(xiv) section 266 (assault),

(xv) section 269 (unlawfully causing bodily harm),

(xvi) section 269.1 (torture),

(xvii) paragraph 270(1)(*a*) (assaulting peace officer),

(xviii) section 273.3 (removal of child from Canada),

(xix) subsection 279(2) (forcible confinement),

(xx) section 279.01 (trafficking in persons),

(xx.1) section 279.011 (trafficking of a person under the age of eighteen years),

(xx.2) section 279.02 (material benefit — trafficking),

(xx.3) section 279.03 (withholding or destroying documents — trafficking),

(xxi) section 279.1 (hostage taking),

(xxii) section 280 (abduction of person under age of 16),

(xxiii) section 281 (abduction of person under age of 14),

(xxiii.1) subsection 286.1(2) (obtaining sexual services for consideration from person under 18 years),

(xxiii.2) section 286.2 (material benefit from sexual services),

(xxiii.3) section 286.3 (procuring),

(xxiii.4) section 320.13 (dangerous operation),

(xxiii.5) subsections 320.14(1), (2) and (3) (operation while impaired),

(xxiii.6) section 320.15 (failure or refusal to comply with demand),

(xxiii.7) section 320.16 (failure to stop after accident),

(xxiii.8) section 320.17 (flight from peace officer),

(xxiv) section 344 (robbery), and

(xxv) section 348 (breaking and entering with intent, committing offence or breaking out),

(*c*) an offence under any of the following provisions of the *Criminal Code*, chapter C-34 of the Revised Statutes of Canada, 1970, as they read from time to time before January 1, 1988:

(i) subsection 146(2) (sexual intercourse with female between ages of 14 and 16),

(ii) section 148 (sexual intercourse with feeble-minded),

(iii) section 166 (parent or guardian procuring defilement), and

(iv) section 167 (householder permitting defilement),

(*c*.1) an offence under any of the following provisions of this Act, as they read from time to time before the day on which this paragraph comes into force:

(i) subsection 212(1) (procuring),

(ii) subsection 212(2) (living on the avails of prostitution of person under 18 years),

(iii) subsection 212(2.1) (aggravated offence in relation to living on the avails of prostitution of person under 18 years), and

(iv) subsection 212(4) (prostitution of person under 18 years); or

(d) an attempt or conspiracy to commit an offence referred to in paragraph (b), (c) or (c.1);

"long-term supervision" means long-term supervision ordered under subsection 753(4), 753.01(5) or (6) or 753.1(3) or subparagraph 759(3)(a)(i);

"primary designated offence" means

(a) an offence under any of the following provisions:

   (i)   section 151 (sexual interference),

   (ii)   section 152 (invitation to sexual touching),

   (iii) section 153 (sexual exploitation),

   (iv)   section 155 (incest),

   (v)   section 239 (attempt to commit murder),

   (vi)   section 244 (discharging firearm with intent),

  (vii) section 267 (assault with weapon or causing bodily harm),

 (viii) section 268 (aggravated assault),

   (ix)   section 271 (sexual assault),

   (x)   section 272 (sexual assault with weapon, threats to third party or causing bodily harm),

  (xi)   section 273 (aggravated sexual assault), and

  (xii) subsection 279(1) (kidnapping),

(b) an offence under any of the following provisions of the *Criminal Code*, chapter C-34 of the Revised Statutes of Canada, 1970, as they read from time to time before January 4, 1983:

   (i)   section 144 (rape),

   (ii)   section 145 (attempt to commit rape),

   (iii) section 149 (indecent assault on female),

   (iv)   section 156 (indecent assault on male),

   (v)   subsection 245(2) (assault causing bodily harm), and

   (vi)   subsection 246(1) (assault with intent) if the intent is to commit an offence referred to in any of subparagraphs (i) to (v) of this paragraph,

(c) an offence under any of the following provisions of the *Criminal Code*, chapter C-34 of the Revised Statutes of Canada, 1970, as enacted by section 19 of *An Act to amend the Criminal Code in relation to sexual offences and other offences against the person and to amend certain other Acts in relation thereto or in consequence thereof*, chapter 125 of the Statutes of Canada, 1980-81-82-83:

   (i)   section 246.1 (sexual assault),

   (ii)   section 246.2 (sexual assault with weapon, threats to third party or causing bodily harm), and

   (iii) section 246.3 (aggravated sexual assault),

(d) an offence under any of the following provisions of the *Criminal Code*, chapter C-34 of the Revised Statutes of Canada, 1970, as they read from time to time before January 1, 1988:

   (i)   subsection 146(1) (sexual intercourse with female under age of 14), and

   (ii)   paragraph 153(1)(a) (sexual intercourse with step-daughter), or (*e*) an attempt or conspiracy to commit an offence referred to in any of paragraphs (*a*) to (*d*);

"serious personal injury offence" means

(*a*) an indictable offence, other than high treason, treason, first degree murder or second degree murder, involving

    (i) the use or attempted use of violence against another person, or

    (ii) conduct endangering or likely to endanger the life or safety of another person or inflicting or likely to inflict severe psychological damage on another person,

and for which the offender may be sentenced to imprisonment for ten years or more, or

(*b*) an offence or attempt to commit an offence mentioned in section 271 (sexual assault), 272 (sexual assault with a weapon, threats to a third party or causing bodily harm) or 273 (aggravated sexual assault). R.S., c. C-34, s. 687; 1976-77, c. 53, s. 14; 1980-81-82-83, c. 125, s. 26; 2008, c. 6, s. 40; 2012, c. 1, s. 35; 2014, c. 25, s. 29; 2018, c. 21, s. 25.

Note: By virtue of s. 179(1)(*b*) of the *Criminal Code*, as re-enacted by R.S.C. 1985, c. 27 (1st Supp.), s. 22, proclaimed in force December 4, 1985, para. (*b*) of the above definition, as it read immediately before January 4, 1983 (the date upon which 1980-81-82, c. 125, s. 26 came into force, amending para. (*b*)) is now relevant to determining whether the offence of vagrancy has been committed. The text of para. (*b*), as it read immediately before January 4, 1983, is as follows:

"(*b*) an offence mentioned in section 144 (rape) or 145 (attempted rape) or an offence or attempt to commit an offence mentioned in section 146 (sexual intercourse with a female under fourteen or between fourteen and sixteen), 149 (indecent assault on a female), 156 (indecent assault on a male) or 157 (gross indecency)."

PROSECUTOR'S DUTY TO ADVISE COURT.

752.01 If the prosecutor is of the opinion that an offence for which an offender is convicted is a serious personal injury offence that is a designated offence and that the offender was convicted previously at least twice of a designated offence and was sentenced to at least two years of imprisonment for each of those convictions, the prosecutor shall advise the court, as soon as feasible after the finding of guilt and in any event before sentence is imposed, whether the prosecutor intends to make an application under subsection 752.1(1). 2008, c. 6, s. 41.

APPLICATION FOR REMAND FOR ASSESSMENT / Report / Extension of time.

752.1 (1) On application by the prosecutor, if the court is of the opinion that there are reasonable grounds to believe that an offender who is convicted of a serious personal injury offence or an offence referred to in paragraph 753.1(2)(*a*) might be found to be a dangerous offender under section 753 or a long-term offender under section 753.1, the court shall, by order in writing, before sentence is imposed, remand the offender, for a period not exceeding 60 days, to the custody of a person designated by the court who can perform an assessment or have an assessment

779

performed by experts for use as evidence in an application under section 753 or 753.1.

(2) The person to whom the offender is remanded shall file a report of the assessment with the court not later than 30 days after the end of the assessment period and make copies of it available to the prosecutor and counsel for the offender.

(3) On application by the prosecutor, the court may extend the period within which the report must be filed by a maximum of 30 days if the court is satisfied that there are reasonable grounds to do so. 1997, c. 17, s. 4; 2008, c. 6, s. 41.

APPLICATION FOR FINDING THAT AN OFFENDER IS A DANGEROUS OFFENDER / Presumption / Time for making application / Application for remand for assessment after imposition of sentence / If offender found to be dangerous offender / Sentence for dangerous offender / If application made after sentencing / If offender not found to be dangerous offender.

753. (1) On application made under this Part after an assessment report is filed under subsection 752.1(2), the court shall find the offender to be a dangerous offender if it is satisfied

(a) that the offence for which the offender has been convicted is a serious personal injury offence described in paragraph (a) of the definition of that expression in section 752 and the offender constitutes a threat to the life, safety or physical or mental well-being of other persons on the basis of evidence establishing

  (i) a pattern of repetitive behaviour by the offender, of which the offence for which he or she has been convicted forms a part, showing a failure to restrain his or her behaviour and a likelihood of causing death or injury to other persons, or inflicting severe psychological damage on other persons, through failure in the future to restrain his or her behaviour,

  (ii) a pattern of persistent aggressive behaviour by the offender, of which the offence for which he or she has been convicted forms a part, showing a substantial degree of indifference on the part of the offender respecting the reasonably foreseeable consequences to other persons of his or her behaviour, or

  (iii) any behaviour by the offender, associated with the offence for which he or she has been convicted, that is of such a brutal nature as to compel the conclusion that the offender's behaviour in the future is unlikely to be inhibited by normal standards of behavioural restraint; or

(b) that the offence for which the offender has been convicted is a serious personal injury offence described in paragraph (b) of the definition of that expression in section 752 and the offender, by his or her conduct in any sexual matter including that involved in the commission of the offence for which he or she has been convicted, has shown a failure to control his or her sexual impulses and a likelihood of causing injury, pain or other evil to other persons through failure in the future to control his or her sexual impulses.

(1.1) If the court is satisfied that the offence for which the offender is convicted is a primary designated offence for which it would be appropriate to impose a sentence of imprisonment of two years or more and that the offender was convicted previously at least twice of a primary designated offence and was sentenced to at least two years of imprisonment for each of those convictions, the conditions in paragraph (1)(*a*) or (*b*), as the case may be, are presumed to have been met unless the contrary is proved on a balance of probabilities.

(2) An application under subsection (1) must be made before sentence is imposed on the offender unless

  (*a*) before the imposition of sentence, the prosecutor gives notice to the offender of a possible intention to make an application under section 752.1 and an application under subsection (1) not later than six months after that imposition; and

  (*b*) at the time of the application under subsection (1) that is not later than six months after the imposition of sentence, it is shown that relevant evidence that was not reasonably available to the prosecutor at the time of the imposition of sentence became available in the interim.

(3) Notwithstanding subsection 752.1(1), an application under that subsection may be made after the imposition of sentence or after an offender begins to serve the sentence in a case to which paragraphs (2)(*a*) and (*b*) apply.

(4) If the court finds an offender to be a dangerous offender, it shall

  (*a*) impose a sentence of detention in a penitentiary for an indeterminate period;

  (*b*) impose a sentence for the offence for which the offender has been convicted — which must be a minimum punishment of imprisonment for a term of two years — and order that the offender be subject to long-term supervision for a period that does not exceed 10 years; or

  (*c*) impose a sentence for the offence for which the offender has been convicted.

(4.1) The court shall impose a sentence of detention in a penitentiary for an indeterminate period unless it is satisfied by the evidence adduced during the hearing of the application that there is a reasonable expectation that a lesser measure under paragraph (4)(*b*) or (*c*) will adequately protect the public against the commission by the offender of murder or a serious personal injury offence.

(4.2) If the application is made after the offender begins to serve the sentence in a case to which paragraphs (2)(*a*) and (*b*) apply, a sentence imposed under paragraph (4)(*a*), or a sentence imposed and an order made under paragraph 4(*b*), replaces the sentence that was imposed for the offence for which the offender was convicted.

(5) If the court does not find an offender to be a dangerous offender,

  (*a*) the court may treat the application as an application to find the offender to be a long-term offender, section 753.1 applies to the application and the court may either find that the offender is a long-term offender or hold another hearing for that purpose; or

(b) the court may impose sentence for the offence for which the offender has been convicted. R.S., c. C-34, s. 688; 1976-77, c. 53, s. 14; 1997, c. 17, s. 4; 2008, c. 6, s. 42.

(6) [*Repealed*, 2008, c. 6, s. 42(5).]

APPLICATION FOR REMAND FOR ASSESSMENT — LATER CONVICTION / Report / Extension of time / Application for new sentence or order / Sentence of indeterminate detention / New long-term supervision

753.01 (1) If an offender who is found to be a dangerous offender is later convicted of a serious personal injury offence or an offence under subsection 753.3(1), on application by the prosecutor, the court shall, by order in writing, before sentence is imposed, remand the offender, for a period not exceeding 60 days, to the custody of a person designated by the court who can perform an assessment or have an assessment performed by experts for use as evidence in an application under subsection (4).

(2) The person to whom the offender is remanded shall file a report of the assessment with the court not later than 30 days after the end of the assessment period and make copies of it available to the prosecutor and counsel for the offender.

(3) On application by the prosecutor, the court may extend the period within which the report must be filed by a maximum of 30 days if the court is satisfied that there are reasonable grounds to do so.

(4) After the report is filed, the prosecutor may apply for a sentence of detention in a penitentiary for an indeterminate period, or for an order that the offender be subject to a new period of long-term supervision in addition to any other sentence that may be imposed for the offence.

(5) If the application is for a sentence of detention in a penitentiary for an indeterminate period, the court shall impose that sentence unless it is satisfied by the evidence adduced during the hearing of the application that there is a reasonable expectation that a sentence for the offence for which the offender has been convicted — with or without a new period of long-term supervision — will adequately protect the public against the commission by the offender of murder or a serious personal injury offence.

(6) If the application is for a new period of long-term supervision, the court shall order that the offender be subject to a new period of long-term supervision in addition to a sentence for the offence for which they have been convicted unless it is satisfied by the evidence adduced during the hearing of the application that there is a reasonable expectation that the sentence alone will adequately protect the public against the commission by the offender of murder or a serious personal injury offence. 2008, c. 6, s. 43.

VICTIM EVIDENCE.

753.02 Any evidence given during the hearing of an application made under subsection 753(1) by a victim of an offence for which the offender was convicted is deemed also to have been given during any hearing held with respect to the offender under paragraph 753(5)(*a*) or subsection 753.01(5) or (6). 2008, c. 6, s. 43.

APPLICATION FOR FINDING THAT AN OFFENDER IS A LONG-TERM OFFENDER / Substantial risk / Sentence for long-term offender / Exception — if application made after sentencing / If offender not found to be long-term offender.

753.1 (1) The court may, on application made under this Part following the filing of an assessment report under subsection 752.1(2), find an offender to be a long-term offender if it is satisfied that

    (*a*) it would be appropriate to impose a sentence of imprisonment of two years or more for the offence for which the offender has been convicted;

    (*b*) there is a substantial risk that the offender will reoffend; and

    (*c*) there is a reasonable possibility of eventual control of the risk in the community.

(2) The court shall be satisfied that there is a substantial risk that the offender will reoffend if

    (*a*) the offender has been convicted of an offence under section 151 (sexual interference), 152 (invitation to sexual touching) or 153 (sexual exploitation), subsection 163.1(2) (making child pornography), 163.1(3) (distribution, etc., of child pornography), 163.1(4) (possession of child pornography) or 163.1(4.1) (accessing child pornography), section 170 (parent or guardian procuring sexual activity), 171 (householder permitting sexual activity), 171.1 (making sexually explicit material available to child), 172.1 (luring a child) or 172.2 (agreement or arrangement — sexual offence against child), subsection 173(2) (exposure) or section 271 (sexual assault), 272 (sexual assault with a weapon) 273 (aggravated sexual assault) or 279.011 (trafficking — person under 18 years) or subsection 279.02(2) (material benefit — trafficking of person under 18 years), 279.03(2) (withholding or destroying documents — trafficking of person under 18 years), 286.1(2) (obtaining sexual services for consideration from person under 18 years), 286.2(2) (material benefit from sexual services provided by person under 18 years) or 286.3(2) (procuring — person under 18 years), or has engaged in serious conduct of a sexual nature in the commission of another offence of which the offender has been convicted; and

    (*b*) the offender

        (i) has shown a pattern of repetitive behaviour, of which the offence for which he or she has been convicted forms a part, that shows a likelihood of the offender's causing death or injury to other persons or inflicting severe psychological damage on other persons, or

CODE

    (ii) by conduct in any sexual matter including that involved in the commission of the offence for which the offender has been convicted, has shown a likelihood of causing injury, pain or other evil to other persons in the future through similar offences.

(3) If the court finds an offender to be a long-term offender, it shall

    (*a*) impose a sentence for the offence for which the offender has been convicted, which must be a minimum punishment of imprisonment for a term of two years; and

    (*b*) order that the offender be subject to long-term supervision for a period that does not exceed 10 years.

(3.1) The court may not impose a sentence under paragraph (3)(*a*) and the sentence that was imposed for the offence for which the offender was convicted stands despite the offender's being found to be a long-term offender, if the application was one that

    (*a*) was made after the offender begins to serve the sentence in a case to which paragraphs 753(2)(*a*) and (*b*) apply; and

    (*b*) was treated as an application under this section further to the court deciding to do so under paragraph 753(5)(*a*).

(4) and (5) [*Repealed*, 2008, c. 6, s. 44(2).]

(6) If the court does not find an offender to be a long-term offender, the court shall impose sentence for the offence for which the offender has been convicted. 1997, c. 17, s. 4; 2002, c. 13, s. 76; 2006, c. 6, s. 44; 2012, c. 1, s. 36; 2014, c. 25, s. 30.

LONG-TERM SUPERVISION / Sentence served concurrently with supervision / Application for reduction in period of long-term supervision.

753.2 (1) Subject to subsection (2), an offender who is subject to long-term supervision shall be supervised in the community in accordance with the *Corrections and Conditional Release Act* when the offender has finished serving

    (*a*) the sentence for the offence for which the offender has been convicted; and

    (*b*) all other sentences for offences for which the offender is convicted and for which sentence of a term of imprisonment is imposed on the offender, either before or after the conviction for the offence referred to in paragraph (*a*).

(2) A sentence imposed on an offender referred to in subsection (1), other than a sentence that requires imprisonment, is to be served concurrently with the long-term supervision.

(3) An offender who is required to be supervised, a member of the Parole Board of Canada or, on approval of that Board, the offender's parole supervisor, as defined in subsection 99(1) of the *Corrections and Conditional Release Act*, may apply to a superior court of criminal jurisdiction for an order reducing the period of long-term supervision or terminating it on the ground that the offender no longer presents a substantial risk of reoffending and thereby being a danger to the community. The onus of proving that ground is on the applicant.

(4) The applicant must give notice of an application under subsection (3) to the Attorney General at the time the application is made. 1997, c. 17, s. 4; 2008, c. 6, s. 45; 2012, c. 1, s. 147; 2012, c. 1, s. 160(*c*)(iv).

BREACH OF LONG-TERM SUPERVISION / Where accused may be tried and punished.

753.3 (1) An offender who, without reasonable excuse, fails or refuses to comply with long-term supervision is guilty of

(*a*) an indictable offence and liable to imprisonment for a term of not more than 10 years; or

(*b*) an offence punishable on summary conviction.

(2) An accused who is charged with an offence under subsection (1) may be tried and punished by any court having jurisdiction to try that offence in the place where the offence is alleged to have been committed or in the place where the accused is found, is arrested or is in custody, but if the place where the accused is found, is arrested or is in custody is outside the province in which the offence is alleged to have been committed, no proceedings in respect of that offence shall be instituted in that place without the consent of the Attorney General of that province. 1997, c. 17, s. 4; 2008, c. 6, s. 46; 2019, c. 25, s. 307.

NEW OFFENCE / Reduction in term of long-term supervision.

753.4 (1) If an offender who is subject to long-term supervision commits one or more offences under this or any other Act and a court imposes a sentence of imprisonment for the offence or offences, the long-term supervision is interrupted until the offender has finished serving all the sentences, unless the court orders its termination.

(2) A court that imposes a sentence of imprisonment under subsection (1) may order a reduction in the length of the period of the offender's long-term supervision. 1997, c. 17, s. 4; 2008, c. 6, s. 47.

HEARING OF APPLICATION / By court alone / When proof unnecessary / Proof of consent.

754. (1) With the exception of an application for remand for assessment, the court may not hear an application made under this Part unless

(*a*) the Attorney General of the province in which the offender was tried has, either before or after the making of the application, consented to the application;

(*b*) at least seven days notice has been given to the offender by the prosecutor, following the making of the application, outlining the basis on which it is intended to found the application; and

(*c*) a copy of the notice has been filed with the clerk of the court or the provincial court judge, as the case may be.

(2) An application under this Part shall be heard and determined by the court without a jury.

(3) For the purposes of an application under this Part, where an offender admits any allegations contained in the notice referred to in paragraph (1)(*b*), no proof of those allegations is required.

(4) The production of a document purporting to contain any nomination or consent that may be made or given by the Attorney General under this Part and purporting to be signed by the Attorney General is, in the absence of any evidence to the contrary, proof of that nomination or consent without proof of the signature or the official character of the person appearing to have signed the document. R.S., c. C-34, s. 689; 1976-77, c. 53, s. 14; R.S.C. 1985, c. 27 (1st Supp.), s. 203; 2008, c. 6, s. 48(1).

---

755. (old provision) [*Repealed*, 1997, c. 17, s. 5.]

EXCEPTION TO LONG-TERM SUPERVISION — LIFE SENTENCE / Maximum length of long-term supervision.

755. (1) The court shall not order that an offender be subject to long-term supervision if they have been sentenced to life imprisonment.

(2) The periods of long-term supervision to which an offender is subject at any particular time must not total more than 10 years. 2008, c. 6, s. 49.

---

756. [*Repealed*, 1997, c. 17, s. 5.]

EVIDENCE OF CHARACTER.

757. Without prejudice to the right of the offender to tender evidence as to their character and repute, if the court thinks fit, evidence of character and repute may be admitted

   (*a*) on the question of whether the offender is or is not a dangerous offender or a long-term offender; and

   (*b*) in connection with a sentence to be imposed or an order to be made under this Part. R.S., c. C-34, s. 692; 1976-77, c. 53, s. 14; 1997, c. 17, s. 5; 2008, c. 6, s. 50.

PRESENCE OF ACCUSED AT HEARING OF APPLICATION / Exception.

758. (1) The offender shall be present at the hearing of the application under this Part and if at the time the application is to be heard

   (*a*) he is confined in a prison, the court may order, in writing, the person having the custody of the accused to bring him before the court; or

   (*b*) he is not confined in a prison, the court shall issue a summons or a warrant to compel the accused to attend before the court and the provisions of Part XVI relating to summons and warrant are applicable with such modifications as the circumstances require.

(2) Notwithstanding subsection (1), the court may

(a) cause the offender to be removed and to be kept out of court, where he misconducts himself by interrupting the proceedings so that to continue the proceedings in his presence would not be feasible; or

(b) permit the offender to be out of court during the whole or any part of the hearing on such conditions as the court considers proper. R.S., c. C-34, s. 693; 1976-77, c. 53, s. 14.

APPEAL — OFFENDER / Appeal — Attorney General / Disposition of appeal / Effect of decision / Commencement of sentence / Part XXI applies.

759. (1) An offender who is found to be a dangerous offender or a long-term offender may appeal to the court of appeal from a decision made under this Part on any ground of law or fact or mixed law and fact.

(2) The Attorney General may appeal to the court of appeal from a decision made under this Part on any ground of law.

(3) The court of appeal may

(a) allow the appeal and

(i) find that an offender is or is not a dangerous offender or a long-term offender or impose a sentence that may be imposed or an order that may be made by the trial court under this Part, or

(ii) order a new hearing, with any directions that the court considers appropriate; or

(b) dismiss the appeal.

(4) A decision of the court of appeal has the same force and effect as if it were a decision of the trial court.

(5) [*Repealed*, 2008, c. 6, s. 51.]

(6) Notwithstanding subsection 719(1), a sentence imposed on an offender by the court of appeal pursuant to this section shall be deemed to have commenced when the offender was sentenced by the court by which he was convicted.

(7) The provisions of Part XXI with respect to procedure on appeals apply, with such modifications as the circumstances require, to appeals under this section. R.S., c. C-34, s. 694; 1976-77, c. 53, s. 14; 1995, c. 22, s. 10; 1997, c. 17, s. 6; 2008, c. 6, s. 51.

DISCLOSURE TO CORRECTIONAL SERVICE OF CANADA.

760. Where a court finds an offender to be a dangerous offender or a long-term offender, the court shall order that a copy of all reports and testimony given by psychiatrists, psychologists, criminologists and other experts and any observations of the court with respect to the reasons for the finding, together with a transcript of the trial of the offender, be forwarded to the Correctional Service of Canada for information. R.S., c. C-34, s. 695; 1976-77, c. 53, s. 14; 1997, c. 17, s. 7.

REVIEW FOR PAROLE / Idem.

761. (1) Subject to subsection (2), where a person is in custody under a sentence of detention in a penitentiary for an indeterminate period, the Parole Board of Canada shall, as soon as possible after the expiration of seven years from the day on which that person was taken into custody and not later than every two years after the previous review, review the condition, history and circumstances of that person for the purpose of determining whether he or she should be granted parole under Part II of the *Corrections and Conditional Release Act* and, if so, on what conditions.

(2) Where a person is in custody under a sentence of detention in a penitentiary for an indeterminate period that was imposed before October 15, 1977, the Parole Board of Canada shall, at least once in every year, review the condition, history and circumstances of that person for the purpose of determining whether he should be granted parole under Part II of the *Corrections and Conditional Release Act* and, if so, on what conditions. 1976-77, c. 53, s. 14; 1992, c. 20, s. 215; 1997, c. 17, s. 8; 2012, c. 1, s. 160(*c*)(v).

PART XXV / EFFECT AND ENFORCEMENT OF UNDERTAKINGS, RELEASE ORDERS AND RECOGNIZANCES

2019, c. 25, s. 308.

APPLICATIONS FOR FORFEITURE / Definitions / "clerk of the court" / "schedule".

762. (1) Applications for the forfeiture of an amount set out in an undertaking, release order or recognizance must be made to the courts designated in column II of the schedule of the respective provinces designated in column I of the schedule.

(2) In this Part,

"clerk of the court" means the officer designated in column III of the schedule in respect of the court designated in column II of the schedule;

"schedule" means the schedule to this Part. R.S., c. C-34, s. 696; 2019, c. 25, s. 309.

UNDERTAKING OR RELEASE BINDING ON PERSON / Summary of certain provisions.

763. (1) If a person is bound by an undertaking, release order or recognizance to appear before a court, provincial court judge or justice for any purpose and the session or sittings of that court or the proceedings are adjourned or an order is made changing the place of trial, that person and their sureties continue to be bound by the undertaking, release order or recognizance as if it had been entered into or issued with respect to the resumed proceedings or the trial at the time and place at which the proceedings are ordered to be resumed or the trial is ordered to be held.

(2) A summary of section 763 must be set out in any undertaking, release order or recognizance. R.S., c. C-34, s. 697; R.S.C. 1985, c. 27 (1st Supp.), s. 203; 2019, c. 25, s. 310.

UNDERTAKING OR RELEASE ORDER BINDING ON ACCUSED / Committal or new sureties / Effect of committal / Summary of certain provisions.

764. (1) If an accused is bound by an undertaking or release order to appear for trial, their arraignment or conviction does not cancel the undertaking or release order, and it continues to bind them and their sureties for their appearance until the accused is discharged or sentenced, as the case may be.

(2) Despite subsection (1), the court, provincial court judge or justice may commit an accused to prison or may require them to furnish new or additional sureties for their appearance until the accused is discharged or sentenced, as the case may be.

(3) The sureties of an accused who is bound by a release order to appear for trial are discharged if the accused is committed to prison under subsection (2).

(4) A summary of subsections (1) to (3) must be set out in any undertaking or release order. R.S., c. C-34, s. 698; 2019, c. 25, s. 310.

EFFECT OF SUBSEQUENT ARREST.

765. If an accused is bound by an undertaking or a release order to appear for trial, their arrest on another charge does not cancel the undertaking or release order, and it continues to bind them and their sureties for their appearance until the accused is discharged or sentenced, as the case may be, in respect of the offence to which the undertaking or release order relates. R.S., c. C-34, s. 699; 2019, c. 25, s. 310.

RENDER OF ACCUSED BY SURETIES / Arrest / Certificate and entry of render / Discharge of sureties.

766. (1) A surety for a person who is subject to a release order or recognizance may, by an application in writing to a court, provincial court judge or justice, apply to be relieved of their obligation under the release order or recognizance, and the court, provincial court judge or justice shall then make an order in writing for committal of that person to the prison named in that order.

(2) An order issued by a court, provincial court judge or justice under subsection (1) must be given to the surety and, on receipt of it, the surety or any peace officer may arrest the person named in the order and deliver that person with the order to the keeper of the prison named in the order, and the keeper shall receive and imprison that person until the person is discharged according to law.

(3) If a court, provincial court judge or justice issues an order under subsection (1) and receives from the sheriff a certificate that the person named in the order has been committed to prison under subsection (2), the court, provincial court judge or justice shall order an entry of the committal to be endorsed on the release order or recognizance, as the case may be.

(4) An endorsement under subsection (3) cancels the release order or recognizance, as the case may be, and discharges the sureties. R.S., c. C-34, s. 700; 2019, c. 25, s. 310.

RENDER OF ACCUSED IN COURT BY SURETIES.

767. A surety for a person who is subject to a release order or recognizance may bring that person before the court where the person is required to appear or where the person entered into the recognizance at any time during the sittings of that court and before the person's trial, and the surety may discharge their obligation under the release order or recognizance by giving that person into the custody of the court. The court shall then commit that person to prison until the person is discharged according to law. R.S., c. C-34, s. 701; 2019, c. 25, s. 310.

SUBSTITUTION OF SURETY / Signing of release order or recognizance by new sureties.

767.1 (1) If a surety for a person who is subject to a release order or recognizance has given the person into the custody of a court under section 767, or a surety applies to be relieved of their obligation under the release order or recognizance under subsection 766(1), the court, justice or provincial court judge, as the case may be, may, instead of committing or issuing an order for the committal of the person to prison, substitute any other suitable person for the surety under the release order or recognizance.

(2) If a person substituted for a surety under a release order or recognizance under subsection (1) signs the release order or recognizance, the original surety is discharged, but the release order or recognizance is not otherwise affected. R.S.C. 1985, c. 27 (1st Supp.), s. 167; 2019, c. 25, s. 310.

RIGHTS OF SURETY PRESERVED.

768. Nothing in this Part limits any right that a surety has of taking and giving into custody any person for whom they are a surety under a release order or recognizance. R.S., c. C-34, s. 702; 2019, c. 25, s. 310.

APPLICATION OF JUDICIAL INTERIM RELEASE PROVISIONS.

769. Where a surety for a person has rendered him into custody and that person has been committed to prison, the provisions of Parts XVI, XXI and XXVII relating to judicial interim release apply, with such modifications as the circumstances require in respect of him and he shall forthwith be taken before a justice or judge as an accused charged with an offence or as an appellant, as the case may be, for the purposes of those provisions. R.S., c. C-34, s. 703; R.S., c. 2 (2nd Supp.), s. 14.

DEFAULT TO BE ENDORSED / Transmission to clerk of court / Certificate is evidence / Transmission of deposit.

770. (1) If, in proceedings to which this Act applies, a person who is subject to an undertaking, release order or recognizance does not comply with any of its conditions, a court, provincial court judge or justice having knowledge of the facts shall endorse or cause to be endorsed on the undertaking, release order or recognizance a certificate in Form 33 setting out

  (a) the nature of the default;
  (b) the reason for the default, if it is known;
  (c) whether the ends of justice have been defeated or delayed by reason of the default; and
  (d) the names and addresses of the principal and sureties.

(2) Once endorsed, the undertaking, release order or recognizance must be sent to the clerk of the court and shall be kept by them with the records of the court.

(3) A certificate that has been endorsed on the undertaking, release order or recognizance is evidence of the default to which it relates.

(4) If, in proceedings to which this section applies, the principal or surety has deposited money as security for the performance of a condition of an undertaking, release order or recognizance, that money must be sent to the clerk of the court with the defaulted undertaking, release order or recognizance, to be dealt with in accordance with this Part. R.S., c. C-34, s. 704; 1997, c. 18, s. 108; 2019, c. 25, s. 311.

PROCEEDINGS IN CASE OF DEFAULT / Order of judge / Judgment debtors of the Crown / Order may be filed / Transfer of deposit.

771. (1) If an undertaking, release order or recognizance has been endorsed with a certificate and has been received by the clerk of the court,

  (a) a judge of the court shall, on the request of the clerk of the court or the Attorney General or counsel acting on the Attorney General's or counsel's behalf, as the case may be, fix a time and place for the hearing of an application for the forfeiture of the amount set out in the undertaking, release order or recognizance; and
  (b) the clerk of the court shall, not less than 10 days before the time fixed under paragraph (a) for the hearing, send by registered mail, or have served in the manner directed by the court or prescribed by the rules of court, to each principal and surety, at the address set out in the certificate, a notice requiring the person to appear at the time and place fixed by the judge to show cause why
    the amount set out in the undertaking, release order or recognizance should not be forfeited.

(2) If subsection (1) has been complied with, the judge may, after giving the parties an opportunity to be heard, in the judge's discretion grant or refuse the application and make any order with respect to the forfeiture of the amount that the judge considers proper.

(3) If a judge orders forfeiture of the amount set out in the undertaking, release order or recognizance, the principal and their sureties become judgment debtors of the Crown, each in the amount that the judge orders them to pay.

(3.1) An order made under subsection (2) may be filed with the clerk of the superior court and if one is filed, the clerk shall issue a writ of *fieri facias* in Form 34 and deliver it to the sheriff of each of the territorial divisions in which the principal or any surety resides, carries on business or has property.

(4) If a deposit has been made by a person against whom an order for forfeiture has been made, no writ of *fieri facias* may be issued, but the amount of the deposit must be transferred by the person who has custody of it to the person who is entitled by law to receive it. R.S., c. C-34, s. 705; 1972, c. 13, s. 60; R.S.C. 1985, c. 27 (1st Supp.), s. 168; 1994, c. 44, s. 78; 1999, c. 5, s. 43; 2019, c. 25, s. 311.

LEVY UNDER WRIT / Costs.

772. (1) Where a writ of *fieri facias* is issued pursuant to section 771, the sheriff to whom it is delivered shall execute the writ and deal with the proceeds thereof in the same manner in which he is authorized to execute and deal with the proceeds of writs of *fieri facias* issued out of superior courts in the province in civil proceedings.

(2) Where this section applies the Crown is entitled to the costs of execution and of proceedings incidental thereto that are fixed, in the Province of Quebec, by any tariff applicable in the Superior Court in civil proceedings, and in any other province, by any tariff applicable in the superior court of the province in civil proceedings, as the judge may direct. R.S., c. C-34, s. 706.

COMMITTAL WHEN WRIT NOT SATISFIED / Notice / Hearing / Warrant to committal / Definition of "Attorney General".

773. (1) Where a writ of *fieri facias* has been issued under this Part and it appears from a certificate in a return made by the sheriff that sufficient goods and chattels, lands and tenements cannot be found to satisfy the writ, or that the proceeds of the execution of the writ are not sufficient to satisfy it, a judge of the court may, upon the application of the Attorney General or counsel acting on his behalf, fix a time and place for the sureties to show cause why a warrant of committal should not be issued in respect of them.

(2) Seven clear days notice of the time and place fixed for the hearing pursuant to subsection (1) shall be given to the sureties.

(3) The judge shall, at the hearing held pursuant to subsection (1), inquire into the circumstances of the case and may in his discretion
   (*a*) order the discharge of the amount for which the surety is liable; or
   (*b*) make any order with respect to the surety and to his imprisonment that he considers proper in the circumstances and issue a warrant of committal in Form 27.

(4) A warrant of committal issued pursuant to this section authorizes the sheriff to take into custody the person in respect of whom the warrant was issued and to

confine him in a prison in the territorial division in which the writ was issued or in the prison nearest to the court, until satisfaction is made or until the period of imprisonment fixed by the judge has expired.

(5) In this section and in section 771, "Attorney General" means, where subsection 734.4(2) applies, the Attorney General of Canada. R.S., c. C-34, s. 707; 1995, c. 22, s. 10.

SCHEDULE TO PART XXII.1
(Section 715.3 and subsections 715.32(2) and 715.43(2) and (3))

1. An offence under any of the following provisions of this Act:
    (a) section 119 or 120 (bribery of officers);
    (b) section 121 (frauds on the government);
    (c) section 123 (municipal corruption);
    (d) section 124 (selling or purchasing office);
    (e) section 125 (influencing or negotiating appointments or dealing in offices);
    (f) subsection 139(3) (obstructing justice);
    (g) section 322 (theft);
    (h) section 330 (theft by person required to account);
    (i) section 332 (misappropriation of money held under direction);
    (j) section 340 (destroying documents of title);
    (k) section 341 (fraudulent concealment);
    (l) section 354 (property obtained by crime);
    (m) section 362 (false pretence or false statement);
    (n) section 363 (obtaining execution of valuable security by fraud);
    (o) section 366 (forgery);
    (p) section 368 (use, trafficking or possession of forged document);
    (q) section 375 (obtaining by instrument based on forged document);
    (r) section 378 (offences in relation to registers);
    (s) section 380 (fraud);
    (t) section 382 (fraudulent manipulation of stock exchange transactions);
    (u) section 382.1 (prohibited insider trading);
    (v) section 383 (gaming in stocks or merchandise);
    (w) section 389 (fraudulent disposal of goods on which money advanced);
    (x) section 390 (fraudulent receipts under *Bank Act*);
    (y) section 392 (disposal of property to defraud creditors);
    (z) section 397 (books and documents);
    (z.1) section 400 (false prospectus);
    (z.2) section 418 (selling defective stores to Her Majesty); and
    (z.3) section 426 (secret commissions);
    (z.4) section 462.31 (laundering proceeds of crime).

2. An offence under any of the following provisions of the *Corruption of Foreign Public Officials Act*:
    (a) section 3 (bribing a foreign public official); and

(b) section 4 (maintenance or destruction of books and records to facilitate or hide the bribing of a foreign public official).

3. A conspiracy or an attempt to commit, being an accessory after the fact in relation to, or any counselling in relation to, an offence referred to in section 1 or 2. 2018, c. 12, s. 405 (Sched. 6).

SCHEDULE TO PART XXV
(Section 762)

Column I	Column II	Column III
Ontario	A judge of the Court of Appeal in respect of a release order or recognizance for the appearance of a person before the Court	The Registrar of the Court of Appeal
	The Superior Court of Justice in respect of undertakings or all other release orders or recognizances	A Registrar of the Superior Court of Justice
Quebec	The Court of Quebec Criminal and Penal Division	The Clerk of the Court
Nova Scotia	The Supreme Court	A Prothonotary of the Supreme Court
New Brunswick	The Court of Queen's Bench	The Registrar of the Court of Queen's Bench
British Columbia	The Supreme Court in respect of an undertaking, release order or recognizance for the appearance of a person before that Court or the Court of Appeal.	The District Registrar of the Supreme Court
	A Provincial Court in respect of an undertaking, release order or recognizance for the appearance of a person before a judge of that Court or a justice.	The Clerk of the Provincial Court
Prince Edward Island	The Supreme Court	The Prothonotory
Manitoba	The Court of Queen's Bench	The registrar or a deputy registrar of the Court of Queen's Bench
Saskatchewan	The Court of Queen's Bench	The Local Registrar of the Court of Queen's Bench
Alberta	The Court of Queen's Bench	The Clerk of the Court of Queen's Bench
Newfoundland and Labrador	The Trial Division of the Supreme Court	The Registrar of the Supreme Court

Yukon......................	The Supreme Court	The Clerk of the Supreme Court
Northwest Territories..........	The Supreme Court	The Clerk of the Supreme Court
Nunavut...................	The Nunavut Court of Justice	The Clerk of the Nunavut Court of Justice

R.S., c. C-46, Sch. to Part XXV; 1985, c. 11, (1st Supp.), s. 2; R.S. 1985, c. 27 (2nd Supp.), s. 10; 1992, c. 1, s. 58; 1992, c. 51, ss. 40 to 42; 1993, c. 28, Sch. III, s. 35.2 (repealed 1999, c. 3, s. 12); 1998, c. 30, s. 14(*d*); 1999, c. 3, ss. 12, 54; c. 5, s. 44; 2002, c. 7, s. 148; 2015, c. 3, ss. 57-59; 2019, c. 25, s. 312.

CODE

PART XXVI / EXTRAORDINARY REMEDIES

APPLICATION OF PART.

774. This Part applies to proceedings in criminal matters by way of *certiorari, habeas corpus, mandamus, procedendo* and prohibition. R.S., c. C-34, s. 708; R.S.C. 1985, c. 27 (1st Supp.), s. 169.

APPEARANCE IN PERSON — HABEAS CORPUS.

774.1 Despite any other provision of this Act, the person who is the subject of a writ of habeas corpus must appear personally in court. 2002, c. 13, s. 77.

DETENTION ON INQUIRY TO DETERMINE LEGALITY OF IMPRISONMENT.

775. Where proceedings to which this Part applies have been instituted before a judge or court having jurisdiction, by or in respect of a person who is in custody by reason that he is charged with or has been convicted of an offence, to have the legality of his imprisonment determined, the judge or court may, without determining the question, make an order for the further detention of that person and direct the judge, justice or provincial court judge under whose warrant he is in custody, or any other judge, justice or provincial court judge, to take any proceedings, hear such evidence or do any other thing that, in the opinion of the judge or court, will best further the ends of justice. R.S., c. C-34, s. 709.

WHERE CONVICTION OR ORDER NOT REVIEWABLE.

776. No conviction or order shall be removed by *certiorari*
  (*a*) where an appeal was taken, whether or not the appeal has been carried to a conclusion; or
  (*b*) where the defendant appeared and pleaded and the merits were tried, and an appeal might have been taken, but the defendant did not appeal. R.S., c. C-34, s. 710.

CONVICTION OR ORDER REMEDIABLE, WHEN / Correcting punishment / Amendment / Sufficiency of statement.

777. (1) No conviction, order or warrant for enforcing a conviction or order shall, on being removed by *certiorari*, be held to be invalid by reason of any irregularity, informality or insufficiency therein, where the court before which or the judge before whom the question is raised, on perusal of the evidence, is satisfied

- (*a*) that an offence of the nature described in the conviction, order or warrant, as the case may be, was committed,
- (*b*) that there was jurisdiction to make the conviction or order or issue the warrant, as the case may be, and
- (*c*) that the punishment imposed, if any, was not in excess of the punishment that might lawfully have been imposed,

but the court or judge has the same powers to deal with the proceedings in the manner that he considers proper that are conferred on a court to which an appeal might have been taken.

(2) Where, in proceedings to which subsection (1) applies, the court or judge is satisfied that a person was properly convicted of an offence but the punishment that was imposed is greater than the punishment that might lawfully have been imposed, the court or judge

- (*a*) shall correct the sentence,
  - (i) where the punishment is a fine, by imposing a fine that does not exceed the maximum fine that might lawfully have been imposed,
  - (ii) where the punishment is imprisonment, and the person has not served a term of imprisonment under the sentence that is equal to or greater than the term of imprisonment that might lawfully have been imposed, by imposing a term of imprisonment that does not exceed the maximum term of imprisonment that might lawfully have been imposed, or
  - (iii) where the punishment is a fine and imprisonment, by imposing a punishment in accordance with subparagraph (i) or (ii), as the case requires; or
- (*b*) shall remit the matter to the convicting judge, justice or provincial court judge and direct him to impose a punishment that is not greater than the punishment that may be lawfully imposed.

(3) Where an adjudication is varied pursuant to subsection (1) or (2), the conviction and warrant of committal, if any, shall be amended to conform to the adjudication as varied.

(4) Any statement that appears in a conviction and is sufficient for the purpose of the conviction is sufficient for the purposes of an information, summons, order or warrant in which it appears in the proceedings. R.S., c. C-34, s. 711.

IRREGULARITIES WITHIN SECTION 777.

778. Without restricting the generality of section 777, that section shall be deemed to apply where (*a*) the statement of the adjudication or of any other matter or thing is in the past tense instead of in the present tense;

(*b*) the punishment imposed is less than the punishment that might by law have been imposed for the offence that appears by the evidence to have been committed; or

(*c*) there has been an omission to negative circumstances, the existence of which would make the act complained of lawful, whether those circumstances are stated by way of exception or otherwise in the provision under which the offence is charged or are stated in another provision. R.S., c. C-34, s. 712.

GENERAL ORDER FOR SECURITY BY RECOGNIZANCE / Provisions of Part XXV.

779. (1) A court that has authority to quash a conviction, order or other proceeding on *certiorari* may prescribe by general order that no motion to quash any such conviction, order or other proceeding removed to the court by *certiorari* shall be heard unless the defendant has entered into a recognizance with one or more sufficient sureties, before one or more justices of the territorial division in which the conviction or order was made or before a judge or other officer, or has made a deposit to be prescribed with a condition that the defendant will prosecute the writ of *certiorari* at his own expense, without wilful delay, and, if ordered, will pay to the person in whose favour the conviction, order or other proceeding is affirmed his full costs and charges to be taxed according to the practice of the court where the conviction, order or proceeding is affirmed.

(2) The provisions of Part XXV relating to forfeiture of an amount set out in a recognizance apply to a recognizance entered into under this section. R.S., c. C-34, s. 713; 2019, c. 25, s. 313.

EFFECT OF ORDER DISMISSING APPLICATION TO QUASH.

780. Where a motion to quash a conviction, order or other proceeding is refused, the order of the court refusing the application is sufficient authority for the clerk of the court forthwith to return the conviction, order or proceeding to the court from which or the person from whom it was removed, and for proceedings to be taken with respect thereto for the enforcement thereof. R.S., c. C-34, s. 714.

WANT OF PROOF OF ORDER IN COUNCIL / Judicial notice.

781. (1) No order, conviction or other proceeding shall be quashed or set aside, and no defendant shall be discharged, by reason only that evidence has not been given

(*a*) of a proclamation or order of the Governor in Council or the lieutenant governor in council;

(*b*) of rules, regulations or by-laws made by the Governor in Council under an Act of Parliament or by the lieutenant governor in council under an Act of the legislature of the province; or (*c*) of the publication of a proclamation, order, rule, regulation or by-law in the *Canada Gazette* or in the official gazette for the province.

(2) Proclamations, orders, rules, regulations and by-laws mentioned in subsection (1) and the publication thereof shall be judicially noticed. R.S., c. C-34, s. 715.

DEFECT IN FORM.

782. No warrant of committal shall, on *certiorari* or *habeas corpus,* be held to be void by reason only of any defect therein, where

(*a*) it is alleged in the warrant that the defendant was convicted; and

(*b*) there is a valid conviction to sustain the warrant. R.S., c. C-34, s. 716.

NO ACTION AGAINST OFFICIAL WHEN CONVICTION, ETC., QUASHED.

783. Where an application is made to quash a conviction, order or other proceeding made or held by a provincial court judge acting under Part XIX or a justice on the ground that he exceeded his jurisdiction, the court to which or the judge to whom the application is made may, in quashing the conviction, order or other proceeding, order that no civil proceedings shall be taken against the justice or provincial court judge or against any officer who acted under the conviction, order or other proceeding or under any warrant issued to enforce it. R.S., c. C-34, s. 717.

APPEAL IN MANDAMUS ETC. / Application of Part XXI / Refusal of application, and appeal / Where writ granted / Appeal from judgment on return of writ / Hearing of appeal.

784. (1) An appeal lies to the court of appeal from a decision granting or refusing the relief sought in proceedings by way of *mandamus, certiorari* or prohibition.

(2) Except as provided in this section, Part XXI applies, with such modifications as the circumstances require, to appeals under this section.

(3) Where an application for a writ of *habeas corpus ad subjiciendum* is refused by a judge of a court having jurisdiction therein, no application may again be made on the same grounds, whether to the same or to another court or judge, unless fresh evidence is adduced, but an appeal from that refusal shall lie to the court of appeal, and where on the appeal the application is refused a further appeal shall lie to the Supreme Court of Canada, with leave of that Court.

(4) Where a writ of *habeas corpus ad subjiciendum* is granted by any judge, no appeal therefrom shall lie at the instance of any party including the Attorney General of the province concerned or the Attorney General of Canada.

(5) Where a judgment is issued on the return of a writ of *habeas corpus ad subjiciendum,* an appeal therefrom lies to the court of appeal, and from a judgment of the court of appeal to the Supreme Court of Canada, with the leave of that Court, at the instance of the applicant or the Attorney General of the province concerned or the Attorney General of Canada, but not at the instance of any other party.

(6) An appeal in *habeas corpus* matters shall be heard by the court to which the appeal is directed at an early date, whether in or out of the prescribed sessions of the court. R.S., c. C-34, s. 719; 1997, c. 18, s. 109.

Part XXVII / SUMMARY CONVICTIONS

Interpretation

DEFINITIONS / "clerk of the appeal court" / "informant" / "information" / "order" / "proceedings" / "prosecutor" / "sentence" / "summary conviction court" / "trial".

785. In this Part,

"clerk of the appeal court" includes a local clerk of the appeal court;

"informant" means a person who lays an information;

"information" includes

    (*a*) a count in an information, and

    (*b*) an order made under subsection 109(1) or 110(1), section 259 or 261, subsection 730(1) or 737(2.1) or (3) or section 738, 739, 742.1 or 742.3,

"order" means any order, including an order for the payment of money;

"proceedings" means

    (*a*) proceedings in respect of offences that are declared by an Act of Parliament or an enactment made thereunder to be punishable on summary conviction, and

    (*b*) proceedings where a justice is authorized by an Act of Parliament or an enactment made thereunder to make an order;

"prosecutor" means the Attorney General or, where the Attorney General does not intervene, the informant, and includes counsel or an agent acting on behalf of either of them;

"sentence" includes

    (*a*) a declaration made under subsection 199(3),

    (*b*) an order made under subsection 109(1) or 110(1), section 320.24, subsection 730(1) or 737(3) or section 738, 739, 742.1 or 742.3,

    (*c*) a disposition made under section 731 or 732 or subsection 732.2(3) or (5), 742.4(3) or 742.6(9),

    (*d*) an order made under subsection 16(1) of the *Controlled Drugs and Substances Act*; and

    (*e*) an order made under subsection 94(1) of the *Cannabis Act*;

"summary conviction court" means a person who has jurisdiction in the territorial division where the subject-matter of the proceedings is alleged to have arisen and who

    (*a*) is given jurisdiction over the proceedings by the enactment under which the proceedings are taken,

(b) is a justice or provincial court judge, where the enactment under which the proceedings are taken does not expressly give jurisdiction to any person or class of persons, or

(c) is a provincial court judge, where the enactment under which the proceedings are taken gives jurisdiction in respect thereof to two or more justices;

"trial" includes the hearing of a complaint. R.S., c. C-34, s. 720; 1972, c. 13, s. 61; 1974-75-76, c. 93, s. 85; 1976-77, c. 53, s. 4; R.S.C. 1985, c. 27 (1st Supp.), s. 170; 1992, c. 1, s. 58; 1995, c. 22, s. 7(1); c. 39, s. 156; 1996, c. 19, s. 76; 1999, c. 25, s. 23; 2002, c. 13, s. 78; 2006, c. 14, s. 7; 2013, c. 11, s. 4; 2018, c. 16, s. 223; 2018, c. 21, s. 26; 2019, c. 25, s. 314.

APPLICATION OF PART / Limitation.

786. (1) Except where otherwise provided by law, this Part applies to proceedings as defined in this Part.

(2) No proceedings shall be instituted more than 12 months after the time when the subject matter of the proceedings arose, unless the prosecutor and the defendant so agree. R.S., c. C-34, 721; 1997, c. 18, s. 110; 2019, c. 25, s. 315.

Punishment

GENERAL PENALTY / Imprisonment in default if not otherwise specified.

787. (1) Unless otherwise provided by law, every person who is convicted of an offence punishable on summary conviction is liable to a fine of not more than $5,000 or to a term of imprisonment of not more than two years less a day, or to both.

(2) If the imposition of a fine or the making of an order for the payment of money is authorized by law, but the law does not provide that imprisonment may be imposed in default of payment of the fine or compliance with the order, the court may order that in default of payment of the fine or compliance with the order, as the case may be, the defendant shall be imprisoned for a term of not more than two years less a day. R.S., c. C-34, s. 722; R.S.C. 1985, c. 27 (1st Supp.), s. 171(1); 2008, c. 18, s. 44; 2019, c. 25, s. 316.

Information

COMMENCEMENT OF PROCEEDINGS / One justice may act before the trial.

788. (1) Proceedings under this Part shall be commenced by laying an information in Form 2.

(2) Notwithstanding any other law that requires an information to be laid before or to be tried by two or more justices, one justice may

(a) receive the information;

(b) issue a summons or warrant with respect to the information; and

(c) do all other things preliminary to the trial. R.S., c. C-34, s. 723.

FORMALITIES OF INFORMATION / No reference to previous convictions.

789. (1) In proceedings to which this Part applies, the information

(a) shall be in writing and under oath; and

(b) may charge more than one offence or relate to more than one matter of complaint, but where more than one offence is charged or the information relates to more than one matter of complaint, each offence or matter of complaint, as the case may be, shall be set out in a separate count.

(2) No information in respect of an offence for which, by reason of previous convictions, a greater punishment may be imposed shall contain any reference to previous convictions. R.S., c. C-34, s. 724.

ANY JUSTICE MAY ACT BEFORE AND AFTER TRIAL / Two or more justices.

790. (1) Nothing in this Act or any other law shall be deemed to require a justice before whom proceedings are commenced or who issues process before or after the trial to be the justice or one of the justices before whom the trial is held.

(2) Where two or more justices have jurisdiction with respect to proceedings, they shall be present and act together at the trial, but one justice may thereafter do anything that is required or is authorized to be done in connection with the proceedings. R.S., c. C-34, s. 725; 1974-75-76, c. 93, s. 86.

(3) and (4) [*Repealed*, R.S.C. 1985, c. 27 (1st Supp.), s. 172.]

---

791. [*Repealed*, R.S.C. 1985, c. 27 (1st Supp.), s. 173.]

---

792. [*Repealed* (with heading), R.S.C. 1985, c. 27 (1st Supp.), s. 174.]

---

793. [*Repealed*, R.S.C. 1985, c. 27 (1st Supp.), s. 175.]

NO NEED TO NEGATIVE EXCEPTION, ETC.

794. (1) No exception, exemption, proviso, excuse or qualification prescribed by law is required to be set out or negatived, as the case may be, in an information. R.S., c. C-34, s. 730; 2018, c. 29, s. 68.

(2) [*Repealed*, 2018, c. 29, s. 68.]

Application

APPLICATION OF PARTS XVI, XVIII, XVIII.1, XX and XX.1.

795. The provisions of Parts XVI and XVIII with respect to compelling the appearance of an accused before a justice, and the provisions of Parts XVIII.1, XX and XX.1, in so far as they are not inconsistent with this Part, apply, with any necessary modifications, to proceedings under this Part. R.S.C. 1985, c. 27 (1st Supp.), s. 176; 1991, c. 43, s. 7; 2011, c. 16, s. 16.

796. [*Repealed*, R.S.C. 1985, c. 27 (1st Supp.), s. 176.]

797. [*Repealed*, R.S.C. 1985, c. 27 (1st Supp.), s. 176.]

Trial

JURISDICTION.

798. Every summary conviction court has jurisdiction to try, determine and adjudge proceedings to which this Part applies in the territorial division over which the person who constitutes that court has jurisdiction. R.S., c. C-34, s. 733.

NON-APPEARANCE OF PROSECUTOR.

799. Where, in proceedings to which this Part applies, the defendant appears for the trial and the prosecutor, having had due notice, does not appear, the summary conviction court may dismiss the information or may adjourn the trial to some other time upon such terms as it considers proper. R.S., c. C-34, s. 734.

WHEN BOTH PARTIES APPEAR / Counsel or agent / Video links / Appearance by organization.

800. (1) Where the prosecutor and defendant appear for the trial, the summary conviction court shall proceed to hold the trial.

(2) A defendant may appear personally or by counsel or agent, but the summary conviction court may require the defendant to appear personally and may, if it thinks fit, issue a warrant in Form 7 for the arrest of the defendant and adjourn the trial to await his appearance pursuant thereto.

(2.1) If the summary conviction court so orders and the defendant agrees, the defendant who is confined in prison may appear by closed-circuit television or videoconference, as long as the defendant is given the opportunity to communicate privately with counsel if they are represented by counsel.

(3) Where the defendant is an organization, it shall appear by counsel or agent and, if it does not appear, the summary conviction court may, on proof of service of the summons, proceed *ex parte* to hold the trial. R.S., c. C-34, s. 735; 1997, c. 18, s. 111; 2003, c. 21, s. 212; 2019, c. 25, s. 317.

ARRAIGNMENT / Finding of guilt, conviction or order if charge admitted / Procedure if charge not admitted.

801. (1) Where the defendant appears for the trial, the substance of the information laid against him shall be stated to him, and he shall be asked, (*a*) whether he pleads guilty or not guilty to the information, where the proceedings are in respect of an offence that is punishable on summary conviction; or

(*b*) whether he has cause to show why an order should not be made against him, in proceedings where a justice is authorized by law to make an order.

(2) Where the defendant pleads guilty or does not show sufficient cause why an order should not be made against him, as the case may be, the summary conviction court shall convict the defendant, discharge the defendant under section 730 or make an order against him accordingly.

(3) Where the defendant pleads not guilty or states that he has cause to show why an order should not be made against him, as the case may be, the summary conviction court shall proceed with the trial, and shall take the evidence of witnesses for the prosecutor and the defendant in accordance with the provisions of Part XVIII relating to preliminary inquiries. R.S., c. C-34, s. 736; R.S.C. 1985, c. 27 (1st Supp.), s. 177(1); 1995, c. 22, s. 10.

(4) and (5) [*Repealed*, R.S.C. 1985, c. 27 (1st Supp.), s. 177(2).]

RIGHT TO MAKE FULL ANSWER AND DEFENCE / Examination of witnesses / On oath.

802. (1) The prosecutor is entitled personally to conduct his case and the defendant is entitled to make his full answer and defence.

(2) The prosecutor or defendant, as the case may be, may examine and cross-examine witnesses personally or by counsel or agent.

(3) Every witness at a trial in proceedings to which this Part applies shall be examined under oath. R.S., c. C-34, s. 737.

LIMITATION ON THE USE OF AGENTS.

802.1 Despite subsections 800(2) and 802(2), a defendant may not appear or examine or cross-examine witnesses by agent if he or she is liable, on summary conviction, to imprisonment for a term of more than six months, unless

(*a*) the defendant is an organization;

(*b*) the defendant is appearing to request an adjournment of the proceedings; or

(*c*) the agent is authorized to do so under a program approved — or criteria established — by the lieutenant governor in council of the province. 2002, c. 13, s. 79; 2019, c. 25, s. 317.1.

ADJOURNMENT / Non-appearance of defendant / Consent of Attorney General required / Non-appearance of prosecutor.

803. (1) The summary conviction court may, in its discretion, before or during the trial, adjourn the trial to a time and place to be appointed and stated in the presence of the parties or their counsel or agents.

(2) If a defendant who is tried alone or together with others does not appear at the time and place appointed for the trial after having been notified of that time and

place, or does not appear for the resumption of a trial that has been adjourned in accordance with subsection (1), the summary conviction court

(a) may proceed *ex parte* to hear and determine the proceedings in the absence of that defendant as if they had appeared; or

(b) may, if it thinks fit, issue a warrant in Form 7 for the arrest of that defendant and adjourn the trial to await their appearance under the warrant.

(3) If the summary conviction court proceeds in the manner described in paragraph (2)(a), no proceedings under section 145 arising out of the defendant's failure to appear at the time and place appointed for the trial or for the resumption of the trial shall, without the consent of the Attorney General, be instituted or be proceeded with.

(4) Where the prosecutor does not appear at the time and place appointed for the resumption of an adjourned trial, the summary conviction court may dismiss the information with or without costs. R.S., c. C-34, s. 738; R.S., c. 2 (2nd Supp.), s. 15; 1972, c. 13, s. 63; 1974-75-76, c. 93, s. 87; 1994, c. 44, s. 79; 1997, c. 18, s. 112; 2008, c. 18, s. 45.

(5) [*Repealed*, 1991, c. 43, s. 9.]

(6) [*Repealed*, 1991, c. 43, s. 9.]

(7) [*Repealed*, 1991, c. 43, s. 9.]

(8) [*Repealed*, 1991, c. 43, s. 9.]

Adjudication

FINDING OF GUILT, CONVICTION, ORDER OR DISMISSAL.

804. When the summary conviction court has heard the prosecutor, defendant and witnesses, it shall, after considering the matter, convict the defendant, discharge him under section 730, make an order against the defendant or dismiss the information, as the case may be. R.S., c. C-34, s. 739; R.S.C. 1985, c. 27 (1st Supp.), s. 178.

805. [*Repealed*, R.S.C. 1985, c. 27 (1st Supp.), s. 179.]

MEMO OF CONVICTION OR ORDER / Warrant of committal / Admissibility of certified copy.

806. (1) If a defendant is convicted or an order is made in relation to the defendant, a minute or memorandum of the conviction or order must be made by the summary conviction court indicating that the matter was dealt with under this Part and, on request by the defendant, the prosecutor or any other person, a conviction or order in Form 35 or 36, as the case may be, and a certified copy of the conviction or order must be drawn up and the certified copy must be delivered to the person making the request.

(2) Where a defendant is convicted or an order is made against him, the summary conviction court shall issue a warrant of committal in Form 21 or 22, and section 528 applies in respect of a warrant of committal issued under this subsection.

(3) If a warrant of committal in Form 21 is signed by a clerk of a court, a copy of the warrant of committal, certified by the clerk, is admissible in evidence in any proceeding. R.S., c. C-34, s. 741; 1972, c. 13, s. 64; 1994, c. 44, s. 80; 2019, c. 25, s. 318(1), (3).

DISPOSAL OF PENALTIES WHEN JOINT OFFENDERS.

807. Where several persons join in committing the same offence and on conviction each is adjudged to pay an amount to a person aggrieved, no more shall be paid to that person than an amount equal to the value of the property destroyed or injured or the amount of the injury done, together with costs, if any, and the residue of the amount adjudged to be paid shall be applied in the manner in which other penalties imposed by law are directed to be applied. R.S., c. C-34, s. 742.

ORDER OF DISMISSAL / Effect of certificate.

808. (1) Where the summary conviction court dismisses an information, it may, if requested by the defendant, draw up an order of dismissal and shall give to the defendant a certified copy of the order of dismissal.

(2) A copy of an order of dismissal, certified in accordance with subsection (1) is, without further proof, a bar to any subsequent proceedings against the defendant in respect of the same cause. R.S., c. C-34, s. 743.

COSTS / Order set out / Costs are part of fine / Where no fine imposed / Definition of "costs".

809. (1) The summary conviction court may in its discretion award and order such costs as it considers reasonable and not inconsistent with such of the fees established by section 840 as may be taken or allowed in proceedings before that summary conviction court, to be paid

(a) to the informant by the defendant, where the summary conviction court convicts or makes an order against the defendant; or

(b) to the defendant by the informant, where the summary conviction court dismisses an information.

(2) An order under subsection (1) shall be set out in the conviction, order or order of dismissal, as the case may be.

(3) Where a fine or sum of money or both are adjudged to be paid by a defendant and a term of imprisonment in default of payment is imposed, the defendant is, in default of payment, liable to serve the term of imprisonment imposed, and for the purposes of this subsection, any costs that are awarded against the defendant shall be deemed to be part of the fine or sum of money adjudged to be paid.

(4) Where no fine or sum of money is adjudged to be paid by a defendant, but costs are awarded against the defendant or informant, the person who is liable to pay them is, in default of payment, liable to imprisonment for one month.

(5) In this section, "costs" includes the costs and charges, after they have been ascertained, of committing and conveying to prison the person against whom costs have been awarded. R.S., c. C-34, s. 744.

Sureties to Keep the Peace

IF INJURY OR DAMAGE FEARED / Duty of justice / Adjudication / Refusal to enter into recognizance / Conditions in recognizance / Conditions / Surrender, etc. / Reasons / Supplementary conditions / Form — warrant of committal / Modification of recognizance / Procedure.

810. (1) An information may be laid before a justice by or on behalf of any person who fears on reasonable grounds that another person

(a) will cause personal injury to them or to their intimate partner or child or will damage their property; or

(b) will commit an offence under section 162.1.

(2) A justice who receives an information under subsection (1) shall cause the parties to appear before him or before a summary conviction court having jurisdiction in the same territorial division.

(3) If the justice or summary conviction court before which the parties appear is satisfied by the evidence adduced that the person on whose behalf the information was laid has reasonable grounds for the fear, the justice or court may order that the defendant enter into a recognizance, with or without sureties, to keep the peace and be of good behaviour for a period of not more than 12 months.

(3.01) The justice or summary conviction court may commit the defendant to prison for a term of not more than 12 months if the defendant fails or refuses to enter into the recognizance.

(3.02) The justice or summary conviction court may add any reasonable conditions to the recognizance that the justice or court considers desirable to secure the good conduct of the defendant, including conditions that require the defendant

(a) to abstain from the consumption of drugs except in accordance with a medical prescription, of alcohol or of any other intoxicating substance;

(b) to provide, for the purpose of analysis, a sample of a bodily substance prescribed by regulation on the demand of a peace officer, a probation officer or someone designated under paragraph 810.3(2)(a) to make a demand, at the place and time and on the day specified by the person making the demand, if that person has reasonable grounds to believe that the defendant has breached a condition of the recognizance that requires them to abstain from the consumption of drugs, alcohol or any other intoxicating substance; or

(c) to provide, for the purpose of analysis, a sample of a bodily substance prescribed by regulation at regular intervals that are specified, in a notice in Form 51 served on the defendant, by a probation officer or a person designated under paragraph 810.3(2)(b) to specify them, if a condition of

the recognizance requires the defendant to abstain from the consumption of drugs, alcohol or any other intoxicating substance.

(3.1) Before making an order under subsection (3), the justice or the summary conviction court shall consider whether it is desirable, in the interests of the safety of the defendant or of any other person, to include as a condition of the recognizance that the defendant be prohibited from possessing any firearm, crossbow, prohibited weapon, restricted weapon, prohibited device, ammunition, prohibited ammunition or explosive substance, or all such things, for any period specified in the recognizance and, where the justice or summary conviction court decides that it is so desirable, the justice or summary conviction court shall add such a condition to the recognizance.

(3.11) Where the justice or summary conviction court adds a condition described in subsection (3.1) to a recognizance order, the justice or summary conviction court shall specify in the order the manner and method by which

   (a) the things referred to in that subsection that are in the possession of the accused shall be surrendered, disposed of, detained, stored or dealt with; and

   (b) the authorizations, licences and registration certificates held by the person shall be surrendered.

(3.12) Where the justice or summary conviction court does not add a condition described in subsection (3.1) to a recognizance order, the justice or summary conviction court shall include in the record a statement of the reasons for not adding the condition.

(3.2) Before making an order under subsection (3), the justice or the summary conviction court shall consider whether it is desirable, in the interests of the safety of the informant, of the person on whose behalf the information was laid or of that person's intimate partner or child, as the case may be, to add either or both of the following conditions to the recognizance,

   (a) a condition prohibiting the defendant from being at, or within a distance specified in the recognizance from, a place specified in the recognizance where the person on whose behalf the information was laid or that person's intimate partner or child, as the case may be, is regularly found; or

   (b) a condition prohibiting the defendant from communicating, in whole or in part, directly or indirectly, with the person on whose behalf the information was laid or that person's intimate partner or child, as the case may be.

(4) A warrant of committal to prison for failure or refusal to enter into the recognizance under subsection (3) may be in Form 23.

(4.1) The justice or the summary conviction court may, on application of the informant or the defendant, vary the conditions fixed in the recognizance.

(5) The provisions of this Part apply, with such modifications as the circumstances require, to proceedings under this section. R.S., c. C-34, s. 745; 1974-75-76, c. 93, s. 88; 1980-81-82-83, c. 125, s. 28; 1991, c. 40, s. 33; 1994, c. 44, s. 81; 1995, c. 22, s. 8, c. 39, s. 157; 2000, c. 12, s. 95(f), (g); 2011, c. 7, s. 7; 2014, c. 31, s. 25; 2019, c. 25, s. 319(1), (4).

FEAR OF CERTAIN OFFENCES / Appearances / Adjudication / Duration extended / Refusal to enter into recognizance / Conditions in recognizance / Conditions — firearms / Surrender, etc. / Reasons / Variance of conditions / Other provisions to apply / Definition of "Attorney General".

810.01 (1) A person who fears on reasonable grounds that another person will commit an offence under section 423.1 or a criminal organization offence may, with the Attorney General's consent, lay an information before a provincial court judge.

(2) A provincial court judge who receives an information under subsection (1) may cause the parties to appear before a provincial court judge.

(3) If the provincial court judge before whom the parties appear is satisfied by the evidence adduced that the informant has reasonable grounds for the fear, the judge may order that the defendant enter into a recognizance to keep the peace and be of good behaviour for a period of not more than 12 months.

(3.1) However, if the provincial court judge is also satisfied that the defendant was convicted previously of an offence referred to in subsection (1), the judge may order that the defendant enter into the recognizance for a period of not more than two years.

(4) The provincial court judge may commit the defendant to prison for a term not exceeding twelve months if the defendant fails or refuses to enter into the recognizance.

(4.1) The provincial court judge may add any reasonable conditions to the recognizance that the judge considers desirable for preventing the commission of an offence referred to in subsection (1), including conditions that require the defendant

    (*a*) to participate in a treatment program;

    (*b*) to wear an electronic monitoring device, if the Attorney General makes the request;

    (*c*) to remain within a specified geographic area unless written permission to leave that area is obtained from the judge;

    (*d*) to return to and remain at their place of residence at specified times;

    (*e*) to abstain from the consumption of drugs, except in accordance with a medical prescription, of alcohol or of any other intoxicating substance;

    (*f*) to provide, for the purpose of analysis, a sample of a bodily substance prescribed by regulation on the demand of a peace officer, a probation officer or someone designated under paragraph 810.3(2)(*a*) to make a demand, at the place and time and on the day specified by the person making the demand, if that person has reasonable grounds to believe that the defendant has breached a condition of the recognizance that requires them to abstain from the consumption of drugs, alcohol or any other intoxicating substance; or

    (*g*) to provide, for the purpose of analysis, a sample of a bodily substance prescribed by regulation at regular intervals that are specified, in a notice in Form 51 served on the defendant, by a probation officer or a person designated under paragraph 810.3(2)(*b*) to specify them, if a condition of

the recognizance requires the defendant to abstain from the consumption of drugs, alcohol or any other intoxicating substance.

(5) The provincial court judge shall consider whether it is desirable, in the interests of the defendant's safety or that of any other person, to prohibit the defendant from possessing any firearm, cross-bow, prohibited weapon, restricted weapon, prohibited device, ammunition, prohibited ammunition or explosive substance, or all of those things. If the judge decides that it is desirable to do so, the judge shall add that condition to the recognizance and specify the period during which the condition applies.

(5.1) If the provincial court judge adds a condition described in subsection (5) to a recognizance, the judge shall specify in the recognizance how the things referred to in that subsection that are in the defendant's possession shall be surrendered, disposed of, detained, stored or dealt with and how the authorizations, licences and registration certificates that are held by the defendant shall be surrendered.

(5.2) If the provincial court judge does not add a condition described in subsection (5) to a recognizance, the judge shall include in the record a statement of the reasons for not adding the condition.

(6) A provincial court judge may, on application of the informant, the Attorney General or the defendant, vary the conditions fixed in the recognizance.

(7) Subsections 810(4) and (5) apply, with any modifications that the circumstances require, to recognizances made under this section.

(8) With respect to proceedings under this section, "Attorney General" means either the Attorney General of Canada or the Attorney General of the province in which those proceedings are taken and includes the lawful deputy of any of them.
1997, c. 23, ss. 19, 26; 2001, c. 32, s. 46 [amended 2001, c. 41, s. 133(21)]; 2001, c. 41, s. 22, 133(19); 2002, c. 13, s. 80; 2009, c. 22, s. 19; 2011, c. 7, s. 8; 2015, c. 20, s. 24.

FEAR OF TERRORISM OFFENCE / Appearances / Adjudication / Duration extended / Refusal to enter into recognizance / Conditions in recognizance / Conditions — firearms / Surrender, etc. / Condition — passport / Condition — specified geographic area / Reasons / Variance of conditions / Other provisions to apply / Definition of "Attorney General" / Annual report.

810.011 (1) A person who fears on reasonable grounds that another person may commit a terrorism offence may, with the Attorney General's consent, lay an information before a provincial court judge.

(2) The provincial court judge who receives an information under subsection (1) may cause the parties to appear before a provincial court judge.

(3) If the provincial court judge before whom the parties appear is satisfied by the evidence adduced that the informant has reasonable grounds for the fear, the judge may order that the defendant enter into a recognizance, with or without sureties, to keep the peace and be of good behaviour for a period of not more than 12 months.

(4) However, if the provincial court judge is also satisfied that the defendant was convicted previously of a terrorism offence, the judge may order that the defendant enter into the recognizance for a period of not more than five years.

(5) The provincial court judge may commit the defendant to prison for a term of not more than 12 months if the defendant fails or refuses to enter into the recognizance.

(6) The provincial court judge may add any reasonable conditions to the recognizance that the judge considers desirable to secure the good conduct of the defendant, including conditions that require the defendant

- (a) to participate in a treatment program;
- (b) to wear an electronic monitoring device, if the Attorney General makes that request;
- (c) to return to and remain at their place of residence at specified times;
- (d) to abstain from the consumption of drugs, except in accordance with a medical prescription, of alcohol or of any other intoxicating substance;
- (e) to provide, for the purpose of analysis, a sample of a bodily substance prescribed by regulation on the demand of a peace officer, a probation officer or someone designated under paragraph 810.3(2)(a) to make a demand, at the place and time and on the day specified by the person making the demand, if that person has reasonable grounds to believe that the defendant has breached a condition of the recognizance that requires them to abstain from the consumption of drugs, alcohol or any other intoxicating substance; or
- (f) to provide, for the purpose of analysis, a sample of a bodily substance prescribed by regulation at regular intervals that are specified, in a notice in Form 51 served on the defendant, by a probation officer or a person designated under paragraph 810.3(2)(b) to specify them, if a condition of the recognizance requires the defendant to abstain from the consumption of drugs, alcohol or any other intoxicating substance.

(7) The provincial court judge shall consider whether it is desirable, in the interests of the defendant's safety or that of any other person, to prohibit the defendant from possessing any firearm, cross-bow, prohibited weapon, restricted weapon, prohibited device, ammunition, prohibited ammunition or explosive substance, or all of those things. If the judge decides that it is desirable to do so, the judge shall add that condition to the recognizance and specify the period during which it applies.

(8) If the provincial court judge adds a condition described in subsection (7) to a recognizance, the judge shall specify in the recognizance how the things referred to in that subsection that are in the defendant's possession shall be surrendered, disposed of, detained, stored or dealt with and how the authorizations, licences and registration certificates that are held by the defendant shall be surrendered.

(9) The provincial court judge shall consider whether it is desirable, to secure the good conduct of the defendant, to include in the recognizance a condition that the defendant deposit, in the specified manner, any passport or other travel document issued in their name that is in their possession or control. If the judge decides that

it is desirable, the judge shall add the condition to the recognizance and specify the period during which it applies.

(10) The provincial court judge shall consider whether it is desirable, to secure the good conduct of the defendant, to include in the recognizance a condition that the defendant remain within a specified geographic area unless written permission to leave that area is obtained from the judge or any individual designated by the judge. If the judge decides that it is desirable, the judge shall add the condition to the recognizance and specify the period during which it applies.

(11) If the provincial court judge does not add a condition described in subsection (7), (9) or (10) to a recognizance, the judge shall include in the record a statement of the reasons for not adding it.

(12) A provincial court judge may, on application of the informant, the Attorney General or the defendant, vary the conditions fixed in the recognizance.

(13) Subsections 810(4) and (5) apply, with any modifications that the circumstances require, to recognizances made under this section.

(14) With respect to proceedings under this section, "Attorney General" means either the Attorney General of Canada or the Attorney General of the province in which those proceedings are taken and includes the lawful deputy of any of them.

(15) Each year, the Attorney General of Canada shall prepare and cause to be laid before each House of Parliament a report setting out the number of recognizances entered into under this section in the previous year. 2015, c. 20, s. 25; 2019, c. 13, s. 153.

FEAR OF FORCED MARRIAGE OR MARRIAGE UNDER AGE OF 16 YEARS / Appearances / Adjudication / Duration extended / Refusal to enter into recognizance / Conditions in recognizance / Conditions — firearms / Surrender, etc. / Variance of conditions.

810.02 (1) A person who fears on reasonable grounds that another person will commit an offence under paragraph 273.3(1)(d) or section 293.1 or 293.2 may lay an information before a provincial court judge.

(2) The judge who receives the information may cause the parties to appear before a provincial court judge.

(3) If the provincial court judge before whom the parties appear is satisfied by the evidence adduced that the informant has reasonable grounds for the fear, the judge may order that the defendant enter into a recognizance to keep the peace and be of good behaviour for a period of not more than 12 months.

(4) However, if the provincial court judge is also satisfied that the defendant was convicted previously of an offence referred to in subsection (1), the judge may order that the defendant enter into the recognizance for a period of not more than two years.

(5) The provincial court judge may commit the defendant to prison for a term not exceeding 12 months if the defendant fails or refuses to enter into the recognizance.

(6) The provincial court judge may add any reasonable conditions to the recognizance that the judge considers desirable to secure the good conduct of the defendant, including conditions that

    (*a*) prohibit the defendant from making agreements or arrangements for the marriage, whether in or outside Canada, of the person in respect of whom it is feared that the offence will be committed;

    (*b*) prohibit the defendant from taking steps to cause the person in respect of whom it is feared that the offence will be committed to leave the jurisdiction of the court;

    (*c*) require the defendant to deposit, in the specified manner, any passport or any other travel document that is in their possession or control, whether or not such passport or document is in their name or in the name of any other specified person;

    (*d*) prohibit the defendant from communicating, directly or indirectly, with any specified person, or refrain from going to any specified place, except in accordance with any specified conditions that the judge considers necessary;

    (*e*) require the defendant to participate in a treatment program, including a family violence counselling program;

    (*f*) require the defendant to remain within a specified geographic area unless written permission to leave that area is obtained from the provincial court judge; and

    (*g*) require the defendant to return to and remain at their place of residence at specified times.

(7) The provincial court judge shall consider whether it is desirable, in the interests of the defendant's safety or that of any other person, to prohibit the defendant from possessing any firearm, cross-bow, prohibited weapon, restricted weapon, prohibited device, ammunition, prohibited ammunition or explosive substance, or all of those things. If the judge decides that it is desirable to do so, the judge shall add that condition to the recognizance and specify the period during which the condition applies.

(8) If the provincial court judge adds a condition described in subsection (7) to a recognizance, the judge shall specify in the recognizance how the things referred to in that subsection that are in the defendant's possession are to be surrendered, disposed of, detained, stored or dealt with and how the authorizations, licences and registration certificates that are held by the defendant are to be surrendered.

(9) A provincial court judge may, on application of the informant or the defendant, vary the conditions fixed in the recognizance. 2015, c. 29, s. 11.

WHERE FEAR OF SEXUAL OFFENCE / Appearances / Adjudication / Duration extended / Conditions in recognizance / Conditions — firearms / Surrender, etc. / Condition — reporting / Refusal to enter into recognizance / Judge may vary recognizance / Other provisions to apply.

810.1 (1) Any person who fears on reasonable grounds that another person will commit an offence under section 151 or 152, subsection 153(1), section 155, subsection 160(2) or (3), section 163.1, 170, 171, 171.1, 172.1 or 172.2, subsection 173(2), section 271, 272, 273 or 279.011, subsection 279.02(2) or 279.03(2), section 280 or 281 or subsection 286.1(2), 286.2(2) or 286.3(2), in respect of one or more persons who are under the age of 16 years, may lay an information before a provincial court judge, whether or not the person or persons in respect of whom it is feared that the offence will be committed are named.

(2) A provincial court judge who receives an information under subsection (1) may cause the parties to appear before a provincial court judge.

(3) If the provincial court judge before whom the parties appear is satisfied by the evidence adduced that the informant has reasonable grounds for the fear, the judge may order that the defendant enter into a recognizance to keep the peace and be of good behaviour for a period that does not exceed 12 months.

(3.01) However, if the provincial court judge is also satisfied that the defendant was convicted previously of a sexual offence in respect of a person who is under the age of 16 years, the judge may order that the defendant enter into the recognizance for a period that does not exceed two years.

(3.02) The provincial court judge may add any reasonable conditions to the recognizance that the judge considers desirable to secure the good conduct of the defendant, including conditions that

    (a) prohibit the defendant from having any contact — including communicating by any means — with a person under the age of 16 years, unless the defendant does so under the supervision of a person whom the judge considers appropriate;

(a.1) prohibit the defendant from using the Internet or other digital network, unless the defendant does so in accordance with conditions set by the judge;

    (b) prohibit the defendant from attending a public park or public swimming area where persons under the age of 16 years are present or can reasonably be expected to be present, or a daycare centre, schoolground or playground;

(b.1) prohibit the defendant from communicating, directly or indirectly, with any person identified in the recognizance, or refrain from going to any place specified in the recognizance, except in accordance with the conditions specified in the recognizance that the judge considers necessary;

    (c) require the defendant to participate in a treatment program;

    (d) require the defendant to wear an electronic monitoring device, if the Attorney General makes the request;

    (e) require the defendant to remain within a specified geographic area unless written permission to leave that area is obtained from the provincial court judge;

    (f) require the defendant to return to and remain at his or her place of residence at specified times;

    (g) require the defendant to abstain from the consumption of drugs except in accordance with a medical prescription, of alcohol or of any other intoxicating substance;

(*h*) require the defendant to provide, for the purpose of analysis, a sample of a bodily substance prescribed by regulation on the demand of a peace officer, a probation officer or someone designated under paragraph 810.3(2)(*a*) to make a demand, at the place and time and on the day specified by the person making the demand, if that person has reasonable grounds to believe that the defendant has breached a condition of the recognizance that requires them to abstain from the consumption of drugs, alcohol or any other intoxicating substance; or

(*i*) require the defendant to provide, for the purpose of analysis, a sample of a bodily substance prescribed by regulation at regular intervals that are specified, in a notice in Form 51 served on the defendant, by a probation officer or a person designated under paragraph 810.3(2)(*b*) to specify them, if a condition of the recognizance requires the defendant to abstain from the consumption of drugs, alcohol or any other intoxicating substance.

(3.03) The provincial court judge shall consider whether it is desirable, in the interests of the defendant's safety or that of any other person, to prohibit the defendant from possessing any firearm, cross-bow, prohibited weapon, restricted weapon, prohibited device, ammunition, prohibited ammunition or explosive substance, or all of those things. If the judge decides that it is desirable to do so, the judge shall add that condition to the recognizance and specify the period during which the condition applies.

(3.04) If the provincial court judge adds a condition described in subsection (3.03) to a recognizance, the judge shall specify in the recognizance how the things referred to in that subsection that are in the defendant's possession should be surrendered, disposed of, detained, stored or dealt with and how the authorizations, licences and registration certificates that are held by the defendant should be surrendered.

(3.05) The provincial court judge shall consider whether it is desirable to require the defendant to report to the correctional authority of a province or to an appropriate police authority. If the judge decides that it is desirable to do so, the judge shall add that condition to the recognizance.

(3.1) The provincial court judge may commit the defendant in prison for a term not exceeding twelve months if the defendant fails or refuses to enter into the recognizance.

(4) A provincial court judge may, on application of the informant or the defendant, vary the conditions fixed in the recognizance.

(5) Subsections 810(4) and (5) apply, with such modifications as the circumstances require, to recognizances made under this section. 1993, c. 45, s. 11; 1997, c. 18, s. 113; 2002, c. 13, s. 81; 2008, c. 6, s. 54; 2008, c. 6, ss. 52, 54(*j*); 2012, c. 1, s. 37; 2011, c. 7, s. 9; 2014, c. 21, s. 4; 2014, c. 25, s. 31; 2019, c. 25, s. 320.

WHERE FEAR OF SERIOUS PERSONAL INJURY OFFENCE / Appearances / Adjudication / Duration extended / Refusal to enter into recognizance / Conditions in recognizance / Condition — firearms / Surrender, etc. / Reasons / Conditions — reporting / Variance of conditions / Other provision to apply.

810.2 (1) Any person who fears on reasonable grounds that another person will commit a serious personal injury offence, as that expression is defined in section 752, may, with the consent of the Attorney General, lay an information before a provincial court judge, whether or not the person or persons in respect of whom it is feared that the offence will be committed are named.

(2) A provincial court judge who receives an information under subsection (1) may cause the parties to appear before a provincial court judge.

(3) If the provincial court judge before whom the parties appear is satisfied by the evidence adduced that the informant has reasonable grounds for the fear, the judge may order that the defendant enter into a recognizance to keep the peace and be of good behaviour for a period that does not exceed 12 months.

(3.1) However, if the provincial court judge is also satisfied that the defendant was convicted previously of an offence referred to in subsection (1), the judge may order that the defendant enter into the recognizance for a period that does not exceed two years.

(4) The provincial court judge may commit the defendant to prison for a term not exceeding twelve months if the defendant fails or refuses to enter into the recognizance.

(4.1) The provincial court judge may add any reasonable conditions to the recognizance that the judge considers desirable to secure the good conduct of the defendant, including conditions that require the defendant

   (a) to participate in a treatment program;

   (b) to wear an electronic monitoring device, if the Attorney General makes the request;

   (c) to remain within a specified geographic area unless written permission to leave that area is obtained from the provincial court judge;

   (d) to return to and remain at his or her place of residence at specified times;

   (e) to abstain from the consumption of drugs except in accordance with a medical prescription, of alcohol or of any other intoxicating substance;

   (f) to provide, for the purpose of analysis, a sample of a bodily substance prescribed by regulation on the demand of a peace officer, a probation officer or someone designated under paragraph 810.3(2)(a) to make a demand, at the place and time and on the day specified by the person making the demand, if that person has reasonable grounds to believe that the defendant has breached a condition of the recognizance that requires them to abstain from the consumption of drugs, alcohol or any other intoxicating substance; or

   (g) to provide, for the purpose of analysis, a sample of a bodily substance prescribed by regulation at regular intervals that are specified, in a notice in Form 51 served on the defendant, by a probation officer or a person designated under paragraph 810.3(2)(b) to specify them, if a condition of

the recognizance requires the defendant to abstain from the consumption of drugs, alcohol or any other intoxicating substance.

(5) The provincial court judge shall consider whether it is desirable, in the interests of the defendant's safety or that of any other person, to prohibit the defendant from possessing any firearm, cross-bow, prohibited weapon, restricted weapon, prohibited device, ammunition, prohibited ammunition or explosive substance, or all of those things. If the judge decides that it is desirable to do so, the judge shall add that condition to the recognizance and specify the period during which the condition applies.

(5.1) If the provincial court judge adds a condition described in subsection (5) to a recognizance, the judge shall specify in the recognizance how the things referred to in that subsection that are in the defendant's possession should be surrendered, disposed of, detained, stored or dealt with and how the authorizations, licences and registration certificates that are held by the defendant should be surrendered.

(5.2) If the provincial court judge does not add a condition described in subsection (5) to a recognizance, the judge shall include in the record a statement of the reasons for not adding the condition.

(6) The provincial court judge shall consider whether it is desirable to require the defendant to report to the correctional authority of a province or to an appropriate police authority. If the judge decides that it is desirable to do so, the judge shall add that condition to the recognizance.

(7) A provincial court judge may, on application of the informant, of the Attorney General or of the defendant, vary the conditions fixed in the recognizance.

(8) Subsections 810(4) and (5) apply, with such modifications as the circumstances require, to recognizances made under this section. 1997, c. 17, s. 9; 2002, c. 13, s. 82; 2008, c. 6, s. 53; 2011, c. 7, s. 10.

AUDIOCONFERENCE OR VIDEOCONFERENCE / Application.

810.21 (1) If a defendant is required to appear under any of sections 83.3 and 810 to 810.2, a provincial court judge may, on application of the prosecutor, order that the defendant appear by audioconference or videoconference.

(2) Despite section 769, sections 714.1 to 714.8 and Part XXII.01 apply, with any necessary modifications, to proceedings under this section. 2015, c. 20, s. 26; 2019, c. 25, s. 321.

TRANSFER OF ORDER / Attorney General's consent / If judge unable to act.

810.22 (1) If a person who is bound by an order under any of sections 83.3 and 810 to 810.2 becomes a resident of — or is charged with, convicted of or discharged under section 730 of an offence, including an offence under section 811, in — a territorial division other than the territorial division in which the order was made, on application of a peace officer or the Attorney General, a provincial court judge may, subject to subsection (2), transfer the order to a provincial court judge in that other territorial division and the order may then be dealt with and enforced by the provincial court judge to whom it is transferred in all respects as if that provincial court judge had made the order.

(2) The transfer may be granted only with
- (a) the consent of the Attorney General of the province in which the order was made, if the two territorial divisions are not in the same province; or
- (b) the consent of the Attorney General of Canada, if the information that led to the issuance of the order was laid with the consent of the Attorney General of Canada.

(3) If the judge who made the order or a judge to whom an order has been transferred is for any reason unable to act, the powers of that judge in relation to the order may be exercised by any other judge of the same court. 2015, c. 20, s. 26.

SAMPLES — DESIGNATIONS AND SPECIFICATIONS / Further designations / Restriction / Destruction of samples / Regulations / Notice — samples at regular intervals.

810.3 (1) For the purposes of sections 810, 810.01, 810.011, 810.1 and 810.2 and subject to the regulations, the Attorney General of a province or the minister of justice of a territory shall, with respect to the province or territory,
- (a) designate the persons or classes of persons that may take samples of bodily substances;
- (b) designate the places or classes of places at which the samples are to be taken;
- (c) specify the manner in which the samples are to be taken;
- (d) specify the manner in which the samples are to be analyzed;
- (e) specify the manner in which the samples are to be stored, handled and destroyed;
- (f) specify the manner in which the records of the results of the analysis of the samples are to be protected and destroyed;
- (g) designate the persons or classes of persons that may destroy the samples; and
- (h) designate the persons or classes of persons that may destroy the records of the results of the analysis of the samples.

(2) Subject to the regulations, the Attorney General of a province or the minister of justice of a territory may, with respect to the province or territory, designate the persons or classes of persons
- (a) to make a demand for a sample of a bodily substance for the purposes of paragraphs 810(3.02)(b), 810.01(4.1)(f), 810.011(6)(e), 810.1(3.02)(h) and 810.2(4.1)(f); and
- (b) to specify the regular intervals at which a defendant must provide a sample of a bodily substance for the purposes of paragraphs 810(3.02)(c), 810.01(4.1)(g), 810.011(6)(f), 810.1(3.02)(i) and 810.2(4.1)(g).

(3) Samples of bodily substances referred to in sections 810, 810.01, 810.011, 810.1 and 810.2 may not be taken, analyzed, stored, handled or destroyed, and the records of the results of the analysis of the samples may not be protected or

destroyed, except in accordance with the designations and specifications made under subsection (1).

(4) The Attorney General of a province or the minister of justice of a territory, or a person authorized by the Attorney General or minister, shall cause all samples of bodily substances provided under a recognizance under section 810, 810.01, 810.011, 810.1 or 810.2 to be destroyed within the period prescribed by regulation unless the samples are reasonably expected to be used as evidence in a proceeding for an offence under section 811.

(5) The Governor in Council may make regulations

- (a) prescribing bodily substances for the purposes of sections 810, 810.01, 810.011, 810.1 and 810.2;
- (b) respecting the designations and specifications referred to in subsections (1) and (2);
- (c) prescribing the periods within which samples of bodily substances are to be destroyed under subsection (4); and
- (d) respecting any other matters relating to the samples of bodily substances.

(6) The notice referred to in paragraph 810(3.02)(c), 810.01(4.1)(g), 810.011(6)(f), 810.1(3.02)(i) or 810.2(4.1)(g) must specify the places and times at which and the days on which the defendant must provide samples of a bodily substance under a condition described in that paragraph. The first sample may not be taken earlier than 24 hours after the defendant is served with the notice, and subsequent samples must be taken at regular intervals of at least seven days. 2011, c. 7, s. 11; 2015, c. 20, s. 34(2)(a)-(e).

PROHIBITION ON USE OF BODILY SUBSTANCE / Prohibition on use or disclosure of result / Exception / Offence.

810.4 (1) No person shall use a bodily substance provided under a recognizance under section 810, 810.01, 810.011, 810.1 or 810.2 except for the purpose of determining whether a defendant is complying with a condition in the recognizance that they abstain from the consumption of drugs, alcohol or any other intoxicating substance.

(2) Subject to subsection (3), no person shall use, disclose or allow the disclosure of the results of the analysis of a bodily substance provided under a recognizance under section 810, 810.01, 810.011, 810.1 or 810.2.

(3) The results of the analysis of a bodily substance provided under a recognizance under section 810, 810.01, 810.011, 810.1 or 810.2 may be disclosed to the defendant to whom they relate, and may also be used or disclosed in the course of an investigation of, or in a proceeding for, an offence under section 811 or, if the results are made anonymous, for statistical or other research purposes.

(4) Every person who contravenes subsection (1) or (2) is guilty of an offence punishable on summary conviction. 2011, c. 7, s. 11; 2015, c. 20, s. 34(2)(f).

ORDERS UNDER SECTIONS 486 TO 486.5 AND 486.7 / Offence — Order Restricting Publication.

810.5 (1) Sections 486 to 486.5 and 486.7 apply, with any necessary modifications, to proceedings under any of sections 83.3 and 810 to 810.2.

(2) Every person who fails to comply with an order made under any of subsections 486.4(1) to (3) or subsection 486.5(1) or (2) in proceedings referred to in subsection (1) is guilty of an offence under section 486.6. 2019, c. 13, s. 154.

BREACH OF RECOGNIZANCE.

811. A person bound by a recognizance under any of sections 83.3 and 810 to 810.2 who commits a breach of the recognizance is guilty of

(a) an indictable offence and is liable to imprisonment for a term of not more than four years; or

(b) an offence punishable on summary conviction. R.S., c. C-34, s. 746; 1993, c. 45, s. 11; 1994, c. 44, s. 82; 1997, c. 17, s. 10; c. 23, ss. 20, 27; 2001, c. 41, s. 23; 2015, c. 20, s. 27(1); c. 23, s. 19; c. 29, s. 12; 2019, c. 25, s. 322.

PROOF OF CERTIFICATE OF ANALYST — BODILY SUBSTANCE / Definition of "analyst" / Notice of intention to produce certificate / Requiring attendance of analyst.

811.1 (1) In a prosecution for breach of a condition in a recognizance under section 810, 810.01, 810.011, 810.1 or 810.2 that a defendant not consume drugs, alcohol or any other intoxicating substance, a certificate purporting to be signed by an analyst that states that the analyst has analyzed a sample of a bodily substance and that states the result of the analysis is admissible in evidence and, in the absence of evidence to the contrary, is proof of the statements contained in the certificate without proof of the signature or official character of the person who appears to have signed the certificate.

(2) In this section, "analyst" has the same meaning as in section 320.11.

(3) No certificate shall be admitted in evidence unless the party intending to produce it has, before the trial, given reasonable notice and a copy of the certificate to the party against whom it is to be produced.

(4) The party against whom a certificate of an analyst is produced may, with leave of the court, require the attendance of the analyst for cross-examination. 2011, c. 7, s. 12; 2015, c. 20, s. 34(3); 2018, c. 21, s. 27.

Appeal

DEFINITION OF "APPEAL COURT".

812. (1) For the purposes of sections 813 to 828 "appeal court" means

(a) in the Province of Ontario, the Superior Court of Justice sitting in the region, district or county or group of counties where the adjudication was made;

    (b) in the Province of Quebec, the Superior Court;
    (c) in the Provinces of Nova Scotia, British Columbia and Prince Edward Island, the Supreme Court;
    (d) in the Provinces of New Brunswick, Manitoba, Saskatchewan and Alberta, the Court of Queen's Bench;
    (e) [*Repealed*, 1992, c. 51, s. 43(2).]
    (f) [*Repealed*. 2015, c. 3, s. 56(2).]
    (g) in the Province of Newfoundland and Labrador, the Trial Division of the Supreme Court;
    (h) in Yukon and the Northwest Territories, a judge of the Supreme Court; and
    (i) in Nunavut, a judge of the Nunavut Court of Justice.

(2) A judge of the Court of Appeal of Nunavut is the appeal court for the purposes of sections 813 to 828 if the appeal is from a conviction, order, sentence or verdict of a summary conviction court consisting of a judge of the Nunavut Court of Justice. R.S., c. C-34, s. 747; 1972, c. 13, s. 65, c. 17, s. 2; 1974-75-76, c. 19, s. 1; 1978-79, c. 11, s. 10; R.S.C. 1985, c. 11 (1st Supp.), s. 2; c. 27 (2nd Supp.), s. 10.; 1990, c. 16, s. 7; 1990, c. 17, s. 15; 1992, c. 51, s. 43; 1993, c. 28, Sch. III, s. 36 (repealed 1999, c. 3, s. 12); 1998, c. 30, s. 14(d); 1999, c. 3, ss. 12, 55; 2002, c. 7, s. 149; 2015, c. 3, s. 56.

APPEAL BY DEFENDANT, INFORMANT OR ATTORNEY GENERAL.

813. Except where otherwise provided by law,
    (a) the defendant in proceedings under this Part may appeal to the appeal court
        (i) from a conviction or order made against him,
        (ii) against a sentence passed on him, or
        (iii) against a verdict of unfit to stand trial or not criminally responsible on account of mental disorder; and
    (b) the informant, the Attorney General or his agent in proceedings under this Part may appeal to the appeal court
        (i) from an order that stays proceedings on an information or dismisses an information,
        (ii) against a sentence passed on a defendant, or
        (iii) against a verdict of not criminally responsible on account of mental disorder or unfit to stand trial,

and the Attorney General of Canada or his agent has the same rights of appeal in proceedings instituted at the instance of the Government of Canada and conducted by or on behalf of that Government as the Attorney General of a province or his agent has under this paragraph. R.S., c. C-34, s. 748; R.S.C. 1985, c. 27 (1st Supp.), s. 180; 1991, c. 43, s. 9.

MANITOBA AND ALBERTA / Saskatchewan / British Columbia / Territories.

814. (1) In the Provinces of Manitoba and Alberta, an appeal under section 813 shall be heard at the sittings of the appeal court that is held nearest to the place where the cause of the proceedings arose, but the judge of the appeal court may, on the application of one of the parties, appoint another place for the hearing of the appeal.

(2) In the Province of Saskatchewan, an appeal under section 813 shall be heard at the sittings of the appeal court at the judicial centre nearest to the place where the adjudication was made, but the judge of the appeal court may, on the application of one of the parties, appoint another place for the hearing of the appeal.

(3) In the Province of British Columbia, an appeal under section 813 shall be heard at the sittings of the appeal court that is held nearest to the place where the adjudication was made, but the judge of the appeal court may, on the application of one of the parties, appoint another place for the hearing of the appeal.

(4) In Yukon, the Northwest Territories and Nunavut, an appeal under section 813 shall be heard at the place where the cause of the proceedings arose or at the place nearest to it where a court is appointed to be held. R.S., c. C-34, s. 749; 1984, c. 41, s. 2; 1993, c. 28, Sch. III, s. 37; 2002, c. 7, s. 150.

NOTICE OF APPEAL / Extension of time.

815. (1) An appellant who proposes to appeal to the appeal court shall give notice of appeal in such manner and within such period as may be directed by rules of court.

(2) The appeal court or a judge thereof may at any time extend the time within which notice of appeal may be given. R.S., c. C-34, s. 750; 1972, c. 13, s. 66; 1974-75-76, c. 93, s. 89.

Interim Release of Appellant

RELEASE ORDER — APPELLANT / Release of appellant / Applicable provisions.

816. (1) A person who was the defendant in proceedings before a summary conviction court and who is an appellant under section 813 shall, if they are in custody, remain in custody unless the appeal court at which the appeal is to be heard makes a release order referred to in section 515, the form of which may be adapted to suit the circumstances, which must include the condition that the person surrender themselves into custody in accordance with the order.

(1.1) The person having the custody of the appellant shall, if the appellant complies with the order, immediately release the appellant.

(2) Sections 495.1, 512.3 and 524 apply, with any modifications that the circumstances require, in respect of any proceedings under this section. R.S., c. C-34, s. 752; R.S., c. 2 (2nd Supp.), s. 16; 1974-75-76, c. 39, s. 91; R.S.C. 1985, c. 27 (1st Supp.), s. 181; 2019, c. 25, s. 323.

RECOGNIZANCE OF PROSECUTOR / Condition / Appeals by Attorney General / Form of undertaking or recognizance.

817. (1) The prosecutor in proceedings before a summary conviction court by whom an appeal is taken under section 813 shall, immediately after filing the notice of appeal and proof of service of the notice in accordance with section 815, appear before a justice, and the justice shall, after giving the prosecutor and the respondent a reasonable opportunity to be heard, order that the prosecutor enter into a recognizance, with or without sureties, in the amount that the justice directs and with or without the deposit of money or other valuable security that the justice directs.

(2) The condition of a recognizance entered into under this section is that the prosecutor will appear personally or by counsel at the sittings of the appeal court at which the appeal is to be heard.

(3) This section does not apply in respect of an appeal taken by the Attorney General or by counsel acting on behalf of the Attorney General. R.S., c. 2 (2nd Supp.), s. 16; 2019, c. 25, s. 324.

(4) [*Repealed*, 2019, c. 25, s. 324(2).]

APPLICATION TO APPEAL COURT FOR REVIEW / Disposition of application by appeal court / Effect of order.

818. (1) Where a justice makes an order under section 817, either the appellant or the respondent may, before or at any time during the hearing of the appeal, apply to the appeal court for a review of the order made by the justice.

(2) On the hearing of an application under this section, the appeal court, after giving the appellant and the respondent a reasonable opportunity to be heard, shall
  (*a*) dismiss the application; or
  (*b*) if the person applying for the review shows cause, allow the application, vacate the order made by the justice and make the order that in the opinion of the appeal court should have been made.

(3) An order made under this section shall have the same force and effect as if it had been made by the justice. R.S., c. 2 (2nd Supp.), s. 16; 1974-75-76, c. 93, s. 91.1.

APPLICATION TO FIX DATE FOR HEARING OF APPEAL / Order fixing date.

819. (1) Where, in the case of an appellant who has been convicted by a summary conviction court and who is in custody pending the hearing of his appeal, the hearing of his appeal has not commenced within thirty days from the day on which notice of his appeal was given in accordance with the rules referred to in section 815, the person having the custody of the appellant shall, forthwith on the expiration of those thirty days, apply to the appeal court to fix a date for the hearing of the appeal.

(2) On receiving an application under subsection (1), the appeal court shall, after giving the prosecutor a reasonable opportunity to be heard, fix a date for the hearing of the appeal and give such directions as it thinks necessary for expediting the hearing of the appeal. R.S., c. 2 (2nd Supp.), s. 16; 1974-75-76, c. 93, s. 92.

PAYMENT OF FINE NOT A WAIVER OF APPEAL / Presumption.

820. (1) A person does not waive his right of appeal under section 813 by reason only that he pays the fine imposed on conviction, without in any way indicating an intention to appeal or reserving the right to appeal.

(2) A conviction, order or sentence shall be deemed not to have been appealed against until the contrary is shown. R.S., c. C-34, s. 753.

Procedure on Appeal

NOTIFICATION AND TRANSMISSION OF CONVICTION, ETC. / Saving / Appellant to furnish transcript of evidence.

821. (1) Where a notice of appeal has been given in accordance with the rules referred to in section 815, the clerk of the appeal court shall notify the summary conviction court that made the conviction or order appealed from or imposed the sentence appealed against of the appeal and on receipt of the notification that summary conviction court shall transmit the conviction, order or order of dismissal and all other material in its possession in connection with the proceedings to the appeal court before the time when the appeal is to be heard, or within such further time as the appeal court may direct, and the material shall be kept by the clerk of the appeal court with the records of the appeal court.

(2) An appeal shall not be dismissed by the appeal court by reason only that a person other than the appellant failed to comply with the provisions of this Part relating to appeals.

(3) Where the evidence on a trial before a summary conviction court has been taken by a stenographer duly sworn or by a sound recording apparatus, the appellant shall, unless the appeal court otherwise orders or the rules referred to in section 815 otherwise provide, cause a transcript thereof, certified by the stenographer or in accordance with subsection 540(6), as the case may be, to be furnished to the appeal court and the respondent for use on the appeal. R.S., c. C-34, s. 754; 1972, c. 13, s. 67; 1974-75-76, c. 93, s. 93.

CERTAIN SECTIONS APPLICABLE TO APPEALS / New trial / Order of detention or release / Trial _de novo_ / Former evidence / Appeal against sentence / General provisions re appeals.

822. (1) Where an appeal is taken under section 813 in respect of any conviction, acquittal, sentence, verdict or order, sections 683 to 689, with the exception of subsections 683(3) and 686(5), apply, with such modifications as the circumstances require.

(2) Where an appeal court orders a new trial, it shall be held before a summary conviction court other than the court that tried the defendant in the first instance, unless the appeal court directs that the new trial be held before the summary conviction court that tried the accused in the first instance.

(3) Where an appeal court orders a new trial, it may make such order for the release or detention of the appellant pending the trial as may be made by a justice

pursuant to section 515 and the order may be enforced in the same manner as if it had been made by a justice under that section, and the provisions of Part XVI apply with such modifications as the circumstances require to the order.

(4) Despite subsections (1) to (3), if an appeal is taken under section 813 and because of the condition of the record of the trial in the summary conviction court or for any other reason, the appeal court, on application of the defendant, the informant, the Attorney General or the Attorney General's agent, is of the opinion that the interests of justice would be better served by hearing and determining the appeal by holding a trial de novo, the appeal court may order that the appeal shall be heard by way of trial de novo in accordance with any rules that may be made under section 482 or 482.1, and for that purpose the provisions of sections 793 to 809 apply, with any modifications that the circumstances require.

(5) The appeal court may, for the purpose of hearing and determining an appeal under subsection (4), permit the evidence of any witness taken before the summary conviction court to be read if that evidence has been authenticated in accordance with section 540 and if

- (*a*)   the appellant and respondent consent,
- (*b*)   the appeal court is satisfied that the attendance of the witness cannot reasonably be obtained, or
- (*c*)   by reason of the formal nature of the evidence or otherwise the court is satisfied that the opposite party will not be prejudiced,

and any evidence that is read under the authority of this subsection has the same force and effect as if the witness had given the evidence before the appeal court.

(6) Where an appeal is taken under subsection (4) against sentence, the appeal court shall, unless the sentence is one fixed by law, consider the fitness of the sentence appealed against and may, on such evidence, if any, as it thinks fit to require or receive, by order,

- (*a*)   dismiss the appeal, or
- (*b*)   vary the sentence within the limits prescribed by law for the offence of which the defendant was convicted,

and in making any order under paragraph (*b*) the appeal court may take into account any time spent in custody by the defendant as a result of the offence.

(7) The following provisions apply in respect of appeals under subsection (4):

- (*a*)   where an appeal is based on an objection to an information or any process, judgment shall not be given in favour of the appellant
  - (i)   for any alleged defect therein in substance or in form, or
  - (ii)   for any variance between the information or process and the evidence adduced at the trial,

  unless it is shown
  - (iii)   that the objection was taken at the trial, and
  - (iv)   that an adjournment of the trial was refused notwithstanding that the variance referred to in subparagraph (ii) had deceived or misled the appellant; and
- (*b*)   where an appeal is based on a defect in a conviction or an order, judgment shall not be given in favour of the appellant, but the court shall make an order curing the defect. R.S., c. C-34, s. 755; R.S., c. 2 (2nd Supp.), s. 17;

1974-75-76, c. 93, s. 94; 1984, c. 40, s. 20; 1991, c. 43, s. 9; 2002, c. 13, s. 83.

823. [*Repealed*, 1991, c. 43, s. 9.]

ADJOURNMENT.

824. The appeal court may adjourn the hearing of the appeal from time to time as may be necessary. R.S., c. C-34, s. 756.

DISMISSAL FOR FAILURE TO APPEAR OR WANT OF PROSECUTION.

825. The appeal court may, on proof that notice of an appeal has been given and that

(a) the appellant has failed to comply with the conditions of a release order made under section 816 or of a recognizance entered into under section 817; or

(b) the appeal has not been proceeded with or has been abandoned,

order that the appeal be dismissed. R.S., c. C-34, s. 757; R.S., c. 2 (2nd Supp.), s. 18; 2019, c. 25, s. 325.

COSTS.

826. Where an appeal is heard and determined or is abandoned or is dismissed for want of prosecution, the appeal court may make any order with respect to costs that it considers just and reasonable. R.S., c. C-34, s. 758.

TO WHOM COSTS PAYABLE, AND WHEN / Certificate of non-payment of costs / Committal.

827. (1) Where the appeal court orders the appellant or respondent to pay costs, the order shall direct that the costs be paid to the clerk of the court, to be paid by him to the person entitled to them, and shall fix the period within which the costs shall be paid.

(2) Where costs are not paid in full within the period fixed for payment and the person who has been ordered to pay them has not been bound by a recognizance to pay them, the clerk of the court shall, on application by the person entitled to the costs, or by any person on his behalf, and on payment of any fee to which the clerk of the court is entitled, issue a certificate in Form 42 certifying that the costs or a part thereof, as the case may be, have not been paid.

(3) A justice having jurisdiction in the territorial division in which a certificate has been issued under subsection (2) may, on production of the certificate, by warrant in Form 26, commit the defaulter to imprisonment for a term not exceeding one month, unless the amount of the costs and, where the justice thinks fit so to order, the costs of the committal and of conveying the defaulter to prison are sooner paid. R.S., c. C-34, s. 759.

ENFORCEMENT OF CONVICTION OR ORDER BY COURT OF APPEAL / Enforcement by justice / Duty of clerk of court.

828. (1) A conviction or order made by the appeal court may be enforced

   (*a*) in the same manner as if it had been made by the summary conviction court; or

   (*b*) by process of the appeal court.

(2) Where an appeal taken against a conviction or order adjudging payment of a sum of money is dismissed, the summary conviction court that made the conviction or order or a justice for the same territorial division may issue a warrant of committal as if no appeal had been taken.

(3) When a conviction or order that has been made by an appeal court is to be enforced by a justice, the clerk of the appeal court shall send to the justice the conviction or order and all writings relating to that conviction or order, except the notice of intention to appeal and any undertaking, release order or recognizance. R.S., c. C-34, s. 760; 2019, c. 25, s. 326.

Summary Appeal on Transcript or Agreed Statement of Facts

DEFINITION OF "APPEAL COURT" / Nunavut.

829. (1) Subject to subsection (2), for the purposes of sections 830 to 838, "appeal court" means, in any province, the superior court of criminal jurisdiction for the province.

(2) If the appeal is from a conviction, judgment, verdict or other final order or determination of a summary conviction court consisting of a judge of the Nunavut Court of Justice, "appeal court" means a judge of the Court of Appeal of Nunavut. R.S.C. 1985, c. 27 (1st Supp.), s. 182; 1999, c. 3, s. 56.

APPEALS / Form of appeal / Rules for appeals / Rights of Attorney General of Canada.

830. (1) A party to proceedings to which this Part applies or the Attorney General may appeal against a conviction, judgment, verdict of acquittal or verdict of not criminally responsible on account of mental disorder or of unfit to stand trial or other final order or determination of a summary conviction court on the ground that

   (*a*) it is erroneous in point of law;

   (*b*) it is in excess of jurisdiction; or

   (*c*) it constitutes a refusal or failure to exercise jurisdiction.

(2) An appeal under this section shall be based on a transcript of the proceedings appealed from unless the appellant files with the appeal court, within fifteen days of the filing of the notice of appeal, a statement of facts agreed to in writing by the respondent.

(3) An appeal under this section shall be made within the period and in the manner directed by any applicable rules of court and where there are no such rules otherwise providing, a notice of appeal in writing shall be served on the respondent and a copy thereof, together with proof of service, shall be filed with the appeal court within thirty days after the date of the conviction, judgment or verdict of acquittal or other final order or determination that is the subject of the appeal.

(4) The Attorney General of Canada has the same rights of appeal in proceedings instituted at the instance of the Government of Canada and conducted by or on behalf of that Government as the Attorney General of a province has under this section. R.S.C. 1985, c. 27 (1st Supp.), s. 182; 1991, c. 43, s. 9.

APPLICATION.

831. The provisions of sections 816, 817, 819 and 825 apply, with such modifications as the circumstances require, in respect of an appeal under section 830, except that on receiving an application by the person having the custody of an appellant described in section 819 to appoint a date for the hearing of the appeal, the appeal court shall, after giving the prosecutor a reasonable opportunity to be heard, give such directions as it thinks necessary for expediting the hearing of the appeal. R.S.C. 1985, c. 27 (1st Supp.), s. 182.

RELEASE ORDER OR RECOGNIZANCE / Attorney General.

832. (1) If a notice of appeal is filed under section 830, the appeal court may, if the defendant is the appellant, make a release order as provided in section 816 or, in any other case, order that the appellant appear before a justice and enter into a recognizance as provided in section 817.

(2) Subsection (1) does not apply where the appellant is the Attorney General or counsel acting on behalf of the Attorney General. R.S.C. 1985, c. 27 (1st Supp.), s. 182; 2019, c. 25, s. 327.

NO WRIT REQUIRED.

833. No writ of *certiorari* or other writ is required to remove any conviction, judgment, verdict or other final order or determination of a summary conviction court for the purpose of obtaining the judgment, determination or opinion of the appeal court. R.S.C. 1985, c. 27 (1st Supp.), s. 182; 1991, c. 43, s. 9.

POWERS OF APPEAL COURT / Authority of judge.

834. (1) When a notice of appeal is filed pursuant to section 830, the appeal court shall hear and determine the grounds of appeal and may

(*a*) affirm, reverse or modify the conviction, judgment, verdict or other final order or determination, or

(*b*) remit the matter to the summary conviction court with the opinion of the appeal court, and may make any other order in relation to the matter or with respect to costs that it considers proper.

(2) Where the authority and jurisdiction of the appeal court may be exercised by a judge of that court, such authority and jurisdiction may, subject to any applicable rules of court, be exercised by a judge of the court sitting in chambers as well as in vacation as in term time. R.S.C. 1985, c. 27 (1st Supp.), s. 182; 1991, c. 43, s. 9.

ENFORCEMENT / Idem.

835. (1) Where the appeal court renders its decision on an appeal, the summary conviction court from which the appeal was taken or a justice exercising the same jurisdiction has the same authority to enforce a conviction, order or determination that has been affirmed, modified or made by the appeal court as the summary conviction court would have had if no appeal had been taken.

(2) An order of the appeal court may be enforced by its own process. R.S.C. 1985, c. 27 (1st Supp.), s. 182.

APPEAL UNDER SECTION 830.

836. Every person who appeals under section 830 from any conviction, judgment, verdict or other final order or determination in respect of which that person is entitled to an appeal under section 813 shall be taken to have abandoned all the person's rights of appeal under section 813. R.S.C. 1985, c. 27 (1st Supp.), s. 182; 1991, c. 43, s. 9.

APPEAL BARRED.

837. Where it is provided by law that no appeal lies from a conviction or order, no appeal under section 830 lies from such a conviction or order. R.S.C. 1985, c. 27 (1st Supp.), s. 182.

EXTENSION OF TIME.

838. The appeal court or a judge thereof may at any time extend any time period referred to in section 830, 831 or 832. R.S.C. 1985, c. 27 (1st Supp.), s. 182.

Appeals to Court of Appeal

APPEAL ON QUESTION OF LAW / Nunavut / Sections applicable / Costs / Enforcement of decision / Right of Attorney General of Canada to appeal.

839. (1) Subject to subsection (1.1), an appeal to the court of appeal as defined in section 673 may, with leave of that court or a judge thereof, be taken on any ground that involves a question of law alone, against

    (*a*) a decision of a court in respect of an appeal under section 822; or

    (*b*) a decision of an appeal court under section 834, except where that court is the court of appeal.

(1.1) An appeal to the Court of Appeal of Nunavut may, with leave of that court or a judge of that court, be taken on any ground that involves a question of law alone, against a decision of a judge of the Court of Appeal of Nunavut acting as an appeal court under subsection 812(2) or 829(2).

(2) Sections 673 to 689 apply with such modifications as the circumstances require to an appeal under this section.

(3) Notwithstanding subsection (2), the court of appeal may make any order with respect to costs that it considers proper in relation to an appeal under this section.

(4) The decision of the court of appeal may be enforced in the same manner as if it had been made by the summary conviction court before which the proceedings were originally heard and determined.

(5) The Attorney General of Canada has the same rights of appeal in proceedings instituted at the instance of the Government of Canada and conducted by or on behalf of that Government as the Attorney General of a province has under this Part. R.S., c. C-34, s. 771; R.S.C. 1985, c. 27 (1st Supp.), s. 183; 1999, c. 3, s. 57.

Fees and Allowances

FEES AND ALLOWANCES / Order of lieutenant governor in council.

840. (1) Subject to subsection (2), the fees and allowances mentioned in the schedule to this Part are the fees and allowances that may be taken or allowed in proceedings before summary conviction courts and justices under this Part.

(2) The lieutenant governor in council of a province may order that all or any of the fees and allowances mentioned in the schedule to this Part shall not be taken or allowed in proceedings before summary conviction courts and justices under this Part in that province and, when the lieutenant governor in council so orders, he or she may fix any other fees and allowances for any items similar to those mentioned in the schedule, or any other items, to be taken or allowed instead. R.S., c. C-34, s. 772; 1994, c. 44, s. 83; 1997, c. 18, s. 114.

SCHEDULE
(Section 840)
FEES AND ALLOWANCES THAT MAY BE CHARGED BY SUMMARY CONVICTION COURTS AND JUSTICES

1. Information	$1.00
2. Summons or warrant.......................................	0.50
3. Warrant where summons issued in first instance	0.30
4. Each necessary copy of summons or warrant	0.30
5. Each subpoena or warrant to or for witnesses...................	0.30
(A subpoena may contain any number of names. Only one subpoena may be issued on behalf of a party in any proceeding, unless the summary conviction court or the justice considers it necessary or desirable that more than one subpoena be issued.)	
6. Information for warrant for witness and warrant for witness ...	1.00

7. Each necessary copy of subpoena to or warrant for witness.... 0.20
8. Each release order or recognizance................................. 1.00
9. Hearing and determining proceeding............................. 1.00
10. Where hearing lasts more than two hours 2.00
11. Where two or more justices hear and determine a proceeding, each is entitled to the fee authorized by item 9.
12. Each warrant of committal 0.50
13. Making up record of conviction or order on request of a party to the proceedings.. 1.00
14. Copy of a writing other than a conviction or order, on request of a party to the proceedings; for each folio of one hundred words

    0.10

15. Bill of costs, when made out in detail upon request of a party to the proceedings.. 0.20
    (Items 14 and 15 may be charged only where there has been an adjudication.)
16. Attending to remand prisoner..................................... 1.00
17. Attending to make a release order or take a recognizance...... 1.00

FEES AND ALLOWANCES THAT MAY BE ALLOWED TO PEACE OFFICERS

18. Arresting a person on a warrant or without a warrant........... $1.50
19. Serving summons or subpoena..................................... 0.50
20. Mileage to serve summons or subpoena or to make an arrest, both ways, for each mile 0.10
    (Where a public conveyance is not used, reasonable costs of transportation may be allowed.)
21. Mileage where service cannot be effected, on proof of a diligent attempt to effect service, each way, for each mile............... 0.10
22. Returning with prisoner after arrest to take him before a summary conviction court or justice at a place different from the place where the peace officer received the warrant to arrest, if the journey is of necessity over a route different from that taken by the peace officer to make the arrest, each way, for each mile

    0.10

23. Taking a prisoner to prison on remand or committal, each way, for each mile.. 0.10
    (Where a public conveyance is not used, reasonable costs of transportation may be allowed. No charge may be made under this item in respect of a service for which a charge is made under item 22.)
24. Attending summary conviction court or justice on summary conviction proceedings, for each day necessarily employed.... 2.00
    (No more than $2.00 may be charged under this item in respect of any day notwithstanding the number of proceedings that the peace officer attended on that day before that summary conviction court or justice.)

FEES AND ALLOWANCES THAT MAY BE ALLOWED TO WITNESSES

| 25. Each day attending trial | $4.00 |
| 26. Mileage travelled to attend trial, each way, for each mile | 0.10 |

FEES AND ALLOWANCES THAT MAY BE ALLOWED TO INTERPRETERS

27. Each half day attending trial	$2.50
28. Actual living expenses when away from ordinary place of residence, not to exceed per day	10.00
29. Mileage travelled to attend trial, each way, for each mile	0.10

R.S., c. C-34, Sch. to Part XXIV; 2019, c. 25, s. 328.

Part XXVIII / MISCELLANEOUS

Electronic Documents

DEFINITIONS / "data" / "electronic document".

841. The definitions in this section apply in this section and in sections 842 to 847.

"data" means representations of information or concepts, in any form.

"electronic document" means data that is recorded or stored on any medium in or by a computer system or other similar device and that can be read or perceived by a person or a computer system or other similar device. It includes a display, printout or other output of the data and any document, record, order, exhibit, notice or form that contains the data.

DEALING WITH DATA IN COURT.

842. Despite anything in this Act, a court may create, collect, receive, store, transfer, distribute, publish or otherwise deal with electronic documents if it does so in accordance with an Act or with the rules of court.

TRANSFER OF DATA / Time of filing.

843. (1) Despite anything in this Act, a court may accept the transfer of data by electronic means if the transfer is made in accordance with the laws of the place where the transfer originates or the laws of the place where the data is received.

(2) If a document is required to be filed in a court and the filing is done by transfer of data by electronic means, the filing is complete when the transfer is accepted by the court.

DOCUMENTS IN WRITING.

844. A requirement under this Act that a document be made in writing is satisfied by the making of the document in electronic form in accordance with an Act or the rules of court.

SIGNATURES.

845. If this Act requires a document to be signed, the court may accept a signature in an electronic document if the signature is made in accordance with an Act or the rules of court.

OATHS.

846. If under this Act an information, an affidavit or a solemn declaration or a statement under oath or solemn affirmation is to be made by a person, the court may accept it in the form of an electronic document if

(*a*) the person states in the electronic document that all matters contained in the information, affidavit, solemn declaration or statement are true to his or her knowledge and belief;

(*b*) the person before whom it is made or sworn is authorized to take or receive informations, affidavits, solemn declarations or statements and he or she states in the electronic document that the information, affidavit, solemn declaration or statement was made under oath, solemn declaration or solemn affirmation, as the case may be; and

(*c*) the electronic document was made in accordance with the laws of the place where it was made.

COPIES.

847. Any person who is entitled to obtain a copy of a document from a court is entitled, in the case of a document in electronic form, to obtain a printed copy of the electronic document from the court on payment of a reasonable fee determined in accordance with a tariff of fees fixed or approved by the Attorney General of the relevant province.

[*Heading repealed*, 2019, c. 25, s. 329.]

848. [*Repealed*, 2019, c. 25, s. 329.]

Forms

FORMS / Seal not required / Official languages.

849. (1) The forms set out in this Part, varied to suit the case, or forms to the like effect are deemed to be good, valid and sufficient in the circumstances for which they are provided.

(2) No justice is required to attach or affix a seal to any writing or process that he or she is authorized to issue and in respect of which a form is provided by this Part.

(3) Any pre-printed portions of a form set out in this Part, varied to suit the case, or of a form to the like effect shall be printed in both official languages. R.S., c. C-34, s. 773; R.S.C. 1985, c. 31 (4th Supp.), s. 97; 2002, c. 13, s. 84.

FORM 1

(*Sections 320.29 and 487*)

Information to obtain a search warrant

Canada,
Province of ....,
(*territorial division*).

This is the information of A.B., of .... in the said (*territorial division*), (*occupation*), hereinafter called the informant, taken before me.

The informant says that (*describe things to be searched for and offence in respect of which search is to be made*), and that he believes on reasonable grounds that the said things, or some part of them, are in the (*dwelling-house, etc.*) of C.D., of .... in the said (*territorial division*). (*Here add the grounds of belief, whatever they may be.*)

Wherefore the informant prays that a search warrant may be granted to search the said (*dwelling-house, etc.*) for the said things.

Sworn before me this ..... day of
......................., A.D. .... ,
at ....

....
(*Signature of Informant*)

....
A Justice of the Peace in and
   for ....

2018, c. 21, s. 28(*a*).

FORM 2

(*Sections 506 and 788*)

Information

Canada,
Province of ....,
(*territorial division*).

This is the information of C.D., of ...., (*occupation*), hereinafter called the informant.

The informant says that (*if the informant has no personal knowledge state that he believes on reasonable grounds and state the offence.*)

Sworn before me this ..... day of
......................., A.D. .... ,
at ....

....
(*Signature of Informant*)

....
A Justice of the Peace in and

833

for ....

Note: The date of birth of the accused may be mentioned on the information or indictment.

FORM 3

[*Repealed, R.S.C. 1985, c. 27 (1st Supp.), s. 184(2).*]

FORM 4

(*Sections 566, 566.1, 580 and 591*)

Heading of Indictment

Canada,
Province of ....,
(*territorial division*).

In the (*set out name of the court*)

Her Majesty the Queen

against

(*name of accused*)

(*Name of accused*) stands charged

1. That he (*state offence*).

2. That he (*state offence*).

Dated this .... day of .... A.D. ...., at ....

....
(*Signature of signing officer, Agent of Attorney General, etc., as the case may be*)

Note: The date of birth of the accused may be mentioned on the information or indictment.

1999, c. 3, s. 58.

FORM 5

(*Sections 320.29 and 487*)

Warrant to search

Canada,
Province of ....,
(*territorial division*).

834

To the peace officers in the said (*territorial division*) or to the (*named public officers*):

Whereas it appears on the oath of A.B., of ..... that there are reasonable grounds for
believing that (*describe things to be searched for and offence in respect of which
search is to be made*) are in .... at ...., hereinafter called the premises;

This is, therefore, to authorize and require you between the hours of (*as
the justice may direct*) to enter into the said premises and to search for the said
things and to bring them before me or some other justice.

Dated this .... day of .... A.D. ...., at ....

....
A Justice of the Peace in
and
for ....

1999, c. 5, s. 45; 2018, c. 21, s. 28(*b*).

FORM 5.001

Preservation Demand

(*Subsection 487.012(1)*)

Canada,
Province of ....
(*territorial division*)

To (*name of person*), of ....:

Because I have reasonable grounds to suspect that the computer data
specified below is in your possession or control and that that computer data
will assist in the investigation of an offence that has been or will be committed
under (*specify the provision of the Criminal Code or other Act of Parliament*),

(*or*)

will assist in the investigation of an offence that has been committed under
(*specify the provision of the law of the foreign state*) that is being conducted by
a person or authority, (*name of person or authority*), with responsibility in
(*specify the name of the foreign state*) for the investigation of such offences,

you are required to preserve (*specify the computer data*) that is in your
possession or control when you receive this demand until (*insert date*) unless,
before that date, this demand is revoked or a document that contains that
data is obtained under a warrant or an order.

This demand is subject to the following conditions:

If you contravene this demand without lawful excuse, you may be subject to a fine.

You are required to destroy the computer data that would not be retained in the ordinary course of business, and any document that is prepared for the purpose of preserving the computer data, in accordance with section 487.0194 of the *Criminal Code*. If you contravene that provision without lawful excuse, you may be subject to a fine, to imprisonment or to both.

....
*(**Signature of peace officer or public officer**)*

2014, c. 31, s. 26.

FORM 5.002

Information to Obtain a Preservation Order

(Subsection 487.013(2))

Canada,

Province of ....

(territorial division)

This is the information of *(name of peace officer or public officer)*, of .... ("the informant").

The informant says that they have reasonable grounds to suspect that an offence has been or will be committed under *(specify the provision of the Criminal Code or other Act of Parliament)* *(or* has been committed under *(specify the provision of the law of the foreign state))* and that *(specify the computer data)* is in the possession or control of (name of the person) and will assist in the investigation of the offence.

The informant also says that a peace officer or public officer intends to apply or has applied for a warrant or order in connection with the investigation to obtain a document that contains the computer data *(and, if applicable,* and that *(name of person or authority)* is conducting the investigation and has responsibility for the investigation of such offences in *(insert the name of the foreign state))*.

The reasonable grounds are: *(including, if applicable, whether a preservation demand was made under section 487.012 of the Criminal Code)*

The informant therefore requests that *(name of the person)* be ordered to preserve *(specify the computer data)* that is in their possession or control when they receive the order for 90 days after the day on which the order is made.

Sworn before me on *(date)*, at *(place)*.

836

....
(*Signature of informant*)

....
(*Signature of justice or judge*)

2014, c. 31, s. 26.

FORM 5.003

Preservation Order

(*Subsection 487.013(4)*)

Canada,
Province of ....
(*territorial division*)

To (name of person), of ....:

Whereas I am satisfied by information on oath of (*name of peace officer or public officer*), of ....,

(*a*) that there are reasonable grounds to suspect that an offence has been or will be committed under (*specify the provision of the Criminal Code or other Act of Parliament*) (*or has been committed under (specify the provision of the law of the foreign state)*) and that (*specify the computer data*) is in your possession or control and will assist in the investigation of the offence; and

(*b*) that a peace officer or public officer intends to apply or has applied for a warrant or order to obtain a document that contains the computer data (*and, if applicable, and that (name of person or authority) is conducting the investigation and has responsibility for the investigation of such offences in (insert the name of the foreign state)*);

Therefore, you are required to preserve the specified computer data that is in your possession or control when you receive this order until (*insert date*) unless, before that date, this order is revoked or a document that contains that data is obtained under a warrant or an order.

This order is subject to the following conditions:

If you contravene this order without lawful excuse, you may be subject to a fine, to imprisonment or to both.

You are required to destroy the computer data that would not be retained in the ordinary course of business, and any document that is prepared for the purpose of preserving the computer data, in accordance with section 487.0194 of the *Criminal Code*. If you contravene that provision without lawful excuse, you may be subject to a fine, to imprisonment or to both.

Dated (*date*), at (*place*).

....
(*Signature of justice or judge*)

2014, c. 31, s. 26.

FORM 5.004

Information to Obtain a Production Order

(*Subsections 487.014(2), 487.015(2), 487.016(2), 487.017(2) and 487.018(3)*)
Canada,
Province of ....
(*territorial division*)

This is the information of (*name of peace officer or public officer*), of
.... ("the informant").

The informant says that they have reasonable grounds to suspect (*or, if the application is for an order under section 487.014 of the Criminal Code, reasonable grounds to believe*)

(*a*) that an offence has been or will be committed under (*specify the provision of the Criminal Code or other Act of Parliament*); and

(*b*) (*if the application is for an order under section 487.014 of the Criminal Code*) that (*specify the document or data*) is in the possession or control of (*name of the person*) and will afford evidence respecting the commission of the offence.

(*or*)

(*b*) (*if the application is for an order under section 487.015 of the Criminal Code*) that the identification of a device or person involved in the transmission of (*specify the communication*) will assist in the investigation of the offence and that (*specify the transmission data*) that is in the possession or control of one or more persons whose identity is unknown will enable that identification.

(*or*)

(*b*) (*if the application is for an order under section 487.016 of the Criminal Code*) that (*specify the transmission data*) is in the possession or control of (*name of the person*) and will assist in the investigation of the offence.

(*or*)

(*b*) (*if the application is for an order under section 487.017 of the Criminal Code*) that (*specify the tracking data*) is in the possession or control of (*name of the person*) and will assist in the investigation of the offence.

(*or*)

(*b*) (*if the application is for an order under section 487.018 of the Criminal Code*) that (*specify the data*) is in the possession or control of (*name of the financial institution, person or entity*) and will assist in the investigation of the offence.

The reasonable grounds are:

The informant therefore requests

(*if the application is for an order under section 487.014 of the Criminal Code*) that (*name of the person*) be ordered to produce a document that is a copy of (*specify the document*) that is in their possession or control when they receive the order (*and/or to prepare and produce a document containing* (*specify the data*) *that is in their possession or control when they receive the order*).

(*or*)

(*if the application is for an order under section 487.015 of the Criminal Code*) that a person who is served with the order in accordance with subsection 487.015(4) of the *Criminal Code* be ordered to prepare and produce a document containing (*specify the transmission data*) that is in their possession or control when they are served with the order.

(*or*)

(*if the application is for an order under section 487.016 of the Criminal Code*) that (*name of the person*) be ordered to prepare and produce a document containing (*specify the transmission data*) that is in their possession or control when they receive the order.

(*or*)

(*if the application is for an order under section 487.017 of the Criminal Code*) that (*name of the person*) be ordered to prepare and produce a document containing (*specify the tracking data*) that is in their possession or control when they receive the order.

(*or*)

(*if the application is for an order under section 487.018 of the Criminal Code*) that (*name of the financial institution, person or entity*) be ordered to prepare and produce a document setting out (*specify the data*) that is in their possession or control when they receive the order.

Sworn before me on (*date*), **at** (*place*).

....
(*Signature of informant*)

....
(Signature of justice or judge)

2014, c. 31, s. 26.

FORM 5.005

Production Order for Documents

(Subsection 487.014(3))

Canada,
Province of ....
(territorial division)

To *(name of person)*, of ....:

Whereas I am satisfied by information on oath of *(name of peace officer or public officer)*, of ...., that there are reasonable grounds to believe that an offence has been or will be committed under *(specify the provision of the Criminal Code or other Act of Parliament)* and that *(specify the document or data)* is in your possession or control and will afford evidence respecting the commission of the offence;

Therefore, you are ordered to

produce a document that is a copy of *(specify the document)* that is in your possession or control when you receive this order

(and/or)

prepare and produce a document containing *(specify the data)* that is in your possession or control when you receive this order.

The document must be produced to *(name of peace officer or public officer)* within *(time)* at *(place)* in *(form)*.

This order is subject to the following conditions:

You have the right to apply to revoke or vary this order.

If you contravene this order without lawful excuse, you may be subject to a fine, to imprisonment or to both.

Dated *(date)*, at *(place)*.

....
(Signature of justice or judge)

2014, c. 31, s. 26.

FORM 5.006

Production Order to Trace a Communication

(*Subsection 487.015(3)*)

Canada,
Province of ....
(*territorial division*)

Whereas I am satisfied by information on oath of (*name of peace officer or public officer*), of ...., that there are reasonable grounds to suspect that an offence has been or will be committed under (*specify the provision of the Criminal Code or other Act of Parliament*), that the identification of a device or person involved in the transmission of (*specify the communication*) will assist in the investigation of the offence and that one or more persons whose identity was unknown when the application was made have possession or control of (*specify the transmission data*) that will enable that identification;

Therefore, on being served with this order in accordance with subsection 487.015(4) of the *Criminal Code*, you are ordered to prepare and produce a document containing (*specify the transmission data*) that is in your possession or control when you are served with this order.

The document must be produced to (*name of peace officer or public officer*) as soon as feasible at (*place*) in (*form*).

This order is subject to the following conditions:

You have the right to apply to revoke or vary this order.

If you contravene this order without lawful excuse, you may be subject to a fine, to imprisonment or to both.

Dated (*date*), at (*place*).

....
(*Signature of justice or judge*)

Served on (*name of person*) on (*date*), at (*place*).

....
(*Signature of peace officer or public officer*)

....
(*Signature of person served*)

2014, c. 31, s. 26.

FORM 5.007

Production Order for Transmission Data or Tracking Data

(Subsections 487.016(3) and 487.017(3))

Canada,
Province of ....
(*territorial division*)

To (*name of person*), of ....:

Whereas I am satisfied by information on oath of (*name of peace officer or public officer*), of ...., that there are reasonable grounds to suspect that an offence has been or will be committed under (*specify the provision of the Criminal Code or other Act of Parliament*) and that (*if the order is made under section 487.016 of the Criminal Code, specify the transmission data*) (*or, if the order is made under section 487.017 of the Criminal Code, specify the tracking data*) is in your possession or control and will assist in the investigation of the offence;

Therefore, you are ordered to prepare and produce a document containing the data specified that is in your possession or control when you receive this order.

The document must be produced to (*name of peace officer or public officer*) within (*time*) at (*place*) in (*form*).

This order is subject to the following conditions:

You have the right to apply to revoke or vary this order.

If you contravene this order without lawful excuse, you may be subject to a fine, to imprisonment or to both.

Dated (*date*), at (*place*).

....
(*Signature of justice or judge*)

2014, c. 31, s. 26.

FORM 5.008

Production Order for Financial Data

(Subsection 487.018(4))

Canada,
Province of ....
(*territorial division*)

To (*name of financial institution, person or entity*), of ....:

Whereas I am satisfied by information on oath of (*name of peace officer or public officer*), of ...., that there are reasonable grounds to suspect that an offence has been or will be committed under (*specify the provision of the Criminal Code or other Act of Parliament*) and that (*specify the data*) is in your possession or control and will assist in the investigation of the offence;

Therefore, you are ordered to prepare and produce a document setting out (*specify the data*) that is in your possession or control when you receive this order.

The document must be produced to (*name of the peace officer or public officer*) within (*time*) at (*place*) in (*form*).

This order is subject to the following conditions:

You have the right to apply to revoke or vary this order.

If you contravene this order without lawful excuse, you may be subject to a fine, to imprisonment or to both.

Dated (*date*), at (*place*).

....
(*Signature of justice or judge*)

2014, c. 31, s. 26.

FORM 5.0081

Information to Revoke or Vary an Order Made under Any of Sections 487.013 to 487.018 of the *Criminal Code*

(*Subsection 487.019(3)*)

Canada,
Province of ....
(*territorial division*)

This is the information of (*name of peace officer or public officer*), of .... ("the informant").

The informant says that on or after (*insert date*) the informant became aware of the following facts that justify the revocation (*or variation*) of an order made on (*insert date*) under (*specify the provision of the Criminal Code*):

....

The informant therefore requests that the order be revoked (*or be varied as follows: ....*).

Sworn before me on (*date*), at (*place*).

....
*(**Signature of informant**)*

....
*(**Signature of justice or judge**)*

2014, c. 31, s. 26.

FORM 5.009

Information to Obtain a Non-Disclosure Order

*(**Subsection 487.0191(2)**)*

Canada,
Province of ....
*(**territorial division**)*

This is the information of *(name of peace officer or public officer)*, of .... ("the informant").

The informant says that they have reasonable grounds to believe that the disclosure of the existence (or any of the contents or any of the following portion or portions) of *(identify the preservation demand made under section 487.012 of the Criminal Code, the preservation order made under section 487.013 of that Act or the production order made under any of sections 487.014 to 487.018 of that Act, as the case may be)* during *(identify the period)* would jeopardize the conduct of the investigation of the offence to which it relates:

(specify portion or portions)

The reasonable grounds are:

The informant therefore requests an order prohibiting *(name of the person, financial institution or entity)* from disclosing the existence (*or* any of the contents or any of the specified portion or portions) of the demand (*or* the order) during a period of *(identify the period)* after the day on which the order is made.

Sworn before me on *(date)*, at *(place)*.

....
*(**Signature of informant**)*

....
*(**Signature of justice or judge**)*

2014, c. 31, s. 26.

FORM 5.0091

Non-Disclosure Order

(*Subsection 487.0191(3)*)

Canada,
Province of ....
(*territorial division*)

To (*name of person, financial institution or entity*), of ....:

Whereas I am satisfied by information on oath of (*name of peace officer or public officer*), of ...., that there are reasonable grounds to believe that the disclosure of the existence (*or* any of the contents or any of the portion or portions, specified in the information,*) of (*identify the preservation demand made under section 487.012 of the Criminal Code, the preservation order made under section 487.013 of that Act or the production order made under any of sections 487.014 to 487.018 of that Act, as the case may be*) during (*identify the period*) would jeopardize the conduct of the investigation of the offence to which it relates;

Therefore, you are prohibited from disclosing the existence (*or* any of the contents or any of the following portion or portions) of the demand (*or* the order) during a period of (*identify the period*) after the day on which this order is made.

(*specify portion or portions*)

You have the right to apply to revoke or vary this order.

If you contravene this order without lawful excuse, you may be subject to a fine, to imprisonment or to both.

Dated (*date*), at (*place*).

....
(*Signature of justice or judge*)

2014, c. 31, s. 26.

FORM 5.01

(*Subsection 487.05(1)*)

Information to Obtain a Warrant to take Bodily Substances for Forensic DNA Analysis

Canada,
Province of ....,
(*territorial division*).

This is the information of (*name of peace officer*), (*occupation*), of .... in the said (*territorial division*), hereinafter called the informant, taken before me.

The informant says that he or she has reasonable grounds to believe

(*a*)   that (*offence*), a designated offence within the meaning of section 487.04 of the *Criminal Code*, has been committed;

(*b*)   that a bodily substance has been found

(i)   at the place where the offence was committed,

(ii)   on or within the body of the victim of the offence,

(iii)   on anything worn or carried by the victim at the time when the offence was committed, or

(iv)   on or within the body of any person or thing or at any place associated with the commission of the offence;

(*c*)   that (*name of person*) was a party to the offence; and

(*d*)   that forensic DNA analysis of a bodily substance from (name of person) will provide evidence about whether the bodily substance referred to in paragraph (*b*) was from that person.

The reasonable grounds are:

The informant therefore requests that a warrant be issued authorizing the taking from (*name of person*) of the number of samples of bodily substances that are reasonably required for forensic DNA analysis, provided that the person taking the samples is able by virtue of training or experience to take them by means of the investigative procedures described in subsection 487.06(1) of the *Criminal Code* and provided that, if the person taking the samples is not a peace officer, he or she take the samples under the direction of a peace officer.

Sworn to before me

this .... day of ...., A.D. ...., at ....

....
(Signature of informant)

....
(*Signature of provincial court judge*)

1998, c. 37, s. 24.

CODE

FORM 5.02

(Subsection 487.05(1))

Warrant Authorizing the Taking of Bodily Substances for Forensic DNA Analysis

Canada,

Province of ....,

(territorial division).

To the peace officers in *(territorial division)*:

Whereas it appears on the oath of (name of peace officer) of .... in the said *(territorial division)*, that there are reasonable grounds to believe

(*a*)   that *(offence)*, a designated offence within the meaning of section 487.04 of the *Criminal Code*, has been committed,

(*b*)   that a bodily substance has been found

  (i)   at the place where the offence was committed,

  (ii)   on or within the body of the victim of the offence,

  (iii)   on anything worn or carried by the victim at the time when the offence was committed, or

  (iv)   on or within the body of any person or thing or at any place associated with the commission of the offence,

(*c*)   that *(name of person)* was a party to the offence, and

(*d*)   that forensic DNA analysis of a bodily substance from *(name of person)* will provide evidence about whether the bodily substance referred to in paragraph (*b*) was from that person;

And whereas I am satisfied that it is in the best interests of the administration of justice to issue this warrant;

This is therefore to authorize and require you to take from (name of person) or cause to be taken by a person acting under your direction, the number of samples of bodily substances that are reasonably required for forensic DNA analysis, provided that the person taking the samples is able by virtue of training or experience to take them by means of the investigative procedures described in subsection 487.06(1) of the *Criminal Code* and provided that, if the person taking the samples is not a peace officer, he or she take the samples under the direction of a peace officer. This warrant is subject to the following terms and conditions that I consider advisable to ensure that the taking of the samples is reasonable in the circumstances:

Dated this .... day of .... A.D. ...., at ....

....

*(**Signature of provincial court judge**)*

1998, c. 37, s. 24.

FORM 5.03

*(**Subsections 487.051(1) and (2)**)*

ORDER AUTHORIZING THE TAKING OF BODILY SUBSTANCES FOR FORENSIC DNA ANALYSIS

Canada

Province of ....

*(**territorial division**)*

To the peace officers in *(**territorial division**)*:

Whereas *(**name of person**)* has been convicted under the *Criminal Code*, discharged under section 730 of that Act or, in the case of a young person, found guilty under the *Young Offenders Act*, chapter Y-1 of the Revised Statutes of Canada, 1985, or the *Youth Criminal Justice Act* of *(**offence**)*, which, on the day on which the person was sentenced or discharged, was a primary designated offence within the meaning of section 487.04 of the *Criminal Code*;

Therefore, you are authorized to take or cause to be taken from *(**name of person**)* the number of samples of bodily substances that is reasonably required for forensic DNA analysis, provided that the person taking the samples is able, by virtue of training or experience, to take them by means of the investigative procedures described in subsection 487.06(1) of the *Criminal Code* and that, if the person taking the samples is not a peace officer, they take them under the direction of a peace officer.

This order is subject to the following terms and conditions that the court considers advisable to ensure that the taking of the samples is reasonable in the circumstances:

Dated *(**date**)*.........., at ....*(**place**)*.

*(**Signature of judge of the court or clerk of the court**)*

**1998, c. 37, s. 24; 2002, c. 1, s. 185; 2005, c. 25, s. 12;
2007, c. 22, s. 23; 2019, c. 25, s. 330.**

FORM 5.04

(Subsection 487.051(3))

ORDER AUTHORIZING THE TAKING OF BODILY SUBSTANCES FOR FORENSIC DNA ANALYSIS

Canada

Province of ....

(territorial division)

To the peace officers in *(territorial division)*:

Whereas *(name of person)*, in this order called the "person",

(a) has been found not criminally responsible on account of mental disorder for *(offence)*, which, on the day on which the finding was made, was a primary designated offence within the meaning of section 487.04 of the *Criminal Code*, or

(b) has been convicted under the *Criminal Code*, discharged under section 730 of that Act or, in the case of a young person, found guilty under the *Young Offenders Act*, chapter Y-1 of the Revised Statutes of Canada, 1985, or the *Youth Criminal Justice Act*, of, or has been found not criminally responsible on account of mental disorder for, *(offence)*, which, on the day on which the person was sentenced or discharged or the finding was made, was one of the following secondary designated offences within the meaning of section 487.04 of the *Criminal Code (check applicable box)*:

☐ (i) an offence under the *Criminal Code* for which the maximum punishment is imprisonment for five years or more and that was prosecuted by indictment,

☐ (i.01) an offence under any of sections 9 to 14 of the *Cannabis Act* for which the maximum punishment is imprisonment for five years or more and that was prosecuted by indictment,

☐ (ii) an offence under any of sections 5 to 7 of the *Controlled Drugs and Substances Act* for which the maximum punishment is imprisonment for five years or more and that was prosecuted by indictment,

☐ (iii) an offence under any of sections 145 to 148, subsection 173(1), sections 264, 264.1, 266 and 270, subsections 286.1(1) and 320.16(1), paragraph 348(1)(e) and sections 349 and 423 of the *Criminal Code*,

☐ (iv) an offence under section 433 or 434 of the *Criminal Code* as that section read from time to time before July 1, 1990,

☐ (iv.1) an offence under section 252 of the *Criminal Code*, as it read from time to time before the day on which section 14 of *An Act to amend the Criminal Code (offences relating to conveyances) and to make consequential amendments to other Acts* comes into force, or

849

☐ **(v) an attempt or a conspiracy to commit an offence referred to in any of subparagraphs (i) to (ii) that was prosecuted by indictment (*or, if applicable*, an attempt or a conspiracy to commit an offence referred to in subparagraph (iii) or (iv));**

Whereas the person's criminal record, the nature of the offence, the circumstances surrounding its commission, whether the person was previously found not criminally responsible on account of mental disorder for a designated offence, and the impact that this order would have on the person's privacy and security have been considered by the court;

And whereas the court is satisfied that it is in the best interests of the administration of justice to make this order;

Therefore, you are authorized to take or cause to be taken from (*name of person*) the number of samples of bodily substances that is reasonably required for forensic DNA analysis, provided that the person taking the samples is able, by virtue of training or experience, to take them by means of the investigative procedures described in subsection 487.06(1) of the *Criminal Code* and that, if the person taking the samples is not a peace officer, they take them under the direction of a peace officer.

This order is subject to the following terms and conditions that the court considers advisable to ensure that the taking of the samples is reasonable in the circumstances:

Dated (*date*)........., at ....(*place*).

(*Signature of judge of the court or clerk of the court*)

> 1998, c. 37, s. 24; 2002, c. 1, s. 186; 2005, c. 25, s. 12; 2007, c. 22, s. 23; 2012, c. 1, s. 38; 2014, c. 25, s. 32; 2018, c. 16, s. 224; 2018, c. 21, s. 29; 2019, c. 25, s. 331.

FORM 5.041

(*Subsections 487.051(4) and 487.055(3.11)*)

ORDER TO A PERSON TO HAVE BODILY SUBSTANCES TAKEN FOR FORENSIC DNA ANALYSIS

Canada
Province of ....
(*territorial division*)

To A.B., of ....,

Whereas an order has been made under section 487.051, or an authorization has been granted under section 487.055, of the *Criminal Code*, to take from you the number of samples of bodily substances that is reasonably required for forensic DNA analysis;

This is therefore to order you, in Her Majesty's name, to appear on ....
(*date*)...................................., at.......... (*hour*), at (..........*place*), for the purpose of
the taking of bodily substances by means of the investigative procedures set
out in subsection 487.06(1) of the *Criminal Code*.

You are warned that failure to appear in accordance with this order may
result in a warrant being issued for your arrest under subsection 487.0551(1)
of the *Criminal Code*. You are also warned that failure to appear, without
reasonable excuse, is an offence under subsection 487.0552(1) of that Act.

Subsection 487.0551(1) of the *Criminal Code* states as follows:

487.0551 (1) If a person fails to appear at the place, day and time set out
in an order made under subsection 487.051(4) or 487.055(3.11) or in a
summons referred to in subsection 487.055(4) or 487.091(3), a justice of the
peace may issue a warrant for their arrest in Form 5.062 to allow samples of
bodily substances to be taken.

Subsection 487.0552(1) of the *Criminal Code* states as follows:

487.0552 (1) Every person who, without reasonable excuse, fails to comply
with an order made under subsection 487.051(4) or 487.055(3.11) of this Act
or under subsection 196.14(4) or 196.24(4) of the *National Defence Act*, or
with a summons referred to in subsection 487.055(4) or 487.091(3) of this
Act, is guilty of

(*a*)   an indictable offence and liable to imprisonment for a term of not
more than two years; or

(*b*)   an offence punishable on summary conviction.

Dated (*date*).........., at ....(*place*).

(*Signature of judge of the court or clerk of the court*)

2005, c. 25, s. 12; 2007, c. 22, s. 23; 2019, c. 25, s. 332.

FORM 5.05

(*Subsection 487.055(1)*)

APPLICATION FOR AN AUTHORIZATION TO TAKE BODILY SUB-STANCES FOR FORENSIC DNA ANALYSIS

Canada
Province of ....
(*territorial division*)

I (*name of peace officer*), (*occupation*), of .... in (*territorial
division*), apply for an authorization to take bodily substances for forensic
DNA analysis. A certificate referred to in paragraph 667(1)(*a*) of the *Criminal
Code* is filed with this application.

Whereas (*name of offender*), before June 30, 2000,

(*a*)   had been declared a dangerous offender under Part XXIV of the *Criminal Code*,

(*b*)   had been declared a dangerous offender or a dangerous sexual offender under Part XXI of the *Criminal Code*, chapter C-34 of the Revised Statutes of Canada, 1970, as it read from time to time before January 1, 1988,

(*c*)   had been convicted of murder,

(*c*.1)   had been convicted of attempted murder or conspiracy to commit murder or to cause another person to be murdered and is currently serving a sentence of imprisonment for that offence,

(*d*)   had been convicted of a sexual offence within the meaning of subsection 487.055(3) of the *Criminal Code* and is currently serving a sentence of imprisonment for that offence, or

(*e*)   had been convicted of manslaughter and is currently serving a sentence of imprisonment for that offence;

Therefore, I request that an authorization be granted under subsection 487.055(1) of the *Criminal Code* to take from (*name of offender*) the number of samples of bodily substances that is reasonably required for forensic DNA analysis, provided that the person taking the samples is able, by virtue of training or experience, to take them by means of the investigative procedures described in subsection 487.06(1) of the *Criminal Code* and that, if the person taking the samples is not a peace officer, they take them under the direction of a peace officer.

Dated this .... day of ...., A.D. ...., at ....

....
(*Signature of applicant*)
Canada

1998, c. 37, s. 24; 2005, c. 25, s. 12; 2007, c. 22, s. 23.

FORM 5.06

(*Subsection 487.055(1)*)

AUTHORIZATION TO TAKE BODILY SUBSTANCES FOR FORENSIC DNA ANALYSIS

Canada
Province of ....
(*territorial division*)

To the peace officers in (*territorial division*):

Whereas (*name of peace officer*), a peace officer in (*territorial division*), has applied for an authorization to take the number of samples of bodily substances from (*name of offender*) that is reasonably required for forensic DNA analysis by means of the investigative procedures described in subsection 487.06(1) of the *Criminal Code*;

Whereas (*name of offender*), before June 30, 2000,

(*a*) had been declared a dangerous offender under Part XXIV of the *Criminal Code*,

(*b*) had been declared a dangerous offender or a dangerous sexual offender under Part XXI of the *Criminal Code*, chapter C-34 of the Revised Statutes of Canada, 1970, as it read from time to time before January 1, 1988,

(*c*) had been convicted of murder,

(*c*.1) had been convicted of attempted murder or conspiracy to commit murder or to cause another person to be murdered and, on the date of the application, was serving a sentence of imprisonment for that offence,

(*d*) had been convicted of a sexual offence within the meaning of subsection 487.055(3) of the *Criminal Code* and, on the date of the application, was serving a sentence of imprisonment for that offence, or

(*e*) had been convicted of manslaughter and, on the date of the application, was serving a sentence of imprisonment for that offence;

And whereas I have considered the offender's criminal record, the nature of the offence, the circumstances surrounding its commission and the impact that this authorization would have on the offender's privacy and security of the person;

Therefore, you are authorized to take those samples or cause them to be taken from (*name of offender*), provided that the person taking the samples is able, by virtue of training or experience, to take them by means of the investigative procedures described in subsection 487.06(1) of the *Criminal Code* and that, if the person taking the samples is not a peace officer, they take them under the direction of a peace officer.

This authorization is subject to the following terms and conditions that I consider advisable to ensure that the taking of the samples is reasonable in the circumstances:

Dated this .... day of ...., A.D. ...., at ....

....
(*Signature of provincial court judge*)
Canada

1998, c. 37, s. 24; 2005, c. 25, s. 12; 2007, c. 22, s. 23.

FORM 5.061

(*Subsections 487.055(4) and 487.091(3)*)

SUMMONS TO A PERSON TO HAVE BODILY SUBSTANCES TAKEN FOR FORENSIC DNA ANALYSIS

Canada
Province of ....
(*territorial division*)

To A.B., of ....,

Whereas an authorization has been granted under section 487.055 or 487.091 of the *Criminal Code* to take from you the number of samples of bodily substances that is reasonably required for forensic DNA analysis;

This is therefore to command you, in Her Majesty's name, to appear on ...., the .... day of ...., A.D. ...., at .... o'clock, at ...., for the purpose of the taking of bodily substances by means of the investigative procedures set out in subsection 487.06(1) of the *Criminal Code*. A peace officer, or a person who is acting under a peace officer's direction, who takes the samples of bodily substances may use as much force as necessary to do so.

You are warned that failure to appear in accordance with this summons may result in a warrant being issued for your arrest under subsection 487.0551(1) of the *Criminal Code*. You are also warned that failure to appear, without reasonable excuse, is an offence under subsection 487.0552(1) of that Act.

Subsection 487.0551(1) of the *Criminal Code* states as follows:

487.0551 (1) If a person fails to appear at the place, day and time set out in an order made under subsection 487.051(4) or 487.055(3.11) or in a summons referred to in subsection 487.055(4) or 487.091(3), a justice of the peace may issue a warrant for their arrest in Form 5.062 to allow samples of bodily substances to be taken.

Subsection 487.0552(1) of the *Criminal Code* states as follows:

487.0552 (1) Every person who, without reasonable excuse, fails to comply with an order made under subsection 487.051(4) or 487.055(3.11) of this Act or under subsection 196.14(4) or 196.24(4) of the *National Defence Act*, or

854

with a summons referred to in subsection 487.055(4) or 487.091(3) of this Act, is guilty of

(*a*)   an indictable offence and liable to imprisonment for a term of not more than two years; or

(*b*)   an offence punishable on summary conviction.

Dated (*date*)..........., at ....(*place*).

(*Signature of judge of the court or clerk of the court*)

2005, c. 25, s. 12; 2007, c. 22, s. 23; 2019, c. 25, s. 333.

CODE

FORM 5.062

(*Subsection 487.0551(1)*)

WARRANT FOR ARREST

Canada
Province of ....
(*territorial division*)

To the peace officers in (*territorial division*):

This warrant is issued for the arrest of A.B., of ...., (*occupation*), in this warrant called the "offender".

Whereas the offender failed to appear at the place, day and time set out in an order made under subsection 487.051(4) or 487.055(3.11), or in a summons referred to in subsection 487.055(4) or 487.091(3), of the *Criminal Code* to submit to the taking of samples of bodily substances;

This is, therefore, to command you, in Her Majesty's name, to arrest the offender without delay in order to allow the samples of bodily substances to be taken.

Dated this .... day of .... , A.D. .... , at ....

....
**A Justice of the Peace in
and for** ....
Canada

2005, c. 25, s. 12; 2007, c. 22, s. 23.

FORM 5.07

(Subsection 487.057(1))

REPORT TO A PROVINCIAL COURT JUDGE OR THE COURT
Canada

Province of ....

(*territorial division*)

☐   To (*name of judge*), a judge of the provincial court who issued a warrant under section 487.05 or granted an authorization under section 487.055 or 487.091 of the *Criminal Code* or to another judge of that court:

☐   To the court that made an order under section 487.051 of the *Criminal Code*:

I (*name of peace officer*), declare that (*state here whether the samples were taken under a warrant issued under section 487.05, an order made under section 487.051 or an authorization granted under section 487.055 or 487.091 of the Criminal Code*).

I have (*state here whether you took the samples yourself or caused them to be taken under your direction*) from (*name of offender*) the number of samples of bodily substances that I believe is reasonably required for forensic DNA analysis, in accordance with (*state whether the samples were taken under a warrant issued or an authorization granted by the judge or another judge of the court or an order made by the court*).

The samples were taken on the .... day of ...., A.D. ...., at .... o'clock.

I (*or state the name of the person who took the samples*) took the following samples from (*name of offender*) in accordance with subsection 487.06(1) of the *Criminal Code* and was able, by virtue of training or experience, to do so (*check applicable box*):

☐   individual hairs, including the root sheath

☐   epithelial cells taken by swabbing the lips, tongue or inside cheeks of the mouth

☐   blood taken by pricking the skin surface with a sterile lancet

Any terms or conditions in the (*warrant, order or authorization*) have been complied with.

Dated this .... day of .... , A.D. .... , at ....

....

(*Signature of peace officer*)

1998, c. 37, s. 24; 2007, c. 22, s. 24.

FORM 5.08

(*Subsection 487.091(1)*)

APPLICATION FOR AN AUTHORIZATION TO TAKE ADDITIONAL SAMPLES OF BODILY SUBSTANCES FOR FORENSIC DNA ANALYSIS

Canada

Province of ....

(*territorial division*)

I (*name of peace officer*), (*occupation*), of .... in (*territorial division*), apply for an authorization to take additional samples of bodily substances for forensic DNA analysis.

Whereas samples of bodily substances were taken from (*name of offender*) for the purpose of forensic DNA analysis under an order made under section 487.051, or an authorization granted under section 487.055, of the *Criminal Code* (*attach a copy of the order or authorization*);

And whereas on (*day/month/year*) it was determined that

(*a*) a DNA profile could not be derived from the samples for the following reasons:

(*b*) the information or bodily substances required by regulations made under the *DNA Identification Act* were not transmitted in accordance with the requirements of the regulations or were lost for the following reasons:

Therefore, I request that an authorization be granted under subsection 487.091(1) of the *Criminal Code* to take from (*name of offender*) the number of additional samples of bodily substances that is reasonably required for forensic DNA analysis, provided that the person taking the samples is able, by virtue of training or experience, to take them by means of the investigative procedures described in subsection 487.06(1) of the *Criminal Code* and that, if the person taking the samples is not a peace officer, they take them under the direction of a peace officer.

Dated this .... day of ...., A.D. ...., at ....

....

(*Signature of applicant*)

Canada

1998, c. 37, s. 24; 2005, c. 25, s. 13; 2007, c. 22, s. 25.

FORM 5.09

(Subsection 487.091(1))

AUTHORIZATION TO TAKE ADDITIONAL SAMPLES OF BODILY SUBSTANCES FOR FORENSIC DNA ANALYSIS

Canada

Province of ....

(territorial division)

To the peace officers in *(territorial division)*:

Whereas samples of bodily substances were taken from *(name of offender)* for the purpose of forensic DNA analysis under an order made under section 487.051 or an authorization granted under section 487.055, of the *Criminal Code*;

Whereas on *(day/month/year)* it was determined that

(*a*)   a DNA profile could not be derived from the samples for the following reasons:

(*b*)   the information or bodily substances required by regulations made under the *DNA Identification Act* were not transmitted in accordance with the requirements of the regulations or were lost for the following reasons:

And whereas *(name of peace officer)*, a peace officer in *(territorial division)*, has applied for an authorization to take the number of additional samples of bodily substances from *(name of offender)* that is reasonably required for forensic DNA analysis by means of the investigative procedures described in subsection 487.06(1) of the *Criminal Code*;

Therefore, you are authorized to take those additional samples, or cause them to be taken, from *(name of offender)*, provided that the person taking the samples is able, by virtue of training or experience, to take them by means of the investigative procedures described in subsection 487.06(1) of the *Criminal Code* and that, if the person taking the samples is not a peace officer, they take them under the direction of a peace officer.

This authorization is subject to the following terms and conditions that I consider advisable to ensure that the taking of the samples is reasonable in the circumstances:

Dated this .... day of ...., A.D. ...., at ....

....
(Signature of provincial court judge)
Canada

1998, c. 37, s. 24; 2005, c. 25, s. 13; 2007, c. 22, s. 25.

FORM 5.1

(Sections 320.29 and 487.1)

Warrant to search

Canada,
Province of [*specify province*].

To A.B. and other peace officers in the [*territorial division in which the warrant is intended for execution*]:

Whereas it appears on the oath of A.B., a peace officer in the [*territorial division in which the warrant is intended for execution*], that there are reasonable grounds for dispensing with an information presented personally and in writing; and that there are reasonable grounds for believing that the following things

[*describe things to be searched for*]

relevant to the investigation of the following indictable offence

[*describe offence in respect of which search is to be made*]

are to be found in the following place or premises

[*describe place or premises to be searched*]:

This is, therefore, to authorize you to enter the said place or premises between the hours of [*as the justice may direct*] and to search for and seize the said things and to report thereon as soon as practicable but within a period not exceeding seven days after the execution of the warrant to the clerk of the court for the [*territorial division in which the warrant is intended for execution*].

Issued at [*time*] on the [*day*] of [*month*] A.D. [*year*], at [*place*].

....
A Judge of the Provincial
Court in and for the
Province of
[*specify province*].

To the Occupant: This search warrant was issued by telephone or other means of telecommunication. If you wish to know the basis on which this warrant was issued, you may apply to the clerk of the court for the territorial division in which the warrant was executed, at [*address*], to obtain a copy of the information on oath.

You may obtain from the clerk of the court a copy of the report filed by the peace officer who executed this warrant. That report will indicate the things, if any, that were seized and the location where they are being held.

R.S.C. 1985, c. 27 (1st Supp.), s. 184(3); R.S.C. 1985,
c. 1 (4th Supp.), s. 17; 2018, c. 1, s. 30.

FORM 5.2

(*Section 489.1*)

REPORT TO A JUSTICE

Canada,
Province of ....,
(*territorial division*).

To the justice who issued a warrant to the undersigned under section 320.29, 487 or 487.1 of the *Criminal Code* (*or another justice for the same territorial division or, if no warrant was issued, any justice having jurisdiction in respect of the matter*).

I, (*name of the peace officer or other person*) have (*state here whether you have acted under a warrant issued under section 320.29, 487 or 487.1 of the Criminal Code or under section 489 of the Criminal Code or otherwise in the execution of duties under the Criminal Code or other Act of Parliament to be specified*)

1 searched the premises situated at ....; and

2 seized the following things and dealt with them as follows:

Property Seized
(*describe each thing seized*)

Disposition
(*state, in respect of each thing seized, whether*

    (*a*) *it was returned to the person lawfully entitled to its possession, in which case the receipt for it shall be attached to this report; or*

    (*b*) *it is being detained to be dealt with according to law, in which case indicate the location and manner in which or, if applicable, the person by whom, it is being detained.*)

1. ....

2. ....

3. ....

4. ....

In the case of a warrant issued by telephone or other means of telecommunication, the statements referred to in subsection 487.1(9) of the *Criminal Code* shall be specified in the report.

Dated (*date*), at (*place*).

....

Signature of the peace officer or other person

R.S.C. 1985, c. 27 (1st Supp.), s. 184(3); R.S.C. 1985, c. 1
(4th Supp.), s. 17; 2018, c. 21, s. 31.

FORM 5.3

(*Section 462.32*)

REPORT TO A JUDGE OF PROPERTY SEIZED

Canada,
Province of ....,
(*territorial division*).

To a judge of the court from which the warrant was issued (*specify court*):

I, (*name of the peace officer or other person*) have acted under a warrant issued under section 462.32 of the *Criminal Code* and have

1. searched the premises situated at ....; and

2. seized the following property:

Property Seized	Location
(*describe each item of property seized*)	(*state, in respect of each item of property seized, the location where it is being detained*).

1.	....
2.	....
3.	....
4.	....

Dated this .... day of .... A.D. ...., at ....

....

Signature of peace officer or other person

R.S.C. 1985, c. 42 (4th Supp.), s. 6.

FORM 6

(*Section 2*)

Summons to a Person Charged with an Offence

Canada,
Province of ....
(*territorial division*).

To (*name of person*), of ...., born on (*date of birth*):

Because you have this day been charged with (set out briefly the offence in respect of which the accused is charged);

Therefore, you are ordered, in Her Majesty's name:

(*a*)   to appear on (*date*) at (*hour*) at (*place*) for the purposes of the *Identification of Criminals Act* (*Ignore, if not filled in*); and

(*b*)   to attend court on (*date*), at (*hour*), at (*place*), or before any justice for the (*territorial division*) who is there, and to attend court at any time after as required by the court, in order to be dealt with according to law.

You are warned that, unless you have a lawful excuse, it is an offence under subsection 145(3) of the *Criminal Code* to fail to appear for the purposes of the *Identification of Criminals Act* or to attend court, as required in this summons.

If you commit an offence under subsection 145(3) of the *Criminal Code*, a warrant for your arrest may be issued (Section 512 or 512.1 of the *Criminal Code*) and you may be liable to a fine or to imprisonment, or to both.

If you do not comply with this summons or are charged with committing an indictable offence after it has been issued to you, this summons may be cancelled and, as a result, you may be detained in custody (Subsection 524(4) of the *Criminal Code*).

Signed on (*date*), at (*place*).

....
(*Signature of judge, justice, clerk of the court or chairperson of the Review Board*)

....
(*Name of the judge, justice or chairperson*)

2018, c. 29, s. 69(1); 2019, c. 25, s. 334.

FORM 7

(Sections 475, 493, 597, 800 and 803)

Warrant for Arrest

Canada,
Province of ....,
(territorial division).

To the peace officers in the *(territorial division)*:

This warrant is issued for the arrest of *(name of person)*, of ...., born on *(date of birth)*, referred to in this warrant as the accused.

Because the accused has been charged with *(set out briefly the offence in respect of which the accused is charged)*;

And because *(check those that are applicable)*:

☐ (a) there are reasonable grounds to believe that it is necessary in the public interest to issue this warrant for the arrest of the accused [507(4), 512(1)];

☐ (b) the accused failed to attend court in accordance with the summons served on the accused [512(2)];

☐ (c) (an appearance notice *or* undertaking) was confirmed and the accused failed to attend court in accordance with it [512(2)];

☐ (d) it appears that a summons cannot be served because the accused is evading service [512(2)];

☐ (e) the accused was ordered to be present at the hearing of an application for a review of an order made by a justice and did not attend the hearing [520(5), 521(5)];

☐ (f) there are reasonable grounds to believe that the accused has contravened or is about to contravene the (summons *or* appearance notice *or* undertaking *or* release order) on which the accused was released [512.3];

☐ (g) there are reasonable grounds to believe that the accused has committed an indictable offence since their release from custody on (summons *or* appearance notice *or* undertaking *or* release order) [512.3];

☐ (h) the accused was required by (appearance notice *or* undertaking *or* summons) to attend at a time and place stated in it for the purposes of the *Identification of Criminals Act* and did not appear at that time and place [512.1, 512.2];

□ **(i)** an indictment has been found against the accused and the accused has not appeared or remained in attendance before the court for their trial [597];

□ **(j)** (*if none of the above applies, reproduce the provisions of the statute that authorize this warrant*).

Therefore, you are ordered, in Her Majesty's name, to immediately arrest the accused and to bring them before (*state court, judge or justice*), **to be dealt with according to law.**

□ (*Check if applicable*) **Because there are reasonable grounds to believe that the accused is or will be present in** (*specify dwelling-house*), **this warrant is also issued to authorize you to enter the dwelling-house for the purpose of arresting the accused, subject to the condition that you may not enter the dwelling-house unless you have, immediately before entering the dwelling-house, reasonable grounds to believe that the person to be arrested is present in the dwelling-house.**

Signed on (*date*), at (*place*).

....
(*Signature of judge, provincial court judge, justice or clerk of the court*)

....
(*Name of the judge, provincial court judge or justice who has issued this warrant*)

1997, c. 39, s. 3; 1999, c. 5, s. 46; 2019, c. 25, s. 335.

FORM 7.1

(*Section 529.1*)

Warrant to Enter Dwelling House

Canada,
Province of ....,
(*territorial division*).

To the peace officers in the said (*territorial division*):

This warrant is issued in respect of the arrest of A.B., or a person with the following description ( ), of ...., (*occupation*).

Whereas there are reasonable grounds to believe:*

   (*a*) a warrant referred to in this or any other Act of Parliament to arrest or apprehend the person is in force anywhere in Canada;

   (*b*) grounds exist to arrest the person without warrant under paragraph 495(1)(*a*) or (*b*) or section 672.91 of the *Criminal Code*; or (*c*) **grounds exist to arrest or apprehend without warrant the person under an Act of Parliament, other than this Act;**

And whereas there are reasonable grounds to believe that the person is or will be present in (*here describe dwelling-house*);

This warrant is issued to authorize you to enter the dwelling-house for the purpose of arresting or apprehending the person.

Dated this .... **day of** .... **A.D.** ...., **at** ....

....
Judge, Clerk of the Court, Provincial Court Judge *or* Justice

★ *Initial applicable recital.*

1997, c. 39, s. 3; 2002, c. 13, s. 85.

FORM 8

(*Sections 493 and 515*)

Warrant for Committal

**Canada,
Province of** ....,
(*territorial division*).

To the peace officers in the (*territorial division*) **and to the keeper of the** (*prison*) **at** ....:

This warrant is issued for the committal of (*name of person*), **of** ...., **born on** (*date of birth*), **referred to in this warrant as the accused.**

Because the accused has been charged with (*set out briefly the offence in respect of which the accused is charged*);

And because (*check those that are applicable*):

☐ (*a*) **the prosecutor has shown cause why the detention of the accused in custody is justified [515(5)];**

☐ (*b*) **a release order has been issued but the accused has not yet complied with the conditions of the order [519(1), 520(9), 521(10), 524(8), 525(6)];★**

☐ (*c*) **the application by the prosecutor for a review of the release order has been allowed and that release order has been vacated, and the prosecutor has shown cause why the detention of the accused in custody is justified [521];**

☐ (d) the accused has contravened or was about to contravene a (summons *or* appearance notice *or* undertaking *or* release order) and it was cancelled, and the detention of the accused in custody is justified [515(10), 523.1(3), 524(3) and (4)];

☐ (e) there are reasonable grounds to believe that the accused has committed an indictable offence after having become subject to the (summons *or* appearance notice *or* undertaking or release order) and the detention of the accused in custody is justified [515(10), 524(3) and (4)];

☐ (f) (*if none of the above applies, reproduce the provisions of the statute that authorize this warrant*).

Therefore, you are ordered, in Her Majesty's name, to arrest the accused and convey them safely to the (*prison*) at ...., and there deliver them to its keeper, with the following order:

You are ordered to receive the accused in your custody in this prison and keep them safely there until they are delivered by due course of law.

Signed on (*date*), at (*place*).

....
(Signature of judge, justice or clerk of the court)

....
(Name of the judge or justice who has issued this warrant)

---

* *If the person having custody of the accused is authorized under paragraph 519(1)(b) of the Criminal Code to release the accused if they comply with a release order, endorse the authorization on this warrant and attach a copy of the order.*

2019, c. 25, s. 336.

FORM 9

(*Section 2*)

Appearance Notice

Canada,
Province of ....
(*territorial division*)

1 *Identification*

Surname: .... Given name(s): ....

Date of Birth: ....

2 *Contact Information*

....

3 *Alleged Offence*

You are alleged to have committed (*set out briefly the substance of the offence, including any failure referred to in section 496, that the accused is alleged to have committed*).

☐ (*Check if applicable*) No new charges are being laid against you at this time but you are required to appear at a judicial referral hearing under section 523.1 for a failure under section 496.

4 *Conditions*

You must attend court as indicated below, and afterwards as required by the court:

Date: ....

Time: ....

Court number: ....

Court address: ....

5 *Appearance for the purposes of the Identification of Criminals Act* (*if applicable*)

☐ You are required to appear on (date) at (hour) at (place) for the purposes of the *Identification of Criminals Act*.

6 *Consequence for non-compliance*

You are warned that,

(a) in the case where charges have been laid against you, unless you have a lawful excuse, you commit an offence under subsection 145(3) of the *Criminal Code* if you fail to appear for the purposes of the *Identification of Criminals Act* or to attend court, as required in this appearance notice;

(b) in the case where no charges have been laid against you and you fail to appear at a judicial referral hearing under section 523.1, as required in this appearance notice, charges may be laid against you for the alleged offence described in item 3 of this notice.

If you commit an offence under subsection 145(3) of the *Criminal Code*, a warrant for your arrest may be issued (section 512 or 512.2 of the *Criminal Code*) and you may be liable to a fine or to imprisonment, or to both.

It is not a lawful excuse to an offence under subsection 145(3) of the *Criminal Code* that this appearance notice does not accurately describe the offence that you are alleged to have committed (subsection 145(6) of the *Criminal Code*).

If you do not comply with this appearance notice or are charged with committing an indictable offence after you have been released, this appearance notice may be cancelled and, as a result, you may be detained in custody (subsection 524(4) of the *Criminal Code*).

7 *Signatures*

ACCUSED:

I understand the contents of this appearance notice and agree to comply with it.

Signed on (*date*), at (*place*).

....
(*Signature of accused*)

PEACE OFFICER:

Signed on (*date*), at (*place*).

....
(*Signature of peace officer*)

....
(*Name of the peace officer*)

1994, c. 44, s. 84; 1997, c. 18, s. 115; 2018, c. 29, s. 70(1); 2019, c. 25, s. 337.

FORM 10

(*Section 2*)

Undertaking

Canada,
Province of ....
(*territorial division*).

1 *Identification*

Surname: .... Given name(s): ....

Date of Birth: ....

2 *Contact Information*

....

3 *Charge(s)*

(*set out briefly the offence in respect of which the accused was charged*)

4 *Mandatory Condition*

You must attend court as indicated below, and afterwards as required by the court:

Date: ....

Time: ....

Court number: ....

Court address: ....

5 *Additional Conditions*

You must also comply with any conditions that are indicated below by a check mark (*check only those that are reasonable in the circumstances of the offence and necessary, to ensure the accused's attendance in court or the safety and security of any victim of or witness to the offence, or to prevent the continuation or repetition of the offence or the commission of another offence*):

☐ (a) You must report to (*name or title*) at (*place*) on (*date or dates*).

☐ (b) You must remain within the following territorial jurisdiction: ....

☐ (c) You must notify (*name, title and phone number*) of any change of your (*address, employment or occupation*).

☐ (d) You must not communicate, directly or indirectly, with ...., except in accordance with the following conditions: ....

☐ (e) You must not go to (*places which are related to the person(s) mentioned in the condition set out in paragraph (d)*), except in accordance with the following conditions: ....

☐ (f) You must not enter the areas (*describe in detail the boundaries of the areas related to the person(s) mentioned in the condition set out in paragraph (d)*), except in accordance with the following conditions: ....

☐ (g) You must deposit all your passports with (*name or title*) at (*place*) before (*date*).

☐ (h) You must reside at (*place*), be at that residence between (*hour*) and (*hour*), and present yourself at the entrance of that residence when a peace officer or (*name and title of another person*) requests you to do so within those hours.

☐ **(i)** You must not possess a firearm, crossbow, prohibited weapon, restricted weapon, prohibited device, ammunition, prohibited ammunition or explosive substance and you must surrender those that are in your possession and also any authorization, licence or registration certificate or other document enabling you to acquire or possess them to (*name or title*) at (*place*).

☐ **(j)** You promise to pay the amount of .... (*not more than $500*), if you fail to comply with a condition of this undertaking.

☐ **(k)** You must deposit money or other valuable security whose value is equal to the amount of .... (*not more than $500*) with (*name or title*), because you are not ordinarily resident in the province or do not reside within 200 km of the place in which you are in custody.

☐ **(l)** You must comply with the following conditions (*conditions for ensuring the safety and security of any victim of or witness to the alleged offence*): ....

6 *Appearance for the purposes of the Identification of Criminals Act*

☐ You are required to appear on (*date*) at (*hour*) at (*place*) for the purposes of the *Identification of Criminals Act*.

7 *Variation and Replacement*

The conditions of this undertaking may be varied with the written consent of the prosecutor and yourself. In addition, you or the prosecutor may apply to a justice of the peace to replace this undertaking with a release order under section 515 of the *Criminal Code*.

8 *Conditions in effect*

The mandatory condition and the conditions indicated by a check mark on this undertaking remain in effect until they are cancelled or changed or until you have been discharged, sentenced or otherwise detained by the court (sections 763 and 764 of the *Criminal Code*).

9 *Consequence for non-compliance*

You are warned that, unless you have a lawful excuse, you commit an offence under section 145 of the *Criminal Code* if you fail to follow any of the conditions set out in this undertaking, including

(a) to fail to attend court as required;

(b) to fail to appear as required for the purposes of the *Identification of Criminals Act*;

(c) to fail to remain in the territorial jurisdiction specified in section 5 of this undertaking (if applicable).

If you commit an offence under section 145 of the *Criminal Code*, a warrant for your arrest may be issued (section 512 or 512.2 of the *Criminal Code*) and you may be liable to a fine or to imprisonment, or to both.

It is not a lawful excuse to an offence under subsection 145(4) of the *Criminal Code* that this undertaking does not accurately describe the offence that you are alleged to have committed (subsection 145(6) of the *Criminal Code*).

If you do not comply with this undertaking or are charged with committing an indictable offence after you have been released, this undertaking may be cancelled and, as a result, you may be detained in custody (subsection 524(4) of the *Criminal Code*).

If you do not comply with this undertaking, the funds or valuable security promised or deposited by you or your surety could be forfeited (subsection 771(2) of the *Criminal Code*).

10 *Signatures*

ACCUSED:

I understand the contents of this undertaking and agree to comply with the mandatory condition and the conditions that are indicated by a check mark.

I understand that I do not have to accept the conditions and that, if I do not accept the conditions, I will be brought to a justice for a bail hearing.

Signed on (*date*), at (*place*).

....
(*Signature of accused*)

PEACE OFFICER:

Signed on (*date*), at (*place*).

....
(*Signature of peace officer*)

....
(*Name of the peace officer*)

1994, c. 44, s. 84; 1997, c. 18, s. 115; 2018, c. 29, s. 70(1);
2019, c. 25, s. 337.

FORM 11

(*Section 2*)

Release Order

Canada,
Province of ....
(*territorial division*).

1 *Identification*

Surname: .... Given name(s): ....

Date of Birth: ....

2 *Contact Information*

....

3 *Charge(s)*

(*set out briefly the offence in respect of which the accused was charged*)

4 *Financial Obligations*

☐   **You do not have any financial obligations under this release order.**

or

In order for you to be released, the obligations that are indicated below by a check mark must be complied with.

☐   **You promise to pay the amount of .... if you fail to comply with a condition of this release order.**

☐   **You must deposit money in the amount of ....or other valuable security whose value does not exceed .... with the clerk of the court.**

☐   **The surety (*name*), born on (*date of birth*), (promises to pay or deposits) to the court the amount of ....**

5 *Conditions*

You must comply with the conditions that are indicated below by a check mark.

☐   **You must report to (*name or title*) at (*place*) on (*date or dates*).**

☐   **You must remain within the territorial jurisdiction of (*province or territory*).**

☐   **You must notify (*name, title and phone number*) of any change of your (*address, employment or occupation*).**

☐   **You must not communicate, directly or indirectly, with (*victims, witnesses or other persons*), except in accordance with the following conditions:**

....

☐ You must not go to (*place*) or enter (*geographic area*), except in accordance with the following conditions: ....

☐ You must deposit all your passports with (*name or title*) at (*place*) before (*date*).

☐ You must not possess a firearm, crossbow, prohibited weapon, restricted weapon, prohibited device, ammunition, prohibited ammunition or explosive substance and you must surrender any of them in your possession and any authorization, licence or registration certificate or other document enabling the acquisition or possession of a firearm to (*name or title*) at (*place*).

☐ You must comply with the following conditions (*conditions for ensuring the safety and security of any victim of or witness to the alleged offence*): ....

☐ You must comply with the following conditions: ....

6 *Variation*

The conditions of this release order may be varied with the written consent of the prosecutor, yourself and your sureties, if any. In addition, you or the prosecutor may apply to a judge to have any condition in this release order cancelled or changed.

7 *Conditions in effect*

The conditions indicated by a check mark on this release order (including any obligations imposed on your sureties) remain in effect until they are cancelled or changed or until you have been discharged, sentenced or otherwise detained by the court (sections 763 and 764 of the *Criminal Code*).

8 *Consequence for non-compliance*

You are warned that, unless you have a lawful excuse, you commit an offence under section 145 of the *Criminal Code* if you fail to follow any of the conditions set out in this release order, including if you fail to attend court as required.

If you commit an offence under section 145 of the *Criminal Code*, a warrant for your arrest may be issued (sections 512 and 512.3 of the *Criminal Code*) and you may be liable to a fine or to imprisonment, or to both.

If you do not comply with this release order or are charged with committing an indictable offence after you have been released, this release order may be cancelled and, as a result, you may be detained in custody (subsection 524(4) of the *Criminal Code*).

If you do not comply with this release order, the money or other valuable security promised or deposited by you or your surety could be forfeited (subsection 771(2) of the *Criminal Code*).

9 *Signatures*

SURETY: (*if applicable*)

I understand my role and my responsibilities under this release order and I agree to act as a surety.

I agree to (*promise or deposit*) to the court the amount of money described in section 4 of this release order.

☐   Surety Declaration is attached (section 515.1 of the *Criminal Code*).

☐   Surety is excepted from providing Surety Declaration (subsection 515.1(2) of the *Criminal Code*).

Signed on (*date*), at (*place*).

....
(*Signature of the surety*)

ACCUSED:

I understand the contents of this form and agree to comply with the conditions that are indicated by a check mark.

I understand that I do not have to accept the conditions and that, if I do not accept the conditions, I will be detained.

Signed on (*date*), at (*place*).

....
(*Signature of accused*)

JUDGE, JUSTICE OR CLERK OF THE COURT:

Signed on (*date*), at (*place*).

....
(*Signature of judge, justice or clerk of the court*)

....
(*Name of judge or justice who has issued this order*)

1992, c. 1, s. 58; 1994, c. 44, s. 84; 1997, c. 18, s. 115;
2018, c. 29, s. 70(1); 2019, c. 25, s. 337.

FORM 11.1
(*Sections 493, 499 and 503*)

[*Repealed, 2019, c. 25, s. 337.*]

FORM 12

(*Section 515.1*)

Surety Declaration

Canada,
Province of ....,
(*territorial division*).

CODE

1 *Identification*

Surname: .... Given name(s): ....

Date of Birth: ....

Home address: ....

Phone number(s): .... (*primary*) ....(*other*)

Other contact information (*if any*): ....

Employment or occupation (*if any*): ....

Name and contact information for employer (*if any*): ....

2 *Information about the Accused*

Surname: .... Given name(s): ....

Date of Birth: ....

Court file number: ....

3 *Other information required*

Relationship to the accused: ....

I am acting as a surety in respect of another accused.

☐ Yes ☐ No

If yes, name and date of birth of any other accused: ....

I have a criminal record or there are outstanding criminal charges against me.

☐ Yes ☐ No

If yes, description of criminal record, if any, and all outstanding criminal charges, specifying offence and year of conviction: ....

4 *Charges against the Accused*

I understand that the accused has been charged with (set out briefly the offence in respect of which the accused was charged).

5 *Other Outstanding Charges against the Accused*

☐   I understand that the accused does not have any other outstanding criminal charges.

☐   I understand that the accused has also been charged with (*set out briefly the offence in respect of which the accused was charged*), but this declaration does not apply to those charges.

6 *Criminal Record of the Accused*

☐   I understand that the accused does not have a criminal record.

☐   I understand that the accused has a criminal record, which is described below or a copy of which I have attached and initialled.

....

7 *Financial Promise or Deposit*

As a surety for the accused, I am willing to (*promise or deposit*) to the court the amount of ....

8 *Acknowledgment*

I understand that failure on the part of the accused to follow any of the conditions in their release order or recognizance could lead to the forfeiture of the amount of money that has been promised or deposited.

I understand that I may, at any time, ask to no longer be a surety by making an application, by bringing the accused to the court in order to be discharged from my obligation (section 767 of the *Criminal Code*) or by taking and giving the accused into custody (section 768 of the *Criminal Code*).

I voluntarily make this declaration and it is my free choice to take on the responsibilities of a surety.

9 *Signature*

Signed on (*date*), at (*place*).

....
(*Signature of the surety*)

Sworn before me on (*date*), at (*place*).

....
(*Signature of the person who is authorized to take or receive statements made under oath, solemn declaration or solemn affirmation*)

1994, c. 44, s. 84; 1999, c. 25, s. 25.; 2008, c. 18, s. 45.1; 2018, c. 29, s. 72; 2019, c. 25, s. 337.

FORM 13

(*Sections 816, 832 and 834*)

[*Repealed, 2019, c. 25, s. 337.*]

FORM 14

(*Section 817*)

[*Repealed, 2019, c. 25, s. 337.*]

CODE

FORM 15

(*Section 543*)

Warrant to Convey Accused Before Justice of Another Territorial Division

Canada,
Province of ....,
(*territorial division*).

To the peace officers in the said (*territorial division*):

Whereas A.B., of .... hereinafter called the accused, has been charged that (*state place of offence and charge*);

And whereas the deposition of X.Y. in respect of the charge has been taken by me (*or if the signatory is not the justice, the justice*);

And Whereas the charge is for an offence committted in the (*territorial division*);

This is to command you, in Her Majesty's name, to convey the said A.B., before a justice of the (*last mentioned territorial division*).

Dated (*date*).........., at ....(*place*).

(*Signature of justice or clerk of the court*)

....

2019, c. 25, s. 338.

FORM 16

(*Section 699*)

Subpoena to a Witness

Canada,
Province of ....,
(*territorial division*).

To E.F., of ...., (*occupation*);

Whereas A.B. has been charged that (*state offence as in the information*), and it has been made to appear that you are likely to give material evidence for (*the prosecution or the defence*);

This is therefore to command you to attend before (set out court or justice), on .... the .... day of .... A.D. ...., at .... o'clock in the .... noon at .... to give evidence concerning the said charge.★

★ Where a witness is required to produce anything, add the following: and to bring with you anything in your possession or under your control that relates to the said charge, and more particularly the following: (*specify any documents, objects or other things required*).

Dated this .... day of .... A.D. ...., at ....

....
A Judge, Justice or Clerk of the court
(*Seal, if required*)

1999, c. 5, s. 47.

FORM 16.1

(*Subsections 278.3(5) and 699(7)*)

SUBPOENA TO A WITNESS IN THE CASE OF PROCEEDINGS IN RESPECT OF AN OFFENCE REFERRED TO IN SUBSECTION 278.2(1) OF THE CRIMINAL CODE

Canada,
Province of ....,
(*territorial division*).

To E.F., of ...., (*occupation*);

Whereas A.B. has been charged that (*state offence as in the information*), and it has been made to appear that you are likely to give material evidence for (*the prosecution or the defence*);

This is therefore to command you to attend before (*set out court or justice*), on .... the .... day of .... A.D. ...., at .... o'clock in the .... noon at .... to give evidence concerning the said charge, and to bring with you anything in your possession or under your control that relates to the said charge, and more particularly the following: (*specify any documents, objects or other things required*).

TAKE NOTE

You are only required to bring the things specified above to the court on the date and at the time indicated, and you are not required to provide the things specified to any person or to discuss their contents with any person unless and until ordered by the court to do so.

If anything specified above is a "record" as defined in section 278.1 of the *Criminal Code*, it may be subject to a determination by the court in accordance with sections 278.1 to 278.91 of the *Criminal Code* as to whether and to what extent it should be produced.

If anything specified above is a "record" as defined in section 278.1 of the *Criminal Code*, the production of which is governed by sections 278.1 to 278.91 of the *Criminal Code*, this subpoena must be accompanied by a copy of an application for the production of the record made pursuant to section 278.3 of the *Criminal Code*, and you will have an opportunity to make submissions to the court concerning the production of the record.

If anything specified above is a "record" as defined in section 278.1 of the *Criminal Code*, the production of which is governed by sections 278.1 to 278.91 of the *Criminal Code*, you are not required to bring it with you until a determination is made in accordance with those sections as to whether and to what extent it should be produced.

As defined in section 278.1 of the *Criminal Code*, "record" means any form of record that contains personal information for which there is a reasonable expectation of privacy and includes, without limiting the generality of the foregoing, medical, psychiatric, therapeutic, counselling, education, employment, child welfare, adoption and social services records, personal journals and diaries, and records containing personal information the production or disclosure of which is protected by any other Act of Parliament or a provincial legislature, but does not include records made by persons responsible for the investigation or prosecution of the offence.

Dated this .... day of .... A.D. ...., at ....

....

Judge, Clerk of the Court,
Provincial Court Judge *or* Justice
(*Seal, if required*)

1997, c. 30, s. 3.

CODE

FORM 17

(*Sections 698 and 705*)

Warrant for witness

Canada,
Province of ....,
(*territorial division*).

To the peace officers in the (*territorial division*):

Whereas A.B. of ...., has been charged that (*state offence as in the information*);

And Whereas it has been made to appear that E.F. of ...., hereinafter called the witness, is likely to give material evidence for (the prosecution *or* the defence) and that★
★*Insert whichever of the following is appropriate*:

(*a*) the said E.F. will not attend unless compelled to do so;

(*b*) the said E.F. is evading service of a subpoena;

(*c*) the said E.F. was duly served with a subpoena and has neglected (to attend at the time and place appointed therein *or* to remain in attendance);

(*d*) the said E.F. was bound by a recognizance to attend and give evidence and has neglected (to attend *or* to remain in attendance).

This is therefore to command you, in Her Majesty's name, to arrest and bring the witness forthwith before (*set out court or justice*) to be dealt with in accordance with section 706 of the *Criminal Code*.

Dated this .... day of .... A.D. ...., at ....

....
A Justice or Clerk of the Court

(*Seal if required*)

FORM 18

(*Section 704*)

Warrant to Arrest an Absconding Witness

Canada,
Province of ....,
(*territorial division*).

To the peace officers in the (*territorial division*):

Whereas A.B., of .... has been charged that (*state offence as in the information*);

And whereas I am (*or if the signatory is not the justice, the justice is*) satisfied by information in writing and under oath that C.D., of ...., in this warrant called the witness, is bound by recognizance to give evidence on the trial of the accused on the charge, and that the witness (*has absconded or is about to abscond*);

This is therefore to command you, in Her Majesty's name, to arrest the witness and bring him forthwith before (*the court, judge, justice or provincial court judge before whom the witness is bound to appear*) to be dealt with in accordance with section 706 of the *Criminal Code*.

Dated (*date*).........., at ....(*place*).

(*Signature of justice or clerk of the court*)

....

2019, c. 25, s. 339.

FORM 19

(*Sections 516 and 537*)

Warrant Remanding a Prisoner

Canada,
Province of ....,
(*territorial division*).

To the peace officers in the (*territorial division*):

You are hereby commanded forthwith to arrest, if necessary, and convey to the (*prison*) at .... the persons named in the following schedule each of whom has been remanded to the time mentioned in the schedule:

Person charged   Offence   Remanded to

And you, the keeper of the prison, are directed to receive each of the persons into your custody in the prison and keep each person safely until the day when that person's remand expires and then to have that person before me or any other justice (*or if the signatory is not the justice, before any justice*) on ....(*date*),.......... at ....(*hour*), at ....(*place*), there to answer to the charge and to be dealt with according to law, unless you are otherwise directed before that time.

Dated (*date*)..........., at ....(*place*).

(*Signature of justice or clerk of the court*)

....

2019, c. 25, s. 340.

FORM 20

(*Section 545*)

Warrant of Committal of Witness for Refusing to Be Sworn or to Give Evidence

Canada,
Province of ....,
(*territorial division*).

To the peace officers in the (*territorial division*):

Whereas A.B. of ...., in this warrant called the accused, has been charged that (*set out offence as in the information*);

And whereas E.F. of ...., in this warrant called the witness, attending before me (*or if the signatory is not the justice*, before the justice) to give evidence for (the prosecution or the defence) concerning the charge against the accused (refused to be sworn or being duly sworn as a witness refused to answer certain questions concerning the charge that were put to them or refused or failed to produce the following writings, namely .... or refused to sign their deposition) having been ordered to do so, without offering any just excuse for that refusal or failure;

This is therefore to direct you, in Her Majesty's name, to arrest, if necessary, and take the witness and convey them safely to the prison at ...., and there deliver them to the keeper of it, together with the following precept:

You, the keeper, are directed to receive the witness into your custody in the prison and safely keep them there for the term of .... days, unless they sooner consent to do what was required of them, and for so doing this is a sufficient warrant.

Dated (*date*)..........., at .... (*place*).

(*Signature of justice or clerk of the court*)

....

2019, c. 25, s. 341.

FORM 21

(Sections 570 and 806)

WARRANT OF COMMITTAL ON CONVICTION

Canada,
Province of ....,
(territorial division).

To the peace officers in *(territorial division)* and to the keeper of *(prison)* at
...................:

Whereas *(name)*, in this Form called the offender, was, on the ....
day of .... 20................, convicted by *(name of judge and court)* of having
committed the following offence(s) and it was adjudged that the offender be
sentenced as follows:

Offence	Sentence	Remarks
(state offence of which offender was convicted)	*(state term of imprisonment for the offence and, in case of imprisonment for default of payment of fine, so indicate together with the amount of it and applicable costs and whether payable immediately or within a time fixed)*	*(state the amount of time spent in custody before sentencing, the term of imprisonment that would have been imposed before any credit was granted under subsection 719(3) or (3.1), the amount of time credited, if any, and whether the sentence is consecutive or concurrent, and specify consecutive to or concurrent with what other sentence)*
1.	....	....
2.	....	....
3.	....	....
4.	....	....

You are hereby commanded, in Her Majesty's name, to arrest the
offender if it is necessary to do so in order to take the offender into custody,
and to take and convey him or her safely to *(prison)* at .... and deliver
him or her to its keeper, who is hereby commanded to receive the accused
into custody and to imprison him or her there for the term(s) of his or her
imprisonment, unless, if a term of imprisonment was imposed only in default
of payment of a fine or costs, those amounts and the costs and charges of the
committal and of conveying the offender to that prison are paid sooner, and
this is a sufficient warrant for so doing.

883

Dated this .... day of .... 20 ...., at ....

....

Clerk of the Court, Justice, Judge *or*
Provincial Court Judge

1995, c. 22, s. 9; 2009, c. 29, s. 4.

FORM 22

(*Section 806*)

Warrant of Committal on an Order for the Payment of Money

Canada,
Province of ....,
(*territorial division*).

To the peace officers in the (*territorial division*) and to the keeper of the (*prison*) at ....:

Whereas A.B., hereinafter called the defendant, was tried on an information alleging that (*set out matter of complaint*), and it was ordered that (*set out the order made*), and in default that the defendant be imprisoned in the (*prison*) at .... for a term of..........;

You are directed, in Her Majesty's name, to arrest, if necessary, and take the defendant and convey them safely to the (*prison*) at ...., and deliver them to the keeper of the prison, together with the following precept:

You, the keeper of the prison, are directed to receive the defendant into your custody in this prison and keep them safely there for the term of ...., unless the amounts and the costs and charges of the committal and of conveying the defendant to the prison are sooner paid, and for so doing this is a sufficient warrant.

Dated (*date*).........., at ....(*place*).

(*Signature of provincial court judge, justice or clerk of the court*)

....

2019, c. 25, s. 342.

CODE

FORM 23

(Sections 810 and 810.1)

Warrant of committal for failure to furnish recognizance to keep the peace

Canada,
Province of ....,
(territorial division).

To the peace officers in the *(territorial division)* and to the keeper of the *(prison)* at ....:

Whereas A.B., hereinafter called the accused, has been ordered to enter into a recognizance to keep the peace and be of good behaviour, and has (refused *or* failed) to enter into a recognizance accordingly;

You are hereby commanded, in Her Majesty's name, to arrest, if necessary, and take the accused and convey him safely to the *(prison)* at .... and deliver him to the keeper thereof, together with the following precept:

You, the said keeper, are hereby commanded to receive the accused into your custody in the said prison and imprison him there until he enters into a recognizance as aforesaid or until he is discharged in due course of law.

Dated this .... day of .... A.D. ...., at ....

....
Clerk of the Court, Justice
or **Provincial Court Judge**

(Seal, if required)

1993, c. 45, s. 12.

FORM 24

(Section 550)

Warrant of Committal of Witness for Failure to Enter into Recognizance

Canada,
Province of ....,
(territorial division).

To the peace officers in the *(territorial division)* and to the keeper of the *(prison)* at ....:

Whereas A.B., in this warrant called the accused, was committed for trial on a charge that *(state offence as in the information)*;

And whereas E.F., in this warrant called the witness, having appeared as a witness on the preliminary inquiry into the charge, and being required to enter into a recognizance to appear as a witness on the trial of the accused on the charge, has (failed or refused) to do so;

This is therefore to direct you, in Her Majesty's name, to arrest, if necessary, and take and safely convey the witness to the (*prison*) at .... and there deliver them to the keeper of it, together with the following precept:

You, the keeper, are directed to receive the witness into your custody in the prison and keep them there safely until the trial of the accused on the charge, unless before that time the witness enters into the recognizance.

Dated (*date*).........., at ....(*place*).

(*Signature of justice or clerk of the court*)

....

2019, c. 25, s. 343.

FORM 25

(*Section 708*)

Warrant of Committal for Contempt

Canada,
Province of ....,
(*territorial division*).

To the peace officers in the (*territorial division*) and to the keeper of the (*prison*) at (*place*)..........:

Because E.F. of ...., in this warrant called the defaulter, was on (*date*).........., at .... (*place*), convicted before .... for contempt because the defaulter did not attend before .... to give evidence on the trial of a charge that (*state offence as in the information*) against A.B. of ...., although (duly subpoenaed or bound by recognizance to appear and give evidence in that regard, *as the case may be*) and did not show any sufficient excuse for the default;

And because, following the conviction it was ordered that the defaulter (*set out the punishment imposed*);

And because the defaulter has not paid the amounts ordered to be paid; (*delete if not applicable*)

Therefore, you are ordered, in Her Majesty's name, to arrest, if necessary, and take the defaulter and convey them safely to the prison at .... and there deliver them to its keeper, together with the following order:

You, the keeper, are ordered to receive the defaulter into your custody in this prison and keep them safely there★ and for so doing this is a sufficient warrant.

★ *Insert whichever of the following is applicable*:

(*a*) for the term of ....;

(*b*) for the term of ...., unless the sums and the costs and charges of the committal and of conveying the defaulter to the prison are sooner paid;

(*c*) for the term of .... and for the term of (*if consecutive so state*) unless the sums and the costs and charges of the committal and of conveying the defaulter to the prison are sooner paid.

Dated (*date*).........., at ....(*place*).

(*Signature of judge, provincial court judge, justice or clerk of the court*)

(*Seal, if required*)

2019, c. 25, s. 344.

CODE

FORM 26

(*Section 827*)

Warrant of committal in default of payment of costs of an appeal
Canada,
Province of ....,
(*territorial division*).

To the peace officers of (*territorial division*) and to the keeper of the (*prison*) at ....:

Whereas it appears that on the hearing of an appeal before the (*set out court*) it was adjudged that A.B., of ...., hereinafter called the defaulter, should pay to the Clerk of the Court the sum of .... dollars in respect of costs;

And Whereas the Clerk of the Court has certified that the defaulter has not paid the sum within the time limited therefor;

I do hereby command you, the said peace officers, in Her Majesty's name, to take the defaulter and safely convey him to the (*prison*) at .... and deliver him to the keeper thereof, together with the following precept:

887

I do hereby command you, the said keeper, to receive the defaulter into your custody in the said prison and imprison him for the term of ...., unless the said sum and the costs and charges of the committal and of conveying the defaulter to the said prison are sooner paid, and for so doing this is a sufficient warrant.

Dated this .... day of .... A.D. ...., at ....

....
A Justice of the Peace in and
      for ....

FORM 27

(Section 773)

Warrant of Committal on Forfeiture of Amounts

Canada,
Province of ....,
(territorial division).

To the sheriff of *(territorial division)* and to the keeper of the *(prison)* at *(place)*.

This warrant of committal is issued for the arrest of *(name of person or persons)*, referred to in this warrant as the defaulter or defaulters, as the case may be.

You are ordered to arrest the defaulter or defaulters and convey them safely to the *(prison)* at ...., and deliver them to its keeper, with the following order:

You, the keeper, are ordered to receive the defaulter or defaulters into your custody in this prison and keep them safely there for a period of .... or until satisfaction is made of a judgment debt of ...., due to Her Majesty the Queen in respect of the forfeiture of an amount set out in (an undertaking entered into or a release order issued or a recognizance entered into) on *(date)*.

Dated *(date)*, at *(place)*.

....
(Signature of judge of the court or clerk of the court)

....
Name of judge who has issued this warrant of committal)

(Seal, if required)

2019, c. 25, s. 345.

FORM 28

(*Section 528*)

Endorsement of Warrant

Canada,
Province of ....,
(*territorial division*).

In accordance with the application this day made to me, I authorize the arrest of the accused (or defendant), within the (*territorial division*).

Dated (*date*).........., at .... (*place*).

.... (*Signature of justice*)

2019, c. 25, s. 346

FORM 28.1

(*Subsection 487.03(2)*)

[*Repealed*, 2007, c. 22, s. 26.]

FORM 29

(*Section 507*)

Endorsement of warrant

Canada,
Province of ....,
(*territorial division*).

Whereas this warrant is issued under section 507, 508 or 512 of the *Criminal Code* in respect of an offence other than an offence mentioned in section 522 of the *Criminal Code*, I hereby authorize the release of the accused pursuant to section 499 of that Act.

Dated this .... day of .... A.D. ...., at ....

....
A Justice of the Peace in and
for ....

1994, c. 44, s. 84.

889

FORM 30

(*Section 537*)

Order for Accused to Be Brought Before Justice Prior to Expiration of Period of Remand

Canada,
Province of ....,
(*territorial division*).

To the keeper of the (*prison*) at ....:

Whereas by warrant dated (*date*), A.B., in this order called the accused, was committed to your custody and you were required to keep them safely until the (*date*)...................................., and then to have them before me or any other justice (*or if the signatory is not the justice*, any justice) at (*place*).......... at .... (*hour*) to answer to the charge against the accused and to be dealt with according to law unless you should be ordered otherwise before that time;

Now, therefore, you are directed to have the accused before .... at (*place*).......... at .... (*hour*) to answer to the charge against them and so they may be dealt with according to law.

Dated (*date*).........., at .... (*place*).

(*Signature of justice or clerk of the court*)

....

2019, c. 25, s. 347.

FORM 31

(*Section 540*)

Deposition of a witness

Canada,
Province of ....,
(*territorial division*).

These are the depositions of X.Y., of ...., and M.N., of ...., taken before me, this .... day of .... A.D., at ...., in the presence and hearing of A.B., hereinafter called the accused, who stands charged (*state offence as in the information*).

X.Y., having been duly sworn, deposes as follows: (*insert deposition as nearly as possible in words of witness*).

M.N., having been duly sworn, deposes as follows:

I certify that the depositions of X.Y., and M.N., written on the several sheets of paper hereto annexed to which my signature is affixed, were taken in the presence and hearing of the accused (and signed by them respectively, in his presence *where they are required to be signed by witness*). In witness whereof I have hereto signed my name.

....

A Justice of the Peace in and
for ....

FORM 32

(Sections 2, 462.34, 490.9, 550, 683, 706, 707, 779, 810, 810.01, 810.1, 810.2, 817 and 832)

Recognizance

Canada,
Province of ....
(territorial division)

1 Identification

Surname: .... Given name(s): ....

Date of birth: ....

Home address: ....

Phone number(s): ....*(primary)*.......... *(other)*

Other contact information *(if any)*: ....

Employment or Occupation *(if any)*: ....

Name and contact information of employer *(if any)*: ....

2 Financial Promise or Deposit

Pursuant to .... *(provision)* of the *Criminal Code*, I agree to *(promise or deposit)* the amount of $ ...., or the other valuable security described here:..........

I understand that if I fail to comply with any of the conditions listed below, this amount or security may be forfeited.

3 Conditions

(List the conditions that have been ordered by the court and indicate the duration for which each condition remains in effect.)

....

4 *Variation*

I understand that I may apply to a judge or a justice of the peace to have any condition in this form cancelled or varied.

5 *Conditions in effect*

I understand that the conditions in this recognizance remain in effect until they are cancelled or changed or until I have been discharged, sentenced or otherwise detained by the court (sections 763 and 764 of the *Criminal Code*).

6 *Signatures*

PERSON WHO IS GIVING RECOGNIZANCE:

I understand the contents of this form and agree to comply with the conditions that are listed above.

Signed on .... (*date*), at ....(*place*).

....
(*Signature of the person*)

....
(*Print name*)

SURETY (*if applicable*):

I understand my role and my responsibilities under this recognizance and I agree to act as a surety.

I agree to (promise or deposit) as security to the court the amount of $...........

I understand that if the person who is giving this recognizance fails to comply with any of the conditions in this recognizance, the money that I have promised or deposited may be forfeited.

Surety Declaration (*if applicable*)

☐ Surety Declaration attached. (Section 515.1 of the *Criminal Code*.)

☐ Surety excepted from providing Surety Declaration. (Subsection 515.1(2) of the *Criminal Code*.)

Signed on .... (*date*), at ....(*place*).

....
(*Signature of the Surety*)

....
(*Print name*)

JUDGE, PROVINCIAL COURT JUDGE, JUSTICE OR CLERK OF THE COURT:

Signed on .... (*date*), at ....(*place*).

....
(*Signature of the judge, provincial court judge, justice or clerk of the court*)

....
(*Print name*)

List of Conditions

(a) **has a surety (sections 462.34, 490.9, 550, 779, 810, 817 and 832 of the *Criminal Code*);**

(b) **agrees to keep the peace and be of good behaviour (sections 83.3, 810, 810.01, 810.1 and 810.2 of the *Criminal Code*);**

(c) **abstains from possessing a firearm, crossbow, prohibited weapon, restricted weapon, prohibited device, ammunition, prohibited ammunition or explosive substance and surrenders those in their possession and surrenders any authorization, licence or registration certificate or other document enabling the acquisition or possession of a firearm (sections 83.3, 810, 810.01, 810.1 and 810.2 of the *Criminal Code*);**

(d) **participates in a treatment program (sections 810.01, 810.1 and 810.2 of the *Criminal Code*);**

(e) **wears an electronic monitoring device (*if the Attorney General makes the request*) (sections 810.01, 810.1 and 810.2 of the *Criminal Code*);**

(f) **remains within a specified geographic area unless written permission to leave that area is obtained from the judge (sections 810.01 and 810.2 of the *Criminal Code*);**

(g) **returns to and remains at their place of residence at specified times (sections 810.01, 810.1 and 810.2 of the *Criminal Code*);**

(h) **abstains from the consumption of drugs, except in accordance with a medical prescription (sections 810.01, 810.1 and 810.2 of the *Criminal Code*);**

(i) **abstains from the consumption of alcohol or of any other intoxicating substance, except in accordance with a medical prescription (sections 810.01, 810.1 and 810.2 of the *Criminal Code*);**

(j) **abstains from any contact — including communicating by any means — with a person under the age of 16 years, unless doing so under the supervision of a person whom the judge considers appropriate (section 810.1 of the *Criminal Code*);**

(k)   abstains from using the Internet or other digital network, unless doing so in accordance with conditions set by the judge (section 810.1 of the *Criminal Code*);

(l)   abstains from attending a public park or public swimming area where persons under the age of 16 years are present or can reasonably be expected to be present, or a daycare centre, school-ground or playground (section 810.1 of the *Criminal Code*);

(m)   appears personally or by counsel at the sittings of the appeal court at which the appeal is to be heard (sections 817 and 832 of the *Criminal Code*);

(n)   appears in court as required (sections 550, 706 and 707 of the *Criminal Code*);

(o)   in the case where a warrant was issued under section 462.32 of the *Criminal Code* or a restraint order was made under subsection 462.33(3) of that Act in relation to any property (*set out a description of the property and its location*), refrains from doing or causing anything to be done that would result, directly or indirectly, in the disappearance, dissipation or reduction in value of the property or otherwise affect the property so that all or a part thereof could not be subject to an order of forfeiture under section 462.37 or 462.38 of that Act or any other provision of that Act or any other Act of Parliament (section 462.34 of the *Criminal Code*);

(p)   agrees to prosecute the writ of certiorari at their own expense, without wilful delay, and, if ordered, to pay to the person in whose favour the conviction, order or other proceeding is affirmed their full costs and charges to be taxed according to the practice of the court where the conviction, order or proceeding is affirmed (section 779 of the *Criminal Code*);

(q)   any other reasonable conditions, including:

–   reports at specified times to peace officer or other person designated;

–   remains within designated territorial jurisdiction;

–   notifies peace officer or other person designated of any change in their address, employment or occupation;

–   abstains from communicating, directly or indirectly, with victim, witness or other specified person except in accordance with conditions specified by judge, provincial court judge or justice; and

–   deposits all their passports as the judge, provincial court judge or justice directs.

R.S.C. 1985, c. 42 (4th Supp.), s. 7; 1993, c. 45, ss. 13, 14; 1999, c. 25, s. 27; 2019, c. 25, s. 348.

FORM 33

(*Section 770*)

Certificate of Default to Be Endorsed

It is certified that A.B. (has not appeared as required by this undertaking, release order or recognizance or has not complied with a condition of this undertaking, release order or recognizance) and that for this reason the ends of justice have been (defeated *or* delayed, *as the case may be*).

The nature of the default is .... and the reason for the default is .... (*state reason if known*).

The names and addresses of the principal and sureties are as follows:

Dated (*date*).........., at .... (*place*).

....

(*Signature of judge, provincial court judge, justice, clerk of the court, peace officer or other person*)

(*Seal, if required*)

1994, c. 44, s. 84; 2019, c. 25, s. 349.

FORM 34

(*Section 771*)

Writ of fieri facias

Elizabeth II by the Grace of God, etc.

To the sheriff of (*territorial division*), GREETING.

You are hereby commanded to levy of the goods and chattels, lands and tenements of each of the following persons the amount set opposite the name of each:

Name   Address   Occupation   Amount

And you are further commanded to make a return of what you have done in execution of this writ.

Dated this .... day of .... A.D. ...., at ....

....
Clerk of the...................

(*Seal*)

FORM 34.1

(*Subsection 737.1(4)*)

STATEMENT ON RESTITUTION

Canada,
Province of ....,
(*territorial division*).

To the court that is sentencing (*name the offender*) who was convicted, or was discharged under section 730 of the *Criminal Code*, of an offence under that Act.

I, (*name of declarant*), declare that (*check the appropriate box*):

☐ (i) I am not seeking restitution for the losses and damages I suffered as the result of the commission of the offence.

☐ (ii) I am seeking restitution in the amount of $.......... for the following losses and damages I suffered as the result of the commission of the offence.

I declare that I have suffered the following losses and damages as the result of the commission of the offence:

(*Complete the following table if seeking restitution.*)

Description	Amount of loss and damage
(*describe each loss and damage*)	(*state the amount of each loss and damage*)
1.	....
2.	....
3.	....
4.	....

I understand that the amount of my losses and damages must be readily ascertainable by the court. For that purpose, I am responsible for providing the court with all necessary documents, including bills, receipts and estimates, in support of my claim for restitution.

Dated this .... day of .... 20 ...., at ....

Signature of declarant

2011, c. 6, s. 5; 2015, c. 13, s. 35.

FORM 34.2

(Subsection 722(4))

VICTIM IMPACT STATEMENT

This form may be used to provide a description of the physical or emotional harm, property damage or economic loss suffered by you as the result of the commission of an

offence, as well as a description of the impact of the offence on you. You may attach additional pages if you need more space.

Your statement must not include

- any statement about the offence or the offender that is not relevant to the harm or loss you suffered;

- any unproven allegations;

- any comments about any offence for which the offender was not convicted;

- any complaint about any individual, other than the offender, who was involved in the investigation or prosecution of the offence; or

- except with the court's approval, an opinion or recommendation about the sentence.

You may present a detailed account of the impact the offence has had on your life. The following sections are examples of information you may wish to include in your statement. You are not required to include all of this information.

Emotional impact

Describe how the offence has affected you emotionally. For example, think of

- your lifestyle and activities;

- your relationships with others such as your spouse, family and friends;

- your ability to work, attend school or study; and

- your feelings, emotions and reactions as they relate to the offence.

_____

_____

_____

_____

Physical impact

Describe how the offence has affected you physically. For example, think of

- ongoing physical pain, discomfort, illness, scarring, disfigurement or physical limitation;

- hospitalization or surgery you have had because of the offence;

- treatment, physiotherapy or medication you have been prescribed;

- the need for any further treatment or the expectation that you will receive further treatment; and

- any permanent or long-term disability.

_____

_____

_____

Economic impact

Describe how the offence has affected you financially. For example, think of

- the value of any property that was lost or damaged and the cost of repairs or replacement;

- any financial loss due to missed time from work;

- the cost of any medical expenses, therapy or counselling;

- any costs or losses that are not covered by insurance.

Please note that this is not an application for compensation or restitution.

_____

_____

_____

_____

Fears for security

Describe any fears you have for your security or that of your family and friends. For example, think of

- concerns with respect to contact with the offender; and

* concerns with respect to contact between the offender and members of your family or close friends.

_____

_____

Drawing, poem or letter

You may use this space to draw a picture or write a poem or letter if it will help you express the impact that the offence has had on you.

☐ I would like to present my statement in court.

To the best of my knowledge, the information contained in this statement is true.

Dated this .... day of .... 20.........., at.......... .

Signature of declarant

If you completed this statement on behalf of the victim, please indicate the reasons why you did so and the nature of your relationship with the victim.

_____

_____

Dated this .... day of .... 20.........., at.......... .

Signature of declarant

2015, c. 13, s. 35.

FORM 34.3

(*Subsection 722.2(2)*)

COMMUNITY IMPACT STATEMENT

This form may be used to provide a description of the harm or loss suffered by a community as the result of the commission of an offence, as well as a description of the impact of the offence on the community. You may attach additional pages if you need more space.

Your statement must not include

* any statement about the offence or the offender that is not relevant to the harm or loss suffered by the community;

- any unproven allegations;

- any comments about any offence for which the offender was not convicted;

- any complaint about any individual, other than the offender, who was involved in the investigation or prosecution of the offence; or

- except with the court's approval, an opinion or recommendation about the sentence.

Name of community on whose behalf the statement is made: ....

Explain how the statement reflects this community's views:

_____

_____

_____

_____

You may present a detailed account of the impact the offence has had on the community.

The following sections are examples of information you may wish to include in your statement. You are not required to include all of this information.

Emotional impact

Describe how the offence has affected community members emotionally. For example, think of

- community members' lifestyles and activities;

- community members' relationships with others in the community and outside it;

- community members' ability to work, attend school or study;

- community members' feelings, emotions and reactions as they relate to the offence; and

- the community's sense of belonging to the region.

_____

_____

_____

Physical impact

Describe how the offence has affected community members physically. For example, think of

- the ability of community members to access services; and

- changes in transportation and routes taken to and from school, work, shopping, etc.

_____

_____

_____

_____

CODE

Economic impact

Describe how the offence has affected the community financially. For example, think of

- any reduction in the number of visitors or tourists to the region;

- the value of any property that was lost or damaged and the cost of repairs or replacement; and

- any costs or losses that are not covered by insurance.

Please note that this is not an application for compensation or restitution.

_____

_____

_____

_____

Fears for security

Describe any fears that community members have for their security or that of their family and friends. For example, think of concerns with respect to contact with the offender.

Drawing, poem or letter

You may use this space to draw a picture or write a poem or letter if it will help you express the impact that the offence has had on the community.

☐ I would like to present this statement in court.

To the best of my knowledge, the information contained in this statement is true.

901

Dated this .... day of .... 20.........., at.......... .

Signature of declarant

2015, c. 13, s. 35.

FORM 35

(*Sections 570 and 806*)

Conviction

Canada,
Province of ....,
(*territorial division*).

Be it remembered that on the .... day of .... at
...................., A.B., (*date of birth*) hereinafter called the accused, was tried
under Part (XIX *or* XXVII) of the *Criminal Code* on the charge that (*state
fully the offence of which accused was convicted*), was convicted of the said
offence and the following punishment was imposed upon him, namely,★

★*Use whichever of the following forms of sentence is applicable*:

(*a*)   that the said accused be imprisoned in the (*prison*) at .... for
the term of ....;

(*b*)   that the said accused forfeit and pay the sum of .... dollars
to be applied according to law and also pay to .... the sum of
.... dollars in respect of costs and in default of payment of
the said sums forthwith (*or within a time fixed, if any*), to be
imprisoned in the (*prison*) at .... for the term of ....
unless the said sums and the costs and charges of the committal and
of conveying the accused to the said prison are sooner paid;

(*c*)   that the said accused be imprisoned in the (*prison*) at .... for
the term of .... and in addition forfeit and pay the sum of
.... dollars to be applied according to law and also pay to
.... the sum of .... dollars in respect of costs and in
default of payment of the said sums (forthwith *or within a time fixed,
if any*), to be imprisoned in the (*prison*) at .... for the term of
.... (*if sentence to be consecutive, state accordingly*) unless the
said sums and the costs and charges of the committal and of
conveying the accused to the said prison are sooner paid.

Dated this .... day of .... A.D. ...., at ....

....
**Clerk of the Court, Justice *or* Provincial
Court Judge**

(*Seal, if required*)

FORM 36

(*Sections 570 and 806*)

Order against an offender

Canada,
Province of ....,
(*territorial division*).

Be it remembered that on the .... day of .... A.D.
..................., at ...., A.B., (*date of birth*) of ...., was tried on
an information (*indictment*) alleging that (*set out matter of complaint or
alleged offence*), and it was ordered and adjudged that (*set out the order
made*).

Dated this .... day of .... A.D. ...., at ....

....
Justice *or* Clerk of the Court

FORM 37

(*Section 570*)

Order acquitting accused

Canada,
Province of ....,
(*territorial division*).

Be it remembered that on the .... day of .... A.D.
..................., at .... A.B., of ...., (*occupation*), (*date of birth*),
was tried on the charge that (*state fully the offence of which accused was
acquitted*) and was found not guilty of the said offence.

Dated this .... day of .... A.D. ...., at ....

....
Provincial Court Judge *or* Clerk of the
Court

(*Seal, if required*)

FORM 38

(*Section 708*)

Conviction for Contempt

Canada,
Province of ....,
(*territorial division*).

Be it remembered that on (*date*).........., at .... (*place*) in the (*territorial division*), E.F. of ...., in this conviction called the defaulter, is convicted for contempt in that they did not attend before (*set out court or justice*) to give evidence on the trial of a charge that (*state fully offence with which accused was charged*), although (duly subpoenaed or bound by recognizance to attend to give evidence, *as the case may be*) and has not shown any sufficient excuse for their default;

The defaulter is therefore convicted for their default, (*set out punishment as authorized and determined in accordance with section 708 of the Criminal Code*).

Dated (*date*).........., at .... (*place*).

(*Signature of judge, provincial court judge, justice or clerk of the court*)

(*Seal, if required*)

2019, c. 25, s. 350.

FORM 39

(*Sections 519 and 550*)

Order for Discharge of a Person in Custody

Canada,
Province of ....,
(*territorial division*).

To the keeper of the (*prison*) at ....:

You are directed to release E.F., detained by you under a (warrant of committal or order) dated (*date*).........., if E.F. is detained by you for no other cause.

(*Signature of judge, justice or clerk of the court*)

(*Seal, if required*)

2019, c. 25, s. 351.

FORM 40

(*Section 629*)

Challenge to array

Canada,
Province of ....,
(*territorial division*).

The Queen

v.

C.D.

The (prosecutor *or* accused) challenges the array of the panel on the ground that X.Y., (sheriff *or* deputy sheriff), who returned the panel, was guilty of (partiality *or* fraud *or* wilful misconduct) on returning it.

Dated this .... day of .... A.D. ...., at ....

....
Counsel for (prosecutor *or* accused)

FORM 41

(*Section 639*)

Challenge for cause

Canada,
Province of ....,
(*territorial division*).

The Queen

v.

C.D.

The (prosecutor *or* accused) challenges G.H. on the ground that (*set out ground of challenge in accordance with subsection 638(1) of the Criminal Code*).

....
Counsel for (prosecutor *or* accused)

FORM 42

(*Section 827*)

Certificate of non-payment of costs of appeal

In the Court of ....

(*Style of Cause*)

I hereby certify that A.B. (the appellant *or* respondent, *as the case may be*) in this appeal, having been ordered to pay costs in the sum of .... dollars, has failed to pay the said costs within the time limited for the payment thereof.

Dated this .... day of .... A.D. ...., at ....

....
Clerk of the Court of...................

(*Seal*)

FORM 43

(*Section 734*)

Jailer's receipt to peace officer for prisoner

I hereby certify that I have received from X.Y., a peace officer for (*territorial division*), one A.B., together with a (warrant *or* order) issued by (*set out court or justice, as the case may be*).★
★*Add a statement of the condition of the prisoner*

Dated this .... day of .... A.D. ...., at ....

....
Keeper of (*prison*)

1995, c. 22, s. 18.

FORM 44

(*Section 667*)

I, (*name*), a fingerprint examiner designated as such for the purposes of section 667 of the *Criminal Code* by the Minister of Public Safety and Emergency Preparedness, do hereby certify that (*name*) also known as (*aliases if any*), FPS Number ...., whose fingerprints are shown reproduced below (*reproduction of fingerprints*) or attached hereto, has been convicted, discharged under section 736 of the *Criminal Code* or convicted and sentenced in Canada as follows:

(*record*)

Dated this .... day of .... A.D. ...., at ....

....
Fingerprint Examiner

1995, c. 22, s. 18; 2005, c. 10, s. 34(1)(*f*)(xiv).

FORM 45
(Section 667)

I, *(name)*, a fingerprint examiner designated as such for the purposes of section 667 of the *Criminal Code* by the Minister of Public Safety and Emergency Preparedness, do hereby certify that I have compared the fingerprints reproduced in or attached to exhibit A with the fingerprints reproduced in or attached to the certificate in Form 44 marked exhibit B and that they are those of the same person.

Dated this .... day of .... A.D. ...., at ....

....
Fingerprint Examiner

2005, c. 10, s. 34(1)(*f*)(xiv).

FORM 46
(Section 732.1)

PROBATION ORDER

Canada,
Province of ....,
(territorial division).

Whereas on the .... day of .... at ...., A.B., hereinafter called the offender, (pleaded guilty to *or* was tried under (*here insert Part XIX, XX or XXVII, as the case may be*) of the *Criminal Code* and was (*here insert convicted or found guilty, as the case may be*) on the charge that (*here state the offence to which the offender pleaded guilty or for which the offender was convicted or found guilty, as the case may be*);

And whereas on the .... day of .... the court adjudged★

★Use whichever of the following forms of disposition is applicable:

(*a*) that the offender be discharged on the following conditions:

(*b*) that the passing of sentence on the offender be suspended and that the said offender be released on the following conditions:

(*c*) that the offender forfeit and pay the sum of .... dollars to be applied according to law and in default of payment of the said sum without delay (*or within a time fixed, if any*), be imprisoned in the (*prison*) at .... for the term of .... unless the said sum and charges of the committal and of conveying the said offender to the said prison are sooner paid, and in addition thereto, that the said offender comply with the following conditions:

907

(d) that the offender be imprisoned in the (*prison*) at .... for the term of .... and, in addition thereto, that the said offender comply with the following conditions:

(e) that following the expiration of the offender's conditional sentence order related to this or another offence, that the said offender comply with the following conditions:

(f) that following the expiration of the offender's sentence of imprisonment related to another offence, that the said offender comply with the following conditions:

(g) when the offender is ordered to serve the sentence of imprisonment intermittently, that the said offender comply with the following conditions when not in confinement:

Now therefore the said offender shall, for the period of .... from the date of
this order (*or, where paragraph (d), (e) or (f) is applicable, the date of expiration of the offender's sentence of imprisonment or conditional sentence order*) comply with the following conditions, namely, that the said offender shall keep the peace and be of good behaviour, appear before the court when required to do so by the court and notify the court or probation officer in advance of any change of name or address and promptly notify the court or probation officer of any change of employment or occupation, and, in addition,

(*here state any additional conditions prescribed pursuant to subsection 732.1(3) of the Criminal Code*).

Dated this .... day of .... A.D. ...., at ....

....

Clerk of the Court,
Justice *or* Provincial Court Judge

1995, c. 22, s. 10; 2004, c. 12, s. 17.

FORM 47

(*Section 462.48*)

ORDER TO DISCLOSE INCOME TAX INFORMATION

Canada,
Province of ....,
(*territorial division*).

To A.B., of .... , (*office or occupation*):

Whereas, it appears on the oath of C.D., of ...., that there are reasonable grounds for believing that E.F., of ...., has committed or benefited from the commission of the offence of .... and that the information or documents (*describe information or documents*) are likely to be of substantial value to an investigation of that offence or a related matter; and

Whereas there are reasonable grounds for believing that it is in the public interest to allow access to the information or documents, having regard to the benefit likely to accrue to the investigation if the access is obtained;

This is, therefore, to authorize and require you between the hours of (*as the judge may direct*), during the period commencing on .... and ending on ...., to produce all the above-mentioned information and documents to one of the following police officers, namely, (*here name police officers*) and allow the police officer to remove the information or documents, or to allow the police officer access to the above-mentioned information and documents and to examine them, *as the judge directs*, subject to the following conditions (*state conditions*): ....

Dated this .... day of .... A.D. ...., at ....

....

Signature of judge

FORM 48

(*Section 672.13*)

ASSESSMENT ORDER OF THE COURT

Canada,
Province of ....,
(*territorial division*).

Whereas I have (*or if the signatory is the clerk of the court*, the judge or justice has) reasonable grounds to believe that evidence of the mental condition of (*name of accused*), who has been charged with ...., may be necessary to determine★

☐ whether the accused is unfit to stand trial

☐ whether the accused suffered from a mental disorder so as to exempt the accused from criminal responsibility by virtue of subsection 16(1) of the *Criminal Code* at the time of the act or omission charged against the accused

☐ whether the balance of the mind of the accused was disturbed at the time of commission of the alleged offence, if accused is a female person charged with an offence arising out of the death of her newly-born child

909

☐ if a verdict of unfit to stand trial or a verdict of not criminally responsible on account of mental disorder has been rendered in respect of the accused, the appropriate disposition to be made in respect of the accused under section 672.54, 672.58 or 672.64 of the *Criminal Code* or whether the court should, under subsection 672.84(3) of that Act, revoke a finding that the accused is a high-risk accused

☐ if a verdict of unfit to stand trial has been rendered in respect of the accused, whether the court should order a stay of proceedings under section 672.851 of the *Criminal Code*

An assessment of the mental condition of (*name of accused*) is ordered to be conducted by/at (*name of person or service by which or place where assessment is to be made*) for a period of .... days.

This order is to be in force for a total of .... days, including travelling time, during which time the accused is to remain ★

☐ in custody at (*place where accused is to be detained*)

☐ out of custody, on the following conditions:

(*set out conditions, if applicable*)

★ Check applicable option.

Dated (*date*).........., at .... (*place*).

(*Signature of judge, provincial court judge, justice or clerk of the court*)

1991, c. 43, s. 8; 1995, c. 22, s. 10 (Sched. I, item 36); 2005, c. 22, s. 40; 2014, c. 6, s. 19; 2019, c. 25, s. 352.

FORM 48.1

(*Section 672.13*)

ASSESSMENT ORDER OF THE REVIEW BOARD

Canada,
Province of ....,
(*territorial division*).

Whereas I have reasonable grounds to believe that evidence of the mental condition of (*name of accused*), who has been charged with ...., may be necessary to ★

☐ if a verdict of unfit to stand trial or a verdict of not criminally responsible on account of mental disorder has been rendered in respect of the accused, make a disposition under section 672.54 of the *Criminal Code* or determine whether the Review Board should, under subsection 672.84(1) of that Act, refer to the superior court of criminal jurisdiction for review a finding that the accused is a high-risk accused

☐ if a verdict of unfit to stand trial has been rendered in respect of the accused, determine whether the Review Board should make a recommendation to the court that has jurisdiction in respect of the offence charged against the accused to hold an inquiry to determine whether a stay of proceedings should be ordered in accordance with section 672.851 of the *Criminal Code*

I hereby order an assessment of the mental condition of (*name of accused*) to be conducted by/at (*name of person or service by whom or place where assessment is to be made*) for a period of .... days.

This order is to be in force for a total of .... days, including travelling time, during which time the accused is to remain *

☐ in custody at (*place where accused is to be detained*)

☐ out of custody, on the following conditions:

(*set out conditions, if applicable*)

* Check applicable option.

* Check applicable option.

Dated this .... day of .... A.D. ...., at ....

....
(*Signature of Chairperson of the Review Board*)
2005, c. 22, s. 40; 2014, c. 6, s. 20.

FORM 48.2

(*Subsection 672.5(14)*)

VICTIM IMPACT STATEMENT — NOT CRIMINALLY RESPONSIBLE

This form may be used to provide a description of the physical or emotional harm, property damage or economic loss suffered by you arising from the conduct for which the accused person was found not criminally responsible on account of mental disorder, as well as a description of the impact that the conduct has had on you. You may attach additional pages if you need more space.

Your statement must not include

• any statement about the conduct of the accused that is not relevant to the harm or loss suffered by you;

- any unproven allegations;

- any comments about any conduct for which the accused was not found not criminally responsible;

- any complaint about any individual, other than the accused, who was involved in the investigation or prosecution of the offence; or

- except with the court's or Review Board's approval, an opinion or recommendation about the disposition.

The following sections are examples of information you may wish to include in your statement. You are not required to include all of this information.

Emotional impact

Describe how the accused's conduct has affected you emotionally. For example, think of

- your lifestyle and activities;

- your relationships with others such as your spouse, family and friends;

- your ability to work, attend school or study; and

- your feelings, emotions and reactions as these relate to the conduct.

_____

_____

_____

_____

Physical impact

Describe how the accused's conduct has affected you physically. For example, think of

- ongoing physical pain, discomfort, illness, scarring, disfigurement or physical limitation;

- hospitalization or surgery you have had because of the conduct of the accused;

- treatment, physiotherapy or medication you have been prescribed;

- the need for any further treatment or the expectation that you will receive further treatment; and

- any permanent or long-term disability.

_____

_____

_____

_____

Economic impact

Describe how the accused's conduct has affected you financially. For example, think of

- the value of any property that was lost or damaged and the cost of repairs or replacement;

- any financial loss due to missed time from work;

- the cost of any medical expenses, therapy or counselling; and

- any costs or losses that are not covered by insurance.

Please note that this is not an application for compensation or restitution.

_____

_____

_____

Fears for security

Describe any fears you have for your security or that of your family and friends. For example, think of

- concerns with respect to contact with the accused; and

- concerns with respect to contact between the accused and members of your family or close friends.

_____

_____

_____

Drawing, poem or letter

You may use this space to draw a picture or write a poem or letter if it will help you express the impact that the accused's conduct has had on you.

☐ I would like to read or present my statement (in court or before the Review Board).

CODE

To the best of my knowledge, the information contained in this statement is true.

Dated this .... day of .... 20.........., at.......... .

Signature of declarant

2015, c. 13, s. 36.

FORM 49

(Section 672.57)

WARRANT OF COMMITTAL

DISPOSITION OF DETENTION

Canada,
Province of ....,
(territorial division).

To the peace officers in the said *(territorial division)* and to the keeper *(administrator, warden)* of the *(prison, hospital or other appropriate place where the accused is detained).*

This warrant is issued for the committal of A.B., of ...., *(occupation),* hereinafter called the accused.

Whereas the accused has been charged that *(set out briefly the offence in respect of which the accused was charged);*

And whereas the accused was found*

☐ .... unfit to stand trial

☐ .... not criminally responsible on account of mental disorder

This is, therefore, to command you, in Her Majesty's name, to take the accused in custody and convey the accused safely to the *(prison, hospital or other appropriate place)* at ...., and there deliver the accused to the keeper *(administrator, warden)* with the following precept:

You, the keeper *(administrator, warden),* are therefore directed to receive the accused in your custody in the *(prison, hospital or other appropriate place)* and to keep the accused safely there until the accused is delivered by due course of law.

The following are the conditions to which the accused shall be subject while in your *(prison, hospital or other appropriate place):*

The following are the powers regarding the restrictions *(and the limits and conditions on those restrictions)* on the liberty of the accused that are hereby delegated to you the said keeper (*administrator, warden*) of the said (*prison, hospital or other appropriate place*):

*Check applicable option.

Dated (*date*)..........., at .... (*place*).

(*Signature of judge, provincial court judge, justice, clerk of the court or chairperson of the review board*)

1991, c. 43, s. 8; 1995, c. 22, s. 10; 2005, c. 22, s. 40; 2014, c. 6, s. 19; 2019, c. 25, s. 353.

CODE

FORM 50

(*Section 672.7(2)*)

WARRANT OF COMMITTAL

PLACEMENT DECISION

Canada,
Province of ....,
(*territorial division*).

To the peace officers in the said (*territorial division*) and to the keeper (*administrator, warden*) of the (*prison, hospital or other appropriate place where the accused is detained*).

This warrant is issued for the committal of A.B., of ...., (*occupation*), hereinafter called the accused.

Whereas the accused has been charged that (*set out briefly the offence in respect of which the accused was charged*);

And whereas the accused was found*

☐ .... unfit to stand trial

☐ .... not criminally responsible on account of mental disorder

And whereas the Review Board had held a hearing and decided that the accused shall be detained in custody;

And whereas the accused is required to be detained in custody pursuant to a warrant of committal issued by (*set out the name of the Judge, Clerk of the Court, Provincial Court Judge or Justice as well as the name of the court and territorial division*), dated the .... day of ...., in respect of the offence that (*set out briefly the offence in respect of which the accused was charged or convicted*);

This is, therefore, to command you, in Her Majesty's name, to★

☐   execute the warrant of committal issued by the court, according to its terms

☐   execute the warrant of committal issued herewith by the Review Board

★Check applicable option.

Dated this .... day of .... A.D. ...., at ....

....
(Signature of chairperson of the
Review Board)
1991, c. 43, s. 8.

FORM 51

(Paragraphs 732.1(3)(c.2), 742.3(2)(a.2), 810(3.02)(c), 810.01(4.1)(g),
810.011(6)(f), 810.1(3.02)(i) and 810.2(4.1)(g))

NOTICE OF OBLIGATION TO PROVIDE SAMPLES OF BODILY SUBSTANCE

To A.B., of ...., (*occupation*), (*address in Canada*), (*date of birth*), (*gender*):

Because, on (*date*), you were ordered, under (*applicable provision*) of the *Criminal Code*, to provide samples of a bodily substance prescribed by regulation at regular intervals for the purpose of analysis;

You are provided with this notice to inform you of your obligations with respect to providing samples.

1. On (*specify a day not earlier than 24 hours after the day on which the notice is served*), you must report, at any time from (*time*) to (*time*), at (*address of place at which sample to be taken, as designated by the Attorney General of the province or Minister of Justice of the territory*), to provide a sample of your (*specify type of bodily substance prescribed by regulation*).

2. Every (*specify a number not less than seven*) days after you first report to provide a sample, you must report, at any time from (*time*) to (*time*), at (*address of place at which sample to be taken, as designated by the Attorney General of the province or Minister of Justice of the territory*), to provide a sample of your (*specify type of bodily substance prescribed by regulation*).

3. You have the right to apply to a court to terminate the obligation to provide samples, and the right to appeal any decision of that court.

4. If you are found to have not complied with your obligation to provide samples as set out in this notice, you may be subject to a fine or imprisonment, or to both (*or, in the case of a conditional sentence*, you may be subject to proceedings under section 742.6 of the *Criminal Code*, the consequences of which may include imprisonment).

5. The results of the analysis of the bodily substances may be used or disclosed in accordance with the *Criminal Code*, including in proceedings against you, the result of which may be that you are subject to a fine or imprisonment, or to both (*or, in the case of a conditional sentence*, including in proceedings under section 742.6 of the *Criminal Code*, the consequences of which may include imprisonment).

Served on (*date*), at (*place the notice is served*).

....

(*Signature of probation officer, supervisor or person designated by the Attorney General or Minister of Justice, as the case may be*)

2005, c. 22, s. 41; 2011, c. 7, s. 13; 2015, c. 20, s. 34(4).

FORM 52

(*Section 490.012*)

ORDER TO COMPLY WITH SEX OFFENDER INFORMATION REGISTRATION ACT

Canada,
Province of ....,
(*territorial division*)

To A.B., of ...., (*occupation*), (*address or address of court if no fixed address*), (*date of birth*), (*gender*):

You have been convicted of or found not criminally responsible on account of mental disorder for (*description of offence(s)*) under (*applicable designated offence provision(s) of the Criminal Code*), a designated offence (*or designated offences*) within the meaning of subsection 490.011(1) of the *Criminal Code*.

1. You must report for the first time to the registration centre referred to in section 7.1 of the *Sex Offender Information Registration Act*, whenever required under subsection 4(1) of that Act.

2. You must subsequently report to the registration centre referred to in section 7.1 of the *Sex Offender Information Registration Act*, whenever required under section 4.1 or 4.3 of that Act, for a period of .... years

after this order is made (*or if paragraph 490.013(2)(c) or any of subsections 490.013(2.1) to (5) of the Criminal Code applies, for life*).

3. Information relating to you will be collected under sections 5 and 6 of the *Sex Offender Information Registration Act* by a person who collects information at the registration centre.

4. Information relating to you will be registered in a database, and may be consulted, disclosed and used in the circumstances set out in the *Sex Offender Information Registration Act.*

5. If you believe that the information registered in the database contains an error or omission, you may ask a person who collects information at the registration centre referred to in section 7.1 of the *Sex Offender Information Registration Act* or, if applicable, the Canadian Forces Provost Marshal, to correct the information.

6. You have the right to apply to a court to terminate this order, and the right to appeal the decision of that court.

7. If you are found to have contravened this order, you may be subject to a fine or imprisonment, or to both.

8. If you are found to have provided false or misleading information, you may be subject to a fine or imprisonment, or to both.

Dated this .... day of .... , at ....

....
(Signature of judge or clerk and name of court)

....
(Signature of person subject to order)

2004, c. 10, s. 21; 2007, c. 5, s. 30; 2010, c. 17, s. 26.

FORM 53

(*Sections 490.019 and 490.032*)

NOTICE OF OBLIGATION TO COMPLY WITH SEX OFFENDER INFORMATION REGISTRATION ACT

Canada,
Province of ....
(*territorial division*).

To A.B., of ...., (*occupation*), a person referred to in subsection 490.02(1) of the *Criminal Code*:

Because, on .... (*insert date(s)*), you were convicted of, or found not criminally responsible on account of mental disorder for, ... (*insert description of offence(s)*), one or more offences referred to in paragraph (*a*), (*c*), (*c*.1), (*d*), (*d*.1) or (*e*) of the definition "designated offence" in subsection 490.011(1) of the *Criminal Code* or in paragraph (*a*) or (*c*) of the definition "designated offence" in section 227 of the *National Defence Act*, under .... (*insert the applicable offence provision(s)*), this is provided to give you notice that you are required to comply with the *Sex Offender Information Registration Act*.

1. You must report for the first time to the registration centre referred to in section 7.1 of the *Sex Offender Information Registration Act*, whenever required under subsection 4(2) of that Act.

2. You must subsequently report to the registration centre referred to in section 7.1 of the *Sex Offender Information Registration Act*, whenever required under section 4.1 or 4.3 of that Act, for a period of .... years after you were sentenced, or found not criminally responsible on account of mental disorder, for the offence (*or if paragraph 490.022(3)(c) or (d) of the Criminal Code applies*, for life) or for any shorter period set out in subsection 490.022(2) of the *Criminal Code*.

3. Information relating to you will be collected under sections 5 and 6 of the *Sex Offender Information Registration Act* by a person who collects information at the registration centre.

4. Information relating to you will be registered in a database, and may be consulted, disclosed and used in the circumstances set out in the *Sex Offender Information Registration Act*.

5. If you believe that the information registered in the database contains an error or omission, you may ask a person who collects information at the registration centre referred to in section 7.1 of the *Sex Offender Information Registration Act* or, if applicable, the Canadian Forces Provost Marshal, to correct the information.

6. You have the right to apply to a court to exempt you from the obligation to comply with the *Sex Offender Information Registration Act*, and the right to appeal any decision of that court.

7. You have the right to apply to a court to terminate the obligation, and the right to appeal any decision of that court.

8. If you are found to have contravened the obligation, you may be subject to a fine or imprisonment, or to both.

9. If you are found to have provided false or misleading information, you may be subject to a fine or imprisonment, or to both.

Dated this .... day of .... , at ....

2004, c. 10, s. 21; 2007, c. 5, s. 31;
2014, c. 25, s. 33.

FORM 54

(Sections 490.02901 to 490.02903, 490.02905 and 490.032)

OBLIGATION TO COMPLY WITH SEX OFFENDER INFORMATION REGISTRATION ACT

To A.B., of ..., (*occupation*), (*address in Canada*), (*date of birth*), (*gender*):

Because, on (*date*), you were convicted of or found not criminally responsible on account of mental disorder for an offence (*or* offences) in (*location of offence(s)*) that the Attorney General of the province, or the minister of justice of the territory, has identified as being equivalent to (*description of offence(s)*) under (*applicable provision(s) of the Criminal Code*), a designated offence (*or* designated offences) as defined in subsection 490.011(1) of the *Criminal Code*;

You are provided with this to inform you that you are required to comply with the *Sex Offender Information Registration Act.*

1. You must report for the first time to the registration centre referred to in section 7.1 of the *Sex Offender Information Registration Act*, whenever required under subsection 4(2) of that Act.

2. You must subsequently report to the registration centre referred to in section 7.1 of the *Sex Offender Information Registration Act*, whenever required under section 4.1 or 4.3 of that Act, for a period of .... years after the day on which you were sentenced or found not criminally responsible on account of mental disorder for the offence (*or if paragraph 490.02904(3)(c) or (d) of the Criminal Code applies,* for life because you were convicted of or found not criminally responsible on account of mental disorder for (*description of offence(s)*) under (*applicable designated offence provision(s) of the Criminal Code*), a designated offence (or designated offences) within the meaning of subsection 490.011(1) of the *Criminal Code*) or for any shorter period determined under subsection 490.02904(2) of the *Criminal Code*.

3. Information relating to you will be collected under sections 5 and 6 of the *Sex Offender Information Registration Act* by a person who collects information at the registration centre.

4. Information relating to you will be registered in a database, and may be consulted, disclosed and used in the circumstances set out in the *Sex Offender Information Registration Act.*

5. If you believe that the information registered in the database contains an error or omission, you may ask a person who collects information at the registration centre referred to in section 7.1 of the *Sex Offender Information Registration Act* to correct the information.

6. You have the right to apply to a court to exempt you from the obligation to comply with the *Sex Offender Information Registration Act*, and the right to appeal the decision of that court.

7. You have the right to apply to a court to terminate the obligation to comply with the *Sex Offender Information Registration Act* and the right to appeal the decision of that court.

8. If you are found to have not complied with the *Sex Offender Information Registration Act*, you may be subject to a fine or imprisonment, or to both.

9. If you are found to have provided false or misleading information, you may be subject to a fine or imprisonment, or to both.

Served on (*date*).

_____

For administrative use only:

Sentence imposed or verdict of not criminally responsible on account of mental disorder rendered on (*date*).

2010, c. 17, s. 27.

6. You have the right to apply to a court to exempt you from the obligation to comply with the Sex Offender Information Registration Act, and the right to appeal the decision of that court.

7. You have the right to apply to a court to terminate the obligation to comply with the Sex Offender Information Registration Act and the right to appeal the decision of that court.

8. If you are found to have not complied with the Sex Offender Information Registration Act, you may be subject to a fine or imprisonment or to both.

9. If you are found to have provided false or misleading information, you may be subject to a fine or imprisonment or to both.

Served on (date):

For administrative use only.

Sentence imposed or verdict of not criminally responsible on account of mental disorder is pieced or varied.

2010, c. 17, s. 27.

CANADA EVIDENCE ACT

R.S.C. 1985, Chap. C-5

Amended R.S.C. 1985, c. 27 (1st Supp.), s. 203(1)

Amended R.S.C. 1985, c. 19 (3rd Supp.), ss. 17 and 18

Amended 1992, c. 1, s. 142(1); Sch. V, item 9(1) in force February 28, 1992; Sch. V, item 9(2) in force September 2, 1994 as provided by s. 142(2)

Amended 1992, c. 47, s. 66; brought into force August 1, 1996 by SI/96-56, *Can. Gaz., Part II*, October 7, 1996

Amended 1993, c. 28, Sch. III, s. 8; in force April 1, 1999

Amended 1993, c. 34, s. 15; in force June 23, 1993

Amended 1994, c. 44, ss. 85 to 93; brought into force February 15, 1995

Amended 1995, c. 28, s. 47; in force July 13, 1995

Amended 1997, c. 18, ss. 116 to 118; in force June 16, 1997

Amended 1998, c. 9, s. 1; brought into force June 30, 1998 by SI/98-79, *Can. Gaz., Part II*, June 24, 1998

Amended 1999, c. 18, ss. 89 to 91; in force June 17, 1999

Amended 1999, c. 28, ss. 149 and 150; brought into force June 28, 1999 by SI/99-70

Amended 2000, c. 5, ss. 52 to 57; brought into force May 1, 2000 by para. (*a*) of SI/2000-29

Amended 2001, c. 41, ss. 43, 44, 124(2) and (3), 140(1), 141(3)(b) and 141(4) to (7); ss. 43 and 44 brought into force December 24, 2001 by SI/2002-16, *Can. Gaz., Part II*, January 2, 2002; s. 141(3)(b) brought into force March 27, 2002 as provided by this section; s. 124(2) and (3) in force June 28, 2002 as provided by this section; ss. 140(1) and 141(4) to (7) in force July 2, 2003 as provided by these sections

Amended 2002, c. 1, s. 166; brought into force April 1, 2003 by SI/2002-91, *Can. Gaz., Part II*, June 19, 2002

Amended 2002, c. 7, s. 96; brought into force April 1, 2003 by SI/2003-48, *Can. Gaz., Part II*, April 9, 2003

Amended 2002, c. 8, ss. 118, 119 and 183(1)(*b*); s. 119 since repealed by 2001, c. 41, s. 141(3)(*b*); remainder brought into force July 2, 2003 by SI/2003-109, *Can. Gaz.*, June 4, 2003

Amended 2003, c. 22, ss. 104 and 105; brought into force April 6, 2005 by SI/2005-24, *Can. Gaz.*, April 6, 2005

Amended SOR/2004-19, s. 1, in force February 12, 2004

Amended 2004, c. 12, ss. 18 and 19, in force on Royal Assent, April 22, 2004

Amended 2005, c. 32, ss. 26 and 27, in force January 2, 2006 as provided by para. (*b*) of SI/2005-104, *Can. Gaz., Part II*, November 16, 2005

Amended 2005, c. 46, s. 56; brought into force April 15, 2007 by SI/2007-43, *Can. Gaz., Part II*, April 4, 2007

Amended SOR/2006-80, s. 1, in force May 1, 2006 as provided by s. 2

Amended 2006, c. 9, s. 222; in force December 12, 2006

Amended SOR/2006-335, s. 1, *Can. Gaz., Part II*, December 27, 2006, in force December 11, 2006 as provided by s. 2

Amended 2008, c. 3, s. 11; brought into force February 22, 2008, by SI/2008-24, *Can. Gaz., Part II*, March 5, 2008

Amended SOR/2012-220, *Can. Gaz., Part II*, October 24, 2012, s. 1; in force October 5, 2012 as provided by s. 2

Amended 2013, c. 9, ss. 17, and 19 to 24; in force July 15, 2013 by SI/2013-67, *Can. Gaz., Part II*, June 19, 2013

Amended 2013, c. 18, ss. 45, 85; in force November 28, 2014 by SI/2014-104, *Can. Gaz., Part II*, December 17, 2014

Amended 2013, c. 40, s. 448; in force November 1, 2014 by SI/2014-84, *Can. Gaz., Part II*, November 5, 2014

Amended 2014, c. 2, s. 5; in force April 1, 2014 by SI/2014-34, *Can. Gaz., Part II*, April 9, 2014

Amended 2014, c. 25, s. 34; in force December 6, 2014

Amended 2014, c. 31, s. 27; in force March 9, 2015

Amended 2015, c. 13, ss. 52 and 53; in force July 22, 2015

Amended 2015, c. 20, s. 13; brought into force August 1, 2015 by SI/2015-64, *Can. Gaz., Part II*, July 15, 2015

Amended 2015, c. 23, s. 20; repealed before coming into force 2015, c. 13, s. 57(2)

Amended 2015, c. 36, s. 43; in force June 23, 2015

Amended 2017, c. 9, s. 41; in force June 19, 2017

Amended 2017, c. 22, s. 2; in force on Royal Assent, October 18, 2017

Amended 2019, c. 13, ss. 20, 61; brought into force July 12, 2019 by SI/2019-67, *Can. Gaz., Part II*, July 24, 2019

Amended 2019, c. 15, ss. 48-54; to come into force by order of the Governor in Council

Amended 2019, c. 18, s. 60; in force June 21, 2019

An Act respecting witnesses and evidence

SHORT TITLE

SHORT TITLE.

1. This Act may be cited as the *Canada Evidence Act*. R.S., c. E-10, s. 1.

Part I / *Application*

APPLICATION.

2. This Part applies to all criminal proceedings and to all civil proceedings and other matters whatever respecting which Parliament has jurisdiction. R.S., c. E-10, s. 2.

Witnesses

INTEREST OR CRIME.

3. A person is not incompetent to give evidence by reason of interest or crime. R.S., c. E-10, s. 3.

ACCUSED AND SPOUSE / Spouse of accused / Communications during marriage / Offences against young persons / Saving / Failure to testify.

4. (1) Every person charged with an offence, and, except as otherwise provided in this section, the wife or husband, as the case may be, of the person so charged, is a competent witness for the defence, whether the person so charged is charged solely or jointly with any other person.

(2) No person is incompetent, or uncompellable, to testify for the prosecution by reason only that they are married to the accused.

(3) No husband is compellable to disclose any communication made to him by his wife during their marriage, and no wife is compellable to disclose any communication made to her by her husband during their marriage.

(4) [*Repealed*, 2015, c. 13, s. 52(2).]

(5) [*Repealed*, 2015, c. 13, s. 52(2).]

(6) The failure of the person charged, or of the wife or husband of that person, to testify shall not be made the subject of comment by the judge or by counsel for the prosecution. R.S., c. E-10, s. 4; 1980-81-82-83, c. 110, s. 71, c. 125, s. 29; 1984, c. 40, s. 27; R.S.C. 1985, c. 19 (3rd Supp.), s. 17; 2002, c. 1, s. 166; 2014, c. 25, s. 34; 2014, c. 31, s. 27; 2015, c. 13, s. 52.

INCRIMINATING QUESTIONS / Answer not admissible against witness.

5. (1) No witness shall be excused from answering any question on the ground that the answer to the question may tend to criminate him, or may tend to establish his liability to a civil proceeding at the instance of the Crown or of any person.

(2) Where with respect to any question a witness objects to answer on the ground that his answer may tend to criminate him, or may tend to establish his liability to a civil proceeding at the instance of the Crown or of any person, and if but for this Act, or the Act of any provincial legislature, the witness would therefore have been excused from answering the question, then although the witness is by reason of this Act or the provincial Act compelled to answer, the answer so given shall not be used or admissible in evidence against him in any criminal trial or other criminal proceeding against him thereafter taking place, other than a prosecution for perjury in the giving of that evidence or for the giving of contradictory evidence. R.S., c. E-10, s. 5; 1997, c. 18, s. 116.

CAN. EV.

925

EVIDENCE OF PERSON WITH PHYSICAL DISABILITY / Evidence of person with mental disability / Inquiry.

6. (1) If a witness has difficulty communicating by reason of a physical disability, the court may order that the witness be permitted to give evidence by any means that enables the evidence to be intelligible.

(2) If a witness with a mental disability is determined under section 16 to have the capacity to give evidence and has difficulty communicating by reason of a disability, the court may order that the witness be permitted to give evidence by any means that enables the evidence to be intelligible.

(3) The court may conduct an inquiry to determine if the means by which a witness may be permitted to give evidence under subsection (1) or (2) is necessary and reliable. R.S., c. E-10, s. 6; 1998, c. 9, s. 1.

IDENTIFICATION OF ACCUSED.

6.1 For greater certainty, a witness may give evidence as to the identity of an accused whom the witness is able to identify visually or in any other sensory manner. 1998, c. 9, s. 1.

EXPERT WITNESSES.

7. Where, in any trial or other proceeding, criminal or civil, it is intended by the prosecution or the defence, or by any party, to examine as witnesses professional or other experts entitled according to the law or practice to give opinion evidence, not more than five of such witnesses may be called on either side without the leave of the court or judge or person presiding. R.S., c. E-10, s. 7.

HANDWRITING COMPARISON.

8. Comparison of a disputed writing with any writing proved to the satisfaction of the court to be genuine shall be permitted to be made by witnesses, and such writings, and the evidence of witnesses respecting those writings, may be submitted to the court and jury as proof of the genuineness or otherwise of the writing in dispute. R.S., c. E-10, s. 8.

ADVERSE WITNESSES / Previous statements by witness not proved adverse.

9. (1) A party producing a witness shall not be allowed to impeach his credit by general evidence of bad character, but if the witness, in the opinion of the court, proves adverse, the party may contradict him by other evidence, or, by leave of the court, may prove that the witness made at other times a statement inconsistent with his present testimony, but before the last mentioned proof can be given the circumstances of the supposed statement, sufficient to designate the particular occasion, shall be mentioned to the witness, and he shall be asked whether or not he did make the statement.

(2) Where the party producing a witness alleges that the witness made at other times a statement in writing, reduced to writing, or recorded on audio tape or

video tape or otherwise, inconsistent with the witness' present testimony, the court may, without proof that the witness is adverse, grant leave to that party to cross-examine the witness as to the statement and the court may consider the cross-examination in determining whether in the opinion of the court the witness is adverse. R.S., c. E-10, s. 9; 1994, c. 44, s. 85.

CROSS-EXAMINATION AS TO PREVIOUS STATEMENTS / Deposition of witness in criminal investigation.

10. (1) On any trial a witness may be cross-examined as to previous statements that the witness made in writing, or that have been reduced to writing, or recorded on audio tape or video tape or otherwise, relative to the subject-matter of the case, without the writing being shown to the witness or the witness being given the opportunity to listen to the audio tape or view the video tape or otherwise take cognizance of the statements, but, if it is intended to contradict the witness, the witness' attention must, before the contradictory proof can be given, be called to those parts of the statement that are to be used for the purpose of so contradicting the witness, and the judge, at any time during the trial, may require the production of the writing or tape or other medium for inspection, and thereupon make such use of it for the purposes of the trial as the judge thinks fit.

(2) A deposition of a witness, purporting to have been taken before a justice on the investigation of a criminal charge and to be signed by the witness and the justice, returned to and produced from the custody of the proper officer shall be presumed, in the absence of evidence to the contrary, to have been signed by the witness. R.S., c. E-10, s. 10; 1994, c. 44, s. 86.

CROSS-EXAMINATION AS TO PREVIOUS ORAL STATEMENTS.

11. Where a witness, on cross-examination as to a former statement made by him relative to the subject-matter of the case and inconsistent with his present testimony, does not distinctly admit that he did make the statement, proof may be given that he did in fact make it, but before that proof can be given the circumstances of the supposed statement, sufficient to designate the particular occasion, shall be mentioned to the witness, and he shall be asked whether or not he did make the statement. R.S., c. E-10, s. 11.

EXAMINATION AS TO PREVIOUS CONVICTION / Proof of previous convictions / How conviction proved.

12. (1) A witness may be questioned as to whether the witness has been convicted of any offence, excluding any offence designated as a contravention under the *Contraventions Act*, but including such an offence where the conviction was entered after a trial on an indictment.

(1.1) If the witness either denies the fact or refuses to answer, the opposite party may prove the conviction.

(2) A conviction may be proved by producing

(a) a certificate containing the substance and effect only, omitting the formal part, of the indictment and conviction, if it is for an indictable offence, or a copy of the summary conviction, if it is for an offence punishable on summary conviction, purporting to be signed by the clerk of the court or other officer having the custody of the records of the court in which the conviction, if on indictment, was had, or to which the conviction, if summary, was returned; and

(b) proof of identity. R.S., c. E-10, s. 12; 1992, c. 47, s. 66.

Oaths and Solemn Affirmations

WHO MAY ADMINISTER OATHS.

13. Every court and judge, and every person having, by law or consent of parties, authority to hear and receive evidence, has power to administer an oath to every witness who is legally called to give evidence before that court, judge or person. R.S., c. E-10, s. 13.

SOLEMN AFFIRMATION BY WITNESS INSTEAD OF OATH / Effect.

14. (1) A person may, instead of taking an oath, make the following solemn affirmation:

> I solemnly affirm that the evidence to be given by me shall be the truth, the whole truth and nothing but the truth.

(2) Where a person makes a solemn affirmation in accordance with subsection (1), his evidence shall be taken and have the same effect as if taken under oath. R.S., c. E-10, s. 14; 1994, c. 44, s. 87.

SOLEMN AFFIRMATION BY DEPONENT / Effect.

15. (1) Where a person who is required or who desires to make an affidavit or deposition in a proceeding or on an occasion on which or concerning a matter respecting which an oath is required or is lawful, whether on the taking of office or otherwise, does not wish to take an oath, the court or judge, or other officer or person qualified to take affidavits or depositions, shall permit the person to make a solemn affirmation in the words following, namely, "I, ..., do solemnly affirm, etc.", and that solemn affirmation has the same force and effect as if that person had taken an oath.

(2) Any witness whose evidence is admitted or who makes a solemn affirmation under this section or section 14 is liable to indictment and punishment for perjury in all respects as if he had been sworn. R.S., c. E-10, s. 15; 1994, c. 44, s. 88.

WITNESS WHOSE CAPACITY IS IN QUESTION / Testimony under oath or solemn affirmation / Testimony on promise to tell truth / No questions regarding understanding of promise / Inability to testify / Burden as to capacity of witness.

16. (1) If a proposed witness is a person of fourteen years of age or older whose mental capacity is challenged, the court shall, before permitting the person to give evidence, conduct an inquiry to determine

  (*a*) whether the person understands the nature of an oath or a solemn affirmation; and

  (*b*) whether the person is able to communicate the evidence.

(2) A person referred to in subsection (1) who understands the nature of an oath or a solemn affirmation and is able to communicate the evidence shall testify under oath or solemn affirmation.

(3) A person referred to in subsection (1) who does not understand the nature of an oath or a solemn affirmation but is able to communicate the evidence may, notwithstanding any provision of any Act requiring an oath or solemn affirmation, testify on promising to tell the truth.

(3.1) A person referred to in subsection (3) shall not be asked any questions regarding their understanding of the nature of the promise to tell the truth for the purpose of determining whether their evidence shall be received by the court.

(4) A person referred to in subsection (1) who neither understands the nature of an oath or a solemn affirmation nor is able to communicate the evidence shall not testify.

(5) A party who challenges the mental capacity of a proposed witness of fourteen years of age or more has the burden of satisfying the court that there is an issue as to the capacity of the proposed witness to testify under an oath or a solemn affirmation. R.S., c. E-10, s. 16; R.S.C. 1985, c. 19 (3rd Supp.), s. 18; 1994, c. 44, s. 89; 2005, c. 32, s. 26; 2015, c. 13, s. 53.

PERSON UNDER FOURTEEN YEARS OF AGE / No oath or solemn affirmation / Evidence shall be received / Burden as to capacity of witness / Court inquiry / Promise to tell truth / Understanding of promise / Effect.

16.1 (1) A person under fourteen years of age is presumed to have the capacity to testify.

(2) A proposed witness under fourteen years of age shall not take an oath or make a solemn affirmation despite a provision of any Act that requires an oath or a solemn affirmation.

(3) The evidence of a proposed witness under fourteen years of age shall be received if they are able to understand and respond to questions.

(4) A party who challenges the capacity of a proposed witness under fourteen years of age has the burden of satisfying the court that there is an issue as to the capacity of the proposed witness to understand and respond to questions.

(5) If the court is satisfied that there is an issue as to the capacity of a proposed witness under fourteen years of age to understand and respond to questions, it shall, before permitting them to give evidence, conduct an inquiry to determine whether they are able to understand and respond to questions.

(6) The court shall, before permitting a proposed witness under fourteen years of age to give evidence, require them to promise to tell the truth.

(7) No proposed witness under fourteen years of age shall be asked any questions regarding their understanding of the nature of the promise to tell the truth for the purpose of determining whether their evidence shall be received by the court.

(8) For greater certainty, if the evidence of a witness under fourteen years of age is received by the court, it shall have the same effect as if it were taken under oath. 2005, c. 32, s. 27.

Judicial Notice

IMPERIAL ACTS, ETC.

17. Judicial notice shall be taken of all Acts of the Imperial Parliament, of all ordinances made by the Governor in Council, or the lieutenant governor in council of any province or colony that, or some portion of which, now forms or hereafter may form part of Canada, and of all the Acts of the legislature of any such province or colony, whether enacted before or after the passing of the *Constitution Act, 1867.* R.S., c. E-10, s. 17.

ACTS OF CANADA.

18. Judicial notice shall be taken of all Acts of Parliament, public or private, without being specially pleaded. R.S., c. E-10, s. 18.

Documentary Evidence

COPIES BY QUEEN'S PRINTER.

19. Every copy of any Act of Parliament, public or private, published by the Queen's Printer, is evidence of that Act and of its contents, and every copy purporting to be published by the Queen's Printer shall be deemed to be so published, unless the contrary is shown. R.S., c. E-10, s. 19; 2000, c. 5, s. 52.

IMPERIAL PROCLAMATIONS, ETC.

20. Imperial proclamations, orders in council, treaties, orders, warrants, licences, certificates, rules, regulations, or other Imperial official records, Acts or documents may be proved

    (a) in the same manner as they may from time to time be provable in any court in England;

(b) by the production of a copy of the *Canada Gazette*, or a volume of the Acts of Parliament purporting to contain a copy of the same or a notice thereof; or

(c) by the production of a copy of them purporting to be published by the Queen's Printer. R.S., c. E-10, s. 20; 2000, c. 5, s. 53.

PROCLAMATIONS, ETC. OF GOVERNOR GENERAL.

21. Evidence of any proclamation, order, regulation or appointment, made or issued by the Governor General or by the Governor in Council, or by or under the authority of any minister or head of any department of the Government of Canada and evidence of a treaty to which Canada is a party, may be given in all or any of the following ways:

(a) by the production of a copy of the *Canada Gazette*, or a volume of the Acts of Parliament purporting to contain a copy of the treaty, proclamation, order, regulation or appointment, or a notice thereof;

(b) by the production of a copy of the proclamation, order, regulation or appointment, purporting to be published by the Queen's Printer;

(c) by the production of a copy of the treaty purporting to be published by the Queen's Printer;

(d) by the production, in the case of any proclamation, order, regulation or appointment made or issued by the Governor General or by the Governor in Council, of a copy or extract purporting to be certified to be true by the clerk or assistant or acting clerk of the Queen's Privy Council for Canada; and

(e) by the production, in the case of any order, regulation or appointment made or issued by or under the authority of any minister or head of a department of the Government of Canada, of a copy or extract purporting to be certified to be true by the minister, by his deputy or acting deputy, or by the secretary or acting secretary of the department over which he presides. R.S., c. E-10, s. 21; 1976-77, c. 28, s. 14; 2000, c. 5, s. 54.

PROCLAMATIONS, ETC., OF LIEUTENANT GOVERNOR / Territories.

22. (1) Evidence of any proclamation, order, regulation or appointment made or issued by a lieutenant governor or lieutenant governor in council of any province, or by or under the authority of any member of the executive council, being the head of any department of the government of the province, may be given in all or any of the following ways:

(a) by the production of a copy of the official gazette for the province purporting to contain a copy of the proclamation, order, regulation or appointment, or a notice thereof;

(b) by the production of a copy of the proclamation, order, regulation or appointment purporting to be published by the government or Queen's Printer for the province; and

(c) by the production of a copy or extract of the proclamation, order, regulation or appointment, purporting to be certified to be true by the clerk or assistant or acting clerk of the executive council, by the head of any department of

931

the government of a province, or by his deputy or acting deputy, as the case may be.

(2) Evidence of any proclamation, order, regulation or appointment made by the Lieutenant Governor or Lieutenant Governor in Council of the Northwest Territories, as constituted prior to September 1, 1905, or by the Legislature of Yukon, of the Northwest Territories or for Nunavut, may be given by the production of a copy of the *Canada Gazette* purporting to contain a copy of the proclamation, order, regulation or appointment, or a notice of it. R.S., c. E-10, s. 22; 1993, c. 28, Sch. III, s. 8; 2000, c. 5, s. 55; 2002, c. 7, s. 96; 2014, c. 2, s. 5.

EVIDENCE OF JUDICIAL PROCEEDINGS, ETC. / Certificate where court has no seal.

23. (1) Evidence of any proceeding or record whatever of, in or before any court in Great Britain, the Supreme Court, the Federal Court of Appeal, the Federal Court or the Tax Court of Canada, any court in a province, any court in a British colony or possession or any court of record of the United States, of a state of the United States or of any other foreign country, or before any justice of the peace or coroner in a province, may be given in any action or proceeding by an exemplification or certified copy of the proceeding or record, purporting to be under the seal of the court or under the hand or seal of the justice, coroner or court stenographer, as the case may be, without any proof of the authenticity of the seal or of the signature of the justice, coroner or court stenographer or other proof whatever.

(2) Where any court, justice or coroner or court stenographer referred to in subsection (1) has no seal, or so certifies, the evidence may be given by a copy purporting to be certified under the signature of a judge or presiding provincial court judge or of the justice or coroner or court stenographer, without any proof of the authenticity of the signature or other proof whatever. R.S., c. E-10, s. 23; 1997, c. 18, s. 117; 2002, c. 8, s. 118.

CERTIFIED COPIES.

24. In every case in which the original record could be admitted in evidence,

   (*a*) a copy of any official or public document of Canada or of any province, purporting to be certified under the hand of the proper officer or person in whose custody the official or public document is placed, or

   (*b*) a copy of a document, by-law, rule, regulation or proceeding, or a copy of any entry in any register or other book of any municipal or other corporation, created by charter or Act of Parliament or the legislature of any province, purporting to be certified under the seal of the corporation, and the hand of the presiding officer, clerk or secretary thereof,

is admissible in evidence without proof of the seal of the corporation, or of the signature or official character of the person or persons appearing to have signed it, and without further proof thereof. R.S., c. E-10, s. 24.

BOOKS AND DOCUMENTS.

25. Where a book or other document is of so public a nature as to be admissible in evidence on its mere production from the proper custody, and no other Act exists that renders its contents provable by means of a copy, a copy thereof or extract therefrom is admissible in evidence in any court of justice or before a person having, by law or by consent of parties, authority to hear, receive and examine evidence, if it is proved that it is a copy or extract purporting to be certified to be true by the officer to whose custody the original has been entrusted. R.S., c. E-10, s. 25.

BOOKS KEPT IN OFFICES UNDER GOVERNMENT OF CANADA / Proof of non-issue of licence or document / Proof of mailing departmental matter / Proof of official character.

26. (1) A copy of any entry in any book kept in any office or department of the Government of Canada, or in any commission, board or other branch in the federal public administration, shall be admitted as evidence of that entry, and of the matters, transactions and accounts therein recorded, if it is proved by the oath or affidavit of an officer of the office or department, commission, board or other branch in the federal public administration that the book was, at the time of the making of the entry, one of the ordinary books kept in the office, department, commission, board or other branch in the federal public administration, that the entry was made in the usual and ordinary course of business of the office, department, commission, board or other branch in the federal public administration and that the copy is a true copy thereof.

(2) Where by any Act of Parliament or regulation made under an Act of Parliament provision is made for the issue by a department, commission, board or other branch in the federal public administration of a licence requisite to the doing or having of any act or thing or for the issue of any other document, an affidavit of an officer of the department, commission, board or other branch in the federal public administration, sworn before any commissioner or other person authorized to take affidavits, setting out that he or she has charge of the appropriate records and that after careful examination and search of those records he or she has been unable to find in any given case that any such licence or other document has been issued, shall be admitted in evidence as proof, in the absence of evidence to the contrary, that in that case no licence or other document has been issued.

(3) Where by any Act of Parliament or regulation made under an Act of Parliament provision is made for sending by mail any request for information, notice or demand by a department or other branch in the federal public administration, an affidavit of an officer of the department or other branch in the federal public administration, sworn before any commissioner or other person authorized to take affidavits, setting out that he or she has charge of the appropriate records, that he or she has a knowledge of the facts in the particular case, that the request, notice or demand was sent by registered letter on a named date to the person or firm to whom it was addressed (indicating that address) and that he or she identifies as exhibits attached to the affidavit the post office certificate of registration of the letter and a true copy of the request, notice or

demand, shall, on production and proof of the post office receipt for the delivery of the registered letter to the addressee, be admitted in evidence as proof, in the absence of evidence to the contrary, of the sending and of the request, notice or demand.

(4) Where proof is offered by affidavit pursuant to this section, it is not necessary to prove the official character of the person making the affidavit if that information is set out in the body of the affidavit. R.S., c. E-10, s. 26; 2003, c. 22, s. 104.

NOTARIAL ACTS IN QUEBEC.

27. Any document purporting to be a copy of a notarial act or instrument made, filed or registered in the Province of Quebec, and to be certified by a notary or prothonotary to be a true copy of the original in his possession as such notary or prothonotary, shall be admitted in evidence in the place and stead of the original and has the same force and effect as the original would have if produced and proved, but it may be proved in rebuttal that there is no such original, that the copy is not a true copy of the original in some material particular or that the original is not an instrument of such nature as may, by the law of the Province of Quebec, be taken before a notary or be filed, enrolled or registered by a notary in that Province. R.S., c. E-10, s. 27.

NOTICE OF PRODUCTION OF BOOK OR DOCUMENT / Not less than 7 days.

28. (1) No copy of any book or other document shall be admitted in evidence, under the authority of section 23, 24, 25, 26 or 27, on any trial, unless the party intending to produce the copy has before the trial given to the party against whom it is intended to be produced reasonable notice of that intention.

(2) The reasonableness of the notice referred to in subsection (1) shall be determined by the court, judge or other person presiding, but the notice shall not in any case be less than seven days. R.S., c. E-10, s. 28.

COPIES OF ENTRIES / Admission in evidence / Cheques, proof of "no account" / Proof of official character / Compulsion of production or appearance / Order to inspect and copy / Warrants to search / Computation of time / Definitions / "court" / "financial institution" / "legal proceeding".

29. (1) Subject to this section, a copy of any entry in any book or record kept in any financial institution shall in all legal proceedings be admitted in evidence as proof, in the absence of evidence to the contrary, of the entry and of the matters, transactions and accounts therein recorded.

(2) A copy of an entry in the book or record described in subsection (1) shall not be admitted in evidence under this section unless it is first proved that the book or record was, at the time of the making of the entry, one of the ordinary books or records of the financial institution, that the entry was made in the usual and ordinary course of business, that the book or record is in the custody or control of

the financial institution and that the copy is a true copy of it, and such proof may be given by any person employed by the financial institution who has knowledge of the book or record or the manager or accountant of the financial institution, and may be given orally or by affidavit sworn before any commissioner or other person authorized to take affidavits.

(3) Where a cheque has been drawn on any financial institution or branch thereof by any person, an affidavit of the manager or accountant of the financial institution or branch, sworn before any commissioner or other person authorized to take affidavits, setting out that he is the manager or accountant, that he has made a careful examination and search of the books and records for the purpose of ascertaining whether or not that person has an account with the financial institution or branch and that he has been unable to find such an account, shall be admitted in evidence as proof, in the absence of evidence to the contrary, that that person has no account in the financial institution or branch.

(4) Where evidence is offered by affidavit pursuant to this section, it is not necessary to prove the signature or official character of the person making the affidavit if the official character of that person is set out in the body of the affidavit.

(5) A financial institution or officer of a financial institution is not in any legal proceedings to which the financial institution is not a party compellable to produce any book or record, the contents of which can be proved under this section, or to appear as a witness to prove the matters, transactions and accounts therein recorded unless by order of the court made for special cause.

(6) On the application of any party to a legal proceeding, the court may order that that party be at liberty to inspect and take copies of any entries in the books or records of a financial institution for the purposes of the legal proceeding, and the person whose account is to be inspected shall be notified of the application at least two clear days before the hearing thereof, and if it is shown to the satisfaction of the court that he cannot be notified personally, the notice may be given by addressing it to the financial institution.

(7) Nothing in this section shall be construed as prohibiting any search of the premises of a financial institution under the authority of a warrant to search issued under any other Act of Parliament, but unless the warrant is expressly endorsed by the person under whose hand it is issued as not being limited by this section, the authority conferred by any such warrant to search the premises of a financial institution and to seize and take away anything in it shall, with respect to the books or records of the institution, be construed as limited to the searching of those premises for the purpose of inspecting and taking copies of entries in those books or records, and section 490 of the *Criminal Code* does not apply in respect of the copies of those books or records obtained under a warrant referred to in this section.

(8) Holidays shall be excluded from the computation of time under this section.

(9) In this section

"court" means the court, judge, arbitrator or person before whom a legal proceeding is held or taken;

"financial institution" means the Bank of Canada, the Business Development Bank of Canada and any institution that accepts in Canada deposits of money from its members or the public, and includes a branch, agency or office of any of those Banks or institutions;

"legal proceeding" means any civil or criminal proceeding or inquiry in which evidence is or may be given, and includes an arbitration. R.S., c. E-10, s. 29; 1974-75-76, c. 14, s. 57; 1994, c. 44, s. 90; 1995, c. 28, s. 47; 1999, c. 28, s. 149.

BUSINESS RECORDS TO BE ADMITTED IN EVIDENCE / Inference where information not in business record / Copy of records / Where record kept in form requiring explanation / Court may order other part of record to be produced / Court may examine record and hear evidence / Notice of intention to produce record or affidavit / Not necessary to prove signature and official character / Examination on record with leave of court / Evidence inadmissible under this section / Construction of this section / Definitions / "business" / "copy" and "photographic film" / "court" / legal proceeding" / "record".

30. (1) Where oral evidence in respect of a matter would be admissible in a legal proceeding, a record made in the usual and ordinary course of business that contains information in respect of that matter is admissible in evidence under this section in the legal proceeding on production of the record.

(2) Where a record made in the usual and ordinary course of business does not contain information in respect of a matter the occurrence or existence of which might reasonably be expected to be recorded in that record, the court may on production of the record admit the record for the purpose of establishing that fact and may draw the inference that the matter did not occur or exist.

(3) Where it is not possible or reasonably practicable to produce any record described in subsection (1) or (2), a copy of the record accompanied by two documents, one that is made by a person who states why it is not possible or reasonably practicable to produce the record and one that sets out the source from which the copy was made, that attests to the copy's authenticity and that is made by the person who made the copy, is admissible in evidence under this section in the same manner as if it were the original of the record if each document is

   (a) an affidavit of each of those persons sworn before a commissioner or other person authorized to take affidavits; or

   (b) a certificate or other statement pertaining to the record in which the person attests that the certificate or statement is made in conformity with the laws of a foreign state, whether or not the certificate or statement is in the form of an affidavit attested to before an official of the foreign state.

(4) Where production of any record or of a copy of any record described in subsection (1) or (2) would not convey to the court the information contained in the record by reason of its having been kept in a form that requires explanation, a transcript of the explanation of the record or copy prepared by a person qualified to make the explanation is admissible in evidence under this section in the same manner as if it were the original of the record if it is accompanied by a document

that sets out the person's qualifications to m..
accuracy of the explanation, and is

  (*a*) an affidavit of that person sworn before a commissioner or ..ts to the
authorized to take affidavits; or

  (*b*) a certificate or other statement pertaining to the recor.. w.. .. .erson
attests that the certificate or statement is made in confor... .y with person
of a foreign state, whether or not the certificate or statemen.. is.... the for...
of an affidavit attested to before an official of the foreign stat..

(5) Where part only of a record is produced under this section by any party, the court may examine any other part of the record and direct that, together with the part of the record previously so produced, the whole or any part of the other part thereof be produced by that party as the record produced by him.

(6) For the purpose of determining whether any provision of this section applies, or for the purpose of determining the probative value, if any, to be given to information contained in any record admitted in evidence under this section, the court may, on production of any record, examine the record, admit any evidence in respect thereof given orally or by affidavit including evidence as to the circumstances in which the information contained in the record was written, recorded, stored or reproduced, and draw any reasonable inference from the form or content of the record.

(7) Unless the court orders otherwise, no record or affidavit shall be admitted in evidence under this section unless the party producing the record or affidavit has, at least seven days before its production, given notice of his intention to produce it to each other party to the legal proceeding and has, within five days after receiving any notice in that behalf given by any such party, produced it for inspection by that party.

(8) Where evidence is offered by affidavit under this section, it is not necessary to prove the signature or official character of the person making the affidavit if the official character of that person is set out in the body of the affidavit.

(9) Subject to section 4, any person who has or may reasonably be expected to have knowledge of the making or contents of any record produced or received in evidence under this section may, with leave of the court, be examined or cross-examined thereon by any party to the legal proceeding.

(10) Nothing in this section renders admissible in evidence in any legal proceeding

  (*a*) such part of any record as is proved to be

    (i) a record made in the course of an investigation or inquiry,

    (ii) a record made in the course of obtaining or giving legal advice or in contemplation of a legal proceeding,

    (iii) a record in respect of the production of which any privilege exists and is claimed, or

    (iv) a record of or alluding to a statement made by a person who is not, or if he were living and of sound mind would not be, competent and compellable to disclose in the legal proceeding a matter disclosed in the record;

  (*b*) any record the production of which would be contrary to public policy; or

937

S. 31 ...ing of evidence taken in the course of another legal

(c) ...transc of this section shall be deemed to be in addition to and not in
proce...

(11) The other r... ...vision of this or any other Act of Parliament respecting the
dem... ...ty in evidence of any record or the proof of any matter; or

(b) ...existing rule of law under which any record is admissible in evidence
or any matter may be proved.

(12) In this section,

"business" means any business, profession, trade, calling, manufacture or
undertaking of any kind carried on in Canada or elsewhere whether for profit or
otherwise, including any activity or operation carried on or performed in Canada
or elsewhere by any government, by any department, branch, board, commission
or agency of any government, by any court or other tribunal or by any other body
or authority performing a function of government;

"copy", in relation to any record, includes a print, whether enlarged or not, from a
photographic film of the record, and "photographic film" includes a photographic
plate, microphotographic film or photostatic negative;

"court" means the court, judge, arbitrator or person before whom a legal
proceeding is held or taken;

"legal proceeding" means any civil or criminal proceeding or inquiry in which
evidence is or may be given, and includes an arbitration;

"record" includes the whole or any part of any book, document, paper, card, tape
or other thing on or in which information is written, recorded, stored or
reproduced, and, except for the purposes of subsections (3) and (4), any copy or
transcript admitted in evidence under this section pursuant to subsection (3) or (4).
R.S., c. E-10, s. 30; 1994, c. 44, s. 91.

**DEFINITIONS / "corporation" / "government" / "photographic film" /
When print admissible in evidence / Evidence of compliance with conditions
/ Proof by notarial copy.**

31. (1) In this section,

"corporation" means any bank, including the Bank of Canada and the Business
Development Bank of Canada, any authorized foreign bank within the meaning of
section 2 of the *Bank Act* and each of the following carrying on business in
Canada, namely, every railway, express, telegraph and telephone company (except
a street railway and tramway company), insurance company or society, trust
company and loan company;

"government" means the government of Canada or of any province and includes
any department, commission, board or branch of any such government;

"photographic film" includes any photographic plate, microphotographic film and
photostatic negative.

(2) A print, whether enlarged or not, from any photographic film of

(a) an entry in any book or record kept by any government or corporation and destroyed, lost or delivered to a customer after the film was taken,

(b) any bill of exchange, promissory note, cheque, receipt, instrument or document held by any government or corporation and destroyed, lost or delivered to a customer after the film was taken, or

(c) any record, document, plan, book or paper belonging to or deposited with any government or corporation,

is admissible in evidence in all cases in which and for all purposes for which the object photographed would have been admitted on proof that

(d) while the book, record, bill of exchange, promissory note, cheque, receipt, instrument or document, plan, book or paper was in the custody or control of the government or corporation, the photographic film was taken thereof in order to keep a permanent record thereof, and

(e) the object photographed was subsequently destroyed by or in the presence of one or more of the employees of the government or corporation, or was lost or was delivered to a customer.

(3) Evidence of compliance with the conditions prescribed by this section may be given by any one or more of the employees of the government or corporation, having knowledge of the taking of the photographic film, of the destruction, loss, or delivery to a customer, or of the making of the print, as the case may be, either orally or by affidavit sworn in any part of Canada before any notary public or commissioner for oaths.

(4) Unless the court otherwise orders, a notarial copy of an affidavit under subsection (3) is admissible in evidence in lieu of the original affidavit. R.S., c. E-10, s. 31; 1974-75-76, c. 14, s. 57; 1992, c. 1, s. 142(1) (Sch. V, item 9(1)); 1995, c. 28, s. 47; 1999, c. 28, s. 150.

CAN. EV.

AUTHENTICATION OF ELECTRONIC DOCUMENTS.

31.1 Any person seeking to admit an electronic document as evidence has the burden of proving its authenticity by evidence capable of supporting a finding that the electronic document is that which it is purported to be. 2000, c. 5, s. 56.

APPLICATION OF BEST EVIDENCE RULE — ELECTRONIC DOCUMENTS / Printouts.

31.2 (1) The best evidence rule in respect of an electronic document is satisfied

(a) on proof of the integrity of the electronic documents system by or in which the electronic document was recorded or stored; or

(b) if an evidentiary presumption established under section 31.4 applies.

(2) Despite subsection (1), in the absence of evidence to the contrary, an electronic document in the form of a printout satisfies the best evidence rule if the printout has been manifestly or consistently acted on, relied on or used as a record of the information recorded or stored in the printout. 2000, c. 5, s. 56.

PRESUMPTION OF INTEGRITY.

31.3 For the purposes of subsection 31.2(1), in the absence of evidence to the contrary, the integrity of an electronic documents system by or in which an electronic document is recorded or stored is proven

  (*a*) by evidence capable of supporting a finding that at all material times the computer system or other similar device used by the electronic documents system was operating properly or, if it was not, the fact of its not operating properly did not affect the integrity of the electronic document and there are no other reasonable grounds to doubt the integrity of the electronic documents system;

  (*b*) if it is established that the electronic document was recorded or stored by a party who is adverse in interest to the party seeking to introduce it; or

  (*c*) if it is established that the electronic document was recorded or stored in the usual and ordinary course of business by a person who is not a party and who did not record or store it under the control of the party seeking to introduce it.

PRESUMPTIONS REGARDING SECURE ELECTRONIC SIGNATURES.

31.4 The Governor in Council may make regulations establishing evidentiary presumptions in relation to electronic documents signed with secure electronic signatures, including regulations respecting

  (*a*) the association of secure electronic signatures with persons; and

  (*b*) the integrity of information contained in electronic documents signed with secure electronic signatures. 2000, c. 5, s. 56.

STANDARDS MAY BE CONSIDERED.

31.5 For the purpose of determining under any rule of law whether an electronic document is admissible, evidence may be presented in respect of any standard, procedure, usage or practice concerning the manner in which electronic documents are to be recorded or stored, having regard to the type of business, enterprise or endeavour that used, recorded or stored the electronic document and the nature and purpose of the electronic document. 2000, c. 5, s. 56.

PROOF BY AFFIDAVIT / Cross-examination.

31.6 (1) The matters referred to in subsection 31.2(2) and sections 31.3 and 31.5 and in regulations made under section 31.4 may be established by affidavit.

(2) A party may cross-examine a deponent of an affidavit referred to in subsection (1) that has been introduced in evidence

  (*a*) as of right, if the deponent is an adverse party or is under the control of an adverse party; and

  (*b*) with leave of the court, in the case of any other deponent. 2000, c. 5, s. 56.

APPLICATION.

31.7 Sections 31.1 to 31.4 do not affect any rule of law relating to the admissibility of evidence, except the rules relating to authentication and best evidence. 2000, c. 5, s. 56.

DEFINITIONS / "Computer system" / "Data" / "Electronic document" / "Electronic documents system" / "Secure electronic signature".

31.8 The definitions in this section apply in sections 31.1 to 31.6.

"computer system" means a device that, or a group of interconnected or related devices one or more of which,

(a) contains computer programs or other data; and

(b) pursuant to computer programs, performs logic and control, and may perform any other function.

"data" means representations of information or of concepts, in any form.

"electronic document" means data that is recorded or stored on any medium in or by a computer system or other similar device and that can be read or perceived by a person or a computer system or other similar device. It includes a display, printout or other output of that data.

"electronic documents system" includes a computer system or other similar device by or in which data is recorded or stored and any procedures related to the recording or storage of electronic documents.

"secure electronic signature" means a secure electronic signature as defined in subsection 31(1) of the *Personal Information Protection and Electronic Documents Act*. 2000, c. 5, s. 56.

ORDER SIGNED BY SECRETARY OF STATE / Copies printed in *Canada Gazette*.

32. (1) An order signed by the Secretary of State of Canada and purporting to be written by command of the Governor General shall be admitted in evidence as the order of the Governor General.

(2) All copies of official and other notices, advertisements and documents published in the *Canada Gazette* are admissible in evidence as proof, in the absence of evidence to the contrary, of the originals and of their contents. R.S., c. E-10, s. 32; 2000, c. 5, s. 57.

PROOF OF HANDWRITING OF PERSON CERTIFYING / Printed or written.

33. (1) No proof shall be required of the handwriting or official position of any person certifying, in pursuance of this Act, to the truth of any copy of or extract from any proclamation, order, regulation, appointment, book or other document.

(2) Any copy or extract referred to in subsection (1) may be in print or in writing, or partly in print and partly in writing. R.S., c. E-10, s. 33.

ATTESTING WITNESS / Instrument, how proved.

34. (1) It is not necessary to prove by the attesting witness any instrument to the validity of which attestation is not requisite.

(2) Any instrument referred to in subsection (1) may be proved by admission or otherwise as if there had been no attesting witness thereto. R.S., c. E-10, s. 34.

IMPOUNDING OF FORGED INSTRUMENT.

35. Where any instrument that has been forged or fraudulently altered is admitted in evidence, the court or the judge or person who admits the instrument may, at the request of any person against whom it is admitted in evidence, direct that the instrument shall be impounded and be kept in the custody of an officer of the court or other proper person for such period and subject to such conditions as to the court, judge or person admitting the instrument seem meet. R.S., c. E-10, s. 35.

CONSTRUCTION.

36. This Part shall be deemed to be in addition to and not in derogation of any powers of proving documents given by any existing Act or existing at law. R.S., c. E-10, s. 36.

Interpretation

DEFINITION OF "OFFICIAL".

36.1 In sections 37 to 38.16, "official" has the same meaning as in section 118 of the *Criminal Code*. 2001, c. 41, s. 43.

Specified Public Interest

OBJECTION TO DISCLOSURE OF INFORMATION / Obligation of court, person or body / Objection made to superior court / Objection not made to superior court / Limitation period / Disclosure order / Disclosure order / Prohibition order / Evidence / When determination takes effect / Introduction into evidence / Relevant factors.

37. (1) Subject to sections 38 to 38.16, a Minister of the Crown in right of Canada or other official may object to the disclosure of information before a court, person or body with jurisdiction to compel the production of information by certifying orally or in writing to the court, person or body that the information should not be disclosed on the grounds of a specified public interest.

(1.1) If an objection is made under subsection (1), the court, person or body shall ensure that the information is not disclosed other than in accordance with this Act.

(2) If an objection to the disclosure of information is made before a superior court, that court may determine the objection.

(3) If an objection to the disclosure of information is made before a court, person or body other than a superior court, the objection may be determined, on application, by

(a) the Federal Court, in the case of a person or body vested with power to compel production by or under an Act of Parliament if the person or body is not a court established under a law of a province; or

(b) the trial division or trial court of the superior court of the province within which the court, person or body exercises its jurisdiction, in any other case.

(4) An application under subsection (3) shall be made within 10 days after the objection is made or within any further or lesser time that the court having jurisdiction to hear the application considers appropriate in the circumstances.

(4.1) Unless the court having jurisdiction to hear the application concludes that the disclosure of the information to which the objection was made under subsection (1) would encroach upon a specified public interest, the court may authorize by order the disclosure of the information.

(5) If the court having jurisdiction to hear the application concludes that the disclosure of the information to which the objection was made under subsection (1) would encroach upon a specified public interest, but that the public interest in disclosure outweighs in importance the specified public interest, the court may, by order, after considering both the public interest in disclosure and the form of and conditions to disclosure that are most likely to limit any encroachment upon the specified public interest resulting from disclosure, authorize the disclosure, subject to any conditions that the court considers appropriate, of all of the information, a part or summary of the information, or a written admission of facts relating to the information.

(6) If the court does not authorize disclosure under subsection (4.1) or (5), the court shall, by order, prohibit disclosure of the information.

(6.1) The court may receive into evidence anything that, in the opinion of the court, is reliable and appropriate, even if it would not otherwise be admissible under Canadian law, and may base its decision on that evidence.

(7) An order of the court that authorizes disclosure does not take effect until the time provided or granted to appeal the order has expired or, if the order is appealed, the time provided or granted to appeal a judgment of an appeal court that confirms the order has expired and no further appeal from a judgment that confirms the order is available.

(8) A person who wishes to introduce into evidence material the disclosure of which is authorized under subsection (5), but who may not be able to do so by reason of the rules of admissibility that apply before the court, person or body with jurisdiction to compel the production of information, may request from the court having jurisdiction under subsection (2) or (3) an order permitting the introduction into evidence of the material in a form or subject to any conditions fixed by that court, as long as that form and those conditions comply with the order made under subsection (5).

(9) For the purpose of subsection (8), the court having jurisdiction under subsection (2) or (3) shall consider all the factors that would be relevant for a

determination of admissibility before the court, person or body. 1980-81-82-83, c. 111, s. 4; 2001, c. 41, ss. 43 and 140(1); 2002, c. 8, s. 183(1)(*b*); 2013, c. 9, s. 17.

APPEAL TO COURT OF APPEAL / Limitation period for appeal.

37.1 (1) An appeal lies from a determination under any of subsections 37(4.1) to (6)

    (*a*) to the Federal Court of Appeal from a determination of the Federal Court; or

    (*b*) to the court of appeal of a province from a determination of a trial division or trial court of a superior court of the province.

(2) An appeal under subsection (1) shall be brought within 10 days after the date of the determination appealed from or within any further time that the court having jurisdiction to hear the appeal considers appropriate in the circumstances. 2001, c. 41, ss. 43 and 141(3)(*b*).

LIMITATION PERIODS FOR APPEALS TO SUPREME COURT OF CANADA.

37.2 Notwithstanding any other Act of Parliament,

    (*a*) an application for leave to appeal to the Supreme Court of Canada from a judgment made under subsection 37.1(1) shall be made within 10 days after the date of the judgment appealed from or within any further time that the court having jurisdiction to grant leave to appeal considers appropriate in the circumstances; and

    (*b*) if leave to appeal is granted, the appeal shall be brought in the manner set out in subsection 60(1) of the *Supreme Court Act* but within the time specified by the court that grants leave. 2001, c. 41, s. 43.

37.21 [*Repealed*, 2004, c. 12, s. 18.]

PROTECTION OF RIGHT TO A FAIR TRIAL / Potential orders.

37.3 (1) A judge presiding at a criminal trial or other criminal proceeding may make any order that he or she considers appropriate in the circumstances to protect the right of the accused to a fair trial, as long as that order complies with the terms of any order made under any of subsections 37(4.1) to (6) in relation to that trial or proceeding or any judgment made on appeal of an order made under any of those subsections.

(2) The orders that may be made under subsection (1) include, but are not limited to, the following orders:

    (*a*) an order dismissing specified counts of the indictment or information, or permitting the indictment or information to proceed only in respect of a lesser or included offence;

    (*b*) an order effecting a stay of the proceedings; and

    (*c*) an order finding against any party on any issue relating to information the disclosure of which is prohibited. 2001, c. 41, s. 43.

International Relations and National Defence and Security

DEFINITIONS / "Judge" / "Participant" / "Potentially injurious information" / "Proceeding" / "Prosecutor" / "Sensitive information".

38. The following definitions apply in this section and in sections 38.01 to 38.15.

"judge" means the Chief Justice of the Federal Court or a judge of that Court designated by the Chief Justice to conduct hearings under section 38.04.

"participant" means a person who, in connection with a proceeding, is required to disclose, or expects to disclose or cause the disclosure of, information.

"potentially injurious information" means information of a type that, if it were disclosed to the public, could injure international relations or national defence or national security.

"proceeding" means a proceeding before a court, person or body with jurisdiction to compel the production of information.

"prosecutor" means an agent of the Attorney General of Canada or of the Attorney General of a province, the Director of Military Prosecutions under the *National Defence Act* or an individual who acts as a prosecutor in a proceeding.

"sensitive information" means information relating to international relations or national defence or national security that is in the possession of the Government of Canada, whether originating from inside or outside Canada, and is of a type that the Government of Canada is taking measures to safeguard. 1980-81-82-83, c. 111, s. 4; 2001, c. 41, ss. 43 and 141(4).

NOTICE TO ATTORNEY GENERAL OF CANADA / During a proceeding / Notice of disclosure from official / During a proceeding / Military proceedings / Exception / Exception / Schedule.

38.01 (1) Every participant who, in connection with a proceeding, is required to disclose, or expects to disclose or cause the disclosure of, information that the participant believes is sensitive information or potentially injurious information shall, as soon as possible, notify the Attorney General of Canada in writing of the possibility of the disclosure, and of the nature, date and place of the proceeding.

(2) Every participant who believes that sensitive information or potentially *injurious information is about to be disclosed*, whether by the participant or another person, in the course of a proceeding shall raise the matter with the person presiding at the proceeding and notify the Attorney General of Canada in writing of the matter as soon as possible, whether or not notice has been given under subsection (1). In such circumstances, the person presiding at the proceeding shall ensure that the information is not disclosed other than in accordance with this Act.

(3) An official, other than a participant, who believes that sensitive information or potentially injurious information may be disclosed in connection with a proceeding may notify the Attorney General of Canada in writing of the possibility of the disclosure, and of the nature, date and place of the proceeding.

(4) An official, other than a participant, who believes that sensitive information or potentially injurious information is about to be disclosed in the course of a proceeding may raise the matter with the person presiding at the proceeding. If the official raises the matter, he or she shall notify the Attorney General of Canada in writing of the matter as soon as possible, whether or not notice has been given under subsection (3), and the person presiding at the proceeding shall ensure that the information is not disclosed other than in accordance with this Act.

(5) In the case of a proceeding under Part III of the *National Defence Act*, notice under any of subsections (1) to (4) shall be given to both the Attorney General of Canada and the Minister of National Defence.

Note: Subsection 38.01(5) replaced, 2019, c. 15, s. 48 (to come into force by order of the Governor in Council):

Military proceedings

(5) In the case of a proceeding under Part III of the *National Defence Act*, other than a "summary hearing" as defined in subsection 2(1) of that Act, notice under any of subsections (1) to (4) shall be given to both the Attorney General of Canada and the Minister of National Defence.

(6) This section does not apply when

    (a) the information is disclosed by a person to their solicitor in connection with a proceeding, if the information is relevant to that proceeding;

    (b) the information is disclosed to enable the Attorney General of Canada, the Minister of National Defence, a judge or a court hearing an appeal from, or a review of, an order of the judge to discharge their responsibilities under section 38, this section and sections 38.02 to 38.13, 38.15 and 38.16;

    (c) disclosure of the information is authorized by the government institution in which or for which the information was produced or, if the information was not produced in or for a government institution, the government institution in which it was first received; or

    (d) the information is disclosed to an entity and, where applicable, for a purpose listed in the schedule.

(7) Subsections (1) and (2) do not apply to a participant if a government institution referred to in paragraph (6)(c) advises the participant that it is not necessary, in order to prevent disclosure of the information referred to in that paragraph, to give notice to the Attorney General of Canada under subsection (1) or to raise the matter with the person presiding under subsection (2).

(8) The Governor in Council may, by order, add to or delete from the schedule a reference to any entity or purpose, or amend such a reference. 2001, c. 41, s. 43.

DISCLOSURE PROHIBITED / Entities / Exceptions.

38.02 (1) Subject to subsection 38.01(6), no person shall disclose in connection with a proceeding

    (a) information about which notice is given under any of subsections 38.01(1) to (4);

    (*b*) the fact that notice is given to the Attorney General of Canada under any of subsections 38.01(1) to (4), or to the Attorney General of Canada and the Minister of National Defence under subsection 38.01(5);

    (*c*) the fact that an application is made to the Federal Court under section 38.04 or that an appeal or review of an order made under any of subsections 38.06(1) to (3) in connection with the application is instituted; or

    (*d*) the fact that an agreement is entered into under section 38.031 or subsection 38.04(6).

(1.1) When an entity listed in the schedule, for any purpose listed there in relation to that entity, makes a decision or order that would result in the disclosure of sensitive information or potentially injurious information, the entity shall not disclose the information or cause it to be disclosed until notice of intention to disclose the information has been given to the Attorney General of Canada and a period of 10 days has elapsed after notice was given.

(2) Disclosure of the information or the facts referred to in subsection (1) is not prohibited if

    (*a*) the Attorney General of Canada authorizes the disclosure in writing under section 38.03 or by agreement under section 38.031 or subsection 38.04(6); or

    (*b*) a judge authorizes the disclosure under subsection 38.06(1) or (2) or a court hearing an appeal from, or a review of, the order of the judge authorizes the disclosure, and either the time provided to appeal the order or judgment has expired or no further appeal is available. 2001, c. 41, ss. 43 and 141(5).

AUTHORIZATION BY ATTORNEY GENERAL OF CANADA / Military proceedings / Notice.

38.03 (1) The Attorney General of Canada may, at any time and subject to any conditions that he or she considers appropriate, authorize the disclosure of all or part of the information and facts the disclosure of which is prohibited under subsection 38.02(1).

(2) In the case of a proceeding under Part III of the *National Defence Act*, the Attorney General of Canada may authorize disclosure only with the agreement of the Minister of National Defence.

Note: Subsection 38.03(2) replaced, 2019, c. 15, s. 49 (to come into force by order of the Governor in Council):

Military proceedings

(2) In the case of a proceeding under Part III of the *National Defence Act*, other than a "summary hearing" as defined in subsection 2(1) of that Act, the Attorney General of Canada may authorize disclosure only with the agreement of the Minister of National Defence.

(3) The Attorney General of Canada shall, within 10 days after the day on which he or she first receives a notice about information under any of subsections 38.01(1) to (4), notify in writing every person who provided notice under section

38.01 about that information of his or her decision with respect to disclosure of the information. 2001, c. 41, s. 43.

DISCLOSURE AGREEMENT / No application to Federal Court.

38.031 (1) The Attorney General of Canada and a person who has given notice under subsection 38.01(1) or (2) and is not required to disclose information but wishes, in connection with a proceeding, to disclose any facts referred to in paragraphs 38.02(1)(*b*) to (*d*) or information about which he or she gave the notice, or to cause that disclosure, may, before the person applies to the Federal Court under paragraph 38.04(2)(*c*), enter into an agreement that permits the disclosure of part of the facts or information or disclosure of the facts or information subject to conditions.

(2) If an agreement is entered into under subsection (1), the person may not apply to the Federal Court under paragraph 38.04(2)(*c*) with respect to the information about which he or she gave notice to the Attorney General of Canada under subsection 38.01(1) or (2). 2001, c. 41, ss. 43 and 141(6).

APPLICATION TO FEDERAL COURT — ATTORNEY GENERAL OF CANADA / Application to Federal Court — general / Notice to Attorney General of Canada / Court records / Procedure / Disclosure agreement / Termination of Court consideration, hearing, review or appeal.

38.04 (1) The Attorney General of Canada may, at any time and in any circumstances, apply to the Federal Court for an order with respect to the disclosure of information about which notice was given under any of subsections 38.01(1) to (4).

(2) If, with respect to information about which notice was given under any of subsections 38.01(1) to (4), the Attorney General of Canada does not provide notice of a decision in accordance with subsection 38.03(3) or, other than by an agreement under section 38.031, does not authorize the disclosure of the information or authorizes the disclosure of only part of the information or authorizes the disclosure subject to any conditions,

    (*a*) the Attorney General of Canada shall apply to the Federal Court for an order with respect to disclosure of the information if a person who gave notice under subsection 38.01(1) or (2) is a witness;

    (*b*) a person, other than a witness, who is required to disclose information in connection with a proceeding shall apply to the Federal Court for an order with respect to disclosure of the information; and

    (*c*) a person who is not required to disclose information in connection with a proceeding but who wishes to disclose it or to cause its disclosure may apply to the Federal Court for an order with respect to disclosure of the information.

(3) A person who applies to the Federal Court under paragraph (2)(*b*) or (*c*) shall provide notice of the application to the Attorney General of Canada.

(4) Subject to paragraph (5)(*a*.1), an application under this section is confidential. During the period when an application is confidential, the Chief Administrator of

the Courts Administration Service may, subject to section 38.12, take any measure that he or she considers appropriate to protect the confidentiality of the application and the information to which it relates.

(5) As soon as the Federal Court is seized of an application under this section, the judge

(*a*) shall hear the representations of the Attorney General of Canada and, in the case of a proceeding under Part III of the *National Defence Act*, the Minister of National Defence, with respect to making the application public;

Note: Paragraph 38.04(5)(*a*) replaced, 2019, c. 15, s. 50(1) (to come into force by order of the Governor in Council):

(*a*) shall hear the representations of the Attorney General of Canada and, in the case of a proceeding under Part III of the *National Defence Act*, other than a "summary hearing" as defined in subsection 2(1) of that Act, the Minister of National Defence, with respect to making the application public;

(*a*.1) shall, if he or she decides that the application should be made public, make an order to that effect;

(*a*.2) shall hear the representations of the Attorney General of Canada and, in the case of a proceeding under Part III of the *National Defence Act*, the Minister of National Defence, concerning the identity of all parties or witnesses whose interests may be affected by either the prohibition of disclosure or the conditions to which disclosure is subject, and concerning the persons who should be given notice of any hearing of the matter;

Note: Paragraph 38.04(5)(*a*.2) replaced, 2019, c. 15, s. 50(2) (to come into force by order of the Governor in Council):

(*a*.2) shall hear the representations of the Attorney General of Canada and, in the case of a proceeding under Part III of the *National Defence Act*, other than a "summary hearing" as defined in subsection 2(1) of that Act, the Minister of National Defence, concerning the identity of all parties or witnesses whose interests may be affected by either the prohibition of disclosure or the conditions to which disclosure is subject, and concerning the persons who should be given notice of any hearing of the matter;

(*b*) shall decide whether it is necessary to hold any hearing of the matter;

(*c*) if he or she decides that a hearing should be held, shall

(i) determine who should be given notice of the hearing,

(ii) order the Attorney General of Canada to notify those persons, and

(iii) determine the content and form of the notice; and

(*d*) if he or she considers it appropriate in the circumstances, may give any person the opportunity to make representations.

(6) After the Federal Court is seized of an application made under paragraph (2)(*c*) or, in the case of an appeal from, or a review of, an order of the judge made under any of subsections 38.06(1) to (3) in connection with that application, before the appeal or review is disposed of,

(*a*) the Attorney General of Canada and the person who made the application may enter into an agreement that permits the disclosure of part of the facts referred to in paragraphs 38.02(1)(*b*) to (*d*) or part of the information, or disclosure of the facts or information subject to conditions; and

CAN. EV.

(*b*) if an agreement is entered into, the Court's consideration of the application or any hearing, review or appeal shall be terminated.

(7) Subject to subsection (6), after the Federal Court is seized of an application made under this section or, in the case of an appeal from, or a review of, an order of the judge made under any of subsections 38.06(1) to (3) before the appeal or review is disposed of, if the Attorney General of Canada authorizes the disclosure of all or part of the information or withdraws conditions to which the disclosure is subject, the Court's consideration of the application or any hearing, appeal or review shall be terminated in relation to that information, to the extent of the authorization or the withdrawal. 2001, c. 41, ss. 43 and 141(7); 2013, c. 9, s. 19.

REPORT RELATING TO PROCEEDINGS.

38.05 If he or she receives notice of a hearing under paragraph 38.04(5)(*c*), a person presiding or designated to preside at the proceeding to which the information relates or, if no person is designated, the person who has the authority to designate a person to preside may, within 10 days after the day on which he or she receives the notice, provide the judge with a report concerning any matter relating to the proceeding that the person considers may be of assistance to the judge. 2001, c. 41, s. 43.

DISCLOSURE ORDER / Disclosure — conditions / Order confirming prohibition / When determination takes effect / Evidence / Introduction into evidence / Relevant factors.

38.06 (1) Unless the judge concludes that the disclosure of the information or facts referred to in subsection 38.02(1) would be injurious to international relations or national defence or national security, the judge may, by order, authorize the disclosure of the information or facts.

(2) If the judge concludes that the disclosure of the information or facts would be injurious to international relations or national defence or national security but that the public interest in disclosure outweighs in importance the public interest in non-disclosure, the judge may by order, after considering both the public interest in disclosure and the form of and conditions to disclosure that are most likely to limit any injury to international relations or national defence or national security resulting from disclosure, authorize the disclosure, subject to any conditions that the judge considers appropriate, of all or part of the information or facts, a summary of the information or a written admission of facts relating to the information.

(3) If the judge does not authorize disclosure under subsection (1) or (2), the judge shall, by order, confirm the prohibition of disclosure.

(3.01) An order of the judge that authorizes disclosure does not take effect until the time provided or granted to appeal the order has expired or, if the order is appealed, the time provided or granted to appeal a judgment of an appeal court that confirms the order has expired and no further appeal from a judgment that confirms the order is available.

(3.1) The judge may receive into evidence anything that, in the opinion of the judge, is reliable and appropriate, even if it would not otherwise be admissible under Canadian law, and may base his or her decision on that evidence.

(4) A person who wishes to introduce into evidence material the disclosure of which is authorized under subsection (2) but who may not be able to do so in a proceeding by reason of the rules of admissibility that apply in the proceeding may request from a judge an order permitting the introduction into evidence of the material in a form or subject to any conditions fixed by that judge, as long as that form and those conditions comply with the order made under subsection (2).

(5) For the purpose of subsection (4), the judge shall consider all the factors that would be relevant for a determination of admissibility in the proceeding. 2001, c. 41, s. 43; 2013, c. 9, s. 20.

NOTICE OF ORDER.

38.07 The judge may order the Attorney General of Canada to give notice of an order made under any of subsections 38.06(1) to (3) to any person who, in the opinion of the judge, should be notified. 2001, c. 41, s. 43.

AUTOMATIC REVIEW.

38.08 If the judge determines that a party to the proceeding whose interests are adversely affected by an order made under any of subsections 38.06(1) to (3) was not given the opportunity to make representations under paragraph 38.04(5)(*d*), the judge shall refer the order to the Federal Court of Appeal for review. 2001, c. 41, s. 43.

APPEAL TO FEDERAL COURT OF APPEAL / Limitation period for appeal.

38.09 (1) An order made under any of subsections 38.06(1) to (3) may be appealed to the Federal Court of Appeal.

(2) An appeal shall be brought within 10 days after the day on which the order is made or within any further time that the Court considers appropriate in the circumstances. 2001, c. 41, s. 43.

LIMITATION PERIODS FOR APPEALS TO SUPREME COURT OF CANADA.

38.1 Notwithstanding any other Act of Parliament,
   (*a*) an application for leave to appeal to the Supreme Court of Canada from a judgment made on appeal shall be made within 10 days after the day on which the judgment appealed from is made or within any further time that the Supreme Court of Canada considers appropriate in the circumstances; and
   (*b*) if leave to appeal is granted, the appeal shall be brought in the manner set out in subsection 60(1) of the *Supreme Court Act* but within the time specified by the Supreme Court of Canada. 2001, c. 41, s. 43.

SPECIAL RULES — HEARING IN PRIVATE / Special rules — hearing in National Capital Region / *Ex parte* representations / *Ex parte* representations — public hearing.

38.11 (1) The judge conducting a hearing under subsection 38.04(5) or the court hearing an appeal or review of an order made under any of subsections 38.06(1) to (3) may make an order that the hearing be held, or the appeal or review be heard, in private.

(1.1) A hearing under subsection 38.04(5) or an appeal or review of an order made under any of subsections 38.06(1) to (3) shall, at the request of either the Attorney General of Canada or, in the case of a proceeding under Part III of the *National Defence Act*, the Minister of National Defence, be held or heard, as the case may be, in the National Capital Region, as described in the schedule to the *National Capital Act*.

Note: Subsection 38.11(1.1) replaced, 2019, c. 15, s. 51 (to come into force by order of the Governor in Council):

Special rules — hearing in National Capital Region

(1.1) A hearing under subsection 38.04(5) or an appeal or review of an order made under any of subsections 38.06(1) to (3) shall, at the request of either the Attorney General of Canada or, in the case of a proceeding under Part III of the *National Defence Act*, other than a "summary hearing" as defined in subsection 2(1) of that Act, the Minister of National Defence, be held or heard, as the case may be, in the National Capital Region, as described in the schedule to the *National Capital Act*.

(2) The judge conducting a hearing under subsection 38.04(5) or the court hearing an appeal or review of an order made under any of subsections 38.06(1) to (3) may give any person who makes representations under paragraph 38.04(5)(*d*), and shall give the Attorney General of Canada and, in the case of a proceeding under Part III of the *National Defence Act*, the Minister of National Defence, the opportunity to make representations *ex parte*.

Note: Subsection 38.11(2) replaced, 2019, c. 15, s. 51 (to come into force by order of the Governor in Council):

Ex parte representations

(2) The judge conducting a hearing under subsection 38.04(5) or the court hearing an appeal or review of an order made under any of subsections 38.06(1) to (3) may give any person who makes representations under paragraph 38.04(5)(*d*), and shall give the Attorney General of Canada and, in the case of a proceeding under Part III of the *National Defence Act*, other than a "summary hearing" as defined in subsection 2(1) of that Act, the Minister of National Defence, the opportunity to make representations *ex parte*.

(3) If a hearing under subsection 38.04(5) is held, or an appeal or review of an order made under any of subsections 38.06(1) to (3) is heard, in public, any *ex parte* representations made in that hearing, appeal or review shall be made in private. 2001, c. 41, s. 43; 2013, c. 9, s. 21.

PROTECTIVE ORDER / Court records.

38.12 (1) The judge conducting a hearing under subsection 38.04(5) or the court hearing an appeal or review of an order made under any of subsections 38.06(1) to (3) may make any order that the judge or the court considers appropriate in the circumstances to protect the confidentiality of any information to which the hearing, appeal or review relates.

(2) The court records relating to a hearing that is held, or an appeal or review that is heard, in private or to any ex parte representations are confidential. The judge or the court may order that the court records, or any part of them, relating to a private or public hearing, appeal or review be sealed and kept in a location to which the public has no access. 2001, c. 41, s. 43; 2013, c. 9, s. 22.

PROHIBITION CERTIFICATE / Military proceedings / Service of certificate / Filing of certificate / Effect of certificate / *Statutory Instruments Act* does not apply / Publication / Restriction / Expiry.

38.13 (1) The Attorney General of Canada may personally issue a certificate that prohibits the disclosure of information in connection with a proceeding for the purpose of protecting information obtained in confidence from, or in relation to, a foreign entity as defined in subsection 2(1) of the *Security of Information Act* or for the purpose of protecting national defence or national security. The certificate may only be issued after an order or decision that would result in the disclosure of the information to be subject to the certificate has been made under this or any other Act of Parliament.

(2) In the case of a proceeding under Part III of the *National Defence Act*, the Attorney General of Canada may issue the certificate only with the agreement, given personally, of the Minister of National Defence.

Note: Subsection 38.13(2) replaced, 2019, c. 15, s. 52 (to come into force by order of the Governor in Council):

Military proceedings

(2) In the case of a proceeding under Part III of the *National Defence Act*, other than a "summary hearing" as defined in subsection 2(1) of that Act, the Attorney General of Canada may issue the certificate only with the agreement, given personally, of the Minister of National Defence.

(3) The Attorney General of Canada shall cause a copy of the certificate to be served on

    (*a*) the person presiding or designated to preside at the proceeding to which the information relates or, if no person is designated, the person who has the authority to designate a person to preside;

    (*b*) every party to the proceeding;

    (*c*) every person who gives notice under section 38.01 in connection with the proceeding;

    (*d*) every person who, in connection with the proceeding, may disclose, is required to disclose or may cause the disclosure of the information about which the Attorney General of Canada has received notice under section 38.01;

(e) every party to a hearing under subsection 38.04(5) or to an appeal of an order made under any of subsections 38.06(1) to (3) in relation to the information;

(f) the judge who conducts a hearing under subsection 38.04(5) and any court that hears an appeal from, or review of, an order made under any of subsections 38.06(1) to (3) in relation to the information; and

(g) any other person who, in the opinion of the Attorney General of Canada, should be served.

(4) The Attorney General of Canada shall cause a copy of the certificate to be filed

(a) with the person responsible for the records of the proceeding to which the information relates; and

(b) in the Registry of the Federal Court and the registry of any court that hears an appeal from, or review of, an order made under any of subsections 38.06(1) to (3).

(5) If the Attorney General of Canada issues a certificate, then, notwithstanding any other provision of this Act, disclosure of the information shall be prohibited in accordance with the terms of the certificate.

(6) The *Statutory Instruments Act* does not apply to a certificate issued under subsection (1).

(7) The Attorney General of Canada shall, without delay after a certificate is issued, cause the certificate to be published in the *Canada Gazette*.

(8) The certificate and any matters arising out of it are not subject to review or to be restrained, prohibited, removed, set aside or otherwise dealt with, except in accordance with section 38.131.

(9) The certificate expires 10 years after the day on which it is issued and may be reissued. 2001, c. 41, s. 43; 2013, c. 8, s. 23.

APPLICATION FOR REVIEW OF CERTIFICATE / Notice to Attorney General of Canada / Military proceedings / Single judge / Admissible information / Special rules and protective order / Expedited consideration / Varying the certificate / Cancelling the certificate / Confirming the certificate / Determination is final / Publication.

38.131 (1) A party to the proceeding referred to in section 38.13 may apply to the Federal Court of Appeal for an order varying or cancelling a certificate issued under that section on the grounds referred to in subsection (8) or (9), as the case may be.

(2) The applicant shall give notice of the application to the Attorney General of Canada.

(3) In the case of proceedings under Part III of the *National Defence Act*, notice under subsection (2) shall be given to both the Attorney General of Canada and the Minister of National Defence.

Note: Subsection 38.131(3) replaced, 2019, c. 15, s. 53 (to come into force by order of the Governor in Council):

Military proceedings

(3) In the case of proceedings under Part III of the *National Defence Act*, other than a "summary hearing" as defined in subsection 2(1) of that Act, notice under subsection (2) shall be given to both the Attorney General of Canada and the Minister of National Defence.

(4) Notwithstanding section 16 of the Federal Court Act, for the purposes of the application, the Federal Court of Appeal consists of a single judge of that Court.

(5) In considering the application, the judge may receive into evidence anything that, in the opinion of the judge, is reliable and appropriate, even if it would not otherwise be admissible under Canadian law, and may base a determination made under any of subsections (8) to (10) on that evidence.

(6) Sections 38.11 and 38.12 apply, with any necessary modifications, to an application made under subsection (1).

(7) The judge shall consider the application as soon as reasonably possible, but not later than 10 days after the application is made under subsection (1).

(8) If the judge determines that some of the information subject to the certificate does not relate either to information obtained in confidence from, or in relation to, a foreign entity as defined in subsection 2(1) of the *Security of Information Act*, or to national defence or national security, the judge shall make an order varying the certificate accordingly.

(9) If the judge determines that none of the information subject to the certificate relates to information obtained in confidence from, or in relation to, a foreign entity as defined in subsection 2(1) of the *Security of Information Act*, or to national defence or national security, the judge shall make an order cancelling the certificate.

(10) If the judge determines that all of the information subject to the certificate relates to information obtained in confidence from, or in relation to, a foreign entity as defined in subsection 2(1) of the *Security of Information Act*, or to national defence or national security, the judge shall make an order confirming the certificate.

(11) Notwithstanding any other Act of Parliament, a determination of a judge under any of subsections (8) to (10) is final and is not subject to review or appeal by any court.

(12) If a certificate is varied or cancelled under this section, the Attorney General of Canada shall, as soon as possible after the decision of the judge and in a manner that mentions the original publication of the certificate, cause to be published in the *Canada Gazette*

    (*a*) the certificate as varied under subsection (8); or

    (*b*) a notice of the cancellation of the certificate under subsection (9). 2001, c. 41, s. 43; 2004, c. 12, s. 19.

CAN. EV.

PROTECTION OF RIGHT TO A FAIR TRIAL / Potential orders.

38.14 (1) The person presiding at a criminal proceeding may make any order that he or she considers appropriate in the circumstances to protect the right of the accused to a fair trial, as long as that order complies with the terms of any order made under any of subsections 38.06(1) to (3) in relation to that proceeding, any judgment made on appeal from, or review of, the order, or any certificate issued under section 38.13.

(2) The orders that may be made under subsection (1) include, but are not limited to, the following orders:

    (*a*) an order dismissing specified counts of the indictment or information, or permitting the indictment or information to proceed only in respect of a lesser or included offence;

    (*b*) an order effecting a stay of the proceedings; and

    (*c*) an order finding against any party on any issue relating to information the disclosure of which is prohibited. 2001, c. 41, s. 43.

FIAT / Effect of fiat / Fiat filed in court / Fiat constitutes conclusive proof / Military proceedings.

38.15 (1) If sensitive information or potentially injurious information may be disclosed in connection with a prosecution that is not instituted by the Attorney General of Canada or on his or her behalf, the Attorney General of Canada may issue a fiat and serve the fiat on the prosecutor.

(2) When a fiat is served on a prosecutor, the fiat establishes the exclusive authority of the Attorney General of Canada with respect to the conduct of the prosecution described in the fiat or any related process.

(3) If a prosecution described in the fiat or any related process is conducted by or on behalf of the Attorney General of Canada, the fiat or a copy of the fiat shall be filed with the court in which the prosecution or process is conducted.

(4) The fiat or a copy of the fiat

    (*a*) is conclusive proof that the prosecution described in the fiat or any related process may be conducted by or on behalf of the Attorney General of Canada; and

    (*b*) is admissible in evidence without proof of the signature or official character of the Attorney General of Canada.

(5) This section does not apply to a proceeding under Part III of the *National Defence Act*. 2001, c. 41, s. 43.

REGULATIONS.

38.16 The Governor in Council may make any regulations that the Governor in Council considers necessary to carry into effect the purposes and provisions of sections 38 to 38.15, including regulations respecting the notices, certificates and the fiat. 2001, c. 41, s. 43.

ANNUAL REPORT.

38.17 Each year the Attorney General of Canada shall prepare and cause to be laid before each House of Parliament a report for the previous year on the operation of sections 38.13 and 38.15 that includes the number of certificates and fiats issued under sections 38.13 and 38.15, respectively. 2013, c. 9, s. 24.

Confidences of the Queen's Privy Council for Canada

OBJECTION RELATING TO A CONFIDENCE OF THE QUEEN'S PRIVY COUNCIL / Definition / Definition of "Council" — Exception.

39. (1) Where a minister of the Crown or the Clerk of the Privy Council objects to the disclosure of information before a court, person or body with jurisdiction to compel the production of information by certifying in writing that the information constitutes a confidence of the Queen's Privy Council for Canada, disclosure of the information shall be refused without examination or hearing of the information by the court, person or body.

(2) For the purpose of subsection (1), "a confidence of the Queen's Privy Council for Canada" includes, without restricting the generality thereof, information contained in

    (*a*) a memorandum the purpose of which is to present proposals or recommendations to Council;

    (*b*) a discussion paper the purpose of which is to present background explanations, analyses of problems or policy options to Council for consideration by Council in making decisions;

    (*c*) an agendum of Council or a record recording deliberations or decisions of Council;

    (*d*) a record used for or reflecting communications or discussions between ministers of the Crown on matters relating to the making of government decisions or the formulation of government policy;

    (*e*) a record the purpose of which is to brief Ministers of the Crown in relation to matters that are brought before, or are proposed to be brought before, Council or that are the subject of communications or discussions referred to in paragraph (*d*); and

    (*f*) draft legislation.

(3) For the purposes of subsection (2), "Council" means the Queen's Privy Council for Canada, committees of the Queen's Privy Council for Canada, Cabinet and committees of Cabinet.

(4) Subsection (1) does not apply in respect of

    (*a*) a confidence of the Queen's Privy Council for Canada that has been in existence for more than twenty years; or

    (*b*) a discussion paper described in paragraph (2)(*b*)

        (i) if the decisions to which the discussion paper relates have been made public, or

CAN. EV.

(ii) where the decisions have not been made public, if four years have passed since the decisions were made. 1980-81-82-83, c. 111, s. 4; 2001, c. 41, s. 43 (title only).

Journalistic Sources

DEFINITIONS / "document" / "journalistic source" / Objection / Former journalist / Power of court, person or body / Objection of court, person or body / Observations / Authorization / Conditions / Burden of proof / Appeal / Limitation period for appeal / Hearing in summary way.

39.1 (1) The following definitions apply in this section.

"document" has the same meaning as in section 487.011 of the *Criminal Code*.

"journalist" means a person whose main occupation is to contribute directly, either regularly or occasionally, for consideration, to the collection, writing or production of information for dissemination by the media, or anyone who assists such a person.

"journalistic source" means a source that confidentially transmits information to a journalist on the journalist's undertaking not to divulge the identity of the source, whose anonymity is essential to the relationship between the journalist and the source.

(2) Subject to subsection (7), a journalist may object to the disclosure of information or a document before a court, person or body with the authority to compel the disclosure of information on the grounds that the information or document identifies or is likely to identify a journalistic source.

(3) For the purposes of subsections (2) and (7), "journalist" includes an individual who was a journalist when information that identifies or is likely to identify the journalistic source was transmitted to that individual.

(4) The court, person or body may raise the application of subsection (2) on their own initiative.

(5) When an objection or the application of subsection (2) is raised, the court, person or body shall ensure that the information or document is not disclosed other than in accordance with this section.

(6) Before determining the question, the court, person or body must give the parties and interested persons a reasonable opportunity to present observations.

(7) The court, person or body may authorize the disclosure of information or a document only if they consider that

(*a*) the information or document cannot be produced in evidence by any other reasonable means; and

(*b*) the public interest in the administration of justice outweighs the public interest in preserving the confidentiality of the journalistic source, having regard to, among other things,

(i) the importance of the information or document to a central issue in the proceeding,

 (ii) freedom of the press, and
 (iii) the impact of disclosure on the journalistic source and the journalist.

(8) An authorization under subsection (7) may contain any conditions that the court, person or body considers appropriate to protect the identity of the journalistic source.

(9) A person who requests the disclosure has the burden of proving that the conditions set out in subsection (7) are fulfilled.

(10) An appeal lies from a determination under subsection (7)
 (*a*) to the Federal Court of Appeal from a determination of the Federal Court;
 (*b*) to the court of appeal of a province from a determination of a superior court of the province;
 (*c*) to the Federal Court from a determination of a court, person or body vested with power to compel production by or under an Act of Parliament if the court, person or body is not established under a law of a province; or
 (*d*) to the trial division or trial court of the superior court of the province within which the court, person or body exercises its jurisdiction, in any other case.

(11) An appeal under subsection (10) shall be brought within 10 days after the date of the determination appealed from or within any further time that the court having jurisdiction to hear the appeal considers appropriate in the circumstances.

(12) An appeal under subsection (10) shall be heard and determined without delay and in a summary way. 2017, c. 22, s. 2.

Provincial Laws of Evidence

HOW APPLICABLE.

40. In all proceedings over which Parliament has legislative authority, the laws of evidence in force in the province in which those proceedings are taken, including the laws of proof of service of any warrant, summons, subpoena or other document, subject to this Act and other Acts of Parliament, apply to those proceedings. R.S., c. E-10, s. 37.

Statutory Declarations

SOLEMN DECLARATION.

41. Any judge, notary public, justice of the peace, provincial court judge, recorder, mayor or commissioner authorized to take affidavits to be used either in the provincial or federal courts, or any other functionary authorized by law to administer an oath in any matter, may receive the solemn declaration of any person voluntarily making the declaration before him, in the following form, in attestation of the execution of any writing, deed or instrument, or of the truth of any fact, or of any account rendered in writing:

   I, ..., solemnly declare that (*state the fact or facts declared to*), and I make this solemn declaration conscientiously believing it to be true, and knowing that it is of the same force and effect as if made under oath.

Declared before me .... at .... this .... day of .... 19 ......

R.S., c. E-10, s. 38; R.S.C. 1985, c. 27 (1st Supp.), s. 203(1).

Insurance Proofs

AFFIDAVITS, ETC.

42. Any affidavit, solemn affirmation or declaration required by any insurance company authorized by law to do business in Canada, in regard to any loss of or injury to person, property or life insured or assured therein, may be taken before any commissioner or other person authorized to take affidavits, before any justice of the peace or before any notary public for any province, and the commissioner, person, justice of the peace or notary public is required to take the affidavit, solemn affirmation or declaration. R.S., c. E-10, s. 39.

Part II / Application

FOREIGN COURTS.

43. This Part applies to the taking of evidence relating to proceedings in courts out of Canada. R.S., c. E-10, s. 40.

Interpretation

DEFINITIONS / "cause" / "court" / "judge" / "oath".

44. In this Part,

"cause" includes a proceeding against a criminal;

"court" means any superior court in any province;

"judge" means any judge of any superior court in any province;

"oath" includes a solemn affirmation in cases in which, by the law of Canada, or of a province, as the case may be, a solemn affirmation is allowed instead of an oath. R.S., c. E-10, s. 41; 1984, c. 40, s. 27.

CONSTRUCTION.

45. This Part shall not be so construed as to interfere with the right of legislation of the legislature of any province requisite or desirable for the carrying out of the objects hereof. R.S., c. E-10, s. 42.

Procedure

ORDER FOR EXAMINATION OF WITNESS IN CANADA / Video links, etc.

46. (1) If, on an application for that purpose, it is made to appear to any court or judge that any court or tribunal outside Canada, before which any civil, commercial or criminal matter is pending, is desirous of obtaining the testimony in relation to that matter of a party or witness within the jurisdiction of the first mentioned court, of the court to which the judge belongs or of the judge, the court or judge may, in its or their discretion, order the examination on oath on interrogatories, or otherwise, before any person or persons named in the order, of that party or witness accordingly, and by the same or any subsequent order may command the attendance of that party or witness for the purpose of being examined, and for the production of any writings or other documents mentioned in the order and of any other writings or documents relating to the matter in question that are in the possession or power of that party or witness.

(2) For greater certainty, testimony for the purposes of subsection (1) may be given by means of technology that permits the virtual presence of the party or witness before the court or tribunal outside Canada or that permits that court or tribunal, and the parties, to hear and examine the party or witness. R.S., c. E-10, s. 43; 1999, c. 18, s. 89.

ENFORCEMENT OF THE ORDER.

47. On the service on the party or witness of an order referred to in section 46, and of an appointment of a time and place for the examination of the party or witness signed by the person named in the order for taking the examination, or, if more than one person is named, by one of the persons named, and on payment or tender of the like conduct money as is properly payable on attendance at a trial, the order may be enforced in like manner as an order made by the court or judge in a cause pending in that court or before that judge. R.S., c. E-10, s. 44.

EXPENSES AND CONDUCT MONEY.

48. Every person whose attendance is required in the manner described is entitled to the like conduct money and payment for expenses and loss of time as on attendance at a trial. R.S., c. E-10, s. 45.

ADMINISTERING OATH.

49. On any examination of parties or witnesses, under the authority of any order made in pursuance of this Part, the oath shall be administered by the person authorized to take the examination, or, if more than one person is authorized, by one of those persons. R.S., c. E-10, s. 46.

RIGHT OF REFUSAL TO ANSWER OR PRODUCE DOCUMENT / Laws about witnesses to apply — video links etc. / Contempt of court in Canada / Nature of right.

50. (1) Any person examined under any order made under this Part has the like right to refuse to answer questions tending to criminate himself, or other questions, as a party or witness, as the case may be, would have in any cause pending in the court by which, or by a judge whereof, the order is made.

(1.1) Despite subsection (1), when a party or witness gives evidence under subsection 46(2), the evidence shall be given as though they were physically before the court or tribunal outside Canada, for the purposes of the laws relating to evidence and procedure but only to the extent that giving the evidence would not disclose information otherwise protected by the Canadian law of non-disclosure of information or privilege.

(1.2) When a party or witness gives evidence under subsection 46(2), the Canadian law relating to contempt of court applies with respect to a refusal by the party or witness to answer a question or to produce a writing or document referred to in subsection 46(1), as ordered under that subsection by the court or judge.

(2) No person shall be compelled to produce, under any order referred to in subsection (1), any writing or other document that he could not be compelled to produce at a trial of such a cause. R.S., c. E-10, s. 47; 1999, c. 18, s. 90.

RULES OF COURT / Letters rogatory.

51. (1) The court may frame rules and orders in relation to procedure and to the evidence to be produced in support of the application for an order for examination of parties and witnesses under this Part, and generally for carrying this Part into effect.

(2) In the absence of any order in relation to the evidence to be produced in support of the application referred to in subsection (1), letters rogatory from a court or tribunal outside Canada in which the civil, commercial or criminal matter is pending, are deemed and taken to be sufficient evidence in support of the application. R.S., c. E-10, s. 48; 1999, c. 18, s. 91.

Part III / *Application*

APPLICATION OF THIS PART.

52. This Part extends to the following classes of persons:

  (*a*) officers of any of Her Majesty's diplomatic or consular services while performing their functions in any foreign country, including ambassadors, envoys, ministers, charges d'affaires, counsellors, secretaries, attaches, consuls general, consuls, vice-consuls, pro-consuls, consular agents, acting consuls general, acting consuls, acting vice-consuls and acting consular agents;

  (*b*) officers of the Canadian diplomatic, consular and representative services while performing their functions in any foreign country or in any part of the

Commonwealth and Dependent Territories other than Canada, including, in addition to the diplomatic and consular officers mentioned in paragraph (*a*), high commissioners, permanent delegates, acting high commissioners, acting permanent delegates, counsellors and secretaries;

(*c*) Canadian Government Trade Commissioners and Assistant Canadian Government Trade Commissioners while performing their functions in any foreign country or in any part of the Commonwealth and Dependent Territories other than Canada;

(*d*) honorary consular officers of Canada while performing their functions in any foreign country or in any part of the Commonwealth and Dependent Territories other than Canada; and

(*e*) judicial officials in a foreign country in respect of oaths, affidavits, solemn affirmations, declarations or similar documents that the official is authorized to administer, take or receive.

(*f*) persons locally engaged and designated by the Deputy Minister of Foreign Affairs or any other person authorized by that Deputy Minister while performing their functions in any foreign country or in any part of the Commonwealth and Dependent Territories other than Canada. R.S., c. E-10, s. 49; 1984, c. 40, s. 27; 1994, c. 44, s. 92; 1997, c. 18, s. 118.

Oaths and Solemn Affirmations

OATHS TAKEN ABROAD.

53. Oaths, affidavits, solemn affirmations or declarations administered, taken or received outside Canada by any person mentioned in section 52 are as valid and effectual and are of the like force and effect to all intents and purposes as if they had been administered, taken or received in Canada by a person authorized to administer, take or receive oaths, affidavits, solemn affirmations or declarations therein that are valid and effectual under this Act. R.S., c. E-10, s. 50.

Documentary Evidence

DOCUMENTS TO BE ADMITTED IN EVIDENCE / Status of statements.

54. (1) Any document that purports to have affixed, impressed or subscribed on it or to it the signature of any person authorized by any of paragraphs 52(*a*) to (*d*) to administer, take or receive oaths, affidavits, solemn affirmations or declarations, together with their seal or with the seal or stamp of their office, or the office to which the person is attached, in testimony of any oath, affidavit, solemn affirmation or declaration being administered, taken or received by the person, shall be admitted in evidence, without proof of the seal or stamp or of the person's signature or official character.

(2) An affidavit, solemn affirmation, declaration or other similar statement taken or received in a foreign country by an official referred to in paragraph 52(*e*) shall be admitted in evidence without proof of the signature or official character of the

963

official appearing to have signed the affidavit, solemn affirmation, declaration or other statement. R.S., c. E-10, s. 51; 1994, c. 44, s. 93.

SCHEDULE

(Paragraph 38.01(6)(d) and subsection 38.01(8))

DESIGNATED ENTITIES

1. A judge of the Federal Court, for the purposes of section 21 of *the Canadian Security Intelligence Service Act*

2. A judge of the Federal Court, for the purposes of sections 6 and 7 of the *Charities Registration (Security Information) Act*, except where the hearing is open to the public

3. A judge of the Federal Court, the Federal Court of Appeal or the Immigration Division or Immigration Appeal Division of the Immigration and Refugee Board, for the purposes of sections 77 to 87.1 of the *Immigration and Refugee Protection Act*

4. A judge of the Federal Court, for the purposes of section 16 of the *Secure Air Travel Act*

5. [*Repealed*, 2001, c. 41, s. 124(3).]

6. [*Repealed*, 2001, c. 41, s. 124(3).]

7. [*Repealed*, 2001, c. 41, s. 124(3).]

8. [*Repealed*, 2001, c. 41, s. 124(3).]

9. A board of inquiry convened under section 45 of the *National Defence Act*

10. A service tribunal or a military judge for the purposes of Part III of the *National Defence Act*

Note: Item 10 of the schedule replaced, 2019, c. 15, s. 54 (to come into force by order of the Governor in Council):

10. A court martial or a military judge for the purposes of Part III of the *National Defence Act*

11. The Federal Public Sector Labour Relations and Employment Board referred to in subsection 4(1) of the *Federal Public Sector Labour Relations and Employment Board Act*, for the purposes of a grievance process under the *Federal Public Sector Labour Relations Act* with respect to an employee of the Canadian Security Intelligence Service, with the exception of any information provided to the Board by the employee

12. The Information Commissioner, for the purposes of the *Access to Information Act*

13. The Privacy Commissioner, for the purposes of the *Privacy Act*

14. The Privacy Commissioner, for the purposes of the *Personal Information Protection and Electronic Documents Act*

15. A judge of the Federal Court, for the purposes of section 41 of the *Access to Information Act*

16. A judge of the Federal Court, for the purpose of sections 41 to 43 of the *Privacy Act*

17. A judge of the Federal Court, for the purpose of sections 14 to 17 of the *Personal Information Protection and Electronic Documents Act*

18. The National Security and Intelligence Review Agency, for the purposes of sections 16 to 19 of the *National Security and Intelligence Review Agency Act*, with the exception of any information provided to the Agency by the complainant or an individual who has been denied a security clearance

19. The Public Sector Integrity Commissioner, for the purposes of sections 26 to 35 of the *Public Servants Disclosure Protection Act*

20. [*Repealed*, 2019, c. 13, s. 61.]

21. A judge of the Federal Court, for the purposes of sections 4 and 6 of the *Prevention of Terrorist Travel Act*

22. The Civilian Review and Complaints Commission for the Royal Canadian Mounted Police, for the purposes of the *Royal Canadian Mounted Police Act*, but only in relation to information that is under the control, or in the possession, of the Royal Canadian Mounted Police. S.C. 2001, c. 41, ss. 44 and 124(2), (3); 2003, c. 22, s. 105; SOR/2004-19; SOR/2006-80, s. 1; SOR/2006-335, s. 1; 2005, c. 46, s. 56; 2006, c. 9, s. 222; SOR/2006-80, s. 1; 2008, c. 3, s. 11; SOR/2012-220, s. 1; 2013, c. 18, ss. 45, 85; c. 40, s. 448; 2015, c. 20, s. 13; c. 36, s. 43; 2017, c. 9, s. 41; 2019, c. 13, ss. 20, 61; 2019, c. 18, s. 60.

CAN. EV.

CANADIAN BILL OF RIGHTS

8-9 Elizabeth II, c. 44 (Canada) (R.S.C. 1985, Appendix III)

Amended 1970-71-72, c. 38, s. 29; proclaimed in force January 1, 1972
Amended 1985, c. 26, s. 105; proclaimed in force August 13, 1985

An Act for the Recognition and Protection of Human Rights and Fundamental Freedoms

PREAMBLE.
The Parliament of Canada, affirming that the Canadian Nation is founded upon principles that acknowledge the supremacy of God, the dignity and worth of the human person and the position of the family in a society of free men and free institutions;

Affirming also that men and institutions remain free only when freedom is founded upon respect for moral and spiritual values and the rule of law;

And being desirous of enshrining these principles and the human rights and fundamental freedoms derived from them, in a Bill of Rights which shall reflect the respect of Parliament for its constitutional authority and which shall ensure the protection of these rights and freedoms in Canada;

Therefore Her Majesty, by and with the advice and consent of the Senate and House of Commons of Canada, enacts as follows:

PART I / BILL OF RIGHTS

RECOGNITION AND DECLARATION OF RIGHTS AND FREEDOMS.

1. It is hereby recognized and declared that in Canada there have existed and shall continue to exist without discrimination by reason of race, national origin, colour, religion or sex, the following human rights and fundamental freedoms, namely,

  (a) the right of the individual to life, liberty, security of the person and enjoyment of property, and the right not to be deprived thereof except by due process of law;

  (b) the right of the individual to equality before the law and the protection of the law;

  (c) freedom of religion;

  (d) freedom of speech;

  (e) freedom of assembly and association; and

  (f) freedom of the press.

967

CONSTRUCTION OF LAW.

2. Every law of Canada shall, unless it is expressly declared by an Act of the Parliament of Canada that it shall operate notwithstanding the *Canadian Bill of Rights*, be so construed and applied as not to abrogate, abridge or infringe or to authorize the abrogation, abridgment or infringement of any of the rights or freedoms herein recognized and declared, and in particular, no law of Canada shall be construed or applied so as to

(*a*) authorize or effect the arbitrary detention, imprisonment or exile of any person;

(*b*) impose or authorize the imposition of cruel and unusual treatment or punishment;

(*c*) deprive a person who has been arrested or detained

(i) of the right to be informed promptly of the reason for his arrest or detention,

(ii) of the right to retain and instruct counsel without delay, or

(iii) of the remedy by way of *habeas corpus* for the determination of the validity of his detention and for his release if the detention is not lawful;

(*d*) authorize a court, tribunal, commission, board or other authority to compel a person to give evidence if he is denied counsel, protection against self crimination or other constitutional safeguards;

(*e*) deprive a person of the right to a fair hearing in accordance with the principles of fundamental justice for the determination of his rights and obligations;

(*f*) deprive a person charged with a criminal offence of the right to be presumed innocent until proved guilty according to law in a fair and public hearing by an independent and impartial tribunal, or of the right to reasonable bail without just cause; or

(*g*) deprive a person of the right to the assistance of an interpreter in any proceedings in which he is involved or in which he is a party or a witness, before a court, commission, board or other tribunal, if he does not understand or speak the language in which such proceedings are conducted.

DUTIES OF MINISTER OF JUSTICE.

3. (1) Subject to subsection (2), the Minister of Justice shall, in accordance with such regulations as may be prescribed by the Governor in Council, examine every regulation transmitted to the Clerk of the Privy Council for registration pursuant to the *Statutory Instruments Act* and every Bill introduced in or presented to the House of Commons by a Minister of the Crown, in order to ascertain whether any of the provisions thereof are inconsistent with the purposes and provisions of this Part and he shall report any such inconsistency to the House of Commons at the first convenient opportunity.

(2) A regulation need not be examined in accordance with subsection (1) if prior to being made it was examined as a proposed regulation in accordance with section 3 of the *Statutory Instruments Act* to ensure that it was not inconsistent with the purposes and provisions of this Part. 1970-71-72, c. 38, s. 29; 1985, c. 26, s. 105.

SHORT TITLE.

4. The provisions of this Part shall be known as the *Canadian Bill of Rights*.

PART II

SAVINGS / "Law of Canada" defined / Jurisdiction of Parliament.

5. (1) Nothing in Part I shall be construed to abrogate or abridge any human right or fundamental freedom not enumerated therein that may have existed in Canada at the commencement of this Act.

(2) The expression "law of Canada" in Part I means an Act of the Parliament of Canada enacted before or after the coming into force of this Act, any order, rule or regulation thereunder, and any law in force in Canada or in any part of Canada at the commencement of this Act that is subject to be repealed, abolished or altered by the Parliament of Canada.

(3) The provisions of Part I shall be construed as extending only to matters coming within the legislative authority of the Parliament of Canada.

BILL OF RIGHTS

CANADIAN CHARTER OF RIGHTS AND FREEDOMS

Being Part I of the Constitution Act, 1982

Enacted by the *Canada Act 1982* (U.K.) c. 11; proclaimed in force April 17, 1982

Amended by the Constitution Amendment Proclamation, 1983, SI/84-102, effective June 21, 1984

Amended by the Constitution Amendment, 1993 (New Brunswick), SI/93-54, *Can. Gaz., Part II*, April 7, 1993, effective March 12, 1993

Whereas Canada is founded upon principles that recognize the supremacy of God and the rule of law:

Guarantee of Rights and Freedoms

RIGHTS AND FREEDOMS IN CANADA.

1. The *Canadian Charter of Rights and Freedoms* guarantees the rights and freedoms set out in it subject only to such reasonable limits prescribed by law as can be demonstrably justified in a free and democratic society.

Fundamental Freedoms

FUNDAMENTAL FREEDOMS.

2. Everyone has the following fundamental freedoms:
- (*a*) freedom of conscience and religion;
- (*b*) freedom of thought, belief, opinion and expression, including freedom of the press and other media of communication;
- (*c*) freedom of peaceful assembly; and
- (*d*) freedom of association.

Democratic Rights

DEMOCRATIC RIGHTS OF CITIZENS.

3. Every citizen of Canada has the right to vote in an election of members of the House of Commons or of a legislative assembly and to be qualified for membership therein.

MAXIMUM DURATION OF LEGISLATIVE BODIES / Continuation in special circumstances.

4. (1) No House of Commons and no legislative assembly shall continue for longer than five years from the date fixed for the return of the writs at a general election of its members.

(2) In time of real or apprehended war, invasion or insurrection, a House of Commons may be continued by Parliament and a legislative assembly may be continued by the legislature beyond five years if such continuation is not opposed by the votes of more than one-third of the members of the House of Commons or the legislative assembly, as the case may be.

ANNUAL SITTING OF LEGISLATIVE BODIES.

5. There shall be a sitting of Parliament and of each legislature at least once every twelve months.

Mobility Rights

MOBILITY OF CITIZENS / Rights to move and gain livelihood / Limitation / Affirmative action programs.

6. (1) Every citizen of Canada has the right to enter, remain in and leave Canada.

(2) Every citizen of Canada and every person who has the status of a permanent resident of Canada has the right
   (*a*) to move to and take up residence in any province; and
   (*b*) to pursue the gaining of a livelihood in any province.

(3) The rights specified in subsection (2) are subject to
   (*a*) any laws or practices of general application in force in a province other than those that discriminate among persons primarily on the basis of province of present or previous residence; and
   (*b*) any laws providing for reasonable residency requirements as a qualification for the receipt of publicly provided social services.

(4) Subsections (2) and (3) do not preclude any law, program or activity that has as its object the amelioration in a province of conditions of individuals in that province who are socially or economically disadvantaged if the rate of employment in that province is below the rate of employment in Canada.

Legal Rights

LIFE, LIBERTY AND SECURITY OF PERSON.

7. Everyone has the right to life, liberty and security of the person and the right not to be deprived thereof except in accordance with the principles of fundamental justice.

SEARCH OR SEIZURE.

8. Everyone has the right to be secure against unreasonable search or seizure.

DETENTION OR IMPRISONMENT.

9. Everyone has the right not to be arbitrarily detained or imprisoned.

ARREST OR DETENTION.

10. Everyone has the right on arrest or detention
    (*a*) to be informed promptly of the reasons therefor;
    (*b*) to retain and instruct counsel without delay and to be informed of that right; and
    (*c*) to have the validity of the detention determined by way of *habeas corpus* and to be released if the detention is not lawful.

PROCEEDINGS IN CRIMINAL AND PENAL MATTERS

11. Any person charged with an offence has the right
    (*a*) to be informed without unreasonable delay of the specific offence;
    (*b*) to be tried within a reasonable time;
    (*c*) not to be compelled to be a witness in proceedings against that person in respect of the offence;
    (*d*) to be presumed innocent until proven guilty according to law in a fair and public hearing by an independent and impartial tribunal;
    (*e*) not to be denied reasonable bail without just cause;
    (*f*) except in the case of an offence under military law tried before a military tribunal, to the benefit of trial by jury where the maximum punishment for the offence is imprisonment for five years or a more severe punishment;
    (*g*) not to be found guilty on account of any act or omission unless, at the time of the act or omission, it constituted an offence under Canadian or international law or was criminal according to the general principles of law recognized by the community of nations;
    (*h*) if finally acquitted of the offence, not to be tried for it again and, if finally found guilty and punished for the offence, not to be tried or punished for it again; and
    (*i*) if found guilty of the offence and if the punishment for the offence has been varied between the time of commission and the time of sentencing, to the benefit of the lesser punishment.

TREATMENT OR PUNISHMENT.

12. Everyone has the right not to be subjected to any cruel and unusual treatment or punishment.

SELF-CRIMINATION.

13. A witness who testifies in any proceedings has the right not to have any incriminating evidence so given used to incriminate that witness in any other proceedings, except in a prosecution for perjury or for the giving of contradictory evidence.

INTERPRETER.

14. A party or witness in any proceedings who does not understand or speak the language in which the proceedings are conducted or who is deaf has the right to the assistance of an interpreter.

Equality Rights

EQUALITY BEFORE AND UNDER LAW AND EQUAL PROTECTION AND BENEFIT OF LAW / Affirmative action programs.

15. (1) Every individual is equal before and under the law and has the right to the equal protection and equal benefit of the law without discrimination and, in particular, without discrimination based on race, national or ethnic origin, colour, religion, sex, age or mental or physical disability.

(2) Subsection (1) does not preclude any law, program or activity that has as its object the amelioration of conditions of disadvantaged individuals or groups including those that are disadvantaged because of race, national or ethnic origin, colour, religion, sex, age or mental or physical disability.

Official Languages of Canada

OFFICIAL LANGUAGES OF CANADA / Official languages of New Brunswick / Advancement of status and use.

16. (1) English and French are the official languages of Canada and have equality of status and equal rights and privileges as to their use in all institutions of the Parliament and government of Canada.

(2) English and French are the official languages of New Brunswick and have equality of status and equal rights and privileges as to their use in all institutions of the legislature and government of New Brunswick.

(3) Nothing in this Charter limits the authority of Parliament or a legislature to advance the equality of status or use of English and French.

ENGLISH AND FRENCH LINGUISTIC COMMUNITIES IN NEW BRUNSWICK / Role of the legislature and government of New Brunswick.

16.1 (1) The English linguistic community and the French linguistic community in New Brunswick have equality of status and equal rights and privileges, including the right to distinct educational institutions and such distinct cultural institutions as are necessary for the preservation and promotion of those communities.

(2) The role of the legislature and government of New Brunswick to preserve and promote the status, rights and privileges referred to in subsection (1) is affirmed.

PROCEEDINGS OF PARLIAMENT / Proceedings of New Brunswick legislature.

17. (1) Everyone has the right to use English or French in any debates and other proceedings of Parliament.

(2) Everyone has the right to use English or French in any debates and other proceedings of the legislature of New Brunswick.

PARLIAMENTARY STATUTES AND RECORDS / New Brunswick statutes and records.

18. (1) The statutes, records and journals of Parliament shall be printed and published in English and French and both language versions are equally authoritative.

(2) The statutes, records and journals of the legislature of New Brunswick shall be printed and published in English and French and both language versions are equally authoritative.

PROCEEDINGS IN COURTS ESTABLISHED BY PARLIAMENT / Proceedings in New Brunswick courts.

19. (1) Either English or French may be used by any person in, or in any pleading in or process issuing from, any court established by Parliament.

(2) Either English or French may be used by any person in, or in any pleading in or process issuing from, any court of New Brunswick.

COMMUNICATIONS BY PUBLIC WITH FEDERAL INSTITUTIONS / Communications by public with New Brunswick institutions.

20. (1) Any member of the public in Canada has the right to communicate with, and to receive available services from, any head or central office of an institution of the Parliament or government of Canada in English or French, and has the same right with respect to any other office of any such institution where
- (a) there is a significant demand for communications with and services from that office in such language; or
- (b) due to the nature of the office, it is reasonable that communications with and services from that office be available in both English and French.

(2) Any member of the public in New Brunswick has the right to communicate with, and to receive available services from, any office of an institution of the legislature or government of New Brunswick in English or French.

CONTINUATION OF EXISTING CONSTITUTIONAL PROVISIONS.

21. Nothing in sections 16 to 20 abrogates or derogates from any right, privilege or obligation with respect to the English and French languages, or either of them, that exists or is continued by virtue of any other provision of the Constitution of Canada.

975

RIGHTS AND PRIVILEGES PRESERVED.

22. Nothing in sections 16 to 20 abrogates or derogates from any legal or customary right or privilege acquired or enjoyed either before or after the coming into force of this Charter with respect to any language that is not English or French.

Minority Language Educational Rights

LANGUAGE OF INSTRUCTION / Continuity of language instruction / Application where numbers warrant.

23. (1) Citizens of Canada

- (*a*) whose first language learned and still understood is that of the English or French linguistic minority population of the province in which they reside, or
- (*b*) who have received their primary school instruction in Canada in English or French and reside in a province where the language in which they received that instruction is the language of the English or French linguistic minority population of the province,

have the right to have their children receive primary and secondary school instruction in that language in that province.

(2) Citizens of Canada of whom any child has received or is receiving primary or secondary school instruction in English or French in Canada, have the right to have all their children receive primary and secondary school instruction in the same language.

(3) The right of citizens of Canada under subsections (1) and (2) to have their children receive primary and secondary school instruction in the language of the English or French linguistic minority population of a province

- (*a*) applies wherever in the province the number of children of citizens who have such a right is sufficient to warrant the provision to them out of public funds of minority language instruction; and
- (*b*) includes, where the number of those children so warrants, the right to have them receive that instruction in minority language educational facilities provided out of public funds.

Enforcement

ENFORCEMENT OF GUARANTEED RIGHTS AND FREEDOMS / Exclusion of evidence bringing administration of justice into disrepute.

24. (1) Anyone whose rights or freedoms, as guaranteed by this Charter, have been infringed or denied may apply to a court of competent jurisdiction to obtain such remedy as the court considers appropriate and just in the circumstances.

(2) Where, in proceedings under subsection (1), a court concludes that evidence was obtained in a manner that infringed or denied any rights or freedoms guaranteed by this Charter, the evidence shall be excluded if it is established that,

having regard to all the circumstances, the admission of it in the proceedings would bring the administration of justice into disrepute.

General

ABORIGINAL RIGHTS AND FREEDOMS NOT AFFECTED BY CHARTER.

25. The guarantee in this Charter of certain rights and freedoms shall not be construed so as to abrogate or derogate from any aboriginal, treaty or other rights or freedoms that pertain to the aboriginal peoples of Canada including

(*a*) any rights or freedoms that have been recognized by the Royal Proclamation of October 7, 1763; and

(*b*) any rights or freedoms that now exist by way of land claims agreements or may be so acquired. SI/84-102, Sch.

OTHER RIGHTS AND FREEDOMS NOT AFFECTED BY CHARTER.

26. The guarantee in this Charter of certain rights and freedoms shall not be construed as denying the existence of any other rights or freedoms that exist in Canada.

MULTICULTURAL HERITAGE.

27. This Charter shall be interpreted in a manner consistent with the preservation and enhancement of the multicultural heritage of Canadians.

RIGHTS GUARANTEED EQUALLY TO BOTH SEXES.

28. Notwithstanding anything in this Charter, the rights and freedoms referred to in it are guaranteed equally to male and female persons.

RIGHTS RESPECTING CERTAIN SCHOOLS PRESERVED.

29. Nothing in this Charter abrogates or derogates from any rights or privileges guaranteed by or under the Constitution of Canada in respect of denominational, separate or dissentient schools.

APPLICATION TO TERRITORIES AND TERRITORIAL AUTHORITIES.

30. A reference in this Charter to a province or to the legislative assembly or legislature of a province shall be deemed to include a reference to the Yukon Territory and the Northwest Territories, or to the appropriate legislative authority thereof, as the case may be.

LEGISLATIVE POWERS NOT EXTENDED.

31. Nothing in this Charter extends the legislative powers of any body or authority.

Application of Charter

APPLICATION OF CHARTER / Exception.

32. (1) This Charter applies

   (*a*) to the Parliament and government of Canada in respect of all matters within the authority of Parliament including all matters relating to the Yukon Territory and Northwest Territories; and

   (*b*) to the legislature and government of each province in respect of all matters within the authority of the legislature of each province.

(2) Notwithstanding subsection (1), section 15 shall not have effect until three years after this section comes into force.

EXCEPTION WHERE EXPRESS DECLARATION / Operation of exception / Five year limitation / Re-enactment / Five year limitation.

33. (1) Parliament or the legislature of a province may expressly declare in an Act of Parliament or of the legislature, as the case may be, that the Act or a provision thereof shall operate notwithstanding a provision included in section 2 or sections 7 to 15 of this Charter.

(2) An Act or a provision of an Act in respect of which a declaration made under this section is in effect shall have such operation as it would have but for the provision of this Charter referred to in the declaration.

(3) A declaration made under subsection (1) shall cease to have effect five years after it comes into force or on such earlier date as may be specified in the declaration.

(4) Parliament or the legislature of a province may re-enact a declaration made under subsection (1).

(5) Subsection (3) applies in respect of a re-enactment made under subsection (4).

Citation

CITATION.

34. This Part may be cited as the *Canadian Charter of Rights and Freedoms*.

. . . . .

CONSTITUTION ACT, 1982
Part VII / GENERAL

PRIMACY OF CONSTITUTION OF CANADA / Constitution of Canada / Amendments to Constitution of Canada.

52. (1) The Constitution of Canada is the supreme law of Canada, and any law that is inconsistent with the provisions of the Constitution is, to the extent of the inconsistency, of no force or effect.

(2) The Constitution of Canada includes

    (*a*) the *Canada Act 1982*, including this Act;

    (*b*) the Acts and orders referred to in the schedule; and

    (*c*) any amendment to any Act or order referred to in paragraph (*a*) or (*b*).

(3) Amendments to the Constitution of Canada shall be made only in accordance with the authority contained in the Constitution of Canada.

CONTROLLED DRUGS AND SUBSTANCES ACT

1996, Chap. 19, ss. 1 to 60 (but see ss. 61 to 63); brought into force May 14, 1997 by SI/97-47, *Can. Gaz.*, *Part II*, May 14, 1997

Amended 1996, c. 8, s. 35; brought into force July 12, 1996 by SI/96-69, *Can. Gaz.*, *Part II*, July 24, 1997

Amended 1996, c. 19, s. 93.2; brought into force May 14, 1997 by SI/97-47, *Can. Gaz.*, *Part II*, May 14, 1997

Amended SOR/97-230, *Can. Gaz.*, *Part II*, May 14, 1997

Amended 1997, c. 18, s. 140; brought into force May 14, 1997 by SI/97-62.

Amended SOR/98-157, *Can. Gaz.*, *Part II*, March 12, 1998

Amended SOR/98-173, *Can. Gaz.*, *Part II*, March 19, 1998

Amended 1999, c. 5, ss. 48 and 49; brought into force May 1, 1999 by para. (*b*) of SI/99-24

Amended SOR/99-371, *Can. Gaz.*, *Part II*, September 29, 1999

Amended SOR/99-421, *Can. Gaz.*, *Part II*, October 21, 1999

Amended SOR/2000-220, *Can. Gaz.*, *Part II*, June 1, 2000; in force September 1, 2000 as provided by s. 3

Amended 2001, c. 32, ss. 47 to 56; ss. 47, 49 to 53, 55, 56 brought into force January 7, 2002 by para. (*a*) of SI/2002-17, *Can. Gaz.*, January 16, 2002; ss. 48, 54 brought into force February 1, 2002 by para. (*b*) of SI/2002-17, *Can. Gaz.*, January 16, 2002

Amended SOR/2002-361, *Can. Gaz.*, September 24, 2002, ss. 1 and 2; in force January 9, 2003 as provided by s. 3

Amended SOR/2003-32, *Can. Gaz.*, January 30, 2003, ss. 1 to 3, 5 to 7; in force January 30, 2003 as provided by s. 8

Amended SOR/2003-37, *Can. Gaz.*, January 30, 2003

Amended SOR/2003-412, *Can. Gaz.*, December 11, 2003

Amended 2005, c. 10, ss. 15, 16 and 34(1)(*d*), brought into force April 4, 2005 by SI/2005-29, *Can. Gaz.*, April 20, 2005

Amended SOR/2005-235, *Can. Gaz.*, August 10, 2005

Amended SOR/2005-271, s. 1, *Can. Gaz.*, in force August 31, 2005 as provided by s. 2

Amended SOR/2005-337, s. 1, *Can. Gaz.*, in force November 15, 2005 as provided by s. 2

Amended SOR/2005-364, ss. 1, 2 and 4, *Can. Gaz.*; s. 1 in force November 21, 2005 as provided by s. 5(1); ss. 2 and 4 in force January 31, 2006 as provided by s. 5(2)

Amended 2005, c. 44, s. 13; in force November 25, 2005

Amended 2011, c. 14, s. 1; in force June 23, 2011

Amended 2012, c. 1, ss. 39 to 46; brought into force November 6, 2012 by SI/2012-48, *Can. Gaz, Part II*, July 4, 2012

Amended SOR/2012-66, *Can. Gaz., Part II*, April 11, 2012, s. 1; in force March 30, 2012 as provided by s. 2

Amended SOR/2012-176, *Can. Gaz., Part II*, October 10, 2012, s. 1; in force September 20, 2012

Amended 2015, c. 22, ss. 2 to 5; brought into force June 30, 2015 by SI/2015-63, *Can. Gaz., Part II*, July 15, 2015

Amended SOR/2015-190, *Can. Gaz., Part II*, July 29, 2015, s. 1; in force January 13, 2016 as provided by s. 2

Amended SOR/2015-192, *Can Gaz., Part II*, July 29, 2015, ss. 1 and 2; in force July 16, 2015 as provided by s. 3

Amended SOR/2015-209, *Can. Gaz., Part II*, August 12, 2015, s. 1; in force February 9, 2016 as provided by s. 2

Amended SOR/2016-13, *Can. Gaz., Part II*, February 24, 2016, s. 1; in force February 5, 2016, as provided by s. 2

Amended SOR/2016-73, *Can. Gaz., Part II*, May 4, 2016, ss. 1 and 2; in force October 31, 2016 as provided by s. 3

Amended SOR/2016-107, *Can. Gaz., Part II*, June 1, 2016, ss. 1 and 2; in force November 28, 2016 as provided by s. 3

Amended SOR/2016-295, *Can. Gaz., Part II*, November 30, 2016, s. 1; in force November 30, 2016 as provided by s. 2

Amended SOR/2017-13, *Can. Gaz., Part II*, February 2, 2017, ss. 1 to 12; in force February 22, 2017 as provided by s. 13

Amended SOR/2017-44, *Can. Gaz., Part II*, April 5, 2017, s. 1; in force May 5, 2017 as provided by s. 2

Amended 2017, c. 4, s. 2; in force May 4, 2017

Amended 2017, c. 7, ss. 1 to 51; ss. 1(3) to (5), 3(1), (3), (4), 4 to 6, 7(2), (4), 9, 25, 26(1), (3), (4), (5), (6), (7), 27(1), (2), 30, 33, 34, 37, 38, 39, 40(1), (3), (6) to (8) (10) to (12), (14) to (19), 41 to 51 in force May 18, 2017; ss. 1(6), 2, 8, 10 to 24, 26(8), 29 brought into force June 21, 2018 by SI/2018-46, *Can. Gaz., Part II*, July 11, 2018; ss. 1(1), 28, 31, 32, 35, 36, 40(12) and (13) to come into force by order of the Governor in Council as provided by s. 73

Amended SOR/2017-249, *Can. Gaz., Part II*, December 13, 2017; in force December 13, 2017 as provided by s. 3

Amended SOR/2017-275, *Can. Gaz., Part II*, December 27, 2017; in force December 8, 2017 as provided by s. 2

Amended SOR/2017-277, *Can. Gaz., Part II*, December 27, 2017; in force December 27, 2017 as provided by s. 3

Amended SOR/2018-70, *Can. Gaz., Part II*, April 18, 2018; in force April 4, 2018 as provided by s. 5

Amended 2018, c. 16, ss. 194 to 206; ss. 194, 200 to 202, 206 in force on Royal Assent, June 21, 2018; ss. 195 to 198, 203 to 205, 206(6) in force October 17, 2018; if Bill C-37, introduced in the 1st session of the 42nd Parliament and entitled *An Act to amend the Controlled Drugs and Substances Act and to make related amendments to other Acts*, receives royal assent, then, on the first day on which both s. 28 of that Act and s. 199(2) of 2018, c. 16 are in force, s. 199(1) will come into force

Amended 2019, c. 25, s. 385; in force September 19, 2019

Editor's Note: The *Controlled Drugs and Substances Act* creates a new scheme for the regulation of certain dangerous drugs and narcotics, now known as "controlled substances". The Act replaces the *Narcotic Control Act*, R.S.C. 1985, c. N-1 and Part III [Controlled Drugs] and Part IV [Restricted Drugs] of the *Food and Drugs Act*, R.S.C. 1985, c. F-27. The essential scheme of the legislation is similar to the former *Narcotic Control Act* and the *Food and Drugs Act*.

Schedules / An important part of the legislation is the schedules to the Act: Schedule I – includes the most dangerous drugs and narcotics, such as phencyclidine, heroin and cocaine. Schedule II – lists cannabis and its derivatives. Schedule III – includes many of the more dangerous drugs which previously were included in schedules G and H to the *Food and Drugs Act*, such as the amphetamines and lysergic acid diethylamide (LSD). Schedule IV – includes many of the drugs formerly included in Schedule G to the *Food and Drugs Act*. These drugs, such as the barbiturates, while dangerous, have therapeutic uses. As was the case under Part III of the *Food and Drugs Act*, simple possession of Schedule IV drugs is not an offence.

Possession / Under s. 4(1), simple possession of any of the drugs and narcotics listed in Schedules I, II and III of the *Controlled Drugs and Substances Act* is an offence unless the person is authorized to be in possession by the regulations. The offence under s. 4(1) is a Crown option offence. The penalty for breach of s. 4(1) depends upon the Schedule in which the substance is included. In addition, a special penalty scheme has been included for possession of small quantities of Schedule II [cannabis] offences. Where the subject matter of the offence is a Schedule II substance in an amount that does not exceed the amount set out in Schedule VIII, then the accused is guilty only of a summary conviction offence and the maximum penalty is a $1,000 fine and/or six months' jail. Further, even where the amounts exceed the Schedule VIII amounts and the Crown proceeds by indictment, the offence is within the absolute jurisdiction of the provincial court where the substance is listed in Schedule II.

"Double-doctoring" / Under s. 4(2), it is an offence to seek or obtain any of the scheduled substances from a practitioner, such as a physician, without disclosing particulars relating to the acquisition of any of the scheduled substances within the preceding 30 days. This is the so-called "double-doctoring" offence which was found in both the *Food and Drugs Act* and the *Narcotic Control Act*. Again, this is a Crown option offence. The maximum penalty for the offence where the Crown proceeds by indictment depends upon the schedule in which the substance is found. If the Crown proceeds by way of summary conviction, then the penalty is the same irrespective of the schedule.

Trafficking / Under s. 5(1), it is an offence to traffic in any of the scheduled substances and under s. 5(2) it is an offence to be in possession for the purpose of trafficking. The definition of "traffic", which of course includes sell, when combined with the definition of "sell" is very broad and covers virtually the same activity as was prohibited under the predecessor legislation. These definitions are found in s. 2. The penalty and classification of the offence depend upon the schedule in which the substance is found. For the Schedule I and II substances, it

DRUGS

983

is a pure indictable offence with a maximum punishment of life imprisonment, except where the offence relates to trafficking in smaller amounts of the Schedule II (cannabis) substance. Under s. 5(4), where the amount of the Schedule II substance does not exceed the amount listed in Schedule VII, the maximum penalty is five years less one day. This offence is also listed in s. 553(*c*) of the *Criminal Code* and thus is within the absolute jurisdiction of the provincial court. For the Schedule III and IV offences, the offence is a Crown-option offence with lesser maximum punishments.

Importing / Section 6 creates the importing offence for substances included in Schedules I to VI. Schedules V and VI list chemicals which can be employed in the manufacture of substances listed in the earlier Schedule. Where the substance is listed in Schedules I and II, the offence is indictable and punishable by life imprisonment. Where the substance is listed in the other schedules, the offence is a Crown-option offence with the maximum penalty depending upon the schedule in which the substance is found.

Production / Section 7 prohibits the production of any of the substances in Schedules I to IV except as authorized by regulations. The term "produce" is defined in s. 2 and includes manufacture and cultivation. For Schedule I and II substances, the offence is indictable with a maximum punishment of life imprisonment unless the substance is marihuana in which case the maximum is seven years. Where the substance is listed in Schedule III or IV, the offence is Crown-option with lesser maximum punishments.

Proceeds of Crime / Sections 8 and 9 recreate the proceeds of crime and money-laundering offences in terms similar to the former provisions of the *Narcotic Control Act* and the *Food and Drugs Act*.

Sentencing / Section 10 sets out the principles of sentencing and includes a list of aggravating circumstances such as that the accused used a weapon in relation to the commission of the offence or committed the trafficking offence near a school. Where one of these aggravating circumstances exists but the judge does not impose a prison term, the judge is required to give reasons for that decision.

Search and Seizure / Sections 11 to 13 set out the powers of search and seizure in respect of offences under this Act. The terms are similar to those found in the *Criminal Code*. In addition, special provision is made in s. 11(7) for a warrantless search in exigent circumstances.

Restraint and Forfeiture / Sections 14 to 23 deal with restraint orders and forfeiture orders in terms similar to Part XII.2 of the *Criminal Code*. This is a departure from the scheme under the *Narcotic Control Act* and the *Food and Drugs Act* which had simply adopted the provisions of Part XII.2 with the necessary modifications. A significant difference between the procedure under this Act and the procedure under the *Criminal Code* is that the Attorney General is not required to give an undertaking as to damages and costs when seeking a restraint order under the Act.

Disposal of seized substances / Part III of the Act deals with the disposal of substances seized or found by a peace officer or inspector. Part IV sets out the scheme for appointment of inspectors and the administrative enforcement of the Act and regulations in terms similar to Part II of the *Food and Drugs Act*. Part V sets out a special scheme for enforcement of "designated regulations". Under this Part, the Minister may make an emergency order where there is a substantial risk of immediate danger to the health or safety of any person.

Miscellaneous / Part VI contains a number of miscellaneous provisions. Most important are those relating to the admissibility of certificates of analysis [ss. 51 and 52], continuity of exhibits [s. 53], admissibility of copies of records seized under the Act or regulations [s. 54], and the limitation period of one year where the Crown proceeds by way of summary conviction [s. 47]. Under s. 48, the evidentiary burden is initially upon the accused to show that any certificate, licence, permit or other qualification operates in the accused's favour. Section 55 gives the Governor in Council wide regulation-making powers.

Section 60 permits the Governor in Council to add or delete items from any of the Schedules. An important innovation in this Act is the concept of "analogue" defined in s. 2 as a substance that, in relation to a controlled substance, has "a substantially similar chemical structure". Thus, for example, Schedule III lists amphetamines, their salts, derivatives, isomers and "analogues". This concept was apparently added to attempt to deal with the problem of chemists manufacturing drugs with a slightly different chemical structure than those actually listed in the schedule. Previously, the government would have been required to amend the schedules to prohibit or regulate the trafficking or production of such substances.

"Controlled substance" / It should also be noted that s. 2(2)(*b*) provides that a reference to a "controlled substance" includes a reference to all synthetic and natural forms of the substances. This specifically meets an argument which had been made under the former *Narcotic Control Act* that certain synthetic forms of narcotics were not covered by the Act.

DRUGS

An act respecting the control of certain drugs, their precursors and other substances and to amend certain other Acts and repeal the Narcotic Control Act in consequence thereof

SHORT TITLE

SHORT TITLE.

1. This Act may be cited as the *Controlled Drugs and Substances Act*.

INTERPRETATION

DEFINITIONS / "adjudicator" / "analogue" / "analyst" / "Attorney General" / "controlled substance" / "designated substance offence" / "inspector" / "judge" / "justice" / "Minister" / "offence-related property" / "possession" / "practitioner" / "precursor" / "prescribed" / "produce" / "provide" / "sell" / "traffic" / Interpretation / Idem.

2. (1) In this Act,

"adjudicator" means a person appointed or employed under the *Public Service Employment Act* who performs the duties and functions of an adjudicator under this Act and the regulations;

Note: Subsection 2(1) amended by repealing the definition "adjudicator", 2017, c. 7, s. 1(1) (to come into force by order of the Governor in Council).

"analogue" means a substance that, in relation to a controlled substance, has a substantially similar chemical structure;

"analyst" means a person who is designated as an analyst under section 44;

"Attorney General" means
(a) the Attorney General of Canada, and includes their lawful deputy, or
(b) with respect to proceedings commenced at the instance of the government of a province and conducted by or on behalf of that government, the Attorney General of that province, and includes their lawful deputy;

"chemical offence-related property" means offence-related property that is a chemical or precursor and includes anything that contains such property or has such property on it;

"controlled substance" means a substance included in Schedule I, II, III, IV or V;

"customs office" has the same meaning as in subsection 2(1) of the *Customs Act*;

"designated device" means a device included in Schedule IX;

"designated substance offence" means
(a) an offence under Part I, except subsection 4(1), or
(b) a conspiracy or an attempt to commit, being an accessory after the fact in relation to, or any counselling in relation to, an offence referred to in paragraph (a);

"inspector" means a person who is designated as an inspector under section 30;

"judge" means a judge as defined in section 552 of the *Criminal Code* or a judge of a superior court of criminal jurisdiction;

"justice" has the same meaning as in section 2 of the *Criminal Code*;

"Minister" means the Minister of Health;

"non-chemical offence-related property" means offence-related property that is not chemical offence-related property;

"offence-related property" means, with the exception of a controlled substance, any property, within or outside Canada, (*a*) by means of or in respect of which a designated substance offence is committed,

(*b*) that is used in any manner in connection with the commission of a designated substance offence, or

(*c*) that is intended for use for the purpose of committing a designated substance offence;

"organization" has the same meaning as in section 2 of the *Criminal Code*;

"person" means an individual or an organization;

"possession" means possession within the meaning of subsection 4(3) of the *Criminal Code*;

"practitioner" means a person who is registered and entitled under the laws of a province to practise in that province the profession of medicine, dentistry or veterinary medicine, and includes any other person or class or persons prescribed as a practitioner;

"precursor" means a substance included in Schedule VI;

"prescribed" means prescribed by the regulations;

"produce" means, in respect of a substance included in any of Schedules I to V, to obtain the substance by any method or process including

(*a*) manufacturing, synthesizing or using any means of altering the chemical or physical properties of the substance, or

(*b*) cultivating, propagating or harvesting the substance or any living thing from which the substance may be extracted or otherwise obtained,

and includes offer to produce;

"provide" means to give, transfer or otherwise make available in any manner, whether directly or indirectly and whether or not for consideration;

"sell" includes offer for sale, expose for sale, have in possession for sale and distribute, whether or not the distribution is made for consideration;

"traffic" means, in respect of a substance included in any of Schedules I to V,

(*a*) to sell, administer, give, transfer, transport, send or deliver the substance,

(*b*) to sell an authorization to obtain the substance, or

(*c*) to offer to do anything mentioned in paragraph (*a*) or (*b*),

otherwise than under the authority of the regulations.

(2) For the purposes of this Act,

(*a*) a reference to a controlled substance includes a reference to any substance that contains a controlled substance; and

(*b*) a reference to a controlled substance includes a reference to

(i) all synthetic and natural forms of the substance, and

(ii) any thing that contains or has on it a controlled substance and that is used or intended or designed for use

(A) in producing the substance, or

(B) in introducing the substance into a human body.

(3) For the purposes of this Act, where a substance is expressly named in any of Schedules I to VI, it shall be deemed not to be included in any other of those

Schedules. 1996, c. 8, s. 35; 2001, c. 32, s. 47; 2017, c. 7, s. 1(3) to (6); 2018, c. 16, s. 194.

INTERPRETATION.

3. (1) Every power or duty imposed under this Act that may be exercised or performed in respect of an offence under this Act may be exercised or performed in respect of a conspiracy, or an attempt to commit, being an accessory after the fact in relation to, or any counselling in relation to, an offence under this Act. 1995, c. 22, s. 18 (Sched. IV, item 26); 2017, c. 7, s. 2.

(2) [*Repealed*, 2017, c. 7, s. 2.]

Part I / OFFENCES AND PUNISHMENT

Particular Offences

POSSESSION OF SUBSTANCE / Obtaining substance / Punishment / Punishment / Punishment / Punishment / Punishment / Determination of amount.

4. (1) Except as authorized under the regulations, no person shall possess a substance included in Schedule I, II or III.

(2) No person shall seek or obtain
  (*a*) a substance included in Schedule I, II, III or IV, or
  (*b*) an authorization to obtain a substance included in Schedule I, II, III or IV

from a practitioner, unless the person discloses to the practitioner particulars relating to the acquisition by the person of every substance in those Schedules, and of every authorization to obtain such substances, from any other practitioner within the preceding thirty days.

(3) Every person who contravenes subsection (1) where the subject-matter of the offence is a substance included in Schedule I
  (*a*) is guilty of an indictable offence and liable to imprisonment for a term not exceeding seven years; or
  (*b*) is guilty of an offence punishable on summary conviction and liable
    (i) for a first offence, to a fine not exceeding one thousand dollars or to imprisonment for a term not exceeding six months, or to both, and
    (ii) for a subsequent offence, to a fine not exceeding two thousand dollars or to imprisonment for a term not exceeding one year, or to both.

(4) Subject to subsection (5), every person who contravenes subsection (1) where the subject-matter of the offence is a substance included in Schedule II
  (*a*) is guilty of an indictable offence and liable to imprisonment for a term not exceeding five years less a day; or
  (*b*) is guilty of an offence punishable on summary conviction and liable
    (i) for a first offence, to a fine not exceeding one thousand dollars or to imprisonment for a term not exceeding six months, or to both, and

(ii) for a subsequent offence, to a fine not exceeding two thousand dollars or to imprisonment for a term not exceeding one year, or to both.

(5) [*Repealed*, 2018, c. 16, s. 195(1).]

(6) Every person who contravenes subsection (1) where the subject-matter of the offence is a substance included in Schedule III

  (*a*) is guilty of an indictable offence and liable to imprisonment for a term not exceeding three years; or

  (*b*) is guilty of an offence punishable on summary conviction and liable

    (i) for a first offence, to a fine not exceeding one thousand dollars or to imprisonment for a term not exceeding six months, or to both, and

    (ii) for a subsequent offence, to a fine not exceeding two thousand dollars or to imprisonment for a term not exceeding one year, or to both.

(7) Every person who contravenes subsection (2)

  (*a*) is guilty of an indictable offence and liable

    (i) to imprisonment for a term not exceeding seven years, where the subject-matter of the offence is a substance included in Schedule I,

    (ii) to imprisonment for a term not exceeding five years less a day, where the subject-matter of the offence is a substance included in Schedule II,

    (iii) to imprisonment for a term not exceeding three years, where the subject-matter of the offence is a substance included in Schedule III, or

    (iv) to imprisonment for a term not exceeding eighteen months, where the subject-matter of the offence is a substance included in Schedule IV; or

  (*b*) is guilty of an offence punishable on summary conviction and liable

    (i) for a first offence, to a fine not exceeding one thousand dollars or to imprisonment for a term not exceeding six months, or to both, and

    (ii) for a subsequent offence, to a fine not exceeding two thousand dollars or to imprisonment for a term not exceeding one year, or to both. 2018, c. 16, s. 195.

(8) [*Repealed*, 2018, c. 16, s. 195(2).]

DEFINITION OF "MEDICAL EMERGENCY" / Exemption — medical emergency / Exemption — persons at the scene / Exemption — evidence / Deeming.

4.1 (1) For the purposes of this section, "medical emergency" means a physiological event induced by the introduction of a psychoactive substance into the body of a person that results in a life-threatening situation and in respect of which there are reasonable grounds to believe that the person requires emergency medical or law enforcement assistance.

(2) No person who seeks emergency medical or law enforcement assistance because that person, or another person, is suffering from a medical emergency is to be charged or convicted of an offence under subsection 4(1) if the evidence in support of that offence was obtained or discovered as a result of that person having sought assistance or having remained at the scene.

DRUGS

(3) The exemption under subsection (2) also applies to any person, including the person suffering from the medical emergency, who is at the scene on the arrival of the emergency medical or law enforcement assistance.

(4) No person who seeks emergency medical or law enforcement assistance because that person, or another person, is suffering from a medical emergency, or who is at the scene on the arrival of the assistance, is to be charged with an offence concerning a violation of any condition of a pre-trial release or probation order relating to an offence under subsection 4(1) if the evidence in support of that offence was obtained or discovered as a result of that person having sought assistance or having remained at the scene.

(5) Any condition of a person's pre-trial release, probation order, conditional sentence or parole relating to an offence under subsection 4(1) that may be violated as a result of the person seeking emergency medical or law enforcement assistance for their, or another person's, medical emergency, or as a result of having been at the scene on the arrival of the assistance, is deemed not to be violated. 2017, c. 4, s. 2; 2018, c. 16, s. 195.1.

TRAFFICKING IN SUBSTANCE / Possession for purpose of trafficking / Punishment / Punishment in respect of specified substance / Interpretation / Idem.

5. (1) No person shall traffic in a substance included in Schedule I, II, III, IV or V or in any substance represented or held out by that person to be such a substance.

(2) No person shall, for the purpose of trafficking, possess a substance included in Schedule I, II, III, IV or V.

(3) Every person who contravenes subsection (1) or (2)

    (a) if the subject matter of the offence is a substance included in Schedule I or II, is guilty of an indictable offence and liable to imprisonment for life, and

        (i) to a minimum punishment of imprisonment for a term of one year if

            (A) the person committed the offence for the benefit of, at the direction of or in association with a criminal organization, as defined in subsection 467.1(1) of the *Criminal Code*,

            (B) the person used or threatened to use violence in committing the offence,

            (C) the person carried, used or threatened to use a weapon in committing the offence, or

            (D) the person was convicted of a designated substance offence, or had served a term of imprisonment for a designated substance offence, within the previous 10 years, or

        (ii) to a minimum punishment of imprisonment for a term of two years if

            (A) the person committed the offence in or near a school, on or near school grounds or in or near any other public place usually frequented by persons under the age of 18 years,

            (B) the person committed the offence in a prison, as defined in section 2 of the *Criminal Code*, or on its grounds, or

      (C) the person used the services of a person under the age of 18 years, or involved such a person, in committing the offence;

  (a.1) [*Repealed*, 2018, c. 16, s. 196(2).]

   (b) if the subject-matter of the offence is a substance included in Schedule III or V,

      (i) is guilty of an indictable offence and liable to imprisonment for a term not exceeding ten years, or

      (ii) is guilty of an offence punishable on summary conviction and liable to imprisonment for a term not exceeding eighteen months; and

   (c) where the subject-matter of the offence is a substance included in Schedule IV,

      (i) is guilty of an indictable offence and liable to imprisonment for a term not exceeding three years, or

      (ii) is guilty of an offence punishable on summary conviction and liable to imprisonment for a term not exceeding one year.

(4) [*Repealed*. 2012, c. 1, s. 39(2).]

(5) For the purposes of applying subsection (3) in respect of an offence under subsection (1), a reference to a substance included in Schedule I, II, III, IV or V includes a reference to any substance represented or held out to be a substance included in that Schedule. 2012, c. 1, s. 39; 2017, c. 7, s. 3(1), (3), (4); 2018, c. 16, s. 196.

(6) [*Repealed*, 2018, c. 16, s. 196(3).]

IMPORTING AND EXPORTING / Possession for the purpose of exporting / Punishment.

6. (1) Except as authorized under the regulations, no person shall import into Canada or export from Canada a substance included in Schedule I, II, III, IV, V or VI.

(2) Except as authorized under the regulations, no person shall possess a substance included in Schedule I, II, III, IV, V or VI for the purpose of exporting it from Canada.

(3) Every person who contravenes subsection (1) or (2)

   (a) if the subject matter of the offence is a substance included in Schedule I in an amount that is not more than one kilogram, or in Schedule II, is guilty of an indictable offence and liable to imprisonment for life, and to a minimum punishment of imprisonment for a term of one year if

      (i) the offence is committed for the purposes of trafficking,

      (ii) the person, while committing the offence, abused a position of trust or authority, or

      (iii) the person had access to an area that is restricted to authorized persons and used that access to commit the offence;

  (a.1) if the subject matter of the offence is a substance included in Schedule I in an amount that is more than one kilogram, is guilty of an indictable offence and liable to imprisonment for life and to a minimum punishment of imprisonment for a term of two years;

DRUGS

   (b) if the subject matter of the offence is a substance included in Schedule III,
V or VI,

      (i) is guilty of an indictable offence and liable to imprisonment for a term
not exceeding ten years, or

      (ii) is guilty of an offence punishable on summary conviction and liable to
imprisonment for a term not exceeding eighteen months; and

   (c) if the subject matter of the offence is a substance included in Schedule IV,

      (i) is guilty of an indictable offence and liable to imprisonment for a term
not exceeding three years, or

      (ii) is guilty of an offence punishable on summary conviction and liable to
imprisonment for a term not exceeding one year. 2012, c. 1, s. 40;
2017, c. 7, s. 4.

PRODUCTION OF SUBSTANCE / Punishment / Factors.

7. (1) Except as authorized under the regulations, no person shall produce a
substance included in Schedule I, II, III, IV or V.

(2) Every person who contravenes subsection (1)

   (a) if the subject matter of the offence is a substance included in Schedule I, is
guilty of an indictable offence and liable to imprisonment for life and to a
minimum punishment of imprisonment for a term of three years if any of
the factors set out in subsection (3) apply and for a term of two years in any
other case;

  (a.1) if the subject matter of the offence is a substance included in Schedule II, is
guilty of an indictable offence and liable to imprisonment for life, and to a
minimum punishment of imprisonment

      (i) for a term of one year if the production is for the purpose of
trafficking, or

      (ii) for a term of 18 months if the production is for the purpose of
trafficking and any of the factors set out in subsection (3) apply;

   (b) [*Repealed*, 2018, c. 16, s. 197(2).]

   (c) if the subject matter of the offence is a substance included in Schedule III
or V,

      (i) is guilty of an indictable offence and liable to imprisonment for a term
not exceeding ten years, or

      (ii) is guilty of an offence punishable on summary conviction and liable to
imprisonment for a term not exceeding eighteen months; and

   (d) where the subject matter of the offence is a substance included in Schedule
IV,

      (i) is guilty of an indictable offence and liable to imprisonment for a term
not exceeding three years, or

      (ii) is guilty of an offence punishable on summary conviction and liable to
imprisonment for a term not exceeding one year.

(3) The following factors must be taken into account in applying paragraphs (2)*(a)*
and (*a*.1):

   (a) the person used real property that belongs to a third party in committing the
offence;

   (*b*) the production constituted a potential security, health or safety hazard to persons under the age of 18 years who were in the location where the offence was committed or in the immediate area;

   (*c*) the production constituted a potential public safety hazard in a residential area; or

   (*d*) the person set or placed a trap, device or other thing that is likely to cause death or bodily harm to another person in the location where the offence was committed or in the immediate area, or permitted such a trap, device or other thing to remain or be placed in that location or area. 2012, c. 1, s. 41; 2017, c. 7, s. 5; 2018, c. 16, s. 197.

POSSESSION, SALE, ETC., FOR USE IN PRODUCTION OF OR TRAFFICKING IN SUBSTANCE / Punishment.

7.1 (1) No person shall possess, produce, sell, import or transport anything intending that it will be used

   (*a*) to produce a controlled substance, unless the production of the controlled substance is lawfully authorized; or

   (*b*) to traffic in a controlled substance.

(2) Every person who contravenes subsection (1)

   (*a*) if the subject matter of the offence is a substance included in Schedule I, II, III or V,

      (i) is guilty of an indictable offence and liable to imprisonment for a term of not more than 10 years, or

      (ii) is guilty of an offence punishable on summary conviction and liable to imprisonment for a term of not more than 18 months; and

   (*b*) if the subject matter of the offence is a substance included in Schedule IV,

      (i) is guilty of an indictable offence and liable to imprisonment for a term of not more than three years, or

      (ii) is guilty of an offence punishable on summary conviction and liable to imprisonment for a term of not more than one year. 2011, c. 14, s. 1; 2017, c. 7, s. 6.

---

8. [*Repealed*, 2001, c. 32, s. 48.]

---

9. [*Repealed*, S.C. 2001, c. 32, s. 48.]

NOTICE

NOTICE.

8. The court is not required to impose a minimum punishment unless it is satisfied that the offender, before entering a plea, was notified of the possible imposition of a minimum punishment for the offence in question and of the Attorney General's intention to prove any factors in relation to the offence that would lead to the imposition of a minimum punishment. 2012, c. 1, s. 42.

DRUGS

REPORT TO PARLIAMENT

REVIEW / Report.

9. (1) Within five years after this section comes into force, a comprehensive review of the provisions and operation of this Act, including a cost-benefit analysis of mandatory minimum sentences, shall be undertaken by any committee of the Senate, of the House of Commons or of both Houses of Parliament that may be designated or established for that purpose.

(2) The committee referred to in subsection (1) shall, within one year after a review is undertaken under that subsection, submit a report to Parliament including a statement of any changes that the committee recommends. 2012, c. 1, s. 42.

Sentencing

PURPOSE OF SENTENCING / Factors to take into consideration / Reasons of court / Drug treatment court program / Minimum punishment.

10. (1) Without restricting the generality of the *Criminal Code*, the fundamental purpose of any sentence for an offence under this Part is to contribute to the respect for the law and the maintenance of a just, peaceful and safe society while encouraging rehabilitation, and treatment in appropriate circumstances, of offenders and acknowledging the harm done to victims and to the community.

(2) If a person is convicted of a designated substance offence for which the court is not required to impose a minimum punishment, the court imposing sentence on the person shall consider any relevant aggravating factors including that the person

(*a*) in relation to the commission of the offence,

    (i) carried, used or threatened to use a weapon,

    (ii) used or threatened to use violence,

    (iii) trafficked in a substance included in Schedule I, II, III, IV or V or possessed such a substance for the purpose of trafficking, in or near a school, on or near school grounds or in or near any other public place usually frequented by persons under the age of 18 years, or

    (iv) trafficked in a substance included in Schedule I, II, III, IV or V, or possessed such a substance for the purpose of trafficking, to a person under the age of 18 years;

(*b*) was previously convicted of a "designated substance offence", as defined in subsection 2(1) of this Act, or a "designated offence", as defined in subsection 2(1) of the *Cannabis Act*.

(*c*) used the services of a person under the age of eighteen years to commit, or involved such a person in the commission of, the offence.

(3) If, under subsection (1), the court is satisfied of the existence of one or more of the aggravating factors enumerated in paragraphs (2)(*a*) to (*c*), but decides not to sentence the person to imprisonment, the court shall give reasons for that decision.

(4) A court sentencing a person who is convicted of an offence under this Part may delay sentencing to enable the offender

    (*a*) to participate in a drug treatment court program approved by the Attorney General; or

    (*b*) to attend a treatment program under subsection 720(2) of the *Criminal Code*.

(5) If the offender successfully completes a program under subsection (4), the court is not required to impose the minimum punishment for the offence for which the person was convicted. 1999, c. 5, s. 49; 2012, c. 1, s. 43; 2017, c. 7, s. 7(2), (4); 2018, c. 16, s. 198.

Part II / ENFORCEMENT

[*Heading repealed*, 2017, c. 7, s. 8.]

INFORMATION FOR SEARCH WARRANT / Application of section 487.1 of the *Criminal Code* / Execution in Canada / Search of person and seizure / Seizure of things not specified / Where warrant not necessary / Seizure of additional things.

11. (1) A justice who, on ex parte application, is satisfied by information on oath that there are reasonable grounds to believe that

    (*a*) a controlled substance or precursor in respect of which this Act has been contravened,

    (*b*) any thing in which a controlled substance or precursor referred to in paragraph (*a*) is contained or concealed,

    (*c*) offence-related property, or

    (*d*) any thing that will afford evidence in respect of an offence under this Act or an offence, in whole or in part in relation to a contravention of this Act, under section 354 or 462.31 of the *Criminal Code*

is in a place may, at any time, issue a warrant authorizing a peace officer, at any time, to search the place for any such controlled substance, precursor, property or thing and to seize it.

(2) For the purposes of subsection (1), an information may be submitted by telephone or other means of telecommunication in accordance with section 487.1 of the *Criminal Code*, with such modifications as the circumstances require.

(3) A warrant issued under subsection (1) may be executed at any place in Canada. Any peace officer who executes the warrant must have authority to act as a peace officer in the place where it is executed.

(4) [*Repealed*, 2019, c. 25, s. 385.]

(5) Where a peace officer who executes a warrant issued under subsection (1) has reasonable grounds to believe that any person found in the place set out in the warrant has on their person any controlled substance, precursor, property or thing set out in the warrant, the peace officer may search the person for the controlled substance, precursor, property or drug and seize it.

DRUGS

(6) A peace officer who executes a warrant issued under subsection (1) may seize, in addition to the things mentioned in the warrant,

- (a) any controlled substance or precursor in respect of which the peace officer believes on reasonable grounds that this Act has been contravened;
- (b) any thing that the peace officer believes on reasonable grounds to contain or conceal a controlled substance or precursor referred to in paragraph (a);
- (c) any thing that the peace officer believes on reasonable grounds is offence-related property; or
- (d) any thing that the peace officer believes on reasonable grounds will afford evidence in respect of an offence under this Act.

(7) A peace officer may exercise any of the powers described in subsection (1), (5) or (6) without a warrant if the conditions for obtaining a warrant exist but by reason of exigent circumstances it would be impracticable to obtain one.

(8) A peace officer who executes a warrant issued under subsection (1) or exercises powers under subsection (5) or (7) may seize, in addition to the things mentioned in the warrant and in subsection (6), any thing that the peace officer believes on reasonable grounds has been obtained by or used in the commission of an offence or that will afford evidence in respect of an offence. 2005, c. 44, s. 13; 2017, c. 7, s. 9; 2019, c. 25, s. 385.

ASSISTANCE AND USE OF FORCE.

12. For the purpose of exercising any of the powers described in section 11, a peace officer may

- (a) enlist such assistance as the officer deems necessary; and
- (b) use as much force as is necessary in the circumstances.

REPORT OF SEIZURE, FINDING, ETC.

12.1 Subject to the regulations, every peace officer, inspector or prescribed person who seizes, finds or otherwise acquires a controlled substance, precursor or chemical offence-related property shall, within 30 days,

- (a) prepare a report setting out
  - (i) the substance, precursor or property,
  - (ii) the amount of it that was seized, found or acquired,
  - (iii) the place where it was seized, found or acquired,
  - (iv) the date on which it was seized, found or acquired,
  - (v) the name of the police force, agency or entity to which the peace officer, inspector or prescribed person belongs,
  - (vi) the number of the file or police report related to the seizure, finding or acquisition, and
  - (vii) any other prescribed information;
- (b) cause the report to be sent to the Minister; and
- (c) in the case of a seizure made under section 11 of this Act, the *Criminal Code* or a power of seizure at common law, cause a copy of the report to be filed with the justice who issued the warrant or another justice for the same

territorial division or, if a warrant was not issued, a justice who would have had jurisdiction to issue a warrant. 2017, c. 7, s. 10.

SECTIONS 489.1 AND 490 OF THE *CRIMINAL CODE* APPLICABLE / Sections 489.1 and 490 of *Criminal Code* applicable / Provisions of this Act applicable / Recognizance.

13. (1) Subject to subsections (2) and (3), sections 489.1 and 490 of the *Criminal Code* apply to any thing seized under this Act.

(2) If a thing seized under this Act is non-chemical offence-related property, sections 489.1 and 490 of the *Criminal Code* apply subject to sections 16 to 22 and subsections 31(6) to (9) of this Act.

(3) If a controlled substance, precursor or chemical offence-related property is seized under this Act, any other Act of Parliament or a power of seizure at common law, the provisions of this Act and the regulations apply in respect of that substance, precursor or property.

(4) If, under this section, an order is made in accordance with paragraph 490(9)(*c*) of the *Criminal Code* for the return of any non-chemical offence-related property seized under this Act, the judge or justice making the order may require the applicant for the order to enter into a recognizance before the judge or justice, with or without sureties, in the amount and with any conditions that the judge or justice directs and, if the judge or justice considers it appropriate, require the applicant to deposit with the judge or justice the sum of money or other valuable security that the judge or justice directs. 2017, c. 7, s. 11.

(5) [*Repealed*, 2017, c. 7, s. 11.]

(6) [*Repealed*, 2017, c. 7, s. 11.]

Division 1

Non-chemical Offence-related Property   2017, c. 7, s. 12.

Restraint Orders

APPLICATION FOR RESTRAINT ORDER / Procedure / Restraint order / Property outside Canada / Conditions / Order in writing / Service of order / Registration of order / Order continues in force / Offence.

14. (1) The Attorney General may make an application in accordance with this section for a restraint order in respect of any non-chemical offence-related property.

(2) The application for a restraint order may be made *ex parte* and shall be made in writing to a judge and be accompanied by an affidavit of the Attorney General or any other person deposing to the following matters

(*a*) the offence to which the property relates;

(*b*) the person who is believed to be in possession of the property; and

DRUGS

(c) a description of the property.

(3) The judge to whom the application is made may, if satisfied that there are reasonable grounds to believe that the property is non-chemical offence-related property, make a restraint order prohibiting any person from disposing of, or otherwise dealing with any interest in, the property specified in the order other than in the manner that is specified in the order.

(4) A restraint order may be issued under this section in respect of property situated outside Canada, with any modifications that the circumstances require.

(5) A restraint order made by a judge under this section may be subject to such reasonable conditions as the judge thinks fit.

(6) A restraint order made under this section shall be made in writing.

(7) A copy of a restraint order made under this section shall be served on the person to whom the order is addressed in such manner as the judge making the order directs or in accordance with the rules of the court.

(8) A copy of a restraint order made under this section shall be registered against any property in accordance with the laws of the province in which the property is situated.

(9) A restraint order made under this section remains in effect until
- (a) an order is made under subsection 19(3) or 19.1(3) of this Act or subsection 490(9) or (11) of the *Criminal Code* in relation to the property; or
- (b) an order of forfeiture of the property is made under subsection 16(1) or 17(2) of this Act or section 490 of the *Criminal Code*.

(10) Any person on whom a restraint order made under this section is served in accordance with this section and who, while the order is in force, acts in contravention of or fails to comply with the order is guilty of an indictable offence or an offence punishable on summary conviction. 1996, c. 16, s. 60; 2001, c. 32, s. 49; 2017, c. 7, s. 13.

14.1 [*Repealed*, 2017, c. 7, s. 14.] 2001, c. 32, s. 50; 2017, c. 7, s. 14.

SECTIONS 489.1 AND 490 OF THE *CRIMINAL CODE* APPLICABLE / Recognizance.

15. (1) Subject to sections 16 to 22, sections 489.1 and 490 of the *Criminal Code* apply, with any modifications that the circumstances require, to any property that is the subject of a restraint order made under section 14.

(2) If, under this section, an order is made in accordance with paragraph 490(9)(c) of the *Criminal Code* for the return of any property that is the subject of a restraint order made under section 14, the judge or justice making the order may require the applicant for the order to enter into a recognizance before the judge or justice, with or without sureties, in the amount and with any conditions that the judge or justice directs and, if the judge or justice considers it appropriate, require the applicant to deposit with the judge or justice the sum of money or other valuable security that the judge or justice directs. 2017, c. 7, s. 14.

Management Orders

MANAGEMENT ORDER / Appointment of Minister of Public Works and Government Services / Power to manage / Application for destruction order / Notice required before destruction / Manner of giving notice / Destruction order / Application for forfeiture order / When management order ceases to have effect / For greater certainty / Application to vary conditions.

15.1 (1) On application of the Attorney General or of any other person with the written consent of the Attorney General, a justice in the case of non-chemical offence-related property seized under section 11 of this Act, the *Criminal Code* or a power of seizure at common law, or a judge in the case of property restrained under section 14, may, if they are of the opinion that the circumstances so require,

    (*a*) appoint a person to take control of and to manage or otherwise deal with all or part of the property in accordance with the directions of the judge or justice; and

    (*b*) require any person having possession of that property to give possession of the property to the person appointed under paragraph (*a*).

(2) If the Attorney General of Canada so requests, a judge or justice appointing a person under subsection (1) shall appoint the Minister of Public Works and Government Services.

(3) The power to manage or otherwise deal with property under subsection (1) includes

    (*a*) the power to make an interlocutory sale of perishable or rapidly depreciating property;

    (*b*) the power to destroy, in accordance with subsections (4) to (7), property that has little or no value; and

    (*c*) the power to have property, other than real property or a conveyance, forfeited to Her Majesty in accordance with subsection (8).

(4) Before a person who is appointed to manage property destroys property that has little or no value, they shall apply to a court for a destruction order.

(5) Before making a destruction order, a court shall require notice in accordance with subsection (6) to be given to and may hear any person who, in the court's opinion, appears to have a valid interest in the property.

(6) A notice shall

    (*a*) be given in the manner that the court directs or that may be specified in the rules of the court; and

    (*b*) specify the effective period of the notice that the court considers reasonable or that may be set out in the rules of the court.

(7) A court shall order that the property be destroyed if it is satisfied that the property has little or no financial or other value.

(8) On application by a person who is appointed to manage the property, a court shall order that the property, other than real property or a conveyance, be forfeited to Her Majesty to be disposed of or otherwise dealt with in accordance with the law if

DRUGS

    (a) a notice is given or published in the manner that the court directs or that may be specified in the rules of the court;

    (b) the notice specifies a period of 60 days during which a person may make an application to the court asserting their interest in the property; and

    (c) during that period, no one makes such an application.

(9) A management order ceases to have effect when the property that is the subject of the management order is returned in accordance with the law, destroyed or forfeited to Her Majesty.

(10) For greater certainty, if property that is the subject of a management order is sold, the management order applies to the net proceeds of the sale.

(11) The Attorney General may at any time apply to the judge or justice to cancel or vary any condition to which a management order is subject but may not apply to vary an appointment made under subsection (2). 2017, c. 7, s. 14.

Forfeiture   2017, c. 7, s. 15.

FORFEITURE OF PROPERTY / Property related to other offences / Property outside Canada / Appeal.

16. (1) Subject to sections 18 to 19.1, if a person is convicted, or discharged under section 730 of the *Criminal Code*, of a designated substance offence and, on application of the Attorney General, the court is satisfied, on a balance of probabilities, that non-chemical offence-related property is related to the commission of the offence, the court shall

    (a) if the prosecution of the offence was commenced at the instance of the government of a province and conducted by or on behalf of that government, order that the property be forfeited to Her Majesty in right of that province to be disposed of or otherwise dealt with in accordance with the law by the Attorney General or Solicitor General of that province; and

    (b) in any other case, order that the property be forfeited to Her Majesty in right of Canada to be disposed of or otherwise dealt with in accordance with the law by the member of the Queen's Privy Council for Canada that is designated by the Governor in Council for the purposes of this paragraph.

(2) Subject to sections 18 to 19.1, if the evidence does not establish to the satisfaction of the court that property in respect of which an order of forfeiture would otherwise be made under subsection (1) is related to the commission of the designated substance offence of which a person is convicted or discharged, but the court is satisfied, beyond a reasonable doubt, that the property is non-chemical offence-related property, the court may make an order of forfeiture under subsection (1) in relation to that property.

(2.1) An order may be issued under this section in respect of property situated outside Canada, with any modifications that the circumstances require.

(3) A person who has been convicted or discharged of a designated substance offence or the Attorney General may appeal to the court of appeal from an order or a failure to make an order under subsection (1) as if the appeal were an appeal against the sentence imposed on the person in respect of the offence. 2001, c. 32, s. 51; 2017, c. 7, s. 16.

APPLICATION FOR *IN REM* FORFEITURE / Order of forfeiture of property / Accused deemed absconded / Who may dispose of forfeited property / Property outside Canada.

17. (1) Where an information has been laid in respect of a designated substance offence, the Attorney General may make an application to a judge for an order of forfeiture under subsection (2).

(2) Subject to sections 18 to 19.1, where an application is made to a judge under subsection (1) and the judge is satisfied

(a) beyond a reasonable doubt that any property is non-chemical offence-related property,

(b) that proceedings were commenced in respect of a designated substance offence to which the property referred to in paragraph (a) is related, and

(c) that the accused charged with the designated substance offence has died or absconded,

the judge shall order that the property be forfeited and disposed of in accordance with subsection (4).

(3) For the purposes of subsection (2), an accused shall be deemed to have absconded in connection with a designated substance offence if

(a) an information has been laid alleging the commission of the offence by the accused,

(b) a warrant for the arrest of the accused has been issued in relation to that information, and

(c) reasonable attempts to arrest the accused pursuant to the warrant have been unsuccessful during a period of six months beginning on the day on which the warrant was issued,

and the accused shall be deemed to have so absconded on the last day of that six month period.

(4) For the purposes of subsection (2),

(a) if the proceedings referred to in paragraph (2)(b) were commenced at the instance of the government of a province, the judge shall order that the property be forfeited to Her Majesty in right of that province and disposed of or otherwise dealt with in accordance with the law by the Attorney General or Solicitor General of that province, and

(b) in any other case, the judge shall order that the property be forfeited to Her Majesty in right of Canada and disposed of or otherwise dealt with in accordance with the law by the member of the Queen's Privy Council for Canada that is designated by the Governor in Council for the purposes of this paragraph.

DRUGS

(5) An order may be issued under this section in respect of property situated outside Canada, with any modifications that the circumstances require. 2001, c. 32, s. 52; 2017, c. 7, s. 17.

VOIDABLE TRANSFERS.

18. A court may, before ordering that property be forfeited under subsection 16(1) or 17(2), set aside any conveyance or transfer of the property that occurred after the property was seized or restrained, unless the conveyance or transfer was for valuable consideration to a person acting in good faith. 2017, c. 7, s. 18.

NOTICE / Manner of giving notice / Order of restoration of property.

19. (1) Before making an order under subsection 16(1) or 17(2) in relation to any property, a court shall require notice in accordance with subsection (2) to be given to, and may hear, any person who, in the opinion of the court, appears to have a valid interest in the property.

(2) A notice shall
  (*a*) be given in the manner that the court directs or that may be specified in the rules of the court;
  (*b*) specify the period that the court considers reasonable or that may be set out in the rules of the court during which a person may make an application to the court asserting their interest in the property; and
  (*c*) set out the designated substance offence charged and a description of the property.

(3) Where a court is satisfied that any person, other than
  (*a*) a person who was charged with a designated substance offence, or
  (*b*) a person who acquired title to or a right of possession of the property from a person referred to in paragraph (*a*) under circumstances that give rise to a reasonable inference that the title or right was transferred for the purpose of avoiding the forfeiture of the property,

is the lawful owner or is lawfully entitled to possession of any property or any part of any property that would otherwise be forfeited pursuant to an order made under subsection 16(1) or 17(2) and that the person appears innocent of any complicity in an offence referred to in paragraph (*a*) or of any collusion in relation to such an offence, the court may order that the property or part be returned to that person. 2017, c. 7, s. 19.

NOTICE / Manner of giving notice / Non-forfeiture of real property / Factors in relation to dwelling-house.

19.1 (1) If all or part of the property that would otherwise be forfeited under subsection 16(1) or 17(2) is a dwelling-house, before making an order of forfeiture, a court shall require notice in accordance with subsection (2) to be given to and may hear any person who resides in the dwelling-house and is a member of the immediate family of the person charged with or convicted, or discharged under section 730 of the *Criminal Code*, of the indictable offence under this Act in relation to which the property would be forfeited.

(2) A notice shall

   (*a*) be given in the manner that the court directs or that may be specified in the rules of the court;

   (*b*) specify the period that the court considers reasonable or that may be set out in the rules of the court during which a member of the immediate family who resides in the dwelling-house may make themselves known to the court; and

   (*c*) set out the offence charged and a description of the property.

(3) Subject to an order made under subsection 19(3), if a court is satisfied that the impact of an order of forfeiture made under subsection 16(1) or 17(2) in respect of real property would be disproportionate to the nature and gravity of the offence, the circumstances surrounding the commission of the offence and the criminal record, if any, of the person charged with or convicted, or discharged under section 730 of the *Criminal Code*, of the offence, as the case may be, it may decide not to order the forfeiture of the property or part of the property and may revoke any restraint order made in respect of that property or part.

(4) Where all or part of the property that would otherwise be forfeited under subsection 16(1) or 17(2) is a dwelling-house, when making a decision under subsection (3), the court shall also consider

   (*a*) the impact of an order of forfeiture on any member of the immediate family of the person charged with or convicted or discharged of the offence, if the dwelling-house was the member's principal residence at the time the charge was laid and continues to be the member's principal residence, and

   (*b*) whether the member referred to in paragraph (*a*) appears innocent of any complicity in the offence or of any collusion in relation to the offence. 2001, c. 32, s. 53; 2017, c. 7, s. 20.

APPLICATION / Fixing day for hearing / Notice / Order declaring interest not affected by forfeiture / Appeal from order made under subsection (4) / Return of property.

20. (1) If any property is forfeited to Her Majesty under an order made under subsection 16(1) or 17(2), any person who claims an interest in the property, other than

   (*a*) in the case of property forfeited under an order made under subsection 16(1), a person who was convicted, or discharged under section 730 of the *Criminal Code*, of the designated substance offence in relation to which the property was forfeited;

   (*b*) in the case of property forfeited pursuant to an order made under subsection 17(2), a person who was charged with the designated substance offence in relation to which the property was forfeited, or

   (*c*) a person who acquired title to or a right of possession of the property from a person referred to in paragraph (*a*) or (*b*) under circumstances that give rise to a reasonable inference that the title or right was transferred from that person for the purpose of avoiding the forfeiture of the property, may, within thirty days after the forfeiture, apply by notice in writing to a judge for an order under subsection (4).

(2) The judge to whom an application is made under subsection (1) shall fix a day not less than thirty days after the date of the filing of the application for the hearing of the application.

(3) An applicant shall serve a notice of the application made under subsection (1) and of the hearing of it on the Attorney General at least fifteen days before the day fixed for the hearing.

(4) Where, on the hearing of an application made under subsection (1), the judge is satisfied that the applicant

(a) is not a persons referred to in paragraph (1)(a), (b) or (c) and appears innocent of any complicity in any designated substance offence that resulted in the forfeiture of the property or of any collusion in relation to such an offence, and

(b) exercised all reasonable care to be satisfied that the property was not likely to have been used in connection with the commission of an unlawful act by the person who was permitted by the applicant to obtain possession of the property or from whom the applicant obtained possession or, where the applicant is a mortgagee or lienholder, by the mortgagor or lien-giver,

the judge may make an order declaring that the interest of the applicant is not affected by the forfeiture and declaring the nature and the extent or value of the interest.

(5) An applicant or the Attorney General may appeal to the court of appeal from an order made under subsection (4), and the provisions of Part XXI of the *Criminal Code* with respect to procedure on appeals apply, with such modifications as the circumstances require, in respect of appeals under this subsection.

(6) The Minister shall, on application made to the Minister by any person in respect of whom a judge has made an order under subsection (4), and where the periods with respect to the taking of appeals from that order have expired and any appeal from that order taken under subsection (5) has been determined, direct that

(a) the property, or the part of it to which the interest of the applicant relates, be returned to the applicant; or

(b) an amount equal to the value of the interest of the applicant, as declared in the order, be paid to the applicant. 2017, c. 7, s. 21.

APPEALS FROM ORDERS UNDER SUBSECTION 17(2).

21. Any person who, in their opinion, is aggrieved by an order made under subsection 17(2) may appeal from the order as if the order were an appeal against conviction or against a judgment or verdict of acquittal, as the case may be, under Part XXI of the *Criminal Code*, and that Part applies, with such modifications as the circumstances require, in respect of such an appeal.

SUSPENSION OF ORDER PENDING APPEAL.

22. Notwithstanding anything in this Act, the operation of an order made in respect of property under subsection 16(1), 17(2) or 20(4) is suspended pending

    (a) any application made in respect of the property under any of those provisions or any other provision of this or any other Act of Parliament that provides for restoration or forfeiture of the property, or

    (b) any appeal taken from an order of forfeiture or restoration in respect of the property,

and the property shall not be disposed of or otherwise dealt with until thirty days have expired after an order is made under any of those provisions.

[*Heading repealed*, 2001, c. 32, s. 54.]

Division 2

Controlled Substances, Precursors and Chemical Offence-related Property

RETURN / Receipt / Report by peace officer.

23. (1) A peace officer, inspector or prescribed person who seizes, finds or otherwise acquires a controlled substance, precursor or chemical offence-related property may return it to the person who is its lawful owner or who is lawfully entitled to its possession if the peace officer, inspector or prescribed person is satisfied

    (a) that there is no dispute as to who is the lawful owner or is lawfully entitled to possession of the substance, precursor or property; and

    (b) that the continued detention of the substance, precursor or property is not required for the purposes of a preliminary inquiry, trial or other proceeding under this Act or any other Act of Parliament.

(2) When the substance, precursor or property is returned, the peace officer, inspector or prescribed person shall obtain a receipt for it.

(3) In the case of a seizure made under section 11 of this Act, the *Criminal Code* or a power of seizure at common law, the peace officer shall make a report about the return to the justice who issued the warrant or another justice for the same territorial division or, if a warrant was not issued, a justice who would have had jurisdiction to issue a warrant. 2017, c. 7, s. 22.

APPLICATION FOR RETURN / Order to return as soon as practicable / Order to return at specified time / Forfeiture order / Payment of compensation in lieu.

24. (1) If a controlled substance, precursor or chemical offence-related property has been seized, found or otherwise acquired by a peace officer, inspector or prescribed person, any person may, within 60 days after the date of the seizure,

DRUGS

finding or acquisition, on prior notification being given to the Attorney General in the prescribed manner, apply, by notice in writing to a justice in the jurisdiction in which it is being detained, for an order to return it to the person.

(2) If, on the hearing of an application made under subsection (1), a justice is satisfied that an applicant is the lawful owner or is lawfully entitled to possession of the substance, precursor or property and the Attorney General does not indicate that it or a portion of it may be required for the purposes of a preliminary inquiry, trial or other proceeding under this Act or any other Act of Parliament, the justice shall, subject to subsection (5), order that it or the portion be returned as soon as practicable to the applicant.

(3) If, on the hearing of an application made under subsection (1), a justice is satisfied that an applicant is the lawful owner or is lawfully entitled to possession of the substance, precursor or property but the Attorney General indicates that it or a portion of it may be required for the purposes of a preliminary inquiry, trial or other proceeding under this Act or any other Act of Parliament, the justice shall, subject to subsection (5), order that it or the portion be returned to the applicant

   (*a*) on the expiry of 180 days after the day on which the application was made, if no proceeding in relation to it has been commenced before that time; or

   (*b*) on the final conclusion of the proceeding or any other proceeding in relation to it, if the applicant is not found guilty in those proceedings of an offence committed in relation to it.

(4) If, on the hearing of an application made under subsection (1), a justice is not satisfied that an applicant is the lawful owner or is lawfully entitled to possession of the substance, precursor or property, and it or a portion of it is not required for the purposes of a preliminary inquiry, trial or other proceeding under this Act or any other Act of Parliament, the justice shall order that it or the portion be forfeited to Her Majesty to be disposed of or otherwise dealt with in accordance with the regulations or, if there are no applicable regulations, in the manner that the Minister directs.

(5) If, on the hearing of an application made under subsection (1), a justice is satisfied that an applicant is the lawful owner or is lawfully entitled to possession of the substance, precursor or property, but it was disposed of or otherwise dealt with under section 26, the justice shall order that an amount equal to its value be paid to the applicant. 2017, c. 7, s. 22.

FORFEITURE IF NO APPLICATION.

25. If no application for the return of a controlled substance, precursor or chemical offence-related property has been made under subsection 24(1) within 60 days after the date of the seizure, finding or acquisition by a peace officer, inspector or prescribed person and it or a portion of it is not required for the purposes of a preliminary inquiry, trial or other proceeding under this Act or any other Act of Parliament, it or the portion is forfeited to Her Majesty and may be disposed of or otherwise dealt with in accordance with the regulations or, if there are no applicable regulations, in the manner that the Minister directs. 2017, c. 7, s. 22.

EXPEDITED DISPOSITION.

26. If a precursor or chemical offence-related property — whose storage or handling poses a risk to health or safety — or a controlled substance, or a portion of any of them, is not required for the purposes of a preliminary inquiry, trial or other proceeding under this Act or any other Act of Parliament, it or the portion may be disposed of or otherwise dealt with by the Minister, a peace officer or a prescribed person in accordance with the regulations or, if there are no applicable regulations, in the manner that the Minister directs. 2017, c. 7, s. 22.

DISPOSITION FOLLOWING PROCEEDINGS.

27. Subject to section 24, if, in a preliminary inquiry, trial or other proceeding under this Act or any other Act of Parliament, the court before which the proceedings have been brought is satisfied that any controlled substance, precursor or chemical offence-related property that is the subject of proceedings before the court is no longer required by that court or any other court, the court

  (a) shall

    (i) if it is satisfied that the person from whom the substance, precursor or property was seized came into possession of it lawfully and continued to deal with it lawfully, order that it be returned to the person, or

    (ii) if it is satisfied that possession of the substance, precursor or property by the person from whom it was seized is unlawful and the person who is the lawful owner or is lawfully entitled to its possession is known, order that it be returned to the person who is the lawful owner or is lawfully entitled to its possession; and

  (b) may, if it is not satisfied that the substance, precursor or property should be returned under subparagraph (a)(i) or (ii) or if possession of it by the person from whom it was seized is unlawful and the person who is the lawful owner or is lawfully entitled to its possession is not known, order that it be forfeited to Her Majesty to be disposed of or otherwise dealt with in accordance with the regulations or, if there are no applicable regulations, in the manner that the Minister directs. 2017, c. 7, s. 23.

DISPOSITION WITH CONSENT.

28. If a controlled substance, precursor or chemical offence-related property has been seized, found or otherwise acquired by a peace officer, inspector or prescribed person and it or a portion of it is not required for the purposes of a preliminary inquiry, trial or other proceeding under this Act or any other Act of Parliament, the person who is its lawful owner may consent to its disposition, and when that consent is given, it or the portion is forfeited to Her Majesty and may be disposed of or otherwise dealt with in accordance with the regulations or, if there are no applicable regulations, in the manner that the Minister directs. 2017, c. 7, s. 24.

DRUGS

REPORT OF DISPOSITION / Interpretation.

29. (1) Subject to the regulations, every peace officer, inspector or prescribed person who disposes of or otherwise deals with a controlled substance, precursor or chemical offence-related property under this Division shall, within 30 days, prepare a report setting out the following information and cause the report to be sent to the Minister:

    (*a*) the substance, precursor or property;

    (*b*) the amount of it that was disposed of or otherwise dealt with;

    (*c*) the manner in which it was disposed of or otherwise dealt with;

    (*d*) the date on which it was disposed of or otherwise dealt with;

    (*e*) the name of the police force, agency or entity to which the peace officer, inspector or prescribed person belongs;

    (*f*) the number of the file or police report related to the disposition of it or other dealing with it; and

    (*g*) any other prescribed information.

(2) For the purposes of subsection (1), dealing with a controlled substance, precursor or chemical offence-related property by a peace officer includes using it to conduct an investigation or for training purposes. 2017, c. 7, s. 24.

Part IV / ADMINISTRATION AND COMPLIANCE

Inspectors

DESIGNATION OF INSPECTORS / Certificate of designation.

30. (1) The Minister may designate, in accordance with the regulations made pursuant to paragraph 55(1)(*n*), any person as an inspector for the purposes of this Act and the regulations.

(2) Every inspector shall be provided with a certificate of designation in a form established by the Minister and, on entering any place under subsection 31(1), shall, on request, produce the certificate to the person in charge of the place. 2015, c. 22, s. 2; 2017, c. 7, s. 25.

POWERS OF INSPECTOR / Place / Means of telecommunication / Limitation — access by means of telecommunication / Person accompanying inspector / Entering private property / Warrant to enter dwelling-house / Authority to issue warrant / Use of force / Assistance to inspector / Storage / Notice / Return by inspector / Return or disposition by Minister.

31. (1) Subject to subsection (2), an inspector may, for a purpose related to verifying compliance or preventing non-compliance with the provisions of this Act or the regulations, enter any place, including a conveyance, referred to in subsection (1.1) and may for that purpose

    (*a*) open and examine any receptacle or package found in that place in which a controlled substance, precursor or designated device may be found;

(b) examine any thing found in that place that is used or may be capable of being used for the production, preservation, packaging or storage of a controlled substance or a precursor;

(c) examine any labels or advertising material or records, books, electronic data or other documents found in that place with respect to any controlled substance, precursor, or designated device other than the records of the medical condition of persons, and make copies thereof or take extracts therefrom;

(d) use or cause to be used any computer system at that place to examine any electronic data referred to in paragraph (c);

(e) reproduce any document from any electronic data referred to in paragraph (c) or cause it to be reproduced, in the form of a printout or other output;

(f) take the labels or advertising material or records, books or other documents referred to in paragraph (c) or the printout or other output referred to in paragraph (e) for examination or copying;

(g) use or cause to be used any copying equipment at that place to make copies of any document;

(g.1) take photographs and make recordings and sketches;

(h) examine any substance found in that place and take, for the purpose of analysis, such samples thereof as are reasonably required; and

(i) seize and detain, in accordance with this Part, any controlled substance, precursor, designated device or conveyance found in that place the seizure and detention of which the inspector believes on reasonable grounds are necessary;

(j) order the owner or person having possession, care or control of any controlled substance, precursor, designated device or other thing to which the provisions of this Act or the regulations apply that is found in that place to move it or, for any time that may be necessary, not to move it or to restrict its movement;

(k) order the owner or person having possession, care or control of any conveyance that is found in that place and that the inspector believes on reasonable grounds contains a controlled substance, precursor or designated device to stop the conveyance, to move it or, for any time that may be necessary, not to move it or to restrict its movement;

(l) order any person in that place to establish their identity to the inspector's satisfaction; and

(m) order a person who, at that place, conducts an activity to which the provisions of this Act or the regulations apply to stop or start the activity.

(1.1) For the purposes of subsection (1), the inspector may only enter a place in which they believe on reasonable grounds

(a) a controlled substance, precursor, designated device or document relating to the administration of this Act or the regulations is located;

(b) an activity could be conducted under a licence, permit, authorization or exemption that is under consideration by the Minister;

(c) an activity to which the provisions of this Act or the regulations apply is being conducted; or

DRUGS

    (d) an activity was being conducted under a licence, permit, authorization or exemption before the expiry or revocation of the licence, permit, authorization or exemption, in which case the inspector may enter the place only within 45 days after the day on which it expired or was revoked.

(1.2) For the purposes of subsections (1) and (1.1), an inspector is considered to have entered a place when they access it remotely by a means of telecommunication.

(1.3) An inspector who enters remotely, by a means of telecommunication, a place that is not accessible to the public must do so with the knowledge of the owner or person in charge of the place and only for the period necessary for any purpose referred to in subsection (1).

(1.4) An inspector may be accompanied by any other person that the inspector believes is necessary to help them exercise their powers or perform their duties or functions under this section.

(1.5) An inspector and any person accompanying them may enter and pass through private property, other than a dwelling-house on that property, in order to gain entry to a place referred to in subsection (1.1).

(2) In the case of a dwelling-house, an inspector may enter it only with the consent of an occupant or under the authority of a warrant issued under subsection (3).

(3) A justice may, on *ex parte* application, issue a warrant authorizing the inspector named in it to enter a place and exercise any of the powers mentioned in paragraphs (1)(*a*) to (*m*), subject to any conditions that are specified in the warrant, if the justice is satisfied by information on oath that

    (a) the place is a dwelling-house but otherwise meets the conditions for entry described in subsections (1) and (1.1);

    (b) entry to the dwelling-house is necessary for the purpose of verifying compliance or preventing non-compliance with the provisions of this Act or the regulations; and

    (c) entry to the dwelling-house has been refused or there are reasonable grounds to believe that entry will be refused.

(4) In executing a warrant issued under subsection (3), an inspector shall not use force unless the inspector is accompanied by a peace officer and the use of force is specifically authorized in the warrant.

(5) The owner or other person in charge of a place entered by an inspector and every person found there shall give the inspector all reasonable assistance in that person's power and provide the inspector with any information that the inspector may reasonably require.

(6) Anything that is seized and detained by an inspector under this section may, at the inspector's discretion, be kept or stored at the place where it was seized or, at the inspector's direction, be removed to any other proper place.

(7) An inspector who seizes anything under this section shall take any measures that are reasonable in the circumstances to give to the owner or other person in charge of the place where the seizure occurred notice of the seizure and of the location where the thing is being kept or stored.

(8) If an inspector determines that to verify compliance or prevent non-compliance with the provisions of this Act or the regulations it is no longer necessary to detain anything seized by the inspector under this section, the inspector shall notify in writing the owner or other person in charge of the place where the seizure occurred of that determination and, on being issued a receipt for it, shall return the thing to that person.

(9) If a period of 120 days has elapsed after the date of a seizure under this section and the thing has not been returned, disposed of or otherwise dealt with in accordance with subsection (8) or any of sections 24 to 27, it shall be returned, disposed of or otherwise dealt with in accordance with the regulations or, if there are no applicable regulations, in the manner that the Minister directs. 2015, c. 22, s. 3; 2017, c. 7, s. 26(1), (3) to (8).

OBSTRUCTING INSPECTOR / False statements / Interference.

32. (1) No person shall, by act or omission, obstruct an inspector who is engaged in the exercise of their powers or the performance of their duties or functions under this Act or the regulations.

(2) No person shall knowingly make any false or misleading statement verbally or in writing to an inspector who is engaged in the exercise of their powers or the performance of their duties or functions under this Act or the regulations.

(3) No person shall, without the authority of an inspector, remove, alter or interfere in any way with anything seized, detained or taken under section 31. 2017, c. 7, s. 27(1), (2).

Part V / ADMINISTRATIVE ORDERS FOR CONTRAVENTIONS OF DESIGNATED REGULATIONS

DESIGNATION OF REGULATIONS.

33. The Governor in Council may, by regulation, designate any regulation made under this Act (in this Part referred to as a "designated regulation") as a regulation the contravention of which shall be dealt with under this Part.

CONTRAVENTION OF DESIGNATED REGULATION.

34. Where the Minister has reasonable grounds to believe that a person has contravened a designated regulation, the Minister shall
  (a) in the prescribed manner, serve a notice to appear on the person; and
  (b) send a copy of the notice to appear to an adjudicator and direct the adjudicator to conduct a hearing to determine whether the contravention has occurred and to notify the Minister of the adjudicator's determination.

Note: If Bill C-37, introduced in the 1st session of the 42nd Parliament and entitled *An Act to amend the Controlled Drugs and Substances Act and to make related amendments to other Acts*, receives royal assent, then, on the first day on which both s. 28 of that Act and s. 199(2) of 2018, c. 16 are in force, s. 34 is amended by enacting subsec. (2), 2018, c. 16, s. 199(1):

Maximum penalty

(2) The maximum penalty for a violation is $1,000,000.

INTERIM ORDER / Idem.

35. (1) Where the Minister has reasonable grounds to believe that a person has contravened a designated regulation and the Minister is of the opinion that, as a result of that contravention, there is a substantial risk of immediate danger to the health or safety of any person, the Minister may, without giving prior notice to the person believed to have contravened the designated regulation, make an interim order in respect of the person

   (a) prohibiting the person from doing anything that the person would otherwise be permitted to do under their licence, permit or authorization, or

   (b) subjecting the doing of anything under the designated regulation by the person to the terms and conditions specified in the interim order,

and may, for that purpose, suspend, cancel or amend the licence, permit or authorization issued or granted to the person or take any other measures set out in the regulations.

(2) Where the Minister makes an interim order under subsection (1), the Minister shall forthwith

   (a) in the prescribed manner, serve the interim order on the person;

   (b) in the prescribed manner, serve a notice to appear on the person; and

   (c) send a copy of the interim order and the notice to appear to an adjudicator and direct the adjudicator to conduct a hearing to determine whether the contravention has occurred and to notify the Minister of the adjudicator's determination.

HEARING BY ADJUDICATOR / Change of hearing date / Proceedings on default / Time and place.

36. (1) Where an adjudicator receives from the Minister a copy of a notice to appear under paragraph 34(b) or 35(2)(c), the adjudicator shall conduct a hearing on a date to be fixed by the adjudicator at the request of the person on whom the notice was served, on two days notice being given to the adjudicator, which hearing date may not

   (a) in the case of a notice served under paragraph 34(a), be less than thirty days, or more than forty-five days, after the day of service of the notice; or

   (b) in the case of a notice served under paragraph 35(2)(b), be less than three days, or more than forty-five days, after the day of service of the notice.

(2) Where the adjudicator is unable to conduct a hearing on the date referred to in subsection (1), the adjudicator shall forthwith notify the person and fix, for the purpose of holding the hearing, the earliest possible date to which the adjudicator and the person agree.

(3) Where an adjudicator has received a copy of a notice to appear referred to in subsection (1) and where the person on whom the notice is served has not requested a date for a hearing within forty-five days after the notice was served on that person, or where the person, having requested a hearing, fails to appear for the hearing, the adjudicator shall proceed to make a determination in the absence of the person.

(4) An adjudicator may, subject to the regulations, determine the time and place of any hearing or other proceeding under this Part.

NOTICE TO APPEAR.

37. A notice to appear served on a person under paragraph 34(*a*) or 35(2)(*b*) shall
- (*a*) specify the designated regulation that the Minister believes the person has contravened;
- (*b*) state the grounds on which the Minister believes the contravention has occurred;
- (*c*) state that the matter has been referred to an adjudicator for a hearing to be conducted on a date within the applicable period described in paragraph 36(1)(*a*) or (*b*); and
- (*d*) set out such other information as is prescribed.

PROOF OF SERVICE.

38. Proof of service of any notice, order or interim order under this Part shall be given in the prescribed manner.

POWERS OF ADJUDICATOR.

39. For the purposes of this Act, an adjudicator has and may exercise the powers of a person appointed as a commissioner under Part I of the *Inquiries Act*.

HEARING PROCEDURE.

40. An adjudicator shall deal with all matters as informally and expeditiously as the circumstances and considerations of fairness and natural justice permit.

DETERMINATION BY ADJUDICATOR / Notice of determination / Ministerial orders / Idem.

41. (1) An adjudicator shall, after the conclusion of a hearing referred to in subsection 36(1) or a proceeding referred to in subsection 36(3), within the prescribed time, make a determination that the person who is the subject of the hearing or proceeding contravened or did not contravene the designated regulation.

(2) Where an adjudicator has made a determination under subsection (1), the adjudicator shall
- (*a*) forthwith notify the person and the Minister of the adjudicator's determination and the reasons; and

(b) where the adjudicator has determined that the person has contravened the designated regulation, notify the person of the opportunity to make representations to the Minister in writing in accordance with the regulations and within the prescribed time.

(3) Where an adjudicator has made a determination referred to in paragraph (2)(b) and the Minister has considered the determination and any representations referred to in that paragraph, the Minister shall forthwith make an order

(a) prohibiting the person from doing anything that they would, if they were in compliance with the designated regulation, be permitted to do, or

(b) subjecting the doing of anything under the designated regulation by the person to the terms and conditions specified in the order,

and may, for that purpose, suspend, cancel or amend any licence, permit or authorization issued or granted to the person under the regulations or take any other measures set out in the regulations.

(4) An order made under subsection (3) shall be served on the person to whom it is directed in the prescribed manner.

EFFECT OF ORDER / Cessation of effect / Application to revoke order / Revocation of order.

42. (1) An interim order made under subsection 35(1) and an order made under subsection 41(3) have effect from the time that they are served on the person to whom they are directed.

(2) An interim order that was made in respect of a person believed to have contravened a designated regulation ceases to have effect

(a) where the Minister makes an order under subsection 41(3), at the time the order is served on the person; and

(b) where an adjudicator has determined that the person did not contravene the designated regulation, at the time the adjudicator makes the determination.

(3) A person in respect of whom an order was made under subsection 41(3) may make an application in writing to the Minister in accordance with the regulations to revoke the order.

(4) The Minister may, in the prescribed circumstances, revoke, in whole or in part, any order made under subsection 41(3).

OFFENCE FOR CONTRAVENTION OF ORDER.

43. Every person commits an offence who contravenes an order or an interim order made under this Part.

Note: Part V replaced, 2017, c. 7, s. 28 (to come into force by order of the Governor in Council):

Administrative Monetary Penalties

Violation

Commission of violation.

33. Every person who contravenes a provision designated by regulations made under paragraph 34(1)(*a*), or contravenes an order made under section 45.1 or 45.2 or reviewed under section 45.4, commits a violation and is liable to the penalty established in accordance with the provisions of this Act and the regulations.

Powers of the Governor in Council and the Minister

Regulations

34. (1) The Governor in Council may make regulations
   (*a*) designating as a violation that may be proceeded with in accordance with this Act the contravention of any specified provision of this Act — except a provision of Part I — or the regulations;
   (*b*) fixing a penalty, or a range of penalties, in respect of each violation;
   (*c*) classifying each violation as a minor violation, a serious violation or a very serious violation; and
   (*d*) respecting the circumstances under which, the criteria by which and the manner in which a penalty may be increased or reduced, including a reduction in the amount that is provided for in a compliance agreement.

Maximum penalty

(2) The maximum penalty for a violation is $30,000.

Criteria for penalty.

35. Unless a penalty is fixed under paragraph 34(1)(*b*), the amount of a penalty shall, in each case, be determined taking into account
   (*a*) the history of compliance with the provisions of this Act or the regulations by the person who committed the violation;
   (*b*) the harm to public health or safety that resulted or could have resulted from the violation;
   (*c*) whether the person made reasonable efforts to mitigate or reverse the violation's effects;
   (*d*) whether the person derived any competitive or economic benefit from the violation; and
   (*e*) any other prescribed criteria.

Notices of violation

36. The Minister may
   (*a*) designate individuals, or classes of individuals, who are authorized to issue notices of violation; and
   (*b*) establish, in respect of each violation, a short-form description to be used in notices of violation.

DRUGS

Proceedings

Issuance of notice of violation

37. (1) If a person who is designated under paragraph 36(*a*) believes on reasonable grounds that a person has committed a violation, the designated person may issue, and shall provide the person with, a notice of violation that
  (*a*) sets out the person's name;
  (*b*) identifies the alleged violation;
  (*c*) sets out the penalty for the violation that the person is liable to pay; and
  (*d*) sets out the particulars concerning the time and manner of payment.

Summary of rights

(2) A notice of violation shall clearly summarize, in plain language, the named person's rights and obligations under this section and sections 38 to 43.7, including the right to have the acts or omissions that constitute the alleged violation or the amount of the penalty reviewed and the procedure for requesting that review.

Penalties

Payment

38. (1) If the person named in the notice pays, in the prescribed time and manner, the amount of the penalty,
  (*a*) they are deemed to have committed the violation in respect of which the amount is paid;
  (*b*) the Minister shall accept that amount as complete satisfaction of the penalty; and
  (*c*) the proceedings commenced in respect of the violation under section 37 are ended.

Alternatives to payment

(2) Instead of paying the penalty set out in a notice of violation, the person named in the notice may, in the prescribed time and manner,
  (*a*) if the penalty is $5,000 or more, request to enter into a compliance agreement with the Minister that ensures the person's compliance with the order or the provision to which the violation relates; or
  (*b*) request a review by the Minister of the acts or omissions that constitute the alleged violation or the amount of the penalty.

Deeming

(3) If the person named in the notice of violation does not pay the penalty in the prescribed time and manner and does not exercise any right referred to in subsection (2) in the prescribed time and manner, they are deemed to have committed the violation identified in the notice.

Compliance Agreements

Compliance agreements

39. (1) After considering a request under paragraph 38(2)(*a*), the Minister may enter into a compliance agreement, as described in that paragraph, with the person making the request on any terms and conditions that are satisfactory to the Minister. The terms and conditions may

   (*a*) include a provision for the giving of reasonable security, in a form and in an amount satisfactory to the Minister, as a guarantee that the person will comply with the compliance agreement; and

   (*b*) provide for the reduction, in whole or in part, of the penalty for the violation.

Deeming

(2) A person who enters into a compliance agreement with the Minister is, on doing so, deemed to have committed the violation in respect of which the compliance agreement was entered into.

Notice of compliance

(3) If the Minister is satisfied that a person who has entered into a compliance agreement has complied with it, the Minister shall cause a notice to that effect to be provided to the person, at which time

   (*a*) the proceedings commenced in respect of the violation under section 37 are ended; and

   (*b*) any security given by the person under the compliance agreement shall be returned to the person.

Notice of default

(4) If the Minister is of the opinion that a person who has entered into a compliance agreement has not complied with it, the Minister shall cause a notice of default to be provided to the person to the effect that

   (*a*) instead of the penalty set out in the notice of violation in respect of which the compliance agreement was entered into, the person is liable to pay, in the prescribed time and manner, twice the amount of that penalty, and, for greater certainty, subsection 34(2) does not apply in respect of that amount; or

   (*b*) the security, if any, given by the person under the compliance agreement shall be forfeited to Her Majesty in right of Canada.

Effect of notice of default

(5) Once provided with the notice of default, the person may not deduct from the amount set out in the notice any amount that they spent under the compliance agreement and

   (*a*) the person is liable to pay the amount set out in the notice; or

   (*b*) if the notice provides for the forfeiture of the security given under the compliance agreement, that security is forfeited to Her Majesty in right of

DRUGS

Canada and the proceedings commenced in respect of the violation under section 37 are ended.

Effect of payment

(6) If a person pays the amount set out in the notice of default in the prescribed time and manner,

    (a) the Minister shall accept the amount as complete satisfaction of the amount owing; and

    (b) the proceedings commenced in respect of the violation under section 37 are ended.

Refusal to enter into compliance agreement

40. (1) If the Minister refuses to enter into a compliance agreement requested under paragraph 38(2)(a), the person who made the request is liable to pay the amount of the penalty in the prescribed time and manner.

Effect of payment

(2) If a person pays the amount referred to in subsection (1),

    (a) they are deemed to have committed the violation in respect of which the payment is made;

    (b) the Minister shall accept the amount as complete satisfaction of the penalty; and

    (c) the proceedings commenced in respect of the violation under section 37 are ended.

Deeming

(3) If a person does not pay the amount referred to in subsection (1) in the prescribed time and manner, they are deemed to have committed the violation identified in the notice of violation.

Review by the Minister

Review — facts

41. (1) On completion of a review requested under paragraph 38(2)(b) with respect to the acts or omissions that constitute the alleged violation, the Minister shall determine whether the person who requested the review committed the violation. If the Minister determines that the person committed the violation but that the amount of the penalty was not established in accordance with the provisions of this Act and the regulations, the Minister shall correct the amount.

Violation not committed — effect

(2) If the Minister determines under subsection (1) that the person who requested the review did not commit the violation, the proceedings commenced in respect of it under section 37 are ended.

Review — penalty

(3) On completion of a review requested under paragraph 38(2)(b) with respect to the amount of the penalty, the Minister shall determine whether the amount of the penalty was established in accordance with the provisions of this Act and the regulations and, if not, the Minister shall correct the amount.

Notice of decision

(4) The Minister shall cause a notice of any decision made under subsection (1) or (3) to be provided to the person who requested the review.

Payment

(5) The person is liable to pay, in the prescribed time and manner, the amount of the penalty that is confirmed or corrected in the Minister's decision made under subsection (1) or (3).

Effect of payment

(6) If a person pays the amount referred to in subsection (5),
  (a) the Minister shall accept the amount as complete satisfaction of the penalty; and
  (b) the proceedings commenced in respect of the violation under section 37 are ended.

Written evidence and submissions

(7) The Minister shall consider only written evidence and written submissions in determining whether a person committed a violation or whether the amount of a penalty was established in accordance with the provisions of this Act and the regulations.

Enforcement

Debts to Her Majesty

42. (1) The following amounts constitute debts due to Her Majesty in right of Canada that may be recovered in the Federal Court:
  (a) the amount of a penalty, from the time the notice of violation setting out the penalty is provided;
  (b) every amount set out in a compliance agreement entered into with the Minister under subsection 39(1), from the time the compliance agreement is entered into;
  (c) the amount set out in a notice of default referred to in subsection 39(4), from the time the notice is provided; and
  (d) the amount of a penalty as set out in a decision of the Minister made under subsection 41(1) or (3), from the time the notice of that decision is provided.

Time limit

(2) No proceedings to recover a debt referred to in subsection (1) may be commenced later than five years after the debt became payable.

Debt final

(3) A debt referred to in subsection (1) is final and not subject to review or to be restrained, prohibited, removed, set aside or otherwise dealt with except to the extent and in the manner provided by sections 38 to 41.

Certificate of default

43. (1) Any debt referred to in subsection 42(1) in respect of which there is a default of payment, or the part of any such debt that has not been paid, may be certified by the Minister.

Judgments

(2) On production to the Federal Court, the certificate shall be registered in that Court and, when registered, has the same force and effect, and all proceedings may be taken on the certificate, as if it were a judgment obtained in that Court for a debt of the amount specified in it and all reasonable costs and charges associated with the registration of the certificate.

Rules About Violations

Certain defences not available

43.1 (1) A person named in a notice of violation does not have a defence by reason that the person
- (*a*) exercised due diligence to prevent the violation; or
- (*b*) reasonably and honestly believed in the existence of facts that, if true, would exonerate the person.

Common law principles

(2) Every rule and principle of the common law that renders any circumstance a justification or excuse in relation to a charge for an offence under this Act applies in respect of a violation to the extent that it is not inconsistent with this Act.

Burden of proof

43.2 In every case when the facts of a violation are reviewed by the Minister, he or she shall determine, on a balance of probabilities, whether the person named in the notice of violation committed the violation identified in the notice.

Violation by corporate officers, etc.

43.3 If a person other than an individual commits a violation under this Act, any of the person's directors, officers, agents or mandataries who directed, authorized, assented to, acquiesced in or participated in the commission of the violation is a party to and liable for the violation whether or not the person who actually committed the violation is proceeded against under this Act.

Vicarious liability — acts of employees and agents

43.4 A person is liable for a violation that is committed by any employee, agent or mandatary of the person acting in the course of the employee's employment or the scope of the agent or mandatary's authority, whether or not the employee, agent or mandatary who actually committed the violation is identified or proceeded against under this Act.

Continuing violation

43.5 A violation that is continued on more than one day constitutes a separate violation in respect of each day on which it is continued.

Other Provisions

Evidence

43.6 In any proceeding in respect of a violation or a prosecution for an offence, a notice of violation purporting to be issued under this Act is admissible in evidence without proof of the signature or official character of the person appearing to have signed the notice of violation.

Time limit

43.7 Proceedings in respect of a violation shall not be commenced later than six months after the Minister becomes aware of the acts or omissions that constitute the alleged violation.

How act or omission may be proceeded with

43.8 If an act or omission may be proceeded with either as a violation or as an offence, proceeding in one manner precludes proceeding in the other.

Certification by Minister

43.9 A document appearing to have been issued by the Minister, certifying the day on which the acts or omissions that constitute the alleged violation became known to the Minister, is admissible in evidence without proof of the signature or official character of the person appearing to have signed the document and, in the absence of evidence to the contrary, is proof that the Minister became aware of the acts or omissions on that day.

Publication of information

43.91 The Minister may, for the purpose of encouraging compliance with the provisions of this Act and the regulations, publish information about any violation after proceedings in respect of it are ended.

DRUGS

Part VI / GENERAL

Analysis

DESIGNATION OF ANALYSTS.

44. The Minister may designate, in accordance with the regulations made pursuant to paragraph 55(1)(*o*), any person as an analyst for the purposes of this Act and the regulations.

ANALYSIS / Report.

45. (1) A peace officer, inspector or prescribed person may submit to an analyst for analysis or examination any substance or sample of it taken by the peace officer, inspector or prescribed person.

(2) An analyst who has made an analysis or examination under subsection (1) may prepare a certificate or report stating that the analyst has analysed or examined a substance or a sample thereof and setting out the results of the analysis or examination. 2017, c. 7, s. 29.

Ministerial Orders

PROVISION OF INFORMATION.

45.1 The Minister may, by order, require a person who is authorized under this Act to conduct activities in relation to controlled substances or precursors or a person who imports designated devices to provide the Minister, in the time and manner that the Minister specifies, with any information respecting those activities that the Minister considers necessary

Note: The portion of s. 45.1 before para. (*a*) replaced, 2017, c. 7, s. 31 (to come into force by order of the Governor in Council):

Provision of information

45.1 Subject to section 24, if, in a preliminary inquiry, trial or other proceeding under this Act or any other Act of Parliament, the court before which the proceedings have been brought is satisfied that any controlled substance, precursor or chemical offence-related property that is the subject of proceedings before the court is no longer required by that court or any other court, the court

   (*a*) to verify compliance or prevent non-compliance with the provisions of this Act or the regulations; or

   (*b*) to address an issue of public health or safety. 2017, c. 7, s. 30.

MEASURES.

45.2 The Minister may, by order, require a person who is authorized under this Act to conduct activities in relation to controlled substances or precursors to take measures, in the time and manner that the Minister specifies, to prevent non-compliance with the provisions of this Act or the regulations or, if the Minister has reasonable grounds to believe that there is such non-compliance, to remedy it. 2017, c. 7, s. 30.

Note: Section 45.2 replaced, 2017, c. 7, s. 32 (to come into force by order of the Governor in Council):

Measures

45.2 The Minister may, by order, require a person who is authorized under this Act to conduct activities in relation to controlled substances or precursors or who conducts activities referred to in section 46.4 in relation to designated devices, to take measures, in the time and manner that the Minister specifies, to prevent non-compliance with the provisions of this Act or the regulations or, if the Minister has reasonable grounds to believe that there is such non-compliance, to remedy it.

REVIEW OFFICER.

45.3 The Minister may designate any qualified individual or class of qualified individuals as review officers for the purpose of reviewing orders under section 45.4. 2017, c. 7, s. 30.

REQUEST FOR REVIEW / Contents of and time for making request / No authority to review / Reasons for refusal / Review initiated by review officer / Order in effect / Completion of review / Extension of period for review / Reasons for extension / Decision on completion of review / Written notice / Effect of amendment.

45.4 (1) Subject to any other provision of this section, an order that is made under section 45.1 or 45.2 shall be reviewed on the written request of the person who was ordered to provide information or to take measures — but only on grounds that involve questions of fact alone or questions of mixed law and fact — by a review officer other than the individual who made the order.

(2) The request shall state the grounds for review and set out the evidence — including evidence that was not considered by the individual who made the order — that supports those grounds and the decision that is sought. It shall be provided to the Minister within seven days after the day on which the order was provided.

(3) The review is not to be done if the request does not comply with subsection (2) or is frivolous, vexatious or not made in good faith.

(4) The person who made the request shall, without delay, be notified in writing of the reasons for not doing the review.

(5) A review officer — other than the individual who made the order — may review an order, whether or not a request is made under subsection (1).

(6) An order continues to apply during a review unless the review officer decides otherwise.

(7) A review officer shall complete the review no later than 30 days after the day on which the request is provided to the Minister.

(8) The review officer may extend the review period by no more than 30 days if they are of the opinion that more time is required to complete the review. They may extend the review period more than once.

(9) If the review period is extended, the person who made the request shall, without delay, be notified in writing of the reasons for extending it.

(10) On completion of a review, the review officer shall confirm, amend, terminate or cancel the order.

(11) The person who made the request or, if there is no request, the person who was ordered to provide information or to take measures shall, without delay, be notified in writing of the reasons for the review officer's decision under subsection (10).

DRUGS

(12) An order that is amended is subject to review under this section. 2017, c. 7, s. 30.

STATUTORY INSTRUMENTS ACT.

45.5 The *Statutory Instruments Act* does not apply in respect of an order made under section 45.1 or 45.2. 2017, c. 7, s. 30.

Offence and Punishment.

PENALTY.

46. Every person who contravenes a provision of this Act for which punishment is not otherwise provided, a provision of a regulation or an order made under section 45.1 or 45.2

    (*a*) is guilty of an indictable offence and liable to a fine of not more than $5,000,000 or to imprisonment for a term not exceeding three years, or to both; or

    (*b*) is guilty of an offence punishable on summary conviction and liable, for a first offence, to a fine of not more than $250,000 or imprisonment for a term of not more than six months, or to both, and, for any subsequent offence, to a fine of not more than $500,000 or imprisonment for a term of not more than 18 months, or to both. 2017, c. 7, s. 33; 2018, c. 16, s. 200.

Prohibitions

OFFENCE OF MAKING FALSE OR DECEPTIVE STATEMENTS.

46.1 No person shall knowingly make, or participate in, assent to or acquiesce in the making of, a false or misleading statement in any book, record, return or other document however recorded, required to be maintained, made or furnished under this Act or the regulations. 2017, c. 7, s. 34.

COMPLIANCE WITH TERMS AND CONDITIONS.

46.2 The holder of a licence, permit, authorization or exemption shall comply with its terms and conditions. 2017, c. 7, s. 34.

IMPORTATION OF DESIGNATED DEVICE / Information for registration / Registration / Proof of registration / Refusal or cancellation / Disclosure of information — designated device / Disclosure of information to police force.

46.3 (1) No person shall import into Canada a designated device unless they register the importation with the Minister.

Note: Section 46.3 amended by replacing subsec. (1), 2017, c. 7, s. 35(1) (to come into force by order of the Governor in Council):

Importation of designated device

46.3 (1) No person shall import into Canada a designated device unless they register the importation with the Minister and the person imports it in accordance with the regulations.

(2) The following information shall be submitted to the Minister for the purpose of registering the importation of a designated device:

(a) the name of the person importing the designated device or, if the person is a corporation, the corporate name and any other name registered with a province, under which the person carries out its activities or identifies itself;

(b) the person's address or, if the person is a corporation, the address of its primary place of business in Canada;

(c) a description of the designated device, including the model number, serial number, and the brand name or trademark associated with it, if any;

(d) the address where the designated device will be delivered as well as the street address of the premises where it will be used by the person importing it;

(e) the name of the customs office where the importation is anticipated; and

(f) the anticipated date of importation.

Note: Subsection 46.3(2) amended by striking out "and" at the end of para. (*e*), by adding "and" to the end of para. (*f*) and by enacting para. (*g*), 2017, c. 7, s. 35(2) (to come into force by order of the Governor in Council):

(g) any other prescribed information.

(3) After the Minister receives the information, the Minister shall register the importation and provide proof of the registration to the person importing the designated device.

(4) The person importing the designated device shall provide the proof of the registration of its importation to the customs office at the time specified by the regulations or, if no time is specified by the regulations, at the time of importation.

(5) The Minister may refuse to register or cancel the registration of the importation of a designated device if the Minister believes on reasonable grounds that false or misleading information was provided, or it is necessary to do so to protect public health or safety or for any other prescribed reason.

(6) The Minister is authorized to disclose to the Canada Border Services Agency or an officer, as defined in section 2(1) of the *Customs Act*, any information submitted under subsection (2) for the purpose of verifying compliance with the provisions of this Act or the regulations.

(7) The Minister is authorized to disclose any information submitted under subsection (2) to a Canadian police force or a member of a Canadian police force who requests the information in the course of an investigation under this Act. 2017, c. 7, s. 34.

Note: Section 46.4 enacted, 2017, c. 7, s. 36 (to come into force by order of the Governor in Council):

DRUGS

Designated device — prescribed activity

46.4 No person shall conduct a prescribed activity in relation to a designated device except in accordance with the regulations.

Evidence and Procedure

TIME LIMIT / Venue.

47. (1) No summary conviction proceedings in respect of an offence under subsection 4(2) or 32(2) or the regulations or in respect of a contravention of an order made under section 45.1 or 45.2 shall be commenced after the expiry of one year after the time when the subject matter of the proceedings arose.

(2) Proceedings in respect of a contravention of any provision of this Act or the regulations or of an order made under section 45.1 or 45.2 may be held in the place where the offence was committed or where the subject matter of the proceedings arose or in any place where the accused is apprehended or happens to be located. 2017, c. 7, s. 37.

BURDEN OF PROVING EXCEPTION, ETC. / Idem.

48. (1) No exception, exemption, excuse or qualification prescribed by law is required to be set out or negatived, as the case may be, in an information or indictment for an offence under this Act or the regulations or under section 463, 464 or 465 of the *Criminal Code* in respect of such an offence.

(2) In any prosecution under this Act, the prosecutor is not required, except by way of rebuttal, to prove that a certificate, licence, permit or other qualification does not operate in favour of the accused, whether or not the qualification is set out in the information or indictment.

COPIES OF DOCUMENTS / Authentication / Evidence inadmissible under this section.

49. (1) A copy of any document filed with a department, ministry, agency, municipality or other body established by or pursuant to a law of a province, or of any statement containing information from the records kept by any such department, ministry, agency, municipality or body, purporting to be certified by any official having custody of that document or those records, is admissible in evidence in any prosecution for an offence referred to in subsection 48(1) and, in the absence of evidence to the contrary, is proof of the facts contained in that document or statement, without proof of the signature or official character of the person purporting to have certified it.

(2) For the purposes of subsection (1), an engraved, lithographed, photocopied, photographed, printed or otherwise electronically or mechanically reproduced facsimile signature of an official referred to in that subsection is sufficient authentication of any copy referred to in that subsection.

(3) Nothing in subsection (1) renders admissible in evidence in any legal proceeding such part of any record as is proved to be a record made in the course of an investigation or inquiry.

CERTIFICATE ISSUED UNDER REGULATIONS / Certificate issued pursuant to regulations.

50. (1) Subject to subsection (2), any certificate or other document issued under regulations made under paragraph 55(2)(*c*) or (2.1)(*c*) is admissible in evidence in a preliminary inquiry, trial or other proceeding under this or any other Act of Parliament and, in the absence of evidence to the contrary, is proof that the certificate or other document was validly issued and of the facts contained in it, without proof of the signature or official character of the person purporting to have certified it.

(2) The defence may, with leave of the court, require that the person who issued the certificate or other document

    (*a*) produce an affidavit or solemn declaration attesting to any of the matters deemed to be proved under subsection (1); or

    (*b*) appear before the court for examination or cross-examination in respect of the issuance of the certificate or other document. 2018, c. 16, s. 201.

CERTIFICATE OR REPORT OF ANALYST / Attendance of analyst.

51. (1) A certificate or report prepared by an analyst under subsection 45(2) is admissible in evidence in any prosecution for an offence under this Act or any other Act of Parliament and, in the absence of evidence to the contrary, is proof of the statements set out in the certificate or report, without proof of the signature or official character of the person appearing to have signed it.

(2) The party against whom a certificate or report of an analyst is produced under subsection (1) may, with leave of the court, require the attendance of the analyst for the purpose of cross-examination. 2017, c. 7, s. 38.

(3) [*Repealed*, 2017, c. 7, s. 38(2).]

PROOF OF NOTICE / Idem.

52. (1) For the purposes of this Act and the regulations, the giving of any notice, whether orally or in writing, or the service of any document may be proved by the oral evidence of, or by the affidavit or solemn declaration of, the persons claiming to have given that notice or served that document.

(2) Notwithstanding subsection (1), the court may require the affiant or declarant to appear before it for examination or cross-examination in respect of the giving of notice or proof of service.

CONTINUITY OF POSSESSION / Alternative method of proof.

53. (1) In any proceeding under this Act or the regulations, continuity of possession of any exhibit tendered as evidence in that proceeding may be proved

DRUGS

by the testimony of, or the affidavit or solemn declaration of, the person claiming to have had it in their possession.

(2) Where an affidavit or solemn declaration is offered in proof of continuity of possession under subsection (1), the court may require the affiant or declarant to appear before it for examination or cross-examination in respect of the issue of continuity of possession.

COPIES OF RECORDS, BOOKS OR DOCUMENTS.

54. Where any record, book, electronic data or other document is examined or seized under this Act or the regulations, the Minister, or the officer by whom the record, book, electronic data or other document is examined or seized, may make or cause to be made one or more copies thereof, and a copy of any such record, book, electronic data or other document purporting to be certified by the Minister or a person authorized by the Minister is admissible in evidence and, in the absence of evidence to the contrary, has the same probative force as the original record, book, electronic data or other document would have had if it had been proved in the ordinary way.

Technical Assistance 2018, c. 16, 202.

ADVICE OF EXPERTS.

54.1 The Minister may engage the services of persons having technical or specialized knowledge to advise the Minister in respect of his or her powers, duties or functions under this Act and, with the approval of the Treasury Board, fix their remuneration. 2018, c. 16, s. 202.

Regulations and Exemptions 2017, c. 7, s. 39.

REGULATIONS / Exception related to paragraph (1)(*z*) / Regulations / Regulations pertaining to law enforcement / Regulations pertaining to law enforcement under other Acts / Incorporation by reference.

55. (1) The Governor in Council may make regulations for carrying out the purposes and provisions of this Act, including the regulation of the medical, scientific and industrial applications and distribution of controlled substances and precursors and the enforcement of this Act, as well as the regulation of designated devices and, without restricting the generality of the foregoing, may make regulations

  (*a*) governing, controlling, limiting, authorizing the importation into Canada, exportation from Canada, production, packaging, sending, transportation, delivery, sale, provision, administration, possession or obtaining of or other dealing in any controlled substances or precursor or any class thereof;

  (*b*) respecting the circumstances in which, the conditions subject to which and the persons or classes of persons by whom any controlled substances or precursor or any class thereof may be imported into Canada, exported from

Canada, produced, packaged, sent, transported, delivered, sold, provided, administered, possessed, obtained or otherwise dealt in, as well as the means by which and the persons or classes of persons by whom such activities may be authorized;

(c) respecting the issuance, suspension, cancellation, duration and terms and conditions of any licence or class of licences for the importation into Canada, exportation from Canada, production, packaging, sale, provision or administration of any substance included in Schedule I, II, III, IV, V or VI or any class of those substances;

(d) respecting the issuance, suspension, cancellation, duration and terms and conditions of any permit for the importation into Canada, exportation from Canada or production of a substance included in Schedule I, II, III, IV, V or VI or any class of those substances as well as the amount of those substances or any class of those substances that may be imported, exported or produced under such a permit;

(d.1) authorizing the Minister to impose terms and conditions on any licence or any permit including existing licences or permits, and to amend those terms and conditions.

(e) prescribing the fees payable on application for any of the licences or permits;

(f) respecting the method of production, preservation, testing, packaging or storage of any controlled substance or precursor or any class thereof;

(g) respecting the premises, processes or conditions for the production or sale of any controlled substance or any class thereof, and deeming such premises, processes or conditions to be or not to be suitable for the purposes of the regulations;

(h) respecting the qualifications of persons who are engaged in the production, preservation, testing, packaging, storage, selling, providing or otherwise dealing in any controlled substance or precursor or any class thereof and who do so under the supervision of a person licensed under the regulations to do any such thing;

(i) prescribing standards of composition, strength, concentration, potency, purity or quality or any other property of any controlled substance or precursor;

(j) respecting the labelling, packaging, size, dimensions, fill and other specifications of packages used for the importation into Canada, exportation from Canada, sending, transportation, delivery, sale or provision of or other dealing in any substance included in Schedule I, II, III, IV, V or VI or any class thereof;

(k) respecting the distribution of samples of any substance included in Schedule I, II, III, IV, V or VI or any class thereof;

(l) controlling and limiting the advertising for sale of any controlled substance or precursor or any class thereof;

(m) respecting records, reports, electronic data or other documents in respect of controlled substances, precursors or designated devices that are required to be kept and provided by any person or class of persons;

DRUGS

(n) respecting the qualifications for inspectors and their powers, duties and functions in relation to verifying compliance or preventing non-compliance with the provisions of this Act or the regulations;

(o) respecting the qualifications for analysts and their powers and duties;

(p) respecting the detention and disposition of or otherwise dealing with any controlled substance, precursor, designated device, offence-related property or conveyance;

(q) [*Repealed*, 2017, c. 7, s. 40(7).];

(r) respecting the taking of samples of substances under paragraph 31(1)(h);

(s) respecting the collection, use, retention, disclosure and disposal of information;

(t) respecting the making, serving, filing and manner of proving service of any notice, order, report or other document required or authorized under this Act or the regulations;

(u) authorizing the Minister to add to or delete from, by order, a schedule to Part J of the *Food and Drug Regulations* any item or portion of an item included in Schedule V;

(v) prescribing forms for the purposes of this Act or the regulations;

(w) establishing classes or groups of controlled substances, precursors or designated devices;

(x) respecting the provision of information under section 45.1;

(y) respecting the measures referred to in section 45.2.

(y.1) respecting the review of orders under section 45.4;

(z) exempting, on any terms and conditions that are specified in the regulations, any person or class of persons or any controlled substance, precursor, designated device or any class of controlled substances, precursors or designated devices from the application of all or any of the provisions of this Act or the regulations;

(z.01) respecting the registration of the importation of any designated device or class of designated devices, including the time that proof of registration must be provided; and

Note: Subsection 55.1(1) amended by striking out "and" at the end of para. (z.01) and by adding paras. (z.02) and (z.03), 2017, c. 7, s. 40(12) (to come into force by order of the Governor in Council):

(z.02) governing, controlling, limiting, authorizing the importation into Canada, exportation from Canada, sale, provision, possession of or other dealing in any designated device or any class of designated devices;

(z.03) respecting the issuance, suspension, cancellation, duration and terms and conditions of any licence or class of licences or of any permit for the importation into Canada, exportation from Canada, sale, provision or possession of any designated device or class of designated devices; and

Note: Subsection 55.1(1) amended by striking out "and" at the end of para. (z.03) and by adding paras. (z.04) to (z.06), 2017, c. 7, s. 40(13) (to come into force by order of the Governor in Council):

(z.04) prescribing exportation from Canada, sale, provision, or possession of any designated device or any class of designated devices as activities for the purpose of section 46.4;

(z.05) respecting the circumstances in which, the conditions subject to which and the persons or classes of persons by whom any designated device or class of designated devices may be exported from Canada, sold, provided or possessed, as well as the means by which and the persons or classes of persons by whom such activities may be authorized;

(z.06) respecting the registration of activities in relation to any designated device or any class of designated devices for the purpose of section 46.4; and

(z.1) prescribing anything that, by this Act, is to be or may be prescribed.

(1.1) [*Repealed*, 2017, c. 7, s. 40(4).]

(1.2) The Governor in Council may make regulations for carrying out the purposes of section 56.1, including

(a) defining terms for the purposes of that section;

(b) [*Repealed*, 2017, c. 7, s. 40(15).];

(c) respecting any information to be submitted to the Minister and the manner in which it is to be submitted;

(d) respecting the circumstances in which an exemption may be granted;

(e) respecting requirements in relation to an application for an exemption made under subsection 56.1(1); and

(f) respecting terms and conditions in relation to an exemption granted under subsection 56.1(1).

(2) The Governor in Council, on the recommendation of the Minister of Public Safety and Emergency Preparedness, may make regulations that pertain to investigations and other law enforcement activities conducted under this Act by a member of a police force or of the military police and other persons acting under the direction and control of the member and, without restricting the generality of the foregoing, may make regulations

(a) authorizing, for the purposes of this subsection,

(i) the Minister of Public Safety and Emergency Preparedness or the provincial minister responsible for policing in a province, as the case may be, to designate a police force within their jurisdiction, or

(ii) the Minister of National Defence to designate military police;

(b) exempting, on any terms and conditions that are specified in the regulations, a member of a police force or of the military police that has been designated under paragraph (a), and other persons acting under the direction and control of the member, from the application of any provision of Part I or the regulations;

(c) respecting the issuance, suspension, cancellation, duration and terms and conditions of a certificate, other document or, in exigent circumstances, an approval to obtain a certificate or other document, that is issued to a member of a police force or of the military police that has been designated under paragraph (a) for the purpose of exempting the member from the application of any provision of this Act or the regulations;

(d) respecting the detention, storage and disposition of or other dealing with any controlled substance or precursor;

(e) respecting records, reports, electronic data or other documents in respect of a controlled substance or precursor that are required to be kept and provided by any person or class of persons; and (*f*) prescribing forms for the purposes of the regulations.

(2.1) The Governor in Council, on the recommendation of the Minister of Public Safety and Emergency Preparedness, may, for the purpose of an investigation or other law enforcement activity conducted under another Act of Parliament, make regulations authorizing a member of a police force or of the military police or other person under the direction and control of the member to commit an act or omission — or authorizing a member of a police force or of the military police to direct the commission of an act or omission — that would otherwise constitute an offence under Part I or the regulations and, without restricting the generality of the foregoing, may make regulations

(*a*) authorizing, for the purposes of this subsection,

   (i) the Minister of Public Safety and Emergency Preparedness or the provincial minister responsible for policing in a province, as the case may be, to designate a police force within their jurisdiction, or

   (ii) the Minister of National Defence to designate military police;

(*b*) exempting, on any terms and conditions that are specified in the regulations, a member of a police force or of the military police that has been designated under paragraph (*a*), and other persons acting under the direction and control of the member, from the application of any provision of Part I or the regulations;

(*c*) respecting the issuance, suspension, cancellation, duration and terms and conditions of a certificate, other document or, in exigent circumstances, an approval to obtain a certificate or other document, that is issued to a member of a police force or of the military police that has been designated under paragraph (*a*) for the purpose of exempting the member from the application of any provision of Part I or the regulations;

(*d*) respecting the detention, storage and disposition of or other dealing with any controlled substance or precursor;

(*e*) respecting records, reports, electronic data or other documents in respect of a controlled substance or precursor that are required to be kept and provided by any person or class of persons; and

(*f*) prescribing forms for the purposes of the regulations.

(3) Any regulations made under this Act incorporating by reference a classification, standard, procedure or other specification may incorporate the classification, standard, procedure or specification as amended from time to time, and, in such a case, the reference shall be read accordingly. 2001, c. 32, s. 55; 2005, c. 10, s. 15; 2015, c. 22, s. 4; 2017, c. 7, s. 40(1), (3), (6) to (8), (11), (14) to (19).

EXEMPTION BY MINISTER / Exception.

56. (1) The Minister may, on any terms and conditions that the Minister considers necessary, exempt from the application of all or any of the provisions of this Act or the regulations any person or class of persons or any controlled substance or precursor or any class of either of them if, in the opinion of the Minister, the exemption is necessary for a medical or scientific purpose or is otherwise in the public interest.

(2) The Minister is not authorized under subsection (1) to grant an exemption for a medical purpose that would allow activities in relation to a controlled substance or precursor that is obtained in a manner not authorized under this Act to take place at a supervised consumption site. 2015, c. 22, s. 5; 2017, c. 7, s. 41.

EXEMPTION FOR MEDICAL PURPOSE — SUPERVISED CONSUMPTION SITE / Application / Subsequent application / Notice / Public decision.

56.1 (1) For the purpose of allowing certain activities to take place at a supervised consumption site, the Minister may, on any terms and conditions that the Minister considers necessary, exempt the following from the application of all or any of the provisions of this Act or the regulations if, in the opinion of the Minister, the exemption is necessary for a medical purpose:

    (*a*) any person or class of persons in relation to a controlled substance or precursor that is obtained in a manner not authorized under this Act; or

    (*b*) any controlled substance or precursor or any class of either of them that is obtained in a manner not authorized under this Act;

(2) An application for an exemption under subsection (1) shall include information, submitted in the form and manner determined by the Minister, regarding the intended public health benefits of the site and information, if any, related to

    (*a*) the impact of the site on crime rates;

    (*b*) the local conditions indicating a need for the site;

    (*c*) the administrative structure in place to support the site;

    (*d*) the resources available to support the maintenance of the site; and

    (*e*) expressions of community support or opposition.

(3) An application for an exemption under subsection (1) that would allow certain activities to continue to take place at a supervised consumption site shall include any update to the information provided to the Minister since the previous exemption was granted, including any information related to the public health impacts of the activities at the site.

(4) The Minister may give notice, in the form and manner determined by the Minister, of any application for an exemption under subsection (1). The notice shall indicate the period of time — not less than 45 days or more than 90 days — in which members of the public may provide the Minister with comments.

(5) After making a decision under subsection (1), the Minister shall, in writing, make the decision public and, if the decision is a refusal, include the reasons for it. 2015, c. 22, s. 5; 2017, c. 7, s. 42.

56.2 A person who is responsible for the direct supervision, at a supervised consumption site, of the consumption of controlled substances, may offer a person using the site alternative pharmaceutical therapy before that person consumes a controlled substance that is obtained in a manner not authorized under this Act. 2017, c. 7, s. 42.

Miscellaneous

POWERS, DUTIES AND FUNCTIONS OF MINISTER OR MINISTER OF PUBLIC SAFETY AND EMERGENCY PREPAREDNESS.

57. The Minister's powers, duties or functions under this Act or the regulations — and those of the Minister of Public Safety and Emergency Preparedness under the regulations — may be exercised or performed by any person designated, or any person occupying a position designated, for that purpose by the relevant Minister. 2005, c. 10, s. 16.

PARAMOUNTCY OF THIS ACT AND THE REGULATIONS.

58. In the case of any inconsistency or conflict between this Act or the regulations made under it, and the *Food and Drugs Act* or the regulations made under that Act, this Act and the regulations made under it prevail to the extent of the inconsistency or conflict.

OFFENCE OF MAKING FALSE OR DECEPTIVE STATEMENTS.

59. [*Repealed*, 2017, c. 7, s. 44.]

Amendments to Schedules

POWER TO AMEND SCHEDULES.

60. The Governor in Council may, by order, amend any of Schedules I to IV, VI and IX by adding to them or deleting from them any item or portion of an item, if the Governor in Council considers the amendment to be necessary in the public interest. 2017, c. 7, s. 45; 2018, c. 16, ss. 203, 206(6).

SCHEDULE V / Deletions.

60.1 (1) The Minister may, by order, add to Schedule V any item or portion of an item for a period of up to one year, or extend that period by up to another year, if the Minister has reasonable grounds to believe that it

    (*a*) poses a significant risk to public health or safety; or

    (*b*) may pose a risk to public health or safety and

        (i) is being imported into Canada with no legitimate purpose, or

        (ii) is being distributed in Canada with no legitimate purpose.

(2) The Minister may, by order, delete any item or portion of an item from Schedule V. 2017, c. 7, s. 45.

REFERENCES TO PRIOR ENACTMENTS.

61. Any reference in a designation by the Minister of Public Safety and Emergency Preparedness under Part VI of the *Criminal Code* to an offence contrary to the *Narcotic Control Act* or Part III or IV of the *Food and Drugs Act* or any conspiracy or attempt to commit or being an accessory after the fact or any counselling in relation to such an offence shall be deemed to be a reference to an offence contrary to section 5 (trafficking), 6 (importing and exporting) or 7 (production) of this Act, as the case may be, or a conspiracy or attempt to commit or being an accessory after the fact or any counselling in relation to such an offence. 2001, c. 32, s. 56; 2005, c. 10, s. 34(1)(*d*).

SCHEDULE I

(Sections 2, 4 to 7.1, 10, 29, 55 and 60)

1. Opium Poppy (*Papaver somniferum*), its preparations, derivatives, alkaloids and salts, including:
    (1) Opium
    (2) Codeine (methylmorphine)
    (3) Morphine (7,8-didehydro-4,5-epoxy-17-methylmorphinan-3,6-diol)
    (4) Thebaine (paramorphine), and the salts, derivatives and salts of derivatives of substances set out in subitems (1) to (4), including:
    (5) Acetorphine (acetyletorphine)
    (6) Acetyldihydrocodeine (4,5-epoxy-3-methoxy-17-methylmorphinan-6-ol acetate)
    (7) Benzylmorphine (7,8-didehydro-4,5-epoxy-17-methyl-3-(phenyl-methoxy) morphinan-6-ol)
    (8) Codoxime (dihydrocodeinone O-(carboxymethyl) oxime)
    (9) Desomorphine (dihydrodeoxymorphine)
    (10) Diacetylmorphine (heroin)
    (11) Dihydrocodeine (4,5-epoxy-3-methoxy-17-methylmorphinan-6-ol)
    (12) Dihydromorphine (4,5-epoxy-17-methylmorphinan-3,6-diol)
    (13) Ethylmorphine (7,8-didehydro-4,5-epoxy-3-ethoxy-17-methylmorphinan-6-ol)
    (14) Etorphine (tetrahydro-7α-(1-hydroxy-1-methylbutyl)-6,14-endo-the-nooripavine)
    (15) Hydrocodone (dihydrocodeinone)
    (16) Hydromorphinol (dihydro-14-hydroxymorphine)
    (17) Hydromorphone (dihydromorphinone)
    (18) Methyldesorphine (Δ6-deoxy-6-methylmorphine)
    (19) Methyldihydromorphine (dihydro-6-methylmorphine)
    (20) Metopon (dihydromethylmorphinone)
    (21) Morphine-N-oxide (morphine oxide)
    (22) Myrophine (benzylmorphine myristate)
    (23) Nalorphine (N-allylnormorphine)
    (24) Nicocodine (6-nicotinylcodeine)
    (25) Nicomorphine (dinicotinylmorphine)
    (26) Norcodeine (N-desmethylcodeine)
    (27) Normorphine (N-desmethylmorphine)
    (28) Oxycodone (dihydrohydroxycodeinone)
    (29) Oxymorphone (dihydrohydroxymorphinone)

DRUGS

(30)   Pholcodine (3-[2-(4-morpholinyl)ethyl]morphine)

(31)   Thebacon (acetyldihydrocodeinone)

but not
including

(32)   Apomorphine (5,6,6a,7-tetrahydro-6-methyl-4H-dibenzo[de,g] quino-line-10,11-diol) and its salts

(33)   Cyprenorphine (N-(cyclopropylmethyl)-6,7,8,14-tetrahydro-7α-(1-hy-droxy-1-methylethyl)-6,14-endo-ethenonororipavine) and its salts

(34)   Nalmefene (17-(cyclopropylmethyl)-4,5α-epoxy-6-methylenemorphi-nan-3,14-diol) and its salts

(34.1)   Naloxone (4,5α-epoxy-3,14-dihydroxy-17-(2-propenyl)morphinan-6-one) and its salts

(34.2)   Naltrexone (17-(cyclopropylmethyl)-4,5α-epoxy-3,14-dihydroxymor-phinan-6-one) and its salts

(34.3)   Methylnaltrexone (17-(cyclopropylmethyl)4,5α-epoxy-3,14-dihy-droxy-17-methyl-6-oxomorphinanium) and its salts

(34.4)   Naloxegol (4,5α-epoxy-6α-(3,6,9,12,15,18,21-heptaoxadocos-1-yloxy)-17-(2-propenyl)morphinan-3,14-diol) and its salts

(35)   Narcotine (6,7-dimethoxy-3-(5,6,7,8-tetrahydro-4-methoxy-6-methyl-1,3-dioxolos[4,5-g]isoquinolin-5-yl)-1(3H)-isobenzofuranone) and its salts

(36)   Papaverine (1-[(3,4-dimethoxyphenyl)methyl]-6,7-dimethoxyisoqui-noline) and its salts

(37)   Poppy seed

2.   Coca (*Erythroxylum*), its preparations, derivatives, alkaloids and salts, including:

(1)   Coca leaves

(2)   Cocaine (benzoylmethylecgonine)

(3)   Ecgonine (3-hydroxy-2-tropane carboxylic acid)

but not
including

(4)   123l-ioflupane

3.   Phenylpiperidines, their intermediates, salts, derivatives and analogues and salts of intermediates, derivatives and analogues, including:

(1)   Allylprodine (3-allyl-1-methyl-4-phenyl-4-piperidinol propionate)

(2)   Alphameprodine (α-3-ethyl-1-methyl-4-phenyl-4-piperidinol propio-nate)

(3)   Alphaprodine (α-1,3-dimethyl-4-phenyl-4-piperidinol propionate)

(4)   Anileridine (ethyl 1-[2-(p-aminophenyl)-4-phenylpiperidine-4-carbox-ylate)

(5)   Betameprodine B-3-ethyl-1-methyl-4-phenyl-4-piperidinol propio-nate)

(6)   Betaprodine (B-1,3-dimethyl-4-phenyl-4-piperidinol propionate)

(7)   Benzethidine (ethyl 1-(2-benzyloxyethyl)-4-phenylpiperidine-4-car-boxylate)

(8)   Diphenoxylate (ethyl 1-(3-cyano-3,3-diphenylpropyl)-4-phenylpiperi-dine-4-carboxylate)

(9) Difenoxin (1-(3-cyano-3,3-diphenylpropyl)-4-phenylpiperidine-4-carboxylate)

(10) Etoxeridine (ethyl 1-[2-(2-hydroxyethoxy) ethyl]-4-phenylpiperidine-4-carboxylate)

(11) Furethidine (ethyl 1-(2-tetrahydrofurfury loxyethyl)-4-phenylpiperidine-4-carboxylate)

(12) Hydroxypethidine (ethyl 4-(m-hydroxyphenyl)-1-methylpiperidine-4-carboxylate)

(13) Ketobemidone (1-[4-(m-hydroxyphenyl)-1-methyl-4-piperidyl]-1-propanone)

(14) Methylphenylisonipecotonitrile (4-cyano-1-methyl-4-phenylpiperidine)

(15) Morpheridine (ethyl 1-(2-morpholinoethyl)-4-phenylpiperidine-4-carboxylate)

(16) Norpethidine (ethyl 4-phenylpiperidine-4-carboxylate)

(17) Pethidine (ethyl 1-methyl-4-phenylpiperidine-4-carboxylate)

(18) Phenoperidine (ethyl 1-(3-hydroxy-3-phenylpropyl)-4-phenylpiperidine-4-carboxylate)

(19) Piminodine (ethyl 1-[3-(phenylamino)propyl]-4-phenylpiperidine-4-carboxylate)

(20) Properidine (isopropyl 1-methyl-4-phenylpiperidine-4-carboxylate)

(21) Trimeperidine (1,2,5-trimethyl-4-phenyl-4-piperidinol propionate)

(22) Pethidine Intermediate C (1-methyl-4-phenylpiperidine-4-carboxylate)

but not
including

(23) Carperidine (ethyl 1-(2-carbamylethyl)-4-phenylpiperidine-4-carboxylate) and its salts

(24) Oxpheneridine (ethyl 1-(2-hydroxy-2-phenylethyl)-4-phenylpiperidine-4-carboxylate) and its salts

4. Phenazepines, their salts, derivatives and salts of derivatives including:

(1) Proheptazine (hexahydro-1,3-dimethyl-4-phenyl-1H-azepin-4-ol propionate)

but not
including

(2) Ethoheptazine (ethyl hexahydro-1-methyl-4-phenyl-azepine-4-carboxylate) and its salts

(3) Metethoheptazine (ethyl hexahydro-1,3-dimethyl-4-phenylazepine-4-carboxylate) and its salts

(4) Metheptazine (ethyl hexahydro-1,2-dimethyl-4-phenylazepine-4-carboxylate) and its salts

5. Amidones, their intermediates, salts, derivatives and salts of intermediates and derivatives including:

(1) Dimethylaminodiphenylbutanonitrile (4-cyano-2-dimethylamino-4,4-diphenylbutane)

(2) Dipipanone (4,4-diphenyl-6-piperidino-3-heptanone)

(3) Isomethadone (6-dimethylamino-5-methyl-4,4-diphenyl-3-hexanone)

(4) Methadone (6-dimethylamino-4,4-diphenyl-3-heptanone)

(5) Normethadone (6-dimethylamino-4,4-diphenyl-3-hexanone)

DRUGS

    (6) Norpipanone (4,4-diphenyl-6-piperidino-3-hexanone)

    (7) Phenadoxone (6-morpholino-4,4-diphenyl-3-heptanone)

6.   Methadols, their salts, derivatives and salts of derivatives including:

    (1) Acetylmethadol (6-dimethylamino-4,4-diphenyl-3-heptanol acetate)

    (2) Alphacetylmethadol (α-6-dimethylamino-4,4-diphenyl-3-heptanol acetate)

    (3) Alphamethadol (α-6-dimethylamino-4,4-diphenyl-3-heptanol)

    (4) Betacetylmethadol (B-6-dimethylamino-4,4-diphenyl-3-heptanol acetate)

    (5) Betamethadol (B-6-dimethylamino-4,4-diphenyl-3-heptanol)

    (6) Dimepheptanol (6-dimethylamino-4,4-diphenyl-3-heptanol)

    (7) Noracymethadol (α-6-methylamino-4,4-diphenyl-3-heptanol acetate)

7.   Phenalkoxams, their salts, derivatives and salts of derivatives including:

    (1) Dimenoxadol (dimethylaminoethyl 1-ethoxy-1,1-diphenylacetate)

    (2) Dioxaphetyl butyrate (ethyl 2,2-diphenyl-4-morpholinobutyrate)

    (3) Dextropropoxyphene ([S-(R★,S★)]-(α-[2-(dimethylamino)-methylethyl]-(α-phenylbenzene-ethanol, propanoate ester)

8.   Thiambutenes, their salts, derivatives and salts of derivatives including:

    (1) Diethylthiambutene (N,N-diethyl-1-methyl-3,3-di-2-thienylallylamine)

    (2) Dimethylthiambutene (N,N,1-trimethyl-3,3-di-2-thienylallylamine)

    (3) Ethylmethylthiambutene (N-ethyl-N,1-dimethyl-3,3-di-2-thienylallylamine)

9.   Moramides, their intermediates, salts, derivatives and salts of intermediates and derivatives including:

    (1) Dextromoramide (d-1-(3-methyl-4-morpholino-2,2-diphenylbutyryl) pyrrolidine)

    (2) Diphenylmorpholinoisovaleric acid (2-methyl-3-morpholino-1,1-diphenylpropionic acid)

    (3) Levomoramide (l-1-(3-methyl-4-morpholino-2,2-diphenylbutyryl) pyrrolidine)

    (4) Racemoramide (d,1-1(3-methyl-4-morpholino-2,2-diphenylbutyryl) pyrrolidine)

10.   Morphinans, their salts, derivatives and salts of derivatives including:

    (1) Buprenorphine (17-(cyclopropylmethyl)-(α-(1,1-dimethylethyl)-4,5-epoxy-18,19-dihydro-3-hydroxy-6-methoxy-(α-methyl-6,14-ethenomorphinan-7-methanol)

    (2) Drotebanol (6(B,14-dihydroxy-3,4-dimethoxy-17-methylmorphinan)

    (3) Levomethorphan (1-3-methoxy-17-methylmorphinan)

    (4) Levorphanol (1-3-hydroxy-17-methylmorphinan)

    (5) Levophenacylmorphan (1-3-hydroxy-17-phenacyl-morphinan)

    (6) Norlevorphanol (1-3-hydroxymorphinan)

    (7) Phenomorphan (3-hydroxy-17-(2-phenylethyl) morphinan)

    (8) Racemethorphan (d,1-3-methoxy-17-methylmorphinan)

    (9) Racemorphan (d, l-3-hydroxy-N-methylmorphinan)

but not
including

    (10) Dextromethorphan (d-1,2,3,9,10,10a-hexahydro-6-methoxy-11-methyl-4H-10,4a-iminoethano-phenanthren) and its salts

    (11) Dextrorphan (d-1,2,3,9,10,10a-hexahydro-11-methyl-4H-10,4a-iminoethanophenanthren-6-ol) and its salts

    (12) Levallorphan (l-11-allyl-1,2,3,9,10,10a-hexahydro-4H-10,4a-iminoethanophenanthren-6ol)

    (13) Levargorphan (l-11-propargyl-1,2,3,9,10,10a-hexahydro-4H-10,4a-iminoethanophenanthren-6-ol) and its salts

    (14) Butorphanol (l-N-(cyclobutylmethyl)-3,14-dihydroxymorphinan) and its salts

    (15) Nalbuphine (N-(cyclobutylmethyl)-4,5-epoxy-morphinan-3,6,14-triol) and its salts

11.   Benzazocines, their salts, derivatives and salts of derivatives including:

    (1) Phenazocine (1,2,3,4,5,6-hexahydro-6,11-dimethyl-3-phenethyl-2,6-methano-3-benzazocin-8-ol)

    (2) Metazocine (1,2,3,4,5,6-hyxahydro-3,6,11-trimethyl-2,6-methano-3-benzazocin-8-ol)

    (3) Pentazocine (1,2,3,4,5,6-hexahydro-6,11-dimethyl-3-(3-methyl-2-butenyl)-2,6-methano-3-benzazocin-8-ol)

but not
including

    (4) Cyclazocine (1,2,3,4,5,6-hexahydro-6,11-dimethyl-3-(cyclopropyl-methyl)-2,6-methano-3-benzazocin-8-ol) and its salts

12.   Ampromides, their salts, derivatives and salts of derivatives including:

    (1) Diampromide (N-[2-(methylphenethylamino) propyl] propionanilide)

    (2) Phenampromide (N-(1-methyl-2-piperidino) ethyl) propionanilide)

    (3) Propiram (N-(1-methyl-2-piperidinoethyl)-N-2-pyridylpropionamide)

13.   Benzimidazoles, their salts, derivatives and salts of derivatives including:

    (1) Clonitazene (2-(p-chlorobenzyl)-1-diethylaminoethyl-5-nitrobenzimidazole)

    (2) Etonitazene (2-(p-ethoxybenzyl)-1-diethylaminoethyl-5-nitrobenzimidazole)

    (3) Bezitramide (1-(3-cyano-3,3-diphenylpropyl)-4-(2-oxo-3-propionyl-1-benzimidazolinyl)-piperidine)

14.   Phencyclidine (1-(1-phenylcyclohexyl)piperidine), its salts, derivatives and analogues and salts of derivatives and analogues, including:

    (1) Ketamine (2-(2-chlorophenyl)-2-(methylamino)cyclohexanone)

15.   Piritramide (1-(3-cyano-3,3-diphenylpropyl)-4-(1-piperidino)piperidine-4-carboxylic acid amide), its salts, derivatives and salts of derivatives

16.   Fentanyls, their salts, derivatives, and analogues and salts of derivatives and analogues, including:

    (1) Accetyl-α-methylfentanyl (N-[1-(α-methylphenethyl)-4-piperidyl] acetanilide)

    (2) Alfentanil (N-[1-[2-(4-ethyl-4,5-dihydro-5-oxo-1H-tetrazol-1-yl) ethyl]-4-(methoxymethyl)-4-piperidyl]propionanilide)

   (3) Carfentanil (methyl 4-[(1-oxopropyl)phenylamino]-1-(2-phenethyl)-4-piperidinecarboxylate)

   (4) p-Fluorofentanyl (4'fluoro-N-(1-phenethyl-4-piperidyl) propionanilide)

   (5) Fentanyl (N-(1-phenethyl-4-piperidyl) propionanilide)

   (6) B-Hydroxyfentanyl (N-[1-(B-hydroxyphenethyl)-4-piperidyl] propionanilide)

   (7) B-Hydroxy-3-methylfentanyl (N-[1-B-hydroxyphenethyl)-3-methyl-4-piperidyl] propionanilide)

   (8) α-Methylfentanyl (N-[1-(α-methylphenethyl)-4-piperidyl] propionanilide)

   (9) α-Methylthiofentanyl (N-[1-methyl-2-(2-thienyl) ethyl]-4-piperidyl] propionanilide)

  (10) 3-Methylfentanyl (N-(3-methyl-1-phenethyl-4-piperidyl) propionanilide)

  (11) 3-Methylthiofentanyl (N-[3-methyl-1-[2-(2-thienyl) ethyl]-4-piperidyl]propionanilide)

 (11.1) Remifentanil (dimethyl 4-carboxy-4-(N-phenylpropionamido)-1-piperidinepropionate)

  (12) Sufentanil (N-[4-(methoxymethyl)-1-[2-(2-thienyl)ethyl]-4-piperidyl] propionanilide)

  (13) Thiofentanyl (N-[1-[2-(2-thienyl)ethyl]-4-piperidyl]propionanilide)

17.   Tilidine (ethyl12-(dimethylamino)-1-phenyl-3-cyclohexene-1-carboxylate), its salts, derivatives and salts of derivatives

17.1   Methylenedioxypyrovalerone (MDPV), its salts, derivatives, isomers and analogues and salts of derivatives, isomers and analogues

18.   Methamphetamine (N,α-dimethylbenzeneethanamine), its salts, derivatives, isomers and analogues and salts of derivatives, isomers and analogues

19.   Amphetamines, their salts, derivatives, isomers and analogues and salts of derivatives, isomers and analogues including:

   (1) amphetamine (a-methylbenzene-ethanamine)

   (2) N-ethylamphetamine (N-ethyl-a-methylbenzeneethanamine)

   (3) 4-methyl-2,5-dimethoxyamphetamine (STP) (2,5-dimethoxy-4,a-dimethylbenzeneethanamine)

   (4) 3,4-methylenedioxyamphetamine (MDA) (a-methyl-1,3-benzodioxole-5-ethanamine)

   (5) 2,5-dimethoxyamphetamine (2,5-dimethoxy-a-methylbenzene-ethanamine)

   (6) 4-methoxyamphetamine (4-methoxy-a-methylbenzeneethanamine)

   (7) 2,4,5-trimethoxyamphetamine (2,4,5-trimethoxy-a-methylbenzeneethanamine)

   (8) N-methyl-3,4-methylenedioxy-amphetamine (N,a-dimethyl-1,3-benzodioxole-5-ethanamine)

   (9) 4-ethoxy-2,5-dimethoxyamphetamine (4-ethoxy-2,5-dimethoxy-a-methylbenzeneethanamine)

  (10) 5-methoxy-3,4-methylenedioxy-amphetamine (7-methoxy-a-methyl-1,3-benzodioxole-5-ethanamine)

(11) N,N-dimethyl-3,4-methylenedioxyamphetamine (N,N, a-trimethyl-1,3-benzodioxole-5-ethanamine)

(12) N-ethyl-3,4-methylenedioxyamphetamine (N-ethyl-a-methyl-1,3-benzodioxole-5-ethanamine)

(13) 4-ethyl-2,5-dimethoxyamphetamine (DOET) (4-ethyl-2,5-dimethoxy-a-methylbenzeneethanamine)

(14) 4-bromo-2,5-dimethoxyamphetamine (4-bromo-2,5-dimethoxy-a-methylbenzeneethanamine)

(15) 4-chloro-2,5-dimethoxyamphetamine (4-chloro-2,5-dimethoxy-a-methyl-benzeneethanamine)

(16) 4-ethoxyamphetamine (4-ethoxy-a-methylbenzeneethanamine)

(17) Benzphetamine (N-benzyl-N,a-dimethylbenzeneethanamine)

(18) N-Propyl-3,4-methylenedioxy-amphetamine (a-methyl-N-propyl-1,3-benzodioxole-5-ethanamine)

(19) N-(2-Hydroxyethyl)-a-meth-ylbenzene-ethanamine

(20) N-hydroxy-3,4-methylenedioxy-amphetamine (N-[a-methyl-3,4-(methylenedioxy)phenethyl]hydroxyla-mine)

(21) 3,4,5-trimethoxyamphetamine (3,4,5-trimethoxy-a-methylbenze-neethanamine)

20. Flunitrazepam (5-(o-fluorophenyl)-1,3-dihydro-1-methyl-7-nitro-2H-1,4-benzodiazepin-2-one) and any of its salts or derivatives

21. 4-hydroxybutanoic acid (GHB) and any of its salts

22. Tapentadol (3-[(1R,2R)-3-(dimethylamino)-1-ethyl-2-methylpropyl]-phenol), its salts, derivatives and isomers and salts of derivatives and isomers

23. AH-7921 (1-(3,4-dichlorobenzamidomethyl)cyclohexyldimethylamine), its salts, isomers and salts of isomers

24. MT-45 (1-cyclohexyl-4-(1,2-diphenylethyl)piperazine), its salts, derivatives, isomers and analogues and salts of derivatives, isomers and analogues, including

(1) Diphenidine (DEP) (1-(1,2-diphenylethyl)piperidine)

(2) Methoxphenidine (2-MeO-Diphenidine, MXP) (1-[1-(2-methoxyphe-nyl)-2-phenylethyl]piperidine)

(3) Ephenidine (NEDPA, EPE) (N-ethyl-1,2-diphenylethylamine)

(4) Isophenidine (NPDPA) (N-isopropyl-1,2-diphenylethylamine)

but not including

(5) Lefetamine ((-)-N,N-dimethyl-α-phenylbenzeneethanamine), its salts, derivatives and isomers and salts of derivatives and isomers

25. W-18 (4-chloro-N-[1-[2-(4-nitrophenyl)ethyl]-2-piperidinylidene]benzene-sulfonamide), its salts, derivatives, isomers and analogues and salts of derivatives, isomers and analogues

26. U-47700 (3,4-dichloro-N-(2-(dimethylamino)cyclohexyl)-N-methylbenza-mide), its salts, derivatives, isomers and analogues, and salts of derivatives, isomers and analogues, including

(1) Bromadoline (4-bromo-N-(2-(dimethylamino)cyclohexyl)benzamide)

(2) U-47109 (3,4-dichloro-N-(2-(dimethylamino)cyclohexyl)benzamide)

(3) U-48520 (4-chloro-N-(2-(dimethylamino)cyclohexyl)-N-methylbenza-mide)

DRUGS

(4) U-50211 (N-(2-(dimethylamino)cyclohexyl)-4-hydroxy-N-methylbenzamide)

(5) U-77891 (3,4-dibromo-N-methyl-N-(1-methyl-1-azaspiro[4.5]decan-6-yl)benzamide). SOR/97-230; SOR/99-371; SOR/99-421; SOR/2005-235, s. 1; SOR/2005-271, s. 1; SOR/2005-337, s. 1; SOR/2012-176, s. 1; 2012, c. 1, s. 44; SOR/2015-190, s. 1; SOR/2016-107, s. 1; SOR/2017-13, ss. 1 to 5; 2017, c. 7, s. 46; SOR/2017-275, s. 1; SOR/2017-277, s. 1; SOR/2018-70, ss. 1, 2.

SCHEDULE II

(Sections 2, 4 to 7.1, 10, 29, 55 and 60)

1. [*Repealed*, 2018, c. 16, s. 204(1).]

2. Synthetic cannabinoid receptor type 1 agonists, their salts, derivatives, isomers, and salts of derivatives and isomers — with the exception of any substance that is identical to any phytocannabinoid and with the exception of ((3S)-2,3-dihydro-5-methyl-3-(4-morpholinylmethyl)pyrrolo[1,2,3-de]-1,4-benzoxazin-6-yl)-1-naphthalenyl-methanone (WIN 55,212-3) and its salts — including those that fall within the following core chemical structure classes:

(1) Any substance that has a 2-(cyclohexyl)phenol structure with substitution at the 1-position of the benzene ring by a hydroxy, ether or ester group and further substituted at the 5-position of the benzene ring, whether or not further substituted on the benzene ring to any extent, and substituted at the 3'-position of the cyclohexyl ring by an alkyl, carbonyl, hydroxyl, ether or ester, and whether or not further substituted on the cyclohexyl ring to any extent, including

(i) Nabilone (±)-trans-3-(1,1-dimethylheptyl)-6,6a,7,8,10,10a-hexahydro-1-hydroxy-6,6-dimethyl-9H-dibenzo[b,d]pyran-9-one)

(ii) Parahexyl (3-hexyl-6,6,9-trimethyl-7,8,9,10-tetrahydro-6H-dibenzo[b,d]pyran-1-ol)

(iii) 3-(1,2-dimethylheptyl)-7,8,9,10-tetrahydro-6,6,9-trimethyl-6H-dibenzo[b,d]pyran-1-ol (DMHP)

(iv) 5-(1,1-dimethylheptyl)-2-(5-hydroxy-2-(3-hydroxypropyl)cyclohexyl)phenol (CP 55,940)

(v) 5-(1,1-dimethylheptyl)-2-(3-hydroxycyclohexyl)phenol (CP 47,497)

(2) Any substance that has a 3-(1-naphthoyl)indole structure with substitution at the nitrogen atom of the indole ring, whether or not further substituted on the indole ring to any extent and whether or not substituted on the naphthyl ring to any extent, including

(i) 1-pentyl-3-(1-naphthoyl)indole (JWH-018)

(ii) 1-butyl-3-(1-naphthoyl)indole (JWH-073)

(iii) 1-pentyl-3-(4-methyl-1-naphthoyl)indole (JWH-122)

(iv) 1-hexyl-3-(1-naphthoyl)indole (JWH-019)

(v) 1-(4-pentenyl)-3-(1-naphthoyl)indole (JWH-022)

(vi) 1-butyl-3-(4-methoxy-1-naphthoyl)indole (JWH-080)

(vii) 1-pentyl-3-(4-methoxy-1-naphthoyl)indole (JWH-081)

(viii) 1-(2-morpholin-4-ylethyl)-3-(1-naphthoyl)indole (JWH-200)

(ix) 1-pentyl-3-(4-ethyl-1-naphthoyl)indole (JWH-210)

(x) 1-pentyl-3-(2-methoxy-1-naphthoyl)indole (JWH-267)

(xi) 1-[(N-methylpiperidin-2-yl)methyl]-3-(1-naphthoyl)indole (AM-1220)

(xii) 1-(5-fluoropentyl)-3-(1-naphthoyl)indole (AM-2201)

(xiii) 1-(5-fluoropentyl)-3-(4-methyl-1-naphthoyl)indole (MAM-2201)

(xiv) 1-(5-fluoropentyl)-3-(4-ethyl-1-naphthoyl)indole (EAM-2201)

(xv) ((3R)-2,3-dihydro-5-methyl-3-(4-morpholinylmethyl)pyrrolo[1,2,3-de]- 1,4-benzoxazin-6-yl)-1-naphthalenyl-methanone (WIN 55,212-2)

(3) Any substance that has a 3-(1-naphthoyl)pyrrole structure with substitution at the nitrogen atom of the pyrrole ring, whether or not further substituted on the pyrrole ring to any extent and whether or not substituted on the naphthyl ring to any extent, including

(i) 1-pentyl-5-(2-fluorophenyl)-3-(1-naphthoyl)pyrrole (JWH-307)

(4) Any substance that has a 3-phenylacetylindole structure with substitution at the nitrogen atom of the indole ring, whether or not further substituted on the indole ring to any extent and whether or not substituted on the phenyl ring to any extent, including

(i) 1-pentyl-3-(2-methoxyphenylacetyl)indole (JWH-250)

(ii) 1-pentyl-3-(2-methylphenylacetyl)indole (JWH-251)

(iii) 1-pentyl-3-(3-methoxyphenylacetyl)indole (JWH-302)

(5) Any substance that has a 3-benzoylindole structure with substitution at the nitrogen atom of the indole ring, whether or not further substituted on the indole ring to any extent and whether or not substituted on the phenyl ring to any extent, including

(i) 1-(1-methylpiperidin-2-ylmethyl)-3-(2-iodobenzoyl)indole (AM-2233)

(6) Any substance that has a 3-methanone(cyclopropyl)indole structure with substitution at the nitrogen atom of the indole ring, whether or not further substituted on the indole ring to any extent and whether or not substituted on the cyclopropyl ring to any extent, including

(i) (1-pentyl-1H-indol-3-yl)(2,2,3,3-tetramethylcyclopropyl)-methanone (UR-144)

(ii) (1-(5-fluoropentyl)-1H-indol-3-yl)(2,2,3,3-tetramethylcyclopropyl)-methanone (5F-UR-144)

(iii) (1-(2-(4-morpholinyl)ethyl)-1H-indol-3-yl)(2,2,3,3-tetramethylcyclo-propyl)-methanone (A-796,260)

(7) Any substance that has a quinolin-8-yl 1H-indole-3-carboxylate structure with substitution at the nitrogen atom of the indole ring, whether or not further substituted on the indole ring to any extent and whether or not substituted on the quinolin-8-yl ring to any extent, including

(i) 1-pentyl-8-quinolinyl ester-1H-indole-3-carboxylic acid (PB-22)

    (ii) 1-(5-fluoropentyl)-8-quinolinyl ester-1H-indole-3-carboxylic acid (5F-PB-22)

(8) Any substance that has a 3-carboxamideindazole structure with substitution at the nitrogen atom of the indazole ring, whether or not further substituted on the indazole ring to any extent and whether or not sub-stituted at the carboxamide group to any extent, including

    (i) N-(adamantan-1-yl)-1-pentyl-1H-indazole-3-carboxamide (AKB48)

    (ii) N-(adamantan-1-yl)-1-(5-fluoropentyl)-1H-indazole-3-carboxamide (5F-AKB48)

    (iii) N-(1-(aminocarbonyl)-2-methylpropyl)-1-(4-fluorobenzyl)-1H-inda-zole-3-carboxamide (AB-FUBINACA)

    (iv) N-(1-amino-3-methyl-1-oxobutan-2-yl)-1-pentyl-1H-indazole-3-car-boxamide (AB-PINACA)

(9) Any substance that has a 3-carboxamideindole structure with substitution at the nitrogen atom of the indole ring, whether or not further substituted on the indole ring to any extent and whether or not substituted at the carboxamide group to any extent, including

    (i) N-(adamantan-1-yl)-1-fluoropentylindole-3-carboxamide (STS-135)

    (ii) N-(adamantan-1-yl)-1-pentylindole-3-carboxamide (APICA). SOR/98-157; SOR/2003-32; SOR/2015-192, ss. 1, 2; 2017, c. 7, s. 47; 2018, c. 16, s. 204.

SCHEDULE III

(Sections 2. 4 to 7.1, 10, 29, 55 and 60)

1.   [*Repealed.* 2012, c. 1, s. 45.]

2.   Methylphenidate (methyl 2-phenyl-2-(piperidin-2-yl)acetate), its salts, derivatives, isomers and analogues and salts of derivatives, isomers and analogues, including

    (1) Ethylphenidate (ethyl 2-phenyl-2-(piperidin-2-yl)acetate)

    (2) Isopropylphenidate (isopropyl 2-phenyl-2-(piperidin-2-yl)acetate)

    (3) Propylphenidate (propyl 2-phenyl-2-(piperidin-2-yl)acetate)

    (4) 3,4-Dichloromethylphenidate (methyl 2-(3,4-dichlorophenyl)-2-(pi-peridin2-yl)acetate)

    (5) 4-Methylmethylphenidate (methyl 2-(4-methylphenyl)-2-(piperidin2-yl)acetate)

    (6) 4-Fluoromethylphenidate (methyl 2-(4-fluorophenyl)-2-(piperidin-2-yl)acetate)

    (7) Methylnaphthidate (methyl 2-(naphthalen-2-yl)-2-(piperidin-2-yl)ace-tate)

    (8) Ethylnaphthidate (ethyl 2-(naphthalen-2-yl)-2-(piperidin-2-yl)acetate)

3.   Methaqualone (2-methyl-3-(2-methylphenyl)-4(3H)-quinazolinone) and any salt thereof

4.   Mecloqualone (2-methyl-3-(2-chlorophenyl)-4(3H)-quinazolinone) and any salt thereof

5. Lysergic acid diethylamide (LSD) (N,N-diethyllysergamide) and any salt thereof

6. N,N-Diethyltryptamine (DET) (3-[2-diethylamino) ethyl]indole) and any salt thereof

7. N,N-Dimethyltryptamine (DMT) (3-[(2-dimethylamino)ethyl]indole) and any salt thereof

8. N-Methyl-3-piperidyl benzilate (3-[(hydroxydiphenylacetyl)oxy]-1-methylpiperidine) and any salt thereof

9. Harmaline (4,9-dihydro-7-methoxy-1-methyl-3H-pyrido(3,4-b)indole) and any salt thereof

10. Harmalol (4,9-dihydro-1-methyl-3H-pyrido (3,4-b)indol-7-ol) and any salt thereof

11. Psilocin (3-[2-(dimethylamino)ethyl]-4-hydroxyindole) and any salt thereof

12. Psilocybin (3-[2-(dimethylamino)ethyl]-4-phosphoryloxyindole) and any salt thereof

13. N-(1-phenylcyclohexyl)ethylamine (PCE) and any salt thereof

14. 1-[1-(2-Thienyl) cyclohexyl]piperidine (TCP) and any salt thereof

15. 1-Phenyl-N-propylcyclohexanamine and any salt thereof

16. Rolicyclidine (1-(1-phenylcyclohexyl) pyrrolidine) and any salt thereof

17. Mescaline (3,4,5-trimethoxybenzeneethanamine) and any salt thereof, but not peyote (lophophora)

18. [*Repealed.* SOR/2017-249, s. 1.]

19. Cathinone ((-)-α-aminopropiophenone) and its salts

20. Fenetylline (d,1-3,7-dihydro-1,3-dimethyl-7-(2-[(1-methyl-2-phenethyl)amino]ethyl)-1H-purine-2,6-dione) and any salt thereof

21. 2-Methylamino-1-phenyl-1-propanone and any salt thereof

22. 1-[1-(Phenylmethyl)cyclohexyl]piperidine and any salt thereof

23. 1-[1-(4-Methylphenyl)cyclohexyl]piperidine and any salt thereof

24. [*Repealed.* SOR/2016-73, s. 1.]

25. [*Repealed.* 2012, c. 1, s. 46.]

26. [*Repealed.* 2012, c. 1, s. 46.]

27. Aminorex (5-phenyl-4,5-dihydro-1,3-oxazol-2-amine), its salts, derivatives, isomers and analogues and salts of derivatives, isomers and analogues, including
    (1) 4-Methylaminorex (4-methyl-5-phenyl-4,5-dihydro-1,3-oxazol-2-amine)
    (2) 4,4'-Dimethylaminorex (4-methyl-5-(4-methylphenyl)-4,5-dihydro-1,3-oxazol-2-amine)

28. Etryptamine (3-(2-aminobutyl)indole) and any salt thereof

29. Lefetamine ((-)-N,N-dimethyl-α-phenylbenzeneethanamine), its salts, derivatives and isomers and salts of derivatives and isomers

30. Mesocarb (3-(α-methylphenethyl)-N-(phenylcarbamoyl)sydnone imine) and any salt thereof

31. Zipeprol (4-(2-methoxy-2-phenylethyl)-α-(methoxyphenylmethyl)-1-piperazineethanol) and any salt thereof

32. Amineptine (7-[(10,11-dihydro-5H-dibenzo[a,d]cyclohepten-5-yl)amino]-heptanoic acid) and any salt thereof

33.   Benzylpiperazine [BZP], namely 1-benzylpiperazine and its salts, isomers and salts of isomers

34.   Trifluoromethylphenylpiperazine [TFMPP], namely 1-(3-trifluoromethyl-phenyl)piperazine and its salts, isomers and salts of isomers

35.   2C-phenethylamines and their salts, derivatives, isomers and salts of derivatives and isomers that correspond to the following chemical description:

any substance that has a 1-amino-2-phenylethane structure substituted at the 2' and 5' or 2' and 6' positions of the benzene ring by an alkoxy or haloalkoxy group, or substituted at two adjacent carbon atoms of the benzene ring which results in the formation of a furan, dihydrofuran, pyran, dihydropyran or methylenedioxy group — whether or not further substituted on the benzene ring to any extent, whether or not substituted at the amino group by one or two, or a combination of, methyl, ethyl, propyl, isopropyl, hydroxyl, benzyl (or benzyl substituted to any extent) or benzylene (or benzylene substituted to any extent) groups and whether or not substituted at the 2-ethyl (beta carbon) position by a hydroxyl, oxo or alkoxy group — and its salts and derivatives and salts of derivatives, including

(1)   4-bromo-2,5-dimethoxy-N-(2-methoxybenzyl)phenethylamine (25B-NBOMe)

(2)   4-chloro-2,5-dimethoxy-N-(2-methoxybenzyl)phenethylamine (25C-NBOMe)

(3)   4-iodo-2,5-dimethoxy-N-(2-methoxybenzyl)phenethylamine (25I-NBOMe)

(4)   4-bromo-2,5-dimethoxybenzeneethanamine (2C-B). SOR/97-230; SOR/98-173; SOR/2000-220; SOR/2003-32; SOR/2003-412; SOR/2005-235, s. 2; SOR/2012-66, s. 1; 2012, c. 1, ss. 45, 46; SOR/2016-73, ss. 1, 2; SOR/2016-107, s. 2; SOR/2017-13, s. 6; 2017, c. 7, s. 48; SOR/2017-249, ss. 1, 2.

SCHEDULE IV

(Sections 2, 4 to 7.1, 10, 29, 55 and 60)

1.   Barbiturates, their salts and derivatives including

(1)   Allobarbital (5,5-diallylbarbituric acid)

(2)   Alphenal (5-allyl-5-phenylbarbituric acid)

(3)   Amobarbital (5-ethyl-5-(3-methylbutyl)barbituric acid)

(4)   Aprobarbital (5-allyl-5-isopropylbarbituric acid)

(5)   Barbital (5,5-diethylbarbituric acid)

(6)   [*Repealed.* SOR/2017-13, s. 7(1).]

(7)   Butabarbital (5-sec-butyl-5-ethylbarbituric acid)

(8)   Butalbital (5-allyl-5-isobutylbarbituric acid)

(9)   Butallylonal (5-(2-bromoallyl)-5-sec-butylbarbituric acid)

(10)   Butethal (5-butyl-5-ethylbarbituric acid)

(11)   Cyclobarbital (5-(1-cyclohexen-1-yl)-5-ethylbarbituric acid)

    (12) Cyclopal (5-allyl-5-(2-cyclopenten-1-yl)barbituric acid)
    (13) Heptabarbital (5-(1-cyclohepten-1-yl)-5-ethylbarbituric acid
    (14) Hexethal (5-ethyl-5-hexylbarbituric acid)
    (15) Hexobarbital (5-(1-cyclohexen-1-yl)-1,5-dimethylbarbituric acid)
    (16) Mephobarbital (5-ethyl-1-methyl-5-phenylbarbituric acid)
    (17) Methabarbital (5,5-diethyl-1-methylbarbituric acid)
    (18) Methylphenobarbital (5-ethyl-1-methyl-5-phenylbarbituric acid)
    (19) Propallylonal (5-(2-bromoallyl)-5-isopropylbarbituric acid)
    (20) Pentobarbital (5-ethyl-5-(1-methylbutyl)barbituric acid)
    (21) Phenobarbital (5-ethyl-5-phenylbarbituric acid)
    (22) Probarbital (5-ethyl-5-isopropylbarbituric acid)
    (23) Phenylmethylbarbituric Acid (5-methyl-5-phenylbarbituric acid)
    (24) Secobarbital (5-allyl-5-(1-methylbutyl)barbituric acid)
    (25) Sigmodal (5-(2-bromoallyl)-5-(1-methylbutyl) barbituric acid
    (26) Talbutal (5-allyl-5-sec-butylbarbituric acid)
    (27) Vinbarbital (5-ethyl-5-(1-methyl-1-butenyl) barbituric acid)
    (28) Vinylbital (5-(1-methylbutyl)-5-vinylbarbituric acid)
but not including
    (29) Barbituric Acid (2,4,6(1H,3H,5H)-pyrimidinetrione) and its salts
    (30) 1,3-dimethylbarbituric acid (1,3-dimethyl-2,4,6(1H,3H,5H)-pyrimidi-netrione) and its salts

2.   Thiobarbiturates, their salts and derivatives including:
    (1) Thialbarbital (5-allyl-5-(2-cyclohexen-1-yl)-2-thiobarbituric acid)
    (2) Thiamylal (5-allyl-5-(1-methylbutyl)-2-thiobarbituric acid)
    (3) Thiobarbituric Acid (2-thiobarbituric acid)
    (4) Thiopental (5-ethyl-5-(1-methylbutyl)-2-thiobarbituric acid)

3.   Chlorphentermine (1-(p-chlorophenyl)-2-methyl-2-aminopropane) and any salt thereof

4.   Diethylpropion (2-(diethylamino)propiophenone) and any salt thereof

5.   Phendimetrazine (d-3,4-dimethyl-2-phenylmorpholine) and any salt thereof

6.   Phenmetrazine (3-methyl-2-phenylmorpholine) and any salt thereof

7.   Pipradol (α,α-diphenyl-2-piperidinemethanol) and its salts

8.   Phentermine (α,α-dimethylbenzeneethanamine) and any salt thereof

9.   Butorphanol (*l*-N-cyclobutylmethyl-3,14-dihydroxymorphinan) and its salts

10.   Nalbuphine (N-cyclobutylmethyl-4,5-epoxy-morphinan-3,6,14-triol) and its salts

11.   Gluethimide (2-ethyl-2-phenylglutarimide)

12.   Clotiazepam (5-(o-chlorophenyl)-7-ethyl-1,3-dihydro-1-methyl-2H-thie-no[2,3-e]-1,4-diazepin-2-one) and any salt thereof

13.   Ethchlorvynol (ethyl-2-chlorovinyl ethynyl carbinol)

14.   Ethinamate (1-ethynylcyclohexanol carbamate)

15.   Mazindol (5-(p-chlorophenyl)-2,5-dihydro-3H-imidazo[2,1-a]isoindol-5-ol)

16.   Meprobamate (2-methyl-2-propyl-1,3-propanediol dicarbamate)

17.   Methyprylon (3,3-diethyl-5-methyl-2,4-piperidinedione)

18.   Benzodiazepines, their salts and derivatives, including:

      (1)   Alprazolam (8-chloro-1-methyl-6-phenyl-4H-s-triazolo[4,3-a][1,4] benzodiazepine)

      (2)   Bromazepam (7-bromo-1,3-dihydro-5-(2-pyridyl)-2H-1, 4-benzodiazepin-2-one)

   (2.1)   Brotizolam (2-bromo-4-(0-chlorophenyl)-9-methyl-6H-thieno[3,2-f]-s-triazolo[4,3-a][1,4]diazepine)

      (3)   Camazepam (7-chloro-1,3-dihydro-3-(N,N-dimethylcarbamoyl)-1-methyl-5-phenyl-2H-1,4-benzodiazepin-2-one)

      (4)   Chlordiazepoxide (7-chloro-2-(methylamino)-5-phenyl-3H-1,4-benzo-diazepine-4-oxide)

      (5)   Clobazam (7-chloro-1-methyl-5-phenyl-1H-1,5-benzodiazepine-2,4(3H,5H)-dione)

      (6)   Clonazepam (5-(o-chlorophenyl)-1,3-dihydro-7-nitro-2H-1,4-benzo-diazepin-2-one)

      (7)   Clorazepate (7-chloro-2,3-dihydro-2,2-dihydroxy-5-phenyl-1H-1,4-benzodiazepine-3-carboxylic acid)

      (8)   Cloxazolam (10-chloro-11b-(0-chlorophenyl)-2,3,7,11b-tetrahydroox-azolo[3,2-d][1,4]benzodiazepin 6-(5H)-one)

      (9)   Delorazepam (7-chloro-5-o-chlorophenyl)-1,3-dihydro-2H-1,4-benzo-diazepin-2-one)

    (10)   Diazepam (7-chloro-1,3-dihydro-1-methyl-5-phenyl-2H-1,4-benzodia-zepin-2-one)

    (11)   Estazolam (8-chloro-6-phenyl-4H-s-triazolo[4,3-a][1,4]benzodiaze-pine)

    (12)   Ethyl Loflazepate (ethyl 7-chloro-5-(o-fluorophenyl)-2,3-dihydro-2-oxo-1H-1,4-benzodiazepine-3-carboxylate)

    (13)   Fludiazepam (7-chloro-5-(o-fluorophenyl)-1,3-dihydro-1-methyl-2H-1,4-benzodiazepin-2-one)

    (14)   [*Repealed*, SOR/98-173, s. 2.]

    (15)   Flurazepam (7-chloro-1-[2-(diethylamino) ethyl]-5-(o-fluorophenyl)-1,3dihydro-2H-1,4-benzodiazepin-2-one)

    (16)   Halazepam (7-chloro-1,3-dihydro-5-phenyl-1-(2, 2,2-trifluoroethyl)-2H-1,4-benzodiazepin-2-one)

    (17)   Haloxazolam (10-bromo-11b-(o-fluorophenyl)-2,3,7,11b-tetrahy-drooxazolo[3,2-d][1,4]benzodiazepin-6(5H)-one)

    (18)   Ketazolam (11-chloro-8,12b-dihydro-2,8-dimethyl-12b-phenyl-4H-[1,3]-oxazino-[3,2-d][1,4] benzodiazepine-4,7(6H)-dione)

    (19)   Loprazolam (6-(o-chlorophenyl)-2,4-dihydro-2-[(4-methyl-1-piperazi-nyl)methylene]-8-nitro-1H-imidazo[1,2-a][1,4]benzodiazepin-1-one)

    (20)   Lorazepam (7-chloro-5-(o-chlorophenyl)-1,3-dihydro-3-hydroxy-2H-1,4-benzodiazepin-2-one)

    (21)   Lormetazepam (7-chloro-5-(o-chlorophenyl)-1,3-dihydro-3-hydroxy-1-methyl-2H-1,4-benzodiazepin-2-one)

    (22)   Medazepam (7-chloro-2,3-dihydro-1-methyl-5-phenyl-1H-1,4-benzo-diazepine)

(22.1) Midazolam (8-chloro-6-(0-fluorophenyl)-1-methyl-4H-imidazo[1,5-9][1,4]benzodiazepine)

(23) Nimetazepam (1,3-dihydro-1-methyl-7-nitro-5-phenyl-2H-1,4-benzodiazepin-2-one)

(24) Nitrazepam (1,3-dihydro-7-nitro-5-phenyl-2H-1,4-benzodiazepin-2-one)

(25) Nordazepam (7-chloro-1,3-dihydro-5-phenyl-2H-1,4-benzodiazepin-2-one)

(26) Oxazepam (7-chloro-1,3-dihydro-3-hydroxy-5-phenyl-2H-1,4-benzodiazepin-2-one)

(27) Oxazolam (10-chloro-2,3,7,11b-tetrahydro-2-methyl-11b-phenyloxazolo [3,2-d][1,4]benzodiazepin-6(5H)-one)

(28) Pinazepam (7-chloro-1,3-dihydro-5-phenyl-1-(2-propynyl)-2H-1, 4-benzodiazepin-2-one)

(29) Prazepam (7-chloro-1-(cyclopropylmethyl)-1,3-dihydro-5-phenyl-2H-1,4-benzodiazepin-2-one)

(29.1) Quazepam (7-chloro-5-(0-fluorophenyl)-1,3-dihydro-1-(2,2,2-trifluoroethyl)-2H-1,4-benzodiazepin-2-thione)

(30) Temazepam (7-chloro-1,3-dihydro-3-hydroxy-1-methyl-5-phenyl-2H-1,4-benzodiazepin-2-one)

(31) Tetrazepam (7-chloro-5-(cyclohexen-1-yl)-1,3-dihdyro-1-methyl-2H-1,4-benzodiazepin-2-one)

(32) Triazolam (8-chloro-6-(o-chlorophenyl)-1-methyl-4H-s-triazolo [4,3-a][1,4]benzodiazepine)

but not including

(32.1) Clozapine (8-chloro-11-(4-methyl-1-piperazinyl)-5H-dibenzo[-b,e][1,4]diazepine) and any salt thereof

(33) Flunitrazepam (5-(o-fluorophenyl)-1,3-dihydro-1-methyl-7-nitro-2H-1,4-benzodiazepin-2-one) and any salts or derivatives thereof

(34) Olanzapine (2-methyl-4-(4-methyl-1-piperazinyl)-10H-thieno[2,3-b][1,5]benzodiazepine) and its salts

(35) Clozapine N-oxide (8-chloro-11-(4-methyl-4-oxido-1-piperazinyl)-5H dibenzo[b,e][1,4]diazepine) and its salts

19. *Catha edulis* Forsk, its preparations, derivatives, alkaloids and salts, including:

(1) Cathine (d-threo-2-amino-1-hydroxy-1-phenylpropane)

20. Fencamfamin (d,1-N-ethyl-3-phenylbicyclo[2,2,1]heptan-2-amine) and any salt thereof

21. Fenproporex (d,1-3-[(α-methylphenethyl)amino]propionitrile) and any salt thereof

22. Mefenorex (d,1-N-(3-chloropropyl)-α-methylbenzeneethanamine) and any salt thereof

23. Anabolic steroids and their derivatives including:

(1) Androisoxazole (17B-hydroxy-17α-methylandrostano[3,2-c]isoxazole)

(2) Androstanolone (17B-hydroxy-5α-androstan-3-one)

(3) Androstenediol (androst-5-ene-3B,17B-diol)

DRUGS

(4)   Bolandiol (estr-4-ene-3B,17B-diol)

(5)   Bolasterone (17B-hydroxy-7α,17-dimethylandrost-4-en-3-one)

(6)   Bolazine (17B-hydroxy-2α-methyl-5B-androstan-3-one azine)

(7)   Boldenone (17B-hydroxyandrosta-1,4-dien-3-one)

(8)   Bolenol (19-nor-17α-pregn-5-en-17-ol)

(9)   Calusterone (17B-hydroxy-7B,17-dimethylandrost-4-en-3-one)

(10) Clostebol (4-chloro-17B-hydroxyandrost-4-en-3-one)

(11) Drostanolone (17B-hydroxy-2α-methyl-5α-androstan-3-one)

(12) Enestebol (4,17B-dihydroxy-17-methylandrosta-1,4-dien-3-one)

(13) Epitiostanol (2α, 3α-epithio-5α-androstan-17B-ol)

(14) Ethylestrenol (19-nor-17α-pregn-4-en-17-ol)

(15) 4-Hydroxy-19-nor testosterone

(16) Fluoxymesterone (9-fluoro-11B,17B-dihydroxy-17-methylandrost-4-en-3-one)

(17) Formebolone (11α,17B-dihydroxy-17-methyl-3-oxoandrosta-1,4 di-2n-2-carboxaldehyde)

(18) Furazabol (17-methol-5α-androstano[2,3-c]furazan-17B-ol)

(19) Mebolazine (17B-hydroxy-2α,17-dimethyl-5α-androstan-3-one azine)

(20) Mesabolone (17B-[(1-methoxycyclohexyl)oxy]-5α-androst-1-en-3-one)

(21) Mesterolone (17B-hydroxy-1α-methyl-5α-androstan-3-one)

(22) Metandienone (17B-hydroxy-17-methylandrosta-1,4-dien-3-one)

(23) Metenolone (17B-hydroxy-1-methyl-5α-androst-1-en-3-one)

(24) Methandriol (17α-methylandrost-5-ene-3B,17B-diol)

(25) Methyltestosterone (17B-hydroxy-17-methylandrost-4-en-3-one)

(26) Metribolone (17B-hydroxy-17-methylestra-4,9,11-trien-3-one)

(27) Mibolerone (17B-hydroxy-7α,170dimethylestr-4-en-3-one)

(28) Nandrolone (17B-hydroxyestr-4-en-3-one)

(29) Norboletone (13-ethyl-17B-hydroxy-18,19-dinorpregn-4-en-3-one)

(30) Norclostebol (4-chloro-17B-hydroxyestr-4-en-3-one)

(31) Norethandrolone (17α-ethyl-17B-hydroxyestr-4-en-3-one)

(32) Oxabolone (4,17B-dihydroxyestr-4-en-3-one)

(33) Oxandrolone (17B-hydroxy-17-methyl-2-oxa-5α-androstan-3-one)

(34) Oxymesterone (4,17B-dihydroxy-17-methylandrost-4-en-3-one)

(35) Oxymetholone (17B-hydroxy-2-(hydroxymethylene)-17-methyl-5α-androstan-3-one)

(36) Prasterone (3B-hydroxyandrost-5-en-17-one)

(37) Quinbolone (17B-(1-cyclopenten-1-yloxy)androsta-1,4-dien-3-one)

(38) Stanozolol (17B-hydroxy-17-methyl-5α-androstano[3,2-c]pyrazole)

(39) Stenbolone (17B-hydroxy-2-methyl-5α-androst-1-en-3-one)

(40) Testosterone (17B-hydroxyandrost-4-en-3-one)

(41) Tibolone ((7α, 17α)-17-hydroxy-7-methyl-19-norpregn-5(10)-en-20-yn-3-one)

(42) Tiomesterone (1α,7α-bis(acetylthio)-17B-hydroxy-17-methylandrost-4-en-3-one)

(43) Trenbolone (17B-hydroxyestra-4,9,11-trien-3-one)

24.   Zeranol (3,4,5,6,7,8,9,10,11,12-decahydro-7,14,16-trihydroxy-3-methyl-1H-2-benzoxacyclotetradecin-1-one)

25. Zolpidem (N,N,6-trimethyl-2-(4-methylphenyl)imidazo [1,2-a]pyridine-3-acetamide) and any salt thereof
25.1 Pemoline (2-amino-5-phenyl-oxazolin-4-one) and any salt thereof
26. Pyrovalerone (4′-methyl-2-(1-pyrrolidinyl) valerophenone) and any salt thereof
27. *Salvia divinorum* (*S. divinorum*), its preparations and derivatives, including:
    (1) Salvinorin A ((2S,4aR,6aR,7R,9S,10aS,10bR)-9-(acetyloxy)-2-(3-furanyl)dodecahydro-6a,10b-dimethyl-4,10-dioxo-2H-naphtho[2,1-c]pyran-7-carboxylic acid methyl ester). SOR/97-230; SOR/98-173; SOR/99-371; SOR/99-421; SOR/2000-220, s. 2; SOR/2003-32, s. 6; SOR/2003-37, s. 1; SOR/2015-209, s. 1; SOR/2017-13, ss. 7 to 12; 2017, c. 7, s. 49.

SCHEDULE V

(Sections 2, 5 to 7.1, 10, 55 and 60.1)

1. [*Repealed*, SOR/2002-361, s. 1.]
2. [*Repealed*, 2017, c. 7, s. 50 (Sched. 1).]
3. [*Repealed*, SOR/2003-32, s. 7.]

SCHEDULE VI

(Sections 2, 6, 55 and 60)

PART 1
CLASS A PRECURSORS[1]
1. Acetic anhydride
2. N-Acetylanthranilic acid (2-acetamidobenzoic acid) and its salts
3. Anthranilic acid (2-aminobenzoic acid) and its salts
4. Ephedrine (erythro-2-(methylamino)-1-phenylpropan-1-ol), its salts and any plant containing ephedrine or any of its salts
5. Ergometrine (9,10-didehydro-N-(2-hydroxy-1-methylethyl)-6-methylergoline-8-carboxamide) and its salts
6. Ergotamine (12-hydroxy-2-methyl-5-(phenylmethyl)ergotaman-3,6,18-trione) and its salts
7. Isosafrole (5-(1-propenyl)-1,3-benzodioxole)
8. Lysergic acid (9,10-didehydro-6-methylergoline-8-carboxylic acid) and its salts
9. 3,4-Methylenedioxyphenyl-2-propanone (1-(1,3-benzodioxole)-2-propanone)
10. Norephedrine (Phenylpropanolamine) and its salts
11. 1-Phenyl-2-propanone
12. Phenylacetic acid and its salts

13.   Piperidine and its salts
14.   Piperonal (1,3-benzodioxole-5-carboxaldehyde)
15.   Potassium permanganate
16.   Pseudoephedrine (threo-2-(methylamino)-1-phenylpropan-1-ol), its salts and any plant containing pseudoephedrine or any of its salts
17.   Safrole (5-(2-propenyl)-1,3-benzodioxole) and any essential oil containing safrole
18.   Gamma-butyrolactone (dihydro-2(3H)-furanone)
19.   1,4-butanediol
20.   Red Phosphorus
21.   White Phosphorus
22.   Hypophosphorous acid, its salts and derivatives
23.   Hydriodic acid
24.   Alpha-phenylacetoacetonitrile and its salts, isomers and salts of isomers
25.   Propionyl chloride
26.   1-Phenethyl-4-piperidone and its salts
27.   4-Piperidone and its salts
28.   Norfentanyl (N-phenyl-N-piperidin-4-ylpropanamide) and its salts
29.   1-Phenethylpiperidin-4-ylidenephenylamine and its salts
30.   N-Phenyl-4-piperidinamine and its salts
31.   N1,N1,N2-trimethylcyclohexane-1,2-diamine and its salts

[1] Each Class A precursor includes synthetic and natural forms.

PART 2
CLASS B PRECURSORS[1]
1.   Acetone
2.   Ethyl ether
3.   Hydrochloric acid
4.   Methyl ethyl ketone
5.   Sulphuric acid
6.   Toluene

[1] Each Class A precursor includes synthetic forms.

PART 3
PREPARATIONS AND MIXTURES
1.   Any preparation or mixture that contains a precursor set out in Part 1, except1 items 20 to 23, or in Part 2. SOR/2002-361, s. 2; SOR/2005-364, ss. 1, 2, 4; SOR/2016-13, s. 1; SOR/2016-295, s. 1.

SCHEDULE VII   [*Repealed*, **2018, c. 16, s. 205.**]

SCHEDULE VIII   [*Repealed*, **2018, c. 16, s. 205.**]

SCHEDULE IX

(Sections 2 and 60)

1.   Manual, semi-automatic or fully automatic device that may be used to compact or mould powdered, granular or semi-solid material to produce coherent solid tablets
2.   Manual, semi-automatic or fully automatic device that may be used to fill capsules with any powdered, granular, semi-solid or liquid material. 2017, c. 7, s. 51 (Sched. 2).

SCHEDULE VII

[repealed, 2018, c. 16, s. 205.]

SCHEDULE VIII

[Repealed 2018, c. 16, s. 204.]

SCHEDULE IX

(Sections 2 and 60)

1. Manual, semi-automatic or fully automatic device that may be used to compact or mould powdered, granular or semi-solid material to produce coherent solid tablet.

2. Manual semi-automatic or fully automatic device that may be used to fill capsules with any powdered, granular, semi-solid or liquid material subject to s. 51.1(3)(a).

CRIMES AGAINST HUMANITY AND WAR CRIMES ACT

S.C. 2000, c. 24

Amended 2001, c. 32, ss. 59 to 61; brought into force February 1, 2002 by SI/
2002-17 by para. (b)
Amended 2019, c. 25, s. 399; in force September 19, 2019

**An Act respecting genocide, crimes against humanity
and war crimes and to implement the Rome Statute of
the International Criminal Court, and to make
consequential amendments to other Acts**

SHORT TITLE

SHORT TITLE.

1. This Act may be cited as the *Crimes Against Humanity and War Crimes Act*.

INTERPRETATION

**DEFINITIONS / "Conventional international law" / "International Criminal
Court" / "Official" / "Rome Statute" / Words and Expressions.**

2. (1) The definitions in this subsection apply in this Act.

"conventional international law" means any convention, treaty or other
international agreement

    (a) that is in force and to which Canada is a party; or

    (b) that is in force and the provisions of which Canada has agreed to accept
and apply in an armed conflict in which it is involved.

"International Criminal Court" means the International Criminal Court established
by the Rome Statute.

"official", in respect of the International Criminal Court, means the Prosecutor,
Registrar, Deputy Prosecutor and Deputy Registrar, and the staff of the organs of
the Court.

"Rome Statute" means the Rome Statute of the International Criminal Court
adopted by the United Nations Diplomatic Conference of Plenipotentiaries on the
Establishment of an International Criminal Court on July 17, 1998, as corrected by
the procès-verbaux of November 10, 1998, July 12, 1999, November 30, 1999 and
May 8, 2000, portions of which are set out in the schedule.

(2) Unless otherwise provided, words and expressions used in this Act have the same meaning as in the *Criminal Code*.

HER MAJESTY

BINDING ON HER MAJESTY.

3. This Act is binding on Her Majesty in right of Canada or a province.

OFFENCES WITHIN CANADA

GENOCIDE, ETC., COMMITTED IN CANADA / Conspiracy, attempt, etc. / Punishment / Definitions / Interpretation — customary international law.

4. (1) Every person is guilty of an indictable offence who commits
  (*a*) genocide;
  (*b*) a crime against humanity; or
  (*c*) a war crime.

(1.1) Every person who conspires or attempts to commit, is an accessory after the fact in relation to, or counsels in relation to, an offence referred to in subsection (1) is guilty of an indictable offence.

(2) Every person who commits an offence under subsection (1) or (1.1)
  (*a*) shall be sentenced to imprisonment for life, if an intentional killing forms the basis of the offence; and
  (*b*) is liable to imprisonment for life, in any other case.

(3) The definitions in this subsection apply in this section.

"crime against humanity" means murder, extermination, enslavement, deportation, imprisonment, torture, sexual violence, persecution or any other inhumane act or omission that is committed against any civilian population or any identifiable group and that, at the time and in the place of its commission, constitutes a crime against humanity according to customary international law or conventional international law or by virtue of its being criminal according to the general principles of law recognized by the community of nations, whether or not it constitutes a contravention of the law in force at the time and in the place of its commission.

"genocide" means an act or omission committed with intent to destroy, in whole or in part, an identifiable group of persons, as such, that, at the time and in the place of its commission, constitutes genocide according to customary international law or conventional international law or by virtue of its being criminal according to the general principles of law recognized by the community of nations, whether or not it constitutes a contravention of the law in force at the time and in the place of its commission.

"war crime" means an act or omission committed during an armed conflict that, at the time and in the place of its commission, constitutes a war crime according to customary international law or conventional international law applicable to armed conflicts, whether or not it constitutes a contravention of the law in force at the time and in the place of its commission.

(4) For greater certainty, crimes described in Articles 6 and 7 and paragraph 2 of Article 8 of the Rome Statute are, as of July 17, 1998, crimes according to customary international law. This does not limit or prejudice in any way the application of existing or developing rules of international law.

BREACH OF RESPONSIBILITY BY MILITARY COMMANDER / Breach of responsibility by a superior / Conspiracy, attempt, etc. / Punishment / Definitions.

5. (1) A military commander commits an indictable offence if

   (*a*) the military commander

     (i) fails to exercise control properly over a person under their effective command and control or effective authority and control, and as a result the person commits an offence under section 4, or

     (ii) fails, after the coming into force of this section, to exercise control properly over a person under their effective command and control or effective authority and control, and as a result the person commits an offence under section 6;

   (*b*) the military commander knows, or is criminally negligent in failing to know, that the person is about to commit or is committing such an offence; and

   (*c*) the military commander subsequently

     (i) fails to take, as soon as practicable, all necessary and reasonable measures within their power to prevent or repress the commission of the offence, or the further commission of offences under section 4 or 6, or

     (ii) fails to take, as soon as practicable, all necessary and reasonable measures within their power to submit the matter to the competent authorities for investigation and prosecution.

(2) A superior commits an indictable offence if

   (*a*) the superior

     (i) fails to exercise control properly over a person under their effective authority and control, and as a result the person commits an offence under section 4, or

     (ii) fails, after the coming into force of this section, to exercise control properly over a person under their effective authority and control, and as a result the person commits an offence under section 6;

   (*b*) the superior knows that the person is about to commit or is committing such an offence, or consciously disregards information that clearly indicates that such an offence is about to be committed or is being committed by the person;

   (*c*) the offence relates to activities for which the superior has effective authority and control; and

   (*d*) the superior subsequently

WAR

    (i) fails to take, as soon as practicable, all necessary and reasonable measures within their power to prevent or repress the commission of the offence, or the further commission of offences under section 4 or 6, or

    (ii) fails to take, as soon as practicable, all necessary and reasonable measures within their power to submit the matter to the competent authorities for investigation and prosecution.

(2.1) Every person who conspires or attempts to commit, is an accessory after the fact in relation to, or counsels in relation to, an offence referred to in subsection (1) or (2) is guilty of an indictable offence.

(3) Every person who commits an offence under subsection (1), (2) or (2.1) is liable to imprisonment for life.

(4) The definitions in this subsection apply in this section.

"military commander" includes a person effectively acting as a military commander and a person who commands police with a degree of authority and control comparable to a military commander.

"superior" means a person in authority, other than a military commander.

OFFENCES OUTSIDE CANADA

GENOCIDE, ETC., COMMITTED OUTSIDE CANADA / Conspiracy, attempt, etc. / Punishment / Definitions / Interpretation — customary international law / Interpretation — crimes against humanity.

6. (1) Every person who, either before or after the coming into force of this section, commits outside Canada

    (*a*) genocide,

    (*b*) a crime against humanity, or

    (*c*) a war crime,

is guilty of an indictable offence and may be prosecuted for that offence in accordance with section 8.

(1.1) Every person who conspires or attempts to commit, is an accessory after the fact in relation to, or counsels in relation to, an offence referred to in subsection (1) is guilty of an indictable offence.

(2) Every person who commits an offence under subsection (1) or (1.1)

    (*a*) shall be sentenced to imprisonment for life, if an intentional killing forms the basis of the offence; and

    (*b*) is liable to imprisonment for life, in any other case.

(3) The definitions in this subsection apply in this section.

"crime against humanity" means murder, extermination, enslavement, deportation, imprisonment, torture, sexual violence, persecution or any other inhumane act or omission that is committed against any civilian population or any identifiable group and that, at the time and in the place of its commission, constitutes a crime against humanity according to customary international law or conventional international law or by virtue of its being criminal according to the general principles of law recognized by the community of nations, whether or not it constitutes a contravention of the law in force at the time and in the place of its commission.

"genocide" means an act or omission committed with intent to destroy, in whole or in part, an identifiable group of persons, as such, that at the time and in the place of its commission, constitutes genocide according to customary international law or conventional international law or by virtue of its being criminal according to the general principles of law recognized by the community of nations, whether or not it constitutes a contravention of the law in force at the time and in the place of its commission.

"war crime" means an act or omission committed during an armed conflict that, at the time and in the place of its commission, constitutes a war crime according to customary international law or conventional international law applicable to armed conflicts, whether or not it constitutes a contravention of the law in force at the time and in the place of its commission.

(4) For greater certainty, crimes described in articles 6 and 7 and paragraph 2 of article 8 of the Rome Statute are, as of July 17, 1998, crimes according to customary international law, and may be crimes according to customary international law before that date. This does not limit or prejudice in any way the application of existing or developing rules of international law.

(5) For greater certainty, the offence of crime against humanity was part of customary international law or was criminal according to the general principles of law recognized by the community of nations before the coming into force of either of the following:

> (a) the Agreement for the prosecution and punishment of the major war criminals of the European Axis, signed at London on August 8, 1945; and
> (b) the Proclamation by the Supreme Commander for the Allied Powers, dated January 19, 1946.

BREACH OF RESPONSIBILITY BY MILITARY COMMANDER / Breach of responsibility by a superior / Conspiracy, attempt, etc. / Jurisdiction / Punishment / Application before coming into force / Definitions.

7. (1) A military commander commits an indictable offence if

> (a) the military commander, outside Canada,
> > (i) fails to exercise control properly over a person under their effective command and control or effective authority and control, and as a result the person commits an offence under section 4, or
> > (ii) fails, before or after the coming into force of this section, to exercise control properly over a person under their effective command and control or effective authority and control, and as a result the person commits an offence under section 6;
> (b) the military commander knows, or is criminally negligent in failing to know, that the person is about to commit or is committing such an offence; and

WAR

  (*c*) the military commander subsequently
- (i) fails to take, as soon as practicable, all necessary and reasonable measures within their power to prevent or repress the commission of the offence, or the further commission of offences under section 4 or 6, or
- (ii) fails to take, as soon as practicable, all necessary and reasonable measures within their power to submit the matter to the competent authorities for investigation and prosecution.

(2) A superior commits an indictable offence if
  (*a*) the superior, outside Canada,
- (i) fails to exercise control properly over a person under their effective authority and control, and as a result the person commits an offence under section 4, or
- (ii) fails, before or after the coming into force of this section, to exercise control properly over a person under their effective authority and control, and as a result the person commits an offence under section 6;

  (*b*) the superior knows that the person is about to commit or is committing such an offence, or consciously disregards information that clearly indicates that such an offence is about to be committed or is being committed by the person;

  (*c*) the offence relates to activities for which the superior has effective authority and control; and

  (*d*) the superior subsequently
- (i) fails to take, as soon as practicable, all necessary and reasonable measures within their power to prevent or repress the commission of the offence, or the further commission of offences under section 4 or 6, or
- (ii) fails to take, as soon as practicable, all necessary and reasonable measures within their power to submit the matter to the competent authorities for investigation and prosecution.

(2.1) Every person who conspires or attempts to commit, is an accessory after the fact in relation to, or counsels in relation to, an offence referred to in subsection (1) or (2) is guilty of an indictable offence.

(3) A person who is alleged to have committed an offence under subsection (1), (2) or (2.1) may be prosecuted for that offence in accordance with section 8.

(4) Every person who commits an offence under subsection (1), (2) or (2.1) is liable to imprisonment for life.

(5) Where an act or omission constituting an offence under this section occurred before the coming into force of this section, subparagraphs (1)(*a*)(ii) and (2)(*a*)(ii) apply to the extent that, at the time and in the place of the act or omission, the act or omission constituted a contravention of customary international law or conventional international law or was criminal according to the general principles of law recognized by the community of nations, whether or not it constituted a contravention of the law in force at the time and in the place of its commission.

(6) The definitions in this subsection apply in this section.

"military commander" includes a person effectively acting as a military commander and a person who commands police with a degree of authority and control comparable to a military commander.

"superior" means a person in authority, other than a military commander.

JURISDICTION.

8. A person who is alleged to have committed an offence under section 6 or 7 may be prosecuted for that offence if

  (a) at the time the offence is alleged to have been committed,
   (i) the person was a Canadian citizen or was employed by Canada in a civilian or military capacity,
   (ii) the person was a citizen of a state that was engaged in an armed conflict against Canada, or was employed in a civilian or military capacity by such a state,
   (iii) the victim of the alleged offence was a Canadian citizen, or
   (iv) the victim of the alleged offence was a citizen of a state that was allied with Canada in an armed conflict; or
  (b) after the time the offence is alleged to have been committed, the person is present in Canada.

PROCEDURE AND DEFENCES

PLACE OF TRIAL / Presence of accused at trial / Personal consent of Attorney General / Consent of Attorney General.

9. (1) Proceedings for an offence under this Act alleged to have been committed outside Canada for which a person may be prosecuted under this Act may, whether or not the person is in Canada, be commenced in any territorial division in Canada and the person may be tried and punished in respect of that offence in the same manner as if the offence had been committed in that territorial division.

(2) For greater certainty, in a proceeding commenced in any territorial division under subsection (1), the provisions of the *Criminal Code* relating to requirements that an accused appear at and be present during proceedings and any exceptions to those requirements apply.

(3) No proceedings for an offence under any of sections 4 to 7 of this Act, or under section 354 or subsection 462.31(1) of the *Criminal Code* in relation to property or proceeds obtained or derived directly or indirectly as a result of the commission of an offence under this Act, may be commenced without the personal consent in writing of the Attorney General or Deputy Attorney General of Canada, and those proceedings may be conducted only by the Attorney General of Canada or counsel acting on their behalf.

(4) No proceedings for an offence under section 18 may be commenced without the consent of the Attorney General of Canada. 2001, c. 32, s. 59.

WAR

EVIDENCE AND PROCEDURE.

10. Proceedings for an offence alleged to have been committed before the coming into force of this section shall be conducted in accordance with the laws of evidence and procedure in force at the time of the proceedings.

DEFENCES.

11. In proceedings for an offence under any of sections 4 to 7, the accused may, subject to sections 12 to 14 and to subsection 607(6) of the *Criminal Code*, rely on any justification, excuse or defence available under the laws of Canada or under international law at the time of the alleged offence or at the time of the proceedings.

WHEN PREVIOUSLY TRIED OUTSIDE CANADA / Exception.

12. (1) If a person is alleged to have committed an act or omission that is an offence under this Act, and the person has been tried and dealt with outside Canada in respect of the offence in such a manner that, had they been tried and dealt with in Canada, they would be able to plead *autrefois acquit*, *autrefois convict* or pardon, the person is deemed to have been so tried and dealt with in Canada.

(2) Despite subsection (1), a person may not plead *autrefois acquit*, *autrefois convict* or pardon in respect of an offence under any of sections 4 to 7 if the person was tried in a court of a foreign state or territory and the proceedings in that court

    (*a*) were for the purpose of shielding the person from criminal responsibility; or

    (*b*) were not otherwise conducted independently or impartially in accordance with the norms of due process recognized by international law, and were conducted in a manner that, in the circumstances, was inconsistent with an intent to bring the person to justice.

CONFLICT WITH INTERNAL LAW.

13. Despite section 15 of the *Criminal Code*, it is not a justification, excuse or defence with respect to an offence under any of sections 4 to 7 that the offence was committed in obedience to or in conformity with the law in force at the time and in the place of its commission.

DEFENCE OF SUPERIOR ORDERS / Interpretation — manifestly unlawful / Limitation — belief of accused.

14. (1) In proceedings for an offence under any of sections 4 to 7, it is not a defence that the accused was ordered by a government or a superior — whether military or civilian — to perform the act or omission that forms the subject-matter of the offence, unless

    (*a*) the accused was under a legal obligation to obey orders of the government or superior;

    (*b*) the accused did not know that the order was unlawful; and

(c) the order was not manifestly unlawful.

(2) For the purpose of paragraph (1)(c), orders to commit genocide or crimes against humanity are manifestly unlawful.

(3) An accused cannot base their defence under subsection (1) on a belief that an order was lawful if the belief was based on information about a civilian population or an identifiable group of persons that encouraged, was likely to encourage or attempted to justify the commission of inhumane acts or omissions against the population or group.

PAROLE ELIGIBILITY

PAROLE ELIGIBILITY / Parole eligibility / Provisions of *Criminal Code* apply / Minimum punishment.

15. (1) The following sentence shall be pronounced against a person who is to be sentenced to imprisonment for life for an offence under section 4 or 6:

   (a) imprisonment for life without eligibility for parole until the person has served 25 years of the sentence, if a planned and deliberate killing forms the basis of the offence;

   (b) imprisonment for life without eligibility for parole until the person has served 25 years of the sentence, if an intentional killing that is not planned and deliberate forms the basis of the offence, and

      (i) the person has previously been convicted of an offence under section 4 or 6 that had, as its basis, an intentional killing, whether or not it was planned and deliberate, or

      (ii) the person has previously been convicted of culpable homicide that is murder, however described in the *Criminal Code*;

   (c) imprisonment for life without eligibility for parole until the person has served at least 10 years of the sentence or any greater number of years, not being more than 25, that has been substituted for it under section 745.4 of the *Criminal Code*, if an intentional killing that is not planned and deliberate forms the basis of the offence; and

   (d) imprisonment for life with normal eligibility for parole, in any other case.

(1.1) The sentence pronounced against a person who is to be sentenced to imprisonment for life for an offence under section 5 or 7 shall be imprisonment for life with normal eligibility for parole.

(2) Sections 745.1 to 746.1 of the *Criminal Code* apply, with any modifications that the circumstances require, to a sentence of life imprisonment imposed under this Act, and, for the purpose of applying those provisions,

   (a) a reference in sections 745.1, 745.3, 745.5 and 746.1 of the *Criminal Code* to first degree murder is deemed to be a reference to an offence under section 4 or 6 of this Act when a planned and deliberate killing forms the basis of the offence;

   (b) a reference in sections 745.1 to 745.5 and 746.1 of the *Criminal Code* to second degree murder is deemed to be a reference to an offence under section 4 or 6 of this Act when an intentional killing that is not planned and deliberate forms the basis of the offence;

(c) a reference in sections 745.4 and 746 of the *Criminal Code* to section 745 of that Act is deemed to be a reference to subsection (1) or (1.1) of this section;

(d) a reference in section 745.6 of the *Criminal Code* to the province in which a conviction took place is deemed, in respect of a conviction that took place outside Canada, to be a reference to the province in which the offender is incarcerated when the offender makes an application under that section; and

(e) a reference in section 745.6 of the *Criminal Code* to murder is deemed to be a reference to an offence under section 4 or 6 of this Act when an intentional killing forms the basis of the offence.

(3) For the purpose of Part XXIII of the *Criminal Code*, the sentence of imprisonment for life prescribed by sections 4 and 6 is a minimum punishment when an intentional killing forms the basis of the offence.

OFFENCES AGAINST THE ADMINISTRATION OF JUSTICE

OBSTRUCTING JUSTICE / When deemed to have obstructed justice.

16. (1) Every person who wilfully attempts in any manner to obstruct, pervert or defeat the course of justice of the International Criminal Court is guilty of an indictable offence and liable to imprisonment for a term of not more than 10 years.

(2) Without restricting the generality of subsection (1), every person is deemed wilfully to attempt to obstruct, pervert or defeat the course of justice who in an existing or proposed proceeding of the International Criminal Court

(a) dissuades or attempts to dissuade a person by threats, bribes or other corrupt means from giving evidence; or

(b) accepts, obtains, agrees to accept or attempts to obtain a bribe or other corrupt consideration to abstain from giving evidence.

OBSTRUCTING OFFICIALS.

17. Every person who resists or wilfully obstructs an official of the International Criminal Court in the execution of their duty or any person lawfully acting in aid of such an official

(a) is guilty of an indictable offence and liable to imprisonment for a term of not more than two years; or

(b) is guilty of an offence punishable on summary conviction.

BRIBERY OF JUDGES AND OFFICIALS.

18. Every person is guilty of an indictable offence and is liable to imprisonment for a term of not more than 14 years who (*a*) being a judge or an official of the International Criminal Court, corruptly accepts, obtains, agrees to accept or attempts to obtain for themselves or any other person any money, valuable consideration, office, place or employment

   (i) in respect of anything done or omitted or to be done or omitted by them in their official capacity, or

   (ii) with intent to interfere in any other way with the administration of justice of the International Criminal Court; or

(*b*) gives or offers, corruptly, to a judge or an official of the International Criminal Court, any money, valuable consideration, office, place or employment

   (i) in respect of anything done or omitted or to be done or omitted by them in their official capacity, or

   (ii) with intent to interfere in any other way with the administration of justice of the International Criminal Court.

PERJURY / Video links, etc. / Punishment / Application / Application.

19. (1) Subject to subsection (5), every person commits perjury who, with intent to mislead, makes a false statement under oath or solemn affirmation, by affidavit, solemn declaration or deposition or orally, knowing that the statement is false, before a judge of the International Criminal Court or an official of that Court who is authorized by the Court to permit statements to be made before them.

(2) Subject to subsection (5), every person who gives evidence under subsection 46(2) of the *Canada Evidence Act*, or gives evidence or a statement under an order made under section 22.2 of the *Mutual Legal Assistance in Criminal Matters Act*, commits perjury who, with intent to mislead, makes a false statement knowing that it is false, whether or not the false statement was made under oath or solemn affirmation in accordance with subsection (1), so long as the false statement was made in accordance with any formalities required by the law of the place outside Canada in which the person is virtually present or heard.

(3) Every person who commits perjury is guilty of an indictable offence and liable to imprisonment for a term of not more than 14 years.

(4) Subsection (1) applies whether or not a statement is made in a judicial proceeding of the International Criminal Court.

(5) Subsections (1) and (2) do not apply to a statement that is made by a person who is not specially permitted, authorized or required by law to make that statement.

WITNESS GIVING CONTRADICTORY EVIDENCE / Evidence in specific cases / Meaning of "evidence" / Proof of former trial.

20. (1) Every person who, being a witness in a proceeding of the International Criminal Court, gives evidence with respect to any matter of fact or knowledge and who later, in a proceeding of that Court, gives evidence that is contrary to their previous evidence, and who, in giving evidence in either proceeding, intends

WAR

to mislead, is guilty of an indictable offence and liable to imprisonment for a term of not more than 14 years, whether or not the prior or later evidence is true.

(2) Evidence given under section 714.1, 714.2 or 714.3 of the *Criminal Code* or subsection 46(2) of the *Canada Evidence Act* or evidence or a statement given under an order made under section 22.2 of the *Mutual Legal Assistance in Criminal Matters Act*, is deemed to be evidence given by a witness in a proceeding for the purpose of subsection (1).

(3) Despite the definition "evidence" in section 118 of the *Criminal Code*, for the purpose of this section, "evidence" does not include evidence that is not material.

(4) If a person is charged with an offence under this section, a certificate that specifies with reasonable particularity the proceeding in which the person is alleged to have given the evidence in respect of which the offence is charged, is evidence that it was given in a proceeding of the International Criminal Court, without proof of the signature or official character of the person by whom the certificate purports to be signed, if it purports to be signed by the Registrar of that Court or another official having the custody of the record of that proceeding or by their lawful deputy. 2019, c. 25, s. 399.

FABRICATING EVIDENCE.

21. Every person who, with intent to mislead, fabricates anything with intent that it be used as evidence in an existing or proposed proceeding of the International Criminal Court, by any means other than perjury or incitement to perjury, is guilty of an indictable offence and liable to imprisonment for a term of not more than 14 years.

OFFENCES RELATING TO AFFIDAVITS.

22. Every person is guilty of an indictable offence and liable to imprisonment for a term of not more than two years who, in respect of an existing or proposed proceeding of the International Criminal Court,

   (*a*) signs a writing that purports to be an affidavit or statutory declaration and to have been sworn or declared before them when the writing was not so sworn or declared or when they know that they have no authority to administer the oath or declaration;

   (*b*) uses or offers for use any writing purporting to be an affidavit or statutory declaration that they know was not sworn or declared, as the case may be, by the affiant or declarant or before a person authorized to administer the oath or declaration; or

   (*c*) signs as affiant or declarant a writing that purports to be an affidavit or statutory declaration and to have been sworn or declared by them, as the case may be, when the writing was not so sworn or declared.

INTIMIDATION.

23. Every person who, wrongfully and without lawful authority, for the purpose of compelling another person to abstain from doing anything that the person has a lawful right to do, or to do anything that the person has a lawful right to abstain from doing, in relation to a proceeding of the International Criminal Court, causes the person reasonably, in all the circumstances, to fear for their safety or the safety of anyone known to them

(*a*) is guilty of an indictable offence and liable to imprisonment for a term of not more than five years; or

(*b*) is guilty of an offence punishable on summary conviction.

MEANING OF "INTERNATIONALLY PROTECTED PERSON".

24. For greater certainty, the definition "internationally protected person" in section 2 of the *Criminal Code* includes judges and officials of the International Criminal Court.

OFFENCES AGAINST THE INTERNATIONAL CRIMINAL COURT — OUTSIDE CANADA / Offences against the International Criminal Court — outside Canada.

25. (1) Every person who, being a Canadian citizen, commits outside Canada an act or omission in relation to the International Criminal Court that if committed in Canada would be an offence under any of sections 16 to 23, or would be contempt of court by virtue of section 9 of the *Criminal Code*, is deemed to have committed that act or omission in Canada.

(2) Every person who, being a Canadian citizen, commits outside Canada an act or omission that if committed in Canada would constitute conspiring or attempting to commit, being an accessory after the fact in relation to, or counselling in relation to, an act or omission that is an offence or a contempt of court under subsection (1) is deemed to have committed that act or omission in Canada.

RETALIATION AGAINST WITNESSES — OUTSIDE CANADA / Retaliation against witnesses — outside Canada.

26. (1) Every person who, being a Canadian citizen, commits outside Canada an act or omission against a person or a member of the person's family in retaliation for the person having given testimony before the International Criminal Court, that if committed in Canada would be an offence under any of sections 235, 236, 264.1, 266 to 269, 271 to 273, 279 to 283, 430, 433 and 434 of the *Criminal Code*, is deemed to have committed that act or omission in Canada.

(2) Every person who, being a Canadian citizen, commits outside Canada an act or omission that if committed in Canada would constitute conspiring or attempting to commit, being an accessory after the fact in relation to, or counselling in relation to, an act or omission that is an offence under subsection (1) is deemed to have committed that act or omission in Canada.

POSSESSION OF PROPERTY OBTAINED BY CERTAIN OFFENCES.

27. [*Repealed*, 2001, c. 32, s. 60, part]

WAR

LAUNDERING PROCEEDS OF CERTAIN OFFENCES.

28. [*Repealed*, 2001, c. 32, s. 60, part]

PART XII.2 OF *CRIMINAL CODE* APPLICABLE.

29. [*Repealed*, 2001, c. 32, s. 60, part]

CRIMES AGAINST HUMANITY FUND

FUND ESTABLISHED / Payment out of Fund / Regulations.

30. (1) There is hereby established a fund, to be known as the Crimes Against Humanity Fund, into which shall be paid

(*a*) all money obtained through enforcement in Canada of orders of the International Criminal Court for reparation or forfeiture or orders of that Court imposing a fine;

(*b*) all money obtained in accordance with section 31; and

(*c*) any money otherwise received as a donation to the Crimes Against Humanity Fund.

(2) The Attorney General of Canada may make payments out of the Crimes Against Humanity Fund, with or without a deduction for costs, to the International Criminal Court, the Trust Fund established under article 79 of the Rome Statute, victims of offences under this Act or of offences within the jurisdiction of the International Criminal Court, and to the families of those victims, or otherwise as the Attorney General of Canada sees fit.

(3) The Governor in Council may make regulations respecting the administration and management of the Crimes Against Humanity Fund.

CREDITS TO FUND.

31. The Minister of Public Works and Government Services shall pay into the Crimes Against Humanity Fund

(*a*) the net amount received from the disposition of any property referred to in subsections 4(1) to (3) of the *Seized Property Management Act* that is

(i) proceeds of crime within the meaning of subsection 462.3(1) of the *Criminal Code*, obtained or derived directly or indirectly as a result of the commission of an offence under this Act, and

(ii) forfeited to Her Majesty and disposed of by that Minister; and

(*b*) any amount paid or recovered as a fine imposed under subsection 462.37(3) of the *Criminal Code* in substitution for the property referred to in paragraph (*a*). 2001, c. 32, s. 61.

PARTIAL EXCLUSION OF *SEIZED PROPERTY MANAGEMENT ACT*.

32. Paragraphs 9(*d*), (*e*) and (*f*) and sections 10, 11 and 13 to 16 of the *Seized Property Management Act* do not apply in respect of any property, proceeds of property or amounts referred to in section 31.

SCHEDULE
(Subsection 2(1))

PROVISIONS OF ROME STATUTE

ARTICLE 6

Genocide

For the purpose of this Statute, "genocide" means any of the following acts committed with intent to destroy, in whole or in part, a national, ethnical, racial or religious group, as such:

   (a) killing members of the group;
   (b) causing serious bodily or mental harm to members of the group;
   (c) deliberately inflicting on the group conditions of life calculated to bring about its physical destruction in whole or in part;
   (d) imposing measures intended to prevent births within the group;
   (e) forcibly transferring children of the group to another group.

ARTICLE 7

Crimes against humanity

1. For the purpose of this Statute, "crime against humanity" means any of the following acts when committed as part of a widespread or systematic attack directed against any civilian population, with knowledge of the attack:

   (a) murder;
   (b) extermination;
   (c) enslavement;
   (d) deportation or forcible transfer of population;
   (e) imprisonment or other severe deprivation of physical liberty in violation of fundamental rules of international law;
   (f) torture;
   (g) rape, sexual slavery, enforced prostitution, forced pregnancy, enforced sterilization, or any other form of sexual violence of comparable gravity;
   (h) persecution against any identifiable group or collectivity on political, racial, national, ethnic, cultural, religious, gender as defined in paragraph 3, or other grounds that are universally recognized as impermissible under international law, in connection with any act referred to in this paragraph or any crime within the jurisdiction of the Court;
   (i) enforced disappearance of persons;
   (j) the crime of apartheid;
   (k) other inhumane acts of a similar character intentionally causing great suffering, or serious injury to body or to mental or physical health.

WAR

2. For the purpose of paragraph 1:

    (*a*) "attack directed against any civilian population" means a course of conduct involving the multiple commission of acts referred to in paragraph 1 against any civilian population, pursuant to or in furtherance of a State or organizational policy to commit such attack;

    (*b*) "extermination" includes the intentional infliction of conditions of life, inter alia the deprivation of access to food and medicine, calculated to bring about the destruction of part of a population;

    (*c*) "enslavement" means the exercise of any or all of the powers attaching to the right of ownership over a person and includes the exercise of such power in the course of trafficking in persons, in particular women and children;

    (*d*) "deportation or forcible transfer of population" means forced displacement of the persons concerned by expulsion or other coercive acts from the area in which they are lawfully present, without grounds permitted under international law;

    (*e*) "torture" means the intentional infliction of severe pain or suffering, whether physical or mental, upon a person in the custody or under the control of the accused; except that torture shall not include pain or suffering arising only from, inherent in or incidental to, lawful sanctions;

    (*f*) "forced pregnancy" means the unlawful confinement of a woman forcibly made pregnant, with the intent of affecting the ethnic composition of any population or carrying out other grave violations of international law. This definition shall not in any way be interpreted as affecting national laws relating to pregnancy;

    (*g*) "persecution" means the intentional and severe deprivation of fundamental rights contrary to international law by reason of the identity of the group or collectivity;

    (*h*) "the crime of apartheid" means inhumane acts of a character similar to those referred to in paragraph 1, committed in the context of an institutionalized regime of systematic oppression and domination by one racial group over any other racial group or groups and committed with the intention of maintaining that regime;

    (*i*) "enforced disappearance of persons" means the arrest, detention or abduction of persons by, or with the authorization, support or acquiescence of, a State or a political organization, followed by a refusal to acknowledge that deprivation of freedom or to give information on the fate or whereabouts of those persons, with the intention of removing them from the protection of the law for a prolonged period of time.

3. For the purpose of this Statute, it is understood that the term "gender" refers to the two sexes, male and female, within the context of society. The term "gender" does not indicate any meaning different from the above.

PARAGRAPH 2 OF ARTICLE 8

War crimes

2. For the purpose of this Statute, "war crimes" means:

  (a) grave breaches of the Geneva Conventions of 12 August 1949, namely, any of the following acts against persons or property protected under the provisions of the relevant Geneva Convention:

     (i) wilful killing;

    (ii) torture or inhuman treatment, including biological experiments;

   (iii) wilfully causing great suffering, or serious injury to body or health;

   (iv) extensive destruction and appropriation of property, not justified by military necessity and carried out unlawfully and wantonly;

    (v) compelling a prisoner of war or other protected person to serve in the forces of a hostile Power;

   (vi) wilfully depriving a prisoner of war or other protected person of the rights of fair and regular trial;

  (vii) unlawful deportation or transfer or unlawful confinement;

 (viii) taking of hostages.

  (b) other serious violations of the laws and customs applicable in international armed conflict, within the established framework of international law, namely, any of the following acts:

     (i) intentionally directing attacks against the civilian population as such or against individual civilians not taking direct part in hostilities;

    (ii) intentionally directing attacks against civilian objects, that is, objects which are not military objectives;

   (iii) intentionally directing attacks against personnel, installations, material, units or vehicles involved in a humanitarian assistance or peacekeeping mission in accordance with the Charter of the United Nations, as long as they are entitled to the protection given to civilians or civilian objects under the international law of armed conflict;

   (iv) intentionally launching an attack in the knowledge that such attack will cause incidental loss of life or injury to civilians or damage to civilian objects or widespread, long-term and severe damage to the natural environment which would be clearly excessive in relation to the concrete and direct overall military advantage anticipated;

    (v) attacking or bombarding, by whatever means, towns, villages, dwellings or buildings which are undefended and which are not military objectives;

   (vi) killing or wounding a combatant who, having laid down his arms or having no longer means of defence, has surrendered at discretion;

  (vii) making improper use of a flag of truce, of the flag or of the military insignia and uniform of the enemy or of the United Nations, as well as of the distinctive emblems of the Geneva Conventions, resulting in death or serious personal injury;

 (viii) the transfer, directly or indirectly, by the Occupying Power of parts of its own civilian population into the territory it occupies, or the deportation or transfer of all or parts of the population of the occupied territory within or outside this territory;

(ix) intentionally directing attacks against buildings dedicated to religion, education, art, science or charitable purposes, historic monuments, hospitals and places where the sick and wounded are collected, provided they are not military objectives;

(x) subjecting persons who are in the power of an adverse party to physical mutilation or to medical or scientific experiments of any kind which are neither justified by the medical, dental or hospital treatment of the person concerned nor carried out in his or her interest, and which cause death to or seriously endanger the health of such person or persons;

(xi) killing or wounding treacherously individuals belonging to the hostile nation or army;

(xii) declaring that no quarter will be given;

(xiii) destroying or seizing the enemy's property unless such destruction or seizure be imperatively demanded by the necessities of war;

(xiv) declaring abolished, suspended or inadmissible in a court of law the rights and actions of the nationals of the hostile party;

(xv) compelling the nationals of the hostile party to take part in the operations of war directed against their own country, even if they were in the belligerent's service before the commencement of the war;

(xvi) pillaging a town or place, even when taken by assault;

(xvii) employing poison or poisoned weapons;

(xviii) employing asphyxiating, poisonous or other gases, and all analogous liquids, materials or devices;

(xix) employing bullets which expand or flatten easily in the human body, such as bullets with a hard envelope which does not entirely cover the core or is pierced with incisions;

(xx) employing weapons, projectiles and material and methods of warfare which are of a nature to cause superfluous injury or unnecessary suffering or which are inherently indiscriminate in violation of the international law of armed conflict, provided that such weapons, projectiles and material and methods of warfare are the subject of a comprehensive prohibition and are included in an annex to this Statute, by an amendment in accordance with the relevant provisions set forth in articles 121 and 123;

(xxi) committing outrages upon personal dignity, in particular humiliating and degrading treatment;

(xxii) committing rape, sexual slavery, enforced prostitution, forced pregnancy, as defined in article 7, paragraph 2(f), enforced sterilization, or any other form of sexual violence also constituting a grave breach of the Geneva Conventions;

(xxiii) utilizing the presence of a civilian or other protected person to render certain points, areas or military forces immune from military operations;

(xxiv) intentionally directing attacks against buildings, material, medical units and transport, and personnel using the distinctive emblems of the Geneva Conventions in conformity with international law;

(xxv) intentionally using starvation of civilians as a method of warfare by depriving them of objects indispensable to their survival, including wilfully impeding relief supplies as provided for under the Geneva Conventions;

(xxvi) conscripting or enlisting children under the age of fifteen years into the national armed forces or using them to participate actively in hostilities.

(c) in the case of an armed conflict not of an international character, serious violations of article 3 common to the four Geneva Conventions of 12 August 1949, namely, any of the following acts committed against persons taking no active part in the hostilities, including members of armed forces who have laid down their arms and those placed hors de combat by sickness, wounds, detention or any other cause:

(i) violence to life and person, in particular murder of all kinds, mutilation, cruel treatment and torture;

(ii) committing outrages upon personal dignity, in particular humiliating and degrading treatment;

(iii) taking of hostages;

(iv) the passing of sentences and the carrying out of executions without previous judgement pronounced by a regularly constituted court, affording all judicial guarantees which are generally recognized as indispensable.

(d) paragraph 2(c) applies to armed conflicts not of an international character and thus does not apply to situations of internal disturbances and tensions, such as riots, isolated and sporadic acts of violence or other acts of a similar nature.

(e) other serious violations of the laws and customs applicable in armed conflicts not of an international character, within the established framework of international law, namely, any of the following acts:

(i) intentionally directing attacks against the civilian population as such or against individual civilians not taking direct part in hostilities;

(ii) intentionally directing attacks against buildings, material, medical units and transport, and personnel using the distinctive emblems of the Geneva Conventions in conformity with international law;

(iii) intentionally directing attacks against personnel, installations, material, units or vehicles involved in a humanitarian assistance or peacekeeping mission in accordance with the Charter of the United Nations, as long as they are entitled to the protection given to civilians or civilian objects under the international law of armed conflict;

(iv) intentionally directing attacks against buildings dedicated to religion, education, art, science or charitable purposes, historic monuments, hospitals and places where the sick and wounded are collected, provided they are not military objectives;

(v) pillaging a town or place, even when taken by assault;

WAR

    (vi)   committing rape, sexual slavery, enforced prostitution, forced pregnancy, as defined in article 7, paragraph 2(f), enforced sterilization, and any other form of sexual violence also constituting a serious violation of article 3 common to the four Geneva Conventions;

    (vii) conscripting or enlisting children under the age of fifteen years into armed forces or groups or using them to participate actively in hostilities;

  (viii) ordering the displacement of the civilian population for reasons related to the conflict, unless the security of the civilians involved or imperative military reasons so demand;

    (ix) killing or wounding treacherously a combatant adversary;

    (x) declaring that no quarter will be given;

    (xi) subjecting persons who are in the power of another party to the conflict to physical mutilation or to medical or scientific experiments of any kind which are neither justified by the medical, dental or hospital treatment of the person concerned nor carried out in his or her interest, and which cause death to or seriously endanger the health of such person or persons;

    (xii) destroying or seizing the property of an adversary unless such destruction or seizure be imperatively demanded by the necessities of the conflict;

 (f) paragraph 2(e) applies to armed conflicts not of an international character and thus does not apply to situations of internal disturbances and tensions, such as riots, isolated and sporadic acts of violence or other acts of a similar nature. It applies to armed conflicts that take place in the territory of a State when there is protracted armed conflict between governmental authorities and organized armed groups or between such groups.

FIREARMS ACT

S.C. 1995, Chap. 39, ss. 1 to 135; ss. 118 and 119 brought into force April 30, 1996; s. 95 brought into force December 18, 1997; ss. 1, 2 and 117 brought into force February 25, 1998; ss. 3, 4, 5(1) and (2), 6, 7(1) to (3), 7(4) except para. (e), 7(5), 8 to 23, 24(1), 24(2) except paras. (c) and (d), 25 to 28, 29(2) to (7), 30, 31, 32 except para. (b), 33, 34, 35(1) except paras. (a)(ii) and (b), 54 to 94, 96, 98 to 116, 120 to 135, 138, 139 (except to the extent that it replaces ss. 85 and 97 of the *Criminal Code*), 140, 151 to 168, 170 to 173, 175 to 193 originally to be brought into force October 1, 1998, however, the coming into force of these sections now deferred to December 1, 1998; s. 97 brought into force December 3, 1998; ss. 5(3), 7(4)(e), 35(1)(a)(ii) and (b), 35(2) to (4) and 36 brought into force January 1, 2001 by SI/2001-4, *Can. Gaz., Part II*, January 3, 2001; s. 29(1) brought into force January 1, 2003 by SI/2002-161, *Can. Gaz., Part II*, December 18, 2002

Amended 1995, c. 39, ss. 136 and 137; s. 136 in force May 14, 1997; s. 137 in force September 3, 1996

Amended 1996, c. 19, s. 76.1; brought into force May 14, 1997 by SI/97-47, *Can. Gaz., Part II*, May 14, 1997

Amended 1999, c. 3, s. 64; in force April 1, 1999

Amended 2000, c. 12, ss. 116 to 118; ss. 117 and 118 brought into force July 31, 2000 by SI/2000-76, *Can. Gaz., Part II*, August 16, 2000; s. 116 brought into force January 1, 2004 by SI/2003-186, *Can. Gaz., Part II*, December 17, 2003

Amended 2001, c. 4, s. 85; brought into force June 1, 2001 by SI/2001-71, *Can. Gaz., Part II*, June 20, 2001

Amended 2001, c. 41, s. 96; brought into force December 24, 2001 by SI/2002-16, *Can. Gaz., Part II*, January 2, 2002

Amended 2003, c. 8, ss. 9 to 21, 23 to 52, 54 and 56; ss. 9(2) and 48 to 50 brought into force May 30, 2003 by SI/2003-114, *Can. Gaz., Part II*, June 18, 2003; ss. 10 to 12, 24, 40(1), 43, 52 and 55 brought into force August 15, 2003 by SI/2003-144, *Can. Gaz., Part II*, August 27, 2003; ss. 9(1) and (3), 13 to 21, 25, 36, 38, 39, 40(2) as it enacts s. 64(3), (4) and (7), 41, 42, 44 to 47, 54 and 56 brought into force April 10, 2005 by para. (a) of SI/2005-27, *Can. Gaz., Part II*, April 6, 2005; ss. 26 to 35, 37, 40(2), 51 repealed before coming into force

2008, c. 20, s. 3; s. 23 brought into force October 31, 2016 by SI/2016-53, *Can. Gaz.*, *Part II*, October 5, 2016

Amended 2003, c. 22, s. 224(z.38); brought into force April 6, 2005 by SI/2005-24, *Can. Gaz., Part II*, April 6, 2005

Amended 2005, c. 10, s. 29; brought into force April 4, 2005 by SI/2005-29, *Can. Gaz., Part II*, April 20, 2005

Amended 2005, c. 38, ss. 139(c), 142(f) and 145(2)(j); ss. 139(c) and 142(f) brought into force December 12, 2005 by SI/2005-119, *Can. Gaz., Part II*, December 14, 2005; s. 145(2)(j) in force December 12, 2005 as provided by the section

Amended 2012, c. 6, ss. 9 to 29; brought into force April 5, 2012 by SI/2012-85, *Can. Gaz.*, *Part II*, April 25, 2012

Amended 2015, c. 27, ss. 2 to 17; 2(2), 3, 4(2), (6) and (9), 5, 7 to 9, 12(1), 13(2), 16 and 17 in force June 18, 2015; ss. 6, 11 and 13(1) brought into force September 2, 2015 by SI/2015-80, *Can. Gaz.*, *Part II*, August 12, 2015; ss. 4(4), (7), (8) and 37 brought into force September 2, 2015 by SI/2015-79, *Can. Gaz., Part II*, August 12, 2015; s. 14 brought into force November 30, 2017 by SI/2017-70, *Can. Gaz.*, *Part II*, November 15, 2017; ss. 10 and 15 to come into force by order of the Governor in Council

Amended 2018, c. 16, s. 182; brought into force October 17, 2018 by SI/2018-52, *Can. Gaz.*, *Part II*, July 11, 2018

Amended 2019, c. 9, ss. 3(1), 4(1), 12, 13(2), 17, 23, 24 in force June 21, 2019; ss. 1, 2, 3(2), 4(2), (3), 5 to 11, 13(1), (3), 14, 15 not in force at date of publication

---

An Act respecting firearms and other weapons

SHORT TITLE

SHORT TITLE.

1. This Act may be cited as the *Firearms Act*.

INTERPRETATION

DEFINITIONS / "authorization to carry" / "authorization to export" / "authorization to import" / "authorization to transport" / "business" / "carrier" / "chief firearms officer" / "commencement day" / "Commissioner" / "common-law partner" / "customs office" / "customs officer" / "federal Minister" / "firearms officer" / "former Act" / "museum" / "non-resident" / "prescribed" / "provincial minister" / "regulations" / To be interpreted with *Criminal Code* / Deemed references to Registrar / Aboriginal and treaty rights.

2. (1) In this Act,

"authorization to carry" means an authorization described in section 20;

"authorization to export" means an authorization referred to in section 44 and includes a permit to export goods that is issued under the *Export and Import Permits Act* and that is deemed by regulations made under para. 117(*a*.1) to be an authorization to export;

"authorization to import" means an authorization referred to in section 46;

"authorization to transport" means an authorization described in section 19;

"business" means a person who carries on a business that includes
- (*a*) the manufacture, assembly, possession, purchase, sale, importation, exportation, display, repair, restoration, maintenance, storage, alteration, pawnbroking, transportation, shipping, distribution or delivery of firearms, prohibited weapons, restricted weapons, prohibited devices or prohibited ammunition,
- (*b*) the possession, purchase or sale of ammunition, or
- (*c*) the purchase of cross-bows

and includes a museum;

"carrier" means a person who carries on a transportation business that includes the transportation of firearms, prohibited weapons, restricted weapons, prohibited devices or prohibited ammunition;

"chief firearms officer" means
- (*a*) in respect of a province, the individual who is designated in writing as the chief firearms officer for the province by the provincial minister of that province,
- (*b*) in respect of a territory, the individual who is designated in writing as the chief firearms officer for the territory by the federal Minister, or
- (*c*) in respect of any matter for which there is no chief firearms officer under paragraph (*a*) or (*b*), the individual who is designated in writing as the chief firearms officer for the matter by the federal Minister;

"commencement day", in respect of a provision of this Act or the expression "former Act" in a provision of this Act, means the day on which the provision comes into force;

"Commissioner" means the Commissioner of Firearms appointed under section 81.1;

"common-law partner", in relation to an individual, means a person who is cohabiting with the individual in a conjugal relationship, having so cohabited for a period of at least one year;

"customs office" has the meaning assigned by subsection 2(1) of the *Customs Act*;

"customs officer" has the meaning assigned to the word "officer" by subsection 2(1) of the *Customs Act*;

"federal Minister" means the Minister of Public Safety and Emergency Preparedness;

"firearms officer" means
- (*a*) in respect of a province, an individual who is designated in writing as a firearms officer for the province by the provincial minister of that province,

FIREARMS

1077

(*b*) in respect of a territory, an individual who is designated in writing as a firearms officer for the territory by the federal Minister, or

(*c*) in respect of any matter for which there is no firearms officer under paragraph (*a*) or (*b*), an individual who is designated in writing as a firearms officer for the matter by the federal Minister;

"former Act" means Part III of the *Criminal Code*, as it read from time to time before the commencement day;

"museum" means a person who operates a museum

(*a*) in which firearms, prohibited weapons, restricted weapons, prohibited devices or prohibited ammunition are possessed, bought, displayed, repaired, restored, maintained, stored or altered, or

(*b*) in which ammunition is possessed or bought;

"non-resident" means an individual who ordinarily resides outside Canada;

"prescribed" means

(*a*) in the case of a form or the information to be included on a form, prescribed by the federal Minister, and

(*b*) in any other case, prescribed by the regulations;

"provincial minister" means

(*a*) in respect of a province, the member of the executive council of the province who is designated by the lieutenant governor in council of the province as the provincial minister,

(*b*) in respect of a territory, the federal Minister, or

(*c*) in respect of any matter for which there is no provincial minister under paragraph (*a*) or (*b*), the federal Minister;

"regulations" means regulations made by the Governor in Council under section 117.

(2) Unless otherwise provided, words and expressions used in this Act have the meanings assigned to them by section 2 or 84 of the *Criminal Code*. Subsections 117.15(3) and (4) of that Act apply to those words and expressions.

Note: Subsection 2(2) replaced, 2019, c. 9, s. 1(1) (to come into force by order of the Governor in Council):
Criminal Code

(2) Unless otherwise provided, words and expressions used in this Act have the meanings assigned to them by section 2 or 84 of the *Criminal Code*.

(2.1) Sections 5, 9, 54 to 58, 67, 68 and 70 to 72 apply in respect of a carrier as if each reference in those sections to a chief firearms officer were a reference to the Registrar and for the purposes of applying section 6 in respect of a carrier, paragraph 113(3)(*b*) of the *Criminal Code* applies as if the reference in that section to a chief firearms officer were a reference to the Registrar.

(3) For greater certainty, nothing in this Act shall be construed so as to abrogate or derogate from any existing aboriginal or treaty rights of the aboriginal peoples of Canada under section 35 of the *Constitution Act, 1982*. 2000, c. 12, s. 116; 2001, c. 4, s. 85; 2003, c. 8, s. 9; 2005, c. 10, s. 29; 2015, c. 27, s. 2(2).

Note: Section 2 amended by enacting subsec. (4), 2019, c. 9, s. 1(2) (to come into force by order of the Governor in Council):
For greater certainty

(4) For greater certainty, nothing in this Act shall be construed so as to permit or require the registration of non-restricted firearms.

HER MAJESTY

BINDING ON HER MAJESTY / Canadian Forces.

3. (1) This Act is binding on Her Majesty in right of Canada or a province.

(2) Notwithstanding subsection (1), this Act does not apply in respect of the Canadian Forces.

PURPOSE

PURPOSE.

4. The purpose of this Act is

    (*a*) to provide, notably by sections 5 to 16 and 54 to 73, for the issuance of

        (i) licences for firearms and authorizations and registration certificates for prohibited firearms or restricted firearms, under which persons may possess firearms in circumstances that would otherwise constitute an offence under subsection 91(1), 92(1), 93(1) or 95(1) of the *Criminal Code*,

        (ii) licences and authorizations under which persons may possess prohibited weapons, restricted weapons, prohibited devices and prohibited ammunition in circumstances that would otherwise constitute an offence under subsection 91(2), 92(2) or 93(1) of the *Criminal Code*, and

        (iii) licences under which persons may sell, barter or give cross-bows in circumstances that would otherwise constitute an offence under subsection 97(1) of the *Criminal Code*;

    (*b*) to authorize,

        (i) notably by sections 5 to 12 and 54 to 73, the manufacture of or offer to manufacture, and

        (ii) notably by sections 21 to 34 and 54 to 73, the transfer of or offer to transfer,

firearms, prohibited weapons, restricted weapons, prohibited devices, ammunition and prohibited ammunition in circumstances that would otherwise constitute an offence under subsection 99(1), 100(1) or 101(1) of the *Criminal Code*; and

    (*c*) to authorize, notably by sections 35 to 73, the importation or exportation of firearms, prohibited weapons, restricted weapons, prohibited devices, ammunition, prohibited ammunition and components and parts designed exclusively for use in the manufacture of or assembly into automatic firearms in circumstances that would otherwise constitute an offence under subsection 103(1) or 104(1) of the *Criminal Code*. 2012, c. 6, s. 9.

AUTHORIZED POSSESSION

Eligibility to Hold Licences
General Rules

PUBLIC SAFETY / Criteria / Exception.

5. (1) A person is not eligible to hold a licence if it is desirable, in the interests of the safety of that or any other person, that the person not possess a firearm, a cross-bow, a prohibited weapon, a restricted weapon, a prohibited device, ammunition or prohibited ammunition.

(2) In determining whether a person is eligible to hold a licence under subsection (1), a chief firearms officer or, on a reference under section 74, a provincial court judge shall have regard to whether the person, within the previous five years,

Note: The portion of subsec. 5(2) before para. (*a*) replaced, 2019, c. 9, s. 2(1) (to come into force by order of the Governor in Council):

Criteria

(2) In determining whether a person is eligible to hold a licence under subsection (1), a chief firearms officer or, on a reference under section 74, a provincial court judge shall have regard to whether the person

(*a*) has been convicted or discharged under section 730 of the *Criminal Code* of

   (i) an offence in the commission of which violence against another person was used, threatened or attempted,

   (ii) an offence under this Act or Part III of the *Criminal Code*,

   (iii) an offence under section 264 of the *Criminal Code* (criminal harassment),

   (iv) an offence relating to the contravention of subsection 5(1) or (2), 6(1) or (2) or 7(1) of the *Controlled Drugs and Substances Act*;

   (v) an offence relating to the contravention of subsection 9(1) or (2), 10(1) or (2), 11(1) or (2), 12(1), (4), (5), (6) or (7), 13(1) or 14(1) of the *Cannabis Act*;

(*b*) has been treated for a mental illness, whether in a hospital, mental institute, psychiatric clinic or otherwise and whether or not the person was confined to such a hospital, institute or clinic, that was associated with violence or threatened or attempted violence on the part of the person against any person; or

(*c*) has a history of behaviour that includes violence or threatened or attempted violence on the part of the person against any person.

Note: Subsection 5(2) amended by striking out "or" at the end of para. (*b*), by replacing para. (*c*) and by enacting paras. (*d*) to (*f*), 2019, c. 9, s. 2(2) (to come into force by order of the Governor in Council):

    (*c*) has a history of behaviour that includes violence or threatened or attempted violence or threatening conduct on the part of the person against any person;

    (*d*) is or was previously prohibited by an order — made in the interests of the safety and security of any person — from communicating with an identified person or from being at a specified place or within a specified distance of that place, and presently poses a threat or risk to the safety and security of any person;

    (*e*) in respect of an offence in the commission of which violence was used, threatened or attempted against the person's intimate partner or former intimate partner, was previously prohibited by a prohibition order from possessing any firearm, cross-bow, prohibited weapon, restricted weapon, prohibited device or prohibited ammunition; or

    (*f*) for any other reason, poses a risk of harm to any person.

Note: Section 5 amended by enacting subsec. (2.1), 2019, c. 9, s. 2(3) (to come into force by order of the Governor in Council):

For greater certainty

(2.1) For greater certainty, for the purposes of paragraph (2)(*c*), threatened violence and threatening conduct include threats or conduct communicated by the person to a person by means of the Internet or other digital network.

(3) Despite subsection (2), in determining whether a non-resident who is eighteen years old or older and by or on behalf of whom an application is made for a sixty-day licence authorizing the non-resident to possess non-restricted firearms is eligible to hold a licence under subsection (1), a chief firearms officer or, on a reference under section 74, a provincial court judge may but need not have regard to the criteria described in subsection (2). 1995, c. 39, ss. 136, 137; 1996, c. 19, s. 76.1; 2003, c. 8, s. 10; 2015, c. 27, s. 3; 2018, c. 16, s. 182.

COURT ORDERS / Exception.

6. (1) A person is eligible to hold a licence only if the person is not prohibited by a prohibition order from possessing any firearm, cross-bow, prohibited weapon, restricted weapon, prohibited device or prohibited ammunition.

(2) Subsection (1) is subject to any order made under section 113 of the *Criminal Code* (lifting of prohibition order for sustenance or employment).

SUCCESSFUL COMPLETION OF SAFETY COURSE / Restricted firearms safety course / After expiration of prohibition order / Exceptions / Further exception.

7. (1) An individual is eligible to hold a licence only if the individual

    (*a*) successfully completes the Canadian Firearms Safety Course, as given by an instructor who is designated by a chief firearms officer, and passes the tests, as administered by an instructor who is designated by a chief firearms officer, that form part of that Course;

FIREARMS

1081

    (*b*) passed, before the commencement day, the tests, as administered by an instructor who is designated by a chief firearms officer, that form part of that Course;

    (*c*) successfully completed, before January 1, 1995, a course that the attorney general of the province in which the course was given had, during the period beginning on January 1, 1993 and ending on December 31, 1994, approved for the purposes of section 106 of the former Act;

    (*d*) passed, before January 1, 1995, a test that the attorney general of the province in which the test was administered had, during the period beginning on January 1, 1993 and ending on December 31, 1994, approved for the purposes of section 106 of the former Act; or

    (*e*) on the commencement day, was an individual referred to in paragraph 7(4)(*c*) as it read immediately before that day and held a licence.

(2) An individual is eligible to hold a licence authorizing the individual to possess prohibited firearms or restricted firearms only if the individual

    (*a*) successfully completes a restricted firearms safety course that is approved by the federal Minister, as given by an instructor who is designated by a chief firearms officer, and passes any tests, as administered by an instructor who is designated by a chief firearms officer, that form part of that course;

    (*b*) passed, before the commencement day, a restricted firearms safety test, as administered by an instructor who is designated by a chief firearms officer, that is approved by the federal Minister; or

    (*c*) on the commencement day, was an individual referred to in paragraph 7(4)(*c*) as it read immediately before that day and held a licence authorizing the individual to possess prohibited firearms or restricted firearms.

(3) An individual against whom a prohibition order was made

    (*a*) is eligible to hold a licence only if the individual has, after the expiration of the prohibition order,

        (i) successfully completed the Canadian Firearms Safety Course, as given by an instructor who is designated by a chief firearms officer, and

        (ii) passed the tests, as administered by an instructor who is designated by a chief firearms officer, that form part of that Course; and

    (*b*) is eligible to hold a licence authorizing the individual to possess restricted firearms only if the individual has, after the expiration of the prohibition order,

        (i) successfully completed a restricted firearms safety course that is approved by the federal Minister, as given by an instructor who is designated by a chief firearms officer, and

        (ii) passed any tests, as administered by an instructor who is designated by a chief firearms officer, that form part of that course.

(4) Subsections (1) and (2) do not apply to an individual who

    (*a*) in the prescribed circumstances, has been certified by a chief firearms officer as meeting the prescribed criteria relating to the safe handling and use of firearms and the laws relating to firearms;

    (*b*) is less than eighteen years old and requires a firearm to hunt or trap in order to sustain himself or herself or his or her family;

(c) [*Repealed*. 2015, c. 27, s. 4(8).]

(d) requires a licence merely to acquire cross-bows; or

(e) is a non-resident who is eighteen years old or older and by or on behalf of whom an application is made for a 60-day licence authorizing the non-resident to possess non-restricted firearms.

(5) Subsection (3) does not apply to an individual in respect of whom an order is made under section 113 of the *Criminal Code* (lifting of prohibition order for sustenance or employment) and who is exempted by a chief firearms officer from the application of that subsection. 2003, c. 8, s. 11; 2015, c. 27, s. 4(2), (4), (6) to (9).

Special Cases — Persons

MINORS / Minors hunting as a way of life / Hunting, etc. / No prohibited or restricted firearms / Consent of parent or guardian.

8. (1) An individual who is less than eighteen years old and who is otherwise eligible to hold a licence is not eligible to hold a licence except as provided in this section.

(2) An individual who is less than eighteen years old and who hunts or traps as a way of life is eligible to hold a licence if the individual needs to hunt or trap in order to sustain himself or herself or his or her family.

(3) An individual who is twelve years old or older but less than eighteen years old is eligible to hold a licence authorizing the individual to possess, in accordance with the conditions attached to the licence, a firearm for the purpose of target practice, hunting or instruction in the use of firearms or for the purpose of taking part in an organized competition.

(4) An individual who is less than eighteen years old is not eligible to hold a licence authorizing the individual to possess prohibited firearms or restricted firearms or to acquire firearms or cross-bows.

(5) An individual who is less than eighteen years old is eligible to hold a licence only if a parent or person who has custody of the individual has consented, in writing or in any other manner that is satisfactory to the chief firearms officer, to the issuance of the licence.

BUSINESSES / Safety courses / Employees — firearms / Employees — prohibited firearms or restricted firearms / Employees — prohibited weapons, restricted weapons, etc. / Exception / Exception / Exception for museums.

9. (1) A business is eligible to hold a licence authorizing a particular activity only if every person who stands in a prescribed relationship to the business is eligible under sections 5 and 6 to hold a licence authorizing that activity or the acquisition of restricted firearms.

FIREARMS

(2) A business other than a carrier is eligible to hold a licence only if

   (a) a chief firearms officer determines that no individual who stands in a prescribed relationship to the business need be eligible to hold a licence under section 7; or

   (b) the individuals who stand in a prescribed relationship to the business and who are determined by a chief firearms officer to be the appropriate individuals to satisfy the requirements of section 7 are eligible to hold a licence under that section.

(3) Subject to subsection (3.1), a business other than a carrier is eligible to hold a licence that authorizes the possession of firearms only if every employee of the business who, in the course of duties of employment, handles or would handle firearms is the holder of a licence authorizing the holder to acquire non-restricted firearms.

(3.1) A business other than a carrier is eligible to hold a licence that authorizes the possession of prohibited firearms or restricted firearms only if every employee of the business who, in the course of duties of employment, handles or would handle firearms is the holder of a licence authorizing the holder to acquire restricted firearms.

(3.2) A business other than a carrier is eligible to hold a licence that authorizes the possession of prohibited weapons, restricted weapons, prohibited devices or prohibited ammunition only if every employee of the business who, in the course of duties of employment, handles or would handle any of those things is eligible under sections 5 and 6 to hold a licence.

(4) In subsection (3), "firearm" does not include a partially manufactured barrelled weapon that, in its unfinished state, is not a barrelled weapon

   (a) from which any shot, bullet or other projectile can be discharged; and

   (b) that is capable of causing serious bodily injury or death to a person.

(5) Subsection (1) does not apply in respect of a person who stands in a prescribed relationship to a business where a chief firearms officer determines that, in all the circumstances, the business should not be ineligible to hold a licence merely because of that person's ineligibility.

(6) Subsection (3) does not apply in respect of an employee of a museum

   (a) who, in the course of duties of employment, handles or would handle only firearms that are designed or intended to exactly resemble, or to resemble with near precision, antique firearms, and who has been trained to handle or use such a firearm; or

   (b) who is designated, by name, by a provincial minister. 2003, c. 8, s. 12; 2015, c. 27, s. 5.

---

10. [*Repealed.* 2003, c. 8, s. 13.]

Special Cases — Prohibited Firearms, Weapons, Devices and Ammunition

PROHIBITED FIREARMS, WEAPONS, DEVICES AND AMMUNITION — BUSINESSES / Prescribed purposes / Carriers.

11. (1) A business that is otherwise eligible to hold a licence is not eligible to hold a licence authorizing the business to possess prohibited firearms, prohibited weapons, prohibited devices or prohibited ammunition except as provided in this section.

(2) A business other than a carrier is eligible to hold a licence authorizing the business to possess prohibited firearms, prohibited weapons, prohibited devices or prohibited ammunition if the business needs to possess them for a prescribed purpose.

(3) A carrier is eligible to hold a licence authorizing the carrier to possess prohibited firearms, prohibited weapons, prohibited devices or prohibited ammunition.

PROHIBITED FIREARMS — INDIVIDUALS / Grandfathered individuals — pre-January 1, 1978 automatic firearms / Grandfathered individuals — pre-August 1, 1992 converted automatic firearms / Grandfathered individuals — *Prohibited Weapons Order, No. 12* / Grandfathered individuals — *Prohibited Weapons Order, No. 13* / Grandfathered individuals — pre-December 1, 1998 handguns / Grandfathered handguns — pre-December 1, 1998 / Next of kin of grandfathered individuals / Grandfathered individuals — regulations re prohibited firearms / Grandfathered individuals — regulations.

12. (1) An individual who is otherwise eligible to hold a licence is not eligible to hold a licence authorizing the individual to possess prohibited firearms except as provided in this section.

(2) An individual is eligible to hold a licence authorizing the individual to possess automatic firearms that, on the commencement day, were registered as restricted weapons under the former Act if the individual

    (*a*) on January 1, 1978 possessed one or more automatic firearms;

    (*b*) on the commencement day held a registration certificate under the former Act for one or more automatic firearms; and

    (*c*) beginning on the commencement day was continuously the holder of a registration certificate for one or more automatic firearms.

(3) An individual is eligible to hold a licence authorizing the individual to possess automatic firearms that have been altered to discharge only one projectile during one pressure of the trigger and that, on the commencement day, were registered as restricted weapons under the former Act if the individual

    (*a*) on August 1, 1992 possessed one or more automatic firearms

        (i) that had been so altered, and

FIREARMS

        (ii) for which on October 1, 1992 a registration certificate under the former Act had been issued or applied for;

    (b) on the commencement day held a registration certificate under the former Act for one or more automatic firearms that had been so altered; and

    (c) beginning on the commencement day was continuously the holder of a registration certificate for one or more automatic firearms that have been so altered.

(4) An individual is eligible to hold a licence authorizing the individual to possess firearms that were declared to be prohibited weapons under the former Act by the *Prohibited Weapons Order, No. 12*, made by Order in Council P.C. 1992-1690 of July 23, 1992 and registered as SOR/92-471 and that, on October 1, 1992, either were registered as restricted weapons under the former Act or were the subject of an application for a registration certificate under the former Act if the individual

    (a) before July 27, 1992 possessed one or more firearms that were so declared;

    (b) on the commencement day held a registration certificate under the former Act for one or more firearms that were so declared; and

    (c) beginning on the commencement day was continuously the holder of a registration certificate for one or more firearms that were so declared.

(5) An individual is eligible to hold a licence authorizing the individual to possess firearms that were declared to be prohibited weapons under the former Act by the *Prohibited Weapons Order, No. 13*, made by Order in Council P.C. 1994-1974 of November 29, 1994 and registered as SOR/94-741 and that, on January 1, 1995, either were registered as restricted weapons under the former Act or were the subject of an application for a registration certificate under the former Act if the individual

    (a) before January 1, 1995 possessed one or more firearms that were so declared;

    (b) on the commencement day held a registration certificate under the former Act for one or more firearms that were so declared; and

    (c) beginning on the commencement day was continuously the holder of a registration certificate for one or more firearms that were so declared.

(6) A particular individual is eligible to hold a licence authorizing that particular individual to possess a handgun referred to in subsection (6.1) if

    (a) on December 1, 1998 the particular individual

        (i) held a registration certificate under the former Act for that kind of handgun, or

        (ii) had applied for a registration certificate that was subsequently issued for that kind of handgun; and

    (b) beginning on December 1, 1998 the particular individual was continuously the holder of a registration certificate for that kind of handgun.

(6.1) Subsection (6) applies in respect of a handgun

    (a) that has a barrel equal to or less than 105 mm in length or that is designed or adapted to discharge a 25 or 32 calibre cartridge; and

    (b) in respect of which

        (i) on December 1, 1998 a registration certificate had been issued to an individual under the former Act,

    (ii) on December 1, 1998 a registration certificate had been applied for by an individual under the former Act, if the certificate was subsequently issued to the individual, or

    (iii) a record was sent before December 1, 1998 to the Commissioner of the Royal Canadian Mounted Police and received by that officer before, on or after that date.

(7) A particular individual is eligible to hold a licence authorizing the particular individual to possess a particular handgun referred to in subsection (6.1) that was manufactured before 1946 if the particular individual is the spouse or common-law partner or a brother, sister, child or grandchild of an individual who was eligible under this subsection or subsection (6) to hold a licence authorizing the individual to possess the particular handgun.

(8) An individual is, in the prescribed circumstances, eligible to hold a licence authorizing the individual to possess firearms prescribed by a provision of regulations made by the Governor in Council under section 117.15 of the *Criminal Code* to be prohibited firearms if the individual

    (*a*) on the day on which the provision comes into force possesses one or more of those firearms; and

    (*b*) beginning on

        (i) the day on which that provision comes into force, or

        (ii) in the case of an individual who on that day did not hold but had applied for a registration certificate for one or more of those firearms, the day on which the registration certificate was issued

was continuously the holder of a registration certificate for one or more of those firearms.

(9) An individual is eligible to hold a licence authorizing the individual to possess prohibited firearms of a prescribed class if the individual

    (*a*) possesses one or more firearms of that class on a day that is prescribed with respect to that class;

    (*b*) holds a registration certificate for one or more firearms of that class in the circumstances prescribed with respect to that class; and

    (*c*) was continuously the holder of a registration certificate for one or more firearms of that class beginning on the day that is prescribed — or that is determined under the regulations — with respect to that class. 2000, c. 12, s. 117; 2003, c. 8, s. 14; 2019, c. 9, s. 3(1).

Note: Section 12 amended by enacting subsecs. (10) to (14), 2019, c. 9, s. 3(2) (to come into force by order of the Governor in Council):

Grandfathered individuals — CZ rifle

(10) An individual is eligible to hold a licence authorizing the individual to possess one or more firearms referred to in subsection (11) if

    (*a*) the individual possessed one or more such firearms on June 30, 2018;

    (*b*) the individual

        (i) held on that day a registration certificate for one or more such firearms, in the case where at least one of those firearms was on that day a restricted firearm, or

      (ii) applies, before the first anniversary of the commencement day, for a registration certificate that is subsequently issued for a firearm referred to in subsection (11), in any other case; and

  (*c*) the individual was continuously the holder of a registration certificate for one or more such firearms beginning on

      (i) June 30, 2018, in the case where at least one of those firearms was on that day a restricted firearm, or

      (ii) the day on which a registration certificate referred to in subparagraph (*b*)(ii) is issued to the individual, in any other case.

Grandfathered firearms — CZ rifle

(11) Subsection (10) applies in respect of a firearm that

  (*a*) is a

      (i) Ceská Zbrojovka (CZ) Model CZ858 Tactical-2P rifle,

      (ii) Ceská Zbrojovka (CZ) Model CZ858 Tactical-2V rifle,

      (iii) Ceská Zbrojovka (CZ) Model CZ858 Tactical-4P rifle, or

      (iv) Ceská Zbrojovka (CZ) Model CZ858 Tactical-4V rifle; and

  (*b*) was registered as a restricted firearm on June 30, 2018 or, in the case of a firearm that was not a restricted firearm on that day, is the subject of an application made before the first anniversary of the commencement day for a registration certificate that is subsequently issued.

For greater certainty

(12) For greater certainty, the firearms referred to in subparagraphs (11)(*a*)(i) to (iv) include only firearms that are prohibited firearms on the commencement day.

Grandfathered individuals — SAN Swiss Arms

(13) An individual is eligible to hold a licence authorizing the individual to possess one or more firearms referred to in subsection (14) if

  (*a*) the individual possessed one or more such firearms on June 30, 2018;

  (*b*) the individual

      (i) held on that day a registration certificate for one or more such firearms, in the case where at least one of those firearms was on that day a restricted firearm, or

      (ii) applies, before the first anniversary of the commencement day, for a registration certificate that was subsequently issued for a firearm referred to in subsection (14), in any other case; and

  (*c*) the individual was continuously the holder of a registration certificate for one or more such firearms beginning on

      (i) June 30, 2018, in the case where at least one of the firearms was on that day a restricted firearm, or

      (ii) the day on which a registration certificate referred to in subparagraph (b)(ii) is issued to the individual, in any other case.

Grandfathered firearms — SAN Swiss Arms

(14) Subsection (13) applies in respect of a firearm that

  (*a*) is a

      (i) SAN Swiss Arms Model Classic Green rifle,

      (ii) SAN Swiss Arms Model Classic Green carbine,

      (iii) SAN Swiss Arms Model Classic Green CQB rifle,

     (iv) SAN Swiss Arms Model Black Special rifle,

     (v) SAN Swiss Arms Model Black Special carbine,

     (vi) SAN Swiss Arms Model Black Special CQB rifle,

     (vii) SAN Swiss Arms Model Black Special Target rifle,

     (viii) SAN Swiss Arms Model Blue Star rifle,

     (ix) SAN Swiss Arms Model Heavy Metal rifle,

     (x) SAN Swiss Arms Model Red Devil rifle,

     (xi) SAN Swiss Arms Model Swiss Arms Edition rifle,

     (xii) SAN Swiss Arms Model Classic Green Sniper rifle,

     (xiii) SAN Swiss Arms Model Ver rifle,

     (xiv) SAN Swiss Arms Model Aestas rifle,

     (xv) SAN Swiss Arms Model Autumnus rifle, or

     (xvi) SAN Swiss Arms Model Hiemis rifle; and

(b) was registered as a restricted firearm on June 30, 2018 or, in the case of a firearm that was not a restricted firearm on that day, is the subject of an application made before the first anniversary of the commencement day for a registration certificate that is subsequently issued.

Registration Certificates

REGISTRATION CERTIFICATE.

12.1 A registration certificate may only be issued for a prohibited firearm or a restricted firearm. 2012, c. 6, s. 10.

REGISTRATION CERTIFICATE.

13. A person is not eligible to hold a registration certificate for a firearm unless the person holds a licence authorizing the person to possess that kind of firearm.

SERIAL NUMBER.

14. A registration certificate may be issued only for a firearm

    (a) that bears a serial number sufficient to distinguish it from other firearms; or

    (b) that is described in the prescribed manner.

EXEMPTED FIREARMS.

15. A registration certificate may not be issued for a firearm that is owned by Her Majesty in right of Canada or a province or by a police force.

ONLY ONE PERSON PER REGISTRATION CERTIFICATE / Exception.

16. (1) A registration certificate for a firearm may be issued to only one person.

(2) Subsection (1) does not apply in the case of a firearm for which a registration certificate referred to in section 127 was issued to more than one person.

FIREARMS

AUTHORIZED TRANSPORTATION OF FIREARMS

PLACES WHERE PROHIBITED AND RESTRICTED FIREARMS MAY BE POSSESSED.

17. Subject to sections 19 and 20, a prohibited firearm or restricted firearm, the holder of the registration certificate for which is an individual, may be possessed only at the dwelling-house of the individual, as recorded in the Canadian Firearms Registry, or at a place authorized by a chief firearms officer. 2003, c. 8, s. 15.

TRANSPORTING AND USING PROHIBITED FIREARMS OR RESTRICTED FIREARMS / Target practice or competition / Exception for prohibited firearms other than prohibited handguns / Automatic authorization to transport — licence renewal / Automatic authorization to transport — transfer / Exceptions / Non-residents.

19. (1) An individual who holds a licence authorizing the individual to possess prohibited firearms or restricted firearms may be authorized to transport a particular prohibited firearm or restricted firearm between two or more specified places for any good and sufficient reason, including, without restricting the generality of the foregoing,

- (*a*) for use in target practice, or a target shooting competition, under specified conditions or under the auspices of a shooting club or shooting range that is approved under section 29; or
- (*a*.1) to provide instructions in the use of firearms as part of a restricted firearms safety course that is approved by the federal Minister;
- (*b*) if the individual
  - (i) changes residence,
  - (ii) wishes to transport the firearm to a peace officer, firearms officer or chief firearms officer for registration or disposal in accordance with this Act or Part III of the *Criminal Code*,
  - (iii) wishes to transport the firearm for repair, storage, sale, exportation or appraisal, or
  - (iv) wishes to transport the firearm to a gun show.

(1.1) In the case of an authorization to transport issued for a reason referred to in paragraph (1)(a) within the province where the holder of the authorization resides, the specified places must — except in the case of an authorization that is issued for a prohibited firearm referred to in subsection 12(9) — include all shooting clubs and shooting ranges that are approved under section 29 and that are located in that province.

Note: Subsection 19(1.1) replaced, 2019, c. 9, s. 4(2) (to come into force by order of the Governor in Council):
Target practice or competition

(1.1) In the case of an authorization to transport issued for a reason referred to in paragraph (1)(*a*) within the province where the holder of the authorization resides, the specified places must — except in the case of an authorization that is issued for a prohibited firearm referred to in subsection 12(9), (11) or (14) — include all shooting clubs and shooting ranges that are approved under section 29 and that are located in that province.

(2) Despite subsection (1), an individual must not be authorized to transport a prohibited firearm — other than a handgun referred to in subsection 12(6.1) or a prohibited firearm referred to in subsection 12(9) — between specified places except for the purposes referred to in paragraph (1)(*b*).

Note: Subsection 19(2) replaced, 2019, c. 9, s. 4(2) (to come into force by order of the Governor in Council):

Exception for prohibited firearms other than prohibited handguns

(2) Despite subsection (1), an individual must not be authorized to transport a prohibited firearm — other than a handgun referred to in subsection 12(6.1) or a prohibited firearm referred to in subsection 12(9), (11) or (14) — between specified places except for the purposes referred to in paragraph (1)(*b*).

(2.1) Subject to subsection (2.3), an individual who holds a licence authorizing the individual to possess prohibited firearms or restricted firearms must, if the licence is renewed, be authorized to transport them within the individual's province of residence

    (*a*) to and from all shooting clubs and shooting ranges that are approved under section 29;

    (*b*) to and from any place a peace officer, firearms officer or chief firearms officer is located, for verification, registration or disposal in accordance with this Act or Part III of the *Criminal Code*;

    (*c*) to and from a business that holds a licence authorizing it to repair or appraise prohibited firearms or restricted firearms;

    (*d*) to and from a gun show; and

    (*e*) to a port of exit in order to take them outside Canada, and from a port of entry.

Note: Subsection 19(2.1) replaced, 2019, c. 9, s. 4(3) (to come into force by order of the Governor in Council):

Automatic authorization to transport — licence renewal

(2.1) An individual who holds a licence authorizing the individual to possess restricted firearms or handguns referred to in subsection 12(6.1) must, if the licence is renewed, be authorized to transport them within the individual's province of residence to and from all shooting clubs and shooting ranges that are approved under section 29. However, the authorization does not apply to a restricted firearm or a handgun referred to in subsection 12(6.1) whose transfer to the individual was approved, in accordance with subparagraph 28(*b*)(ii), for the purpose of having it form part of a gun collection.

(2.2) Subject to subsection (2.3), if a chief firearms officer has authorized the transfer of a prohibited firearm or a restricted firearm to an individual who holds a licence authorizing the individual to possess prohibited firearms or restricted firearms, the individual must be authorized

    (*a*) to transport the firearm within the individual's province of residence from the place where the individual acquires it to the place where they may possess it under section 17; and

FIREARMS

(*b*) to transport their prohibited firearms and restricted firearms within the individual's province of residence to and from the places referred to in any of paragraphs (2.1)(*a*) to (*e*).

Note: Subsection 19(2.2) replaced, 2019, c. 9, s. 4(3) (to come into force by order of the Governor in Council):

Automatic authorization to transport — transfer

(2.2) If a chief firearms officer has authorized the transfer of a prohibited firearm or a restricted firearm to an individual who holds a licence authorizing the individual to possess prohibited firearms or restricted firearms, the individual must be authorized to transport the firearm within the individual's province of residence from the place where they acquire it to the place where they may possess it under section 17.

(2.3) An individual must not be authorized under subsection (2.1) or (2.2) to transport the following firearms to or from the places referred to in paragraph (2.1)(*a*)

(*a*) a prohibited firearm, other than a handgun referred to in subsection 12(6.1); and

(*b*) a restricted firearm or a handgun referred to in subsection 12(6.1) whose transfer was approved, in accordance with subparagraph 28(*b*)(ii), for the purpose of forming part of a gun collection.

Note: Subsection 19(2.3) replaced, 2019, c. 9, s. 4(3) (to come into force by order of the Governor in Council):

Automatic authorization to transport — transfer

(2.3) If a chief firearms officer has authorized the transfer of a restricted firearm or a handgun referred to in subsection 12(6.1) to an individual who holds a licence authorizing the individual to possess a restricted firearm or such a handgun, the individual must be authorized to transport their restricted firearm or handgun within the individual's province of residence to and from all shooting clubs and shooting ranges that are approved under section 29, unless the transfer of the restricted firearm or handgun was approved, in accordance with subparagraph 28(*b*)(ii), for the purpose of having it form part of a gun collection.

(3) A non-resident may be authorized to transport a particular restricted firearm between specified places in accordance with sections 35 and 35.1. 2003, c. 8, s. 16; 2015, c. 27, s. 6; 2019, c. 9, s. 4(1).

CARRYING RESTRICTED FIREARMS AND PRE-DECEMBER 1, 1998 HANDGUNS.

20. An individual who holds a licence authorizing the individual to possess restricted firearms or handguns referred to in subsection 12(6.1) (pre-December 1, 1998 handguns) may be authorized to possess a particular restricted firearm or handgun at a place other than the place at which it is authorized to be possessed if the individual needs the particular restricted firearm or handgun

(*a*) to protect the life of that individual or of other individuals; or

(*b*) for use in connection with his or her lawful profession or occupation. 2003, c. 8, s. 56.

AUTHORIZED TRANSFERS AND LENDING

General Provisions

DEFINITION OF "TRANSFER".
21. For the purposes of sections 22 to 32, "transfer" means sell, barter or give.

MENTAL DISORDER, ETC.
22. A person may transfer or lend a firearm to an individual only if the person has no reason to believe that the individual
    (*a*) has a mental illness that makes it desirable, in the interests of the safety of that individual or any other person, that the individual not possess a firearm; or
    (*b*) is impaired by alcohol or a drug.

Authorized Transfers

AUTHORIZATION TO TRANSFER NON-RESTRICTED FIREARMS.
23. A person may transfer a non-restricted firearm if, at the time of the transfer,
    (*a*) the transferee holds a licence authorizing the transferee to acquire and possess that kind of firearm; and
    (*b*) the transferor has no reason to believe that the transferee is not authorized to acquire and possess that kind of firearm. 2003, c. 8, s. 17; 2012, c. 6, s. 11; 2015, c. 27, s. 7.

Note: Section 23 replaced, 2019, c. 9, s. 5 (to come into force by order of the Governor in Council):

AUTHORIZATION TO TRANSFER NON-RESTRICTED FIREARMS / Information — transferee's licence / Reference number / Period of validity / Registrar not satisfied.

23. (1) A person may transfer one or more non-restricted firearms if, at the time of the transfer,
    (*a*) the transferee holds a licence authorizing the transferee to acquire and possess a non-restricted firearm;
    (*b*) the Registrar has, at the transferor's request, issued a reference number for the transfer and provided it to the transferor; and
    (*c*) the reference number is still valid.

(2) The transferee shall provide to the transferor the prescribed information that relates to the transferee's licence, for the purpose of enabling the transferor to request that the Registrar issue a reference number for the transfer.

FIREARMS

(3) The Registrar shall issue a reference number if he or she is satisfied that the transferee holds and is still eligible to hold a licence authorizing them to acquire and possess a non-restricted firearm.

(4) A reference number is valid for the prescribed period.

(5) If the Registrar is not satisfied as set out in subsection (3), he or she may so inform the transferor.

VOLUNTARY REQUEST TO REGISTRAR / No record of request.

23.1 (1) A transferor referred to in section 23 may request that the Registrar inform the transferor as to whether the transferee, at the time of the transfer, holds and is still eligible to hold the licence referred to in paragraph 23(*a*), and if such a request is made, the Registrar or his or her delegate, or any other person that the federal Minister may designate, shall so inform the transferor.

(2) Despite sections 12 and 13 of the *Library and Archives of Canada Act* and subsections 6(1) and (3) of the *Privacy Act*, neither the Registrar or his or her delegate nor a designated person shall retain any record of a request made under subsection (1). 2012, c. 6, s. 11.

Note: Section 23.1 repealed, 2019, c. 9, s. 5 (to come into force by order of the Governor in Council).

AUTHORIZATION TO TRANSFER PROHIBITED OR RESTRICTED FIREARMS / Notice.

23.2 (1) A person may transfer a prohibited firearm or a restricted firearm if, at the time of the transfer,

- (*a*) the transferee holds a licence authorizing the transferee to acquire and possess that kind of firearm;
- (*b*) the transferor has no reason to believe that the transferee is not authorized to acquire and possess that kind of firearm;
- (*c*) the transferor informs the Registrar of the transfer;
- (*d*) if the transferee is an individual, the transferor informs a chief firearms officer of the transfer and obtains the authorization of the chief firearms officer for the transfer;
- (*e*) a new registration certificate for the firearm is issued in accordance with this Act; and
- (*f*) the prescribed conditions are met.

(2) If, after being informed of a proposed transfer of a firearm, the Registrar decides to refuse to issue a registration certificate for the firearm, the Registrar shall inform a chief firearms officer of that decision. 2012, c. 6, s. 11.

AUTHORIZATION TO TRANSFER PROHIBITED WEAPONS, DEVICES AND AMMUNITION / Conditions.

24. (1) Subject to section 26, a person may transfer a prohibited weapon, prohibited device or prohibited ammunition only to a business.

(2) A person may transfer a prohibited weapon, prohibited device, ammunition or prohibited ammunition to a business only if

- (a) the business holds a licence authorizing the business to acquire and possess prohibited weapons, prohibited devices, ammunition or prohibited ammunition, as the case may be;
- (b) [Repealed. 2003, c. 8, s. 18.]
- (c) the person has no reason to believe that the business is not authorized to acquire and possess prohibited weapons, prohibited devices, ammunition or prohibited ammunition, as the case may be; and
- (d) the prescribed conditions are complied with. 2003, c. 8, s. 18.

AUTHORIZATION TO TRANSFER AMMUNITION TO INDIVIDUALS.

25. A person may transfer ammunition that is not prohibited ammunition to an individual only if the individual

- (a) until January 1, 2001, holds a licence authorizing him or her to possess firearms or a prescribed document; or
- (b) after January 1, 2001, holds a licence authorizing him or her to possess firearms.

AUTHORIZATION TO TRANSFER PROHIBITED OR RESTRICTED FIREARMS TO CROWN, ETC. / Authorization to transfer prohibited weapons, etc., to the Crown, etc.

26. (1) A person may transfer a prohibited firearm or a restricted firearm to Her Majesty in right of Canada or a province, to a police force or to a municipality if the person informs the Registrar of the transfer and complies with the prescribed conditions.

(2) A person may transfer a prohibited weapon, restricted weapon, prohibited device, ammunition or prohibited ammunition to Her Majesty in right of Canada or a province, to a police force or to a municipality if the person informs a chief firearms officer of the transfer and complies with the prescribed conditions. 2003, c. 8, s. 19; 2012, c. 6, s. 12.

CHIEF FIREARMS OFFICER.

27. On being informed of a proposed transfer of a prohibited firearm or restricted firearm under section 23.2, a chief firearms officer shall

- (a) verify
  - (i) whether the transferee or individual holds a licence,
  - (ii) whether the transferee or individual is still eligible to hold that licence, and
  - (iii) whether the licence authorizes the transferee or individual to acquire that kind of firearm or to acquire prohibited weapons, prohibited devices, ammunition or prohibited ammunition, as the case may be;
- (b) in the case of a proposed transfer of a restricted firearm or a handgun referred to in subsection 12(6.1) (pre-December 1, 1998 handguns), verify the purpose for which the transferee or individual wishes to acquire the

FIREARMS

restricted firearm or handgun and determine whether the particular restricted firearm or handgun is appropriate for that purpose;

(c) decide whether to approve the transfer and inform the Registrar of that decision; and

(d) take the prescribed measures. 2003, c. 8, s. 20; 2012, c. 6, s. 13.

PERMITTED PURPOSES.

28. A chief firearms officer may approve the transfer to an individual of a restricted firearm or a handgun referred to in subsection 12(6.1) (pre-December 1, 1998 handguns) only if the chief firearms officer is satisfied

(a) that the individual needs the restricted firearm or handgun

    (i) to protect the life of that individual or of other individuals, or

    (ii) for use in connection with his or her lawful profession or occupation; or

(b) that the purpose for which the individual wishes to acquire the restricted firearm or handgun is

    (i) for use in target practice, or a target shooting competition, under conditions specified in an authorization to transport or under the auspices of a shooting club or shooting range that is approved under section 29, or

    (ii) to form part of a gun collection of the individual, in the case of an individual who satisfies the criteria described in section 30. 2003, c. 8, s. 21.

SHOOTING CLUBS AND SHOOTING RANGES / Approval / Revocation / Delegation / Notice of refusal to approve or revocation / Material to accompany notice / Non-disclosure of information.

29. (1) No person shall operate a shooting club or shooting range except under an approval of the provincial minister for the province in which the premises of the shooting club or shooting range are located.

(2) A provincial minister may approve a shooting club or shooting range for the purposes of this Act if

(a) the shooting club or shooting range complies with the regulations made under paragraph 117(e); and

(b) the premises of the shooting club or shooting range are located in that province.

(3) A provincial minister who approves a shooting club or shooting range for the purposes of this Act may revoke the approval for any good and sufficient reason including, without limiting the generality of the foregoing, where the shooting club or shooting range contravenes a regulation made under paragraph 117(e).

(4) A chief firearms officer who is authorized in writing by a provincial minister may perform such duties and functions of the provincial minister under this section as are specified in the authorization.

(5) Where a provincial minister decides to refuse to approve or to revoke an approval of a shooting club or shooting range for the purposes of this Act, the

provincial minister shall give notice of the decision to the shooting club or shooting range.

(6) A notice given under subsection (5) must include reasons for the decision disclosing the nature of the information relied on for the decision and must be accompanied by a copy of sections 74 to 81.

(7) A provincial minister need not disclose any information the disclosure of which could, in the opinion of the provincial minister, endanger the safety of any person.

GUN COLLECTORS.

30. The criteria referred to in subparagraph 28(*b*)(ii) are that the individual
   (*a*) has knowledge of the historical, technological or scientific characteristics that relate or distinguish the restricted firearms or handguns that he or she possesses;
   (*b*) has consented to the periodic inspection, conducted in a reasonable manner, of the premises in which the restricted firearms or handguns are to be kept; and
   (*c*) has complied with such other requirements as are prescribed respecting knowledge, secure storage and the keeping of records in respect of restricted firearms or handguns.

REGISTRAR / Transfers of firearms to the Crown, etc.

31. (1) On being informed of a proposed transfer of a firearm, the Registrar may
   (*a*) issue a new registration certificate for the firearm in accordance with this Act; and
   (*b*) revoke any registration certificate for the firearm held by the transferor.

(2) On being informed of a transfer of a firearm to Her Majesty in right of Canada or a province, to a police force or to a municipality, the Registrar shall revoke any registration certificate for the firearm. 2003, c. 8, s. 23.

MAIL-ORDER TRANSFERS OF FIREARMS.

32. A person may transfer a firearm by mail only if
   (*a*) the verifications, notifications, issuances and authorizations referred to in sections 21 to 28, 30, 31, 40 to 43 and 46 to 52 take place within a reasonable period before the transfer in the prescribed manner; and
   (*b*) [*Repealed. 2003, c. 8, s. 24.*]
   (*c*) the prescribed conditions are complied with. 2003, c. 8, s. 24.

Authorized Lending

AUTHORIZATION TO LEND.

33. Subject to section 34, a person may lend a firearm only if
   (*a*) the person

FIREARMS

      (i) has reasonable grounds to believe that the borrower holds a licence authorizing the borrower to possess that kind of firearm, and

      (ii) in the case of a prohibited firearm or a restricted firearm, lends the registration certificate for it to the borrower; or

  (*b*) the borrower uses the firearm under the direct and immediate supervision of the person in the same manner in which the person may lawfully use it. 2012, c. 6, s. 14.

AUTHORIZATION TO LEND FIREARMS, ETC., TO THE CROWN, ETC.

34. A person may lend a firearm, prohibited weapon, restricted weapon, prohibited device, ammunition or prohibited ammunition to Her Majesty in right of Canada or a province, to a police force or to a municipality if

  (*a*) in the case of a prohibited firearm or a restricted firearm, the transferor lends the registration certificate for it to the borrower; and

  (*b*) the prescribed conditions are complied with. 2003, c. 8, s. 25; 2012, c. 6, s. 15.

AUTHORIZED EXPORTATION AND IMPORTATION

Individuals

AUTHORIZATION FOR NON-RESIDENTS WHO DO NOT HOLD A LICENCE TO IMPORT FIREARMS THAT ARE NOT PROHIBITED FIREARMS / Non-compliance / Disposal of firearm / Non-compliance.

35. (1) A non-resident who does not hold a licence may import a firearm that is not a prohibited firearm if, at the time of the importation,

  (*a*) the non-resident

      (i) is eighteen years old or older,

      (ii) declares the firearm to a customs officer in the prescribed manner and, in the case of a declaration in writing, completes the prescribed form containing the prescribed information, and

      (iii) in the case of a restricted firearm, produces an authorization to transport the restricted firearm; and

  (*b*) a customs officer confirms in the prescribed manner the declaration referred to in subparagraph (*a*)(ii) and the authorization to transport referred to in subparagraph (*a*)(iii).

(2) Where a firearm is declared at a customs office to a customs officer but the requirements of subparagraphs (1)(*a*)(ii) and (iii) are not complied with, the customs officer may authorize the firearm to be exported from that customs office or may detain the firearm and give the non-resident a reasonable time to comply with those requirements.

(3) Where those requirements are not complied with within a reasonable time and the firearm is not exported, the firearm shall be disposed of in the prescribed manner.

(4) If a non-restricted firearm is declared at a customs office to a customs officer and

    (*a*) the non-resident has not truthfully completed the prescribed form, or

    (*b*) the customs officer has reasonable grounds to believe that it is desirable, in the interests of the safety of the non-resident or any other person, that the declaration not be confirmed,

the customs officer may refuse to confirm the declaration and may authorize the firearm to be exported from that customs office. 2015, c. 27, s. 8.

TEMPORARY LICENCE AND REGISTRATION CERTIFICATE / Renewal / Electronic or other means.

36. (1) A declaration that is confirmed under paragraph 35(1)(*b*) has the same effect after the importation of the firearm as a licence authorizing the non-resident to possess only that firearm and, in the case of a restricted firearm, as a registration certificate for the firearm until

    (*a*) the expiry of 60 days after the importation, in the case of a non-restricted firearm; or

    (*b*) the earlier of the expiry of 60 days after the importation and the expiry of the authorization to transport, in the case of a restricted firearm.

(2) A chief firearms officer may renew the confirmation of a declaration for one or more periods of sixty days.

(3) For greater certainty, an application for a renewal of the confirmation of a declaration may be made by telephone or other electronic means or by mail and a chief firearms officer may renew that confirmation by electronic means or by mail. 2012, c. 6, s. 16; 2015, c. 27, s. 9.

37 to 42. [*Repealed before coming into force*, 2008, c. 20, s. 3.]

Note: Section 42.2 enacted, 2015, c. 27, s. 10 (to come into force by order of the Governor in Council):

OBLIGATION TO PROVIDE INFORMATION / Information sharing.

42.2 (1) A business may import a prohibited firearm or a restricted firearm only if the business completes the prescribed form containing the prescribed information and provides it by electronic or other means to the Registrar before the importation and to a customs officer before or at the time of the importation.

(2) The Registrar and a customs officer may provide each other with any form or information that they receive under subsection (1).

43 to 53. [*Repealed before coming into force*, 2008, c. 20, s. 3.]

LICENCES, REGISTRATION CERTIFICATES AND AUTHORIZATIONS

Applications

APPLICATIONS / To whom made / Pre-commencement restricted firearms and handguns.

54. (1) A licence, registration certificate or authorization, other than an authorization referred to in subsection 19(2.1) or (2.2), may be issued only on application made in the prescribed form — which form may be in writing or electronic — or in the prescribed manner. The application must set out the prescribed information and be accompanied by payment of the prescribed fees.

Note: Subsection 54(1) replaced, 2019, c. 9, s. 6 (to come into force by order of the Governor in Council):

Applications

(1) A licence, registration certificate or authorization, other than an authorization referred to in subsection 19(2.1), (2.2) or (2.3), may be issued only on application made in the prescribed form — which form may be in writing or electronic — or in the prescribed manner. The application must set out the prescribed information and be accompanied by payment of the prescribed fees.

(2) An application for a licence, registration certificate or authorization must be made to

(*a*) a chief firearms officer, in the case of a licence, an authorization to carry or an authorization to transport; or

(*b*) the Registrar, in the case of a registration certificate, an authorization to export or an authorization to import.

(3) An individual who, on the commencement day, possesses one or more restricted firearms or one or more handguns referred to in subsection 12(6.1) (pre-December 1, 1998 handguns) must specify, in any application for a licence authorizing the individual to possess restricted firearms or handguns that are so referred to,

(*a*) except in the case of a firearm described in paragraph (*b*), for which purpose described in section 28 the individual wishes to continue to possess restricted firearms or handguns that are so referred to; and

(*b*) for which of those firearms was a registration certificate under the former Act issued because they were relics, were of value as a curiosity or rarity or were valued as a memento, remembrance or souvenir. 2003, c. 8, ss. 36, 56; 2015, c. 27, s. 11.

FURTHER INFORMATION / Investigation.

55. (1) A chief firearms officer or the Registrar may require an applicant for a licence or authorization to submit such information, in addition to that included in the application, as may reasonably be regarded as relevant for the purpose of determining whether the applicant is eligible to hold the licence or authorization.

(2) Without restricting the scope of the inquiries that may be made with respect to an application for a licence, a chief firearms officer may conduct an investigation of the applicant, which may consist of interviews with neighbours, community workers, social workers, individuals who work or live with the applicant, spouse or common-law partner, former spouse or common-law partner, dependants or whomever in the opinion of the chief firearms officer may provide information pertaining to whether the applicant is eligible under section 5 to hold a licence. 2000, c. 12, s. 118.

Issuance

LICENCES / Only one licence per individual / Separate licence for each location.

56. (1) A chief firearms officer is responsible for issuing licences.

(2) Only one licence may be issued to any one individual.

(3) A business other than a carrier requires a separate licence for each place where the business is carried on.

AUTHORIZATIONS TO CARRY OR TRANSPORT.

57. A chief firearms officer is responsible for issuing authorizations to carry and authorizations to transport.

CONDITIONS / Exception — licence or authorization / Minors / Minors.

58. (1) A chief firearms officer who issues a licence, an authorization to carry or an authorization to transport may attach any reasonable condition to it that the chief firearms officer considers desirable in the particular circumstances and in the interests of the safety of the holder or any other person.

(1.1) However, a chief firearms officer's power to attach a condition to a licence, an authorization to carry or an authorization to transport is subject to the regulations.

(2) Before attaching a condition to a licence that is to be issued to an individual who is less than eighteen years old and who is not eligible to hold a licence under subsection 8(2) (minors hunting as a way of life), a chief firearms officer must consult with a parent or person who has custody of the individual.

(3) Before issuing a licence to an individual who is less than eighteen years old and who is not eligible to hold a licence under subsection 8(2) (minors hunting as a way of life), a chief firearms officer shall have a parent or person who has custody of the individual sign the licence, including any conditions attached to it. 2015, c. 27, s. 12(1).

Note: Section 58.1 added, 2019, c. 9, s. 7 (to come into force by order of the Governor in Council):

FIREARMS

CONDITIONS — LICENCE ISSUED TO BUSINESS / Destruction of records.

58.1 (1) A chief firearms officer who issues a licence to a business must attach the following conditions to the licence:

   (*a*) the business must record and, for the prescribed period, keep the prescribed information that relates to the business' possession and disposal of non-restricted firearms;

   (*b*) the business must record and — for a period of 20 years from the day on which the business transfers a non-restricted firearm, or for a longer period that may be prescribed — keep the following information in respect of the transfer:

      (i) the reference number issued by the Registrar,

      (ii) the day on which the reference number was issued,

      (iii) the transferee's licence number, and

      (iv) the firearm's make, model and type and, if any, its serial number; and

   (*c*) the business must, unless otherwise directed by a chief firearms officer, transmit any records containing the information referred to in paragraph (*a*) or (*b*) to a prescribed official if it is determined that the business will cease to be a business.

(2) The prescribed official may destroy the records transmitted to them under paragraph (1)(*c*) at the times and in the circumstances that may be prescribed.

DIFFERENT REGISTERED OWNER.

59. An individual who holds an authorization to carry or authorization to transport need not be the person to whom the registration certificate for the particular prohibited firearm or restricted firearm was issued.

REGISTRATION CERTIFICATES AND AUTHORIZATIONS TO EXPORT OR IMPORT.

60. The Registrar is responsible for issuing registration certificates for prohibited firearms and restricted firearms and assigning firearms identification numbers to them and for issuing authorizations to export and authorizations to import. 2012, c. 6, s. 19.

FORM / Form of authorizations / Condition attached to licence / Automatic authorization to transport / Businesses.

61. (1) A licence or registration certificate must be issued in the prescribed form — which form may be in writing or electronic — or in the prescribed manner, and include the prescribed information, including any conditions attached to it.

(2) An authorization to carry, authorization to transport, authorization to export or authorization to import may be issued in the prescribed form — which form may be in writing or electronic — or in the prescribed manner, and include the prescribed information, including any conditions attached to it.

(3) An authorization to carry or authorization to transport may take the form of a condition attached to a licence.

(3.1) An authorization to transport referred to in subsection 19(1.1), (2.1) or (2.2) must take the form of a condition attached to a licence.

Note: Subsection 61(3.1) replaced, 2019, c. 9, s. 8 (to come into force by order of the Governor in Council):
Automatic authorization to transport

(3.1) An authorization to transport referred to in subsection 19(1.1), (2.1), (2.2) or (2.3) must take the form of a condition attached to a licence.

(4) A licence that is issued to a business must specify each particular activity that the licence authorizes in relation to prohibited firearms, restricted firearms, firearms that are neither prohibited firearms nor restricted firearms, cross-bows, prohibited weapons, restricted weapons, prohibited devices, ammunition or prohibited ammunition. 2003, c. 8, s. 38; 2015, c. 27, s. 13.

NOT TRANSFERABLE.

62. Licences, registration certificates, authorizations to carry, authorizations to transport, authorizations to export and authorizations to import are not transferable.

GEOGRAPHICAL EXTENT / Authorizations to carry.

63. (1) Licences, registration certificates, authorizations to transport, authorizations to export and authorizations to import are valid throughout Canada.

(2) [*Repealed.* 2003, c. 8, s. 39.]

(3) Authorizations to carry are not valid outside the province in which they are issued. 2003, c. 8, s. 39.

Term

TERM OF LICENCES / Extension period / No use or acquisition / Authorizations — no extension / Authorizations — issuance / Minors / Businesses / Businesses that sell only ammunition / Notice to holder.

64. (1) A licence that is issued to an individual who is eighteen years old or older expires on the earlier of
  (a) five years after the birthday of the holder next following the day on which it is issued, and
  (b) the expiration of the period for which it is expressed to be issued.

(1.1) Despite subsection (1), if a licence for firearms is not renewed before it expires, the licence is extended for a period of six months beginning on the day on which it would have expired under that subsection.

(1.2) The holder of a licence that is extended under subsection (1.1) must not, until the renewal of their licence, use their firearms or acquire any firearms or ammunition.

(1.3) The extension of a licence under subsection (1.1) does not result in the extension of any authorization to carry or authorization to transport beyond the day on which the licence would have expired under subsection (1).

(1.4) During the extension period, the following authorizations must not be issued to the holder of the licence:
  (*a*) an authorization to carry; and
  (*b*) an authorization to transport, unless it is issued
      (i) for a reason referred to in subparagraph 19(1)(*b*)(i) or (ii), or
      (ii) because the holder wishes to transport a firearm for disposal through sale or exportation.

(2) A licence that is issued to an individual who is less than eighteen years old expires on the earlier of
  (*a*) the day on which the holder attains the age of eighteen years, and
  (*b*) the expiration of the period for which it is expressed to be issued.

(3) A licence that is issued to a business other than a business referred to in subsection (4) expires on the earlier of
  (*a*) three years after the day on which it is issued, and
  (*b*) the expiration of the period for which it is expressed to be issued.

(4) A licence that is issued to a business that sells ammunition but is not authorized to possess firearms, prohibited weapons, restricted weapons, prohibited devices or prohibited ammunition expires on the earlier of
  (*a*) five years after the day on which it is issued, and
  (*b*) the expiration of the period for which it is expressed to be issued.

(5) and (6) [*Repealed* before coming into force, 2008, c. 20, s. 3.]

(7) The chief firearms officer shall give notice of every extension under this section to the holder of the licence. 2003, c. 8, s. 40; 2015, c. 27, s. 14.

TERM OF AUTHORIZATIONS / Authorizations to transport / Authorizations to transport / Authorizations to carry.

65. (1) Subject to subsections (2) to (4), an authorization expires on the expiration of the period for which it is expressed to be issued.

(2) Subject to subsection (3), an authorization to transport that takes the form of a condition attached to a licence expires on the earlier of
  (*a*) the expiration of the period for which the condition is expressed to be attached, and
  (*b*) the expiration of the licence.

(3) An authorization to transport a prohibited firearm, except for an automatic firearm, or a restricted firearm for use in target practice, or a target shooting competition, under specified conditions or under the auspices of a shooting club or shooting range that is approved under section 29, whether or not the authorization takes the form of a condition attached to the licence of the holder of the authorization, expires on the earlier of
  (*a*) the expiration of the period for which the authorization is expressed to be issued, which period may be no more than five years, and

(*b*) the expiration of the licence.

(4) An authorization to carry expires

(*a*) in the case of an authorization to carry that takes the form of a condition attached to a licence, on the earlier of

(i) the expiration of the period for which the condition is expressed to be attached, which period may not be more than two years, and

(ii) the expiration of the licence; and

(*b*) in the case of an authorization to carry that does not take the form of a condition attached to a licence, on the expiration of the period for which the authorization is expressed to be issued, which period may not be more than two years. 2003, c. 8, s. 41.

TERM OF REGISTRATION CERTIFICATES.

66. A registration certificate for a prohibited firearm or a restricted firearm expires when

(*a*) the holder of the registration certificate ceases to be the owner of the firearm; or

(*b*) the firearm ceases to be a firearm. 2012, c. 6, s. 20.

RENEWAL / Restricted firearms and pre-December 1, 1998 handguns / Registrar / Relics / Material to accompany notice.

67. (1) A chief firearms officer may renew a licence, authorization to carry or authorization to transport in the prescribed manner.

(2) On renewing a licence authorizing an individual to possess restricted firearms or handguns referred to in subsection 12(6.1) (pre-December 1, 1998 handguns), a chief firearms officer shall decide whether any of those firearms or handguns that the individual possesses are being used for a purpose described in section 28.

(*a*) the purpose described in section 28 for which the individual acquired the restricted firearms or handguns; or

(*b*) in the case of any of those firearms or handguns that were possessed by the individual on the commencement day, the purpose described in that section that was specified by the individual in the licence application.

(3) A chief firearms officer who decides that any restricted firearms or any handguns referred to in subsection 12(6.1) (pre-December 1, 1998 handguns) that are possessed by an individual are not being used for that purpose shall

(*a*) give notice of that decision in the prescribed form to the individual; and

(*b*) inform the Registrar of that decision.

(4) Subsections (2) and (3) do not apply to a firearm

(*a*) that is a relic, is of value as a curiosity or rarity or is valued as a memento, remembrance or souvenir;

(*b*) that was specified in the licence application as being a firearm for which a registration certificate under the former Act was issued because the firearm was a relic, was of value as a curiosity or rarity or was valued as a memento, remembrance or souvenir;

FIREARMS

(*c*) for which a registration certificate under the former Act was issued because the firearm was a relic, was of value as a curiosity or rarity or was valued as a memento, remembrance or souvenir; and

(*d*) in respect of which an individual, on the commencement day, held a registration certificate under the former Act.

(5) A notice given under paragraph (3)(*a*) must include the reasons for the decision and be accompanied by a copy of sections 74 to 81. 2003, c. 8, ss. 42, 56.

Refusal to Issue and Revocation

LICENCES AND AUTHORIZATIONS.

68. A chief firearms officer shall refuse to issue a licence if the applicant is not eligible to hold one and may refuse to issue an authorization to carry or authorization to transport for any good and sufficient reason.

REGISTRATION CERTIFICATES.

69. The Registrar may refuse to issue a registration certificate, authorization to export or authorization to import for any good and sufficient reason including, in the case of an application for a registration certificate, where the applicant is not eligible to hold a registration certificate.

REVOCATION OF LICENCE OR AUTHORIZATION / Registrar.

70. (1) A chief firearms officer may revoke a licence, an authorization to carry or an authorization to transport for any good and sufficient reason including, without limiting the generality of the foregoing,

(*a*) where the holder of the licence or authorization

(i) is no longer or never was eligible to hold the licence or authorization,

Note: Subparagraph 70(1)(*a*)(i.1) added, 2019, c. 9, s. 9 (to come into force by order of the Governor in Council):

(i.1) transfers, as defined in section 21, a non-restricted firearm other than in accordance with section 23,

(ii) contravenes any condition attached to the licence or authorization, or

(iii) has been convicted or discharged under section 730 of the *Criminal Code* of an offence referred to in paragraph 5(2)(*a*); or

(*b*) where, in the case of a business, a person who stands in a prescribed relationship to the business has been convicted or discharged under section 730 of the *Criminal Code* of any such offence.

(2) The Registrar may revoke an authorization to export or authorization to import for any good and sufficient reason. 1995, c. 39, s. 137; 2003, c. 8, s. 43.

REVOCATION OF REGISTRATION CERTIFICATE / Automatic revocation of registration certificate.

71. (1) The Registrar

(a) may revoke a registration certificate for a prohibited firearm or a restricted firearm for any good and sufficient reason; and

(b) shall revoke a registration certificate for a firearm held by an individual where the Registrar is informed by a chief firearms officer under section 67 that the firearm is not being used for a purpose described in section 28.

(2) A registration certificate for a prohibited firearm referred to in subsection 12(3) (pre-August 1, 1992 converted automatic firearms) is automatically revoked on the change of any alteration in the prohibited firearm that was described in the application for the registration certificate. 2003, c. 8, s. 44; 2012, c. 6, s. 21.

NOTICE OF REFUSAL TO ISSUE OR REVOCATION / When notice not required / Material to accompany notice / Non-disclosure of information / Disposal of firearms / Disposal of firearms — registration certificate / Reference.

72. (1) Subject to subsection (1.1), if a chief firearms officer decides to refuse to issue or to revoke a licence or authorization to transport or the Registrar decides to refuse to issue or to revoke a registration certificate, authorization to export or authorization to import, the chief firearms officer or Registrar shall give notice of the decision in the prescribed form to the applicant for or holder of the licence, registration certificate or authorization.

(1.1) Notice under subsection (1) need not be given in any of the following circumstances:

(a) if the holder has requested that the licence, registration certificate or authorization be revoked; or

(b) if the revocation is incidental to the issuance of a new licence, registration certificate or authorization.

(2) A notice given under subsection (1) must include reasons for the decision disclosing the nature of the information relied on for the decision and must be accompanied by a copy of sections 74 to 81.

(3) A chief firearms officer or the Registrar need not disclose any information the disclosure of which could, in the opinion of the chief firearms officer or the Registrar, endanger the safety of any person.

(4) A notice given under subsection (1) in respect of a licence must specify a reasonable period during which the applicant for or holder of the licence may deliver to a peace officer or a firearms officer or a chief firearms officer or otherwise lawfully dispose of any firearm, prohibited weapon, restricted weapon, prohibited device or prohibited ammunition that the applicant for or holder of the licence possesses and during which sections 91, 92 and 94 of the *Criminal Code* do not apply to the applicant or holder.

(5) A notice given under subsection (1) in respect of a registration certificate for a prohibited firearm or a restricted firearm must specify a reasonable period during which the applicant for or holder of the registration certificate may deliver to a peace officer or a firearms officer or a chief firearms officer or otherwise lawfully dispose of the firearm to which the registration certificate relates and during which

sections 91, 92 and 94 of the *Criminal Code* do not apply to the applicant or holder.

(6) If the applicant for or holder of the licence or registration certificate refers the refusal to issue it or revocation of it to a provincial court judge under section 74, the reasonable period of time does not begin until after the reference is finally disposed of. 2003, c. 8, s. 45; 2012, c. 6, s. 22.

References to Provincial Court Judge

REFERENCE TO JUDGE OF REFUSAL TO ISSUE OR REVOCATION, ETC. / Limitation period.

74. (1) Subject to subsection (2), where

    (*a*) a chief firearms officer or the Registrar refuses to issue or revokes a licence, registration certificate, authorization to transport, authorization to export or authorization to import,

    (*b*) a chief firearms officer decides under section 67 that a firearm possessed by an individual who holds a licence is not being used for a purpose described in section 28, or

    (*c*) a provincial minister refuses to approve or revokes the approval of a shooting club or shooting range for the purposes of this Act,

the applicant for or holder of the licence, registration certificate, authorization or approval may refer the matter to a provincial court judge in the territorial division in which the applicant or holder resides.

(2) An applicant or holder may only refer a matter to a provincial court judge under subsection (1) within thirty days after receiving notice of the decision of the chief firearms officer, Registrar or provincial minister under section 29, 67 or 72 or within such further time as is allowed by a provincial court judge, whether before or after the expiration of those thirty days. 2003, c. 8, s. 47.

HEARING OF REFERENCE / Evidence / Burden of proof / Where hearing may proceed *ex parte*.

75. (1) On receipt of a reference under section 74, the provincial court judge shall fix a date for the hearing of the reference and direct that notice of the hearing be given to the chief firearms officer, Registrar or provincial minister and to the applicant for or holder of the licence, registration certificate, authorization or approval, in such manner as the provincial court judge may specify.

(2) At the hearing of the reference, the provincial court judge shall hear all relevant evidence presented by or on behalf of the chief firearms officer, Registrar or provincial minister and the applicant or holder.

(3) At the hearing of the reference, the burden of proof is on the applicant or holder to satisfy the provincial court judge that the refusal to issue or revocation of the licence, registration certificate or authorization, the decision or the refusal to approve or revocation of the approval was not justified.

(4) A provincial court judge may proceed *ex parte* to hear and determine a reference in the absence of the applicant or holder in the same circumstances as those in which a summary conviction court may, under Part XXVII of the *Criminal Code*, proceed with a trial in the absence of the defendant.

DECISION BY PROVINCIAL COURT JUDGE.

76. On the hearing of a reference, the provincial court judge may, by order,

- (*a*) confirm the decision of the chief firearms officer, Registrar or provincial minister;
- (*b*) direct the chief firearms officer or Registrar to issue a licence, registration certificate or authorization or direct the provincial minister to approve a shooting club or shooting range; or
- (*c*) cancel the revocation of the licence, registration certificate, authorization or approval or the decision of the chief firearms officer under section 67.

Appeals to Superior Court and Court of Appeal

NUNAVUT / "provincial court judge" / "superior court judge".

76.1 With respect to Nunavut, the following definitions apply for the purpose of sections 77 to 81.

"provincial court judge" means a judge of the Nunavut Court of Justice.

"superior court [judge]" means a judge of the Court of Appeal of Nunavut. 1999, c. 3, s. 64.

APPEAL TO SUPERIOR COURT / Appeal by Attorney General.

77. (1) Subject to section 78, where a provincial court judge makes an order under paragraph 76(*a*), the applicant for or holder of the licence, registration certificate, authorization or approval, as the case may be, may appeal to the superior court against the order.

(2) Subject to section 78, where a provincial court judge makes an order under paragraph 76(*b*) or (*c*),

- (*a*) the Attorney General of Canada may appeal to the superior court against the order, if the order is directed to a chief firearms officer who was designated by the federal Minister, to the Registrar or to the federal Minister; or
- (*b*) the attorney general of the province may appeal to the superior court against the order, in the case of any other order made under paragraph 76(*b*) or (*c*).

FIREARMS

NOTICE OF APPEAL / Extension of time / Contents of notice / Service of notice.

78. (1) An appellant who proposes to appeal an order made under section 76 to the superior court must give notice of appeal not later than thirty days after the order is made.

(2) The superior court may, either before or after the expiration of those thirty days, extend the time within which notice of appeal may be given.

(3) A notice of appeal must set out the grounds of appeal, together with such further material as the superior court may require.

(4) A copy of any notice of appeal filed with the superior court under subsection (1) and of any further material required to be filed with it shall be served within fourteen days after the filing of the notice, unless before or after the expiration of those fourteen days further time is allowed by the superior court, on
- (a) the Attorney General of Canada, in the case of an appeal of an order made under paragraph 76(*a*) confirming a decision of a chief firearms officer who was designated by the federal Minister, of the Registrar or of the federal Minister;
- (b) the attorney general of the province, in the case of an appeal against any other order made under paragraph 76(*a*);
- (c) the applicant for or holder of the licence, registration certificate, authorization or approval, in the case of an appeal against an order made under paragraph 76(*b*) or (*c*); and
- (d) any other person specified by the superior court.

DISPOSITION OF APPEAL / Burden on applicant.

79. (1) On the hearing of an appeal, the superior court may
- (a) dismiss the appeal; or
- (b) allow the appeal and, in the case of an appeal against an order made under paragraph 76(*a*),
  - (i) direct the chief firearms officer or Registrar to issue a licence, registration certificate or authorization or direct the provincial minister to approve a shooting club or shooting range, or
  - (ii) cancel the revocation of the licence, registration certificate, authorization or approval or the decision of the chief firearms officer under section 67.

(2) A superior court shall dispose of an appeal against an order made under paragraph 76(*a*) by dismissing it, unless the appellant establishes to the satisfaction of the court that a disposition referred to in paragraph (1)(*b*) is justified.

APPEAL TO COURT OF APPEAL.

80. An appeal to the court of appeal may, with leave of that court or of a judge of that court, be taken against a decision of a superior court under section 79 on any ground that involves a question of law alone.

APPLICATION OF PART XXVII OF THE *CRIMINAL CODE*.

81. Part XXVII of the *Criminal Code*, except sections 785 to 812, 816 to 819 and 829 to 838, applies in respect of an appeal under this Act, with such modifications as the circumstances require and as if each reference in that Part to the appeal court were a reference to the superior court.

Commissioner of Firearms

APPOINTMENT.

81.1 The Governor in Council may appoint a person to be known as the Commissioner of Firearms to hold office during pleasure. The Commissioner shall be paid such remuneration as the Governor in Council may fix. 2003, c. 8, s. 48.

DUTIES, FUNCTIONS AND POWERS.

81.2 Subject to any direction that the federal Minister may give, the Commissioner may exercise the powers and shall perform the duties and functions relating to the administration of this Act that are delegated to the Commissioner by the federal Minister. 2003, c. 8, s. 48.

DELEGATION — FEDERAL MINISTER.

81.3 The federal Minister may delegate to the Commissioner any duty, function or power conferred on the federal Minister under this Act, except the power to delegate under this section and the power under subsections 97(2) and (3). 2003, c. 8, s. 48.

INCAPACITY OR VACANCY.

81.4 In the event of the absence or incapacity of, or vacancy in the office of, the Commissioner, the federal Minister may appoint a person to perform the duties and functions and exercise the powers of the Commissioner, but no person may be so appointed for a term of more than 60 days without the approval of the Governor in Council. 2003, c. 8, s. 48.

SUPERANNUATION AND COMPENSATION.

81.5 The Commissioner shall be deemed to be a person employed in the Public Service for the purposes of the *Public Service Superannuation Act* and to be employed in the public service of Canada for the purposes of the *Government Employees Compensation Act* and any regulations made pursuant to section 9 of the *Aeronautics Act*. 2003, c. 8, s. 48.

FIREARMS

CANADIAN FIREARMS REGISTRATION SYSTEM

Registrar of Firearms

REGISTRAR OF FIREARMS.

82. An individual to be known as the Registrar of Firearms shall be appointed or deployed in accordance with the *Public Service Employment Act*. 2003, c. 8, s. 49(1).

INCAPACITY OR VACANCY.

82.1 In the event of the absence or incapacity of, or vacancy in the position of, the Registrar, the Commissioner may perform the duties and functions and exercise the powers of the Registrar. 2003, c. 8, s. 49(1).

Records of the Registrar

CANADIAN FIREARMS REGISTRY / Operation.

83. (1) The Registrar shall establish and maintain a registry, to be known as the Canadian Firearms Registry, in which shall be kept a record of

- (*a*) every licence, every registration certificate for a prohibited firearm or a restricted firearm and every authorization that is issued or revoked by the Registrar;
- (*b*) every application for a licence, a registration certificate for a prohibited firearm or a restricted firearm or an authorization that is refused by the Registrar;
- (*c*) every transfer of a firearm of which the Registrar is informed under section 26 or 27;
- (*d*) every exportation from or importation into Canada of a firearm of which the Registrar is informed under section 42 or 50;

Note: Subsection 83(1) amended by enacting para. (*d*.1), 2015, c. 27, s. 15 (to come into force by order of the Governor in Council):

- (*d*.1) all information provided to the Registrar under section 42.2;
- (*e*) every loss, finding, theft or destruction of a firearm of which the Registrar is informed under section 88; and
- (*f*) such other matters as may be prescribed.

(2) The Registrar is responsible for the day-to-day operation of the Canadian Firearms Registry. 2012, c. 6, s. 23.

DESTRUCTION OF RECORDS.

84. The Registrar may destroy records kept in the Canadian Firearms Registry at such times and in such circumstances as may be prescribed.

OTHER RECORDS OF REGISTRAR / Reporting of acquisitions and transfers / Destruction of records.

85. (1) The Registrar shall establish and maintain a record of
 (*a*) firearms acquired or possessed by the following persons and used by them in the course of their duties or for the purposes of their employment, namely,
  (i) peace officers,
  (ii) persons training to become police officers or peace officers under the control and supervision of
   (A) a police force, or
   (B) a police academy or similar institution designated by the federal Minister or the lieutenant governor in council of a province,
  (iii) persons or members of a class of persons employed in the federal public administration or by the government of a province or municipality who are prescribed by the regulations made by the Governor in Council under Part III of the *Criminal Code* to be public officers, and
  (iv) chief firearms officers and firearms officers; and
 (*b*) firearms acquired or possessed by individuals on behalf of, and under the authority of, a police force or a department of the Government of Canada or of a province.

Note: Subsection 85(1) amended by striking out "and" at the end of para. (*a*) and by enacting paras. (*c*) and (*d*), 2019, c. 9, s. 10(3) (to come into force by order of the Governor in Council):
 (*c*) every request for a reference number made to the Registrar under section 23 and, if the request is refused, the reasons for refusing the request; and
 (*d*) every reference number that is issued by the Registrar under subsection 23(3) and, with respect to each reference number, the day on which it was issued and the licence numbers of the transferor and transferee.

(2) A person referred to in subsection (1) who acquires or transfers a firearm shall have the Registrar informed of the acquisition or transfer.

Note: Subsection 85(2) replaced, 2019, c. 9, s. 10(4) (to come into force by order of the Governor in Council):
Reporting of acquisitions and transfers

(2) A person referred to in paragraph (1)(*a*) or (*b*) who acquires or transfers a firearm shall have the Registrar informed of the acquisition or transfer.

(3) The Registrar may destroy any record referred to in subsection (1) at such times and in such circumstances as may be prescribed. 2003, c. 22, s. 224(*z*.38).

RECORDS TO BE TRANSFERRED.

86. The records kept in the registry maintained pursuant to section 114 of the former Act that relate to registration certificates shall be transferred to the Registrar.

Records of Chief Firearms Officers

RECORDS OF CHIEF FIREARMS OFFICERS / Destruction of records.

87. (1) A chief firearms officer shall keep a record of

- (*a*) every licence and authorization that is issued or revoked by the chief firearms officer;
- (*b*) every application for a licence or authorization that is refused by the chief firearms officer;
- (*c*) every prohibition order of which the chief firearms officer is informed under section 89; and
- (*d*) such other matters as may be prescribed.

(2) A chief firearms officer may destroy any record referred to in subsection (1) at such times and in such circumstances as may be prescribed.

REPORTING OF LOSS, FINDING, THEFT AND DESTRUCTION.

88. A chief firearms officer to whom the loss, finding, theft or destruction of a prohibited firearm or a restricted firearm is reported shall have the Registrar informed without delay of the loss, finding, theft or destruction. 2012, c. 6, s. 24.

Reporting of Prohibition Orders

REPORTING OF PROHIBITION ORDERS.

89. Every court, judge or justice that makes, varies or revokes a prohibition order shall have a chief firearms officer informed without delay of the prohibition order or its variation or revocation.

Access to Records

RIGHT OF ACCESS.

90. The Registrar has a right of access to records kept by a chief firearms officer under section 87 and a chief firearms officer has a right of access to records kept by the Registrar under section 83 or 85 and to records kept by other chief firearms officers under section 87.

RIGHT OF ACCESS — SUBSECTION 23.1(1).

90.1 For the purpose of subsection 23.1(1), the person responding to a request made under that subsection has a right of access to records kept by a chief firearms officer under section 87. 2012, c. 6, s. 25.

Note: Section 90.1 repealed, 2019, c. 9, s. 11 (to come into force by order of the Governor in Council).

Electronic Filing

ELECTRONIC FILING / Time of receipt.

91. (1) Subject to the regulations, notices and documents that are sent to or issued by the Registrar pursuant to this or any other Act of Parliament may be sent or issued in electronic or other form in any manner specified by the Registrar.

(2) For the purposes of this Act and Part III of the *Criminal Code*, a notice or document that is sent or issued in accordance with subsection (1) is deemed to have been received at the time and date provided by the regulations.

RECORDS OF REGISTRAR / Storage of documents or information in electronic or other form / Probative value.

92. (1) Records required by section 83 or 85 to be kept by the Registrar may
   (*a*) be in bound or loose-leaf form or in photographic film form; or
   (*b*) be entered or recorded by any system of mechanical or electronic data processing or by any other information storage device that is capable of reproducing any required information in intelligible written or printed form within a reasonable time.

(2) Subject to the regulations, a document or information received by the Registrar under this Act in electronic or other form may be entered or recorded by any information storage device, including any system of mechanical or electronic data processing, that is capable of reproducing stored documents or information in intelligible written or printed form within a reasonable time.

(3) Where the Registrar maintains a record of a document otherwise than in written or printed form, an extract from that record that is certified by the Registrar has the same probative value as the document would have had if it had been proved in the ordinary way.

Reports

REPORT TO FEDERAL MINISTER / Report to be laid before Parliament.

93. (1) The Commissioner shall, as soon as possible after the end of each calendar year and at any other times that the federal Minister may in writing request, submit to the federal Minister a report, in the form and including the information that the federal Minister may direct, with regard to the administration of this Act.

(2) The federal Minister shall have each report laid before each House of Parliament on any of the first 15 days on which that House is sitting after the federal Minister receives it. 2003, c. 8, s. 50.

INFORMATION TO BE SUBMITTED TO COMMISSIONER.

94. A chief firearms officer shall submit to the Commissioner the prescribed information with regard to the administration of this Act at the prescribed time and

FIREARMS

1115

in the prescribed form for the purpose of enabling the Commissioner to compile the reports referred to in section 93. 2003, c. 8, s. 50.

GENERAL

Agreements with Provinces

AGREEMENTS WITH PROVINCES.

95. The federal Minister may, with the approval of the Governor in Council, enter into agreements with the governments of the provinces

- (a) providing for payment of compensation by Canada to the provinces in respect of administrative costs actually incurred by the provinces in relation to processing licences, registration certificates and authorizations and applications for licences, registration certificates and authorizations and the operation of the Canadian Firearms Registration System; and
- (b) notwithstanding subsections 17(1) and (4) of the *Financial Administration Act*, authorizing the governments of the provinces to withhold those costs, in accordance with the terms and conditions of the agreement, from fees under paragraph 117(*p*) collected or received by the governments of the provinces.

Other Matters

OTHER OBLIGATIONS NOT AFFECTED.

96. The issuance of a licence, registration certificate or authorization under this Act does not affect the obligation of any person to comply with any other Act of Parliament or any regulation made under an Act of Parliament respecting firearms or other weapons.

EXEMPTIONS — GOVERNOR IN COUNCIL / Exemptions — federal Minister / Exemptions — provincial minister / Public safety / Conditions.

97. (1) Subject to subsection (4), the Governor in Council may exempt any class of non-residents from the application of any provision of this Act or the regulations, or from the application of any of sections 91 to 95, 99 to 101, 103 to 107 and 117.03 of the *Criminal Code*, for any period specified by the Governor in Council.

(2) Subject to subsection (4), the federal Minister may exempt any non-resident from the application of any provision of this Act or the regulations, or from the application of any of sections 91 to 95, 99 to 101, 103 to 107 and 117.03 of the *Criminal Code*, for any period not exceeding one year.

(3) Subject to subsection (4), a provincial minister may exempt from the application in that province of any provision of this Act or the regulations or Part III of the *Criminal Code*, for any period not exceeding one year, the employees, in respect of any thing done by them in the course of or for the purpose of their duties

or employment, of any business that holds a licence authorizing the business to acquire prohibited firearms, prohibited weapons, prohibited devices or prohibited ammunition.

(4) Subsections (1) to (3) do not apply if it is not desirable, in the interests of the safety of any person, that the exemption be granted.

(5) The authority granting an exemption may attach to it any reasonable condition that the authority considers desirable in the particular circumstances and in the interests of the safety of any person. 2001, c. 41, s. 96.

DELEGATION

AUTHORIZED CHIEF FIREARMS OFFICER MAY PERFORM FUNCTIONS OF PROVINCIAL MINISTER.

98. A chief firearms officer of a province who is authorized in writing by a provincial minister may perform the function of the provincial minister of designating firearms officers for the province.

DESIGNATED OFFICERS MAY PERFORM FUNCTIONS OF CHIEF FIREARMS OFFICERS.

99. A firearms officer who is designated in writing by a chief firearms officer may perform any of the duties and functions of the chief firearms officer under this Act or Part III of the *Criminal Code* that are specified in the designation. 2003, c. 8, s. 52.

DESIGNATED OFFICERS MAY PERFORM FUNCTIONS OF REGISTRAR.

100. A person who is designated in writing by the Registrar for the purpose of this section may perform such duties and functions of the Registrar under this Act or Part III of the *Criminal Code* as are specified in the designation.

INSPECTION

DEFINITION OF "INSPECTOR".

101. In sections 102 to 105, "inspector" means a firearms officer and includes, in respect of a province, a member of a class of individuals designated by the provincial minister.

INSPECTION / Operation of data processing systems and copying equipment / Use of force / Receipt for things taken / Definition of "business".

102. (1) Subject to section 104, for the purpose of ensuring compliance with this Act and the regulations, an inspector may at any reasonable time enter and inspect any place where the inspector believes on reasonable grounds a business is being

FIREARMS

carried on or there is a record of a business, any place in which the inspector believes on reasonable grounds there is a gun collection or a record in relation to a gun collection or any place in which the inspector believes on reasonable grounds there is a prohibited firearm or there are more than 10 firearms and may

  (*a*) open any container that the inspector believes on reasonable grounds contains a firearm or other thing in respect of which this Act or the regulations apply;

  (*b*) examine any firearm and examine any other thing that the inspector finds and take samples of it;

  (*c*) conduct any tests or analyses or take any measurements; and

  (*d*) require any person to produce for examination or copying any records, books of account or other documents that the inspector believes on reasonable grounds contain information that is relevant to the enforcement of this Act or the regulations.

(2) In carrying out an inspection of a place under subsection (1), an inspector may

  (*a*) use or cause to be used any data processing system at the place to examine any data contained in or available to the system;

  (*b*) reproduce any record or cause it to be reproduced from the data in the form of a print-out or other intelligible output and remove the print-out or other output for examination or copying; and

  (*c*) use or cause to be used any copying equipment at the place to make copies of any record, book of account or other document.

(3) In carrying out an inspection of a place under subsection (1), an inspector may not use force.

(4) An inspector who takes any thing while carrying out an inspection of a place under subsection (1) must give to the owner or occupant of the place at the time that the thing is taken a receipt for the thing that describes the thing with reasonable precision, including, in the case of a firearm, the serial number if available of the firearm.

(5) For greater certainty, in this section, "business" has the meaning assigned by subsection 2(1).

DUTY TO ASSIST INSPECTORS.

103. The owner or person in charge of a place that is inspected by an inspector under section 102 and every person found in the place shall

  (*a*) give the inspector all reasonable assistance to enable him or her to carry out the inspection and exercise any power conferred by section 102; and

  (*b*) provide the inspector with any information relevant to the enforcement of this Act or the regulations that he or she may reasonably require.

INSPECTION OF DWELLING-HOUSE / Authority to issue warrant / Areas that may be inspected.

104. (1) An inspector may not enter a dwelling-house under section 102 except

  (*a*) on reasonable notice to the owner or occupant, except where a business is being carried on in the dwelling-house; and (*b*) with the consent of the occupant or under a warrant.

(2) A justice who on *ex parte* application is satisfied by information on oath

(*a*) that the conditions for entry described in section 102 exist in relation to a dwelling-house,

(*b*) that entry to the dwelling-house is necessary for any purpose relating to the enforcement of this Act or the regulations, and

(*c*) that entry to the dwelling-house has been refused or that there are reasonable grounds for believing that entry will be refused

may issue a warrant authorizing the inspector named in it to enter that dwelling-house subject to any conditions that may be specified in the warrant.

(3) For greater certainty, an inspector who is carrying out an inspection of a dwelling-house may enter and inspect only

(*a*) that part of a room of the dwelling-house in which the inspector believes on reasonable grounds there is a firearm, prohibited weapon, restricted weapon, prohibited device, prohibited ammunition, a record in relation to a gun collection or all or part of a device or other thing required by a regulation made under paragraph 117(*h*) respecting the storage of firearms and restricted weapons; and

(*b*) in addition, in the case of a dwelling-house where the inspector believes on reasonable grounds a business is being carried on, that part of a room in which the inspector believes on reasonable grounds there is ammunition or a record of the business.

DEMAND TO PRODUCE FIREARM.

105. An inspector who believes on reasonable grounds that a person possesses a firearm may, by demand made to that person, require that person, within a reasonable time after the demand is made, to produce the firearm in the manner specified by the inspector for the purpose of verifying the serial number or other identifying features of the firearm and of ensuring that, in the case of a prohibited firearm or a restricted firearm, the person is the holder of the registration certificate for it. 2012, c. 6, s. 26.

OFFENCES

FALSE STATEMENTS TO PROCURE LICENCES, ETC. / False statements to procure customs confirmations / Definition of "statement".

106. (1) Every person commits an offence who, for the purpose of procuring a licence, registration certificate or authorization for that person or any other person, knowingly makes a statement orally or in writing that is false or misleading or knowingly fails to disclose any information that is relevant to the application for the licence, registration certificate or authorization.

(2) Every person commits an offence who, for the purpose of procuring the confirmation by a customs officer of a document under this Act for that person or any other person, knowingly makes a statement orally or in writing that is false or

misleading or knowingly fails to disclose any information that is relevant to the document.

(3) In this section, "statement" means an assertion of fact, opinion, belief or knowledge, whether material or not and whether admissible or not.

TAMPERING WITH LICENCES, ETC.

107. Every person commits an offence who, without lawful excuse the proof of which lies on the person, alters, defaces or falsifies

- (*a*) a licence, registration certificate or authorization; or
- (*b*) a confirmation by a customs officer of a document under this Act.

UNAUTHORIZED POSSESSION OF AMMUNITION.

108. Every business commits an offence that possesses ammunition, unless the business holds a licence under which it may possess ammunition.

PUNISHMENT.

109. Every person who commits an offence under section 106, 107 or 108, who contravenes subsection 29(1) or who contravenes a regulation made under paragraph 117(*d*), (*e*), (*f*), (*g*), (*i*), (*j*), (*k*.2), (*l*), (*m*) or (*n*) the contravention of which has been made an offence under paragraph 117(*o*)

- (*a*) is guilty of an indictable offence and liable to imprisonment for a term not exceeding five years; or
- (*b*) is guilty of an offence punishable on summary conviction. 2019, c. 9, s. 12.

CONTRAVENTION OF CONDITIONS OF LICENCES, ETC.

110. Every person commits an offence who, without lawful excuse, contravenes a condition of a licence, registration certificate or authorization held by the person.

PUNISHMENT.

111. Every person who commits an offence under section 110 or who does not comply with section 103

- (*a*) is guilty of an indictable offence and liable to imprisonment for a term not exceeding two years; or
- (*b*) is guilty of an offence punishable on summary conviction.

112. [*Repealed.* 2012, c. 6, s. 27.]

NON-COMPLIANCE WITH DEMAND TO PRODUCE FIREARM.

113. Every person commits an offence who, without reasonable excuse, does not comply with a demand made to the person by an inspector under section 105.

FAILURE TO DELIVER UP REVOKED LICENCE, ETC.

114. Every person commits an offence who, being the holder of a licence, a registration certificate for a prohibited firearm or a restricted firearm or an authorization that is revoked, does not deliver it up to a peace officer or firearms officer without delay after the revocation. 2012, c. 6, s. 28.

PUNISHMENT.

115. Every person who commits an offence under section 113 or 114 is guilty of an offence punishable on summary conviction. 2012, c. 6, s. 28.

ATTORNEY GENERAL OF CANADA MAY ACT.

116. Any proceedings in respect of an offence under this Act may be commenced at the instance of the Government of Canada and conducted by or on behalf of that government.

Regulations

REGULATIONS.

117. The Governor in Council may make regulations
- (*a*) regulating the issuance of licences, registration certificates and authorizations, including regulations respecting the purposes for which they may be issued under any provision of this Act and prescribing the circumstances in which persons are or are not eligible to hold licences;
- (*a*.1) deeming permits to export goods, or classes of permits to export goods, that are issued under the *Export and Import Permits Act* to be authorizations to export for the purposes of this Act;
- (*b*) regulating the revocation of licences, registration certificates and authorizations;
- (*c*) prescribing the circumstances in which an individual does or does not need firearms
  - (i) to protect the life of that individual or of other individuals, or
  - (ii) for use in connection with his or her lawful profession or occupation;

Note: Section 117 amended by enacting para. (*c*.1), 2019, c. 9, s. 13(1) (to come into force by order of the Governor in Council):
- (*c*.1) regulating, for the purpose of issuing a reference number under section 23, the provision of information by a transferor, a transferee and the Registrar;
- (*d*) regulating the use of firearms in target practice or target shooting competitions;
- (*e*) regulating
  - (i) the establishment and operation of shooting clubs and shooting ranges,
  - (ii) the activities that may be carried on at shooting clubs and shooting ranges,
  - (iii) the possession and use of firearms at shooting clubs and shooting ranges, and

FIREARMS

     (iv) the keeping and destruction of records in relation to shooting clubs and shooting ranges and members of those clubs and ranges;

  (f) regulating the establishment and maintenance of gun collections and the acquisition and disposal or disposition of firearms that form part or are to form part of a gun collection;

  (g) regulating the operation of gun shows, the activities that may be carried on at gun shows and the possession and use of firearms at gun shows;

  (h) regulating the storage, handling, transportation, shipping, display, advertising and mail-order sale of firearms and restricted weapons and defining the expression "mail-order sale" for the purposes of this Act;

  (i) regulating the storage, handling, transportation, shipping, possession for a prescribed purpose, transfer, exportation or importation of

     (i) prohibited firearms, prohibited weapons, restricted weapons, prohibited devices and prohibited ammunition, or

    (ii) components or parts of prohibited firearms, prohibited weapons, restricted weapons, prohibited devices and prohibited ammunition;

  (j) regulating the possession and use of restricted weapons;

(j.1) respecting the possession and transportation of firearms during the extension period referred to in subsection 64(1.1);

  (k) for authorizing

     (i) the possession at any place, or

    (ii) the manufacture or transfer, whether or not for consideration, or offer to manufacture or transfer, whether or not for consideration, of firearms, prohibited weapons, restricted weapons, prohibited devices, ammunition, prohibited ammunition and components and parts designed exclusively for use in the manufacture of or assembly into firearms;

(k.1) respecting the importation or exportation of firearms, prohibited weapons, restricted weapons, prohibited devices, ammunition, prohibited ammunition and components and parts designed exclusively for use in the manufacture of or assembly into firearms;

(k.2) respecting the marking of firearms manufactured in Canada or imported into Canada and the removal, alteration, obliteration and defacing of those markings;

(k.3) respecting the confirmation of declarations and authorizations to transport for the purposes of paragraph 35(1)(d), the confirmation of declarations for the purposes of paragraph 35.1(2)(d) and the confirmation of authorizations to import for the purposes of paragraph 40(2)(e);

  (l) regulating the storage, handling, transportation, shipping, acquisition, possession, transfer, exportation, importation, use and disposal or disposition of firearms, prohibited weapons, restricted weapons, prohibited devices, prohibited ammunition and explosive substances

     (i) by the following persons in the course of their duties or for the purposes of their employment, namely,

      (A) peace officers,

   (B) persons training to become police officers or peace officers under the control and supervision of a police force or a police academy or similar institution designated by the federal Minister or the lieutenant governor in council of a province,

   (C) persons or members of a class of persons employed in the federal public administration or by the government of a province or municipality who are prescribed by the regulations made by the Governor in Council under Part III of the *Criminal Code* to be public officers, and

   (D) chief firearms officers and firearms officers, and

  (ii) by individuals on behalf of, and under the authority of, a police force or a department of the Government of Canada or of a province;

 (m) regulating the keeping, transmission and destruction of records in relation to firearms, prohibited weapons, restricted weapons, prohibited devices and prohibited ammunition;

 (n) regulating the keeping and destruction of records by businesses in relation to ammunition;

Note: Section 117 amended by enacting para. (*n*.1), 2019, c. 9, s. 13(3) (to come into force by order of the Governor in Council):

 (n.1) regulating the transmission of records under paragraph 58.1(1)(*c*) by a business to a prescribed official;

 (o) creating offences consisting of contraventions of the regulations made under paragraph (*d*), (*e*), (*f*), (*g*), (*i*), (*j*), (*k*.1), (*k*.2), (*l*), (*m*) or (*n*);

 (p) prescribing the fees that are to be paid to Her Majesty in right of Canada for licences, registration certificates, authorizations, approvals of transfers and importations of firearms and confirmations by customs officers of documents under this Act;

 (q) waiving or reducing the fees payable under paragraph (*p*) in such circumstances as may be specified in the regulations;

 (r) prescribing the charges that are to be paid to Her Majesty in right of Canada in respect of costs incurred by Her Majesty in right of Canada in storing goods that are detained by customs officers or in disposing of goods;

 (s) respecting the operation of the Canadian Firearms Registry;

 (t) regulating the sending or issuance of notices and documents in electronic or other form, including

  (i) the notices and documents that may be sent or issued in electronic or other form,

  (ii) the persons or classes of persons by whom they may be sent or issued,

  (iii) their signature in electronic or other form or their execution, adoption or authorization in a manner that pursuant to the regulations is to have the same effect for the purposes of this Act as their signature, and

  (iv) the time and date when they are deemed to be received;

 (u) respecting the manner in which any provision of this Act or the regulations applies to any of the aboriginal peoples of Canada, and adapting any such provision for the purposes of that application;

FIREARMS

 (*v*) repealing

  (i) section 4 of the *Cartridge Magazine Control Regulations*, made by Order in Council P.C. 1992-1660 of July 16, 1992 and registered as SOR/92- 460, and the heading before it,

  (ii) the *Designated Areas Firearms Order*, C.R.C., chapter 430,

  (iii) section 4 of the *Firearms Acquisition Certificate Regulations*, made by Order in Council P.C. 1992-1663 of July 16, 1992 and registered as SOR/92-461, and the heading before it,

  (iv) section 7 of the *Genuine Gun Collector Regulations*, made by Order in Council P.C. 1992-1661 of July 16, 1992 and registered as SOR/92-435, and the heading before it,

  (v) sections 8 and 13 of the *Prohibited Weapons Control Regulations*, made by Order in Council P.C. 1991-1925 of October 3, 1991 and registered as SOR/91- 572, and the headings before them,

  (vi) the *Restricted Weapon Registration Certificate for Classes of Persons other than Individuals Regulations*, made by Order in Council P.C. 1993- 766 of April 20, 1993 and registered as SOR/93-200, and

  (vii) sections 7, 15 and 17 of the *Restricted Weapons and Firearms Control Regulations*, made by Order in Council P.C. 1978-2572 of August 16, 1978 and registered as SOR/78-670, and the headings before them; and

 (*w*) prescribing anything that by any provision of this Act is to be prescribed by regulation. 2003, c. 8, s. 54; 2003, c. 22, s. 224(z.38); 2015, c. 27, s. 16; 2019, c. 9, s. 13(2).

LAYING OF PROPOSED REGULATIONS / Idem / Report by committee / Making of regulations / Definition of "sitting day".

118. (1) Subject to subsection (2), the federal Minister shall have each proposed regulation laid before each House of Parliament.

(2) Where a proposed regulation is laid pursuant to subsection (1), it shall be laid before each House of Parliament on the same day.

(3) Each proposed regulation that is laid before a House of Parliament shall, on the day it is laid, be referred by that House to an appropriate committee of that House, as determined by the rules of that House, and the committee may conduct inquiries or public hearings with respect to the proposed regulation and report its findings to that House.

(4) A proposed regulation that has been laid pursuant to subsection (1) may be made

 (*a*) on the expiration of thirty sitting days after it was laid; or

 (*b*) where, with respect to each House of Parliament,

  (i) the committee reports to the House, or

  (ii) the committee decides not to conduct inquiries or public hearings.

(5) For the purpose of this section, "sitting day" means a day on which either House of Parliament sits.

EXCEPTION / Exception — minor changes / Exception — urgency / Notice of opinion / Exception — prescribed dates / Part III of the *Criminal Code*.

119. (1) No proposed regulation that has been laid pursuant to section 118 need again be laid under that section, whether or not it has been altered.

(2) A regulation made under section 117 may be made without being laid before either House of Parliament if the federal Minister is of the opinion that the changes made by the regulation to an existing regulation are so immaterial or insubstantial that section 118 should not be applicable in the circumstances.

(3) A regulation made under paragraph 117(*i*), (*l*), (*m*), (*n*), (*o*), (*q*), (*s*) or (*t*) may be made without being laid before either House of Parliament if the federal Minister is of the opinion that the making of the regulation is so urgent that section 118 should not be applicable in the circumstances.

(4) Where the federal Minister forms the opinion described in subsection (2) or (3), he or she shall have a statement of the reasons why he or she formed that opinion laid before each House of Parliament.

(5) A regulation may be made under paragraph 117(*w*) prescribing a date for the purposes of the application of any provision of this Act without being laid before either House of Parliament.

(6) For greater certainty, a regulation may be made under Part III of the *Criminal Code* without being laid before either House of Parliament.

TRANSITIONAL PROVISIONS

Licences

FIREARMS ACQUISITION CERTIFICATES / Authorizations / Expiration / Lost, stolen and destroyed firearms acquisition certificates.

120. (1) A firearms acquisition certificate is deemed to be a licence if it
  (*a*) was issued under section 106 or 107 of the former Act;
  (*b*) had not been revoked before the commencement day; and
  (*c*) was valid pursuant to subsection 106(11) of the former Act, or pursuant to that subsection as applied by subsection 107(1) of the former Act, on the commencement day.

(2) A firearms acquisition certificate that is deemed to be a licence authorizes the holder
  (*a*) to acquire and possess any firearms other than prohibited firearms that are acquired by the holder on or after the commencement day and before the expiration or revocation of the firearms acquisition certificate;
  (*b*) in the case of an individual referred to in subsection 12(2), (3), (4), (5), (6) or (8), to acquire and possess any prohibited firearms referred to in that subsection that are acquired by the holder on or after the commencement day; and

  (*c*) in the case of a particular individual who is eligible under subsection 12(7) to hold a licence authorizing the particular individual to possess a handgun referred to in subsection 12(6.1) (pre-December 1, 1998 handguns) in the circumstances described in subsection 12(7), to acquire and possess such a handgun in those circumstances, if the particular handgun is acquired by the particular individual on or after the commencement day.

(3) A firearms acquisition certificate that is deemed to be a licence expires on the earlier of

  (*a*) five years after the day on which it was issued, and

  (*b*) the issuance of a licence to the holder of the firearms acquisition certificate.

(4) Where a firearms acquisition certificate that is deemed to be a licence is lost, stolen or destroyed before its expiration under subsection (3), a person who has authority under this Act to issue a licence may issue a replacement firearms acquisition certificate that has the same effect as the one that was lost, stolen or destroyed. 2003, c. 8, s. 56.

MINORS' PERMITS / Authorizations / Geographical extent / Expiration.

121. (1) A permit is deemed to be a licence if it

  (*a*) was issued under subsection 110(6) or (7) of the former Act to a person who was under the age of eighteen years;

  (*b*) had not been revoked before the commencement day; and

  (*c*) remained in force pursuant to subsection 110(8) of the former Act on the commencement day.

(2) A permit that is deemed to be a licence authorizes the holder to possess non-restricted firearms.

(3) A permit that is deemed to be a licence is valid only in the province in which it was issued, unless the permit was endorsed pursuant to subsection 110(10) of the former Act as being valid within the provinces indicated in the permit, in which case it remains valid within those provinces.

(4) A permit that is deemed to be a licence expires on the earliest of

  (*a*) the expiration of the period for which it was expressed to be issued,

  (*b*) the day on which the person to whom it was issued attains the age of eighteen years, and

  (*c*) five years after the birthday of the person next following the day on which it was issued, if that fifth anniversary occurs on or after the commencement day. 2015, c. 27, s. 17.

MUSEUM APPROVALS / Expiration.

122. (1) An approval of a museum, other than a museum established by the Chief of the Defence Staff, is deemed to be a licence if the approval

  (*a*) was granted under subsection 105(1) of the former Act; and

  (*b*) had not been revoked before the commencement day.

(2) An approval of a museum that is deemed to be a licence expires on the earlier of

(a) the expiration of the period for which the approval was expressed to be granted, and

(b) three years after the commencement day.

PERMITS TO CARRY ON BUSINESS / Expiration.

123. (1) A permit to carry on a business described in paragraph 105(1)(*a*) or (*b*) or subparagraph 105(2)(*b*)(i) of the former Act is deemed to be a licence if it

(a) was
   (i) issued under subsection 110(5) of the former Act, or
   (ii) continued under subsection 6(2) of the *Criminal Law Amendment Act, 1968-69*, chapter 38 of the Statutes of Canada, 1968-69, or subsection 48(1) of the *Criminal Law Amendment Act, 1977*, chapter 53 of the Statutes of Canada, 1976- 77;

(b) had not been revoked before the commencement day;

(c) had not ceased to be in force or have any effect on October 30, 1992 under section 34 of *An Act to amend the Criminal Code and the Customs Tariff in consequence thereof*, chapter 40 of the Statutes of Canada, 1991; and

(d) remained in force pursuant to subsection 110(5) of the former Act on the commencement day.

(2) A permit that is deemed to be a licence expires on the earlier of

(a) the expiration of the period for which the permit was expressed to be issued, and

(b) one year after the commencement day.

GEOGRAPHICAL EXTENT.

124. A permit or an approval of a museum that is deemed to be a licence under section 122 or 123 is valid only for the location of the business or museum for which it was issued.

INDUSTRIAL PURPOSE DESIGNATIONS / Geographical extent / Expiration.

125. (1) A designation of a person is deemed to be a licence if it

(a) was made under subsection 90(3.1) or paragraph 95(3)(*b*) of the former Act, and

(b) had not been revoked before the commencement day.

(2) A designation of a person that is deemed to be a licence is valid only in the province in which it was made.

(3) A designation of a person that is deemed to be a licence expires on the earliest of

(a) the expiration of the period for which it was expressed to be made,

(b) one year after the commencement day, and

(c) in the case of a designation of a person who holds a permit that is deemed to be a licence under section 123, the expiration of the permit.

FIREARMS

PENDING APPLICATIONS.

126. Every application that was pending on the commencement day for a document that would be a document referred to in any of sections 120 to 125 had it been issued before the commencement day shall be dealt with and disposed of under and in accordance with the former Act, except that

    (*a*) a licence shall be issued instead of issuing a firearms acquisition certificate or a permit or making an approval or designation; and

    (*b*) only a person who has authority under this Act to issue a licence may finally dispose of the application.

Note: Section 126.1 added, 2019, c. 9, s. 14 (to come into force by order of the Governor in Council):

LICENCE OF BUSINESS — DEEMED CONDITIONS.

126.1 Every licence of a business that is valid on the commencement day is deemed to include the conditions set out in paragraphs 58.1(1)(*a*) to (*c*).

Registration Certificates

REGISTRATION CERTIFICATES / Expiration.

127. (1) A registration certificate is deemed to be a registration certificate issued under section 60 if it

    (*a*) was

        (i) issued under subsection 109(7) of the former Act, or

        (ii) continued under subsection 6(2) of the *Criminal Law Amendment Act, 1968-69*, chapter 38 of the Statutes of Canada, 1968-69, or subsection 48(2) of the *Criminal Law Amendment Act, 1977*, chapter 53 of the Statutes of Canada, 1976- 77; and

    (*b*) had not been revoked before the commencement day.

(2) A registration certificate that is deemed to be a registration certificate issued under section 60 expires on the earlier of

    (*a*) its expiration under section 66, and

    (*b*) December 31, 2002, or such other date as is prescribed.

PENDING APPLICATIONS.

128. Every application for a registration certificate that was pending on the commencement day shall be dealt with and disposed of under and in accordance with the former Act, except that only a person who has authority under this Act to issue a registration certificate may finally dispose of the application.

Authorized Transportation of Firearms

PERMIT TO CARRY / Geographical extent / Expiration.

129. (1) A permit authorizing a person to possess a particular prohibited firearm or restricted firearm is deemed to be an authorization to carry or authorization to transport if it

(*a*) was

(i) issued under subsection 110(1) of the former Act, or

(ii) continued under subsection 6(2) of the *Criminal Law Amendment Act, 1968-69*, chapter 38 of the Statutes of Canada, 1968-69, or subsection 48(1) of the *Criminal Law Amendment Act, 1977*, chapter 53 of the Statutes of Canada, 1976-77;

(*b*) had not been revoked before the commencement day; and

(*c*) remained in force pursuant to subsection 110(1) of the former Act on the commencement day.

(2) A permit that is deemed to be an authorization to carry or authorization to transport is valid only in the province in which the permit was issued, unless it was endorsed pursuant to subsection 110(10) of the former Act as being valid within the provinces indicated in the permit, in which case it remains valid within those provinces.

(3) A permit that is deemed to be an authorization to carry or authorization to transport expires on the earlier of

(*a*) the expiration of the period for which it was expressed to be issued, and

(*b*) two years after the commencement day.

TEMPORARY PERMIT TO CARRY.

130. A permit authorizing a person who does not reside in Canada to possess and carry a particular prohibited firearm or restricted firearm is deemed to be an authorization to transport if it

(*a*) was issued under subsection 110(2.1) of the former Act;

(*b*) had not been revoked before the commencement day; and

(*c*) remained in force pursuant to that subsection on the commencement day.

PERMIT TO TRANSPORT OR CONVEY.

131. A permit authorizing a person to transport or to convey to a local registrar of firearms a particular prohibited firearm or restricted firearm is deemed to be an authorization to transport if it

(*a*) was

(i) issued under subsection 110(3) or (4) of the former Act, or

(ii) continued under subsection 6(2) of the *Criminal Law Amendment Act, 1968-69*, chapter 38 of the Statutes of Canada, 1968-69, or subsection 48(1) of the *Criminal Law Amendment Act, 1977*, chapter 53 of the Statutes of Canada, 1976- 77;

(*b*) had not been revoked before the commencement day; and

FIREARMS

(c) remained in force pursuant to subsection 110(3) or (4) of the former Act on the commencement day.

EXPIRATION.

132. A permit that is deemed to be an authorization to transport under section 130 or 131 expires on the expiration of the period for which the permit was expressed to be issued.

PENDING APPLICATIONS.

133. Every application that was pending on the commencement day for a document that would be a document referred to in any of sections 129 to 131 had it been issued before the commencement day shall be dealt with and disposed of under and in accordance with the former Act, except that

(a) an authorization to carry or authorization to transport shall be issued or a condition shall be attached to a licence instead of issuing a permit; and

(b) only a person who has authority under this Act to issue an authorization to carry or authorization to transport may finally dispose of the application.

SHOOTING CLUB APPROVALS / Expiration.

134. (1) An approval of a shooting club is deemed to be an approval granted under this Act if the approval

(a) was granted under subparagraph 109(3)(c)(iii) or paragraph 110(2)(c) of the former Act; and

(b) had not been revoked before the commencement day.

(2) An approval of a shooting club that is deemed to be an approval granted under this Act expires on the earlier of

(a) the expiration of the period for which it was expressed to be granted, and

(b) one year after the commencement day.

TEMPORARY STORAGE PERMIT.

135. Every permit authorizing a person to temporarily store a particular prohibited firearm or restricted firearm

(a) that was issued under subsection 110(3.1) of the former Act,

(b) that had not been revoked before the commencement day, and

(c) that remained in force pursuant to subsection 110(3.3) of the former Act on the commencement day

continues in force until the expiration of the period for which it was expressed to be issued, unless the permit is revoked by a chief firearms officer for any good and sufficient reason.

Note: Section 135.1 added, 2019, c. 9, s. 15 (to come into force by order of the Governor in Council):

REVOCATION OF AUTHORIZATION TO TRANSPORT.

135.1 All of the following authorizations to transport a prohibited firearm or a restricted firearm are revoked:

(a) authorizations issued under any of paragraphs 19(2.1)(b) to (e), as those paragraphs read immediately before the commencement day; and

(b) authorizations issued under paragraph 19(2.2)(b), as that paragraph read immediately before the commencement day, in respect of transportation to and from the places referred to in any of the paragraphs that are set out in paragraph (a).

IDENTIFICATION OF CRIMINALS ACT

R.S.C. 1985, Chap. I-1

Amended 1992, c. 47, ss. 73 to 76; brought into force August 1, 1996

Amended 1996, c. 7, ss. 39 and 40; in force July 31, 1996

Amended 1999, c. 18, s. 88; in force June 17, 1999

Amended 2001, c. 41, ss. 23.1 and 35; brought into force December 24, 2001 by SI/2002-16, *Can. Gaz., Part II*, January 2, 2002

Amended 2018, c. 16, ss. 166, 167; brought into force October 17, 2018 by SI/2018-52, *Can. Gaz., Part II*, July 11, 2018

Amended 2019, c. 25, s. 388; s. 388(1) in force September 19, 2019; s. 388(2) in force December 18, 2019

An Act respecting the identification of criminals

SHORT TITLE

SHORT TITLE.

1. This Act may be cited as the *Identification of Criminals Act*. R.S., c. I-1, s. 1.

HER MAJESTY

BINDING ON HER MAJESTY.

1.1 This Act is binding on Her Majesty in right of Canada or a province. 1992, c. 47, s. 73.

IDENTIFICATION OF CRIMINALS

FINGERPRINTS AND PHOTOGRAPHS / Use of force / Publication.

2. (1) The following persons may be fingerprinted or photographed or subjected to such other measurements, processes and operations having the object of identifying persons as are approved by order of the Governor in Council:

    (*a*) any person who is in lawful custody charged with or convicted of

        (i) an indictable offence, other than an offence that is designated as a contravention under the *Contraventions Act* in respect of which the Attorney General, within the meaning of that Act, has made an election under section 50 of that Act,

        (ii) an offence under the *Security of Information Act*, or

        (iii) an offence punishable on summary conviction if that offence may also be prosecuted as an indictable offence described in subparagraph (i);

   (*b*) any person who has been apprehended under the *Extradition Act*;

   (*c*) any person alleged to have committed an indictable offence, other than an offence that is designated as a contravention under the *Contraventions Act* in respect of which the "*Attorney General*", within the meaning of that Act, has made an election under section 50 of that Act, who is required under subsection 500(3), 501(4) or 509(5) of the *Criminal Code* to appear for the purposes of this Act by an appearance notice, undertaking or summons; or

   (*d*) any person who is in lawful custody pursuant to section 83.3 of the *Criminal Code*.

(2) Such force may be used as is necessary to the effectual carrying out and application of the measurements, processes and operations described under subsection (1).

(3) The results of the measurements, processes and operations to which a person has been subjected pursuant to subsection (1) may be published for the purpose of affording information to officers and others engaged in the execution or administration of the law. 1992, c. 47, s. 74; 1996, c. 7, s. 39; 1999, c. 18, s. 88; 2001, c. 41, ss. 23.1, 35; 2018, c. 16, s. 166; 2019, c. 25, s. 388.

NO LIABILITY FOR ACTING UNDER ACT.

3. No liability, civil or criminal, for anything lawfully done under this Act shall be incurred by any person

   (*a*) having custody of a person described in subsection 2(1);

   (*b*) acting in the aid or under the direction of a person having such custody; or

   (*c*) concerned in the publication of results under subsection 2(3). R.S., c. I-1, s. 3; 1992, c. 47, s. 75.

DESTRUCTION OF FINGERPRINTS AND PHOTOGRAPHS

DESTRUCTION OF FINGERPRINTS AND PHOTOGRAPHS.

4. Where a person charged with an offence that is designated as a contravention under the *Contraventions Act* is fingerprinted or photographed and the Attorney General, within the meaning of that Act, makes an election under section 50 of that Act, the fingerprints or photographs shall be destroyed. 1992, c. 47, s. 76; 1996, c. 7, s. 40.

DESTRUCTION OF FINGERPRINTS AND PHOTOGRAPHS — *CANNABIS ACT*.

5. If a person charged with an offence referred to in any of paragraphs 51(2)(*a*) to (*j*) of the *Cannabis Act* is fingerprinted or photographed and the Attorney General, within the meaning of that Act, makes an election under section 58 of that Act, the fingerprints or photographs shall be destroyed. 2018, c. 16, s. 167.

INTERPRETATION ACT

R.S.C. 1985, Chap. I-21

Amended R.S.C. 1985, c. 11 (1st Supp.), s. 2(1)
Amended R.S.C. 1985, c. 27 (1st Supp.), s. 203
Amended R.S.C. 1985, c. 27 (2nd Supp.), s. 10
Amended 1986, SOR/86-532, *Can. Gaz. Part II*, May 28, 1986
Amended 1990, c. 17, s. 26; brought into force September 1, 1990 by SI/90-106, *Can. Gaz., Part II*, August 29, 1990 (but see s. 45)
Amended 1992, c. 1, ss. 87 to 91; in force February 28, 1992
Amended 1992, c. 47, s. 79; in force October 15, 1992
Amended 1992, c. 51, s. 56; brought into force January 30, 1993
Amended 1993, c. 28, Sch. III, s. 82; however s. 82 amended by 1998, c. 15, s. 28 (in force June 11, 1998); in force April 1, 1999; however, s. 82(3) repealed 1999, c. 3, s. 12 (in force March 11, 1999)
Amended 1993, c. 34, s. 88; in force June 23, 1993
Amended 1993, c. 38, s. 87; brought into force October 25, 1993
Amended 1995, c. 39, s. 174; in force December 5, 1995
Amended 1996, c. 31, ss. 86 and 87; brought into force January 31, 1997 by SI/97-21, *Can. Gaz., Part II*, February 5, 1997
Amended 1997, c. 39, s. 4; in force December 18, 1997
Amended 1998, c. 30, s. 15(*i*); brought into force April 19, 1999 by SI/99-37, *Can. Gaz., Part II*, April 28, 1999
Amended 1999, c. 3, s. 71; in force April 1, 1999
Amended 1999, c. 28, s. 168; brought into force June 28, 1999 by SI/99-70, *Can. Gaz., Part II*, July 7, 1999
Amended 1999, c. 31, s. 146; in force June 17, 1999
Amended 2001, c. 4, s. 8; in force June 1, 2001
Amended 2002, c. 7, s. 188; brought into force April 1, 2003 by SI/2003-48, *Can. Gaz., Part II*, April 9, 2003
Amended 2002, c. 8, s. 151; brought into force July 2, 2003 by SI/2003-109, *Can. Gaz., Part II*, June 4, 2003
Amended 2003, c. 22, s. 224(*z*.43); brought into force April 1, 2005 by para. (*b*) of SI/2005-24, *Can. Gaz., Part II*, April 6, 2005
Amended 2014, c. 2, s. 14; brought into force April 1, 2014 by SI/2014-34, *Can. Gaz., Part II*, April 09, 2014
Amended 2015, c. 3, s. 124; in force February 26, 2015

An Act respecting the interpretation of statutes and regulations

SHORT TITLE

SHORT TITLE.

1. This Act may be cited as the *Interpretation Act*. R.S., c. I-23.

INTERPRETATION

DEFINITIONS / "Act" / "enact" / "enactment" / "public officer" / "regulation" / "repeal" / Expired enactment.

2. (1) In this Act,

"Act" means an Act of Parliament;

"enact" includes to issue, make or establish;

"enactment" means an Act or regulation or any portion of an Act or regulation;

"public officer" includes any person in the federal public administration who is authorized by or under an enactment to do or enforce the doing of an act or thing or to exercise a power, or on whom a duty is imposed by or under an enactment;

"regulation" includes an order, regulation, rule, rule of court, form, tariff of costs or fees, letters patent, commission, warrant, proclamation, by-law, resolution or other instrument issued, made or established

    (*a*) in the execution of a power conferred by or under the authority of an Act, or

    (*b*) by or under the authority of the Governor in Council;

"repeal" includes revoke or cancel.

(2) For the purposes of this Act, an enactment that has been replaced is repealed and an enactment that has expired, lapsed or otherwise ceased to have effect is deemed to have been repealed. R.S., I-23, s. 2; 1993, c. 34, s. 88; 1999, c. 31, s. 146; 2003, c. 22, s. 224(*z*.43).

APPLICATION

APPLICATION / Application to this Act / Rules of construction not excluded.

3. (1) Every provision of this Act applies, unless a contrary intention appears, to every enactment, whether enacted before or after the commencement of this Act.

(2) The provisions of this Act apply to the interpretation of this Act.

(3) Nothing in this Act excludes the application to an enactment of a rule of construction applicable to that enactment and not inconsistent with this Act. R.S., c. I-23, s. 3.

ENACTING CLAUSE OF ACTS

ENACTING CLAUSE / Order of clauses.

4. (1) The enacting clause of an Act may be in the following form:

"Her Majesty, by and with the advice and consent of the Senate and House of Commons of Canada, enacts as follows:".

(2) The enacting clause of an Act shall follow the preamble, if any, and the various provisions within the purview or body of the Act shall follow in a concise and enunciative form. R.S., c. I-23, s. 4.

OPERATION

Royal Assent

ROYAL ASSENT / Date of commencement / Commencement provision / Commencement when no date fixed.

5. (1) The Clerk of the Parliaments shall endorse on every Act, immediately after its title, the day, month and year when the Act was assented to in Her Majesty's name and the endorsement shall be a part of the Act.

(2) If no date of commencement is provided for in an Act, the date of commencement of that Act is the date of assent to the Act.

(3) Where an Act contains a provision that the Act or any portion thereof is to come into force on a day later than the date of assent to the Act, that provision is deemed to have come into force on the date of assent to the Act.

(4) Where an Act provides that certain provisions thereof are to come or are deemed to have come into force on a day other than the date of assent to the Act, the remaining provisions of the Act are deemed to have come into force on the date of assent to the Act. R.S., c. I-23, s. 5.

Day Fixed for Commencement or Repeal

OPERATION WHEN DATE FIXED FOR COMMENCEMENT OR REPEAL / When no date fixed / Judicial notice.

6. (1) Where an enactment is expressed to come into force on a particular day, it shall be construed as coming into force on the expiration of the previous day, and where an enactment is expressed to expire, lapse or otherwise cease to have effect on a particular day, it shall be construed as ceasing to have effect on the commencement of the following day.

(2) Every enactment that is not expressed to come into force on a particular day shall be construed as coming into force

- (a) in the case of an Act, on the expiration of the day immediately before the day the Act was assented to in Her Majesty's name; and
- (b) in the case of a regulation, on the expiration of the day immediately before the day the regulation was registered pursuant to section 6 of the *Statutory Instruments Act* or, if the regulation is of a class that is exempted from the application of subsection 5(1) of that Act, on the expiration of the day immediately before the day the regulation was made.

(3) Judicial notice shall be taken of a day for the coming into force of an enactment that is fixed by a regulation that has been published in the *Canada Gazette*. R.S., c. I-23, s. 6; R.S., c. 29 (2nd Supp.), s. 1; 1992, c. 1, s. 87.

Regulation Prior to Commencement

PRELIMINARY PROCEEDINGS.

7. Where an enactment is not in force and it contains provisions conferring power to make regulations or do any other thing, that power may, for the purpose of making the enactment effective on its commencement, be exercised at any time before its commencement, but a regulation so made or a thing so done has no effect until the commencement of the enactment except in so far as may be necessary to make the enactment effective on its commencement. R.S., c. I-23, s. 7.

Territorial Operation

TERRITORIAL OPERATION / Amending enactment / Exclusive economic zone of Canada / Continental shelf of Canada / Extra-territorial operation.

8. (1) Every enactment applies to the whole of Canada, unless a contrary intention is expressed in the enactment.

(2) Where an enactment that does not apply to the whole of Canada is amended, no provision in the amending enactment applies to any part of Canada to which the amended enactment does not apply, unless it is provided the amending enactment that it applies to that part of Canada or to the whole of Canada.

(2.1) Every enactment that applies in respect of exploring or exploiting, conserving or managing natural resources, whether living or non-living, applies, in addition to its application to Canada, to the exclusive economic zone of Canada, unless a contrary intention is expressed in the enactment.

(2.2) Every enactment that applies in respect of exploring or exploiting natural resources that are

- (a) mineral or other non-living resources of the seabed or subsoil, or

(b) living organisms belonging to sedentary species, that is to say, organisms that, at the harvestable stage, either are immobile on or under the seabed or are unable to move except in constant physical contact with the seabed or subsoil

applies, in addition to its application to Canada, to the continental shelf of Canada, unless a contrary intention is expressed in the enactment.

(3) Every Act now in force enacted prior to December 11, 1931 that expressly or by necessary or reasonable implication was intended, as to the whole or any part thereof, to have extra-territorial operation shall be construed as if, at the date of its enactment, the Parliament of Canada had full power to make laws having extra-territorial operation as provided by the *Statute of Westminster, 1931*. R.S., c. I-23, s. 8; 1996, c. 31, s. 86.

RULES OF CONSTRUCTION

Property and Civil Rights

DUALITY OF LEGAL TRADITIONS AND APPLICATION OF PROVINCIAL LAW.

8.1 Both the common law and the civil law are equally authoritative and recognized sources of the law of property and civil rights in Canada and, unless otherwise provided by law, if in interpreting an enactment it is necessary to refer to a province's rules, principles or concepts forming part of the law of property and civil rights, reference must be made to the rules, principles and concepts in force in the province at the time the enactment is being applied. 2001, c. 4, s. 8.

TERMINOLOGY.

8.2 Unless otherwise provided by law, when an enactment contains both civil law and common law terminology, or terminology that has a different meaning in the civil law and the common law, the civil law terminology or meaning is to be adopted in the Province of Quebec and the common law terminology or meaning is to be adopted in the other provinces. 2001, c. 4, s. 8.

Private Acts

PROVISIONS IN PRIVATE ACTS.

9. No provision in a private Act affects the rights of any person, except as therein mentioned or referred to. R.S., c. I-23, s. 9.

Law Always Speaking

LAW ALWAYS SPEAKING.

10. The law shall be considered as always speaking, and where a matter or thing is expressed in the present tense, it shall be applied to the circumstances as they arise, so that effect may be given to the enactment according to its true spirit, intent and meaning. R.S., c. I-23, s. 10.

Imperative and Permissive Construction

"SHALL" AND "MAY".

11. The expression "shall" is to be construed as imperative and the expression "may" as permissive. R.S., c. I-23, s. 28.

Enactments Remedial

ENACTMENTS DEEMED REMEDIAL.

12. Every enactment is deemed remedial, and shall be given such fair, large and liberal construction and interpretation as best ensures the attainment of its objects. R.S., I-23, s. 11.

Preambles and Marginal Notes

PREAMBLE.

13. The preamble of an enactment shall be read as a part of the enactment intended to assist in explaining its purport and object. R.S., I-23, s. 12.

MARGINAL NOTES AND HISTORICAL REFERENCES.

14. Marginal notes and references to former enactments that appear after the end of a section or other division in an enactment form no part of the enactment, but are inserted for convenience of reference only. R.S., I-23, s. 13.

Application of Interpretation Provisions

APPLICATION OF DEFINITIONS AND INTERPRETATION RULES / Interpretation sections subject to exceptions.

15. (1) Definitions or rules of interpretation in an enactment apply to all the provisions of the enactment, including the provisions that contain those definitions or rules of interpretation.

(2) Where an enactment contains an interpretation section or provision, it shall be read and construed

- (*a*) as being applicable only if a contrary intention does not appear, and
- (*b*) as being applicable to all other enactments relating to the same subject-matter unless a contrary intention appears. R.S., c. I-23, s. 14.

WORDS IN REGULATIONS.

16. Where an enactment confers power to make regulations, expressions used in the regulations have the same respective meanings as in the enactment conferring the power. R.S., I-23, s. 15.

INTER.

Her Majesty

HER MAJESTY NOT BOUND OR AFFECTED UNLESS STATED.

17. No enactment is binding on Her Majesty or affects Her Majesty or Her Majesty's rights or prerogatives in any manner, except as mentioned or referred to in the enactment. R.S., c. I-23, s. 16.

Proclamations

PROCLAMATION / Proclamation to be issued on advice / Effective day of proclamations.

18. (1) Where an enactment authorizes the issue of a proclamation, the proclamation shall be understood to be a proclamation of the Governor in Council.

(2) Where the Governor General is authorized to issue a proclamation, the proclamation shall be understood to be a proclamation issued under an order of the Governor in Council, but it is not necessary to mention in the proclamation that it is issued under such an order.

(3) A proclamation that is issued under an order of the Governor in Council may purport to have been issued on the day of the order or on any subsequent day and, if so, takes effect on that day. R.S., c. I-23; 1992, c. 1, s. 88.

(4) [*Repealed*. 1992, c. 1, s. 88.]

Oaths

ADMINISTRATION OF OATHS / Where justice of peace empowered.

19. (1) Where, by an enactment or by a rule of the Senate or House of Commons, evidence under oath is authorized or required to be taken, or an oath is authorized or directed to be made, taken or administered, the oath may be administered, and a certificate of its having been made, taken or administered may be given by

- (*a*) any person authorized by the enactment or rule to take the evidence; or

(b) a judge of any court, a notary public, a justice of the peace or a commissioner for taking affidavits, having authority or jurisdiction within the place where the oath is administered.

(2) Where power is conferred on a justice of the peace to administer an oath or solemn affirmation or to take an affidavit or declaration, the power may be exercised by a notary public or a commissioner for taking oaths. R.S., c. I-23, s. 18.

Reports to Parliament

REPORTS TO PARLIAMENT.

20. Where an Act requires a report or other document to be laid before Parliament and, in compliance with the Act, a particular report or document has been laid before Parliament at a session thereof, nothing in the Act shall be construed as requiring the same report or document to be laid before Parliament at any subsequent session. R.S., c. I-23, s. 19.

Corporations

POWERS VESTED IN CORPORATIONS / Corporate name / Banking business.

21. (1) Words establishing a corporation shall be construed

(a) as vesting in the corporation power to sue and be sued, to contract and be contracted with by its corporate name, to have a common seal and to alter or change it at pleasure, to have perpetual succession, to acquire and hold personal property for the purposes for which the corporation is established and to alienate that property at pleasure;

(b) in the case of a corporation having a name consisting of an English and a French form or a combined English and French form, to vest in the corporation power to use either the English or the French form of its name or both forms and to show on its seal both the English and French forms of its name or have two seals, one showing the English and the other showing the French form of its name;

(c) as vesting in a majority of the members of the corporation the power to bind the others by their acts; and

(d) as exempting from personal liability for its debts, obligations or acts such individual members of the corporation who do not contravene the provisions of the enactment establishing the corporation.

(2) Where an enactment establishes a corporation and in each of the English and French versions of the enactment the name of the corporation is in the form only of the language of that version, the name of the corporation shall consist of the form of its name in each of the versions of the enactment.

(3) No corporation is deemed to be authorized to carry on the business of banking unless that power is expressly conferred on it by the enactment establishing the corporation. R.S., c. I-23, s. 20.

Majority and Quorum

MAJORITIES / Quorum of board, court, commission, etc.

22. (1) Where an enactment requires or authorizes more than two persons to do an act or thing, a majority of them may do it.

(2) Where an enactment establishes a board, court, commission or other body consisting of three or more members in this section called an "association",

(*a*) at a meeting of the association, a number of members of the association equal to,

(i) if the number of members provided for by the enactment is a fixed number, at least one-half of the number of members, and

(ii) if the number of members provided for by the enactment is not a fixed number but is within a range having a maximum or minimum, at least one-half of the number of members in office if that number is within the range,

constitutes a quorum;

(*b*) an act or thing done by a majority of the members of the association present at a meeting, if the members present constitute a quorum, shall be deemed to have been done by the association; and

(*c*) a vacancy in the membership of the association does not invalidate the constitution of the association or impair the right of the members in office to act, if the number of members in office is not less than a quorum. R.S., c. I-23, s. 21.

Appointment, Retirement and Powers of Officers

PUBLIC OFFICERS HOLD OFFICE DURING PLEASURE / Effective day of appointments / Appointment or engagement otherwise than under Great Seal / Remuneration / Commencement of appointments or retirements.

23. (1) Every public officer appointed by or under the authority of an enactment or otherwise is deemed to have been appointed to hold office during pleasure only, unless it is otherwise expressed in the enactment, commission or instrument of appointment.

(2) Where an appointment is made by instrument under the Great Seal, the instrument may purport to have been issued on or after the day its issue was authorized, and the day on which it so purports to have been issued is deemed to be the day on which the appointment takes effect.

(3) Where there is authority to appoint a person to a position or to engage the services of a person, otherwise than by instrument under the Great Seal, the instrument of appointment or engagement may be expressed to be effective on or

after the day on which that person commenced the performance of the duties of the position or commenced the performance of the services, and the day on which it is so expressed to be effective, unless that day is more than sixty days before the day on which the instrument is issued, is deemed to be the day on which the appointment or engagement takes effect.

(4) Where a person is appointed to an office, the appointing authority may fix, vary or terminate his remuneration.

(5) Where a person is appointed to an office effective on a specified day, or where the appointment of a person is terminated effective on a specified day, the appointment or termination is deemed to have been effected immediately on the expiration of the previous day. R.S., c. I-23, s. 22.

IMPLIED POWERS RESPECTING PUBLIC OFFICERS / Power to act for ministers / Restriction as to public servants / Successors to and deputy of public officer / Powers of holder of public office.

24. (1) Words authorizing the appointment of a public officer to hold office during pleasure include, in the discretion of the authority in whom the power of appointment is vested, the power to
    (*a*) terminate the appointment or remove or suspend the public officer;
    (*b*) re-appoint or reinstate the public officer; and
    (*c*) appoint another person in the stead of, or to act in the stead of, the public officer.

(2) Words directing or empowering a minister of the Crown to do an act or thing, regardless of whether the act or thing is administrative, legislative or judicial, or otherwise applying to that minister as the holder of the office, include
    (*a*) a minister acting for that minister, or, if the office is vacant, a minister designated to act in the office by or under the authority of an order in council;
    (*b*) the successors of that minister in the office;
    (*c*) his or their deputy; and
    (*d*) notwithstanding paragraph (*c*), a person appointed to serve, in the department or ministry of state over which the minister presides, in a capacity appropriate to the doing of the act or thing, or to the words so applying.

(3) Nothing in paragraph (2)(*c*) or (*d*) shall be construed as authorizing the deputy to exercise any authority conferred on a minister to make a regulation as defined in the *Statutory Instruments Act*.

(4) Words directing or empowering any public officer, other than a minister of the Crown, to do any act or thing, or otherwise applying to the public officer by his name of office, include his successors in the office and his or their deputy.

(5) Where a power is conferred or a duty imposed on the holder of an office, the power may be exercised and the duty shall be performed by the person for the time being charged with the execution of the powers and duties of the office. R.S., c. I-23, s. 23; R.S., c. 29 (2nd Supp.), s. 1; 1992, c. 1, s. 89.

Evidence

DOCUMENTARY EVIDENCE / Queen's Printer.

25. (1) Where an enactment provides that a document is evidence of a fact without anything in the context to indicate that the document is conclusive evidence, then, in any judicial proceedings, the document is admissible in evidence and the fact is deemed to be established in the absence of any evidence to the contrary.

(2) Every copy of an enactment having printed thereon what purports to be the name or title of the Queen's Printer and Controller of Stationery or the Queen's Printer is deemed to be a copy purporting to be printed by the Queen's Printer for Canada. R.S., c. I-23, s. 24.

Computation of Time

TIME LIMITS AND HOLIDAYS.

26. Where the time limited for the doing of a thing expires or falls on a holiday, the thing may be done on the day next following that is not a holiday. R.S., c. I-23, s. 25.

CLEAR DAYS / Not clear days / Beginning and ending of prescribed periods / After specified day / Within a time.

27. (1) Where there is a reference to a number of clear days or "at least" a number of days between two events, in calculating that number of days the days on which the events happen are excluded.

(2) Where there is a reference to a number of days, not expressed to be clear days, between two events, in calculating that number of days the day on which the first event happens is excluded and the day on which the second event happens is included.

(3) Where a time is expressed to begin or end at, on or with a specified day, or to continue to or until a specified day, the time includes that day.

(4) Where a time is expressed to begin after or to be from a specified day, the time does not include that day.

(5) Where anything is to be done within a time after, from, of or before a specified day, the time does not include that day. R.S., c. I-23, s. 25.

CALCULATION OF A PERIOD OF MONTHS AFTER OR BEFORE A SPECIFIED DAY.

28. Where there is a reference to a period of time consisting of a number of months after or before a specified day, the period is calculated by

    (*a*) counting forward or backward from the specified day the number of months, without including the month in which that day falls;

    (*b*) excluding the specified day; and

(c) including in the last month counted under paragraph (a) the day that has the same calendar number as the specified day or, if that month has no day with that number, the last day of that month. R.S., c. I-23, s. 25.

TIME OF THE DAY.

29. Where there is a reference to time expressed as a specified time of the day, the time is taken to mean standard time. R.S., c. I-23, s. 25.

TIME WHEN SPECIFIED AGE ATTAINED.

30. A person is deemed not to have attained a specified number of years of age until the commencement of the anniversary, of the same number, of the day of that person's birth. R.S., c. I-23, s. 25.

Miscellaneous Rules

REFERENCE TO PROVINCIAL COURT JUDGE, ETC. / Ancillary powers / Powers to be exercised as required / Power to repeal.

31. (1) Where anything is required or authorized to be done by or before a judge, provincial court judge, justice of the peace or any functionary or officer, it shall be done by or before one whose jurisdiction or powers extend to the place where the thing is to be done.

(2) Where power is given to a person, officer or functionary to do or enforce the doing of any act or thing, all such powers as are necessary to enable the person, officer or functionary to do or enforce the doing of the act or thing are deemed to be also given.

(3) Where a power is conferred or a duty imposed, the power may be exercised and the duty shall be performed from time to time as occasion requires.

(4) Where a power is conferred to make regulations, the power shall be construed as including a power, exercisable in the same manner and subject to the same consent and conditions, if any, to repeal, amend or vary the regulations and make others. R.S., c. I-23, s. 26; R.S.C. 1985, c. 27 (1st Supp.), s. 203.

FORMS.

32. Where a form is prescribed, deviations from that form, not affecting the substance or calculated to mislead, do not invalidate the form used. R.S., c. I-23, s. 26.

GENDER / Number / Parts of speech and grammatical forms.

33. (1) Words importing female persons include male persons and corporations and words importing male persons include female persons and corporations.

(2) Words in the singular include the plural, and words in the plural include the singular.

(3) Where a word is defined, other parts of speech and grammatical forms of the same word have corresponding meanings. R.S., c. I-23, s. 26; 1992, c. 1, s. 90.

Offences

INDICTABLE AND SUMMARY CONVICTION OFFENCES / *Criminal Code* to apply / Documents similarly construed.

34. (1) Where an enactment creates an offence,

    (*a*) the offence is deemed to be an indictable offence if the enactment provides that the offender may be prosecuted for the offence by indictment;

    (*b*) the offence is deemed to be one for which the offender is punishable on summary conviction if there is nothing in the context to indicate that the offence is an indictable offence; and

    (*c*) if the offence is one for which the offender may be prosecuted by indictment or for which the offender is punishable on summary conviction, no person shall be considered to have been convicted of an indictable offence by reason only of having been convicted of the offence on summary conviction.

(2) All the provisions of the *Criminal Code* relating to indictable offences apply to indictable offences created by an enactment, and all the provisions of that *Code* relating to summary conviction offences apply to all other offences created by an enactment, except to the extent that the enactment otherwise provides.

(3) In a commission, proclamation, warrant or other document relating to criminal law or procedure in criminal matters

    (*a*) a reference to an offence for which the offender may be prosecuted by indictment shall be construed as a reference to an indictable offence; and

    (*b*) a reference to any other offence shall be construed as a reference to an offence for which the offender is punishable on summary conviction. R.S., c. I-23, s. 27.

Powers to Enter Dwelling-houses to Carry out Arrests

AUTHORIZATION TO ENTER DWELLING-HOUSE.

34.1 Any person who may issue a warrant to arrest or apprehend a person under any Act of Parliament, other than the *Criminal Code*, has the same powers, subject to the same terms and conditions, as a judge or justice has under the *Criminal Code*

    (*a*) to authorize the entry into a dwelling-house described in the warrant for the purpose of arresting or apprehending the person, if the person issuing the warrant is satisfied by information on oath that there are reasonable grounds to believe that the person is or will be present in the dwelling-house; and

    (*b*) to authorize the entry into the dwelling-house without prior announcement if the requirement of subsection 529.4(1) is met. 1997, c. 39, s. 4.

DEFINITIONS

GENERAL DEFINITIONS / "Act" / "bank" / "British Commonwealth" or "British Commonwealth of Nations" / "broadcasting" / "Canada" / "Canadian waters" / "Clerk of the Privy Council" or "Clerk of the Queen's Privy Council" / "Commencement" / "Commonwealth" or "Commonwealth of Nations" / "Commonwealth and Dependent Territories" / "contiguous zone" / "continental shelf" / "contravene" / "corporation" / "county" / "diplomatic or consular officer" / "exclusive economic zone" / "Governor", "Governor General" or "Governor of Canada" / "Governor General in Council" or "Governor in Council" / "Great Seal" / "Her Majesty", "His Majesty", "the Queen", "the King" or "the Crown" / "Her Majesty's Realms and Territories" or "His Majesty's Realms and Territories" / "herein" / "holiday" / "internal waters" / "legislative assembly" or "legislature" / "lieutenant governor" / "lieutenant governor in council" / "local time" / "military" / "month" / "oath" and "sworn" / "Parliament" / "person" / "proclamation" / "province" / "radio" or "radiocommunication" / "regular force" / "reserve force" / "security" and "sureties" / "standard time" / "statutory declaration" / "superior court" / "telecommunication" / "territorial sea" / "territory" / "two justices" / "United Kingdom" / "United States" / "writing" / Governor in Council may amend schedule.

35. (1) In every enactment,

"Act", in respect of an Act of a legislature, includes a law of the Legislature of Yukon, of the Northwest Territories or for Nunavut;

"bank" means a bank listed in Schedule I or II to the *Bank Act*;

"British Commonwealth" or "British Commonwealth of Nations" has the same meaning as "Commonwealth".

"broadcasting" means any radiocommunication in which the transmissions are intended for direct reception by the general public;

"Canada", for greater certainty, includes the internal waters of Canada and the territorial sea of Canada;

"Canadian waters" includes the territorial sea of Canada and the internal waters of Canada;

"Clerk of the Privy Council" or "Clerk of the Queen's Privy Council" means the Clerk of the Privy Council and Secretary to the Cabinet;

"commencement", when used with reference to an enactment, means the time at which the enactment comes into force;

"Commonwealth" or "Commonwealth of Nations" means the association of countries named in the schedule;

"Commonwealth and Dependent Territories" means the several Commonwealth countries and their colonies, possessions, dependencies, protectorates, protected states, condominiums and trust territories;

"contiguous zone",

  (*a*) in relation to Canada, means the contiguous zone of Canada as determined
     under the *Oceans Act*, and

  (*b*) in relation to any other state, means the contiguous zone of the other state
     as determined in accordance with international law and the domestic laws
     of that other state;

"continental shelf",

  (*a*) in relation to Canada, means the continental shelf of Canada as determined
     under the *Oceans Act*, and

  (*b*) in relation to any other state, means the continental shelf of the other state
     as determined in accordance with international law and the domestic laws
     of that other state;

"contravene" includes fail to comply with;

"corporation" does not include a partnership that is considered to be a legal entity
under provincial law;

"county" includes two or more counties united for purposes to which the
enactment relates;

"county court", [*Repealed.* 1990, c. 17, s. 26(1).]

"diplomatic or consular officer" includes an ambassador, envoy, minister, charge
d'affaires, counsellor, secretary, attaché, consul-general, consul, vice-consul, pro-
consul, consular agent, acting consul-general, acting consul, acting vice-consul,
acting consular agent, high commissioner, permanent delegate, adviser, acting
high commissioner, and acting permanent delegate;

"exclusive economic zone",

  (*a*) in relation to Canada, means the exclusive economic zone of Canada as
     determined under the *Oceans Act* and includes the seabed and subsoil
     below that zone, and

  (*b*) in relation to any other state, means the exclusive economic zone of the
     other state as determined in accordance with international law and the
     domestic laws of that other state;

"Federal Court" [*Repealed.* 2002, c. 8, s. 151(1).]

"Federal Court — Appeal Division" or "Federal Court of Appeal" [*Repealed.*
2002, c. 8, s. 151(1).]

"Federal Court — Trial Division" [*Repealed.* 2002, c. 8, s. 151(1).]

"Governor", "Governor General" or "Governor of Canada" means the Governor
General of Canada or other chief executive officer or administrator carrying on the
Government of Canada on behalf and in the name of the Sovereign, by whatever
title that officer is designated;

"Governor General in Council" or "Governor in Council" means the Governor
General of Canada, acting by and with the advice of, or by and with the advice and
consent of, or in conjunction with the Queen's Privy Council for Canada;

"Great Seal" means the Great Seal of Canada;

"Her Majesty", "His Majesty", "the Queen", "the King" or "the Crown" means the Sovereign of the United Kingdom, Canada and Her or His other Realms and Territories, and Head of the Commonwealth;

"Her Majesty's Realms and Territories" or "His Majesty's Realms and Territories" means all realms and territories under the sovereignty of Her or His Majesty;

"herein" used in any section shall be understood to relate to the whole enactment, and not to that section only;

"holiday" means any of the following days, namely, Sunday; New Year's Day; Good Friday; Easter Monday; Christmas Day; the birthday or the day fixed by proclamation for the celebration of the birthday of the reigning Sovereign; Victoria Day; Canada Day; the first Monday in September, designated Labour Day; Remembrance Day; any day appointed by proclamation to be observed as a day of general prayer or mourning or day of public rejoicing or thanksgiving; and any of the following additional days, namely:

  (*a*) in any province, any day appointed by proclamation of the lieutenant governor of the province to be observed as a public holiday or as a day of general prayer or mourning or day of public rejoicing or thanksgiving within the province, and any day that is a non-juridical day by virtue of an Act of the legislature of the province, and

  (*b*) in any city, town, municipality or other organized district, any day appointed to be observed as a civic holiday by resolution of the council or other authority charged with the administration of the civic or municipal affairs of the city, town, municipality or district;

"internal waters",

  (*a*) in relation to Canada, means the internal waters of Canada as determined under the *Oceans Act* and includes the airspace above and the bed and subsoil below those waters, and

  (*b*) in relation to any other state, means the waters on the landward side of the baselines of the territorial sea of the other state;

"legislative assembly", "legislative council" or "legislature" [*Repealed*. 2014, c. 2, s. 14(1).]

"legislative assembly" or "legislature" includes the Lieutenant Governor in Council and the Legislative Assembly of the Northwest Territories, as constituted before September 1, 1905, and the Legislature of Yukon, of the Northwest Territories or for Nunavut;

"lieutenant governor" means the lieutenant governor or other chief executive officer or administrator carrying on the government of the province indicated by the enactment, by whatever title that officer is designated, and in Yukon, the Northwest Territories and Nunavut means the Commissioner;

"lieutenant governor in council" means

  (*a*) the lieutenant governor of the province indicated by the enactment acting by and with the advice of, by and with the advice and consent of, or in conjunction with, the executive council,

(b) in Yukon, the Commissioner of Yukon acting with the consent of the Executive Council of Yukon,

(c) in the Northwest Territories, the Commissioner of the Northwest Territories acting with the consent of the Executive Council of the Northwest Territories, and

(d) in Nunavut, the Commissioner;

"local time", in relation to any place, means the time observed in that place for the regulation of business hours;

"military" shall be construed as relating to all or any part of the Canadian Forces;

"month" means a calendar month;

"oath" includes a solemn affirmation or declaration, when the context applies to any person by whom and to any case in which a solemn affirmation or declaration may be made instead of an oath, and in the same cases the expression "sworn" includes the expression "affirmed" or "declared";

"Parliament" means the Parliament of Canada;

"person" or any word or expression descriptive of a person, includes a corporation;

"proclamation" means a proclamation under the Great Seal;

"province" means a province of Canada, and includes Yukon, the Northwest Territories and Nunavut;

"radio" or "radiocommunication" means any transmission, emission or reception of signs, signals, writing, images, sounds or intelligence of any nature by means of electro magnetic waves of frequencies lower than 3000 CHz propagated in space without artificial guide;

"regular force" means the component of the Canadian Forces that is referred to in the *National Defence Act* as the regular force;

"reserve force" means the component of the Canadian Forces that is referred to in the *National Defence Act* as the reserve force;

"security" means sufficient security, and "sureties" means sufficient sureties, and when those words are used one person is sufficient therefor, unless otherwise expressly required;

"standard time", except as otherwise provided by any proclamation of the Governor in Council which may be issued for the purposes of this definition in relation to any province or territory or any part thereof, means

(a) in relation to the Province of Newfoundland and Labrador, Newfoundland standard time, being three hours and thirty minutes behind Greenwich time,

(b) in relation to the Provinces of Nova Scotia, New Brunswick and Prince Edward Island, that part of the Province of Quebec lying east of the sixty-third meridian of west longitude, and that part of Nunavut lying east of the sixty-eighth meridian of west longitude, Atlantic standard time, being four hours behind Greenwich time,

(c) in relation to that part of the Province of Quebec lying west of the sixty-third meridian of west longitude, that part of the Province of Ontario lying between the sixty-eighth and the ninetieth meridians of west longitude, Southampton Island and the islands adjacent to Southampton Island, and that part of Nunavut lying between the sixty-eighth and the eighty-fifth meridians of west longitude, eastern standard time, being five hours behind Greenwich time,

(*d*) in relation to that part of the Province of Ontario lying west of the ninetieth meridian of west longitude, the Province of Manitoba, and that part of Nunavut, except Southampton Island and the islands adjacent to Southampton Island, lying between the eighty-fifth and the one hundred and second meridians of west longitude, central standard time, being six hours behind Greenwich time,

(*e*) in relation to the Provinces of Saskatchewan and Alberta, the Northwest Territories and that part of Nunavut lying west of the one hundred and second meridian of west longitude, mountain standard time, being seven hours behind Greenwich time,

(*f*) in relation to the Province of British Columbia, Pacific standard time, being eight hours behind Greenwich time, and

(*g*) in relation to Yukon, Yukon standard time, being nine hours behind Greenwich time;

"statutory declaration" means a solemn declaration made pursuant to section 41 of the *Canada Evidence Act*;

"superior court" means

(*a*) in the Province of Newfoundland and Labrador, the Supreme Court,

(*a*.1) in the Province of Ontario, the Court of Appeal for Ontario and the Superior Court of Justice,

(*b*) in the Province of Quebec, the Court of Appeal and the Superior Court in and for the Province,

(*c*) in the Province of New Brunswick, Manitoba, Saskatchewan or Alberta, the Court of Appeal for the Province and the Court of Queen's Bench for the Province, and

(*d*) in the Provinces of Nova Scotia, British Columbia and Prince Edward Island, the Court of Appeal and the Supreme Court of the Province, and

(*e*) the Supreme Court of Yukon, the Supreme Court of the Northwest Territories and the Nunavut Court of Justice

and includes the Supreme Court of Canada, the Federal Court of Appeal, the Federal Court and the Tax Court of Canada;

"telecommunications" means the emission, transmission or reception of signs, signals, writing, images, sounds or intelligence of any nature by any wire, cable, radio, optical or other electromagnetic system, or by any similar technical system;

"territorial sea",

(*a*) in relation to Canada, means the territorial sea of Canada as determined under the *Oceans Act* and includes the airspace above and the seabed and subsoil below that sea, and

(*b*) in relation to any other state, means the territorial sea of the other state as determined in accordance with international law and the domestic laws of that other state;

"territory" means Yukon, the Northwest Territories and Nunavut;

"two justices" means two or more justices of the peace, assembled or acting together;

"United Kingdom" means the United Kingdom of Great Britain and Northern Ireland;

"United States" means the United States of America;

"writing", or any term of like import, includes words printed, typewritten, painted, engraved, lithographed, photographed, or represented or reproduced by any mode of representing or reproducing words in visible form;

(2) The Governor in Council may, by order, amend the schedule by adding thereto the name of any country recognized by the order to be a member of the Commonwealth or deleting therefrom the name of any country recognized by the order to be no longer a member of the Commonwealth. R.S., c. I-23, s. 28; R.S., c. 10 (2nd Supp.), s. 65; 1972, c. 17, s. 2; 1974-75-76, c. 16, s. 4, c. 19, s. 2; 1978-79, c. 11, s. 10; R.S.C. 1985, c. 11 (1st Supp.), s. 2(1); R.S.C. 1985, c. 27 (2nd Supp.), s. 10; 1990, c. 17, s. 26; 1992, c. 1, s. 91; 1992, c. 47, s. 79; 1993, c. 38, s. 87; 1993, c. 28, s. 78; 1996, c. 31, s. 87; 1998, c. 30, s. 15(*i*); 1999, c. 3, s. 71; 1999, c. 28, s. 168; 2002, c. 7, s. 188; 2002, c. 8, s. 151; 2014, c. 2, s. 14; 2015, c. 3, s. 124.

CONSTRUCTION OF "TELEGRAPH".

36. The expression "telegraph" and its derivatives, in an enactment or in an Act of the legislature of any province enacted before that province became part of Canada on any subject that is within the legislative powers of Parliament, are deemed not to include the word "telephone" or its derivatives. R.S., c. I-23, s. 29.

CONSTRUCTION OF "YEAR" / Governor in Council may define year.

37. (1) The expression "year" means any period of twelve consecutive months, except that a reference

- (*a*) to a "calendar year" means a period of twelve consecutive months commencing on January 1;
- (*b*) to a "financial year" or "fiscal year" means, in relation to money provided by Parliament, or the Consolidated Revenue Fund, or the accounts, taxes or finances of Canada, the period beginning on April 1 in one calendar year and ending on March 31 in the next calendar year; and
- (*c*) by number to a Dominical year means the period of twelve consecutive months commencing on January 1 of that Dominical year.

(2) Where in an enactment relating to the affairs of Parliament or the Government of Canada there is a reference to a period of a year without anything in the context to indicate beyond doubt whether a financial or fiscal year, any period of twelve consecutive months or a period of twelve consecutive months commencing on January 1 is intended, the Governor in Council may prescribe which of those periods of twelve consecutive months shall constitute a year for the purposes of the enactment. R.S., c. I-23, ss. 28, 31.

COMMON NAMES.

38. The name commonly applied to any country, place, body, corporation, society, officer, functionary, person, party or thing means the country, place, body, corporation, society, officer, functionary, person, party or thing to which the name is commonly applied, although the name is not the formal or extended designation thereof. R.S., c. I-23, s. 30.

AFFIRMATIVE AND NEGATIVE RESOLUTIONS / Effect of negative resolution.

39. (1) In every Act,

   (*a*) the expression "subject to affirmative resolution of Parliament", when used in relation to any regulation, means that the regulation shall be laid before Parliament within fifteen days after it is made or, if Parliament is not then sitting, on any of the first fifteen days next thereafter that Parliament is sitting and shall not come into force unless and until it is affirmed by a resolution of both Houses of Parliament introduced and passed in accordance with the rules of those Houses;

   (*b*) the expression "subject to affirmative resolution of the House of Commons", when used in relation to any regulation, means that the regulation shall be laid before the House of Commons within fifteen days after it is made or, if the House is not then sitting, on any of the first fifteen days next thereafter that the House is sitting and shall not come into force unless and until it is affirmed by a resolution of the House of Commons introduced and passed in accordance with the rules of that House;

   (*c*) the expression "subject to negative resolution of Parliament", when used in relation to any regulation, means that the regulation shall be laid before Parliament within fifteen days after it is made or, if Parliament is not then sitting, on any of the first fifteen days next thereafter that Parliament is sitting and may be annulled by a resolution of both Houses of Parliament introduced and passed in accordance with the rules of those Houses; and

   (*d*) the expression "subject to negative resolution of the House of Commons", when used in relation to any regulation, means that the regulation shall be laid before the House of Commons within fifteen days after it is made or, if the House is not then sitting, on any of the first fifteen days next thereafter that the House is sitting and may be annulled by a resolution of the House of Commons introduced and passed in accordance with the rules of that House.

(2) Where a regulation is annulled by a resolution of Parliament or of the House of Commons, it is deemed to have been revoked on the day the resolution is passed and any law that was revoked or amended by the making of that regulation is deemed to be revived on the day the resolution is passed, but the validity of any action taken or not taken in compliance with a regulation so deemed to have been revoked shall not be affected by the resolution. R.S., c. 29, (2nd Supp.), s. 1.

REFERENCES AND CITATIONS

CITATION OF ENACTMENT / Citation includes amendment.

40. (1) In an enactment or document

    (*a*) an Act may be cited by reference to its chapter number in the Revised Statutes, by reference to its chapter number in the volume of Acts for the year or regnal year in which it was enacted or by reference to its long title or short title, with or without reference to its chapter number; and

    (*b*) a regulation may be cited by reference to its long title or short title, by reference to the Act under which it was made or by reference to the number or designation under which it was registered by the Clerk of the Privy Council.

(2) A citation of or reference to an enactment is deemed to be a citation of or reference to the enactment as amended. R.S., c. I-23, s. 32.

REFERENCE TO TWO OR MORE PARTS, ETC. / Reference in enactment to parts, etc. / Reference in enactment to subsections, etc. / Reference to regulations / Reference to another enactment.

41. (1) A reference in an enactment by number or letter to two or more parts, divisions, sections, subsections, paragraphs, subparagraphs, clauses, subclauses, schedules, appendices or forms shall be read as including the number or letter first mentioned and the number or letter last mentioned.

(2) A reference in an enactment to a part, division, section, schedule, appendix or form shall be read as a reference to a part, division, section, schedule, appendix or form of the enactment in which the reference occurs.

(3) A reference in an enactment to a subsection, paragraph, sub-paragraph, clause or subclause shall be read as a reference to a subsection, paragraph, subparagraph, clause or subclause of the section, subsection, paragraph, subparagraph or clause, as the case may be, in which the reference occurs.

(4) A reference in an enactment to regulations shall be read as a reference to regulations made under the enactment in which the reference occurs.

(5) A reference in an enactment by number or letter to any section, subsection, paragraph, subparagraph, clause, subclause or other division or line of another enactment shall be read as a reference to the section, subsection, paragraph, subparagraph, clause, subclause or other division or line of such other enactment as printed by authority of law. R.S., c. I-23, s. 33.

REPEAL AND AMENDMENT

POWER OF REPEAL OR AMENDMENT RESERVED / Amendment or repeal at same session / Amendment part of enactment.

42. (1) Every Act shall be so construed as to reserve to Parliament the power of repealing or amending it, and of revoking, restricting or modifying any power, privilege or advantage thereby vested in or granted to any person.

(2) An Act may be amended or repealed by an Act passed in the same session of Parliament.

(3) An amending enactment, as far as consistent with the tenor thereof, shall be construed as part of the enactment that it amends. R.S., c. I-23, s. 34.

EFFECT OF REPEAL.

43. Where an enactment is repealed in whole or in part, the repeal does not
  (a) revive any enactment or anything not in force or existing at the time when the repeal takes effect,
  (b) affect the previous operation of the enactment so repealed or anything duly done or suffered thereunder,
  (c) affect any right, privilege, obligation or liability acquired, accrued, accruing or incurred under the enactment so repealed,
  (d) affect any offence committed against or contravention of the provisions of the enactment so repealed, or any punishment, penalty or forfeiture incurred under the enactment so repealed, or
  (e) affect any investigation, legal proceeding or remedy in respect of any such right, privilege, obligation, liability referred to in paragraph (c) or in respect of any punishment, penalty or forfeiture referred to in paragraph (d),

and an investigation, legal proceeding or remedy as described in paragraph (e) may be instituted, continued or enforced, and the punishment, penalty or forfeiture may be imposed as if the enactment had not been so repealed. R.S., c. I-23, s. 35.

REPEAL AND SUBSTITUTION.

44. Where an enactment in this section called the "former enactment", is repealed and another enactment, in this section called the "new enactment" is substituted therefor,
  (a) every person acting under the former enactment shall continue to act, as if appointed under the new enactment, until another is appointed in the stead of that person;
  (b) every bond and security given by a person appointed under the former enactment remains in force, and all books, papers, forms and things made or used under the former enactment shall continue to be used as before the repeal in so far as they are consistent with the new enactment;

(c) every proceeding taken under the former enactment shall be taken up and continued under and in conformity with the new enactment so far as it may be done consistently with the new enactment;

(d) the procedure established by the new enactment shall be followed as far as it can be adapted thereto

   (i) in the recovery or enforcement of fines, penalties and forfeitures imposed under the former enactment,

   (ii) in the enforcement of rights, existing or accruing under the former enactment,

   (iii) in a proceeding in relation to matters that have happened before the repeal;

(e) when any punishment, penalty or forfeiture is reduced or mitigated by the new enactment, the punishment, penalty or forfeiture if imposed or adjudged after the repeal shall be reduced or mitigated accordingly;

(f) except to the extent that the provisions of the new enactment are not in substance the same as those of the former enactment, the new enactment shall not be held to operate as new law, but shall be construed and have effect as a consolidation and as declaratory of the law as contained in the former enactment;

(g) all regulations made under the repealed enactment remain in force and are deemed to have been made under the new enactment, in so far as they are not inconsistent with the new enactment, until they are repealed or others made in their stead; and

(h) any reference in an unrepealed enactment to the former enactment shall, with respect to a subsequent transaction, matter or thing, be read and construed as a reference to the provisions of the new enactment relating to the same subject-matter as the former enactment, but where there are no provisions in the new enactment relating to the same subject-matter, the former enactment shall be read as unrepealed in so far as is necessary to maintain or give effect to the unrepealed enactment. R.S., c. I-23, s. 36.

REPEAL DOES NOT IMPLY ENACTMENT WAS IN FORCE / Amendment does not imply change in law / Repeal does not declare previous law / Judicial construction not adopted.

45. (1) The repeal of an enactment in whole or in part shall not be deemed to be or to involve a declaration that such enactment was previously in force or was considered by Parliament or other body or person by whom the enactment was enacted to have been previously in force.

(2) The amendment of an enactment shall not be deemed to be or to involve a declaration that the law under that enactment was or was considered by Parliament or other body or person by whom the enactment was enacted to have been different from the law as it is under the enactment as amended.

(3) The repeal or amendment of an enactment in whole or in part shall not be deemed to be or to involve any declaration as to the previous state of the law.

(4) A re-enactment, revision, consolidation or amendment of an enactment shall not be deemed to be or to involve an adoption of the construction that has by

judicial decision or otherwise been placed on the language used in the enactment or on similar language. R.S., c. I-23, s. 37.

DEMISE OF CROWN

EFFECT OF DEMISE / Continuation of proceedings.

46. (1) Where there is a demise of the Crown,

- (*a*) the demise does not affect the holding of any office under the Crown in right of Canada; and
- (*b*) it is not necessary by reason of the demise that the holder of any such office again be appointed thereto or, having taken an oath of office or allegiance before the demise, again take that oath.

(2) No writ, action or other process or proceeding, civil or criminal, in or issuing out of any court established by an Act is, by reason of a demise of the Crown, determined, abated, discontinued or affected, but every such writ, action, process or proceeding remains in full force and may be enforced, carried on or otherwise proceeded with or completed as though there had been no such demise. R.S., c. I-23, s. 38.

SCHEDULE

(Section 35)

Antigua and Barbuda
Australia
The Bahamas
Bangladesh
Barbados
Belize
Botswana
Brunei Darussalam
Canada
Cyprus
Dominica
Fiji
Gambia
Ghana
Grenada
Guyana
India
Jamaica
Kenya
Kiribati

Lesotho
Malawi
Malaysia
Maldives
Malta
Mauritius
Nauru
New Zealand
Nigeria
Papua New Guinea
St. Christopher and Nevis
St. Lucia
St. Vincent and the Grenadines
Seychelles
Sierra Leone
Singapore
Solomon Islands
Sri Lanka
Swaziland
Tanzania
Tonga
Trinidad and Tobago
Tuvalu
Uganda
United Kingdom
Vanuatu
Western Samoa
Zambia
Zimbabwe

R.S., c. I-23, Sch.; SI/72-93; SOR/74-287; SOR/77-394; SI/80-136; SOR/81-208; SOR/84-186; SOR/86-532.

YOUTH CRIMINAL JUSTICE ACT

S.C. 2002, c. 1, in force April 1, 2003

Amended 2002, c. 7, s. 274; brought into force April 1, 2003 as provided by the section

Amended 2002, c. 13, s. 91(1); brought into force June 1, 2004, as provided by s. 91(2), by SI/2003-182, *Can. Gaz.*, December 3, 2003

Amended 2004, c. 11, ss. 48 and 49; brought into force May 21, 2004 by SI/2004-58, *Can. Gaz.*, Part II, June 2, 2004

Amended 2005, c. 22, s. 63; brought into force June 30, 2005 by para. (*a*) of SI/2005-56, *Can. Gaz.*, Part II, June 15, 2005

Amended 2012, c. 1, ss. 156 to 159, 160(*l*), 167 to 188(2), 189, 190, and 192 to 195; ss. 156 to 159 in force March 13, 2012; ss. 167 to 188(2), 189 and 190, and 192 to 195 in force October 23, 2012 by SI/2012-48, *Can. Gaz.*, *Part II*, July 4, 2012; s. 160(*l*) brought into force February 28, 2013 by SI/2013-13, *Can. Gaz.*, *Part II*, February 27, 2013

Amended 2014, c. 2, s. 52; in force April 1, 2014 by SI/2014-34, *Can. Gaz.*, *Part II*, April 9, 2014

Amended 2014, c. 25, s. 43; in force December 6, 2014

Amended 2015, c. 20, ss. 32, 33, 36(8) and (9); in force July 18, 2015

Amended 2015, c. 29, ss. 14 and 15; brought into force July 16, 2015 by SI/2015-67, *Can. Gaz.*, *Part II*, July 17, 2015; however, replaced by 2015, c. 20, s. 36(8) and (9)

Amended 2018, c. 16, s. 184; in force October 17, 2018

Amended 2019, c. 13, ss. 159-167; in force June 21, 2019

Amended 2019, c. 25, ss. 361-383; ss. 370(1), 376-379, 382 in force September 19, 2019; s. 383 in force June 21, 2019; ss. 361-365, 367-369, 370(2), 371-375, 380, 381 in force December 18, 2019; s. 366 repealed before coming into force 2019, c. 25, s. 404(5)

An Act in respect of criminal justice for young persons and to amend and repeal other Acts

---

PREAMBLE

WHEREAS members of society share a responsibility to address the developmental challenges and the needs of young persons and to guide them into adulthood;

WHEREAS communities, families, parents and others concerned with the development of young persons should, through multi-disciplinary approaches, take reasonable steps to prevent youth crime by addressing its underlying causes, to respond to the needs of young persons, and to provide guidance and support to those at risk of committing crimes;

WHEREAS information about youth justice, youth crime and the effectiveness of measures taken to address youth crime should be publicly available;

WHEREAS Canada is a party to the United Nations Convention on the Rights of the Child and recognizes that young persons have rights and freedoms, including those stated in the *Canadian Charter of Rights and Freedoms* and the *Canadian Bill of Rights*, and have special guarantees of their rights and freedoms;

AND WHEREAS Canadian society should have a youth criminal justice system that commands respect, takes into account the interests of victims, fosters responsibility and ensures accountability through meaningful consequences and effective rehabilitation and reintegration, and that reserves its most serious intervention for the most serious crimes and reduces the over-reliance on incarceration for non-violent young persons;

NOW, THEREFORE, Her Majesty, by and with the advice and consent of the Senate and House of Commons of Canada, enacts as follows:

SHORT TITLE

SHORT TITLE.

1. This Act may be cited as the *Youth Criminal Justice Act.*

INTERPRETATION

DEFINITIONS / "adult" / "adult sentence" / "Attorney General" / "child" / "conference" / "confirmed delivery service" / "custodial portion" / "disclosure" / "extrajudicial measures" / "extrajudicial sanction" / "offence" / "parent" / "pre-sentence report" / "provincial director" / "publication" / "record" / "review board" / "serious offence" / "serious violent offence" / "violent offence" / "young person" / "youth custody facility" / "youth justice court" / "youth justice court judge" / "youth sentence" / "youth worker" / Words and expressions / Descriptive cross-references.

2. (1) The definitions in this subsection apply in this Act.

"adult" means a person who is neither a young person nor a child.

"adult sentence", in the case of a young person who is found guilty of an offence, means any sentence that could be imposed on an adult who has been convicted of the same offence.

"Attorney General" means the Attorney General as defined in section 2 of the *Criminal Code*, read as if the reference in that definition to "proceedings" were a reference to "proceedings or extrajudicial measures", and includes an agent or delegate of the Attorney General.

"child" means a person who is or, in the absence of evidence to the contrary, appears to be less than twelve years old.

"conference" means a group of persons who are convened to give advice in accordance with section 19.

"confirmed delivery service" means certified or registered mail or any other method of service that provides proof of delivery.

"custodial portion", with respect to a youth sentence imposed on a young person under paragraph 42(2)(n), (o), (q) or (r), means the period of time, or the portion of the young person's youth sentence, that must be served in custody before he or she begins to serve the remainder under supervision in the community subject to conditions under paragraph 42(2)(n) or under conditional supervision under paragraph 42(2)(o), (q) or (r).

"disclosure" means the communication of information other than by way of publication.

"extrajudicial measures" means measures other than judicial proceedings under this Act used to deal with a young person alleged to have committed an offence and includes extrajudicial sanctions.

"extrajudicial sanction" means a sanction that is part of a program referred to in section 10.

"offence" means an offence created by an Act of Parliament or by any regulation, rule, order, by-law or ordinance made under an Act of Parliament other than a law of the Legislature of Yukon, of the Northwest Territories or for Nunavut.

"parent" includes, in respect of a young person, any person who is under a legal duty to provide for the young person or any person who has, in law or in fact, the custody or control of the young person, but does not include a person who has the custody or control of the young person by reason only of proceedings under this Act.

"pre-sentence report" means a report on the personal and family history and present environment of a young person made in accordance with section 40.

"presumptive offence" [Repealed, 2012, c. 1, s. 167(1).]

"provincial director" means a person, a group or class of persons or a body appointed or designated by or under an Act of the legislature of a province or by the lieutenant governor in council of a province or his or her delegate to perform in that province, either generally or in a specific case, any of the duties or functions of a provincial director under this Act.

"publication" means the communication of information by making it known or accessible to the general public through any means, including print, radio or television broadcast, telecommunication or electronic means.

"record" includes any thing containing information, regardless of its physical form or characteristics, including microform, sound recording, videotape, machine-readable record, and any copy of any of those things, that is created or kept for the purposes of this Act or for the investigation of an offence that is or could be prosecuted under this Act.

"review board" means a review board referred to in subsection 87(2).

"serious offence" means an indictable offence under an Act of Parliament for which the maximum punishment is imprisonment for five years or more.

"serious violent offence" means an offence under one of the following provisions of the *Criminal Code*:

   (*a*)   section 231 or 235 (first degree murder or second degree murder);

   (*b*)   section 239 (attempt to commit murder);

   (*c*)   section 232, 234 or 236 (manslaughter); or

   (*d*)   section 273 (aggravated sexual assault).

"violent offence" means

   (*a*)   an offence committed by a young person that includes as an element the causing of bodily harm;

   (*b*)   an attempt or a threat to commit an offence referred to in paragraph (*a*); or

   (*c*)   an offence in the commission of which a young person endangers the life or safety of another person by creating a substantial likelihood of causing bodily harm.

"young person" means a person who is or, in the absence of evidence to the contrary, appears to be twelve years old or older, but less than eighteen years old and, if the context requires, includes any person who is charged under this Act with having committed an offence while he or she was a young person or who is found guilty of an offence under this Act.

"youth custody facility" means a facility designated under subsection 85(2) for the placement of young persons and, if so designated, includes a facility for the secure restraint of young persons, a community residential centre, a group home, a child care institution and a forest or wilderness camp.

"youth justice court" means a youth justice court referred to in section 13.

"youth justice court judge" means a youth justice court judge referred to in section 13.

"youth sentence" means a sentence imposed under section 42, 51 or 59 or any of sections 94 to 96 and includes a confirmation or a variation of that sentence.

"youth worker" means any person appointed or designated, whether by title of youth worker or probation officer or by any other title, by or under an Act of the legislature of a province or by the lieutenant governor in council of a province or his or her delegate to perform in that province, either generally or in a specific case, any of the duties or functions of a youth worker under this Act.

(2) Unless otherwise provided, words and expressions used in this Act have the same meaning as in the *Criminal Code*.

(3) If, in any provision of this Act, a reference to another provision of this Act or a provision of any other Act is followed by words in parentheses that are or purport to be descriptive of the subject-matter of the provision referred to, those words form no part of the provision in which they occur but are inserted for convenience of reference only. 2002, c. 7, s. 274; 2012, c. 1, s. 167; 2014, c. 2, s. 52.

DECLARATION OF PRINCIPLE

POLICY FOR CANADA WITH RESPECT TO YOUNG PERSONS / Act to be liberally construed.

3. (1) The following principles apply in this Act:

(*a*) the youth criminal justice system is intended to protect the public by

    (i) holding young persons accountable through measures that are proportionate to the seriousness of the offence and the degree of responsibility of the young person,

    (ii) promoting the rehabilitation and reintegration of young persons who have committed offences, and

    (iii) supporting the prevention of crime by referring young persons to programs or agencies in the community to address the circumstances underlying their offending behaviour;

(*b*) the criminal justice system for young persons must be separate from that of adults, must be based on the principle of diminished moral blameworthiness or culpability and must emphasize the following:

    (i) rehabilitation and reintegration,

    (ii) fair and proportionate accountability that is consistent with the greater dependency of young persons and their reduced level of maturity,

    (iii) enhanced procedural protection to ensure that young persons are treated fairly and that their rights, including their right to privacy, are protected,

    (iv) timely intervention that reinforces the link between the offending behaviour and its consequences, and

    (v) the promptness and speed with which persons responsible for enforcing this Act must act, given young persons' perception of time;

(*c*) within the limits of fair and proportionate accountability, the measures taken against young persons who commit offences should

    (i) reinforce respect for societal values,

    (ii) encourage the repair of harm done to victims and the community,

    (iii) be meaningful for the individual young person given his or her needs and level of development and, where appropriate, involve the parents, the extended family, the community and social or other agencies in the young person's rehabilitation and reintegration, and

    (iv) respect gender, ethnic, cultural and linguistic differences and respond to the needs of aboriginal young persons and of young persons with special requirements; and

(*d*) special considerations apply in respect of proceedings against young persons and, in particular,

    (i) young persons have rights and freedoms in their own right, such as a right to be heard in the course of and to participate in the processes, other than the decision to prosecute, that lead to decisions that affect them, and young persons have special guarantees of their rights and freedoms,

YOUTH

    (ii) victims should be treated with courtesy, compassion and respect for their dignity and privacy and should suffer the minimum degree of inconvenience as a result of their involvement with the youth criminal justice system,

    (iii) victims should be provided with information about the proceedings and given an opportunity to participate and be heard, and

    (iv) parents should be informed of measures or proceedings involving their children and encouraged to support them in addressing their offending behaviour.

(2) This Act shall be liberally construed so as to ensure that young persons are dealt with in accordance with the principles set out in subsection (1). 2012, c. 1, s. 168.

PART 1 / EXTRAJUDICIAL MEASURES

Principles and Objectives

DECLARATION OF PRINCIPLES.

4. The following principles apply in this Part in addition to the principles set out in section 3:

    (*a*) extrajudicial measures are often the most appropriate and effective way to address youth crime;

    (*b*) extrajudicial measures allow for effective and timely interventions focused on correcting offending behaviour;

    (*c*) extrajudicial measures are presumed to be adequate to hold a young person accountable for his or her offending behaviour if the young person has committed a non-violent offence and has not previously been found guilty of an offence; and

    (*d*) extrajudicial measures should be used if they are adequate to hold a young person accountable for his or her offending behaviour and, if the use of extrajudicial measures is consistent with the principles set out in this section, nothing in this Act precludes their use in respect of a young person who

      (i) has previously been dealt with by the use of extrajudicial measures, or

      (ii) has previously been found guilty of an offence.

CERTAIN OFFENCES — EXTRAJUDICIAL MEASURES DEEMED ADEQUATE / Certain offences — various measures

4.1 (1) Extrajudicial measures are presumed to be adequate to hold a young person accountable for a failure or refusal referred to in section 137 and for a failure referred to in section 496 of the *Criminal Code* unless

    (*a*) the young person has a history of repetitive failures or refusals; or

    (*b*) the young person's failure or refusal caused harm, or a risk of harm, to the safety of the public.

(2) In the cases referred to in paragraphs (1)(*a*) and (*b*),
  (*a*) extrajudicial measures should be used if they are adequate to hold the young person accountable for the failure or refusal; and
  (*b*) if the use of extrajudicial measures would not be adequate under paragraph (*a*), but issuing an appearance notice under section 496 (judicial referral hearing) of the *Criminal Code* or making an application for review of the youth sentence referred to in section 59(1) as an alternative to proceeding by charge would be adequate, then the applicable alternative should be used.

OBJECTIVES.

5. Extrajudicial measures should be designed to
  (*a*) provide an effective and timely response to offending behaviour outside the bounds of judicial measures;
  (*b*) encourage young persons to acknowledge and repair the harm caused to the victim and the community;
  (*c*) encourage families of young persons — including extended families where appropriate — and the community to become involved in the design and implementation of those measures;
  (*d*) provide an opportunity for victims to participate in decisions related to the measures selected and to receive reparation; and
  (*e*) respect the rights and freedoms of young persons and be proportionate to the seriousness of the offence.

Warnings, Cautions and Referrals

WARNINGS, CAUTIONS AND REFERRALS / Saving.

6. (1) A police officer shall, before starting judicial proceedings or taking any other measures under this Act against a young person alleged to have committed an offence, consider whether it would be sufficient, having regard to the principles set out in sections 4 and 4.1, to take no further action, warn the young person, administer a caution, if a program has been established under section 7, or, with the consent of the young person, refer the young person to a program or agency in the community that may assist the young person not to commit offences.

(2) The failure of a police officer to consider the options set out in subsection (1) does not invalidate any subsequent charges against the young person for the offence. 2019, c. 25, s. 362.

POLICE CAUTIONS.

7. The Attorney General, or any other minister designated by the lieutenant governor of a province, may establish a program authorizing the police to administer cautions to young persons instead of starting judicial proceedings under this Act.

CROWN CAUTIONS.

8. The Attorney General may establish a program authorizing prosecutors to administer cautions to young persons instead of starting or continuing judicial proceedings under this Act.

EVIDENCE OF MEASURES IS INADMISSIBLE.

9. Evidence that a young person has received a warning, caution or referral mentioned in section 6, 7 or 8 or that a police officer has taken no further action in respect of an offence, and evidence of the offence, is inadmissible for the purpose of proving prior offending behaviour in any proceedings before a youth justice court in respect of the young person.

Extrajudicial Sanctions

EXTRAJUDICIAL SANCTIONS / Conditions / Restriction on use / Admissions not admissible in evidence / No bar to judicial proceedings / Laying of information, etc.

10. (1) An extrajudicial sanction may be used to deal with a young person alleged to have committed an offence only if the young person cannot be adequately dealt with by a warning, caution or referral mentioned in section 6, 7 or 8 because of the seriousness of the offence, the nature and number of previous offences committed by the young person or any other aggravating circumstances.

(2) An extrajudicial sanction may be used only if

   (*a*) it is part of a program of sanctions that may be authorized by the Attorney General or authorized by a person, or a member of a class of persons, designated by the lieutenant governor in council of the province;

   (*b*) the person who is considering whether to use the extrajudicial sanction is satisfied that it would be appropriate, having regard to the needs of the young person and the interests of society;

   (*c*) the young person, having been informed of the extrajudicial sanction, fully and freely consents to be subject to it;

   (*d*) the young person has, before consenting to be subject to the extrajudicial sanction, been advised of his or her right to be represented by counsel and been given a reasonable opportunity to consult with counsel;

   (*e*) the young person accepts responsibility for the act or omission that forms the basis of the offence that he or she is alleged to have committed;

   (*f*) there is, in the opinion of the Attorney General, sufficient evidence to proceed with the prosecution of the offence; and

   (*g*) the prosecution of the offence is not in any way barred at law.

(3) An extrajudicial sanction may not be used in respect of a young person who

   (*a*) denies participation or involvement in the commission of the offence; or

   (*b*) expresses the wish to have the charge dealt with by a youth justice court.

(4) Any admission, confession or statement accepting responsibility for a given act or omission that is made by a young person as a condition of being dealt with by

extrajudicial measures is inadmissible in evidence against any young person in civil or criminal proceedings.

(5) The use of an extrajudicial sanction in respect of a young person alleged to have committed an offence is not a bar to judicial proceedings under this Act, but if a charge is laid against the young person in respect of the offence,

    (*a*) the youth justice court shall dismiss the charge if it is satisfied on a balance of probabilities that the young person has totally complied with the terms and conditions of the extrajudicial sanction; and

    (*b*) the youth justice court may dismiss the charge if it is satisfied on a balance of probabilities that the young person has partially complied with the terms and conditions of the extrajudicial sanction and if, in the opinion of the court, prosecution of the charge would be unfair having regard to the circumstances and the young person's performance with respect to the extrajudicial sanction.

(6) Subject to subsection (5) and section 24 (private prosecutions only with consent of Attorney General), nothing in this section shall be construed as preventing any person from laying an information or indictment, obtaining the issue or confirmation of any process or proceeding with the prosecution of any offence in accordance with law.

NOTICE TO PARENT.

11. If a young person is dealt with by an extrajudicial sanction, the person who administers the program under which the sanction is used shall inform a parent of the young person of the sanction.

VICTIM'S RIGHT TO INFORMATION.

12. If a young person is dealt with by an extrajudicial sanction, a police officer, the Attorney General, the provincial director or any organization established by a province to provide assistance to victims shall, on request, inform the victim of the identity of the young person and how the offence has been dealt with.

PART 2 / ORGANIZATION OF YOUTH CRIMINAL JUSTICE SYSTEM

Youth Justice Court

DESIGNATION OF YOUTH JUSTICE COURT / Deemed youth justice court / Deemed youth justice court / Court of record.

13. (1) A youth justice court is any court that may be established or designated by or under an Act of the legislature of a province, or designated by the Governor in Council or the lieutenant governor in council of a province, as a youth justice court for the purposes of this Act, and a youth justice court judge is a person who may be appointed or designated as a judge of the youth justice court or a judge sitting in a court established or designated as a youth justice court.

(2) When a young person elects to be tried by a judge without a jury, the judge shall be a judge as defined in section 552 of the *Criminal Code*, or if it is an offence set out in section 469 of that Act, the judge shall be a judge of the superior court of criminal jurisdiction in the province in which the election is made. In either case, the judge is deemed to be a youth justice court judge and the court is deemed to be a youth justice court for the purpose of the proceeding.

(3) When a young person elects or is deemed to have elected to be tried by a court composed of a judge and jury, the superior court of criminal jurisdiction in the province in which the election is made or deemed to have been made is deemed to be a youth justice court for the purpose of the proceeding, and the superior court judge is deemed to be a youth justice court judge.

(4) A youth justice court is a court of record.

EXCLUSIVE JURISDICTION OF YOUTH JUSTICE COURT / Orders / Prosecution prohibited / Continuation of proceedings / Young persons over the age of eighteen years / Powers of youth justice court judge / Powers of a judge of a superior court.

14. (1) Despite any other Act of Parliament but subject to the *Contraventions Act* and the *National Defence Act*, a youth justice court has exclusive jurisdiction in respect of any offence alleged to have been committed by a person while he or she was a young person, and that person shall be dealt with as provided in this Act.

(2) A youth justice court has exclusive jurisdiction to make orders against a young person under sections 83.3 (recognizance — terrorist activity), 810 (recognizance — fear of injury or damage), 810.01 (recognizance — fear of certain offences), 810.011 (recognizance — fear of terrorism offence), 810.02 (recognizance — fear of forced marriage or marriage under age of 16 years) and 810.2 (recognizance — fear of serious personal injury offence) of the *Criminal Code* and the provisions of this Act apply, with any modifications that the circumstances require. If the young person fails or refuses to enter into a recognizance referred to in any of those sections, the court may impose any one of the sanctions set out in subsection 42(2) (youth sentences) except that, in the case of an order under paragraph 42(2)(n) (custody and supervision order), it shall not exceed 30 days.

(3) Unless the Attorney General and the young person agree, no extrajudicial measures shall be taken or judicial proceedings commenced under this Act in respect of an offence after the end of the time limit set out in any other Act of Parliament or any regulation made under it for the institution of proceedings in respect of that offence.

(4) Extrajudicial measures taken or judicial proceedings commenced under this Act against a young person may be continued under this Act after the person attains the age of eighteen years.

(5) This Act applies to persons eighteen years old or older who are alleged to have committed an offence while a young person.

(6) For the purpose of carrying out the provisions of this Act, a youth justice court judge is a justice and a provincial court judge and has the jurisdiction and powers of a summary conviction court under the *Criminal Code*.

(7) A judge of a superior court of criminal jurisdiction, when deemed to be a youth justice court judge for the purpose of a proceeding, retains the jurisdiction and powers of a superior court of criminal jurisdiction. 2015, c. 20, ss. 32, 36(8); c. 29, s. 14; 2019, c. 13, s. 159.

CONTEMPT AGAINST YOUTH JUSTICE COURT / Jurisdiction of youth justice court / Concurrent jurisdiction of youth justice court / Youth sentence — contempt.

15. (1) Every youth justice court has the same power, jurisdiction and authority to deal with and impose punishment for contempt against the court as may be exercised by the superior court of criminal jurisdiction of the province in which the court is situated.

(2) A youth justice court has jurisdiction in respect of every contempt of court committed by a young person against the youth justice court whether or not committed in the face of the court, and every contempt of court committed by a young person against any other court otherwise than in the face of that court.

(3) A youth justice court has jurisdiction in respect of every contempt of court committed by a young person against any other court in the face of that court and every contempt of court committed by an adult against the youth justice court in the face of the youth justice court, but nothing in this subsection affects the power, jurisdiction or authority of any other court to deal with or impose punishment for contempt of court.

(4) When a youth justice court or any other court finds a young person guilty of contempt of court, it may impose as a youth sentence any one of the sanctions set out in subsection 42(2) (youth sentences), or any number of them that are not inconsistent with each other, but no other sentence. Section 708 of *Criminal Code* applies in respect of adults (5) Section 708 (contempt) of the *Criminal Code* applies in respect of proceedings under this section in youth justice court against adults, with any modifications that the circumstances require.

STATUS OF OFFENDER UNCERTAIN.

16. When a person is alleged to have committed an offence during a period that includes the date on which the person attains the age of eighteen years, the youth justice court has jurisdiction in respect of the offence and shall, after putting the person to their election under section 67 (adult sentence) if applicable, and on finding the person guilty of the offence,

    (*a*) if it has been proven that the offence was committed before the person attained the age of eighteen years, impose a sentence under this Act;

    (*b*) if it has been proven that the offence was committed after the person attained the age of eighteen years, impose any sentence that could be imposed under the *Criminal Code* or any other Act of Parliament on an adult who has been convicted of the same offence; and

(c) if it has not been proven that the offence was committed after the person attained the age of eighteen years, impose a sentence under this Act.

YOUTH JUSTICE COURT MAY MAKE RULES / Rules of court / Publication of rules.

17. (1) The youth justice court for a province may, subject to the approval of the lieutenant governor in council of the province, establish rules of court not inconsistent with this Act or any other Act of Parliament or with any regulations made under section 155 regulating proceedings within the jurisdiction of the youth justice court.

(2) Rules under subsection (1) may be made

   (a) generally to regulate the duties of the officers of the youth justice court and any other matter considered expedient to attain the ends of justice and carry into effect the provisions of this Act;

   (b) subject to any regulations made under paragraph 155(b), to regulate the practice and procedure in the youth justice court; and

   (c) to prescribe forms to be used in the youth justice court if they are not otherwise provided for by or under this Act.

(3) Rules of court that are made under the authority of this section shall be published in the appropriate provincial gazette.

Youth Justice Committees

YOUTH JUSTICE COMMITTEES / Role of committee.

18. (1) The Attorney General of Canada or a province or any other minister that the lieutenant governor in council of the province may designate may establish one or more committees of citizens, to be known as youth justice committees, to assist in any aspect of the administration of this Act or in any programs or services for young persons.

(2) The functions of a youth justice committee may include the following:

   (a) in the case of a young person alleged to have committed an offence,

      (i) giving advice on the appropriate extrajudicial measure to be used in respect of the young person,

      (ii) supporting any victim of the alleged offence by soliciting his or her concerns and facilitating the reconciliation of the victim and the young person,

      (iii) ensuring that community support is available to the young person by arranging for the use of services from within the community, and enlisting members of the community to provide short-term mentoring and supervision, and

      (iv) when the young person is also being dealt with by a child protection agency or a community group, helping to coordinate the interaction of the agency or group with the youth criminal justice system;

(*b*) advising the federal and provincial governments on whether the provisions of this Act that grant rights to young persons, or provide for the protection of young persons, are being complied with;

(*c*) advising the federal and provincial governments on policies and procedures related to the youth criminal justice system;

(*d*) providing information to the public in respect of this Act and the youth criminal justice system;

(*e*) acting as a conference; and

(*f*) any other functions assigned by the person who establishes the committee.

Conferences

YOUTH

CONFERENCES MAY BE CONVENED / Mandate of a conference / Rules for conferences / Rules to apply.

19. (1) A youth justice court judge, the provincial director, a police officer, a justice of the peace, a prosecutor or a youth worker may convene or cause to be convened a conference for the purpose of making a decision required to be made under this Act.

(2) The mandate of a conference may be, among other things, to give advice on appropriate extrajudicial measures, conditions for judicial interim release, sentences, including the review of sentences, and reintegration plans.

(3) The Attorney General or any other minister designated by the lieutenant governor in council of a province may establish rules for the convening and conducting of conferences other than conferences convened or caused to be convened by a youth justice court judge or a justice of the peace.

(4) In provinces where rules are established under subsection (3), the conferences to which those rules apply must be convened and conducted in accordance with those rules.

Justices of the Peace

CERTAIN PROCEEDINGS MAY BE TAKEN BEFORE JUSTICES / Orders under section 810 of *Criminal Code*.

20. (1) Any proceeding that may be carried out before a justice under the *Criminal Code*, other than a plea, a trial or an adjudication, may be carried out before a justice in respect of an offence alleged to have been committed by a young person, and any process that may be issued by a justice under the *Criminal Code* may be issued by a justice in respect of an offence alleged to have been committed by a young person.

(2) Despite subsection 14(2), a justice has jurisdiction to make an order under section 810 (recognizance — fear of injury or damage) of the *Criminal Code* in respect of a young person. If the young person fails or refuses to enter into a

recognizance referred to in that section, the justice shall refer the matter to a youth justice court. 2019, c. 13, s. 160.

Clerks of the Court

POWERS OF CLERKS.

21. In addition to any powers conferred on a clerk of a court by the *Criminal Code*, a clerk of the youth justice court may exercise the powers ordinarily exercised by a clerk of a court, and, in particular, may

- (*a*) administer oaths or solemn affirmations in all matters relating to the business of the youth justice court; and
- (*b*) in the absence of a youth justice court judge, exercise all the powers of a youth justice court judge relating to adjournment.

Provincial Directors

POWERS, DUTIES AND FUNCTIONS OF PROVINCIAL DIRECTORS.

22. The provincial director may authorize any person to exercise the powers or perform the duties or functions of the provincial director under this Act, in which case the powers, duties or functions are deemed to have been exercised or performed by the provincial director.

PART 3 / JUDICIAL MEASURES

Consent to Prosecute

PRE-CHARGE SCREENING / Pre-charge screening program.

23. (1) The Attorney General may establish a program of pre-charge screening that sets out the circumstances in which the consent of the Attorney General must be obtained before a young person is charged with an offence.

(2) Any program of pre-charge screening of young persons that is established under an Act of the legislature of a province or by a directive of a provincial government, and that is in place before the coming into force of this section, is deemed to be a program of pre-charge screening for the purposes of subsection (1).

PRIVATE PROSECUTIONS.

24. No prosecutions may be conducted by a prosecutor other than the Attorney General without the consent of the Attorney General.

Certain Offences — Review of Charges by Attorney General
2019, c. 25, s. 363.

REVIEW REQUIRED.

24.1 If a charge for which an appearance notice, summons or release order was issued, or an undertaking was given, is dismissed, withdrawn or stayed, or the young person is acquitted of that charge, the Attorney General must review any charge pending against the young person under any of subsections 145(2) to (5) of the *Criminal Code* for failure to comply with the appearance notice, summons, release order or undertaking in order to determine whether the prosecution of the charge should proceed. 2019, c. 25, s. 363.

Right to Counsel

YOUTH

RIGHT TO COUNSEL / Arresting officer to advise young person of right to counsel / Justice, youth justice court or review board to advise young person of right to counsel / Trial, hearing or review before youth justice court or review board / Appointment of counsel / Release hearing before justice / Young person may be assisted by adult / Counsel independent of parents / Statement of right to counsel / Recovery of costs of counsel / Exception for persons over the age of twenty.

25. (1) A young person has the right to retain and instruct counsel without delay, and to exercise that right personally, at any stage of proceedings against the young person and before and during any consideration of whether, instead of starting or continuing judicial proceedings against the young person under this Act, to use an extrajudicial sanction to deal with the young person.

(2) Every young person who is arrested or detained shall, on being arrested or detained, be advised without delay by the arresting officer of the right to retain and instruct counsel, and be given an opportunity to obtain counsel.

(3) When a young person is not represented by counsel
- (*a*) at a hearing at which it will be determined whether to release the young person or detain the young person in custody,
- (*a*.1) at a hearing held in relation to an order referred to in subsection 14(2) or 20(2),
- (*b*) at a hearing held under section 71 (hearing — adult sentences),
- (*c*) at trial,
- (*d*) at any proceedings held under subsection 98(3) (continuation of custody), 103(1) (review by youth justice court), 104(1) (continuation of custody), 105(1) (conditional supervision) or 109(1) (review of decision),
- (*e*) at a review of a youth sentence held before a youth justice court under this Act, or
- (*f*) at a review of the level of custody under section 87,

the justice or youth justice court before which the hearing, trial or review is held, or the review board before which the review is held, shall advise the young person

1175

of the right to retain and instruct counsel and shall give the young person a reasonable opportunity to obtain counsel.

(4) When a young person at trial or at a hearing or review referred to in subsection (3) wishes to obtain counsel but is unable to do so, the youth justice court before which the hearing, trial or review is held or the review board before which the review is held

(a) shall, if there is a legal aid program or an assistance program available in the province where the hearing, trial or review is held, refer the young person to that program for the appointment of counsel; or

(b) if no legal aid program or assistance program is available or the young person is unable to obtain counsel through the program, may, and on the request of the young person shall, direct that the young person be represented by counsel.

(5) When a direction is made under paragraph (4)(b) in respect of a young person, the Attorney General shall appoint counsel, or cause counsel to be appointed, to represent the young person.

(6) When a young person, at a hearing referred to in paragraph (3)(a) or (a.1) that is held before a justice who is not a youth justice court judge, wishes to obtain counsel but is unable to do so, the justice shall

(a) if there is a legal aid program or an assistance program available in the province where the hearing is held,

(i) refer the young person to that program for the appointment of counsel, or

(ii) refer the matter to a youth justice court to be dealt with in accordance with paragraph (4)(a) or (b); or

(b) if no legal aid program or assistance program is available or the young person is unable to obtain counsel through the program, refer the matter without delay to a youth justice court to be dealt with in accordance with paragraph (4)(b).

(7) When a young person is not represented by counsel at trial or at a hearing or review referred to in subsection (3), the justice before whom or the youth justice court or review board before which the proceedings are held may, on the request of the young person, allow the young person to be assisted by an adult whom the justice, court or review board considers to be suitable.

(8) If it appears to a youth justice court judge or a justice that the interests of a young person and the interests of a parent are in conflict or that it would be in the best interests of the young person to be represented by his or her own counsel, the judge or justice shall ensure that the young person is represented by counsel independent of the parent.

(9) A statement that a young person has the right to be represented by counsel shall be included in

(a) any appearance notice or summons issued to the young person;

(b) any warrant to arrest the young person;

(c) any undertaking entered into before a peace officer by the young person;

(d) [*Repealed*, 2019, c. 25, s. 364(2).]

(e) any notice given to the young person in relation to any proceedings held under subsection 98(3) (continuation of custody), 103(1) (review by youth justice court), 104(1) (continuation of custody), 105(1) (conditional supervision) or 109(1) (review of decision); or

(f) any notice of a review of a youth sentence given to the young person.

(10) Nothing in this Act prevents the lieutenant governor in council of a province or his or her delegate from establishing a program to authorize the recovery of the costs of a young person's counsel from the young person or the parents of the young person. The costs may be recovered only after the proceedings are completed and the time allowed for the taking of an appeal has expired or, if an appeal is taken, all proceedings in respect of the appeal have been completed.

(11) Subsections (4) to (9) do not apply to a person who is alleged to have committed an offence while a young person, if the person has attained the age of twenty years at the time of his or her first appearance before a youth justice court in respect of the offence; however, this does not restrict any rights that a person has under the law applicable to adults. 2019, c. 13, s. 161; 2019, c. 25, s. 364.

YOUTH

Notices to Parents

NOTICE IN CASE OF ARREST AND DETAINED / Notice in other cases / Notice to parent in case of ticket / Notice to relative or other adult / Notice on direction of youth justice court judge or justice / Contents of notice / Notice of ticket under Contraventions Act / Service of notice / Proceedings not invalid / Exception / Where notice is not served / Exception for persons over the age of twenty.

26. (1) Subject to subsection (4), if a young person is arrested and detained in custody pending their appearance in court, a peace officer shall, as soon as possible after the young person is detained, give or cause to be given to a parent of the young person, orally or in writing, notice of the arrest stating the place of detention and the reason for the arrest.

(2) Subject to subsection (4), if a summons or an appearance notice is issued in respect of a young person, the person who issued the summons or appearance notice, or, if a young person is released on an undertaking, a peace officer, shall, as soon as possible, give or cause to be given to a parent of the young person notice in writing of the summons, appearance notice or undertaking.

(3) Subject to subsection (4), a person who serves a ticket under the *Contraventions Act* on a young person, other than a ticket served for a contravention relating to parking a vehicle, shall, as soon as possible, give or cause to be given notice in writing of the ticket to a parent of the young person.

(4) If the whereabouts of the parents of a young person are not known or it appears that no parent is available, a notice under this section may be given to an adult relative of the young person who is known to the young person and is likely to assist the young person or, if no such adult relative is available, to any other adult

who is known to the young person and is likely to assist the young person and who the person giving the notice considers appropriate.

(5) If doubt exists as to the person to whom a notice under this section should be given, a youth justice court judge or, if a youth justice court judge is, having regard to the circumstances, not reasonably available, a justice may give directions as to the person to whom the notice should be given, and a notice given in accordance with those directions is sufficient notice for the purposes of this section.

(6) Any notice under this section shall, in addition to any other requirements under this section, include

    (*a*) the name of the young person in respect of whom it is given;

    (*b*) the charge against the young person and, except in the case of a notice of a ticket served under the *Contraventions Act*, the time and place of appearance; and

    (*c*) a statement that the young person has the right to be represented by counsel.

(7) A notice under subsection (3) shall include a copy of the ticket.

(8) Subject to subsections (10) and (11), a notice under this section that is given in writing may be served personally or be sent by confirmed delivery service.

(9) Subject to subsections (10) and (11), failure to give a notice in accordance with this section does not affect the validity of proceedings under this Act.

(10) Failure to give a notice under subsection (2) in accordance with this section in any case renders invalid any subsequent proceedings under this Act relating to the case unless

    (*a*) a parent of the young person attends court with the young person; or

    (*b*) a youth justice court judge or a justice before whom proceedings are held against the young person

        (i) adjourns the proceedings and orders that the notice be given in the manner and to the persons that the judge or justice directs, or

        (ii) dispenses with the notice if the judge or justice is of the opinion that, having regard to the circumstances, the notice may be dispensed with.

(11) Where there has been a failure to give a notice under subsection (1) or (3) in accordance with this section and none of the persons to whom the notice may be given attends court with the young person, a youth justice court judge or a justice before whom proceedings are held against the young person may

    (*a*) adjourn the proceedings and order that the notice be given in the manner and to the persons that the judge or justice directs; or

    (*b*) dispense with the notice if the judge or justice is of the opinion that, having regard to the circumstances, the notice may be dispensed with.

(12) This section does not apply to a person who is alleged to have committed an offence while a young person, if the person has attained the age of twenty years at the time of his or her first appearance before a youth justice court in respect of the offence. 2019, c. 25, s. 365.

ORDER REQUIRING ATTENDANCE OF PARENT / No order in ticket proceedings / Service of order / Failure to attend / Warrant to arrest parent.

27. (1) If a parent does not attend proceedings held before a youth justice court in respect of a young person, the court may, if in its opinion the presence of the parent is necessary or in the best interests of the young person, by order in writing require the parent to attend at any stage of the proceedings.

(2) Subsection (1) does not apply in proceedings commenced by filing a ticket under the *Contraventions Act*.

(3) A copy of the order shall be served by a peace officer or by a person designated by a youth justice court by delivering it personally to the parent to whom it is directed, unless the youth justice court authorizes service by confirmed delivery service.

(4) A parent who is ordered to attend a youth justice court under subsection (1) and who fails without reasonable excuse, the proof of which lies on the parent, to comply with the order

    (*a*) is guilty of contempt of court;

    (*b*) may be dealt with summarily by the court; and

    (*c*) is liable to the punishment provided for in the *Criminal Code* for a summary conviction offence.

(5) If a parent who is ordered to attend a youth justice court under subsection (1) does not attend when required by the order or fails to remain in attendance as required and it is proved that a copy of the order was served on the parent, a youth justice court may issue a warrant to compel the attendance of the parent.

Detention and Release   [*Heading amended* 2019, c. 13, s. 162.]

APPLICATION OF PART XVI OF CRIMINAL CODE.

28. Except to the extent that they are inconsistent with or excluded by this Act, the provisions of Part XVI (compelling appearance of an accused and interim release) of the *Criminal Code* apply to the detention and release of young persons under this Act.

SUBSTITUTE FOR SOCIAL MEASURES PROHIBITED.

28.1 A peace officer, youth justice court judge or justice shall not detain a young person in custody, or impose a condition in respect of a young person's release by including it in an undertaking or release order, as a substitute for appropriate child protection, mental health or other social measures. 2019, c. 25, s. 367.

RELEASE ORDER WITH CONDITIONS / Justification for detention in custody / Onus.

29. (1) A youth justice court judge or a justice may impose a condition set out in subsections 515(4) to (4.2) of the *Criminal Code* in respect of a release order only if they are satisfied that

1179

   (*a*) the condition is necessary to ensure the young person's attendance in court or for the protection or safety of the public, including any victim of or witness to the offence;

   (*b*) the condition is reasonable having regard to the circumstances of the offending behaviour; and

   (*c*) the young person will reasonably be able to comply with the condition.

(2) A youth justice court judge or a justice may order that a young person be detained in custody only if

   (*a*) the young person has been charged with

      (i) a serious offence, or

      (ii) an offence other than a serious offence, if they have a history that indicates a pattern of either outstanding charges or findings of guilt;

   (*b*) the judge or justice is satisfied, on a balance of probabilities,

      (i) that there is a substantial likelihood that, before being dealt with according to law, the young person will not appear in court when required by law to do so,

      (ii) that detention is necessary for the protection or safety of the public, including any victim of or witness to the offence, having regard to all the circumstances, including a substantial likelihood that the young person will, if released from custody, commit a serious offence, or

      (iii) in the case where the young person has been charged with a serious offence and detention is not justified under subparagraph (i) or (ii), that there are exceptional circumstances that warrant detention and that detention is necessary to maintain confidence in the administration of justice, having regard to the principles set out in section 3 and to all the circumstances, including

         (A) the apparent strength of the prosecution's case,

         (B) the gravity of the offence,

         (C) the circumstances surrounding the commission of the offence, including whether a firearm was used, and

         (D) the fact that the young person is liable, on being found guilty, for a potentially lengthy custodial sentence; and

   (*c*) the judge or justice is satisfied, on a balance of probabilities, that no condition or combination of conditions of release would, depending on the justification on which the judge or justice relies under paragraph (*b*),

      (i) reduce, to a level below substantial, the likelihood that the young person would not appear in court when required by law to do so,

      (ii) offer adequate protection to the public from the risk that the young person might otherwise present, or

      (iii) maintain confidence in the administration of justice.

(3) The onus of satisfying the youth justice court judge or the justice as to the matters referred to in subsection (2) is on the Attorney General. 2012, c. 1, s. 169; 2019, c. 13, s. 163; 2019, c. 25, s. 368.

DESIGNATED PLACE OF TEMPORARY DETENTION / Exception / Detention separate from adults / Transfer to adult facility / When young person is twenty years old or older / Transfer by provincial director / Exception relating to temporary detention / Authorization of provincial authority for detention / Determination by provincial authority of place of detention.

30. (1) Subject to subsection (7), a young person who is detained in custody in relation to any proceedings against the young person shall be detained in a safe, fair and humane manner in any place of temporary detention that may be designated by the lieutenant governor in council of the province or his or her delegate or in a place within a class of places so designated.

(2) A young person who is detained in a place of temporary detention under subsection (1) may, in the course of being transferred from that place to the court or from the court to that place, be held under the supervision and control of a peace officer.

(3) A young person referred to in subsection (1) shall be held separate and apart from any adult who is detained or held in custody unless a youth justice court judge or a justice is satisfied that, having regard to the best interests of the young person,

   (a) the young person cannot, having regard to his or her own safety or the safety of others, be detained in a place of detention for young persons; or

   (b) no place of detention for young persons is available within a reasonable distance.

(4) When a young person is detained under subsection (1), the youth justice court may, on application of the provincial director made at any time after the young person attains the age of eighteen years, after giving the young person an opportunity to be heard, authorize the provincial director to direct, despite subsection (3), that the young person be temporarily detained in a provincial correctional facility for adults, if the court considers it to be in the best interests of the young person or in the public interest.

(5) When a young person is twenty years old or older at the time his or her temporary detention under subsection (1) begins, the young person shall, despite subsection (3), be temporarily detained in a provincial correctional facility for adults.

(6) A young person who is detained in custody under subsection (1) may, during the period of detention, be transferred by the provincial director from one place of temporary detention to another.

(7) Subsections (1) and (3) do not apply in respect of any temporary restraint of a young person under the supervision and control of a peace officer after arrest, but a young person who is so restrained shall be transferred to a place of temporary detention referred to in subsection (1) as soon as is practicable, and in no case later than the first reasonable opportunity after the appearance of the young person before a youth justice court judge or a justice under section 503 of the *Criminal Code*.

(8) In any province for which the lieutenant governor in council has designated a person or a group of persons whose authorization is required, either in all circumstances or in circumstances specified by the lieutenant governor in council, before a young person who has been arrested may be detained in accordance with this section, no young person shall be so detained unless the authorization is obtained.

(9) In any province for which the lieutenant governor in council has designated a person or a group of persons who may determine the place where a young person who has been arrested may be detained in accordance with this section, no young person may be so detained in a place other than the one so determined. 2019, c. 13, s. 164.

REVIEW OF DETENTION — 30-DAY PERIOD.

30.1 For the purposes of section 525 of the *Criminal Code* with respect to a young person who has been charged with an offence for which they are being prosecuted in proceedings by way of summary conviction, every reference in that provision to "90 days" or "90-day" is to be read and construed as a reference to "30 days" or "30-day" respectively. 2019, c. 25, s. 369.

PLACEMENT OF YOUNG PERSON IN CARE OF RESPONSIBLE PERSON / Inquiry as to availability of a responsible person / Condition of placement / Removing young person from care / Order / Effect of arrest.

31. (1) A young person who has been arrested may be placed in the care of a responsible person instead of being detained in custody if a youth justice court or a justice is satisfied that

- (a) the young person would, but for this subsection, be detained in custody under section 515 (judicial interim release) of the *Criminal Code*;
- (b) the person is willing and able to take care of and exercise control over the young person; and
- (c) the young person is willing to be placed in the care of that person.

(2) If a young person would, in the absence of a responsible person, be detained in custody, the youth justice court or the justice shall inquire as to the availability of a responsible person and whether the young person is willing to be placed in that person's care.

(3) A young person shall not be placed in the care of a person under subsection (1) unless

- (a) that person undertakes in writing to take care of and to be responsible for the attendance of the young person in court when required and to comply with any other conditions that the youth justice court judge or the justice may specify; and
- (b) the young person undertakes in writing to comply with the arrangement and to comply with any other conditions that the youth justice court judge or the justice may specify.

(4) A young person, a person in whose care a young person has been placed or any other person may, by application in writing to a youth justice court judge or a justice, apply for an order under subsection (5) if

    (*a*) the person in whose care the young person has been placed is no longer willing or able to take care of or exercise control over the young person; or

    (*b*) it is, for any other reason, no longer appropriate that the young person remain in the care of the person with whom he or she has been placed.

(5) When a youth justice court judge or a justice is satisfied that a young person should not remain in the custody of the person in whose care he or she was placed under subsection (1), the judge or justice shall

    (*a*) make an order relieving the person and the young person of the obligations undertaken under subsection (3); and

    (*b*) issue a warrant for the arrest of the young person.

(6) If a young person is arrested in accordance with a warrant issued under paragraph (5)(*b*), the young person shall be taken before a youth justice court judge or a justice without delay and dealt with under this section and sections 28 to 30.

Appearance

APPEARANCE BEFORE JUDGE OR JUSTICE / Waiver / Young person not represented by counsel / If youth justice court not satisfied / If youth justice court not satisfied.

32. (1) A young person against whom an information or indictment is laid must first appear before a youth justice court judge or a justice, and the judge or justice shall

    (*a*) cause the information or indictment to be read to the young person;

    (*b*) if the young person is not represented by counsel, inform the young person of the right to retain and instruct counsel; and

    (*c*) if notified under subsection 64(2) (intention to seek adult sentence) or if section 16 (status of accused uncertain) applies, inform the young person that the youth justice court might, if the young person is found guilty, order that an adult sentence be imposed.

    (*d*) [*Repealed*, 2012, c. 1, s. 170.]

(2) A young person may waive the requirements of subsection (1) if the young person is represented by counsel and counsel advises the court that the young person has been informed of that provision.

(3) When a young person is not represented by counsel, the youth justice court, before accepting a plea, shall

    (*a*) satisfy itself that the young person understands the charge;

    (*b*) if the young person is liable to an adult sentence, explain to the young person the consequences of being liable to an adult sentence and the procedure by which the young person may apply for an order that a youth sentence be imposed; and (*c*) explain that the young person may plead guilty or not guilty to the charge or, if subsection 67(1) (election of court for trial — adult sentence) or (3) (election of court for trial in Nunavut — adult sentence) applies, explain that the young person may elect to be tried by a youth justice court judge without a jury and without having a preliminary inquiry, or to have a preliminary inquiry and be tried by a judge without a jury, or to have a preliminary inquiry and be tried by a court composed of a judge and jury and, in either of the latter two cases, a preliminary inquiry will only be conducted if requested by the young person or the prosecutor.

(4) If the youth justice court is not satisfied that a young person understands the charge, the court shall, unless the young person must be put to his or her election under subsection 67(1) (election of court for trial — adult sentence) or, with respect to Nunavut, subsection 67(3) (election of court for trial in Nunavut — adult sentence), enter a plea of not guilty on behalf of the young person and proceed with the trial in accordance with subsection 36(2) (young person pleads not guilty).

(5) If the youth justice court is not satisfied that a young person understands the matters set out in subsection (3), the court shall direct that the young person be represented by counsel. 2002, c. 13, s. 91(1)(*a*); 2012, c. 1, s. 170.

Application for Release from or Detention in Custody   [*Heading amended,* 2019, c. 13, s. 165.]

APPLICATION FOR RELEASE FROM OR DETENTION IN CUSTODY / Notice to prosecutor / Notice to young person / Waiver of notice / Application for review under section 520 or 521 of *Criminal Code* / Nunavut / No review / Interim release by youth justice court judge only / Review by court of appeal.

33. (1) If an order is made under section 515 (judicial interim release) of the *Criminal Code* in respect of a young person by a justice who is not a youth justice court judge, an application may, at any time after the order is made, be made to a youth justice court for the release from or detention in custody of the young person, as the case may be, and the youth justice court shall hear the matter as an original application.

(2) An application under subsection (1) for release from custody shall not be heard unless the young person has given the prosecutor at least two clear days notice in writing of the application.

(3) An application under subsection (1) for detention in custody shall not be heard unless the prosecutor has given the young person at least two clear days notice in writing of the application.

(4) The requirement for notice under subsection (2) or (3) may be waived by the prosecutor or by the young person or his or her counsel, as the case may be.

(5) An application under section 520 or 521 of the *Criminal Code* for a review of an order made in respect of a young person by a youth justice court judge who is a judge of a superior court shall be made to a judge of the court of appeal.

(6) Despite subsection (5), an application under section 520 or 521 of the *Criminal Code* for a review of an order made in respect of a young person by a youth justice court judge who is a judge of the Nunavut Court of Justice shall be made to a judge of that court.

(7) No application may be made under section 520 or 521 of the *Criminal Code* for a review of an order made in respect of a young person by a justice who is not a youth justice court judge.

(8) If a young person against whom proceedings have been taken under this Act is charged with an offence referred to in section 522 of the *Criminal Code*, a youth justice court judge, but no other court, judge or justice, may release the young person from custody under that section.

(9) A decision made by a youth justice court judge under subsection (8) may be reviewed in accordance with section 680 of the *Criminal Code* and that section applies, with any modifications that the circumstances require, to any decision so made.

Medical and Psychological Reports

MEDICAL OR PSYCHOLOGICAL ASSESSMENT / Purpose of assessment / Custody for assessment / Presumption against custodial remand / Report of qualified person in writing / Application to vary assessment order if circumstances change / Disclosure of report / Cross-examination / Non-disclosure in certain cases / Non-disclosure in certain cases / Exception — interests of justice / Report to be part of record / Disclosure by qualified person/Definition of "qualified person".

34. (1) A youth justice court may, at any stage of proceedings against a young person, by order require that the young person be assessed by a qualified person who is required to report the results in writing to the court,

    (*a*) with the consent of the young person and the prosecutor; or

    (*b*) on its own motion or on application of the young person or the prosecutor, if the court believes a medical, psychological or psychiatric report in respect of the young person is necessary for a purpose mentioned in paragraphs (2)(*a*) to (*g*) and

        (i) the court has reasonable grounds to believe that the young person may be suffering from a physical or mental illness or disorder, a psychological disorder, an emotional disturbance, a learning disability or a mental disability,

        (ii) the young person's history indicates a pattern of repeated findings of guilt under this Act or the *Young Offenders Act*, chapter Y-1 of the Revised Statutes of Canada, 1985, or

        (iii) the young person is alleged to have committed a serious violent offence.

(2) A youth justice court may make an order under subsection (1) in respect of a young person for the purpose of

    (*a*) considering an application under section 33 (release from or detention in custody);

    (*b*) making its decision on an application heard under section 71 (hearing — adult sentences);

    (*c*) making or reviewing a youth sentence;

    (*d*) considering an application under subsection 104(1) (continuation of custody);

    (*e*) setting conditions under subsection 105(1) (conditional supervision);

    (*f*) making an order under subsection 109(2) (conditional supervision); or

    (*g*) authorizing disclosure under subsection 127(1) (information about a young person).

(3) Subject to subsections (4) and (6), for the purpose of an assessment under this section, a youth justice court may remand a young person to any custody that it directs for a period not exceeding thirty days.

(4) A young person shall not be remanded in custody in accordance with an order made under subsection (1) unless

    (*a*) the youth justice court is satisfied that

        (i) on the evidence custody is necessary to conduct an assessment of the young person, or

        (ii) on the evidence of a qualified person detention of the young person in custody is desirable to conduct the assessment of the young person, and the young person consents to custody; or

    (*b*) the young person is required to be detained in custody in respect of any other matter or by virtue of any provision of the *Criminal Code*.

(5) For the purposes of paragraph (4)(*a*), if the prosecutor and the young person agree, evidence of a qualified person may be received in the form of a report in writing.

(6) A youth justice court may, at any time while an order made under subsection (1) is in force, on cause being shown, vary the terms and conditions specified in the order in any manner that the court considers appropriate in the circumstances.

(7) When a youth justice court receives a report made in respect of a young person under subsection (1),

    (*a*) the court shall, subject to subsection (9), cause a copy of the report to be given to

        (i) the young person,

        (ii) any parent of the young person who is in attendance at the proceedings against the young person,

        (iii) any counsel representing the young person, and

        (iv) the prosecutor; and

    (*b*) the court may cause a copy of the report to be given to

        (i) a parent of the young person who is not in attendance at the proceedings if the parent is, in the opinion of the court, taking an active interest in the proceedings, or

(ii) despite subsection 119(6) (restrictions respecting access to certain records), the provincial director, or the director of the provincial correctional facility for adults or the penitentiary at which the young person is serving a youth sentence, if, in the opinion of the court, withholding the report would jeopardize the safety of any person.

(8) When a report is made in respect of a young person under subsection (1), the young person, his or her counsel or the adult assisting the young person under subsection 25(7) and the prosecutor shall, subject to subsection (9), on application to the youth justice court, be given an opportunity to cross-examine the person who made the report.

(9) A youth justice court shall withhold all or part of a report made in respect of a young person under subsection (1) from a private prosecutor, if disclosure of the report or part, in the opinion of the court, is not necessary for the prosecution of the case and might be prejudicial to the young person.

(10) A youth justice court shall withhold all or part of a report made in respect of a young person under subsection (1) from the young person, the young person's parents or a private prosecutor if the court is satisfied, on the basis of the report or evidence given in the absence of the young person, parents or private prosecutor by the person who made the report, that disclosure of the report or part would seriously impair the treatment or recovery of the young person, or would be likely to endanger the life or safety of, or result in serious psychological harm to, another person.

(11) Despite subsection (10), the youth justice court may release all or part of the report to the young person, the young person's parents or the private prosecutor if the court is of the opinion that the interests of justice make disclosure essential.

(12) A report made under subsection (1) forms part of the record of the case in respect of which it was requested.

(13) Despite any other provision of this Act, a qualified person who is of the opinion that a young person held in detention or committed to custody is likely to endanger his or her own life or safety or to endanger the life of, or cause bodily harm to, another person may immediately so advise any person who has the care and custody of the young person whether or not the same information is contained in a report made under subsection (1).

(14) In this section, "qualified person" means a person duly qualified by provincial law to practice medicine or psychiatry or to carry out psychological examinations or assessments, as the circumstances require, or, if no such law exists, a person who is, in the opinion of the youth justice court, so qualified, and includes a person or a member of a class of persons designated by the lieutenant governor in council of a province or his or her delegate.

Referral to Child Welfare Agency

REFERRAL TO CHILD WELFARE AGENCY.

35. In addition to any order that it is authorized to make, a youth justice court may, at any stage of proceedings against a young person, refer the young person to a child welfare agency for assessment to determine whether the young person is in need of child welfare services.

Adjudication

WHEN YOUNG PERSON PLEADS GUILTY / When young person pleads not guilty.

36. (1) If a young person pleads guilty to an offence charged against the young person and the youth justice court is satisfied that the facts support the charge, the court shall find the young person guilty of the offence.

(2) If a young person charged with an offence pleads not guilty to the offence or pleads guilty but the youth justice court is not satisfied that the facts support the charge, the court shall proceed with the trial and shall, after considering the matter, find the young person guilty or not guilty or make an order dismissing the charge, as the case may be.

Appeals

APPEALS / Appeals for contempt of court / Appeal / Appeals heard together / Appeals for summary conviction offences / Appeals where offences are tried jointly / Deemed election / If the youth justice court is a superior court / Nunavut / Appeal to the Supreme Court of Canada / No appeal from youth sentence on review.

37. (1) An appeal in respect of an indictable offence or an offence that the Attorney General elects to proceed with as an indictable offence lies under this Act in accordance with Part XXI (appeals — indictable offences) of the *Criminal Code*, which Part applies with any modifications that the circumstances require.

(2) A finding of guilt under section 15 for contempt of court or a sentence imposed in respect of the finding may be appealed as if the finding were a conviction or the sentence were a sentence in a prosecution by indictment.

(3) Section 10 of the *Criminal Code* applies if a person is convicted of contempt of court under subsection 27(4) (failure of parent to attend court).

(4) An order under subsection 72(1) or (1.1) (adult or youth sentence) or 76(1) (placement when subject to adult sentence) may be appealed as part of the sentence and, unless the court to which the appeal is taken otherwise orders, if more than one of these is appealed they must be part of the same appeal proceeding.

(5) An appeal in respect of an offence punishable on summary conviction or an offence that the Attorney General elects to proceed with as an offence punishable on summary conviction lies under this Act in accordance with Part XXVII (summary conviction offences) of the *Criminal Code*, which Part applies with any modifications that the circumstances require.

(6) An appeal in respect of one or more indictable offences and one or more summary conviction offences that are tried jointly or in respect of which youth sentences are jointly imposed lies under this Act in accordance with Part XXI (appeals — indictable offences) of the *Criminal Code*, which Part applies with any modifications that the circumstances require.

(7) For the purpose of appeals under this Act, if no election is made in respect of an offence that may be prosecuted by indictment or proceeded with by way of summary conviction, the Attorney General is deemed to have elected to proceed with the offence as an offence punishable on summary conviction.

(8) In any province where the youth justice court is a superior court, an appeal under subsection (5) shall be made to the court of appeal of the province.

(9) Despite subsection (8), if the Nunavut Court of Justice is acting as a youth justice court, an appeal under subsection (5) shall be made to a judge of the Nunavut Court of Appeal, and an appeal of that judge's decision shall be made to the Nunavut Court of Appeal in accordance with section 839 of the *Criminal Code*.

(10) No appeal lies under subsection (1) from a judgment of the court of appeal in respect of a finding of guilt or an order dismissing an information or indictment to the Supreme Court of Canada unless leave to appeal is granted by the Supreme Court of Canada.

(11) No appeal lies from a youth sentence under section 59 — other than subsection 59(10) — or under any of sections 94 to 96. 2012, c. 1, s. 171; 2019, c. 25, s. 370.

PART 4 / SENTENCING

Purpose and Principles

PURPOSE / Sentencing principles / Factors to be considered.

38. (1) The purpose of sentencing under section 42 (youth sentences) is to hold a young person accountable for an offence through the imposition of just sanctions that have meaningful consequences for the young person and that promote his or her rehabilitation and reintegration into society, thereby contributing to the long-term protection of the public.

(2) A youth justice court that imposes a youth sentence on a young person shall determine the sentence in accordance with the principles set out in section 3 and the following principles:

    (a) the sentence must not result in a punishment that is greater than the punishment that would be appropriate for an adult who has been convicted of the same offence committed in similar circumstances;

    (b) the sentence must be similar to the sentences imposed in the region on similar young persons found guilty of the same offence committed in similar circumstances;

    (c) the sentence must be proportionate to the seriousness of the offence and the degree of responsibility of the young person for that offence;

    (d) all available sanctions other than custody that are reasonable in the circumstances should be considered for all young persons, with particular attention to the circumstances of aboriginal young persons;

    (e) subject to paragraph (c), the sentence must

       (i) be the least restrictive sentence that is capable of achieving the purpose set out in subsection (1),

       (ii) be the one that is most likely to rehabilitate the young person and reintegrate him or her into society, and

      (iii) promote a sense of responsibility in the young person, and an acknowledgement of the harm done to victims and the community;

(e.1) if this Act provides that a youth justice court may impose conditions as part of the sentence, a condition may be imposed only if

       (i) the imposition of the condition is necessary to achieve the purpose set out in subsection 38(1),

      (ii) the young person will reasonably be able to comply with the condition, and

      (iii) the condition is not used as a substitute for appropriate child protection, mental health or other social measures; and

    (f) subject to paragraph (c), the sentence may have the following objectives:

       (i) to denounce unlawful conduct, and

      (ii) to deter the young person from committing offences.

(3) In determining a youth sentence, the youth justice court shall take into account

    (a) the degree of participation by the young person in the commission of the offence;

    (b) the harm done to victims and whether it was intentional or reasonably foreseeable;

    (c) any reparation made by the young person to the victim or the community;

    (d) the time spent in detention by the young person as a result of the offence;

    (e) the previous findings of guilt of the young person; and

    (f) any other aggravating and mitigating circumstances related to the young person or the offence that are relevant to the purpose and principles set out in this section. 2012, c. 1, s. 172; 2019, c. 25, s. 371.

COMMITTAL TO CUSTODY / Alternatives to custody / Factors to be considered / Imposition of same sentence / Custody as social measure prohibited / Pre-sentence report / Report dispensed with / Length of custody / Reasons.

39. (1) A youth justice court shall not commit a young person to custody under section 42 (youth sentences) unless

(a) the young person has committed a violent offence;

(b) the young person has previously been found guilty of an offence under section 137 in relation to more than one sentence and, if the court is imposing a sentence for an offence under subsections 145(2) to (5) of the *Criminal Code* or section 137, the young person caused harm, or a risk of harm, to the safety of the public in committing that offence;

(c) the young person has committed an indictable offence for which an adult would be liable to imprisonment for a term of more than two years and has a history that indicates a pattern of either extrajudicial sanctions or of findings of guilt

or of both under this Act or the *Young Offenders Act*, chapter Y-1 of the Revised Statutes of Canada, 1985; or

(d) in exceptional cases where the young person has committed an indictable offence, the aggravating circumstances of the offence are such that the imposition of a non-custodial sentence would be inconsistent with the purpose and principles set out in section 38.

(2) If any of paragraphs (1)(a) to (c) apply, a youth justice court shall not impose a custodial sentence under section 42 (youth sentences) unless the court has considered all alternatives to custody raised at the sentencing hearing that are reasonable in the circumstances, and determined that there is not a reasonable alternative, or combination of alternatives, that is in accordance with the purpose and principles set out in section 38.

(3) In determining whether there is a reasonable alternative to custody, a youth justice court shall consider submissions relating to

(a) the alternatives to custody that are available;

(b) the likelihood that the young person will comply with a non-custodial sentence, taking into account his or her compliance with previous non-custodial sentences; and

(c) the alternatives to custody that have been used in respect of young persons for similar offences committed in similar circumstances.

(4) The previous imposition of a particular non-custodial sentence on a young person does not preclude a youth justice court from imposing the same or any other non-custodial sentence for another offence.

(5) A youth justice court shall not use custody as a substitute for appropriate child protection, mental health or other social measures.

(6) Before imposing a custodial sentence under section 42 (youth sentences), a youth justice court shall consider a pre-sentence report and any sentencing proposal made by the young person or his or her counsel.

(7) A youth justice court may, with the consent of the prosecutor and the young person or his or her counsel, dispense with a pre-sentence report if the court is satisfied that the report is not necessary.

(8) In determining the length of a youth sentence that includes a custodial portion, a youth justice court shall be guided by the purpose and principles set out in section 38, and shall not take into consideration the fact that the supervision portion of the sentence may not be served in custody and that the sentence may be reviewed by the court under section 94.

(9) If a youth justice court imposes a youth sentence that includes a custodial portion, the court shall state the reasons why it has determined that a non-custodial sentence is not adequate to achieve the purpose set out in subsection 38(1), including, if applicable, the reasons why the case is an exceptional case under paragraph (1)(*d*). 2012, c. 1, s. 173; 2019, c. 25, s. 372.

Pre-sentence Report

PRE-SENTENCE REPORT / Contents of report / Oral report with leave / Report forms part of record / Copies of pre-sentence report / Cross-examination / Report may be withheld from private prosecutor / Report disclosed to other persons / Disclosure by the provincial director / Inadmissibility of statements.

40. (1) Before imposing sentence on a young person found guilty of an offence, a youth justice court

- (*a*) shall, if it is required under this Act to consider a pre-sentence report before making an order or a sentence in respect of a young person, and
- (*b*) may, if it considers it advisable, require the provincial director to cause to be prepared a pre-sentence report in respect of the young person and to submit the report to the court.

(2) A pre-sentence report made in respect of a young person shall, subject to subsection (3), be in writing and shall include the following, to the extent that it is relevant to the purpose and principles of sentencing set out in section 38 and to the restrictions on custody set out in section 39:

- (*a*) the results of an interview with the young person and, if reasonably possible, the parents of the young person and, if appropriate and reasonably possible, members of the young person's extended family;
- (*b*) the results of an interview with the victim in the case, if applicable and reasonably possible;
- (*c*) the recommendations resulting from any conference referred to in section 41;
- (*d*) any information that is applicable to the case, including
  - (i) the age, maturity, character, behaviour and attitude of the young person and his or her willingness to make amends,
  - (ii) any plans put forward by the young person to change his or her conduct or to participate in activities or undertake measures to improve himself or herself,

    (iii) subject to subsection 119(2) (period of access to records), the history of previous findings of delinquency under the *Juvenile Delinquents Act*, chapter J-3 of the Revised Statutes of Canada, 1970, or previous findings of guilt for offences under the *Young Offenders Act*, chapter Y-1 of the Revised Statutes of Canada, 1985, or under this or any other Act of Parliament or any regulation made under it, the history of community or other services rendered to the young person with respect to those findings and the response of the young person to previous sentences or dispositions and to services rendered to him or her,

    (iv) subject to subsection 119(2) (period of access to records), the history of alternative measures under the *Young Offenders Act*, chapter Y-1 of the Revised Statutes of Canada, 1985, or extrajudicial sanctions used to deal with the young person and the response of the young person to those measures or sanctions,

    (v) the availability and appropriateness of community services and facilities for young persons and the willingness of the young person to avail himself or herself of those services or facilities,

    (vi) the relationship between the young person and the young person's parents and the degree of control and influence of the parents over the young person and, if appropriate and reasonably possible, the relationship between the young person and the young person's extended family and the degree of control and influence of the young person's extended family over the young person, and

    (vii) the school attendance and performance record and the employment record of the young person;

  (*e*) any information that may assist the court in determining under subsection 39(2) whether there is an alternative to custody; and

  (*f*) any information that the provincial director considers relevant, including any recommendation that the provincial director considers appropriate.

(3) If a pre-sentence report cannot reasonably be committed to writing, it may, with leave of the youth justice court, be submitted orally in court.

(4) A pre-sentence report shall form part of the record of the case in respect of which it was requested.

(5) If a pre-sentence report made in respect of a young person is submitted to a youth justice court in writing, the court

  (*a*) shall, subject to subsection (7), cause a copy of the report to be given to
    (i) the young person,
    (ii) any parent of the young person who is in attendance at the proceedings against the young person,
    (iii) any counsel representing the young person, and
    (iv) the prosecutor; and

  (*b*) may cause a copy of the report to be given to a parent of the young person who is not in attendance at the proceedings if the parent is, in the opinion of the court, taking an active interest in the proceedings.

(6) If a pre-sentence report made in respect of a young person is submitted to a youth justice court, the young person, his or her counsel or the adult assisting the

young person under subsection 25(7) and the prosecutor shall, subject to subsection (7), on application to the court, be given the opportunity to cross-examine the person who made the report.

(7) If a pre-sentence report made in respect of a young person is submitted to a youth justice court, the court may, when the prosecutor is a private prosecutor and disclosure of all or part of the report to the prosecutor might, in the opinion of the court, be prejudicial to the young person and is not, in the opinion of the court, necessary for the prosecution of the case against the young person,

  (*a*) withhold the report or part from the prosecutor, if the report is submitted in writing; or

  (*b*) exclude the prosecutor from the court during the submission of the report or part, if the report is submitted orally in court.

(8) If a pre-sentence report made in respect of a young person is submitted to a youth justice court, the court

  (*a*) shall, on request, cause a copy or a transcript of the report to be supplied to
    (i)   any court that is dealing with matters relating to the young person, and
    (ii) any youth worker to whom the young person's case has been assigned; and

  (*b*) may, on request, cause a copy or a transcript of all or part of the report to be supplied to any person not otherwise authorized under this section to receive a copy or a transcript of the report if, in the opinion of the court, the person has a valid interest in the proceedings.

(9) A provincial director who submits a pre-sentence report made in respect of a young person to a youth justice court may make all or part of the report available to any person in whose custody or under whose supervision the young person is placed or to any other person who is directly assisting in the care or treatment of the young person.

(10) No statement made by a young person in the course of the preparation of a pre-sentence report in respect of the young person is admissible in evidence against any young person in civil or criminal proceedings except those under section 42 (youth sentences), 59 (review of non-custodial sentence) or 71 (hearing — adult sentences) or any of sections 94 to 96 (reviews and other proceedings related to custodial sentences).

Youth Sentences

RECOMMENDATION OF CONFERENCE.

41. When a youth justice court finds a young person guilty of an offence, the court may convene or cause to be convened a conference under section 19 for recommendations to the court on an appropriate youth sentence.

CONSIDERATIONS AS TO YOUTH SENTENCE / Youth sentence / Agreement of provincial director / Youth justice court statement / Deferred custody and supervision order / Application of sections 106 to 109 / Intensive rehabilitative custody and supervision order / Safeguard of rights / Determination by court / Appeals / Inconsistency / Coming into force of youth sentence / Consecutive youth sentences / Duration of youth sentence for a single offence / Duration of youth sentence for different offences / Duration of youth sentences made at different times / Sentence continues when adult.

42. (1) A youth justice court shall, before imposing a youth sentence, consider any recommendations submitted under section 41, any pre-sentence report, any representations made by the parties to the proceedings or their counsel or agents and by the parents of the young person, and any other relevant information before the court.

(2) When a youth justice court finds a young person guilty of an offence and is imposing a youth sentence, the court shall, subject to this section, impose any one of the following sanctions or any number of them that are not inconsistent with each other and, if the offence is first degree murder or second degree murder within the meaning of section 231 of the *Criminal Code*, the court shall impose a sanction set out in paragraph (*q*) or subparagraph (*r*)(ii) or (iii) and may impose any other of the sanctions set out in this subsection that the court considers appropriate:

(*a*) reprimand the young person;

(*b*) by order direct that the young person be discharged absolutely, if the court considers it to be in the best interests of the young person and not contrary to the public interest;

(*c*) by order direct that the young person be discharged on any conditions imposed by the court in accordance with paragraph 38(2)(*e*.1) and may require the young person to report to and be supervised by the provincial director;

(*d*) impose on the young person a fine not exceeding $1,000 to be paid at the time and on the terms that the court may fix;

(*e*) order the young person to pay to any other person at the times and on the terms that the court may fix an amount by way of compensation for loss of or damage to property or for loss of income or support, or an amount for, in the Province of Quebec, pre-trial pecuniary loss or, in any other province, special damages, for personal injury arising from the commission of the offence if the value is readily ascertainable, but no order shall be made for other damages in the Province of Quebec or for general damages in any other province;

(*f*) order the young person to make restitution to any other person of any property obtained by the young person as a result of the commission of the offence within the time that the court may fix, if the property is owned by the other person or was, at the time of the offence, in his or her lawful possession;

(*g*) if property obtained as a result of the commission of the offence has been sold to an innocent purchaser, where restitution of the property to its owner or any other person has been made or ordered, order the young person to pay the purchaser, at the time and on the terms that the court may fix, an amount not exceeding the amount paid by the purchaser for the property;

(*h*) subject to section 54, order the young person to compensate any person in kind or by way of personal services at the time and on the terms that the court may fix for any loss, damage or injury suffered by that person in respect of which an order may be made under paragraph (*e*) or (*g*);

(*i*) subject to section 54, order the young person to perform a community service at the time and on the terms that the court may fix, and to report to and be supervised by the provincial director or a person designated by the youth justice court;

(*j*) subject to section 51 (mandatory prohibition order), make any order of prohibition, seizure or forfeiture that may be imposed under any Act of Parliament or any regulation made under it if an accused is found guilty or convicted of that offence, other than an order under section 161 of the *Criminal Code*;

(*k*) place the young person on probation in accordance with sections 55 and 56 (conditions and other matters related to probation orders) for a specified period not exceeding two years;

(*l*) subject to subsection (3) (agreement of provincial director), order the young person into an intensive support and supervision program approved by the provincial director;

(*m*) subject to subsection (3) (agreement of provincial director) and section 54, order the young person to attend a non-residential program approved by the provincial director, at the times and on the terms that the court may fix, for a maximum of two hundred and forty hours, over a period not exceeding six months;

(*n*) make a custody and supervision order with respect to the young person, ordering that a period be served in custody and that a second period — which is one half as long as the first — be served, subject to sections 97 (conditions to be included) and 98 (continuation of custody), under supervision in the community subject to conditions, the total of the periods not to exceed two years from the date of the coming into force of the order or, if the young person is found guilty of an offence for which the punishment provided by the *Criminal Code* or any other Act of Parliament is imprisonment for life, three years from the date of coming into force of the order;

(*o*) in the case of an offence set out in section 239 (attempt to commit murder), 232, 234 or 236 (manslaughter) or 273 (aggravated sexual assault) of the *Criminal Code*, make a custody and supervision order in respect of the young person for a specified period not exceeding three years from the date of committal that orders the young person to be committed into a continuous period of custody for the first portion of the sentence and, subject to subsection 104(1) (continuation of custody), to serve the remainder of the sentence under conditional supervision in the community in accordance with section 105;

(*p*) subject to subsection (5), make a deferred custody and supervision order that is for a specified period not exceeding six months, subject to the conditions set out in subsection 105(2), and to any conditions set out in subsection 105(3) that the court considers appropriate;

(*q*) order the young person to serve a sentence not to exceed

   (i) in the case of first degree murder, ten years comprised of

     (A) a committal to custody, to be served continuously, for a period that must not, subject to subsection 104(1) (continuation of custody), exceed six years from the date of committal, and

     (B) a placement under conditional supervision to be served in the community in accordance with section 105, and

   (ii) in the case of second degree murder, seven years comprised of

     (A) a committal to custody, to be served continuously, for a period that must not, subject to subsection 104(1) (continuation of custody), exceed four years from the date of committal, and

     (B) a placement under conditional supervision to be served in the community in accordance with section 105;

(*r*) subject to subsection (7), make an intensive rehabilitative custody and supervision order in respect of the young person

   (i) that is for a specified period that must not exceed

     (A) two years from the date of committal, or

     (B) if the young person is found guilty of an offence for which the punishment provided by the *Criminal Code* or any other Act of Parliament is imprisonment for life, three years from the date of committal,

and that orders the young person to be committed into a continuous period of intensive rehabilitative custody for the first portion of the sentence and, subject to subsection 104(1) (continuation of custody), to serve the remainder under conditional supervision in the community in accordance with section 105,

   (ii) that is for a specified period that must not exceed, in the case of first degree murder, ten years from the date of committal, comprising

     (A) a committal to intensive rehabilitative custody, to be served continuously, for a period that must not exceed six years from the date of committal, and

     (B) subject to subsection 104(1) (continuation of custody), a placement under conditional supervision to be served in the community in accordance with section 105, and

   (iii) that is for a specified period that must not exceed, in the case of second degree murder, seven years from the date of committal, comprising

     (A) a committal to intensive rehabilitative custody, to be served continuously, for a period that must not exceed four years from the date of committal, and

     (B) subject to subsection 104(1) (continuation of custody), a placement under conditional supervision to be served in the community in accordance with section 105; and

(*s*) impose on the young person, in accordance with paragraph 38(2)(*e*.1), any other conditions that the court considers appropriate.

(3) A youth justice court may make an order under paragraph (2)(*l*) or (*m*) only if the provincial director has determined that a program to enforce the order is available.

(4) When the youth justice court makes a custody and supervision order with respect to a young person under paragraph (2)(*n*), the court shall state the following with respect to that order:

> You are ordered to serve (state the number of days or months to be served) in custody, to be followed by (state one-half of the number of days or months stated above) to be served under supervision in the community subject to conditions.
>
> If you breach any of the conditions while you are under supervision in the community, you may be brought back into custody and required to serve the rest of the second period in custody as well.
>
> You should also be aware that, under other provisions of the Youth Criminal Justice Act, a court could require you to serve the second period in custody as well.
>
> The periods in custody and under supervision in the community may be changed if you are or become subject to another sentence.

(5) The court may make a deferred custody and supervision order under paragraph (2)(*p*) if

   (*a*) the young person is found guilty of an offence other than one in the commission of which a young person causes or attempts to cause serious bodily harm; and

   (*b*) it is consistent with the purpose and principles set out in section 38 and the restrictions on custody set out in section 39.

(6) Sections 106 to 109 (suspension of conditional supervision) apply to a breach of a deferred custody and supervision order made under paragraph (2)(*p*) as if the breach were a breach of an order for conditional supervision made under subsection 105(1) and, for the purposes of sections 106 to 109, supervision under a deferred custody and supervision order is deemed to be conditional supervision.

(7) A youth justice court may make an intensive rehabilitative custody and supervision order under paragraph (2)(*r*) in respect of a young person only if

   (*a*) either

      (i) the young person has been found guilty of a serious violent offence, or

      (ii) the young person has been found guilty of an offence, in the commission of which the young person caused or attempted to cause serious bodily harm and for which an adult is liable to imprisonment for a term of more than two years, and the young person had previously been found guilty at least twice of such an offence;

   (*b*) the young person is suffering from a mental illness or disorder, a psychological disorder or an emotional disturbance;

   (*c*) a plan of treatment and intensive supervision has been developed for the young person, and there are reasonable grounds to believe that the plan might reduce the risk of the young person repeating the offence or committing a serious violent offence; and (*d*) the provincial director has determined that an intensive rehabilitative custody and supervision program is available and that the young person's participation in the program is appropriate.

(8) Nothing in this section abrogates or derogates from the rights of a young person regarding consent to physical or mental health treatment or care.

(9) and (10) [*Repealed*, 2012, c. 1, s. 174(4).]

(11) An order may not be made under paragraphs (2)(*k*) to (*m*) in respect of an offence for which a conditional discharge has been granted under paragraph (2)(*c*).

(12) A youth sentence or any part of it comes into force on the date on which it is imposed or on any later date that the youth justice court specifies.

(13) Subject to subsections (15) and (16), a youth justice court that sentences a young person may direct that a sentence imposed on the young person under paragraph (2)(*n*), (*o*), (*q*) or (*r*) be served consecutively if the young person
(*a*) is sentenced while under sentence for an offence under any of those paragraphs; or
(*b*) is found guilty of more than one offence under any of those paragraphs.

(14) No youth sentence, other than an order made under paragraph (2)(*j*), (*n*), (*o*), (*q*) or (*r*), shall continue in force for more than two years. If the youth sentence comprises more than one sanction imposed at the same time in respect of the same offence, the combined duration of the sanctions shall not exceed two years, unless the sentence includes a sanction under paragraph (2)(*j*), (*n*), (*o*), (*q*) or (*r*) that exceeds two years.

(15) Subject to subsection (16), if more than one youth sentence is imposed under this section in respect of a young person with respect to different offences, the continuous combined duration of those youth sentences shall not exceed three years, except if one of the offences is first degree murder or second degree murder within the meaning of section 231 of the *Criminal Code*, in which case the continuous combined duration of those youth sentences shall not exceed ten years in the case of first degree murder, or seven years in the case of second degree murder.

(16) If a youth sentence is imposed in respect of an offence committed by a young person after the commencement of, but before the completion of, any youth sentences imposed on the young person,
(*a*) the duration of the sentence imposed in respect of the subsequent offence shall be determined in accordance with subsections (14) and (15);
(*b*) the sentence may be served consecutively to the sentences imposed in respect of the previous offences; and
(*c*) the combined duration of all the sentences may exceed three years and, if the offence is, or one of the previous offences was,
   (i) first degree murder within the meaning of section 231 of the *Criminal Code*, the continuous combined duration of the youth sentences may exceed ten years, or
   (ii) second degree murder within the meaning of section 231 of the *Criminal Code*, the continuous combined duration of the youth sentences may exceed seven years.

(17) Subject to sections 89, 92 and 93 (provisions related to placement in adult facilities) of this Act and section 743.5 (transfer of jurisdiction) of the *Criminal Code*, a youth sentence imposed on a young person continues in effect in accordance with its terms after the young person becomes an adult. 2012, c. 1, s. 174; 2019, c. 25, s. 373.

ADDITIONAL YOUTH SENTENCES.

43. Subject to subsection 42(15) (duration of youth sentences), if a young person who is subject to a custodial sentence imposed under paragraph 42(2)(*n*), (*o*), (*q*) or (*r*) that has not expired receives an additional youth sentence under one of those paragraphs, the young person is, for the purposes of the *Corrections and Conditional Release Act*, the *Criminal Code*, the *Prisons and Reformatories Act* and this Act, deemed to have been sentenced to one youth sentence commencing at the beginning of the first of those youth sentences to be served and ending on the expiry of the last of them to be served.

CUSTODIAL PORTION IF ADDITIONAL YOUTH SENTENCE.

44. Subject to subsection 42(15) (duration of youth sentences) and section 46 (exception when youth sentence in respect of earlier offence), if an additional youth sentence under paragraph 42(2)(*n*), (*o*), (*q*) or (*r*) is imposed on a young person on whom a youth sentence had already been imposed under one of those paragraphs that has not expired and the expiry date of the youth sentence that includes the additional youth sentence, as determined in accordance with section 43, is later than the expiry date of the youth sentence that the young person was serving before the additional youth sentence was imposed, the custodial portion of the young person's youth sentence is, from the date the additional sentence is imposed, the total of

    (*a*) the unexpired portion of the custodial portion of the youth sentence before the additional youth sentence was imposed, and

    (*b*) the relevant period set out in subparagraph (i), (ii) or (iii):

        (i) if the additional youth sentence is imposed under paragraph 42(2)(*n*), the period that is two thirds of the period that constitutes the difference between the expiry of the youth sentence as determined in accordance with section 43 and the expiry of the youth sentence that the young person was serving before the additional youth sentence was imposed,

       (ii) if the additional youth sentence is a concurrent youth sentence imposed under paragraph 42(2)(*o*), (*q*) or (*r*), the custodial portion of the youth sentence imposed under that paragraph that extends beyond the expiry date of the custodial portion of the sentence being served before the imposition of the additional sentence, or

      (iii) if the additional youth sentence is a consecutive youth sentence imposed under paragraph 42(2)(*o*), (*q*) or (*r*), the custodial portion of the additional youth sentence imposed under that paragraph.

SUPERVISION WHEN ADDITIONAL YOUTH SENTENCE EXTENDS THE PERIOD IN CUSTODY / Supervision when additional youth sentence does not extend the period in custody / Supervision when youth sentence additional to supervision.

45. (1) If a young person has begun to serve a portion of a youth sentence in the community subject to conditions under paragraph 42(2)(*n*) or under conditional supervision under paragraph 42(2)(*o*), (*q*) or (*r*) at the time an additional youth sentence is imposed under one of those paragraphs, and, as a result of the application of section 44, the custodial portion of the young person's youth sentence ends on a day that is later than the day on which the young person received the additional youth sentence, the serving of a portion of the youth sentence under supervision in the community subject to conditions or under conditional supervision shall become inoperative and the young person shall be committed to custody under paragraph 102(1)(*b*) or 106(*b*) until the end of the extended portion of the youth sentence to be served in custody.

(2) If a youth sentence has been imposed under paragraph 42(2)(*n*), (*o*), (*q*) or (*r*) on a young person who is under supervision in the community subject to conditions under paragraph 42(2)(*n*) or under conditional supervision under paragraph 42(2)(*o*), (*q*) or (*r*), and the additional youth sentence would not modify the expiry date of the youth sentence that the young person was serving at the time the additional youth sentence was imposed, the young person may be remanded to the youth custody facility that the provincial director considers appropriate. The provincial director shall review the case and, no later than forty-eight hours after the remand of the young person, shall either refer the case to the youth justice court for a review under section 103 or 109 or release the young person to continue the supervision in the community or the conditional supervision.

(3) If a youth sentence has been imposed under paragraph 42(2)(*n*), (*o*), (*q*) or (*r*) on a young person who is under conditional supervision under paragraph 94(19)(*b*) or subsection 96(5), the young person shall be remanded to the youth custody facility that the provincial director considers appropriate. The provincial director shall review the case and, no later than forty-eight hours after the remand of the young person, shall either refer the case to the youth justice court for a review under section 103 or 109 or release the young person to continue the conditional supervision.

EXCEPTION WHEN YOUTH SENTENCE IN RESPECT OF EARLIER OFFENCE.

46. The total of the custodial portions of a young person's youth sentences shall not exceed six years calculated from the beginning of the youth sentence that is determined in accordance with section 43 if

(*a*) a youth sentence is imposed under paragraph 42(2)(*n*), (*o*), (*q*) or (*r*) on the young person already serving a youth sentence under one of those paragraphs; and

(*b*) the later youth sentence imposed is in respect of an offence committed before the commencement of the earlier youth sentence.

COMMITTAL TO CUSTODY DEEMED CONTINUOUS / Intermittent custody / Availability of place of intermittent custody.

47. (1) Subject to subsections (2) and (3), a young person who is sentenced under paragraph 42(2)(*n*) is deemed to be committed to continuous custody for the custodial portion of the sentence.

(2) If the sentence does not exceed ninety days, the youth justice court may order that the custodial portion of the sentence be served intermittently if it is consistent with the purpose and principles set out in section 38.

(3) Before making an order of committal to intermittent custody, the youth justice court shall require the prosecutor to make available to the court for its consideration a report of the provincial director as to the availability of a youth custody facility in which an order of intermittent custody can be enforced and, if the report discloses that no such youth custody facility is available, the court shall not make the order.

REASONS FOR THE SENTENCE.

48. When a youth justice court imposes a youth sentence, it shall state its reasons for the sentence in the record of the case and shall, on request, give or cause to be given a copy of the sentence and the reasons for the sentence to

- (*a*) the young person, the young person's counsel, a parent of the young person, the provincial director and the prosecutor; and
- (*b*) in the case of a committal to custody under paragraph 42(2)(*n*), (*o*), (*q*) or (*r*), the review board.

WARRANT OF COMMITTAL / Custody during transfer / Subsection 30(3) applies.

49. (1) When a young person is committed to custody, the youth justice court shall issue or cause to be issued a warrant of committal.

(2) A young person who is committed to custody may, in the course of being transferred from custody to the court or from the court to custody, be held under the supervision and control of a peace officer or in any place of temporary detention referred to in subsection 30(1) that the provincial director may specify.

(3) Subsection 30(3) (detention separate from adults) applies, with any modifications that the circumstances require, in respect of a person held in a place of temporary detention under subsection (2).

APPLICATION OF PART XXIII OF CRIMINAL CODE / Section 787 of *Criminal Code* does not apply / Reasons for the prohibition order / Reasons / Application of *Criminal Code*.

50. (1) Subject to section 74 (application of *Criminal Code* to adult sentences), Part XXIII (sentencing) of the *Criminal Code* does not apply in respect of proceedings under this Act except for paragraph 718.2(*e*) (sentencing principle for aboriginal offenders), sections 722 (victim impact statements), 722.1 (copy of statement) and 722.2 (inquiry by court), subsection 730(2) (court process continues in force) and sections 748 (pardons and remissions), 748.1 (remission by the Governor in Council) and 749 (royal prerogative) of that Act, which provisions apply with any modifications that the circumstances require.

(2) Section 787 (general penalty) of the *Criminal Code* does not apply in respect of proceedings under this Act.

MANDATORY PROHIBITION ORDER / Duration of prohibition order / Discretionary prohibition order / Duration of prohibition order / Report.

51. (1) Despite section 42 (youth sentences), when a young person is found guilty of an offence referred to in any of paragraphs 109(1)(*a*) to (*d*) of the *Criminal Code*, the youth justice court shall, in addition to imposing a sentence under section 42 (youth sentences), make an order prohibiting the young person from possessing any firearm, cross-bow, prohibited weapon, restricted weapon, prohibited device, ammunition, prohibited ammunition or explosive substance during the period specified in the order as determined in accordance with subsection (2).

(2) An order made under subsection (1) begins on the day on which the order is made and ends not earlier than two years after the young person has completed the custodial portion of the sentence or, if the young person is not subject to custody, after the time the young person is found guilty of the offence.

(3) Despite section 42 (youth sentences), where a young person is found guilty of an offence referred to in paragraph 110(1)(*a*) or (*b*) of the *Criminal Code*, the youth justice court shall, in addition to imposing a sentence under section 42 (youth sentences), consider whether it is desirable, in the interests of the safety of the young person or of any other person, to make an order prohibiting the young person from possessing any firearm, cross-bow, prohibited weapon, restricted weapon, prohibited device, ammunition, prohibited ammunition or explosive substance, or all such things, and where the court decides that it is so desirable, the court shall so order.

(4) An order made under subsection (3) against a young person begins on the day on which the order is made and ends not later than two years after the young person has completed the custodial portion of the sentence or, if the young person is not subject to custody, after the time the young person is found guilty of the offence.

(5) When a youth justice court makes an order under this section, it shall state its reasons for making the order in the record of the case and shall give or cause to be given a copy of the order and, on request, a transcript or copy of the reasons to the young person against whom the order was made, the counsel and a parent of the young person and the provincial director.

(6) When the youth justice court does not make an order under subsection (3), or when the youth justice court does make such an order but does not prohibit the possession of everything referred to in that subsection, the youth justice court shall include in the record a statement of the youth justice court's reasons.

(7) Sections 113 to 117 (firearm prohibition orders) of the *Criminal Code* apply in respect of any order made under this section.

(8) Before making an order referred to in section 113 (lifting firearms order) of the *Criminal Code* in respect of a young person, the youth justice court may require the provincial director to cause to be prepared, and to submit to the youth justice court, a report on the young person.

REVIEW OF ORDER MADE UNDER SECTION 51 / Grounds / Decision of review / New order not to be more onerous / Application of provisions.

52. (1) A youth justice court may, on application, review an order made under section 51 at any time after the end of the period set out in subsection 119(2) (period of access to records) that applies to the record of the offence that resulted in the order being made.

(2) In conducting a review under this section, the youth justice court shall take into account
- (a) the nature and circumstances of the offence in respect of which the order was made; and
- (b) the safety of the young person and of other persons.

(3) When a youth justice court conducts a review under this section, it may, after giving the young person, a parent of the young person, the Attorney General and the provincial director an opportunity to be heard,
- (a) confirm the order;
- (b) revoke the order; or
- (c) vary the order as it considers appropriate in the circumstances of the case.

(4) No variation of an order made under paragraph (3)(c) may be more onerous than the order being reviewed.

(5) Subsections 59(3) to (5) apply, with any modifications that the circumstances require, in respect of a review under this section.

FUNDING FOR VICTIMS / Victim fine surcharge.

53. (1) The lieutenant governor in council of a province may order that, in respect of any fine imposed in the province under paragraph 42(2)(d), a percentage of the fine as fixed by the lieutenant governor in council be used to provide such assistance to victims of offences as the lieutenant governor in council may direct from time to time.

(2) If the lieutenant governor in council of a province has not made an order under subsection (1), a youth justice court that imposes a fine on a young person under paragraph 42(2)(d) may, in addition to any other punishment imposed on the young person, order the young person to pay a victim fine surcharge in an amount not exceeding fifteen per cent of the fine. The surcharge shall be used to provide such assistance to victims of offences as the lieutenant governor in council of the province in which the surcharge is imposed may direct from time to time.

WHERE A FINE OR OTHER PAYMENT IS ORDERED / Discharge of fine or surcharge / Rates, crediting and other matters / Representations respecting orders under paragraphs 42(2)(*e*) to (*h*) / Notice of orders under paragraphs 42(2)(*e*) to (*h*) / Consent of person to be compensated / Orders under paragraph 42(2)(*h*), (*i*) or (*m*) / Duration of order for service / Community service order / Application for further time to complete youth sentence.

54. (1) The youth justice court shall, in imposing a fine under paragraph 42(2)(*d*) or in making an order under paragraph 42(2)(*e*) or (*g*), have regard to the present and future means of the young person to pay.

(2) A young person on whom a fine is imposed under paragraph 42(2)(*d*), including any percentage of a fine imposed under subsection 53(1), or on whom a victim fine surcharge is imposed under subsection 53(2), may discharge the fine or surcharge in whole or in part by earning credits for work performed in a program established for that purpose

    (*a*) by the lieutenant governor in council of the province in which the fine or surcharge was imposed; or

    (*b*) by the lieutenant governor in council of the province in which the young person resides, if an appropriate agreement is in effect between the government of that province and the government of the province in which the fine or surcharge was imposed.

(3) A program referred to in subsection (2) shall determine the rate at which credits are earned and may provide for the manner of crediting any amounts earned against the fine or surcharge and any other matters necessary for or incidental to carrying out the program.

(4) In considering whether to make an order under any of paragraphs 42(2)(*e*) to (*h*), the youth justice court may consider any representations made by the person who would be compensated or to whom restitution or payment would be made.

(5) If the youth justice court makes an order under any of paragraphs 42(2)(*e*) to (*h*), it shall cause notice of the terms of the order to be given to the person who is to be compensated or to whom restitution or payment is to be made.

(6) No order may be made under paragraph 42(2)(*h*) unless the youth justice court has secured the consent of the person to be compensated.

(7) No order may be made under paragraph 42(2)(*h*), (*i*) or (*m*) unless the youth justice court is satisfied that

    (*a*) the young person against whom the order is made is a suitable candidate for such an order; and

    (*b*) the order does not interfere with the normal hours of work or education of the young person.

(8) No order may be made under paragraph 42(2)(*h*) or (*i*) to perform personal or community services unless those services can be completed in two hundred and forty hours or less and within twelve months after the date of the order.

(9) No order may be made under paragraph 42(2)(*i*) unless

    (*a*) the community service to be performed is part of a program that is approved by the provincial director; or

YOUTH

(b)   the youth justice court is satisfied that the person or organization for whom the community service is to be performed has agreed to its performance.

(10) A youth justice court may, on application by or on behalf of the young person in respect of whom a youth sentence has been imposed under any of paragraphs 42(2)(d) to (i), allow further time for the completion of the sentence subject to any regulations made under paragraph 155(b) and to any rules made by the youth justice court under subsection 17(1).

CONDITION THAT MUST APPEAR IN ORDERS / Conditions that may appear in orders.

55. (1) The youth justice court shall prescribe, as a condition of an order made under paragraph 42(2)(k) or (l), that the young person appear before the youth justice court when required by the court to do so.

(2) A youth justice court may, in accordance with paragraph 38(2)(e.1), prescribe as conditions of an order made under paragraph 42(2)(k) or (l) that a young person do one or more of the following:

(a)   report to and be supervised by the provincial director or a person designated by the youth justice court;

(b)   notify the clerk of the youth justice court, the provincial director or the youth worker assigned to the case of any change of address or any change in the young person's place of employment, education or training;

(c)   remain within the territorial jurisdiction of one or more courts named in the order;

(d)   make reasonable efforts to obtain and maintain suitable employment;

(e)   attend school or any other place of learning, training or recreation that is appropriate, if the youth justice court is satisfied that a suitable program for the young person is available there;

(f)   reside with a parent, or any other adult that the youth justice court considers appropriate, who is willing to provide for the care and maintenance of the young person;

(g)   reside at a place that the provincial director may specify;

(h)   comply with any other conditions set out in the order that the youth justice court considers appropriate; and

(i)   not own, possess or have the control of any weapon, ammunition, prohibited ammunition, prohibited device or explosive substance, except as authorized by the order. 2019, c. 25, s. 374.

COMMUNICATION OF ORDER / Copy of order to parent / Endorsement of order by young person / Validity of order / Commencement of order / Effect of order in case of custody / Notice to appear / Warrant in default of appearance.

56. (1) A youth justice court that makes an order under paragraph 42(2)(k) or (l) shall

(a)   cause the order to be read by or to the young person bound by it;

(*b*) explain or cause to be explained to the young person the purpose and effect of the order, and confirm that the young person understands it; and

(*c*) cause a copy of the order to be given to the young person, and to any parent of the young person who is in attendance at the sentencing hearing.

(2) A youth justice court that makes an order under paragraph 42(2)(*k*) or (*l*) may cause a copy to be given to a parent of the young person who is not in attendance at the proceedings if the parent is, in the opinion of the court, taking an active interest in the proceedings.

(3) After the order has been read and explained under subsection (1), the young person shall endorse on the order an acknowledgement that the young person has received a copy of the order and had its purpose and effect explained.

(4) The failure of a young person to endorse the order or of a parent to receive a copy of the order does not affect the validity of the order.

(5) An order made under paragraph 42(2)(*k*) or (*l*) comes into force

(*a*) on the date on which it is made; or

(*b*) if a young person receives a sentence that includes a period of continuous custody and supervision, at the end of the period of supervision.

(6) If a young person is subject to a sentence that includes both a period of continuous custody and supervision and an order made under paragraph 42(2)(*k*) or (*l*), and the court orders under subsection 42(12) a delay in the start of the period of custody, the court may divide the period that the order made under paragraph 42(2)(*k*) or (*l*) is in effect, with the first portion to have effect from the date on which it is made until the start of the period of custody, and the remainder to take effect at the end of the period of supervision.

(7) A young person may be given notice either orally or in writing to appear before the youth justice court under paragraph 55(1)(*b*).

(8) If service of a notice in writing is proved and the young person fails to attend court in accordance with the notice, a youth justice court may issue a warrant to compel the appearance of the young person.

TRANSFER OF YOUTH SENTENCE / No transfer outside province before appeal completed / Transfer to a province when person is adult.

57. (1) When a youth sentence has been imposed under any of paragraphs 42(2)(*d*) to (*i*), (*k*), (*l*) or (*s*) in respect of a young person and the young person or a parent with whom the young person resides is or becomes a resident of a territorial division outside the jurisdiction of the youth justice court that imposed the youth sentence, whether in the same or in another province, a youth justice court judge in the territorial division in which the youth sentence was imposed may, on the application of the Attorney General or on the application of the young person or the young person's parent, with the consent of the Attorney General, transfer to a youth justice court in another territorial division the youth sentence and any portion of the record of the case that is appropriate. All subsequent proceedings relating to the case shall then be carried out and enforced by that court.

(2) No youth sentence may be transferred from one province to another under this section until the time for an appeal against the youth sentence or the finding on which the youth sentence was based has expired or until all proceedings in respect of any such appeal have been completed.

(3) When an application is made under subsection (1) to transfer the youth sentence of a young person to a province in which the young person is an adult, a youth justice court judge may, with the consent of the Attorney General, transfer the youth sentence and the record of the case to the youth justice court in the province to which the transfer is sought, and the youth justice court to which the case is transferred shall have full jurisdiction in respect of the youth sentence as if that court had imposed the youth sentence. The person shall be further dealt with in accordance with this Act.

INTERPROVINCIAL ARRANGEMENTS / Youth justice court retains jurisdiction / Waiver of jurisdiction.

58. (1) When a youth sentence has been imposed under any of paragraphs 42(2)(*k*) to (*r*) in respect of a young person, the youth sentence in one province may be dealt with in any other province in accordance with any agreement that may have been made between those provinces.

(2) Subject to subsection (3), when a youth sentence imposed in respect of a young person is dealt with under this section in a province other than that in which the youth sentence was imposed, the youth justice court of the province in which the youth sentence was imposed retains, for all purposes of this Act, exclusive jurisdiction over the young person as if the youth sentence were dealt with within that province, and any warrant or process issued in respect of the young person may be executed or served in any place in Canada outside the province where the youth sentence was imposed as if it were executed or served in that province.

(3) When a youth sentence imposed in respect of a young person is dealt with under this section in a province other than the one in which the youth sentence was imposed, the youth justice court of the province in which the youth sentence was imposed may, with the consent in writing of the Attorney General of that province and the young person, waive its jurisdiction, for the purpose of any proceeding under this Act, to the youth justice court of the province in which the youth sentence is dealt with, in which case the youth justice court in the province in which the youth sentence is dealt with shall have full jurisdiction in respect of the youth sentence as if that court had imposed the youth sentence.

REVIEW OF YOUTH SENTENCES NOT INVOLVING CUSTODY / Grounds for review / Progress report / Subsections 94(10) to (12) apply / Subsections 94(7) and (14) to (18) apply / Compelling appearance of young person / Decision of the youth justice court after review / New youth sentence not to be more onerous / Exception / Exception — paragraph (2)(*c*).

59. (1) When a youth justice court has imposed a youth sentence in respect of a young person, other than a youth sentence under paragraph 42(2)(*n*), (*o*), (*q*) or (*r*), the youth justice court shall, on the application of the young person, the young person's parent, the Attorney General or the provincial director, review the youth sentence if the court is satisfied that there are grounds for a review under subsection (2).

(2) A review of a youth sentence may be made under this section

  (*a*) on the ground that the circumstances that led to the youth sentence have changed materially;

  (*b*) on the ground that the young person in respect of whom the review is to be made is unable to comply with or is experiencing serious difficulty in complying with the terms of the youth sentence;

  (*c*) on the ground that the young person in respect of whom the review is to be made has contravened a condition of an order made under paragraph 42(2)(*k*) or (*l*) without reasonable excuse;

  (*d*) on the ground that the terms of the youth sentence are adversely affecting the opportunities available to the young person to obtain services, education or employment; or

  (*e*) on any other ground that the youth justice court considers appropriate.

(3) The youth justice court may, before reviewing under this section a youth sentence imposed in respect of a young person, require the provincial director to cause to be prepared, and to submit to the youth justice court, a progress report on the performance of the young person since the youth sentence took effect.

(4) Subsections 94(10) to (12) apply, with any modifications that the circumstances require, in respect of any progress report required under subsection (3).

(5) Subsections 94(7) and (14) to (18) apply, with any modifications that the circumstances require, in respect of reviews made under this section and any notice required under subsection 94(14) shall also be given to the provincial director.

(6) The youth justice court may, by summons or warrant, compel a young person in respect of whom a review is to be made under this section to appear before the youth justice court for the purposes of the review.

(7) When a youth justice court reviews under this section a youth sentence imposed in respect of a young person, it may, after giving the young person, a parent of the young person, the Attorney General and the provincial director an opportunity to be heard,

  (*a*) confirm the youth sentence;

  (*b*) terminate the youth sentence and discharge the young person from any further obligation of the youth sentence; or

  (*c*) vary the youth sentence or impose any new youth sentence under section 42, other than a committal to custody, for any period of time, not exceeding the remainder of the period of the earlier youth sentence, that the court considers appropriate in the circumstances of the case.

(8) Subject to subsections (9) and (10), when a youth sentence imposed in respect of a young person is reviewed under this section, no youth sentence imposed under subsection (7) shall, without the consent of the young person, be more onerous than the remainder of the youth sentence reviewed.

(9) A youth justice court may under this section extend the time within which a youth sentence imposed under paragraphs 42(2)(*d*) to (*i*) is to be complied with by a young person if the court is satisfied that the young person requires more time to comply with the youth sentence, but in no case shall the extension be for a period of time that expires more than twelve months after the date the youth sentence would otherwise have expired.

(10) In the case of a review of a youth sentence made on the ground set out in paragraph (2)(*c*), the youth justice court may, in accordance with paragraph 38(2)(*e*.1), impose on the young person additional or more onerous conditions if it is of the opinion that the conditions

   (*a*) would better protect against the risk of harm to the safety of the public that the young person might otherwise present; or

   (*b*) would assist the young person to comply with any conditions previously imposed as part of that sentence. 2019, c. 25, s. 375.

PROVISIONS APPLICABLE TO YOUTH SENTENCES ON REVIEW.

60. This Part and Part 5 (custody and supervision) apply with any modifications that the circumstances require to orders made in respect of reviews of youth sentences under sections 59 and 94 to 96.

Adult Sentence and Election

61. [*Repealed.* 2012, c. 1, s. 175.]

62. [*Repealed.* 2012, c. 1, s. 175.]

63. [*Repealed.* 2012, c. 1, s. 175.]

APPLICATION BY ATTORNEY GENERAL / Obligation / Order fixing age / Notice of intention to seek adult sentence / Notice to young person.

64. (1) The Attorney General may, before evidence is called as to sentence or, if no evidence is called, before submissions are made as to sentence, make an application to the youth justice court for an order that a young person is liable to an adult sentence if the young person is or has been found guilty of an offence for which an adult is liable to imprisonment for a term of more than two years and that was committed after the young person attained the age of 14 years.

(1.1) [*Repealed,* 2019, c. 25, s. 376.]

(1.2) [*Repealed,* 2019, c. 25, s. 376.]

(2) If the Attorney General intends to seek an adult sentence for an offence by making an application under subsection (1), the Attorney General shall, before the young person enters a plea or with leave of the youth justice court before the commencement of the trial, give notice to the young person and the youth justice court of the intention to seek an adult sentence.

(3) A notice of intention to seek an adult sentence given in respect of an offence is notice in respect of any included offence of which the young person is found guilty for which an adult is liable to imprisonment for a term of more than two years. 2012, c. 1, s. 176; 2019, c. 25, s. 376.

(4) and (5) [*Repealed*. 2012, c. 1, s. 176(2).]

65. [*Repealed*. 2012, c. 1, s. 177.]

66. [*Repealed*. 2012, c. 1, s. 177.]

ELECTION — ADULT SENTENCE / Wording of election / Election — Nunavut / Wording of election / Mode of trial where co-accused are young persons / Attorney General may require trial by jury / Preliminary inquiry / Preliminary inquiry if two or more accused / When no request for preliminary inquiry / Preliminary inquiry provisions of *Criminal Code* / Parts XIX and XX of *Criminal Code*.

67. (1) The youth justice court shall, before a young person enters a plea, put the young person to his or her election in the words set out in subsection (2) if

    (a)   [*Repealed*, 2012, c. 1, s. 178(1).]

    (b)   the Attorney General has given notice under subsection 64(2) of the intention to seek an adult sentence for an offence committed after the young person has attained the age of fourteen years;

    (c)   the young person is charged with first or second degree murder within the meaning of section 231 of the *Criminal Code*; or

    (d)   the person to whom section 16 (status of accused uncertain) applies is charged with having, after attaining the age of fourteen years, committed an offence for which an adult would be entitled to an election under section 536 of the *Criminal Code*, or over which a superior court of criminal jurisdiction would have exclusive jurisdiction under section 469 of that Act.

(2) The youth justice court shall put the young person to his or her election in the following words:

> You have the option to elect to be tried by a youth justice court judge without a jury and without having had a preliminary inquiry; or you may elect to be tried by a judge without a jury; or you may elect to be tried by a court composed of a judge and jury. If you do not elect now, you are deemed to have elected to be tried by a court composed of a judge and jury. If you elect to be tried by a judge without a jury or by a court composed of a judge and jury or if you are deemed to have elected to be tried by a court composed of a judge and jury, you will have a preliminary inquiry only if you or the prosecutor requests one. How do you elect to be tried?

(3) In respect of proceedings in Nunavut, the youth justice court shall, before a young person enters a plea, put the young person to his or her election in the words set out in subsection (4) if

    (a)   [*Repealed*, 2012, c. 1, s. 178(2).]

- (b) the Attorney General has given notice under subsection 64(2) of the intention to seek an adult sentence for an offence committed after the young person has attained the age of fourteen years;
- (c) the young person is charged with first or second degree murder within the meaning of section 231 of the *Criminal Code*; or
- (d) the person to whom section 16 (status of accused uncertain) applies is charged with having, after attaining the age of fourteen years, committed an offence for which an adult would be entitled to an election under section 536.1 of the *Criminal Code*.

(4) The youth justice court shall put the young person to his or her election in the following words:

> You have the option to elect to be tried by a judge of the Nunavut Court of Justice alone, acting as a youth justice court without a jury and without a preliminary inquiry; or you may elect to be tried by a judge of the Nunavut Court of Justice, acting as a youth justice court without a jury; or you may elect to be tried by a judge of the Nunavut Court of Justice, acting as a youth justice court with a jury. If you elect to be tried by a judge without a jury or by a judge, acting as a youth justice court, with a jury or if you are deemed to have elected to be tried by a judge, acting as a youth justice court, with a jury, you will have a preliminary inquiry only if you or the prosecutor requests one. How do you elect to be tried?

(5) When two or more young persons who are charged with the same offence, who are jointly charged in the same information or indictment or in respect of whom the Attorney General seeks joinder of counts that are set out in separate informations or indictments are put to their election, then, unless all of them elect or re-elect or are deemed to have elected, as the case may be, the same mode of trial, the youth justice court judge

- (a) may decline to record any election, re-election or deemed election for trial by a youth justice court judge without a jury, a judge without a jury or, in Nunavut, a judge of the Nunavut Court Justice without a jury; and
- (b) if the judge declines to do so, shall hold a preliminary inquiry, if requested to do so by one of the parties, unless a preliminary inquiry has been held prior to the election, re-election or deemed election.

(6) The Attorney General may, even if a young person elects under subsection (1) or (3) to be tried by a youth justice court judge without a jury or a judge without a jury, require the young person to be tried by a court composed of a judge and jury.

(7) When a young person elects to be tried by a judge without a jury, or elects or is deemed to have elected to be tried by a court composed of a judge and jury, the youth justice court referred to in subsection 13(1) shall, on the request of the young person or the prosecutor made at that time or within the period fixed by rules of court made under section 17 or 155 or, if there are no such rules, by the youth justice court judge, conduct a preliminary inquiry and if, on its conclusion, the young person is ordered to stand trial, the proceedings shall be conducted

- (a) before a judge without a jury or a court composed of a judge and jury, as the case may be; or (*b*) in Nunavut, before a judge of the Nunavut Court of Justice acting as a youth justice court, with or without a jury, as the case may be.

(7.1) If two or more young persons are jointly charged in an information and one or more of them make a request for a preliminary inquiry under subsection (7), a preliminary inquiry must be held with respect to all of them.

(7.2) If no request for a preliminary inquiry is made under subsection (7), the youth justice court shall fix the date for the trial or the date on which the young person must appear in the trial court to have the date fixed.

(8) The preliminary inquiry shall be conducted in accordance with the provisions of Part XVIII (procedure on preliminary inquiry) of the *Criminal Code*, except to the extent that they are inconsistent with this Act.

(9) Proceedings under this Act before a judge without a jury or a court composed of a judge and jury or, in Nunavut, a judge of the Nunavut Court of Justice acting as a youth justice court, with or without a jury, as the case may be, shall be conducted in accordance with the provisions of Parts XIX (indictable offences — trial without jury) and XX (procedure in jury trials and general provisions) of the *Criminal Code*, with any modifications that the circumstances require, except that

(*a*) the provisions of this Act respecting the protection of privacy of young persons prevail over the provisions of the *Criminal Code*; and

(*b*) the young person is entitled to be represented in court by counsel if the young person is removed from court in accordance with subsection 650(2) of the *Criminal Code*. 2002, c. 13, s. 91(1)(*b*) to (*e*); 2012, c. 1, s. 178; 2019, c. 13, s. 166.

---

68. [*Repealed*. 2012, c. 1, s. 179.]

INCLUDED OFFENCES.

69. (1) [*Repealed*. 2012, c. 1, s. 180(1).]

(2) If the Attorney General has given notice under subsection 64(2) of the intention to seek an adult sentence and the young person is found guilty of an included offence for which an adult is liable to imprisonment for a term of more than two years, committed after he or she has attained the age of 14 years, the Attorney General may make an application under subsection 64(1) (application for adult sentence). 2012, c. 1, s. 180.

---

70. [*Repealed*. 2012, c. 1, s. 181.]

HEARING — ADULT SENTENCES.

71. The youth justice court shall, at the commencement of the sentencing hearing, hold a hearing in respect of an application under subsection 64(1) (application for adult sentence), unless the court has received notice that the application is not opposed. Both parties and the parents of the young person shall be given an opportunity to be heard at the hearing. 2012, c. 1, s. 182.

ORDER OF ADULT SENTENCE / Order of youth sentence / Onus / Pre-sentence report / Court to state reasons / Appeal.

72. (1) The youth justice court shall order that an adult sentence be imposed if it is satisfied that

    (*a*) the presumption of diminished moral blameworthiness or culpability of the young person is rebutted; and

    (*b*) a youth sentence imposed in accordance with the purpose and principles set out in subparagraph 3(1)(*b*)(ii) and section 38 would not be of sufficient length to hold the young person accountable for his or her offending behaviour.

(1.1) If the youth justice court is not satisfied that an order should be made under subsection (1), it shall order that the young person is not liable to an adult sentence and that a youth sentence must be imposed.

(2) The onus of satisfying the youth justice court as to the matters referred to in subsection (1) is on the Attorney General.

(3) In making an order under subsection (1) or (1.1), the youth justice court shall consider the pre-sentence report.

(4) When the youth justice court makes an order under this section, it shall state the reasons for its decision.

(5) For the purposes of an appeal in accordance with section 37, an order under subsection (1) or (1.1) is part of the sentence. 2012, c. 1, s. 183.

COURT MUST IMPOSE ADULT SENTENCE / Court must impose youth sentence.

73. (1) When the youth justice court makes an order under subsection 72(1) in respect of a young person, the court shall, on a finding of guilt, impose an adult sentence on the young person.

(2) When the youth justice court makes an order under subsection 72(1.1) in respect of a young person, the court shall, on a finding of guilt, impose a youth sentence on the young person. 2012, c. 1, s. 184.

APPLICATION OF PARTS XXIII AND XXIV OF CRIMINAL CODE / Finding of guilt becomes a conviction / Interpretation.

74. (1) Parts XXIII (sentencing) and XXIV (dangerous and long-term offenders) of the *Criminal Code* apply to a young person in respect of whom the youth justice court has ordered that an adult sentence be imposed.

(2) A finding of guilt for an offence in respect of which an adult sentence is imposed becomes a conviction once the time allowed for the taking of an appeal has expired or, if an appeal is taken, all proceedings in respect of the appeal have been completed and the appeal court has upheld an adult sentence.

(3) This section does not affect the time of commencement of an adult sentence under subsection 719(1) of the *Criminal Code*.

75. [*Repealed*, 2019, c. 25, s. 377.]

PLACEMENT WHEN SUBJECT TO ADULT SENTENCE / Young person under age of 18 / Opportunity to be heard / Report / Appeals / Review / Who may make application / Notice / Limit — age twenty.

76. (1) Subject to subsections (2) and (9) and sections 79 and 80 and despite anything else in this Act or any other Act of Parliament, when a young person who is subject to an adult sentence in respect of an offence is sentenced to a term of imprisonment for the offence, the youth justice court shall order that the young person serve any portion of the imprisonment in

 (a) a youth custody facility separate and apart from any adult who is detained or held in custody;

 (b) a provincial correctional facility for adults; or

 (c) if the sentence is for two years or more, a penitentiary.

(2) No young person who is under the age of 18 years is to serve any portion of the imprisonment in a provincial correctional facility for adults or a penitentiary.

(3) Before making an order under subsection (1), the youth justice court shall give the young person, a parent of the young person, the Attorney General, the provincial director and representatives of the provincial and federal correctional systems an opportunity to be heard.

(4) Before making an order under subsection (1), the youth justice court may require that a report be prepared for the purpose of assisting the court.

(5) For the purposes of an appeal in accordance with section 37, an order under subsection (1) is part of the sentence.

(6) On application, the youth justice court shall review the placement of a young person under this section and, if satisfied that the circumstances that resulted in the initial order have changed materially, and after having given the young person, a parent of the young person, the Attorney General, the provincial director and the representatives of the provincial and federal correctional systems an opportunity to be heard, the court may order that the young person be placed in

 (a) a youth custody facility separate and apart from any adult who is detained or held in custody;

 (b) a provincial correctional facility for adults; or

 (c) if the sentence is for two years or more, a penitentiary.

(7) An application referred to in this section may be made by the young person, one of the young person's parents, the provincial director, representatives of the provincial and federal correctional systems and the Attorney General, after the time for all appeals has expired.

(8) When an application referred to in this section is made, the applicant shall cause a notice of the application to be given to the other persons referred to in subsection (7).

(9) No young person shall remain in a youth custody facility under this section after the young person attains the age of twenty years, unless the youth justice court that makes the order under subsection (1) or reviews the placement under

subsection (6) is satisfied that remaining in the youth custody facility would be in the best interests of the young person and would not jeopardize the safety of others. 2012, c. 1, s. 186; 2019, c. 25, s. 378.

OBLIGATION TO INFORM — PAROLE / Applicability of Corrections and Conditional Release Act / Appropriate parole board.

77. (1) When a young person is ordered to serve a portion of a sentence in a youth custody facility under paragraph 76(1)(*a*) (placement when subject to adult sentence), the provincial director shall inform the appropriate parole board.

(2) For greater certainty, Part II of the *Corrections and Conditional Release Act* applies, subject to section 78, with respect to a young person who is the subject of an order under subsection 76(1) (placement when subject to adult sentence).

(3) The appropriate parole board for the purposes of this section is

 (*a*) if subsection 112(1) of the *Corrections and Conditional Release Act* would apply with respect to the young person but for the fact that the young person was ordered into a youth custody facility, the parole board mentioned in that subsection; and

 (*b*) in any other case, the Parole Board of Canada. 2012, c. 1, s. 160(*l*)(i).

RELEASE ENTITLEMENT / Release entitlement.

78. (1) For greater certainty, section 6 of the Prisons and Reformatories Act applies to a young person who is ordered to serve a portion of a sentence in a youth custody facility under paragraph 76(1)(*a*) (placement when subject to adult sentence) only if section 743.1 (rules respecting sentences of two or more years) of the *Criminal Code* would direct that the young person serve the sentence in a prison.

(2) For greater certainty, section 127 of the *Corrections and Conditional Release Act* applies to a young person who is ordered to serve a portion of a sentence in a youth custody facility under paragraph 76(1)(a) (placement when subject to adult sentence) only if section 743.1 (rules respecting sentences of two or more years) of the *Criminal Code* would direct that the young person serve the sentence in a penitentiary.

IF PERSON CONVICTED UNDER ANOTHER ACT.

79. If a person who is serving all or a portion of a sentence in a youth custody facility under paragraph 76(1)(*a*) (placement when subject to adult sentence) is sentenced to a term of imprisonment under an Act of Parliament other than this Act, the remainder of the portion of the sentence being served in the youth custody facility shall be served in a provincial correctional facility for adults or a penitentiary, in accordance with section 743.1 (rules respecting sentences of two or more years) of the *Criminal Code*.

IF PERSON WHO IS SERVING A SENTENCE UNDER ANOTHER ACT IS SENTENCED TO AN ADULT SENTENCE.

80. If a person who has been serving a sentence of imprisonment under an Act of Parliament other than this Act is sentenced to an adult sentence of imprisonment under this Act, the sentences shall be served in a provincial correctional facility for adults or a penitentiary, in accordance with section 743.1 (rules respecting sentences of two or more years) of the *Criminal Code*.

PROCEDURE FOR APPLICATION OR NOTICE.

81. An application or a notice to the court under section 64 or 76 must be made or given orally, in the presence of the other party, or in writing with a copy served personally on the other party. 2012, c. 1, s. 187.

Effect of Termination of Youth Sentence

EFFECT OF ABSOLUTE DISCHARGE OR TERMINATION OF YOUTH SENTENCE / Disqualifications removed / Applications for employment / Finding of guilt not a previous conviction.

82. (1) Subject to section 12 (examination as to previous convictions) of the Canada Evidence Act, if a young person is found guilty of an offence, and a youth justice court directs under paragraph 42(2)(*b*) that the young person be discharged absolutely, or the youth sentence, or any disposition made under the *Young Offenders Act*, chapter Y-1 of the Revised Statutes of Canada, 1985, has ceased to have effect, other than an order under section 51 (mandatory prohibition order) of this Act or section 20.1 (mandatory prohibition order) of the *Young Offenders Act*, the young person is deemed not to have been found guilty or convicted of the offence except that

(*a*) the young person may plead autrefois convict in respect of any subsequent charge relating to the offence;

(*b*) a youth justice court may consider the finding of guilt in considering an application under subsection 64(1) (application for adult sentence);

(*c*) any court or justice may consider the finding of guilt in considering an application for judicial interim release or in considering what sentence to impose for any offence; and

(*d*) the Parole Board of Canada or any provincial parole board may consider the finding of guilt in considering an application for conditional release or for a record suspension under the *Criminal Records Act*.

(2) For greater certainty and without restricting the generality of subsection (1), an absolute discharge under paragraph 42(2)(*b*) or the termination of the youth sentence or disposition in respect of an offence for which a young person is found guilty removes any disqualification in respect of the offence to which the young person is subject under any Act of Parliament by reason of a finding of guilt.

(3) No application form for or relating to the following shall contain any question that by its terms requires the applicant to disclose that he or she has been charged

with or found guilty of an offence in respect of which he or she has, under this Act or the *Young Offenders Act*, chapter Y-1 of the Revised Statutes of Canada, 1985, been discharged absolutely, or has completed the youth sentence under this Act or the disposition under the *Young Offenders Act*:

- (a) employment in any department, as defined in section 2 of the *Financial Administration Act*;
- (b) employment by any Crown corporation, as defined in section 83 of the *Financial Administration Act*;
- (c) enrolment in the Canadian Forces; or
- (d) employment on or in connection with the operation of any work, undertaking or business that is within the legislative authority of Parliament.

(4) A finding of guilt under this Act is not a previous conviction for the purposes of any offence under any Act of Parliament for which a greater punishment is prescribed by reason of previous convictions, except for

- (a) [*Repealed.* 2012, c. 1, s. 188(2).]
- (b) the purpose of determining the adult sentence to be imposed. 2012, c. 1, s. 156; 2012, c. 1, s. 188; 2012, c. 1, s. 160(*l*)(ii).

PART 5 / CUSTODY AND SUPERVISION

PURPOSE / Principles to be used.

83. (1) The purpose of the youth custody and supervision system is to contribute to the protection of society by

- (a) carrying out sentences imposed by courts through the safe, fair and humane custody and supervision of young persons; and
- (b) assisting young persons to be rehabilitated and reintegrated into the community as law-abiding citizens, by providing effective programs to young persons in custody and while under supervision in the community.

(2) In addition to the principles set out in section 3, the following principles are to be used in achieving that purpose:

- (a) that the least restrictive measures consistent with the protection of the public, of personnel working with young persons and of young persons be used;
- (b) that young persons sentenced to custody retain the rights of other young persons, except the rights that are necessarily removed or restricted as a consequence of a sentence under this Act or another Act of Parliament;
- (c) that the youth custody and supervision system facilitate the involvement of the families of young persons and members of the public;
- (d) that custody and supervision decisions be made in a forthright, fair and timely manner, and that young persons have access to an effective review procedure; and
- (e) that placements of young persons where they are treated as adults not disadvantage them with respect to their eligibility for and conditions of release.

1218

YOUNG PERSON TO BE HELD APART FROM ADULTS.

84. Subject to subsection 30(3) (pre-trial detention), paragraphs 76(1)(*b*) and (*c*) (placement in adult facilities with adult sentence) and sections 89 to 93 (placement in adult facilities with youth sentence), a young person who is committed to custody shall be held separate and apart from any adult who is detained or held in custody.

LEVELS OF CUSTODY / Designation of youth custody facilities/Provincial director to specify custody level — committal to custody / Provincial director to specify custody level — transfer / Factors / Placement and transfer at appropriate level / Notice.

85. (1) In the youth custody and supervision system in each province there must be at least two levels of custody for young persons distinguished by the degree of restraint of the young persons in them.

(2) Every youth custody facility in a province that contains one or more levels of custody shall be designated by

    (*a*) in the case of a youth custody facility with only one level of custody, being the level of custody with the least degree of restraint of the young persons in it, the lieutenant governor in council or his or her delegate; and

    (*b*) in any other case, the lieutenant governor in council.

(3) The provincial director shall, when a young person is committed to custody under paragraph 42(2)(*n*), (*o*), (*q*) or (*r*) or an order is made under subsection 98(3), paragraph 103(2)(*b*), subsection 104(1) or paragraph 109(2)(*b*), determine the level of custody appropriate for the young person, after having taken into account the factors set out in subsection (5).

(4) The provincial director may determine a different level of custody for the young person when the provincial director is satisfied that the needs of the young person and the interests of society would be better served by doing so, after having taken into account the factors set out in subsection (5).

(5) The factors referred to in subsections (3) and (4) are

    (*a*) that the appropriate level of custody for the young person is the one that is the least restrictive to the young person, having regard to

        (i) the seriousness of the offence in respect of which the young person was committed to custody and the circumstances in which that offence was committed,

        (ii) the needs and circumstances of the young person, including proximity to family, school, employment and support services,

        (iii) the safety of other young persons in custody, and

        (iv) the interests of society;

    (*b*) that the level of custody should allow for the best possible match of programs to the young person's needs and behaviour, having regard to the findings of any assessment in respect of the young person; and

    (*c*) the likelihood of escape.

(6) After the provincial director has determined the appropriate level of custody for the young person under subsection (3) or (4), the young person shall be placed

YOUTH

in the youth custody facility that contains that level of custody specified by the provincial director.

(7) The provincial director shall cause a notice in writing of a determination under subsection (3) or (4) to be given to the young person and a parent of the young person and set out in that notice the reasons for it.

PROCEDURAL SAFEGUARDS / Withholding of information.

86. (1) The lieutenant governor in council of a province shall ensure that procedures are in place to ensure that the due process rights of the young person are protected with respect to a determination made under subsection 85(3) or (4), including that the young person be

- (a) provided with any relevant information to which the provincial director has access in making the determination, subject to subsection (2);
- (b) given the opportunity to be heard; and
- (c) informed of any right to a review under section 87.

(2) Where the provincial director has reasonable grounds to believe that providing the information referred to in paragraph (1)(a) would jeopardize the safety of any person or the security of a facility, he or she may authorize the withholding from the young person of as much information as is strictly necessary in order to protect such safety or security.

REVIEW / Procedural safeguards / Withholding of information / Factors / Decision is final.

87. (1) A young person may apply for a review under this section of a determination

- (a) under subsection 85(3) that would place the young person in a facility at a level of custody that has more than a minimal degree of restraint; or
- (b) under subsection 85(4) that would transfer a young person to a facility at a level of custody with a higher degree of restraint or increase the degree of restraint of the young person in the facility.

(2) The lieutenant governor in council of a province shall ensure that procedures are in place for the review under subsection (1), including that

- (a) the review board that conducts the review be independent;
- (b) the young person be provided with any relevant information to which the review board has access, subject to subsection (3); and
- (c) the young person be given the opportunity to be heard.

(3) Where the review board has reasonable grounds to believe that providing the information referred to in paragraph (2)(b) would jeopardize the safety of any person or the security of a facility, it may authorize the withholding from the young person of as much information as is strictly necessary in order to protect such safety or security.

(4) The review board shall take into account the factors referred to in subsection 85(5) in reviewing a determination.

(5) A decision of the review board under this section in respect of a particular determination is final.

FUNCTIONS TO BE EXERCISED BY YOUTH JUSTICE COURT.

88. The lieutenant governor in council of a province may order that the power to make determinations of the level of custody for young persons and to review those determinations be exercised in accordance with the *Young Offenders Act*, chapter Y-1 of the Revised Statutes of Canada, 1985. The following provisions of that Act apply, with any modifications that the circumstances require, to the exercise of those powers:

  (*a*) the definitions "review board" and "progress report" in subsection 2(1);
  (*b*) section 11;
  (*c*) sections 24.1 to 24.3; and
  (*d*) sections 28 to 31.

EXCEPTION IF YOUNG PERSON IS TWENTY YEARS OLD OR OLDER / If serving youth sentence in a provincial correctional facility / Provisions to apply.

89. (1) When a young person is twenty years old or older at the time the youth sentence is imposed on him or her under paragraph 42(2)(*n*), (*o*), (*q*) or (*r*), the young person shall, despite section 85, be committed to a provincial correctional facility for adults to serve the youth sentence.

(2) If a young person is serving a youth sentence in a provincial correctional facility for adults pursuant to subsection (1), the youth justice court may, on application of the provincial director at any time after the young person begins to serve a portion of the youth sentence in a provincial correctional facility for adults, after giving the young person, the provincial director and representatives of the provincial and federal correctional systems an opportunity to be heard, authorize the provincial director to direct that the young person serve the remainder of the youth sentence in a penitentiary if the court considers it to be in the best interests of the young person or in the public interest and if, at the time of the application, that remainder is two years or more.

(3) If a young person is serving a youth sentence in a provincial correctional facility for adults or a penitentiary under subsection (1) or (2), the *Prisons and Reformatories Act* and the *Corrections and Conditional Release Act*, and any other statute, regulation or rule applicable in respect of prisoners or offenders within the meaning of those Acts, statutes, regulations and rules, apply in respect of the young person except to the extent that they conflict with Part 6 (publication, records and information) of this Act, which Part continues to apply to the young person.

YOUTH WORKER / Role of youth worker when young person in the community.

90. (1) When a youth sentence is imposed committing a young person to custody, the provincial director of the province in which the young person received the youth sentence and was placed in custody shall, without delay, designate a youth worker to work with the young person to plan for his or her reintegration into the community, including the preparation and implementation of a reintegration plan that sets out the most effective programs for the young person in order to maximize his or her chances for reintegration into the community.

(2) When a portion of a young person's youth sentence is served in the community in accordance with section 97 or 105, the youth worker shall supervise the young person, continue to provide support to the young person and assist the young person to respect the conditions to which he or she is subject, and help the young person in the implementation of the reintegration plan.

REINTEGRATION LEAVE / Renewal of reintegration leave / Revocation of authorization / Arrest and return to custody.

91. (1) The provincial director of a province may, subject to any terms or conditions that he or she considers desirable, authorize, for a young person committed to a youth custody facility in the province further to an order under paragraph 76(1)(*a*) (placement when subject to adult sentence) or a youth sentence imposed under paragraph 42(2)(*n*), (*o*), (*q*) or (*r*),

- (*a*) a reintegration leave from the youth custody facility for a period not exceeding thirty days if, in the opinion of the provincial director, it is necessary or desirable that the young person be absent, with or without escort, for medical, compassionate or humanitarian reasons or for the purpose of rehabilitating the young person or reintegrating the young person into the community; or
- (*b*) that the young person be released from the youth custody facility on the days and during the hours that the provincial director specifies in order that the young person may
  - (i) attend school or any other educational or training institution,
  - (ii) obtain or continue employment or perform domestic or other duties required by the young person's family,
  - (iii) participate in a program specified by the provincial director that, in the provincial director's opinion, will enable the young person to better carry out employment or improve his or her education or training, or
  - (iv) attend an out-patient treatment program or other program that provides services that are suitable to addressing the young person's needs.

(2) A reintegration leave authorized under paragraph (1)(*a*) may be renewed by the provincial director for one or more thirty-day periods on reassessment of the case.

(3) The provincial director of a province may, at any time, revoke an authorization made under subsection (1).

(4) If the provincial director revokes an authorization under subsection (3) or if a young person fails to comply with any term or condition of a reintegration leave or a release from custody under this section, the young person may be arrested without warrant and returned to custody.

TRANSFER TO ADULT FACILITY / If serving youth sentence in a provincial correctional facility / Provisions to apply / Placement when adult and youth sentences / Youth sentence and adult sentence.

92. (1) When a young person is committed to custody under paragraph 42(2)(*n*), (*o*), (*q*) or (*r*), the youth justice court may, on application of the provincial director made at any time after the young person attains the age of eighteen years, after giving the young person, the provincial director and representatives of the provincial correctional system an opportunity to be heard, authorize the provincial director to direct that the young person, subject to subsection (3), serve the remainder of the youth sentence in a provincial correctional facility for adults, if the court considers it to be in the best interests of the young person or in the public interest.

(2) The youth justice court may authorize the provincial director to direct that a young person, subject to subsection (3), serve the remainder of a youth sentence in a penitentiary

    (*a*) if the youth justice court considers it to be in the best interests of the young person or in the public interest;

    (*b*) if the provincial director applies for the authorization at any time after the young person begins to serve a portion of a youth sentence in a provincial correctional facility for adults further to a direction made under subsection (1);

    (*c*) if, at the time of the application, that remainder is two years or more; and

    (*d*) so long as the youth justice court gives the young person, the provincial director and representatives of the provincial and federal correctional systems an opportunity to be heard.

(3) If the provincial director makes a direction under subsection (1) or (2), the *Prisons and Reformatories Act* and the *Corrections and Conditional Release Act*, and any other statute, regulation or rule applicable in respect of prisoners and offenders within the meaning of those Acts, statutes, regulations and rules, apply in respect of the young person except to the extent that they conflict with Part 6 (publication, records and information) of this Act, which Part continues to apply to the young person.

(4) If a person is subject to more than one sentence, at least one of which is a youth sentence imposed under paragraph 42(2)(*n*), (*o*), (*q*) or (*r*) and at least one of which is a sentence referred to in either paragraph (*b*) or (*c*), he or she shall serve, in a provincial correctional facility for adults or a penitentiary in accordance with section 743.1 (rules respecting sentences of two or more years) of the *Criminal Code*, the following:

    (*a*) the remainder of any youth sentence imposed under paragraph 42(2)(*n*), (*o*), (*q*) or (*r*);

    (*b*) an adult sentence to which an order under paragraph 76(1)(*b*) or (*c*) (placement in adult facility) applies; and

    (*c*) any sentence of imprisonment imposed otherwise than under this Act.

(5) If a young person is committed to custody under a youth sentence under paragraph 42(2)(*n*), (*o*), (*q*) or (*r*) and is also already subject to an adult sentence to which an order under paragraph 76(1)(*a*) (placement when subject to adult

sentence) applies, the young person may, in the discretion of the provincial director, serve the sentences, or any portion of the sentences, in a youth custody facility, in a provincial correctional facility for adults or, if the unexpired portion of the sentence is two years or more, in a penitentiary.

WHEN YOUNG PERSON REACHES TWENTY YEARS OF AGE / If serving youth sentence in a provincial correctional facility / Provisions to apply.

93. (1) When a young person who is committed to custody under paragraph 42(2)(*n*), (*o*), (*q*) or (*r*) is in a youth custody facility when the young person attains the age of twenty years, the young person shall be transferred to a provincial correctional facility for adults to serve the remainder of the youth sentence, unless the provincial director orders that the young person continue to serve the youth sentence in a youth custody facility.

(2) If a young person is serving a portion of a youth sentence in a provincial correctional facility for adults pursuant to a transfer under subsection (1), the youth justice court may, on application of the provincial director after the transfer, after giving the young person, the provincial director and representatives of the provincial and federal correctional systems an opportunity to be heard, authorize the provincial director to direct that the young person serve the remainder of the youth sentence in a penitentiary if the court considers it to be in the best interests of the young person or in the public interest and if, at the time of the application, that remainder is two years or more.

(3) If the provincial director makes the direction, the Prisons and Reformatories Act and the Corrections and Conditional Release Act, and any other statute, regulation or rule applicable in respect of prisoners and offenders within the meaning of those Acts, statutes, regulations and rules, apply in respect of the young person except to the extent that they conflict with Part 6 (publication, records and information) of this Act, which Part continues to apply to the young person.

ANNUAL REVIEW / Annual review / Optional review / Time for optional review / Review / Grounds for review / No review if appeal pending / Youth justice court may order appearance of young person for review / Progress report / Additional information in progress report / Written or oral report / Subsections 40(4) to (10) to apply / Notice of review from provincial director / Notice of review from person requesting it / Statement of right to counsel / Service of notice / Notice may be waived / If notice not given / Decision of the youth justice court after review.

94. (1) When a young person is committed to custody pursuant to a youth sentence under paragraph 42(2)(*n*), (*o*), (*q*) or (*r*) for a period exceeding one year, the provincial director of the province in which the young person is held in custody shall cause the young person to be brought before the youth justice court without delay at the end of one year from the date of the most recent youth sentence imposed in respect of the offence — and at the end of every subsequent year from that date — and the youth justice court shall review the youth sentence.

(2) When a young person is committed to custody pursuant to youth sentences imposed under paragraph 42(2)(*n*), (*o*), (*q*) or (*r*) in respect of more than one offence for a total period exceeding one year, the provincial director of the province in which the young person is held in custody shall cause the young person to be brought before the youth justice court without delay at the end of one year from the date of the earliest youth sentence imposed — and at the end of every subsequent year from that date — and the youth justice court shall review the youth sentences.

(3) When a young person is committed to custody pursuant to a youth sentence imposed under paragraph 42(2)(*n*), (*o*), (*q*) or (*r*) in respect of an offence, the provincial director may, on the provincial director's own initiative, and shall, on the request of the young person, the young person's parent or the Attorney General, on any of the grounds set out in subsection (6), cause the young person to be brought before a youth justice court to review the youth sentence,

- (*a*) when the youth sentence is for a period not exceeding one year, once at any time after the expiry of the greater of
  - (i) thirty days after the date of the youth sentence imposed under subsection 42(2) in respect of the offence, and
  - (ii) one third of the period of the youth sentence imposed under subsection 42(2) in respect of the offence; and
- (*b*) when the youth sentence is for a period exceeding one year, at any time after six months after the date of the most recent youth sentence imposed in respect of the offence.

(4) The young person may be brought before the youth justice court at any other time, with leave of the youth justice court judge.

(5) If a youth justice court is satisfied that there are grounds for review under subsection (6), the court shall review the youth sentence.

(6) A youth sentence imposed in respect of a young person may be reviewed under subsection (5)

- (*a*) on the ground that the young person has made sufficient progress to justify a change in the youth sentence;
- (*b*) on the ground that the circumstances that led to the youth sentence have changed materially;
- (*c*) on the ground that new services or programs are available that were not available at the time of the youth sentence;
- (*d*) on the ground that the opportunities for rehabilitation are now greater in the community; or
- (*e*) on any other ground that the youth justice court considers appropriate.

(7) Despite any other provision of this section, no review of a youth sentence in respect of which an appeal has been taken shall be made under this section until all proceedings in respect of any such appeal have been completed.

(8) When a provincial director is required under subsections (1) to (3) to cause a young person to be brought before the youth justice court and fails to do so, the youth justice court may, on application made by the young person, his or her parent or the Attorney General, or on its own motion, order the provincial director to cause the young person to be brought before the youth justice court.

1225

(9) The youth justice court shall, before reviewing under this section a youth sentence imposed in respect of a young person, require the provincial director to cause to be prepared, and to submit to the youth justice court, a progress report on the performance of the young person since the youth sentence took effect.

(10) A person preparing a progress report in respect of a young person may include in the report any information relating to the personal and family history and present environment of the young person that he or she considers advisable.

(11) A progress report shall be in writing unless it cannot reasonably be committed to writing, in which case it may, with leave of the youth justice court, be submitted orally in court.

(12) Subsections 40(4) to (10) (procedures respecting pre-sentence reports) apply, with any modifications that the circumstances require, in respect of progress reports.

(13) When a youth sentence imposed in respect of a young person is to be reviewed under subsection (1) or (2), the provincial director shall cause any notice that may be directed by rules of court applicable to the youth justice court or, in the absence of such a direction, at least five clear days notice of the review to be given in writing to the young person, a parent of the young person and the Attorney General.

(14) When a review of a youth sentence imposed in respect of a young person is requested under subsection (3), the person requesting the review shall cause any notice that may be directed by rules of court applicable to the youth justice court or, in the absence of such a direction, at least five clear days notice of the review to be given in writing to the young person, a parent of the young person and the Attorney General.

(15) A notice given to a parent under subsection (13) or (14) shall include a statement that the young person whose youth sentence is to be reviewed has the right to be represented by counsel.

(16) A notice under subsection (13) or (14) may be served personally or may be sent by confirmed delivery service.

(17) Any of the persons entitled to notice under subsection (13) or (14) may waive the right to that notice.

(18) If notice under subsection (13) or (14) is not given in accordance with this section, the youth justice court may

    (*a*) adjourn the proceedings and order that the notice be given in the manner and to the persons that it directs; or

    (*b*) dispense with the notice if, in the opinion of the court, having regard to the circumstances, notice may be dispensed with.

(19) When a youth justice court reviews under this section a youth sentence imposed in respect of a young person, it may, after giving the young person, a parent of the young person, the Attorney General and the provincial director an opportunity to be heard, having regard to the needs of the young person and the interests of society,

    (*a*) confirm the youth sentence;

    (*b*) release the young person from custody and place the young person under conditional supervision in accordance with the procedure set out in section 105, with any modifications that the circumstances require, for a period not exceeding the remainder of the youth sentence that the young person is then serving; or

    (*c*) if the provincial director so recommends, convert a youth sentence under paragraph 42(2)(*r*) to a youth sentence under paragraph 42(2)(*q*) if the offence was murder or to a youth sentence under paragraph 42(2)(*n*) or (*o*), as the case may be, if the offence was an offence other than murder.

ORDERS ARE YOUTH SENTENCES.

95. Orders under subsections 97(2) (conditions) and 98(3) (continuation of custody), paragraph 103(2)(*b*) (continuation of custody), subsections 104(1) (continuation of custody) and 105(1) (conditional supervision) and paragraph 109(2)(*b*) (continuation of suspension of conditional supervision) are deemed to be youth sentences for the purposes of section 94 (reviews).

RECOMMENDATION OF PROVINCIAL DIRECTOR FOR CONDITIONAL SUPERVISION OF YOUNG PERSON / Notice / Application to court for review of recommendation / Subsections 94(7), (9) to (12) and (14) to (19) apply / If no application for review made under subsection (3) / Notice when no release ordered / Provincial director may request review / When provincial director requests a review.

96. (1) When a young person is held in custody pursuant to a youth sentence under paragraph 42(2)(*n*), (*o*), (*q*) or (*r*), the provincial director may, if satisfied that the needs of the young person and the interests of society would be better served by doing so, make a recommendation to the youth justice court that the young person be released from custody and placed under conditional supervision.

(2) If the provincial director makes a recommendation, the provincial director shall cause a notice to be given in writing that includes the reasons for the recommendation and the conditions that the provincial director would recommend be set under section 105 to the young person, a parent of the young person and the Attorney General and give a copy of the notice to the youth justice court.

(3) If notice of a recommendation is made under subsection (2) with respect to a youth sentence imposed on a young person, the youth justice court shall, if an application for review is made by the young person, the young person's parent or the Attorney General within ten days after service of the notice, review the youth sentence without delay.

(4) Subject to subsection (5), subsections 94(7) (no review of appeal pending), (9) to (12) (progress reports) and (14) to (19) (provisions respecting notice and decision of the youth justice court) apply, with any modifications that the circumstances require, in respect of reviews made under this section and any notice required under subsection 94(14) shall also be given to the provincial director.

(5) A youth justice court that receives a notice under subsection (2) shall, if no application for a review is made under subsection (3),

- (*a*) order the release of the young person and place the young person under conditional supervision in accordance with section 105, having regard to the recommendations of the provincial director; or
- (*b*) if the court considers it advisable, order that the young person not be released.

For greater certainty, an order under this subsection may be made without a hearing.

(6) When a youth justice court orders that the young person not be released under paragraph (5)(*b*), it shall cause a notice of its order to be given to the provincial director without delay.

(7) When the provincial director is given a notice under subsection (6), he or she may request a review under this section.

(8) When the provincial director requests a review under subsection (7),

- (*a*) the provincial director shall cause any notice that may be directed by rules of court applicable to the youth justice court or, in the absence of such a direction, at least five clear days notice of the review to be given in writing to the young person, a parent of the young person and the Attorney General; and
- (*b*) the youth justice court shall review the youth sentence without delay after the notice required under paragraph (*a*) is given.

CONDITIONS TO BE INCLUDED IN CUSTODY AND SUPERVISION ORDER / Other conditions / Communication of conditions / Provisions to apply.

97. (1) Every youth sentence imposed under paragraph 42(2)(*n*) shall contain the following conditions, namely, that the young person, while serving the portion of the youth sentence under supervision in the community,

- (*a*) keep the peace and be of good behaviour;
- (*b*) report to the provincial director and then be under the supervision of the provincial director;
- (*c*) inform the provincial director immediately on being arrested or questioned by the police;
- (*d*) report to the police, or any named individual, as instructed by the provincial director;
- (*e*) advise the provincial director of the young person's address of residence and report immediately to the provincial director any change
  - (i) in that address,
  - (ii) in the young person's normal occupation, including employment, vocational or educational training and volunteer work,
  - (iii) in the young person's family or financial situation, and
  - (iv) that may reasonably be expected to affect the young person's ability to comply with the conditions of the sentence; and

(f) not own, possess or have the control of any weapon, ammunition, prohibited ammunition, prohibited device or explosive substance, except as authorized in writing by the provincial director for the purposes of the young person participating in a program specified in the authorization.

(2) The provincial director may set additional conditions that support and address the needs of the young person, promote the reintegration of the young person into the community and offer adequate protection to the public from the risk that the young person might otherwise present. The provincial director shall, in setting the conditions, take into account the needs of the young person, the most effective programs for the young person in order to maximize his or her chances for reintegration into the community, the nature of the offence and the ability of the young person to comply with the conditions.

(3) The provincial director shall
    (a) cause the conditions to be read by or to the young person bound by them;
    (b) explain or cause to be explained to the young person the purpose and effect of the conditions, and confirm that the young person understands them; and
    (c) cause a copy of the conditions to be given to the young person, and to a parent of the young person.

(4) Subsections 56(3) (endorsement of order by young person) and (4) (validity of order) apply, with any modifications that the circumstances require, in respect of conditions under this section.

APPLICATION FOR CONTINUATION OF CUSTODY / Continuation of custody / Decision / Factors.

98. (1) Within a reasonable time before the expiry of the custodial portion of a young person's youth sentence, the Attorney General or the provincial director may apply to the youth justice court for an order that the young person remain in custody for a period not exceeding the remainder of the youth sentence.

(2) If the hearing for an application under subsection (1) cannot be completed before the expiry of the custodial portion of the youth sentence, the court may order that the young person remain in custody pending the determination of the application if the court is satisfied that the application was made in a reasonable time, having regard to all the circumstances, and that there are compelling reasons for keeping the young person in custody.

(3) The youth justice court may, after giving both parties and a parent of the young person an opportunity to be heard, order that a young person remain in custody for a period not exceeding the remainder of the youth sentence, if it is satisfied that there are reasonable grounds to believe that
    (a) the young person is likely to commit a serious violent offence before the expiry of the youth sentence he or she is then serving; and
    (b) the conditions that would be imposed on the young person if he or she were to serve a portion of the youth sentence in the community would not be adequate to prevent the commission of the offence.

(4) For the purpose of determining an application under subsection (1), the youth justice court shall take into consideration any factor that is relevant to the case of the young person, including

(a) evidence of a pattern of persistent violent behaviour and, in particular,

    (i)   the number of offences committed by the young person that caused physical or psychological harm to any other person,

    (ii) the young person's difficulties in controlling violent impulses to the point of endangering the safety of any other person,

    (iii) the use of weapons in the commission of any offence,

    (iv) explicit threats of violence,

    (v)   behaviour of a brutal nature associated with the commission of any offence, and

    (vi) a substantial degree of indifference on the part of the young person as to the reasonably foreseeable consequences, to other persons, of the young person's behaviour;

(b) psychiatric or psychological evidence that a physical or mental illness or disorder of the young person is of such a nature that the young person is likely to commit, before the expiry of the youth sentence the young person is then serving, a serious violent offence;

(c) reliable information that satisfies the youth justice court that the young person is planning to commit, before the expiry of the youth sentence the young person is then serving, a serious violent offence;

(d) the availability of supervision programs in the community that would offer adequate protection to the public from the risk that the young person might otherwise present until the expiry of the youth sentence the young person is then serving;

(e) whether the young person is more likely to reoffend if he or she serves his or her youth sentence entirely in custody without the benefits of serving a portion of the youth sentence in the community under supervision; and

(f) evidence of a pattern of committing violent offences while he or she was serving a portion of a youth sentence in the community under supervision.

REPORT / Written or oral report / Provisions apply/Notice of hearing / Statement of right to counsel / Service of notice / When notice not given.

99. (1) For the purpose of determining an application under section 98 (application for continuation of custody), the youth justice court shall require the provincial director to cause to be prepared, and to submit to the youth justice court, a report setting out any information of which the provincial director is aware with respect to the factors set out in subsection 98(4) that may be of assistance to the court.

(2) A report referred to in subsection (1) shall be in writing unless it cannot reasonably be committed to writing, in which case it may, with leave of the youth justice court, be submitted orally in court.

(3) Subsections 40(4) to (10) (procedures respecting pre-sentence reports) apply, with any modifications that the circumstances require, in respect of a report referred to in subsection (1).

(4) When an application is made under section 98 (application for continuation of custody) in respect of a young person, the provincial director shall cause to be given, to the young person and to a parent of the young person, at least five clear days notice of the hearing in writing.

(5) Any notice given to a parent under subsection (4) shall include a statement that the young person has the right to be represented by counsel.

(6) A notice under subsection (4) may be served personally or may be sent by confirmed delivery service.

(7) When notice under subsection (4) is not given in accordance with this section, the youth justice court may

(a) adjourn the hearing and order that the notice be given in any manner and to any person that it directs; or

(b) dispense with the giving of the notice if, in the opinion of the youth justice court, having regard to the circumstances, the giving of the notice may be dispensed with.

YOUTH

REASONS.

100. When a youth justice court makes an order under subsection 98(3) (decision for continued custody), it shall state its reasons for the order in the record of the case and shall provide, or cause to be provided, to the young person in respect of whom the order was made, the counsel and a parent of the young person, the Attorney General and the provincial director

(a) a copy of the order; and

(b) on request, a transcript or copy of the reasons for the order.

REVIEW OF YOUTH JUSTICE COURT DECISION / Extension of time to make application / Notice of application.

101. (1) An order made under subsection 98(3) (decision for continued custody) in respect of a young person, or the refusal to make such an order, shall, on application of the young person, the young person's counsel, the Attorney General or the provincial director made within thirty days after the decision of the youth justice court, be reviewed by the court of appeal, and that court may, in its discretion, confirm or reverse the decision of the youth justice court.

(2) The court of appeal may, at any time, extend the time within which an application under subsection (1) may be made.

(3) A person who proposes to apply for a review under subsection (1) shall give notice of the application in the manner and within the period of time that may be directed by rules of court.

BREACH OF CONDITIONS / Provisions apply.

102. (1) If the provincial director has reasonable grounds to believe that a young person has breached or is about to breach a condition to which he or she is subject under section 97 (conditions to be included in custody and supervision orders), the provincial director may, in writing,

   (a) permit the young person to continue to serve a portion of his or her youth sentence in the community, on the same or different conditions; or

   (b) if satisfied that the breach is a serious one that increases the risk to public safety, order that the young person be remanded to any youth custody facility that the provincial director considers appropriate until a review is conducted.

(2) Sections 107 (apprehension) and 108 (review by provincial director) apply, with any modifications that the circumstances require, to an order under paragraph (1)(b).

REVIEW BY YOUTH JUSTICE COURT / Order / Provisions apply.

103. (1) When the case of a young person is referred to the youth justice court under section 108 (review by provincial director), the provincial director shall, without delay, cause the young person to be brought before the youth justice court, and the youth justice court shall, after giving the young person an opportunity to be heard,

   (a) if the court is not satisfied on reasonable grounds that the young person has breached or was about to breach one of the conditions under which he or she was being supervised in the community, order that the young person continue to serve a portion of his or her youth sentence in the community, on the same or different conditions; or

   (b) if the court is satisfied on reasonable grounds that the young person has breached or was about to breach one of the conditions under which he or she was being supervised in the community, make an order under subsection (2).

(2) On completion of a review under subsection (1), the youth justice court

   (a) shall order that the young person continue to serve the remainder of the youth sentence the young person is then serving in the community, and when the court does so, the court may vary the existing conditions or impose new conditions; or

   (b) shall, despite paragraph 42(2)(n) (custody and supervision order), order that the young person remain in custody for a period that does not exceed the remainder of the youth sentence the young person is then serving, if the youth justice court is satisfied that the breach of the conditions was serious.

(3) Subsections 109(4) to (8) apply, with any modifications that the circumstances require, in respect of a review under this section.

CONTINUATION OF CUSTODY / Continuation of custody / Factors / Youth justice court to order appearance of young person / Provisions to apply / If application denied.

104. (1) When a young person on whom a youth sentence under paragraph 42(2)(o), (q) or (r) has been imposed is held in custody and an application is made to the youth justice court by the Attorney General, within a reasonable time before the expiry of the custodial portion of the youth sentence, the provincial director of the province in which the young person is held in custody shall cause the young person to be brought before the youth justice court and the youth justice court may, after giving both parties and a parent of the young person an opportunity to be heard and if it is satisfied that there are reasonable grounds to believe that the young person is likely to commit an offence causing the death of or serious harm to another person before the expiry of the youth sentence the young person is then serving, order that the young person remain in custody for a period not exceeding the remainder of the youth sentence.

(2) If the hearing of an application under subsection (1) cannot be completed before the expiry of the custodial portion of the youth sentence, the court may order that the young person remain in custody until the determination of the application if the court is satisfied that the application was made in a reasonable time, having regard to all the circumstances, and that there are compelling reasons for keeping the young person in custody.

(3) For the purpose of determining an application under subsection (1), the youth justice court shall take into consideration any factor that is relevant to the case of the young person, including

(*a*) evidence of a pattern of persistent violent behaviour and, in particular,

    (i) the number of offences committed by the young person that caused physical or psychological harm to any other person,

    (ii) the young person's difficulties in controlling violent impulses to the point of endangering the safety of any other person,

    (iii) the use of weapons in the commission of any offence,

    (iv) explicit threats of violence,

    (v) behaviour of a brutal nature associated with the commission of any offence, and

    (vi) a substantial degree of indifference on the part of the young person as to the reasonably foreseeable consequences, to other persons, of the young person's behaviour;

(*b*) psychiatric or psychological evidence that a physical or mental illness or disorder of the young person is of such a nature that the young person is likely to commit, before the expiry of the youth sentence the young person is then serving, an offence causing the death of or serious harm to another person;

(*c*) reliable information that satisfies the youth justice court that the young person is planning to commit, before the expiry of the youth sentence the young person is then serving, an offence causing the death of or serious harm to another person; and

(*d*) the availability of supervision programs in the community that would offer adequate protection to the public from the risk that the young person might otherwise present until the expiry of the youth sentence the young person is then serving.

(4) If a provincial director fails to cause a young person to be brought before the youth justice court under subsection (1), the youth justice court shall order the provincial director to cause the young person to be brought before the youth justice court without delay.

(5) Sections 99 to 101 apply, with any modifications that the circumstances require, in respect of an order made, or the refusal to make an order, under this section.

(6) If an application under this section is denied, the court may, with the consent of the young person, the Attorney General and the provincial director, proceed as though the young person had been brought before the court as required under subsection 105(1).

CONDITIONAL SUPERVISION / Conditions to be included in order / Other conditions / Temporary conditions / Conditions to be set at first opportunity / Report / Provisions apply / Provisions apply.

105. (1) The provincial director of the province in which a young person on whom a youth sentence under paragraph 42(2)(*o*), (*q*) or (*r*) has been imposed is held in custody or, if applicable, with respect to whom an order has been made under subsection 104(1) (continuation of custody), shall cause the young person to be brought before the youth justice court at least one month before the expiry of the custodial portion of the youth sentence. The court shall, after giving the young person an opportunity to be heard, by order, set the conditions of the young person's conditional supervision.

(2) The youth justice court shall include in the order under subsection (1) the following conditions, namely, that the young person
    (*a*) keep the peace and be of good behaviour;
    (*b*) appear before the youth justice court when required by the court to do so;
    (*c*) report to the provincial director immediately on release, and then be under the supervision of the provincial director or a person designated by the youth justice court;
    (*d*) inform the provincial director immediately on being arrested or questioned by the police;
    (*e*) report to the police, or any named individual, as instructed by the provincial director;
    (*f*) advise the provincial director of the young person's address of residence on release and after release report immediately to the clerk of the youth justice court or the provincial director any change
        (i) in that address,
        (ii) in the young person's normal occupation, including employment, vocational or educational training and volunteer work,
        (iii) in the young person's family or financial situation, and
        (iv) that may reasonably be expected to affect the young person's ability to comply with the conditions of the order;
    (*g*) not own, possess or have the control of any weapon, ammunition, prohibited ammunition, prohibited device or explosive substance, except as authorized by the order; and
    (*h*) comply with any reasonable instructions that the provincial director considers necessary in respect of any condition of the conditional supervision in order to prevent a breach of that condition or to protect society.

(3) In setting conditions for the purposes of subsection (1), the youth justice court may include in the order the following conditions, namely, that the young person

- (a) on release, travel directly to the young person's place of residence, or to any other place that is noted in the order;
- (b) make reasonable efforts to obtain and maintain suitable employment;
- (c) attend school or any other place of learning, training or recreation that is appropriate, if the court is satisfied that a suitable program is available for the young person at such a place;
- (d) reside with a parent, or any other adult that the court considers appropriate, who is willing to provide for the care and maintenance of the young person;
- (e) reside in any place that the provincial director may specify;
- (f) remain within the territorial jurisdiction of one or more courts named in the order;
- (g) comply with conditions set out in the order that support and address the needs of the young person and promote the reintegration of the young person into the community; and
- (h) comply with any other conditions set out in the order that the court considers appropriate, including conditions for securing the young person's good conduct and for preventing the young person from repeating the offence or committing other offences.

(4) When a provincial director is required under subsection (1) to cause a young person to be brought before the youth justice court but cannot do so for reasons beyond the young person's control, the provincial director shall so advise the youth justice court and the court shall, by order, set any temporary conditions for the young person's conditional supervision that are appropriate in the circumstances.

(5) When an order is made under subsection (4), the provincial director shall bring the young person before the youth justice court as soon after the order is made as the circumstances permit and the court shall then set the conditions of the young person's conditional supervision.

(6) For the purpose of setting conditions under this section, the youth justice court shall require the provincial director to cause to be prepared, and to submit to the youth justice court, a report setting out any information that may be of assistance to the court.

(7) Subsections 99(2) to (7) (provisions respecting reports and notice) and 104(4) (ordering appearance of young person) apply, with any modifications that the circumstances require, in respect of any proceedings held under subsection (1).

(8) Subsections 56(1) to (4) (provisions respecting probation orders), (7) (notice to appear) and (8) (warrant in default) and section 101 (review of youth justice court decision) apply, with any modifications that the circumstances require, in respect of an order made under subsection (1).

SUSPENSION OF CONDITIONAL SUPERVISION.

106. If the provincial director has reasonable grounds to believe that a young person has breached or is about to breach a condition of an order made under subsection 105(1), the provincial director may, in writing,

   (*a*) suspend the conditional supervision; and

   (*b*) order that the young person be remanded to any youth custody facility that the provincial director considers appropriate until a review is conducted under section 108 and, if applicable, section 109.

APPREHENSION / Warrants / Peace officer may arrest / Requirement to bring before provincial director / Release or remand in custody.

107. (1) If the conditional supervision of a young person is suspended under section 106, the provincial director may issue a warrant in writing, authorizing the apprehension of the young person and, until the young person is apprehended, the young person is deemed not to be continuing to serve the youth sentence the young person is then serving.

(2) A warrant issued under subsection (1) shall be executed by any peace officer to whom it is given at any place in Canada and has the same force and effect in all parts of Canada as if it had been originally issued or subsequently endorsed by a provincial court judge or other lawful authority having jurisdiction in the place where it is executed.

(3) If a peace officer believes on reasonable grounds that a warrant issued under subsection (1) is in force in respect of a young person, the peace officer may arrest the young person without the warrant at any place in Canada.

(4) If a young person is arrested under subsection (3) and detained, the peace officer making the arrest shall cause the young person to be brought before the provincial director or a person designated by the provincial director

   (*a*) if the provincial director or the designated person is available within a period of twenty-four hours after the young person is arrested, without unreasonable delay and in any event within that period; and

   (*b*) if the provincial director or the designated person is not available within that period, as soon as possible.

(5) If a young person is brought before the provincial director or a person designated by the provincial director under subsection (4), the provincial director or the designated person

   (*a*) if not satisfied that there are reasonable grounds to believe that the young person is the young person in respect of whom the warrant referred to in subsection (1) was issued, shall release the young person; or

   (*b*) if satisfied that there are reasonable grounds to believe that the young person is the young person in respect of whom the warrant referred to in subsection (1) was issued, may remand the young person in custody to await execution of the warrant, but if no warrant for the young person's arrest is executed within a period of forty-eight hours after the time the young person is remanded in custody, the person in whose custody the young person then is shall release the young person.

REVIEW BY PROVINCIAL DIRECTOR.

108. Without delay after the remand to custody of a young person whose conditional supervision has been suspended under section 106, or without delay after being informed of the arrest of such a young person, the provincial director shall review the case and, within forty-eight hours, cancel the suspension of the conditional supervision or refer the case to the youth justice court for a review under section 109.

REVIEW BY YOUTH JUSTICE COURT / Order / Custody and supervision order / Factors to be considered / Reasons / Report / Provisions apply / Provisions apply.

109. (1) If the case of a young person is referred to the youth justice court under section 108, the provincial director shall, without delay, cause the young person to be brought before the youth justice court, and the youth justice court shall, after giving the young person an opportunity to be heard,

    (a) if the court is not satisfied on reasonable grounds that the young person has breached or was about to breach a condition of the conditional supervision, cancel the suspension of the conditional supervision; or

    (b) if the court is satisfied on reasonable grounds that the young person has breached or was about to breach a condition of the conditional supervision, review the decision of the provincial director to suspend the conditional supervision and make an order under subsection (2).

(2) On completion of a review under subsection (1), the youth justice court shall order

    (a) the cancellation of the suspension of the conditional supervision, and when the court does so, the court may vary the conditions of the conditional supervision or impose new conditions;

    (b) in a case other than a deferred custody and supervision order made under paragraph 42(2)(p), the continuation of the suspension of the conditional supervision for any period of time, not to exceed the remainder of the youth sentence the young person is then serving, that the court considers appropriate, and when the court does so, the court shall order that the young person remain in custody; or

    (c) in the case of a deferred custody and supervision order made under paragraph 42(2)(p), that the young person serve the remainder of the order as if it were a custody and supervision order under paragraph 42(2)(n).

(3) After a court has made a direction under paragraph (2)(c), the provisions of this Act applicable to orders under paragraph 42(2)(n) apply in respect of the deferred custody and supervision order.

(4) In making its decision under subsection (2), the court shall consider the length of time the young person has been subject to the order, whether the young person has previously contravened it, and the nature of the contravention, if any.

(5) When a youth justice court makes an order under subsection (2), it shall state its reasons for the order in the record of the case and shall give, or cause to be

1237

given, to the young person in respect of whom the order was made, the counsel and a parent of the young person, the Attorney General and the provincial director,

    (*a*) a copy of the order; and

    (*b*) on request, a transcript or copy of the reasons for the order.

(6) For the purposes of a review under subsection (1), the youth justice court shall require the provincial director to cause to be prepared, and to submit to the youth justice court, a report setting out any information of which the provincial director is aware that may be of assistance to the court.

(7) Subsections 99(2) to (7) (provisions respecting reports and notice) and 105(6) (report for the purpose of setting conditions) apply, with any modifications that the circumstances require, in respect of a review under this section.

(8) Section 101 (review of youth justice court decision) applies, with any modifications that the circumstances require, in respect of an order made under subsection (2).

PART 6 / PUBLICATION, RECORDS AND INFORMATION

Protection of Privacy of Young Persons

IDENTITY OF OFFENDER NOT TO BE PUBLISHED / Limitation / Exception / *Ex parte* application for leave to publish / Order ceases to have effect / Application for leave to publish.

110. (1) Subject to this section, no person shall publish the name of a young person, or any other information related to a young person, if it would identify the young person as a young person dealt with under this Act.

(2) Subsection (1) does not apply

    (*a*) in a case where the information relates to a young person who has received an adult sentence; or

    (*b*) [*Repealed*, 2019, c. 25, s. 379.]

    (*c*) in a case where the publication of information is made in the course of the administration of justice, if it is not the purpose of the publication to make the information known in the community.

(3) A young person referred to in subsection (1) may, after he or she attains the age of eighteen years, publish or cause to be published information that would identify him or her as having been dealt with under this Act or the *Young Offenders Act*, chapter Y-1 of the Revised Statutes of Canada, 1985, provided that he or she is not in custody pursuant to either Act at the time of the publication.

(4) A youth justice court judge shall, on the *ex parte* application of a peace officer, make an order permitting any person to publish information that identifies a young person as having committed or allegedly committed an indictable offence, if the judge is satisfied that

(*a*) there is reason to believe that the young person is a danger to others; and

(*b*) publication of the information is necessary to assist in apprehending the young person.

(5) An order made under subsection (4) ceases to have effect five days after it is made.

(6) The youth justice court may, on the application of a young person referred to in subsection (1), make an order permitting the young person to publish information that would identify him or her as having been dealt with under this Act or the *Young Offenders Act*, chapter Y-1 of the Revised Statutes of Canada, 1985, if the court is satisfied that the publication would not be contrary to the young person's best interests or the public interest. 2012, c. 1, s. 189; 2019, c. 25, s. 379.

IDENTITY OF VICTIM OR WITNESS NOT TO BE PUBLISHED / Exception / Application for leave to publish.

111. (1) Subject to this section, no person shall publish the name of a child or young person, or any other information related to a child or a young person, if it would identify the child or young person as having been a victim of, or as having appeared as a witness in connection with, an offence committed or alleged to have been committed by a young person.

(2) Information that would serve to identify a child or young person referred to in subsection (1) as having been a victim or a witness may be published, or caused to be published, by

(*a*) that child or young person after he or she attains the age of eighteen years or before that age with the consent of his or her parents; or

(*b*) the parents of that child or young person if he or she is deceased.

(3) The youth justice court may, on the application of a child or a young person referred to in subsection (1), make an order permitting the child or young person to publish information that would identify him or her as having been a victim or a witness if the court is satisfied that the publication would not be contrary to his or her best interests or the public interest.

NON-APPLICATION.

112. Once information is published under subsection 110(3) or (6) or 111(2) or (3), subsection 110(1) (identity of offender not to be published) or 111(1) (identity of victim or witness not to be published), as the case may be, no longer applies in respect of the information.

Fingerprints and Photographs

IDENTIFICATION OF CRIMINALS ACT APPLIES / Limitation.

113. (1) The *Identification of Criminals Act* applies in respect of young persons.

(2) No fingerprint, palmprint or photograph or other measurement, process or operation referred to in the *Identification of Criminals Act* shall be taken of, or

applied in respect of, a young person who is charged with having committed an offence except in the circumstances in which an adult may, under that Act, be subjected to the measurements, processes and operations.

Records That May Be Kept

YOUTH JUSTICE COURT, REVIEW BOARD AND OTHER COURTS.

114. A youth justice court, review board or any court dealing with matters arising out of proceedings under this Act may keep a record of any case that comes before it arising under this Act.

POLICE RECORDS / Extrajudicial measures / Police records / Records held by R.C.M.P.

115. (1) A record relating to any offence alleged to have been committed by a young person, including the original or a copy of any fingerprints or photographs of the young person, may be kept by any police force responsible for or participating in the investigation of the offence.

(1.1) The police force shall keep a record of any extrajudicial measures that they use to deal with young persons.

(2) When a young person is charged with having committed an offence in respect of which an adult may be subjected to any measurement, process or operation referred to in the *Identification of Criminals Act*, the police force responsible for the investigation of the offence may provide a record relating to the offence to the Royal Canadian Mounted Police. If the young person is found guilty of the offence, the police force shall provide the record.

(3) The Royal Canadian Mounted Police shall keep the records provided under subsection (2) in the central repository that the Commissioner of the Royal Canadian Mounted Police may, from time to time, designate for the purpose of keeping criminal history files or records of offenders or keeping records for the identification of offenders. 2012, c. 1, s. 190.

GOVERNMENT RECORDS / Other records.

116. (1) A department or an agency of any government in Canada may keep records containing information obtained by the department or agency

- (*a*) for the purposes of an investigation of an offence alleged to have been committed by a young person;
- (*b*) for use in proceedings against a young person under this Act;
- (*c*) for the purpose of administering a youth sentence or an order of the youth justice court;
- (*d*) for the purpose of considering whether to use extrajudicial measures to deal with a young person; or
- (*e*) as a result of the use of extrajudicial measures to deal with a young person.

(2) A person or organization may keep records containing information obtained by the person or organization

- (*a*) as a result of the use of extrajudicial measures to deal with a young person; or
- (*b*) for the purpose of administering or participating in the administration of a youth sentence.

Access to Records

EXCEPTION — ADULT SENTENCE.

117. Sections 118 to 129 do not apply to records kept in respect of an offence for which an adult sentence has been imposed once the time allowed for the taking of an appeal has expired or, if an appeal is taken, all proceedings in respect of the appeal have been completed and the appeal court has upheld an adult sentence. The record shall be dealt with as a record of an adult and, for the purposes of the *Criminal Records Act*, the finding of guilt in respect of the offence for which the record is kept is deemed to be a conviction.

NO ACCESS UNLESS AUTHORIZED / Exception for employees.

118. (1) Except as authorized or required by this Act, no person shall be given access to a record kept under sections 114 to 116, and no information contained in it may be given to any person, where to do so would identify the young person to whom it relates as a young person dealt with under this Act.

(2) No person who is employed in keeping or maintaining records referred to in subsection (1) is restricted from doing anything prohibited under subsection (1) with respect to any other person so employed.

PERSONS HAVING ACCESS TO RECORDS / Period of access / Prohibition orders not included / Extrajudicial measures / Exception / Records of assessments or forensic DNA analysis / Introduction into evidence / Disclosures for research or statistical purposes / Application of usual rules / Records of offences that result in a prohibition order.

119. (1) Subject to subsections (4) to (6), from the date that a record is created until the end of the applicable period set out in subsection (2), the following persons, on request, shall be given access to a record kept under section 114, and may be given access to a record kept under sections 115 and 116:

- (*a*) the young person to whom the record relates;
- (*b*) the young person's counsel, or any representative of that counsel;
- (*c*) the Attorney General;
- (*d*) the victim of the offence or alleged offence to which the record relates;
- (*e*) the parents of the young person, during the course of any proceedings relating to the offence or alleged offence to which the record relates or during the term of any youth sentence made in respect of the offence;

(f) any adult assisting the young person under subsection 25(7), during the course of any proceedings relating to the offence or alleged offence to which the record relates or during the term of any youth sentence made in respect of the offence;

(g) any peace officer for
  (i) law enforcement purposes, or
  (ii) any purpose related to the administration of the case to which the record relates, during the course of proceedings against the young person or the term of the youth sentence;

(h) a judge, court or review board, for any purpose relating to proceedings against the young person, or proceedings against the person after he or she becomes an adult, in respect of offences committed or alleged to have been committed by that person;

(i) the provincial director, or the director of the provincial correctional facility for adults or the penitentiary at which the young person is serving a sentence;

(j) a person participating in a conference or in the administration of extrajudicial measures, if required for the administration of the case to which the record relates;

(k) a person acting as ombudsman, privacy commissioner or information commissioner, whatever his or her official designation might be, who in the course of his or her duties under an Act of Parliament or the legislature of a province is investigating a complaint to which the record relates;

(l) a coroner or a person acting as a child advocate, whatever his or her official designation might be, who is acting in the course of his or her duties under an Act of Parliament or the legislature of a province;

(m) a person acting under the *Firearms Act*;

(n) a member of a department or agency of a government in Canada, or of an organization that is an agent of, or under contract with, the department or agency, who is
  (i) acting in the exercise of his or her duties under this Act,
  (ii) engaged in the supervision or care of the young person, whether as a young person or an adult, or in an investigation related to the young person under an Act of the legislature of a province respecting child welfare,
  (iii) considering an application for conditional release, or for a record suspension under the *Criminal Records Act*, made by the young person, whether as a young person or an adult,
  (iv) administering a prohibition order made under an Act of Parliament or the legislature of a province, or
  (v) administering a youth sentence, if the young person has been committed to custody and is serving the custody in a provincial correctional facility for adults or a penitentiary;

(o) a person, for the purpose of carrying out a criminal record check required by the Government of Canada or the government of a province or a municipality for purposes of employment or the performance of services, with or without remuneration;

(*p*) an employee or agent of the Government of Canada, for statistical purposes under the *Statistics Act*;

(*p*.1) an employee of a department or agency of the Government of Canada, for the purpose of administering the *Canadian Passport Order*;

(*q*) an accused or his or her counsel who swears an affidavit to the effect that access to the record is necessary to make a full answer and defence;

(*r*) a person or a member of a class of persons designated by order of the Governor in Council, or the lieutenant governor in council of the appropriate province, for a purpose and to the extent specified in the order; and

(*s*) any person or member of a class of persons that a youth justice court judge considers has a valid interest in the record, to the extent directed by the judge, if the judge is satisfied that access to the record is

    (i) desirable in the public interest for research or statistical purposes, or

    (ii) desirable in the interest of the proper administration of justice.

(2) The period of access referred to in subsection (1) is

(*a*) if an extrajudicial sanction is used to deal with the young person, the period ending two years after the young person consents to be subject to the sanction in accordance with paragraph 10(2)(*c*);

(*b*) if the young person is acquitted of the offence otherwise than by reason of a verdict of not criminally responsible on account of mental disorder, the period ending two months after the expiry of the time allowed for the taking of an appeal or, if an appeal is taken, the period ending three months after all proceedings in respect of the appeal have been completed;

(*c*) if the charge against the young person is dismissed for any reason other than acquittal, the charge is withdrawn, or the young person is found guilty of the offence and a reprimand is given, the period ending two months after the dismissal, withdrawal, or finding of guilt;

(*d*) if the charge against the young person is stayed, with no proceedings being taken against the young person for a period of one year, at the end of that period;

(*d*.1) if an order referred to in subsection 14(2) or 20(2) is made against a young person, the period ending six months after the expiry of the order;

(*e*) if the young person is found guilty of the offence and the youth sentence is an absolute discharge, the period ending one year after the young person is found guilty;

(*f*) if the young person is found guilty of the offence and the youth sentence is a conditional discharge, the period ending three years after the young person is found guilty;

(*g*) subject to paragraphs (*i*) and (*j*) and subsection (9), if the young person is found guilty of the offence and it is a summary conviction offence, the period ending three years after the youth sentence imposed in respect of the offence has been completed;

(*h*) subject to paragraphs (*i*) and (*j*) and subsection (9), if the young person is found guilty of the offence and it is an indictable offence, the period ending five years after the youth sentence imposed in respect of the offence has been completed;

   (*i*) subject to subsection (9), if, during the period calculated in accordance with paragraph (*g*) or (*h*), the young person is found guilty of an offence punishable on summary conviction committed when he or she was a young person, the latest of

      (i) the period calculated in accordance with paragraph (*g*) or (*h*), as the case may be, and

      (ii) the period ending three years after the youth sentence imposed for that offence has been completed; and

   (*j*) subject to subsection (9), if, during the period calculated in accordance with paragraph (*g*) or (*h*), the young person is found guilty of an indictable offence committed when he or she was a young person, the period ending five years after the sentence imposed for that indictable offence has been completed.

(3) Prohibition orders made under an Act of Parliament or the legislature of a province, including any order made under section 51, shall not be taken into account in determining any period referred to in subsection (2).

(4) Access to a record kept under section 115 or 116 in respect of extrajudicial measures, other than extrajudicial sanctions, used in respect of a young person shall be given only to the following persons for the following purposes:

   (*a*) a peace officer or the Attorney General, in order to make a decision whether to again use extrajudicial measures in respect of the young person;

   (*b*) a person participating in a conference, in order to decide on the appropriate extrajudicial measure;

   (*c*) a peace officer, the Attorney General or a person participating in a conference, if access is required for the administration of the case to which the record relates; and

   (*d*) a peace officer for the purpose of investigating an offence.

(5) When a youth justice court has withheld all or part of a report from any person under subsection 34(9) or (10) (nondisclosure of medical or psychological report) or 40(7) (nondisclosure of pre-sentence report), that person shall not be given access under subsection (1) to that report or part.

(6) Access to a report made under section 34 (medical and psychological reports) or a record of the results of forensic DNA analysis of a bodily substance taken from a young person in execution of a warrant issued under section 487.05 of the *Criminal Code* may be given only under paragraphs (1)(*a*) to (*c*), (*e*) to (*h*) and (*q*) and subparagraph (1)(*s*)(ii).

(7) Nothing in paragraph (1)(*h*) or (*q*) authorizes the introduction into evidence of any part of a record that would not otherwise be admissible in evidence.

(8) When access to a record is given to a person under paragraph (1)(*p*) or subparagraph (1)(*s*)(i), the person may subsequently disclose information contained in the record, but shall not disclose the information in any form that would reasonably be expected to identify the young person to whom it relates.

(9) If, during the period of access to a record under any of paragraphs (2)(*g*) to (*j*), the young person is convicted of an offence committed when he or she is an adult,

(a) section 82 (effect of absolute discharge or termination of youth sentence) does not apply to the young person in respect of the offence for which the record is kept under sections 114 to 116;

(b) this Part no longer applies to the record and the record shall be dealt with as a record of an adult; and

(c) for the purposes of the *Criminal Records Act*, the finding of guilt in respect of the offence for which the record is kept is deemed to be a conviction.

(10) Despite anything in this Act, when a young person is found guilty of an offence that results in a prohibition order being made, and the order is still in force at the end of the applicable period for which access to a record kept in respect of the order may be given under subsection (2),

(a) the record kept by the Royal Canadian Mounted Police pursuant to subsection 115(3) may be disclosed only to establish the existence of the order for purposes of law enforcement; and

(b) the record referred to in section 114 that is kept by the youth justice court may be disclosed only to establish the existence of the order in any offence involving a breach of the order. 2012, c. 1, s. 157; 2019, c. 13, s. 167.

YOUTH

ACCESS TO R.C.M.P. RECORDS / Access for identification purposes / Period of access / Subsequent offences as young person / Disclosure for research or statistical purposes / Subsequent offences as adult.

120. (1) The following persons may, during the period set out in subsection (3), be given access to a record kept under subsection 115(3) in respect of an offence set out in the schedule:

(a) the young person to whom the record relates;

(b) the young person's counsel, or any representative of that counsel;

(c) an employee or agent of the Government of Canada, for statistical purposes under the *Statistics Act*;

(d) any person or member of a class of persons that a youth justice court judge considers has a valid interest in the record, to the extent directed by the judge, if the judge is satisfied that access is desirable in the public interest for research or statistical purposes;

(e) the Attorney General or a peace officer, when the young person is or has been charged with another offence set out in the schedule or the same offence more than once, for the purpose of investigating any offence that the young person is suspected of having committed, or in respect of which the young person has been arrested or charged, whether as a young person or as an adult;

(f) the Attorney General or a peace officer to establish the existence of an order in any offence involving a breach of the order; and

(g) any person for the purposes of the *Firearms Act*.

(2) During the period set out in subsection (3), access to the portion of a record kept under subsection 115(3) that contains the name, date of birth and last known address of the young person to whom the fingerprints belong, may be given to a person for identification purposes if a fingerprint identified as that of the young

person is found during the investigation of an offence or during an attempt to identify a deceased person or a person suffering from amnesia.

(3) For the purposes of subsections (1) and (2), the period of access to a record kept under subsection 115(3) in respect of an offence is the following:

(a) if the offence is an indictable offence, other than an offence referred to in paragraph (b), the period starting at the end of the applicable period set out in paragraphs 119(2)(h) to (j) and ending five years later; and

(b) if the offence is a serious violent offence for which the Attorney General has given notice under subsection 64(2) (intention to seek adult sentence), the period starting at the end of the applicable period set out in paragraphs 119(2)(h) to (j) and continuing indefinitely.

(4) If a young person was found guilty of an offence set out in the schedule is, during the period of access to a record under subsection (3), found guilty of an additional offence set out in the schedule, committed when he or she was a young person, access to the record may be given to the following additional persons:

(a) a parent of the young person or any adult assisting the young person under subsection 25(7);

(b) a judge, court or review board, for a purpose relating to proceedings against the young person under this Act or any other Act of Parliament in respect of offences committed or alleged to have been committed by the young person, whether as a young person or as an adult; or

(c) a member of a department or agency of a government in Canada, or of an organization that is an agent of, or is under contract with, the department or agency, who is

 (i) preparing a report in respect of the young person under this Act or for the purpose of assisting a court in sentencing the young person after the young person becomes an adult,

 (ii) engaged in the supervision or care of the young person, whether as a young person or as an adult, or in the administration of a sentence in respect of the young person, whether as a young person or as an adult, or

 (iii) considering an application for conditional release, or for a record suspension under the *Criminal Records Act*, made by the young person after the young person becomes an adult.

(5) A person who is given access to a record under paragraph (1)(c) or (d) may subsequently disclose information contained in the record, but shall not disclose the information in any form that would reasonably be expected to identify the young person to whom it relates.

(6) If, during the period of access to a record under subsection (3), the young person is convicted of an additional offence set out in the schedule, committed when he or she was an adult,

(a) this Part no longer applies to the record and the record shall be dealt with as a record of an adult and may be included on the automated criminal conviction records retrieval system maintained by the Royal Canadian Mounted Police; and (*b*) for the purposes of the *Criminal Records Act*, the finding of guilt in respect of the offence for which the record is kept is deemed to be a conviction. 2012, c. 1, ss. 158, 192.

DEEMED ELECTION.

121. For the purposes of sections 119 and 120, if no election is made in respect of an offence that may be prosecuted by indictment or proceeded with by way of summary conviction, the Attorney General is deemed to have elected to proceed with the offence as an offence punishable on summary conviction.

DISCLOSURE OF INFORMATION AND COPIES OF RECORD.

122. A person who is required or authorized to be given access to a record under section 119, 120, 123 or 124 may be given any information contained in the record and may be given a copy of any part of the record.

YOUTH

WHERE RECORDS MAY BE MADE AVAILABLE / Restriction for paragraph (1)(*a*) / Notice / Where notice not required / Use of record / Disclosure for research or statistical purposes.

123. (1) A youth justice court judge may, on application by a person after the end of the applicable period set out in subsection 119(2), order that the person be given access to all or part of a record kept under sections 114 to 116 or that a copy of the record or part be given to that person,

    (*a*) if the youth justice court judge is satisfied that

        (i) the person has a valid and substantial interest in the record or part,

        (ii) it is necessary for access to be given to the record or part in the interest of the proper administration of justice, and

        (iii) disclosure of the record or part or the information in it is not prohibited under any other Act of Parliament or the legislature of a province; or

    (*b*) if the youth court judge is satisfied that access to the record or part is desirable in the public interest for research or statistical purposes.

(2) Paragraph (1)(*a*) applies in respect of a record relating to a particular young person or to a record relating to a class of young persons only if the identity of young persons in the class at the time of the making of the application referred to in that paragraph cannot reasonably be ascertained and the disclosure of the record is necessary for the purpose of investigating any offence that a person is suspected on reasonable grounds of having committed against a young person while the young person is, or was, serving a sentence.

(3) Subject to subsection (4), an application for an order under paragraph (1)(*a*) in respect of a record shall not be heard unless the person who makes the application has given the young person to whom the record relates and the person or body that has possession of the record at least five days notice in writing of the application, and the young person and the person or body that has possession have had a reasonable opportunity to be heard.

(4) A youth justice court judge may waive the requirement in subsection (3) to give notice to a young person when the judge is of the opinion that

    (a) to insist on the giving of the notice would frustrate the application; or

    (b) reasonable efforts have not been successful in finding the young person.

(5) In any order under subsection (1), the youth justice court judge shall set out the purposes for which the record may be used.

(6) When access to a record is given to any person under paragraph (1)*(b)*, that person may subsequently disclose information contained in the record, but shall not disclose the information in any form that would reasonably be expected to identify the young person to whom it relates.

ACCESS TO RECORD BY YOUNG PERSON.

124. A young person to whom a record relates and his or her counsel may have access to the record at any time.

Disclosure of Information in a Record

DISCLOSURE BY PEACE OFFICER DURING INVESTIGATION / Disclosure by Attorney General / Information that may be disclosed to a foreign state / Disclosure to insurance company / Preparation of reports / Schools and others / Information to be kept separate / Time limit.

125. (1) A peace officer may disclose to any person any information in a record kept under section 114 (court records) or 115 (police records) that it is necessary to disclose in the conduct of the investigation of an offence.

(2) The Attorney General may, in the course of a proceeding under this Act or any other Act of Parliament, disclose the following information in a record kept under section 114 (court reports) or 115 (police records):

    (a) to a person who is a co-accused with the young person in respect of the offence for which the record is kept, any information contained in the record; and

    (b) to an accused in a proceeding, if the record is in respect of a witness in the proceeding, information that identifies the witness as a young person who has been dealt with under this Act.

(3) The Attorney General or a peace officer may disclose to the Minister of Justice of Canada information in a record that is kept under section 114 (court records) or 115 (police records) to the extent that it is necessary to deal with a request to or by a foreign state under the *Mutual Legal Assistance in Criminal Matters Act*, or for the purposes of any extradition matter under the *Extradition Act*. The Minister of Justice of Canada may disclose the information to the foreign state in respect of which the request was made, or to which the extradition matter relates, as the case may be.

(4) A peace officer may disclose to an insurance company information in a record that is kept under section 114 (court records) or 115 (police records) for the

purpose of investigating a claim arising out of an offence committed or alleged to have been committed by the young person to whom the record relates.

(5) The provincial director or a youth worker may disclose information contained in a record if the disclosure is necessary for procuring information that relates to the preparation of a report required by this Act.

(6) The provincial director, a youth worker, the Attorney General, a peace officer or any other person engaged in the provision of services to young persons may disclose to any professional or other person engaged in the supervision or care of a young person — including a representative of any school board or school or any other educational or training institution — any information contained in a record kept under sections 114 to 116 if the disclosure is necessary

   (a) to ensure compliance by the young person with an authorization under section 91 or an order of the youth justice court;
   (b) to ensure the safety of staff, students or other persons; or
   (c) to facilitate the rehabilitation of the young person.

(7) A person to whom information is disclosed under subsection (6) shall
   (a) keep the information separate from any other record of the young person to whom the information relates;
   (b) ensure that no other person has access to the information except if authorized under this Act, or if necessary for the purposes of subsection (6); and
   (c) destroy their copy of the record when the information is no longer required for the purpose for which it was disclosed.

(8) No information may be disclosed under this section after the end of the applicable period set out in subsection 119(2) (period of access to records).

RECORDS IN THE CUSTODY, ETC., OF ARCHIVISTS.

126. When records originally kept under sections 114 to 116 are under the custody or control of the Librarian and Archivist of Canada or the archivist for any province, that person may disclose any information contained in the records to any other person if

   (a) a youth justice court judge is satisfied that the disclosure is desirable in the public interest for research or statistical purposes; and
   (b) the person to whom the information is disclosed undertakes not to disclose the information in any form that could reasonably be expected to identify the young person to whom it relates. 2004, c. 11, s. 48.

DISCLOSURE WITH COURT ORDER / Opportunity to be heard / *Ex parte* application / Time limit.

127. (1) The youth justice court may, on the application of the provincial director, the Attorney General or a peace officer, make an order permitting the applicant to disclose to the person or persons specified by the court any information about a young person that is specified, if the court is satisfied that the disclosure is necessary, having regard to the following circumstances:

   (a) the young person has been found guilty of an offence involving serious personal injury;

   (b) the young person poses a risk of serious harm to persons; and

   (c) the disclosure of the information is relevant to the avoidance of that risk.

(2) Subject to subsection (3), before making an order under subsection (1), the youth justice court shall give the young person, a parent of the young person and the Attorney General an opportunity to be heard.

(3) An application under subsection (1) may be made *ex parte* by the Attorney General where the youth justice court is satisfied that reasonable efforts have been made to locate the young person and that those efforts have not been successful.

(4) No information may be disclosed under subsection (1) after the end of the applicable period set out in subsection 119(2) (period of access to records).

Disposition or Destruction of Records and Prohibition on Use and Disclosure

EFFECT OF END OF ACCESS PERIODS / Disposal of records / Disposal of R.C.M.P. records / Purging CPIC / Exception / Authority to inspect / Definition of "destroy".

128. (1) Subject to sections 123, 124 and 126, after the end of the applicable period set out in section 119 or 120 no record kept under sections 114 to 116 may be used for any purpose that would identify the young person to whom the record relates as a young person dealt with under this Act or the *Young Offenders Act*, chapter Y-1 of the Revised Statutes of Canada, 1985.

(2) Subject to paragraph 125(7)(*c*), any record kept under sections 114 to 116, other than a record kept under subsection 115(3), may, in the discretion of the person or body keeping the record, be destroyed or transmitted to the Librarian and Archivist of Canada or the archivist for any province, at any time before or after the end of the applicable period set out in section 119.

(3) All records kept under subsection 115(3) shall be destroyed or, if the Librarian and Archivist of Canada requires it, transmitted to the Librarian and Archivist, at the end of the applicable period set out in section 119 or 120.

(4) The Commissioner of the Royal Canadian Mounted Police shall remove a record from the automated criminal conviction records retrieval system maintained by the Royal Canadian Mounted Police at the end of the applicable period referred to in section 119; however, information relating to a prohibition order made under an Act of Parliament or the legislature of a province shall be removed only at the end of the period for which the order is in force.

(5) Despite subsections (1), (2) and (4), an entry that is contained in a system maintained by the Royal Canadian Mounted Police to match crime scene information and that relates to an offence committed or alleged to have been committed by a young person shall be dealt with in the same manner as

information that relates to an offence committed by an adult for which a record suspension ordered under the *Criminal Records Act* is in effect.

(6) The Librarian and Archivist of Canada may, at any time, inspect records kept under sections 114 to 116 that are under the control of a government institution as defined in section 2 of the *Library and Archives of Canada Act*, and the archivist for a province may at any time inspect any records kept under those sections that the archivist is authorized to inspect under any Act of the legislature of the province.

(7) For the purposes of subsections (2) and (3), "destroy", in respect of a record, means

    (*a*) to shred, burn or otherwise physically destroy the record, in the case of a record other than a record in electronic form; and

    (*b*) to delete, write over or otherwise render the record inaccessible, in the case of a record in electronic form. 2004, c. 11, s. 49; 2012, c. 1, s. 159.

NO SUBSEQUENT DISCLOSURE.

129. No person who is given access to a record or to whom information is disclosed under this Act shall disclose that information to any other person unless the disclosure is authorized under this Act.

PART 7 / GENERAL PROVISIONS

Disqualification of Judge

DISQUALIFICATION OF JUDGE / Exception.

130. (1) Subject to subsection (2), a youth justice court judge who, prior to an adjudication in respect of a young person charged with an offence, examines a pre-sentence report made in respect of the young person in connection with that offence or has, after a guilty plea or a finding of guilt, heard submissions as to sentence and then there has been a change of plea, shall not in any capacity conduct or continue the trial of the young person for the offence and shall transfer the case to another judge to be dealt with according to law.

(2) A youth justice court judge may, in the circumstances referred to in subsection (1), with the consent of the young person and the prosecutor, conduct or continue the trial of the young person if the judge is satisfied that he or she has not been predisposed by a guilty plea or finding of guilt, or by information contained in the pre-sentence report or submissions as to sentence.

Substitution of Judge

POWERS OF SUBSTITUTE YOUTH JUSTICE COURT JUDGE / Transcript of evidence already given.

131. (1) A youth justice court judge who acts in the place of another youth justice court judge under subsection 669.2(1) (continuation of proceedings) of the *Criminal Code* shall

    (*a*) if an adjudication has been made, proceed to sentence the young person or make the order that, in the circumstances, is authorized by law; or

    (*b*) if no adjudication has been made, recommence the trial as if no evidence had been taken.

(2) A youth justice court judge who recommences a trial under paragraph (1)(*b*) may, if the parties consent, admit into evidence a transcript of any evidence already given in the case.

Exclusion from Hearing

EXCLUSION FROM HEARING / Exception / Exclusion after adjudication or during review / Exception.

132. (1) Subject to subsection (2), a court or justice before whom proceedings are carried out under this Act may exclude any person from all or part of the proceedings if the court or justice considers that the person's presence is unnecessary to the conduct of the proceedings and the court or justice is of the opinion that

    (*a*) any evidence or information presented to the court or justice would be seriously injurious or seriously prejudicial to

        (i) the young person who is being dealt with in the proceedings,

        (ii) a child or young person who is a witness in the proceedings, or

        (iii) a child or young person who is aggrieved by or the victim of the offence charged in the proceedings; or

    (*b*) it would be in the interest of public morals, the maintenance of order or the proper administration of justice to exclude any or all members of the public from the court room.

(2) Subject to section 650 (accused to be present) of the *Criminal Code* and except if it is necessary for the purposes of subsection 34(9) (nondisclosure of medical or psychological report) of this Act, a court or justice may not, under subsection (1), exclude from proceedings under this Act

    (*a*) the prosecutor;

    (*b*) the young person who is being dealt with in the proceedings, the counsel or a parent of the young person or any adult assisting the young person under subsection 25(7);

    (*c*) the provincial director or his or her agent; or

    (*d*) the youth worker to whom the young person's case has been assigned.

(3) A youth justice court, after it has found a young person guilty of an offence, or a youth justice court or a review board, during a review, may, in its discretion, exclude from the court or from a hearing of the review board any person other than the following, when it is being presented with information the knowledge of which might, in its opinion, be seriously injurious or seriously prejudicial to the young person:

    (*a*) the young person or his or her counsel;

    (*b*) the provincial director or his or her agent;

    (*c*) the youth worker to whom the young person's case has been assigned; and

    (*d*) the Attorney General.

(4) The exception set out in paragraph (3)(*a*) is subject to subsection 34(9) (nondisclosure of medical or psychological report) of this Act and section 650 (accused to be present) of the *Criminal Code*.

Transfer of Charges

TRANSFER OF CHARGES.

133. Despite subsections 478(1) and (3) of the *Criminal Code*, a young person charged with an offence that is alleged to have been committed in one province may, if the Attorney General of the province consents, appear before a youth justice court of any other province and

    (*a*) if the young person pleads guilty to that offence and the youth justice court is satisfied that the facts support the charge, the court shall find the young person guilty of the offence alleged in the information or indictment; and

    (*b*) if the young person pleads not guilty to that offence, or pleads guilty but the court is not satisfied that the facts support the charge, the young person shall, if he or she was detained in custody prior to the appearance, be returned to custody and dealt with according to law.

Forfeiture of Recognizances

APPLICATIONS FOR FORFEITURE.

134. Applications for the forfeiture of amounts set out in undertakings, release orders or recognizances binding young persons shall be made to the youth justice court. 2019, c. 25, s. 380.

PROCEEDINGS IN CASE OF DEFAULT / Order for forfeiture / Judgment debtors of the Crown / Order may be filed / If a deposit has been made / Subsections 770(2) and (4) of *Criminal Code* do not apply / Sections 772 and 773 of *Criminal Code* apply.

135. (1) If an undertaking, release order or recognizance binding a young person has been endorsed with a certificate under subsection 770(1) of the *Criminal Code*, a youth justice court judge shall

(a) on the request of the Attorney General, fix a time and place for the hearing of an application for the forfeiture of the amount set out in the undertaking, release order or recognizance; and

(b) after fixing a time and place for the hearing, cause to be sent by confirmed delivery service, not less than 10 days before the time so fixed, to each principal and surety named in the undertaking, release order or recognizance, directed to their latest known address, a notice requiring them to appear at the time and place fixed by the judge to show cause why the amount set out in the undertaking, release order or recognizance should not be forfeited.

(2) When subsection (1) is complied with, the youth justice court judge may, after giving the parties an opportunity to be heard, in the judge's discretion grant or refuse the application and make any order with respect to the forfeiture of the amount that the judge considers proper.

(3) If, under subsection (2), a youth justice court judge orders the forfeiture of the amount, the principal and their sureties become judgment debtors of the Crown, each in the amount that the judge orders them to pay.

(4) An order made under subsection (2) may be filed with the clerk of the superior court or, in the province of Quebec, the prothonotary and, if an order is filed, the clerk or the prothonotary shall issue a writ of fieri facias in Form 34 set out in the *Criminal Code* and deliver it to the sheriff of each of the territorial divisions in which any of the principal and his or her sureties resides, carries on business or has property.

(5) If a deposit has been made by a person against whom an order for forfeiture has been made, no writ of *fieri facias* shall issue, but the amount of the deposit shall be transferred by the person who has custody of it to the person who is entitled by law to receive it.

(6) Subsections 770(2) (transmission to clerk of the court) and (4) (transmission of deposit) of the *Criminal Code* do not apply in respect of proceedings under this Act.

(7) Sections 772 (levy under writ) and 773 (committal when writ not satisfied) of the *Criminal Code* apply in respect of writs of fieri facias issued under this section as if they were issued under section 771 (proceedings in case of default) of that Act. 2019, c. 25, s. 381.

Offences and Punishment

INDUCING A YOUNG PERSON, ETC. / Absolute jurisdiction of provincial court judge.

136. (1) Every person who

(a) induces or assists a young person to leave unlawfully a place of custody or other place in which the young person has been placed in accordance with a youth sentence or a disposition imposed under the *Young Offenders Act*, chapter Y-1 of the Revised Statutes of Canada, 1985, (*b*) unlawfully removes a young person from a place referred to in paragraph (*a*),

   (*c*) knowingly harbours or conceals a young person who has unlawfully left a place referred to in paragraph (*a*),

   (*d*) wilfully induces or assists a young person to breach or disobey a term or condition of a youth sentence or other order of the youth justice court, or a term or condition of a disposition or other order under the *Young Offenders Act*, chapter Y-1 of the Revised Statutes of Canada, 1985, or

   (*e*) wilfully prevents or interferes with the performance by a young person of a term or condition of a youth sentence or other order of the youth justice court, or a term or condition of a disposition or other order under the *Young Offenders Act*, chapter Y-1 of the Revised Statutes of Canada, 1985,

is guilty of an indictable offence and liable to imprisonment for a term not exceeding two years or is guilty of an offence punishable on summary conviction.

(2) The jurisdiction of a provincial court judge to try an adult charged with an indictable offence under this section is absolute and does not depend on the consent of the accused.

YOUTH

FAILURE TO COMPLY WITH SENTENCE OR DISPOSITION.

137. Every person who is subject to a youth sentence imposed under any of paragraphs 42(2)(*c*) to (*m*) or (*s*) of this Act, to a victim fine surcharge ordered under subsection 53(2) of this Act or to a disposition made under any of paragraphs 20(1)(a.1) to (*g*), (*j*) or (*l*) of the *Young Offenders Act*, chapter Y-1 of the Revised Statutes of Canada, 1985, and who wilfully fails or refuses to comply with that sentence, surcharge or disposition is guilty of an offence punishable on summary conviction.

OFFENCES / Provincial court judge has absolute jurisdiction on indictment.

138. (1) Every person who contravenes subsection 110(1) (identity of offender not to be published), 111(1) (identity of victim or witness not to be published), 118(1) (no access to records unless authorized) or 128(3) (disposal of R.C.M.P. records) or section 129 (no subsequent disclosure) of this Act, or subsection 38(1) (identity not to be published), (1.12) (no subsequent disclosure), (1.14) (no subsequent disclosure by school) or (1.15) (information to be kept separate), 45(2) (destruction of records) or 46(1) (prohibition against disclosure) of the *Young Offenders Act*, chapter Y-1 of the Revised Statutes of Canada, 1985,

   (*a*) is guilty of an indictable offence and liable to imprisonment for a term not exceeding two years; or

   (*b*) is guilty of an offence punishable on summary conviction.

(2) The jurisdiction of a provincial court judge to try an adult charged with an offence under paragraph (1)(*a*) is absolute and does not depend on the consent of the accused.

OFFENCE AND PUNISHMENT / Offence and punishment / Punishment.

139. (1) Every person who wilfully fails to comply with section 30 (designated place of temporary detention), or with an undertaking entered into under subsection 31(3) (condition of placement),

- (*a*) is guilty of an indictable offence and liable to imprisonment for a term not exceeding two years; or
- (*b*) is guilty of an offence punishable on summary conviction.

(2) Every person who wilfully fails to comply with section 7 (designated place of temporary detention) of the *Young Offenders Act*, chapter Y-1 of the Revised Statutes of Canada, 1985, or with an undertaking entered into under subsection 7.1(2) (condition of placement) of that Act is guilty of an offence punishable on summary conviction.

(3) Any person who uses or authorizes the use of an application form in contravention of subsection 82(3) (application for employment) is guilty of an offence punishable on summary conviction.

Application of *Criminal Code*

APPLICATION OF CRIMINAL CODE.

140. Except to the extent that it is inconsistent with or excluded by this Act, the provisions of the *Criminal Code* apply, with any modifications that the circumstances require, in respect of offences alleged to have been committed by young persons.

SECTIONS OF CRIMINAL CODE APPLICABLE / Notice and copies to counsel and parents / Proceedings not invalid / Exception / No hospital order assessments / Considerations of court or Review Board making a disposition / Cap applicable to young persons / Application to increase cap of unfit young person subject to adult sentence / Consideration of youth justice court for increase in cap / *Prima facie* case to be made every year / Designation of hospitals for young persons / Definition of "Review Board".

141. (1) Except to the extent that they are inconsistent with or excluded by this Act, section 16 (defence of mental disorder) and Part XX.1 (mental disorder) of the *Criminal Code* apply, with any modifications that the circumstances require, in respect of proceedings under this Act in relation to offences alleged to have been committed by young persons.

(2) For the purposes of subsection (1),

- (*a*) wherever in Part XX.1 (mental disorder) of the *Criminal Code* a reference is made to a copy to be sent or otherwise given to an accused or a party to the proceedings, the reference shall be read as including a reference to a copy to be sent or otherwise given to
  - (i) any counsel representing the young person,
  - (ii) a parent of the young person who is in attendance at the proceedings against the young person, and

(iii) a parent of the young person not in attendance at the proceedings who is, in the opinion of the youth justice court or Review Board, taking an active interest in the proceedings; and

(b) wherever in Part XX.1 (mental disorder) of the *Criminal Code* a reference is made to notice to be given to an accused or a party to proceedings, the reference shall be read as including a reference to notice to be given to a parent of the young person and any counsel representing the young person.

(3) Subject to subsection (4), failure to give a notice referred to in paragraph (2)(*b*) to a parent of a young person does not affect the validity of proceedings under this Act.

(4) Failure to give a notice referred to in paragraph (2)(*b*) to a parent of a young person in any case renders invalid any subsequent proceedings under this Act relating to the case unless

(a) a parent of the young person attends at the court or Review Board with the young person; or

(b) a youth justice court judge or Review Board before whom proceedings are held against the young person

(i) adjourns the proceedings and orders that the notice be given in the manner and to the persons that the judge or Review Board directs, or

(ii) dispenses with the notice if the youth justice court or Review Board is of the opinion that, having regard to the circumstances, the notice may be dispensed with.

(5) [*Repealed*, 2005, c. 22, s. 63(2).]

(6) Before making or reviewing a disposition in respect of a young person under Part XX.1 (mental disorder) of the *Criminal Code*, a youth justice court or Review Board shall consider the age and special needs of the young person and any representations or submissions made by a parent of the young person.

(7) to (9) [*Repealed*, 2005, c. 22, s. 63(3).]

(10) For the purpose of applying subsection 672.33(1) (fitness to stand trial) of the *Criminal Code* to proceedings under this Act in relation to an offence alleged to have been committed by a young person, wherever in that subsection a reference is made to two years, there shall be substituted a reference to one year.

(11) A reference in Part XX.1 (mental disorder) of the *Criminal Code* to a hospital in a province shall be construed as a reference to a hospital designated by the Minister of Health for the province for the custody, treatment or assessment of young persons.

(12) In this section, "Review Board" has the meaning assigned by section 672.1 of the *Criminal Code*. 2005, c. 22, s. 63.

PART XXVII AND SUMMARY CONVICTION TRIAL PROVISIONS OF CRIMINAL CODE TO APPLY / Indictable offences / Attendance of young person / Limitation period / Costs.

142. (1) Subject to this section and except to the extent that they are inconsistent with this Act, the provisions of Part XXVII (summary conviction offences) of the

Criminal Code, and any other provisions of that Act that apply in respect of summary conviction offences and relate to trial proceedings, apply to proceedings under this Act

(a) in respect of an order under section 83.3 (recognizance — terrorist activity), 810 (recognizance — fear of injury or damage), 810.01 (recognizance — fear of certain offences), 810.011 (recognizance — fear of terrorism offence), 810.02 (recognizance — fear of forced marriage or marriage under age of 16 years) or 810.2 (recognizance — fear of serious personal injury offence) of that Act or an offence under section 811 (breach of recognizance) of that Act;

(b) in respect of a summary conviction offence; and

(c) in respect of an indictable offence as if it were defined in the enactment creating it as a summary conviction offence.

(2) For greater certainty and despite subsection (1) or any other provision of this Act, an indictable offence committed by a young person is, for the purposes of this Act or any other Act of Parliament, an indictable offence.

(3) Section 650 of the *Criminal Code* applies in respect of proceedings under this Act, whether the proceedings relate to an indictable offence or an offence punishable on summary conviction.

(4) In proceedings under this Act, subsection 786(2) of the *Criminal Code* does not apply in respect of an indictable offence.

(5) Section 809 of the *Criminal Code* does not apply in respect of proceedings under this Act. 2015, c. 20, ss. 33, 36(9); c. 29, s. 15.

Procedure

COUNTS CHARGED IN INFORMATION.

143. Indictable offences and offences punishable on summary conviction may under this Act be charged in the same information or indictment and tried jointly.

ISSUE OF SUBPOENA / Service of subpoena.

144. (1) If a person is required to attend to give evidence before a youth justice court, the subpoena directed to that person may be issued by a youth justice court judge, whether or not the person whose attendance is required is within the same province as the youth justice court.

(2) A subpoena issued by a youth justice court and directed to a person who is not within the same province as the youth justice court shall be served personally on the person to whom it is directed.

WARRANT.

145. A warrant issued by a youth justice court may be executed anywhere in Canada.

Evidence

GENERAL LAW ON ADMISSIBILITY OF STATEMENTS TO APPLY / When statements are admissible / Exception in certain cases for oral statements / Waiver of right to consult / Waiver of right to consult / Admissibility of statements / Statements made under duress are inadmissible / Misrepresentation of age / Parent, etc., not a person in authority.

146. (1) Subject to this section, the law relating to the admissibility of statements made by persons accused of committing offences applies in respect of young persons.

(2) No oral or written statement made by a young person who is less than eighteen years old, to a peace officer or to any other person who is, in law, a person in authority, on the arrest or detention of the young person or in circumstances where the peace officer or other person has reasonable grounds for believing that the young person has committed an offence is admissible against the young person unless

  (*a*) the statement was voluntary;

  (*b*) the person to whom the statement was made has, before the statement was made, clearly explained to the young person, in language appropriate to his or her age and understanding, that

    (i) the young person is under no obligation to make a statement,

    (ii) any statement made by the young person may be used as evidence in proceedings against him or her,

    (iii) the young person has the right to consult counsel and a parent or other person in accordance with paragraph (*c*), and

    (iv) any statement made by the young person is required to be made in the presence of counsel and any other person consulted in accordance with paragraph (*c*), if any, unless the young person desires otherwise;

  (*c*) the young person has, before the statement was made, been given a reasonable opportunity to consult

    (i) with counsel, and

    (ii) with a parent or, in the absence of a parent, an adult relative or, in the absence of a parent and an adult relative, any other appropriate adult chosen by the young person, as long as that person is not a co-accused, or under investigation, in respect of the same offence; and

  (*d*) if the young person consults a person in accordance with paragraph (*c*), the young person has been given a reasonable opportunity to make the statement in the presence of that person.

(3) The requirements set out in paragraphs (2)(*b*) to (*d*) do not apply in respect of oral statements if they are made spontaneously by the young person to a peace officer or other person in authority before that person has had a reasonable opportunity to comply with those requirements.

(4) A young person may waive the rights under paragraph (2)(*c*) or (*d*) but any such waiver

  (*a*) must be recorded on video tape or audio tape; or

1259

(*b*) must be in writing and contain a statement signed by the young person that he or she has been informed of the right being waived.

(5) When a waiver of rights under paragraph (2)(*c*) or (*d*) is not made in accordance with subsection (4) owing to a technical irregularity, the youth justice court may determine that the waiver is valid if it is satisfied that the young person was informed of his or her rights, and voluntarily waived them.

(6) When there has been a technical irregularity in complying with paragraphs (2)(*b*) to (*d*), the youth justice court may admit into evidence a statement referred to in subsection (2), if satisfied that the admission of the statement would not bring into disrepute the principle that young persons are entitled to enhanced procedural protection to ensure that they are treated fairly and their rights are protected.

(7) A youth justice court judge may rule inadmissible in any proceedings under this Act a statement made by the young person in respect of whom the proceedings are taken if the young person satisfies the judge that the statement was made under duress imposed by any person who is not, in law, a person in authority.

(8) A youth justice court judge may in any proceedings under this Act rule admissible any statement or waiver by a young person if, at the time of the making of the statement or waiver,

(*a*) the young person held himself or herself to be eighteen years old or older;

(*b*) the person to whom the statement or waiver was made conducted reasonable inquiries as to the age of the young person and had reasonable grounds for believing that the young person was eighteen years old or older; and

(*c*) in all other circumstances the statement or waiver would otherwise be admissible.

(9) For the purpose of this section, a person consulted under paragraph (2)(*c*) is, in the absence of evidence to the contrary, deemed not to be a person in authority.

STATEMENTS NOT ADMISSIBLE AGAINST YOUNG PERSON / Exceptions.

147. (1) Subject to subsection (2), if a young person is assessed in accordance with an order made under subsection 34(1) (medical or psychological assessment), no statement or reference to a statement made by the young person during the course and for the purposes of the assessment to the person who conducts the assessment or to anyone acting under that person's direction is admissible in evidence, without the consent of the young person, in any proceeding before a court, tribunal, body or person with jurisdiction to compel the production of evidence.

(2) A statement referred to in subsection (1) is admissible in evidence for the purposes of

(*a*) making a decision on an application heard under section 71 (hearing — adult sentences);

(*b*) determining whether the young person is unfit to stand trial;

(*c*) determining whether the balance of the mind of the young person was disturbed at the time of commission of the alleged offence, if the young person is a female person charged with an offence arising out of the death of her newly-born child;

(*d*) making or reviewing a sentence in respect of the young person;

(*e*) determining whether the young person was, at the time of the commission of an alleged offence, suffering from automatism or a mental disorder so as to be exempt from criminal responsibility by virtue of subsection 16(1) of the *Criminal Code*, if the accused puts his or her mental capacity for criminal intent into issue, or if the prosecutor raises the issue after verdict;

(*f*) challenging the credibility of a young person in any proceeding if the testimony of the young person is inconsistent in a material particular with a statement referred to in subsection (1) that the young person made previously;

(*g*) establishing the perjury of a young person who is charged with perjury in respect of a statement made in any proceeding;

(*h*) deciding an application for an order under subsection 104(1) (continuation of custody);

(*i*) setting the conditions under subsection 105(1) (conditional supervision);

(*j*) conducting a review under subsection 109(1) (review of decision); or

(*k*) deciding an application for a disclosure order under subsection 127(1) (information about a young person).

TESTIMONY OF A PARENT / Evidence of age by certificate or record / Other evidence / When age may be inferred.

148. (1) In any proceedings under this Act, the testimony of a parent as to the age of a person of whom he or she is a parent is admissible as evidence of the age of that person.

(2) In any proceedings under this Act,

(*a*) a birth or baptismal certificate or a copy of it purporting to be certified under the hand of the person in whose custody those records are held is evidence of the age of the person named in the certificate or copy; and

(*b*) an entry or record of an incorporated society that has had the control or care of the person alleged to have committed the offence in respect of which the proceedings are taken at or about the time the person came to Canada is evidence of the age of that person, if the entry or record was made before the time when the offence is alleged to have been committed.

(3) In the absence of any certificate, copy, entry or record mentioned in subsection (2), or in corroboration of that certificate, copy, entry or record, the youth justice court may receive and act on any other information relating to age that it considers reliable.

(4) In any proceedings under this Act, the youth justice court may draw inferences as to the age of a person from the person's appearance or from statements made by the person in direct examination or cross-examination.

ADMISSIONS / Other party may adduce evidence.

149. (1) A party to any proceedings under this Act may admit any relevant fact or matter for the purpose of dispensing with proof of it, including any fact or matter the admissibility of which depends on a ruling of law or of mixed law and fact.

(2) Nothing in this section precludes a party to a proceeding from adducing evidence to prove a fact or matter admitted by another party.

MATERIAL EVIDENCE.

150. Any evidence material to proceedings under this Act that would not but for this section be admissible in evidence may, with the consent of the parties to the proceedings and if the young person is represented by counsel, be given in such proceedings.

EVIDENCE OF A CHILD OR YOUNG PERSON.

151. The evidence of a child or a young person may be taken in proceedings under this Act only after the youth justice court judge or the justice in the proceedings has
- (*a*) if the witness is a child, instructed the child as to the duty to speak the truth and the consequences of failing to do so; and
- (*b*) if the witness is a young person and the judge or justice considers it necessary, instructed the young person as to the duty to speak the truth and the consequences of failing to do so.

PROOF OF SERVICE / Proof of signature and official character unnecessary.

152. (1) For the purposes of this Act, service of any document may be proved by oral evidence given under oath by, or by the affidavit or statutory declaration of, the person claiming to have personally served it or sent it by confirmed delivery service.

(2) If proof of service of any document is offered by affidavit or statutory declaration, it is not necessary to prove the signature or official character of the person making or taking the affidavit or declaration, if the official character of that person appears on the face of the affidavit or declaration.

SEAL NOT REQUIRED.

153. It is not necessary to the validity of any information, indictment, summons, warrant, minute, sentence, conviction, order or other process or document laid, issued, filed or entered in any proceedings under this Act that any seal be attached or affixed to it.

Forms, Regulations and Rules of Court

FORMS / If forms not prescribed.

154. (1) The forms prescribed under section 155, varied to suit the case, or forms to the like effect, are valid and sufficient in the circumstances for which they are provided.

(2) In any case for which forms are not prescribed under section 155, the forms set out in Part XXVIII of the *Criminal Code*, with any modifications that the circumstances require, or other appropriate forms, may be used.

REGULATIONS.

155. The Governor in Council may make regulations

- (a) prescribing forms that may be used for the purposes of this Act;
- (b) establishing uniform rules of court for youth justice courts across Canada, including rules regulating the practice and procedure to be followed by youth justice courts; and
- (c) generally for carrying out the purposes and provisions of this Act.

Agreements with Provinces

AGREEMENTS WITH PROVINCES.

156. Any minister of the Crown may, with the approval of the Governor in Council, enter into an agreement with the government of any province providing for payments by Canada to the province in respect of costs incurred by the province or a municipality in the province for care of and services provided to young persons dealt with under this Act.

Programs

COMMUNITY-BASED PROGRAMS.

157. The Attorney General of Canada or a minister designated by the lieutenant governor in council of a province may establish the following types of community-based programs:

- (a) programs that are an alternative to judicial proceedings, such as victim-offender reconciliation programs, mediation programs and restitution programs;
- (b) programs that are an alternative to detention before sentencing, such as bail supervision programs; and
- (c) programs that are an alternative to custody, such as intensive support and supervision programs, and programs to carry out attendance orders.

PART 8 / TRANSITIONAL PROVISIONS

PROHIBITION ON PROCEEDINGS.

158. On and after the coming into force of this section, no proceedings may be commenced under the *Young Offenders Act*, chapter Y-1 of the Revised Statutes of Canada, 1985, in respect of an offence within the meaning of that Act, or under the

Juvenile Delinquents Act, chapter J-3 of the Revised Statutes of Canada, 1970, in respect of a delinquency within the meaning of that Act.

PROCEEDINGS COMMENCED UNDER YOUNG OFFENDERS ACT/ Proceedings commenced under *Juvenile Delinquents Act.*

159. (1) Subject to section 161, where, before the coming into force of this section, proceedings are commenced under the *Young Offenders Act*, chapter Y-1 of the Revised Statutes of Canada, 1985, in respect of an offence within the meaning of that Act alleged to have been committed by a person who was at the time of the offence a young person within the meaning of that Act, the proceedings and all related matters shall be dealt with in all respects as if this Act had not come into force.

(2) Subject to section 161, where, before the coming into force of this section, proceedings are commenced under the *Juvenile Delinquents Act*, chapter J-3 of the Revised Statutes of Canada, 1970, in respect of a delinquency within the meaning of that Act alleged to have been committed by a person who was at the time of the delinquency a child as defined in that Act, the proceedings and all related matters shall be dealt with under this Act as if the delinquency were an offence that occurred after the coming into force of this section.

OFFENCES COMMITTED BEFORE THIS SECTION IN FORCE.

160. [*Repealed*, 2012, c. 1, s. 193.]

APPLICABLE SENTENCE / Dispositions under paragraph 20(1)(*k*) or (*k*.1) of *Young Offenders Act* / Review of sentence.

161. (1) A person referred to in section 159 who is found guilty of an offence or delinquency, other than a person convicted of an offence in ordinary court, as defined in subsection 2(1) of the *Young Offenders Act*, chapter Y-1 of the Revised Statutes of Canada, 1985, shall be sentenced under this Act, except that

(*a*) [*Repealed*, 2019, c. 25, s. 382.]

(*b*) paragraph 42(2)(*r*) applies in respect of the offence or delinquency only if the young person consents to its application.

The provisions of this Act applicable to sentences imposed under section 42 apply in respect of the sentence.

(2) Where a young person is to be sentenced under this Act while subject to a disposition under paragraph 20(1)(*k*) or (*k*.1) of the *Young Offenders Act*, chapter Y-1 of the Revised Statutes of Canada, 1985, on the application of the Attorney General or the young person, a youth justice court shall, unless to do so would bring the administration of justice into disrepute, order that the remaining portion of the disposition made under that Act be dealt with, for all purposes under this Act or any other Act of Parliament, as if it had been a sentence imposed under paragraph 42(2)(*n*) or (*q*) of this Act, as the case may be.

(3) For greater certainty, for the purpose of determining when the sentence is reviewed under section 94, the relevant date is the one on which the disposition

came into force under the *Young Offenders Act*, chapter Y-1 of the Revised Statutes of Canada, 1985. 2019, c. 25, s. 382.

COMMENCEMENT OF PROCEEDINGS.

162. For the purposes of sections 158 and 159, proceedings are commenced by the laying of an information or indictment. 2012, c. 1, s. 194.

APPLICATION TO DELINQUENCY AND OTHER OFFENDING BEHAVIOUR.

163. Sections 114 to 129 apply, with any modifications that the circumstances require, in respect of records relating to the offence of delinquency under the *Juvenile Delinquents Act*, chapter J-3 of the Revised Statutes of Canada, 1970, and in respect of records kept under sections 40 to 43 of the *Young Offenders Act*, chapter Y-1 of the Revised Statutes of Canada, 1985.

AGREEMENTS CONTINUE IN FORCE.

164. Any agreement made under the *Young Offenders Act*, chapter Y-1 of the Revised Statutes of Canada, 1985, remains in force until it expires, unless it is amended or a new agreement is made under this Act.

DESIGNATION OF YOUTH JUSTICE COURT / Designation of youth justice court judges / Designation of provincial directors and youth workers / Designation of review boards and youth justice committees / Alternative measures continued as extrajudicial sanctions / Designation of places of temporary detention and youth custody / Exception / Designation of other persons.

165. (1) Any court established or designated as a youth court for the purposes of the *Young Offenders Act*, chapter Y-1 of the Revised Statutes of Canada, 1985, is deemed, as of the coming into force of this section, to have been established or designated as a youth justice court for the purposes of this Act.

(2) Any person appointed to be a judge of the youth court for the purposes of the *Young Offenders Act*, chapter Y-1 of the Revised Statutes of Canada, 1985, is deemed, as of the coming into force of this section, to have been appointed as a judge of the youth justice court for the purposes of this Act.

(3) Any person, group or class of persons or body appointed or designated as a provincial director for the purposes of the *Young Offenders Act*, chapter Y-1 of the Revised Statutes of Canada, 1985, and any person appointed or designated as a youth worker for the purposes of that Act is deemed, as of the coming into force of this section, to have been appointed or designated as a provincial director or youth worker, as the case may be, for the purposes of this Act.

(4) Any review board established or designated for the purposes of the *Young Offenders Act*, chapter Y-1 of the Revised Statutes of Canada, 1985, and any youth justice committee established for the purposes of that Act is deemed, as of the coming into force of this section, to have been established or designated as a

review board or a youth justice committee, as the case may be, for the purposes of this Act.

(5) Any program of alternative measures authorized for the purposes of the *Young Offenders Act*, chapter Y-1 of the Revised Statutes of Canada, 1985, is deemed, as of the coming into force of this section, to be a program of extrajudicial sanctions authorized for the purposes of this Act.

(6) Subject to subsection (7), any place that was designated as a place of temporary detention or open custody for the purposes of the *Young Offenders Act*, chapter Y-1 of the Revised Statutes of Canada, 1985, and any place or facility designated as a place of secure custody for the purposes of that Act is deemed, as of the coming into force of this section, to have been designated for the purposes of this Act as

- (*a*) in the case of a place of temporary detention, a place of temporary detention; and
- (*b*) in the case of a place of open custody or secure custody, a youth custody facility.

(7) If the lieutenant governor in council of a province makes an order under section 88 that the power to make determinations of the level of custody for young persons and to review those determinations be exercised in accordance with the *Young Offenders Act*, chapter Y-1 of the Revised Statutes of Canada, 1985, the designation of any place as a place of open custody or secure custody for the purposes of that Act remains in force for the purposes of section 88, subject to revocation or amendment of the designation.

(8) Any person designated as a clerk of the youth court for the purposes of the *Young Offenders Act*, chapter Y-1 of the Revised Statutes of Canada, 1985, or any person or group of persons who were designated under that Act to carry out specified functions and duties are deemed, as of the coming into force of this section, to have been designated as a clerk of the youth justice court, or to carry out the same functions and duties, as the case may be, under this Act.

Note: Sections 166 to 199 of the *Youth Criminal Justice Act* make consequential amendments to other Acts. These sections are not reproduced here.

COMING INTO FORCE.

200. The provisions of this Act come into force on a day or days to be fixed by order of the Governor in Council.

SCHEDULE
(Subsections 120(1), (4) and (6))

1. An offence under any of the following provisions of the *Criminal Code*:
   - (*a*) paragraph 81(2)(*a*) (using explosives);
   - (*b*) subsection 85(1) (using firearm in commission of offence);
   - (*c*) section 151 (sexual interference);
   - (*d*) section 152 (invitation to sexual touching);

(e) section 153 (sexual exploitation);

(f) section 155 (incest);

(g) [Repealed, 2019, c. 25, s. 383.]

(h) section 170 (parent or guardian procuring sexual activity by child);

(i) [Repealed, 2014, c. 25, s. 43(1).]

(j) [Repealed, 2014, c. 25, s. 43(1).]

(k) section 231 or 235 (first degree murder or second degree murder within the meaning of section 231);

(l) section 232, 234 or 236 (manslaughter);

(m) section 239 (attempt to commit murder);

(n) section 267 (assault with a weapon or causing bodily harm);

(o) section 268 (aggravated assault);

(p) section 269 (unlawfully causing bodily harm);

(q) section 271 (sexual assault);

(r) section 272 (sexual assault with a weapon, threats to a third party or causing bodily harm);

(s) section 273 (aggravated sexual assault);

(t) section 279 (kidnapping);

(t.1) section 279.011 (trafficking — person under 18 years);

(t.2) subsection 279.02(2) (material benefit — trafficking of person under 18 years);

(t.3) subsection 279.03(2) (withholding or destroying documents — trafficking of person under 18 years);

(t.4) subsection 286.1(2) (obtaining sexual services for consideration from person under 18 years);

(t.5) subsection 286.2(2) (material benefit from sexual services provided by person under 18 years);

(t.6) subsection 286.3(2) (procuring — person under 18 years);

(u) section 344 (robbery);

(v) section 433 (arson — disregard for human life);

(w) section 434.1 (arson — own property);

(x) section 436 (arson by negligence); and

(y) paragraph 465(1)(a) (conspiracy to commit murder).

1.1 An offence under one of the following provisions of the *Criminal Code*, as they read from time to time before the day on which this section comes into force:

(a) subsection 212(2) (living on the avails of prostitution of person under 18 years); and

(b) subsection 212(4) (prostitution of person under 18 years).

2. An offence under any of the following provisions of the *Criminal Code*, as they read immediately before July 1, 1990:

(a) section 433 (arson);

(b) section 434 (setting fire to other substance); and

(c) section 436 (setting fire by negligence).

3. An offence under any of the following provisions of the *Criminal Code*, chapter C-34 of the Revised Statutes of Canada, 1970, as they read immediately before January 4, 1983:

(a) section 144 (rape);

    (*b*) section 145 (attempt to commit rape);
    (*c*) section 149 (indecent assault on female);
    (*d*) section 156 (indecent assault on male); and
    (*e*) section 246 (assault with intent).

4. An offence under any of the following provisions of the *Controlled Drugs and Substances Act*:
    (*a*) section 5 (trafficking);
    (*b*) section 6 (importing and exporting); and
    (*c*) section 7 (production of substance).

5.   An offence under any of the following provisions of the *Cannabis Act*:
    (*a*) section 9 (distribution and possession for purpose of distributing);
    (*b*) section 10 (selling and possession for purpose of selling);
    (*c*) section 11 (importing and exporting and possession for purpose of exporting);
    (*d*) section 12 (production); and
    (*e*) section 14 (use of young person). 2014, c. 25, s. 43; 2018, c. 16, s. 184; 2019, c. 25, s. 383.

INDEX

NOTE: All references are to sections of the *Criminal Code* unless preceded by the following abbreviations:

BR = Canadian Bill of Rights
CD = Controlled Drugs and Substances Act
CE = Canada Evidence Act
CH = Canadian Charter of Rights and Freedoms
FIR = Firearms Act
IDENT = Identification of Criminals Act
INT = Interpretation Act
WC = Crimes Against Humanity and War Crimes Act
YC = Youth Criminal Justice Act

NOTE: *Italicized* section numbers in bold face type refer to section numbers that were not yet or no longer in effect when this index was published.

INDEX

INDEX

INDEX

INDEX

INDEX

INDEX

INDEX

INDEX

INDEX

INDEX

INDEX

INDEX

INDEX

INDEX

INDEX

INDEX

INDEX

INDEX TO FORMS FOR THE CRIMINAL CODE

Warrant of committal on conviction (ss. 570 and 806), Form 21

Warrant of committal on forfeiture of a recognizance (s. 773), Form 27

Warrant remanding a prisoner (ss. 516 and 537), Form 19

Warrant to arrest an absconding witness (s. 704), Form 18

Warrant to convey accused before justice of another territorial division (s. 543), Form 15

Warrant to enter dwelling house (s. 529.1), Form 7.1

Warrant to search (s. 487), Form 5

Warrant to search (ss. 320.29 and 487.1), Form 5.1

Writ of fieri facias (s. 771), Form 34

APPENDIX

FORMS OF CHARGES

APPENDIX

FORMS OF CHARGES

INTRODUCTORY NOTE

The Appendix contains a collection of suggested forms of charges pursuant to Form 2 of the *Criminal Code* for the offences most commonly encountered by police officers, and suggested forms of charges under the *Controlled Drugs and Substances Act*. It is suggested that the Crown Attorney or appropriate counterpart be consulted in the case of offences not included in these pages, and in all cases where the facts are complicated.

The charges are arranged under the sections of the Code to which they relate, in numerical sequence. If the particular section number is not known, it can be readily found by reference to the Index preceding these pages. The section numbers of the Code and the subject-matter of each charge are printed in bold face type.

The use of square brackets and italic type should be explained. Square brackets are used either to set out editorial instructions, which are in all cases printed in italics, or to indicate alternate words or phrases which are printed in ordinary type. See, for example, the first form of charge for an offence under s. 57(1)(*a*), the opening charge, in which the editorial instruction "specify the forged passport" is printed in italics within square brackets, and the charge under s. 81(1)(*a*) in which the alternate words "was likely to cause serious damage to property" are printed in ordinary type within square brackets preceded by the word "or" which is printed in italics to indicate that it is not part of the charge. Round brackets within square brackets indicate an alternative within the alternative (see, for example, the charge under s. 81(1)(*b*)(ii)).

It will be noted that every charge ends with the word "contrary *etc.*". This phrase has been used to avoid needless repetition, but the actual charge should state the section of the Code under which it is laid, *e.g.*, ". . . contrary to section 81(1)(*a*) of the *Criminal Code*".

FORMS OF CHARGES UNDER THE *CRIMINAL CODE*

57(1)(*a*) Forging a passport

A.B. on .... at .... did forge a passport [*specify the forged passport*] contrary *etc*.

57(1)(*b*) Uttering a forged passport

A.B. on .... at .... did knowingly

(i) use [*or* deal with *or* act on] a forged passport to wit [*specify the forged passport*] as if it were genuine contrary *etc*.

or

(ii) cause [*or* attempt to cause] C.D. to use [*or* deal with *or* act upon] a forged passport to wit [*specify the forged document*] as if it were genuine contrary *etc*.

57(2) False statement for passport

A.B. on .... at .... did for the purpose of procuring a passport for himself [*or* C.D.] make a written [*or* oral] statement to wit [*specify the statement*] that he knew was false [*or* misleading] contrary *etc*.

or

A.B. on .... at .... did for the purpose of procuring a material alteration [*or* addition] to a passport for himself [*or* C.D.] make a written [*or* oral] statement to wit [*specify the statement*] that he knew was false [*or* misleading] contrary *etc*.

57(3) Possession of forged passport

A.B. on .... at .... did without lawful excuse have in his possession a forged passport to wit [*specify the forged passport*] contrary *etc*.

65 Participating in riot

A.B. on .... at .... did take part in a riot [*specify time and place*] contrary *etc*.

66 Unlawful assembly

A.B. on .... at .... was a member of an unlawful assembly [*specify time and place*] contrary *etc*.

72(1) Forcible entry

A.B. on .... at .... did commit forcible entry on the real property of C.D. at [*insert address*] contrary *etc*.

72(2) Forcible detainer

A.B. on .... at .... did commit forcible detainer of the real property known as [*insert address*] against C.D. the person entitled by law to possession of it, contrary *etc*.

76 Hijacking

A.B. on .... at .... did by force [*or* by threat of force *or* specify form of intimidation*] seize [*or* exercise control of] an aircraft [*specify*] with intent

(a)   to cause C.D. on board the said aircraft to be confined [*or* imprisoned] against his will contrary *etc.*

or

(b)   to cause C.D. on board the said aircraft to be transported against his will to [*specify place*] which place was other than [*specify*], the then next scheduled place of landing of the said aircraft contrary *etc.*

or

(c)   to hold C.D. on board the said aircraft for ransom [*or* to service against his will] contrary, *etc.*

or

(d)   to cause the said aircraft to deviate in a material respect [*specify*] from its flight plan [*specify*] contrary *etc.*

77(a) Assault in aircraft in flight

A.B. on .... on board aircraft [*specify*] was in flight over the Province of .... between [*specify by longitudes and latitudes or geographical locations*] did commit an assault on C.D., which assault was likely to endanger the safety of the said aircraft contrary *etc.*

77(c) Damage to aircraft in service

A.B. on .... at .... did cause damage [*specify*] to a [*specify*] aircraft in service that rendered the said aircraft incapable of flight [*or* was likely to endanger the safety of the said aircraft in flight] contrary *etc.*

77(d) Placing dangerous substance on an aircraft

A.B. on .... at .... did place [*or* cause to be placed] on board a [*specify*] aircraft in service a [*specify*] that was likely to cause damage to the said aircraft that would render it incapable of flight [*or* that was likely to endanger the safety of the said aircraft in flight] contrary *etc.*

77(e) Damaging or interfering with a navigation facility

A.B. on .... at .... did cause damage to [*or* interfere with the operation of] a [*specify*] air navigation facility, which damage [*or* interference] was likely to endanger the safety of aircraft in flight contrary *etc.*

77(g) Endangering aircraft by false information

A.B. on .... at .... did endanger the safety of a [*specify*] aircraft in flight between .... and .... in the Province of .... by communicating to C.D. information that [*specify*], which information he knew was false, contrary *etc.*

78(1) Offensive weapon or explosive substance on aircraft

A.B. on .... at .... did take on board a [*specify*] aircraft an offensive weapon [*or* an explosive substance] [*specify*]

(a)   without the consent of the owner or the operator or any person duly authorized by the owner or the operator to consent thereto contrary *etc.*

or

(b)   with the consent of the owner [*or* the operator *or* C.D., a person duly
authorized by the owner (*or* the operator) to consent thereto] but
without complying with the term [*or* condition] [*specify*] on which
consent was given contrary *etc.*

78.1(1) Seizing control of ship or fixed platform

A.B. on .... at .... did by force [*or* by threat of force *or*
specify form of intimidation] seize [*or* exercise control of] a ship [*or* fixed
platform] [*specify*] contrary *etc.*

78.1(2)(*a*) Violence on ship or fixed platform

A.B. on .... did commit an act of violence against C.D. on board
ship [*or* fixed platform] [*specify*] between [*specify by longitudes and latitudes or
geographical locations*] which act was likely to endanger the safe navigation of
the said ship [*or* safety of the said fixed platform] contrary *etc.*

78.1(2)(*b*) Damage to ship or fixed platform

A.B. on .... did cause damage to ship [*or* the cargo of ship or fixed
platform] [*specify*] between [*specify by longitudes and latitudes or geographical
locations*] which damage was likely to endanger the safe navigation of the said
ship [*or* safety of the said fixed platform] contrary *etc.*

78.1(2)(*c*) Damage to navigational facility

A.B. on .... did destroy [*or* cause serious damage] to a maritime
navigational facility between [*specify by longitudes and latitudes or geographical locations*] which destruction [*or* damage] was likely to endanger the safe
navigation of a ship [*or* the safety of a fixed platform] contrary *etc.*

78.1(2)(*d*) Placing dangerous substance on a ship or fixed platform

A.B. on .... at .... did place [*or* cause to be placed] on board
ship [*or* fixed platform] [*specify*] a [*specify dangerous substance etc.*] that was
likely to cause damage to the said ship [*or* the cargo of the said ship or the said
fixed platform] and to endanger the safe navigation of the ship [*or* the safety
of the fixed platform] contrary *etc.*

78.1(3) Endangering ship by false information

A.B. on .... at .... did endanger the safe navigation of ship
[*specify*] between [*specify by longitudes and latitudes or geographical locations*]
by communicating to C.D. information that [*specify*], which information he
knew was false, contrary *etc.*

78.1(4) Threat to commit offence

A.B. on .... did threaten to commit an act of violence against C.D.
on board ship [*or* fixed platform] [*specify*] between [*specify by longitudes and
latitudes or geographical locations*] which threat was likely to endanger the safe
navigation of the said ship [*or* the safety of the said fixed platform] contrary
etc.

or

A.B. on .... did threaten to cause damage to the ship [*or* the cargo of the ship or fixed platform] [*specify*] between [*specify by longitudes and latitudes or geographical locations*] which threat was likely to endanger the safe navigation of the said ship [*or* safety of the said fixed platform] contrary *etc.*

or

A.B. on .... did threaten to destroy [*or* cause serious damage] to a maritime navigational facility between [*specify by longitudes and latitudes or geographical locations*] which destruction [*or* damage] was likely to endanger the safe navigation of a ship [*or* the safety of a fixed platform] contrary *etc.*

81(1)(a) Explosives: intent to cause explosion

A.B. on .... at .... with intent to cause an explosion of an explosive substance, to wit .... that was likely to cause serious bodily harm or death to persons [*or* was likely to cause serious damage to property] did [*specify act done*] contrary *etc.*

81(1)(b) Explosives: intent to cause bodily harm

A.B. on .... at .... with intent to do bodily harm to C.D. did

(i) cause an explosive substance, to wit .... to explode contrary *etc.*

or

(ii) send [*or* deliver] to C.D. [*or* cause C.D. to take (*or* receive)] an explosive substance [*or other dangerous substance or thing*] to wit .... contrary *etc.*

or

(iii) place upon [*or* throw upon *or* throw at] C.D. a corrosive fluid [*or* explosive substance *or* dangerous substance *or* dangerous thing] to wit .... contrary *etc.*

81(1)(c) Explosives: intent to cause damage to property

A.B. on .... at .... with intent to destroy or damage the property of C.D. and without lawful excuse did place [*or* throw] an explosive substance, to wit .... upon [*or* at] a [*specify property, e.g., building, motor vehicle, etc.*] of the said C.D. contrary, *etc.*

81(1)(d) Explosives: making or possession of substance; intending bodily harm or property damage

A.B. on .... at .... did make [*or* have in his possession *or* have under his care *or* have under his control] an explosive substance to wit .... with intent thereby

(i) to endanger life [*or* to cause serious damage to property] contrary *etc.*

or

(ii) to enable C.D. to endanger life [*or* to cause serious damage to property] contrary *etc.*

82(1) Explosives: making or possession for unlawful purpose
 A.B. on .... at .... without lawful excuse did make [*or* have in his possession *or* have under his care or have under his control] an explosive substance to wit .... contrary *etc.*

82(2) Explosives: making or possession for benefit of criminal organization
 A.B. on .... at .... without lawful excuse did make [*or* have in his possession *or* have under his care or have under his control] an explosive substance to wit .... for the benefit of [*or* at the direction of or in association with] a criminal organization [*specify*] contrary *etc.*

85(1)(*a*) Firearm: use while committing offence
 A.B. on .... at .... did use a firearm to wit .... while committing the indictable offence of [*specify offence, e.g., break and enter with intent to commit an indictable offence*] contrary *etc.*

85(1)(*b*) Firearm: use while attempting to commit offence
 A.B. on .... at .... did use a firearm to wit .... while attempting to commit the indictable offence of [*specify offence, e.g., break and enter with intent to commit an indictable offence*] contrary *etc.*

85(1)(*c*) Firearm: use during flight
 A.B. on .... at .... did use a firearm to wit .... during his flight after committing [*or* attempting to commit] the indictable offence of [*specify offence, e.g., break and enter with intent to commit an indictable offence*] contrary *etc.*

85(2)(*a*) Imitation firearm: use while committing offence
 A.B. on .... at .... did use an imitation firearm to wit .... while committing the indictable offence of [*specify offence, e.g., robbery*] contrary *etc.*

85(2)(*b*) Imitation firearm: use while attempting to commit offence
 A.B. on .... at .... did use an imitation firearm to wit .... while attempting to commit the indictable offence of [*specify offence, e.g., robbery*] contrary *etc.*

85(2)(*c*) Imitation firearm: use during flight
 A.B. on .... at .... did use an imitation firearm to wit .... during his flight after committing [*or* attempting to commit] the indictable offence of [*specify offence, e.g., robbery*] contrary *etc.*

86(1) Firearm, weapon, ammunition: careless use etc.
 A.B. on .... at .... did, without lawful excuse, use [*or* carry, *or* handle, *or* ship *or* transport, *or* store] a firearm [*or* a prohibited weapon, *or* a restricted weapon, *or* a prohibited device *or* ammunition, *or* prohibited ammunition], to wit .... in a careless manner [*or* without reasonable precaution for the safety of other persons] contrary *etc.*

86(2) Firearm regulations

A.B. on .... at .... did [*specify manner of breach of regulation made under s. 117(h) of the Firearms Act e.g. store a loaded shotgun*] thereby contravening [*specify regulation e.g. s. 5(1)(a) of the Storage, Display, Transportation and Handling of Firearms by Individuals Regulations*] contrary *etc.*

87 Firearm: pointing

A.B. on .... at .... did, without lawful excuse, point a firearm to wit .... at C.D. contrary *etc.*

88 Weapon etc.: possession for dangerous purpose

A.B. on .... at .... did carry [*or* have in his possession] a weapon [*or* an imitation of a weapon *or* a prohibited device *or* ammunition *or* prohibited ammunition], to wit .... , for a purpose dangerous to the public peace [*or* for the purpose of committing an offence] contrary *etc.*

89 Weapon etc.: carrying at public meeting

A.B. on .... at .... did without lawful excuse carry a weapon [*or* a prohibited device *or* ammunition *or* prohibited ammunition], to wit .... while attending [*or* on his way to attend] a public meeting at [*specify meeting place*] contrary *etc.*

90 Weapon: carrying concealed weapon

A.B. on .... at .... not being authorized under the *Firearms Act* to carry concealed a weapon [*or* a prohibited device *or* prohibited ammunition], to wit .... did carry it concealed contrary *etc.*

91(1) Firearm: unauthorized possession

A.B. on .... at .... did possess a firearm, to wit .... without being the holder of a licence under which he may possess it [*or* the holder of a registration certificate for the firearm] contrary *etc.*

91(2) Weapon: unauthorized possession

A.B. on .... at .... did have in his possession a prohibited weapon, [*or* a restricted weapon *or* a prohibited device *or* prohibited ammunition] to wit .... without being the holder of a licence under which he may possess it contrary *etc.*

92(1) Firearm: knowledge of unauthorized possession

A.B. on .... at .... did possess a firearm, to wit .... knowing that he was not the holder of a licence under which he may possess it [*or* the holder of a registration certificate for the firearm] contrary *etc.*

92(2) Weapon: knowledge of unauthorized possession

A.B. on .... at .... did have in his possession a prohibited weapon, [*or* a restricted weapon *or* a prohibited device *or* prohibited ammunition] to wit .... knowing that he was not the holder of a licence under which he may possess it contrary *etc.*

93 Firearm etc.: possession at unauthorized place

A.B. being the holder of an authorization [*or* a licence] under which he was entitled to possess a firearm [*or* a prohibited weapon, *or* a restricted weapon, *or* a prohibited device, *or* prohibited ammunition], to wit .... did have it in his possession on .... at ....

(*a*) a place at which he was not entitled to possess it as indicated in the authorization [*or* licence] issued therefore

or

(*b*) being a place other than the place where he was entitled to possess it as indicated in the authorization [*or* licence] therefore

or

(*c*) being a place other than a place where he was entitled to possess it under the *Firearms Act*

contrary *etc.*

94 Firearm etc.: in motor vehicle

A.B. on .... at .... was an occupant of a motor vehicle, to wit .... in which he knew that there was at that time a firearm [*or* prohibited weapon *or* restricted weapon *or* prohibited device *or* prohibited ammunition], to wit .... contrary *etc.*

95 Prohibited or restricted firearm: with ammunition

A.B. on .... at .... did possess

(*a*) a loaded prohibited [*or* restricted] firearm

or

(*b*) a prohibited [*or* restricted] firearm together with readily accessible ammunition capable of being discharged in the said firearm

and was not the holder of an authorization or licence under which he may possess the said firearm in that place [*or* the registration certificate for the said firearm] contrary *etc.*

96 Possession of weapon obtained by crime

A.B. on .... at .... did have in his possession a firearm [*or* a prohibited weapon, *or* a restricted weapon, *or* a prohibited device, *or* prohibited ammunition], to wit .... or knowing that it was obtained

(*a*) by the commission in Canada of an offence

or

(*b*) by an act [*or* omission] in [*specify place e.g. the State of New York*] which act [*or* omission] had it occurred in Canada would have constituted an offence,

contrary *etc.*

98(1)(a) Breaking and entering with intent to steal firearm

A.B. on .... at .... did break and enter a certain place to wit [*specify type of place, e.g., a dwelling house or store or factory*] situate at

A/11

.... with intent to steal a firearm located in it contrary to s. 98 of the *Criminal Code*

98(1)(b) Breaking, entering and stealing firearm

A.B. on .... at .... did break and enter a certain place to wit [*specify type of place, e.g., a dwelling house, store, factory etc.*] situate at .... and did steal a firearm located in it contrary to s. 98 of the *Criminal Code*

98(1)(c) Breaking out

A.B. on .... at .... did break out of a certain place to wit [*specify type of place, e.g., a dwelling house, store etc.*] situate at .... after stealing a firearm located in it contrary to s. 98 of the *Criminal Code*

or

A.B. on .... at .... did break out of a certain place to wit [*specify type of place*] situate at .... after having entered the said place with intent to steal a firearm located in it contrary to s. 98 of the *Criminal Code*

NOTE: Because of the similarity of this offence to the offence in s. 348, it is suggested that the section number be specified in the information.

98.1 Robbery of firearm

A.B. on .... at .... did steal a firearm from C.D. and at the time thereof did use violence [*or* threats of violence] to C.D. contrary to s. 98.1 of the *Criminal Code*

or

A.B. on .... at .... did steal a firearm from C.D. and at the time thereof [*or* immediately before *or* immediately thereafter] did wound [*or* beat *or* strike *or specify personal violence used*] C.D. contrary to s. 98.1 of the *Criminal Code*

or

A.B. on .... at .... did assault C.D. with intent to steal a firearm from him contrary to s. 98.1 of the *Criminal Code*

or

A.B. on .... at .... did steal from C.D. a firearm while armed with an offensive weapon [*or* imitation of an offensive weapon] to wit [*specify weapon*] contrary to s. 98.1 of the *Criminal Code*

or

(General Charge)

A.B. on .... at .... did rob C.D. of a firearm contrary to s. 98.1 of the *Criminal Code*

NOTE: Because of the similarity of this offence to the offence in s. 344, it is suggested that the section number be specified in the information.

99 Weapon or firearm: trafficking

A.B. on .... at .... did [*or* did offer to] manufacture [*or* transfer] a firearm [*or* a prohibited weapon, *or* a restricted weapon, *or* a

prohibited device *or* ammunition, *or* prohibited ammunition], to wit
.... knowing that he was not authorized to do so, contrary *etc.*

99(2) Firearm etc. trafficking

A.B. on .... at .... did [*or* did offer to] manufacture [*or* transfer] a firearm [*or* a prohibited device, *or* ammunition, *or* prohibited ammunition], to wit .... knowing that he was not authorized to do so, contrary *etc.*

99(3) Other weapons

A.B. on .... at .... did [*or* did offer to] manufacture [*or* transfer] a prohibited weapon [*or* a restricted weapon], to wit .... knowing that he was not authorized to do so, contrary *etc.*

100 Weapon or firearm: possession for purpose of trafficking

A.B. on .... at .... did have in his possession a firearm [*or* a prohibited weapon, *or* a restricted weapon, *or* a prohibited device *or* ammunition, *or* prohibited ammunition], to wit .... for the purpose of transferring [*or* offering to transfer] it knowing that he was not authorized to do so, contrary *etc.*

100(2) Firearm etc.: possession for purpose of trafficking

A.B. on .... at .... did have in his possession a firearm [*or* a prohibited device, *or* ammunition, *or* prohibited ammunition], to wit .... for the purpose of transferring [*or* offering to transfer] it knowing that he was not authorized to do so, contrary *etc.*

100(3) Other weapons: possession for the purpose of trafficking

A.B. on .... at .... did have in his possession a prohibited weapon [*or* a restricted weapon], to wit .... for the purpose of transferring [*or* offering to transfer] it knowing that he was not authorized to do so, contrary *etc.*

101 Weapon or firearm: transfer without authority

A.B. on .... at .... did without lawful authority transfer a firearm [*or* a prohibited weapon, *or* a restricted weapon, *or* a prohibited device *or* ammunition, *or* prohibited ammunition], to wit .... to C.D., contrary *etc.*

102 Making automatic firearm

A.B. on .... at .... did without lawful excuse alter [*or* manufacture or assemble] a firearm, to wit .... so that the said firearm is capable of discharging a projectile in rapid succession during one pressure of the trigger contrary *etc.*

103(1) Firearm or weapon: importing etc.

A.B. on .... at .... did import into Canada [*or* export from Canada]:

(*a*)   a firearm [*or* a prohibited weapon, *or* a restricted weapon, *or* a prohibited device, *or* prohibited ammunition], to wit ....

A / 13

or

(**b**) a component [or part] to wit .... designed exclusively for use in the manufacture of [or assembly into] an automatic weapon
knowing that he was not authorized to do so, contrary *etc.*

103(2) Firearm etc.: importing etc.

A.B. on .... at .... did import into Canada [or export from Canada] a firearm [or a prohibited device, or prohibited ammunition], to wit .... knowing that he was not authorized to do so, contrary *etc.*

103(2.1) Other weapons: importing etc.

A.B. on .... at .... did import into Canada [or export from Canada]

(**a**) a prohibited weapons [or a restricted weapon], to wit ....

(**b**) a component [or part], to wit .... designed exclusively for use in the manufacture of [or assembly into] an automatic firearm
knowing that he was not authorized to do so, contrary *etc.*

104(1) Firearm or weapon: importing etc. without authority

A.B. on .... at .... did without lawful authority import into Canada [or export from Canada]:

(**a**) a firearm [or a prohibited weapon, or a restricted weapon, or a prohibited device, or prohibited ammunition], to wit ....

or

(**b**) a component [or part] to wit .... designed exclusively for use in the manufacture of [or assembly into] an automatic weapon
contrary *etc.*

105(1) Firearm or weapon: losing or finding

(**a**) A.B. having lost [or had stolen from his possession] on .... at .... a firearm [or a prohibited weapon, or a restricted weapon, or a prohibited device, or prohibited ammunition or an authorization or a licence or a registration certificate], to wit .... failed to report the loss to a peace officer, firearms officer or chief firearms officer with reasonable despatch contrary *etc.*

(**b**) A.B. on .... at .... having found a firearm [or a prohibited weapon, or a restricted weapon, or a prohibited device, or prohibited ammunition], to wit .... that he had reasonable grounds to believe had been lost or abandoned failed to deliver it [or report its finding] to a peace officer, firearms officer or chief firearms officer with reasonable despatch contrary *etc.*

106(1) Firearm or weapon: destroying

(*a*) A.B. having destroyed on .... at .... a firearm [*or* a prohibited weapon, *or* a restricted weapon, *or* a prohibited device, *or* prohibited ammunition], to wit .... failed to report the destruction to a peace officer, firearms officer or chief firearms officer with reasonable despatch contrary *etc.*

(*b*) A.B. on .... at .... having become aware of the destruction of a firearm [*or* a prohibited weapon, *or* a restricted weapon, *or* a prohibited device, *or* prohibited ammunition], to wit .... failed to report the destruction to a peace officer, firearms officer or chief firearms officer with reasonable despatch contrary *etc.*

107(1) Firearm or weapon: false statements concerning loss etc.

A.B. on .... at .... did knowingly make a false report [*or* statement] concerning the loss [*or* theft *or* destruction] of a firearm [*or* a prohibited weapon, *or* a restricted weapon, *or* a prohibited device, *or* prohibited ammunition *or* an authorization *or* a licence *or* a registration certificate], to wit [*specify statement or report alleged to be false*] to C.D. a peace officer [*or* firearms officer *or* chief firearms officer] contrary *etc.*

108(1) Firearm: tampering with serial number

(*a*) A.B. on .... at .... did without lawful excuse alter [*or* deface *or* remove] a serial number on a firearm to wit .... contrary etc.

(*b*) A.B. on .... at .... was without lawful excuse in possession of a firearm to wit .... knowing that the serial number on it had been altered [*or* defaced *or* removed] contrary etc.

117.01(1) Firearm or weapon: possession contrary to prohibition order

A.B. on .... at .... did have in his possession a firearm [*or* a cross-bow *or* a prohibited weapon, *or* a restricted weapon, *or* a prohibited device, *or* ammunition *or* prohibited ammunition *or* an explosive substance] while he was prohibited from doing so by reason of an order made pursuant to [*here specify basis for prohibition e.g. section 109(1) of the Criminal Code and identify order e.g. at Montreal on January 5, 1999*] contrary *etc.*

120(*a*) Bribery: officers accepting bribes

A.B. on .... at .... being a justice [*or* police comissioner *or* peace officer *or* public officer *or* officer of a juvenile court *or* being employed in the administration of criminal law] to wit [*specify position held*] did corruptly

accept [*or* obtain]

or

agree to accept

APP

or

attempt to obtain

for himself [*or* C.D.] a sum of money [*or* valuable consideration, *or* office, *or* place *or* employment] to wit [*specify item sought*] with intent

(i)   to interfere with the administration of justice by [*specify details*] contrary *etc*.

or

(ii)   to procure or facilitate the commission of the offence of .... contrary *etc*.

or

(iii)   to protect from detection [*or* punishment] E.F. who had committed [*or* who had intended to commit] the offence of .... contrary *etc*.

120(*b*) Bribery of officers

A.B. on .... at .... did corruptly give [*or* offer] C.D., a justice [*or* police commissioner, *or* peace officer *or* public officer *or* officer of a juvenile court *or* a person employed in the administration of criminal law], to wit [*specify position held*] a sum of money [*or* valuable consideration *or* office *or* place *or* employment] to wit .... with intent that C.D. should

(*a*)   interfere with the administration of justice [*specify interference contemplated*] contrary *etc*.

or

(*b*)   procure or facilitate the commission of the offence of .... contrary *etc*.

or

(*c*)   protect A.B. [*or* E.F.] who had committed [*or* who had intended to commit] the offence of .... from detection or punishment for such offence contrary *etc*.

121(1) Frauds on the government

121(1)(*a*) Giving a benefit to an official/accepting a benefit

(i)   A.B. on .... at .... did give [*or* offer *or* agree to give *or* agree to offer] to C.D. [*or* E.F. a member of the family of C.D. *or* G.H. for the benefit of C.D.] an official [*specify nature of office*]

or

(ii)   C.D., being an official [*specify nature of office*] on .... at .... did demand [*or* accept *or* offer to accept *or* agree to accept] from A.B. for himself [*or* E.F.]

a loan [*or* reward *or* advantage *or* benefit] to wit [*specify loan etc.*] as consideration for cooperation, assistance, exercise of influence or an act or omission in connection with

(iii)   the transaction of business with [*or* a matter of business relating to] the government [*specify*] contrary *etc.*

or

(iv)   a claim against Her Majesty [*or* a benefit that Her Majesty is authorized or is entitled to bestow] to wit [*specify*] contrary *etc.*

121(1)(b) Conferring a benefit by person having dealings with government

A.B. a person having dealings with the government of [*specify*] on .... at .... did, without the consent in writing of the head of the branch of that government, pay a commission to [*or* reward to *or* confer an advantage or benefit on] C.D. [*or* E.F. a member of the family of C.D. *or* G.H. for the benefit of C.D.] an official [*or* employee] of the government of [*specify*] with respect to those dealings contrary *etc.*

121(1)(c) Accepting a benefit from person having dealings with government

C.D. being an official [*or* employee] of the government of [*specify*] on .... at .... did, for his benefit and without the consent in writing of the head of the branch of that government of which he is an official [*or* that employs him], demand [*or* accept *or* offer to accept *or* agree to accept] a commission [*or* reward *or* an advantage or benefit] of [*specify*] from A.B. a person having dealings with the government of [*specify*] contrary *etc.*

121(1)(d) Influence peddling

C.D. a person having or pretending to have influence with the government [*or* with E.F. a minister of the government] of [*specify*] on .... at .... did demand [*or* accept *or* offer to accept *or* agree to accept] a commission [*or* reward *or* an advantage or benefit] of [*specify*] for himself [*or* G.H.] from A.B. as consideration for cooperation, assistance, exercise of influence or an act or omission [*specify*] in connection with

the transaction of business with [*or* a matter of business relating to] the government [*specify*] contrary *etc.*

or

a claim against Her Majesty [*or* a benefit that Her Majesty is authorized or is entitled to bestow] to wit [*specify*] contrary *etc.*

121(1)(e) Offering benefit for exercise of influence

A.B. on .... at .... did give [*or* offer *or* agree to give *or* agree to offer] to C.D. a Minister [*or* official] of the government of [*specify*] as consideration for cooperation, assistance, exercise of influence or an act or omission [*specify*] in connection with

the transaction of business with [*or* a matter of business relating to] the government [*specify*] contrary *etc.*

or

a claim against Her Majesty [*or* a benefit that Her Majesty is authorized or is entitled to bestow] to wit [*specify*] contrary *etc.*

or

his appointment [*or* the appointment of E.F.] to an office to wit [*specify*] contrary *etc.*

121(1)(f) Fraud in relation to government tenders

A.B. having made a tender to obtain a contract [*specify*] with the government of [*specify*] on .... at .... did,

(i)   give [*or* offer to give] to C.D. [*or* E.F. a member of the family of C.D. *or* G.H. for the benefit of C.D.], a person who has also made a tender to obtain the contract, a reward [*or* an advantage or benefit] of [*specify*] as consideration for C.D. withdrawing his tender contrary *etc*.

or

(ii)   demand [*or* accept *or* offer to accept *or* agree to accept] from C.D. a person who has also made a tender to obtain the contract a reward [*or* an advantage or benefit] of [*specify*] as consideration for withdrawing his tender contrary *etc*.

121(2) Contractor subscribing to election fund

A.B. in order to obtain [*or* retain] a contract [*specify*] with the government of [*specify*] on .... at .... did subscribe [*or* give *or* agree to give *or* agree to subscribe] to C.D. the sum of [*specify*]

(a)   for the purpose of promoting the election of E.F. a candidate [*or*, *specify class or party*] to Parliament [*or*, *specify provincial legislature*] contrary *etc*.

or

(b)   with the intention of influencing or affecting the result of the election held [*or* to be held] on .... for the purpose of electing persons to serve in Parliament [*or*, *specify provincial legislature*] contrary *etc*.

122 Breach of trust by public officer

A.B. on .... at .... being an official [*specify nature of office*] did commit a fraud [*or* a breach of trust] in connection with the duties of his office by [*specify fraud or breach of trust*] contrary *etc*.

123(1) Municipal corruption
    Corruption of municipal official

(a)   A.B. on .... at .... did give [*or* offer *or* agree to give *or* agree to offer] to C.D. a municipal official to wit [*specify nature of office*]

or

(b)   C.D., being a municipal official [*specify nature of office*] on .... at .... did demand [*or* accept *or* offer to accept *or* agree to accept] from A.B.

a loan [*or* reward *or* advantage *or* benefit] to wit [*specify loan etc.*] as consideration for C.D.

or

(c)   abstaining from voting at a meeting of the municipal council [*or specify committee of council e.g. the committee of adjustment*] in relation to [*specify e.g. severance of the property of A.B. at ....*] contrary *etc.*

or

(d)   voting in favour of [*or against*] a measure [*or motion or resolution*] to wit [*specify the measure, motion or resolution*] contrary *etc.*

or

(e)   aiding [*or procuring or preventing*] the adoption of a measure [*or motion or resolution*] to wit [*specify the measure, motion or resolution*] contrary *etc.*

or

(f)   performing [*or failing to perform*] an official act, to wit, [*specify*] contrary *etc.*

123(2) Influencing municipal official

(a)   A.B. being under a duty to disclose the truth did on .... at .... suppress the truth in relation to [*specify*]

or

(b)   A.B. on .... at .... by threats [*or deceit*] [*specify*]

or

(c)   A.B. on .... at .... by [*specify unlawful means*] influenced or attempted to influence C.D. a municipal official to wit [*specify nature of office*] to

        abstain from voting at a meeting of the municipal council [*or specify committee of council e.g. the committee of adjustment*] in relation to [*specify e.g. severance of the property of A.B. at ....*] contrary *etc.*

or

        vote in favour of [*or against*] a measure [*or motion or resolution*] to wit [*specify the measure, motion or resolution*] contrary *etc.*

or

        aid in [*or procure or prevent*] the adoption of a measure [*or motion or resolution*] to wit [*specify the measure, motion or resolution*] contrary *etc.*

or

        perform [*or fail to perform*] an official act, to wit [*specify*] contrary *etc.*

125 Influencing or negotiating appointments or dealing in offices

(a)   A.B. on .... at .... did receive from C.D. [*or agree to receive from C.D. or give to C.D. or agree to give to C.D. or procure to be given to C.D.*] a reward [*or an advantage or benefit*] of [*specify*] as consideration for the cooperation [*or assistance or exercise of influence*] by [*specify e.g. A.B. or C.D. as the case may be*] to secure the

A / 19

appointment of [*specify person to be appointed*] to the office of [*specify nature of office*] contrary *etc.*

or

(b) A.B. on .... at .... did in the expectation of a reward [*or an advantage or benefit*] of [*specify*] solicit [*or recommend or* negotiate] the appointment of C.D. to [*or resignation of C.D. from*] the office of [*specify*] contrary *etc.*

or

(c) A.B. on .... did without lawful authority keep premises at .... for the purpose of transacting or negotiating business in relation to the filling of vacancies in [*or the sale of or* purchase of *or the appointment to or* resignation from] offices of [*specify*] contrary *etc.*

127 Disobeying court order
A.B. on .... at .... did without lawful excuse disobey the lawful order made by [*specify judge and court or other body authorized by an act of Parliament or the Legislature*] to [*specify order*] contrary *etc.*

128 Misconduct of officers in executing process
A.B. on .... at .... being a peace officer [*or coroner*] for [*specify police force or as the case may be*] and being entrusted with the execution of a process, to wit [*specify process e.g. execution of a warrant of committal for C.D.*] wilfully

(a) misconducted himself in the execution of that process contrary *etc.*

or

(b) made a false return to that process contrary *etc.*

129(a) Resisting or obstructing public or peace officer
A.B. on .... at .... did resist [*or wilfully obstruct*] C.D. a public [*or peace*] officer to wit [*describe C.D., e.g., a police constable for the City of* ....] engaged in the execution of his duty [*specify act C.D. engaged in*] by [*specify manner of resistance or obstruction*] contrary *etc.*

or

E.F. a person acting in aid of C.D. [a police constable for the City of ....] engaged in the execution of his duty [*specify C.D.'s duty*] by [*specify manner of resistance or obstruction*] contrary *etc.*

129(b) Omitting to assist peace officer
A.B. on .... at .... did omit without reasonable excuse, to assist C.D., a public [*or peace*] officer to wit [*describe C.D.*] engaged in the execution of his duty in arresting E.F. [*or in preserving the peace*] after having reasonable notice that he was required to do so contrary *etc.*

129(c) Obstructing or resisting bailiff, etc.
A.B. on .... at .... did resist [*or wilfully obstruct*] C.D., a person engaged in the lawful execution of a process issued out of [*specify court*] against the lands [*or goods*] of A.B. [*or E.F.*] contrary *etc.*

or

C.D. a person engaged in the making of a lawful distress [*or* seizure] upon [*specify subject-matter*] contrary *etc.*

130 Personating peace officer

(a)   A.B. on .... at .... did falsely represent himself to be a peace [*or* public] officer to wit [*specify, e.g., a police constable for the City of* ....] to C.D. contrary *etc.*

or

(b)   A.B. on .... at .... not being a peace [*or* public] officer did use a badge [*or* article of uniform *or* equipment] to wit .... in a manner that was likely to cause C.D. to believe that A.B. was [*specify, e.g., a police constable for the City of* ....] contrary *etc.*

131(1) Perjury

A.B. on .... at .... did commit perjury at the trial in the [*specify court and place and time of sitting*] between [*state full style of cause of the judicial proceeding*] by swearing falsely and with intent to mislead the court that [*recite evidence verbatim*] contrary *etc.*

or

A.B. on .... at .... being specially permitted [*or* authorized *or* required] by law to make a statement by affidavit [*or* solemn declaration *or* solemn affirmation *or* orally under oath] to wit [*specify, e.g., an affidavit under the Marriage Act*] did make a false statement to wit [*specify false statement, e.g., that he had not been previously married*] knowing that such statement was false contrary *etc.*

134(1) Statements not specially permitted

A.B. on .... at .... not being specially permitted, authorized or required by law to make a statement under oath or solemn affirmation, did make such a statement, by affidavit [*or* solemn declaration *or* disposition *or* orally] to wit [*specify*] before C.D. who was authorized by law to permit it to be made before him, knowing that the statement was false contrary *etc.*

136(1) Witness giving contradictory evidence

A.B. on .... at .... being a witness at [*specify judicial proceeding e.g. the trial of C.D. on a charge of first degree murder before the Honourable Madam Justice Smith in the Court of Queens Bench*] gave evidence that [*specify testimony of matter of fact or knowledge*] which was contrary to the evidence he gave on .... at .... while a witness at [*specify earlier judicial proceeding e.g. the preliminary hearing of C.D. on a charge of first degree murder before His Honour Judge Jones in the Manitoba Provincial Court*] contrary *etc.*

137 Fabricating evidence

A.B. on .... at .... did with intent to mislead fabricate [*specify item fabricated, e.g., a photograph*] with intent that it should be used as evidence in an existing [*or* proposed] judicial proceeding contrary *etc.*

138(a) Swearing pretended affidavit

A.B. on .... at .... did sign a writing that purported to be an affidavit [*or* statutory declaration] subscribed to by C.D. and dated the .... day of ...., 19................, and to have been sworn [*or* declared] before him when the writing was not so sworn [*or* declared] contrary *etc.*

or

A.B. on .... at .... did unlawfully sign a writing that purported to be an affidavit [*or* statutory declaration] subscribed to by C.D. and dated the .... day of ...., 19................, when he knew that he had no authority to administer the oath [*or* declaration] contrary *etc.*

138(b) Using pretended affidavit

A.B. on .... at .... did [offer for] use a writing that purported to be an affidavit [*or* statutory declaration] dated the .... day of ...., 19................,

that he knew was not sworn [*or* declared] by C.D. the affiant [*or* declarant] therein contrary *etc.*

or

that he knew was not sworn [*or* declared] before a person authorized to administer the oath [*or* declaration] contrary *etc.*

138(c) Signing pretended affidavit

A.B. on .... at .... did sign a writing that purported to be an affidavit dated the .... day of ...., 19................, and to have been sworn [*or* declared] before C.D. by him as affiant [*or* declarant] when the writing was not so sworn contrary *etc.*

139(1) Obstructing justice

A.B. on .... at .... did wilfully attempt to obstruct [*or* pervert *or* defeat] the course of justice in a judicial proceeding by [*specify act done*] contrary *etc.*

140(1) Public mischief

A.B. on .... at .... did commit public mischief in that with intent to mislead he caused C.D. a peace officer [*describe C.D., e.g., a police constable for the City of ....*] to enter upon [*or* continue] an investigation by

(*a*) making a false statement to [*specify*] that accused E.F. of having committed the offence of [*specify offence*] contrary *etc.*

or

(*b*) [*specify act done by A.B., e.g., placing counterfeit twenty dollar bills in the seat lining of E.F.'s automobile*], which act was intended to cause E.F. to be suspected of having committed an offence which E.F. had not committed [*or* to divert suspicion from himself*] contrary *etc.*

or

A /22

(c)   reporting that the offence .... had been committed when it had not been committed contrary *etc.*

or

(d)   reporting [*or* making it known] that he had died [*or* that E.F. had died when E.F. had not died] contrary *etc.*

141 Compounding indictable offence

A.B. on .... at .... did ask for [*or* obtain *or* agree to receive or obtain] [*specify valuable consideration, e.g., the sum of fifty dollars*] from C.D. for himself [*or* E.F.] by agreeing to compound [*or* conceal] the indictable offence of .... committed by the said C.D. [*or* X.Y.] contrary *etc.*

142 Corruptly taking reward for recovery of goods

A.B. on .... at .... did corruptly and directly [*or* indirectly] accept a valuable consideration from C.D. to wit [*specify consideration, e.g., the sum of fifty dollars*] under pretence [*or* upon account] of helping C.D. [*or* E.F.] to recover [*specify article*] obtained by the commission of an indictable offence to wit [*specify offence, e.g., robbery*] contrary *etc.*

144 Prison-breach

(a)   A.B. on .... at .... did by force [*or* violence] break a prison to wit [*specify prison*] with intent to set at liberty himself [*or* C.D. a person confined therein] contrary *etc.*

or

(b)   A.B. on .... at .... did with intent to escape forcibly break out of [*or* make a breach in] a cell [*or* specify other place*] within a prison to wit [*specify prison*] in which he was confined contrary *etc.*

145(1)(a) Escape from lawful custody

A.B. on .... at .... did escape from lawful custody at [*specify manner of custody*] contrary *etc.*

145(1)(b) Being unlawfully at large

A.B. on .... at .... was, before the expiration of a term of imprisonment to which he was sentenced, at large within Canada without lawful excuse contrary *etc.*

145(2) Failing to attend court when at large on undertaking or recognizance: failing to surrender

A.B. on .... at .... unlawfully

(a)   did being at large on his undertaking [*or* recognizance] given to [*or* entered into before] a justice [*or* a judge] without lawful excuse fail to attend court [*specify court, e.g., Courtroom 21, 1000 Eagle Street*] in accordance therewith, contrary *etc.*

or

APP

(b)   [did, fail to surrender himself in accordance with the order of [*here specify Judge*] at [*specify place of surrender*] contrary *etc.*

or

A.B. on .... at .... having appeared before a court [*or justice or judge*] to wit [*specify, e.g., Provincial Court Judge C.D.*] on [*specify date of last appearance*] did unlawfully fail to attend court on [*specify date that failed to appear*] at .... as required by the said court [*or justice or judge*] contrary *etc.*

145(3) Failing to comply with direction in detention order

A.B. on .... at .... being detained by the order of a justice [*or judge*] made on .... at .... and being bound to comply with a direction of the said justice [*or judge*] did fail without lawful excuse to comply with the direction not to communication with C.D. contrary *etc.*

145(3) Failing to comply with condition of undertaking or recognizance

A.B. on .... at .... did being at large on his undertaking [*or recognizance*] given to [*or entered into before*] a justice [*or a judge*] and being bound to comply with a condition of that undertaking [*or recognizance*] [*here specify condition e.g. that he not communicate with C.D.*] without lawful excuse failed to comply with that condition by [*here specify breach e.g. by telephoning C.D.*] contrary *etc.*

145(4) Failing to appear or to comply with summons

A.B. having been served with a summons did fail without lawful excuse

(a)   to appear on .... at .... for the purposes of the *Identification of Criminals Act* in accordance therewith, contrary *etc.*

or

(b)   to attend on .... at [*specify courtroom*] in accordance therewith, contrary *etc.*

145(5) Failing to appear or to comply with appearance notice, promise to appear or recognizance

A.B. on .... at .... unlawfully did having been named in an appearance notice [*or promise to appear or recognizance entered into before an officer in charge*] that has been confirmed by a justice under s. 508 of the *Criminal Code* fail without lawful excuse

(a)   to appear in accordance therewith on .... at .... for the purposes of the *Identification of Criminals Act*, contrary *etc.*

or

(b)   to attend court in accordance therewith by not appearing in [*specify courtroom*] on .... contrary *etc.*

145(5.1) Failing to comply with condition of undertaking given to officer in charge or peace officer

A.B. on .... at .... did being at large on his undertaking given to an officer in charge [*or* a peace officer] and being bound to comply with a condition of that undertaking directed by the said officer in charge [*or* peace officer] fail without lawful excuse to comply with that condition to wit: [*specify condition, e.g., to abstain from the consumption of alcohol or other intoxicating substances*] contrary *etc.*

146 Escape: permitting, assisting in, or procuring

A.B. on .... at .... did

(*a*)   permit C.D. whom he had in lawful custody to escape by failing to perform a legal duty imposed on him to wit [*specify failure of specific legal duty*] contrary *etc.*

or

(*b*)   convey [*or* cause to be conveyed by E.F.] [*specify item, e.g., a revolver*] into [*specify prison*] with intent to facilitate the escape of C.D. imprisoned therein contrary *etc.*

or

(*c*)   direct [*or* procure] under colour of pretended authority [*specify pretended authority*] the discharge of C.D., a prisoner not entitled to be discharged contrary *etc.*

147(*a*) Escape: rescuing or assisting

A.B. on .... at .... did

rescue C.D. from lawful custody to wit [*specify manner of custody*] contrary *etc.*

or

assist C.D. in escaping [*or* attempting to escape] from lawful custody to wit [*specify manner of custody*] contrary *etc.*

147(*b*) Escape: peace officer permitting

A.B. on .... at .... did

being a peace officer to wit [*describe A.B., e.g., a police officer for the City of ....*] wilfully permit C.D., a person in his lawful custody, to escape contrary *etc.*

147(*c*) Escape: prison officer permitting

A.B. on .... at .... did

being an officer of [*or* an employee in] a prison to wit [*specify prison*] wilfully permit C.D. to escape from lawful custody therein contrary *etc.*

151 Sexual interference

A.B., on .... at .... did for a sexual purpose touch C.D. a person under the age of sixteen years directly [*or indirectly*]

A/25

with a part of his body, to wit [*specify the part of the body*] contrary *etc.*

or

with an object, to wit [*specify the object*] contrary *etc.*

152 Invitation to sexual touching

A.B. on .... at .... did for a sexual purpose invite [*or* counsel *or* incite] C.D. a person under the age of sixteen years to touch directly [*or* indirectly] with a part of his body [*or* with an object] to wit [*specify the part of the body or the object used*] the body of A.B. [*or* the said C.D. *or* E.F. *as the case may be*] contrary *etc.*

153 Sexual exploitation

A.B. on .... at ...., being in a position of trust or authority towards C.D. a young person, [*or* being a person with whom C.D., a young person, was in a relationship of dependency] did

(*a*)   for a sexual purpose, touch directly [*or* indirectly] the body of C.D., a young person, with a part of his body [*or* with an object] to wit [*specify the part of the body of A.B. or the object used*] contrary *etc.*

or

(*b*)   for a sexual purpose invite [*or* counsel *or* incite] C.D. a young person to touch directly [*or* indirectly] with a part of his body [*or* with an object] to wit [*specify the part of the body or the object used*] the body of A.B. [*or* the said C.D. *or* E.F. *as the case may be*] contrary *etc.*

153.1 Sexual exploitation of person with disability

A.B. on .... at .... , being in a position of trust or authority towards C.D. a person with a mental [*or* physical] disability, [*or* being a person with whom C.D., a person with a mental [*or* physical] disability was in a relationship of dependency,] did without the consent of C.D. for a sexual purpose counsel [*or* incite] C.D. to touch directly [*or* indirectly] with a part of his body [*or* with an object] to wit [specify the part of the body or the object used] the body of A.B. [*or* the said C.D. *or* E.F. as the case may be] contrary etc.

155 Incest
Single charge

A.B. on .... at .... did have sexual intercourse with C.D. while knowing that C.D. was his [*or* her] [*specify blood relationship e.g., daughter*] contrary *etc.*

Joint charge

A.B. and C.D. on .... at .... did have sexual intercourse with each other while knowing that they were related by blood relationship to wit [*specify blood relationship e.g., father and daughter*] contrary *etc.*

160(1) Bestiality

A.B. on .... at .... did commit bestiality with [*specify e.g., an animal e.g. a cow*] contrary *etc.*

160(2) Compelling bestiality

A.B. on .... at .... did compel C.D. to commit bestiality with [*specify e.g., an animal e.g. a cow*] contrary *etc.*

160(3) Bestiality in presence of person under sixteen years etc.

A.B. on .... at .... did commit bestiality with [*specify e.g., an animal e.g. a cow*] in the presence of C.D. a person under the age of sixteen years contrary *etc.*

or

A.B. on .... at .... did incite C.D., a person under the age of sixteen years, to commit bestiality with [*specify e.g., an animal e.g. a cow*] contrary *etc.*

161(4) Breach of prohibition order in relation to children

A.B. on .... at .... being a person bound by an Order of Prohibition made on .... at .... by [*specify judge who made order*] prohibiting him from [*specify terms of Order eg. attending a public park or public swimming area where persons under the age of 14 are present or can reasonably be expected to be present etc.*] did fail to comply with the said Order by [*specify nature of failure to comply eg. attending the public park at 1000 Eagle Street where persons under the age of 14 were present*] contrary *etc.*

163(1) Obscene matter
Making, etc.

A.B. on .... at .... did make [*or* print *or* publish *or* distribute *or* circulate] obscene matter [*or* an obscene picture *or* model *or* phonograph record *etc.*] to wit [*specify item*] contrary *etc.*

or

Possessing

A.B. on .... at .... unlawfully did have in his possession for the purpose of publication [*or* distribution *or* circulation] obscene written matter [*or* an obscene picture *or* model *or* phonograph record *etc.*] to wit [*specify item*] contrary *etc.*

163(2) Obscene matter: selling, exposing or exhibiting

A.B. on .... at .... knowingly and without lawful justification or excuse did

(*a*) sell [*or* expose to public view *or* have in his possession for the purpose of selling (*or* exposing to public view)] obscene written matter [*or* an obscene picture *or* model *or* phonograph record *etc.*] to wit [*specify item*] contrary *etc.*

or

(*b*) publicly exhibit a disgusting object [*or* an indecent show] to wit [*specify object or show*] contrary *etc.*

APP

163.1(2) Child pornography: printing and publishing

A.B. on .... at .... did make [*or* print *or* publish *or* have in his possession for the purpose of publication] child pornography to wit [*specify item*] contrary *etc.*

163.1(3) Child pornography: importing and distributing

A.B. on .... at .... did import [*or* distribute *or* sell *or* have in his possession for the purpose of distribution *or* sale] child pornography to wit [*specify item*] contrary *etc.*

163.1(4) Child pornography: possession

A.B. on .... at .... did have in his possession child pornography to wit [*specify item*] contrary *etc.*

167 Immoral theatrical performance

A.B. on .... at .... being the lessee [*or* manager *or* agent *or* person in charge] of a theatre to wit [*specify*] did present [*or* give *or* allow to be presented therein] an immoral [*or* indecent *or* obscene] performance [*or* entertainment *or* representation] to wit [*specify*] contrary *etc.*

or

A.B. on .... at .... did unlawfully take part [*or* appear as an actor *or* performer *or* assistant (*state capacity*)] in an immoral [*or* indecent *or* obscene] performance [*or* entertainment *or* representation] to wit [*specify, e.g., a play*] in a theatre to wit [*specify*] contrary *etc.*

168 Obscene matter: mailing

A.B. on .... at .... did make use of the mails for the purpose of transmitting [*or* delivering] obscene [*or* indecent *or* scurrilous] matter to wit [*specify item mailed*] contrary *etc.*

170 Parent or guardian procuring sexual activity

A.B. on .... at .... being the parent [*or* guardian] of C.D., a person under the age of eighteen years, did procure the said C.D. for the purpose of engaging in sexual activity to wit [*specify the prohibited sexual activity e.g. anal intercourse*] prohibited by section [*specify the section number e.g. 159*] of the *Criminal Code*, with E.F. contrary *etc.*

171 Householder permitting sexual activity

A.B. on .... at ....

(a) being the owner [*or* occupier *or* manager] of premises to wit [*specify*]

or

(b) having control [*or* assisting in the management (*or* control)] of premises to wit [*specify*]

did knowingly permit C.D., a person aged [*specify age under eighteen years*] to resort to [*or* to be in *or* upon] such premises for the purpose of engaging in sexual activity to wit [*specify the prohibited sexual activity e.g. anal intercourse*] prohibited by section [*specify the section number e.g. 159*] of the *Criminal Code*, thereby committing an offence contrary *etc.*

173(1) Indecent acts

A.B. on .... at .... wilfully did an indecent act to wit [*specify act, e.g., expose his private person*]

(a) in a public place to wit [*specify*] in the presence of C.D. [*or* of one or more persons] contrary *etc.*

or

(b) at [*specify place*] with intent thereby to insult [*or* offend] C.D. contrary *etc.*

173(2) Exposure to person under age of sixteen years

A.B. on .... at .... did for a sexual purpose expose his [*or* her] genital organs to C.D. a person under the age of sixteen years contrary *etc.*

174(1) Nudity

A.B. on .... at ...., without lawful excuse was

(a) nude in a public place to wit [*specify the place*] contrary *etc.*

or

(b) exposed to public view while nude on private property to wit [*specify the place*] contrary *etc.*

175(1) Causing disturbance; indecent exhibition; loitering

A.B. on .... at ....

(a) not being in a dwelling house did cause a disturbance in or near a public place to wit [*specify*]

    (i) by fighting [*or* screaming *or* shouting *or* swearing *or* singing *or* using insulting (*or* obscene) language] contrary *etc.*

or

    (ii) by being drunk contrary *etc.*

or

    (iii) by impeding [*or* molesting] other persons contrary *etc.*

(b) did openly expose [*or* exhibit] an indecent exhibition to wit [*specify*] in a public place to wit [*specify*] contrary *etc.*

or

(c) did loiter in a public place to wit [*specify*] and obstruct persons who were there contrary *etc.*

or

(d) did disturb the peace and quiet of the occupants of a dwelling house to wit [*specify address*] by discharging firearms [*or specify type of disorderly conduct*] in a public place to wit [*specify*] contrary *etc.*

or

APP

not being an occupant thereof did disturb the peace and quiet of the occupants of a dwelling house [*specify address*] comprised in a structure [*specify address*] by discharging firearms [*or specify disorderly conduct*] in a part of the said structure contrary *etc.*

176(1)(a) Obstructing officiating clergyman

A.B. on .... at .... did

by threats [*or force*] unlawfully obstruct [*or prevent or endeavour to obstruct or endeavour to prevent*] C.D., a clergyman [*or minister*], from celebrating divine service [*or performing the function of* .... *in connection with his calling*] contrary *etc.*

176(1)(b) Violence to or arrest of officiating clergyman

A.B. on .... at .... did

knowing that C.D., a clergyman [*or minister*], was about to perform [*or on his way to perform or returning from performing*] a divine service [*or the function of* .... *in connection with his calling*] assaulted [*or offered violence to or arrested upon a civil process or arrested under the pretense of executing a civil process*] the said C.D. contrary *etc.*

177 Trespassing or prowling at night near dwelling

A.B. on .... at .... without lawful excuse did loiter [*or prowl*] at night upon the property of C.D. situate at [*specify address*] near a dwelling house situated thereon contrary *etc.*

179(1)(a) Vagrancy: living off gaming or crime

A.B. having no lawful profession or calling by which to maintain himself, did within the period between the .... day of .... 19............... and the .... day of .... 19............... support himself in whole [*or in part*] by gaming [*or crime*] contrary *etc.*

180(1) Common nuisance

(*a*) A.B. on .... at .... did commit a common nuisance by [*specify unlawful act done or legal duty not complied with, e.g., by discharging a tear gas bomb in the* .... *Theatre on First St.*] and did thereby endanger the lives [*or safety or health or property or comfort*] of the public contrary *etc.*

or

(*b*) A.B. on .... at .... did commit a common nuisance and thereby did cause physical injury to C.D. by [*specify unlawful act or legal duty not complied with*] contrary *etc.*

182(a) Dead body: neglect duty

A.B. on .... at .... did neglect, without lawful excuse, to perform a duty imposed upon him by law [*or that he undertook*] with reference to the burial of the human remains of C.D. to wit [*specify legal duty or duty undertaken, e.g., to bury the body of his wife C.D.*] contrary *etc.*

182(*b*) Dead body: indignity to

A.B. on .... at .... did improperly [*or* indecently] interfere with [*or* offer an indignity to] the human remains of C.D. by [*specify interference or indignity*] contrary *etc.*

184(1) Interception of private communication

A.B. on .... at .... by means of an electromagnetic [*or* acoustic *or* mechanical] device to wit [*specify type etc.*] wilfully intercepted a private communication by telephone [*or* radio-telephone *or* orally, etc.] between C.D. and E.F. contrary *etc.*

191(1) Possession of devices for surreptitious interception of private communication

A.B. on .... at .... unlawfully did possess [*or* sell *or* purchase] an electromagnetic device [*or* acoustic device *or* mechanical device, *or* component of an electromagnetic device etc.] knowing that the design thereof rendered it primarily useful for the surreptitious interception of private communications, to wit: [*describe device or component*], contrary *etc.*

193(1) Disclosure of private communication

A.B. on .... at .... without the express consent of C.D. the originator thereof, or of E.F. the person C.D. intended to receive it, wilfully used [*or* disclosed] a private communication between the said C.D. and E.F. contrary *etc.*

201(1) Common gaming or betting house: keeping

A.B. on .... at .... did keep a common gaming [*or* betting] house at [*specify address*] contrary *etc.*

201(2)(*a*) Common gaming or betting house: found in

A.B. on .... at .... was found, without lawful excuse, in a common gaming [*or* betting] house to wit [*specify address*] contrary *etc.*

201(2)(*b*) Common gaming or betting house: owner, etc.

A.B. on .... at .... being the owner [*or* landlord *or* lessor *or* tenant *or* occupier *or* agent] of a place known as [*specify address*] did knowingly permit such place to be let [*or* used] for the purposes of a common gaming [*or* betting] house contrary *etc.*

202(1) Betting, pool-selling, book-making, etc.

A.B. on .... at ....

(*a*) did use [*or* allow to be used] a place under his control to wit [*specify address*] for the purpose of recording [*or* registering] bets [*or* selling a pool] contrary *etc.*

or

(*b*) did import [*or* make *or* buy *or* sell *or* rent *or* lease *or* hire *or* keep *or* exhibit *or* employ *or* knowingly allow to be kept *or* exhibited *or* employed in a place under his control to wit (*specify address*)] a device [*or* apparatus] for the purpose of recording [*or* registering] bets [*or*

APP

selling a pool] [_or_ a machine _or_ device for gambling _or_ betting to wit (_specify_)] contrary _etc._

_or_

(**c**)   did have under his control a sum of money [_or specify other property_] relating to [_specify an offence under s. 202(1), e.g., pool-selling_] contrary _etc._

_or_

(**d**)   did unlawfully record [_or_ register] a bet [_or_ sell a pool] to wit (_specify e.g., on the result of a horse race at ...._)] contrary _etc._

_or_

(**e**)   did engage in pool-selling [_or_ book-making _or_ the business _or_ occupation of betting] [_or_ did make an agreement for the purchase (_or_ sale) of betting (_or_ gaming) privileges _or_ for the purchase (_or_ sale) of information that was intended to assist in book-making (_or_ pool-selling _or_ betting) to wit (_specify subject matter of agreement_)] contrary _etc._

NOTE: Section 202(1)(_f_) to (_j_) relate to offences as follows:

(**f**)   printing or providing book-making, pool-selling or betting information on horse-races, fights, games or sports;

(**g**)   importing information or writing to promote gambling, book-making, pool-selling or betting;

(**h**)   advertising, printing, publishing, exhibiting or posting up for contests;

(**i**)   sending, transmitting or delivering messages by radio, telegraph, telephone, mail or express that convey information relating to these matters;

(**j**)   aiding or assisting in anything that is an offence under this section.

203(_a_) Betting: off-track

A.B. on .... at .... did place [_or_ offer to place _or_ agree to place] a bet on behalf of C.D., to wit .... for a consideration paid [_or_ to be paid] by or on behalf of C.D. contrary _etc._

206(1)(_a_) Lottery scheme: publishing

A.B. on .... at .... did make [_or_ print _or_ advertise _or_ publish _or_ cause to be made _or_ printed _or_ advertised _or_ published] a proposal [_or_ scheme _or_ plan] for advancing [_or_ lending _or_ giving _or_ selling] the disposal of property to wit [_specify property, e.g., an automobile_] by lots [_or_ cards _or_ tickets (_or specify other mode of chance_)] contrary _etc._

209 Cheating at play

A.B. on .... at .... did, with intent to defraud C.D., cheat while playing the game of .... [_or_ in holding the stakes for a game of .... _or_ in betting (_specify, e.g., on a horse-race at etc._)] contrary _etc._

210(1) Common bawdy-house: keeping

A.B. on .... at .... did keep a common bawdy-house located at [*specify address*] contrary *etc.*

210(2)(*a*) Common bawdy-house: inmate

A.B. on .... at .... was an inmate of a common bawdy-house at [*specify address*] contrary *etc.*

210(2)(*b*) Common bawdy-house: found in

A.B. on .... at .... was found without lawful excuse in a common bawdy-house at [*specify address*] contrary *etc.*

210(2)(*c*) Common bawdy-house: owner, *etc.*

A.B. on .... at .... being the owner [*or* landlord *or* tenant *or* occupier *or* having charge *or* control] of premises [*specify address*] did knowingly permit [a part of] such premises to be let [*or* used] for the purposes of a common bawdy-house contrary *etc.*

211 Common bawdy-house: transporting person to

A.B. on .... at .... did knowingly take [*or* transport *or* direct *or* offer to take *or* transport *or* direct] C.D. to a common bawdy-house at [*specify address*] contrary *etc.*

212(1) Procuring

A.B. on .... at .... did

(*a*) procure [*or* attempt to procure *or* solicit] C.D. to have illicit sexual intercourse with E.F. at [*specify address*] contrary *etc.*

(*b*) inveigle [*or* entice] C.D., not a prostitute [*or* not of known immoral character], to a common bawdy-house [*or* house of assignation] at [*specify address*] for the purpose of illicit sexual intercourse [*or* prostitution] contrary *etc.*

(*c*) knowingly conceal C.D. in a common bawdy-house [*or* house of assignation] at [*specify address*] contrary *etc.*

(*d*) procure [*or* attempt to procure] C.D. to become a prostitute contrary *etc.*

(*g*) procure C.D. to enter [*or* leave] Canada for the purpose of prostitution contrary *etc.*

(*h*) for the purpose of gain, exercise control [*or* direction *or* influence] over the movements of C.D. in such manner as to show that he was aiding [*or* abetting *or* compelling] C.D. to engage in [*or* carry on] prostitution with E.F. [*or* generally] contrary *etc.*

(*i*) apply [*or* administer] to C.D. [*or* cause C.D. to take] a drug [*or* intoxicating liquor *or specify item*] with intent to stupefy [*or* overpower] him and to enable himself [*or* E.F.] to have illicit sexual intercourse with him contrary *etc.*

APP

212(2.1) Living on avails of juvenile prostitution and using violence
  A.B. at .... between the .... day of .... 19 .... ,
and the .... day of .... 19 .... , did live wholly [*or* partly]
on the avails of prostitution of C.D. a person under the age of eighteen years
and for the purposes of profit did aid [*or* abet *or* counsel or compel] C.D. to
engage in prostitution [*or* carry on prostitution] and used [*or* threatened to use
or attempt to use] violence [*or* intimidation *or* coercion] in relation to C.D.
contrary *etc.*

212(4) Juvenile prostitution
  A.B. on .... at .... did obtain [*or* attempt to obtain] for
consideration, the sexual services of C.D., a person under the age of eighteen
years, contrary *etc.*

213(1) Prostitution offences
  A.B. on .... at .... a public place [*or* a place open to public
view] did

(a)   stop [*or* attempt to stop] motor vehicles
                        or

(b)   impede the free flow of pedestrian traffic [*or* vehicular traffic *or* ingress
       to adjacent premises to wit .... *or* egress from adjacent premises
       to wit ....]

                        or

for the purpose of engaging in prostitution [*or* of obtaining the sexual services
of a prostitute] contrary *etc.*

215(2)(a) Necessaries of life: failure to provide to child or spouse
  A.B. on .... [*or* between the .... day of ....
19................ and the .... day of .... 19................] at
................, being the parent of C.D. a child under the age of sixteen years
[*or* the spouse of E.F.], did fail without lawful excuse to provide the
necessaries of life to C.D. [*or* E.F.]

(i)   C.D. [*or* E.F.] then being in destitute [*or* necessitous] circumstances
       contrary *etc.*

                        or

(ii)   and did thereby endanger the life of C.D. [*or* E.F.] contrary *etc.*
                        or

       thereby causing [*or* being likely to cause] the health of C.D. [*or* E.F.] to
       be endangered permanently contrary *etc.*

215(2)(b) Necessaries of life: failure to provide to person under charge
  A.B. on .... [*or* between the .... day of ....
19................ , and the .... day of .... 19................] at
.... did fail without lawful excuse to provide the necessaries of life to
C.D., a person under his charge and unable, by reason of detention [*or* age *or*
illness *or* insanity *or* specify other reason] to withdraw himself from such

charge, and to provide himself with such necessaries and did thereby endanger the life of C.D. [*or* cause *or* likely cause the health of C.D. to be injured permanently] contrary *etc.*

218 Abandoning child

A.B. on .... at .... did unlawfully abandon [*or* expose] C.D., a child under the age of ten years, and did thereby endanger its life [*or* which abandoning *or* exposing was likely to endanger its life] contrary *etc.*

or

A.B. on .... at .... did unlawfully abandon [*or* expose] C.D., a child under the age of ten years, which abandoning [*or* exposing] permanently injured [*or* was likely to permanently injure] its health contrary *etc.*

220(a) Criminal negligence causing death by use of firearm

A.B. on .... at .... did use a firearm to wit .... in the commission of the offence of criminal negligence [*specify act done e.g. by discharging the said firearm at C.D.*] thereby causing the death of C.D. contrary *etc.*

220(b) Criminal negligence causing death

A.B. on .... at .... did by criminal negligence to wit [*specify act done or duty not complied with, e.g., by operating a motor vehicle at an excessive rate of speed on First St.*] cause the death of C.D. contrary *etc.*

221 Criminal negligence causing bodily harm

A.B. on .... at .... did by criminal negligence to wit [*specify act done or duty not complied with, e.g., by administering drug "A" for drug "B"*] cause bodily harm to C.D. contrary *etc.*

or

A.B. on .... at .... was criminally negligent in the operation of a motor vehicle on [*name of street*] and did thereby cause bodily harm to C.D. contrary *etc.*

233 Infanticide

A.B., a female person, on .... at .... did cause the death of her newly-born child by a wilful act [*or* omission] to wit [*specify act or omission, e.g., by suffocation*] contrary *etc.*

235(1) Murder

A.B. on .... at .... did commit first degree [*or* second degree] murder on the person of C.D. contrary *etc.*

236(a) Manslaughter while using firearm

A.B. on .... at .... did unlawfully kill C.D. while using a firearm to wit [*specify*] and thereby commit manslaughter contrary *etc.*

236(b) Manslaughter

A.B. on .... at .... did unlawfully kill C.D. and thereby commit manslaughter contrary *etc.*

239(1)(a) Attempted murder while using certain firearms etc.
A.B. on .... at .... did attempt to murder C.D.

while using a restricted firearm [*or* a prohibited firearm] [*specify means used e.g. by discharging the firearm at the said C.D.*] contrary *etc.*

or

while using a firearm and did so for the benefit of [*or* at the direction of *or* in association with] a criminal organization to wit .... contrary *etc.*

239(1)(a.1) Attempted murder while using other firearms
A.B. on .... at .... did attempt to murder C.D. while using a firearm [*specify means used e.g. by discharging a shotgun at the said C.D.*] contrary *etc.*

239(1)(b) Attempted murder
A.B. on .... at .... did attempt to murder C.D. [*specify means used*] contrary *etc.*

240 Accessory after fact to murder
A.B. on .... at .... knowing that C.D. had murdered E.F. did receive [*or* comfort *or* assist] C.D. for the purpose of enabling C.D. to escape contrary *etc.*

241(a) Suicide: counselling
A.B. on .... at .... counsel C.D. to commit suicide contrary *etc.*

241(b) Suicide: aiding or abetting
A.B. on .... at .... did unlawfully aid [*or* abet] C.D. to commit suicide contrary *etc.*

243 Concealing body of child
A.B. on .... at .... did dispose of the dead body of a child with intent to conceal the fact that she [*or* C.D.] had been delivered of it by [*specify manner of disposal, e.g., secretly burying it*] contrary *etc.*

244 Discharging firearm with intent
A.B. on .... at .... with intent

(a)   to wound [*or* maim *or* disfigure] C.D.

or

(b)   to endanger the life of C.D.

or

(c)   to prevent the arrest [*or* detention] of E.F.
did discharge a firearm [*specify*] at C.D. [*or* any other person] contrary *etc.*

244.1 Discharging air gun or pistol with intent
A.B. on .... at .... with intent

(a)   to wound [*or* maim *or* disfigure] C.D.

or

(b)   to endanger the life of C.D.

or

(c)   to prevent the arrest [*or* detention] of E.F.
did discharge an air [*or* compressed gas] gun [*or* pistol] at C.D. [*or* any other person] contrary *etc.*

245 Bodily harm: administering noxious thing

A.B. on .... at .... did administer [*or* cause to be administered] to C.D. [*or* cause C.D. to take] poison [*or* a destructive *or* noxious thing] to wit [*specify*] with intent thereby

(a)   to endanger the life of [*or* cause bodily harm to] C.D. contrary *etc.*

or

(b)   to aggrieve [*or* annoy] C.D. contrary *etc.*

246 Bodily harm: overcoming resistance to commission of offence

A.B. on .... at .... with intent to enable [*or* assist] himself [*or* C.D.] to commit the indictable offence of .... did

(a)   attempt to choke [*or* suffocate *or* strangle] C.D. by [*specify means used, e.g., a light cord*] contrary *etc.*

or

attempt to render C.D. insensible [*or* unconscious *or* incapable of resistance] by choking [*or* suffocating *or* strangling] C.D. with [*specify means used*] contrary *etc.*

or

(b)   administer [*or* cause to be administered *or* attempt to administer] to C.D. [*or* cause *or* attempt to cause C.D. to take] a stupefying [*or* overpowering] drug [*or* specify other matter or thing] contrary *etc.*

247 Setting trap likely to cause death or bodily harm

(1)(*a*)   A.B. on .... at .... with intent to cause death [*or* bodily harm] to any person did set [*or* place] a trap [*or* device *or* other thing] to wit [*specify or describe, e.g., a spring gun*] which trap [*or* device] was likely to cause death [*or* bodily harm] to a person contrary *etc.*

(1)(*b*)   A.B. on .... at .... being in occupation [*or* possession] of the said premises with intent to cause death [*or* bodily harm] to any person knowingly permitted a trap [*or* device *or* other thing] to wit [*specify or describe, e.g., a spring gun*] which trap [*or* device] was likely to cause death [*or* bodily harm] to a person contrary *etc.*

(2)   A.B. on .... at .... with intent to cause death [*or* bodily harm] to any person did set [*or* place] a trap [*or* device *or* other thing] to

APP

wit [*specify or describe, e.g., a spring gun*] which trap [*or device*] was likely to cause death [*or bodily harm*] to a person and thereby caused bodily harm to C.D. contrary *etc.*

or

A.B. on .... at .... being in occupation [*or possession*] of the said premises with intent to cause death [*or bodily harm*] to any person knowingly permitted a trap [*or device or other thing*] to wit [*specify or describe, e.g., a spring gun*] which trap [*or device*] was likely to cause death [*or bodily harm*] to a person and thereby caused bodily harm to C.D. contrary *etc.*

(3) A.B. on .... at .... which place was kept or used for the purpose of committing another indictable offence [*specify e.g. producing Cannabis marihuana*] with intent to cause death [*or bodily harm*] to any person did set [*or place*] a trap [*or device or other thing*] to wit [*specify or describe, e.g., a spring gun*] which trap [*or device*] was likely to cause death [*or bodily harm*] to a person contrary *etc.*

or

A.B. on .... at .... being in occupation [*or possession*] of the said premises which premises were kept or used for the purpose of committing another indictable offence [*specify e.g. producing Cannabis marihuana*] did with intent to cause death [*or bodily harm*] to any person knowingly permit a trap [*or device or other thing*] to wit [*specify or describe, e.g., a spring gun*] which trap [*or device*] was likely to cause death [*or bodily harm*] to a person contrary *etc.*

(4) A.B. on .... at .... which place was kept or used for the purpose of committing another indictable offence [*specify e.g. producing Cannabis marihuana*] with intent to cause death [*or bodily harm*] to any person did set [*or place*] a trap [*or device or other thing*] to wit [*specify or describe, e.g., a spring gun*] which trap [*or device*] was likely to cause death [*or bodily harm*] to a person and thereby caused bodily harm to C.D. contrary *etc.*

or

A.B. on .... at .... being in occupation [*or possession*] of the said premises which premises were kept or used for the purpose of committing another indictable offence [*specify e.g. producing Cannabis marihuana*] did with intent to cause death [*or bodily harm*] to any person knowingly permit a trap [*or device or other thing*] to wit [*specify or describe, e.g., a spring gun*] which trap [*or device*] was likely to cause death [*or bodily harm*] to a person and thereby caused bodily harm to C.D. contrary *etc.*

(5) A.B. on .... at .... with intent to cause death [*or bodily harm*] to any person did set [*or place*] a trap [*or device or other thing*] to wit [*specify or describe, e.g., a spring gun*] which trap [*or device*] was likely to cause death [*or* bodily harm] to a person and thereby caused the death of C.D. contrary *etc.*

or

A.B. on .... at .... being in occupation [*or* possession] of the said premises with intent to cause death [*or* bodily harm] to any person knowingly permitted a trap [*or* device *or* other thing] to wit [*specify or describe, e.g., a spring gun*] which trap [*or* device] was likely to cause death [*or* bodily harm] to a person and thereby caused the death of C.D. contrary *etc.*

263(2) Duty to safeguard excavation

A.B. on .... at .... being the owner of [*or* being in charge of *or* being the supervisor of*] certain land to wit [*here specify*] on which he left an excavation did fail to guard the excavation in a manner adequate to warn persons that the excavation [*or* to prevent persons from falling in by accident] contrary *etc.*

264(1), (2) Criminal harassment

A.B. on .... [*or* between .... and ....] at .... knowing that C.D. is harassed or being reckless as to whether C.D. is harassed did without lawful authority

(2)(a) repeatedly follow C.D. [*or* E.F., a person known to C.D.] from place to place

or

(2)(b) repeatedly communicate directly or indirectly with C.D. [*or* E.F., a person known to C.D.]

or

(2)(c) beset or watch

(i) the dwelling-house of C.D. [*or* residence of C.D. *or* place of work of C.D. *or* place where C.D. carries on business *or* place where C.D. happens to be] at .... [*here specify the place e.g. by address*]

or

(ii) the dwelling-house of E.F. a person know to C.D. [*or* residence of E.F. a person known to C.D. *or* place of work of E.F. a person known to C.D. *or* place where E.F. a person known to C.D. carries on business *or* place where E.F. a person known to C.D. happens to be] at .... [*here specify the place e.g. by address*]

or

(2)(d) engage in threatening conduct directed at C.D. [*or* G.H. a member of the family of C.D.]

thereby causing C.D. to reasonably, in all the circumstances, fear for her safety [*or* the safety of E.F. a person known to C.D.] contrary *etc.*

264.1(1) Uttering threats

A.B. on .... at .... did by [*specify means, e.g., telephone*] knowingly utter a threat to C.D. [*or* convey a threat to C.D. *or* cause C.D. to receive a threat] to

(a)   cause death [*or* bodily harm] to C.D. [*or* E.F.] contrary *etc.*

or

(b)   burn [*or* destroy *or* damage] real [*or* personal] property of C.D. [*or* E.F.] to wit [*specify, e.g., his dwelling house or automobile*] contrary *etc.*

or

(c)   kill [*or* poison *or* injure] an animal [*or* bird] of C.D. to wit [*specify animal or bird, e.g., cattle*] contrary *etc.*

266 Assault

A.B. on .... at .... did commit an assault on C.D. contrary *etc.*

267(a) Assault with weapon

A.B. on .... at .... did in committing an assault on C.D. carry [*or* use *or* threaten to use] a weapon [*or* an imitation of a weapon] to wit [*here specify*] contrary *etc.*

267(b) Assault causing bodily harm

A.B. on .... at .... did in committing an assault upon C.D. cause bodily harm to him contrary *etc.*

268 Aggravated assault

A.B. on .... at .... did wound [*or* maim *or* disfigure *or* endanger the life of] C.D. thereby committing an aggravated assault contrary *etc.*

269 Unlawfully causing bodily harm

A.B. on .... at .... did unlawfully cause bodily harm to C.D. by [*e.g., throwing acid upon the person of C.D.*] contrary *etc.*

269.1 Torture

A.B. on .... at ....

being an official to wit [*specify e.g. a peace officer*]

or

acting at the instigation of [*or* with the consent of *or* the acquiescence of] C.D. an official

did inflict torture on C.D. by [*here specify act or omission constituting torture as defined in s. 269.1(2) e.g. beating the said C.D. and thereby intentionally causing him severe pain, for the purpose of obtaining a statement from C.D. as to his alleged involvement in a robbery*] contrary *etc.*

270(1) Assaulting a peace officer

(a)   Assaulting peace officer

A.B. on .... at .... did assault C.D., a public [*or* peace] officer [*describe* C.D.] engaged in the execution of his duty [*or* E.F. a person acting in aid of C.D. a public (*or* peace) officer engaged in the execution of his duty] contrary *etc.*

(b)   Assault with intent to resist arrest

A.B. on .... at .... did assault C.D. with intent to resist [*or* prevent] the lawful arrest [*or* detention] of himself [*or* X.Y.] contrary *etc.*

(c)   Assault to prevent execution of process

A.B. on .... at .... did

(i)   assault C.D., a person engaged in the lawful execution of a process against lands [*or* goods] [*or* engaged in making a lawful distress *or* seizure] contrary *etc.*

or

(ii)   assault C.D. with intent to rescue property to wit [*specify*] taken under a lawful process [*or* distress *or* seizure] contrary *etc.*

271 Sexual assault

A.B. on .... at .... did commit a sexual assault on C.D. contrary *etc.*

272(2)(a) Miscellaneous sexual assaults while using certain firearm

(a)   Sexual assault with weapon

A.B. on .... at .... did in committing a sexual assault on C.D. carry [*or* use *or* threaten to use] a restricted [*or* prohibited] firearm to wit [*here specify*] contrary *etc.*

(b)   Sexual assault with threat to third party

A.B. on ...., at .... did use a restricted [*or* prohibited] firearm to wit [*here specify*] and threaten to cause bodily harm to E.F. in committing a sexual assault on C.D. contrary *etc.*

(c)   Sexual assault causing bodily harm

A.B. on .... at .... did use a restricted [*or* prohibited] firearm in committing a sexual assault on C.D. and causing bodily harm to him contrary *etc.*

(d)   Gang sexual assault

A.B. on .... at .... did use a restricted [*or* prohibited] firearm in committing a sexual assault on C.D. to which sexual assault E.F. was also a party contrary to *etc.*

272(2)(*a*) Miscellaneous sexual assaults while using firearm: criminal organization

(*a*)   Sexual assault with weapon

A.B. on .... at .... did in committing a sexual assault on C.D. carry [*or* use *or* threaten to use] a firearm to wit [*here specify*] which offence was committed for the benefit of [*or* at the direction of *or* in association with] a criminal organization to wit .... contrary *etc.*

(*b*)   Sexual assault with threat to third party

A.B. on .... at .... did use a firearm to wit [*here specify*] and threaten to cause bodily harm to E.F. in committing a sexual assault on C.D. contrary *etc.*

(*c*)   Sexual assault causing bodily harm

A.B. on .... at .... did use a firearm in committing a sexual assault on C.D. and causing bodily harm to him contrary *etc.*

(*d*)   Gang sexual assault

A.B. on .... at .... did use a firearm in committing a sexual assault on C.D. to which sexual assault E.F. was also a party contrary to *etc.*

272(2)(*a*.1) Miscellaneous sexual assaults while using firearm

(*a*)   Sexual assault with weapon

A.B. on .... at .... did in committing a sexual assault on C.D. carry [*or* use *or* threaten to use] a firearm to wit [*here specify*] contrary *etc.*

(*b*)   Sexual assault with threat to third party

A.B. on .... at .... did use a firearm to wit [*here specify*] and threaten to cause bodily harm to E.F. in committing a sexual assault on C.D. contrary *etc.*

(*c*)   Sexual assault causing bodily harm

A.B. on .... at .... did use a firearm in committing a sexual assault on C.D. and causing bodily harm to him contrary *etc.*

(*d*)   Gang sexual assault

A.B. on .... at .... did use a firearm in committing a sexual assault on C.D. to which sexual assault E.F. was also a party contrary to *etc.*

272(2)(*b*) Miscellaneous sexual assaults

(*a*)   Sexual assault with weapon

A.B. on .... at .... did in committing a sexual assault on C.D. carry [*or* use *or* threaten to use] a weapon [*or* an imitation of a weapon] to wit [*here specify*] contrary *etc.*

(*b*)   Sexual assault with threat to third party

A.B. on .... at .... did in committing a sexual assault on C.D. threaten to cause bodily harm to E.F. contrary *etc.*

(c)   Sexual assault causing bodily harm

A.B. on .... at .... did in committing a sexual assault on C.D. cause bodily harm to him contrary *etc.*

(d)   Gang sexual assault

A.B. on .... at .... did commit a sexual assault on C.D. to which sexual assault E.F. was also a party contrary to *etc.*

NOTE: To ensure that there is no doubt as to which form of sexual assault is charged it is strongly recommended that the particular Code section, subsection and paragraph be specified.

273(2)(*a*) Aggravated sexual assault while using certain firearms

A.B. on .... at .... did use a restricted [*or* prohibited] firearm [*here specify*] in committing a sexual assault on C.D. and wound [*or* maim *or* disfigure or endanger the life of] the said C.D. thereby committing an aggravated sexual assault contrary *etc.*

273(2)(*a*.1) Aggravated sexual assault while using firearm: criminal organization

A.B. on .... at .... did use a firearm [*here specify*] in committing a sexual assault on C.D. and wound [*or* maim *or* disfigure or endanger the life of] the said C.D. thereby committing an aggravated sexual assault which offence was committed for the benefit of [*or* at the direction of *or* in association with] a criminal organization to wit .... contrary *etc.*

273(2)(*b*) Aggravated sexual assault

A.B. on .... at .... did in committing a sexual assault on C.D. wound [*or* maim *or* disfigure or endanger the life of] the said C.D. thereby committing an aggravated sexual assault contrary *etc.*

273.3(1) Removal of child from Canada

(*a*)   A.B. on .... at .... with the intention of committing an act outside Canada that if it were committed in Canada would be an offence against section 151 [*or* 152 *or* 160(3) *or* 173(2)] of the *Criminal Code* in respect of C.D. a person ordinarily resident in Canada, and under the age of sixteen years, did [*specify act done e.g. obtain false identification for C.D.*] for the purpose of removing C.D. from Canada contrary *etc.*

(*b*)   A.B. on .... at .... with the intention of committing an act outside Canada that if it were committed in Canada would be an offence against section 153 of the *Criminal Code* in respect of C.D. a person ordinarily resident in Canada, and over the age of sixteen years and under the age of eighteen years, did [*specify act done e.g. obtain false identification for C.D.*] for the purpose of removing C.D. from Canada contrary *etc.*

(*c*)   A.B. on .... at .... with the intention of committing an act outside Canada that if it were committed in Canada would be an offence against section 155 [*or* 159 *or* 160(2) *or* 170 *or* 171 *or* 267 *or* 268 *or* 269 *or* 271 *or* 272 *or* 273] of the *Criminal Code* in respect of C.D. a person ordinarily resident in Canada, and under the age of eighteen years, did [*specify act done e.g. obtain false identification for C.D.*] for the purpose of removing C.D. from Canada contrary *etc.*

276.3(1) Prohibited publication of complainant's sexual activity
    A.B. on .... at .... did publish in a newspaper [*or* broadcast] to wit [*here specify*]

(*a*)   the contents of an application made under s. 276.1 of the *Criminal Code* at the trial of C.D. to determine the admissibility of evidence of the sexual activity of E.F. to wit [*here specify matter published or broadcast*] contrary *etc.*

or

(*b*)   the evidence taken [*or* the information given *or* the representations made] at an application made under s. 276.1 [*or* a hearing under s. 276.2] of the *Criminal Code* at the trial of C.D. to determine the admissibility of evidence of the sexual activity of E.F. to wit [*here specify matter published or broadcast*] contrary *etc.*

or

(*c*)   the decision of [*here specify judge, provincial court judge or justice*] made under subsection 276.1(4) of the *Criminal Code* at the trial of C.D. that a hearing be held into the admissibility of evidence of the sexual activity of E.F. to wit [*here specify matter published or broadcast*] contrary *etc.*

or

(*d*)   the determination made [*or* the reasons given] by [*here specify judge, provincial court judge or justice*] made under subsection 276.2 of the *Criminal Code* at the trial of C.D. as to the admissibility of the evidence of the sexual activity of E.F. to wit [*here specify matter published or broadcast*] contrary *etc.*

278.9(1) Prohibited publication of personal information records
    A.B. on .... at .... did publish in a newspaper [*or* broadcast] to wit [*here specify*]

(*a*)   the contents of an application made under s. 278.3 of the *Criminal Code* at the trial of C.D. for production of records containing personal information concerning E.F. to wit [*here specify matter published or broadcast*] contrary *etc.*

or

(*b*)   the evidence taken [*or* the information given *or* the submissions made] at a hearing under s. 278.4(1) [*or* s. 278.6(2)] of the *Criminal Code* at the trial of C.D. to determine whether records containing personal information concerning E.F. should be produced to the court [*or* produced to the said C.D.] to wit [*here specify matter published or broadcast*] contrary *etc.*

or

(c) the determination made [*or* the reasons given] by [*here specify judge, provincial court judge or justice*] made under subsection 278.5 [*or* subsection 278.7(1) *or* s. 278.8] of the *Criminal Code* at the trial of C.D. as to the production of records containing personal information concerning E.F. to wit [*here specify matter published or broadcast*] contrary *etc.*

279(1.1)(a) Kidnapping while using certain firearms

A.B. on .... at .... did use a restricted [*or* prohibited] firearm to wit [*here specify*] in kidnapping C.D. with intent

(a) to cause him to be confined [*or* imprisoned] against his will contrary *etc.*

or

(b) to cause him to be unlawfully sent [*or* transported] out of Canada against his will contrary *etc.*

or

(c) to hold him for ransom [*or* to service against his will] contrary *etc.*

279(1.1)(a) Kidnapping while using firearm: criminal organization

A.B. on .... at .... did use a firearm to wit [*here specify*] in kidnapping C.D. with intent

(a) to cause him to be confined [*or* imprisoned] against his will which offence was committed for the benefit of [*or* at the direction of *or* in association with] a criminal organization to wit .... contrary *etc.*

or

(b) to cause him to be unlawfully sent [*or* transported] out of Canada against his will which offence was committed for the benefit of [*or* at the direction of *or* in association with] a criminal organization to wit .... contrary *etc.*

or

(c) to hold him for ransom [*or* to service against his will] which offence was committed for the benefit of [*or* at the direction of *or* in association with] a criminal organization to wit .... contrary *etc.*

279(1.1)(a.1) Kidnapping while using firearm

A.B. on .... at .... did use a firearm to wit [*here specify*] in kidnapping C.D. with intent

(a) to cause him to be confined [*or* imprisoned] against his will contrary *etc.*

or

(b)   to cause him to be unlawfully sent [*or* transported] out of Canada against his will contrary *etc.*

or

(c)   to hold him for ransom [*or* to service against his will] contrary *etc.*

279(1.1)(b) Kidnapping

A.B. on .... at .... did kidnap C.D. with intent

(a)   to cause him to be confined [*or* imprisoned] against his will contrary *etc.*

or

(b)   to cause him to be unlawfully sent [*or* transported] out of Canada against his will contrary *etc.*

or

(c)   to hold him for ransom [*or* to service against his will] contrary *etc.*

279(2) Forcible confinement etc.

A.B. on .... at .... did without lawful authority confine [*or* imprison *or* forcibly seize] C.D. contrary *etc.*

279.1(2)(a) Hostage taking using certain firearms

A.B. on .... at .... did use a restricted [*or* prohibited] firearm to wit [*specify*] in taking hostage C.D. by confining [*or* imprisoning *or* forcibly seizing *or* detaining] C.D. and uttering [*or* conveying *or* causing any person to receive] a threat to cause the death of C.D. [*or* cause bodily harm to C.D. *or* continue the confinement, imprisonment *or* detention of C.D.] with the intent to induce E.F. [*or* specify the group, state, etc.] to [*specify the demand, e.g., release G.H. from Kingston Penitentiary*] as a condition of the release of C.D. contrary *etc.*

279.1(2)(a) Hostage taking using firearm: criminal organization

A.B. for the benefit of [*or* at the direction of *or* in association with] a criminal organization to wit .... on .... at .... did use a firearm to wit [*specify*] in taking hostage C.D. by confining [*or* imprisoning *or* forcibly seizing *or* detaining] C.D. and uttering [*or* conveying *or* causing any person to receive] a threat to cause the death of C.D. [*or* cause bodily harm to C.D. *or* continue the confinement, imprisonment *or* detention of C.D.] with the intent to induce E.F. [*or* specify the group, state, etc.] to [*specify the demand, e.g., release G.H. from Kingston Penitentiary*] as a condition of the release of C.D. contrary *etc.*

279.1(2)(a.1) Hostage taking using firearm

A.B. on .... at .... did use a firearm to wit [*specify*] in taking hostage C.D. by confining [*or* imprisoning *or* forcibly seizing *or* detaining] C.D. and uttering [*or* conveying *or* causing any person to receive] a threat to cause the death of C.D. [*or* cause bodily harm to C.D. *or* continue the confinement, imprisonment *or* detention of C.D.] with the intent to induce

E.F. [*or* specify the group, state, etc.] to [*specify the demand, e.g., release G.H. from Kingston Penitentiary*] as a condition of the release of C.D. contrary *etc.*

279.1(2)(*b*) Hostage taking

A.B. on .... at .... did take hostage C.D. by confining [*or* imprisoning *or* forcibly seizing *or* detaining] C.D. and uttering [*or* conveying *or* causing any person to receive] a threat to cause the death of C.D. [*or* cause bodily harm to C.D. *or* continue the confinement, imprisonment *or* detention of C.D.] with the intent to induce E.F. [*or* specify the group, state, etc.] to [*specify the demand, e.g., release G.H. from Kingston Penitentiary*] as a condition of the release of C.D. contrary *etc.*

280(1) Abduction of person under sixteen

A.B. on .... at .... without lawful authority did take [*or* cause to be taken] C.D., an unmarried person under the age of sixteen years, out of possession of and against the will of E.F., his parent [*or* guardian *or* specify other person*], who had lawful care [*or* charge] of him contrary *etc.*

281 Abduction of person under fourteen

A.B. not being the parent [*or* guardian *or* specify other applicable person*] having lawful care [*or* charge] of E.F., a person under the age of fourteen years, on .... at .... with intent to deprive C.D., the parent [*or* guardian *or* specify other applicable person*] of the said E.F. of the possession of E.F. did unlawfully

take [or entice away or detain or conceal] the said E.F. contrary etc.

or

receive [or harbour] the said E.F. contrary etc.

282(1) Abduction in contravention of custody order

A.B. being the parent [*or* guardian *or* specify other applicable person*] having lawful care [*or* charge] of E.F. a person under the age of fourteen years on .... at .... in contravention of the custody provisions of a custody order in relation to the said E.F. made by [*specify full title of court*] at [*specify place where court order made*] on [*insert date of order*] with intent to deprive C.D. the parent [*or* guardian *or* specify other applicable person*] of E.F. of the possession of E.F. did

(*a*)   take [*or* entice away *or* detain *or* conceal] the said E.F. contrary *etc.*

or

(*b*)   receive [*or* harbour] the said E.F. contrary *etc.*

283(1) Abduction

A.B. being the parent [*or* guardian *or* specify other applicable person*] having lawful care [*or* charge] of E.F. a person under the age of fourteen years on .... at .... with intent to deprive C.D. the parent [*or* guardian *or* specify other applicable person*] having lawful care [*or* charge] of E.F. of the possession of E.F. did (*a*)   take [*or* entice away *or* detain *or* conceal] the said E.F. contrary *etc.*

or

(*b*)   receive [*or* harbour] the said E.F. contrary *etc.*

287(1) Procuring miscarriage of another

A.B. on .... at .... with intent to procure the miscarriage of C.D., did [*specify means used, e.g., use manipulation or an instrument or administer a drug*] for such purpose contrary *etc.*

287(2) Self-procured miscarriage

A.B., a female person being pregnant, on .... at .... with intent to procure her own miscarriage did [*specify means used, e.g., use an instrument or drug or noxious thing or manipulation*] [*or did permit (specify means, e.g., an instrument or drug or noxious thing or manipulation) to be used for such purpose*] contrary *etc.*

291 Bigamy

(*a*)   A.B. on .... at .... then being married to C.D. [*or knowing E.F. to be married to G.H.*] did go through a form of marriage with E.F. and did thereby commit bigamy contrary *etc.*

or

A.B. on .... at .... did on the same day to wit [*specify date*] [*or simultaneously*] go through a form of marriage with C.D. and E.F. and did thereby commit bigamy contrary *etc.*

(*b*)   A.B. on .... at ...., being then married to C.D. and being a Canadian citizen resident in Canada, did leave Canada with intent to go through a form of marriage with E.F. and did on the .... day of .... 19................, [at the City of Reno in the State of Nevada, one of the United States of America] go through a form of marriage with E.F. and did thereby commit bigamy contrary *etc.*

NOTE: Charge [b] above may be adapted according to the facts to comply with the provisions of s. 290(1)(*a*)(ii) or (iii)

292 Procuring feigned marriage

A.B. on .... at .... did procure [*or* knowingly aid in procuring] a feigned marriage between himself and C.D. contrary *etc.*

293 Polygamy

A.B., a male person, on .... at .... with C.D., a female person, did practice [*or* enter into *or* agree to practice *or* enter into] a form of polygamy contract *etc.*

294 Pretending to solemnize marriage

(*a*)   A.B. on .... at .... without lawful authority did [pretend to] solemnize a marriage between C.D. and E.F. contrary *etc.*

or

(*b*)   A.B. on .... at .... did procure C.D. to solemnize a marriage between E.F. and G.H. knowing that C.D. was not lawfully authorized to solemnize the marriage contrary *etc.*

295 Solemnizing marriage contrary to law

A.B. on .... at ...., being lawfully authorized to solemnize a marriage, did knowingly and wilfully solemnize a marriage between C.D. and E.F. in violation of the laws of the Province of .... [*specify violation, e.g., without publication of banns and without any licence*] as required by section .... of the [*specify provincial Act in full*] of the said province contrary *etc.*

300 Defamatory libel known to be false

A.B. on .... at .... did publish a defamatory libel, knowing that it was false, by [*specify means e.g. delivering to C.D. a pamphlet entitled etc.*] contrary *etc.*

301 Defamatory libel

A.B. on .... at .... did publish a defamatory libel by [*specify means e.g. delivering to C.D. a pamphlet entitled etc.*] contrary *etc.*

302(1) Extortion by libel

A.B. on .... at .... with intent

(*a*)   to extort money from C.D.

or

(*b*)   to induce C.D. to confer on E.F. [*or* procure for E.F.] an appointment [*or* office] of profit [*or* trust] to wit [*specify appointment or office*]

did publish [*or* threaten to publish *or* offer to abstain from publishing *or* offer to prevent the publication of] a defamatory libel, to wit [*specify defamatory libel e.g. a pamphlet entitled etc.*] contrary *etc.*

318(1) Advocating genocide

A.B. on .... at .... did advocate [*or* promote] genocide [*specify means, e.g., by publishing a newsletter entitled* "................" *containing a statement* "................"] contrary *etc.*

319(1) Public incitement of hatred

A.B. on .... at ...., in a public place to wit [*specify*], did by communicating statements [*specify*] incite hatred against an identifiable group to wit [*specify the group*] with a likelihood of leading to a breach of the peace contrary *etc.*

319(2) Wilful promotion of hatred

A.B. on .... at .... did by communicating statements [*specify*] wilfully promote hatred against an identifiable group to wit [*specify the group*] contrary *etc.*

320.13(1) Dangerous operation

A.B. on .... at .... did operate a conveyance in a manner that was dangerous to the public contrary *etc.*

320.13(2) Dangerous operation causing bodily harm

NOTE: Where the dangerous operation has caused bodily harm, prior to the word "contrary" insert "and thereby caused bodily harm to C.D."

320.13(3) Dangerous operation causing death

NOTE: Where the dangerous operation has caused death, prior to the word "contrary" insert "and thereby caused the death of C.D."

320.14(1)(*a*) Operating while impaired

A.B. on .... at .... while his ability to operate a conveyance was impaired by alcohol [*or* a drug *or* a combination of alcohol and a drug] did operate a conveyance contrary *etc.*

320.14(1)(*b*) Operating with over 80 mgs. of alcohol

A.B. on .... at .... did within two hours of ceasing to operate a conveyance have a blood alcohol concentration that was equal to or exceeded eighty milligrams of alcohol in one hundred millilitres of blood contrary *etc.*

320.14(1)(*c*) Operating with excessive blood drug concentration

A.B. on .... at .... did within two hours of ceasing to operate a conveyance have a blood drug concentration that was equal to or exceeded the blood drug concentration prescribed by [*state applicable regulation*] contrary *etc.*

320.14(1)(*d*) Operating with excessive blood alcohol and blood drug concentration

A.B. on .... at .... did within two hours of ceasing to operate a conveyance have a blood alcohol concentration and blood drug concentration that was equal to or exceeded the blood drug concentration prescribed by [*state applicable regulation*] contrary *etc.*

320.14(2) Impaired operation (or operation over legal limit) causing bodily harm

NOTE: Where the impaired operation or operation with excess blood alcohol and/or blood drug concentration has caused bodily harm, prior to the word "contrary" insert "and thereby caused bodily harm to C.D."

320.14(3) Impaired operation (or operation over legal limit) causing death

NOTE: Where the impaired operation or operation with excess blood alcohol and/or blood drug concentration has caused death, prior to the word "contrary" insert "and thereby caused the death of C.D."

320.14(4) Operating with low blood drug concentration (summary conviction offence)

A.B. on .... at .... did within two hours of ceasing to operate a conveyance have a blood drug concentration that was equal to or exceeded the blood drug concentration prescribed by [*specify applicable regulation*] contrary *etc.*

320.15(1) Failure or refusal to comply with breath screening demand

A.B. on .... at .... did without reasonable excuse fail [*or* refuse] to comply with a demand made to him by C.D., a peace officer, under s. 320.27 of the *Criminal Code*

(*a*)   to immediately provide the samples of his breath as in the opinion of C.D. was necessary to enable a proper analysis of his breath to be made by means of an approved screening device contrary *etc.*

or

(*b*)   to accompany C.D. for the purpose of enabling the samples of his breath as in the opinion of C.D. were necessary to be taken for analysis by means of an approved screening device contrary *etc.*

320.15(1) Failure or refusal to comply with bodily substance screening demand

A.B. on .... at .... did without reasonable excuse fail [*or* refuse] to comply with a demand made to him by C.D., a peace officer, under s. 320.27 of the *Criminal Code*

(*a*)   to immediately provide the samples of a bodily substance as in the opinion of C.D. were necessary to enable a proper analysis to be made by means of approved drug screening equipment contrary *etc.*

or

(*b*)   to accompany C.D. for the purpose of enabling the samples of a bodily substance as in the opinion of C.D. were necessary to be taken for analysis by means of approved drug screening equipment contrary *etc.*

320.15(1) Failure or refusal to comply with physical coordination test demand

A.B. on .... at .... did without reasonable excuse fail [*or* refuse] to comply with a demand made to him by C.D., a peace officer, under s. 320.27 of the *Criminal Code*

(*a*)   to immediately perform the physical coordination tests prescribed by [*specify applicable regulation*] contrary *etc.*

or

(*b*)   to accompany C.D. for the purpose of performing physical coordination tests prescribed by [*specify applicable regulation*] contrary *etc.*

320.15(1) Failure or refusal to comply with breath demand

A.B. on .... at .... did without reasonable excuse fail [*or* refuse] to comply with a demand made to him by C.D., a peace officer, under s. 320.28 of the *Criminal Code*

APP

(*a*)   to provide then or as soon thereafter as was practicable samples of his breath as in the opinion of a qualified technician were necessary to enable a proper analysis to be made in order to determine the concentration, if any, of alcohol in his blood contrary *etc.*

or

(*b*)   to accompany C.D. for the purpose of enabling samples of his breath to be taken contrary *etc.*

320.15(1) Failure or refusal to comply with drug evaluation demand

A.B. on .... at .... did without reasonable excuse fail [*or* refuse] to comply with a demand made to him by C.D., a peace officer, under s. 320.28 of the *Criminal Code*

(*a*)   to submit then or as soon thereafter was practicable to an evaluation conducted by an evaluating officer to determine whether his ability to operate a conveyance was impaired by a drug or by a combination of alcohol and a drug contrary *etc.*

or

(*a*)   to accompany C.D. for the purpose of enabling an evaluation officer to determine whether his ability to operate a conveyance was impaired by a drug or by a combination of alcohol and a drug contrary *etc.*

320.15(1) Failure or refusal to comply with blood demand

A.B. on .... at .... did without reasonable excuse fail [*or* refuse] to comply with a demand made to him by C.D., a peace officer, under s. 320.28 of the *Criminal Code*

(*a*)   to provide then or as soon thereafter as was practicable samples of his blood as in the opinion of a qualified technician [*or* qualified medical practitioner] were necessary to enable a proper analysis to be made in order to determine A.B.'s blood alcohol concentration [*and/or* blood drug concentration] contrary *etc.*

or

(*b*)   to accompany C.D. for the purpose of enabling a qualified technician [*or* qualified medical practitioner] to take blood samples contrary *etc.*

320.15(2) Failure to comply with demand after accident resulting in bodily harm

NOTE: Where the failure or refusal has followed an accident resulting in bodily harm, prior to the words "without reasonable excuse", insert "knowing at the time of the failure [*or* refusal], or being reckless as to whether, he was involved in an accident that resulted in bodily harm to another person . . ."

320.15(3) Failure to comply with demand after accident resulting in death

NOTE: Where the failure or refusal has followed an accident causing death, prior to the words "without reasonable excuse", insert "knowing at the time of the failure [*or refusal*], or being reckless as to whether, he was involved in an accident that resulted the death of another person . . ."

320.16(1) Failure to stop after accident

A.B. on .... at .... while operating a conveyance and knowing, or being reckless to whether, the conveyance had been involved in an accident with a person or another conveyance, failed without reasonable excuse to stop the conveyance, give their name and address and, if any person has been injured or appeared to require assistance, offer assistance.

320.16(2) Failure to stop after accident resulting in bodily harm

NOTE: Where the failure to stop followed an accident causing bodily harm, prior to the words "failed without reasonable excuse", insert "and knowing at the time of the failure, or being reckless as to whether, the accident caused bodily harm to another person . . ."

320.16(3) Failure to stop after accident resulting in death

NOTE: Where the failure to stop followed an accident causing death, prior to the words "failed without reasonable excuse," insert "and knowing at the time of the failure, or being reckless as to whether, the accident caused the death of another person . . ."

320.17 Flight from peace officer

A.B. on .... at .... while operating a motor vehicle [*or vessel*] and being pursued by a peace officer, did fail without reasonable excuse to stop his vehicle [*or vessel*] as soon as was reasonable in the circumstances contrary *etc.*

320.18(1) Operating while prohibited

A.B. on .... at ....did operate a conveyance while prohibited from so doing by reason of

(*a*) an order pursuant to s. 320.24 of the *Criminal Code* contrary *etc.*

or

(*b*) the legal disqualification [*or restriction*] in the Province of .... of his right or privilege to operate a [*specify type of conveyance*] contrary *etc.*

333.1 Motor Vehicle Theft

A.B. on .... at .... did steal a motor vehicle [*specify the vehicle e.g. by licence plate number*] the property of C.D. and did thereby commit theft contrary to s. 333.1 of the *Criminal Code of Canada.*

NOTE: We advise specifying the section number so that the accused is aware that he or she is not charged under the general theft section in s. 334.]

334 Theft

A.B. on .... at .... did steal [*specify item*], the property of C.D. of a value [not] exceeding five thousand dollars contrary *etc.*

NOTE: It is suggested that this general form of charge may be used for the specific forms of theft referred to in ss. 323, 328, 330, 331 and 332. The particular type of theft may be subsequently proved. Two alternate forms for the types of theft referred to in s. 326 follow.

Theft of Electricity or Gas (s. 326(1)(*a*))

A.B. on .... at .... did fraudulently [*or* maliciously *or* without colour of right] consume [*or* abstract *or* use] electricity [*or* gas] the property of .... of a value [not] exceeding five thousand dollars and did thereby commit theft contrary *etc.*

or

Theft of Telecommunications Service (s. 326(1)(*b*))

A.B. on .... at .... did fraudulently [*or* maliciously *or* without colour of right] use a telecommunication wire [*or* cable] the property of .... the value of such use [not] exceeding five thousand dollars and did thereby commit theft contrary *etc.*

335(1) Taking motor vehicle or vessel without consent (joy-riding)

A.B. on .... at .... did take a motor vehicle to wit [*specify vehicle*] without the consent of C.D., the owner thereof, with intent to drive [*or* use] it [*or* cause it to be driven *or* used] contrary *etc.*

or

A.B. on .... at .... did take a vessel to wit [*specify*] without the consent of C.D., the owner thereof, with intent to navigate [*or* operate] it [*or* cause it to be navigated or operated] contrary *etc.*

335(1) Occupant of motor vehicle or vessel without consent

A.B. on .... at .... did occupy a motor vehicle [*or* vessel] to wit [*specify motor vehicle or vessel*] knowing that it was taken without the consent of the owner thereof contrary *etc.*

341 Fraudulent concealment

A.B. on .... at .... did for a fraudulent purpose take [*or* obtain *or* remove *or* conceal] certain property of C.D. to wit [*specify property, e.g., a bicycle*] contrary *etc.*

342(1) Theft, forgery, etc. of credit card

(*a*)   A.B. on .... at .... did steal a credit card [*specify credit card, e.g., a Toronto-Dominion VISA card #x*] from C.D. contrary *etc.*

or

(*b*)   A.B. on .... at .... did forge [*or* falsify] a credit card [*specify credit card*] by [*specify means, e.g., by altering the numbers on the said card*] contrary *etc.*

or

(*c*)

    (i)   A.B. on .... at .... did have in his possession [*or* used *or* trafficked in] a credit card [*specify credit card*] knowing that the said card was obtained by the commission in Canada of an offence contrary *etc.*

or

    (ii)   A.B. on .... at .... did have in his possession [*or* used *or* trafficked in] a credit card [*specify credit card*] knowing that the said card was obtained in [*specify, e.g., the State of New York*] by the commission of an offence which had it occurred in Canada would have constituted an offence contrary *etc.*

or

(*d*)   A.B. on .... at .... used a credit card [*specify credit card*] knowing that the said credit card had been revoked [*or* cancelled] contrary *etc.*

342(3) Possess, traffic etc. in credit card data

A.B. on .... at .... did fraudulently and without colour of right have in his [*or* her] possession credit card data that would enable a person to use a credit card [*here specify credit card*] [*or* obtain the services that are provided by the issuer of a credit card [*here specify issuer*] to credit card holders] contrary *etc.*

or

A.B. on .... at .... did fraudulently and without colour of right use credit card data that would enable a person to use a credit card [*here specify credit card*] [*or* obtain the services that are provided by the issuer of a credit card [*here specify issuer*] to credit card holders] contrary *etc.*

or

A.B. on .... at .... did fraudulently and without colour of right traffic in credit card data that would enable a person to use a credit card [*here specify credit card*] [*or* obtain the services that are provided by the issuer of a credit card [*here specify issuer*] to credit card holders] contrary *etc.*

or

A.B. on .... at .... did fraudulently and without colour of right permit C.D. to use credit card data that would enable a person to use a credit card [*here specify credit card*] [*or* obtain the services that are provided by the issuer of a credit card [*here specify issuer*] to credit card holders] contrary *etc.*

342.01 Instrument for use in forging credit card

A.B. on .... at .... did without lawful justification or excuse make [*or* repair *or* buy *or* sell *or* export from Canada *or* import into Canada *or* have in his possession] an instrument [*or* device *or* apparatus *or* material *or* thing] to wit .... that he knew had been used [*or* was adapted for use *or* intended for use] in forging [*or* falsifying] credit cards contrary *etc.*

342.1(1) Unauthorized use of computer

A.B. on .... at .... did fraudulently and without colour of right

(a) obtain, directly or indirectly a computer service to wit [*specify computer service e.g., the data processing facility at the University of Toronto*] contrary *etc.*

(b) by means of an electromagnetic [*or* acoustic *or* mechanical] device to wit [*specify type etc.*] intercepted [*or* caused to be intercepted], directly or indirectly, a function of a computer system to wit [*specify computer system e.g. the mainframe computer facility of the Public Utilities Commission*] contrary *etc.*

(c) used [*or* caused to be used] directly or indirectly, a computer system [*specify computer system*] with intent to

obtain, directly or indirectly a computer service to wit [*specify computer service*] contrary *etc.*

intercept [*or* cause to be intercepted], directly or indirectly a function of a computer system to wit [*specify computer system*] by means of an electromagnetic [*or* acoustic *or* mechanical] device to wit [*specify type etc.*] contrary *etc.*

commit the offence contrary to [*specify offence contrary to s. 430 in relation to data or a computer system e.g. s. 430(1.1)(a) of the Criminal Code*] by wilfully destroying data to wit [*specify data*] contrary *etc.*

(d) use [*or* have in his possession *or* traffic in *or* permit C.D. to have access to*] a computer password that would enable him [*or* C.D. *or* E.F.] to commit the offence [*here specify offence contrary to paragraph (a), (b) or (c) e.g. contrary to s. 342(1)(a) of the Criminal Code of fraudulently and without colour of right obtaining directly or indirectly the data processing facilty at the University of Toronto*] contrary *etc.*

342.2 Instrument for obtaining authorized use of computer etc.

A.B. on .... at .... did without lawful justification or excuse make an instrument [*or* device *or* component of an instrument *or* component of a device] to wit .... the design of which rendered it primarily useful for committing the offence [*here specify offence under s. 342.1 e.g. contrary to s. 342.1(1)(a) of the Criminal Code of fraudulently and without colour of right obtaining directly or indirectly a computer service*] under circumstances that gave rise to a reasonable inference that the instrument [*or* device *or* component of an instrument *or* component of a device] had been used [*or* is intended for use *or* was intended for use] to commit the said offence contrary *etc.*

344(1)(a) Robbery using certain firearms

A.B. on .... at .... did use a restricted [*or* prohibited] firearm to wit [*here specify firearm*] in robbing C.D. of [*specify property taken, e.g., a wallet containing personal papers and the sum of fifty dollars*] contrary *etc.*

344(1)(a) Robbery using firearm: criminal organization

A.B. for the benefit of [*or* at the direction of *or* in association with] a criminal organization to wit .... on .... at .... did use a firearm to wit [*here specify firearm*] in robbing C.D. of [*specify property taken, e.g., a wallet containing personal papers and the sum of fifty dollars*] contrary *etc.*

344(1)(a.1) Robbery using firearm

A.B. on .... at .... did use a firearm to wit [*here specify firearm*] in robbing C.D. of [*specify property taken, e.g., a wallet containing personal papers and the sum of fifty dollars*] contrary *etc.*

344(1)(b) Robbery

A.B. on .... at .... did steal [*specify property stolen, e.g., the sum of fifty dollars*] from C.D. and at the time thereof did use violence [*or* threats of violence] to C.D. contrary *etc.*

or

A.B. on .... at .... did steal [*specify property stolen, e.g., a gold wrist watch*] from C.D. and at the time thereof [*or* immediately before *or* immediately thereafter] did wound [*or* beat *or* strike *or* specify personal violence used] C.D. contrary *etc.*

or

A.B. on .... at .... did assault C.D. with intent to steal from him contrary *etc.*

or

A.B. on .... at .... did steal from C.D. [*specify property stolen, e.g., the sum of fifty dollars*] while armed with an offensive weapon [*or* imitation of an offensive weapon] to wit [*specify weapon*] contrary *etc.*

NOTE: Robbery is defined in s. 343(*a*)-(*d*), with which the above four charges comply.

or
(General Charge)

A.B. on .... at .... did rob C.D. of [*specify property taken, e.g., a wallet containing personal papers and the sum of fifty dollars*] contrary *etc.*

345 Stopping mail with intent

A.B. on .... at .... did stop a mail conveyance to wit [*specify type of conveyance, e.g., truck or train*] with intent to rob [*or* search] it contrary *etc.*

346(1.1)(a) Extortion using certain firearms

A.B. on .... at .... without reasonable justification or excuse and with intent to obtain [*specify item requested, e.g., the sum of $1,000*] did

A/57

use a restricted [*or* prohibited] firearm to wit [*specify firearm*] and induce [*or* attempt to induce] C.D. by threats [*or accusations or* menaces *or* violence] to [*specify act done or caused to be done by C.D., e.g., pay the said sum of $1,000 to A.B.*] contrary *etc.*

346(1.1)(*a*) Extortion using firearm: criminal organization

A.B. for the benefit of [*or* at the direction of *or* in association with] a criminal organization to wit .... on .... at .... without reasonable justification or excuse and with intent to obtain [*specify item requested, e.g., the sum of $1,000*] did use a firearm to wit [*specify firearm*] and induce [*or* attempt to induce] C.D. by threats [*or accusations or* menaces *or* violence] to [*specify act done or caused to be done by C.D., e.g., pay the said sum of $1,000 to A.B.*] contrary *etc.*

346(1.1)(*a.1*) Extortion using firearm

A.B. on .... at .... without reasonable justification or excuse and with intent to obtain [*specify item requested, e.g., the sum of $1,000*] did use a firearm to wit [*specify firearm*] and induce [*or* attempt to induce] C.D. by threats [*or accusations or* menaces *or* violence] to [*specify act done or caused to be done by C.D., e.g., pay the said sum of $1,000 to A.B.*] contrary *etc.*

346(1.1)(*b*) Extortion

A.B. on .... at .... without reasonable justification or excuse and with intent to obtain [*specify item requested, e.g., the sum of $1,000*] did induce [*or* attempt to induce] C.D. by threats [*or accusations or* menaces *or* violence] to [*specify act done or caused to be done by C.D., e.g., pay the said sum of $1,000 to A.B.*] contrary *etc.*

or

A.B. on .... at .... without reasonable justification or excuse and with intent to obtain .... dollars from C.D. did [*accuse C.D. of committing the offence of bigamy*] and did receive from C.D. the said sum of .... dollars contrary *etc.*

347(1) Criminal interest rate

(*a*)   A.B. on .... at .... entered into an agreement [*or* arrangement] with C.D. to wit [*specify agreement, e.g., for a loan of $1,000 secured by a promissory note dated Aug. 1, 1981*] to receive interest at a criminal rate, namely [*specify rate, e.g., an effective annual rate of interest of 75 per cent on the sum of $1,000 advanced under the agreement*] contrary *etc.*

or

(*b*)   A.B. on .... at .... received a payment [*or* partial payment] of interest of [*specify amount, e.g., $750*] from C.D. at a criminal rate to wit, [*specify rate and transaction, e.g., an effective annual rate of interest of 75 per cent on the advance of $1,000 on Aug. 1, 1981*] contrary *etc.*

348(1)(a) Breaking and entering with intent

A.B. on .... at .... did break and enter a certain place to wit [*specify type of place, e.g., a dwelling house or store or factory*] situate at .... with intent to commit an indictable offence therein contrary *etc.*

348(1)(b) Breaking, entering and committing

A.B. on .... at .... did break and enter a certain place to wit [*specify type of place, e.g., a dwelling house, store, factory etc.*] situate at .... and did commit therein the indictable offence of .... contrary *etc.*

348(1)(c) Breaking out

A.B. on .... at .... did break out of a certain place to wit [*specify type of place, e.g., a dwelling house, store etc.*] situate at .... after committing therein the indictable offence of .... contrary *etc.*

or

A.B. on .... at .... did break out of a certain place to wit [*specify type of place*] situate at .... after having entered the said place with intent to commit an indictable offence therein contrary *etc.*

349(1) Being unlawfully in dwelling house

A.B. on .... at .... without lawful excuse did enter [*or* was in] the dwelling house of C.D. situate at .... with intent to commit an indictable offence therein contrary *etc.*

351(1) Possession of break-in instruments

A.B. on .... at .... without lawful excuse did have in his possession [an] instrument[s] suitable for the purpose of breaking into a place [*or* into vehicle *or* vault *or* safe] to wit [*specify instrument(s), e.g., nitro-glycerine etc.*] under circumstances [*specify, e.g., mode of concealment, type of instrument*] that gave rise to a reasonable inference that the said instrument had been used [*or* was intended to be used] for such purpose contrary *etc.*

351(2) Disguise with intent

A.B. on .... at .... with intent to commit an indictable offence did have his face masked [*or* coloured *or specify manner of disguise*] contrary *etc.*

352 Possession of coin-operated device breaking instrument

A.B. on .... at .... did without lawful excuse have in his possession an instrument, to wit .... suitable for breaking into a coin-operated device [*or* a currency exchange device] under circumstances [*specify, e.g., mode of concealment, type of instrument*] that gave rise to a reasonable inference that the said instrument had been used [*or* was intended to be used] for breaking into a coin-operated device [*or* a currency exchange device] contrary *etc.*

353(1)(a) Automobile master key: selling or advertising

A.B. on .... at .... did sell [*or* offer for sale *or* advertise] in the Province of .... an automobile master key, to wit .... other than under the authority of a licence issued by the Attorney General of that province contrary *etc.*

353(1)(b) Automobile master key: buying or possessing

A.B. on .... at .... did purchase [*or* have in his possession] in the Province of .... an automobile master key, to wit .... other than under the authority of a licence issued by the Attorney General of that province contrary *etc.*

353(4) Automobile master key: record of sale

A.B. on .... at .... did, having sold an automobile master key, to wit .... fail to

(*a*)   keep a record of the said transaction showing the name [and address] of the purchaser [and the particulars of the licence issued to the purchaser as described in s. 353(1)(b) of the *Criminal Code*] contrary *etc.*

and

(*b*)   produce at the request of C.D., a peace officer, the record described in s. 353(3)(a) of the *Criminal Code* of the said transaction contrary *etc.*

353.1 Tampering with Vehicle Identification Number

A.B. on . . . . at . . . . did without lawful excuse alter [*or remove or obliterate*] a vehicle identification number on a motor vehicle [*specify the vehicle e.g. by licence plate number*] contrary *etc.*

354(1) Possession of property obtained by crime

(*a*)   A.B. on .... at .... did have in his possession property [*or* proceeds of property] [*specify item(s)*] of a value [not] exceeding five thousand dollars knowing that all [*or* part] of the property [*or* proceeds of the property] was obtained [*or* derived directly *or* indirectly] by the commission in Canada of an offence punishable by indictment contrary *etc.*

or

(*b*)   A.B. on .... at .... did have in his possession property [*or* proceeds of property] [*specify item(s)*] of a value [not] exceeding five thousand dollars knowing that all [*or* part] of the property [*or* proceeds of the property] was obtained [*or* derived directly *or* indirectly] by the commission of the offence of .... in [the State of New York] [*set out method of obtaining that would constitute an indictable offence in Canada*], which offence had it occurred in Canada would have been punishable by indictment, contrary *etc.*

356(1)(a) Theft from mail

A.B. on .... at .... did steal

(i)   [*specify item, e.g., a letter or parcel*] sent by post, after it was deposited at a post office and before it was delivered contrary *etc.*

or

(ii) a bag [*or* sack *or* container *or* covering] in which mail is conveyed [*or* containing mail] contrary *etc.*

or

(iii) a key suited to a lock adopted for use by the Canada Post Office contrary *etc.*

356(1)(*b*) Theft from mail: possession of article stolen from mail

A.B. on .... at .... did have in his possession [*specify item set out in* s. 356(1)(*a*)] knowing that an offence under section 356(1)(*a*) of the *Criminal Code* had been committed with respect thereto contrary *etc.*

357 Bringing into Canada property obtained by crime

A.B. on .... at .... did bring into [*or* have in] Canada [*specify item, e.g., an automobile*] that he had obtained outside of Canada by an act that if committed in Canada would have been the offence of theft [*or* an offence under s. 354 of the *Criminal Code*] contrary *etc.*

362(1)(*a*) Obtaining by false pretences

A.B. on .... at .... did by a false pretence [with intent to defraud] [*or* through the medium of a contract obtained by false pretence] obtain from C.D. [*specify item obtained, e.g., a car radio*] of a value [not] exceeding five thousand dollars contrary *etc.*

or

A.B. on .... at .... did by a false pretence [with intent to defraud] [*or* through the medium of a contract obtained by false pretence] cause C.D. to deliver to E.F. [*specify item*] of a value [not] exceeding five thousand dollars contrary *etc.*

362(1)(*b*) Obtaining credit by fraud or false pretence

A.B. on .... at .... did by a false pretence [*or* by fraud] obtain credit from C.D. in the amount of .... dollars contrary *etc.*

362(1)(*c*) False statement in writing

A.B. on .... at .... did knowingly make [*or* cause to be made] directly [*or* indirectly] a false statement in writing with intent that it should be relied upon to wit

[*specify type of statement, e.g., a statement of assets and liabilities*] respecting his [*or* E.F.'s] financial position for the purpose of procuring from C.D. for his own benefit [*or* for the benefit of E.F.]

(i) the delivery of personal property to wit [*specify, e.g., an automobile*] contrary *etc.*

or

(ii) the payment of money to wit [*specify sum*] contrary *etc.*

or

(iii) the making of a loan [*specify amount*] contrary *etc.*

or

APP

(iv)   the grant [*or* extension] of credit to the value of [*specify amount*] [*or specify item referred to in s. 362(1)(c)(v) and (vi)*] contrary *etc.*

363 Obtaining execution of valuable security by fraud

A.B. on .... at .... with intent to defraud [*or* injure] C.D. did by a false pretence, cause [*or* induce] C.D. [*or* E.F.]

(*a*)   to execute [*or* make *or* accept *or* endorse *or* destroy the whole (*or* any part of)] a valuable security to wit [*specify, e.g., a promissory note, bond etc.*] contrary *etc.*

or

(*b*)   to write [*or* impress *or* affix] a name [*or* seal] on a paper (*or* parchment) to wit [*specify document*] in order that it might afterwards be made into [*or* converted into *or* used *or* dealt with as*] a valuable security contrary *etc.*

364 Fraudulently obtaining food and lodging

A.B. on .... at .... did fraudulently obtain food [*or* lodging *or* other accommodation*] from C.D. at [*specify restaurant, hotel etc.*] situate at .... contrary *etc.*

367 Forgery

A.B. on .... at .... did knowingly make a false document to wit [*specify, e.g., a cheque dated .... for $100 payable to C.D. and signed E.F.*] with intent that it be acted upon as genuine and did thereby commit forgery contrary *etc.*

or

A.B. on .... at .... did knowingly make a false document to wit [*specify, e.g., a cheque dated .... for $100 payable to C.D. and signed E.F.*] by forging the endorsement of C.D. thereon with intent that it be acted upon as genuine and did thereby commit forgery contrary *etc.*

368(1) Uttering forged document

A.B. on .... at .... did knowingly

(*a*)   use [*or* deal with *or* act upon] a forged document to wit [*specify, e.g., a cheque and give particulars thereof*] as if it were genuine contrary *etc.*

or

(*b*)   cause [*or* attempt to cause] C.D. to use [*or* deal with *or* act upon] a forged document to wit [*specify, e.g., a cheque and give particulars thereof*] as if it were genuine contrary *etc.*

or

A.B. on .... at .... knowing a [*specify document, e.g., vacation-with-pay stamp book*] in the name of C.D. to be forged did cause E.F. to act upon such book as if it were genuine contrary *etc.*

369(*a*) Exchequer bill or bank note paper

A.B. on .... at .... did make [*or* use *or* knowingly have in his possession]

(i) exchequer bill paper [*or* revenue paper *or* paper that is used to make bank notes] contrary *etc.*

or

(ii) paper that was intended to resemble exchequer bill paper [*or* revenue paper *or* paper that is used to make bank notes] contrary *etc.*

369(*b*) Instruments for forgery

A.B. on .... at .... did make [*or* offer *or* dispose of *or* knowingly have in his possession] a plate [*or* die *or* machinery *or* instrument *or* specify other writing *or* material] that was adapted and intended to be used to commit forgery contrary *etc.*

372(1) False message

A.B. on .... at .... did with intent to injure [*or* alarm] C.D. convey [*or* cause *or* procure to be conveyed] by letter [*or* telegram *or* telephone *or* cable *or* radio *or* otherwise] to C.D. information that he knew to be false to wit [*specify information*] contrary *etc.*

372(2) Indecent telephone calls

A.B. on .... at .... did with intent to alarm [*or* annoy] C.D. make an indecent telephone call to C.D. contrary *etc.*

372(3) Harassing telephone calls

A.B. on ...., at .... did, without lawful excuse and with intent to harass C.D., make [*or* cause to be made] repeated telephone calls, to wit .... to C.D. contrary *etc.*

374 Drawing document without authority

(*a*) A.B. on .... at .... with intent to defraud and without lawful authority did make [*or* execute *or* draw *or* sign *or* accept *or* endorse] a document to wit [*specify*] in the name [*or* on the account] of C.D. contrary *etc.*

(*b*) A.B. on .... at .... did make use of [*or* utter] a document to wit [*specify*] knowing that it had been made [*or* executed *or* signed *or* accepted *or* endorsed] with intent to defraud and without lawful authority, in the name [*or* on the account] of C.D. contrary *etc.*

375 Obtaining, *etc.*, by instrument based on forged document

A.B. on .... at .... did demand [*or* receive *or* obtain] goods [*or* specify] under [*or* on *or* by virtue of] an instrument issued under the authority of law, knowing that the instrument was based on a forged document to wit [*specify document*] contrary *etc.*

or

A.B. on .... at .... did cause [*or procure*] goods [*or specify*] to be delivered [*or paid*] to C.D. under [*or on or by virtue of*] an instrument issued under the authority of law, knowing that the instrument was based on a forged document contrary *etc.*

376(1) Counterfeiting stamp

A.B. on .... at .... did

(*a*)   fraudulently use [*or mutilate or affix or remove or counterfeit*] a stamp [*or part of a stamp*] to wit [*specify*] contrary *etc.*

or

(*b*)   knowingly and without lawful excuse have in his possession a counterfeit stamp [*or a stamp that has been fraudulently mutilated or a document bearing a stamp of which a part has been fraudulently erased (or removed or concealed) or without lawful excuse made or knowingly had in his possession a die or instrument capable of making the impression of a stamp or part of a stamp*] contrary *etc.*

or

(*c*)   without lawful excuse make [*or knowingly have in his possession*] a die [*or instrument*] capable of making the impression of a stamp [*or a part of a stamp*] to wit [*specify*] contrary *etc.*

377(1)(*b*) False entry in official register

A.B. on .... at .... did unlawfully insert in a register of births [*or baptisms or marriages or deaths or burials*] that was required by law to be kept in Canada, an entry that he knew to be false relating to the birth [*or baptism or marriage or death or burial*] of C.D. to wit [*specify entry made*] contrary *etc.*

380(1) Fraud

A.B. on .... at .... did by deceit, falsehood or other fraudulent means defraud C.D. of [*specify property, money or valuable security or service, e.g., the sum of $1,000*] by [*specify fraud*] contrary *etc.*

380(2) Fraud: affecting public market

A.B. on .... at .... did by deceit, falsehood or other means, with intent to defraud, affect the public market price of stocks [*or shares, merchandise, securities, articles*] by [*specify act done, e.g., publishing false reports of the value of mineral rights leased by United Moose Pastures Limited, whose common stock was then traded on the Toronto Stock Exchange*] contrary *etc.*

381 Using mails to defraud

A.B. on .... at .... did make use of the mails for the purpose of transmitting [*or delivering*] letters [*or circulars*] concerning schemes devised [*or intended*] to defraud [*or for the purpose of obtaining money under false pretences from*] the public by [*e.g., posting to divers members of the public letters soliciting subscriptions for the common stock of United Moose Pastures Limited] contrary *etc.*

382 Fraudulent manipulation of stock exchange transactions

A.B. and C.D. on .... at .... did through the facility of a stock exchange [*or* curb market *or* over the counter market] with intent to create a false [*or* misleading] appearance of active public trading in [*specify security*] [*or* with intent to create a false (*or* misleading) appearance with respect to the market price of (*specify security*)],

(*a*)   effect a transaction in the said security that involved no change in the beneficial ownership thereof contrary *etc.*

or

(*b*)   enter an order for the purchase of [*specify security*] knowing that an order of substantially the same size at substantially the same time and at substantially the same price for the sale of the said security had been [would be] entered by [for] the said A.B. and C.D. [*or* other persons] contrary *etc.*

or

(*c*)   enter an order for the sale of [*specify security*] knowing that an order of substantially the same size at substantially the same time and at substantially the same price for the purchase of the said security had been [would be] entered by [for] the said A.B. and C.D. [*or* other persons] contrary *etc.*

390(*a*) Fraudulent receipts under *Bank Act*

A.B. on .... at .... did wilfully make a false statement in a receipt [*or* certificate *or* acknowledgement] for property that may be used for a purpose mentioned in the *Bank Act* contrary *etc.*

392 Defrauding creditors

(*a*)   **Disposing of property**

A.B. on .... at .... did with intent to defraud his creditors

(i)   make [*or* cause to be made] a gift [*or* conveyance *or* assignment *or* sale *or* transfer *or* delivery] of his property to wit [*specify property transferred*] to C.D. contrary *etc.*

or

(ii)   remove [*or* conceal *or* dispose of] his property to wit [*specify property concealed etc.*] contrary *etc.*

(*b*)   **Receiving property**

A.B. on .... at .... with intent that C.D. should defraud his creditors did receive from C.D. certain property of C.D. to wit [*specify property received*] by means of [*or* in relation to] which an offence under s. 392(*a*) of the *Criminal Code* had been committed contrary *etc.*

393(1) Fraud in relation to fares etc.

A.B. on .... at .... being under the duty to collect a fare [*or* toll *or* ticket *or* admission] did wilfully

(*a*)   fail to collect it from C.D. contrary *etc.*

or

(*b*)   collect less than the proper amount payable in respect thereof from C.D. contrary *etc.*

or

(*c*)   accept a valuable consideration to wit [*specify consideration received*] for failing to collect such fare [*or* for collecting less than the proper amount payable in respect thereof] from C.D. contrary *etc.*

393(3) Obtaining transportation by fraud

A.B. on .... at .... did by a false pretence [*or* fraud] to wit [*specify false pretence or fraud*] obtain transportation by land [*or* water *or* air] to wit [*specify, e.g., by taxi-cab*] to the value of .... dollars from C.D. contrary *etc.*

396(1) Offences in relation to mines

(*a*)   A.B. on .... at .... with the fraudulent intent to affect the result of an assay, [*or* test *or* valuation] that has been made [*or* was to be made] with respect to a mine [*or* prospective mine *or* mining claim *or* oil well] to wit [*specify*] did add [*specify e.g. gold ore*] to [*or* remove (*specify*) from] the mine [*or* mining claim *or* oil well] contrary *etc.*

or

(*b*)   A.B. on .... at .... did add [*specify e.g. gold ore*] to [*or* remove (*specify*) from *or* tamper with] a sample [*or* material] that was taken [*or* about to be taken] from a mine [*or* prospective mine *or* mining claim *or* oil well] to wit [*specify*] for the purpose of being assayed [*or* tested *or* otherwise valued] with the fraudulent intent to affect the result of the assay [*or* test *or* valuation] contrary *etc.*

397(1) Falsification of books and documents

A.B. on .... at .... with intent to defraud C.D. did

(*a*)   destroy [*or* mutilate *or* alter *or* falsify *or* make a false entry in]

or

(*b*)   omit a material particular from [*or* alter a material particular in] to wit [*specify item omitted or altered*]

a book [*or* paper *or* writing *or* valuable security *or* document] to wit [*specify book etc.*] contrary *etc.*

398 Falsifying employment record

A.B. on .... at .... with intent to deceive did falsify an employment record to wit [*specify, e.g., company pay sheet*] by [*specify means used*] contrary *etc.*

400(1) False prospectus

A.B. on .... at .... did make [*or* circulate *or* publish] a prospectus [*or* statement *or* account] which he knew was false in a material particular to wit [*specify false particular*] with intent

(*a*)   to induce persons to become shareholders or partners in [*specify company*] contrary *etc.*

or

(*b*)   to deceive [*or* defraud] the member [*or* shareholders *or* creditors] of [*specify company*] contrary *etc.*

or

(*c*)(i)   to induce C.D. to entrust [*or* advance] a sum of money [*or specify*] to [*specify company*] contrary *etc.*

or

(*c*)(ii)   to enter into a security for the benefit of [*specify company*] contrary *etc.*

401(1) Obtaining carriage by false billing

A.B. on .... at .... did knowingly, by means of a false [*or* misleading] representation to wit [*specify*], obtain [*or* attempt to obtain] the carriage of [*specify goods*] by [*specify carrier*] into [*specify province, country or district or other place*], the transportation [*or* importation] of those goods into the said province [*or* country *or* district *or as the case may be*] being unlawful contrary *etc.*

402.2(1) Identity Theft

A.B. on . . . . , at . . . . did knowingly obtain [*or* possess] C.D.'s identity information [*specify information e.g. American Express credit card number (see definition in s. 402.1)*] in circumstances giving rise to a reasonable inference that the information was intended to be used to commit the indictable offence of [*specify offence e.g. theft of credit cards*] contrary *etc.*

402.2(2) Trafficking in Identity Information

A.B. on . . . . at . . . . did transmit [*or* make available *or* distribute *or* sell *or* offer for sale] C.D.'s identity information [*specify information e.g. American Express credit card number (see definition in s. 402.1)*] knowing that or being reckless as to whether the information would be used to commit the indictable offence of [*specify offence e.g. theft of credit cards*] contrary *etc.*

or

A.B. on . . . . at . . . . did have in his possession for the purpose of transmitting *or* making available *or* distributing *or* selling *or* offering for sale] C.D.'s identity information [*specify information e.g. American Express credit card number (see definition in s. 402.1)*] knowing that or being reckless as to whether the information would be used to commit the indictable offence of [*specify offence e.g. theft of credit cards*] contrary *etc.*

403 Identity Fraud

A.B. on . . . . at . . . . did fraudulently personate C.D.

(a) with intent to gain advantage for himself [*or* E.F.] to wit . . . . contrary *etc.*

or

(b) with intent to obtain certain [*or* an interest in] property to wit . . . . contrary *etc.*

or

(c) with intent to cause disadvantage to C.D. [*or* E.F.] contrary *etc.*

or

(d) with intent to avoid arrest [*or* prosecution *or* obstruct, prevent *or* defeat the course of justice] contrary *etc.*

419 Unlawful use of military uniforms or certificates

A.B. on .... at .... without lawful excuse did

(a) wear a uniform of the Canadian [*or name other country, e.g., American*] Forces to wit [*specify uniform worn, e.g., the uniform of a Captain in the Canadian (or American) Army*] contrary *etc.*

[*or* wear a uniform so similar to the uniform of the Canadian [*or name other country*] Forces to wit [*specify*] that it was likely to be mistaken therefor contrary *etc.*]

or

(b) wear [an imitation of] a distinctive mark relating to wounds received [*or* a military medal *or* ribbon *or* badge *or* chevron *or* decoration *or* order] to wit [*specify item worn, e.g., the Victoria Cross*] contrary *etc.* [*or* wear a mark [*or* device *or* thing] that was likely to be mistaken for [*specify item imitated*] contrary *etc.*

or

(c) have in his possession a certificate of discharge [*or* certificate of release *or* statement of service *or* identity card] from the Canadian Forces [*or specify other country*] that was not issued to and did not belong to him contrary *etc.*

422(1) Criminal breach of contract

A.B. on .... at .... wilfully broke a contract with [*or between (specify)*] knowing or having reasonable cause to believe that the probable consequence of doing so would be

(a) to endanger human life contrary *etc.*

or

(b) to cause serious bodily injury contrary *etc.*

or

(c) to expose valuable property to destruction or serious injury contrary *etc.*

or

(d) to deprive the inhabitants of the City of [*or specify*] wholly or to a great extent, of their supply of light [*or power or gas or water*] contrary *etc.*

or

(e) to delay or prevent the running of a locomotive engine [*or tender or freight or passenger train or car*] on the [*specify railway which is common carrier*] contrary *etc.*

423(1) Intimidation

A.B. on .... at .... did wrongfully and without lawful authority for the purpose of compelling C.D. to abstain from [*or to do*] [*specify act, e.g., work at the X.Y.Z. Plant*] which C.D. had a lawful right to do [*or to abstain from doing*]

(a) use violence [*or threats of violence*] to the person of C.D. [*or to the wife or husband or children of C.D.*] [*or did injure his property to wit (specify property damaged)*] contrary *etc.*

or

(c) persistently follow C.D. about from place to place contrary *etc.*

or

(e) with E.F. and G.H. follow C.D. in a disorderly manner, on a highway to wit [*specify highway*] contrary *etc.*

423.1 Intimidation of justice system participant or journalist

(a) A.B. on .... at .... did without lawful authority, intending to provoke a state of fear in the general public [*or identify group of persons*] and to impede the administration of criminal justice

or

(b) A.B. on .... at .... did without lawful authority, intending to provoke a state of fear in C.D. a justice system participant in order to impede him [*or her*] in the performance of his [*or her*] duties

or

(c) A.B. on .... at .... did without lawful authority, intending to provoke a state of fear in C.D. a journalist in order to impede him [*or her*] in the transmission to the public of information in relation to a criminal organization [*specify criminal organization*]

   (a) use violence against [*or destroy the property of or cause damage to the property of*] C.D. a justice system participant [*or a journalist*] contrary *etc.*

or

use violence against [*or* destroy the property of *or* cause damage to the property of] E.F. a person known to C.D. a justice system participant [*or* a journalist] contrary *etc.*

or

(b) threaten to use violence against [*or* destroy the property of *or* cause damage to the property of] C.D. a justice system participant [*or* a journalist] contrary *etc.*

or

threaten to use violence against [*or* destroy the property of *or* cause damage to the property of] E.F. a person known to C.D. a justice system participant [*or* a journalist] contrary *etc.*

or

(c) persistently [*or* repeatedly] followed C.D. a justice system participant [*or* a journalist] from place to place [*or* in a disorderly manner on a highway to wit *specify highway*] contrary *etc.*

or

persistently [*or* repeatedly] followed E.F. a person known to C.D. a justice system participant [*or* a journalist] from place to place [*or* in a disorderly manner on a highway to wit *specify highway*] contrary *etc.*

or

(d) repeatedly communicated directly or indirectly with C.D. a justice system participant [*or* a journalist] contrary *etc.*

or

repeatedly communicated with E.F. a person known to C.D. a justice system participant [*or* a journalist] contrary *etc.*

or

(e) beset [*or* watched] [*specify place*] where C.D. a justice system participant [*or* a journalist] resides [*or* works *or* attends school *or* carries on business *or* happened to be] contrary *etc.*

or

beset [*or* watched] [*specify place*] where E.F. a person known to C.D. a justice system participant [*or* a journalist] resides [*or* works *or* attends school *or* carries on business *or* happened to be] contrary *etc.*

424 Threat to commit offence against internationally protected person

A.B. on .... at .... did threaten to commit the offence of murder contrary to s. 235 [*or specify offence contrary to s. 266, 267, 268, 269, 269.1, 271, 272, 273, 279 or 279.1*] of the *Criminal Code* against C.D. an internationally protected person contrary *etc.*

or

A.B. on .... at .... did threaten to commit the offence contrary to s. 431 of the Criminal Code by threatening to attack the official premises [*or* private accommodation *or* means of transport] of C.D. an

internationally protected person, such attack being likely to endanger the life
or liberty of C.D. contrary *etc.*

426(1)(*a*) Bribery of agent

A.B. on .... at .... did corruptly

give [*or* offer *or* agree to give *or* offer] to C.D. an agent for X.Y.

or

being an agent for X.Y. demand [*or* accept *or* offer *or* agree to accept]
from C.D.

a reward [*or* advantage *or* benefit] to wit [*specify, e.g., the sum of one
hundred dollars*] as consideration for doing [*or* forbearing to do *or*
for having done *or* forborne to do] an act relating to the affairs *or*
business of X.Y. to wit [*specify act done or to be done or as care may
be*] contrary *etc.*

or

a reward [*or* advantage *or* benefit] to wit [*specify, e.g., the sum of one
hundred dollars*] for showing [*or* forbearing to show] favour [*or*
disfavour] to A.B. [*or* C.D.] with relation to the affairs [*or* business]
of X.Y. contrary *etc.*

426(1)(*b*) False account to deceive a principal

A.B. on .... at .... with intent to deceive X.Y. did give to
C.D., an agent for X.Y. [*or* A.B., being an agent for X.Y. did use with intent
to deceive X.Y.] a receipt [*or* account *or* other writing] to wit [*specify
document*] in which X.Y. had an interest that contained a false [*or* erroneous
or defective] statement in a material particular that was intended to mislead
X.Y. to wit [*specify incorrect statement in document*] contrary *etc.*

430(2) Mischief endangering life

A.B. on .... at .... did commit mischief by wilfully damaging
without legal justification or excuse and without colour of right the [*specify
property damaged, e.g., the dwelling house of C.D. situate at* ....] by
[*specify means used, e.g., planting an explosive*] and did thereby endanger the
life of C.D. contrary *etc.*

430(3) Mischief over $5,000: to testamentary instrument

A.B. on .... at .... did commit mischief by wilfully ....
[*specify act of mischief as described in subsec. (1), e.g., damaging*] without legal
justification or excuse and without colour of right property to wit

[*specify property damaged etc., e.g., the automobile*] of C.D. the value of
which exceeded five thousand dollars contrary *etc.*

or

[*specify testamentary document, e.g., the codicil dated January 1st, 1986
to the last will and testament*] of C.D.

430(4) Mischief not exceeding $5,000

A.B. on .... at .... did commit mischief by wilfully .... [*specify act of mischief as described in subsec. (1), e.g., damaging*] without legal justification or excuse and without colour of right property to wit [*specify property damaged etc., e.g., the bicycle*] of C.D. the value of which did not exceed five thousand dollars contrary *etc.*

430(4.1) Mischief relating to religious property

A.B. on .... at .... did commit mischief by wilfully .... and for reasons of bias, prejudice or hate based on religion [*or* race *or* colour *or* national *or* ethnic origin] [specify act of mischief as described in subsec. (1), e.g., damaging] without legal justification or excuse and without colour of right property that is primarily used for religious worship to wit [*specify church, mosque, synagogue or temple or object associated with religious worship located in or on the grounds of such building or cemetery*] the value of which did not exceed five thousand dollars contrary etc.

430(5) Mischief to data

A.B. on .... at .... did commit mischief in relation to data by wilfully without legal justification or excuse and without colour of right [*specify act of mischief as described in subsec. (1.1), e.g., destroying or rendering meaningless, useless or ineffective*] data to wit [*specify data*] contrary *etc.*

431 Attack on premises, residence or transport of internationally protected person

A.B. on .... at .... did attack the official premises [*or* private accommodation *or* means of transport] of C.D. an internationally protected person, in manner likely to endanger the life or liberty of C.D. contrary *etc.*

433 Arson: disregard for human life

(*a*)   A.B. on .... at .... did intentionally or recklessly cause damage by fire [*or* explosion] to [*specify property damaged, e.g., a dwelling house*] situate at .... knowing that or being reckless with respect whether the said property was inhabited or occupied contrary *etc.*

or

(*b*)   A.B. on .... at .... did intentionally or recklessly cause damage by fire [*or* explosion] to [*specify property damaged, e.g., a dwelling house*] situate at .... which fire [*or* explosion] did cause bodily harm to C.D. contrary *etc.*

434 Arson: damage to property

A.B. on .... at .... did intentionally or recklessly cause damage by fire [*or* explosion] to [*specify property damaged, e.g., a dwelling house*] the property of C.D. situate at .... contrary *etc.*

434.1 Arson: damage to own property

A.B. on .... at .... did intentionally or recklessly cause damage by fire [*or* explosion] to [*specify property damaged, e.g., a dwelling house*] owned by the said A.B. situate at .... which fire [*or* explosion] seriously threatened the health [*or* safety, *or* property situate at ....] of C.D. contrary *etc.*

435(1) Arson for fraudulent purpose

A.B. on .... at .... did with intent to defraud C.D. cause damage by fire [*or* explosion] to [*specify property damaged, e.g., a dwelling house*] the property of C.D. situate at .... contrary *etc.*

436(1) Arson by negligence

A.B. on .... at .... did as a result of a marked departure from the standard of care that a reasonably prudent person would use to prevent or control the spread of fires [*or* to prevent explosions] cause a fire [*or* explosion] in [*specify property damaged, e.g., a dwelling house*] owned [*or* controlled] by the said A.B. situate at .... which fire [*or* explosion] did cause bodily harm to [*or* damage the property of] C.D. contrary *etc.*

436.1 Possession of incendiary material

A.B. on .... at .... did possess an incendiary material [*or* incendiary device *or* explosive substance] to wit [*specify material, device or substance*] for the purpose of committing the offence of [*specify an offence contrary to s. 433 to 436, e.g., arson contrary to s. 433(a)*] contrary *etc.*

437 False alarm of fire

A.B. on .... at .... did wilfully without reasonable cause by outcry [*or* ringing bells *or* using a fire alarm *or* telephone *or* telegraph *or* specify other means used*] make [*or* circulate *or* cause to be made *or* circulated] an alarm of fire at [*specify premises where fire purported to be*] contrary *etc.*

or

A.B. on .... at .... did wilfully without reasonable cause make an alarm of fire by using a fire alarm signal box on .... Street contrary *etc.*

445 Killing or injuring animals

A.B. on .... at .... did wilfully and without lawful cause

(*a*) kill [*or* maim *or* wound *or* poison *or* injure] [*specify bird or animal, e.g., a dog*] the property of C.D. that was kept for a lawful purpose contrary *etc.*

or

(*b*) place poison in such a position that it might easily be consumed by dogs, birds, or animals that were kept for a lawful purpose to wit [*specify where poison placed, e.g., at the base of a tree on the front lawn of the premises situate at ....*] contrary *etc.*

445.1 Cruelty to animals

A.B. on .... at ....

(a) did wilfully cause [*or* being the owner did wilfully permit to be caused] unnecesssary pain [*or* suffering *or* injury] to [*specify animal or bird*] by [*specify means used*] contrary *etc.*

(b) did encourage, aid or assist at the fighting [*or* baiting] of [*specify animals or birds*] contrary *etc.*

(c) did willfully and without reasonable excuse administer a poisonous [*or* injurious] drug [*or* substance] to wit .... to a domestic animal [*or* bird *or* an animal or bird wild by nature that is kept in captivity] to wit .... contrary *etc.*

or

did being the owner of a domestic animal [*or* bird *or* an animal or bird wild by nature that is kept in captivity] to wit .... willfully permit a poisonous [*or* injurious] drug [*or* substance] to wit .... to be administered to it, contrary *etc.*

(d) did promote [*or* arrange, *or* conduct *or* assist in *or* receive money for *or* take part in] a meeting [*or* competition *or* exhibition *or* pastime *or* practice *or* display *or* event] at [*or* in the course of] which captive birds were liberated by [*here specify means e.g. by hand*] for the purpose of being shot when they were liberated contrary *etc.*

(e) being the owner [*or* occupier *or* person in charge] of [*specify premises*] permitted those premises to be used for the purpose of promoting [*or* arranging, *or* conducting *or* assisting in *or* receiving money for *or* taking part in] a meeting [*or* competition *or* exhibition *or* pastime *or* practice *or* display *or* event] at [*or* in the course of] which captive bird were liberated by [*herer specify means e.g. by hand*] for the purpose of being shot when they were liberated contrary *etc.*

446 Causing damage or injury to animals or birds

A.B. on .... at ....

(a) by willful neglect did cause damage [*or* injury] to [*specify animals or birds*] while they were being driven [*or* conveyed] by A.B. to wit by [*specify neglect, e.g., failure to water them*] contrary *etc.*

(b) being the owner [*or* the person having the custody *or* control] of a domestic animal [*or* bird *or* an animal *or* bird wild by nature that was in capativity] to wit [*specify, e.g., a dog*] did willfully neglect [*or* fail] to provide suitable and adequate food [*or* water *or* shelter *or* care] for such [*specify animal or bird*] contrary *etc.*

447.1 Animals: breach of order prohibiting keeping

A.B. on .... at .... did, while prohibited from doing so by an order made under s. 447.1(1)(a) of the *Criminal Code*, own [*or* have the custody of *or* have control of *or* reside in the same premises as] an animal [*or* bird] to wit .... contrary *etc.*

449 Counterfeit money: making
A.B. on .... at .... did [*or* did begin to] make counterfeit money to wit [*specify, e.g., a counterfeit ten dollar Bank of Canada bill*] contrary *etc.*

450 Counterfeit money: buying, receiving, possessing or importing
A.B. on .... at .... without lawful justification or excuse did

(*a*) buy [*or* receive *or* offer to buy *or* receive] from C.D.
or

(*b*) have in his custody [*or* possession]
or

(*c*) introduce into Canada
counterfeit money to wit: [*specify coin or paper*] contrary *etc.*

452 Counterfeit money: uttering, using and exporting
A.B. on .... at .... without lawful justification or excuse did

(*a*) utter [*or* offer to utter *or* use] counterfeit money to wit [*specify, e.g., a counterfeit ten dollar Bank of Canada bill*] as if it were genuine contrary *etc.*
or

(*b*) export [*or* send *or* take] counterfeit money to wit [*specify, e.g., counterfeit ten dollar Bank of Canada bills*] out of Canada contrary *etc.*

453(*a*) Coin not current: uttering
A.B. on .... at .... with intent to defraud C.D. did knowingly utter a coin that was not current contrary *etc.*

453(*b*) Counterfeit coin: uttering
A.B. on .... at .... with intent to defraud C.D. did knowingly utter a piece of metal [*or* mixed metals] that resembled in size, figure and colour a current gold [*or* silver] coin but of less value than the current coin for which it was uttered to wit [*specify, e.g., a current twenty-five cent piece*] contrary *etc.*

454 Fraudulent use of slugs
A.B. on .... at .... did

(*a*) manufacture [*or* produce *or* sell]
or

(*b*) have in his possession
a [*specify article*] that was intended to be fraudulently used in substitution for a coin [*or* token of value] that any coin- [*or* token-] operated device is designed to receive contrary *etc.*

456 Defacing current coin

A.B. on .... at .... did

(a)   deface [*specify*], a current coin contrary *etc.*

or

(b)   utter [*specify*], a current coin that had been defaced contrary *etc.*

457 Printing circulars etc. in likeness of notes

(1) A.B. on .... at .... did design [*or* engrave *or* print *or* make *or* execute *or* issue *or* distribute *or* circulate *or* use] a business [*or* professional] card [*or* notice *or* placard *or* circular *or* handbill *or* advertisement] in the likeness [*or* appearance] of [*specify*]

(a)   a current bank-note [*or* paper money] contrary *etc.*

or

(b)   an obligation [*or* security] of the Government of [*specify*] [*or the Bank of (specify)*] contrary *etc.*

(2) A.B. on .... at .... did publish [*or* print] [*specify*] in the likeness [*or* appearance] of [*specify*] being

(a)   a current bank-note [*or* paper money] contrary *etc.*

or

(b)   an obligation [*or* security] of the Government of [*specify*] [*or the Bank of (specify)*] contrary *etc.*

458 Counterfeiting: instruments for

A.B. on .... at .... without lawful justification or excuse did

(a)   make [*or* repair]

or

(b)   begin [*or* proceed] to make [*or* repair]

or

(c)   buy [*or* sell]

or

(d)   have in his custody [*or* possession]

a machine [*or* engine *or* tool *or* instrument *or* material *or* thing] that he knew had been used [*or* had been adapted and intended for use] in making counterfeit money [*or* counterfeit tokens of value] contrary *etc.*

462.2 Promoting illicit drug use

A.B. on .... at .... did knowingly

(a)   import into Canada [*or* export from Canada *or* manufacture *or* promote *or* sell] an instrument to wit [*specify instrument*] which instrument was designed primarily [*or* intended] under the circumstances for consuming [*or* facilitating the consumption of] an illicit drug to wit [*specify illicit drug*] contrary *etc.*

or

(b) import into Canada [*or* export from Canada *or* manufacture *or* promote *or* sell] literature to wit [*specify literature*] which literature describes [*or* depicts] the production [*or* preparation *or* consumption] of an illicit drug and is designed primarily [*or* intended] under the circumstances to promote [*or* encourage *or* advocate] the production [*or* preparation *or* consumption of] an illicit drug to wit [*specify illicit drug*] contrary *etc.*

462.31(1) Laundering proceeds of crime

(1) A.B. on .... at .... did use [*or* transfer the possession of *or* transport *or* transmit *or* dispose of *or* otherwise deal with] property [*or* proceeds of any property] to wit [*specify property*] with intent to conceal or convert that property [*or* those proceeds] knowing or believing that all [*or* part] of the property [*or* proceeds of the property] was obtained [*or* derived directly or indirectly] as a result of

(a) the commission in Canada of the designated offence of [*specify designated offence*] contrary *etc.*

or

(b) an act [*or* omission] in [*specify place e.g. State of New York*] namely [*specify act or omission e.g. uttering counterfeit money which would constitute designated offence if committed in Canada*] which offence had it occurred in Canada would have constituted the designated offence of [*specify designated offence*], contrary *etc.*

or

(2) A.B. on .... at .... did send [*or* deliver] to [*specify person or place*] property [*or* proceeds of any property] to wit [*specify property*] with intent to conceal or convert that property [*or* those proceeds] knowing or believing that all [*or* part] of the property [*or* proceeds of the property] was obtained [*or* derived directly or indirectly] as a result of

(a) the commission in Canada of the designated offence of [*specify designated offence*] contrary *etc.*

or

(b) an act [*or* omission] in [*specify place e.g. State of New York*] namely [*specify act or omission e.g. uttering counterfeit money which would constitute designated offence if committed in Canada*] which offence had it occurred in Canada would have constituted the designated offence of [*specify designated offence*], contrary *etc.*

464 Counselling offence that is not committed: indictable and summary

(a) **Indictable offence**

A.B. on .... at .... did counsel C.D. to commit the indictable offence .... which offence was not committed contrary *etc.*

(*b*)   Summary offence

A.B. on .... at .... did counsel C.D. to commit an offence punishable on summary conviction to wit [*specify offence, e.g., pretend to use witchcraft*] which offence was not committed contrary *etc.*

465(1)(*a*) Conspiracy to murder

A.B. and C.D. on .... at .... did conspire together to murder E.F. [*or* to cause E.F. to be murdered] contrary *etc.*

465(1)(*c*) Conspiracy to commit indictable offence

A.B. and C.D. on .... at .... did conspire together to commit the indictable offence of .... by [*state sufficient particulars to enable accused to identify the agreement and know nature of charge he has to meet*] contrary *etc.*

465(1)(*d*) Conspiracy to commit summary conviction offence

A.B. and C.D. on .... at .... did conspire together to commit the summary conviction offence of .... by [*state sufficient particulars to enable accused to identify the agreement and know nature of charge they have to meet*] contrary *etc.*

467.11(1) Participation in criminal organization

A.B. on .... at .... did participate in [*or* contribute to] the activities of a criminal organization to wit [*here specify organization*] for the purpose of enhancing the ability of the said organization to facilitate [*or* commit] the indictable offence of [*here specify offence under Criminal Code or other Federal legislation*] contrary *etc.*

467.12(1) Commission of offence for criminal organization

A.B. on .... at .... did commit the indictable offence of [*specify indictable offence*] for the benefit of [*or* at the direction of *or* in association with] a criminal organization to wit [*here specify organization*] [here specify offence] contrary *etc.*

467.13(1) Instructing commission of offence for criminal organization

A.B. being one of the persons constituting the criminal organization of [*here specify organization*] on .... at .... did knowingly directly or indirectly instruct a person [*here specify the person if known*] to commit the indictable offence of [*here specify offence*] for the benefit of [*or* at the direction of *or* in association with] the said criminal organization to wit contrary *etc.*

733.1(1) Probation order: non-compliance

A.B. on [*or* between] .... at .... did, while bound by a probation order made by [*insert full title of the court making the order*] .... on [*insert date of order*]................, fail [*or* refuse] without reasonable excuse to comply with such order, to wit [*here recite the non-complied with condition of the order*] .... contrary *etc.*

810(1) Fear of injury or damage by another person

A.B. fears that X.Y. will cause personal injury to him [*or to his spouse or to his children*] in that X.Y. did on .... at .... utter the words [*specify, e.g., "I will kill you"*] contrary *etc.*

or

A.B. fears that X.Y. will cause personal injury to his property [*specify, e.g., dwelling house situate at 4 Main Street*] in that X.Y. did on .... at .... utter the words [*specify, e.g., "I will burn your house down"*] contrary *etc.*

810.01 Where fear of criminal organization offence

A.B. fears that X.Y. will commit the offence of .... contrary to s. 423.1 [*or specify criminal organization offence or terrorism offence as defined in s. 2*]

810.1 Where fear of sexual offence

A.B. fears that X.Y. will commit an offence under section 151 [*or 152 or 155 or 159 or 160(2) or (3) or 170 or 171 or 173(2) or 271 or 272 or 273*] of the *Criminal Code* in respect of C.D. a person under the age of fourteen years in that X.Y. did on .... at .... [*specify grounds for fear*]

FORMS OF CHARGES UNDER THE *CONTROLLED DRUGS AND SUB-STANCES ACT*

4(1) Possession of substance included in Schedule I, II or III

A.B. on .... at .... did unlawfully possess a substance included in Schedule I [*or* II *or* III] to wit . . . . . [*specify substance*] contrary to s. 4 of the *Controlled Drugs and Substances Act.*

4(2) Seeking or obtaining substance or authorization to obtain substance included in Schedule I, II, III or IV from practitioner

A.B. on .... at .... did seek [*or* obtain] a substance [*or* an authorization to obtain a substance] included in Schedule I [*or* II *or* III *or* IV] to wit . . . . . [*specify substance*] from Dr. C.D. a practitioner without disclosing to the said practitioner particulars relating to the acquisition within the preceding thirty days by A.B. from another practitioner Dr. E.F. of a substance in Schedule I, [*or* II, III and IV *or* every authorization to obtain such substances] namely [*here specify particulars not disclosed to practitioner*] contrary to s. 4 of the *Controlled Drugs and Substances Act.*

5(1) Trafficking

A.B. on .... at .... did traffic in a substance

included in Schedule I [*or* II *or* III *or* IV *or* V] to wit .... [*specify substance*] contrary to s. 5 of the *Controlled Drugs and Substances Act.*

or

represented [*or* held out to be] a substance included in Schedule I [*or* II *or* III *or* IV *or* V] to wit .... [*specify substance*] contrary to s. 5 of the *Controlled Drugs and Substances Act.*

5(2) Possession for the purpose of trafficking

A.B. on .... at .... did possess a substance included in Schedule I [*or* II *or* III *or* IV *or* V] to wit .... [*specify substance*] for the purpose of trafficking contrary to s. 5 of the *Controlled Drugs and Substances Act.*

6(1) Importing and exporting

A.B. on .... at .... did unlawfully import into [*or* export from] Canada a substance included in Schedule I [*or* II *or* III *or* IV *or* V *or* VI] to wit .... [*specify substance*] contrary to s. 6 of the *Controlled Drugs and Substances Act.*

6(2) Possession for the purpose of exporting

A.B. on .... at .... did unlawfully possess a substance included in Schedule I [*or* II *or* III *or* IV *or* V *or* VI] to wit .... [*specify substance*] for the purpose of exporting it from Canada contrary to s. 6 of the *Controlled Drugs and Substances Act.*

7 Production of substance

A.B. on .... at .... did unlawfully produce a substance included in Schedule I [*or* II *or* III *or* IV *or* V] to wit .... [*specify substance*] contrary to s. 7 of the *Controlled Drugs and Substances Act*.